SIR WALTER SCOTT

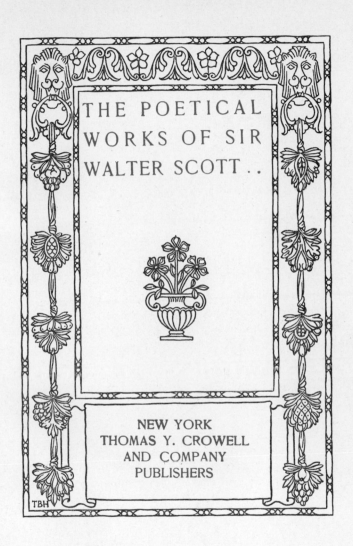

THE POETICAL WORKS OF SIR WALTER SCOTT ..

NEW YORK
THOMAS Y. CROWELL
AND COMPANY
PUBLISHERS

THE

COMPLETE POETICAL WORKS

OF

SIR WALTER SCOTT

WITH AN INTRODUCTION

BY

CHARLES ELIOT NORTON

BIOGRAPHICAL SKETCH

BY

NATHAN HASKELL DOLE

NEW YORK
THOMAS Y. CROWELL & CO.
PUBLISHERS

INTRODUCTION.

In looking back over this century, which is now so near its close, there is none among its conspicuous figures of pleasanter aspect than that of Scott; and of all the men who have lived during its course there is not one who has contributed more largely to the pleasure of its successive generations. This is a high eulogy; no man could desire a better. To amuse men rationally, to give them wholesome entertainment, is to do them a great service; and to do this through a lifetime more successfully than any one else, is to be worthy of lasting gratitude. This is what Scott did for our fathers, and has done for many of us, and will continue to do for many of our children. At this moment, more than sixty years after the last of his novels was written, two popular editions of them are in course of publication; while his poems, ninety years after the " Lay of the Last Minstrel " was first published, are still the delight of youthful readers, and still charm readers of all ages by the interest of their animated narrative, the ease of their versification, and the manliness of their spirit.

" Scott," said Mr. Emerson, " is the most lovable of men, and entitled to the world's gratitude for the entertainment he has given to solitude, the relief to headache and heartache. But," he adds, " he is not sufficiently alive to ideas to be a great man."

" Into the question whether Scott was a great man or not, we do not propose," says Carlyle, " to enter deeply. It is, as too usual, a question about words. There can be no doubt that many men have been named and printed *great* who were vastly smaller than he; as little doubt, moreover, that of the specially *good*, a very large portion, according to any genuine standard of man's worth, were worthless in comparison with him. . . . The truth is, our best definition of Scott were perhaps even this, that he was, if no great man, then something much pleasanter to be, — a robust, thoroughly healthy, and withal very prosperous and victorious man. An eminently well-conditioned man, healthy in body, healthy in soul; we will call him one of the healthiest of men."

iii

And it is this sound, healthy human nature, on good terms with itself and with the world, with easy mastery of its own faculties, open, sympathetic, cordial, — it is this large, genial nature with which his work, whether in prose or poetry, is inspired. Let us be grateful for such a gift. There is space even on the narrow shelves of the immortals for books such as his. Shakespeare, Milton, Wordsworth, may rest on a higher shelf, but Scott will be nearer at hand for the multitude of readers, and his volumes will require more frequent rebinding.

He was past thirty years old before his poetic genius found its full expression. He was born in 1771, and it was in 1805 that his first long poem, " The Lay of the Last Minstrel," was published and sprang into the popularity which it has never lost. It was largely a piece of improvisation. It was no poem the writing of which " made him lean for many years." Once fairly entered upon, it was soon finished, " proceeding," as he tell us, " at about the rate of a canto per week." In a letter written within a month or two after its publication, he wrote, " It is deficient in that sort of continuity which a story ought to have, and which, were it to write again, I would endeavor to give it. . . . The sixth canto is altogether redundant." Composed as it was at breakneck speed, it is not surprising that the diction is often careless, that the facile couplets are too apt to drop heavily to a prosaic level, and that there is little depth in the reflections which occasionally intervene in the story. But, on the other hand, the narrative flows with rapid current, the story is full of picturesque and lively scenes, and the verse has what Wordsworth well called " an easy, glowing energy." The account of William of Deloraine's ride by night quickens the blood till its beat keeps time with the gallop ; and, though the last canto be redundant, it contains in the Ballad of Rosabelle one of those fine lyrics within the limits of which Scott's improvising genius seems often to find its best expression. In his modest introduction to his final edition of the Lay in 1830, he gives an interesting account of its origin and composition ; but neither he nor his critics have done justice to the chief distinction of the poem, that its mode was practically a new invention, reclaiming poetry from the tediousness of the then prevailing artificial style, to its place as an art of entertainment in the spirited romantic delineation of nature and of life. There had been nothing like it in English literature. It was an extension of the delightful realm of poetry, and in its kind there has been nothing better.

Scott was in no hurry to take advantage of the popularity of his first long poem, and he determined that his second should be less hasty in its composition. " Accordingly," to cite his own words, " particular passages of a poem which was finally called ' Marmion ' were labored with a good deal of care by one by whom much care was seldom bestowed ; " and he adds in words which it is pleasant to recall, and which in part account for the excellence of the poem, " The period of its composition was a very happy one in life." But " Marmion " was finished in haste, perhaps in too much haste ; and yet Scott was right in thinking well of the last canto, of which he wrote to one of his correspondents, " I have succeeded better than I ventured to hope." He was, indeed, in this canto at his best ; and when " Scott's poetry is at its best," says Matthew Arnold, " it is undoubtedly very good indeed." The description of the Battle of Flodden Field is a splendid piece of verse. " My heart is a soldier's, and always has been," Scott once wrote ; and his soldier's heart beats in the thick of the battle he describes. After the words I have just cited, Matthew Arnold quotes these verses : —

> " Tunstall lies dead upon the field,
> His life-blood stains the spotless shield :
> Edmund is down : — my life is reft ;
> The Admiral alone is left.
> Let Stanley charge with spur of fire, —
> With Chester charge, and Lancashire,
> Full upon Scotland's central host,
> Or victory and England's lost."

And then he adds, " That is, no doubt, as vigorous as possible, as spirited as possible ; it is exceedingly fine poetry." And there is much hardly less good.

In thanking Scott for a copy of Marmion, Wordsworth wrote to him, with characteristic directness, " I think your end has been attained. That it is not the end which I should wish you to propose to yourself, you will be well aware from what you know of my notions of composition, both as to matter and manner." In view of their relative positions in popular esteem at the time, Scott may well have been more amused than annoyed at his brother poet's unsympathetic disapproval, and have asked him in reply, " Can the Ethiopian change his skin ? " Scott's poetic method, and his view of man and nature, were, indeed, widely different from Wordsworth's. But " because thou art virtuous shall there be no more cakes and ale ? " He was not given to introspection or meditation ; he sympathized with men more than he studied them, and was more interested in their actions and their earthly fates than in their spiritual elements. He cared little for the order and significance of nature, but delighted in its infinite variety of aspect ; and used it in his poems as a picturesque background for his characters, the scenery of the stage on which they played their parts.

"Marmion" was published in 1808; and its success was so great from the first, that Scott more than half resolved not to write another long poem, for fear of hazard to his popularity. But this resolution did not last long; and, citing to himself the words of the great Marquis of Montrose, —

> "He either fears his fate too much,
>   Or his deserts are small,
> Who dares not put it to the touch,
>   To win or lose it all,"

he began the "Lady of the Lake," which was to achieve, on its publication in 1810, as instant and as great a success as either of its predecessors, and was to maintain its popularity as firmly and as long. No one of Scott's poems is fuller of movement, of the health of the open air and the charm of the wild landscape than this; and no one of them contains more verses which have become part of the familiar possessions of the English-speaking race. "I like it myself," wrote Scott, "as well as any of my former attempts;" and his judgment has been confirmed by the verdict of three generations. Fitz-James's horn still wakes a ready echo in the adventurous heart of youth, and many a maiden, on many a lake, wears the form of Katrine's lady in her lover's eyes,

It has, indeed, rarely happened in the history of literature, that poems written off-hand like these, with so little pains and so little revision, have gained more than a brief lease of life. Scott himself, with his delightful modesty, did not look for permanent fame as a poet. "I have enjoyed too extensive popularity in this generation to be entitled to draw long-dated bills on the applause of the next," he wrote in a letter, just before the "Lady of the Lake" was published. And twenty years afterward he said, in his preface to the last edition which he was to oversee, "I can, with honest truth, exculpate myself from having been at any time a partisan of my own poetry, even when it was in the highest fashion with the million." In all that he anywhere says of his poetry his words are quite sound, simple, and unpretending. He recognized the limits of his power and the sources of his popularity; he was pleased, but not elated, by success. Success could, indeed, do nothing but good to so manly and healthy a nature. The real and abiding charm of his verse consists not in its style, nor its stock of ideas, nor in any significance underlying the narrative, but in qualities which depend upon personal character. It is the expression of a generous nature, with a lively interest in the outward spectacle of the world, a quick sympathy with the actors in the long drama of life, and a keen sense of relation to the earth and enjoyment of it. It is the expression of a lover of his own land, of its mountains and glens, and rivers and lakes, dearer for the sake of the story of its people, a story as varied and picturesque as the scenery itself. The literary critic will find a hundred faults in his poems; but the boy, entranced by the tale, does not know they are there; and the man, jaded with care and weary of books, does not mind them, finding refreshment in verse inspired with the breath of the open air, unstudied in its animation, unforced in its sentiment, and making simple appeal to his memory and imagination.

Scott was almost forty years old when the " Lady of the Lake" was written. His later poems, " Rokeby," " The Lord of the Isles," and others, have less of the freshness of youth, and have never possessed the popualrity of his earlier work. In his preface in 1830 to " Rokeby" he gives some of the reasons of their comparative lack of success. Fortunately for the lasting pleasure of mankind, he turned from poetry to prose, and wrote the Waverley novels.

Every year there is jettison of part of the cargo with which the good ship of literature is overladen. Some of Scott's poetry has already gone overboard, and the time may come when more of it must follow; but it will not all suffer this fate. Even if the rest should go, some of his lyrics, at least, are sure to be saved. What he once called " The only good song I ever wrote," the " Pibroch of Donald Dhu," with its spirited rallying cry, —

> " Come as the winds come, when
> Forests are rended;
> Come as the waves come, when
> Navies are stranded,"

this will not be lost; nor will the " Coronach," from the " Lady of the Lake." Some hearts would not forget the ballad of " Alice Brand; " and some memories are sure to hold Cleveland's song; and more will recall the stately measure and the pathos of " I climbed the dark brow of the mighty Helvellyn; " and others still, the wild ballad of Elspeth, in " The Antiquary," —

> " The herring loves the merry moonlight,
> The mackerel loves the wind."

And so long as any of his poems shall last, the memory of Scott himself will be cherished in the hearts of men whom he has entertained, and to whom he has not only given pleasure, but done good. For to become friends with him in his books is to become friends with one of the pleasantest of men, with whom we cannot keep up acquaintance without, let us hope, gaining something of his own simplicity, geniality, kindliness, modesty, and manliness.

Among the last verses which Tennyson wrote there is a stanza of singularly felicitous simplicity and strength, which in its personal tribute expresses a common sentiment, —

> " O great and gallant Scott!
>   True gentleman, heart, blood, and bone,
>   I would it had been my lot
>   To have seen thee, and heard thee, and known."

It is fortunate that in the " Life of Scott," by his son-in-law, Lockhart, and in his own Journal and Letters, we have such a picture of him as exists of few other men, and in all its features consistent with the attractive image that the reader of his poems and novels forms for himself of their large-hearted and lovable author.

1894.   CHARLES ELIOT NORTON.

BIOGRAPHICAL SKETCH.

"EVERY Scottishman," wrote Sir Walter Scott in his fragment of autobiography, "has a pedigree. It is a national prerogative as inalienable as his pride and his poverty."

Scott was proud of the fact that in his veins flowed the mingled blood of two hostile clans, the Scotts and the Haliburtons. He claimed no more than "gentle" birth, but few men in Scotland were connected with so many "stocks of historical distinction."

On his father's side he traced his lineage through seven generations to Auld Watt of Harden, and "his fair dame, the Flower of Yarrow." On his mother's side were the "Bauld Rutherfords, that were sae stout," and the knightly family of Swintons, through whom he claimed kinship with Sir William Alexander, first Earl of Sterling, the Marquess of Douglas, and Sir Robert Sinclair of Longformacus.

Robert Scott, his grandfather, was bred for the sea, but exchanged the tiller for the plough, and engaged in stock farming with considerable success. He married Barbara Haliburton, through whom would have come to him the patrimony of Dryburgh, comprising the ruins of the ancient abbey, had not the childless proprietor, whose heir he was, fallen into pecuniary difficulties, and been obliged to sell his estate.

His son Walter, the oldest of "a numerous progeny," married Anne, eldest daughter of Dr. John Rutherford, Professor of Medicine in Edinburgh University.

Of their twelve children, the first six died in infancy. Walter, the third son, was born in Edinburgh, August 15, 1771. Till he was eighteen months old he "showed every sign of health and strength." Then fever caused the lameness from which he suffered all his life. After trying various remedies, his parents sent him to his grandfather's at Sandy-Knowe, to get the benefit of the country air. He distinctly remembered being stript and swathed in the warm skin of a sheep just flayed, and his grandfather, a venerable, white-haired man, using every incitement to make him try to crawl on the floor of the little farm-house parlor, while a distant kinsman, Sir Henry Hay MacDougal, drest in an embroidered scarlet waistcoat and a light-colored coat, with milk-white locks tied in military fashion, knelt on the floor before him, dragging his watch along the carpet as a sort of bait. Walter Scott was only four when his grandfather died, but he continued to live at the farm, gradually becoming rugged, though his leg was somewhat shrunken and wasted. He was a remarkably precocious boy; and the reading which he heard, and the stories of Border adventure which were related for his amusement, and the influences of the romantic neighborhood, with its ruined towers, stately castles, purple mountains, and glorious rivers, were a far more important factor in his education than the formal teaching which he received at the hands of his "kind and affectionate aunt, Miss Janet Scott," or at the day-school at Bath, whither he was sent for a year when he was five.

The change from the solitude of the Sandy-Knowe farm to his father's home in Edinburgh was very great; but except for the too rigid Presbyterian strictness of his parents, which made Sundays especially irksome, the discipline was probably good for him. He was sent to the High School, and also received private lessons; but, as he himself said, he glanced like a meteor from one end of the class to the other, and commonly disgusted his kind master as much by negligence and frivolity, as he occasionally pleased him by flashes of intellect and talent; while he won favor with his companions not only by his inexhaustible fund of stories, but also by his address in all sorts of out-door games, and in the " bickers " which occurred between the school boys and the town boys.

Toward the end of his course in the High School, under the direct tuition of the Rector, Dr. Adam, he began to grow sensible of the beauties of Latin, and even distinguished himself " by some attempts at poetical versions " from Horace and Vergil. He felt that the rector's judicious mixture of praise and blame went far to counteract his habits of indolence and inattention.

His health growing delicate again, he was not immediately sent to college, but spent six months with his Aunt Janet at Kelso, on the Tweed. Here he had excellent instruction, and made the acquaintance of Dr. Blacklock, the friend of Burns; and through his recommendation became intimate with Ossian and Spenser. Spenser he especially delighted in, and could repeat incredible quantities of his verse. A respectable subscription library, a circulating library, and several private book-shelves being open to him, he declared that he waded into the stream like a blind man into a ford. His appetite for books was as ample and indiscriminating as it was indefatigable; and he many times afterwards repeated that few had ever read so much, or to so little purpose.

At the University, Scott entirely neglected Greek, much to his later regret, largely forgot his Latin, and made small progress in mathematics. In the other branches he was more fortunate, though in ethics, history, and law, he always felt that his learning was flimsy and inaccurate, and he would, even at the height of his popularity, have sacrificed half of his reputation, if by so doing he could have rested what was left on a solid foundation of learning and science.

Scott's father was a writer to the Signet, a branch of the law comprising the duties of the solicitor or attorney with those of the man of business. His practice had at one time been extensive, but a rather too simple and confiding nature, and over zeal for clients' interests to the detriment of his own, had somewhat diminished it. When Scott left the University in 1786, he was indentured to him for five years, and at the age of sixteen " entered upon the dry and barren wilderness of forms and conveyances."

Though he rebelled against the drudgery and confinement, he felt a rational pride in rendering himself useful to his father; and when actually at the oar, he says no one could pull harder than he, sometimes writing upwards of one hundred and twenty folio pages at a sitting, thereby earning at least thirty shillings. The duties of his apprenticeship often required him to make expeditions to the Highlands and elsewhere; and many of the most effective scenes of his poems and novels were inspired by his adventures in those wild and unknown regions.

For recreation he read indefatigably; and as his constitution hardened, he made long trips both on horseback and on foot, sometimes, in spite of his lameness, walking twenty or thirty miles a day. Thus he stored his mind with pictures of romantic or historic interest. And as he was unable to draw, he kept a sort of log-book of his rambles; wherever he went, he cut a branch from a tree, and thus fixed the scene in his memory.

He endeavored to educate his eye by taking lessons in oil painting, " from a little Jew animalcule, a smouch called Burrell," but he afterwards regretfully wrote in his diary that he made no progress : " Nature denied me correctness of eye and neatness of hand."

Still he drew the Castle of Hermitage at Liddesdale so accurately that Clerk put it into regular form, H. W. Williams copied it, and his drawing was engraved for the frontispiece of the first volume of the Kelso Edition of the Minstrelsy.

In music he was less talented. He wrote : " My ear appears to me as dull as my voice is incapable of musical expression." It is related of his early Edinburgh days, that being one time present at a drinking bout, when the conviviality was prolonged till late, or rather early, Scott fell asleep, and on waking was convinced by his friends that he had sung a song in the course of the evening, and had sung it extremely well. But it is probable that none of them was a very good judge in the circumstances.

In respect to lack of musical ear, Scott was like Burns and Byron and many of the great poets. Fortunately, poetry depends rather upon a sense of time than of genuine musical feeling, and many of his halting lines may be attributed to carelessness and haste.

In later days some of the reviews, while giving credit to Scott's abundant vivacity and verve of style, complained that it seemed impossible for him to write good English.

Scott, in his diary, under date of April 22, 1826, thus comments on his early neglect of fundamentals : —

" I write grammar as I speak, to make my meaning known; and a solecism in point of composition, like a Scotch word in speaking, is indifferent to me. I never learned grammar; and not only Sir Hugh Evans, but even Mrs. Quickly, might puzzle me about Giney's [Jenny's] case, and horum, harum, horum. I believe the bailiff in ' The Good Natured Man ' is not far wrong when he says: 'One man has one way of expressing himself, and another another, and that is all the difference between them.' "

The grave Presbyterian father was somewhat scandalized by his son's erratic ways, though it is said he also read romances on the sly, and was guilty of playing on the 'cello. One time Walter came home after one of his protracted absences. His father impatiently demanded how he had managed to live without any supply of pocket money; and when Walter expressed his regret that he had not Goldsmith's art, so as to tramp like poor George Primrose from cottage to cottage over the world, his father replied : —

" I greatly doubt, sir, you were born for nae better than a gangrel scrape gut ! "

In spite of the dangerous habits of young Scotch noblemen and gentlemen, Scott's character was not permanently vitiated by his intercourse with them. Indeed, he often exercised a restraining influence upon them. In his later life he was more than once heard to remark: " Depend upon it, of all vices drinking is the most incompatible with greatness." The terrible example of his brother Daniel's fate was perhaps salutary to him.

Scott had by this time outgrown all trace of early ill-health. He was so strong that he could lift a smith's anvil by the horn with one hand. He is described as about six feet in stature, with a fresh, brilliant complexion, clear, open eyes, perfect teeth, and a noble brow, and with great vivacity of expression. His upper lip was long, and his nose was far from classic, but his head was well set, and he was eminently formed (with the exception of the blemish in one leg) to attract the attention of the fair.

Lockhart says that it was the united testimony of his associates that Scott was remarkably free from the more rakish indiscretions of young manhood; and he partially explains it by reference to a secret attachment, " which continued through all the most perilous stage of life to act as a romantic charm in safeguard of virtue."

His earliest love, whom he himself compares to Byron's Mary Duff, was " a very good-natured, pretty girl," a Miss Dalrymple, daughter of Lord Westhall, and her daughter afterwards became the spouse of his colleague, Robert Hamilton.

When he was sixty he wrote: —

" I was a mere child, and could feel none of the passion which Byron alleges, yet the recollec tion of this good-humored companion of my childhood is like that of a morning dream."

But while he was still serving his apprenticeship, it happened that one Sunday, as the congregation were dispersing from Gray Friars, it began to rain, and Scott offered his umbrella to Miss Williamina Belches, a beautiful girl, the daughter of a gentleman who afterwards became Sir John Stuart of Fettercairn. The acquaintance thus begun ripened into friendship, and speedily, on Scott's part, into an undying love, which, though ultimately disappointed, was advantageous in more ways than one. Lockhart says it "had a powerful influence in nerving Scott's mind for the sedulous diligence with which he pursued his proper legal studies during the two or three years that preceded his call to the bar."

Scott's father, discovering his attachment, felt it his duty to warn the young lady's father, since she had "prospects of future far above his son's." She finally married Sir William Forbes, who in the time of Scott's adversity befriended him in many ways.

It was evident that Scott's pride was piqued, if his heart was broken, by her conduct; but when he had acquired name and fame he renewed relations with Lady Jane Stuart, the young lady's mother; and as late as 1827, on receiving an affectionate letter from her, felt his heart stirred to its deepest depths, and he wrote in his diary, "Alas! alas! — but why alas?"

He determined not to enter into partnership with his father, but to embrace the more ambitious profession of the bar; and with that object in view he was *eydent* in his studies for four years, and on the 11th of July, 1792, he "assumed the gown, with all its duties and honors." At the dinner which he gave, as was customary on such occasions, his father was one of the happiest of guests. "On a festival occasion," says Scott in his autobiography, "there were few whom a moderate glass of wine exhilarated to such a lively degree."

On the first day of his presence at Court, a friendly solicitor gave him a guinea, with which he purchased a new night-cap; but his first important fee was spent for a silver candlestick for his mother. He was afterwards offered employment at the Circuit Court at Jedburgh; but, as he wrote his friend Clerk, " durst not venture."

He still kept up his habit of making what he called "raids" into unexplored districts; and with his friend Robert Shortreid as guide, for seven successive years explored every nook and corner of Liddesdale, where, till Scott's appearance, a wheeled carriage had never been seen. To these rambles he owed much of the material collected in "The Minstrelsy of the Scottish Border."

Among the lawyers of the Outer House, many of whom afterwards attained distinction, but who were now light-hearted loungers of " the mountain," *Duns Scotus*, as they called Scott, was regarded as the prince of story-tellers. Nearly all of them united to form a class for the study of German; and to this circumstance may be traced Scott's first entrance upon the field of literature. He had already shown a natural facility for rhyming, and at the age of sixteen is said to have composed a poem in four books on the Conquest of Granada; but this was immediately burnt, and not a line is known to have survived, unless in one of the extemporized mottoes to the novels.

Bürger's " Lenore " first stimulated him to more serious verse. Having heard about the poem, which was brought to Edinburgh by Mrs. Barbauld in 1795, Scott obtained the original, and translated it at a sitting. His friend Miss Cranstoun, who was in the secret of his love for Miss Belches, had the ballad printed in " most elegant style," and sent a copy " richly bound and blazoned " to her at the country house where she and Scott were both visiting. The young lady had undoubtedly "high admiration of Scott's abilities," but not even this new proof of his talent won her love.

Mrs. Scott of Harden, who was of noble German birth, supplied him with many standard German books, and he translated a number of prose dramas and some of Goethe's lyrics.

The "Lenore" and "Wild Huntsman" were published in a thin quarto, without Scott's name, in 1796, the year of Burns's death, — and was welcomed as a remarkable production by many good critics, but proved pecuniarily a dead loss.

Meantime, his practice was slowly increasing, — in his first year he made a little more than twenty-four pounds, in his fifth he made £144 10s., — and his spare time was largely occupied by his efforts in the formation of a body of volunteer cavalry, in which he occupied at first the triple functions of paymaster, quartermaster, and secretary. He was the very life of the "Light Horse," and was familiarly known as *Earl Walter.*

During his summer vacation in 1797 he made a tour of the English lakes, where he afterwards laid the scene of "Triermain" and "St. Ronan's Well;" and here he met Miss Charlotte Margaret Carpenter, or Charpentier, a young lady of English origin, but born in France. Her guardian was the Marquess of Downshire, but the report that he was her father was disbelieved by Lockhart.

After a brief courtship, and some opposition on the part of Scott's family, he became engaged to her. He married her on the 24th of December, 1797. The following year their first-born son died the day after his birth, and Scott completed his translation of Goethe's "Goetz von Berlichingen," which, when published in February, 1799, brought him twenty-five guineas from a London bookseller. They hired a pretty cottage at Lasswade, which they occupied for several summers; and here amid the most romantic scenery of Scotland were thrown off those ballads which Scott called "his first serious attempts in verse." He was also occupied in making his collections for the subsequently published volumes of "The Scottish Minstrelsy of the Border."

One of the advantages of his residence at Lasswade was his acquaintance with the houses of Melville and Buccleuch; and when the office of sheriff-depute of Selkirkshire became vacant in 1799, Scott, through the Duke of Buccleuch, was appointed to this position. The duties were almost nominal, and the salary £300 a year. This, in addition to what he had received from his father's estate, his wife's income, and his own professional earnings, placed him on a secure footing, and gave him, at least during his vacations, time to cultivate literature.

Among Scott's schoolmates at Lancelot Whale's School in 1783, was James Ballantyne, who had now become a printer, and was publishing a weekly newspaper at Kelso. Scott then proposed to him to print off a dozen or so copies of his ballads. This was done, and the pamphlet containing "William and Ellen," "The Fire King," "The Chase," and a few others, was published under the title, "Apology for Tales of Terror." At the same time the scheme of a collection of Old Border Ballads was broached.

In April, 1800, he wrote to Ballantyne, asking him to Edinburgh, to engage in a general printing business, to include a newspaper, a monthly journal, an annual register, the execution of session papers, and, lastly, the publication of books.

It was two years, however, before Ballantyne emigrated; but in the meantime he had won golden opinions by the beautiful style in which he had brought out the first two volumes of "The Border Minstrelsy." Scott's share of the profits of these was £78 10s. He had already begun that pecuniary assistance to Ballantyne which, in 1805, resulted in a secret partnership, and his ultimate ruin. The third volume of the "Minstrelsy" was well received. The London publisher, Longman, issued one thousand copies of the first two, and fifteen hundred of the third. Scott's entire profits were £600.

His first contributions to the *Edinburgh Review* were printed in 1803, in which year he was mainly engaged in editing the ancient manuscript of "Sir Tristrem, by Thomas the Rhymer." This was published in May, 1804, in an edition of only one hundred and fifty copies, at the high price of two guineas each.

The same month he took a lease of the house and farm of Ashestiel, on the south bank of the Tweed, and about a month later his uncle, Captain Robert Scott, died, leaving him his beautiful little villa and thirty acres of land, besides £600 in cash. He sold Rosebank for £5,000, and was now assured of an annual income of £1,000, besides his practice at the Bar (which, for instance, in 1803 brought him over £228) and his literary profits.

He had been scarcely more than a week in possession of his beautiful new residence when he was called upon to try a poacher. The man's pitiful story and clever humor moved the sheriff; he not only let him off, but took him into his service as *grieve*, or bailiff. From that time forth Tom Purdie was his faithful henchman and trusted friend till he died. It was he who, when Scott received his baronetcy, proceeded to add an S to every sheep on the estate; and this mark, S. W. S., so delighted Scott, that he frequently used it as a signature.

The romantic and retired situation of Ashestiel offered Scott abundant inspiration and leisure for writing; and here he finished "The Lay of the Last Minstrel," begun some time before in an attempt to write a ballad to be called "The Goblin Page." It was published in January, 1805, seven hundred and fifty copies in quarto, at £1 5s. a copy. Nearly forty-four thousand copies were disposed of before he superintended the edition of 1830, not counting various pirated editions in America and elsewhere. Scott's profits on the first edition were £169 6s. The publishers, Longman & Co., of London, offered him £500 for the copyright, and afterwards added £100.

It was shortly after this that the poet, instead of buying the estate of Long-meadows, on the Yarrow, as he was tempted to do, invested all his capital in Ballantyne's concern, whereby he acquired a third interest.

The success of the "Lay" determined Scott to quit the Bar and devote himself to literature. His first great scheme was a complete edition of British poets, ancient and modern; but finding that Thomas Campbell was engaged upon a similar work, he took upon himself only the new edition and biography of Dryden. Thus he combined, to use Lockhart's words, "the conscientious magistrate, the martinet quartermaster, the speculative printer, and the ardent lover of literature for its own sake." He might have added also laird and forester and farmer.

This same year he began the story of Waverley, but laid it aside till a later day. In 1806 he was appointed clerk of sessions, in place of George Home, who had held the office for upwards of thirty years. By special arrangement, which Scott considered a hard bargain, he undertook the duties, but waived the salary during Home's life. The duties required his attendance at court from four to six hours a day five or six days a week during about six months in the year, and the salary was £1,300. This position Scott filled for twenty-five years, not slighting any of the "really base drudgery" of the work, or giving to its more exacting claims any but his best talents and skill.

During the whole of 1806 and 1807 he gave most of his spare moments to his editorial work on Dryden, but he was also enlisted in several contributions to the *Edinburgh Review*, and finished "Marmion." Constable offered one thousand guineas for it before he had seen a single line of it. It was published in February, 1808, in "a splendid quarto, price one guinea and a half," and the legitimate sale of the work in England alone reached fifty thousand copies by 1836.

"Marmion" was followed in April by the edition of Dryden on which Scott had been working so long. It was in eighteen volumes, and the editor's fee was £756. The work, in spite of many prognostications of failure, was a distinguished success.

Scott's industry at this period of his life was scarcely less remarkable than it was when he was struggling to pay off his debts. He edited Strutt's "Queenhoo Hall," adding the concluding chapters. The State papers of Ralph Sadler, which ultimately extended to thirteen ponderous quarto volumes, and were not completed till 1812; a new edition of "Captain Carleton's Memoirs;" a similar one of the "Memoirs of Robert Cary, Earl of Monmouth;" and a complete edition of the works of Swift, for which he was promised £1,500, were among his labors.

He afterwards confessed that this "tumult of engagements" was enough to tear him to pieces, but that he was saved by "the wonderful exhilaration about it all," which kept his blood at a fever-pitch, and made him feel as though he could grapple with anything and everything.

In a letter to his friend Morritt, he gives a lively picture of his occupations: —

"I have been Secretary to the Judicature Commission, which sat daily during all the Christmas Vacation. I have been editing Swift, and correcting the press at the rate of six sheets [90 pages] a week. I have been editing Somers at the rate of four ditto ditto; I have written reviews, I have written songs, I have made selections, I have superintended rehearsals, and all this independent of visiting and of my official duty . . . . and independent of a new poem with which I am threatening the world. This last employment is not the most prudent, but I really cannot well help myself. My office, though a very good one for Scotland, is only held in reversion; nor do I at present derive a shilling from it. I must expect that a fresh favorite of the public will supersede me, and my philosophy being very great on the point of poetical fame, I would fain, at the risk of hastening my own downfall, avail myself of the favorable moment, to make some further provision for my little people."

His "little people" were four in number: Charlotte Sophia, afterwards Mrs. Lockhart, born 1799; Walter, 1801; Anne, 1803; and Charles, 1805. Lockhart gives a delightful picture of Scott's treatment of his children. He himself confessed in his diary that he did not like babies, yet to use the words of his son-in-law : —

"No father ever devoted more time and tender care to his offspring, than he did to each of his, as they successively reached the age when they could listen to him and understand his talk. Like their mute playmates, Camp and the greyhounds, they had at all times free access to his study; he never considered their tattle as any disturbance; they went and came as pleased their fancy; he was always ready to answer their questions ; and when they, unconscious how he was engaged, entreated him to lay down his pen and tell them a story, he would take them on his knee, repeat a ballad or a legend, kiss them, and set them down again to their marbles or ninepins, and resume his labor, as if refreshed by the interruption."

His accomplishment of so much was due to his habit of early rising, and, as he expressed it, "breaking the neck of the day's work" before breakfast. This left him time for his visits and his visitors, for his various out-door avocations, and the manifold duties and pleasures that filled his day. Moreover he was able to compose while walking or riding.

In this incessant round of occupations the years passed rapidly. Unfortunately, his zeal was enlisted in furthering the interests of numberless mediocrities who appealed to him; and when, on account of political differences, he quarrelled with the shrewd and enterprising Constable, and entered with the Ballantyne brothers into a rival publishing business, he sowed the seeds of disaster. Lockhart says that, though they would have shed their heart's blood in his service, yet, as men of affairs, they deeply injured him, and he adds:—

"The day that brought John into pecuniary connection with him was the blackest in his calendar."

The two brothers whom Scott called respectively Aldiborontiphoscophornio and Rigdumfunnidos, entered rashly upon all sorts of engagements, and Scott the silent, secret partner, who furnished the most of the capital, was even more ready to suggest the publication of works which were foredoomed to failure.

The bond of copartnership dated from 1809, if not earlier, and in May of the following year, the "Lady of the Lake" was published also, in a majestic quarto at two guineas, and had a phenomenal success. Within a few months twenty thousand copies of different editions had been sold, and the legitimate sale by July, 1836, was reckoned as exceeding fifty thousand copies.

A curious effect followed the publication of this poem; attention was drawn to the beauties of the Scottish Lake region, and the cost of post-horse service rose in an extraordinary degree.

Scott himself increased his acquaintance with the Highlands during the summer of 1810. At first he had thought of going to the peninsula, where the British army then was, but an invitation from the Laird of Staffa changed his mind, and he betook himself to the Hebrides with his dog Wallace, his wife, his eldest daughter, and several friends. This locality he afterwards chose as the scene of his last important poem. On his return he resumed the composition of "Waverley;" but at the desire of Ballantyne it was laid aside once more. It is interesting to know that while the publishing affairs of Scott's firm were going from bad to worse, owing to his imprudent enterprises, he was tempted "to pitch the Court of Session and the booksellers to the Devil," and go out to India. Had Mr. Dundas (afterward Lord Melville), been appointed Governor-General of India, there is little doubt that he would have accepted a situation as Indian Secretary or Judge.

The year 1811 was distinguished by the publication of the "Vision of Don Roderick;" the proceeds of this he applied as his subscription for the relief of the Portuguese, who had suffered so bitterly in Massena's campaign. Far more important was his first purchase of land. He was about to come into a salary of £1300 as Clerk of Sessions, and his lease of Ashestiel had run out. He therefore bought for £4000 a little farm stretching half a mile along the "Tweed's Fair River." The land comprised the scene of the last clan Battle of the Borders,

> "Where gallant Cessford's life-blood dear
> Reeked on dark Elliot's border spear."

It consisted of a rich meadow or intervale, and a hundred acres of undulating land, "a bank and haugh as poor and bare as Sir John Falstaff's regiment," undrained and unplanted except with heath, while in front of the wretched little farm-house was a stagnant pond called Clarty Hole. He gives in his diary a comic picture of the hegira from Ashestiel to his new domain, a whole troupe carrying old swords, lances, targets, bows, a family of turkeys in a helmet, and dozens of peasant children bringing up the rear.

The whole region had originally belonged to the Abbey of Melrose, the ruins of which were visible from the hillocks near the house. He immediately christened the estate Abbotsford, and felt no little pride in being greeted as the *Laird!* He immediately began to plant trees, an occupation most fascinating to him. He also, like Gladstone, took pleasure in wielding the axe. His passion for acquiring land was ultimately gratified. His hundred acres grew into a domain of over a thousand, and the cottage which he planned became twelve years later a baronial castle. The estate was acquired by means of borrowed money, half of the amount being advanced on the security of the poem "Rokeby," which indeed was not written, but as yet only planned.

The following summer was among the busiest of Scott's life. As he wrote Mr.

Morritt, a dozen masons were hammering at his new house, and his "poor noddle" at the poem. Indeed, he was also at work at "Triermain," which he hoped to bring out anonymously at the same time as "Rokeby."

"Rokeby" was issued early in January, 1813. Nearly thirty-two hundred copies at two guineas were sold in two days, and ten thousand of the later editions in three months, but its popularity was much inferior to his two preceding poems. Two months later "Triermain" appeared, but its anonymity did not play the expected deception on Jeffrey, for whom the trap was chiefly laid; he had gone to America. The *Quarterly Review*, however, was completely deceived.

Amid dark anxieties, and most humiliating demands upon him by his partners for meeting notes and claims against the publishing-house, which seemed to be losing at the rate of £200 a month, and was indeed reported to be on the verge of bankruptcy, Scott received from the Prince Regent the offer of the Laureateship. This he declined.

In July, 1814, Scott's "Life and Works of Swift," in nineteen octavo volumes, were published in an edition of twelve hundred and fifty copies, which took just ten years to sell; and on the very day of their issue he finished "Waverley," having spent less than a month on the last two volumes. Constable, with whom, now that he and the Ballantynes had forsworn publishing, he was again on friendly terms, at first offered him £700 for the copyright, but afterwards decided on an equal division of profits.

"Waverley" was published anonymously, and was the first of that long series which procured for its author the title of "The Great Unknown," and "The Wizard of the North." Though thirty persons were in the secret, it was kept tolerably well, and not even the personal efforts of the Prince Regent induced Scott to drop the mask. The failure of the Ballantynes revealed the real state of things, and at a dinner of the Theatrical Fund in 1827 Scott made his memorable confession.

Without waiting to see how his anonymous venture should succeed, Scott almost immediately proceeded on what in his diary he calls a "voyage in the Lighthouse Yacht to Nova Zembla and the lord knows where." This voyage gave the finishing touches to "The Lord of the Isles," and furnished abundant material for the scenery of "The Pirate." On his return, early in September, he arranged with Constable for the publication of "The Lord of the Isles." He received fifteen hundred guineas for one half of the copyright. The death of the Duchess of Buccleuch, "a beautiful, affectionate, and generous friend," to whom he was sincerely attached, dashed his enthusiasm for this poem, which was accordingly finished rather as a task than as a labor of love, which it would otherwise have been. It was composed with the utmost speed — the last three cantos occupying less than a month. It was published on January 18, 1815; and only a month later came the second of the Waverley Novels, "Guy Mannering," which Scott said was "the work of six weeks at Christmas." And this in addition to a most voluminous correspondence and other literary work, besides his anxious superintendence of the affairs of the Ballantynes, whose erratic business manager was constantly keeping them on a dangerous lee-shore.

The sum received for "Guy Mannering" served for a time to keep the sinking ship from the reefs of disaster. The first edition of two thousand copies at a guinea each was sold in two days, and ten thousand were distributed before a collected edition of the novels was made.

With the publication of "The Lord of the Isles" Scott's poetical career practically ended; for "The Field of Waterloo" and the few lyrics which he wrote during a visit to the Continent in 1815, or "Harold the Dauntless," and the poems that occur in the novels are of small consequence compared with his previous masterpieces.   Scott wrote his friend Morritt in 1817, announcing "Harold the Daunt-less," and " a doggrel tale called the ' Search after Happiness ' ": —

" I begin to get too old and stupid, I think, for poetry, and will certainly never again adventure on a grand scale.

Indeed, Scott's gift as a poet lay in the province of improvisation, and had all the shortcomings, as well as the excellencies, characteristic of such verse.

Scott made one attempt to be promoted as Baron of Exchequer, but it fell through.   While it was still pending, he had a terrible attack of cramps in the stomach, which caused his friends much anxiety.   They were due to gallstones; and their effect was such that at the end of a year they left him looking twenty years older, with scanty hair pure white, and with the fire of his eyes dimmed. He came out of it; but, as he wrote one of his friends, he could for some time " neither stir for weakness and giddiness, nor read for dazzling in his eyes, nor listen for a whizzing sound in his ears, nor even think for lack of the power of arranging his ideas."

The attacks kept increasing in violence, and they were so agonizing that his screams were heard beyond the house.   Nevertheless, in their intervals he wrote " Rob Roy," [2] " Old Mortality," and in June, 1818, he finished "The Heart of Mid-Lothian," and began " The Bride of Lammermoor."   He was informed that his friend, the Prince Regent, was going to grant him a baronetcy; but just as he was about to start for London to receive it, a still worse attack of his disorder occurred, and he thought that he was dying.   He gave his children his parting blessing, and turned his face to the wall.   Instead of dying, he fell into a deep sleep, and when he woke the crisis had past.

The publication of " Ivanhoe " in December, 1819, marked the acme of Scott's popularity.   Twelve thousand copies at ten shillings were almost instantly sold. Unfortunately, his publishers refrained from telling him of the falling off in popu-larity of the succeeding novels.   And Scott, whose literary income had been for some time upwards of £10,000 a year, believing that the golden stream was in-exhaustible, entered deeper and deeper into the expenditures caused by the building of Abbotsford, and the constant acquisition of land at exorbitant prices.

During his visit to London, in 1820, Sir Thomas Lawrence painted his portrait for the King's Gallery, and Mr. Chantrey made the bust, which, according to Lock-hart, " alone preserves for posterity the cast of expression most fondly remembered by all who ever mingled in his domestic circle."

Scott was then gazetted as a baronet; and the king remarked to him at the levee, " I shall always reflect with pleasure on Sir Walter Scott's having been the first creation of my reign."

Scott, whose Tory proclivities were always shown, and who, in the reform meas-ures of a few years later, saw nothing but destruction, was naturally much pleased by this doubtful distinction.   The same year both the English universities conferred upon him the honorary degree of Doctor in Civil Law.

All the time that he was pouring out his romances at the rate of twelve volumes a year, his hospitality was burdened with an unending multitude of visitors who made his castle a hotel.   Lockhart says that the most princely nobleman of his age did not exceed him in the number of his distinguished visitors.

The next year John Ballantyne died, much to the regret of Scott, to whom he left two thousand pounds by will.   Unfortunately, instead of being possessed of

---

[2] He sent the final sheets with this doggrel rhyme : —

> "With great joy
>   I send you Roy.
> 'Twas a tough job,
>   But we're done with Rob."

property, the reckless fellow was deep in debt. Scott was still blinded to the real state of affairs. So assured was he of possessing unlimited means and unlimited resources, that he "exchanged instruments, and received his booksellers' bills for no less than four 'works of fiction,' not one of them otherwise described in the deeds of agreement, to be produced in unbroken succession."

Nor did his genius or fortune fail him. "The Fortunes of Nigel" were followed by "Peveril of the Peak," "Quentin Durward," "St. Ronan's Well," and "Red Gauntlet," and Abbotsford was complete!

He was happy in his family; his eldest son independent in fortune; his second talented and on the road to promotion in the army; his daughter married to Lockhart, who was a rising young man with fine prospects as editor of *Murray's Quarterly*. This was the grand climax!

In Dec. 18, 1825, occurs this entry in Scott's diary: —

"My extremity has come. Cadell has received letters from London which all but positively announce the failure of Hurst and Robinson, so that Constable and Co. must follow, and I must go with poor James Ballantyne for company. I suppose it will involve my all. But if they leave me £500, I can still make it £1000 or £1200 a year.

At the thought of his dogs and tenants and trees his heart was crushed within him. Lady Scott, pleasure-loving, easy-going, extravagant, was incredulous and critical. For a time it seemed as though the blow might be avoided, and possibly it might if Constable had hastened to London; but he delayed, and the crash came. The total liabilities of the three allied firms was about half a million pounds, of which Scott's share was £130,000. He wrote in his diary: —

"I have walked the last on the domains I have planted — sate the last time in the halls I have built. . . . I find my eyes moistening, and that will not do. I will not yield without a fight for it. . . . In prosperous times I have sometimes felt my fancy and powers of language flag, but adversity is to me, at least, a tonic and bracer; the fountain is awakened from its inmost recesses, as if the spirit of affliction had troubled it in his passage."

As soon as his misfortune was known, friends and strangers sprang with one impulse to his aid. One anonymous correspondent was anxious to send him £30,000, and he was greatly touched by the offer of his daughter's harp-teacher to contribute £500 or £600, "probably his all."

A woman of rank offered to marry him, and some "unutterable idiot of a privy counsellor" tried to bring about a match with a dowager duchess.

But Scott declined all aid. He buckled down to the colossal work of paying this indebtedness by his own exertions. His creditors, with the exception of one grasping Jew, who demanded his pound of flesh, were willing to grant him every facility.

He had once written, "I cannot pull well when the draught is too far behind me. I love to have the press thumping, clattering, banging in my rear; it creates the necessity which almost always makes me work best." And to his factor, Laidlaw, he wrote, "For myself I feel like the Eildon Hills — quite firm, though a little cloudy. . . . I do not dislike the path that lies before me. I have seen all that society can show, and enjoyed all that wealth can give me, and I am satisfied much is vanity, if not vexation of spirit."

Also in his diary he made the best of the matter, "I think, now the shock of the discovery is past and over, I am much better off on the whole; I am as if I had shaken off from my shoulders a great mass of garments, rich indeed, but cumbrous, and always more a burden than a comfort."

By "Woodstock," the fruit of less than three months later, he won what he calls "the matchless sum" of £8,228.

Amid these terrible labors other misfortunes came upon him; ill-health and failure of eyesight, the fatal illness of his grandson, Johnnie Lockhart, for whom he felt a peculiar tenderness, as the little fellow had a lameness similar to his own; it was for him that he wrote the "Tales of a Grandfather." Lady Scott also fell into ill-health and died while her husband was in Edinburgh. He entered into his diary his conviction that she was still "sentient and conscious of his emotions — somewhere — somehow — where we cannot tell, how we cannot tell" — and he spoke with warmth of "the mysterious yet certain hope that he should see her in a better world."

"Grief," he wrote, "makes me a housekeeper, and to labor is my only resource." Yet he had written a year or two earlier in his diary that "never did a being hate task work as he had hated it from his infancy up." "It is not that I am idle in my nature either. But propose to me to do one thing, and it is inconceivable the desire I have to do something else — not that it is more easy or more pleasant, but just because it is escaping from an imposed task."

The Bank of Scotland threatened to push him, and then for the first time he turned and declared that if they used the sword of the Law, he would grasp the shield. He rightly felt that he ought to be left free to write under fitting conditions.

During the two years preceding January, 1828, he earned by his pen nearly £40,000!

How pathetic is this entry in his diary: —

"What a life mine has been ! — half-educated, almost wholly neglected or left to myself, stuffing my head with most nonsensical trash, and undervalued in society for a time by most of my companions, getting forward and held a bold and clever fellow contrary to the opinion of all who thought me a mere dreamer, broken-hearted for two years, my heart handsomely pieced again, but the crack will remain till my dying day. Rich and poor four or five times, once on the verge of ruin, yet opened new sources of wealth almost overflowing. Now taken in my pitch of pride and nearly winged."

The gallant struggle which he made is almost unique in the history of literature. It became a passion with him to be at his desk "feaguing it away," to use his own expression. But like Carlyle, he had little respect for that "dear *publicum*" whom he was doomed to amuse.

When the debt was reduced to £60,000, the creditors signified their sense of his labors by surrendering his books, furniture, plate, and curiosities. Some of his friends thought it was not very handsomely done, but Scott was extremely gratified.

In five years his debt was reduced to £54,000, and if he had lived till 1833 it would have been entirely cleared. But his health was yielding under the strain. In November, 1830, he resigned from the Court of Sessions on a pension of £840. The following May he often wished he might lie down and sleep without waking. His bodily strength was greatly weakened; fear that his mental faculties were failing haunted him. To linger on like Swift, "a driveller and a show," seemed a terrible fate.

It had been decided that he should try the effect of a winter in Italy; and in September, just before he started, "the old splendor of Abbotsford" was revived for the last time. Captain Glencairn Burns, the son of the poet, came to see him. The neighbors were assembled, and Sir Walter did the honors of the table. Two days later Wordsworth came to bid him farewell. On the 29th of October he sailed for Malta on a government frigate. He was conscious that his days were numbered; he wrote in his diary, "I am perhaps setting."

At Malta he made a round of visits with old friends, and was greatly gratified at a grand ball given in his honor. Four hundred gentlemen, mostly English officers, were present.

At Naples his son Charles was awaiting him; and there was a fine eruption of Vesuvius, which Scott thought, if it portended his death, did him too much honor. He went to the Palazzo on the king's birthday dressed like a brigadier-general of Archers' Guards; he wore " a decent green uniform, laced at the cuffs," and was " sworded and feathered."

Here he refused to listen to the remonstrances of his friends and the warning of his physicians, but began a new novel, and planned to close the series of Waverley with a poem in the style of "the Lay" or "the Lady of the Lake:" the subject, a curious tale of chivalry belonging to Rhodes. In order to carry out this dream, Sir Frederick Adams offered him a steamboat that should carry him to Greece. But this plan was abandoned.

Accordingly Sir Walter bought a small closing carriage, and on the 16th of April started for Rome.

He grew more and more impatient to get home. He had looked forward to meeting Goethe in Germany. This hope also was disappointed. " He at least died at home," he said — " let us to Abbotsford."

He seemed to enjoy the steamboat trip down the Rhine; but on the 9th of June he was attacked by apoplexy, combined with paralysis. He was brought to London a week later, and it was not until the middle of July that he was allowed to return to Abbotsford, which he so longed to see.

He lingered until the 21st of September, when he peacefully died in the presence of all his children.

His two sons died childless. Lockhart's daughter Charlotte married James Hope, whose daughter, Mary Monica, became the wife of the Honorable Joseph Maxwell, the present possessor of Abbotsford. They have six children.

Lockhart's biography of Scott is justly regarded as a model of fairness and ability. It has been since supplemented by the publication of Scott's letters, and of the diary from which Lockhart made limited extracts. The result is that Scott's life lies before us with the utmost distinctness: his generosity, his modesty, his lofty principle and piety, modified, as in the case of all human beings, by his individuality, his toryism, his outspoken frankness, his occasional narrowness. He had his faults, but few men could better afford to allow the world to balance them with his noble qualities.

We have the vividest pen-pictures of Scott's daily life; we know his methods of composition, his disposition of time, his ideas of hospitality.

Few men were ever more honored. In 1827 he was appointed Professor of Antiquities at the Royal Academy, and, writing of his honorary titles, he remarked jocosely : —

" What a tail of the alphabet I should draw after me were I to sign with the indications of the different societies I belong to, beginning with President of the Royal Society of Edinburgh and ending with umpire of the Six-foot-high Club ! "

There oftentimes arises discussion as to the immortality of Scott; but while we may readily acknowledge his faults as a man, as a novelist, and as a poet, still we may be justified in asserting that it will be a sad day, should it ever come, when the young do not feel their hearts glow with enthusiasm alike for Scott's honorable life and for his varied and splendid works.

NATHAN HASKELL DOLE.

CONTENTS.

CONTENTS. xxvii

THE
LAY OF THE LAST MINSTREL:

A POEM IN SIX CANTOS.

*Dum relego, scripsisse pudet ; quia plurima cerno,
Me quoque, qui feci, judice, digna lini.*

TO THE RIGHT HONORABLE

CHARLES, EARL OF DALKEITH,

THIS POEM IS INSCRIBED BY

THE AUTHOR.

PREFACE TO THE FIRST EDITION.

The Poem, now offered to the Public, is intended to illustrate the customs and manners which anciently prevailed on the Borders of England and Scotland. The inhabitants living in a state partly pastoral and partly warlike, and combining habits of constant depredation with the influence of a rude spirit of chivalry, were often engaged in scenes highly susceptible of poetical ornament. As the description of scenery and manners was more the object of the Author than a combined and regular narrative, the plan of the ancient Metrical Romance was adopted, which allows greater latitude, in this respect, than would be consistent with the dignity of a regular Poem. The same model offered other facilities, as it permits an occasional alteration of measure, which, in some degree, authorizes the change of rhythm in the text. The machinery, also adopted from popular belief, would have seemed puerile in a Poem which did not partake of the rudeness of the old Ballad, or Metrical Romance.

For these reasons, the Poem was put into the mouth of an ancient Minstrel, the last of the race, who, as he is supposed to have survived the Revolution, might have caught somewhat of the refinement of modern poetry, without losing the simplicity of his original model. The date of the Tale itself is about the middle of the sixteenth century, when most of the personages actually flourished. The time occupied by the action is Three Nights and Three Days.

INTRODUCTION TO EDITION 1830.

A POEM of nearly thirty years' standing may be supposed hardly to need an Introduction, since, without one, it has been able to keep itself afloat through the best part of a generation. Nevertheless, as, in the edition of the Waverley Novels now in course of publication [1830], I have imposed on myself the task of saying something concerning the purpose and history of each, in their turn, I am desirous that the Poems for which I first received some marks of the public favor, should also be accompanied with such scraps of their literary history as may be supposed to carry interest along with them. Even if I should be mistaken in thinking that the secret history of what was once so popular, may still attract public attention and curiosity, it seems to me not without its use to record the manner and circumstances under which the present, and other Poems on the same plan, attained for a season an extensive reputation.

I must resume the story of my literary labors at the period at which I broke off in the Essay on the Imitation of Popular Poetry, when I had enjoyed the first gleam of public favor, by the success of the first edition of the Minstrelsy of the Scottish Border. The second edition of that work, published in 1803, proved, in the language of the trade, rather a heavy concern. The demand in Scotland had been supplied by the first edition, and the curiosity of the English was not much awakened by poems in the rude garb of antiquity, accompanied with notes referring to the obscure feuds of barbarous clans, of whose very names civilized history was ignorant. It was, on the whole, one of those books which are more praised than they are read.

At this time I stood personally in a different position from that which I occupied when I first dipt my desperate pen in ink for other purposes than those of my profession. In 1796, when I first published the Translations from Bürger, I was an insulated individual, with only my own wants to provide for, and having, in a great measure, my own inclinations alone to consult. In 1803, when the second edition of the Minstrelsy appeared, I had arrived at a period of life when men, however thoughtless, encounter duties and circumstances which press consideration and plans of life upon the most careless minds. I had been for some time married — was the father of a rising family — and, though fully enabled to meet the consequent demands upon me, it was my duty and desire to place myself in a situation which would enable me to make honorable provision against the various contingencies of life.

It may be readily supposed that the attempts which I had made in literature had been unfavorable to my success at the Bar. The goddess Themis is at Edinburgh, and I suppose every where else, of a peculiarly jealous disposition. She will not readily consent to share her authority, and sternly demands from her votaries, not only that real duty be carefully attended to and discharged, but that a certain air of business shall be observed even in the midst of total idleness. It is prudent, if not absolutely necessary, in a young barrister, to appear completely engrossed by his profession ; however destitute of employment he may in reality be, he ought to preserve, if possible, the appearance of full occupation. He should, therefore, seem perpetually engaged among his law papers, dusting them, as it were ; and, as Ovid advises the fair,

" Si nullus erit pulvis, tamen excute nullum." [1]

Perhaps such extremity of attention is more especially required, considering the great number of counsellors who are called to the Bar, and how very small a proportion of them are finally disposed, or find encouragement, to follow the law as a profession. Hence the number of deserters is so great, that the least lingering look behind occasions a young novice to be set down as one of the intending fugitives. Certain it is, that the Scottish Themis was at this time peculiarly jealous of any flirtation with the Muses, on the part of those who had ranged themselves under her banners. This was probably owing to her consciousness of the superior attractions of her rivals. Of late, however, she has relaxed in some instances in this particular — an eminent example of which has been shown in the case of my friend, Mr. Jeffrey, who, after long conducting one of the most influential literary periodicals of the age with unquestionable ability, has been, by the general consent of his

---

[1] " If dust be none, yet brush that none away."

brethren, recently elected to be their Dean of Faculty, or President — being the highest acknowledgment of his professional talents which they had it in their power to offer. But this is an incident much beyond the ideas of a period of thirty years' distance, when a barrister who really possessed any turn for lighter literature, was at as much pains to conceal it as if it had in reality been something to be ashamed of; and I could mention more than one instance in which literature and society have suffered much loss, that jurisprudence might be enriched.

Such, however, was not my case; for the reader will not wonder that my open interference with matters of light literature diminished my employment in the weightier matters of the law. Nor did the solicitors, upon whose choice the counsel takes rank in his profession, do me less than justice, by regarding others among my contemporaries as fitter to discharge the duty due to their clients, than a young man who was taken up with running after ballads, whether Teutonic or National. My profession and I, therefore, came to stand nearly upon the footing which honest Slender consoled himself on having established with Mistress Anne Page: "There was no great love between us at the beginning, and it pleased Heaven to decrease it on farther acquaintance." I became sensible that the time was come when I must either buckle myself resolutely to the "toil by day, the lamp by night," renouncing all the Delilahs of my imagination, or bid adieu to the profession of the law, and hold another course.

I confess my own inclination revolted from the more severe choice, which might have been deemed by many the wiser alternative. As my transgressions had been numerous, my repentance must have been signalized by unusual sacrifices. I ought to have mentioned, that since my fourteenth or fifteenth year, my health, originally delicate, had become extremely robust. From infancy I had labored under the infirmity of a severe lameness, but, as I believe is usually the case with men of spirit who suffer under personal inconveniences of this nature, I had, since the improvement of my health, in defiance of this incapacitating circumstance distinguished myself by the endurance of toil on foot or horseback, having often walked thirty miles a day, and rode upwards of a hundred, without resting. In this manner I made many pleasant journeys through parts of the country then not very accessible, gaining more amusement and instruction than I have been able to acquire since I have travelled in a more commodious manner. I practised most sylvan sports also, with some success, and with great delight. But these pleasures must have been all resigned, or used with great moderation, had I determined to regain my station at the Bar. It was even doubtful whether I could, with perfect character as a jurisconsult, retain a situation in a volunteer corps of cavalry, which I then held. The threats of invasion were at this time instant and menacing; the call by Britain on her children was universal, and was answered by some, who, like myself, consulted rather their desire than their ability to bear arms. My services, however, were found useful in assisting to maintain the discipline of the corps, being the point on which their constitution rendered them most amenable to military criticism. In other respects, the squadron was a fine one, consisting chiefly of handsome men, well mounted and armed at their own expense. My attention to the corps took up a good deal of time; and while it occupied many of the happiest hours of my life, it furnished an additional reason for my reluctance again to encounter the severe course of study indispensable to success in the juridical profession.

On the other hand, my father, whose feelings might have been hurt by my quitting the Bar, had been for two or three years dead, so that I had no control to thwart my own inclination; and my income being equal to all the comforts, and some of the elegancies, of life, I was not pressed to an irksome labor by necessity, that most powerful of motives; consequently, I was the more easily seduced to choose the employment which was most agreeable to me. This was yet the easier, that in 1800 I had obtained the preferment of Sheriff of Selkirkshire, about £300 a year in value, and which was the more agreeable to me, as in that country, I had several friends and relations. But I did not abandon the profession to which I had been educated without certain prudential resolutions, which, at the risk of some egotism, I will here mention; not without the hope that they may be useful to young persons who may stand in circumstances similar to those in which I then stood.

In the first place, upon considering the lives and fortunes of persons who had given themselves up to literature, or to the task of pleasing the public, it seemed to me, that the circumstances which chiefly affected their happiness and character, were those from which Horace has bestowed upon authors the epithet of the Irritable Race. It requires no depth of philosophic reflection to perceive, that the petty warfare of Pope with the Dunces of his period could not have been carried on without his suffering the most acute torture, such as a man must endure from mosquitoes, by whose stings he suffers agony, although he can crush them in his grasp by myriads. Nor is it necessary to call to memory the many humiliating instances in which men of the greatest genius have, to avenge some pitiful quarrel, made themselves ridiculous during their lives, to become the still more degraded objects of pity to future times.

Upon the whole, as I had no pretension to the genius of the distinguished persons who had fallen into such errors, I concluded there could be no occasion for imitating them in their mistakes, or what I considered as such; and, in adopting literary pursuits as the principal occupation of my future life, I resolved, if possible, to avoid those weaknesses of temper which seemed to have most easily beset my more celebrated predecessors.

With this view, it was my first resolution to keep as far as was in my power abreast of society, continuing to maintain my place in general company, without yielding to the very natural temptation of narrowing myself to what is called literary society. By doing so, I imagined I should escape the besetting sin of listening to language, which, from one motive or other, is apt to ascribe a very undue degree of consequence to literary pursuits, as if they were, indeed, the business, rather than the amusement, of life. The opposite course can only be compared to the injudicious conduct of one who pampers himself with cordial and luscious draughts, until he is unable to endure wholesome bitters. Like Gil Blas, therefore, I resolved to stick by the society of my *commis*, instead of seeking that of a more literary cast, and to maintain my general interest in what was going on around me, reserving the man of letters for the desk and the library.

My second resolution was a corollary from the first. I determined that, without shutting my ears to the voice of true criticism, I would pay no regard to that which assumes the form of satire. I therefore resolved to arm myself with that triple brass of Horace, of which those of my profession are seldom held deficient, against all the roving warfare of satire, parody, and sarcasm; to laugh if the jest was a good one, or, if otherwise, to let it hum and buzz itself to sleep.

It is to the observance of these rules (according to my best belief) that, after a life of thirty years engaged in literary labors of various kinds, I attribute my never having been entangled in any literary quarrel or controversy; and, which is a still more pleasing result, that I have been distinguished by the personal friendship of my most approved contemporaries of all parties.

I adopted at the same time another resolution, on which it may doubtless be remarked, that it was well for me that I had it·in my power to do so, and that, therefore, it is a line of conduct which, depending upon accident, can be less generally applicable in other cases. Yet I fail not to record this part of my plan, convinced that, though it may not be in every one's power to adopt exactly the same resolution, he may nevertheless, by his own exertions, in some shape or other, attain the object on which it was founded, namely, to secure the means of subsistence without relying exclusively on literary talents. In this respect I determined that literature should be my staff, but not my crutch, and that the profits of my literary labor, however convenient otherwise, should not, if I could help it, become necessary to my ordinary expenses. With this purpose I resolved, if the interest of my friends could so far favor me, to retire upon any of the respectable offices of the law, in which persons of that profession are glad to take refuge when they feel themselves, or are judged by others, incompetent to aspire to its higher honors. Upon such a post an author might hope to retreat, without any perceptible alteration of circumstances, whenever the time should arrive that the public grew weary of his endeavors to please, or he himself should tire of the pen. At this period of my life, I possessed so many friends capable of assisting me in this object of ambition, that I could hardly overrate my own prospects of obtaining the preferment to which I limited my wishes; and, in fact, I obtained in no long period the reversion of a situation which completely met them.

Thus far all was well, and the author had been guilty, perhaps, of no great imprudence when he relinquished his forensic practice with the hope of making some figure in the field of literature. But an established character with the public, in my new capacity, still remained to be acquired. I have noticed that the translations from Bürger had been unsuccessful, nor had the original poetry which appeared under the auspices of Mr. Lewis, in the "Tales of Wonder," in any great degree raised my reputation. It is true, I had private friends disposed to second me in my efforts to obtain popularity. But I was sportsman enough to know, that if the greyhound does not run well, the halloos of his patrons will obtain nothing for him.

Neither was I ignorant that the practice of ballad-writing was for the present out of fashion, and that any attempt to revive it, or to found a poetical character upon it, would certainly fail of success. The ballad measure itself, which was once listened to as to an enchanting melody, had become hackneyed and sickening, from its being the accompaniment of every grinding hand-organ; and besides, a long work in quatrains, whether those of the common ballad, or such as are termed elegiac, has an effect upon the mind like that of the bed of Procrustes upon the human body; for, as it must be both awkward and difficult to carry on a long sentence from one stanza to another, it follows that the meaning of each period must be comprehended within four lines, and equally so that it must be extended so as to fill that space. The alternate dilation and contraction thus rendered necessary is singularly unfavorable to narrative composition; and the "Gondibert" of Sir William D'Avenant, though containing many striking passages, has never become popular owing chiefly to its being told in this species of elegiac verse.

In the dilemma occasioned by this objection, the idea occurred to the author of using the measured short line, which forms the structure of so much minstrel poetry, that it may be properly termed the Romantic stanza by way of distinction, and which appears so natural to our language, that the very best of our poets have not been able to protract it into the verse properly called Heroic, without the use of epithets which are, to say the least, unnecessary. But, on the other hand, the extreme facility of the short couplet, which seems congenial to our language, and was, doubtless, for that reason so popular with our old minstrels, is, for the same reason, apt to prove a snare to the composer who uses it in more modern days, by encouraging him in a habit of slovenly composition. The necessity of occasional pauses often forces the young poet to pay more attention to sense, as the boy's kite rises highest when the train is loaded by a due counterpoise. The author was, therefore, intimidated by what Byron calls the "fatal facility" of the octo-syllabic verse, which was otherwise better adapted to his purpose of imitating the more ancient poetry.

I was not less at a loss for a subject which might admit of being treated with the simplicity and wildness of the ancient ballad. But accident dictated both a theme and measure, which decided the subject, as well as the structure of the poem.

The lovely young Countess of Dalkeith, afterwards Harriet, Duchess of Buccleuch, had come to the land of her husband with the desire of making herself acquainted with its traditions and customs, as well as its manners and history. All who remember this lady will agree that the intellectual character of her extreme beauty, the amenity and courtesy of her manners, the soundness of her understanding, and her unbounded benevolence, gave more the idea of an angelic visitant than of a being belonging to this nether world; and such a thought was but too consistent with the short space she was permitted to tarry among us. Of course, where all made it a pride and pleasure to gratify her wishes, she soon heard enough of Border lore; among others, an aged gentleman of property,[1] near Langholm, communicated to her ladyship the story of Gilpin Horner, a tradition in which the narrator, and many more of that country, were firm believers. The young Countess, much delighted with the legend, and the gravity and full confidence with which it was told, enjoined on me as a task to compose a ballad on the subject. Of course, to hear was to obey; and thus the goblin story, objected to by several critics as an excrescence upon the poem, was, in fact, the occasion of its being written.

A chance similar to that which dictated the subject, gave me also the hint of a new mode of treating it. We had at that time the lease of a pleasant cottage, near Lasswade, on the romantic banks of the Esk, to which we escaped when the vacations of the Court permitted me so much leisure. Here I had the pleasure to receive a visit from Mr. Stoddart (now Sir John Stoddart, Judge-Advocate at Malta), who was at that time collecting the particulars which he afterwards embodied in his Remarks on Local Scenery in Scot-

---

[1] This was Mr. Beattie of Mickledale, a man then considerably upwards of eighty, of a shrewd and sarcastic temper, which he did not at all times suppress, as the following anecdote will show: A worthy clergyman, now deceased, with better good-will than tact, was endeavoring to push the senior forward in his recollection of Border ballads and legends, by expressing reiterated surprise at his wonderful memory. "No, sir," said old Mickledale; "my memory is good for little, for it cannot retain what ought to be preserved. I can remember all these stories about the auld riding days, which are of no earthly importance; but were you, reverend sir, to repeat your best sermon in this drawing-room, I could not tell you half an hour afterwards what you had been speaking about."

land. I was of some use to him in procuring the information which he desired, and guiding him to the scenes which he wished to see. In return, he made me better acquainted than I had hitherto been with the poetic effusions which have since made the lakes of Westmoreland, and the authors by whom they have been sung, so famous wherever the English tongue is spoken.

I was already acquainted with the "Joan of Arc," the " Thalaba," and the "Metrical Ballads" of Mr. Southey, which had found their way to Scotland, and were generally admired. But Mr. Stoddart, who had the advantage of personal friendship with the authors, and who possessed a strong memory, with an excellent taste, was able to repeat to me many long specimens of their poetry, which had not yet appeared in print. Amongst others, was the striking fragment called "Christabel," by Mr. Coleridge, which, from the singularly irregular structure of the stanzas, and the liberty which it allowed the author to adapt the sound to the sense, seemed to be exactly suited to such an extravaganza as I meditated on the subject of Gilpin Horner. As applied to comic and humorous poetry, this mescolanza of measures had been already used by Anthony Hall, Anstey, Dr. Wolcott, and others; but it was in "Christabel" that I first found it used in serious poetry, and it is to Mr. Coleridge that I am bound to make the acknowledgment due from the pupil to his master. I observe that Lord Byron, in noticing my obligations to Mr. Coleridge, which I have been always most ready to acknowledge, expressed, or was understood to express, a hope that I did not write an unfriendly review on Mr. Coleridge's productions. On this subject I have only to say, that I do not even know the review which is alluded to; and were I ever to take the unbecoming freedom of censuring a man of Mr. Coleridge's extraordinary talents, it would be on account of the caprice and indolence with which he has thrown from him, as if in mere wantonness, those unfinished scraps of poetry, which, like the Torso of antiquity, defy the skill of his poetical brethren to complete them. The charming fragments which the author abandons to their fate are surely too valuable to be treated like the proofs of careless engravers, the sweepings of whose studios often make the fortune of some painstaking collector.

I did not immediately proceed upon my projected labor, though I was now furnished with a subject, and with a structure of verse which might have the effect of novelty to the public ear, and afford the author an opportunity of varying his measure with the variations of a romantic theme. On the contrary, it was, to the best of my recollection, more than a year after Mr. Stoddart's visit, that, by way of experiment, I composed the first two or three stanzas of "The Lay of the Last Minstrel." I was shortly afterwards visited by two intimate friends, one of whom still survives. They were men whose talents might have raised them to the highest station in literature, had they not preferred exerting them in their own profession of the law, in which they attained equal preferment. I was in the habit of consulting them on my attempts at composition, having equal confidence in their sound taste and friendly sincerity.[1] In this specimen I had, in the phrase of the Highland servant, packed all that was my own *at least*, for I had also included a line of invocation, a little softened, from Coleridge —

> "Mary, mother, shield us well."

As neither of my friends said much to me on the subject of the stanzas I showed them before their departure, I had no doubt that their disgust had been greater than their good nature chose to express. Looking upon them, therefore, as a failure, I threw the manuscript into the fire, and thought as little more as I could of the matter. Some time afterwards I met one of my two counsellors, who inquired, with considerable appearance of interest, about the progress of the romance I had commenced, and was greatly surprised at learning its fate. He confessed that neither he nor our mutual friend had been at first able to give a precise opinion on a poem so much out of the common road; but that as they walked home together to the city, they had talked much on the subject, and the result was an earnest desire that I would proceed with the composition. He also added, that some sort of prologue might be necessary, to place the mind of the hearers in the situation

---

[1] One of these, William Erskine, Esq. (Lord Kinnedder), I have often had occasion to mention and though I may hardly be thanked for disclosing the name of the other, yet I cannot but state that the second is George Cranstoun, Esq., now a Senator of the College of Justice, by the title of Lord Corehouse. 1831.

'o understand and enjoy the poem, and recommended the adoption of such quaint mottoes as Spenser has used to announce the contents of the chapters of the Faery Queen, such as —

> " Babe's bloody hands may not be cleansed.
> The face of golden Mean :
> Her sisters two, Extremities,
> Strive her to banish clean."

I entirely agreed with my friendly critic in the necessity of having some sort of pitch-pipe which might make readers aware of the object, or rather the tone, of the publication. But I doubted whether, in assuming the oracular style of Spenser's mottoes, the interpreter might not be censured as the harder to be understood of the two. I therefore introduced the Old Minstrel, as an appropriate prolocutor, by whom the Lay might be sung or spoken, and the introduction of whom betwixt the cantos might remind the reader, at intervals, of the time, place, and circumstances of the recitation. This species of *cadre* or frame, afterwards afforded the poem its name of " The Lay of the Last Minstrel."

The work was subsequently shown to other friends during its progress, and received the *imprimatur* of Mr. Francis Jeffrey, who had been already for some time distinguished by his critical talent.

The poem, being once licensed by the critics as fit for the market, was soon finished, proceeding at about the rate of a canto per week. There was, indeed, little occasion for pause or hesitation, when a troublesome rhyme might be accommodated by an alteration of the stanza, or where an incorrect measure might be remedied by a variation of the rhyme. It was finally published in 1805, and may be regarded as the first work in which the writer, who has been since so voluminous, laid his claim to be considered as an original author.

The book was published by Longman and Company, and Archibald Constable and Company. The principal of the latter firm was then commencing that course of bold and liberal industry which was of so much advantage to his country, and might have been so to himself, but for causes which it is needless to enter into here. The work, brought out on the usual terms of division of profits between the author and publishers, was not long after purchased by them for £500, to which Messrs. Longman and Company afterwards added £100, in their own unsolicited kindness, in consequence of the uncommon success of the work. It was handsomely given to supply the loss of a fine horse, which broke down suddenly while the author was riding with one of the worthy publishers.

It would be great affectation not to own frankly, that the author expected some success from " The Lay of the last Minstrel." The attempt to return to a more simple and natural style of poetry was likely to be welcomed at a time when the public had become tired of heroic hexameters, with all the buckram and binding which belong to them of later days. But whatever might have been his expectations, whether moderate or unreasonable, the result left them far behind, for among those who smiled on the adventurous Minstrel were numbered the great names of William Pitt and Charles Fox. Neither was the extent of the sale inferior to the character of the judges who received the poem with approbation. Upwards of thirty thousand copies of the Lay were disposed of by the trade ; and the author had to perfom a task difficult to human vanity, when called upon to make the necessary deductions from his own merits, in a calm attempt to account for his popularity.

A few additional remarks on the author's literary attempts after this period will be found in the introduction to the Poem of Marmion.

ABBOTSFORD, *April*, 1830.

THE LAY OF THE LAST MINSTREL

INTRODUCTION.

THE way was long, the wind was cold,
The Minstrel was infirm and old;
His withered cheek, and tresses gray,
Seem'd to have known a better day;
The harp, his sole remaining joy,
Was carried by an orphan boy.
The last of all the Bards was he,
Who sung of Border chivalry;
For, welladay! their date was fled,
His tuneful brethren all were dead;
And he, neglected and oppress'd,
Wish'd to be with them, and at rest.
No more on prancing palfrey borne,
He caroll'd, light as lark at morn;
No longer courted and caress'd,
High placed in hall, a welcome guest,
He pour'd, to lord and lady gay,
The unpremeditated lay:
Old times were changed, old manners gone;
A stranger filled the Stuarts' throne;
The bigots of the iron time
Had call'd his harmless art a crime.
A wandering Harper, scorn'd and poor,
He begg'd his bread from door to door.
And tuned, to please a peasant's ear,
The harp a king had loved to hear.

He pass'd where Newark's * stately tower
Looks out from Yarrow's birchen bower:
The Minstrel gazed with wishful eye —
No humbler resting-place was nigh,
With hesitating step at last,
The embattled portal arch he pass'd,

Whose ponderous grate and massy bar
Had oft roll'd back the tide of war,
But never closed the iron door
Against the desolate and poor.
The Duchess † mark'd his weary pace,
His timid mien, and reverend face,
And bade her page the menials tell,
That they should tend the old man well:
For she had known adversity,
Though born in such a high degree;
In pride of power, in beauty's bloom,
Had wept o'er Monmouth's bloody tomb!

When kindness had his wants supplied,
And the old man was gratified,
Began to rise his minstrel pride:
And he began to talk anon,
Of good Earl Francis,‡ dead and gone,
And of Earl Walter,§ rest him, God!
A braver ne'er to battle rode;
And how full many a tale he knew,
Of the old warriors of Buccleuch:
And, would the noble Duchess deign
To listen to an old man's strain,
Though stiff his hand, his voice though weak,
He thought even yet, the sooth to speak,
That, if she loved the harp to hear,
He could make music to her ear.

The humble boon was soon obtain'd;
The aged Minstrel audience gain'd.

---

* Newark's stately tower.   A large square tower now in ruins; situated three miles from Selkirk, on the right bank of the Yarrow.

† The Duchess.   Anne, the heiress of Buccleuch, who had been married to the unhappy Duke of Monmouth, son of Charles II.   He was beheaded for rebellion against James II., 1685.

‡ Earl Francis.   The Duchess's late father.

§ Walter, Earl of Buccleuch, grandfather of the Duchess, and a celebrated warrior.

But, when he reach'd the room of state,
Where she, with all her ladies, sate,
Perchance he wished his boon denied:
For, when to tune his harp he tried,
His trembling hand had lost the ease,
Which marks security to please;
And scenes, long past, of joy and pain,
Came wildering o'er his aged brain —
He tried to tune his harp in vain!
The pitying Duchess praised its chime,
And gave him heart, and gave him time,
Till every string's according glee
Was blended into harmony.
And then, he said, he would full fain
He could recall an ancient strain,
He never thought to sing again.
It was not framed for village churls,
But for high dames and mighty earls;
He had play'd it to King Charles the Good,
When he kept court in Holyrood;
And much he wish'd, yet fear'd to try
The long-forgotten melody.
Amid the strings his fingers stray'd,
And an uncertain warbling made,
And oft he shook his hoary head.
But when he caught the measure wild,
The old man raised his face, and smiled;
And lighten'd up his faded eye,
With all a poet's ecstasy!
In varying cadence, soft or strong,
He swept the sounding chords along;
The present scene, the future lot,
His toils, his wants, were all forgot:
Cold diffidence, and age's frost,
In the full tide of song were lost;
Each blank in faithless memory void,
The poet's glowing thought supplied;
And, while his harp responsive rung,
'Twas thus the LATEST MINSTREL sung.

CANTO FIRST.

I.

THE feast was over in Branksome tower,[1]
And the Ladye had gone to her secret
      bower;
Her bower that was guarded by word and
      by spell,
Deadly to hear, and deadly to tell —
Jesu Maria, shield us well!

No living wight, save the Ladye alone,
Had dared to cross the threshold stone.

II.

The tables were drawn, it was idlesse all;
   Knight, and page, and household squire,
Loiter'd through the lofty hall,
   Or crowded round the ample fire:
The staghounds, weary with the chase,
   Lay stretch'd upon the rushy floor,
And urged, in dreams, the forest race,
   From Teviot-stone to Eskdale-moor.

III.

Nine-and-twenty knights of fame
   Hung their shields in Branksome Hall,[2]
Nine-and-twenty squires of name
   Brought them their steeds to bower
      from stall;
   Nine-and-twenty yeomen tall
   Waited, duteous, on them all;
   They were all knights of mettle true,
   Kinsmen to the bold Buccleuch.

IV.

Ten of them were sheathed in steel,
With belted sword, and spur on heel:
They quitted not their harness bright,
Neither by day, nor yet by night;
      They lay down to rest,
      With corselet laced,
Pillow'd on buckler cold and hard;
      They carved at the meal
      With gloves of steel,
And they drank the red wine through the
      helmet barr'd.

V.

Ten squires, ten yeomen, mail-clad men,
Waited the beck of the warders ten;
Thirty steeds, both fleet and wight,
Stood saddled in stable day and night,
Barbed with frontlet of steel, I trow,
And with Jedwood-axe at saddlebow;[3]
A hundred more fed free in stall: —
Such was the custom of Branksome Hall.

VI.

Why do these steeds stand ready dight?
Why watch these warriors, arm'd, by
      night? —

They watch, to hear the blood-hound
  baying;
They watch to hear the war-horn braying;
To see St. George's red cross streaming,
To see the midnight beacon gleaming:
They watch, against Southern force and
  guile,
  Lest Scroop, or Howard, or Percy's
    powers,
  Threaten Branksome's lordly towers,
From Warkworth, or Naworth, or merry
    Carlisle.[4]

VII.

Such is the custom of Branksome Hall —
  Many a valiant knight is here;
But he, the chieftain of them all,
His sword hangs rusting on the wall,
  Beside his broken spear.
  Bards long shall tell
  How Lord Walter fell! [5]
  When startled burghers fled, afar,
  The furies of the Border war;
  When the streets of high Dunedin *
  Saw lances gleam and falchions redden,
  And heard the slogan's † deadly yell —
  Then the Chief of Branksome fell.

VIII.

Can piety the discord heal,
  Or stanch the death-feud's enmity?
Can Christian lore, can patriot zeal,
  Can love of blessed charity?
No! vainly to each holy shrine,
  In mutual pilgrimage they drew;
Implored, in vain, the grace divine
  For chiefs, their own red falchions slew;
While Cessford owns the rule of Carr,
  While Ettrick boasts the line of Scott,
The slaughter'd chiefs, the mortal jar,
The havoc of the feudal war,
  Shall never, never be forgot! [6]

IX.

In sorrow o'er Lord Walter's bier
  The warlike foresters had bent;
And many a flower, and many a tear,
  Old Teviot's maids and matrons lent:
But o'er her warrior's bloody bier
The Ladye dropp'd nor flower nor tear!

* Edinburgh.
† The war-cry, or gathering word, of a Border
clan.

Vengeance, deep-brooding o'er the slain,
  Had lock'd the source of softer woe;
And burning pride, and high disdain,
  Forbade the rising tear to flow;
Until, amid his sorrowing clan,
  Her son lisp'd from the nurse's knee —
" And if I live to be a man,
  My father's death revenged shall be ! "
Then fast the mother's tears did seek
To dew the infant's kindling cheek.

X.

All loose her negligent attire,
  All loose her golden hair,
Hung Margaret o'er her slaughter'd sire,
  And wept in wild despair:
But not alone the bitter tear
  Had filial grief supplied;
For hopeless love, and anxious fear,
  Had lent their mingled tide;
Nor in her mother's alter'd eye
Dared she to look for sympathy.
Her lover, 'gainst her father's clan,
  With Carr in arms had stood,[7]
When Mathouse-burn to Melrose ran,
  All purple with their blood;
And well she knew, her mother dread,
Before Lord Cranstoun [8] she should wed,
Would see her on her dying bed.

XI.

Of noble race the Ladye came,
Her father was a clerk of fame,
  Of Bethune's line of Picardie: [9]
He learn'd the art that none may name,
  In Padua, far beyond the sea.[10]
Men said, he changed his mortal frame
  By feat of magic mystery;
For when, in studious mode, he paced
  St. Andrew's cloister'd hall,
His form no darkening shadow traced
  Upon the sunny wall! [11]

XII.

And of his skill, as bards avow,
  He taught that Ladye fair,
Till to her bidding she could bow
  The viewless forms of air.
And now she sits in secret bower,
In old Lord David's western tower,
  And listens to a heavy sound,
That moans the mossy turrets round

Is it the roar of Teviot's tide,
That chafes against the scaur's * red side?
Is it the wind that swings the oaks?
Is it the echo from the rocks?
What may it be, the heavy sound,
That moans old Branksome's turrets
  round?

XIII.

At the sullen, moaning sound,
  The ban-dogs bay and howl;
And, from the turrets round,
  Loud whoops the startled owl.
In the hall, both squire and knight
Swore that a storm was near,
And looked forth to view the night;
  But the night was still and clear!

XIV.

From the sound of Teviot's tide,
Chafing with the mountain's side,
From the groan of the wind-swung oak,
From the sullen echo of the rock,
From the voice of the coming storm,
  The Ladye knew it well!
It was the Spirit of the Flood that spoke,
And he call'd on the Spirit of the Fell.

XV.

RIVER SPIRIT.

" Sleep'st thou, brother?"

MOUNTAIN SPIRIT.

    — " Brother, nay —
On my hills the moon-beams play.
From Craik-cross to Skelfhill-pen,
By every rill, in every glen,
  Merry elves their morris pacing,
    To aërial minstrelsy,
  Emerald rings on brown heath tracing,
    Trip it deft and merrily.
Up, and mark their nimble feet!
Up, and list their music sweet!" —

XVI.

RIVER SPIRIT.

" Tears of an imprison'd maiden
  Mix with my polluted stream;
Margaret of Branksome, sorrow-laden,
  Mourns beneath the moon's pale beam.

* A steep bank.

Tell me, thou, who view'st the stars,
When shall cease these feudal jars?
What shall be the maiden's fate?
Who shall be the maiden's mate?"

XVII.

MOUNTAIN SPIRIT.

" Arthur's slow wain his course doth roll,
In utter darkness round the pole;
The Northern Bear lowers black and grim;
Orion's studded belt is dim;
Twinkling faint, and distant far,
Shimmers through mist each planet star;
  Ill may I read their high decree!
But no kind influence deign they shower
On Teviot's tide, and Branksome's tower,
  Till pride be quell'd, and love be free."

XVIII.

The unearthly voices ceast,
  And the heavy sound was still;
It died on the river's breast,
  It died on the side of the hill.
But round Lord David's tower
  The sound still floated near;
For it rung in the Ladye's bower,
  And it rung in the Ladye's ear.
She raised her stately head,
  And her heart throbb'd high with
    pride: —
" Your mountains shall bend,
  And your streams ascend,
Ere Margaret be our foeman's bride!"

XIX.

The Ladye sought the lofty hall,
  Where many a bold retainer lay,
And, with jocund din, among them all,
  Her son pursued his infant play.
A fancied moss-trooper,† the boy
  The truncheon of a spear bestrode,
And round the hall, right merrily,
  In mimic foray rode.
Even bearded knights, in arms grown old,
  Share in his frolic gambols bore,
Albeit their hearts, of rugged mould,
  Were stubborn as the steel they wore.

† Moss-trooper, a borderer, whose profession
was pillage of the English. These marauders
were called *moss-troopers* because they dwelt
in the mosses, and rode, on their incursions, in
troops.

For the gray warriors prophesied
　How the brave boy, in future war,
Should tame the Unicorn's pride,*
　Exalt the Crescent and the Star.†

XX.

The Ladye forgot her purpose high,
　One moment, and no more;
One moment gazed with a mother's eye,
　As she paused at the arched door;
Then from amid the armed train
She call'd to her William of Deloraine.

XXI.

A stark moss-trooping Scott was he,
As e'er couch'd Border lance by knee;
Through Solway sands, through Tarras
　moss,
Blindfold, he knew the paths to cross;
By wily turns, by desperate bounds,
Had baffled Percy's best blood-hounds;[12]
In Eske or Liddel, fords were none,
But he would ride them, one by one;
Alike to him was time or tide,
December's snow, or July's pride;
Alike to him was tide or time,
Moonless midnight, or matin prime;
Steady of heart, and stout of hand,
As ever drove prey from Cumberland;
Five times outlaw'd had he been,
By England's King, and Scotland's
　Queen.

XXII.

" Sir William of Deloraine, good at need,
Mount thee on the wightest steed;
Spare not to spur, nor stint to ride,
Until thou come to fair Tweedside;
And in Melrose's holy pile
Seek thou the monk of St. Mary's aisle.
　Greet the Father well from me;
　　Say that the fated hour is come,
　And to-night he shall watch with thee,
　　To win the treasure of the tomb;
For this will be St. Michael's night,
And, though stars be dim, the moon is
　bright;

And the cross, of bloody red,
Will point to the grave of the mighty
　dead.

XXIII.

" What he gives thee, see thou keep;
Stay not thou for food or sleep;
Be it scroll, or be it book,
Into it, Knight, thou must not look;
If thou readest, thou art lorn !
Better hadst thou ne'er been born." —

XXIV.

" O swiftly can speed my dapple-gray
　steed,
　Which drinks of the Teviot clear;
Ere break of day," the Warrior 'gan say,
　" Again will I be here:
And safer by none may thy errand be
　done,
　Than, noble dame, by me;
Letter nor line know I never a one,
　Wer't my neck-verse at Hairibee." ‡

XXV.

Soon in his saddle sate he fast,
And soon the steep descent he past,
Soon cross'd the sounding barbican,§
And soon the Teviot side he won.
Eastward the wooded path he rode,
Green hazels o'er his basnet nod;
He pass'd the Peel of Goldiland,‖
And cross'd old Borthwick's roaring
　strand;
Dimly he view'd the Moat-hill's mound,
Where Druid shades still flitted round;
In Hawick twinkled many a light;
Behind him soon they set in night;
And soon he spurr'd his courser keen
Beneath the tower of Hazeldean.

* The Unicorn Head was the crest of the Carrs, or Kerrs, of Cessford, the enemies of the child's late father.

† The Crescent and the Star were armorial bearings of the Scotts of Buccleuch.

‡ *Hairibee*, the place on Carlisle wall where the moss-troopers, if caught, were hung. The neck-verse was the first verse of Psalm 51. If a criminal claimed on the scaffold " benefit of his clergy," a priest instantly presented him with a Psalter, and he read his neck-verse. The power of reading it entitled him to his life, which was spared; but he was banished the kingdom. See Palgrave's " Merchant and Friar."

§ *Barbican*, the defence of the outer gate of a feudal castle.

‖ *Peel*, a Border tower.

XXVI.

The clattering hoofs the watchmen mark; —
"Stand, ho!" thou courier of the dark." —
"For Branksome, ho!" the knight rejoin'd,
And left the friendly tower behind.
    He turn'd him now from Teviotside,
        And, guided by the tinkling rill,
    Northward the dark ascent did ride,
        And gain'd the moor at Horsliehill;
Broad on the left before him lay,
For many a mile, the Roman way.*

XXVII.

A moment now he slack'd his speed,
A moment breathed his panting steed;
Drew saddle-girth and corslet band,
And loosen'd in the sheath his brand.
On Minto-crags the moonbeams glint,
Where Barnhill hew'd his bed of flint;
Who flung his outlaw'd limbs to rest,
Where falcons hang their giddy nest,
Mid cliffs, from whence his eagle eye
For many a league his prey could spy;
Cliffs, doubling, on their echoes borne,
The terrors of the robber's horn,
Cliffs, which, for many a later year,
The warbling Doric reed shall hear,
When some sad swain shall teach the grove,
Ambition is no cure for love!

XXVIII.

Unchallenged, thence pass'd Deloraine,
To ancient Riddel's fair domain,
    Where Aill, from mountains freed,
Down from the lakes did raving come;
Each wave was crested with tawny foam,
    Like the mane of a chestnut steed.
In vain! no torrent, deep or broad,
Might bar the bold moss-trooper's road.

XXIX.

At the first plunge the horse sunk low,
And the water broke o'er the saddlebow;
Above the foaming tide, I ween,
Scarce half the charger's neck was seen;

* An ancient Roman road, crossing through part of Roxburghshire.

For he was barded † from counter to tail,
And the rider was armed complete in mail;
Never heavier man and horse
Stemm'd a midnight torrent's force.
The warrior's very plume, I say,
Was daggled by the dashing spray:
Yet, through good heart, and Our Ladye's grace,
At length he gain'd the landing-place.

XXX.

Now Bowden Moor the march-man won,
    And sternly shook his plumed head,
As glanced his eyes o'er Halidon;‡
    For on his soul the slaughter red
Of that unhallow'd morn arose,
When first the Scott and Carr were foes;
When royal James beheld the fray,
Prize to the victor of the day;
When Home and Douglas, in the van,
Bore down Buccleuch's retiring clan,
Till gallant Cessford's heart-blood dear
Reek'd on dark Elliot's Border spear.

XXXI.

In bitter mood he spurred fast,
And soon the hated heath was past;
And far beneath, in lustre wan,
Old Melros' rose, and fair Tweed ran:
Like some tall rock with lichens gray,
Seem'd dimly huge, the dark Abbaye.
When Hawick he pass'd, had curfew rung,
Now midnight lauds § were in Melrose sung.
The sound, upon the fitful gale,
In solemn wise did rise and fail,
Like that wild harp, whose magic tone
Is waken'd by the winds alone.
But when Melrose he reach'd, 'twas silence all;
He meetly stabled his steed in stall,
And sought the convent's lonely wall.[13]

———

HERE paused the harp; and with its swell
The Master's fire and courage fell;

† *Barded*, or barbed, applied to a horse accoutred with defensive armor.

‡ Halidon was an ancient seat of the Kerrs of Cessford, now demolished.

§ *Lauds*, the midnight service of the Catholic Church.

Dejectedly, and low, he bow'd,
And, gazing timid on the crowd,
He seem'd to seek, in every eye,
If they approved his minstrelsy;
And, diffident of present praise,
Somewhat he spoke of former days,
And how old age, and wand'ring long,
Had done his hand and harp some wrong.
The Duchess, and her daughters fair,
And every gentle lady there,
Each after each, in due degree,
Gave praises to his melody;
His hand was true, his voice was clear,
And much they long'd the rest to hear.
Encouraged thus, the Aged Man,
After meet rest, again began.

CANTO SECOND.

I.

IF thou would'st view fair Melrose aright,
Go visit it by the pale moonlight;
For the gay beams of lightsome day
Gild, but to flout, the ruins gray.
When the broken arches are black in night,
And each shafted oriel glimmers white;
When the cold light's uncertain shower
Streams on the ruin'd central tower;
When buttress and buttress, alternately,
Seem framed of ebon and ivory;
When silver edges the imagery,
And the scrolls that teach thee to live and
     die; [14]
When distant Tweed is heard to rave,
And the owlet to hoot o'er the dead man's
     grave,
Then go — but go alone the while —
Then view St. David's ruin'd pile;
And, home returning, soothly swear,
Was never scene so sad and fair !

II.

Short halt did Deloraine make there;
Little reck'd he of the scene so fair;
With dagger's hilt, on the wicket strong,
He struck full loud, and struck full long.
The porter hurried to the gate : —
" Who knocks so loud, and knocks so
     late ? "
" From Branksome I," the warrior cried;
And straight the wicket open'd wide :

For Branksome's Chiefs had in battle stood
     To fence the rights of fair Melrose;
And lands and livings, many a rood,
     Had gifted the shrine for their souls'
     repose.

III.

Bold Deloraine his errand said;
The porter bent his humble head;
With torch in hand, and feet unshod,
And noiseless step, the path he trod,
The arched cloister, far and wide,
Rang to the warrior's clanking stride,
Till, stooping low his lofty crest,
He enter'd the cell of the ancient priest,
And lifted his barred aventayle,*
To hail the Monk of St. Mary's aisle.

IV.

" The Ladye of Branksome greets thee by
     me,
     Says, that the fated hour is come,
And that to-night I shall watch with thee,
     To win the treasure of the tomb."
From sackcloth couch the Monk arose,
     With toil his stiffen'd limbs he rear'd;
A hundred years had flung their snows
     On his thin locks and floating beard.

V.

And strangely on the Knight look'd he,
     And his blue eyes gleam'd wild and
     wide : —
" And darest thou, Warrior ! seek to see
     What heaven and hell alike would hide ?
My breast, in belt of iron pent,
     With shirt of hair and scourge of
     thorn;
For threescore years, in penance spent,
     My knees those flinty stones have worn :
Yet all too little to atone
For knowing what should ne'er be known.
     Would'st thou thy every future year
          In ceaseless prayer and penance drie,
     Yet wait thy latter end with fear —
          Then, daring Warrior, follow me ! "

VI.

" Penance, father, will I none;
Prayer know I hardly one;

---

* *Aventayle*, visor of the helmet.

For mass or prayer can I rarely tarry
Save to patter an Ave Mary,
When I ride on a Border foray.
Other prayer can I none;
So speed me my errand, and let me be
    gone.'' —

VII.

Again on the Knight looked the Church-
    man old,
    And again he sighed heavily;
For he had himself been a warrior bold,
    And fought in Spain and Italy.
And he thought on the days that were long
    since by,
When his limbs were strong, and his cour-
    age was high : —
Now, slow and faint, he led the way,
Where, cloister'd round, the garden lay;
The pillar'd arches were over their head,
And beneath their feet were the bones of
    the dead.

VIII

Spreading herbs, and flowerets bright,
Glisten'd with the dew of night;
Nor herb, nor floweret, glisten'd there,
But was carved in the cloister-arches as
    fair.
    The Monk gazed long on the lovely
        moon,
    Then into the night he looked forth;
    And red and bright the streamers light
        Were dancing in the glowing north.
So had he seen, in fair Castile,
    The youth in glittering squadrons
        start;
Sudden the flying jennet wheel,
    And hurl the unexpected dart.
He knew, by the streamers that shot so
    bright,
That spirits were riding the northern light.

IX.

By a steel-clenched postern door,
    They enter'd now the chancel tall;
The darken'd roof rose high aloof
    On pillars lofty, and light, and small:
The key-stone, that lock'd each ribbed
    aisle,
Was a fleur-de-lys, or a quatre-feuille;
The corbels were carved grotesque and
    grim;

And the pillars, with cluster'd shafts so
    trim,
With base and with capital flourish'd
    around,
Seem'd bundles of lances which garlands
    had bound.

X.

Full many a scutcheon and banner riven,
Shook to the cold night-wind of heaven,
    Around the screened altar's pale;
And there the dying lamps did burn,
Before thy low and lonely urn,
O gallant Chief of Otterburne ! [15]
    And thine, dark Knight of Liddes-
        dale ! [16]
O fading honors of the dead !
O high ambition, lowly laid !

XI.

The moon on the east oriel shone
Through slender shafts of shapely stone,
    By foliaged tracery combined;
Thou would'st have thought some fairy's
    hand
'Twixt poplars straight the osier wand,
    In many a freakish knot, had twined;
Then framed a spell, when the work was
    done,
And changed the willow-wreaths to stone.
The silver light, so pale and faint,
Show'd many a prophet, and many a saint,
    Whose image on the glass was dyed;
Full in the midst, his Cross of Red
Triumphant Michael brandished,
    And trampled the Apostate's pride.
The moon-beam kiss'd the holy pane,
And threw on the pavement a bloody
    stain.

XII.

They sate them down on a marble stone,
    (A Scottish monarch slept below;) *
Thus spoke the Monk, in solemn tone: —
    '' I was not always a man of woe;
For Paynim countries I have trod,
And fought beneath the Cross of God:
Now, strange to my eyes thine arms ap-
    pear,
And their iron clang sounds strange to my
    ear.

        * Alexander II.

XIII.

"In these far climes it was my lot
To meet the wondrous Michael Scott,[17]
A wizard, of such dreaded fame,
That when, in Salamanca's cave,
Him listed his magic wand to wave,
  The bells would ring in Notre Dame!
Some of his skill he taught to me;
And, Warrior, I could say to thee
The words that cleft Eildon hills in three,[18]
  And bridled the Tweed with a curb of
    stone:
But to speak them were a deadly sin;
And for having but thought them my heart
    within,
  A treble penance must be done.

XIV.

"When Michael lay on his dying bed,
His conscience was awakened:
He bethought him of his sinful deed,
And he gave me a sign to come with speed;
I was in Spain when the morning rose,
But I stood by his bed ere evening close.
The words may not again be said,
That he spoke to me, on death-bed laid;
They would rend this Abbaye's massy
    nave,
And pile it in heaps above his grave.

XV.

"I swore to bury his Mighty Book,
That never mortal might therein look;
And never to tell where it was hid,
Save at his Chief of Branksome's need:
And when that need was past and o'er,
Again the volume to restore.
I buried him on St. Michael's night,
When the bell toll'd one, and the moon
    was bright,
And I dug his chamber among the dead,
When the floor of the chancel was stained
    red,
That his patron's cross might over him
    wave,
And scare the fiends from the Wizard's
    grave.

XVI.

"It was a night of woe and dread,
When Michael in the tomb I laid!
Strange sounds along the chancel pass'd,
The banners waved without a blast;"—

—Still spoke the Monk, when the bell
    toll'd one!—
I tell you, that a braver man
Than William of Deloraine, good at need,
Against a foe ne'er spurr'd a steed;
Yet somewhat was he chill'd with dread,
And his hair did bristle upon his head.

XVII.

"Lo, Warrior! now, the Cross of Red
Points to the grave of the mighty dead;
Within it burns a wondrous light,
To chase the spirits that love the night:
That lamp shall burn unquenchably,
Until the eternal doom shall be."*—
Slow moved the Monk to the broad flag-
    stone,
Which the bloody Cross was traced upon:
He pointed to a secret nook;
An iron bar the Warrior took;
And the Monk made a sign with his
    wither'd hand,
The grave's huge portal to expand.

XVIII.

With beating heart to the task he went;
His sinewy frame o'er the grave-stone
    bent;
With bar of iron heaved amain,
Till the toil-drops fell from his brows, like
    rain.
It was by dint of passing strength,
That he moved the massy stone at length.
I would you had been there, to see
How the light broke forth so gloriously,
Stream'd upward to the chancel roof,
And through the galleries far aloof!
No earthly flame blazed e'er so bright:
It shone like heaven's own blessed light,
  And, issuing from the tomb,
Show'd the Monk's cowl, and visage pale,
Danced on the dark-brow'd Warrior's
    mail,
  And kiss'd his waving plume.

XIX.

Before their eyes the Wizard lay,
As if he had not been dead a day.
His hoary beard in silver roll'd,
He seem'd some seventy winters old;

* It was a belief of the Middle Ages, that
eternal lamps were to be found burning in
ancient sepulchres.

A palmer's amice wrapp'd him round,
With a wrought Spanish baldric bound,
    Like a pilgrim from beyond the sea;
His left hand held his Book of Might;
A silver cross was in his right;
    The lamp was placed beside his knee;
High and majestic was his look,
At which the fellest fiends had shook,
And all unruffled was his face:
They trusted his soul had gotten grace.

XX.

Often had William of Deloraine
Rode through the battle's bloody plain,
And trampled down the warriors slain,
    And neither known remorse nor awe;
Yet now remorse and awe he own'd;
His breath came thick, his head swam
    round,
    When this strange scene of death he
    saw,
Bewilder'd and unnerved he stood,
And the priest pray'd fervently and loud:
With eyes averted prayed he;
He might not endure the sight to see,
Of the man he had loved so brotherly.

XXI.

And when the priest his death-prayer had
    pray'd,
Thus unto Deloraine he said: —
" Now, speed thee what thou hast to do,
Or, Warrior, we may dearly rue;
For those, thou may'st not look upon,
Are gathering fast round the yawning
    stone! " —
Then Deloraine, in terror, took
From the cold hand the Mighty Book,
With iron clasp'd, and with iron bound:
He thought, as he took it, the dead man
    frown'd;
But the glare of the sepulchral light,
Perchance, had dazzled the warrior's sight.

XXII.

When the huge stone sunk o'er the tomb,
The night return'd in double gloom;
For the moon had gone down, and the
    stars were few;
And, as the Knight and Priest withdrew,
With wavering steps and dizzy brain,
They hardly might the postern gain.

'Tis said, as through the aisles they pass'd,
They heard strange noises on the blast;
And through the cloister-galleries small,
Which at mid-height thread the chancel
    wall,
Loud sobs, and laughter louder, ran,
And voices unlike the voice of man;
As if the fiends kept holiday,
Because these spells were brought to day.
I cannot tell how the truth may be;
I say the tale as 'twas said to me.

XXIII.

" Now, hie thee hence," the Father said,
" And when we are on death-bed laid,
O may our dear Ladye, and sweet St.
    John,
Forgive our souls for the deed we have
    done ! "
    The Monk return'd him to his cell,
        And many a prayer and penance
        sped;
    When the convent met at the noontide
    bell —
        The Monk of St. Mary's aisle was
        dead !
Before the cross was the body laid,
With hands clasp'd fast, as if still he
    pray'd.

XXIV.

The Knight breathed free in the morning
    wind,
And strove his hardihood to find.
He was glad when he pass'd the tomb-
    stones gray,
Which girdle round the fair Abbaye;
For the mystic Book, to his bosom prest,
Felt like a load upon his breast,
And his joints, with nerves of iron twined,
Shook, like the aspen leaves in wind.
Full fain was he when the dawn of day
Began to brighten Cheviot gray;
He joy'd to see the cheerful light,
And he said Ave Mary as well as he
    might.

XXV.

The sun had brighten'd Cheviot gray,
    The sun had brighten'd the Carter's *
    side;

* A mountain on the Border of England,
above Jedburgh.

And soon beneath the rising day
  Smiled Branksome Towers and Teviot's
    tide.
The wild birds told their warbling tale,
  And waken'd every flower that blows;
And peeped forth the violet pale,
  And spread her breast the mountain
    rose.
And lovelier than the rose so red,
  Yet paler than the violet pale,
She early left her sleepless bed,
  The fairest maid of Teviotdale.

XXVI.

Why does fair Margaret so early awake?
  And don her kirtle so hastilie;
And the silken knots, which in hurry she
    would make,
  Why tremble her slender fingers to tie;
Why does she stop, and look often around,
  As she glides down the secret stair;
And why does she pat the shaggy blood-
    hound,
  As he rouses him up from his lair;
And, though she passes the postern alone,
Why is not the watchman's bugle blown?

XXVII.

The Ladye steps in doubt and dread,
Lest her watchful mother hear her tread;
The Ladye caresses the rough blood-
    hound,
Lest his voice should waken the castle
    round,
The watchman's bugle is not blown,
For he was her foster-father's son;
And she glides through the greenwood at
    dawn of light
To meet Baron Henry, her own true
    knight.

XXVIII.

The Knight and Ladye fair are met,
And under the hawthorn's boughs are set.
A fairer pair were never seen
To meet beneath the hawthorn green.
He was stately, and young, and tall;
Dreaded in battle, and loved in hall;
And she, when love, scarce told, scarce
    hid,
Lent to her cheek a livelier red;
When the half sigh her swelling breast
Against the silken ribbon prest;

When her blue eyes their secret told,
Though shaded by her locks of gold —
Where would you find the peerless fair,
With Margaret of Branksome might com-
    pare?

XXIX.

And now, fair dames, methinks I see
You listen to my minstrelsy;
Your waving locks ye backward throw,
And sidelong bend your necks of snow;
Ye ween to hear a melting tale,
Of two true lovers in a dale;
  And how the Knight, with tender fire
    To paint his faithful passion strove;
  Swore he might at her feet expire,
    But never, never, cease to love;
And how she blush'd, and how she sigh'd,
And, half consenting, half denied,
And said that she would die a maid; —
Yet, might the bloody feud be stay'd,
Henry of Cranstoun, and only he,
Margaret of Branksome's choice should
    be.

XXX.

Alas! fair dames, your hopes are vain!
My harp has lost the enchanting strain;
  Its lightness would my age reprove:
My hairs are gray, my limbs are old,
My heart is dead, my veins are cold;
  I may not, must not, sing of love.

XXXI.

Beneath an oak, moss'd o'er by eld,
The Baron's Dwarf his courser held,[19]
  And held his crested helm and spear:
That Dwarf was scarce an earthly man,
If the tales were true that of him ran
  Through all the Border, far and near.
'Twas said, when the Baron a-hunting
    rode,
Through Redesdale's glens, but rarely
    trode,
  He heard a voice cry, "Lost! lost!
    lost!"
  And, like tennis-ball by racket toss'd,
    A leap, of thirty feet and three,
Made from the gorse this elfin shape,
Distorted like some dwarfish ape,
  And lighted at Lord Cranstoun's
    knee.

Lord Cranstoun was some whit dis-
      may'd;
'Tis said that five good miles he rade,
   To rid him of his company;
But where he rode one mile, the Dwarf
   ran four,
And the Dwarf was first at the castle
   door.

XXXII.

Use lessens marvel, it is said:
This elvish Dwarf with the Baron staid;
Little he ate, and less he spoke,
Nor mingled with the menial flock:
And oft apart his arms he toss'd,
And often mutter'd "Lost! lost! lost!"
   He was waspish, arch, and litherlie,*
But well Lord Cranstoun served he:
And he of his service was full fain;
For once he had been ta'en or slain,
   An it had not been for his ministry.
All between Home and Hermitage,
Talk'd of Lord Cranstoun's Goblin-Page.

XXXIII.

For the Baron went on Pilgrimage,
And took with him this elvish Page,
   To Mary's Chapel of the Lowes;
For there beside our Ladye's lake,
An offering he had sworn to make,
   And he would pay his vows.
But the Ladye of Branksome gather'd a
   band
Of the best that would ride at her com-
   mand:
   The trysting place was Newark Lee.
Wat of Harden came thither amain,
And thither came John of Thirlestane,
And thither came William of Deloraine;
   They were three hundred spears and
      three.
Through Douglas-burn, up Yarrow
   stream,
Their horses prance, their lances gleam.
They came to St. Mary's lake ere day;
But the chapel was void, and the Baron
   away.
They burn'd the chapel for very rage,
And cursed Lord Cranstoun's Goblin-
   Page.

* Idle.

XXXIV.

And now, in Branksome's good green-
   wood,
As under the aged oak he stood,
The Baron's courser pricks his ears,
As if a distant noise he hears.
The Dwarf waves his long lean arm on
   high,
And signs to the lovers to part and fly;
No time was then to vow or sigh.
Fair Margaret through the hazel grove,
Flew like the startled cushat-dove:
The Dwarf the stirrup held and rein;
Vaulted the Knight on his steed amain,
And, pondering deep that morning's
   scene,
Rode eastward through the hawthorns
   green.

———

WHILE thus he pour'd the lengthen'd tale
The Minstrel's voice began to fail:
Full slyly smiled the observant page,
And gave the wither'd hand of age
A goblet crown'd with mighty wine,
The blood of Velez' scorched vine.
He raised the silver cup on high,
And, while the big drop fill'd his eye,
Pray'd God to bless the Duchess long,
And all who cheer'd a son of song.
The attending maidens smiled to see
How long, how deep, how zealously,
The precious juice the Minstrel quaff'd;
And he, embolden'd by the draught,
Look'd gayly back to them, and laugh'd.
The cordial nectar of the bowl
Swell'd his old veins, and cheer'd his soul;
A lighter, livelier prelude ran,
Ere thus his tale again began.

———

CANTO THIRD.

I.

AND said I that my limbs were old,
And said I that my blood was cold,
And that my kindly fire was fled,
And my poor wither'd heart was dead,
   And that I might not sing of love? —
How could I to the dearest theme,
That ever warm'd a minstrel's dream,
   So foul, so false a recreant prove!

How could I name love's very name,
Nor wake my heart to notes of flame !

II.

In peace, Love tunes the shepherd's reed;
In war, he mounts the warrior's steed;
In halls, in gay attire is seen;
In hamlets, dances on the green.
Love rules the court, the camp, the grove,
And men below, and saints above;
For love is heaven, and heaven is love.

III.

So thought Lord Cranstoun, as I ween,
While, pondering deep the tender scene,
He rode through Branksome's hawthorn
    green.
    But the Page shouted wild and shrill,
        And scarce his helmet could he don,
    When downward from the shady hill
        A stately knight came pricking on.
That warrior's steed, so dapple-gray,
Was dark with sweat, and splash'd with
    clay;
    His armor red with many a stain;
He seem'd in such a weary plight,
As if he had ridden the live-long night;
    For it was William of Deloraine.

IV.

But no whit weary did he seem,
When, dancing in the sunny beam,
He mark'd the crane on the baron's
    crest; *
For his ready spear was in his rest.
    Few were the words, and stern and
        high,
        That mark'd the foemen's feudal
        hate;
    For question fierce, and proud reply,
        Gave signal soon of dire debate.
Their very coursers seem'd to know
That each was other's mortal foe,
And snorted fire, when wheel'd around,
To give each knight his vantage-ground.

* The crest of the Cranstouns, in allusion to
their name, is a crane, dormant, holding a stone
in his foot, with an emphatic Border motto,
Thou shalt want ere I want. Arms thus pun-
ning on the name, are said heraldically to be
" canting."

V.

In rapid round the Baron bent;
    He sigh'd a sigh, and pray'd a prayer;
The prayer was to his patron saint,
    The sigh was to his ladye fair.
Stout Deloraine nor sigh'd nor pray'd,
Nor saint, nor ladye, call'd to aid;
But he stoop'd his head, and couch'd his
    spear,
And spurr'd his steed to full career.
The meeting of these champions proud
Seem'd like the bursting thunder-cloud.

VI.

Stern was the dint the Borderer lent !
The stately Baron backwards bent;
Bent backwards to his horse's tail,
And his plumes went scattering on the
    gale.
The tough ash spear, so stout and true,
Into a thousand flinders flew.
But Cranstoun's lance, of more avail,
Pierced through, like silk, the Borderer's
    mail;
Through shield, and jack, and acton, past,
Deep in his bosom, broke at last. —
Still sate the warrior saddle-fast,
Till, stumbling in the mortal shock,
Down went the steed, the girthing broke,
Hurl'd on a heap lay man and horse.
The Baron onward pass'd his course ;
Nor knew — so giddy roll'd his brain —
His foe lay stretch'd upon the plain.

VII.

But when he rein'd his courser round,
And saw his foeman on the ground
    Lie senseless as the bloody clay,
He bade his page to stanch the wound,
    And there beside the warrior stay,
And tend him in his doubtful state,
And lead him to Branksome castle-gate:
His noble mind was inly moved
For the kinsman of the maid he loved.
" This shalt thou do without delay:
No longer here myself may stay ;
Unless the swifter I speed away,
Short shrift will be at my dying day."

VIII.

Away in speed Lord Cranstoun rode;
The Goblin-Page behind abode;

His lord's command he ne'er withstood,
Though small his pleasure to do good.
As the corslet off he took,
The Dwarf espied the Mighty Book!
Much he marvell'd a knight of pride,
Like a book-bosom'd priest should ride ; *
He thought not to search or stanch the
   wound,
Until the secret he had found.

IX.

The iron band, the iron clasp,
Resisted long the elfin grasp:
For when the first he had undone,
It closed as he the next begun.
Those iron clasps, that iron band,
Would not yield to unchristen'd hand,
Till he smear'd the cover o'er
With the Borderer's curdled gore;
A moment then the volume spread,
And one short spell therein he read,
It had much of glamour † might,
Could make a ladye seem a knight;
The cobwebs on a dungeon wall
Seem tapestry in lordly hall;
A nut-shell seem a gilded barge,
A sheeling ‡ seem a palace large,
And youth seem age, and age seem
   youth —
All was delusion, naught was truth.[20]

X.

He had not read another spell,
When on his cheek a buffet fell,
So fierce, it stretch'd him on the plain,
Beside the wounded Deloraine.
From the ground he rose dismay'd,
And shook his huge and matted head;
One word he mutter'd, and no more,
" Man of age, thou smitest sore ! " —
No more the Elfin Page durst try
Into the wondrous Book to pry;
The clasps, though smear'd with Chris-
   tian gore,
Shut faster than they were before.
He hid it underneath his cloak. —
Now, if you ask who gave the stroke,

* Priests were wont to carry their mass-book,
for burying and marrying, etc., in their bosoms.

† Magical delusion.

‡ A shepherd's hut.

I cannot tell, so mot I thrive;
It was not given by man alive.

XI.

Unwillingly himself he address'd,
To do his master's high behest :
He lifted up the living corse,
And laid it on the weary horse;
He led him into Branksome Hall,
Before the beards of the warders all;
And each did after swear and say,
There only pass'd a wain of hay.
He took him to Lord David's tower,
Even to the Ladye's secret bower;
And, but that stronger spells were spread,
And the door might not be opened,
He had laid him on her very bed.
Whate'er he did of gramarye,§
Was always done maliciously;
He flung the warrior on the ground,
And the blood well'd freshly from the
   wound.

XII.

As he repass'd the outer court,
He spied the fair young child at sport;
He thought to train him to the wood;
For, at a word, be it understood,
He was always for ill, and never for good.
Seem'd to the boy, some comrade gay
Led him forth to the woods to play;
On the drawbridge the warders stout
Saw a terrier and lurcher passing out.

XIII.

He led the boy o'er bank and fell,
   Until they came to a woodland brook; [21]
The running stream dissolved the spell,
   And his own elvish shape he took.
Could he have had his pleasure vilde,
He had crippled the joints of the noble
   child;
Or, with his fingers long and lean,
Had strangled him in fiendish spleen;
But his awful mother he had in dread,
And also his power was limited;
So he but scowl'd on the startled child,
And darted through the forest wild;
The woodland brook he bounding cross'd,
And laugh'd, and shouted, " Lost ! lost !
   lost ! " —

§ Magic.

XIV.

Full sore amazed at the wondrous change,
    And frighten'd as a child might be,
At the wild yell and visage strange,
    And the dark words of gramarye,
The child, amidst the forest bower,
Stood rooted like a lily flower;
    And when, at length, with trembling
        pace,
        He sought to find where Branksome
            lay,
    He fear'd to see that grisly face
    Glare from some thicket on his way.
Thus, starting oft, he journey'd on,
And deeper in the wood is gone, —
For aye the more he sought his way,
The farther still he went astray, —
Until he heard the mountains round
Ring to the baying of a hound.

XV.

And hark! and hark! the deep-mouth'd
        bark
    Comes nigher still, and nigher:
Bursts on the path a dark blood-hound,
His tawny muzzle track'd the ground,
    And his red eye shot fire.
Soon as the wilder'd child saw he,
He flew at him right furiouslie.
I ween you would have seen with joy
The bearing of the gallant boy,
When, worthy of his noble sire,
His wet cheek glow'd 'twixt fear and ire!
He faced the blood-hound manfully,
And held his little bat on high;
So fierce he struck, the dog, afraid,
At cautious distance hoarsely bay'd,
    But still in act to spring;
When dash'd an archer through the glade,
And when he saw the hound was stay'd,
    He drew his tough bow-string;
But a rough voice cried, "Shoot not, hoy!
Ho! shoot not, Edward — 'Tis a boy!"

XVI.

The speaker issued from the wood,
And check'd his fellow's surly mood,
    And quell'd the ban-dog's ire:
He was an English yeoman good,
    And born in Lancashire,
Well could he hit a fallow-deer

Five hundred feet him fro;
With hand more true, and eye more clear,
    No archer bended bow.
His coal-black hair, shorn round and
        close,
    Set off his sun-burn'd face:
Old England's sign, St. George's cross,
    His barret-cap did grace;
His bugle-horn hung by his side,
All in a wolf-skin baldric tied;
And his short falchion, sharp and clear,
Had pierced the throat of many a deer.

XVII.

His kirtle, made of forest green,
    Reach'd scantly to his knee;
And, at his belt, of arrows keen
    A furbish'd sheaf bore he;
His buckler, scarce in breadth a span,
    No larger fence had he;
He never counted him a man,
    Would strike below the knee;[22]
His slacken'd bow was in his hand,
And the leash, that was his blood-hound's
        band.

XVIII.

He would not do the fair child harm,
But held him with his powerful arm,
That he might neither fight nor flee;
For when the Red-Cross spied he,
The boy strove long and violently.
Now, by St. George," the archer cries,
"Edward, methinks we have a prize!
This boy's fair face, and courage free,
Show he is come of high degree." —

XIX.

"Yes! I am come of high degree,
    For I am the heir of bold Buccleuch,
And, if thou dost not set me free,
    False Southron, thou shalt dearly rue!
For Walter of Harden shall come with
        speed,
And William of Deloraine, good at need,
And every Scott, from Esk to Tweed;
And, if thou dost not let me go,
Despite thy arrows, and thy bow,
I'll have thee hang'd to feed the
    crow!" —

XX.

"Gramercy,* for thy good-will, fair boy!
My mind was never set so high;
But if thou art chief of such a clan,
And art the son of such a man,
And ever comest to thy command,
  Our wardens had need to keep good
    order;
My bow of yew to a hazel wand,
  Thou'lt make them work upon the
    Border.
Meantime, be pleased to come with me,
For good Lord Dacre shalt thou see;
I think our work is well begun,
When we have taken thy father's son."

XXI.

Although the child was led away,
In Branksome still he seem'd to stay,
For so the Dwarf his part did play;
And, in the shape of that young boy,
He wrought the castle much annoy.
The comrades of the young Buccleuch
He pinch'd, and beat, and overthrew;
Nay, some of them he wellnigh slew.
He tore Dame Maudlin's silken tire,
And, as Sym Hall stood by the fire,
He lighted the match of his bandelier,†
And wofully scorch'd the hackbuteer.‡
It may be hardly thought or said,
The mischief that the urchin made,
Till many of the castle guess'd
That the young Baron was possess'd!

XXII.

Well I ween the charm he held
The noble Ladye had soon dispelled;
But she was deeply busied then
To tend the wounded Deloraine.
  Much she wonder'd to find him lie,
    On the stone threshold stretch'd
      along;
  She thought some spirit of the sky
    Had done the bold moss-trooper
      wrong;
Because, despite her precept dread,
Perchance he in the Book had read;
But the broken lance in his bosom stood,
And it was earthly steel and wood.

* *Grand merci,* thanks.
† *Bandelier,* belt for carrying ammunition.
‡ *Hackbuteer,* musketeer.

XXIII.

She drew the splinter from the wound,
  And with a charm she stanch'd the
    blood;
She bade the gash be cleansed and bound:
  No longer by his couch she stood;
But she has ta'en the broken lance,
  And wash'd it from the clotted gore,
  And salved the splinter o'er and o'er. §
William of Deloraine, in trance,
  Whene'er she turned it round and
    round,
  Twisted as if she gall'd his wound.
  Then to her maidens she did say,
  That he should be whole man and
    sound,
  Within the course of a night and day.
Full long she toil'd; for she did rue
Mishap to friend so stout and true.

XXIV.

So pass'd the day — the evening fell,
'Twas near the time of curfew bell;
The air was mild, the wind was calm,
The stream was smooth, the dew was
  balm;
E'en the rude watchman, on the tower,
Enjoy'd and bless'd the lovely hour.
Far more fair Margaret loved and bless'd
The hour of silence and of rest.
On the high turret sitting lone,
She waked at times the lute's soft tone,
Touch'd a wild note, and all between
Thought of the bower of hawthorns green.
Her golden hair stream'd free from band,
Her fair cheek rested on her hand,
Her blue eyes sought the west afar,
For lovers love the western star.

XXV.

Is yon the star, o'er Penchryst Pen,
That rises slowly to her ken,
And, spreading broad its wavering light,
Shakes its loose tresses on the night?
Is yon red glare the western star? —
O, 'tis the beacon-blaze of war!
Scarce could she draw her tighten'd
  breath,
For well she knew the fire of death!

§ This was called the cure by sympathy.
Sir Kenelm Digby was wont occasionally to
practise it.

XXVI.

The Warder view'd it blazing strong,
And blew his war-note loud and long,
Till, at the high and haughty sound,
Rock, wood, and river rung around.
The blast alarm'd the festal hall,
And startled forth the warriors all,
Far downward, in the castle-yard,
Full many a torch and cresset glared;
And helms and plumes, confusedly toss'd,
Were in the blaze half-seen, half-lost;
And spears in wild disorder shook,
Like reeds beside a frozen brook.

XXVII.

The Seneschal, whose silver hair
Was redden'd by the torches' glare,
Stood in the midst, with gesture proud,
And issued forth his mandates loud:
" On Penchryst glows a bale * of fire,
And three are kindling on Priesthaugh-
   swire;
     Ride out, ride out,
     The foe to scout!
Mount, mount for Branksome,† every
   man.
Thou, Todrig, warn the Johnstone clan,
   That ever are true and stout —
Ye need not send to Liddesdale;
For when they see the blazing bale,
Elliots and Armstrongs never fail. —
Ride, Alton, ride, for death and life!
And warn the Warder of the strife,
Young Gilbert, let our beacon blaze,
Our kin and clan and friends to raise."

XXVIII.

Fair Margaret from the turret head,
Heard, far below, the coursers' tread,
   While loud the harness rung,
As to their seats, with clamor dread,
   The ready horsemen sprung:
And trampling hoofs, and iron coats,
And leaders' voices, mingled notes,
     And out! and out!
     In hasty rout,
   The horsemen gallop'd forth;
Dispersing to the south to scout,
   And east, and west, and north,
To view their coming enemies,
And warn their vassals and allies.

XXIX.

The ready page, with hurried hand,
Awaked the need-fire's ‡ slumbering
   brand,
   And ruddy blush'd the heaven:
For a sheet of flame, from the turret high,
Waved like a blood-flag on the sky,
   All flaring and uneven;
And soon a score of fires, I ween,
From height, and hill, and cliff, were
   seen;
Each with warlike tidings fraught,
Each from each the signal caught;
Each after each they glanced to sight,
As stars arise upon the night.
They gleam'd on many a dusky tarn,§
Haunted by the lonely earn; ‖
On many a cairn's gray pyramid,
Where urns of mighty chiefs lie hid; 23
Till high Dunedin the blazes saw,
From Soltra and Dumpender Law;
And Lothian heard the Regent's order,
That all should boune ¶ them for the
   Border.

XXX.

The livelong night in Branksome rang
   The ceaseless sound of steel;
The castle-bell, with backward clang,
   Sent forth the larum peal;
Was frequent heard the heavy jar,
Where massy stone and iron bar
Were piled on echoing keep and tower,
To whelm the foe with deadly shower;
Was frequent heard the changing guard,
And watchword from the sleepless ward;
While, wearied by the endless din,
Blood-hound and ban-dog yell'd within.

XXXI.

The noble Dame, amid the broil,
Shared the gray Seneschal's high toil,
And spoke of danger with a smile;

---

* A Border beacon.

† *Mount for Branksome* was the gathering
word of the Scotts.

‡ *Need-fire,* beacon.

§ *Tarn,* a mountain lake.

‖ *Earn,* a Scottish eagle.

¶ *Boune,* make ready.

Cheer'd the young knights, and council
    sage
Held with the chiefs of riper age.
No tidings of the foe were brought,
Nor of his numbers knew they aught,
Nor what in time of truce he sought.
    Some said, that there were thousands
    ten;
And others ween'd that it was naught
    But Leven Clans, or Tynedale men,
Who came to gather in black-mail;*
And Liddesdale, with small avail,
    Might drive them lightly back agen.
So pass'd the anxious night away,
And welcome was the peep of day.

Ceased the high sound — the listening
    throng
Applaud the Master of the Song;
And marvel much, in helpless age,
So hard should be his pilgrimage.
Had he no friend — no daughter dear,
His wandering toil to share and cheer;
No son to be his father's stay,
And guide him on the rugged way?
' Ay, once he had — but he was dead!'
Upon the harp he stoop'd his head,
And busied himself the strings withal,
To hide the tear that fain would fall.
In solemn measure, soft and slow,
Arose a father's notes of woe.

CANTO FOURTH.

I.

Sweet Teviot! on thy silver tide
    The glaring bale-fires blaze no more;
No longer steel-clad warriors ride
    Along thy wild and willow'd shore;
Where'er thou wind'st, by dale or hill,
All, all is peaceful, all is still.
    As if thy waves, since Time was born,
Since first they roll'd upon the Tweed,
Had only heard the shepherd's reed,
    Nor started at the bugle-horn.

II.

Unlike the tide of human time,
    Which, though it change in ceaseless
    flow,

Retains each grief, retains each crime,
    Its earliest course was doom'd to know;
And, darker as it downward bears,
Is stain'd with past and present tears.
    Low as that tide has ebb'd with me,
It still reflects to Memory's eye
The hour my brave, my only boy,
    Fell by the side of great Dundee.†
Why, when the volleying musket play'd
Against the bloody Highland blade,
Why was not I beside him laid! —
Enough — he died the death of fame!
Enough — he died with conquering
    Græme!

III.

Now over Border, dale, and fell,
    Full wide and far was terror spread;
For pathless marsh, and mountain cell,
    The peasant left his lowly shed.[24]
The frighten'd flocks and herds were pent
Beneath the peel's rude battlement;
And maids and matrons dropp'd the tear,
While ready warriors seized the spear.
From Branksome's towers, the watch-
    man's eye
Dun wreaths of distant smoke can spy,
Which, curling in the rising sun,
Show'd southern ravage was begun.

IV.

Now loud the heedful gate-ward cried:—
    " Prepare ye all for blows and blood!
Watt Tinlinn,[25] from the Liddel-side,
    Comes wading through the flood.
Full oft the Tynedale snatchers knock
At his lone gate, and prove the lock;
It was but last St. Barnabright ‡
They sieged him a whole summer night,
But fled at morning; well they knew,
In vain he never twang'd the yew.
Right sharp has been the evening
    shower,
That drove him from his Liddel tower;
And by my faith," the gate-ward said,
" I think 'twill prove a Warden-Raid." §

---

† Claverhouse, Viscount of Dundee, slain in
the battle of Killicrankie.

‡ St. Barnabas's day, June 11. It is still called
Barnaby Bright in Hants, from its being generally a bright, sunshiny day.

§ An inroad commanded by the Warden in
person.

V.

While thus he spoke, the bold yeoman
Enter'd the echoing barbican.
He led a small and shaggy nag,
That through a bog, from hag to hag,*
Could bound like any Billhope stag.
It bore his wife and children twain;
A half-clothed serf † was all their train;
His wife, stout, ruddy, and dark-brow'd,
Of silver brooch and bracelet proud,
Laugh'd to her friends among the crowd.
He was of stature passing tall,
But sparely form'd, and lean withal;
A batter'd morion on his brow;
A leather jack, as fence enow,
On his broad shoulders loosely hung;
A border axe behind was slung;
  His spear, six Scottish ells in length,
    Seem'd newly dyed with gore;
  His shafts and bow, of wondrous
    strength,
    His hardy partner bore.

VI.

Thus to the Ladye did Tinlinn show
The tidings of the English foe:—
"Belted Will Howard [26] is marching
  here,
And hot Lord Dacre [27] with many a spear,
And all the German hackbut-men,[28]
Who have long lain at Askerten:
They cross'd the Liddel at curfew hour,
And burn'd my little lonely tower:
The fiend receive their souls therefor!
It had not been burnt this year and more.
Barn-yard and dwelling, blazing bright,
Served to guide me on my flight;
But I was chased the livelong night.
Black John of Akeshaw, and Fergus
  Græme,
Fast upon my traces came,
Until I turn'd at Priesthaugh Scrogg,
And shot their horses in the bog,
Slew Fergus with my lance outright —
I had him long at high despite:
He drove my cows last Fastern's
  night." ‡

* The broken ground in a bog.
† Bondsman.
‡ Shrove Tuesday, the eve of the great Spring
fast.

VII.

Now weary scouts from Liddesdale,
Fast hurrying in, confirm'd the tale;
  As far as they could judge by ken,
    Three hours would bring to Teviot's
      strand
  Three thousand armed Englishmen —
    Meanwhile, full many a warlike
      band,
From Teviot, Aill, and Ettrick shade,
Came in, their Chief's defence to aid.
  There was saddling and mounting in
    haste,
    There was pricking o'er moor and
      lea;
  He that was last at the trysting place
    Was but lightly held of his gaye
      ladye.

VIII.

From fair St. Mary's silver wave,
  From dreary Gamescleugh's dusky
    height,
His ready lances Thirlestane brave
  Array'd beneath a banner bright.
The tressured fleur-de-luce he claims,
To wreathe his shield, since royal James,
Encamp'd by Fala's mossy wave,
  The proud distinction grateful gave,
    For faith mid feudal jars;
What time, save Thirlestane alone,
Of Scotland's stubborn barons none
  Would march to southern wars;
And hence, in fair remembrance worn,
Yon sheaf of spears his crest has borne;
Hence his high motto shines reveal'd —
"Ready, aye ready," for the field.[29]

IX.

An aged Knight, to danger steel'd,
  With many a moss-trooper, came on:
And azure in a golden field,
  The stars and crescent graced his shield,
    Without the bend of Murdieston.
Wide lay his lands round Oakwood tower,
And wide round haunted Castle-Ower;
High over Borthwick's mountain flood,
His wood-embosom'd mansion stood,
In the dark glen, so deep below,
The herds of plunder'd England low;
His bold retainers' daily food,

And bought with danger, blows, and
    blood.
Marauding chief ! his sole delight
The moonlight raid, the morning fight;
Not even the Flower of Yarrow's charms,
In youth, might tame his rage for arms;
And still, in age, he spurn'd at rest,
And still his brows the helmet press'd,
Albeit the blanched locks below
Were white as Dinlay's spotless snow;
    Five stately warriors drew the sword
    Before their father's band;
    A braver knight than Harden's lord
    Ne'er belted on a brand.*

x.

Scotts of Eskdale, a stalwart band,
    Came trooping down the Todshawhill;
By the sword they won their land,
    And by the sword they hold it still.
Harken, Ladye, to the tale,
How thy sires won fair Eskdale. —
Earl Morton was lord of that valley fair,
The Beattisons were his vassals there.
The Earl was gentle, and mild of mood,
The vassals were warlike, and fierce, and
    rude;
High of heart, and haughty of word,
Little they reck'd of a tame liege lord.
The Earl into fair Eskdale came,
Homage and seignory to claim:
Of Gilbert the Galliard a heriot † he
    sought,
Saying, " Give thy best steed, as a vassal
    ought."
— " Dear to me is my bonny white steed,
Oft has he help'd me at pinch of need;
Lord and Earl though thou be, I trow,
I can rein Bucksfoot better than thou."
Word on word gave fuel to fire,
Till so highly blazed the Beattison's ire,
But that the Earl the flight had ta'en,
The vassals there their lord had slain.
Sore he plied both whip and spur,
As he urged his steed through Eskdale
    muir;
And it fell down a weary weight,
Just on the threshold of Branksome gate.

* This knight was the ancestor of Sir Walter
Scott.

† The feudal superior, in certain cases, was entitled to the best horse of the vassal, in name
of Heriot, or Herezeld.

XI.

The Earl was a wrathful man to see,
Full fain avenged would he be.
In haste to Branksome's Lord he spoke,
Saying — " Take these traitors to the
    yoke;
For a cast of hawks, and a purse of gold,
All Eskdale I'll sell thee, to have and
    hold;
Beshrew thy heart, of the Beattisons' clan
If thou leavest on Esk a landed man;
But spare Woodkerrick's lands alone,
For he lent me his horse to escape upon.'
A glad man then was Branksome bold,
Down he flung him the purse of gold;
To Eskdale soon he spurr'd amain,
And with him five hundred riders has
    ta'en.
He left his merrymen in the mist of the
    hill,
And bade them hold them close and still;
And alone he wended to the plain,
To meet with the Galliard and all his
    train.
To Gilbert the Galliard thus he said:—
" Know thou me for thy liege lord and
    head,
Deal not with me as with Morton tame,
For Scotts play best at the roughest game.
Give me in peace my heriot due,
Thy bonny white steed, or thou shalt rue.
If my horn I three times wind,
Eskdale shall long have the sound in
    mind."

XII.

Loudly the Beattison laugh'd in scorn:—
" Little care we for thy winded horn.
Ne'er shall it be the Galliard's lot,
To yield his steed to a haughty Scott.
Wend thou to Branksome back on foot,
With rusty spur and miry boot." —
He blew his bugle so loud and hoarse,
That the dun deer started at fair Craik-
    cross:
He blew again so loud and clear,
Through the gray mountain-mist there did
    lances appear:
And the third blast rang with such a din,
That the echoes answer'd from Pent-un-
    linn,
And all his riders came lightly in.

Then had you seen a gallant shock,
When saddles were emptied, and lances
   broke !
For each scornful word the Galliard had
   said,
A Beattison on the field was laid.
His own good sword the Chieftain drew,
And he bore the Galliard through and
   through :
Where the Beattison's blood mix'd with
   the rill,
The Galliard's-Haugh men call it still.
The Scotts have scatter'd the Beattison
   clan,
In Eskdale they left but one landed man.
The valley of Esk, from the mouth to the
   source,
Was lost and won for that bonny white
   horse.

XIII.

Whitslade the Hawk, and Headshaw
   came,
And warriors more than I may name;
From Yarrow-cleugh to Hindhaugh-
   swair,
   From Woodhouselie to Chester-glen,
Troop'd man and horse, and bow and
   spear;
   Their gathering word was Bellenden.[30]
And better hearts o'er Border sod
To siege or rescue never rode.
   The Ladye mark'd the aids come in,
   And high her heart of pride arose :
She bade her youthful son attend,
That he might know his father's friend,
   And learn to face his foes.
" The boy is ripe to look on war;
   I saw him draw a cross-bow stiff,
And his true arrow struck afar
   The raven's nest upon the cliff;
The red cross, on a southern breast,
Is broader than a raven's nest :
Thou, Whitslade, shalt teach him his wea-
   pon to wield,
And o'er him hold his father's shield."

XIV.

Well may you think, the wily page
Cared not to face the Ladye sage.
He counterfeited childish fear,
And shriek'd and shed full many a tear,

And moan'd and plain'd in manner
   wild.
   The attendants to the Ladye told,
Some fairy, sure had changed the child,
   That wont to be so free and bold.
Then wrathful was the noble dame;
She blush'd blood-red for very shame :—
" Hence ! ere the clan his faintness view;
Hence with the weakling to Buccleuch ! —
Watt Tinlinn, thou shalt be his guide
To Rangleburn's lonely side. —
Sure some fell fiend has cursed our line,
That coward should e'er be son of mine ! "

XV.

A heavy task Watt Tinlinn had,
To guide the counterfeited lad.
Soon as the palfrey felt the weight
Of that ill-omen'd elvish freight,
He bolted, sprung, and rear'd amain,
Nor heeded bit, nor curb, nor rein.
   It cost Watt Tinlinn mickle toil
   To drive him but a Scottish mile;
   But as a shallow brook they cross'd,
The elf, amid the running stream,
His figure changed, like form in dream,
   And fled, and shouted, " Lost ! lost !
   lost ! "
Full fast the urchin ran and laugh'd,
But faster still a cloth-yard shaft
Whistled from startled Tinlinn's yew,
And pierced his shoulder through and
   through.
Although the imp might not be slain,
And though the wound soon heal'd again,
Yet as he ran, he yell'd for pain;
And Watt of Tinlinn, much aghast,
Rode back to Branksome fiery fast.

XVI.

Soon on the hill's steep verge he stood,
That looks o'er Branksome's towers and
   wood;
And martial murmurs, from below,
Proclaim'd the approaching southern foe.
Through the dark wood, in mingled tone,
Were Border pipes and bugles blown,
The coursers' neighing he could ken,
A measured tread of marching men;
While broke at times the solemn hum,
The Almayn's sullen kettle-drum;

And banners tall, of crimson sheen,
 Above the copse appear;
And, glistening through the hawthorns
  green,
 Shine helm, and shield, and spear.

XVII.

Light forayers, first, to view the ground,
Spurr'd their fleet coursers loosely round;
 Behind, in close array, and fast,
  The Kendal archers, all in green,
 Obedient to the bugle blast,
  Advancing from the wood were seen.
To back and guard the archer band,
Lord Dacre's bill-men were at hand:
A hardy race, on Irthing bred,
With kirtles white, and crosses red,
Array'd beneath the banner tall,
That stream'd o'er Acre's conquer'd wall;
And minstrels, as they march'd in order,
Play'd " Noble Lord Dacre, he dwells on
 the Border."

XVIII.

Behind the English bill and bow,
The mercenaries, firm and slow,
 Moved on to fight, in dark array,
By Conrad led of Wolfenstein,
Who brought the band from distant Rhine,
 And sold their blood for foreign pay.
The camp their home, their law the sword,
They knew no country, own'd no lord:
They were not arm'd like England's sons,
But bore the levin-darting guns;
Buff-coats, all frounced and broider'd
 o'er,
And morsing-horns * and scarfs they wore;
Each better knee was bared, to aid
The warriors in the escalade;
All, as they march'd, in rugged tongue,
Songs of Teutonic feuds they sung.

XIX.

But louder still the clamor grew,
And louder still the minstrels blew,
When, from beneath the greenwood tree,
Rode forth Lord Howard's chivalry;
His men-at-arms, with glaive and spear,
Brought up the battle's glittering rear,

* Powder-flasks.

There many a youthful knight, full keen
To gain his spurs, in arms was seen;
With favor in his crest, or glove,
Memorial of his ladye-love.
So rode they forth in fair array,
Till full their lengthen'd lines display;
Then call'd a halt, and made a stand,
And cried, " St. George, for merry Eng-
 land ! "

XX.

Now every English eye, intent
On Branksome's armed towers were bent;
So near they were, that they might know
The straining harsh of each cross-bow;
On battlement and bartizan
Gleam'd axe and spear and partisan;
Falcon and culver,† on each tower,
Stood prompt their deadly hail to shower;
And flashing armor frequent broke
From eddying whirls of sable smoke,
Where upon tower and turret head,
The seething pitch and molten lead
Reek'd, like a witch's caldron red.
While yet they gaze, the bridges fall,
The wicket opes, and from the wall
Rides forth the hoary Seneschal.

XXI.

Armed he rode, all save the head,
His white beard o'er his breast-plate
 spread;
Unbroke by age, erect his seat,
He ruled his eager courser's gait;
Forced him, with chasten'd fire, to prance,
And, high curvetting, slow advance:
In sign of truce, his better hand
Display'd a peeled willow wand;
His squire, attending in the rear,
Bore high a gauntlet on a spear. ‡
When they espied him riding out,
Lord Howard and Lord Dacre stout
Sped to the front of their array,
To hear what this old knight should say:—

† Ancient pieces of artillery.

‡ A glove upon a lance was the emblem of
faith among the ancient Borderers, who were
wont, when any one broke his word, to expose
this emblem, and proclaim him a faithless villain at the first Border meeting. This ceremony was much dreaded. — *See* LESLEY.

XXII.

" Ye English warden lords, of you
Demands the Ladye of Buccleuch,
Why, 'gainst the truce of Border tide,
In hostile guise ye dare to ride,
With Kendal bow, and Gilsland brand,
And all yon mercenary band,
Upon the bounds of fair Scotland?
My Ladye redes you swith * return;
And, if but one poor straw you burn,
Or do our towers so much molest,
As scare one swallow from her nest,
St. Mary ! but we'll light a brand
Shall warm your hearths in Cumberland.''

XXIII.

A wrathful man was Dacre's lord,
But calmer Howard took the word:
" May't please thy Dame, Sir Seneschal,
To seek the castle's outward wall,
Our pursuivant-at-arms shall show
Both why we came, and when we go.'' —
The message sped, the noble Dame
To the wall's outward circle came;
Each chief around lean'd on his spear,
To see the pursuivant appear.
All in Lord Howard's livery dress'd,
The lion argent deck'd his breast;
He led a boy of blooming hue —
O sight to meet a mother's view !
It was the heir of great Buccleuch.
Obeisance meet the herald made,
And thus his master's will he said: —

XXIV.

" It irks, high Dame, my noble Lords,
'Gainst ladye fair to draw their swords:
But yet they may not tamely see,
All through the Western Wardenry,
Your law-contemning kinsmen ride,
And burn and spoil the Border-side;
And ill beseems your rank and birth
To make your towers a flemens-firth.†
We claim from thee William of Deloraine,
That he may suffer march-treason [31] pain.
It was but last St. Cuthbert's even
He prick'd to Stapleton on Leven,
Harried‡ the lands of Richard Musgrave,
And slew his brother by dint of glaive.

* *Swith*, instantly.
† An asylum for outlaws.
‡ Plundered.

Then, since a lone and widow'd Dame
These restless riders may not tame,
Either receive within thy towers
Two hundred of my master's powers,
Or straight they sound their warrison,§
And storm and spoil thy garrison:
And this fair boy, to London led,
Shall good King Edward's page be bred.''

XXV.

He ceased — and loud the boy did cry,
And stretch'd his little arms on high;
Implored for aid each well-known face,
And strove to seek the Dame's embrace.
A moment changed that Ladye's cheer,
Gush'd to her eye the unbidden tear;
She gazed upon the leaders round,
And dark and sad each warrior frown'd;
Then, deep within her sobbing breast
She lock'd the struggling sigh to rest;
Unalter'd and collected stood,
And thus replied, in dauntless mood: —

XXVI.

" Say to your Lords of high emprize,
Who war on women and on boys,
That either William of Deloraine
Will cleanse him, by oath, of march-
treason stain,
Or else he will the combat take
'Gainst Musgrave, for his honor's sake.
No knight in Cumberland so good,
But William may count with him kin and
blood.
Knighthood he took of Douglas' sword,[32]
When English blood swell'd Ancram's
ford; [33]
And but Lord Dacre's steed was wight,
And bare him ably in the flight,
Himself had seen him dubb'd a knight.
For the young heir of Branksome's line,
God be his aid, and God be mine;
Through me no friend shall meet his
doom;
Here, while I live, no foe finds room.
   Then, if thy Lords their purpose urge,
   Take our defiance loud and high;
   Our slogan is their lyke-wake ‖ dirge,
   Our moat, the grave where they shall
     lie.''

§ Note of assault.
‖ Watching a corpse all night.

XXVII.

Proud she look'd round, applause to
        claim —
Then lighten'd Thirlestane's eye of flame;
    His bugle Watt of Harden blew;
Pensils and pennons wide were flung,
To heaven the Border slogan rung,
    "St. Mary for the young Buccleuch!"
The English war-cry answer'd wide,
    And forward bent each southern spear;
Each Kendal archer made a stride,
    And drew the bowstring to his ear;
Each minstrel's war-note loud was blown:
But, ere a gray-goose shaft had flown,
A horseman gallop'd from the rear.

XXVIII.

"Ah! noble Lords!" he breathless said,
"What treason has your march betray'd?
What make you here, from aid so far,
Before you walls, around you war?
Your foemen triumph in the thought,
That in the toils the lion's caught.
Already on dark Ruberslaw
The Douglas holds his weapon-schaw;*
The lances, waving in his train,
Clothe the dun heath like autumn grain;
And on the Liddel's northern strand,
To bar retreat to Cumberland,
Lord Maxwell ranks his merry-men good,
Beneath the eagle and the rood;
    And Jedwood, Esk, and Teviotdale,
        Have to proud Angus come;
    And all the Merse and Lauderdale
        Have risen with haughty Home.
An exile from Northumberland,
    In Liddesdale I've wander'd long;
    But still my heart was with merry Eng-
        land,
        And cannot brook my country's
            wrong;
And hard I've spurr'd all night to show
The mustering of the coming foe."

XXIX.

"And let them come!" fierce Dacre
        cried;
"For soon yon crest, my father's pride,
That swept the shores of Judah's sea,
And waved in gales of Galilee,

* *Weapon-schaw* — military gathering of a
chief's followers, or the army of a county.

From Branksome's highest towers dis-
        play'd,
Shall mock the rescue's lingering aid! —
Level each harquebuss on row;
Draw, merry archers, draw the bow;
Up, bill-men, to the walls, and cry,
Dacre for England, win or die!"

XXX.

"Yet hear," quoth Howard, "calmly
        hear,
Nor deem my words the words of fear:
For who, in field or foray slack,
Saw the blanche lion e'er fall back? [34]
But thus to risk our Border flower
In strife against a kingdom's power,
Ten thousand Scots 'gainst thousands
        three,
Certes, were desperate policy.
Nay, take the terms the Ladye made,
Ere conscious of the advancing aid:
Let Musgrave meet fierce Deloraine
In single fight, and, if he gain,
He gains for us; but if he's cross'd,
'Tis but a single warrior lost:
The rest, retreating as they came,
Avoid defeat, and death, and shame."

XXXI.

Ill could the haughty Dacre brook
His brother Warden's sage rebuke;
And yet his forward step he staid,
And slow and sullenly obey'd.
But ne'er again the Border side
Did these two lords in friendship ride;
And this slight discontent, men say,
Cost blood upon another day.

XXXII.

The pursuivant-at-arms again
    Before the castle took his stand;
His trumpet call'd, with parleying strain,
    The leaders of the Scottish band;
And he defied, in Musgrave's right,
Stout Deloraine to single fight;
A gauntlet at their feet he laid,
And thus the terms of fight he said: —
"If in the lists good Musgrave's sword
    Vanquish the Knight of Deloraine,
Your youthful chieftain, Branksome's
        Lord
    Shall hostage for his clan remain:

If Deloraine foil good Musgrave,
The boy his liberty shall have.
Howe'er it falls, the English band,
Unharming Scots, by Scots unharm'd,
In peaceful march, like men unarm'd,
    Shall straight retreat to Cumberland."

XXXIII.

Unconscious of the near relief,
The proffer pleased each Scottish chief,
    Though much the Ladye sage gain-
        say'd;
For though their hearts were brave and
        true,
From Jedwood's recent sack they knew,
    How tardy was the Regent's aid:
And you may guess the noble Dame
    Durst not the secret prescience own,
Sprung from the art she might not name,
    By which the coming help was known.
Closed was the compact, and agreed
That lists should be enclosed with speed,
    Beneath the castle, on a lawn:
They fix'd the morrow for the strife,
On foot, with Scottish axe and knife,
    At the fourth hour from peep of dawn;
When Deloraine, from sickness freed,
Or else a champion in his stead,
Should for himself and chieftain stand,
Against stout Musgrave, hand to hand.

XXXIV.

I know right well, that, in their lay,
Full many minstrels sing and say,
    Such combat should be made on horse,
On foaming steed, in full career,
With brand to aid, when as the spear
    Should shiver in the course:
But he, the jovial Harper, taught
Me, yet a youth, how it was fought,
    In guise which now I say;
He knew each ordinance and clause
Of Black Lord Archibald's battle-laws,
    In the old Douglas' day.
He brook'd not, he, that scoffing tongue
Should tax his minstrelsy with wrong,
    Or call his song untrue:
For this, when they the goblet plied,
And such rude taunt had chafed his pride,
    The Bard of Reull he slew.
On Teviot's side, in fight they stood,

And tuneful hands were stain'd with
        blood;
Where still the thorn's white branches
        wave,
Memorial o'er his rival's grave.

XXXV.

Why should I tell the rigid doom,
That dragg'd my master to his tomb;
    How Ousenam's maidens tore their
        hair,
Wept till their eyes were dead and dim,
And wrung their hands for love of him,
    Who died at Jedwood Air?
He died! — his scholars, one by one,
To the cold silent grave are gone;
And I, alas! survive alone,
To muse o'er rivalries of yore,
And grieve that I shall hear no more
The strains, with envy heard before;
For, with my minstrel brethren fled,
My jealousy of song is dead.

———

He paused: the listening dames again
Applaud the hoary Minstrel's strain.
With many a word of kindly cheer, —
In pity half, and half sincere, —
Marvell'd the Duchess how so well
His legendary song could tell —
Of ancient deeds, so long forgot;
Of feuds, whose memory was not;
Of forests, now laid waste and bare;
Of towers, which harbor now the hare;
Of manners, long since changed and gone;
Of chiefs, who under their gray stone
So long had slept, that fickle Fame
Had blotted from her rolls their name,
And twined round some new minion's
        head
The fading wreath for which they bled;
In sooth, 'twas strange, this old man's
        verse
Could call them from their marble hearse.

The Harper smiled, well-pleased; for
        ne'er
Was flattery lost on poet's ear:
A simple race! they waste their toil
For the vain tribute of a smile;

E'en when in age their flame expires,
Her dulcet breath can fan its fires:
Their drooping fancy wakes at praise,
And strives to trim the short-lived blaze.
    Smiled then, well-pleased, the Aged Man,
And thus his tale continued ran.

CANTO FIFTH.

I.

CALL it not vain: — they do not err,
    Who say, that when the Poet dies,
Mute Nature mourns her worshipper,
    And celebrates his obsequies:
Who say, tall cliff, and cavern lone,
For the departed Bard make moan;
That mountains weep in crystal rill;
That flowers in tears of balm distil;
Through his loved groves that breezes sigh,
And oaks, in deeper groan, reply;
And rivers teach their rushing wave
To murmur dirges round his grave.

II.

Not that, in sooth, o'er mortal urn
Those things inanimate can mourn;
But that the stream, the wood, the gale,
Is vocal with the plaintive wail
Of those, who, else forgotten long,
Lived in the poet's faithful song,
And, with the poet's parting breath,
Whose memory feels a second death.
The Maid's pale shade, who wails her lot,
That love, true love, should be forgot,
From rose and hawthorn shakes the tear
Upon the gentle Minstrel's bier:
The phantom Knight, his glory fled,
Mourns o'er the field he heap'd with dead;
Mounts the wild blast that sweeps amain,
And shrieks along the battle-plain.
The Chief, whose antique crownlet long
Still sparkled in the feudal song,
Now, from the mountain's misty throne,
Sees, in the thanedom once his own,
His ashes undistinguish'd lie,
His place, his power, his memory die:

His groans the lonely caverns fill,
His tears of rage impel the rill:
All mourn the Minstrel's harp unstrung,
Their name unknown, their praise unsung.

III.

Scarcely the hot assault was staid,
The terms of truce were scarcely made,
When they could spy from Branksome's towers
The advancing march of martial powers.
Thick clouds of dust afar appear'd,
And trampling steeds were faintly heard;
Bright spears, above the columns dun,
Glanced momentary to the sun;
And feudal banners fair display'd
The bands that moved to Branksome's aid.

IV.

Vails not to tell each hardy clan,
    From the fair Middle Marches came;
The Bloody Heart blazed in the van,
    Announcing Douglas, dreaded name ! [35]
Vails not to tell what steeds did spurn,
Where the Seven Spears of Wedderburne*
    Their men in battle-order set;
And Swinton laid the lance in rest,
That tamed of yore the sparkling crest
    Of Clarence's Plantagenet. [36]
Nor list I say what hundreds more,
From the rich Merse and Lammermore,
And Tweed's fair borders, to the war,
Beneath the crest of Old Dunbar,
    And Hepburn's mingled banners come,
Down the steep mountain glittering far,
    And shouting still, "A Home! a Home!" [37]

V.

Now squire and knight, from Branksome sent,
On many a courteous message went;
To every chief and lord they paid
Meet thanks for prompt and powerful aid;
And told them, — how a truce was made,
    And how a day of fight was ta'en
'Twixt Musgrave and stout Deloraine;

* Sir David Home of Wedderburne, who was slain in the fatal battle of Flodden, left seven sons, who were called the Seven Spears of Wedderburne.

And how the Ladye pray'd them dear,
That all would stay the fight to see,
And deign, in love and courtesy,
    To taste of Branksome cheer.
Nor, while they bade to feast each Scot,
Were England's noble lords forgot.
Himself, the hoary Seneschal,
Rode forth, in seemly terms to call
Those gallant foes to Branksome Hall.
Accepted Howard, than whom knight
Was never dubb'd more bold in fight;
Nor, when from war and armor free,
More famed for stately courtesy;
But angry Dacre rather chose
In his pavilion to repose.

VI.

Now, noble Dame, perchance you ask,
    How these two hostile armies met?
Deeming it were no easy task
    To keep the truce which here was set;
Where martial spirits, all on fire,
Breathed only blood and mortal ire.—
By mutual inroads, mutual blows,
By habit, and by nation, foes,
    They met on Teviot's strand;
They met and sate them mingled down,
Without a threat, without a frown,
    As brothers meet in foreign land:
The hands, the spear that lately grasp'd,
Still in the mailed gauntlet clasp'd,
    Were interchanged in greeting dear;
Visors were raised, and faces shown,
And many a friend, to friend made known,
Partook of social cheer.
Some drove the jolly bowl about;
    With dice and draughts some chased
        the day;
And some, with many a merry shout,
In riot, revelry, and rout,
    Pursued the foot-ball play.

VII.

Yet, be it known, had bugles blown,
    Or sign of war been seen,
Those bands, so fair together ranged,
Those hands, so frankly interchanged,
    Had dyed with gore the green:
The merry shout by Teviotside
Had sunk in war-cries wild and wide,
    And in the groan of death:

And whingers * now in friendship bare,
The social meal to part and share,
    Had found a bloody sheath.
'Twixt truce and war, such sudden change
Was not infrequent, nor held strange,
    In the old Border-day : 38
But yet on Branksome's towers and town,
In peaceful merriment, sunk down
    The sun's declining ray.

VIII.

The blithesome signs of wassail gay
Decay'd not with the dying day;
Soon through the latticed windows tall
Of lofty Branksome's lordly hall,
Divided square by shafts of stone,
Huge flakes of ruddy lustre shone;
Nor less the gilded rafters rang
With merry harp and beakers' clang:
    And frequent, on the darkening plain,
        Loud hollo, whoop, or whistle ran,
    As bands, their stragglers to regain,
        Give the shrill watchword of their
            clan; 39
And revellers, o'er their bowls, proclaim
Douglas or Dacre's conquering name.

IX.

Less frequent heard, and fainter still,
    At length the various clamors died:
And you might hear, from Branksome hill,
    No sound but Teviot's rushing tide;
Save when the changing sentinel
The challenge of his watch could tell;
And save where, through the dark pro-
        found,
The clanging axe and hammer's sound
    Rung from the nether lawn;
For many a busy hand toil'd there,
Strong pales to shape, and beams to
        square,
The lists' dread barriers to prepare
    Against the morrow's dawn.

X.

Margaret from hall did soon retreat,
    Despite the Dame's reproving eye;
Nor mark'd she, as she left her seat,
    Full many a stifled sigh;

* Large knives.

For many a noble warrior strove
To win the Flower of Teviot's love,
    And many a bold ally. —
With throbbing head and anxious heart,
All in her lonely bower apart,
    In broken sleep she lay;
By times, from silken couch she rose;
While yet the banner'd hosts repose,
    She view'd the dawning day;
Of all the hundreds sunk to rest,
First woke the loveliest and the best.

XI.

She gazed upon the inner court,
    Which in the tower's tall shadow lay;
Where coursers' clang, and stamp, and snort,
    Had rung the livelong yesterday;
Now still as death; till stalking slow, —
    The jingling spurs announced his tread,
A stately warrior pass'd below;
    But when he raised his plumed head —
    Bless'd Mary! can it be? —
Secure, as if in Ousenam bowers,
He walks through Branksome's hostile towers,
    With fearless step and free.
She dared not sign, she dared not speak,
Oh! if one page's slumbers break,
    His blood the price must pay!
Not all the pearls Queen Mary wears,
Not Margaret's yet more precious tears,
    Shall buy his life a day.

XII.

Yet was his hazard small; for well
You may bethink you of the spell
    Of that sly urchin page;
This to his lord he did impart,
And made him seem, by glamour art,
    A knight from Hermitage.
Unchallenged thus, the warder's post,
The court, unchallenged, thus he cross'd,
    For all the vassalage:
But O! what magic's quaint disguise
Could blind fair Margaret's azure eyes!
    She started from her seat;
While with surprise and fear she strove,
And both could scarcely master love —
    Lord Henry's at her feet.

XIII.

Oft have I mused, what purpose bad
That foul malicious urchin had
    To bring this meeting round;
For happy love's a heavenly sight,
And by a vile malignant sprite
    In such no joy is found;
And oft I've deem'd, perchance he thought
Their erring passion might have wrought
    Sorrow, and sin, and shame;
And death to Cranstoun's gallant Knight,
And to the gentle ladye bright,
    Disgrace, and loss of fame.
But earthly spirit could not tell
The heart of them that loved so well.
True love's the gift which God has given
To man alone beneath the heaven;
    It is not fantasy's hot fire,
    Whose wishes, soon as granted, fly;
    It liveth not in fierce desire,
    With dead desire it doth not die;
It is the secret sympathy,
The silver link, the silken tie,
Which heart to heart, and mind to mind,
In body and in soul can bind.
Now leave we Margaret and her Knight,
To tell you of the approaching fight.

XIV.

Their warning blasts the bugles blew,
    The pipe's shrill port* aroused each clan;
In haste, the deadly strife to view,
    The trooping warriors eager ran:
Thick round the lists their lances stood,
Like blasted pines in Ettrick wood;
To Branksome many a look they threw,
The combatants' approach to view,
And bandied many a word of boast,
About the knight each favor'd most.

XV.

Meantime full anxious was the Dame;
For now arose disputed claim,
Of who should fight for Deloraine,
'Twixt Harden and 'twixt Thirlestane:
They 'gan to reckon kin and rent,
And frowning brow on brow was bent;

---

* A martial piece of music, adapted to the bagpipes.

But yet not long the strife — for, lo !
Himself, the Knight of Deloraine,
Strong, as it seem'd, and free from pain,
In armor sheath'd from top to toe,
Appear'd, and craved the combat due.
The Dame her charm successful knew,
And the fierce chiefs their claims withdrew.

XVI.

When for the lists they sought the plain,
The stately Ladye's silken rein
  Did noble Howard hold;
Unarmed by her side he walk'd,
And much, in courteous phrase, they
    talk'd
  Of feats of arms of old.
Costly his garb — his Flemish ruff
Fell o'er his doublet, shaped of buff,
  With satin slash'd and lined;
Tawny his boot, and gold his spur,
His cloak was all of Poland fur,
  His hose with silver twined;
His Bilboa blade, by Marchmen felt,
Hung in a broad and studded belt;
Hence, in rude phrase, the Borderers still
Call'd noble Howard, Belted Will.

XVII.

Behind Lord Howard and the Dame,
Fair Margaret on her palfrey came,
  Whose foot-cloth swept the ground:
White was her wimple, and her veil,
And her loose locks a chaplet pale
  Of whitest roses bound;
The lordly Angus, by her side,
In courtesy to cheer her tried;
Without his aid, her hand in vain
Had strove to guide her broider'd rein.
He deem'd she shudder'd at the sight
Of warriors met for mortal fight;
But cause of terror, all unguess'd,
Was fluttering in her gentle breast,
When, in their chairs of crimson placed,
The Dame and she the barriers graced.

XVIII.

Prize of the field, the young Buccleuch,
An English knight led forth to view:
Scarce rued the boy his present plight,
So much he longed to see the fight.
Within the lists, in knightly pride,
High Home and haughty Dacre ride;

Their leading staffs of steel they wield,
As marshals of the mortal field;
While to each knight their care assign'd
Like vantage of the sun and wind.
The heralds hoarse did loud proclaim,
In King and Queen and Warden's name,
  That none, while lasts the strife,
Should dare, by look, or sign, or word,
Aid to a champion to afford,
  On peril of his life;
And not a breath the silence broke,
Till thus the alternate Heralds spoke: —

XIX.

ENGLISH HERALD.

" Here standeth Richard of Musgrave,
  Good knight and true, and freely born,
    Amends from Deloraine to crave,
  For foul despiteous scathe and scorn.
He sayeth, that William of Deloraine
Is traitor false by Border laws;
This with his sword he will maintain,
  So help him God, and his good cause ! "

XX.

SCOTTISH HERALD.

" Here standeth William of Deloraine,
Good knight and true, of noble strain,
Who sayeth, that foul treason's stain,
  Since he bore arms, ne'er soil'd his
      coat,
    And that, so help him God above !
    He will on Musgrave's body prove,
He lies most foully in his throat."

LORD DACRE.

" Forward, brave champions, to the fight !
Sound trumpets ! " ——

LORD HOME.

—— " God defend the right ! "
Then, Teviot ! how thine echoes rang,
When bugle-sound and trumpet clang
  Let loose the martial foes,
And in mid list with shield poised high,
And measured step and wary eye,
  The combatants did close.

XXI.

Ill would it suit your gentle ear,
Ye lovely listeners, to hear

How to the axe the helms did sound,
And blood pour'd down from many a
    wound;
For desperate was the strife and long,
And either warrior fierce and strong,
But, were each dame a listening knight,
I well could tell how warriors fight !
For I have seen war's lightning flashing,
Seen the claymore with bayonet clashing,
Seen through red blood the war-horse
    dashing,
And scorn'd, amid the reeling strife,
To yield a step for death or life. —

XXII.

'Tis done, 'tis done ! that fatal blow
    Has stretch'd him on the bloody plain !
He strives to rise — Brave Musgrave, no !
    Thence never shalt thou rise again !
He chokes in blood — some friendly hand
Undo the visor's barred band,
Unfix the gorget's iron clasp,
And give him room for life to gasp ! —
O, bootless aid ! — haste, holy Friar,
Haste, ere the sinner shall expire !
Of all his guilt let him be shriven,
And smooth his path from earth to heaven !

XXIII.

In haste the holy Friar sped; —
His naked foot was dyed with red,
    As through the lists he ran;
Unmindful of the shouts on high,
That hail'd the conqueror's victory,
    He raised the dying man;
Loose waved his silver beard and hair,
As o'er him he kneel'd down in prayer;
And still the crucifix on high
He holds before his darkening eye;
And still he bends an anxious ear,
His faltering penitence to hear;
Still props him from the bloody sod,
Still, even when soul and body part,
Pours ghostly comfort on his heart,
    And bids him trust in God !
Unheard he prays; — the death-pang's
    o'er !
Richard of Musgrave breathes no more.

XXIV.

As if exhausted in the fight,
Or musing o'er the piteous sight,

    The silent victor stands;
His beaver did he not unclasp,
Mark'd not the shouts, felt not the grasp
    Of gratulating hands.
When lo ! strange cries of wild surprise
Mingled with seeming terror, rise
    Among the Scottish bands;
And all, amid the throng'd array,
In panic haste gave open way
To a half-naked ghastly man,
Who downward from the castle ran.
He cross'd the barriers at a bound,
And wild and haggard look'd around,
    As dizzy, and in pain;
And all, upon the armed ground,
    Knew William of Deloraine !
Each lady sprung from seat with speed;
Vaulted each marshal from his steed;
    " And who art thou," they cried,
" Who hast this battle fought and won ? "
His plumed helm was soon undone —
    " Cranstoun of Teviot-side !
For this fair prize I've fought and won,"
And to the Ladye led her son.

XXV.

Full oft the rescued boy she kiss'd,
And often press'd him to her breast;
For, under all her dauntless show,
Her heart had throbb'd at every blow;
Yet not Lord Cranstoun deign'd she greet,
Though low he kneeled at her feet.
Me lists not tell what words were made,
What Douglas, Home, and Howard, said
—For Howard was a generous foe —
And how the clan united pray'd
    The Ladye would the feud forego,
And deign to bless the nuptial hour
Of Cranstoun's Lord and Teviot's Flower.

XXVI.

She look'd to river, look'd to hill,
    Thought on the Spirit's prophecy,
Then broke her silence stern and still,—
    " Not you, but Fate, has vanquish'd me.
Their influence kindly stars may shower
On Teviot's tide and Branksome's tower,
    For pride is quell'd, and love is free."—
She took fair Margaret by the hand,
Who, breathless, trembling, scarce might
    stand,

That hand to Cranstoun's Lord gave
      she:
"As I am true to thee and thine,
Do thou be true to me and mine!
This clasp of love our bond shall be;
For this is your betrothing day,
And all these noble lords shall stay,
    To grace it with their company."

XXVII.

All as they left the listed plain,
Much of the story she did gain;
How Cranstoun fought with Deloraine,
And of his page, and of the Book
Which from the wounded knight he took;
And how he sought her castle high,
That morn, by help of gramarye;
How, in Sir William's armor dight,
Stolen by his page, while slept the knight,
He took on him the single fight.
But half his tale he left unsaid,
And linger'd till he join'd the maid. —
Cared not the Ladye to betray
Her mystic arts in view of day;
But well she thought, ere midnight came,
Of that strange page the pride to tame,
From his foul hands the Book to save,
And send it back to Michael's grave.—
Needs not to tell each tender word
'Twixt Margaret and 'twixt Cranstoun's
      Lord;
Nor how she told of former woes,
And how her bosom fell and rose,
While he and Musgrave bandied blows.—
Needs not these lovers' joys to tell:
One day, fair maids, you'll know them
      well.

XXVIII.

William of Deloraine, some chance
Had wakened from his death-like trance;
    And taught that, in the listed plain,
Another, in his arms and shield,
Against fierce Musgrave axe did wield,
    Under the name of Deloraine.
Hence, to the field, unarm'd, he ran,
And hence his presence scared the clan,
Who held him for some fleeting wraith,*
And not a man of blood and breath.
    Not much this new ally he loved,
    Yet, when he saw what hap had proved,
    He 'greeted him right heartilie:

* The spectral apparition of a living person.

He would not waken old debate,
For he was void of rancorous hate,
    Though rude and scant of courtesy;
In raids he spilt but seldom blood,
Unless when men-at-arms withstood,
Or, as was meet for deadly feud.
He ne'er bore grudge for stalwart blow,
Ta'en in fair fight from gallant foe;
    And so 'twas seen of him, e'en now,
      When on dead Musgrave he look'd
        down;
    Grief darken'd on his rugged brow,
      Though half disguised with a frown;
And thus, while sorrow bent his head,
His foeman's epitaph he made:—

XXIX.

"Now, Richard Musgrave, liest thou here!
    I ween my deadly enemy;
For, if I slew thy brother dear,
    Thou slew'st a sister's son to me;
And when I lay in dungeon dark,
    Of Naworth Castle, long months three,
Till ransom'd for a thousand mark,
    Dark Musgrave, it was long of thee.
And, Musgrave, could our fight be tried,
    And thou wert now alive as I,
No mortal man should us divide,
    Till one, or both of us, did die:
Yet rest thee God! for well I know
I ne'er shall find a nobler foe.
In all the northern counties here,
Whose word is Snaffle, spur, and spear,
Thou wert the best to follow gear!
'Twas pleasure, as we look'd behind,
To see how thou the chase could'st wind,
Cheer the dark blood-hound on his way,
And with the bugle rouse the fray!
I'd give the lands of Deloraine,
Dark Musgrave were alive again."

XXX.

So mourn'd he, till Lord Dacre's band
Were bouning back to Cumberland.
They raised brave Musgrave from the field,
And laid him on his bloody shield;
On levell'd lances, four and four,
By turns the noble burden bore.
Before, at times, upon the gale,
Was heard the Minstrel's plaintive wail;
Behind, four priests, in sable stole,
Sung requiem for the warrior's soul:

Around, the horsemen slowly rode;
With trailing pikes the spearmen trode;
And thus the gallant knight they bore,
Through Liddesdale to Leven's shore;
Thence to Holme Coltrame's lofty nave,
And laid him in his father's grave.

THE harp's wild notes, though hush'd
   the song,
The mimic march of death prolong;
Now seems it far, and now a-near,
Now meets, and now eludes the ear;
Now seems some mountain-side to sweep,
Now faintly dies in valley deep;
Seems now as if the Minstrel's wail,
Now the sad requiem, loads the gale;
Last, o'er the warrior's closing grave,
Rung the full choir in choral stave.

After due pause, they bade him tell,
Why he, who touch'd the harp so well,
Should thus, with ill-rewarded toil,
Wander a poor and thankless soil,
When the more generous Southern Land
Would well requite his skilful hand.

The Aged Harper, howsoe'er
His only friend, his harp, was dear,
Liked not to hear it rank'd so high
Above his flowing poesy:
Less liked he still, that scornful jeer
Misprised the land he loved so dear;
High was the sound, as thus again
The Bard resumed his minstrel strain.

CANTO SIXTH.

I.

BREATHES there the man, with soul so
   dead,
Who never to himself hath said,
   This is my own, my native land!
Whose heart hath ne'er within him burn'd,
As home his footsteps he hath turn'd,
   From wandering on a foreign strand!
If such there breathe, go, mark him well;
For him no Minstrel raptures swell;
High though his titles, proud his name,
Boundless his wealth as wish can claim;
Despite those titles, power, and pelf,
The wretch, concentred all in self,

Living, shall forfeit fair renown,
And, doubly dying, shall go down
To the vile dust, from whence he sprung,
Unwept, unhonor'd, and unsung.

II.

O Caledonia! stern and wild,
Meet nurse for a poetic child!
Land of brown heath and shaggy wood,
Land of the mountain and the flood,
Land of my sires! what mortal hand
Can e'er untie the filial band,
That knits me to thy rugged strand!
Still, as I view each well-known scene,
Think what is now, and what hath been,
Seems as, to me, of all bereft,
Sole friends thy woods and streams were
      left;
And thus I love them better still,
Even in extremity of ill.
By Yarrow's streams still let me stray,
Though none should guide my feeble way;
Still feel the breeze down Ettrick break,
Although it chill my wither'd cheek;*
Still lay my head by Teviot Stone,
Though there, forgotten and alone,
The Bard may draw his parting groan.

III.

Not scorn'd like me! to Branksome Hall
The Minstrels came, at festive call;
Trooping they came, from near and far,
The jovial priests of mirth and war;
Alike for feast and fight prepared,
Battle and banquet both they shared.
Of late, before each martial clan,
They blew their death-note in the van,
But now, for every merry mate,
Rose the portcullis' iron grate;
They sound the pipe, they strike the
   string,
They dance, they revel, and they sing,
Till the rude turrets shake and ring.

IV.

Me lists not at this tide declare
   The splendor of the spousal rite,
How muster'd in the chapel fair
      Both maid and matron, squire and
      knight;

* The preceding four lines now form the inscription on the monument of Sir Walter Scott
in the market-place of Selkirk.

Me lists not tell of owches rare,
Of mantles green, and braided hair,
And kirtles furr'd with miniver;
What plumage waved the altar round,
How spurs and ringing chainlets sound;
And hard it were for bard to speak
The changeful hue of Margaret's cheek;
That lovely hue which comes and flies,
As awe and shame alternate rise!

V.

Some bards have sung, the Ladye high
Chapel or altar came not nigh;
Nor durst the rights of spousal grace,
So much she fear'd each holy place.
False slanders these: — I trust right well
She wrought not by forbidden spell;[40]
For mighty words and signs have power
O'er sprites in planetary hour:
Yet scarce I praise their venturous part,
Who tamper with such dangerous art.
   But this for faithful truth I say,
   The Ladye by the altar stood,
Of sable velvet her array,
   And on her head a crimson hood,
With pearls embroider'd and entwined,
Guarded with gold, with ermine lined;
A merlin sat upon her wrist[41]
Held by a leash of silken twist.

VI.

The spousal rites were ended soon:
'Twas now the merry hour of noon,
And in the lofty arched hall
Was spread the gorgeous festival.
Steward and squire, with heedful haste,
Marshall'd the rank of every guest;
Pages, with ready blade, were there,
The mighty meal to carve and share.
O'er capon, heron-shew, and crane,
And princely peacock's gilded train,[42]
And o'er the boar-head, garnish'd brave,
And cygnet from St. Mary's wave;*
O'er ptarmigan and venison,
The priest had spoke his benison.
Then rose the riot and the din,
Above, beneath, without, within!
For, from the lofty balcony,
Rung trumpet, shalm, and psaltery:

* Flights of wild swans are often seen on St. Mary's Lake, which is at the head of the Yarrow.

Their clanging bowls old warriors quaff'd,
Loudly they spoke, and loudly laugh'd;
Whisper'd young knights, in tone more mild,
To ladies fair, and ladies smiled.
The hooded hawks, high perch'd on beam,
The clamor join'd with whistling scream,
And flapp'd their wings, and shook their bells,
In concert with the stag-hound's yells.
Round go the flasks of ruddy wine,
From Bordeaux, Orléans, or the Rhine.
Their tasks the busy sewers ply,
And all is mirth and revelry.

VII.

The Goblin Page, omitting still
No opportunity of ill,
Strove now, while blood ran hot and high,
To rouse debate and jealousy;
Till Conrad, Lord of Wolfenstein,
By nature fierce, and warm with wine,
And now in humor highly cross'd,
About some steeds his band had lost,
High words to words succeeding still,
Smote, with his gauntlet, stout Hunthill;[43]
A hot and hardy Rutherford,
Whom men called Dickon Draw-the-Sword.
He took it on the page's saye,
Hunthill had driven these steeds away.
Then Howard, Home, and Douglas rose,
The kindling discord to compose:
Stern Rutherford right little said,
But bit his glove,[44] and shook his head.
A fortnight thence, in Inglewood,
Stout Conrad, cold, and drench'd in blood,
His bosom gored with many a wound,
Was by a woodman's lyme-dog found;
Unknown the manner of his death,
Gone was his brand, both sword and sheath:
But ever from that time, 'twas said,
That Dickon wore a Cologne blade.

VIII.

The dwarf, who fear'd his master's eye
Might his foul treachery espie,
Now sought the castle buttery,
Where many a yeoman, bold and free,
Revell'd as merrily and well
As those that sat in lordly selle.

Watt Tinlinn, there, did frankly raise
The pledge to Arthur Fire-the-Braes;*
And he, as by his breeding bound,
To Howard's merry-men sent it round.
To quit them, on the English side,
Red Roland Forster loudly cried,
" A deep carouse to yon fair bride ! " —
At every pledge, from vat and pail,
Foam'd forth in floods the nut-brown ale;
While shout the riders every one;
Such day of mirth ne'er cheer'd their clan,
Since old Buccleuch the name did gain,
When in the cleuch the buck was ta'en.

IX.

The wily page, with vengeful thought,
Remember'd him of Tinlinn's yew.
And swore, it should be dearly bought
That ever he the arrow drew.
First, he the yeoman did molest,
With bitter gibe and taunting jest;
Told, how he fled at Solway strife,
And how Hob Armstrong cheer'd his wife;
Then, shunning still his powerful arm,
At unawares he wrought him harm;
From trencher stole his choicest cheer,
Dash'd from his lips his can of beer;
Then, to his knee sly creeping on,
With bodkin pierced him to the bone:
The venom'd wound, and festering joint,
Long after rued that bodkin's point.
The startled yeoman swore and spurn'd,
And board and flagons overturn'd.
Riot and clamor wild began;
Back to the hall the Urchin ran;
Took in a darkling nook his post,
And grinn'd, and mutter'd " Lost ! lost !
    lost !"

X.

By this, the Dame, lest farther fray
Should mar the concord of the day,
Had bid the Minstrels tune their lay.
And first stept forth old Albert Græme,
The Minstrel of that ancient name : 45
Was none who struck the harp so well,
Within the Land Debateable.
Well friended, too, his hardy kin,
Whoever lost, were sure to win;

They sought the beeves that made their
    broth,
In Scotland and in England both.
In homely guise, as nature bade,
His simple song the Borderer said.

XI.

ALBERT GRÆME.

It was an English ladye bright,
    (The sun shines fair on Carlisle wall,†)
And she would marry a Scottish knight,
    For Love will still be lord of all.

Blithely they saw the rising sun,
    When he shone fair on Carlisle wall;
But they were sad ere day was done,
    Though Love was still the lord of all.

Her sire gave brooch and jewel fine,
    Where the sun shines fair on Carlisle
        wall;
Her brother gave but a flask of wine,
    For ire that Love was lord of all.

For she had lands, both meadow and lea,
    Where the sun shines fair on Carlisle
        wall,
And he swore her death, ere he would see
    A Scottish knight the lord of all !

XII.

That wine she had not tasted well,
    (The sun shines fair on Carlisle wall,)
When dead, in her true love's arms, she
        fell,
    For Love was still the lord of all !

He pierced her brother to the heart,
    Where the sun shines fair on Carlisle
        wall:
So perish all would true love part,
    That Love may still be lord of all !

And then he took the cross divine,
    (Where the sun shines fair on Carlisle
        wall,)
And died for her sake in Palestine,
    So Love was still the lord of all.

Now all ye lovers, that faithful prove,
    (The sun shines fair on Carlisle wall,)
Pray for their souls who died for love,
    For Love shall still be lord of all !

---

* The person bearing this redoutable *nom de guerre* was an Elliott, and resided at Thorleshope, in Liddesdale. He occurs in the list of Border riders, in 1597.

† This burden is from an old Scottish song.

XIII.

As ended Albert's simple lay,
    Arose a bard of loftier port;
For sonnet, rhyme, and roundelay,
    Renown'd in haughty Henry's court:
There rung thy harp, unrivall'd long,
Fitztraver of the silver song!
    The gentle Surrey loved his lyre —
        Who has not heard of Surrey's
            fame? [46]
    His was the hero's soul of fire,
        And his the bard's immortal name,
And his was love, exalted high
By all the glow of chivalry.

XIV.

They sought, together, climes afar,
    And oft, within some olive grove,
When even came with twinkling star,
    They sung of Surrey's absent love.
His step the Italian peasant stay'd,
    And deem'd, that spirits from on high,
Round where some hermit saint was laid,
    Were breathing heavenly melody;
So sweet did harp and voice combine
To praise the name of Geraldine.

XV.

Fitztraver! O what tongue may say
    The pangs thy faithful bosom knew,
When Surrey, of the deathless lay,
    Ungrateful Tudor's sentence slew?
Regardless of the tyrant's frown,
His harp call'd wrath and vengeance
        down.
He left, for Naworth's iron towers,
Windsor's green glades, and courtly
        bowers,
And faithful to his patron's name,
With Howard still Fitztraver came;
Lord William's foremost favorite he,
And chief of all his minstrelsy.

XVI.

FITZTRAVER.

'Twas All-souls' eve, and Surrey's heart
        beat high;
    He heard the midnight bell with anx-
        ious start,
Which told the mystic hour, approaching
        nigh,
    When wise Cornelius promised, by his
        art,

To show to him the ladye of his heart,
    Albeit betwixt them roar'd the ocean
        grim;
Yet so the sage had hight to play his part,
    That he should see her form in life
        and limb,
And mark, if still she loved, and still she
        thought of him.

XVII.

Dark was the vaulted room of gramarye,
    To which the wizard led the gallant
        Knight,
Save that before a mirror, huge and high,
    A hallow'd taper shed a glimmering
        light
On mystic implements of magic might;
    On cross, and character, and talisman,
And altmagest, and altar, nothing bright:
    For fitful was the lustre, pale and wan,
As watchlight by the bed of some de-
        parting man.

XVIII.

But soon, within that mirror huge and high,
    Was seen a self-emitted light to gleam;
And forms upon its breast the Earl 'gan
        spy,
    Cloudy and indistinct, as feverish
        dream,
Till, slow arranging, and defined, they
        seem
To form a lordly and a lofty room,
    Part lighted by a lamp with silver beam,
Placed by a couch of Agra's silken
        loom,
And part by moonshine pale, and part
        was hid in gloom.

XIX.

Fair all the pageant—but how passing fair
    The slender form, which lay on couch
        of Ind!
O'er her white bosom stray'd her hazel
        hair,
    All in her night-robe loose she lay re-
        clined.
    Pale her dear cheek, as if for love she
        pined;
And, pensive, read from tablet eburnine
Some strain that seem'd her inmost soul
        to find; —

That favor'd strain was Surrey's raptured line,
That fair and lovely form, the Lady Geraldine !

XX.

Slow roll'd the clouds upon the lovely
form,
   And swept the goodly vision all away —
So royal envy roll'd the murky storm
   O'er my beloved Master's glorious day.
Thou jealous, ruthless tyrant ! Heaven
repay
   On thee, and on thy children's latest
line,
The wild caprice of thy despotic sway,
   The gory bridal bed, the plunder'd
shrine,
The murder'd Surrey's blood, the tears of
Geraldine.

XXI.

Both Scots and Southern chiefs prolong
Applauses of Fitztraver's song;
These hated Henry's name as death,
And those still held the ancient faith —
Then, from his seat, with lofty air,
Rose Harold, bard of brave St. Clair;
St. Clair, who, feasting high at Home,
Had with that lord to battle come.
Harold was born where restless seas
Howl round the storm-swept Orcades;
Where erst St. Clairs held princely sway
O'er isle and islet, strait and bay; —
Still nods their palace to its fall,
Thy pride and sorrow, fair Kirkwall ! —
Thence oft he mark'd fierce Pentland rave,
As if grim Odin rode her wave;
And watch'd, the whilst, with visage pale,
And throbbing heart, the struggling sail;
For all of wonderful and wild
Had rapture for the lonely child.

XXII.

And much of wild and wonderful
In these rude isles might fancy cull !
For thither came, in times afar,
Stern Lochlin's sons of roving war,
The Norsemen, train'd to spoil and blood,
Skill'd to prepare the raven's food;
Kings of the main their leaders brave,
Their barks the dragons of the wave.

And there, in many a stormy vale,
The Scald had told his wondrous tale;
And many a Runic column high
Had witness'd grim idolatry.
And thus had Harold, in his youth,
Learn'd many a Saga's rhyme uncouth,—
Of that Sea-Snake * tremendous curl'd,
Whose monstrous circle girds the world;
Of those dread Maids † whose hideous yell
Maddens the battle's bloody swell;
Of Chiefs, who, guided through the gloom
By the pale death-lights of the tomb,
Ransack'd the graves of warriors old,
Their falchions wrench'd from corpses'
hold,
Waked the deaf tomb with war's alarms,
And bade the dead arise to arms !
With war and wonder all on flame,
To Roslin's bowers young Harold came,
Where, by sweet glen and greenwood
tree,
He learn'd a milder minstrelsy;
Yet something of the Northern spell
Mix'd with the softer numbers well.

XXIII.

HAROLD.

O listen, listen, ladies gay !
   No haughty feat of arms I tell;
Soft is the note, and sad the lay,
   That mourns the lovely Rosabelle.

— " Moor, moor the barge, ye gallant
crew !
   And, gentle ladye, deign to stay,
Rest thee in Castle Ravensheuch,
   Nor tempt the stormy firth to-day.

"The blackening wave is edged with
white :
   To inch ‡ and rock the sea-mews fly;
The fishers have heard the Water-Sprite,
   Whose screams forebode that wreck is
nigh.

* The *jormungandr* or snake of the ocean,
whose folds surround the earth. It was very
nearly caught by the god Thor, who went to fish
for it with a hook baited with a bull's head. See
the "Edda," or Mallet's "Northern Antiquities," p. 445.

† The *Valkyriur* or Scandinavian Fates, or
Fatal Sisters.

‡ *Inch*, an island.

" Last night the gifted Seer did view
  A wet shroud swathed round ladye gay;
Then stay thee, Fair, in Ravensheuch:
  Why cross the gloomy firth to-day ? " —

" 'Tis not because Lord Lindesay's heir
  To-night at Roslin leads the ball,
But that my ladye-mother there
  Sits lonely in her castle-hall.

" 'Tis not because the ring they ride,
  And Lindesay at the ring rides well,
But that my sire the wine will chide,
  If 'tis not fill'd by Rosabelle." —

O'er Roslin all that dreary night
  A wondrous blaze was seen to gleam;
'Twas broader than the watch-fire's light,
  And redder than the bright moonbeam.

It glared on Roslin's castled rock,
  It ruddied all the copse-wood glen,
'Twas seen from Dryden's groves of oak,
  And seen from cavern'd Hawthornden.

Seem'd all on fire that chapel proud,
  Where Roslin's chiefs uncoffin'd lie,
Each Baron, for a sable shroud,
  Sheathed in his iron panoply.

Seem'd all on fire, within, around,
  Deep sacristy and altar's pale,
Shone every pillar foliage-bound,
  And glimmer'd all the dead men's mail.

Blazed battlement and pinnet high,
  Blazed every rose-carved buttress fair —
So still they blaze, when fate is nigh
  The lordly line of high St. Clair.

There are twenty of Roslin's barons bold
  Lie buried within that proud chapelle;
Each one the holy vault doth hold —
  But the sea holds lovely Rosabelle !

And each St. Clair was buried there,
  With candle, with book, and with knell;
But the sea-caves rung, and the wild
    winds sung,
  The dirge of lovely Rosabelle.

XXIV.

So sweet was Harold's piteous lay,
  Scarce mark'd the guests the darken'd
    hall,
Though, long before the sinking day,
  A wondrous shade involved them all:
It was not eddying mist or fog,
Drain'd by the sun from fen or bog;
  Of no eclipse had sages told;
And yet, as it came on apace,
Each one could scarce his neighbor's face,
  Could scarce his own stretch'd hand
    behold.
A secret horror check'd the feast,
And chill'd the soul of every guest;
Even the high Dame stood half aghast,
She knew some evil on the blast;
The elvish page fell to the ground,
And, shuddering, mutter'd, " Found !
    found ! found ! "

XXV.

Then sudden, through the darken'd air,
  A flash of lightning came;
So broad, so bright, so red the glare,
  The castle seem'd on flame.
Glanced every rafter of the hall,
Glanced every shield upon the wall;
Each trophied beam, each sculptured
    stone,
Were instant seen, and instant gone:
Full through the guests' bedazzled band
Resistless flash'd the levin-brand,
And fill'd the hall with smouldering
    smoke,
As on the elvish page it broke.
  It broke, with thunder long and loud,
  Dismay'd the brave, appall'd the
    proud, —
  From sea to sea the larum rung;
  On Berwick wall, and at Carlisle withal,
  To arms the startled warders sprung:
When ended was the dreadful roar,
The elvish dwarf was seen no more.

XXVI.

Some heard a voice in Branksome Hall,
Some saw a sight, not seen by all;
That dreadful voice was heard by some,
Cry, with loud summons, " GYLBIN,
    COME ! "

And on the spot where burst the brand,
　Just where the page had flung him
　　down,
Some saw an arm, and some a hand,
　And some the waving of a gown.
The guests in silence pray'd and shook,
And terror dimm'd each lofty look.
But none of all the astonish'd train
Was so dismay'd as Deloraine;
His blood did freeze, his brain did burn,
'Twas fear'd his mind would ne'er return;
For he was speechless, ghastly, wan,
Like him of whom the story ran,
　Who spoke the spectre-hound in Man.
At length, by fits, he darkly told,
With broken hint, and shuddering cold —
　That he had seen, right certainly,
A shape with amice wrapp'd around,
With a wrought Spanish baldric bound,
Like pilgrim from beyond the sea ;
And knew — but how it matter'd not —
It was the wizard, Michael Scott.

XXVII.

The anxious crowd, with horror pale,
All trembling heard the wondrous tale;
　No sound was made, no word was spoke,
　Till noble Angus silence broke;
　　And he a solemn sacred plight
　　Did to St. Bride of Douglas make,
　　That he a pilgrimage would take
　　To Melrose Abbey, for the sake
　　　Of Michael's restless sprite.
Then each, to ease his troubled breast,
To some bless'd saint his prayers ad-
　　dress'd :
Some to St. Modan made their vows,
Some to St. Mary of the Lowes,
Some to the Holy Rood of Lisle,
Some to our Ladye of the Isle;
Each did his patron witness make,
That he such pilgrimage would take,
And monks should sing, and bells should
　　toll,
All for the weal of Michael's soul.
While vows were ta'en, and prayers
　　were pray'd,
'Tis said the noble dame, dismay'd,
Renounced, for aye, dark magic's aid.

XXVIII.

Naught of the bridal will I tell,
Which after in short space befell;

Nor how brave sons and daughters fair
Bless'd Teviot's Flower, and Cranstoun's
　　heir :
After such dreadful scene, 'twere vain
To wake the note of mirth again.
　More meet it were to mark the day
　　Of penitence and prayer divine
　　When pilgrim chiefs, in sad array,
　　Sought Melrose' holy shrine.

XXIX.

With naked foot, and sackcloth vest,
And arms enfolded on his breast,
　Did every pilgrim go;
The standers-by might hear uneath,[*]
Footstep, or voice, or high-drawn breath,
　Through all the lengthen'd row.
No lordly look, nor martial stride,
Gone was their glory, sunk their pride,
　Forgotten their renown;
Silent and slow, like ghosts they glide
To the high altar's hallow'd side,
　And there they knelt them down :
Above the suppliant chieftains wave
The banners of departed brave;
Beneath the letter'd stones were laid
The ashes of their fathers dead;
From many a garnish'd niche around,
Stern saints and tortured martyrs frown'd

XXX.

And slow up the dim aisle afar,
With sable cowl and scapular,
And snow-white stoles, in order due,
The holy Fathers, two and two,
　In long procession came;
Taper, and host, and book they bare,
And holy banner, flourish'd fair
　With the Redeemer's name.
Above the prostrate pilgrim band
The mitred Abbot stretch'd his hand,
　And bless'd them as they kneel'd;
With holy cross he sign'd them all,
And pray'd they might be sage in hall,
　And fortunate in field.
Then mass was sung and prayers were said,
And solemn requiem for the dead;
And bells toll'd out their mighty peal,
For the departed spirit's weal;
And ever in the office close
The hymn of intercession rose :

---

[*] Scarcely hear.

And far the echoing aisles prolong
The awful burden of the song, —
   DIES IRÆ, DIES ILLA,
   SOLVET SÆCLUM IN FAVILLA;
While the pealing organ rung.
   Were it meet with sacred strain
   To close my lay, so light and vain,
Thus the holy Fathers sung: —

XXXI.

HYMN FOR THE DEAD.

That day of wrath, that dreadful day,
When heaven and earth shall pass away,
What power shall be the sinner's stay?
How shall he meet that dreadful day?

When, shrivelling like a parched scroll,
The flaming heavens together roll;
When louder yet, and yet more dread,
Swells the high trump that wakes the dead,

Oh! on that day, that wrathful day,
When man to judgment wakes from clay,
Be THOU the trembling sinner's stay,
Though heaven and earth shall pass away.

HUSH'D is the harp—the Minstrel gone,
And did he wander forth alone?
Alone, in indigence and age,
To linger out his pilgrimage?
No; close beneath proud Newark's tower,
Arose the Minstrel's lowly bower;
A simple hut; but there was seen
The little garden hedged with green,
The cheerful hearth, and lattice clean.
There shelter'd wanderers, by the blaze,
Oft heard the tale of other days;
For much he loved to ope his door,
And give the aid he begg'd before.
So pass'd the winter's day; but still,
When summer smiled on sweet Bowhill,
And July's eve, with balmy breath,
Waved the blue-bells on Newark heath;
When throstles sung in Harehead-shaw,
And corn was green on Carterhaugh,
And flourish'd, broad, Blackandro's oak,
The aged Harper's soul awoke!
Then would he sing achievements high,
And circumstance of chivalry.
Till the rapt traveller would stay,
Forgetful of the closing day;
And noble youths, the strain to hear,
Forsook the hunting of the deer;
And Yarrow, as he roll'd along,
Bore burden to the Minstrel's song.

MARMION:

A TALE OF FLODDEN FIELD.

IN SIX CANTOS.

Alas! that Scottish maid should sing
The combat where her lover fell!
That Scottish Bard should wake the string,
The triumph of our foes to tell!

LEYDEN.

TO THE RIGHT HONORABLE

HENRY LORD MONTAGU, ETC., ETC., ETC.,

THIS ROMANCE IS INSCRIBED BY

THE AUTHOR.

ADVERTISEMENT TO THE FIRST EDITION.

It is hardly to be expected that an author whom the Public have honored with some degree of applause should not be again a trespasser on their kindness. Yet the Author of MARMION *must be supposed to feel some anxiety concerning its success, since he is sensible that he hazards by this second intrusion, any reputation which his first poem may have procured him. The present story turns upon the private adventures of a fictitious character; but is called a Tale of Flodden Field, because the hero's fate is connected with that memorable defeat, and the causes which led to it. The design of the Author was, if possible, to apprise his readers, at the outset, of the date of his Story, and to prepare them for the manners of the Age in which it is laid. Any Historical Narrative, far more an attempt at Epic composition, exceeded his plan of a Romantic Tale; yet he may be permitted to hope, from the popularity of* THE LAY OF THE LAST MINSTREL, *that an attempt to paint the manners of the feudal times, upon a broader scale, and in the course of a more interesting story, will not be unacceptable to the Public.*

The Poem opens about the commencement of August, and concludes with the defeat of Flodden, 9th September, 1513.

ASHESTIEL, 1808.

INTRODUCTION TO EDITION 1830.

WHAT I have to say respecting this Poem may be briefly told. In the Introduction to the "Lay of the Last Minstrel," I have mentioned the circumstances, so far as my literary life is concerned, which induced me to resign the active pursuit of an honorable profession, for the more precarious resources of literature. My appointment to the Sheriffdom of Selkirk called for a change of residence. I left, therefore, the pleasant cottage I had upon the side of the Esk for the "pleasanter banks of the Tweed," in order to comply with the law, which requires that the Sheriff shall be resident, at least during a certain number of months, within his jurisdiction. We found a delightful retirement, by my becoming the tenant of my intimate friend and cousin-german, Colonel Russell, in his mansion of Ashestiel, which was unoccupied, during his absence on military service in India. The house was adequate to our accommodation, and the exercise of a limited hospitality. The situation is uncommonly beautiful, by the side of a fine river, whose streams are there very favorable for angling, surrounded by the remains of natural woods, and by hills abounding in game. In point of society, according to the heartfelt phrase of Scripture, we dwelt "amongst our own people;" and as the distance from the metropolis was only thirty miles, we were not out of reach of our Edinburgh friends, in which city we spent the terms of the summer and winter Sessions of the Court, that is, five or six months in the year.

An important circumstance had, about the same time, taken place in my life. Hopes had been held out to me from an influential quarter, of a nature to relieve me from the anxiety which I must have otherwise felt, as one upon the precarious tenure of whose own life rested the principal prospects of his family, and especially as one who had necessarily some dependence upon the favor of the public, which is proverbially capricious; though it is but justice to add that, in my own case, I have not found it so. Mr. Pitt had expressed a wish to my personal friend, the Right Honorable William Dundas, now Lord Clerk Register of Scotland, that some fitting opportunity should be taken to be of service to me, and as my views and wishes pointed to a future rather than an immediate provision, an opportunity of accomplishing this was soon found. One of the Principal Clerks of Session, as they are called (official persons who occupy an important and responsible situation, and enjoy a considerable income), who had served upwards of thirty years, felt himself, from age, and the infirmity of deafness with which it was accompanied, desirous of retiring from his official situation. As the law then stood, such official persons were entitled to bargain with their successors, either for a sum of money, which was usually a considerable one, or for an interest in the emoluments of the office during their life. My predecessor, whose services had been unusually meritorious, stipulated for the emoluments of his office during his life, while I should enjoy the survivorship, on the condition that I discharged the duties of the office in the meantime. Mr. Pitt, however, having died in the interval, his administration was dissolved, and was succeeded by that known by the name of the Fox and Grenville Ministry. My affair was so far completed, that my commission lay in the office subscribed by his majesty; but, from hurry or mistake, the interest of my predecessor was not expressed in it, as had been usual in such cases. Although, therefore, it only required payment of the fees, I could not in honor take out the commission in the present state, since in the event of my dying before him, the gentleman whom I succeeded must have lost the vested interest which he had stipulated to retain. I had the honor of an interview with Earl Spencer on the subject, and he, in the most handsome manner, gave directions that the commission should issue as originally intended; adding, that the matter having received the royal assent, he regarded only as a claim of justice what he would have willingly done as an act of favor. I never saw Mr. Fox on this, or on any other occasion, and never made any application to him, conceiving that in doing so I might have been supposed to express political opinions contrary to those which I had always professed. In his private capacity, there is no man to whom I would have been more proud to owe an obligation, had I been so distinguished.

By this arrangement I obtained the survivorship of an office, the emoluments of which were fully adequate to my wishes; and as the law respecting the mode of providing for superannuated officers was, about five or six years after, altered from that which admitted the arrangement of assistant and successor, my colleague very handsomely took the opportunity of the alteration, to accept of the retiring annuity provided in such cases, and admitted me to the full benefit of the office.

But although the certainty of succeeding to a considerable income, at the time I obtained it, seemed to assure me of a quiet harbor in my old age, I did not escape my share of inconvenience from the contrary tides and currents by which we are so often encountered in our journey through life. Indeed the publication of my next poetical attempt was prematurely accelerated, from one of those unpleasant accidents which can neither be foreseen nor avoided.

I had formed the prudent resolution to endeavor to bestow a little more labor than I had yet done on my productions, and to be in no hurry again to announce myself as a candidate for literary fame. Accordingly, particular passages of a poem, which was finally called " Marmion," were labored with a good deal of care by one by whom much care was seldom bestowed. Whether the work was worth the labor or not I am no competent judge ; but I may be permitted to say, that the period of its composition was a very happy one in my life ; so much so, that I remember with pleasure, at this moment, some of the spots in which particular passages were composed. It is probably owing to this, that the Introductions to the several Cantos assumed the form of familiar epistles to my intimate friends, in which I alluded, perhaps more than was necessary or graceful, to my domestic occupations and amusements — a loquacity which may be excused by those who remember that I was still young, light-headed, and happy, and that " out of the abundance of the heart the mouth speaketh."

The misfortunes of a near relation and friend, which happened at this time, led me to alter my prudent determination, which had been, to use great precaution in sending this poem into the world ; and made it convenient at least, if not absolutely necessary, to hasten its publication. The publishers of " The Lay of the Last Minstrel," emboldened by the success of that poem, willingly offered a thousand pounds for " Marmion." The transaction, being no secret, afforded Lord Byron, who was then at general war with all who blacked paper, an apology for including me in his satire, entitled " English Bards and Scotch Reviewers." I never could conceive how an arrangement between an author and his publishers, if satisfactory to the persons concerned, could afford matter of censure to any third party. I had taken no unusual or ungenerous means of enhancing the value of my merchandise — I had never higgled a moment about the bargain, but accepted at once what I considered the handsome offer of my publishers. These gentlemen, at least, were not of opinion that they had been taken advantage of in the transaction, which, indeed, was one of their own framing ; on the contrary, the sale of the Poem was so far beyond their expectation, as to induce them to supply the Author's cellars with what is always an acceptable present to a young Scottish housekeeper, namely, a hogshead of excellent claret.

The Poem was finished in too much haste to allow me an opportunity of softening down, if not removing, some of its most prominent defects. The nature of Marmion's guilt, although similar instances were found, and might be quoted, as existing in feudal times, was nevertheless not sufficiently peculiar to be indicative of the character of the period, forgery being the crime of a commercial, rather than of a proud and warlike age. This gross defect ought to have been remedied or palliated. Yet I suffered the tree to lie as it had fallen. I remember my friend, Dr. Leyden, then in the East, wrote me a furious remonstrance on the subject. I have, nevertheless, always been of opinion, that corrections, however in themselves judicious, have a bad effect — after publication. An author is never so decidedly condemned as on his own confession, and may long find apologists and partisans, until he gives up his own cause. I was not, therefore, inclined to afford matter for censure out of my own admissions ; and, by good fortune, the novelty of the subject, and, if I may so say, some force and vivacity of description, were allowed to atone for many imperfections. Thus the second experiment on the public patience, generally the most perilous, — for the public are then most apt to judge with rigor, what in the first instance they had received, perhaps, with imprudent generosity, — was in my case decidedly successful. I had the good fortune to pass this ordeal favorably, and the return of sales before me makes the copies amount to thirty-six thousand printed between 1808 and 1825, besides a considerable sale since that period. I shall here pause upon the subject of " Marmion," and, in a few prefatory words to " The Lady of the Lake," the last poem of mine which obtained eminent success, I will continue the task which I have imposed on myself respecting the origin of my productions.

ABBOTSFORD, *April*, 1830.

MARMION.

INTRODUCTION TO CANTO FIRST.

TO

WILLIAM STEWART ROSE, ESQ.

Ashestiel, Ettrick Forest.

NOVEMBER'S sky is chill and drear,
November's leaf is red and sear:
Late, gazing down the steepy linn,
That hems our little garden in,
Low in its dark and narrow glen,
You scarce the rivulet might ken,
So thick the tangled greenwood grew,
So feeble trill'd the streamlet through:
Now murmuring hoarse, and frequent
     seen
Through bush and brier, no longer green,
An angry brook, it sweeps the glade,
Brawls over rock and wild cascade,
And, foaming brown with doubled speed,
Hurries its waters to the Tweed.

No longer Autumn's glowing red
Upon our Forest hills is shed;
No more, beneath the evening beam,
Fair Tweed reflects their purple gleam;
Away hath pass'd the heather-bell
That bloom'd so rich on Needpath-fell;
Sallow his brow, and russet bare
Are now the sister-heights of Yair.
The sheep, before the pinching heaven,
To shelter'd dale and down are driven,
Where yet some faded herbage pines,
And yet a watery sunbeam shines:
In meek despondency they eye
The wither'd sward and wintry sky
And far beneath their summer hill,
Stray sadly by Glenkinnon's rill:
The shepherd shifts his mantle's fold,
And wraps him closer from the cold;
His dogs no merry circles wheel,
But, shivering, follow at his heel;
A cowering glance they often cast,
As deeper moans the gathering blast.

My imps, though hardy, bold, and wild,
As best befits the mountain child,
Feel the sad influence of the hour,
And wail the daisy's vanish'd flower:
Their summer gambols tell, and mourn,
And anxious ask, — Will spring return,
And birds and lambs again be gay,
And blossoms clothe the hawthorn spray?

Yes, prattlers, yes. The daisy's flower
Again shall paint your summer bower;
Again the hawthorn shall supply
The garlands you delight to tie;
The lambs upon the lea shall bound,
The wild birds carol to the round,
And while you frolic light as they,
Too short shall seem the summer day.

To mute and to material things
New life revolving summer brings;
The genial call dead Nature hears,
And in her glory reappears.
But oh! my country's wintry state
What second spring shall renovate?
What powerful call shall bid arise
The buried warlike and the wise;
The mind that thought for Britain's weal,
The hand that grasp'd the victor steel?
The vernal sun new life bestows
Even on the meanest flower that blows;
But vainly, vainly may he shine,
Where glory weeps o'er NELSON's shrine;
And vainly pierce the solemn gloom,
That shrouds, O PITT, thy hallow'd tomb!

Deep graved in every British heart,
O never let those names depart!
Say to your sons, — Lo, here his grave,
Who victor died on Gadite wave;*
To him, as to the burning levin,
Short, bright, resistless course was given,

* Nelson. *Gadite wave*, sea of Cadiz, or
Gades.

Where'er his country's foes were found,
Was heard the fated thunder's sound.
Till burst the bolt on yonder shore,
Roll'd, blazed, destroy'd, — and was no
　　more.

Nor mourn ye less his perish'd worth,
Who bade the conqueror go forth,
And launch'd that thunderbolt of war
On Egypt, Hafnia,* Trafalgar;
Who, born to guide such high emprize,
For Britain's weal was early wise;
Alas! to whom the Almighty gave,
For Britain's sins, an early grave!
His worth, who, in his mightiest hour,
A bauble held the pride of power,
Spurn'd at the sordid lust of pelf,
And served his Albion for herself;
Who, when the frantic crowd amain
Strain'd at subjection's bursting rein,
O'er their wild mood full conquest gain'd,
The pride, he would not crush, restrain'd,
Show'd their fierce zeal a worthier cause,
And brought the freeman's arm, to aid
　　the freeman's laws.

Had'st thou but lived, though stripp'd
　　of power,
A watchman on the lonely tower,
Thy thrilling trump had roused the land,
When fraud or danger were at hand;
By thee, as by the beacon-light,
Our pilots had kept course aright;
As some proud column, though alone,
Thy strength had propp'd the tottering
　　throne:
Now is the stately column broke,
The beacon-light is quench'd in smoke,
The trumpet's silver sound is still,
The warder silent on the hill!

Oh think, how to his latest day,
When Death, just hovering, claim'd his
　　prey,
With Palinure's unalter'd mood,
Firm at his dangerous post he stood;
Each call for needful rest repell'd,
With dying hand the rudder held,
Till, in his fall, with fateful sway,
The steerage of the realm gave way!
Then, while on Britain's thousand plains,
One unpolluted church remains,

* Copenhagen.

Whose peaceful bells ne'er sent around
The bloody tocsin's maddening sound,
But still, upon the hallow'd day,
Convoke the swains to praise and pray;
While faith and civil peace are dear,
Grace this cold marble with a tear, —
He, who preserved them, PITT, lies here!

Nor yet suppress the generous sigh,
Because his rival slumbers nigh;
Nor be thy *requiescat* dumb,
Lest it be said o'er Fox's tomb.
For talents mourn, untimely lost,
When best employ'd, and wanted most;
Mourn genius high, and lore profound,
And wit that loved to play, not wound;
And all the reasoning powers divine,
To penetrate, resolve, combine;
And feelings keen, and fancy's glow, —
They sleep with him who sleeps below:
And, if thou mourn'st they could not save
From error him who owns this grave,
Be every harsher thought suppress'd,
And sacred be the last long rest.
Here, where the end of earthly things
Lays heroes, patriots, bards, and kings;
Where stiff the hand, and still the tongue,
Of those who fought, and spoke, and sung;
Here, where the fretted aisles prolong
The distant notes of holy song,
As if some angel spoke agen,
" All peace on earth, good-will to men;"
If ever from an English heart,
O *here* let prejudice depart,
And, partial feeling cast aside,
Record, that Fox a Briton died!
When Europe crouch'd to France's yoke,
And Austria bent, and Prussia broke,
And the firm Russian's purpose brave,
Was barter'd by a timorous slave,
Even then dishonor's peace he spurn'd,
The sullied olive-branch return'd,
Stood for his country's glory fast,
And nail'd her colors to the mast!
Heaven, to reward his firmness, gave
A portion in this honor'd grave,
And ne'er held marble in its trust
Of two such wondrous men the dust.

With more than mortal powers en-
　　dow'd,
How high they soar'd above the crowd!

Theirs was no common party race,
Jostling by dark intrigue for place;
Like fabled Gods, their mighty war
Shook realms and nations in its jar;
Beneath each banner proud to stand,
Look'd up the noblest of the land,
Till through the British world were known
The names of PITT and FOX alone.
Spells of such force no wizard grave
E'er framed in dark Thessalian cave,
Though his could drain the ocean dry,
And force the planets from the sky.
These spells are spent, and, spent with
    these,
The wine of life is on the lees,
Genius, and taste, and talent gone,
Forever tomb'd beneath the stone,
Where — taming thought to human
    pride ! —
The mighty chiefs sleep side by side.
Drop upon FOX'S grave the tear,
'Twill trickle to his rival's bier;
O'er PITT'S the mournful requiem sound,
And FOX'S shall the notes rebound.
The solemn echo seems to cry, —
" Here let their discord with them die.
Speak not for those a separate doom,
Whom Fate made Brothers in the tomb;
But search the land of living men,
Where wilt thou find their like agen ? "

Rest, ardent Spirits ! till the cries
Of dying Nature bid you rise;
Not even your Britain's groans can pierce
The leaden silence of your hearse;
Then, O, how impotent and vain
This grateful tributary strain !
Though not unmark'd from northern
    clime,
Ye heard the Border Minstrel's rhyme :
His Gothic harp has o'er you rung;
The Bard you · deign'd to praise, your
    deathless names has sung.

Stay yet, illusion, stay a while,
My wilder'd fancy still beguile !
From this high theme how can I part,
Ere half unloaded is my heart !
For all the tears e'er sorrow drew,
And all the raptures fancy knew,
And all the keener rush of blood,
That throbs through bard in bard-like
    mood,

Were here a tribute mean and low,
Though all their mingled streams could
    flow —
Woe, wonder, and sensation high,
In one spring-tide of ecstasy ! —
It will not be — it may not last —
The vision of enchantment's past :
Like frostwork in the morning ray,
The fancied fabric melts away;
Each Gothic arch, memorial-stone,
And long, dim, lofty aisle, are gone;
And, lingering last, deception dear,
The choir's high sounds die on my ear.
Now slow return the lonely down,
The silent pastures bleak and brown,
The farm begirt with copsewood wild,
The gambols of each frolic child,
Mixing their shrill cries with the tone
Of Tweed's dark waters rushing on.

Prompt on unequal tasks to run,
Thus Nature disciplines her son :
Meeter, she says, for me to stray,
And waste the solitary day,
In plucking from yon fen the reed,
And watch it floating down the Tweed;
Or idly list the shrilling lay,
With which the milkmaid cheers her way.
Marking its cadence rise and fail,
As from the field, beneath her pail,
She trips it down the uneven dale:
Meeter for me, by yonder cairn,
The ancient shepherd's tale to learn;
Though oft he stop in rustic fear,
Lest his old legends tire the ear
Of one, who, in his simple mind,
May boast of book-learn'd taste refined.

But thou, my friend, canst fitly tell,
(For few have read romance so well),
How still the legendary lay
O'er poet's bosom holds its sway;
How on the ancient minstrel strain
Time lays his palsied hand in vain;
And how our hearts at doughty deeds
By warriors wrought in steely weeds,
Still throb for fear and pity's sake;
As when the champion of the Lake
Enters Morgana's fated house,
Or in the Chapel Perilous,
Despising spells and demons' force,
Holds converse with the unburied corse; I

Or when, Dame Ganore's grace to move,
(Alas, that lawless was their love!)
He sought proud Tarquin in his den,
And freed full sixty knights; or when,
A sinful man, and unconfess'd,
He took the Sangreal's holy quest,
And, slumbering, saw the vision high,
He might not view with waking eye. [2]

The mightiest chiefs of British song
Scorn'd not such legends to prolong:
They gleam through Spenser's elfin
    dream,
And mix in Milton's heavenly theme;
And Dryden, in immortal strain,
Had raised the Table Round again, [3]
But that a ribald King and Court
Bade him toil on, to make them sport;
Demanded for their niggard pay,
Fit for their souls, a looser lay,
Licentious satire, song, and play;
The world defrauded of the high design,
Profaned the God-given strength, and
    marr'd the lofty line.

Warm'd by such names, well may we
    then
Though dwindled souls of little men,
Essay to break a feeble lance
In the fair fields of old romance;
Or seek the moated castle's cell,
Where long through talisman and spell,
While tyrants ruled, and damsels wept,
Thy Genius, Chivalry, hath slept:
There sound the harpings of the North,
Till he awake and sally forth,
On venturous quest to prick again,
In all his arms, with all his train,
Shield, lance, and brand, and plume, and
    scarf,
Fay, giant, dragon, squire, and dwarf,
And wizard with his wand of might,
And errant maid on palfrey white.
Around the Genius weave their spells,
Pure Love, who scarce his passion tells;
Mystery, half veil'd and half reveal'd;
And Honor, with his spotless shield;
Attention, with fix'd eye; and Fear,
That loves the tale she shrinks to hear;
And gentle Courtesy; and Faith,
Unchanged by sufferings, time, or death;
And Valor, lion-mettled lord,
Leaning upon his own good sword.

Well has thy fair achievement shown,
A worthy meed may thus be won;
Ytene's * oaks — beneath whose shade
Their theme the merry minstrels made,
Of Ascapart, and Bevis bold, [4]
And that Red King, [†] who, while of old,
Through Boldrewood the chase he led,
By his loved huntsman's arrow bled —
Ytene's oaks have heard again
Renew'd such legendary strain;
For thou hast sung, how He of Gaul,
That Amadis so famed in hall,
For Oriana, foil'd in fight
The Necromancer's felon might;
And well in modern verse hast wove
Partenopex's mystic love: [‡]
Hear, then, attentive to my lay,
A knightly tale of Albion's elder day.

CANTO FIRST.

THE CASTLE.

I.

Day set on Norham's castled steep, [5]
And Tweed's fair river, broad and deep,
    And Cheviot's mountains lone:
The battled towers, the donjon keep, [6]
The loophole grates, where captives weep,
The flanking walls that round it sweep,
    In yellow lustre shone.
The warriors on the turrets high,
Moving athwart the evening sky,
    Seem'd forms of giant height:
Their armor, as it caught the rays,
Flash'd back again the western blaze,
    In lines of dazzling light.

II.

Saint George's banner, broad and gay,
Now faded, as the fading ray
    Less bright, and less, was flung:
The evening gale had scarce the power
To wave it on the Donjon Tower,
    So heavily it hung.

* *Ytene*, ancient name of the New Forest,
Hants.

† William Rufus.

‡ *Partenopex*, a poem by W. S. Rose.

The scouts had parted on their search,
  The Castle gates were barr'd;
Above the gloomy portal arch,
Timing his footsteps to a march,
  The Warder kept his guard;
Low humming, as he paced along,
Some ancient Border gathering song.

III.

A distant trampling sound he hears;
He looks abroad, and soon appears
  O'er Horncliff-hill a plump of spears,*
    Beneath a pennon gay;
A horseman, darting from the crowd,
Like lightning from a summer cloud,
Spurs on his mettled courser proud,
    Before the dark array.
Beneath the sable palisade,
That closed the Castle barricade,
    His bugle-horn he blew;
The warder hasted from the wall,
And warn'd the Captain in the hall,
    For well the blast he knew;
And joyfully that knight did call,
To sewer, squire, and seneschal.

IV

" Now broach ye a pipe of Malvoisie,†
  Bring pasties of the doe,
And quickly make the entrance free,
And bid my heralds ready be,
And every minstrel sound his glee,
And all our trumpets blow;
And, from the platform, spare ye not
To fire a noble salvo-shot;
  Lord MARMION waits below ! "
Then to the Castle's lower ward
  Sped forty yeomen tall,
The iron-studded gates unbarr'd,
Raised the portcullis' ponderous guard,
The lofty palisade unspar'd
  And let the drawbridge fall.

V.

Along the bridge Lord Marmion rode,
Proudly his red-roan charger trode,
He was a stalworth knight, and keen,
And had in many a battle been;

* Body of men-at-arms. " Plump " properly
applies to a flight of water-fowl ; but is used by
analogy for a body of horse.
  † Malmsey.

The scar on his brown cheek reveal'd
A token true of Bosworth field:
His helm hung at the saddlebow;
Well by his visage you might know
His eyebrow dark, and eye of fire,
Show'd spirit proud, and prompt to ire;
Yet lines of thought upon his cheek
Did deep design and counsel speak.
His forehead, by his casque worn bare,
His thick mustache, and curly hair,
Coal-black, and grizzled here and there.
  But more through toil than age;
His square-turn'd joints, and strength of
    limb,
Show'd him no carpet knight so trim,
But in close fight a champion grim,
    In camps a leader sage.

VI.

Well was he arm'd from head to heel,
In mail and plate of Milan steel;[7]
But his strong helm, of mighty cost,
Was all with burnish'd gold emboss'd:
Amid the plumage of the crest,
A falcon hover'd on her nest,
With wings outspread,and forward breast;
E'en such a falcon, on his shield,
Soar'd sable in an azure field:
The golden legend bore aright,
𝔚𝔥𝔬 𝔠𝔥𝔢𝔠𝔨𝔰 𝔞𝔱 𝔪𝔢, 𝔱𝔬 𝔡𝔢𝔞𝔱𝔥 𝔦𝔰 𝔡𝔦𝔤𝔥𝔱.[8]
Blue was the charger's broider'd rein;
Blue ribbons deck'd his arching mane;
The knightly housing's ample fold
Was velvet blue, and trapp'd with gold.

VII.

Behind him rode two gallant squires,
Of noble name, and knightly sires;
They burn'd the gilded spurs to claim,
For well could each a war-horse tame,
Could draw the bow,the sword could sway,
And lightly bear the ring away;
Nor less with courteous precepts stored,
Could dance in hall, and carve at board,
And frame love-ditties passing rare,
And sing them to a lady fair.

VIII.

Four men-at-arms came at their backs,
With halbert, bill, and battle-axe;
They bore Lord Marmion's lance so
    strong,
And led his sumpter mules along,

And ambling palfrey, when at need
Him listed ease his battle-steed.
The last and trustiest of the four,
On high his forky pennon bore;
Like swallow's tale, in shape and hue,
Flutter'd the streamer glossy blue,
Where, blazon'd sable, as before,
The towering falcon seem'd to soar.
Last, twenty yemen, two and two,
In hosen black and jerkins blue,
With falcons broider'd on each breast,
Attended on their lord's behest.
Each, chosen for an archer good,
Knew hunting-craft by lake or wood;
Each one a six-foot bow could bend,
And far a cloth-yard shaft could send;
Each held a boar-spear tough and strong,
And at their belts their quivers rung.
Their dusty palfreys, and array,
Show'd they had march'd a weary way.

IX.

'Tis meet that I should tell you now,
How fairly arm'd, and order'd how,
  The soldiers of the guard,
With musket, pike, and morion,
To welcome noble Marmion,
  Stood in the Castle-yard;
Minstrels and trumpeters were there,
The gunner held his linstock yare,
  For welcome-shot prepared;
Enter'd the train, and such a clang,
As then through all his turrets rang,
  Old Norham never heard.

X.

The guards their morrice-pikes advanced,
  The trumpets flourish'd brave,
The cannon from the ramparts glanced,
  And thundering welcome gave.
A blithe salute, in martial sort,
  The minstrels well might sound,
For, as Lord Marmion cross'd the court,
  He scatter'd angels * round.
" Welcome to Norham, Marmion !
  Stout heart, and open hand !
Well dost thou brook thy gallant roan,
  Thou flower of English land ! "

* A gold coin of the period, value about ten
shillings.

XI.

Two pursuivants, whom tabarts † deck,
With silver scutcheon round their neck,
  Stood on the steps of stone,
By which you reach the donjon gate,
And there, with herald pomp and state,
  They hail'd Lord Marmion:
They hail'd him Lord of Fontenaye,
Of Lutterward, and Scrivelbaye,
  Of Tamworth tower and town; [9]
And he, their courtesy to requite,
Gave them a chain of twelve marks'
  weight,
  All as he lighted down.
" Now, largesse, largesse, ‡ Lord Mar-
  mion,
  Knight of the crest of gold !
A blazon'd shield, in battle won,
  Ne'er guarded heart so bold. "

XII.

They marshall'd him to the Castle-hall,
  Where the guests stood all aside,
And loudly flourish'd the trumpet-call,
  And the heralds loudly cried: —
" Room, lordings, room for Lord Mar-
  mion,
  With the crest and helm of gold !
Full well we know the trophies won
  In the lists of Cottiswold:
There, vainly Ralph de Wilton strove,
  'Gainst Marmion's force to stand;
To him he lost his lady-love,
  And to the King his land.
Ourselves beheld the listed field,
  A sight both sad and fair;
We saw Lord Marmion pierce his shield,
  And saw his saddle bare;
We saw the victor win the crest
  He wears with worthy pride;
And on the gibbet-tree, reversed,
  His foeman's scutcheon tied.
Place, nobles, for the Falcon-Knight !
  Room, room, ye gentles gay,
For him who conquer'd in the right,
  Marmion of Fontenaye ! "

† The embroidered overcoat of the heralds,
etc., also spelt tabard and taberd.

‡ The cry by which the bounty of knights and
nobles was thanked. The cry is still used in the
hop gardens of Kent and Sussex, as a demand
for payment from strangers entering them.

XIII.

Then stepp'd to meet that noble Lord,
  Sir Hugh the Heron bold,
Baron of Twisell, and of Ford,
  And Captain of the Hold.[10]
He led Lord Marmion to the dais,
  Raised o'er the pavement high,
And placed him in the upper place —
  They feasted full and high:
The whiles a Northern harper rude
Chanted a rhyme of deadly feud,
  " *How the fierce Thirwalls, and Rid-
      leys all,*
    Stout Willimondswick,
    And Hardriding Dick,
  *And Hughie of Hawdon, and Will o'
      the Wall,*
Have set on Sir Albany Featherstonhaugh,
*And taken his life at the Deadman's-
      shaw.*"
  Scantly Lord Marmion's ear could
      brook
    The harper's barbarous lay;
  Yet much he praised the pains he took,
    And well those pains did pay:
For lady's suit, and minstrel's strain,
By knight should ne'er be heard in vain.

XIV.

"Now, good Lord Marmion," Heron
      says,
    " Of your fair courtesy,
I pray you bide some little space
  In this poor tower with me.
Here may you keep your arms from rust,
  May breathe your war-horse well;
Seldom hath pass'd a week but giust
  Or feat of arms befell:
The Scots can rein a mettled steed;
  And love to couch a spear; —
Saint George! a stirring life they lead,
  That have such neighbors near.
Then stay with us a little space,
  Our northern wars to learn;
I pray you, for your lady's grace! "
  Lord Marmion's brow grew stern.

XV.

The Captain mark'd his alter'd look,
  And gave a squire the sign;
A mighty wassail-bowl he took,
  And crown'd it high in wine.

"Now pledge me here, Lord Marmion:
  But first I pray thee fair,
Where hast thou left that page of thine,
  That used to serve thy cup of wine,
    Whose beauty was so rare?
When last in Raby towers we met,
  The boy I closely eyed,
And often mark'd his cheeks were wet,
  With tears he fain would hide:
His was no rugged horse-boy's hand,
To burnish shield or sharpen brand,
  Or saddle battle-steed;
But meeter seem'd for lady fair,
To fan her cheek, or curl her hair,
Or through embroidery, rich and rare,
  The slender silk to lead;
His skin was fair, his ringlets gold,
  His bosom — when he sigh'd,
The russet doublet's rugged fold
  Could scarce repel its pride!
Say, hast thou given that lovely youth
  To serve in lady's bower?
Or was the gentle page, in sooth,
  A gentle paramour? "

XVI.

Lord Marmion ill could brook such jest;
  He roll'd his kindling eye,
With pain his rising wrath suppress'd,
  Yet made a calm reply:
" That boy thou thought'st so goodly
      fair,
He might not brook the northern air;
More of his fate if thou wouldst learn,
I left him sick in Lindisfarne.*
Enough of him. — But, Heron, say,
Why does thy lovely lady gay
Disdain to grace the hall to-day?
Or has that dame, so fair and sage,
Gone on some pious pilgrimage? " —
He spoke in covert scorn, for fame
Whisper'd light tales of Heron's dame.

XVII.

Unmark'd, at least unreck'd, the taunt;
  Careless the Knight replied,
" No bird, whose feathers gayly flaunt,
  Delights in cage to bide:
Norham is grim and grated close,
Hemm'd in by battlement and fosse,

* See note 24.

And many a darksome tower;
And better loves my lady bright
To sit in liberty and light,
    In fair Queen Margaret's bower.
We hold our greyhound in our hand,
    Our falcon on our glove;
But where shall we find leash or band,
    For dame that loves to rove?
Let the wild falcon soar her swing,
She'll stoop when she has tired her wing."

XVIII.

" Nay, if with Royal James's bride
The lovely Lady Heron bide,
Behold me here a messenger,
Your tender greetings prompt to bear;
For, to the Scottish court address'd,
I journey at our King's behest,
And pray you, of your grace, provide
For me, and mine, a trusty guide.
I have not ridden in Scotland since
James back'd the cause of that mock prince
Warbeck, that Flemish counterfeit,
Who on the gibbet paid the cheat.
Then did I march with Surrey's power,
What time we razed old Ayton tower."[11]

XIX.

" For such-like need, my lord, I trow,
Norham can find you guides enow;
For here be some have prick'd as far,
On Scottish ground, as to Dunbar;
Have drunk the monks of St. Bothan's ale,
And driven the beeves of Lauderdale;
Harried the wives of Greenlaw's goods,
And given them light to set their hoods."[12]

XX.

" Now, in good sooth," Lord Marmion
    cried,
" Were I in warlike wise to ride,
A better guard I would not lack,
Than your stout forayers at my back;
But, as in form of peace I go,
A friendly messenger, to know,
Why through all Scotland, near and far,
Their King is mustering troops for war,
The sight of plundering border spears
Might justify suspicious fears,
And deadly feud, or thirst of spoil,
Break out in some unseemly broil:

A herald were my fitting guide;
Or friar, sworn in peace to bide;
Or pardoner, or travelling priest,
Or strolling pilgrim, at the least."

XXI.

The Captain mused a little space,
And pass'd his hand across his face.
— " Fain would I find the guide you want,
But ill may spare a pursuivant,
The only men that safe can ride
Mine errands on the Scottish side:
And though a bishop built this fort,
Few, holy brethren here resort;
Even our good chaplain, as I ween,
Since our last siege, we have not seen:
The mass he might not sing or say,
Upon one stinted meal a-day;
So, safe he sat in Durham aisle,
And pray'd for our success the while.
Our Norman vicar, woe betide!
Is all too well in case to ride;
The priest of Shoreswood[13] — he could
    rein
The wildest war-horse in your train;
But then, no spearman in the hall
Will sooner swear, or stab, or brawl.
Friar John of Tilmouth were the man:
A blithesome brother at the can,
A welcome guest in hall and bower,
He knows each castle, town, and tower,
In which the wine and ale is good,
'Twixt Newcastle and Holy-Rood.
But that good man, as ill befalls,
Hath seldom left our castle walls,
Since, on the vigil of St. Bede,
In evil hour, he cross'd the Tweed,
To teach Dame Alison her creed.
Old Bughtrig found him with his wife;
And John, an enemy to strife,
Sans frock and hood, fled for his life.
The jealous churl hath deeply swore,
That, if again he venture o'er,
He shall shrive penitent no more.
Little he loves such risks, I know;
Yet, in your guard, perchance will go."

XXII.

Young Selby, at the fair hall-board,
Carved to his uncle and that lord,
And reverently took up the word: —
" Kind uncle, woe were we each one,
If harm should hap to brother John.

He is a man of mirthful speech,
Can many a game and gambol teach;
Full well at tables can he play,
And sweep at bowls the stake away.
None can a lustier carol bawl,
The needfullest among us all,
When time hangs heavy in the hall,
And snow comes thick at Christmas tide,
And we can neither hunt, nor ride
A foray on the Scottish side.
The vow'd revenge of Bughtrig rude,
May end in worse than loss of hood.
Let Friar John, in safety, still
In chimney-corner snore his fill,
Roast hissing crabs, or flagons swill.
Last night, to Norham there came one,
Will better guide Lord Marmion." —
" Nephew," quoth Heron, " by my fay,
Well hast thou spoke; say forth thy say."

XXIII.

" Here is a holy Palmer come,
From Salem first, and last from Rome;
One, that hath kiss'd the blessed tomb,
And visited each holy shrine
In Araby and Palestine;
On hills of Armenie hath been,
Where Noah's ark may yet be seen;
By that Red Sea, too, hath he trod,
Which parted at the prophet's rod;
In Sinai's wilderness he saw
The Mount, where Israel heard the law,
Mid thunder-dint, and flashing levin,
And shadows, mists, and darkness, given.
He shows Saint James's cockle-shell,
Of fair Montserrat, too, can tell;
    And of that Grot where Olives nod,
Where, darling of each heart and eye,
From all the youth of Sicily,
    Saint Rosalie retired to God.[14]

XXIV.

"To stout Saint George of Norwich merry,
Saint Thomas, too, of Canterbury,
Cuthbert of Durham and Saint Bede,
For his sins' pardon hath he pray'd.
He knows the passes of the North,
And seeks far shrines beyond the Forth;
Little he eats, and long will wake,
And drinks but of the stream or lake.
This were a guide o'er moor and dale;
But, when our John hath quaff'd his ale,

As little as the wind that blows,
And warms itself against his nose,
Kens he, or cares, which way he goes." —

XXV.

" Gramercy!" quoth Lord Marmion,
" Full loth were I, that Friar John,
That venerable man, for me,
Were placed in fear of jeopardy.
If this same Palmer will me lead
    From hence to Holy-Rood,
Like his good saint, I'll pay his meed,
Instead of cockle-shell, or bead,
    With angels fair and good.
I love such holy ramblers; still
They know to charm a weary hill,
    With song, romance, or lay:
Some jovial tale, or glee, or jest,
Some lying legend, at the least,
    They bring to cheer the way." —

XXVI.

" Ah! noble sir," young Selby said,
And finger on his lip he laid,
" This man knows much, perchance e'en
    more
Than he could learn by holy lore.
Still to himself he's muttering,
And shrinks as at some unseen thing.
Last night we listen'd at his cell;
Strange sounds we heard, and, sooth to
    tell,
He murmur'd on till morn, howe'er
No living mortal could be near.
Sometimes I thought I heard it plain,
As other voices spoke again.
I cannot tell — I like it not —
Friar John hath told us it is wrote,
No conscience clear, and void of wrong,
Can rest awake, and pray so long.
Himself still sleeps before his beads
Have mark'd ten aves, and two creeds."[15]

XXVII.

— " Let pass," quoth Marmion; " by my
    fay,
This man shall guide me on my way,
Although the great arch fiend and he
Had sworn themselves of company.
So please you, gentle youth, to call
This Palmer to the Castle-hall."
The summon'd Palmer came in place:[16]
His sable cowl o'erhung his face;

In his black mantle was he clad,
With Peter's keys, in cloth of red,
  On his broad shoulders wrought;
The scallop-shell his cap did deck;
The crucifix around his neck
  Was from Loretto brought;
His sandals were with travel tore,
Staff, budget, bottle, scrip, he wore;
The faded palm-branch in his hand
Show'd pilgrim from the Holy Land.

XXVIII.

When as the Palmer came in hall,
No lord, nor knight, was there more tall,
Nor had a statelier step withal,
  Or look'd more high and keen;
For no saluting did he wait,
But strode across the hall of state,
And fronted Marmion where he sate,
  As he his peer had been.
But his gaunt frame was worn with toil;
His cheek was sunk, alas the while!
And when he struggled at a smile,
  His eye look'd haggard wild:
Poor wretch! the mother that him bare,
If she had been in presence there,
In his wan face, and sun-burn'd hair,
  She had not known her child.
Danger, long travel, want, or woe,
Soon change the form that best we
    know —
For deadly fear can time outgo,
  And blanch at once the hair;
Hard toil can roughen form and face,
And want can quench the eye's bright
    grace,
Nor does old age a wrinkle trace
  More deeply than despair.
Happy whom none of these befall,
But this poor Palmer knew them all.

XXIX.

Lord Marmion then his boon did ask;
The Palmer took on him the task,
So he would march with morning tide,
To Scottish court to be his guide.
" But I have solemn vows to pay,
And may not linger by the way,
  To fair St. Andrew's bound,
Within the ocean-cave to pray,
Where good Saint Rule his holy lay,
From midnight to the dawn of day,
  Sung to the billows' sound;[17]

Thence to Saint Fillan's blessed well,
Whose spring can frenzied dreams dispel,
  And the crazed brain restore:[18]
Saint Mary grant, that cave or spring
Could back to peace my bosom bring,
  Or bid it throb no more ! "

XXX.

And now the midnight draught of
    sleep,
Where wine and spices richly steep,
In massive bowl of silver deep,
  The page presents on knee.
Lord Marmion drank a fair good rest,
The Captain pledged his noble guest,
The cup went through among the rest,
  Who drain'd it merrily;
Alone the Palmer pass'd it by,
Though Selby press'd him courteously.
This was a sign the feast was o'er;
It hush'd the merry wassail roar,
  The minstrels ceased to sound.
Soon in the castle naught was heard,
But the slow footstep of the guard,
  Pacing his sober round.

XXXI.

With early dawn Lord Marmion rose:
And first the chapel doors unclose;
Then, after morning rites were done,
(A hasty mass from Friar John,)
And knight and squire had broke their
    fast
On rich substantial repast,
Lord Marmion's bugles blew to horse:
Then came the stirrup-cup in course:
Between the Baron and his host,
No point of courtesy was lost;
High thanks were by Lord Marmion
    paid,
Solemn excuse the Captain made,
Till, filing from the gate, had pass'd
That noble train, their Lord the last.
Then loudly rung the trumpet call;
Thunder'd the cannon from the wall,
  And shook the Scottish shore;
Around the castle eddied slow,
Volumes of smoke as white as snow,
  And hid its turrets hoar;
Till they roll'd forth upon the air,
And met the river breezes there,
Which gave again the prospect fair.

INTRODUCTION TO CANTO SECOND.

TO

THE REV. JOHN MARRIOTT, A.M.

Ashestiel, Ettrick Forest.

THE scenes are desert now, and bare,
Where flourish'd once a forest fair,[19]
When these waste glens with copse were
    lined,
And peopled with the hart and hind.
Yon Thorn — perchance whose prickly
    spears
Have fenced him for three hundred years,
While fell around his green compeers —
Yon lonely Thorn, would he could tell
The changes of his parent dell,
Since he, so gray and stubborn now,
Waved in each breeze a sapling bough;
Would he could tell how deep the shade
A thousand mingled branches made;
How broad the shadows of the oak,
How clung the rowan * to the rock,
And through the foliage show'd his head,
With narrow leaves and berries red;
What pines on every mountain sprung,
O'er every dell what birches hung,
In every breeze what aspens shook,
What alders shaded every brook!

" Here, in my shade, ' methinks he'd
    say,
"The mighty stag at noon-tide lay:
The wolf I've seen, a fiercer game,
(The neighboring dingle bears his name,)
With lurching step around me prowl,
And stop, against the moon to howl;
The mountain-boar, on battle set,
His tusks upon my stem would whet;
While doe, and roe, and red deer good,
Have bounded by, through gay green-
    wood.
Then oft, from Newark's riven tower,
Sallied a Scottish monarch's power:
A thousand vassals muster'd round,
With horse, and hawk, and horn, and
    hound;
And I might see the youth intent,
Guard every pass with crossbow bent;
And through the brake the rangers stalk,
And falc'ners hold the ready hawk;

* Mountain ash.

And foresters, in green-wood trim,
Lead in the leash the gazehounds grim,
Attentive, as the bratchet's † bay
From the dark covert drove the prey,
To slip them as he broke away.
The startled quarry bounds amain,
As fast the gallant greyhounds strain;
Whistles the arrow from the bow,
Answers the harquebuss below;
While all the rocking hills reply,
To hoof-clang, hound, and hunters' cry,
And bugles ringing lightsomely.''

Of such proud huntings, many tales
Yet linger in our lonely dales,
Up pathless Ettrick and on Yarrow,
Where erst the outlaw drew his arrow.‡
But not more blithe that silvan court,
Than we have been at humbler sport;
Though small our pomp, and mean our
    game,
Our mirth, dear Marriott, was the same.
Remember'st thou my greyhounds true?
O'er holt or hill there never flew,
From slip or leash there never sprang,
More fleet of foot, or sure of fang.
Nor dull, between each merry chase,
Pass'd by the intermitted space;
For we had fair resource in store,
In Classic and in Gothic lore:
We mark'd each memorable scene,
And held poetic talk between;
Nor hill, nor brook, we paced along,
But had its legend or its song.
All silent now — for now are still
Thy bowers, untenanted Bowhill!§
No longer, from thy mountains dun,
The yeoman hears the well-known gun,
And while his honest heart grows warm,
At thought of his parental farm,
Round to his mates a brimmer fills,
And drinks, "The Chieftain of the
    Hills!''
No fairy forms, in Yarrow's bowers,
Trip o'er the walks, or tend the flowers,
Fair as the elves whom Janet saw
By moonlight dance on Carterhaugh;

† Slowhound.

‡ Murray, the Robin Hood of Ettrick, but
inferior in good qualities to the famous English
archer.

§ A seat of the Duke of Buccleuch on th
Yarrow.

No youthful Baron's left to grace
The Forest-Sheriff's lonely chase,
And ape, in manly step and tone,
The majesty of Oberon :
And she is gone, whose lovely face
Is but her least and lowest grace;
Though if to Sylphid Queen 'twere given,
To show our earth the charms of Heaven,
She could not glide along the air,
With form more light, or face more fair.
No more the widow's deafen'd ear
Grows quick that lady's step to hear :
At noon-tide she expects her not,
Nor busies her to trim the cot;
Pensive she turns her humming wheel,
Or pensive cooks her orphans' meal;
Yet blesses, ere she deals their bread,
The gentle hand by which they're fed.

From Yair,— which hills so closely bind,
Scarce can the Tweed his passage find,
Though much he fret, and chafe, and toil,
Till all his eddying currents boil, —
Her long descended lord is gone,*
And left us by the stream alone.
And much I miss those sportive boys,
Companions of my mountain joys,
Just at the age 'twixt boy and youth,
When thought is speech, and speech is
    truth.
Close to my side with what delight
They press'd to hear of Wallace wight,
When, pointing to his airy mound,
I call'd his ramparts holy ground !
Kindled their brows to hear me speak;
And I have smiled, to feel my cheek,
Despite the difference of our years,
Return again the glow of theirs.
Ah, happy boys ! such feelings pure,
They will not, cannot, long endure !
Condemn'd to stem the world's rude tide,
You may not linger by the side;
For Fate shall thrust you from the shore,
And Passion ply the sail and oar.
Yet cherish the remembrance still,
Of the lone mountain, and the rill;
For trust, dear boys, the time will come,
When fiercer transports shall be dumb,
And you will think right frequently,
But well, I hope, without a sigh,
On the free hours that we have spent
Together, on the brown hill's bent.

*The late Alex. Pringle, Esq., of Whytbank.

When, musing on companions gone,
We doubly feel ourselves alone,
Something, my friend, we yet may gain;
There is a pleasure in this pain :
It soothes the love of lonely rest,
Deep in each gentler heart impress'd.
'Tis silent amid worldly toils,
And stifled soon by mental broils,
But in a bosom thus prepared,
Its still small voice is often heard,
Whispering a mingled sentiment,
'Twixt resignation and content.
Oft in my mind such thoughts awake,
By lone St. Mary's silent lake;[2]
Thou know'st it well,—nor fen,nor sedge,
Pollute the pure lake's crystal edge;
Abrupt and sheer, the mountains sink
At once upon the level brink;
And just a trace of silver sand
Marks where the water meets the land.
Far in the mirror, bright and blue,
Each hill's huge outline you may view,
Shaggy with heath, but lonely bare,
Nor tree, nor bush, nor brake, is there,
Save where, of land, yon slender line
Bears thwart the lake the scatter'd pine.
Yet even this nakedness has power,
And aids the feeling of the hour :
Nor thicket, dell, nor copse you spy,
Where living thing conceal'd might lie;
Nor point, retiring, hides a dell,
Where swain, or woodman lone, might
    dwell;
There's nothing left to fancy's guess,
You see that all is loneliness :
And silence aids — though the steep hills
Send to the lake a thousand rills;
In summer tide, so oft they weep,
The sound but lulls the ear asleep;
Your horse's hoof-tread sounds too rude,
So stilly is the solitude.

Naught living meets the eye or ear,
But well I ween the dead are near;
For though, in feudal strife, a foe
Hath laid Our Lady's chapel low,[21]
Yet still, beneath the hallow'd soil,
The peasant rests him from his toil,
And, dying, bids his bones be laid,
Where erst his simple fathers pray'd.

If age had tamed the passions' strife,
And fate had cut my ties to life,

Here, have I thought, 'twere sweet to
        dwell,
And rear again the chaplain's cell,
Like that same peaceful hermitage,
Where Milton long'd to spend his age.
'Twere sweet to mark the setting day,
On Bourhope's lonely top decay;
And, as it faint and feeble died
On the broad lake, and mountain's side,
To say, " Thus pleasures fade away;
Youth, talents, beauty, thus decay,
And leave us dark, forlorn, and gray;"
Then gaze on Dryhope's ruin'd tower,
And think on Yarrow's faded Flower:
And when that mountain-sound I heard,
Which bids us be for storm prepared,
The distant rustling of his wings,
As up his force the Tempest brings,
'Twere sweet, ere yet his terrors rave,
To sit upon the Wizard's grave;
That Wizard Priest's, whose bones are
        thrust
From company of holy dust;[22]
On which no sunbeam ever shines —
(So superstition's creed divines) —
Thence view the lake, with sullen roar,
Heave her broad billows to the shore;
And mark the wild-swans mount the gale,
Spread wide through mist their snowy sail,
And ever stoop again, to lave
Their bosoms on the surging wave.
Then, when against the driving hail
No longer might my plaid avail,
Back to my lonely home retire,
And light my lamp, and trim my fire;
There ponder o'er some mystic lay,
Till the wild tale had all its sway.
And, in the bittern's distant shriek,
I heard unearthly voices speak,
And thought the Wizard Priest was come,
To claim again his ancient home !
And bade my busy fancy range,
To frame him fitting shape and strange,
Till from the task my brow I clear'd,
And smiled to think that I had fear'd.

But chief, 'twere sweet to think such
        life,
(Though but escape from fortune's strife,)
Something most matchless good and wise,
A great and grateful sacrifice;
And deem each hour to musing given,
A step upon the road to heaven.

Yet him, whose heart is ill at ease,
Such peaceful solitudes displease:
He loves to drown his bosom's jar
Amid the elemental war:
And my black Palmer's choice had been
Some ruder and more savage scene,
Like that which frowns round dark Loch-
        skene.[23]
There eagles scream from isle to shore;
Down all the rocks the torrents roar;
O'er the black waves incessant driven,
Dark mists infect the summer heaven;
Through the rude barriers of the lake,
Away its hurrying waters break,
Faster and whiter dash and curl,
Till down yon dark abyss they hurl.
Rises the fog-smoke white as snow,
Thunders the viewless stream below,
Diving, as if condemned to lave
Some demon's subterranean cave,
Who, prison'd by enchanter's spell,
Shakes the dark rock with groan and yell.
And well that Palmer's form and mien
Had suited with the stormy scene,
Just on the edge, straining his ken
To view the bottom of the den,
Where, deep deep down, and far within,
Toils with the rocks the roaring linn;
Then, issuing forth one foamy wave,
And wheeling round the Giant's Grave,
White as the snowy charger's tail,
Drives down the pass of Moffatdale.

Marriott, thy harp, on Isis strung,
To many a Border theme has rung;
Then list to me, and thou shalt know
Of this mysterious Man of Woe.

CANTO SECOND.

THE CONVENT.

I.

THE breeze which swept away the smoke
        Round Norham Castle roll'd,
When all the loud artillery spoke,
With lightning-flash and thunder-stroke,
        As Marmion left the Hold.
It curl'd not Tweed alone, that breeze,
For, far upon Northumbrian seas,
        It freshly blew, and strong,

Where, from high Whitby's cloister'd pile,
Bound to St. Cuthbert's Holy Isle,[24]
   It bore a bark along.
Upon the gale she stoop'd her side,
And bounded o'er the swelling tide,
   As she were dancing home;
The merry seamen laugh'd, to see
Their gallant ship so lustily
   Furrow the green sea-foam.
Much joy'd they in their honor'd freight,
For, on the deck, in chair of state,
The Abbess of Saint Hilda placed,
With five fair nuns, the galley graced.

II.

'Twas sweet to see these holy maids,
Like birds escaped to green-wood shades,
   Their first flight from the cage,
How timid, and how curious too,
For all to them was strange and new,
And all the common sights they view,
   Their wonderment engage.
One eyed the shrouds and swelling sail,
   With many a benedicite;
One at the rippling surge grew pale,
   And would for terror pray;
Then shriek'd, because the sea-dog, nigh,
His round black head, and sparkling eye,
   Rear'd o'er the foaming spray;
And one would still adjust her veil,
Disorder'd by the summer gale,
Perchance lest some more worldly eye
Her dedicated charms might spy;
Perchance, because such action graced
Her fair-turn'd arm and slender waist.
Light was each simple bosom there,
Save two, who ill might pleasure share,—
The Abbess and the Novice Clare.

III.

The Abbess was of noble blood,
But early took the veil and hood,
Ere upon life she cast a look,
Or knew the world that she forsook.
Fair too she was, and kind had been
As she was fair, but ne'er had seen
For her a timid lover sigh,
Nor knew the influence of her eye.
Love, to her ear, was but a name
Combined with vanity and shame;
Her hopes, her fears, her joys, were all
Bounded within the cloister wall:

The deadliest sin her mind could reach,
Was of monastic rule the breach;
And her ambition's highest aim
To emulate Saint Hilda's fame.
For this she gave her ample dower,
To raise the convent's eastern tower;
For this, with carving rare and quaint,
She deck'd the chapel of the saint,
And gave the relic-shrine of cost,
With ivory and gems emboss'd.
The poor her Convent's bounty blest,
The pilgrim in its halls found rest.

IV.

Black was her garb, her rigid rule
Reform'd on Benedictine school;
Her cheek was pale, her form was spare;
Vigils, and penitence austere,
Had early quench'd the light of youth,
But gentle was the dame, in sooth;
Though, vain of her religious sway,
She loved to see her maids obey.
Yet nothing stern was she in cell,
And the nuns loved their Abbess well.
Sad was this voyage to the dame;
Summon'd to Lindisfarne, she came,
There, with Saint Cuthbert's Abbot old,
And Tynemouth's Prioress, to hold
A chapter of St. Benedict,
For inquisition stern and strict,
On two apostates from the faith,
And, if need were, to doom to death.

V.

Naught say I here of Sister Clare,
Save this, that she was young and fair;
As yet, a novice unprofess'd,
Lovely and gentle, but distress'd.
She was betroth'd to one now dead,
Or worse, who had dishonor'd fled.
Her kinsmen bade her give her hand
To one, who loved her for her land:
Herself, almost heart-broken now,
Was bent to take the vestal vow,
And shroud within Saint Hilda's gloom,
Her blasted hopes and wither'd bloom.

VI.

She sate upon the galley's prow,
And seem'd to mark the waves below;
Nay, seem'd, so fix'd her look and eye,
To count them as they glided by.

She saw them not — 'twas seeming all —
Far other scene her thoughts recall,—
A sun-scorch'd desert, waste and bare,
Nor waves, nor breezes, murmur'd there;
There saw she, where some careless hand
O'er a dead corpse had heap'd the sand,
To hide it till the jackals come,
To tear it from the scanty tomb.—
See what a woful look was given,
As she raised up her eyes to heaven!

VII.

Lovely, and gentle, and distress'd —
These charms might tame the fiercest
    breast;
Harpers have sung, and poets told,
That he, in fury uncontroll'd,
The shaggy monarch of the wood,
Before a virgin, fair and good,
Hath pacified his savage mood.
But passions in the human frame,
Oft put the lion's rage to shame:
And jealousy, by dark intrigue,
With sordid avarice in league,
Had practised with their bowl and knife,
Against the mourner's harmless life.
This crime was charged 'gainst those who
    lay
Prison'd in Cuthbert's islet gray.

VIII.

And now the vessel skirts the strand
Of mountainous Northumberland;
Towns, towers, and halls, successive rise,
And catch the nuns' delighted eyes.
Monk-Wearmouth soon behind them lay;
And Tynemouth's priory and bay;
They mark'd, amid her trees, the hall
Of lofty Seaton-Delaval;
They saw the Blythe and Wansbeck floods
Rush to the sea through sounding woods;
They pass'd the tower of Widderington,
Mother of many a valiant son;
At Coquet-isle their beads they tell
To the good Saint who own'd the cell;
Then did the Alne attention claim,
And Warkworth, proud of Percy's name;
And next, they cross'd themselves, to
    hear
The whitening breakers sound so near,
Where, boiling thro' the rocks, they roar,
On Dunstanborough's cavern'd shore;

Thy tower, proud Bamborough, mark'd
    they there,
King Ida's castle, huge and square,
From its tall rock look grimly down,
And on the swelling ocean frown;
Then from the coast they bore away,
And reach'd the Holy Island's bay.

IX.

The tide did now its flood-mark gain,
And girdled in the Saint's domain:
For, with the flow and ebb, its style
Varies from continent to isle;
Dry-shod, o'er sands, twice every day,
The pilgrims to the shrine find way;
Twice every day, the waves efface
Of staves and sandall'd feet the trace.
As to the port the galley flew,
Higher and higher rose to view
The Castle with its battled walls,
The ancient monastery's halls,
A solemn, huge, and dark-red pile,
Placed on the margin of the isle.

X.

In Saxon strength that abbey frown'd,
With massive arches broad and round,
    That rose alternate, row and row,
      On ponderous columns, short and low,
        Built ere the art was known,
    By pointed aisle, and shafted stalk,
    The arcades of an alley'd walk
      To emulate in stone.
On the deep walls, the heathen Dane
Had pour'd his impious rage in vain;
And needful was such strength to these,
Exposed to the tempestuous seas,
Scourged by the winds' eternal sway,
Open to rovers fierce as they,
Which could twelve hundred years with-
    stand
Winds, waves, and northern pirates'
    hand.
Not but that portions of the pile,
Rebuilded in a later style,
Show'd where the spoiler's hand had
    been;
Not but the wasting sea-breeze keen
Had worn the pillar's carving quaint,
And moulder'd in his niche the saint,
And rounded, with consuming power,
The pointed angles of each tower;

Yet still entire the Abbey stood,
Like veteran, worn, but unsubdued.

XI.

Soon as they near'd his turrets strong,
The maidens raised Saint Hilda's song,
And with the sea-wave and the wind,
Their voices, sweetly shrill, combined,
And made harmonious close;
Then, answering from the sandy shore,
Half drown'd amid the breakers' roar,
According chorus rose:
Down to the haven of the Isle,
The monks and nuns in order file,
From Cuthbert's cloisters grim;
Banner, and cross, and relics there,
To meet St. Hilda's maids, they bare;
And, as they caught the sounds on air,
They echoed back the hymn.
The islanders, in joyous mood,
Rush'd emulously through the flood,
To hale the bark to land;
Conspicuous by her veil and hood,
Signing the cross, the Abbess stood,
And bless'd them with her hand.

XII.

Suppose we now the welcome said,
Suppose the Convent banquet made:
All through the holy dome,
Through cloister, aisle, and gallery
Wherever vestal maid might pry,
Nor risk to meet unhallow'd eye,
The stranger sisters roam;
Till fell the evening damp with dew,
And the sharp sea-breeze coldly blew,
For there, even summer night is chill.
Then, having stray'd and gazed their fill,
They closed around the fire;
And all, in turn, essay'd to paint
The rival merits of their saint,
A theme that ne'er can tire
A holy maid; for, be it known,
That their saint's honor is their own.

XIII.

Then Whitby's nuns exulting told,
How to their house three Barons bold
Must menial service do;
While horns blow out a note of shame,
And monks cry "Fie upon your name!
In wrath, for loss of sylvan game,
Saint Hilda's priest ye slew."

"This, on Ascension-day, each year,
While laboring on our harbor-pier,
Must Herbert, Bruce, and Percy hear."
They told, how in their convent cell
A Saxon princess once did dwell,
The lovely Edelfled; 25
And how, of thousand snakes, each one
Was changed into a coil of stone,
When holy Hilda pray'd!
Themselves, within their holy bound,
Their stony folds had often found.
They told, how sea-fowls' pinions fail
As over Whitby's towers they sail,26
And, sinking down, with flutterings faint,
They do their homage to the saint.

XIV.

Nor did St. Cuthbert's daughters fail
To vie with these in holy tale;
His body's resting-place, of old,
How oft their patron changed, they
told; 27
How, when the rude Dane burn'd their
pile,
The monks fled forth from Holy Isle;
O'er northern mountain, marsh, and
moor,
From sea to sea, from shore to shore,
Seven years Saint Cuthbert's corpse they
bore.
They rested them in fair Melrose;
But though, alive, he loved it well,
Not there his relics might repose;
For, wondrous tale to tell!
In his stone coffin forth he rides,
A ponderous bark for river tides,
Yet light as gossamer it glides,
Downward to Tilmouth cell.
Nor long was his abiding there,
For southward did the saint repair;
Chester-le-Street and Rippon saw
His holy corpse, ere Wardilaw
Hail'd him with joy and fear;
And, after many wanderings past,
He chose his lordly seat at last,
Where his cathedral, huge and vast,
Looks down upon the Wear:
There, deep in Durham's Gothic shade,
His relics are in secret laid;
But none may know the place,
Save of his holiest servants three,
Deep sworn to solemn secrecy,
Who share that wondrous grace.

XV.

Who may his miracles declare !
Even Scotland's dauntless king, and heir,
  (Although with them they led
Galwegians, wild as ocean's gale,
And Lodon's knights, all sheathed in
    mail,
And the bold men of Teviotdale,)
  Before his standard fled.[28]
'Twas he, to vindicate his reign,
Edged Alfred's falchion on the Dane,
And turn'd the Conqueror back again,[29]
When, with his Norman bowyer band,
He came to waste Northumberland.

XVI.

But fain Saint Hilda's nuns would learn
If, on a rock by Lindisfarne,
Saint Cuthbert sits, and toils to frame
The sea-born beads that bear his name : [30]
Such tales had Whitby's fishers told,
And said they might his shape behold,
  And hear his anvil sound;
A deaden'd clang, — a huge dim form,
Seen but, and heard, when gathering
    storm
  And night were closing round.
But this, as tale of idle fame,
The nuns of Lindisfarne disclaim.

XVII.

While round the fire such legends go,
Far different was the scene of woe,
Where, in a secret aisle beneath,
Council was held of life and death.
It was more dark and lone that vault,
  Than the worst dungeon cell:
Old Colwulf [31] built it, for his fault,
  In penitence to dwell,
When he, for cowl and beads, laid down
The Saxon battle-axe and crown,
This den, which, chilling every sense
Of feeling, hearing, sight,
Was call'd the Vault of Penitence,
  Excluding air and light,
Was, by the prelate Sexhelm, made
A place of burial for such dead,
As, having died in mortal sin,
Might not be laid the church within.
'Twas now a place of punishment;
Whence if so loud a shriek were sent,

As reach'd the upper air,
The hearers bless'd themselves, and said,
The spirits of the sinful dead
  Bemoan'd their torments there.

XVIII.

But though, in the monastic pile,
Did of this penitential aisle
  Some vague tradition go,
Few only, save the Abbot, knew
Where the place lay; and still more few
Were those, who had from him the clew
  To that dread vault to go.
Victim and executioner
Were blindfold when transported there.
In low dark rounds the arches hung,
From the rude rock the side-walls sprung;
The grave-stones, rudely sculptured o'er,
Half sunk in earth, by time half wore,
Were all the pavement of the floor:
The mildew-drops fell one by one,
With tinkling plash, upon the stone.
A cresset, * in an iron chain,
Which served to light this drear domain,
With damp and darkness seem'd to strive,
As if it scarce might keep alive;
And yet it dimly served to show
The awful conclave met below.

XIX.

There, met to doom in secrecy,
Were placed the heads of convents three :
All servants of St. Benedict,
The statutes of whose orders strict
  On iron table lay;
In long black dress, on seats of stone,
Behind were these three judges shown
  By the pale cresset's ray:
The Abbess of Saint Hilda's, there,
Sat for a space with visage bare,
Until, to hide her bosom's swell,
And tear-drops that for pity fell,
  She closely drew her veil :
Yon shrouded figure, as I guess,
By her proud mien and flowing dress,
Is Tynemouth's haughty Prioress,[32]
  And she with awe looks pale:
And he, that Ancient Man, whose sight
Has long been quench'd by age's night,
Upon whose wrinkled brow alone,
Nor ruth, nor mercy's trace, is shown,

* Antique chandelier.

Whose look is hard and stern, —
Saint Cuthbert's Abbot is his style;
For sanctity call'd, through the isle,
  The Saint of Lindisfarne.

XX.

Before them stood a guilty pair;
But, though an equal fate they share,
Yet one alone deserves our care.
Her sex a page's dress belied;
The cloak and doublet, loosely tied,
Obscured her charms, but could not hide.
  Her cap down o'er her face she drew;
    And, on her doublet breast,
  She tried to hide the badge of blue,
    Lord Marmion's falcon crest.
But, at the prioress' command,
A Monk undid the silver band,
  That tied her tresses fair,
And raised the bonnet from her head,
And down her slender form they spread,
  In ringlets rich and rare.
Constance de Beverley they know,
Sister profess'd of Fontevraud,
Whom the church number'd with the
    dead,
For broken vows, and convent fled.

XXI.

When thus her face was given to view,
(Although so pallid was her hue,
It did a ghastly contrast bear
To those bright ringlets glistering fair,)
Her look composed, and steady eye,
Bespoke a matchless constancy;
And there she stood so calm and pale,
That, but her breathing did not fail,
And motion slight of eye and head,
And of her bosom, warranted
That neither sense nor pulse she lacks,
You might have thought a form of wax,
Wrought to the very life, was there;
So still she was, so pale, so fair.

XXII.

Her comrade was a sordid soul,
  Such as does murder for a meed;
Who, but of fear, knows no control,
Because his conscience, sear'd and foul,
  Feels not the import of his deed;
One, whose brute-feeling ne'er aspires
Beyond his own more brute desires.

Such tools the Tempter ever needs,
To do the savagest of deeds;
For them no vision'd terrors daunt,
Their nights no fancied spectres haunt,
One fear with them, of all most base,
The fear of death, — alone finds place.
This wretch was clad in frock and cowl,
And shamed not loud to moan and howl,
His body on the floor to dash,
And crouch, like hound beneath the lash,
While his mute partner, standing near,
Waited her doom without a tear.

XXIII.

Yet well the luckless wretch might shriek,
Well might her paleness terror speak!
For there were seen in that dark wall,
Two niches, narrow, deep, and tall;—
Who enters at such grisly door,
Shall ne'er, I ween, find exit more.
In each a slender meal was laid,
Of roots, of water, and of bread:
By each, in Benedictine dress,
Two haggard monks stood motionless;
Who, holding high a blazing torch,
Show'd the grim entrance of the porch:
Reflecting back the smoky beam,
The dark-red walls and arches gleam.
Hewn stones and cement were display'd,
And building tools in order laid.

XXIV.

These executioners were chose,
As men who were with mankind foes,
And with despite and envy fired,
Into the cloister had retired;
  Or who, in desperate doubt of grace,
  Strove, by deep penance, to efface
    Of some foul crime the stain;
For, as the vassals of her will,
Such men the Church selected still,
  As either joy'd in doing ill,
  Or thought more grace to gain,
If, in her cause, they wrestled down,
Feelings their nature strove to own.
By strange device were they brought
    there,
They knew not how, nor knew not where.

XXV.

And now that blind old Abbot rose,
  To speak the Chapter's doom,

On those the wall was to enclose,
    Alive, within the tomb,[38]
But stopp'd, because that woful Maid,
Gathering her powers, to speak essay'd.
Twice she essay'd, and twice in vain;
Her accents might no utterance gain;
Naught but imperfect murmurs slip
From her convulsed and quivering lip;
    'Twixt each attempt all was so still,
    You seem'd to hear a distant rill —
        'Twas ocean's swells and falls;
    For though this vault of sin and fear
    Was to the sounding surge so near,
    A tempest there you scarce could hear,
        So massive were the walls.

XXVI.

At length, an effort sent apart
The blood that curdled to her heart,
    And light came to her eye,
And color dawn'd upon her cheek,
A hectic and a flutter'd streak,
Like that left on the Cheviot peak,
    By Autumn's stormy sky;
And when her silence broke at length,
Still as she spoke she gather'd strength,
    And arm'd herself to bear.
It was a fearful sight to see
Such high resolve and constancy,
    In form so soft and fair.

XXVII.

' I speak not to implore your grace;
Well know I, for one minute's space
    Successless might I sue:
Nor do I speak your prayers to gain;
For if a death of lingering pain,
To cleanse my sins, be penance vain,
    Vain are your masses too. —
I listen'd to a traitor's tale,
I left the convent and the veil;
For three long years I bow'd my pride,
A horse-boy in his train to ride;
And well my folly's meed he gave,
And forfeited, to be his slave,
All here, and all beyond the grave. —
He saw young Clara's face more fair,
He knew her of broad lands the heir,
Forgot his vows, his faith forswore,
And Constance was beloved no more. —
'Tis an old tale, and often told;
    But did my fate and wish agree,

Ne'er had been read, in story old,
Of maiden true betray'd for gold,
    That loved, or was avenged, like me.

XXVIII.

"The King approved his favorite's aim;
In vain a rival barr'd his claim,
    Whose fate with Clare's was plight,
For he attaints that rival's fame
With treason's charge —and on they came
    In mortal lists to fight.
    Their oaths are said,
    Their prayers are pray'd,
    Their lances in the rest are laid,
    They meet in mortal shock;
And, hark! the throng, with thundering cry,
Shout ' Marmion, Marmion! to the sky,
    De Wilton to the block! '
Say ye, who preach Heaven shall decide
When in the lists two champions ride,
    Say, was Heaven's justice here!
When, loyal in his love and faith,
Wilton found overthrow or death,
    Beneath a traitor's spear?
How false the charge, how true he fell,
This guilty packet best can tell." —
Then drew a packet from her breast,
Paused, gather'd voice, and spoke the rest: —

XXIX.

" Still was false Marmion's bridal staid;
To Whitby's convent fled the maid,
    The hated match to shun.
' Ho! shifts she thus? ' King Henry cried,
' Sir Marmion, she shall be thy bride,
    If she were sworn a nun.'
One way remain'd — the King's command
Sent Marmion to the Scottish land:
I linger'd here, and rescue plann'd
    For Clara and for me:
This caitiff Monk, for gold, did swear,
He would to Whitby's shrine repair,
And, by his drugs, my rival fair
    A saint in heaven should be.
But ill the dastard kept his oath,
Whose cowardice has undone us both.

XXX.

" And now my tongue the secret tells,
Not that remorse my bosom swells,

But to assure my soul that none
Shall ever wed with Marmion.
Had fortune my last hope betray'd,
This packet, to the King convey'd,
Had given him to the headsman's stroke,
Although my heart that instant broke. —
Now, men of death, work forth your
     will,
For I can suffer, and be still;
And come he slow, or come he fast,
It is but Death who comes at last.

XXXI.

" Yet dread me, from my living tomb,
Ye vassal slaves of bloody Rome!
If Marmion's late remorse should wake,
Full soon such vengeance will he take,
That you shall wish the fiery Dane
Had rather been your guest again.
Behind, a darker hour ascends!
The altars quake, the crosier bends,
The ire of a despotic King
Rides forth upon destruction's wing;
Then shall these vaults, so strong and
     deep,
Burst open to the sea-winds' sweep;
Some traveller then shall find my bones
Whitening amid disjointed stones,
And, ignorant of priests' cruelty,
Marvel such relics here should be."

XXXII.

Fix'd was her look, and stern her air:
Back from her shoulders stream'd her
     hair;
The locks, that wont her brow to shade,
Stared up erectly from her head;
Her figure seem'd to rise more high;
Her voice, despair's wild energy
Had given a tone of prophecy.
Appall'd the astonish'd conclave sate;
With stupid eyes, the men of fate
Gazed on the light inspired form,
And listen'd for the avenging storm;
The judges felt the victim's dread;
No hand was moved, no word was said,
Till thus the Abbot's doom was given,
Raising his sightless balls to heaven: —
" Sister, let thy sorrows cease;
Sinful brother, part in peace!"
     From that dire dungeon, place of doom,
Of execution too, and tomb,

Paced forth the judges three;
Sorrow it were, and shame, to tell
The butcher-work that there befell,
When they had glided from the cell
     Of sin and misery.

XXXIII.

A hundred winding steps convey
That conclave to the upper day;
But, ere they breathed the fresher air,
They heard the shriekings of despair,
     And many a stifled groan:
With speed their upward way they take,
(Such speed as age and fear can make,)
And cross'd themselves for terror's sake,
     As hurrying, tottering on:
Even in the vesper's heavenly tone,
They seem'd to hear a dying groan,
And bade the passing knell to toll
For welfare of a parting soul.
Slow o'er the midnight wave it swung,
Northumbrian rocks in answer rung;
To Warkworth cell the echoes roll'd,
His beads the wakeful hermit told,
The Bamborough peasant raised his head,
But slept ere half a prayer he said;
So far was heard the mighty knell,
The stag sprung up on Cheviot Fell,
Spread his broad nostril to the wind,
Listed before, aside, behind,
Then couch'd him down beside the hind,
And quaked among the mountain fern,
To hear that sound so dull and stern.

———

INTRODUCTION TO CANTO THIRD.

TO WILLIAM ERSKINE, ESQ.*

Ashestiel, Ettrick Forest.

LIKE April morning clouds, that pass,
With varying shadow, o'er the grass,
And imitate, on field and furrow,
Life's chequer'd scene of joy and sorrow;
Like streamlet of the mountain north,
Now in a torrent racing forth,
Now winding slow its silver train,
And almost slumbering on the plain;

* A Judge of the Court of Sessions, after
wards, by title, Lord Kinnedder. He died in
1822.

Like breezes of the autumn day,
Whose voice inconstant dies away,
And ever swells again as fast,
When the ear deems its murmur past;
Thus various, my romantic theme
Flits, winds, or sinks, a morning dream.
Yet pleased, our eye pursues the trace
Of Light and Shade's inconstant race;
Pleased, views the rivulet afar,
Weaving its maze irregular;
And pleased, we listen as the breeze
Heaves its wild sigh through Autumn
    trees;
Then, wild as cloud, or stream, or gale,
Flow on, flow unconfined, my Tale!

Need I to thee, dear Erskine, tell
I love the license all too well,
In sounds now lowly, and now strong,
To raise the desultory song? —
Oft, when mid such capricious chime,
Some transient fit of lofty rhyme
To thy kind judgment seem'd excuse
For many an error of the muse,
Oft hast thou said, "If, still misspent,
Thine hours to poetry are lent,
Go, and to tame thy wandering course,
Quaff from the fountain at the source;
Approach those masters, o'er whose tomb
Immortal laurels ever bloom,
Instructive of the feebler bard,
Still from the grave their voice is heard,
From them, and from the paths they
    show'd,
Choose honor'd guide and practised road;
Nor ramble on through brake and maze,
With harpers rude, of barbarous days.

"Or deem'st thou not our later time
Yields topic meet for classic rhyme?
Hast thou no elegiac verse
For Brunswick's venerable hearse?*
What, not a line, a tear, a sigh,
When valor bleeds for liberty? —
Oh, hero of that glorious time,
When, with unrivall'd light sublime, —
Though martial Austria, and though all
The might of Russia, and the Gaul,
Though banded Europe stood her foes —
The star of Brandenburgh arose!
Thou could'st not live to see her beam
Forever quench'd in Jena's stream.

* Killed at Auerstadt, 1806.

Lamented chief! — It was not given
To thee to change the doom of Heaven,
And crush that dragon in its birth,
Predestined scourge of guilty earth.
Lamented chief! — not thine the power,
To save in that presumptuous hour,
When Prussia hurried to the field,
And snatch'd the spear, but left the shield;
Valor and skill 'twas thine to try,
And, tried in vain, 'twas thine to die.
Ill had it seem'd thy silver hair
The last, the bitterest pang to share,
For princedoms reft, and scutcheons riven,
And birthrights to usurpers given;
Thy land's, thy children's wrongs to feel,
And witness woes thou could'st not heal.
On thee relenting Heaven bestows
For honor'd life an honor'd close;
And when revolves, in time's sure change,
The hour of Germany's revenge,
When, breathing fury for her sake,
Some new Arminius shall awake,
Her champion, ere he strike, shall come
To whet his sword on BRUNSWICK's tomb.

"Or of the Red-Cross hero † teach,
Dauntless in dungeon as on breach:
Alike to him, the sea, the shore,
The brand, the bridle, or the oar:
Alike to him the war that calls
Its votaries to the shatter'd walls,
Which the grim Turk, besmear'd with
    blood,
Against the Invincible made good;
Or that, whose thundering voice would
    wake
The silence of the polar lake,
When stubborn Russ, and metall'd
    Swede,
On the warp'd wave their death-game
    play'd;
Or that, where Vengeance and Affright
Howl'd round the father of the fight,
Who snatch'd, on Alexandria's sand,
The conqueror's wreath with dying hand.‡
"Or, if to touch such cord be thine,
Restore the ancient tragic line,
And emulate the notes that rung
From the wild harp, which silent hung
By silver Avon's holy shore,
Till twice an hundred years roll'd o'er;

† Sir Sidney Smith.
‡ Sir Ralph Abercromby.

When she, the bold Enchantress,* came,
With fearless hand and heart on flame!
From the pale willow snatch'd the treas-
    ure,
And swept it with a kindred measure,
Till Avon's swans, while rung the grove
With Montfort's hate and Basil's love,
Awakening at the inspired strain,
Deem'd their own Shakespeare lived
    again.''
  Thy friendship thus thy judgment
    wronging,
With praises not to me belonging,
In task more meet for mightiest powers,
Wouldst thou engage my thriftless hours.
But say, my Erskine, hast thou weigh'd
That secret power by all obey'd,
Which warps not less the passive mind,
Its source conceal'd or undefined;
Whether an impulse, that has birth
Soon as the infant wakes on earth,
One with our feelings and our powers,
And rather part of us than ours;
Or whether fitlier term'd the sway
Of habit form'd in early day?
Howe'er derived, its force confest
Rules with despotic sway the breast,
And drags us on by viewless chain,
While taste and reason plead in vain.
Look east, and ask the Belgian why,
Beneath Batavia's sultry sky,
He seeks not eager to inhale
The freshness of the mountain gale,
Content to rear his whiten'd wall
Beside the dank and dull canal?
He'll say, from youth he loved to see
The white sail gliding by the tree.
Or see yon weatherbeaten hind,
Whose sluggish herds before him wind,
Whose tatter'd plaid and rugged cheek
His northern clime and kindred speak:
Through England's laughing meads he
    goes,
And England's wealth around him flows;
Ask, if it would content him well,
At ease in those gay plains to dwell,
Where hedge-rows spread a verdant
    screen,
And spires and forests intervene,
And the neat cottage peeps between?
No! not for these will he exchange
His dark Lochaber's boundless range:

* Joanna Baillie.

Not for fair Devon's meads forsake
Bennevis gray, and Garry's lake.

  Thus, while I ape the measure wild
Of tales that charm'd me yet a child,
Rude though they be, still with the chime
Return the thoughts of early time;
And feelings, roused in life's first day,
Glow in the line, and prompt the lay.
Then rise those crags, that mountain
    tower,
Which charm'd my fancy's wakening hour.
Though no broad river swept along,
To claim, perchance, heroic song;
Though sigh'd no groves in summer gale,
To prompt of love a softer tale:
Though scarce a puny streamlet's speed
Claim'd homage from a shepherd's reed;
Yet was poetic impulse given,
By the green hill and clear blue heaven.
It was a barren scene, and wild,
Where naked cliffs were rudely piled;
But ever and anon between
Lay velvet tufts of loveliest green;
And well the lonely infant knew
Recesses where the wall-flower grew,
And honey-suckle loved to crawl
Up the low crag and ruin'd wall.
I deem'd such nooks the sweetest shade
The sun in all its round survey'd;
And still I thought that shatter'd tower†
The mightiest work of human power;
And marvell'd as the aged hind
With some strange tale bewitch'd m
    mind,
Of forayers, who, with headlong force,
Down from that strength had spurr'
    their horse,
Their southern rapine to renew,
Far in the distant Cheviots blue,
And, home returning, fill'd the hall
With revel, wassail-rout, and brawl.
Methought that still with trump and clar
The gateway's broken arches rang;
Methought grim features, seam'd wit
    scars,
Glared through the window's rusty bar
And ever, by the winter hearth,
Old tales I heard of woe or mirth,
Of lovers' slights, of ladies' charms,
Of witches' spells, of warriors' arms;

† Smailholm tower, in Berwickshire.

Of patriot battles, won of old
By Wallace wight and Bruce the bold;
Of later fields of feud and fight,
When, pouring from their Highland
　　height,
The Scottish clans, in headlong sway,
Had swept the scarlet ranks away.
While stretch'd at length upon the floor,
Again I fought each combat o'er,
Pebbles and shells, in order laid,
The mimic ranks of war display'd;
And onward still the Scottish Lion bore,
And still the scatter'd Southron fled before.

Still, with vain fondness, could I trace,
Anew, each kind familiar face,
That brighten'd at our evening fire!
From the thatch'd mansion's gray-hair'd
　　Sire,*
Wise without learning, plain and good,
And sprung of Scotland's gentler blood;
Whose eye, in age, quick, clear, and keen,
Show'd what in youth its glance had been;
Whose doom discording neighbors sought,
Content with equity unbought;
To him the venerable Priest,
Our frequent and familiar guest,
Whose life and manners well could paint
Alike the student and the saint;
Alas! whose speech too oft I broke
With gambol rude and timeless joke:
For I was wayward, bold, and wild,
A self-will'd imp, a grandame's child;
But half a plague, and half a jest,
Was still endured, beloved, caress'd.

For me, thus nurtured, dost thou ask
The classic poet's well-conn'd task?
Nay, Erskine, nay. — On the wild hill
Let the wild heath-bell flourish still;
Cherish the tulip, prune the vine,
But freely let the woodbine twine,
And leave untrimm'd the eglantine;
Nay, my friend, nay. — Since oft thy
　　praise
Hath given fresh vigor to my lays;
Since oft thy judgment could refine
My flatten'd thought, or cumbrous line;
Still kind, as is thy wont, attend,
And in the minstrel spare the friend.

* Robert Scott of Sandyknows, the grandfather of the poet.

Though wild as cloud, as stream, as gale,
Flow forth, flow unrestrain'd, my Tale!

CANTO THIRD.

THE HOSTEL, OR INN.

I.

THE lifelong day Lord Marmion rode:
The mountain path the Palmer show'd,
By glen and streamlet winded still,
Where stunted birches hid the rill.
They might not choose the lowland road,
For the Mersc forayers were abroad,
Who, fired with hate and thirst of prey,
Had scarcely fail'd to bar their way.
Oft on the trampling band, from crown
Of some tall cliff, the deer look'd down;
On wing of jet, from his repose
In the deep heath, the black-cock rose;
Sprung from the gorse the timid roe,
Nor waited for the bending bow;
And when the stony path began,
By which the naked peak they wan,
Up flew the snowy ptarmigan.
The noon had long been pass'd before
They gain'd the height of Lammermoor;
Thence winding down the northern way
Before them, at the close of day,
Old Gifford's towers and hamlet lay.

II.

No summons calls them to the tower,
To spend the hospitable hour.
To Scotland's camp the Lord was gone;
His cautious dame, in bower alone,
Dreaded her castle to unclose,
So late, to unknown friends or foes.
On through the hamlet as they paced,
Before a porch, whose front was graced
With bush and flagon trimly placed,
　　Lord Marmion drew his rein:
The village inn seem'd large, though
　　rude; [34]
Its cheerful fire and hearty food
　　Might well relieve his train.
Down from their seats the horsemen
　　sprung,
With jingling spurs the court-yard rung;

They bind their horses to the stall,
For forage, food, and firing call,
And various clamor fills the hall:
Weighing the labor with the cost,
Toils everywhere the bustling host.

III.

Soon, by the chimney's merry blaze,
Through the rude hostel might you gaze;
Might see, where, in dark nook aloof,
The rafters of the sooty roof
  Bore wealth of winter cheer;
Of sea-fowl dried, and solands store,
And gammons of the tusky boar,
  And savory haunch of deer,
The chimney arch projected wide;
Above, around it, and beside,
  Were tools for housewives' hand;
Nor wanted, in that martial day,
The implements of Scottish fray,
  The buckler, lance, and brand.
Beneath its shade, the place of state,
On oaken settle Marmion sate,
And view'd around the blazing hearth.
His followers mix in noisy mirth;
Whom with brown ale, in jolly tide,
From ancient vessels ranged aside,
Full actively their host supplied.

IV.

Theirs was the glee of martial breast,
And laughter theirs at little jest;
And oft Lord Marmion deign'd to aid,
And mingle in the mirth they made;
For though with men of high degree,
The proudest of the proud was he,
Yet, train'd in camps, he knew the art
To win the soldier's hardy heart.
They love a captain to obey,
Boisterous as March, yet fresh as May;
With open hand and brow as free,
Lover of wine and minstrelsy;.
Ever the first to scale a tower,
As venturous in a lady's bower:—
Such buxom chief shall lead his host
From India's fires to Zembla's frost.

V.

Resting upon his pilgrim staff,
  Right opposite the Palmer stood;
His thin dark visage seen but half,
  Half hidden by his hood.

Still fix'd on Marmion was his look,
Which he, who ill such gaze could brook,
  Strove by a frown to quell;
But not for that, though more than once
Full met their stern encountering glance,
  The Palmer's visage fell.

VI.

By fits less frequent from the crowd
Was heard the burst of laughter loud;
For still, as squire and archer stared
On that dark face and matted beard,
  Their glee and game declined.
All gazed at length in silence drear,
Unbroke, save when in comrade's ear
Some yeoman, wondering in his fear,
  Thus whisper'd forth his mind:—
"Saint Mary! saw'st thou e'er such sight?
How pale his cheek, his eye how bright,
Whene'er the firebrand's fickle light,
  Glances beneath his cowl!
Full on our Lord he sets his eye;
For his best palfrey, would not I
  Endure that sullen scowl."

VII.

But Marmion, as to chase the awe
Which thus had quell'd their hearts, who saw
The ever-varying firelight show
That figure stern and face of woe,
  Now call'd upon a squire:—
"Fitz-Eustace, know'st thou not some lay,
To speed the lingering night away?
  We slumber by the fire." —

VIII.

"So please you," thus the youth rejoin'd
"Our choicest minstrel's left behind.
Ill may we hope to please your ear,
Accustom'd Constant's strain to hear.
The harp full deftly can he strike,
And wake the lover's lute alike;
To dear Saint Valentine, no thrush
Sings livelier from a spring-tide bush,
No nightingale her lovelorn tune
More sweetly warbles to the moon.
Woe to the cause, whate'er it be,
Detains from us his melody,
Lavish'd on rocks, and billows stern,
Or duller monks of Lindisfarne.

Now must I venture, as I may,
To sing his favorite roundelay."

IX.

A mellow voice Fitz-Eustace had,
The air he chose was wild and sad;
Such have I heard, in Scottish land,
Rise from the busy harvest band,
When falls before the mountaineer,
On Lowland plains the ripen'd ear.
Now one shrill voice the notes prolong,
Now a wild chorus swells the song:
Oft have I listen'd and stood still,
As it came soften'd up the hill,
And deem'd it the lament of men
Who languish'd for their native glen;
And thought how sad would be such
    sound
On Susquehanna's swampy ground,
Kentucky's wood-encumber'd brake,
Or wild Ontario's boundless lake,
Where heart-sick exiles, in the strain,
Recall'd fair Scotland's hills again!

X.

SONG.

Where shall the lover rest,
    Whom the fates sever
From his true maiden's breast,
    Parted forever?
Where, through groves deep and high,
    Sounds the far billow,
Where early violets die,
    Under the willow.

CHORUS.

Eleu loro, etc.   Soft shall be his pillow.

There, through the summer day,
    Cool streams are laving;
There, while the tempests sway,
    Scarce are boughs waving;
There, thy rest shalt thou take,
    Parted forever,
Never again to wake,
    Never, O never!

CHORUS.

Eleu loro, etc.   Never, O never!

XI.

Where shall the traitor rest,
    He, the deceiver,
Who could win maiden's breast,
    Ruin, and leave her?
In the lost battle,
    Borne down by the flying,
Where mingles war's rattle
    With groans of the dying.

CHORUS.

Eleu loro, etc.   There shall he be lying

Her wing shall the eagle flap
    O'er the false-hearted;
His warm blood the wolf shall lap,
    Ere life be parted.
Shame and dishonor sit
    By his grave ever,
Blessing shall hallow it, —
    Never, O never!

CHORUS.

Eleu loro, etc.   Never, O never!

XII.

It ceased, the melancholy sound;
And silence sunk on all around.
The air was sad; but sadder still
    It fell on Marmion's ear,
And plain'd as if disgrace and ill,
    And shameful death, were near.
He drew his mantle past his face,
    Between it and the band,
And rested with his head a space,
    Reclining on his hand.
His thoughts I scan not; but I ween,
That, could their import have been seen,
The meanest groom in all the hall,
That e'er tied courser to a stall,
Would scarce have wish'd to be their prey,
For Lutterward and Fontenaye.

XIII.

High minds, of native pride and force,
Most deeply feel thy pangs, Remorse!
Fear, for their scourge, mean villains have,
Thou art the torturer of the brave!
Yet fatal strength they boast to steel
Their minds to bear the wounds they feel,

Even while they writhe beneath the smart
Of civil conflict in the heart.
For soon Lord Marmion raised his head,
And, smiling, to Fitz-Eustace said, —
" Is it not strange, that, as ye sung,
Seem'd in mine ear a death-peal rung,
Such as in nunneries they toll
For some departing sister's soul?
   Say, what may this portend? " —
Then first the Palmer silence broke,
(The livelong day he had not spoke,)
   " The death of a dear friend." ³⁵

XIV.

Marmion, whose steady heart and eye
Ne'er changed in worst extremity;
Marmion, whose soul could scantly brook,
Even from his King, a haughty look;
Whose accent of command controll'd,
In camps, the boldest of the bold —
Thought, look, and utterance fail'd him now,
Fall'n was his glance, and flush'd his brow;
   For either in the tone,
Or something in the Palmer's look,
So full upon his conscience strook,
   That answer he found none.
Thus oft it haps, that when within
They shrink at sense of secret sin,
   A feather daunts the brave;
A fool's wild speech confounds the wise,
And proudest princes vail their eyes
   Before their meanest slave.

XV.

Well might he falter ! — By his aid
Was Constance Beverley betray'd.
Not that he augur'd of the doom,
Which on the living closed the tomb:
But, tired to hear the desperate maid
Threaten by turns, beseech, upbraid;
And wroth, because, in wild despair,
She practised on the life of Clare;
Its fugitive the Church he gave,
Though not a victim, but a slave;
And deem'd restraint in convent strange
Would hide her wrongs, and her revenge.
Himself, proud Henry's favorite peer,
Held Romish thunders idle fear,
Secure his pardon he might hold,
For some slight mulct of penance-gold.
This judging, he gave secret way,
When the stern priests surprised their prey.

His train but deem'd the favorite page
Was left behind, to spare his age;
Or other if they deem'd, none dared
To mutter what he thought and heard:
Woe to the vassal, who durst pry
Into Lord Marmion's privacy !

XVI.

His conscience slept — he deem'd her well,
And safe secured in distant cell:
But, waken'd by her favorite lay,
And that strange Palmer's boding say,
That fell so ominous and drear,
Full on the object of his fear,
To aid remorse's venom'd throes,
Dark tales of convent-vengeance rose;
And Constance, late betray'd and scorn'd,
All lovely on his soul return'd;
Lovely as when, at treacherous call,
She left her convent's peaceful wall
Crimson'd with shame, with terror mute,
Dreading alike escape, pursuit,
Till love, victorious o'er alarms,
Hid fears and blushes in his arms.

XVII.

" Alas ! " he thought, " how changed that mien !
How changed these timid looks have been,
Since years of guilt, and of disguise,
Have steel'd her brow, and arm'd her eyes !
No more of virgin terror speaks
The blood that mantles in her cheeks;
Fierce, and unfeminine, are there,
Frenzy for joy, for grief despair;
And I the cause — for whom were given
Her peace on earth, her hopes in heaven!—
Would," thought he, as the picture grows,
" I on its stalk had left the rose !
Oh, why should man's success remove
The very charms that wake his love !
Her convent's peaceful solitude
Is now a prison harsh and rude.
And, pent within the narrow cell,
How will her spirit chafe and swell !
How brook the stern monastic laws !
The penance how — and I the cause !
Vigil and scourge — perchance even worse ! " —
And twice he rose to cry, " To horse ! " —

And twice his Sovereign's mandate came,
Like damp upon a kindling flame;
And twice he thought, "Gave I not charge
She should be safe, though not at large?
They durst not, for their island, shred
One golden ringlet from her head."

XVIII.

While thus in Marmion's bosom strove
Repentance and reviving love,
Like whirlwinds, whose contending sway
I've seen Loch Vennachar obey,
Their Host the Palmer's speech had heard,
And, talkative, took up the word:
"Ay, reverend Pilgrim, you, who stray
From Scotland's simple land away,
To visit realms afar,
Full often learn the art to know
Of future weal, or future woe,
By word, or sign, or star;
Yet might a knight his fortune hear,
If, knight-like, he despises fear,
Not far from hence; — if fathers old
Aright our hamlet legend told." —
These broken words the menials move,
(For marvels still the vulgar love,)
And, Marmion giving license cold,
His tale the host thus gladly told: —

XIX.

THE HOST'S TALE.

"A Clerk could tell what years have flown
Since Alexander fill'd our throne,
(Third monarch of that warlike name,)
And eke the time when here he came
To seek Sir Hugo, then our lord:
A braver never drew a sword;
A wiser never, at the hour
Of midnight, spoke the word of power:
The same, whom ancient records call
The founder of the Goblin-Hall.[36]
I would, Sir Knight, your longer stay
Gave you that cavern to survey.
Of lofty roof, and ample size,
Beneath the castle deep it lies:
To hew the living rock profound,
The floor to pave, the arch to round,
There never toil'd a mortal arm,
It all was wrought by word and charm;
And I have heard my grandsire say,
That the wild clamor and affray
Of those dread artisans of hell,
Who labor'd under Hugo's spell,

Sounded as loud as ocean's war,
Among the caverns of Dunbar.

XX.

"The King Lord Gifford's castle sought,
Deep laboring with uncertain thought;
Even then her muster'd all his host,
To meet upon the western coast:
For Norse and Danish galleys plied
Their oars within the frith of Clyde.
There floated Haco's banner trim,[37]
Above Norweyan warriors grim,
Savage of heart, and large of limb;
Threatening both continent and isle,
Bute, Arran, Cunninghame, and Kyle.
Lord Gifford, deep beneath the ground,
Heard Alexander's bugle sound,
And tarried not his garb to change,
But, in his wizard habit strange,
Came forth, — a quaint and fearful sight;
His mantle lined with fox-skins white;
His high and wrinkled forehead bore
A pointed cap, such as of yore
Clerks say that Pharaoh's Magi wore:
His shoes were mark'd with cross and spell,
Upon his breast a pentacle;[38]
His zone, of virgin parchment thin,
Or, as some tell, of dead man's skin,
Bore many a planetary sign,
Combust, and retrograde, and trine;
And in his hand he held prepared,
A naked sword without a guard.

XXI.

"Dire dealings with the fiendish race
Had mark'd strange lines upon his face;
Vigil and fast had worn him grim,
His eyesight dazzled seem'd and dim,
As one unused to upper day;
Even his own menials with dismay
Beheld, Sir Knight, the grisly Sire,
In his unwonted wild attire;
Unwonted, for traditions run,
He seldom thus beheld the sun. —
'I know,' he said — his voice was hoarse,
And broken seem'd its hollow force, —
'I know the cause, although untold,
Why the King seeks his vassal's hold:
Vainly from me my liege would know
His kingdom's future weal or woe;
But yet, if strong his arm and heart,
His courage may do more than art.

XXII.

" ' Of middle air the demons proud,
Who ride upon the racking cloud,
Can read, in fix'd or wandering star,
The issue of events afar;
But still their sullen aid withhold,
Save when by mightier force controll'd.
Such late I summon'd to my hall;
And though so potent was the call,
That scarce the deepest nook of hell
I deem'd a refuge from the spell,
Yet, obstinate in silence still,
The haughty demon mocks my skill.
But thou — who little know'st thy might,
As born upon that blessed night [39]
When yawning graves, and dying groan,
Proclaim'd hell's empire overthrown, —
With untaught valor shall compel
Response denied to magic spell.'
' Gramercy,' quoth our Monarch free,
' Place him but front to front with me,
And, by this good and honor'd brand,
The gift of Cœur-de-Lion's hand,
Soothly I swear, that, tide what tide,
The demon shall a buffet bide.' —
His bearing bold the wizard view'd,
And thus, well pleased, his speech re-
    new'd : —
' There spokè the blood of Malcolm ! —
    mark :
Forth pacing hence, at midnight dark,
The rampart seek, whose circling crown
Crests the ascent of yonder down :
A southern entrance shalt thou find;
There halt, and there thy bugle wind,
And trust thine elfin foe to see,
In guise thy worst enemy:
Couch then thy lance, and spur thy steed,
Upon him ! and Saint George to speed !
If he go down, thou soon shalt know
Whate'er these airy sprites can show; —
If thy heart fail thee in the strife,
I am no warrant for thy life.'

XXIII.

" Soon as the midnight bell did ring,
Alone, and arm'd, forth rode the King
To that old camp's deserted round :
Sir Knight, you well might mark the
    mound,
Left hand the town, — the Pictish race,
The trench, long since, in blood did trace;

The moor around is brown and bare,
The space within is green and fair,
The spot our village children know,
For there the earliest wild-flowers grow;
But woe betide the wandering wight,
That treads its circle in the night !
The breadth across, a bowshot clear,
Gives ample space for full career :
Opposed to the four points of heaven,
By four deep gaps are entrance given.
The southernmost our Monarch past,
Halted, and blew a gallant blast;
And on the north, within the ring,
Appear'd the form of England's King,
Who then, a thousand leagues afar,
In Palestine waged holy war :
Yet arms like England's did he wield,
Alike the leopards in the shield,
Alike his Syrian courser's frame,
The rider's length of limb the same :
Long afterwards did Scotland know,
Fell Edward * was her deadliest foe.

XXIV.

" The vision made our Monarch start,
But soon he mann'd his noble heart,
And in the first career they ran,
The Elfin Knight fell, horse and man;
Yet did a splinter of his lance
Through Alexander's visor glance,
And razed the skin — a puny wound.
The King, light leaping to the ground,
With naked blade his phantom foe
Compell'd the future war to show.
Of Largs he saw the glorious plain,
Where still gigantic bones remain,
    Memorial of the Danish war;
Himself he saw, amid the field,
On high his brandish'd war-axe wield,
    And strike proud Haco from his car,
While all around the shadowy Kings
Denmark's grim ravens cower'd their
    wings.
'Tis said, that, in that awful night,
Remoter visions met his sight,
Foreshowing future conquests far,
When our sons' sons wage northern
    war;
A royal city, tower and spire,
Redden'd the midnight sky with fire,

* Edward I. of England, surnamed "Long-
shanks."

And shouting crews her navy bore,
Triumphant, to the victor shore.*
Such signs may learned clerks explain,
They pass the wit of simple swain.

XXV.

"The joyful King turn'd home again,
Headed his host, and quell'd the Dane;
But yearly, when return'd the night
Of his strange combat with the sprite,
	His wound must bleed and smart;
Lord Gifford then would gibing say,
'Bold as ye were, my liege, ye pay
	The penance of your start.'
Long since, beneath Dunfermline's nave,
King Alexander fills his grave,
	Our Lady give him rest!
Yet still the knightly spear and shield
The Elfin Warrior doth wield,
	Upon the brown hill's breast; 40
And many a knight hath proved his chance,
In the charm'd ring to break a lance,
	But all have foully sped;
Save two, as legends tell, and they
Were Wallace wight, and Gilbert Hay. —
	Gentles, my tale is said."

XXVI.

The quaighs† were deep, the liquor strong,
And on the tale the yeoman-throng
Had made a comment sage and long,
	But Marmion gave a sign:
And, with their lords, the squires retire;
The rest, around the hostel fire,
	Their drowsy limbs recline:
For pillow, underneath each head,
The quiver and the targe were laid.
Deep slumbering on the hostel floor,
Oppress'd with toil and ale, they snore:
The dying flame, in fitful change,
Threw on the group its shadows strange.

XXVII.

Apart, and nestling in the hay
Of a waste loft, Fitz-Eustace lay;
Scarce, by the pale moonlight, were seen
The foldings of his mantle green:

Lightly he dreamt, as youth will dream
Of sport by thicket, or by stream.
Of hawk or hound, of ring or glove,
Or, lighter yet, of lady's love.
A cautious tread his slumber broke,
And, close beside him, when he woke,
In moonbeam half, and half in gloom,
Stood a tall form, with nodding plume;
But, ere his dagger Eustace drew,
His master Marmion's voice he knew.

XXVIII.

— "Fitz-Eustace! rise, I cannot rest;
Yon churl's wild legend haunts my breast,
And graver thoughts have chafed my mood:
The air must cool my feverish blood;
And fain would I ride forth, to see
The scene of Elfin chivalry.
Arise, and saddle me my steed;
And, gentle Eustace, take good heed
Thou dost not rouse these drowsy slaves;
I would not, that the prating knaves
Had cause for saying, o'er their ale,
That I could credit such a tale." —
Then softly down the steps they slid,
Eustace the stable-door undid,
And, darkling, Marmion's steed array'd,
While, whispering, thus the Baron said:—

XXIX.

"Did'st never, good my youth, hear tell,
	That on the hour when I was born,
Saint George, who graced my sire's chapelle,
Down from his steed of marble fell,
	A weary wight forlorn?
The flattering chaplains all agree,
The champion left his steed to me.
I would, the omen's truth to show,
That I could meet this Elfin Foe!
Blithe would I battle, for the right
To ask one question at the sprite: —
Vain thought! for elves, if elves there be,
An empty race, by fount or sea,
To dashing waters dance and sing,
Or round the green oak wheel their ring."
Thus speaking, he his steed bestrode,
And from the hostel slowly rode.

---

* An allusion to the battle of Copenhagen, 1801.

† *Quaigh*, a wooden cup.

XXX.

Fitz-Eustace follow'd him abroad,
And mark'd him pace the village
    road,
    And listen'd to his horse's tramp,
    Till, by the lessening sound,
    He judged that of the Pictish camp
    Lord Marmion sought the round.
Wonder it seem'd, in the squire's
    eyes,
That one, so wary held, and wise, —
Of whom 'twas said, he scarce received
For gospel, what the church believed, —
    Should, stirr'd by idle tale,
Ride forth in silence of the night,
As hoping half to meet a sprite,
    Array'd in plate and mail.
For little did Fitz-Eustace know,
That passions in contending flow,
    Unfix the strongest mind;
Wearied from doubt to doubt to flee,
We welcome fond credulity,
    Guide confident, though blind.

XXXI.

Little for this Fitz-Eustace cared,
But, patient, waited till he heard,
At distance, prick'd to utmost speed,
The foot-tramp of a flying steed,
    Come town-ward rushing on;
First, dead, as if on turf it trode,
Then, clattering on the village road, —
In other pace than forth he yode,*
    Return'd Lord Marmion.
Down hastily he sprung from selle,
And, in his haste, wellnigh he fell;
To the squire's hand the rein he
    threw,
And spoke no word as he withdrew:
But yet the moonlight did betray,
The falcon-crest was soil'd with clay;
And plainly might Fitz-Eustace see,
By stains upon the charger's knee,
And his left side, that on the moor
He had not kept his footing sure.
Long musing on these wondrous signs,
At length to rest the squire reclines,
Broken and short; for still, between,
Would dreams of terror intervene:
Eustace did ne'er so blithely mark
The first notes of the morning lark.

* *Yode,* used by old poets for *went.*

INTRODUCTION TO CANTO FOURTH.

TO JAMES SKENE, ESQ.†

Ashestiel, Ettrick Forest.

An ancient Minstrel sagely said,
" Where is the life which late we led? "
That motley clown in Arden wood,
Whom humorous Jacques with envy
    view'd,
Not even that clown could amplify,
On this trite text, so long as I.
Eleven years we now may tell,
Since we have known each other well;
Since, riding side by side, our hand
First drew the voluntary brand,
And sure, through many a varied scene,
Unkindness never came between.
Away these winged years have flown,
To join the mass of ages gone;
And though deep mark'd, like all below,
With chequer'd shades of joy and woe;
Though thou o'er realms and seas hast
    ranged,
Mark'd cities lost, and empires changed,
While here, at home, my narrower ken
Somewhat of manners saw, and men;
Though varying wishes, hopes, and fears,
Fever'd the progress of these years,
Yet now, days, weeks, and months, but
    seem
The recollection of a dream,
So still we glide down to the sea
Of fathomless eternity.

Even now it scarcely seems a day,
Since first I tuned this idle lay;
A task so often thrown aside,
When leisure graver cares denied,
That now, November's dreary gale,
Whose voice inspired my opening tale,
That same November gale once more
Whirls the dry leaves on Yarrow shore.
Their vex'd boughs streaming to the sky,
Once more our naked birches sigh,
And Blackhouse heights, and Ettrick Pen,
Have donn'd their wintry shrouds again:
And mountain dark, and flooded mead,
Bid us forsake the banks of Tweed.
Earlier than wont along the sky,
Mix'd with the rack, the snow mists fly:

† James Skene, Esq., of Rubislaw, Aberdeen
shire.

The shepherd, who in summer sun,
Had something of our envy won,
As thou with pencil, I with pen,
The features traced of hill and glen; —
He who, outstretch'd the live-long day,
At ease among the heath-flowers lay,
View'd the light clouds with vacant look,
Or slumber'd o'er his tatter'd book,
Or idly busied him to guide
His angle o'er the lessen'd tide, —
At midnight now, the snowy plain
Finds sterner labor for the swain.

When red hath set the beamless sun,
Through heavy vapors dark and dun;
When the tired ploughman, dry and warm,
Hears, half asleep, the rising storm
Hurling the hail, and sleeted rain,
Against the casement's tinkling pane;
The sounds that drive wild deer, and fox,
To shelter in the brake and rocks,
Are warnings which the shepherd ask
To dismal and to dangerous task.
Oft he looks forth, and hopes, in vain,
The blast may sink in mellowing rain;
Till, dark above, and white below,
Decided drives the flaky snow,
And forth the hardy swain must go.
Long, with dejected look and whine,
To leave his hearth his dogs repine;
Whistling and cheering them to aid,
Around his back he wreathes the plaid :
His flock he gathers, and he guides,
To open downs, and mountain sides,
Where, fiercest though the tempest blow,
Least deeply lies the drift below.
The blast, that whistles o'er the fells,
Stiffens his locks to icicles;
Oft he looks back, while streaming far,
His cottage window seems a star, —
Loses its feeble gleam, — and then
Turns patient to the blast again,
And, facing to the tempest's sweep,
Drives through the gloom his lagging
      sheep.
If fails his heart, if his limbs fail,
Benumbing death is in the gale:
His paths, his landmarks, all unknown
Close to the hut, no more his own,
Close to the aid he sought in vain,
The morn may find the stiffen'd swain :[41]
The widow sees, at dawning pale,
His orphans raise their feeble wail;

And, close beside him, in the snow,
Poor Yarrow, partner of their woe,
Couches upon his master's breast,
And licks his cheek to break his rest.

Who envies now the shepherd's lot,
His healthy fare, his rural cot,
His summer couch by greenwood tree,
His rustic kirn's * loud revelry,
His native hill-notes, tuned on high,
To Marion of the blithesome eye;
His crook, his scrip, his oaten reed,
And all Arcadia's golden creed?

Changes not so with us, my Skene,
Of human life the varying scene?
Our youthful summer oft we see
Dance by on wings of game and glee,
While the dark storm reserves its rage,
Against the winter of our age:
As he, the ancient Chief of Troy,
His manhood spent in peace and joy;
But Grecian fires, and loud alarms,
Call'd ancient Priam forth to arms.
Then happy those, since each must drain
His share of pleasure, share of pain, —
Then happy those, beloved of Heaven,
To whom the mingled cup is given;
Whose lenient sorrows find relief,
Whose joys are chasten'd by their grief.
And such a lot, my Skene, was thine,
When thou of late, wert doom'd to twine,
Just when thy bridal hour was by, —
The cypress with the myrtle tie.
Just on thy bride her Sire had smiled,
And bless'd the union of his child,
When love must change its joyous cheer
And wipe affection's filial tear.
Nor did the actions next his end,
Speak more the father than the friend.
Scarce had lamented Forbes [42] paid
The tribute to his Minstrel's shade;
The tale of friendship scarce was told,
Ere the narrator's heart was cold —
Far may we search before we find
A heart so manly and so kind !
But not around his honor'd urn,
Shall friends alone and kindred mourn;
The thousand eyes his care had dried,
Pour at his name a bitter tide;

* Scottish harvest-home.

And frequent falls the grateful dew,
For benefits the world ne'er knew.
If mortal charity dare claim
The Almighty's attributed name,
Inscribe above his mouldering clay,
" The widow's shield, the orphan's stay."
Nor, though it wake thy sorrow, deem
My verse intrudes on this sad theme;
For sacred was the pen that wrote,
" Thy father's friend forget thou not :"
And grateful title may I plead,
For many a kindly word and deed,
To bring my tribute to his grave :—
'Tis little — but 'tis all I have.

To thee, perchance, this rambling strain
Recalls our summer walks again;
When, doing naught,—and, to speak true,
Not anxious to find aught to do, —
The wild unbounded hills we ranged,
While oft our talk its topic changed,
And, desultory as our way,
Ranged, unconfined, from grave to gay.
Even when it flagg'd, as oft will chance,
No effort made to break its trance,
We could right pleasantly pursue
Our sports in social silence too;
Thou bravely laboring to portray
The blighted oak's fantastic spray;
I spelling o'er, with much delight,
The legend of that antique knight,
Tirante by name, yclep'd the White.
At either's feet a trusty squire,
Pandour and Camp,* with eyes of fire,
Jealous, each other's motions view'd,
And scarce suppress'd their ancient feud.
The laverock † whistled from the cloud;
The stream was lively, but not loud;
From the whitethorn the May-flower shed
Its dewy fragrance round our head :
Not Ariel lived more merrily
Under the blossom'd bough, than we.

And blithesome nights, too, have been
    ours,
When Winter stript the summer's bowers.
Careless we heard, what now I hear,
The wild blast sighing deep and drear,
When fires were bright, and lamps beam'd
    gay,
And ladies tuned the lovely lay;

* A favorite bull-terrier of Sir Walter's.
† *Laverock,* the lark.

And he was held a laggard soul,
Who shunn'd to quaff the sparkling bowl.
Then he, whose absence we deplore, ‡
Who breathes the gales of Devon's shore,
The longer miss'd, bewail'd the more;
And thou, and I, and dear loved R——,§
And one whose name I may not say,— ‖
For not mimosa's tender tree
Shrinks sooner from the touch than he,—
In merry chorus well combined,
With laughter drown'd the whistling wind.
Mirth was within; and Care without
Might gnaw her nails to hear our shout.
Not but amid the buxom scene
Some grave discourse might intervene —
Of the good horse that bore him best,
His shoulder, hoof, and arching crest :
For, like mad Tom's,¶ our chiefest care,
Was horse to ride, and weapon wear.
Such nights we've had; and, though the
    game
Of manhood be more sober tame,
And though the field-day, or the drill,
Seem less important now — yet still
Such may we hope to share again.
The sprightly thought inspires my strain !
And mark, how, like a horseman true,
Lord Marmion's march I thus renew.

CANTO FOURTH.

THE CAMP.

I.

EUSTACE, I said, did blithely mark
The first notes of the merry lark.
The lark sang shrill, the cock he crew,
And loudly Marmion's bugles blew,
And with their light and lively call,
Brought groom and yeomen to the stall.
  Whistling they came, and free of heart,
      But soon their mood was changed;
  Complaint was heard on every part,
      Of something disarranged.

‡ Colin Mackenzie, of Portmore.
§ Sir William Rae, Bart., of St. Catharine's.
‖ Sir William Forbes, Bart., of Pitsligo. Son
of the author of the Life of Beattie and brother-
in-law of James Skene.

¶ Common name for an idiot; assumed by
Edgar in King Lear.

Some clamor'd loud for armor lost;
Some brawl'd and wrangled with the host;
" By Becket's bones," cried one, " I fear,
That some false Scot has stolen my spear ! "—
Young Blount, Lord Marmion's second squire,
Found his steed wet with sweat and mire;
Although the rated horse-boy sware,
Last night he dressed him sleek and fair.
While chafed the impatient squire, like thunder
Old Hubert shouts, in fear and wonder,—
"Help, gentle Blount ! help, comrades all !
Bevis lies dying in his stall:"
To Marmion who the plight dare tell,
Of the good steed he loves so well?
Gaping for fear and ruth, they saw
The charger panting on his straw;
Till one, who would seem wisest, cried: —
" What else but evil could betide,
With that cursed Palmer for our guide?
Better we had through mire and bush
Been lantern-led by Friar Rush." [43]

II.

Fitz-Eustace, who the cause but guess'd,
    Nor wholly understood,
His comrades' clamorous plaints suppress'd;
    He knew Lord Marmion's mood.
Him, ere he issued forth, he sought,
And found deep plunged in gloomy thought,
    And did his tale display
Simply as if he knew of naught
    To cause such disarray.
Lord Marmion gave attention cold,
Nor marvell'd at the wonders told, —
Pass'd them as accidents of course,
And bade his clarions sound to horse.

III.

Young Henry Blount, meanwhile, the cost
Had reckon'd with their Scottish host;
And, as the charge he cast and paid,
" Ill thou deserv'st thy hire," he said ;
" Dost see, thou knave, my horse's plight?
Fairies have ridden him all the night,
And left him in a foam !
I trust that soon a conjuring band,
With English cross and blazing brand,
Shall drive the devils from this land,
    To their infernal home:
For in this haunted den, I trow,
All night they trample on and fro."
The laughing host look'd on the hire: —
" Gramercy, gentle southern squire,
And if thou comest among the rest,
With Scottish broadsword to be blest,
Sharp be the brand, and sure the blow,
And short the pang to undergo."
Here stay'd their talk,— for Marmion
Gave now a signal to set on.
The Palmer showing forth the way,
They journey'd all the morning day.

IV.

The green-sward way was smooth and good,
Through Humbie's and through Saltoun's wood;
A forest glade, which, varying still,
Here gave a view of dale and hill,
There narrower closed, till over-head
A vaulted screen the branches made.
" A pleasant path," Fitz-Eustace said;
" Such as where errant-knights might see
Adventures of high chivalry;
Might meet some damsel flying fast,
With hair unbound and looks aghast;
And smooth and level course were here,
In her defence to break a spear.
Here, too, are twilight nooks and dells;
And oft, in such, the story tells,
The damsel kind, from danger freed,
Did grateful pay her champion's meed."
He spoke to cheer Lord Marmion's mind:
Perchance to show his lore design'd;
    For Eustace much had pored
Upon a huge romantic tome,
In the hall window of his home,
Imprinted at the antique dome
    Of Caxton, or De Worde.*
Therefore he spoke, — but spoke in vain,
For Marmion answer'd naught again.

* William Caxton was the earliest English printer ; born in Kent, A.D. 1412, died 1491 ; Wynken de Worde was his successor.

v.

Now sudden, distant trumpets shrill,
In notes prolong'd by wood and hill,
　Were heard to echo far;
Each ready archer grasp'd his bow,
But by the flourish soon they know,
　They breathed no point of war.
Yet cautious, as in foeman's land,
Lord Marmion's order speeds the band,
　Some opener ground to gain;
And scarce a furlong had they rode,
When thinner trees, receding, show'd
　A little woodland plain.
Just in that advantageous glade,
The halting troop a line had made,
As forth from the opposing shade
　Issued a gallant train.

vi.

First came the trumpets at whose clang
So late the forest echoes rang;
On prancing steeds they forward press'd,
With scarlet mantle, azure vest;
Each at his trump a banner wore,
Which Scotland's royal scutcheon bore:
Heralds and pursuivants, by name
Bute, Islay, Marchmount, Rothsay, came,
In painted tabards, proudly showing
Gules, Argent, Or, and Azure glowing,
　Attendant on a King-at-arms,
Whose hand the armorial truncheon held
That feudal strife had often quell'd,
　When wildest its alarms.

vii.

He was a man of middle age;
In aspect manly, grave, and sage,
　As on King's errand come;
But in the glances of his eye,
A penetrating, keen, and sly
　Expression found its home;
The flash of that satiric rage,
Which, bursting on the early stage,
Branded the vices of the age,
　And broke the keys of Rome.
On milk-white palfrey forth he paced;
His cap of maintenance was graced
　With the proud heron-plume.
From his steed's shoulder, loin, and
　breast,
Silk housings swept the ground,
With Scotland's arms, device, and crest,
　Embroider'd round and round.

The double tressure might you see,
　First by Achaius borne,
The thistle and the fleur-de-lis,
　And gallant unicorn.
So bright the King's armorial coat,
That scarce the dazzled eye could note,
In living colors, blazon'd brave,
The Lion, which his title gave;
A train which well beseem'd his state,
But all unarm'd, around him wait.
　Still is thy name in high account,
　　And still thy verse has charms,
　Sir David Lindesay of the Mount,
　　Lord Lion King-at-arms![44]

viii.

Down from his horse did Marmion spring,
Soon as he saw the Lion-King;
For well the stately Baron knew
To him such courtesy was due,
Whom royal James himself had crown'd,
And on his temples placed the round
　Of Scotland's ancient diadem:
And wet his brow with hallow'd wine,
And on his finger given to shine
　The emblematic gem.
Their mutual greetings duly made,
The Lion thus his message said: —
" Though Scotland's King hath deeply
　swore
Ne'er to knit faith with Henry more,
And strictly hath forbid resort
From England to his royal court;
Yet, for he knows Lord Marmion's name,
And honors much his warlike fame,
My liege hath deem'd it shame, and lack
Of courtesy, to turn him back;
And, by his order, I, your guide,
Must lodging fit and fair provide,
Till finds King James meet time to see
The flower of English chivalry."

ix.

Though inly chafed at this delay,
Lord Marmion bears it as he may.
The Palmer, his mysterious guide,
Beholding thus his place supplied,
　Sought to take leave in vain;
Strict was the Lion King's command,
That none, who rode in Marmion's band,
　Should sever from the train: —
" England has here enow of spies
In Lady Heron's witching eyes;"

To Marchmount thus, apart, he said,
But fair pretext to Marmion made.
The right-hand path they now decline,
And trace against the stream the Tyne.

x.

At length up that wild dale they wind,
   Where Crichtoun Castle[45] crowns the
     bank;
For there the Lion's care assign'd
   A lodging meet for Marmion's rank.
That Castle rises on the steep
   Of the green vale of Tyne:
And far beneath, where slow they creep,
From pool to eddy, dark and deep,
Where alders moist, and willows weep,
   You hear her streams repine.
The towers in different ages rose;
Their various architecture shows
   The builders' various hands;
A mighty mass, that could oppose,
When deadliest hatred fired its foes,
   The vengeful Douglas bands.

XI.

Crichtoun! though now thy miry court
   But pens the lazy steer and sheep,
Thy turrets rude, and totter'd Keep,
Have been the minstrel's loved resort.
Oft have I traced, within thy fort,
   Of mouldering shields the mystic sense,
   Scutcheons of honor, or pretence,
Quarter'd in old armorial sort,
   Remains of rude magnificence.
Nor wholly yet had time defaced
Thy lordly gallery fair;
Nor yet the stony cord unbraced,
Whose twisted knots, with roses laced,
   Adorn thy ruin'd stair;
Still rises unimpair'd below,
The court-yard's graceful portico:
Above its cornice, row and row
Of fair hewn facets richly show
   Their pointed diamond form,
Though there but houseless cattle go,
   To shield them from the storm.
   And, shuddering, still may we explore,
     Where oft whilom were captives pent,
   The darkness of thy Massy More;
Or, from thy grass-grown battlement,
May trace, in undulating line,
The sluggish mazes of the Tyne.

XII.

Another aspect Crichtoun show'd,
As through its portals Marmion rode;
But yet 'twas melancholy state
Received him at the outer gate;
For none were in the Castle then,
But women, boys, or aged men.
With eyes scarce dried, the sorrowing
   dame,
To welcome noble Marmion, came;
Her son, a stripling twelve years old,
Proffer'd the Baron's rein to hold;
For each man that could draw a sword
Had march'd that morning with their lord,
Earl Adam Hepburn,[46] he who died
On Flodden, by his sovereign's side.
Long may his Lady look in vain!
She ne'er shall see his gallant train
Come sweeping back through Crichtoun-
   Dean,
'Twas a brave race, before the name
Of hated Bothwell stain'd their fame.

XIII.

And here two days did Marmion rest,
   With every rite that honor claims,
Attended as the King's own guest: —
   Such the command of royal James,
Who marshall'd then his land's array,
Upon the Borough-moor that lay.
Perchance he would not foeman's eye
Upon his gathering host should pry,
Till full prepared was every band
To march against the English land.
Here while they dwelt, did Lindesay's wit
Oft cheer the Baron's moodier fit;
And, in his turn, he knew to prize
Lord Marmion's powerful mind, and wise,
Train'd in the lore of Rome and Greece,
And policies of war and peace.

XIV.

It chanced, as fell the second night,
   That on the battlements they walk'd,
And, by the slowly fading light,
   Of varying topics talk'd;
And, unaware, the Herald-bard
Said, Marmion might his toil have spared,
   In travelling so far;
For that a messenger from heaven
In vain to James had counsel given
   Against the English war; [47]

And, closer question'd, thus he told
A tale, which chronicles of old
In Scottish story have enroll'd: —

XV.

SIR DAVID LINDESAY'S TALE.

"Of all the palaces so fair,
  Built for the royal dwelling,
In Scotland, far beyond compare
  Linlithgow is excelling;
And in its park in jovial June,
How sweet the merry linnet's tune,
  How blithe the blackbird's lay!
The wild-buck bells [48] from ferny brake,
The coot dives merry on the lake,
The saddest heart might pleasure take
  To see all nature gay.
But June is to our sovereign dear
The heaviest month in all the year:
Too well his cause of grief you know,
June saw his father's overthrow.[49]
Woe to the traitors, who could bring
The princely boy against his King!
Still in his conscience burns the sting.
In offices as strict as Lent,
King James's June is ever spent.

XVI.

"When last this ruthful month was come,
And in Linlithgow's holy dome
  The King, as wont, was praying;
While, for his royal father's soul,
The chanters sung, the bells did toll,
  The Bishop mass was saying —
For now the year brought round again
The day the luckless king was slain —
In Katharine's aisle the Monarch knelt,
With sackcloth-shirt, and iron belt,
  And eyes with sorrow streaming;
Around him in their stalls of state,
The Thistle's Knight-Companions sate,
  Their banners o'er them beaming.
I too was there, and, sooth to tell,
Bedeafen'd with the jangling knell,
Was watching where the sunbeams fell,
  Through the stain'd casement gleaming;
But, while I mark'd what next befell,
  It seem'd as I were dreaming.
Stepp'd from the crowd a ghostly wight,
In azure gown, with cincture white;
His forehead bald, his head was bare,
Down hung at length his yellow hair. —

Now, mock me not, when, good my Lord,
I pledge to you my knightly word,
That, when I saw his placid grace,
  His simple majesty of face,
  His solemn bearing, and his pace
    So stately gliding on, —
Seem'd to me ne'er did limner paint
So just an image of the Saint,
Who propp'd the Virgin in her faint, —
  The loved Apostle John!

XVII.

"He stepp'd before the Monarch's chair,
And stood with rustic plainness there,
  And little reverence made;
Nor head, nor body, bow'd nor bent,
But on the desk his arm he leant,
  And words like these he said,
In a low voice, but never tone
So thrill'd through vein, and nerve and
  bone: —
'My mother sent me from afar,
Sir King, to warn thee not to war, —
  Woe waits on thine array;
If war thou wilt, of woman fair,
Her witching wiles and wanton snare,
James Stuart, doubly warn'd, beware:
  God keep thee as he may!'
    The wondering Monarch seem'd to
      seek
      For answer, and found none;
    And when he raised his head to
      speak,
      The monitor was gone;
The Marshal and myself had cast
To stop him as he outward pass'd;
But, lighter than the whirlwind's blast,
  He vanish'd from our eyes,
Like sunbeam on the billow cast,
  That glances but, and dies."

XVIII.

While Lindesay told his marvel strange,
  The twilight was so pale,
He mark'd not Marmion's color change,
  While listening to the tale;
But, after a suspended pause,
The Baron spoke:—"Of Nature's laws
So strong I held the force,
That never superhuman cause
  Could e'er control their course.
And, three days since, had judged your aim
Was but to make your guest your game.

But I have seen, since past the Tweed,
What much has changed my skeptic creed,
And made me credit aught." — He staid,
And seem'd to wish his words unsaid:
But, by that strong emotion press'd,
Which prompts us to unload our breast,
    Even when discovery's pain,
To Lindesay did at length unfold
The tale his village host had told,
    At Gifford, to his train.
Naught of the Palmer says he there,
And naught of Constance or of Clare;
The thoughts, which broke his sleep, he seems
To mention but as feverish dreams.

XIX.

" In vain," said he, " to rest I spread
My burning limbs, and couch'd my head:
    Fantastic thoughts return'd;
And, by their wild dominion led,
    My heart within me burn'd.
So sore was the delirious goad,
I took my steed, and forth I rode,
And, as the moon shone bright and cold,
Soon reach'd the camp upon the wold.
The southern entrance I pass'd through,
And halted, and my bugle blew.
Methought an answer met my ear, —
    Yet was the blast so low and drear,
So hollow, and so faintly blown,
It might be echo of my own.

XX.

"Thus judging, for a little space
I listen'd, ere I left the place;
    But scarce could trust my eyes,
Nor yet can think they served me true,
When sudden in the ring I view,
In form distinct of shape and hue,
    A mounted champion rise. —
I've fought, Lord Lion, many a day,
In single fight, and mix'd affray,
And ever, I myself may say,
    Have borne me as a knight;
But when this unexpected foe
Seem'd starting from the gulf below, —
I care not though the truth I show, —
    I trembled with affright;
And as I placed in rest my spear,
My hand so shook for very fear,
    I scarce could couch it right.

XXI.

" Why need my tongue the issue tell?
We ran our course, — my charger fell: —
What could he 'gainst the shock of hell? —
    I roll'd upon the plain.
High o'er my head, with threatening hand,
The spectre shook his naked brand, —
    Yet did the worst remain:
My dazzled eyes I upward cast. —
Not opening hell itself could blast
    Their sight, like what I saw !
Full on his face the moonbeam strook, —
    A face could never be mistook !
I knew the stern vindictive look,
    And held my breath for awe.
I saw the face of one who, fled
To foreign climes, has long been dead, —
    I well believe the last;
For ne'er, from vizor raised, did stare
A human warrior, with a glare,
    So grimly and so ghast.
Thrice o'er my head he shook the blade;
But when to good Saint George I pray'd,
(The first time e'er I ask'd his aid,)
    He plunged it in the sheath;
And, on his courser mounting light,
He seem'd to vanish from my sight:
The moonbeam droop'd, and deepest night
    Sunk down upon the heath. —
    'Twere long to tell what cause I have
    To know his face, that met me there,
    Call'd by his hatred from the grave,
        To cumber upper air:
Dead or alive, good cause had he
To be my mortal enemy."

XXII.

Marvell'd Sir David of the Mount;
Then, learn'd in story, 'gan recount
    Such chance had happ'd of old,
When once, near Norham, there did fight
A spectre fell of fiendish might,
In likeness of a Scottish knight,
    With Brian Bulmer bold,
And train'd him nigh to disallow
The aid of his baptismal vow.
" And such a phantom, too, 'tis said,
With Highland broadsword, targe, and plaid.

And fingers, red with gore,
Is seen in Rothiemurcus glade,
Or where the sable pine-trees shade
Dark Tomantoul, and Auchnaslaid,
   Dromouchty, or Glenmore.*
And yet, whate'er such legends say,
Of warlike demon, ghost, or fay,
   On mountain, moor, or plain,
Spotless in faith, in bosom bold,
True son of chivalry should hold
   These midnight terrors vain;
For seldom have such spirits power
To harm, save in the evil hour,
When guilt we meditate within,
Or harbor unrepented sin " —
Lord Marmion turn'd him half aside,
And twice to clear his voice he tried,
   Then press'd Sir David's hand, —
But naught, at length, in answer said;
And here their farther converse staid,
   Each ordering that his band
Should boune them with the rising day,
To Scotland's camp to take their way. —
Such was the King's command.

XXIII.

Early they took Dun-Edin's road,
And I could trace each step they trode.
Hill, brook, nor dell, nor rock, nor stone,
Lies on the path to me unknown.
Much might it boast of storied lore;
But, passing such digression o'er,
Suffice it that the route was laid
Across the furzy hills of Braid.
They pass'd the glen and scanty rill,
And climb'd the opposing bank, until
They gain'd the top of Blackford Hill.

XXIV.

Blackford! on whose uncultured breast,
   Among the broom, and thorn, and whin,
A truant-boy, I sought the nest,
Or listed, as I lay at rest,
   While rose, on breezes thin,
The murmur of the city crowd,
And, from his steeple jangling loud,
   Saint Giles's mingling din.
Now, from the summit to the plain,
Waves all the hill with yellow grain;

* See note 40.

And o'er the landscape as I look,
Naught do I see unchanged remain,
Save the rude cliffs and chiming brook.
To me they make a heavy moan,
Of early friendships past and gone.

XXV.

But different far the change has been,
   Since Marmion, from the crown
Of Blackford, saw that martial scene
   Upon the bent so brown:
Thousand pavilions, white as snow,
Spread all the Borough-moor[50] below,
   Upland, and dale, and down: —
A thousand did I say? I ween,
Thousands on thousands there were seen,
That chequer'd all the heath between
   The streamlet and the town;
In crossing ranks extending far,
Forming a camp irregular;
Oft giving way, where still there stood
Some relics of the old oak wood,
That darkly huge did intervene,
And tamed the glaring white with green:
In these extended lines there lay
A martial kingdom's vast array.

XXVI.

For from Hebudes,† dark with rain,
To eastern Lodon's fertile plain,
And from the Southern Redswire edge,
To farthest Rosse's rocky ledge;
From west to east, from south to north,
Scotland sent all her warriors forth.
Marmion might hear the mingled hum
Of myriads up the mountain come;
The horses' tramp, and tingling clank,
Where chiefs review'd their vassal rank,
   And charger's shrilling neigh;
And see the shifting lines advance,
While frequent flash'd, from shield and lance,
   The sun's reflected ray.

XXVII.

Thin curling in the morning air,
The wreaths of failing smoke declare
To embers now the brands decay'd,
Where the night-watch their fires had made.

† The ancient name of the Hebrides.

They saw, slow rolling on the plain,
Full many a baggage-cart and wain,
And dire artillery's clumsy car,
By sluggish oxen tugg'd to war;
And there were Borthwick's Sisters Seven,*
And culverins which France had given.
Ill-omen'd gift! the guns remain
The conqueror's spoil on Flodden plain.

XXVIII.

Nor mark'd they less, where in the air
A thousand streamers flaunted fair;
　　Various in shape, device, and hue,
　　Green, sanguine, purple, red, and blue,
Broad, narrow, swallow-tail'd, and square,
Scroll, pennon, pensil, bandrol, there
　　O'er the pavilions flew.
Highest and midmost, was descried
The royal banner floating wide;
　　The staff, a pine-tree, strong and straight,
Pitch'd deeply in a massive stone,
Which still in memory is shown,
　　Yet bent beneath the standard's weight
　　Whene'er the western wind unroll'd,
　　With toil, the huge and cumbrous fold,
And gave to view the dazzling field,
Where, in proud Scotland's royal shield,
　　The ruddy lion ramp'd in gold.[51]

XXIX.

Lord Marmion view'd the landscape bright, —
He view'd it with a chief's delight, —
　　Until within him burn'd his heart,
　　And lightning from his eye did part,
　　　As on the battle-day;
　　Such glance did falcon never dart,
　　　When stooping on his prey.
"Oh! well, Lord-Lion, hast thou said,
Thy King from warfare to dissuade
　Were but a vain essay:
For, by St. George, were that host mine,
Not power infernal nor divine,
Should once to peace my soul incline,
Till I had dimm'd their armor's shine
　In glorious battle-fray!"
Answer'd the Bard, of milder mood:
" Fair is the sight, — and yet 'twere good,

That kings would think withal,
When peace and wealth their land has bless'd,
'Tis better to sit still at rest,
　Than rise, perchance to fall."

XXX.

Still on the spot Lord Marmion stay'd,
For fairer scene he ne'er survey'd.
　　When sated with the martial show
　　That peopled all the plain below,
　　The wandering eye could o'er it go
　　And mark the distant city glow
　　　With gloomy splendor red;
　　For on the smoke-wreaths, huge and slow,
　　That round her sable turrets flow,
　　　The morning beams were shed,
　　And tinged them with a lustre proud,
　　Like that which streaks a thunder-cloud.
Such dusky grandeur clothed the height,
Where the huge Castle holds its state,
　And all the steep slope down,
Whose ridgy back heaves to the sky,
Piled deep and massy, close and high,
　Mine own romantic town!
But northward far, with purer blaze,
On Ochil mountains fell the rays,
And as each heathy top they kiss'd,
It gleam'd a purple amethyst.
Yonder the shores of Fife you saw;
Here Preston-Bay and Berwick-Law:
　And, broad between them roll'd,
The gallant Frith the eye might note
Whose islands on its bosom float,
　Like emeralds chased in gold.
Fitz-Eustace' heart felt closely pent;
As if to give his rapture vent,
The spur he to his charger lent,
　And raised his bridle hand,
And, making demi-volte in air,
Cried, "Where's the coward that would not dare
　To fight for such a land?"
The Lindesay smiled his joy to see;
Nor Marmion's frown repressed his glee.

XXXI.

Thus while they look'd, a flourish proud,
Where mingled trump and clarion loud,

* Seven culverins, so called from him who cast them.

And fife, and kettle-drum,
And sackbut deep, and psaltery,
And war-pipe with discordant cry,
And cymbal clattering to the sky,
Making wild music bold and high,
    Did up the mountain come;
The whilst the bells, with distant chime,
Merrily told the hour of prime,
And thus the Lindesay spoke: —
" Thus clamor still the war-notes when
The king to mass his way has ta'en,
Or to St. Katharine's of Sienne,
    Or Chapel of Saint Rocque.
To you they speak of martial fame;
But me remind of peaceful game,
    When blither was their cheer,
Thrilling in Falkland-woods the air,
In signal none his steed should spare,
But strive which foremost might repair
    To the downfall of the deer.

XXXII.

" Nor less," he said, — " when looking
        forth,
I view yon Empress of the North
    Sit on her hilly throne;
Her palace's imperial bowers,
Her castle, proof to hostile powers,
Her stately halls and holy towers —
    Nor less," he said, " I moan,
To think what woe mischance may bring,
And how these merry bells may ring
The death-dirge of our gallant king;
    Or with the 'larum call
The burghers forth to watch and ward,
'Gainst southern sack and fires to guard
    Dun-Edin's leaguer'd wall. —
But not for my presaging thought,
Dream conquest sure, or cheaply bought !
Lord Marmion, I say nay:
God is the guider of the field,
He breaks the champion's spear and
        shield, —
But thou thyself shalt say,
When joins yon host in deadly stowre,
That England's dames must weep in
        bower,
    Her monks the death-mass sing;
For never saw'st thou such a power
    Led on by such a King."—
And now, down winding to the plain,
The barriers of the camp they gain,

And there they made a stay. —
There stays the Minstrel till he fling
His hand o'er every Border string,
And fit his harp the pomp to sing,
Of Scotland's ancient Court and King,
    In the succeeding lay.

INTRODUCTION TO CANTO FIFTH.

TO GEORGE ELLIS, ESQ.*

Edinburgh.

WHEN dark December glooms the day,
And takes our autumn joys away;
When short and scant the sunbeam
        throws,
Upon the weary waste of snows,
A cold and profitless regard,
Like patron on a needy bard;
When silvan occupation's done,
And o'er the chimney rests the gun,
And hang, in idle trophy, near,
The game-pouch, fishing-rod, and spear;
When wiry terrier, rough and grim,
And greyhound, with his length of limb,
And pointer, now employ'd no more,
Cumber our parlor's narrow floor;
When in his stall the impatient steed
Is long condemned to rest and feed;
When from our snow-encircled home,
Scarce cares the hardiest step to roam,
Since path is none, save that to bring
The needful water from the spring;
When wrinkled news-page, thrice conn'd
        o'er,
Beguiles the dreary hour no more,
And darkling politician, cross'd,
Inveighs against the lingering post,
And answering housewife sore complains
Of carriers' snow-impeded wains;
When such the country cheer, I come,
Well pleased, to seek our city home:
For converse, and for books, to change
The Forest's melancholy range,
And welcome, with renew'd delight,
The busy day and social night.

* The learned editor of the " Specimens of
Ancient English Romances." He died April
10, 1815, aged 70.

Not here need my desponding rhyme
Lament the ravages of time,
As erst by Newark's riven towers,
And Ettrick stripp'd of forest bowers.
True, — Caledonia's Queen is changed,[52]
Since on her dusky summit ranged,
Within its steepy limits pent,
By bulwark, line, and battlement,
And flanking towers, and laky flood,
Guarded and garrison'd she stood,
Denying entrance or resort,
Save at each tall embattled port;
Above whose arch, suspended, hung
Portcullis spiked with iron prong.
That long is gone, — but not so long
Since, early closed, and opening late,
Jealous revolved the studded gate,
Whose task, from eve to morning tide,
A wicket churlishly supplied.
Stern, then, and steel-girt was thy brow,
Dun-Edin ! O, how alter'd now,
When safe amid thy mountain court
Thou sit'st, like Empress at her sport,
And liberal, unconfined, and free,
Flinging thy white arms to the sea.
For thy dark cloud, with umber'd lower,
That hung o'er cliff, and lake, and tower,
Thou gleam'st against the western ray
Ten thousand lines of brighter day.

Not she, the Championess of old,
In Spenser's magic tale enroll'd,
She, for the charmed spear renown'd,
Which forced each knight to kiss the
        ground, —
Not she more changed, when, placed at
        rest,
What time she was Malbecco's guest,
She gave to flow her maiden vest;
When from the corslet's grasp relieved,
Free to the sight her bosom heaved;
Sweet was her blue eye's modest smile,
Erst hidden by the aventayle;
And down her shoulders graceful roll'd,
Her locks profuse, of paly gold.
They who whilom, in midnight fight,
Had marvell'd at her matchless might,
No less her maiden charms approved,
But looking liked, and liking loved.
The sight could jealous pangs beguile,
And charm Malbecco's cares a while;
And he, the wandering Squire of Dames,
Forgot his Columbella's claims,

And passion, erst unknown, could gain
The breast of blunt Sir Satyrane;
Nor durst light Paridel advance,
Bold as he was, a looser glance.
She charm'd at once, and tamed the
        heart,
Incomparable Britomarte ! *

So thou, fair City ! disarray'd
Of battled wall, and rampart's aid,
As stately seem'st, but lovelier far
Than in that panoply of war.
Nor deem that from thy fenceless throne
Strength and security are flown;
Still, as of yore, Queen of the North !
Still canst thou send thy children forth.
Ne'er readier at alarm-bell's call
Thy burghers rose to man thy wall,
Than now, in danger, shall be thine,
Thy dauntless voluntary line;
For fosse and turret proud to stand,
Their breasts the bulwarks of the land.
Thy thousands, trained to martial toil,
Full red would stain their native soil,
Ere from thy mural crown there fell
The slightest knosp or pinnacle.
And if it come, — as come it may,
Dun-Edin ! that eventful day, —
Renown'd for hospitable deed,
That virtue much with Heaven may plead,
In patriarchal times whose care
Descending angels deign'd to share;
That claim may wrestle blessings down
On those who fight for The Good Town,
Destined in every age to be
Refuge of injured royalty;
Since first, when conquering York arose,
To Henry meek she gave repose,†
Till late, with wonder, grief, and awe,
Great Bourbon's relics, sad she saw.‡

* The Maiden Knight in Spenser's " Faërie
Queen," book iii. canto 9.

† Henry VI. of England, who with his Queen,
his heir, and the chiefs of his family, sought
refuge in Scotland after the fatal battle of Tow-
ton. "The Meek Usurper," see Gray.

‡ In January, 1796, the exiled Comte d'Artois,
afterwards Charles X. of France, took up his
residence at Holy-Rood, where he remained till
August, 1799. When again driven from his country by the Revolution of 1830, the same unfortunate Prince, with all the immediate members of
his family, sought refuge once more in the ancient
palace of the Stuarts, and remained there till
Sept. 18. 1842.

Truce to these thoughts ! — For, as they
    rise,
How gladly I avert mine eyes,
Bodings, or true or false, to change,
For Fiction's fair romantic range,
Or for Tradition's dubious light,
That hovers 'twixt the day and night:
Dazzling alternately and dim,
Her wavering lamp I'd rather trim,
Knights, squires, and lovely dames to
    see,
Creation of my fantasy,
Than gaze abroad on reeky fen,
And make of mists invading men.
Who loves not more the night of June
Than dull December's gloomy noon?
The moonlight than the fog of frost?
And can we say, which cheats the most?

But who shall teach my harp to gain
A sound of the romantic strain,
Whose Anglo-Norman tones whilere
Coul ' win the royal Henry's ear,
Famed Beauclerc call'd, for that he loved
The minstrel * and his lay approved?
Who shall these lingering notes redeem,
Decaying on Oblivion's stream;
Such notes as from the Breton tongue
Marie † translated, Blondel sung? —
O ! born, Time's ravage to repair,
And make the dying Muse thy care;
Who, when his scythe her hoary foe
Was poising for the final blow,
The weapon from his hand could wring,
And break his glass, and shear his wing,
And bid, reviving in his strain,
The gentle poet live again;
Thou, who canst give to lightest lay
An unpedantic moral gay,
Nor less the dullest theme bid flit
On wings of unexpected wit;
In letters as in life approved,
Example honor'd, and beloved, —
Dear ELLIS ! to the bard impart
A lesson of thy magic art,
To win at once the head and heart. —
At once to charm, instruct, and mend,
My guide, my pattern, and my friend !

* Philip de Than.

† Marie of France, who translated the " Lais "
of Brittany into French.   She resided at the
Court of Henry III. of England, to whom she
dedicated her book.

Such minstrel lesson to bestow
Be long thy pleasing task, — but, O !
No more by thy example teach,
— What few can practise, all can
    preach, —
With even patience to endure
Lingering disease, and painful cure,
And boast affliction's pangs subdued
By mild and manly fortitude.
Enough, the lesson has been given:
Forbid the repetition, Heaven !

Come listen, then ! for thou hast known,
And loved the Minstrel's varying tone,
Who, like his Border sires of old,
Waked a wild measure rude and bold,
Till Windsor's oaks, and Ascot plain,
With wonder heard the northern strain.
Come listen ! bold in thy applause,
The bard shall scorn pedantic laws;
And, as the ancient art could stain
Achievements on the storied pane,
Irregularly traced and plann'd,
But yet so glowing and so grand, —
So shall he strive, in changeful hue,
Field, feast, and combat, to renew,
And loves, and arms, and harpers' glee,
And all the pomp of chivalry.

' CANTO FIFTH

THE COURT.

I.

THE train has left the hills of Braid;
The barrier guard have open made
(So Lindesay bade) the palisade,
    That closed the tented ground;
Their men the warders backward drew,
And carried pikes as they rode through,
    Into its ample bound.
Fast ran the Scottish warriors there,
Upon the Southern band to stare,
And envy with their wonder rose,
To see such well-appointed foes;
Such length of shafts, such mighty bows,
So huge, that many simply thought,
But for a vaunt such weapons wrought;
And little deem'd their force to feel,
Through links of mail, and plates of steel,
When rattling upon Flodden vale,
The cloth-yard arrows flew like hail.[53]

II.

Nor less did Marmion's skilful view
Glance every line and squadron through,
And much he marvell'd one small land
Could marshal forth such various band:
    For men-at-arms were here,
Heavily sheathed in mail and plate,
Like iron towers for strength and weight,
On Flemish steeds of bone and height,
    With battle-axe and spear.
Young knights and squires, a lighter train,
Practised their chargers on the plain,
By aid of leg, of hand, and rein,
    Each warlike feat to show,
To pass, to wheel, the croupe to gain,
And high curvett, that not in vain
The sword sway might descend amain
    On foeman's casque below.
He saw the hardy burghers there
March arm'd, on foot, with faces bare,[54]
    For vizor they wore none,
Nor waving plume, nor crest of knight;
But burnished were their corslets bright,
Their brigantines, and gorgets light,
    Like very silver shone.
Long pikes they had for standing fight,
    Two-handed swords they wore,
And many wielded mace of weight,
    And bucklers bright they bore.

III.

On foot the yeoman too, but dress'd
In his steel-jack, a swarthy vest,
    With iron quilted well;
Each at his back (a slender store)
His forty days' provision bore,
    As feudal statutes tell.
His arms were halbert, axe, or spear,[55]
A crossbow there, a hagbut here,
    A dagger-knife, and brand.
Sober he seem'd, and sad of cheer,
As loth to leave his cottage dear,
    And march to foreign strand;
Or musing, who would guide his steer,
    To till the fallow land.
Yet deem not in his thoughtful eye
Did aught of dastard terror lie;
    More dreadful far his ire,
Than theirs, who, scorning danger's name,
In eager mood to battle came,
Their valor like light straw on flame,
    A fierce but fading fire.

IV.

Not so the Borderer: — bred to war,
He knew the battle's din afar,
    And joy'd to hear it swell.
His peaceful day was slothful ease;
Nor harp, nor pipe, his ear could please
    Like the loud slogan yell.
On active steed, with lance and blade,
The light-arm'd pricker plied his trade, —
    Let nobles fight for fame;
Let vassals follow where they lead,
Burghers to guard their townships bleed,
    But war's the Borderer's game.
Their gain, their glory, their delight,
To sleep the day, maraud the night,
    O'er mountain, moss, and moor;
Joyful to fight they took their way,
Scarce caring who might win the day,
    Their booty was secure.
These, as Lord Marmion's train pass'd by,
Look'd on at first with careless eye,
Nor marvell'd aught, well taught to know
The form and force of English bow.
But when they saw the Lord array'd
In splendid arms and rich brocade,
Each Borderer to his kinsman said; —
    " Hist, Ringan! seest thou there!
Canst guess which road they'll homeward ride? —
O! could we but on Border side,
By Eusedale's glen, or Liddell's tide,
    Beset a prize so fair!
That fangless Lion, too, their guide,
Might chance to lose his glistering hide;
Brown Maudlin, of that doublet pied,
    Could make a kirtle rare."

V.

Next, Marmion mark'd the Celtic race,
Of different language, form, and face,
    A various race of man;
Just then the Chiefs their tribes array'd,
And wild and garish semblance made,
The chequer'd trews, and belted plaid,
And varying notes the war-pipes bray'd
    To every varying clan;
Wild through their red or sable hair
Look'd out their eyes with savage stare,
    On Marmion as he pass'd;
Their legs above the knee were bare;
Their frame was sinewy, short, and spare
    And harden'd to the blast;

Of taller race, the chiefs they own
Were by the eagle's plumage known.
The hunted red deer's undress'd hide
Their hairy buskins well supplied;
The graceful bonnet deck'd their head:
Back from their shoulders hung the plaid;
A broadsword of unwieldy length,
A dagger proved for edge and strength,
　A studded targe they wore,
And quivers, bows, and shafts, — but, O!
Short was the shaft, and weak the bow,
　To that which England bore.
The Isles-men carried at their backs
The ancient Danish battle-axe.
They raised a wild and wondering cry,
As with his guide rode Marmion by.
Loud were their clamoring tongues, as
　when
The clanging sea-fowl leave the fen,
And, with their cries discordant mix'd,
Grumbled and yell'd the pipes betwixt.

VI.

Thus through the Scottish camp they
　pass'd,
And reach'd the City gate at last,
Where all around, a wakeful guard,
Arm'd burghers kept their watch and
　ward.
Well had they cause of jealous fear,
When lay encamp'd, in field so near,
The Borderer and the Mountaineer.
As through the bustling streets they
　go,
All was alive with martial show:
At every turn, with dinning clang,
The armorer's anvil clash'd and rang;
Or toil'd the swarthy smith, to wheel
The bar that arms the charger's heel;
Or axe, or falchion, to the side
Of jarring grindstone was applied.
Page, groom, and squire, with hurrying
　pace,
Through street, and lane, and market-
　place,
　Bore lance, or casque, or sword;
While burghers, with important face,
　Described each new-come lord,
Discuss'd his lineage, told his name,
His following, and his warlike fame.
The Lion led to lodging meet,
Which high o'erlook'd the crowded
　street;

There must the Baron rest,
Till past the hour of vesper tide,
And then to Holy-Rood must ride, —
　Such was the King's behest.
Meanwhile the Lion's care assigns
A banquet rich, and costly wines,
　To Marmion and his train; 56
And when the appointed hour succeeds,
The Baron dons his peaceful weeds,
And following Lindesay as he leads,
　The palace-halls they gain.

VII.

Old Holy-Rood rung merrily
That night, with wassail, mirth, and glee;
King James within her princely bower,
Feasted the Chiefs of Scotland's power,
Summon'd to spend the parting hour;
For he had charged, that his array　.
Should southward march by break of
　day.
Well loved that splendid monarch aye
　The banquet and the song,
By day the tourney, and by night
The merry dance, traced fast and light,
The maskers quaint, the pageant bright,
　The revel loud and long.
This feast outshone his banquets past,
It was his blithest — and his last.
The dazzling lamps, from gallery gay,
Cast on the Court a dancing ray;
Here to the harp did minstrels sing;
There ladies touch'd a softer string;
With long-ear'd cap, and motley vest
The licensed fool retail'd his jest;
His magic tricks the juggler plied;
At dice and draughts the gallants vied;
While some, in close recess apart,
Courted the ladies of their heart,
　Nor courted them in vain;
For often, in the parting hour,
Victorious Love asserts his power
　O'er coldness and disdain;
And flinty is her heart, can view
To battle march a lover true —
Can hear, perchance, his last adieu,
　Nor own her share of pain.

VIII.

Through this mix'd crowd of glee and
　game,
The King to greet Lord Marmion came,

While, reverent, all made room.
An easy task it was, I trow,
King James's manly form to know.
Although, his courtesy to show,
He doff'd to Marmion bending low,
    His broider'd cap and plume.
For royal was his garb and mien,
    His cloak, of crimson velvet piled,
    Trimm'd with the fur of marten wild;
His vest of changeful satin sheen,
    The dazzled eye beguiled;
His gorgeous collar hung adown,
Wrought with the badge of Scotland's
    crown,
The thistle brave, of old renown: ·
His trusty blade, Toledo right,
Descended from a baldric bright;
White were his buskins, on the heel
His spurs inlaid of gold and steel;
His bonnet, all of crimson fair,
Was button'd with a ruby rare:
And Marmion deem'd he ne'er had seen
A prince of such a noble mien.

IX.

The monarch's form was middle size;
For feat of strength, or exercise,
    Shaped in proportion fair;
And hazel was his eagle eye,
And auburn of the darkest dye,
    His short curl'd beard and hair.
Light was his footstep in the dance,
    And firm his stirrup in the lists;
And, oh! he had that merry glance,
    That seldom lady's heart resists.
Lightly from fair to fair he flew,
And loved to plead, lament, and sue; —
Suit lightly won, and short-lived pain,
For monarchs seldom sigh in vain.
    I said he joy'd in banquet bower;
But mid his mirth, 'twas often strange,
How suddenly his cheer would change,
    His look o'ercast and lower,
If, in a sudden turn, he felt
The pressure of his iron belt,
That bound his breast in penance-pain,
In memory of his father slain.[57]
Even so 'twas strange how evermore,
Soon as the passing pang was o'er
Forward he rush'd, with double glee,
Into the stream of revelry:
Thus, dim-seen object of affright
Startles the courser in his flight,

And half he halts, half springs aside;
But feels the quickening spur applied,
And, straining on the tighten'd rein,
Scours doubly swift o'er hill and plain.

x.

O'er James's heart, the courtiers say,
Sir Hugh the Heron's wife held sway: [58]
    To Scotland's Court she came,
To be a hostage for her lord,
Who Cessford's gallant heart had gored,
And with the King to make accord,
    Had sent his lovely dame.
Nor to that lady free alone
Did the gay King allegiance own;
    For the fair Queen of France
Sent him a turquois ring and glove,
And charged him, as her knight and love,
    For her to break a lance; [59]
And strike three strokes with Scottish
    brand,
And march three miles on Southron land,
And bid the banners of his band
    In English breezes dance.
And thus, for France's Queen he drest
His manly limbs in mailed vest;
And thus admitted English fair
His inmost counsels still to share;
And thus for both, he madly plann'd
The ruin of himself and land!
    And yet, the sooth to tell,
Nor England's fair, nor France's Queen,
Were worth one pearl-drop, bright and
    sheen,
From Margaret's eyes that fell, —
His own Queen Margaret, who, in Lith-
    gow's bower,
All lonely sat, and wept the weary hour.

xi.

The Queen sits lone in Lithgow pile,
    And weeps the weary day,
The war against her native soil,
Her monarch's risk in battle broil: —
And in gay Holy-Rood, the while,
Dame Heron rises with a smile
    Upon the harp to play.
Fair was her rounded arm, as o'er
    The strings her fingers flew;
And as she touch'd and tuned them all,
Even her bosom's rise and fall
    Was plainer given to view;

For, all for heat, was laid aside
Her wimple, and her hood untied.
And first she pitch'd her voice to sing,
Then glanced her dark eye on the King,
And then around the silent ring;
And laugh'd, and blush'd, and oft did
    say
Her pretty oath, by Yea and Nay,
She could not, would not, durst not play!
At length, upon the harp, with glee,
Mingled with arch simplicity,
A soft, yet lively air she rung,
While thus the wily lady sung: —

XII.

LOCHINVAR.*

LADY HERON'S SONG.

O, young Lochinvar is come out of the
    west,
Through all the wide Border his steed was
    the best;
And save his good broadsword he wea-
    pons had none,
He rode all unarm'd, and he rode all
    alone.
So faithful in love, and so dauntless in
    war,
There never was knight like the young
    Lochinvar.

He staid not for brake, and he stopp'd
    not for stone,
He swam the Esk river where ford there
    was none;
But ere he alighted at Netherby gate,
The bride had consented, the gallant came
    late:
For a laggard in love, and a dastard in
    war,
Was to wed the fair Ellen of brave Loch-
    invar.

So boldly he enter'd the Netherby Hall,
Among bride's-men, and kinsmen, and
    brothers, and all:
Then spoke the bride's father, his hand
    on his sword,
(For the poor craven bridegroom said
    never a word,)

* See the ballad called "Katharine Janfarie,"
in "Minstrelsy of the Scottish Border," vol. iii.

"O come ye in peace here, or come ye in
    war,
Or to dance at our bridal, young Lord
    Lochinvar?" —

"I long woo'd your daughter, my suit
    you denied; —
Love swells like the Solway, but ebbs like
    its tide —
And now am I come, with this lost love
    of mine,
To lead but one measure, drink one cup of
    wine.
There are maidens in Scotland more love-
    · ly by far,
That would gladly be bride to the young
    Lochinvar."

The bride kiss'd the goblet: the knight
    took it up,
He quaff'd off the wine, and he threw
    down the cup.
She look'd down to blush, and she look'd
    up to sigh,
With a smile on her lips, and a tear in her
    eye.
He took her soft hand, ere her mother
    could bar, —
"Now tread we a measure!" said young
    Lochinvar.

So stately his form, and so lovely her
    face,
That never a hall such a galliard did
    grace;
While her mother did fret, and her father
    did fume,
And the bridegroom stood dangling his
    bonnet and plume;
And the bride-maidens whisper'd,
    "'Twere better by far,
To have match'd our fair cousin with
    young Lochinvar."

One touch to her hand, and one word in
    her ear,
When they reach'd the hall-door, and the
    charger stood near;
So light to the croupe the fair lady he
    swung,
So light to the saddle before her he
    sprung!

" She is won! we are gone, over bank,
        bush, and scaur;
They'll have fleet steeds that follow,"
        quoth young Lochinvar.

There was mounting 'mong Græmes of
        the Netherby clan;
Forsters, Fenwicks, and Musgraves, they
        rode and they ran;
There was racing and chasing, on Canno-
        bie Lee,
But the lost bride of Netherby ne'er did
        they see.
So daring in love, and so dauntless in war,
Have ye e'er heard of gallant like young
        Lochinvar?

XIII.

The Monarch o'er the siren hung
And beat the measure as she sung;
And, pressing closer, and more near,
He whisper'd praises in her ear.
In loud applause the courtiers vied;
And ladies wink'd, and spoke aside.
The witching dame to Marmion threw
        A glance, where seem'd to reign
The pride that claims applauses due,
        And of her royal conquest too,
        A real or feign'd disdain:
Familiar was the look, and told,
Marmion and she were friends of old.
The King observed their meeting eyes,
With something like displeased surprise;
For monarchs ill can rivals brook,
Even in a word, or smile, or look.
Straight took he forth the parchment
        broad
Which Marmion's high commission
        show'd:
" Our Borders sack'd by many a raid,
Our peaceful liege-men robb'd," he said:
" On day of truce our Warden slain,
Stout Barton kill'd, his vassals ta'en —
Unworthy were we here to reign,
Should these for vengeance cry in vain;
Our full defiance, hate, and scorn,
Our herald has to Henry borne."

XIV.

He paused, and led where Douglas stood,
And with stern eye the pageant view'd:
I mean that Douglas, sixth of yore,
Who coronet of Angus bore,

And, when his blood and heart were
        high,
Did the third James in camp defy,
And all his minions led to die
        On Lauder's dreary flat:
Princes and favorites long grew tame,
And trembled at the homely name
        Of Archibald Bell-the-cat; [60]
The same who left the dusky vale
Of Hermitage in Liddisdale,
        Its dungeons, and its towers,
Where Bothwell's turrets brave the air,
And Bothwell bank is blooming fair,
        To fix his princely bowers.
Though now, in age, he had laid down
His armor for the peaceful gown,
        And for a staff his brand,
Yet often would flash forth the fire,
That could, in youth, a monarch's ire
        And minion's pride withstand:
And even that day, at council board,
        Unapt to soothe his sovereign's mood,
        Against the war had Angus stood,
And chafed his royal lord.[61]

XV.

His giant-form, like ruin'd tower,
Though fall'n its muscles' brawny vaunt,
Huge-boned, and tall, and grim, and
        gaunt,
        Seem'd o'er the gaudy scene to lower:
His locks and beard in silver grew;
His eyebrows kept their sable hue.
Near Douglas when the Monarch stood,
His bitter speech he thus pursued: —
" Lord Marmion, since these letters say
That in the North you needs must stay,
        While slightest hopes of peace remain,
Uncourteous speech it were, and stern,
To say — Return to Lindisfarne,
        Until my herald come again. —
Then rest you in Tantallon Hold;[62]
Your host shall be the Douglas bold, —
A chief unlike his sires of old.
He wears their motto on his blade,[63]
Their blazon o'er his towers display'd;
Yet loves his sovereign to oppose,
More than to face his country's foes.
And, I bethink me, by St. Stephen,
But e'en this morn to me was given
A prize, the first-fruits of the war,
Ta'en by a galley from Dunbar,
A bevy of the maids of Heaven.

Under your guard, these holy maids
Shall safe return to cloister shades,
And, while they at Tantallon stay,
Requiem for Cochran's soul may say."
And, with the slaughter'd favorite's name,
Across the Monarch's brow there came
A cloud of ire, remorse, and shame.

XVI.

In answer naught could Angus speak;
His proud heart swell'd wellnigh to break:
He turn'd aside, and down his cheek
    A burning tear there stole.
His hand the Monarch sudden took,
That sight his kind heart could not brook:
    "Now, by the Bruce's soul,
Angus, my hasty speech forgive!
For sure as doth his spirit live,
As he said of the Douglas old,
    I well may say of you, —
That never king did subject hold,
In speech more free, in war more bold,
    More tender and more true:
Forgive me, Douglas, once again."
And, while the King his hand did strain,
The old man's tears fell down like rain.
To seize the moment Marmion tried,
And whisper'd to the King aside:
"Oh! let such tears unwonted plead
For respite short from dubious deed!
A child will weep a bramble smart,
A maid to see her sparrow part,
A stripling for a woman's heart;
But woe awaits a country, when
She sees the tears of bearded men.
Then, oh! what omen, dark and high,
When Douglas wets his manly eye!"

XVII.

Displeased was James, that stranger view'd
And tamper'd with his changing mood.
"Laugh those that can, weep those that
    may,"
Thus did the fiery Monarch say,
"Southward I march by break of day;
And if within Tantallon strong,
The good Lord Marmion tarries long,
Perchance our meeting next may fall
At Tamworth, in his castle-hall." —
The haughty Marmion felt the taunt,
And answer'd, grave, the royal vaunt: —

"Much honor'd were my humble home,
If in its halls King James should come;
But Nottingham has archers good,
And Yorkshire men are stern of mood;
Northumbrian prickers wild and rude.
On Derby Hills the paths are steep;
In Ouse and Tyne the fords are deep;
And many a banner will be torn,
And many a knight to earth be borne,
And many a sheaf of arrows spent,
Ere Scotland's King shall cross the Trent.
Yet pause, brave Prince, while yet you
    may!" —
The Monarch lightly turn'd away,
And to his nobles loud did call, —
"Lords, to the dance, — a hall! a hall!"*
Himself his cloak and sword flung by,
And led Dame Heron gallantly;
And minstrels, at the royal order,
Rung out — "Blue Bonnets o'er the
    Border."

XVIII.

Leave we these revels now, to tell
What to Saint Hilda's maids befell,
Whose galley, as they sail'd again
To Whitby, by a Scot was ta'en.
Now at Dun-Edin did they bide,
Till James should of their fate decide;
    And soon, by his command,
Were gently summon'd to prepare
To journey under Marmion's care,
As escort honor'd, safe, and fair,
    Again to English land.
The Abbess told her chaplet o'er,
Nor knew which saint she should implore,
For, when she thought of Constance,
    sore
    She feared Lord Marmion's mood.
And judge what Clara must have felt!
The sword, that hung in Marmion's belt,
    Had drunk De Wilton's blood.
Unwittingly, King James had given,
    As guard to Whitby's shades,
The man most dreaded under Heaven
    By these defenceless maids:
Yet what petition could avail,
Or who would listen to the tale
Of woman, prisoner, and nun,
Mid bustle of a war begun?

---

* The ancient cry to make room for a dance,
or pageant.

They deem'd it hopeless to avoid
The convoy of their dangerous guide.

XIX.

Their lodging, so the King assign'd,
To Marmion's, as their guardian, join'd;
And thus it fell, that passing nigh,
The Palmer caught the Abbess' eye,
Who warn'd him by a scroll,
She had a secret to reveal,
That much concern'd the Church's weal,
    And health of sinner's soul;
And, with deep charge of secrecy,
    She named a place to meet,
Within an open balcony,
That hung from dizzy pitch, and high,
    Above the stately street;
To which, as common to each home,
At night they might in secret come.

XX.

At night, in secret there they came,
The Palmer and the holy Dame.
The moon among the clouds rode high,
And all the city hum was by.
Upon the street, where late before
Did din of war and warriors roar,
    You might have heard a pebble fall,
A beetle hum, a cricket sing,
An owlet flap his boding wing
    On Giles's steeple tall.
The antique buildings, climbing high,
Whose Gothic frontlets sought the sky,
    Were here wrapt deep in shade;
There on their brows the moon-beam broke,
Through the faint wreaths of silvery smoke,
    And on the casements play'd.
And other light was none to see,
    Save torches gliding far,
Before some chieftain of degree,
Who left the royal revelry
    To boune him for the war. —
A solemn scene the Abbess chose;
A solemn hour, her secret to disclose.

XXI.

" O, holy Palmer ! " she began, —
" For sure he must be sainted man,
Whose blessed feet have trod the ground
Where the Redeemer's tomb is found, —

For His dear Church's sake, my tale
Attend, nor deem of light avail,
Though I must speak of worldly love, —
How vain to those who wed above ! —
De Wilton and Lord Marmion woo'd
Clara de Clare of Gloster's blood;
(Idle it were of Whitby's dame,
To say of that same blood I came;)
And once, when jealous rage was high,
Lord Marmion said despiteously,
Wilton was traitor in his heart,
And had made league with Martin Swart,[64]
When he came here on Simnel's part;
And only cowardice did restrain
His rebel aid on Stokefield's plain, —
And down he threw his glove: — the thing
Was tried, as wont, before the King;
Where frankly did De Wilton own,
That Swart in Gueldres he had known;
And that between them then there went
Some scroll of courteous compliment.
For this he to his castle sent;
But when his messenger return'd,
Judge how De Wilton's fury burn'd !
For in his packet there were laid
Letters that claim'd disloyal aid,
And proved King Henry's cause betray'd.
His fame, thus blighted, in the field
He strove to clear, by spear and shield;
To clear his fame in vain he strove,
For wondrous are His ways above !
Perchance some form was unobserved;
Perchance in prayer or faith he swerved;
Else how could guiltless champion quail,
Or how the blessed ordeal fail?

XXII.

" His squire, who now De Wilton saw
As recreant doom'd to suffer law,
    Repentant, own'd in vain,
That, while he had the scrolls in care,
A stranger maiden, passing fair,
Had drench'd him with a beverage rare;
    His words no faith could gain.
With Clare alone he credence won,
Who, rather than wed Marmion,
Did to Saint Hilda's shrine repair,
To give our house her livings fair
And die a vestal vot'ress there.
The impulse from the earth was given,
But bent her to the paths of heaven.

A purer heart, a lovelier maid,
Ne'er shelter'd her in Whitby's shade,
No, not since Saxon Edelfled;
 Only one trace of earthly strain,
  That for her lover's loss
 She cherishes a sorrow vain,
  And murmurs at the cross. —
 And then her heritage; it goes
  Along the banks of Tame;
Deep fields of grain the reaper mows,
In meadows rich the heifer lows,
The falconer and huntsman knows
  Its woodlands for the game.
Shame were it to Saint Hilda dear,
And I, her humble vot'ress here,
 Should do a deadly sin,
Her temple spoil'd before mine eyes,
If this false Marmion such a prize
 By my consent should win;
Yet hath our boisterous monarch sworn
That Clare shall from our house be
  torn,
And grievous cause have I to fear
Such mandate doth Lord Marmion bear.

XXIII.

" Now, prisoner, helpless, and betray'd
To evil power, I claim thine aid,
 By every step that thou hast trod
To holy shrine and grotto dim,
By every martyr's tortured limb,
By angel, saint, and seraphim,
 And by the Church of God!
For mark: — When Wilton was betray'd,
And with his squire forged letters laid,
She was, alas! that sinful maid,
 By whom the deed was done, —
O! shame and horror to be said! —
 She was a perjured nun!
No clerk in all the land, like her,
Traced quaint and varying character.
Perchance you may a marvel deem,
 That Marmion's paramour
(For such vile thing she was) should
  scheme
 Her lover's nuptial hour;
But o'er him thus she hoped to gain
As privy to his honor's stain,
 Illimitable power:
For this she secretly retain'd
 Each proof that might the plot reveal,
 Instructions with his hand and seal;
And thus Saint Hilda deign'd,

Through sinner's perfidy impure,
 Her house's glory to secure,
And Clare's immortal weal.

XXIV.

" 'Twere long, and needless, here to tell,
How to my hand these papers fell;
 With me they must not stay.
Saint Hilda keep her Abbess true!
Who knows what outrage he might do,
 While journeying by the way ? —
O, blessed Saint, if e'er again
I venturous leave thy calm domain,
To travel or by land or main,
 Deep penance may I pay! —
Now, saintly Palmer, mark my prayer:
I give this packet to thy care,
For thee to stop they will not dare;
 And O! with cautious speed,
To Wolsey's hand the papers bring,
That he may show them to the King:
 And, for thy well-earn'd meed,
Thou holy man, at Whitby's shrine
A weekly mass shall still be thine,
 While priests can sing and read. —
What ail'st thou? — Speak! " For as he
  took
The charge, a strong emotion shook
 His frame; and, ere reply,
They heard a faint, yet shrilly tone,
Like distant clarion feebly blown,
 That on the breeze did die;
And loud the Abbess shriek'd in fear: —
" Saint Withold, save us! — What is here!
 Look at yon City Cross!
See on its battled tower appear
Phantoms, that scutcheons seem to rear,
 And blazon'd banners toss! "

XXV.

Dun-Edin's Cross, a pillar'd stone,[65]
Rose on a turret octagon;
(But now is razed that monument,
 Whence royal edict rang,
And voice of Scotland's law was sent
 In glorious trumpet-clang.
O! be his tomb as lead to lead,
Upon its dull destroyer's head!
A minstrel's malison * is said.)
Then on its battlements they saw
A vision, passing Nature's law,

---

* Curse.

Strange, wild, and dimly seen;
Figures that seem'd to rise and die,
Gibber and sign, advance and fly,
While naught confirm'd could ear or eye
    Discern of sound or mien.
Yet darkly did it seem, as there
Heralds and Pursuivants prepare,
With trumpet sound and blazon fair,
    A summons to proclaim;
But indistinct the pageant proud,
As fancy forms of midnight cloud,
When flings the moon upon her shroud
    A wavering tinge of flame;
It flits, expands, and shifts, till loud,
From midmost of the spectre crowd,
    This awful summons came:[66]—

XXVI.

' Prince, prelate, potentate, and peer,
    Whose names I now shall call,
Scottish, or foreigner, give ear;
Subjects of him who sent me here,
At his tribunal to appear,
    I summon one and all:
I cite you by each deadly sin,
That e'er hath soil'd your hearts within:
I cite you by each brutal lust,
That e'er defiled your earthly dust, —
    By wrath, by pride, by fear,
By each o'er-mastering passion's tone,
By the dark grave, and dying groan!
When forty days are pass'd and gone,
I cite you, at your Monarch's throne,
    To answer and appear."
Then thunder'd forth a roll of names:
The first was thine, unhappy James!
    Then all thy nobles came;
Crawford, Glencairn, Montrose, Argyle,
Ross, Bothwell, Forbes, Lennox, Lyle, —
Why should I tell their separate style?
    Each chief of birth and fame,
Of Lowland, Highland, Border, Isle,
Fore-doom'd to Flodden's carnage pile,
    Was cited there by name;
And Marmion, Lord of Fontenaye,
Of Lutterward, and Scrivelbaye;
De Wilton, erst of Aberley,
The self-same thundering voice did say. —
    But then another spoke: —
' Thy fatal summons I deny,
And thine infernal Lord defy,
Appealing me to Him on High,
    Who burst the sinner's yoke."

At that dread accent, with a scream,
Parted the pageant like a dream,
    The summoner was gone.
Prone on her face the Abbess fell,
And fast, and fast, her beads did tell;
Her nuns came, startled by the yell,
    And found her there alone.
She mark'd not, at the scene aghast,
What time, or how, the Palmer pass'd.

XXVII.

Shift we the scene. — The camp doth
    move,
Dun-Edin's streets are empty now,
Save when, for weal of those they love,
    To pray the prayer, and vow the vow,
The tottering child, the anxious fair,
The gray-hair'd sire, with pious care,
To chapels and to shrines repair —
Where is the Palmer now? and where
The Abbess, Marmion, and Clare? —
Bold Douglas! to Tantallon fair
    They journey in thy charge:
Lord Marmion rode on his right hand,
The Palmer still was with the band;
Angus, like Lindesay, did command,
    That none should roam at large.
But in that Palmer's altered mien
A wondrous change might now be seen,
    Freely he spoke of war,
Of marvels wrought by single hand,
When lifted for a native land;
And still look'd high, as if he plann'd
    Some desperate deed afar.
His courser would he feed and stroke,
And, tucking up his sable frock,
Would first his mettle bold provoke,
    Then soothe or quell his pride.
Old Hubert said, that never one
He saw, except Lord Marmion,
    A steed so fairly ride.

XXVIII.

Some half-hour's march behind, there
    came
    By Eustace govern'd fair,
A troop escorting Hilda's Dame,
    With all her nuns, and Clare.
No audience had Lord Marmion sought;
    Ever he fear'd to aggravate
    Clara de Clare's suspicious hate;
And safer 'twas, he thought,

To wait till, from the nuns removed,
The influence of kinsmen loved,
And suit by Henry's self-approved,
Her slow consent had wrought.
  His was no flickering flame, that dies
Unless when fann'd by looks and sighs,
And lighted oft at lady's eyes;
He long'd to stretch his wide command
O'er luckless Clara's ample land:
Besides, when Wilton with him vied,
Although the pang of humbled pride
The place of jealousy supplied,
Yet conquest by that meanness won
He almost loath'd to think upon,
Led him, at times, to hate the cause,
Which made him burst through honor's
    laws.
If e'er he loved, 'twas her alone,
Who died within that vault of stone.

XXIX.

And now, when close at hand they saw
North Berwick's town, and lofty Law,
Fitz-Eustace bade them pause awhile,
Before a venerable pile,*
  Whose turrets view'd, afar,
The lofty Bass, the Lambie Isle,
  The ocean's peace or war.
At tolling of a bell, forth came
The convent's venerable Dame,
And pray'd Saint Hilda's Abbess rest
With her, a loved and honor'd guest,
Till Douglas should a bark prepare
To waft her back to Whitby fair.
Glad was the Abbess, you may guess,
And thank'd the Scottish Prioress;
And tedious were to tell, I ween,
The courteous speech that pass'd between.
  O'erjoy'd the nuns their palfreys leave;
But when fair Clara did intend,
Like them, from horseback to descend,
  Fitz-Eustace said, — " I grieve,
Fair lady, grieve e'en from my heart,
Such gentle company to part; —
  Think not discourtesy,
But lords' commands must be obey'd;
And Marmion and the Douglas said,
  That you must wend with me.
Lord Marmion hath a letter broad,
Which to the Scottish Earl he show'd,
Commanding that, beneath his care,

* A convent of Cistertian nuns, founded by
Duncan, Earl of Fife, in 1216.

Without delay, you shall repair
To your good kinsman, Lord Fitz-Clare.'

XXX.

The startled Abbess loud exclaim'd;
But she, at whom the blow was aim'd,
Grew pale as death, and cold as lead, —
She deem'd she heard her death-doom
    read.
" Cheer thee, my child ! " the Abbess
    said,
" They dare not tear thee from my hand
To ride alone with armed band."
  " Nay, holy mother, nay,"
Fitz-Eustace said, " the lovely Clare
Will be in Lady Angus' care,
  In Scotland while we stay;
And, when we move, an easy ride
Will bring us to the English side,
Female attendance to provide
  Befitting Gloster's heir:
Nor thinks nor dreams my noble lord,
By slightest look, or act, or word,
  To harass Lady Clare.
Her faithful guardian he will be,
Nor sue for slightest courtesy
  That e'en to stranger falls,
Till he shall place her, safe and free,
  Within her kinsman's halls."
He spoke, and blush'd with earnest
    grace;
His faith was painted on his face,
  And Clare's worst fear relieved.
The Lady Abbess loud exclaim'd
On Henry, and the Douglas blamed,
  Entreated, threaten'd, grieved;
To martyr, saint, and prophet pray'd,
Against Lord Marmion inveigh'd,
And call'd the Prioress to aid,
To curse with candle, bell, and book.
Her head the grave Cistertian shook:
" The Douglas, and the King," she said,
" In their commands will be obey'd;
Grieve not, nor dream that harm can fa
The maiden in Tantallon hall."

XXXI.

The Abbess, seeing strife was vain,
Assumed her wonted state again, —
  For much of state she had, —
Composed her veil, and raised her head
And — " Bid," in solemn voice she said
  " Thy master, bold and bad,

The records of his house turn o'er,
  And, when he shall there written
     see,
  That one of his own ancestry
  Drove the Monks forth of Coventry, 67
Bid him his fate explore!
  Prancing in pride of earthly trust,
  His charger hurl'd him to the dust,
  And, by a base plebeian thrust,
He died his band before.
  God judge 'twixt Marmion and me;
  He is a Chief of high degree,
And I a poor recluse:
  Yet oft, in holy writ, we see
  Even such weak minister as me
May the oppressor bruise:
  For thus, inspired, did Judith slay
    The mighty in his sin,
  And Jael thus, and Deborah " —
    Here hasty Blount broke in:
' Fitz-Eustace, we must march our band;
St. Anton' fire thee! wilt thou stand
All day, with bonnet in thy hand,
  To hear the lady preach?
By this good light! if thus we stay,
Lord Marmion, for our fond delay,
  Will sharper sermon teach.
Come, don thy cap, and mount thy
    horse;
The dame must patience take perforce."

XXXII.

" Submit we then to force," said Clare,
" But let this barbarous lord despair
  His purposed aim to win;
Let him take living, land, and life:
But to be Marmion's wedded wife
  In me were deadly sin:
And if it be the King's decree;
  That I must find no sanctuary,
In that inviolable dome,
Where even a homicide might come,
  And safely rest his head,
Though at its open portals stood,
Thirsting to pour forth blood for blood,
  The kinsmen of the dead;
Yet one asylum is my own
  Against the dreaded hour;
A low, a silent, and a lone,
  Where kings have little power.
One victim is before me there. —
Mother, your blessing; and in prayer,
Remember your unhappy Clare!' "

Loud weeps the Abbess, and bestows
  Kind blessings many a one:
Weeping and wailing loud arose,
Round patient Clare, the clamorous woes
  Of every simple nun.
His eyes the gentle Eustace dried,
And scarce rude Blount the sight could bide.
Then took the squire her rein,
  And gently led away her steed,
And, by each courteous word and deed,
  To cheer her strove in vain.

XXXIII.

But scant three miles the band had rode
  When o'er a height they pass'd,
And, sudden, close before them show'd
  His towers, Tantallon vast;
Broad, massive, high, and stretching far,
And held impregnable in war.
On a projecting rock they rose,
And round three sides the ocean flows,
The fourth did battled walls enclose,
  And double mound and fosse.
By narrow drawbridge, outworks strong,
Through studded gates, and entrance
    long,
  To the main court they cross.
It was a wide and stately square:
  Around were lodgings, fit and fair,
    And towers of various form,
Which on the court projected far,
And broke its lines quadrangular.
Here was square keep, there turret high,
Or pinnacle that sought the sky,
Whence oft the wanderer could descry
  The gathering ocean-storm.

XXXIV.

Here did they rest. — The princely care
Of Douglas, why should I declare,
  Or say they met reception fair;
    Or why the tidings say,
Which, varying, to Tantallon came,
By hurrying posts or fleeter fame, ·
    With every varying day?
And, first three heard King James had won
  Etall, and Wark, and Ford; and then,
  That Norham Castle strong was ta'en.
At that sore marvell'd Marmion; —
And Douglas hoped his monarch's hand
Would soon subdue Northumberland:
  But whisper'd news there came,

That, while his host inactive lay,
And melted by degrees away,
King James was dallying off the day
   With Heron's wily dame. —
Such acts to chronicles I yield;
   Go seek them there, and see:
Mine is a tale of Flodden Field,
   And not a history. —
At length they heard the Scottish host
On that high ridge had made their post,
   Which frowns o'er Millfield Plain;
And that brave Surrey many a band
Had gather'd in the Southern land,
And march'd into Northumberland,
   And camp at Wooler ta'en.
Marmion, like charger in the stall,
That hears, without, the trumpet-call,
   Began to chafe, and swear: —
"A sorry thing to hide my head
In castle, like a fearful maid,
   When such a field is near!
Needs must I see this battle-day:
Death to my fame if such a fray
Were fought, and Marmion away!
The Douglas, too, I wot not why,
Hath 'bated of his courtesy:
No longer in his halls I'll stay."
Then bade his band they should array
For march against the dawning day.

INTRODUCTION TO CANTO SIXTH.

TO RICHARD HEBER, ESQ.

Mertoun House, * Christmas.*

HEAP on more wood! — the wind is chill;
But let it whistle as it will,
We'll keep our Christmas merry still.
Each age has deem'd the new-born year
The fittest time for festal cheer:
Even, heathen yet, the savage Dane
At Iol more deep the mead did drain; 68
High on the beach his galleys drew,
And feasted all his pirate crew;
Then in his low and pine-built hall,
Where shields and axes deck'd the wall,
They gorged upon the half-dress'd steer;
Caroused in seas of sable beer;

While round, in brutal jest, were thrown
The half-gnaw'd rib and marrow-bone:
Or listen'd all, in grim delight,
While Scalds yell'd out the joys of fight
Then forth, in frenzy, would they hie,
While wildly-loose their red locks fly,
And dancing round the blazing pile,
They make such barbarous mirth,the while
As best might to the mind recall
The boisterous joys of Odin's hall.

   And well our Christian sires of old
Loved when the year its course had roll'd
And brought blithe Christmas back again
With all his hospitable train.
Domestic and religious rite
Gave honor to the holy night;
On Christmas eve the bells were rung;
On Christmas eve the mass was sung;
That only night in all the year,
Saw the stoled priest the chalice rear.†
The damsel donn'd her kirtle sheen;
The hall was dress'd with holly green;
Forth to the wood did merry-men go,
To gather in the mistletoe.
Then open'd wide the Baron's hall
To vassal, tenant, serf, and all;
Power laid his rod of rule aside,
And Ceremony doff'd his pride.
The heir with roses in his shoes,
That night might village partner choose;
The Lord, underogating, share
The vulgar game of "post and pair."‡
All hail'd with uncontroll'd delight,
And general voice, the happy night,
That to the cottage, as the crown,
Brought tidings of salvation down.

   The fire, with well-dried logs supplied
Went roaring up the chimney wide;
The huge hall-table's oaken face,
Scrubb'd till it shone, the day to grace,
Bore then upon its massive board
No mark to part the squire and lord.
Then was brought in the lusty brawn,
By old blue-coated serving man;
Then the grim boar's head frown'd on high
Crested with bays and rosemary.
Well can the green-garb'd ranger tell,
How, when, and where, the monster fell

---

* Mertoun-House, the seat of Hugh Scott,
Esq., of Harden, is beautifully situated on the
Tweed about two miles below Dryburgh Abbey.

† In the Roman Catholic Church mass
never said at night except on Christmas Eve.

‡ An old game at cards.

What dogs before his death he tore,
And all the baiting of the boar.
The wassel round, in good brown bowls,
Garnish'd with ribbons, blithely trowls.
There the huge sirloin reek'd; hard by
Plum-porridge stood, and Christmas pie;
Nor fail'd old Scotland to produce,
At such high tide, her savory goose.
Then came the merry maskers in,
And carols roar'd with blithesome din;
If unmelodious was the song,
It was a hearty note, and strong.
Who lists may in their mumming see
Traces of ancient mystery;[69]
White shirts supplied the masquerade,
And smutted cheeks the visors made;
But, O! what maskers, richly dight,
Can boast of bosoms half so light!
England was merry England, when
Old Christmas brought his sports again.
'Twas Christmas broach'd the mightiest
  ale;
'Twas Christmas told the merriest tale;
A Christmas gambol oft could cheer
The poor man's heart through half the
  year.

Still linger, in our northern clime,
Some remnants of the good old time;
And still, within our valleys here,
We hold the kindred title dear,
Even when, perchance, its far-fetch'd
  claim
To Southron ear sounds empty name;
For course of blood, our proverbs deem,
Is warmer than the mountain-stream.*
And thus, my Christmas still I hold
Where my great grandsire came of old,
With amber beard, and flaxen hair,
And reverend apostolic air —
The feast and holy-tide to share,
And mix sobriety with wine,
And honest mirth with thoughts divine:
Small thought was his, in after time
E'er to be hitch'd into a rhyme.
The simple sire could only boast,
That he was loyal to his cost;
The banish'd race of kings revered,
And lost his land, — but kept his beard.

In these dear halls, where welcome kind
Is with fair liberty combined;

Where cordial friendship gives the hand,
And flies constraint the magic wand
Of the fair dame that rules the land.†
Little we heed the tempest drear,
While music, mirth, and social cheer,
Speed on their wings the passing year.
And Mertoun's halls are fair e'en now,
When not a leaf is on the bough.
Tweed loves them well, and turns again,
As loth to leave the sweet domain,
And holds his mirror to her face,
And clips her with a close embrace: —
Gladly as he, we seek the dome,
And as reluctant turn us home.

How just that, at this time of glee,
My thoughts should, Heber, turn to thee!
For many a merry hour we've known,
And heard the chimes of midnight tone.
Cease, then, my friend! a moment cease,
And leave these classic tomes in peace!
Of Roman and of Grecian lore,
Sure mortal brain can hold no more.
These ancients, as Noll Bluff might say,
" Were pretty fellows in their day;"
But time and tide o'er all prevail —
On Christmas eve a Christmas tale —
Of wonder and of war — "Profane!
What! leave the lofty Latian strain,
Her stately prose, her verse's charms,
To hear the clash of rusty arms:
In Fairy Land or Limbo lost,
To jostle conjurer and ghost,
Goblin and witch!" — Nay, Heber dear,
Before you touch my charter, hear:
Though Leyden aids, alas! no more,
My cause with many-languaged lore,
This may I say: — in realms of death
Ulysses meets Alcides' *wraith;*
Æneas, upon Thracia's shore,
The ghost of murder'd Polydore;
For omens, we in Livy cross,
At every turn, *locutus Bos.*
As grave and duly speaks that ox,
As if he told the price of stocks;
Or held, in Rome republican,
The place of common-councilman.

All nations have their omens drear,
Their legends wild of woe and fear.

* " Blood is warmer than water."

† A lady of noble German descent, born
Countess Harriet Brühl of Martinskirchen, and
married to H. Scott, Esq., of Harden.

To Cambria look — the peasant see,
Bethink him of Glendowerdy,
And shun " the spirit's Blasted Tree." *
The Highlander, whose red claymore
The battle turn'd on Maida's shore,
Will, on a Friday morn, look pale,
If ask'd to tell a fairy tale: [70]
He fears the vengeful Elfin King,
Who leaves that day his grassy ring:
Invisible to human ken,
He walks among the sons of men.

Didst e'er, dear Heber, pass along
Beneath the towers of Franchémont,
Which, like an eagle's nest in air,
Hang o'er the stream and hamlet fair?
Deep in their vaults, the peasants say,
A mighty treasure buried lay,
Amass'd through rapine and through
wrong,
By the last Lord of Franchémont. [71]
The iron chest is bolted hard,
A huntsman sits its constant guard;
Around his neck his horn is hung,
His hanger in his belt is slung;
Before his feet his blood-hounds lie.
An 'twere not for his gloomy eye,
Whose withering glance no heart can brook,
As true a huntsman doth he look,
As bugle e'er in brake did sound,
Or ever halloo'd to a hound.
To chase the fiend, and win the prize,
In that same dungeon ever tries
An aged necromantic priest;
It is a hundred years at least,
Since 'twixt them first the strife begun,
And neither yet has lost nor won.
And oft the Conjurer's words will make
The stubborn Demon groan and quake;
And oft the bands of iron break,
Or bursts one lock, that still amain,
Fast as 'tis open'd, shuts again.
That magic strife within the tomb
May last until the day of doom,
Unless the adept shall learn to tell
The very word that clench'd the spell,
When Franch'mont lock'd the treasure
cell.
A hundred years are pass'd and gone,
And scarce three letters has he won.

* Alluding to the Welsh tradition of Howel
Sell and Owen Glendwr. Howel fell in single
combat against Glendwr, and his body was
concealed in a hollow oak.

Such general superstition may
Excuse for old Pitscottie say;
Whose gossip history has given
My song the messenger from Heaven,
That warn'd, in Lithgow, Scotland's
King,
Nor less the infernal summoning;
May pass the Monk of Durham's tale,
Whose demon fought in Gothic mail;
May pardon plead for Fordun grave,
Who told of Gifford's Goblin-Cave.
But why such instances to you,
Who, in an instant, can renew
Your treasured hoards of various lore,
And furnish twenty thousand more;
Hoards, not like theirs whose volumes
rest
Like treasures in the Franch'mont chest,
While gripple owners still refuse
To others what they cannot use;
Give them the priest's whole century,
They shall not spell you letters three:
Their pleasure in the books the same
The magpie takes in pilfer'd gem.
Thy volumes, open as thy heart,
Delight, amusement, science, art,
To every ear and eye impart;
Yet who of all who thus employ them,
Can like the owner's self enjoy them? —
But, hark! I hear the distant drum!
The day of Flodden Field is come. —
Adieu, dear Heber! life and health,
And store of literary wealth.

CANTO SIXTH.

THE BATTLE.

I.

WHILE great events were on the gale,
And each hour brought a varying tale,
And the demeanor, changed and cold,
Of Douglas, fretted Marmion bold,
And, like the impatient steed of war,
He snuff'd the battle from afar;
And hopes were none, that back again
Herald should come from Terouenne,
Where England's King in leaguer lay,
Before decisive battle-day;
Whilst these things were, the mournful
Clare
Did in the Dame's devotions share:

For the good Countess ceaseless pray'd
To heaven and Saints, her sons to aid,
And, with short interval, did pass
From prayer to book, from book to mass,
And all in high Baronial pride, —
A life both dull and dignified;
Yet as Lord Marmion nothing press'd
Upon her intervals of rest,
Dejected Clara well could bear
The formal state, the lengthen'd prayer,
Though dearest to her wounded heart
The hours that she might spend apart.

II.

said, Tantallon's dizzy steep
Hung o'er the margin of the deep.
Many a rude tower and rampart there
Repell'd the insult of the air,
Which, when the tempest vex'd the sky,
Half breeze, half spray, came whistling by.
Above the rest, a turret square
Did o'er its Gothic entrance bear,
Of sculpture rude, a stony shield;
The Bloody Heart was in the Field,
And in the chief three mullets stood,
The cognizance of Douglas blood.
The turret held a narrow stair,
Which, mounted, gave you access where
A parapet's embattled row
Did seaward round the castle go.
Sometimes in dizzy steps descending,
Sometimes in narrow circuit bending,
Sometimes in platform broad extending,
Its varying circle did combine
Bulwark, and bartizan, and line,
And bastion, tower, and vantage-coign;
Above the booming ocean leant
The far-projecting battlement;
The billows burst, in ceaseless flow,
Upon the precipice below.
Where'er Tantallon faced the land,
Gate-works, and walls, were strongly
　　　mann'd;
No need upon the sea-girt side;
The steepy rock, and frantic tide,
Approach of human step denied;
And thus these lines and ramparts rude,
Were left in deepest solitude.

III.

And, for they were so lonely, Clare
Would to these battlements repair,
And muse upon her sorrows there,
And list the sea-bird's cry;
Or slow, like noontide ghost, would glide,
Along the dark-gray bulwarks' side,
And ever on the heaving tide
　　　Look down with weary eye.
Oft did the cliff and swelling main,
Recall the thoughts of Whitby's fane, —
A home she ne'er might see again;
　　　For she had laid adown,
So Douglas bade, the hood and veil,
And frontlet of the cloister pale,
　　　And Benedictine gown:
It were unseemly sight, he said,
A novice out of convent shade. —
Now her bright locks, with sunny glow,
Again adorn'd her brow of snow;
Her mantle rich, whose borders, round,
A deep and fretted broidery bound,
In golden foldings sought the ground;
Of holy ornament, alone
Remain'd a cross with ruby stone;
　　　And often did she look
On that which in her hand she bore,
With velvet bound, and broider'd o'er,
　　　Her breviary book.
In such a place, so lone, so grim,
At dawning pale, or twilight dim,
　　　It fearful would have been
To meet a form so richly dress'd,
With book in hand, and cross on breast,
　　　And such a woeful mien.
Fitz-Eustace, loitering with his bow,
To practise on the gull and crow,
Saw her, at distance, gliding slow,
　　　And did by Mary swear, —
Some love-lorn Fay she might have been,
Or, in Romance, some spell-bound
　　　Queen;
Nor ne'er, in work-day world, was seen
　　　A form so witching fair.

IV.

Once walking thus, at evening tide,
It chanced a gliding sail she spied,
And, sighing, thought: — "The Abbess
　　　there,
Perchance, does to her home repair;
Her peaceful rule, where Duty, free,
Walks hand in hand with Charity;
Where oft Devotion's tranced glow
Can such a glimpse of heaven bestow,
That the enraptured sisters see
High vision and deep mystery;

The very form of Hilda fair,
Hovering upon the sunny air,
And smiling on her votaries' prayer.
O! wherefore, to my duller eye,
Did still the Saint her form deny;
Was it, that, sear'd by sinful scorn,
My heart could neither melt nor burn?
Or lie my warm affections low,
With him, that taught them first to
     glow?
Yet, gentle Abbess, well I knew,
To pay thy kindness grateful due,
And well could brook the mild command,
That ruled thy simple maiden band.
How different now! condemn'd to bide
My doom from this dark tyrant's pride. —
But Marmion has to learn, ere long,
That constant mind, and hate of wrong,
Descended to a feeble girl,
From Red De Clare, stout Gloster's Earl:
Of such a stem, a sapling weak,
He ne'er shall bend, although he break.

v.

" But see! what makes this armor
     here?" —
     For in her path there lay
Targe, corslet, helm; — she view'd them
     near. —
" The breast-plate pierced! — Ay, much
     I fear,
Weak fence wert thou 'gainst foeman's
     spear,
That hath made fatal entrance here,
     As these dark blood-gouts say. —
Thus Wilton! — Oh! not corslet's ward,
Not truth, as diamond pure and hard,
Could be thy manly bosom's guard,
     On yon disastrous day!" —
She raised her eyes in mournful mood, —
WILTON himself before her stood!
It might have seem'd his passing ghost,
For every youthful grace was lost;
And joy unwonted, and surprise,
Gave their strange wildness to his eyes. —
Expect not, noble dames and lords,
That I can tell such scene in words:
What skilful limner e'er would choose
To paint the rainbow's varying hues,
Unless to mortal it were given
To dip his brush in dyes of heaven?
Far less can my weak line declare
     Each changing passion's shade;

Brightening to rapture from despair,
Sorrow, surprise, and pity there,
And joy, with her angelic air,
And hope that paints the future fair,
     Their varying hues display'd:
Each o'er its rival's ground extending,
Alternate conquering, shifting, blending,
Till all, fatigued, the conflict yield,
And mighty Love retains the field.
Shortly I tell what then he said,
By many a tender word delay'd,
And modest blush, and bursting sigh,
And question kind, and fond reply: —

VI.

DE WILTON'S HISTORY.

" Forget we that disastrous day,
When senseless in the lists I lay.
     Thence dragg'd, — but how I cannot
          know,
     For sense and recollection fled, —
I found me on a pallet low,
     Within my ancient beadsman's shed.
Austin, — remember'st thou, my Clare,
How thou didst blush, when the old man,
When first our infant love began,
     Said we would make a matchless pair?
Menials, and friends, and kinsmen fled
From the degraded traitor's bed, —
He only held my burning head,
And tended me for many a day,
While wounds and fever held their sway.
But far more needful was his care,
When sense return'd to wake despair;
     For I did tear the closing wound,
     And dash me frantic on the ground,
If e'er I heard the name of Clare.
At length, to calmer reason brought,
Much by his kind attendance wrought,
     With him I left my native strand,
And, in a Palmer's weeds array'd,
My hated name and form to shade,
     I journey'd many a land;
No more a lord of rank and birth,
But mingled with the dregs of earth.
     Oft Austin for my reason fear'd,
When I would sit and deeply brood
On dark revenge, and deeds of blood,
     Or wild mad schemes uprear'd.
My friend at length fell sick, and said,
     God would remove him soon;
And, while upon his dying bed,
     He begg'd of me a boon —

If e'er my deadliest enemy
Beneath my brand should conquer'd lie,
Even then my mercy should awake,
And spare his life for Austin's sake.

VII.

"Still restless as a second Cain,
To Scotland next my route was ta'en,
    Full well the paths I knew.
Fame of my fate made various sound,
That death in pilgrimage I found,
That I had perish'd of my wound,
    None cared which tale was true;
And living eye could never guess
De Wilton in his Palmer's dress;
For now that sable slough is shed,
And trimm'd my shaggy beard and head,
I scarcely know me in the glass.
A chance most wondrous did provide,
That I should be that Baron's guide —
    I will not name his name! —
Vengeance to God alone belongs;
But, when I think of all my wrongs,
    My blood is liquid flame!
And ne'er the time shall I forget,
When, in a Scottish hostel set,
    Dark looks we did exchange:
What were his thoughts I cannot tell;
But in my bosom muster'd Hell
    Its plans of dark revenge.

VIII.

"A word of vulgar augury,
That broke from me, I scarce knew
        why,
    Brought on a village tale;
Which wrought upon his moody sprite,
And sent him armed forth by night.
    I borrow'd steed and mail,
And weapons, from his sleeping band;
    And, passing from a postern door,
We met, and 'counter'd hand to hand, —
    He fell on Gifford moor.
For the death-stroke my brand I drew,
(O then my helmed head he knew,
    The Palmer's cowl was gone,)
Then had three inches of my blade
The heavy debt of vengeance paid, —
My hand the thought of Austin staid; —
    I left him there alone. —
O good old man! even from the grave
Thy spirit could thy master save:

If I had slain my foeman, ne'er
Had Whitby's Abbess, in her fear,
Given to my hand this packet dear,
Of power to clear my injured fame,
And vindicate De Wilton's name. —
Perchance you heard the Abbess tell
Of the strange pageantry of Hell,
    That broke our secret speech —
It rose from the infernal shade,
Or featly was some juggle play'd,
    A tale of peace to teach.
Appeal to Heaven I judged was best,
When my name came among the rest.

IX.

"Now here, within Tantallon Hold,
To Douglas late my tale I told,
To whom my house was known of old.
Won by my proofs, his falchion bright
This eve anew shall dub me knight.
These were the arms that once did turn
The tide of fight on Otterbourne,
And Harry Hotspur forced to yield,
When the Dead Douglas won the field. *
These Angus gave — his armorer's care,
Ere morn shall every breach repair;
For naught, he said, was in his halls,
But ancient armor on the walls,
And aged chargers in his stalls,
And women, priests, and gray-hair'd
        men;
The rest were all in Twisel glen.†
And now I watch my armor here,
By law of arms, till midnight's near;
Then, once again a belted knight,
Seek Surrey's camp with dawn of light.

X.

"There soon again we meet, my Clare!
This Baron means to guide thee there:
Douglas reveres his King's command,
Else would he take thee from his band.
And there thy kinsman, Surrey, too,
Will give De Wilton justice due.
Now meeter far for martial broil,
Firmer my limbs, and strung by toil,
Once more "—"O Wilton! must we then
Risk new-found happiness again,

---

* See the ballad of Otterbourne, in the
"Border Minstrelsy," vol. i. p. 345.

† Where James encamped before taking post
on Flodden.

Trust fate of arms once more?
And is there not a humble glen,
  Where we, content and poor,
Might build a cottage in the shade,
A shepherd thou, and I to aid
  Thy task on dale and moor? —
That reddening brow! — too well I know,
Not even thy Clare can peace bestow,
  While falsehood stains thy name;
Go then to fight! Clare bids thee go!
Clare can a warrior's feelings know,
  And weep a warrior's shame;
Can Red Earl Gilbert's spirit feel,
Buckle the spurs upon thy heel,
And belt thee with thy brand of steel,
  And send thee forth to fame!"

XI.

That night, upon the rocks and bay,
The midnight moon-beam slumbering lay,
And pour'd its silver light, and pure,
Through loop-hole, and through embra-
      zure,
  Upon Tantallon tower and hall;
But chief where arched windows wide
Illuminate the chapel's pride,
  The sober glances fall.
Much was their need; though seam'd
    with scars,
Two veterans of the Douglas' wars,
  Though two gray priests were there,
And each a blazing torch held high,
You could not by their blaze descry
  The chapel's carving fair.
Amid that dim and smoky light,
Chequering the silver moon-shine bright,
  A bishop by the altar stood,*
  A noble lord of Douglas blood,
With mitre sheen, and rocquet white.
Yet show'd his meek and thoughtful eye
But little pride of prelacy;
More pleased that, in a barbarous age,
He gave rude Scotland Virgil's page,
Than that beneath his rule he held
The bishopric of fair Dunkeld.
Beside him ancient Angus stood,
Doff'd his furr'd gown and sable hood:

* The well-known Gawain Douglas, Bishop of
Dunkeld, son of Archibald Bell-the-Cat, Earl of
Angus. He was author of a Scottish metrical
version of the Æneid, and of many other poetical
pieces of great merit. He had not at this period
attained the mitre.

O'er his huge form and visage pale,
He wore a cap and shirt of mail;
And lean'd his large and wrinkled hand
Upon the huge and sweeping brand
Which wont of yore, in battle fray,
His foeman's limbs to shred away,
As wood-knife lops the sapling spray.[72]
He seem'd as, from the tombs around
    Rising at judgment-day,
Some giant Douglas may be found
    In all his old array;
So pale his face, so huge his limb,
So old his arms, his look so grim.

XII.

Then at the altar Wilton kneels,
And Clare the spurs bound on his heels,
And think what next he must have felt,
At buckling of the falchion belt!
  And judge how Clara changed her hue,
While fastening to her lover's side
A friend, which, though in danger tried,
  He once had found untrue!
Then Douglas struck him with his blade:
" Saint Michael and Saint Andrew aid,
  I dub thee knight.
Arise, Sir Ralph, De Wilton's heir!
For King, for Church, for Lady fair,
  See that thou fight." —
And Bishop Gawain, as he rose,
Said—"Wilton! grieve not for thy woes,
  Disgrace, and trouble;
For He, who honor best bestows,
  May give thee double."
De Wilton sobb'd, for sob he must —
" Where'er I meet a Douglas, trust
  That Douglas is my brother!" —
" Nay, nay," old Angus said, "not so;
To Surrey's camp thou now must go,
  Thy wrongs no longer smother.
I have two sons in yonder field;
And, if thou meet'st them under shield,
Upon them bravely — do thy worst;
And foul fall him that blenches first!"

XIII.

Not far advanced was morning day,
When Marmion did his troop array
  To Surrey's camp to ride;
He had safe conduct for his band,
Beneath the royal seal and hand,
  And Douglas gave a guide:

The ancient Earl, with stately grace,
Would Clara on her palfrey place,
And whisper'd in an under tone,
"Let the hawk stoop, his prey is
    flown." —
The train from out the castle drew,
But Marmion stopp'd to bid adieu: —
    "Though something I might plain,"
    he said,
"Of cold respect to stranger guest,
Sent hither by your King's behest,
    While in Tantallon's towers I staid;
Part we in friendship from your land,
And, noble Earl, receive my hand." —
But Douglas round him drew his cloak,
Folded his arms, and thus he spoke: —
"My manors, halls, and bowers, shall still
Be open, at my Sovereign's will,
To each one whom he lists, howe'er
Unmeet to be the owner's peer.
My castles are my King's alone,
From turret to foundation-stone —
The hand of Douglas is his own;
And never shall in friendly grasp
The hand of such as Marmion clasp." —

XIV.

Burn'd Marmion's swarthy cheek like fire,
And shook his very frame for ire,
    And — "This to me!" he said, —
"An 'twere not for thy hoary beard,
Such hand as Marmion's had not spared
To cleave the Douglas' head!
And, first, I tell thee, haughty Peer,
He, who does England's message here,
Although the meanest in her state,
May well, proud Angus, be thy mate:
And, Douglas, more I tell thee here,
    Even in thy pitch of pride,
Here in thy hold, thy vassals near,
(Nay, never look upon your lord,
And lay your hands upon your sword,)
    I tell thee thou'rt defied!
And if thou saidst I am not peer
To any lord in Scotland here,
Lowland or Highland, far or near,
    Lord Angus, thou hast lied!"
On the Earl's cheek the flush of rage
O'ercame the ashen hue of age:
Fierce he broke forth, — "And darest
    thou, then,
To beard the lion in his den,
    The Douglas in his hall?

And hopest thou hence unscathed to
    go? —
No, by Saint Bride of Bothwell, no!
Up drawbridge, grooms — what, Warder,
    ho!
    Let the portcullis fall." [73]
Lord Marmion turn'd, — well was his
    need,
And dash'd the rowels in his steed,
Like arrow through the archway sprung,
The ponderous gate behind him rung:
To pass there was such scanty room,
The bars, descending, razed his plume.

XV.

The steed along the drawbridge flies,
Just as it trembled on the rise;
Nor lighter does the swallow skim
Along the smooth lake's level brim:
And when Lord Marmion reach'd his
    band,
He halts, and turn'd with clenched hand,
And shout of loud defiance pours,
And shook his gauntlet at the towers.
"Horse! horse!" the Douglas cried,
    "and chase!" —
But soon he rein'd his fury's pace:
"A royal messenger he came,
Though most unworthy of the name. —
A letter forged! Saint Jude to speed!
Did ever knight so foul a deed! [74]
At first in heart it liked me ill,
When the King praised his clerkly skill.
Thanks to Saint Bothan, son of mine,
Save Gawain, ne'er could pen a line.
So swore I, and I swear it still,
Let my boy-bishop fret his fill. —
Saint Mary mend my fiery mood!
Old age ne'er cools the Douglas blood,
I thought to slay him where he stood.
'Tis pity of him too," he cried:
"Bold can he speak, and fairly ride,
I warrant him a warrior tried."
With this his mandate he recalls,
And slowly seeks his castle halls.

XVI.

The day in Marmion's journey wore;
Yet, ere his passion's gust was o'er,
They cross'd the heights of Stanrig-Moor.
His troop more closely there he scann'd,
And miss'd the Palmer from the band. —

" Palmer or not," young Blount did say,
" He parted at the peep of day;
Good sooth, it was in strange array."
" In what array? " said Marmion quick.
" My lord, I ill can spell the trick;
But all night long, with clink and bang,
Close to my couch did hammers clang;
At dawn the falling drawbridge rang,
And from a loop-hole while I peep,
Old Bell-the-Cat came from the Keep,
Wrapp'd in a gown of sables fair,
As fearful of the morning air;
Beneath, when that was blown aside,
A rusty shirt of mail I spied,
By Archibald won in bloody work,
Against the Saracen and Turk:
Last night it hung not in the hall;
I thought some marvel would befall.
And next I saw them saddled lead
Old Cheviot forth, the Earl's best steed;
A matchless horse, though something old,
Prompt in his paces, cool and bold.
I heard the Sheriff Sholto say,
The Earl did much the Master * pray
To use him on the battle-day;
But he preferr'd —" "Nay, Henry, cease!
Thou sworn horse-courser, hold thy peace.
Eustace, thou bear'st a brain — I pray
What did Blount see at break of day? " —

XVII.

" In brief, my lord, we both descried
(For then I stood by Henry's side)
The Palmer mount, and outwards ride,
Upon the Earl's own favorite steed:
All sheathed he was in armor bright,
And much resembled that same knight,
Subdued by you in Cotswold fight:
Lord Angus wish'd him speed." —
The instant that Fitz-Eustace spoke,
A sudden light on Marmion broke:—
" Ah! dastard fool, to reason lost!"
He mutter'd; " 'Twas nor fay nor ghost
I met upon the moonlight wold,
But living man of earthly mould. —
   O dotage blind and gross!
Had I but fought as wont, one thrust
Had laid De Wilton in the dust,
   My path no more to cross. —
How stand we now? — he told his tale
To Douglas; and with some avail;

* His eldest son, the Master of Angus.

'Twas therefore gloom'd his rugged
   brow. —
Will Surrey dare to entertain,
'Gainst Marmion, charge disproved and
   vain?
   Small risk of that, I trow.
Yet Clare's sharp questions must I shun;
Must separate Constance from the Nun —
O, what a tangled web we weave, ·
When first we practise to deceive!
A Palmer too! — no wonder why
I felt rebuked beneath his eye:
I might have known there was but one
Whose look could quell Lord Marmion."

XVIII.

Stung with these thoughts, he urged to
   speed
His troop, and reach'd at eve, the Tweed,
Where Lennel's convent † closed their
   march.
(There now is left but one frail arch;
   Yet mourn thou not its cells;
Our time a fair exchange has made;
Hard by, in hospitable shade,
   A reverend pilgrim dwells,
Well worth the whole Bernardine brood,
That e'er wore sandal, frock, or hood.)
Yet did St. Bernard's Abbot there
Give Marmion entertainment fair,
And lodging for his train and Clare.
Next morn the Baron climb'd the tower,
To view afar the Scottish power,
   Encamp'd on Flodden edge:
The white pavilions made a show,
Like remnants of the winter snow,
   Along the dusky ridge.
Lord Marmion look'd: — at length his eye
Unusual movement might descry
   Amid the shifting lines:
The Scottish host drawn out appears,
For, flashing on the hedge of spears
   The eastern sunbeam shines.
Their front now deepening, now extend-
   ing;
Their flank inclining, wheeling, bending,
Now drawing back, and now descending,
The skilful Marmion well could know,
They watch'd the motions of some foe,
Who traversed on the plain below.

† A Cistertian convent.   At Lennel House
resided Patrick Brydone, Scott's venerable
friend.

XIX.

Even so it was.　From Flodden ridge
　The Scots beheld the English host
Leave Barmore-wood, their evening
　　post,
　And heedful watch'd them as they
　　cross'd
The Till by Twisel Bridge.[75]
　High sight it is, and haughty, while
They dive into the deep defile;
　Beneath the cavern'd cliff they fall,
　Beneath the castle's airy wall.
By rock, by oak, by hawthorn-tree,
　Troop after troop are disappearing;
　Troop after troop their banners rearing,
Upon the eastern bank you see.
Still pouring down the rocky den,
　Where flows the sullen Till,
And rising from the dim-wood glen,
　Standards on standards, men on men,
　In slow succession still,
And, sweeping o'er the Gothic arch,
And pressing on, in ceaseless march,
　To gain the opposing hill.
That morn, to many a trumpet clang,
Twisel! thy rock's deep echo rang;
And many a chief of birth and rank;
Saint Helen! at thy fountain drank.
Thy hawthorn glade, which now we
　　see
In spring-tide bloom so lavishly,
Had then from many an axe its doom,
To give the marching columns room.

XX.

And why stands Scotland idly now,
Dark Flodden! on thy airy brow,
Since England gains the pass the while,
And struggles through the deep defile?
What checks the fiery soul of James?
Why sits that champion of the dames
　Inactive on his steed,
And sees between him and his land,
Between him and Tweed's southern
　　strand,
His host Lord Surrey lead?
What 'vails the vain knight-errant's
　　brand?
— O, Douglas, for thy leading wand!
　Fierce Randolph, for thy speed!
O for one hour of Wallace wight,
Or well-skill'd Bruce to rule the fight,
And cry—"Saint Andrew and our right!"

Another sight had seen that morn,
From Fate's dark book a leaf been torn,
And Flodden had been Bannock-
　　bourne! —
The precious hour has pass'd in vain,
And England's host has gain'd the plain:
Wheeling their march, and circling still,
Around the base of Flodden hill.

XXI.

Ere yet the bands met Marmion's eye,
Fitz-Eustace shouted loud and high: —
"Hark! hark! my lord, an English drum!
And see ascending squadrons come
　Between Tweed's river and the hill,
Foot, horse, and cannon: — hap what
　　hap,
My basnet to a prentice cap,
　Lord Surrey's o'er the Till!
Yet more! yet more! — how far array'd
They file from out the hawthorn shade,
　And sweep so gallant by:
With all their banners bravely spread,
　And all their armor flashing high,
Saint George might waken from the dead,
　To see fair England's standards fly." —
"Stint in thy prate," quoth Blount,
　　"thou'dst best,
And listen to our lord's behest." —
With kindling brow Lord Marmion
　　said :—
"This instant be our band array'd,
The river must be quickly cross'd,
That we may join Lord Surrey's host.
If fight King James, — as well I trust,
That fight he will, and fight he must, —
The Lady Clare behind our lines
Shall tarry, while the battle joins.'

XXII.

Himself he swift on horseback threw,
Scarce to the Abbot bade adieu;
Far less would listen to his prayer,
To leave behind the helpless Clare.
Down to the Tweed his band he drew,
And mutter'd as the flood they view,
"The pheasant in the falcon's claw,
He scarce will yield to please a daw:
Lord Angus may the Abbot awe,
So Clare shall bide with me."
Then on that dangerous ford, and deep,
Where to the Tweed Leat's eddies creep,
　He ventured desperately:

And not a moment will he bide,
Till squire, or groom, before him ride;
Headmost of all he stems the tide;
  And stems it gallantly.
Eustace held Clare upon her horse,
  Old Hubert led her rein,
Stoutly they braved the current's course,
And, though far downward driven per
    force
The southern bank they gain;
Behind them straggling, came to shore,
  As best they might, the train:
Each o'er his head his yew-bow bore,
  A caution not in vain;
Deep need that day that every string,
By wet unharm'd, should sharply ring.
A moment then Lord Marmion staid,
And breathed his steed, his men array'd,
  Then forward moved his band,
Until, Lord Surrey's rear-guard won,
He halted by a Cross of Stone,
That, on a hillock standing lone,
  Did all the field command.

XXIII.

Hence might they see the full array
Of either host, for deadly fray; [76]
Their marshall'd lines stretch'd east and
    west,
  And fronted north and south,
And distant salutation pass'd
  From the loud cannon mouth,
Not in the close successive rattle,
That breathes the voice of modern battle,
  But slow and far between. —
The hillock gain'd, Lord Marmion staid:
"Here by this Cross," he gently said:
  "You well may view the scene.
Here shalt thou tarry, lovely Clare:
O! think of Marmion in thy prayer! —
Thou wilt not? — well, — no less my
    care
Shall, watchful, for thy weal prepare. —
You, Blount and Eustace, are her
    guard,
  With ten pick'd archers of my train;
With England if the day go hard,
  To Berwick speed amain. —
But if we conquer, cruel maid,
My spoils shall at your feet be laid,
  When here we meet again."
He waited not for answer there,
And would not mark the maid's despair,

Nor heed the discontented look
From either squire; but spurr'd amain,
And, dashing through the battle plain,
  His way to Surrey took.

XXIV.

" —— The good Lord Marmion, by my
    life!
Welcome to danger's hour!
Short greeting serves in time of strife!
  Thus have I ranged my power: —
Myself will rule this central host,
  Stout Stanley fronts their right,
My sons command the vaward post,
  With Brian Tunstall, stainless knight,[77]
Lord Dacre, with his horsemen light,
  Shall be in rear-ward of the fight,
And succor those that need it most.
  Now, gallant Marmion, well I know,
  Would gladly to the vanguard go;
Edmund, the Admiral, Tunstall there,
With thee their charge will blithely share;
There fight thine own retainers too,
Beneath De Burg, thy steward true."
" Thanks, noble Surrey! " Marmion said,
Nor farther greeting there he paid;
But, parting like a thunderbolt,
First in the vanguard made a halt,
  Where such a shout there rose
Of " Marmion! Marmion! " that the cry,
Up Flodden mountains shrilling high,
  Startled the Scottish foes.

XXV.

Blount and Fitz-Eustace rested still
With Lady Clare upon the hill!
On which (for far the day was spent)
The western sunbeams now were bent.
The cry they heard, its meaning knew,
Could plain their distant comrades view;
Sadly to Blount did Eustace say: —
" Unworthy office here to stay!
No hope of gilded spurs to-day. —
But see! look up — on Flodden bent
The Scottish foe has fired his tent."
  And sudden, as he spoke,
From the sharp ridges of the hill,
All downward to the banks of Till,
  Was wreathed in sable smoke.
Volumed and fast, and rolling far,
The cloud enveloped Scotland's war,
  As down the hill they broke;

Nor martial shout, nor minstrel tone,
Announced their march; their tread alone,
At times one warning trumpet blown,
    At times a stifled hum,
Told England, from his mountain-throne
    King James did rushing come. —
Scarce could they hear or see their foes,
    Until at weapon-point they close. —
They close, in clouds of smoke and dust,
With sword-sway, and with lance's thrust;
    And such a yell was there,
Of sudden and portentous birth,
As if men fought upon the earth,
    And fiends in upper air;
O life and death were in the shout,
Recoil and rally, charge and rout,
    And triumph and despair.
Long look'd the anxious squires; their eye
Could in the darkness naught descry.

XXVI.

At length the freshening western blast
Aside the shroud of battle cast;
And, first, the ridge of mingled spears
Above the brightening cloud appears;
And in the smoke the pennons flew,
As in the storm the white sea-mew.
Then mark'd they, dashing broad and far,
The broken billows of the war,
And plumed crests of chieftains brave,
Floating like foam upon the wave;
    But naught distinct they see:
Wide raged the battle on the plain;
Spears shook, and falchions flash'd amain,
Fell England's arrow-flight like rain;
Crests rose, and stoop'd, and rose again,
    Wild and disorderly.
Amid the scene of tumult, high
They saw Lord Marmion's falcon fly:
And stainless Tunstall's banner white,
And Edmund Howard's lion bright,
Still bare them bravely in the fight,
    Although against them come,
Of gallant Gordons many a one,
And many a stubborn Badenoch-man,
And many a rugged Border clan,
    With Huntly, and with Home.

XXVII.

Far on the left, unseen the while,
Stanley broke Lennox and Argyle;
Though there the western mountaineer
Rush'd with bare bosom on the spear,

And flung the feeble targe aside,
And with both hands the broadsword
    plied,
'Twas vain: — But Fortune, on the right,
With fickle smile, cheer'd Scotland's
    fight.
Then fell that spotless banner white,
    The Howard's lion fell;
Yet still Lord Marmion's falcon flew
With wavering flight, while fiercer grew
    Around the battle-yell.
The Border slogan rent the sky!
A Home! a Gordon! was the cry:
Loud were the clanging blows;
Advanced, — forced back, — now low,
    now high,
The pennon sunk and rose;
As bends the bark's mast in the gale,
When rent are rigging, shrouds, and sail,
    It waver'd mid the foes.
No longer Blount the view could bear: —
" By Heaven, and all its saints! I swear
    I will not see it lost!
Fitz-Eustace, you with Lady Clare
May bid your beads, and patter prayer, —
    I gallop to the host."
And to the fray he rode amain,
Follow'd by all the archer train.
The fiery youth, with desperate charge,
Made, for a space, an opening large, —
    The rescued banner rose, —
But darkly closed the war around,
Like pine-tree, rooted from the ground,
    It sunk among the foes.
Then Eustace mounted too: — yet staid
As loth to leave the helpless maid,
    When, fast as shaft can fly,
Blood-shot his eyes, his nostrils spread,
The loose rein dangling from his head,
Housing and saddle bloody red,
    Lord Marmion's steed rush'd by;
And Eustace, maddening at the sight,
    A look and sign to Clara cast
    To mark he would return in haste,
Then plunged into the fight.

XXVIII.

Ask me not what the maiden feels,
    Left in that dreadful hour alone:
Perchance her reason stoops, or reels;
    Perchance a courage, not her own,
    Braces her mind to desperate tone. —
The scatter'd van of England wheels: —

She only said, as loud in air
  The tumult roar'd, "Is   Wilton
  there?" —
They fly, or madden'd by despair,
  Fight but to die, — "Is Wilton
  there?"
With that, straight up the hill there rode
Two horsemen drench'd with gore,
And in their arms, a helpless load,
  A wounded knight they bore.
His hand still strain'd the broken brand;
His arms were smear'd with blood and
  sand.
Dragg'd from among the horses' feet,
With dinted shield, and helmet beat,
The falcon-crest and plumage gone,
Can that be haughty Marmion! . . .
Young Blount his armor did unlace,
And, gazing on his ghastly face,
  Said — "By Saint George, he's gone!
That spear-wound has our master sped,
And see the deep cut on his head!
  Good-night to Marmion." —
"Unnurtured Blount! thy brawling cease:
He opes his eyes," said Eustace;
  "peace!"

XXIX.

When, doff'd his casque, he felt free air,
Around 'gan Marmion wildly stare: —
"Where's Harry Blount? Fitz-Eustace
  where?
Linger ye here, ye hearts of hare!
Redeem my pennon, — charge again!
Cry — 'Marmion to the rescue!' —
  Vain!
Last of my race, on battle-plain
That shout shall ne'er be heard again!
Yet my last thought is England's — fly,
  To Dacre bear my signet-ring:
Tell him his squadrons up to bring. —
Fitz-Eustace, to Lord Surrey hie;
  Tunstall lies dead upon the field,
  His life-blood stains the spotless shield.
Edmund is down : — my life is reft;
The Admiral alone is left.
Let Stanley charge with spur of fire, —
With Chester charge, and Lancashire,
Full upon Scotland's central host,
Or victory and England's lost. —
Must I bid twice? — hence, varlets!
  fly!
Leave Marmion here alone — to die."

They parted, and alone he lay;
  Clare drew her from the sight away,
Till pain wrung forth a lowly moan,
And half he murmur'd, — "Is there none
  Of all my halls have nurst,
Page, squire, or groom, one cup to bring
Of blessed water from the spring,
  To slake my dying thirst!"

XXX.

O, Woman! in our hours of ease,
Uncertain, coy, and hard to please,
And variable as the shade
By the light quivering aspen made;
When pain and anguish wring the brow,
A ministering angel thou! —
Scarce were the piteous accents said,
When, with the Baron's casque, the maid
  To the nigh streamlet ran:
Forgot were hatred, wrongs, and fears;
The plaintive voice alone she hears,
  Sees but the dying man.
She stoop'd her by the runnel's side,
  But in abhorrence backward drew;
For, oozing from the mountain's side,
  Where raged the war, a dark-red tide
Was curdling in the streamlet blue.
Where shall she turn? — behold her
  mark
  A little fountain cell,
Where water, clear as diamond-spark,
  In a stone basin fell.
Above, some half-worn letters say,

𝔇𝔯𝔦𝔫𝔨. 𝔴𝔢𝔞𝔯𝔶. 𝔭𝔦𝔩𝔤𝔯𝔦𝔪. 𝔡𝔯𝔦𝔫𝔨. 𝔞𝔫𝔡. 𝔭𝔯𝔞𝔶.
𝔉𝔬𝔯. 𝔱𝔥𝔢. 𝔨𝔦𝔫𝔡. 𝔰𝔬𝔲𝔩. 𝔬�. 𝔖𝔶𝔟𝔦𝔩. 𝔊𝔯𝔢𝔶.
𝔚𝔥𝔬. 𝔟𝔲𝔦𝔩𝔱. 𝔱𝔥𝔦𝔰. 𝔠𝔯𝔬𝔰𝔰. 𝔞𝔫𝔡. 𝔴𝔢𝔩𝔩.

She fill'd the helm, and back she hied,
And with surprise and joy espied
  A monk supporting Marmion's head:
A pious man, whom duty brought
To dubious verge of battle fought,
  To shrieve the dying, bless the dead.

XXI.

Deep drank Lord Marmion of the wave,
And, as she stoop'd his brow to lave —
"Is it the hand of Clare," he said,
"Or injured Constance, bathes my
  head?"
Then, as remembrance rose, —
"Speak not to me of shrift or prayer!
I must redress her woes.

Short space, few words, are mine to
    spare;
Forgive and listen, gentle Clare ! " —
" Alas ! " she said, " the while, —
O, think of your immortal weal !
In vain for Constance is your zeal;
   She —— died at Holy Isle." —
Lord Marmion started from the ground,
As light as if he felt no wound;
Though in the action burst the tide,
In torrents, from his wounded side.
" Then it was truth,"—he said—"I knew
That the dark presage must be true. —
I would the Fiend, to whom belongs
The vengeance due to all her wrongs,
   Would spare me but a day !
For wasting fire, and dying groan,
And priests slain on the altar-stone,
   Might bribe him for delay.
It may not be ! — this dizzy trance —
Curse on yon base marauder's lance,
And doubly cursed my failing brand !
A sinful heart makes feeble hand."
Then, fainting, down on earth he sunk,
Supported by the trembling monk.

XXXII.

With fruitless labor, Clara bound,
And strove to stanch the gushing wound;
The Monk, with unavailing cares,
Exhausted all the Church's prayers.
Ever, he said, that, close and near,
A lady's voice was in his ear,
And that the priest he could not hear,
   For that she ever sung,
" *In the lost battle, borne down by the*
    flying,
Where mingles war's rattle with groans
    of the dying ! "
   So the notes rung; —
" Avoid thee, Fiend ! — with cruel hand,
Shake not the dying sinner's sand ! —
O, look, my son, upon yon sign
Of the Redeemer's grace divine;
O, think on faith and bliss ! —
By many a death-bed I have been,
And many a sinner's parting seen,
   But never aught like this." —
The war, that for a space did fail,
Now trebly thundering swell'd the gale,
   And — STANLEY ! was the cry;
A light on Marmion's visage spread,
   And fired his glazing eye;

With dying hand, above his head,
He shook the fragment of his blade,
   And shouted " Victory ! —
Charge, Chester, charge ! On, Stanley,
   on ! "
Were the last words of Marmion.

XXXIII.

By this, though deep the evening fell,
Still rose the battle's deadly swell,
For still the Scots, around their King,
Unbroken, fought in desperate ring.
Where's now their victor vaward wing,
   Where Huntly, and where Home? —
O, for a blast of that dread horn,
On Fontarabian echoes borne,
   That to King Charles did come,
When Rowland brave, and Olivier,
And every paladin and peer,
   On Roncesvalles died !
Such blasts might warn them, not in vain,
To quit the plunder of the slain,
And turn the doubtful day again,
   While yet on Flodden side,
Afar, the Royal Standard flies,
And round it toils, and bleeds, and dies,
   Our Caledonian pride !
In vain the wish — for far away,
While spoil and havoc mark their way,
Near Sybil's Cross the plunderers stray.—
" O, Lady," cried the Monk, " away ! "
   And placed her on her steed,
And led her to the chapel fair,
   Of Tillmouth upon Tweed.
There all the night they spent in prayer,
And at the dawn of morning, there
She met her kinsman, Lord Fitz-Clare.

XXXIV.

But as they left the dark'ning heath,
More desperate grew the strife of death.
The English shafts in volleys hail'd,
In headlong charge their horse assail'd;
Front, flank, and rear, the squadrons
   sweep
To break the Scottish circle deep,
   That fought around their King.
But yet, though thick the shafts as snow,
Though charging knights like whirlwinds
   go,
Though bill-men ply the ghastly blow,
   Unbroken was the ring;

The stubborn spear-men still made good
Their dark impenetrable wood,
Each stepping where his comrade stood,
　The instant that he fell.
No thought was there of dastard flight;
Link'd in the serried phalanx tight,
Groom fought like noble, squire like knight
　As fearlessly and well;
Till utter darkness closed her wing
O'er their thin host and wounded King.
Then skilful Surrey's sage commands
Led back from strife his shatter'd bands,
And from the charge they drew,
As mountain-waves, from wasted lands,
　Sweep back to ocean blue.
Then did their loss his foeman know;
Their King, their Lords, their mightiest
　low,
They melted from the field, as snow,
When streams are swoln and south winds
　blow,
　Dissolves in silent dew.
Tweed's echoes heard the ceaseless plash,
　While many a broken band,
Disorder'd, through her currents dash,
　To gain the Scottish land;
To town and tower, to down and dale,
To tell red Flodden's dismal tale,
And raise the universal wail.
Tradition, legend, tune, and song,
Shall many an age that wail prolong:
Still from the sire the son shall hear
Of the stern strife, and carnage dear,
　Of Flodden's fatal field,
Where shiver'd was fair Scotland's spear,
And broken was her shield!

XXXV.

Day dawns upon the mountain's side:—
There, Scotland! lay thy bravest pride,
Chiefs, knights, and nobles, many a one:
The sad survivors all are gone—
View not that corpse mistrustfully,
Defaced and mangled though it be;
Nor to yon Border Castle high,
Look northward with upbraiding eye;
　Nor cherish hope in vain,
That journeying far on foreign strand,
The Royal Pilgrim to his land
　May yet return again.
He saw the wreck his rashness wrought;
Reckless of life, he desperate fought,
　And fell on Flodden plain;

And well in death his trusty brand,
Firm clench'd within his manly hand,
　Beseem'd the monarch slain.[78]
But, O! how changed since yon blithe
　night!—
Gladly I turn me from the sight,
　Unto my tale again.

XXXVI.

Short is my tale: — Fitz-Eustace' care
A pierced and mangled body bare
To moated Litchfield's lofty pile;
And there, beneath the southern aisle,
A tomb, with Gothic sculpture fair,
Did long Lord Marmion's image bear,
(Now vainly for its sight you look;
'Twas levell'd when fanatic Brook
The fair cathedral storm'd and took;[79]
But, thanks to Heaven and good Saint
　Chad,
A guerdon meet the spoiler had!)
There erst was martial Marmion found,
His feet upon a couchant hound.
　His hands to heaven upraised;
And all around, on scutcheon rich,
And tablet carved, and fretted niche,
　His arms and feats were blazed.
And yet, though all was carved so fair,
And priest for Marmion breathed the
　prayer,
The last Lord Marmion lay not there.
From Ettrick woods a peasant swain
Follow'd his lord to Flodden plain,—
One of those flowers, whom plaintive
　lay
In Scotland mourns as " wede away: "
Sore wounded, Sybil's Cross he spied,
And dragg'd him to its foot, and died,
Close by the noble Marmion's side.
The spoilers stripp'd and gash'd the slain,
And thus their corpses were mista'en;
And thus, in the proud Baron's tomb,
The lowly woodsman took the room.

XXXVII.

Less easy task it were, to show
Lord Marmion's nameless grave, and low.
　They dug his grave e'en where he lay,
　　But every mark is gone;
　Time's wasting hand has done away
　The simple cross of Sybil Grey,
　　And broke her font of stone:

But yet from out the little hill
Oozes the slender springlet still.
　Oft halts the stranger there,
For thence may best his curious eye
The memorable field descry;
　And shepherd boys repair
To seek the water-flag and rush,
And rest them by the hazel bush,
　And plait their garlands fair;
Nor dream they sit upon the grave,
That holds the bones of Marmion brave.—
When thou shalt find the little hill,
With thy heart commune, and be still
If ever in temptation strong,
Thou left'st the right path for the wrong;
If every devious step, thus trod,
Still led thee farther from the road;
Dread thou to speak presumptuous doom
On noble Marmion's lowly tomb;
But say, " He died a gallant knight,
With sword in hand for England's right."

XXXVIII.

I do not rhyme to that dull elf,
Who cannot image to himself,
That all through Flodden's dismal night,
Wilton was foremost in the fight;
That, when brave Surrey's steed was slain,
'Twas Wilton mounted him again;
'Twas Wilton's brand that deepest hew'd,
Amid the spearmen's stubborn wood;
Unnamed by Holinshed or Hall,
He was the living soul of all:
That, after fight, his faith made plain,
He won his rank and lands again;
And charged his old paternal shield
With bearings won on Flodden field.
Nor sing I to that simple maid,
To whom it must in terms be said,
That King and kinsmen did agree,
To bless fair Clara's constancy;

Who cannot, unless I relate,
Paint to her mind the bridal's state;
That Wolsey's voice the blessing spoke,
More, Sands, and Denny, pass'd the joke,
That bluff King Hal the curtain drew,
And Catherine's hand the stocking
　　threw;
And afterwards, for many a day,
That it was held enough to say,
In blessing to a wedded pair,
" Love they like Wilton and like Clare ! "

L'ENVOY.

TO THE READER.

WHY then a final note prolong,
Or lengthen out a closing song,
Unless to bid the gentles speed,
Who long have listed to my rede? *
To Statesmen grave, if such may deign
To read the Minstrel's idle strain,
Sound head, clean hands, and piercing
　　wit,
And patriotic heart — as PITT !
A garland for the hero's crest,
And twined by her he loves the best;
To every lovely lady bright,
What can I wish but faithful knight?
To every faithful lover too,
What can I wish but lady true?
And knowledge to the studious sage;
And pillow to the head of age.
To thee, dear school-boy, whom my lay
Has cheated of thy hour of play,
Light task, and merry holiday !
To all, to each, a fair good-night,
And pleasing dreams, and slumbers light !

* Story.

THE

LADY OF THE LAKE:

A POEM IN SIX CANTOS.

TO THE MOST NOBLE

JOHN JAMES, MARQUIS OF ABERCORN,

ETC., ETC., ETC.

THIS POEM IS INSCRIBED BY

THE AUTHOR.

INTRODUCTION TO EDITION 1830.

AFTER the success of " Marmion," I felt inclined to exclaim with Ulysses in the " Odyssey " —

Οὗτος μὲν δὴ ἆεθλος ἀάατος ἐκτετέλεσται.
Νῦν αὖτε σκοπὸν ἄλλον. — Odys. χ. 5. 6.

" One venturesome game my hand has won to-day —
Another, gallants, yet remains to play."

The ancient manners, the habits and customs, of the aboriginal race by whom the Highlands of Scotland were inhabited, had always appeared to me peculiarly adapted to poetry. The change in their manners, too, had taken place almost within my own time, or at least I had learned many particulars concerning the ancient state of the Highlands from the old men of the last generation. I had always thought the old Scottish Gael highly adapted for poetical composition. The feuds and political dissensions, which, half a century earlier, would have rendered the richer and wealthier part of the kingdom indisposed to countenance a poem the scene of which was laid in the Highlands, were now sunk in the generous compassion which the English, more than any other nation, feel for the misfortunes of an honorable foe. The Poems of Ossian had, by their popularity, sufficiently shown, that if writings on Highland subjects were qualified to interest the reader, mere national prejudices were, in the present day, very unlikely to interfere with their success.

I had also read a great deal, seen much, and heard more, of that romantic country, where I was in the habit of spending some time every autumn ; and the scenery of Loch

120

Katrine was connected with the recollection of many a dear friend and merry expedition of former days. This poem, the action of which lay among scenes so beautiful, and so deeply imprinted on my recollection, was a labor of love, and it was no less so to recall the manners and incidents introduced. The frequent custom of James IV., and particularly of James V., to walk through their kingdom in disguise, afforded me the hint of an incident, which never fails to be interesting, if managed with the slightest address or dexterity.

I may now confess, however, that the employment, though attended with great pleasure, was not without its doubts and anxieties. A lady, to whom I was nearly related, and with whom I lived, during her whole life, on the most brotherly terms of affection, was residing with me at the time when the work was in progress, and used to ask me, what I could possibly do to rise so early in the morning (that happening to be the most convenient time to me for composition). At last I told her the subject of my meditations; and I can never forget the anxiety and affection expressed in her reply. "Do not be so rash," she said, "my dearest cousin. You are already popular — more so, perhaps, than you yourself will believe, or that even I, or other partial friends, can fairly allow to your merit. You stand high — do not rashly attempt to climb higher, and incur the risk of a fall; for, depend upon it, a favorite will not be permitted even to stumble with impunity." I replied to this affectionate expostulation in the words of Montrose —

> " He either fears his fate too much,
>   Or his deserts are small,
> Who dares not put it to the touch
>   To gain or lose it all."

"If I fail," I said, for the dialogue is strong in my recollection, "it is a sign that I ought never to have succeeded, and I will write prose for life: you shall see no change in my temper, nor will I eat a single meal the worse. But if I succeed,

> ' Up with the bonnie blue bonnet,
>   The dirk, and the feather, and a'!'"

Afterwards I showed my affectionate and anxious critic the first canto of the poem, which reconciled her to my imprudence. Nevertheless, although I answered thus confidently, with the obstinacy often said to be proper to those who bear my surname, I acknowledge that my confidence was considerably shaken by the warning of her excellent taste and unbiassed friendship. Nor was I much comforted by her retraction of the unfavorable judgment, when I recollected how likely a natural partiality was to affect that change of opinion. In such cases, affection rises like a light on the canvas, improves any favorable tints which it formerly exhibited, and throws its defects into the shade.

I remember that about the same time a friend started in to "heeze up my hope," like the "sportsman with his cutty-gun," in the old song. He was bred a farmer, but a man of powerful understanding, natural good taste, and warm poetical feeling, perfectly competent to supply the wants of an imperfect or irregular education. He was a passionate admirer of field-sports, which we often pursued together.

As this friend happened to dine with me at Ashestiel one day, I took the opportunity of reading to him the first canto of "The Lady of the Lake," in order to ascertain the effect the poem was likely to produce upon a person who was but too favorable a representative of readers at large. It is, of course, to be supposed, that I determined rather to guide my opinion by what my friend might appear to feel, than by what he might think fit to say. His reception of my recitation, or prelection, was rather singular. He placed his hand across his brow, and listened with great attention through the whole account of the stag-hunt, till the dogs threw themselves into the lake to follow their master, who embarks with Ellen Douglas. He then started up with a sudden exclamation, struck his hand on the table, and declared, in a voice of censure calculated for the occasion, that the dogs must have been totally ruined by being permitted to take the water after such a severe chase. I own I was much encouraged by the species of reverie which had possessed so zealous a follower of the sports of the ancient Nimrod, who had been completely surprised out of all doubts of the reality of the tale. Another of his remarks gave me less pleasure. He detected the identity of the King with the wandering knight, Fitz-James, when he winds his bugle to summon his attendants. He was probably thinking of the lively, but somewhat licentious, old ballad, in which the dénouement of a royal intrigue takes place as follows : —

> " He took a bugle frae his side,
>   He blew both loud and shrill,
> And four-and-twenty belted knights
>   Came skipping ower the hill ;
> Then he took out a little knife,
>   Let a' his duddies fa',
> And he was the brawest gentleman
>   That was amang them a':
>   And we'll go no more a-roving," etc.[1]

This discovery, as Mr. Pepys says of the rent in his camlet cloak, was but a trifle, yet it troubled me ; and I was at a good deal of pains to efface any marks by which I thought my secret could be traced before the conclusion, when I relied on it with the same hope of producing effect, with which the Irish postboy is said to reserve a " trot for the avenue."

I took uncommon pains to verify the accuracy of the local circumstances of this story. I recollect, in particular, that to ascertain whether I was telling a probable tale, I went into Perthshire, to see whether King James could actually have ridden from the banks of Loch Vennachar to Stirling Castle within the time supposed in the Poem, and had the pleasure to satisfy myself that it was quite practicable.

After a considerable delay, " The Lady of the Lake " appeared in May, 1810 ; and its success was certainly so extraordinary as to induce me for the moment to conclude that I had at last fixed a nail in the proverbially inconstant wheel of Fortune, whose stability in behalf of an individual who had so boldly courted her favors for three successive times had not as yet been shaken. I had attained, perhaps, that degree of public reputation at which prudence, or certainly timidity, would have made a halt, and discontinued efforts by which I was far more likely to diminish my fame than to increase it. But, as the celebrated John Wilkes is said to have explained to his late Majesty, that he himself, amid his full tide of popularity, was never a Wilkite, so I can, with the honest truth, exculpate myself from having been at any time a partisan of my own poetry, even when it was in the highest fashion with the million. It must not be supposed that I was either so ungrateful, or so superabundantly candid, as to despise or scorn the value of those whose voice had elevated me so much higher than my own opinion told me I deserved. I felt, on the contrary, the more grateful to the public, as receiving that from partiality to me, which I could not have claimed from merit ; and I endeavored to deserve the partiality, by continuing such exertions as I was capable of for their amusement.

It may be that I did not, in this continued course of scribbling, consult either the interest of the public or my own. But the former had effectual means of defending themselves, and could, by their coldness, sufficiently check any approach to intrusion ; and for myself, I had now for several years dedicated my hours so much to literary labor, that I should have felt difficulty in employing myself otherwise ; and so, like Dogberry, I generously bestowed all my tediousness on the public, comforting myself with the reflection that if posterity should think me undeserving of the favor with which I was regarded by my contemporaries, " they could not but say I *had* the crown," and had enjoyed for a time that popularity which is so much coveted.

I conceived, however, that I held the distinguished situation I had obtained, however unworthily, rather like the champion of pugilism, on the condition of being always ready to show proofs of my skill, than in the manner of the champion of chivalry, who performs his duties only on rare and solemn occasions. I was in any case conscious that I could not long hold a situation which the caprice, rather than the judgment, of the public, had bestowed upon me, and preferred being deprived of my precedence by some more worthy rival, to sinking into contempt for my indolence, and losing my reputation by what Scottish lawyers call the *negative prescription.* Accordingly, those who choose to look at the Introduction to Rokeby, in the present edition, will be able to trace the steps by which I declined as a poet to figure as a novelist ; as the ballad says, Queen Eleanor sunk at Charing-Cross to rise again at Queenhithe.

It only remains for me to say, that, during my short pre-eminence of popularity, I faithfully observed the rules of moderation which I had resolved to follow before I began my

---

1 " The Jolly Beggar," attributed to King James V. — *Herd's Collection*, 1776.

course as a man of letters. If a man is determined to make a noise in the world, he is as sure to encounter abuse and ridicule, as he who gallops furiously through a village must reckon on being followed by the curs in full cry. Experienced persons know, that in stretching to flog the latter, the rider is very apt to catch a bad fall; nor is an attempt to chastise a malignant critic attended with less danger to the author. On this principle, I let parody, burlesque, and squibs, find their own level; and while the latter hissed most fiercely, I was cautious never to catch them up, as schoolboys do, to throw them back against the naughty boy who fired them off, wisely remembering that they are, in such cases, apt to explode in the handling. Let me add, that my reign (since Byron has so called it) was marked by some instances of good-nature as well as patience. I never refused a literary person of merit such services in smoothing his way to the public as were in my power: and I had the advantage, rather an uncommon one with our irritable race, to enjoy general favor, without incurring permanent ill-will, so far as is known to me, among any of my contemporaries.

W. S.

Abbotsford, *April*, 1830.

ARGUMENT.

The Scene of the following Poem is laid chiefly in the vicinity of Loch Katrine, in the Western Highlands of Perthshire. The time of action includes six days, and the transactions of each day occupy a Canto.

THE LADY OF THE LAKE.

CANTO FIRST.

THE CHASE.

HARP of the North! that mouldering
        long hast hung
    On the witch-elm that shades Saint
        Fillan's spring,
And down the fitful breeze thy numbers
        flung,
    Till envious ivy did around thee
        cling, —
Muffling with verdant ringlet every string,
    O minstrel Harp, still must thine ac-
        cents sleep?
Mid rustling leaves and fountains mur-
        muring,
    Still must thy sweeter sounds their
        silence keep,
Nor bid a warrior smile, nor teach a maid
    to weep?

Not thus, in ancient days of Caledon,
    Was thy voice mute amidst the festal
        crowd,
When lay of hopeless love, or glory
        won,
    Aroused the fearful, or subdued the
        proud.
At each according pause, was heard aloud
    Thine ardent symphony sublime and
        high!
Fair dames and crested chiefs attention
        bow'd;
    For still the burden of thy minstrelsy
Was Knighthood's dauntless deed, and
    Beauty's matchless eye.

O wake once more! how rude soe'er the
        hand
    That ventures o'er thy magic maze to
        stray;

O wake once more! though scarce my
        skill command
    Some feeble echoing of thine earlier
        lay:
Though harsh and faint, and soon to die
        away,
    And all unworthy of thy nobler strain,
Yet if one heart throb higher at its sway,
    The wizard note has not been touch'd
        in vain.
Then silent be no more! Enchantress,
    wake again!

I.

The stag at eve had drunk his fill,
Where danced the moon on Monan's rill,
And deep his midnight lair had made
In lone Glenartney's hazel shade;
But, when the sun his beacon red
Had kindled on Benvoirlich's head,*
The deep-mouth'd bloodhound's heavy
        bay
Resounded up the rocky way,
And faint, from farther distance borne,
Were heard the clanging hoof and horn.

II.

As Chief, who hears his warder call,
"To arms! the foemen storm the wall,"
The antler'd monarch of the waste
Sprung from his heathery couch in haste
But, ere his fleet career he took,
The dew-drops from his flanks he shook;
Like crested leader proud and high,
Toss'd his beam'd frontlet to the sky;
A moment gazed adown the dale,
A moment snuff'd the tainted gale,

* One of the Grampian chain of mountains a
the head of the Valley of the Garry.

A moment listen'd to the cry,
That thicken'd as the chase drew nigh;
Then, as the headmost foes appear'd,
With one brave bound the copse he
    clear'd,
And, stretching forward free and far,
Sought the wild heaths of Uam-Var.

III.

Yell'd on the view the opening pack;
Rock, glen, and cavern paid them back;
To many a mingled sound at once
The awaken'd mountain gave response.
A hundred dogs bay'd deep and strong,
Clatter'd a hundred steeds along,
Their peal the merry horns rung out,
A hundred voices join'd the shout;
With hark and whoop and wild halloo,
No rest Benvoirlich's echoes knew.
Far from the tumult fled the roe,
Close in her covert cower'd the doe,
The falcon, from her cairn on high,
Cast on the rout a wondering eye,
Till far beyond her piercing ken
The hurricane had swept the glen.
Faint and more faint, its failing din
Return'd from cavern, cliff, and linn,
And silence settled, wide and still,
On the lone wood and mighty hill.

IV.

Less loud the sounds of sylvan war
Disturb'd the heights of Uam-Var,
And roused the cavern, where 'tis told,
A giant made his den of old;[1]
For ere that steep ascent was won,
High in his pathway hung the sun,
And many a gallant, stay'd perforce,
Was fain to breathe his faltering horse,
And of the trackers of the deer,
Scarce half the lessening pack was near;
So shrewdly on the mountain side
Had the bold burst their mettle tried.

V.

The noble stag was pausing now,
Upon the mountain's southern brow,
Where broad extended, far beneath,
The varied realms of fair Menteith.
With anxious eye he wander'd o'er
Mountain and meadow, moss and moor,
And ponder'd refuge from his toil,
By far Lochard or Aberfoyle.
But nearer was the copsewood gray,
That waved and wept on Loch-Achray,
And mingled with the pine-trees blue
On the bold cliffs of Benvenue.
Fresh vigor with the hope return'd,
With flying foot the heath he spurn'd,
Held westward with unwearied race,
And left behind the panting chase.

VI.

'Twere long to tell what steeds gave o'er,
As swept the hunt through Cambus-more;
What reins were tighten'd in despair,
When rose Benledi's ridge in air;[*]
Who flagg'd upon Bochastle's heath,
Who shunn'd to stem the flooded
    Teith,[†] —
For twice that day, from shore to shore,
The gallant stag swam stoutly o'er.
Few were the stragglers following far,
That reach'd the lake of Venachar;
And when the Brigg[‡] of Turk was won,
The headmost horseman rode alone.

VII.

Alone, but with unbated zeal,
That horseman plied the scourge and steel:
For jaded now, and spent with toil,
Emboss'd with foam, and dark with soil,
While every gasp with sobs he drew,
The laboring stag strain'd full in view.
Two dogs of black Saint Hubert's breed,
Unmatch'd for courage, breath, and speed,[2]
Fast on his flying traces came,
And all but won that desperate game;
For, scarce a spear's length from his
    haunch,
Vindictive toil'd the bloodhounds stanch;
Nor nearer might the dogs attain,
Nor farther might the quarry strain.
Thus up the margin of the lake,
Between the precipice and brake,
O'er stock and rock their race they take.

* Benledi is a high mountain on the north-
west of Callender. Its name signifies the mountain of God.

  † A river which gives its name to the territory
of Menteith.

  ‡ *Brigg,* a bridge.

VIII.

The Hunter mark'd that mountain high,
The lone lake's western boundary,
And deem'd the stag must turn to bay,
Where that huge rampart barr'd the way;
Already glorying in the prize,
Measured his antlers with his eyes;
For the death-wound and death-halloo,
Muster'd his breath, his whinyard
    drew;[3] —
But thundering as he came prepared,
With ready arm and weapon bared,
The wily quarry shunn'd the shock,
And turn'd him from the opposing rock;
Then, dashing down a darksome glen,
Soon lost to hound and hunter's ken,
In the deep Trosach's wildest nook
His solitary refuge took.
There, while close couch'd, the thicket shed
Cold dews and wild-flowers on his head,
He heard the baffled dogs in vain
Rave through the hollow pass amain,
Chiding the rocks that yell'd again.

IX.

Close on the hounds the Hunter came,
To cheer them on the vanish'd game;
But, stumbling in the rugged dell,
The gallant horse exhausted fell.
The impatient rider strove in vain
To rouse him with the spur and rein,
For the good steed, his labors o'er,
Stretch'd his stiff limbs to rise no more;
Then, touch'd with pity and remorse,
He sorrow'd o'er the expiring horse: —
" I little thought when first thy rein
I slack'd upon the banks of Seine,
That Highland eagle e'er should feed
On thy fleet limbs, my matchless steed.
Woe worth the chase, woe worth the day,
That costs thy life, my gallant gray! "

X.

Then through the dell his horn resounds,
From vain pursuit to call the hounds.
Back limp'd, with slow and crippled pace,
The sulky leaders of the chase;
Close to their master's side they press'd,
With drooping tail and humbled crest;
But still the dingle's hollow throat
Prolong'd the swelling bugle-note.

The owlets started from their dream,
The eagles answer'd with their scream,
Round and around the sounds were cast,
Till echo seem'd an answering blast;
And on the Hunter hied his way,
To join some comrades of the day;
Yet often paused, so strange the road,
So wondrous were the scenes it show'd.

XI.

The western waves of ebbing day
Roll'd o'er the glen their level way;
Each purple peak, each flinty spire,
Was bathed in floods of living fire.
But not a setting beam could glow
Within the dark ravines below,
Where twined the path in shadow hid,
Round many a rocky pyramid,
Shooting abruptly from the dell
Its thunder-splinter'd pinnacle;
Round many an insulated mass,
The native bulwarks of the pass,
Huge as the tower * which builders vain
Presumptuous piled on Shinar's plain.
The rocky summits, split and rent,
Form'd turret, dome, or battlement,
Or seem'd fantastically set
With cupola or minaret,
Wild crests as pagod ever deck'd,
Or mosque of Eastern architect.
Nor were these earth-born castles bare,
Nor lack'd they many a banner fair;
For, from their shiver'd brows display'd,
Far o'er the unfathomable glade,
All twinkling with the dew-drops sheen,
The brier-rose fell in streamers green,
And creeping shrubs, of thousand dyes,
Waved in the west-wind's summer sighs.

XII.

Boon nature scatter'd, free and wild,
Each plant or flower, the mountain's
    child.
Here eglantine embalm'd the air,
Hawthorn and hazel mingled there;
The primrose pale and violet flower,
Found in each cleft a narrow bower;
Fox-glove and night-shade, side by side,
Emblems of punishment and pride,
Group'd their dark hues with every stain
The weather-beaten crags retain.

* The Tower of Babel. — Genesis xi. 1-9.

With boughs that quaked at every breath
Gray birch and aspen wept beneath;
Aloft, the ash and warrior oak
Cast anchor in the rifted rock;
And, higher yet, the pine-tree hung
His shatter'd trunk, and frequent flung,
Where seem'd the cliffs to meet on high,
His boughs athwart the narrow'd sky.
Highest of all, where white peaks glanced,
Where glist'ning streamers waved and
        danced,
The wanderer's eye could barely view
The summer heaven's delicious blue;
So wondrous wild, the whole might seem
The scenery of a fairy dream.

XIII.

Onward, amid the copse 'gan peep
A narrow inlet, still and deep,
Affording scarce such breadth of brim,
As served the wild duck's brood to swim,
Lost for a space, through thickets veering,
But broader when again appearing,
Tall rocks and tufted knolls their face
Could on the dark-blue mirror trace;
And farther as the hunter stray'd,
Still broader sweeps its channels made.
The shaggy mounds no longer stood,
Emerging from entangled wood,
But, wave encircled, seem'd to float,
Like castle girdled with its moat;
Yet broader floods extending still
Divide them from their parent hill,
Till each, retiring, claims to be
An islet in an inland sea.

XIV.

And now, to issue from the glen,
No pathway meets the wanderer's ken,
Unless he climb, with footing nice,
A far projecting precipice.[4]
The broom's tough roots his ladder made,
The hazel saplings lent their aid;
And thus an airy point he won,
Where, gleaming with the setting sun,
One burnish'd sheet of living gold,
Loch Katrine lay beneath him roll'd,
In all her length far winding lay,
With promontory, creek, and bay,
And islands that, empurpled bright,
Floated amid the livelier light,
And mountains, that like giants stand,
To sentinel enchanted land.

High on the south, huge Benvenue
Down on the lake in masses threw
Crags, knolls, and mounds, confusedly
        hurl'd,
The fragments of an earlier world;
A wildering forest feather'd o'er
His ruin'd sides and summit hoar,
While on the north, through middle air,
Benan heaved high his forehead bare.

XV.

From the steep promontory gazed
The stranger, raptured and amazed.
And, "What a scene were here," he
        cried,
"For princely pomp, or churchman's
        pride!
On this bold brow, a lordly tower;
In that soft vale, a lady's bower;
On yonder meadow, far away,
The turrets of a cloister gray;
How blithely might the bugle-horn
Chide, on the lake, the lingering morn!
How sweet, at eve, the lover's lute
Chime, when the groves were still and
        mute!
And, when the midnight moon should
        lave
Her forehead in the silver wave,
How solemn on the ear would come
The holy matins' distant hum,
While the deep peal's commanding tone
Should wake, in yonder islet lone,
A sainted hermit from his cell,
To drop a bead with every knell —
And bugle, lute, and bell, and all,
Should each bewilder'd stranger call
To friendly feast, and lighted hall.

XVI.

"Blithe were it then to wander here!
But now, — beshrew yon nimble deer, —
Like that same hermit's, thin and spare,
The copse must give my evening fare;
Some mossy bank my couch must be,
Some rustling oak my canopy.
Yet pass we that; the war and chase
Give little choice of resting-place; —
A summer night, in greenwood spent,
Were but to-morrow's merriment:
But hosts may in these wilds abound,
Such as are better miss'd than found;

To meet with Highland plunderers here,
Were worse than loss of steed or deer. — 5
I am alone, — my bugle strain
May call some straggler of the train;
Or, fall the worst that may betide,
Ere now this falchion has been tried."

XVII.

But scarce again his horn he wound,
When lo! forth starting at the sound,
From underneath an aged oak,
That slanted from the islet rock,
A damsel guider of its way,
A little skiff shot to the bay,
That round the promontory steep
Led its deep line in graceful sweep.
Eddying in almost viewless wave,
The weeping willow-twig to lave,
And kiss, with whispering sound and
    slow,
The beach of pebbles bright as snow.
The boat had touch'd this silver strand,
Just as the hunter left his stand,
And stood conceal'd amid the brake,
To view this Lady of the Lake.
The maiden paused, as if again
She thought to catch the distant strain.
With head up-raised, and look intent,
And eye and ear attentive bent,
And locks flung back, and lips apart,
Like monument of Grecian art,
In listening mood, she seem'd to stand,
The guardian Naiad of the strand.

XVIII.

And ne'er did Grecian chisel trace
A Nymph, a Naiad, or a Grace,
Of finer form, or lovelier face:
What though the sun, with ardent frown,
Had slightly tinged her cheek with
    brown, —
The sportive toil, which, short and light,
Had dyed her glowing hue so bright,
Served too in hastier swell to show
Short glimpses of a breast of snow:
What though no rule of courtly grace
To measured mood had trained her pace,
A foot more light, a step more true,
Ne'er from the heath-flower dash'd the
    dew;
E'en the slight harebell raised its head,
Elastic from her airy tread:

What though upon her speech there hung
The accents of the mountain tongue, —
Those silver sounds, so soft, so clear,
The listener held his breath to hear!

XIX.

A Chieftain's daughter seem'd the maid,
Her satin snood,* her silken plaid,
Her golden brooch, such birth betray'd.
And seldom was a snood amid
Such wild luxuriant ringlets hid,
Whose glossy black to shame might bring
The plumage of the raven's wing;
And seldom o'er a breast so fair,
Mantled a plaid with modest care,
And never brooch the folds combined
Above a heart more good and kind.
Her kindness and her worth to spy,
You need but gaze on Ellen's eye;
Not Katrine, in her mirror blue,
Gives back the shaggy banks more true,
Than every free-born glance confess'd
The guileless movements of her breast;
Whether joy danced in her dark eye,
Or woe or pity claim'd a sigh,
Or filial love was glowing there,
Or meek devotion pour'd a prayer,
Or tale of injury call'd forth
The indignant spirit of the North.
One only passion unreveal'd,
With maiden pride the maid conceal'd,
Yet not less purely felt the flame; —
O need I tell that passion's name!

XX.

Impatient of the silent horn,
Now on the gale her voice was borne —
"Father!" she cried; the rocks around
Loved to prolong the gentle sound.
Awhile she paused, no answer came:—
"Malcolm, was thine the blast?"—The
    name
Less resolutely utter'd fell,
The echoes could not catch the swell.
"A stranger I," the Huntsman said,
Advancing from the hazel shade.
The maid, alarm'd, with hasty oar,
Push'd her light shallop from the shore,
And when a space was gain'd between,
Closer she drew her bosom's screen;

* *Snood,* the fillet worn round the hair of
maidens.

(So forth the startled swan would swing,
So turn to prune his ruffled wing,)
Then safe, though flutter'd and amazed,
She paused and on the stranger gazed.
Not his the form, nor his the eye,
That youthful maidens wont to fly.

XXI.

On his bold visage middle age
Had slightly press'd its signet sage,
Yet had not quench'd the open truth
And fiery vehemence of youth;
Forward and frolic glee was there,
The will to do, the soul to dare,
The sparkling glance, soon blown to fire,
Of hasty love, or headlong ire.
His limbs were cast in manly mould,
For hardy sports or contest bold;
And though in peaceful garb array'd,
And weaponless, except his blade,
His stately mien as well implied
A high-born heart, a martial pride,
As if a Baron's crest he wore,
And sheathed in armor trod the shore.
Slighting the petty need he show'd,
He told of his benighted road;
His ready speech flow'd fair and free,
In phrase of gentlest courtesy;
Yet seem'd that tone, and gesture bland,
Less used to sue than to command.

XXII.

A while the maid the stranger eyed,
And, reassured, at length replied,
That Highland halls were open still
To wilder'd wanderers of the hill.
"Nor think you unexpected come
To yon lone isle, our desert home;
Before the heath had lost the dew,
This morn, a couch was pull'd for you;
On yonder mountain's purple head
Have ptarmigan and heath-cock bled,
And our broad nets have swept the mere
To furnish forth your evening cheer."—
"Now, by the rood, my lovely maid,
Your courtesy has err'd," he said;
"No right have I to claim, misplaced,
The welcome of expected guest.
A wanderer, here by fortune tost,
My way, my friends, my courser, lost,
I ne'er before, believe me, fair,
Have ever drawn your mountain air,

Till on this lake's romantic strand,
I found a fay in fairy land!"—

XXIII.

"I well believe," the maid replied,
As her light skiff approach'd the side,—
"I well believe, that ne'er before
Your foot has trod Loch Katrine's shore,
But yet, as far as yesternight,
Old Allan-Bane foretold your plight,—
A gray-hair'd sire, whose eye intent
Was on the vision'd future bent.[6]
He saw your steed, a dappled gray,
Lie dead beneath the birchen way:
Painted exact your form and mien,
Your hunting suit of Lincoln green,
That tassell'd horn so gayly gilt,
That falchion's crooked blade and hilt,
That cap with heron plumage trim,
And yon two hounds so dark and grim.
He bade that all should ready be,
To grace a guest of fair degree,
But light I held his prophecy,
And deem'd it was my father's horn,
Whose echoes o'er the lake were borne."

XXIV.

The stranger smil'd: "Since to your home
A destined errant-knight I come,
Announced by prophet sooth and old,
Doom'd, doubtless, for achievement bold,
I'll lightly front each high emprise,
For one kind glance of those bright eyes.
Permit me, first, the task to guide
Your fairy frigate o'er the tide."
The maid with smile suppress'd and sly
The toil unwonted saw him try;
For seldom sure, if e'er before,
His noble hand had grasp'd an oar:
Yet with main strength his strokes he
    drew,
And o'er the lake the shallop flew;
With heads erect, and whimpering cry,
The hounds behind their passage ply.
Nor frequent does the bright oar break
The dark'ning mirror of the lake,
Until the rocky isle they reach,
And moor their shallop on the beach.

XXV.

The stranger view'd the shore around,
'Twas all so close with copsewood bound,

Nor track nor pathway might declare
That human foot frequented there,
Until the mountain-maiden show'd
A clambering, unsuspected road,
That winded through the tangled screen,
And open'd on a narrow green,
Where weeping birch and willow round
With their long fibres swept the ground.
Here, for retreat in dangerous hour,
Some chief had framed a rustic bower.[7]

XXVI.

It was a lodge of ample size,
But strange of structure and device,
Of such materials, as around
The workman's hands had readiest found.
Lopp'd off their boughs, their hoar trunks bared,
And by the hatchet rudely squared,
To give the walls their destined height,
The sturdy oak and ash unite;
While moss and clay and leaves combined
To fence each crevice from the wind.
The lighter pine-trees over-head,
Their slender length for rafters spread,
And wither'd heath and rushes dry
Supplied a russet canopy.
Due westward, fronting to the green,
A rural portico was seen,
Aloft on native pillars borne,
Of mountain fir, with bark unshorn,
Where Ellen's hand had taught to twine
The ivy and Idæan vine,
The clematis, the favor'd flower
Which boasts the name of virgin-bower,
And every hardy plant could bear
Loch Katrine's keen and searching air.
An instant in this porch she staid,
And gayly to the stranger said:—
" On heaven and on thy lady call,
And enter the enchanted hall ! "

XXVII.

" My hope, my heaven, my trust must be,
My gentle guide, in following thee."
He cross'd the threshold — and a clang
Of angry steel that instant rang.
To his bold brow his spirit rush'd,
But soon for vain alarm he blush'd,
When on the floor he saw display'd,
Cause of the din, a naked blade

Dropp'd from the sheath, that careless flung
Upon a stag's huge antlers swung;
For all around, the walls to grace,
Hung trophies of the fight or chase:
A target there, a bugle here,
A battle-axe, a hunting-spear,
And broadswords, bows, and arrows store,
With the tusk'd trophies of the boar.
Here grins the wolf as when he died,
And there the wild-cat's brindled hide
The frontlet of the elk adorns,
Or mantles o'er the bison's horns;
Pennons and flags defaced and stain'd,
That blackening streaks of blood retain'd,
And deer-skins, dappled, dun, and white,
With otter's fur and seal's unite,
In rude and uncouth tapestry all,
To garnish forth the sylvan hall.

XXVIII.

The wondering stranger round him gazed,
And next the fallen weapon raised: —
Few were the arms whose sinewy strength
Sufficed to stretch it forth at length,
And as the brand he poised and sway'd,
" I never knew but one," he said,
" Whose stalwart arm might brook to wield
A blade like this in battle-field."
She sigh'd, then smiled and took the word:
" You see the guardian champion's sword:
As light it trembles in his hand,
As in my grasp a hazel wand;
My sire's tall form might grace the part
Of Ferragus or Ascabart;[8]
But in the absent giant's hold
Are women now, and menials old."

XXIX.

The mistress of the mansion came,
Mature of age, a graceful dame;
Whose easy step and stately port
Had well become a princely court,
To whom, though more than kind-ed knew,
Young Ellen gave a mother's due.
Meet welcome to her guest she made,
And every courteous rite was paid,

That hospitality could claim,
Though all unask'd his birth and name.[9]
Much then the reverence to a guest,
That fellest foe might join the feast,
And from his deadliest foeman's door
Unquestion'd turn, the banquet o'er.
At length his rank the stranger names:—
The Knight of Snowdoun, James Fitz-
James;
Lord of a barren heritage,
Which his brave sires, from age to age,
By their good swords had held with toil;
His sire had fallen in such turmoil,
And he, God wot, was forced to stand
Oft for his right with blade in hand.
This morning, with Lord Moray's train,
He chased a stalwart stag in vain,
Outstripp'd his comrades, miss'd the deer,
Lost his good steed, and wander'd here.''

XXX.

Fain would the knight in turn require
The name and state of Ellen's sire.
Well show'd the elder lady's mien,
That courts and cities she had seen;
Ellen, though more her looks display'd
The simple grace of sylvan maid,
In speech and gesture, form and face,
Show'd she was come of gentle race.
'Twere strange, in ruder rank to find,
Such looks, such manners, and such
mind.
Each hint the Knight of Snowdoun gave,
Dame Margaret heard with silence grave;
Or Ellen, innocently gay,
Turn'd all inquiry light away: —
" Weird women we ! by dale and down
We dwell, afar from tower and town.
We stem the flood, we ride the blast,
On wandering knights our spells we cast;
While viewless minstrels touch the string,
'Tis thus our charmed rhymes we sing.''
She sung, and still a harp unseen
Fill'd up the symphony between.

XXXI.
SONG.

" Soldier, rest ! thy warfare o'er,
  Sleep the sleep that knows not breaking;
Dream of battled fields no more,
  Days of danger, nights of waking.

In our isle's enchanted hall,
  Hands unseen thy couch are strewing,
Fairy strains of music fall,
  Every sense in slumber dewing.
Soldier, rest ! thy warfare o'er,
Dream of fighting fields no more:
Sleep the sleep that knows not breaking.
Morn of toil, nor night of waking.

" No rude sound shall reach thine ear,
  Armor's clang, nor war-steed champing,
Trump nor pibroch summon here
  Mustering clan, or squadron tramping;
Yet the lark's shrill fife may come
  At the day-break from the fallow,
And the bittern sound his drum,
  Booming from the sedgy shallow.
Ruder sounds shall none be near,
Guards nor warders challenge here;
Here's no war-steed's neigh and champing,
Shouting clans, or squadrons stamping.''

XXXII.

She paused — then, blushing, led the
  lay
To grace the stranger of the day.
Her mellow notes awhile prolong
The cadence of the flowing song,
Till to her lips in measured frame
The minstrel verse spontaneous came:—

SONG CONTINUED.

" Huntsman, rest ! thy chase is done,
  While our slumb'rous spells assail ye,
Dream not, with the rising sun,
  Bugles here shall sound reveillé.
Sleep ! the deer is in his den;
  Sleep ! thy hounds are by thee lying;
Sleep ! nor dream in yonder glen,
  How thy gallant steed lay dying.
Huntsman, rest ! thy chase is done,
Think not of the rising sun,
For at dawning to assail ye,
Here no bugles sound reveillé.''

XXXIII.

The hall was clear'd — the stranger's bed
Was there of mountain heather spread,
Where oft a hundred guests had lain,
And dream'd their forest sports again.
But vainly did the heath-flower shed
Its moorland fragrance round his head;

Not Ellen's spell had lull'd to rest
The fever of his troubled breast.
In broken dreams the image rose
Of varied perils, pains, and woes:
His steed now flounders in the brake,
Now sinks his barge upon the lake;
Now leader of a broken host,
His standard falls, his honor's lost.
Then, — from my couch may heavenly
    might
Chase that worst phantom of the night ! —
Again return'd the scenes of youth,
Of confident undoubting truth;
Again his soul he interchanged
With friends whose hearts were long es-
    tranged.
They come, in dim procession led,
The cold, the faithless, and the dead;
As warm each hand, each brow as gay,
As if they parted yesterday.
And doubt distracts him at the view.
O, were his senses false or true?
Dream'd he of death, or broken vow,
Or is it all a vision now?

XXXIV.

At length, with Ellen in a grove
He seem'd to walk, and speak of love;
She listen'd with a blush and sigh,
His suit was warm, his hopes were high,
He sought her yielded hand to clasp,
And a cold gauntlet met his grasp:
The phantom's sex was changed and
    gone,
Upon its head a helmet shone;
Slowly enlarged to giant size,
With darken'd cheek and threatening
    eyes,
The grisly visage, stern and hoar,
To Ellen still a likeness bore. —
He woke, and panting with affright,
Recall'd the vision of the night.
The hearth's decaying brands were red,
And deep and dusky lustre shed,
Half showing, half concealing, all
The uncouth trophies of the hall.
Mid those the stranger fix'd his eye,
Where that huge falchion hung on high,
And thoughts on thoughts, a countless
    throng,
Rush'd, chasing countless thoughts along,
Until, the giddy whirl to cure,
He rose, and sought the moonshine pure.

XXXV.

The wild rose, eglantine, and broom,
Wafted around their rich perfume;
The birch-trees wept in fragrant balm,
The aspens slept beneath the calm;
The silver light, with quivering glance,
Play'd on the water's still expanse, —
Wild were the heart whose passion's sway
Could rage beneath the sober ray !
He felt its calm, that warrior guest,
While thus he commuued with his
    breast : —
" Why is it, at each turn I trace
Some memory of that exiled race !
Can I not mountain-maiden spy,
But she must bear the Douglas eye?
Can I not view a Highland brand,
But it must match the Douglas hand?
Can I not frame a fever'd dream,
But still the Douglas is the theme?
I'll dream no more — by manly mind
Not even in sleep is will resign'd.
My midnight orisons said o'er,
I'll turn to rest, and dream no more.''
His midnight orisons he told,
A prayer with every bead of gold.
Consign'd to heaven his cares and woes,
And sunk in undisturb'd repose;
Until the heath-cock shrilly crew,
And morning dawn'd on Benvenue.

CANTO SECOND.

THE ISLAND.

I.

At morn the black-cock trims his jetty
    wing,
    'Tis morning prompts the linnet's
        blithest lay,
All Nature's children feel the matin spring
    Of life reviving, with reviving day;
And while yon little bark glides down
    the bay,
    Wafting the stranger on his way again
Morn's genial influence roused a minstrel
    gray,
    And sweetly o'er the lake was heard
    thy strain,
Mix'd with the sounding harp, O white-
    hair'd Allan-Bane ! [10]

II.

SONG.

'Not faster yonder rowers' might
 Flings from their oars the spray,
Not faster yonder rippling bright,
That tracks the shallop's course in light,
 Melts in the lake away,
Than men from memory erase
 The benefits of former days;
Then, stranger, go! good speed the while,
Nor think again of the lonely isle.

'High place to thee in royal court,
 High place in battle line,
Good hawk and hound for sylvan sport,
Where beauty sees the brave resort,
 The honor'd meed be thine!
True be thy sword, thy friend sincere,
Thy lady constant, kind, and dear,
And lost in love and friendship's smile
Be memory of the lonely isle.

III.

SONG CONTINUED.

'But if beneath yon southern sky
 A plaided stranger roam,
Whose drooping crest and stifled sigh,
And sunken cheek and heavy eye,
 Pine for his Highland home;
Then, warrior, then be thine to show
The care that soothes a wanderer's woe;
Remember then thy hap erewhile,
A stranger in the lonely isle.

'Or if on life's uncertain main
 Mishap shall mar thy sail;
If faithful, wise, and brave in vain,
Woe, want, and exile thou sustain
 Beneath the fickle gale;
Waste not a sigh on fortune changed,
On thankless courts, or friends estranged,
But come where kindred worth shall smile,
To greet thee in the lonely isle.''

IV.

As died the sounds upon the tide,
The shallop reach'd the mainland side,
And ere his onward way he took,
The stranger cast a lingering look,
Where easily his eye might reach
The Harper on the islet beach,
Reclined against a blighted tree,
As wasted, gray, and worn as he.
To minstrel meditation given,
His reverend brow was raised to heaven,
As from the rising sun to claim
A sparkle of inspiring flame.
His hand, reclined upon the wire,
Seem'd watching the awakening fire;
So still he sate, as those who wait
Till judgment speak the doom of fate;
So still, as if no breeze might dare
To lift one lock of hoary hair;
So still, as life itself were fled,
In the last sound his harp had sped.

V.

Upon a rock with lichens wild,
Beside him Ellen sate and smiled. —
Smiled she to see the stately drake
Lead forth his fleet upon the lake,
While her vex'd spaniel from the beach
Bay'd at the prize beyond his reach?
Yet tell me, then, the maid who knows,
Why deepen'd on her cheek the rose? —
Forgive, forgive, Fidelity!
Perchance the maiden smiled to see
Yon parting lingerer wave adieu,
And stop and turn to wave anew;
And, lovely ladies, ere your ire
Condemn the heroine of my lyre,
Show me the fair would scorn to spy,
And prize such conquest of her eye!

VI.

While yet he loiter'd on the spot,
It seem'd as Ellen mark'd him not;
But when he turn'd him to the glade,
One courteous parting sign she made;
And after oft the Knight would say,
That not when prize of festal day
Was dealt him by the brightest fair
Who e'er wore jewel in her hair,
So highly did his bosom swell,
As at that simple mute farewell.
Now with a trusty mountain-guide,
And his dark stag-hounds by his side,
He parts — the maid, unconscious still,
Watch'd him wind slowly round the hill;
But when his stately form was hid,
The guardian in her bosom chid —

" Thy Malcolm! vain and selfish maid!"
'Twas thus upbraiding conscience said, —
" Not so had Malcolm idly hung
On the smooth phrase of southern tongue;
Not so had Malcolm strain'd his eye,
Another step than thine to spy.
Wake, Allan-Bane," aloud she cried,
To the old Minstrel by her side, —
" Arouse thee from thy moody dream!
I'll give thy harp heroic theme,
And warm thee with a noble name;
Pour forth the glory of the Græme!" [11]
Scarce from her lip the word had rush'd,
When deep the conscious maiden blush'd;
For of his clan, in hall and bower,
Young Malcolm Græme was held the
    flower.

VII.

The Minstrel waked his harp—three times
Arose the well-known martial chimes,
And thrice their high heroic pride
In melancholy murmurs died.
" Vainly thou bid'st, O noble maid,"
Clasping his wither'd hands, he said,
" Vainly thou bid'st me wake the strain,
Though all unwont to bid in vain.
Alas! than mine a mightier hand
Has tuned my harp, my strings has
    spann'd!
I touch the chords of joy, but low
And mournful answer notes of woe;
And the proud march, of which victors
    tread,
Sinks in the wailing for the dead.
O well for me, if mine alone
That dirge's deep prophetic tone!
If, as my tuneful fathers said,
This harp, which erst Saint Modan
    sway'd,[12]
Can thus its master's fate foretell,
Then welcome be the minstrel's knell!

VIII.

" But ah! dear lady, thus it sigh'd
The eve thy sainted mother died;
And such the sounds which, while I strove
To wake a lay of war or love,
Came marring all the festal mirth,
Appalling me who gave them birth,
And, disobedient to my call,
Wail'd loud through Bothwell's banner'd
    hall,

Ere Douglases, to ruin driven,[13]
Were exiled from their native heaven. —
Oh! if yet worse mishap and woe
My master's house must undergo,
Or aught but weal to Ellen fair
Brood in these accents of despair,
No future bard, sad Harp! shall fling
Triumph or rapture from thy string;
One short, one final strain shall flow,
Fraught with unutterable woe,
Then shiver'd shall thy fragments lie,
Thy master cast him down and die!"

IX.

Soothing she answer'd him: —" Assuage
Mine honor'd friend, the fears of age;
All melodies to thee are known,
That harp has rung, or pipe has blown,
In Lowland vale or Highland glen,
From Tweed to Spey—what marvel, then
At times, unbidden notes should rise,
Confusedly bound in memory's ties,
Entangling, as they rush along,
The war-march with the funeral song?—
Small ground is now for boding fear;
Obscure, but safe, we rest us here.
My sire, in native virtue great,
Resigning lordship, lands, and state,
Not then to fortune more resign'd
Than yonder oak might give the wind;
The graceful foliage storms may reave,
The noble stem they cannot grieve.
For me," — she stoop'd, and, looking
    round,
Pluck'd a blue hare-bell from the ground,
" For me, whose memory scarce conveys
An image of more splendid days,
This little flower, that loves the lea,
May well my simple emblem be;
It drinks heaven's dew as blithe as rose
That in the King's own garden grows;
And when I place it in my hair,
Allan, a bard is bound to swear
He ne'er saw coronet so fair."
Then playfully the chaplet wild
She wreath'd in her dark locks, and
    smiled.

X.

Her smile, her speech, with winning sway
Wiled the old harper's mood away.
With such a look as hermits throw,
When angels stoop to soothe their woe,

He gazed, till fond regret and pride
Thrill'd to a tear, then thus replied:—
' Loveliest and best! thou little know'st
The rank, the honors, thou hast lost!
O might I live to see thee grace,
In Scotland's court, thy birth-right place,
To see my favorite's step advance,
The lightest in the courtly dance,
The cause of every gallant's sigh,
And leading star of every eye,
And theme of every minstrel's art,
The lady of the Bleeding Heart!'' *—

XI.

' Fair dreams are these,'' the maiden
    cried
 Light was her accent, yet she sigh'd;)
' Yet is this mossy rock to me
Worth splendid chair and canopy;
Nor would my footsteps spring more gay
In courtly dance than blithe strathspey,
Nor half so pleased mine ear incline
To royal minstrel's lay as thine.
And then for suitors proud and high,
To bend before my conquering eye, —
Thou, flattering bard! thyself wilt say,
That grim Sir Roderick owns its sway.
The Saxon scourge, Clan-Alpine's pride,
The terror of Loch Lomond's side,
Would, at my suit, thou know'st, delay
A Lennox foray — for a day.'' —

XII.

The ancient bard her glee repress'd:—
'' Ill hast thou chosen theme for jest!
For who, through all this western wild,
Named Black Sir Roderick e'er, and
    smiled!
In Holy-Rood a knight he slew;[14]
I saw, when back the dirk he drew,
Courtiers give place before the stride
Of the undaunted homicide:
And since, though outlaw'd, hath his hand
Full sternly kept his mountain land.
Who else dared give — ah! woe the day,
That I such hated truth should say —
The Douglas, like a stricken deer,
Disown'd by every noble peer,[15]
Even the rude refuge we have here?
Alas, this wild marauding Chief
Alone might hazard our relief,

* The cognizance of the Douglas family.

And now thy maiden charms expand,
Looks for his guerdon in thy hand;
Full soon may dispensation sought,
To back his suit, from Rome be brought.
Then, though an exile on the hill,
Thy father, as the Douglas, still
Be held in reverence and fear;
And though to Roderick thou'rt so
    dear,
That thou might'st guide with silken
    thread,
Slave of thy will, this chieftain dread;
Yet, O loved maid, thy mirth refrain!
Thy hand is on a lion's mane.'' —

XIII.

'' Minstrel,'' the maid replied, and high
Her father's soul glanced from her eye,
'' My debts to Roderick's house I know:
All that a mother could bestow,
To Lady Margaret's care I owe,
Since first an orphan in the wild
She sorrow'd o'er her sister's child;
To her brave chieftain son, from ire
Of Scotland's king who shrouds my sire,
A deeper, holier debt is owed;
And, could I pay it with my blood,
Allan! Sir Roderick should command
My blood, my life, — but not my hand.
Rather will Ellen Douglas dwell
A votaress in Maronnan's cell;[16]
Rather through realms beyond the sea,
Seeking the world's cold charity,
Where ne'er was spoke a Scottish word
And ne'er the name of Douglas heard,
An outcast pilgrim will she rove,
Than wed the man she cannot love.

XIV.

'' Thou shakest, good friend, thy tresses
    gray, —
That pleading look, what can it say
But what I own? — I grant him brave,
But wild as Bracklinn's thundering
    wave;[17]
And generous — save vindictive mood,
Or jealous transport, chafe his blood.
I grant him true to friendly band,
As his claymore is to his hand;
But O! that very blade of steel
More mercy for a foe would feel:
I grant him liberal, to fling
Among his clan the wealth they bring,

When back by lake and glen they wind,
And in the Lowland leave behind,
Where once some pleasant hamlet stood,
A mass of ashes slaked with blood.
The hand that for my father fought,
I honor, as his daughter ought;
But can I clasp it reeking red
From peasants slaughter'd in their shed?
No! wildly while his virtues gleam,
They make his passions darker seem,
And flash along his spirit high,
Like lightning o'er the midnight sky.
While yet a child, — and children know,
Instinctive taught, the friend and foe, —
I shudder'd at his brow of gloom,
His shadowy plaid, and sable plume;
A maiden grown, I ill could bear
His haughty mien and lordly air:
But, if thou join'st a suitor's name,
In serious mood, to Roderick's name,
I thrill with anguish! or, if e'er
A Douglas knew the word, with fear.
To change such odious theme were best,—
What think'st thou of our stranger
    guest?" —

XV.

"What think I of him? — woe the while
That brought such wanderer to our isle!
Thy father's battle-brand, of yore
For Tine-man forged by fairy lore,[18]
What time he leagued, no longer foes,
His border spears with Hotspur's bows,
Did, self-unscabbarded, foreshow
The footstep of a secret foe.[19]
If courtly spy hath harbor'd here,
What may we for the Douglas fear?
What for this island, deem'd of old
Clan-Alpine's last and surest hold?
If neither spy nor foe, I pray,
What yet may jealous Roderick say?
— Nay, wave not thy disdainful head,
Bethink thee of the discord dread
That kindled, when at Beltane game
Thou ledst the dance with Malcolm
    Græme:
Still, though thy sire the peace renew'd,
Smoulders in Roderick's breast the feud;
Beware! — But hark, what sounds are
    these?
My dull ears catch no faltering breeze,
No weeping birch nor aspens wake,
Nor breath is dimpling in the lake,

Still is the canna's* hoary beard,
Yet, by my minstrel faith, I heard —
And hark again! some pipe of war
Sends the bold pibroch from afar."

XVI.

Far up the lengthen'd lake were spied
Four darkening specks upon the tide,
That, slow enlarging on the view,
Four mann'd and masted barges grew,
And, bearing downwards from Glengyle
Steer'd full upon the lonely isle;
The point of Brianchoil they pass'd,
And, to the windward, as they cast,
Against the sun they gave to shine
The bold Sir Roderick's banner'd Pine.
Nearer and nearer as they bear,
Spears, pikes, and axes flash in air.
Now might you see the Tartans brave,
And plaids and plumage dance and wave
Now see the bonnets sink and rise,
As his tough oar the rower plies;
See, flashing at each sturdy stroke,
The wave ascending into smoke;
See the proud pipers on the bow,
And mark the gaudy streamers flow
From their loud chanters† down, and
    sweep
The furrow'd bosom of the deep,
As, rushing through the lake amain,
They plied the ancient Highand strain.

XVII.

Ever, as on they bore, more loud
And louder rung the pibroch proud.
At first the sound, by distance tame,
Mellow'd along the waters came,
And, lingering long by cape and bay,
Wail'd every harsher note away;
Then bursting bolder on the ear,
The clan's shrill Gathering they could
    hear;
Those thrilling sounds, that call the might
Of old Clan-Alpine to the fight.[20]
Thick beat the rapid notes, as when
The mustering hundreds shake the glen.
And, hurrying at the signal dread,
The batter'd earth returns their tread.
Then prelude light, of livelier tone,
Express'd their merry marching on,

* Cotton grass.
† The pipe of the bagpipe.

re peal of closing battle rose,
With mingled outcry, shrieks, and blows;
And mimic din of stroke and ward,
As broadsword upon target jarr'd;
And groaning pause, ere yet again,
Condensed, the battle yell'd amain;
The rapid charge, the rallying shout,
Retreat borne headlong into rout,
And bursts of triumph, to declare
Clan-Alpine's conquest — all were there.
Nor ended thus the strain; but slow,
sunk in a moan prolong'd and low,
And changed the conquering clarion
swell,
'or wild lament o'er those that fell.

XVIII.

The war-pipes ceased: but lake and hill
Were busy with their echoes still;
And, when they slept, a vocal strain
Bade their hoarse chorus wake again,
While loud a hundred clansmen raise
Their voices in their Chieftain's praise.
Each boatman, bending to his oar,
With measured sweep the burden bore,
In such wild cadence, as the breeze
Makes through December's leafless trees.
The chorus first could Allan know,
Roderigh Vich Alpine, ho! iro!"
And near, and nearer as they row'd,
Distinct the martial ditty flow'd.

XIX.

BOAT SONG.

Hail to the Chief who in triumph advances!
Honor'd and bless'd be the ever-green
Pine!
Long may the tree, in his banner that
glances,
Flourish, the shelter and grace of our
line.
Heaven send it happy dew,
Earth lend it sap anew,
Gayly to bourgeon, and broadly to grow,
While every Highland glen
Sends our shout back agen,
"Roderigh Vich Alpine dhu, ho!
iero!" [21]

urs is no sapling, chance-sown by the
fountain,
Blooming at Beltane, in winter to fade;

When the whirlwind has stripp'd every
leaf on the mountain,
The more shall Clan-Alpine exult in
her shade.
Moor'd in the rifted rock,
Proof to the tempest's shock,
Firmer he roots him the ruder it blow;
Menteith and Breadalbane, then,
Echo his praise agen,
"Roderigh Vich Alpine dhu, ho!
iero!"

XX.

Proudly our pibroch * has thrill'd in Glen
Fruin,
And Bannochar's groans to our slogan †
replied;
Glen Luss and Ross-dhu, they are smok-
ing in ruin,
And the best of Loch Lomond lie dead
on her side.
Widow and Saxon maid
Long shall lament our raid,
Think of Clan-Alpine with fear and
with woe;
Lennox and Leven-glen
Shake when they hear agen,
"Roderigh Vich Alpine dhu, ho!
iero!"

Row, vassals, row, for the pride of the
Highlands!
Stretch to your oars for the ever-green
Pine!
O! that the rosebud that graces yon
islands,
Were wreathed in a garland around
him to twine!
O that some seedling gem,
Worthy such noble stem,
Honor'd and bless'd in their shadow
might grow!
Loud should Clan-Alpine then
Ring from the deepmost glen,
"Roderigh Vich Alpine dhu, ho!
iero!"

XXI.

With all her joyful female band,
Had Lady Margaret sought the strand,

---

* Bagpipe air belonging to a clan.
† *Slogan*, a war-cry.

Loose on the breeze their tresses flew,
And high their snowy arms they threw,
As echoing back with shrill acclaim,
And chorus wild, the Chieftain's name;
While, prompt to please, with mother's art,
The darling passion of his heart,
The Dame call'd Ellen to the strand,
To greet her kinsman ere he land: —
" Come, loiterer, come ! a Douglas thou,
And shun to wreathe a victor's brow? " —
Reluctantly and slow, the maid
The unwelcome summoning obey'd,
And, when a distant bugle rung,
In the mid-path aside she sprung: —
" List, Allan-Bane ! From mainland cast
I hear my father's signal blast.
Be ours," she cried, " the skiff to guide,
And waft him from the mountain side."
Then, like a sunbeam, swift and bright,
She darted to her shallop light,
And, eagerly, while Roderick scann'd,
For her dear form, his mother's band,
The islet far behind her lay,
And she had landed in the bay.

XXII.

Some feelings are to mortals given,
With less of earth in them than heaven.
And if there be a human tear
From passion's dross refined and clear,
A tear so limpid and so meek,
It would not stain an angel's cheek,
'Tis that which pious fathers shed
Upon a duteous daughter's head !
And as the Douglas to his breast
His darling Ellen closely press'd,
Such holy drops her tresses steep'd,
Though 'twas a hero's eye that weep'd,
Nor while on Ellen's faltering tongue
Her filial welcomes crowded hung,
Mark'd she, that fear (affection's proof)
Still held a graceful youth aloof;
No ! not till Douglas named his name,
Although the youth was Malcolm Græme.

XXIII.

Allan, with wistful look the while,
Mark'd Roderick landing on the isle;
His master piteously he eyed,
Then gazed upon the Chieftain's pride.
Then dash'd, with hasty hand, away
From his dimm'd eye the gathering spray;

And Douglas, as his hand he laid
On Malcolm's shoulder, kindly said: —
" Canst thou, young friend, no meaning spy
In my poor follower's glistening eye?
I'll tell thee: — he recalls the day,
When in my praise he led the lay
O'er the arch'd gate of Bothwell proud,
While many a minstrel answer'd loud,
When Percy's Norman pennon, won
In bloody field, before me shone,
And twice ten knights, the least a name
As mighty as yon Chief may claim,
Gracing my pomp, behind me came.
Yet trust me, Malcolm, not so proud
Was I of all that marshall'd crowd,
Though the waned crescent own'd m might,
And in my train troop'd lord and knight
Though Blantyre hymn'd her holiest lays
And Bothwell's bards flung back my praise
As when this old man's silent tear,
And this poor maid's affection dear,
A welcome give more kind and true,
Then aught my better fortunes knew.
Forgive, my friend, a father's boast,
O ! it out-beggars all I lost ! "

XXIV.

Delightful praise ! — Like summer rose,
That brighter in the dew-drop glows,
The bashful maiden's cheek appear'd,
For Douglas spoke, and Malcolm heard
The flush of shame-faced joy to hide,
The hounds, the hawk, her cares divide
The loved caresses of the maid
The dogs with crouch and whimper paid
And, at her whistle, on her hand
The falcon took her favorite stand,
Closed his dark wing, relax'd his eye,
Nor, though unhooded, sought to fly.
And, trust, while in such guise she stood
Like fabled Goddess of the wood,
That if a father's partial thought
O'erweigh'd her worth and beauty aught
Well might the lover's judgment fail
To balance with a juster scale;
For with each secret glance he stole,
The fond enthusiast sent his soul.

XXV.

Of stature tall, and slender frame,
But firmly knit, was Malcolm Græme.

The belted plaid and tartan hose
Did ne'er more graceful limbs disclose;
His flaxen hair of sunny hue,
Curl'd closely round his bonnet blue.
Train'd to the chase, his eagle eye
The ptarmigan in snow could spy:
Each pass, by mountain, lake, and heath,
He knew, through Lennox and Menteith:
Vain was the bound of dark-brown doe,
When Malcolm bent his sounding bow,
And scarce that doe, though wing'd with fear,
Outstripp'd in speed the mountaineer:
Right up Ben-Lomond could he press,
And not a sob his toil confess.
His form accorded with a mind
Lively and ardent, frank and kind;
A blither heart, till Ellen came,
Did never love nor sorrow tame;
It danced as lightsome in his breast,
As play'd the feather on his crest.
Yet friends who nearest knew the youth,
His scorn of wrong, his zeal for truth,
And bards, who saw his features bold,
When kindled by the tales of old,
Said, were that youth to manhood grown,
Not long should Roderick Dhu's renown
Be foremost voiced by mountain fame,
But quail to that of Malcolm Græme.

XXVI.

Now back they wend their watery way,
And, " O my sire!" did Ellen say,
' Why urge thy chase so far astray?
And why so late return'd? And why — "
The rest was in her sparkling eye.
" My child, the chase I follow far;
'Tis mimicry of noble war,
And with that gallant pastime reft,
Were all of Douglas I have left.
I met young Malcolm as I stray'd
Far eastward, in Glenfinlas' shade,
Nor stray'd I safe: for, all around,
Hunters and horsemen scour'd the ground.
This youth, though still a royal ward,
Risk'd life and land to be my guard,
And through the passes of the wood,
Guided my steps not unpursued;
And Roderick shall his welcome make,
Despite old spleen, for Douglas' sake.
Then must he seek Strath-Endrick glen,
Nor peril aught for me agen."

XXVII.

Sir Roderick, who to meet them came,
Redden'd at sight of Malcolm Græme,
Yet, not in action, word, or eye,
Fail'd aught in hospitality.
In talk and sport they wiled away
The morning of that summer day;
But at high noon a courier light
Held secret parley with the knight,
Whose moody aspect soon declared,
That evil were the news he heard.
Deep thought seem'd toiling in his head:
Yet was the evening banquet made,
Ere he assembled round the flame,
His mother, Douglas, and the Græme,
And Ellen, too; then cast around
His eyes, then fix'd them on the ground,
As studying phrase that might avail
Best to convey unpleasant tale.
Long with his dagger's hilt he play'd,
Then raised his haughty brow and said: —

XXVIII.

" Short be my speech, — nor time affords,
Nor my plain temper, glozing words.
Kinsman and father, — if such name
Douglas vouchsafe to Roderick's claim;
Mine honored mother; — Ellen — why,
My cousin, turn away thine eye? —
And Græme; in whom I hope to know
Full soon a noble friend or foe,
When age shall give thee thy command,
And leading in thy native land, —
List all! — The King's vindictive pride
Boasts to have tamed the Border-side,
Where chiefs, with hound and hawk who came
To share their monarch's sylvan game,
Themselves in bloody toils were snared;
And when the banquet they prepared,
And wide their loyal portals flung,
O'er their own gateway struggling hung.
Loud cries their blood from Meggat's mead,
From Yarrow braes, and banks of Tweed,
Where the lone streams of Ettrick glide,
And from the silver Teviot's side;
The dales, where martial clans did ride,
Are now one sheep-walk, waste and wide.
This tyrant of the Scottish throne,
So faithless and so ruthless known,
Now hither comes; his end the same,
The same pretext of sylvan game;

What grace for Highland Chiefs, judge ye
By fate of Border chivalry.
Yet more; amid Glenfinlas green,
Douglas, thy stately form was seen.
This by espial sure I know;
Your counsel in the streight I show."

XXIX.

Ellen and Margaret fearfully
Sought comfort in each other's eye,
Then turn'd their ghastly look, each one,
This to her sire — that to her son.
The hasty color went and came
In the bold cheek of Malcolm Græme,
But from his glance it well appear'd,
'Twas but for Ellen that he fear'd;
While sorrowful, but undismay'd,
The Douglas thus his counsel said: —
"Brave Roderick, though the tempest roar,
It may but thunder and pass o'er;
Nor will I here remain an hour,
To draw the lightning on thy bower;
For well thou know'st, at this gray head
The royal bolt were fiercest sped.
For thee, who, at thy King's command,
Canst aid him with a gallant band,
Submission, homage, humbled pride,
Shall turn the Monarch's wrath aside.
Poor remnants of the Bleeding Heart,
Ellen and I will seek, apart,
The refuge of some forest cell,
There, like the hunted quarry, dwell,
Till on the mountain and the moor,
The stern pursuit be pass'd and o'er."

XXX.

"No, by mine honor," Roderick said,
"So help me, heaven, and my good blade;
No, never! Blasted be yon Pine,
My fathers' ancient crest and mine,
If from its shade in danger part
The lineage of the Bleeding Heart!
Hear my blunt speech: Grant me this maid
To wife, thy council to mine aid;
To Douglas, leagued with Roderick Dhu,
Will friends and allies flock enow;
Like cause of doubt, distrust, and grief,
Will bind to us each Western Chief.
When the loud pipes my bridal tell,
The Links of Forth shall hear the knell,
The guards shall start in Stirling's porch;
And, when I light the nuptial torch,

A thousand villages in flames,
Shall scare the slumbers of King James!
— Nay, Ellen, blench not thus away,
And, mother, cease these signs I pray;
I meant not all my heat might say. —
Small need of inroad, or of fight,
When the sage Douglas may unite
Each mountain clan in friendly band,
To guard the passes of their land,
Till the foil'd king, from pathless glen,
Shall bootless turn him home agen."

XXXI.

There are who have, at midnight hour,
In slumber scaled a dizzy tower,
And, on the verge that beetled o'er
The ocean-tide's incessant roar,
Dream'd calmly out their dangerous
      dream;
Till waken'd by the morning beam;
When, dazzled by the eastern glow,
Such startler cast his glance below,
And saw unmeasured depth around,
And heard unintermitted sound,
And thought the battled fence so frail,
It waved like cobweb in the gale;
Amid his senses' giddy wheel,
Did he not desperate impulse feel,
Headlong to plunge himself below,
And meet the worst his fears foreshow? —
Thus, Ellen, dizzy and astound,
As sudden ruin yawn'd around,
By crossing terrors wildly toss'd,
Still for the Douglas fearing most,
Could scarce the desperate thought with-
      stand
To buy his safety with her hand.

XXXII.

Such purpose dread could Malcolm spy
In Ellen's quivering lip and eye,
And eager rose to speak — but ere
His tongue could hurry forth his fear,
Had Douglas mark'd the hectic strife,
Where death seemed combating with life;
For to her cheek, in feverish flood,
One instant rush'd the throbbing blood,
Then ebbing back, with sudden sway,
Left its domain as wan as clay.
"Roderick, enough! enough!" he cried,
"My daughter cannot be thy bride;
Not that the blush to wooer dear,
Nor paleness that of maiden fear.

It may not be — forgive her, Chief,
Nor hazard aught for our relief.
Against his sovereign, Douglas ne'er
Will level a rebellious spear.
'Twas I that taught his youthful hand
To rein a steed and wield a brand;
I see him yet, the princely boy!
Not Ellen more my pride and joy;
I love him still, despite my wrongs,
By hasty wrath, and slanderous tongues.
O seek the grace you well may find,
Without a cause to mine combined."

XXXIII.

Twice through the hall the Chieftain strode;
The waving of his tartans broad,
And darken'd brow, where wounded pride
With ire and disappointment vied,
Seem'd, by the torch's gloomy light,
Like the ill Demon of the night,
Stooping his pinions' shadowy sway
Upon the nighted pilgrim's way:
But, unrequited Love! thy dart
Plunged deepest its envenom'd smart,
And Roderick, with thine anguish stung,
At length the hand of Douglas wrung,
While eyes, that mock'd at tears before,
With bitter drops were running o'er.
The death-pangs of long-cherish'd hope
Scarce in that ample breast had scope,
But, struggling with his spirit proud,
Convulsive heaved its checker'd shroud,
While every sob — so mute were all —
Was heard distinctly through the hall.
The son's despair, the mother's look,
Ill might the gentle Ellen brook;
She rose, and to her side there came,
To aid her parting steps, the Græme.

XXXIV.

Then Roderick from the Douglas broke —
As flashes flame through sable smoke,
Kindling its wreaths, long, dark, and low,
To one broad blaze of ruddy glow,
So the deep anguish of despair
Burst, in fierce jealousy, to air.
With stalwart grasp his hand he laid
On Malcolm's breast and belted plaid: —
"Back, beardless boy!" he sternly said,
"Back, minion! hold'st thou thus at naught
The lesson I so lately taught?

This roof, the Douglas, and that maid,
Thank thou for punishment delay'd."
Eager as greyhound on his game,
Fiercely with Roderick grappled Græme.
"Perish my name, if aught afford
Its Chieftain safety save his sword!"
Thus, as they strove, their desperate hand
Griped to the dagger or the brand,
And death had been — but Douglas rose,
And thrust between the struggling foes
His giant strength: — "Chieftains, forego!
I hold the first who strikes, my foe. —
Madmen, forbear your frantic jar!
What! is the Douglas fall'n so far,
His daughter's hand is deem'd the spoil
Of such dishonorable broil!"
Sullen and slowly they unclasp,
As struck with shame, their desperate grasp,
And each upon his rival glared,
With foot advanced, and blade half-bared.

XXXV.

Ere yet the brands aloft were flung,
Margaret on Roderick's mantle hung,
And Malcolm heard his Ellen's scream,
As falter'd through terrific dream.
Then Roderick plunged in sheath his sword,
And veil'd his wrath in scornful word: —
"Rest safe till morning; pity 'twere
Such cheek should feel the midnight air!
Then mayest thou to James Stuart tell,
Roderick will keep the lake and fell,
Nor lackey with his freeborn clan,
The pageant pomp of earthly man.
More would he of Clan-Alpine know,
Thou canst our strength and passes show. —
Malise, what ho!" — his henchman * came;
"Give our safe-conduct to the Græme."
Young Malcolm answer'd, calm and bold,
"Fear nothing for thy favorite hold;
The spot an angel deign'd to grace
Is bless'd, though robbers haunt the place.
Thy churlish courtesy for those
Reserve, who fear to be thy foes.

* A henchman was the confidential attendant or gilly of a chief. His standing behind his lord at festivals originated the name of haunchman or henchman.

As safe to me the mountain way
At midnight as in blaze of day,
Though with his boldest at his back
Even Roderick Dhu beset the track. —
Brave Douglas, — lovely Ellen, — nay,
Naught here of parting will I say.
Earth does not hold a lonesome glen,
So secret, but we meet agen. —
Chieftain ! we too shall find an hour."
He said, and left the sylvan bower.

Old Allan follow'd to the strand,
(Such was the Douglas's command,)
And anxious told, how, on the morn,
The stern Sir Roderick deep had sworn,
The Fiery Cross should circle o'er
Dale, glen, and valley, down, and
   moor.
Much were the peril to the Græme,
From those who to the signal came;
Far up the lake 'twere safest land,
Himself would row him to the strand.
He gave his counsel to the wind,
While Malcolm did, unheeding, bind,
Round dirk and pouch and broadsword
   roll'd,
His ample plaid in tighten'd fold,
And stripp'd his limbs to such array,
As best might suit the watery way, —

XXXVII.

Then spoke abrupt : " Farewell to thee,
Pattern of old fidelity ! "
The Minstrel's hand he kindly press'd, —
" O ! could I point a place of rest !
My sovereign holds in ward my land,
My uncle leads my vassal band;
To tame his foes, his friends to aid,
Poor Malcolm has but heart and blade.
Yet, if there be one faithful Græme,
Who loves the Chieftain of his name,
Not long shall honor'd Douglas dwell,
Like hunted stag in mountain cell;
Nor, ere yon pride-swoll'n robber dare —
I may not give the rest to air !
Tell Roderick Dhu, I owe him naught,
Not the poor service of a boat,
To waft me to yon mountain-side."
Then plunged he in the flashing tide.
Bold o'er the flood his head he bore,
And stoutly steer'd him from the shore;
And Allan strain'd his anxious eye,
Far mid the lake his form to spy.

Darkening across each puny wave,
To which the moon her silver gave,
Fast as the cormorant could skim,
The swimmer plied each active limb;
Then landing in the moonlight dell,
Loud shouted of his weal to tell.
The Minstrel heard the far halloo,
And joyful from the shore withdrew.

CANTO THIRD.

THE GATHERING.

I.

TIME rolls his ceaseless course. The race
   of yore,
   Who danced our infancy upon their
    knee,
And told our marvelling boyhood legends
   store,
   Of their strange ventures happ'd by
    land or sea,
How are they blotted from the things
   that be !
   How few, all weak, and wither'd of
    their force,
Wait on the verge of dark eternity,
   Like stranded wrecks, the tide return-
    ing hoarse,
To sweep them from our sight ! Time
   rolls his ceaseless course.

Yet live there still who can remember
   well,
   How, when a mountain chief his bugle
    blew,
Both field and forest, dingle, cliff, and
   dell,
   And solitary heath, the signal knew;
And fast the faithful clan around him
   drew,
   What time the warning note was
    keenly wound,
What time aloft their kindred banner flew,
   While clamorous war-pipes yell'd the
    gathering sound,
And while the Fiery Cross glanced, like
   a meteor, round.[22]

II.

The Summer dawn's reflected hue
To purple changed Loch Katrine blue;

Mildly and soft the western breeze
Just kiss'd the lake, just stirr'd the
      trees.
And the pleased lake, like maiden coy,
Trembled but dimpled not for joy;
The mountain-shadows on her breast
Were neither broken nor at rest;
In bright uncertainty they lie,
Like future joys, to Fancy's eye.
The water-lily to the light
Her chalice rear'd of silver bright;
The doe awoke, and to the lawn,
Begemm'd with dew-drops, led her fawn;
The gray mist left the mountain-side,
The torrent show'd its glistening pride;
Invisible in flecked sky,
The lark sent down her revelry;
The blackbird and the speckled thrush
Good-morrow gave from brake and bush;
In answer coo'd the cushat dove
Her notes of peace, and rest, and love.

III.

No thought of peace, no thought of rest,
Assuaged the storm in Roderick's breast.
With sheathed broadsword in his hand,
Abrupt he paced the islet strand,
And eyed the rising sun, and laid
His hand on his impatient blade.
Beneath a rock, his vassals' care
Was prompt the ritual to prepare,
With deep and deathful meaning fraught;
For such Antiquity had taught
Was preface meet, ere yet abroad
The Cross of Fire should take its road.
The shrinking band stood oft aghast
At the impatient glance he cast; —
Such glance the mountain-eagle threw,
As from the cliffs of Benvenue,
She spread her dark sails on the wind,
And, high in middle heaven, reclined,
With her broad shadow on the lake,
Silenced the warblers of the brake.

IV.

A heap of wither'd boughs was piled,
Of juniper and rowan wild,
Mingled with shivers from the oak,
Rent by the lightning's recent stroke.
Brian, the Hermit, by it stood,
Barefooted, in his frock and hood.
His grizzled beard and matted hair
Obscured a visage of despair;

His naked arms and legs, seam'd o'er,
The scars of frantic penance bore.
That monk, of savage form and face,[23]
The impending danger of his race
Had drawn from deepest solitude,
Far in Benharrow's bosom rude.
Not his the mien of Christian priest,
But Druid's, from the grave released,
Whose harden'd heart and eye might
      brook
On human sacrifice to look;
And much, 'twas said, of heathen lore
Mix'd in the charms he mutter'd o'er.
The hallow'd creed gave only worse
And deadlier emphasis of curse;
No peasant sought that Hermit's prayer,
His cave the pilgrim shunn'd with care,
The eager huntsman knew his bound,
And in mid chase call'd off his hound;
Or if, in lonely glen or strath,
The desert-dweller met his path,
He pray'd, and sign'd the cross between,
While terror took devotion's mien.

v.

Of Brian's birth strange tales were told;[24]
His mother watch'd a midnight fold,
Built deep within a dreary glen,
Where scatter'd lay the bones of men,
In some forgotten battle slain,
And bleach'd by drifting wind and rain.
It might have tamed a warrior's heart,
To view such mockery of his art!
The knot-grass fetter'd there the hand,
Which once could burst an iron band;
Beneath the broad and ample bone,
That buckler'd heart to fear unknown,
A feeble and a timorous guest,
The field-fare framed her lowly nest,
There the slow blind-worm left his slime,
On the fleet limbs that mock'd at time;
And there, too, lay the leader's skull,
Still wreathed with chaplet, flush'd and full,
For heath-bell with her purple bloom
Supplied the bonnet and the plume.
All night, in this sad glen, the maid
Sate, shrouded in her mantle's shade:
— She said, no shepherd sought her side,
No hunter's hand her snood untied,
Yet ne'er again to braid her hair
The virgin snood did Alice wear;[25]
Gone was her maiden glee and sport,
Her maiden girdle all too short,

Nor sought she, from that fatal night,
Or holy church or blessed rite,
But lock'd her secret in her breast,
And died in travail, unconfess'd.

VI.

Alone, among his young compeers,
Was Brian from his infant years;
A moody and heart-broken boy,
Estranged from sympathy and joy,
Bearing each taunt which careless tongue
On his mysterious lineage flung.
Whole nights he spent by moonlight pale,
To wood and stream his hap to wail,
Till, frantic, he as truth received
What of his birth the crowd believed,
And sought, in mist and meteor fire,
To meet and know his Phantom Sire!
In vain, to soothe his wayward fate,
The cloister oped her pitying gate;
In vain, the learning of the age
Unclasp'd the sable-letter'd page;
Even in its treasures he could find
Food for the fever of his mind.
Eager he read whatever tells
Of magic, cabala, and spells,
And every dark pursuit allied
To curious and presumptuous pride;
Till with fired brain and nerves o'erstrung,
And heart with mystic horrors wrung,
Desperate he sought Benharrow's den,
And hid him from the haunts of men.

VII.

The desert gave him visions wild,
Such as might suit the Spectre's child.
Where with black cliffs the torrents toil,
He watch'd the wheeling eddies boil,
Till, from their foam, his dazzled eyes
Beheld the River Demon rise;
The mountain mist took form and limb,
Of noontide hag, or goblin grim;
The midnight wind came wild and dread,
Swell'd with the voices of the dead;
Far on the future battle-heath
His eye beheld the ranks of death:
Thus the lone Seer, from mankind hurl'd,
Shaped forth a disembodied world.
One lingering sympathy of mind
Still bound him to the mortal kind;
The only parent he could claim
Of ancient Alpine's lineage came.

Late had he heard, in prophet's dream,
The fatal Ben-Shie's boding scream;[26]
Sounds, too, had come in midnight blast,
Of charging steeds, careering fast
Along Benharrow's shingly side,
Where mortal horsemen ne'er might
　　　ride;[27]
The thunderbolt had split the pine, —
All augur'd ill to Alpine's line.
He girt his loins, and came to show
The signals of impending woe,
And now stood prompt to bless or ban,
As bade the Chieftain of his clan.

VIII.

'Twas all prepared:—and from the rock,
A goat, the patriarch of the flock,
Before the kindling pile was laid,
And pierced by Roderick's ready blade.
Patient the sickening victim eyed
The life-blood ebb in crimson tide,
Down his clogg'd beard and shaggy limb,
Till darkness glazed his eyeballs dim.
The grisly priest, with murmuring prayer,
A slender crosslet fram'd with care,
A cubit's length in measure due;
The shaft and limbs were rods of yew,
Whose parents in Inch-Cailliach wave
Their shadows o'er Clan-Alpine's grave,
And, answering Lomond's breezes deep,
Soothe many a chieftain's endless sleep.
The Cross, thus form'd, he held on high,
With wasted hand, and haggard eye,
And strange and mingled feelings woke,
While his anathema he spoke: —

IX.

"Woe to the clansman, who shall view
This symbol of sepulchral yew,
Forgetful that its branches grew
Where weep the heavens their holiest dew,
　　　On Alpine's dwelling low!
Deserter of his Chieftain's trust,
He ne'er shall mingle with their dust,
But, from his sires and kindred thrust,
Each clansman's execration just
　　　Shall doom him wrath and woe!"
He paused;—the word the vassals took,
With forward step and fiery look,
On high their naked brands they shook,
Their clattering targets wildly strook;
　　　And first in murmur low,

Then, like the billow in his course,
That far to seaward finds his source,
And flings to shore his muster'd force,
Burst, with loud roar, their answer hoarse,
    " Woe to the traitor, woe ! "
Ben-an's gray scalp the accents knew,
The joyous wolf from covert drew,
The exulting eagle scream'd afar, —
They knew the voice of Alpine's war.

X.

The shout was hush'd on lake and fell,
The Monk resumed his mutter'd spell :
Dismal and low its accent came,
The while he scathed the Cross with
    flame,
And the few words that reach'd the air,
Although the holiest name was there,
Had more of blasphemy than prayer.
But when he shook above the crowd
Its kindled points, he spoke aloud :—
" Woe to the wretch who fails to rear
At this dread sign the ready spear !
For, as the flames this symbol sear,
His home, the refuge of his fear,
    A kindred fate shall know ;
Far o'er its roof the volumed flame
Clan-Alpine's vengeance shall proclaim,
While maids and matrons on his name
Shall call down wretchedness and shame,
    And infamy and woe."
Then rose the cry of females, shrill
As goss-hawk's whistle on the hill,
Denouncing misery and ill,
Mingled with childhood's babbling trill
    Of curses stammer'd slow ;
Answering, with imprecation dread :—
" Sunk be his home in embers red !
And cursed be the meanest shed
That e'er shall hide the houseless head,
    We doom to want and woe ! "
A sharp and shrieking echo gave,
Coir-Uriskin, thy goblin cave !
And the gray pass where birches wave,
    On Beala-nam-bo.

XI.

Then deeper paused the priest anew,
And hard his laboring breath he drew,
While, with set teeth and clenched hand,
And eyes that glow'd like fiery brand,
He meditated curse more dread,
And deadlier, on the clansman's head,

Who, summon'd to his Chieftain's aid,
The signal saw and disobey'd.
The crosslet's points of sparkling wood,
He quench'd among the bubbling blood,
And, as again the sign he rear'd,
Hollow and hoarse his voice was heard :—
" When flits this Cross from man to man,
Vich-Alpine's summons to his clan,
Burst be the ear that fails to heed !
Palsied the foot that shuns to speed !
May ravens tear the careless eyes,
Wolves make the coward heart their
    prize !
As sinks that blood-stream in the earth,
So may his heart's-blood drench his
    hearth !
As dies in hissing gore the spark,
Quench thou his light, destruction dark,
And be the grace to him denied,
Bought by this sign to all beside ! "
He ceased ; no echo gave agen
The murmur of the deep " Amen."

XII.

Then Roderick, with impatient look,
From Brian's hand the symbol took :
" Speed, Malise, speed ! " he said, and
    gave
The crosslet to his henchman brave.
" The muster-place be Lanrick mead —
Instant the time — speed, Malise, speed ! "
Like heath-bird when the hawks pursue,
A barge across Loch Katrine flew ;
High stood the henchman on the prow ;
So rapidly the barge-men row,
The bubbles, where they launch'd the boat,
Were all unbroken and afloat,
Dancing in foam and ripple still,
When it had near'd the mainland hill ;
And from the silver beach's side
Still was the prow three fathom wide,
When lightly bounded to the land
The messenger of blood and brand.

XIII.

Speed, Malise, speed ! the dun deer's hide
On fleeter foot was never tied.[28]
Speed, Malise, speed ! such cause of haste
Thine active sinews never braced.
Bend 'gainst the steepy hill thy breast,
Burst down like torrent from its crest ;
With short and springing footstep pass
The trembling bog and false morass,

Across the brook like roebuck bound,
And thread the brake like questing hound;
The crag is high, the scaur is deep,
Yet shrink not from the desperate leap:
Parch'd are thy burning lips and brow,
Yet by the fountain pause not now;
Herald of battle, fate, and fear,
Stretch onward in thy fleet career!
The wounded hind thou track'st not
      now,
Pursuest not maid through greenwood
      bough,
Nor pliest thou now thy flying pace,
With rivals in the mountain race;
But danger, death, and warrior deed,
Are in thy course — speed, Malise, speed!

XIV.

Fast as the fatal symbol flies,
In arms the huts and hamlets rise,
From winding glen, from upland brown,
They pour'd each hardy tenant down.
Nor slack'd the messenger his pace;
He show'd the sign, he named the place,
And, pressing forward like the wind,
Left clamor and surprise behind.
The fisherman forsook the strand,
The swarthy smith took dirk and brand;
With changed cheer, the mower blithe
Left in the half-cut swathe the scythe;
The herds without a keeper stray'd,
The plough was in mid-furrow staid,
The falc'ner toss'd his hawk away,
The hunter left the stag at bay;
Prompt at the signal of alarms,
Each son of Alpine rush'd to arms;
So swept the tumult and affray
Along the margin of Achray.
Alas! thou lovely lake! that e'er
Thy banks should echo sounds of fear!
The rocks, the bosky thickets, sleep
So stilly on thy bosom deep,
The lark's blithe carol, from the cloud,
Seems for the scene too gayly loud.

XV.

Speed, Malise, speed! the lake is past,
Duncraggan's huts appear at last,
And peep, like moss-grown rocks, half
      seen,
Half hidden in the copse so green;
There may'st thou rest, thy labor done,
Their Lord shall speed the signal on. —

As stoops the hawk upon his prey,
The henchman shot him down the way.
— What woeful accents load the gale?
The funeral yell, the female wail!
A gallant hunter's sport is o'er,
A valiant warrior fights no more.
Who, in the battle or the chase,
At Roderick's side shall fill his place! —
Within the hall, where torches' ray
Supplies the excluded beams of day,
Lies Duncan on his lowly bier,
And o'er him streams his widow's tear.
His stripling son stands mournful by,
His youngest weeps, but knows not why;
The village maids and matrons round
The dismal coronach resound.[29]

XVI.

CORONACH.

He is gone on the mountain,
   He is lost to the forest,
Like a summer-dried fountain,
   When our need was the sorest.
The font, reappearing,
   From the rain-drops shall borrow,
But to us comes no cheering,
   To Duncan no morrow!

The hand of the reaper
   Takes the ears that are hoary,
But the voice of the weeper
   Wails manhood in glory.
The autumn winds rushing
   Waft the leaves that are searest,
But our flower was in flushing,
   When blighting was nearest.

Fleet foot on the correi,*
   Sage counsel in cumber,
Red hand in the foray,
   How sound is thy slumber!
Like the dew on the mountain,
   Like the foam on the river,
Like the bubble on the fountain,
   Thou art gone, and forever!

XVII.

See Stumah,† who, the bier beside,
His master's corpse with wonder eyed,

* *Correi*, the hollow side of the hill where
game usually lies.

† The name of a dog. The word is Celtic for
"faithful."

Poor Stumah! whom his least halloo
Could send like lightning o'er the dew,
Bristles his crest, and points his ears,
As if some stranger step he hears.
'Tis not a mourner's muffled tread,
Who comes to sorrow o'er the dead,
But headlong haste, or deadly fear,
Urge the precipitate career.
All stand aghast:— unheeding all,
The henchman bursts into the hall;
Before the dead man's bier he stood;
Held forth the Cross besmear'd with blood:
"The muster-place is Lanrick mead;
Speed forth the signal! clansmen, speed!"

XVIII.

Angus, the heir of Duncan's line,
Sprung forth and seized the fatal sign.
In haste the stripling to his side
His father's dirk and broadsword tied;
But when he saw his mother's eye
Watch him in speechless agony,
Back to her open'd arms he flew,
Press'd on her lips a fond adieu —
"Alas!" she sobb'd,—"and yet, be gone,
And speed thee forth, like Duncan's son!"
One look he cast upon the bier,
Dash'd from his eye the gathering tear,
Breathed deep to clear his laboring breast,
And toss'd aloft his bonnet crest.
Then, like the high-bred colt, when, freed,
First he essays his fire and speed,
He vanish'd, and o'er moor and moss
Sped forward with the Fiery Cross.
Suspended was the widow's tear,
While yet his footsteps she could hear;
And when she mark'd the henchman's eye
Wet with unwonted sympathy,
"Kinsman," she said, "his race is run,
That should have sped thine errand on;
The oak has fall'n, — the sapling bough
Is all Duncraggan's shelter now.
Yet trust I well, his duty done,
The orphan's God will guard my son. —
And you, in many a danger true,
At Duncan's hest your blades that drew,
To arms, and guard that orphan's head!
Let babes and women wail the dead."
Then weapon-clang, and martial call,
Resounded through the funeral hall,
While from the walls the attendant band
Snatch'd sword and targe, with hurried
        hand;

And short and flitting energy
Glanced from the mourner's sunken eye,
As if the sounds to warrior dear,
Might rouse her Duncan from his bier.
But faded soon that borrow'd force,
Grief claim'd his right, and tears their
        course.

XIX.

Benledi saw the Cross of Fire;
It glanced like lightning up Strath-Ire.
O'er dale and hill the summons flew,
Nor rest nor pause young Angus knew;
The tear that gather'd in his eye
He left the mountain breeze to dry;
Until, where Teith's young waters roll,
Betwixt him and a wooded knoll,
That graced the sable strath with green,
The chapel of St. Bride was seen.
Swoln was the stream, remote the bridge,
But Angus paused not on the edge;
Though the dark waves danced dizzily,
Though reel'd his sympathetic eye,
He dash'd amid the torrent's roar:
His right hand high the crosslet bore,
His left the pole-axe grasp'd, to guide
And stay his footing in the tide.
He stumbled twice — the foam splash'd
        high,
With hoarser swell the stream raced by;
And had he fall'n, — forever there,
Farewell Duncraggan's orphan heir!
But still, as if in parting life,
Firmer he grasp'd the Cross of strife,
Until the opposing bank he gain'd,
And up the chapel pathway strain'd.

XX.

A blithesome rout, that morning tide,
Had sought the chapel of St. Bride.
Her troth Tombea's Mary gave
To Norman, heir of Armandave,
And, issuing from the Gothic arch,
The bridal now resumed their march.
In rude, but glad procession, came
Bonneted sire and coif-clad dame;
And plaided youth, with jest and jeer,
Which snooded maiden would not hear;
And children, that, unwitting why,
Lent the gay shout their shrilly cry;
And minstrels, that in measures vied
Before the young and bonny bride,
Whose downcast eye and cheek disclose
The tear and blush of morning rose

With virgin step, and bashful hand,
She held the 'kerchief's snowy band;
The gallant bridegroom by her side,
Beheld his prize with victor's pride,
And the glad mother in her ear
Was closely whispering word of cheer.

XXI.

Who meets them at the churchyard gate?
The messenger of fear and fate!
Haste in his hurried accent lies,
And grief is swimming in his eyes.
All dripping from the recent flood,
Panting and travel-soil'd he stood,
The fatal sign of fire and sword
Held forth, and spoke the appointed
          word: —
" The muster-place is Lanrick mead;
Speed forth the signal! Norman, speed! "
And must he change so soon the hand,
Just link'd to his by holy band,
For the fell Cross of blood and brand?
And must the day, so blithe that rose,
And promised rapture in the close,
Before its setting hour, divide
The bridegroom from the plighted bride?
O fatal doom! — it must! it must!
Clan-Alpine's cause, her Chieftain's trust,
Her summons dread, brook no delay;
Stretch to the race — away! away!

XXII.

Yet slow he laid his plaid aside,
And, lingering, eyed his lovely bride,
Until he saw the starting tear
Speak woe he might not stop to cheer;
Then, trusting not a second look,
In haste he sped him up the brook,
Nor backward glanced, till on the heath
Where Lubnaig's lake supplies the Teith.
— What in the racer's bosom stirr'd?
The sickening pang of hope deferr'd,
And memory, with a torturing train
Of all his morning visions vain.
Mingled with love's impatience, came
The manly thirst for martial fame;
The stormy joy of mountaineers,
Ere yet they rush upon the spears;
And zeal for Clan and Chieftain burning,
And hope, from well-fought field return-
          ing,
With war's red honors on his crest,
To clasp his Mary to his breast.

Stung by such thoughts, o'er bank and
          brae,
Like fire from flint he glanced away,
While high resolve, and feeling strong,
Burst into voluntary song.

XXIII.

SONG.

The heath this night must be my bed,
The bracken* curtain for my head,
My lullaby the warder's tread,
     Far, far from love and thee, Mary;
To-morrow eve, more stilly laid,
My couch may be my bloody plaid,
My vesper song, thy wail, sweet maid!
     It will not waken me, Mary!
I may not, dare not, fancy now
The grief that clouds thy lovely brow;
I dare not think upon thy vow,
     And all it promised me, Mary.
No fond regret must Norman know;
When bursts Clan-Alpine on the foe,
His heart must be like bended bow,
     His foot like arrow free, Mary.

A time will come with feeling fraught,
For, if I fall in battle fought,
Thy hapless lover's dying thought
     Shall be a thought on thee, Mary.
And if return'd from conquer'd foes,
How blithely will the evening close,
How sweet the linnet sing repose,
     To my young bride and me, Mary!

XXIV.

Not faster o'er thy heathery braes,
Balquidder, speeds the midnight blaze,[30]
Rushing, in conflagration strong,
Thy deep ravines and dells along,
Wrapping thy cliffs in purple glow,
And reddening the dark lakes below;
Nor faster speeds it, nor so far,
As o'er thy heaths the voice of war.
The signal roused to martial coil
The sullen margin of Loch Voil,
Waked still Loch Doine, and to the
          source
Alarm'd, Balvaig, thy swampy course;
Thence southward turn'd its rapid road
Adown Strath-Gartney's valley broad,

* Fern.

ill rose in arms each man might claim
A portion in Clan-Alpine's name,
From the gray sire, whose trembling hand
Could hardly buckle on his brand,
To the raw boy, whose shaft and bow
Were yet scarce terror to the crow.
Each valley, each sequester'd glen,
Muster'd its little horde of men,
That met as torrents from the height
In Highland dales their streams unite,
Still gathering, as they pour along,
A voice more loud, a tide more strong,
Till at the rendezvous they stood,
By hundreds, prompt for blows and blood;
Each train'd to arms since life began,
Owning no tie but to his clan,
No oath, but by his Chieftain's hand,
No law, but Roderick Dhu's command.

XXV.

That summer morn had Roderick Dhu
Survey'd the skirts of Benvenue,
And sent his scouts o'er hill and heath,
To view the frontiers of Menteith.
All backward came with news of truce;
Still lay each martial Græme and Bruce,
In Rednock courts no horsemen wait,
No banner waved on Cardross gate,
On Duchray's towers no beacon shone,
Nor scared the herons from Loch Con;
All seem'd at peace. — Now, wot ye why
The chieftain, with such anxious eye,
Ere to the muster he repair,
This western frontier scann'd with
    care? —
In Benvenue's most darksome cleft,
A fair, though cruel, pledge was left;
For Douglas, to his promise true,
That morning from the isle withdrew,
And in a deep sequester'd dell
Had sought a low and lonely cell.
By many a bard, in Celtic tongue,
Has Coir-nan-Uriskin been sung; [31]
A softer name the Saxons gave,
And call'd the grot the Goblin-cave.

XXVI.

It was a wild and strange retreat,
As e'er was trod by outlaw's feet.
The dell, upon the mountain's crest,
Yawn'd like a gash on warrior's breast;
Its trench had staid full many a rock,
Hurl'd by primeval earthquake shock

From Benvenue's gray summit wild,
And here, in random ruin piled,
They frown'd incumbent o'er the spot,
And form'd the rugged sylvan grot.
The oak and birch, with mingled shade,
At noontide there a twilight made,
Unless when short and sudden shone
Some straggling beam on cliff or stone,
With such a glimpse as prophet's eye
Gains on thy depth, Futurity.
No murmur waked the solemn still,
Save tinkling of a fountain rill;
But when the wind chafed with the lake,
A sullen sound would upward break,
With dashing hollow voice, that spoke
The incessant war of wave and rock.
Suspended clifts with hideous sway
Seem'd nodding o'er the cavern gray.
From such a den the wolf had sprung,
In such the wild-cat leaves her young;
Yet Douglas and his daughter fair
Sought for a space their safety there.
Gray Superstition's whisper dread
Debarr'd the spot to vulgar tread:
For there, she said, did fays resort,
And satyrs * hold their sylvan court,
By moonlight tread their mystic maze,
And blast the rash beholder's gaze.

XXVII.

Now eve, with western shadows long,
Floated on Katrine bright and strong,
When Roderick, with a chosen few,
Repass'd the heights of Benvenue.
Above the Goblin-cave they go,
Through the wild pass of Beal-nam-bo:
The prompt retainers speed before,
To launch the shallop from the shore,
For 'cross Loch Katrine lies his way
To view the passes of Achray,
And place his clansmen in array.
Yet lags the chief in musing mind,
Unwonted sight, his men behind.
A single page, to bear his sword,
Alone attended on his lord;
The rest their way through thickets break,
And soon await him by the lake.
It was a fair and gallant sight,
To view them from the neighboring
    height,

---

* The Highlanders had a mythological satyr
called *urisk.*

By the low-levell'd sunbeam's light!
For strength and stature, from the clan
Each warrior was a chosen man,
As even afar might well be seen,
By their proud step and martial mien.
Their feathers dance, their tartans float,
Their targets gleam, as by the boat
A wild and war-like group they stand,
That well became such mountain-strand.

XXVIII.

The Chief, with step reluctant, still
Was lingering on the craggy hill,
Hard by where turn'd apart the road
To Douglas's obscure abode.
It was but with that dawning morn,
That Roderick Dhu had proudly sworn
To drown his love in war's wild roar,
Nor think of Ellen Douglas more;
But he who stems a stream with sand,
And fetters flame with flaxen band,
Has yet a harder task to prove —
By firm resolve to conquer love!
Eve finds the Chief, like restless ghost,
Still hovering near his treasure lost;
For though his haughty heart deny
A parting meeting to his eye,
Still fondly strains his anxious ear,
The accents of her voice to hear,
And inly did he curse the breeze
That waked to sound the rustling trees.
But hark! what mingles in the strain?
It is the harp of Allan-Bane,
That wakes its measure slow and high,
Attuned to sacred minstrelsy.
What melting voice attends the strings?
'Tis Ellen, or an angel, sings.

XXIX.
HYMN TO THE VIRGIN.

Ave Maria! maiden mild!
  Listen to a maiden's prayer!
Thou canst hear though from the wild,
  Thou canst save amid despair.
Safe may we sleep beneath thy care,
  Though banish'd, outcast, and reviled,
Maiden! hear a maiden's prayer;
  Mother, hear a suppliant child!
                    Ave Maria!
Ave Maria! undefiled!
  The flinty couch we now must share
Shall seem with down of eider piled,
  If thy protection hover there.

The murky cavern's heavy air
  Shall breathe of balm if thou has
    smiled;
Then, Maiden! hear a maiden's prayer;
  Mother, list a suppliant child!
                    Ave Maria
Ave Maria! stainless styled!
  Foul demons of the earth and air,
From this their wanton haunt exiled,
  Shall flee before thy presence fair.
We bow us to our lot of care,
  Beneath thy guidance reconciled;
Hear for a maid a maiden's prayer,
  And for a father hear a child!
                    Ave Maria

XXX.

Died on the harp the closing hymn. —
Unmoved in attitude and limb,
As list'ning still, Clan-Alpine's lord
Stood leaning on his heavy sword,
Until the page, with humble sign,
Twice pointed to the sun's decline.
Then while his plaid he round him cast,
" It is the last time — 'tis the last,"
He mutter'd thrice, — " the last time
    e'er
That angel voice shall Roderick hear!"
It was a goading thought — his stride
Hied hastier down the mountain-side;
Sullen he flung him in the boat,
And instant 'cross the lake it shot.
They landed in that silvery bay,
And eastward held their hasty way,
Till with the latest beams of light,
The band arrived on Lanrick height,
Where muster'd, in the vale below,
Clan-Alpine's men in martial show

XXXI.

A various scene the clansmen made;
Some sate, some stood, some slowly
    stray'd;
But most with mantles folded round,
Were couch'd to rest upon the ground,
Scarce to be known by curious eye,
From the deep heather where they lie,
So well was match'd the tartan screen
With heath-bell dark and brackens green;
Unless where, here and there, a blade,
Or lance's point, a glimmer made,
Like glow-worm twinkling through the
    shade.

ut when, advancing through the gloom,
hey saw the Chieftain's eagle-plume,
heir shout of welcome, shrill and wide,
nook the steep mountain's steady side.
hrice it arose, and lake and fell
hree times return'd the martial yell;
 died upon Bochastle's plain,
nd Silence claim'd her evening reign.

CANTO FOURTH.

THE PROPHECY.

I.

THE rose is fairest when 'tis budding
 new,
 And hope is brightest when it dawns
 from fears;
he rose is sweetest wash'd with morning dew,
nd love is loveliest when embalm'd in
 tears.
 wilding rose, whom fancy thus endears,
 I bid your blossoms in my bonnet
 wave,
mblem of hope and love through future
 years!"
 Thus spoke young Norman, heir of
 Armandave,
What time the sun arose on Vennachar's
 broad wave.

II.

uch fond conceit, half said, half sung,
ove prompted to the bridegroom's
 tongue.
ll while he stripp'd the wild-rose spray,
 is axe and bow beside him lay,
or on a pass 'twixt lake and wood,
 wakeful sentinel he stood.
 ark! on the rock a footstep rung,
nd instant to his arms he sprung.
 Stand, or thou diest! — What, Malise?
 — soon
 rt thou return'd from Braes of Doune.
 y thy keen step and glance I know,
hou bring'st us tidings of the foe," —
 For while the Fiery Cross hied on,
 n distant scout had Malise gone.)
 Where sleeps the Chief?" the henchman said. —
 Apart, in yonder misty glade.

To his lone couch I'll be your guide." —
Then call'd a slumberer by his side,
And stirr'd him with his slacken'd bow —
"Up, up, Glentarkin! rouse thee, ho!
We seek the Chieftain; on the track,
Keep eagle watch till I come back."

III.

Together up the pass they sped:
"What of the foemen?" Norman said. —
"Varying reports from near and far;
This certain — that a band of war
Has for two days been ready boune,
At prompt command, to march from
 Doune;
King James, the while with princely
 powers,
Holds revelry in Stirling towers.
Soon will this dark and gathering cloud
Speak on our glens in thunder loud.
Inured to bide such bitter bout,
The warrior's plaid may bear it out;
But, Norman, how wilt thou provide
A shelter for thy bonny bride?"
"What! know ye not that Roderick's
 care
To the lone isle hath caused repair
Each maid and matron of the clan,
And every child and aged man
Unfit for arms; and given his charge,
Nor skiff nor shallop, boat nor barge,
Upon these lakes shall float at large,
But all beside the islet moor,
That such dear pledge may rest secure?"

IV.

" 'Tis well advised—the Chieftain's plan
Bespeaks the father of his clan.
But wherefore sleeps Sir Roderick Dhu
Apart from all his followers true?" —
"It is because last evening-tide
Brian an augury hath tried,
Of that dread kind which must not be
Unless in dread extremity,
The Taghairm call'd; by which, afar,
Our sires foresaw the events of war.[32]
Duncraggan's milk-white bull they slew.'

MALISE.

"Ah! well the gallant brute I knew!
The choicest of the prey we had,
When swept our merry-men Gallangad.

His hide was snow, his horns were dark,
His red eye glow'd like fiery spark;
So fierce, so tameless, and so fleet,
Sore did he cumber our retreat,
And kept our stoutest kernes in awe,
Even at the pass of Beal 'maha.
But steep and flinty was the road,
And sharp the hurrying pikemen's goad,
And when we came to Dennan's Ròw,
A child might scatheless stroke his brow.''

V.

NORMAN.

"That bull was slain: his reeking hide
They stretch'd the cataract beside,
Whose waters their wild tumult toss
Adown the black and craggy boss
Of that huge cliff, whose ample verge
Tradition calls the Hero's Targe.[33]
Couch'd on a shelve beneath its brink,
Close where the thundering torrents sink,
Rocking beneath their headlong sway,
And drizzled by the ceaseless spray,
Midst groan of rock, and roar of stream,
The wizard waits prophetic dream.
Nor distant rests the Chief; — but hush!
See, gliding slow through mist and bush,
The hermit gains yon rock, and stands
To gaze upon our slumbering bands.
Seems he not, Malise, like a ghost,
That hovers o'er a slaughter'd host?
Or raven on the blasted oak,
That, watching while the deer is broke,
His morsel claims with sullen croak?''

MALISE.

"Peace! peace! to other than to me,
Thy words were evil augury;
But still I hold Sir Roderick's blade
Clan-Alpine's omen and her aid,
Not aught that, glean'd from heaven or hell,
Yon fiend-begotten monk can tell.
The Chieftain joins him, see — and now,
Together they descend the brow.''

VI.

And as they came, with Alpine's Lord
The Hermit Monk held solemn word: —
"Roderick! it is a fearful strife,
For man endow'd with mortal life,
Whose shroud of sentient clay can still
Feel feverish pang and fainting chill,

Whose eye can stare in stony trance,
Whose hair can rouse like warrior's lance
'Tis hard for such to view unfurl'd
The curtain of the future world.
Yet, witness every quaking limb,
My sunken pulse, my eyeballs dim,
My soul with harrowing anguish torn,—
This for my Chieftain have I borne! —
The shapes that sought my fearful couch
A human tongue may ne'er avouch;
No mortal man, — save he, who bred
Between the living and the dead,
Is gifted beyond nature's law, —
Had e'er survived to say he saw.
At length the fatal answer came,
In characters of living flame!
Not spoke in word, nor blazed in scroll,
But borne and branded on my soul; —
WHICH SPILLS THE FOREMOST FOEMAN'S
LIFE,
THAT PARTY CONQUERS IN TH
STRIFE!''[34]

VII.

"Thanks, Brian, for thy zeal and care!
Good is thine augury, and fair.
Clan-Alpine ne'er in battle stood,
But first our broadswords tasted blood.
A surer victim still I know,
Self-offer'd to the auspicious blow;
A spy has sought my land this morn, —
No eve shall witness his return!
My followers guard each pass's mouth,
To east, to westward, and to south;
Red Murdoch, bribed to be his guide,
Has charge to lead his steps aside,
Till, in deep path or dingle brown,
He light on those shall bring him down
— But see, who comes his news to show
Malise! what tidings of the foe?''

VIII.

"At Doune, o'er many a spear and glaive
Two Barons proud their banners wave.
I saw the Moray's silver star,
And mark'd the sable pale of Mar.'' —
"By Alpine's soul, high tidings those!
I love to hear of worthy foes.
When move they on?'' — "To-morrow's
noon
Will see them here for battle boune.'' *—

* Ready.

Then shall it see a meeting stern ! —
ut, for the place—say, couldst thou learn
aught of the friendly clans of Earn?
trengthen'd by them, we well might bide
he battle on Benledi's side.
hou couldst not? —Well ! Clan-Alpine's
   men
hall man the Trosachs' shaggy glen;
'ithin Loch Katrine's gorge we'll fight,
ll in our maids' and matrons' sight,
ach for his hearth and household fire,
ather for child, and son for sire, —
over for maid beloved ! — But why —
s it the breeze affects mine eye?
r dost thou come, ill-omen'd tear !
messenger of doubt or fear?
o ! sooner may the Saxon lance
nfix Benledi from his stance,
han doubt or terror can pierce through
he unyielding heart of Roderick Dhu !
Tis stubborn as his trusty targe. —
Cach to his post !—all know their charge."
he pibroch sounds, the bands advance,
he broadswords gleam, the banners
   dance,
Obedient to the Chieftain's glance.
—I turn me from the martial roar,
nd seek Coir-Uriskin once more.

IX.

Vhere is the Douglas? — he is gone;
And Ellen sits on the gray stone
'ast by the cave, and makes her moan;
While vainly Allan's words of cheer
Are pour'd on her unheeding ear. —
' He will return — Dear lady, trust ! —
Vith joy return; — he will — he must.
Well was it time to seek, afar,
Some refuge from impending war,
When e'en Clan-Alpine's rugged swarm
Are cow'd by the approaching storm.
saw their boats with many a light,
'loating the livelong yesternight,
Shifting like flashes darted forth
By the red streamers of the north;
mark'd at morn how close they ride,
Thick moor'd by the lone islet's side,
Like wild-ducks couching in the fen,
When stoops the hawk upon the glen.
Since this rude race dare not abide
The peril on the mainland side,
Shall not thy noble father's care
Some safe retreat for thee prepare?" —

X.

ELLEN.

" No, Allan, no ! Pretext so kind
My wakeful terrors could not blind.
When in-such tender tone, yet grave,
Douglas a parting blessing gave,
The tear that glisten'd in his eye
Drown'd not his purpose fix'd on high.
My soul, though feminine and weak,
Can image his; e'en as the lake,
Itself disturbed by slightest stroke,
Reflects the invulnerable rock.
He hears report of battle rife,
He deems himself the cause of strife.
I saw him redden, when the theme
Turn'd, Allan, on thine idle dream,
Of Malcolm Græme, in fetters bound,
Which I, thou saidst, about him wound.
Think'st thou he trow'd thine omen
   aught?
Oh no ! 'twas apprehensive thought
For the kind youth, — for Roderick too—
(Let me be just) that friend so true;
In danger both, and in our cause !
Minstrel, the Douglas dare not pause.
Why else that solemn warning given,
' If not on earth, we meet in heaven ! '
Why else, to Cambuskenneth's fane,
If eve return him not again,
Am I to hie, and make me known?
Alas ! he goes to Scotland's throne,
Buys his friend's safety with his own; —
He goes to do — what I had done,
Had Douglas' daughter been his son ! "

XI.

" Nay, lovely Ellen ! — dearest, nay !
If aught should his return delay,
He only named yon holy fane
As fitting place to meet again.
Be sure he's safe; and for the Græme,
Heaven's blessing on his gallant name ! —
My vision'd sight may yet prove true,
Nor bode of ill to him or you.
When did my gifted dream beguile?
Think of the stranger at the isle,
And think upon the harpings slow,
That presaged this approaching woe?
Sooth was my prophecy of fear;
Believe it when it augurs cheer.
Would we had left this dismal spot !
Ill luck still haunts a fairy grot.

Of such a wondrous tale I know —
Dear lady, change that look of woe,
My harp was wont thy grief to cheer."—

ELLEN.

" Well, be it as thou wilt; I hear,
But cannot stop the bursting tear."
The Minstrel tried his simple art,
But distant far was Ellen's heart.

XII.

BALLAD.

Alice Brand.

Merry it is in the good greenwood,
    Where the mavis * and merle † are
      singing,
When the deer sweeps by, and the hounds
      are in cry,
    And the hunter's horn is ringing.

" O Alice Brand, my native land
    Is lost for love of you;
And we must hold by wood and wold,
    As outlaws wont to do.

" O Alice, 'twas all for thy locks so bright,
    And 'twas all for thine eyes so blue,
That on the night of our luckless flight,
    Thy brother bold I slew.

" Now must I teach to hew the beech
    The hand that held the glaive,
For leaves to spread our lowly bed,
    And stakes to fence our cave.

" And for vest of pall, thy fingers small,
    That wont on harp to stray,
A cloak must sheer from the slaughter'd
      deer,
    To keep the cold away." —

" O Richard ! if my brother died,
    'Twas but a fatal chance,
For darkling was the battle tried,
    And fortune sped the lance.

" If pall and vair no more I wear,
    Nor thou the crimson sheen,
As warm, we'll say, is the russet gray.
    As gay the forest green.

      * *Mavis*, a thrush.
      † *Merle*, a blackbird.

" And, Richard, if our lot be hard,
    And lost thy native land,
Still Alice has her own Richard,
    And he his Alice Brand."

XIII.

BALLAD CONTINUED.

'Tis merry, 'tis merry, in good greenwoo
    So blithe Lady Alice is singing;
On the beech's pride, and oak's brown sid
    Lord Richard's axe is ringing.

Up spoke the moody Elfin King,
    Who wonn'd within the hill, —
Like wind in the porch of a ruin'd churc
    His voice was ghostly shrill.

"Why sounds yon stroke on beech and oak
    Our moonlit circle's screen ?
Or who comes here to chase the deer,
    Beloved of our Elfin Queen ? [35]
Or who may dare on wold to wear
    The fairies' fatal green ? [36]

"Up, Urgan, up ! to yon mortal hie,
    For thou wert christen'd man; [37]
For cross or sign thou wilt not fly,
    For mutter'd word or ban.

"Lay on him the curse of the wither'd
      heart,
    The curse of the sleepless eye;
Till he wish and pray that his life would
      part,
    Nor yet find leave to die."

XIV.

BALLAD CONTINUED.

'Tis merry, 'tis merry, in good greenwood
    Though the birds have still'd their sing
      ing;
The evening blaze doth Alice raise,
    And Richard is fagots bringing.

Up Urgan starts, that hideous dwarf
    Before Lord Richard stands,
And, as he cross'd and bless'd himself,
    " I fear not sign," quoth the grisly elf,
      " That is made with bloody hands."

But out then spoke she, Alice Brand,
    That woman void of fear, —
" And if there's blood upon his hand,
    'Tis but the blood of deer." —

Now loud thou liest, thou bold of mood!
It cleaves unto his hand,
he stain of thine own kindly blood,
The blood of Ethert Brand."

hen forward stepp'd she, Alice Brand,
And made the holy sign, —
And if there's blood on Richard's hand,
A spotless hand is mine.

And I conjure thee, thou Demon elf,
By Him whom Demons fear,
o show us whence thou art thyself,
And what thine errand here?" —

XV.

BALLAD CONTINUED.

'Tis merry, 'tis merry in Fairy-land,
When fairy birds are singing,
/hen the court doth ride by their monarch's side,
With bit and bridle ringing;

And gayly shines the Fairy-land —
But all is glistening show,
ike the idle gleam that December's beam
Can dart on ice and snow.

And fading, like that varied gleam,
Is our inconstant shape,
/ho now like knight and lady seem,
And now like dwarf and ape.

It was between the night and day,
When the Fairy King has power,
hat I sunk down in a sinful fray,
nd 'twixt life and death, was snatch'd
away
To the joyless Elfin bower.

But wist I of a woman bold,
Who thrice my brow durst sign,
might regain my mortal mould,
As fair a form as thine."

he cross'd him once — she cross'd him
twice —
That lady was so brave;
he fouler grew his goblin hue,
The darker grew the cave.

he cross'd him thrice, that lady bold;
He rose beneath her hand
he fairest knight on Scottish mould,
Her brother, Ethert Brand!

Merry it is in good greenwood,
When the mavis and merle are singing,
But merrier were they in Dunfermline
gray,
When all the bells were ringing.

XVI.

Just as the minstrel sounds were staid,
A stranger climb'd the steepy glade:
His martial step, his stately mien,
His hunting suit of Lincoln green,
His eagle glance, remembrance claims —
'Tis Snowdoun's Knight, 'tis James Fitz-
James.
Ellen beheld as in a dream,
Then, starting, scarce suppress'd a
scream:
" O stranger! in such hour of fear,
What evil hap has brought thee here?" —
" An evil hap how can it be,
That bids me look again on thee?
By promise bound, my former guide
Met me betimes this morning tide,
And marshall'd, over bank and bourne,
The happy path of my return." —
"The happy path! — what I said he naught
Of war, of battle to be fought,
Of guarded pass?" — " No, by my faith!
Nor saw I aught could augur scathe." —
" O haste thee, Allan, to the kern,
— Yonder his tartans I discern;
Learn thou his purpose, and conjure
That he will guide the stranger sure! —
What prompted thee, unhappy man?
The meanest serf in Roderick's clan
Had not been bribed by love or fear,
Unknown to him to guide thee here." —

XVII.

" Sweet Ellen, dear my life must be,
Since it is worthy care from thee;
Yet life I hold but idle breath,
When love or honor's weigh'd with death.
Then let me profit by my chance,
And speak my purpose bold at once.
I come to bear thee from a wild,
Where ne'er before such blossom smiled,
By this soft hand to lead thee far
From frantic scenes of feud and war.
Near Bochastle my horses wait;
They bear us soon to Stirling gate,
I'll place thee in a lovely bower,
I'll guard thee like a tender flower" —

"O! hush, Sir Knight! 'twere female art,
To say I do not read thy heart;
Too much, before, my selfish ear
Was idly soothed my praise to hear.
That fatal bait hath lured thee back,
In deathful hour, o'er dangerous track;
And how, O how, can I atone
The wreck my vanity brought on!
One way remains — I'll tell him all —
Yes! struggling bosom, forth it shall!
Thou, whose light folly bears the blame,
Buy thine own pardon with thy shame!
But first — my father is a man
Outlaw'd and exiled, under ban;
The price of blood is on his head,
With me 'twere infamy to wed. —
Still wouldst thou speak? — then hear the
　　　　truth!
Fitz-James, there is a noble youth, —
If yet he is! — exposed for me
And mine to dread extremity —
Thou hast the secret of my heart:
Forgive, be generous, and depart!"

XVIII.

Fitz-James knew every wily train
A lady's fickle heart to gain;
But here he knew and felt them vain.
There shot no glance from Ellen's eye,
To give her steadfast speech the lie;
In maiden confidence she stood,
Though mantled in her cheek the blood,
And told her love with such a sigh
Of deep and hopeless agony,
As death had seal'd her Malcolm's doom,
And she sat sorrowing on his tomb.
Hope vanish'd from Fitz-James's eye,
But not with hope fled sympathy.
He proffer'd to attend her side,
As brother would a sister guide. —
"O! little know'st thou Roderick's heart,
Safer for both we go apart.
O haste thee, and from Allan learn,
If thou may'st trust yon wily kern."
With hand upon his forehead laid,
The conflict of his mind to shade,
A parting step or two he made;
Then, as some thought had cross'd his brain,
He paused, and turn'd, and came again:—

XIX.

"Hear, lady, yet a parting word! —
It chanced in fight that my poor sword

Preserved the life of Scotland's lord.
This ring the grateful monarch gave,
And bade when I had boon to crave,
To bring it back, and boldly claim
The recompense that I would name.
Ellen, I am no courtly lord,
But one who lives by lance and sword,
Whose castle is his helm and shield,
His lordship the embattled field.
What from a prince can I demand,
Who neither reck of state nor land?
Ellen, thy hand — the ring is thine;
Each guard and usher knows the sign.
Seek thou the king without delay;
This signet shall secure thy way;
And claim thy suit, whate'er it be,
As ransom of his pledge to me."
He placed the golden circlet on,
Paused — kiss'd her hand — and then
　　　　was gone.
The aged Minstrel stood aghast,
So hastily Fitz-James shot past.
He join'd his guide, and wending down
The ridges of the mountain brown,
Across the stream they took their way,
That joins Loch Katrine to Achray.

XX.

All in the Trosachs' glen was still,
Noontide was sleeping on the hill;
Sudden his guide whoop'd loud and
　　　　high. —
"Murdoch! was that a signal cry?" —
He stammer'd forth, — "I shout to scare
Yon raven from his dainty fare."
He look'd — he knew the raven's prey,
His own brave steed: — "Ah! gallant
　　　　gray!
For thee — for me, perchance — 'twere
　　　　well
We ne'er had seen the Trosachs' dell. —
Murdoch, move first — but silently;
Whistle or whoop, and thou shalt die!"
Jealous and sullen on they fared,
Each silent, each upon his guard.

XXI.

Now wound the path its dizzy ledge
Around a precipice's edge,
When lo! a wasted female form,
Blighted by wrath of sun and storm,
In tatter'd weeds and wild array,
Stood on a cliff beside the way,

And glancing round her restless eye,
Upon the wood, the rock, the sky,
Seem'd naught to mark, yet all to spy.
Her brow was wreath'd with gaudy
    broom;
With gesture wild she waved a plume
Of feathers, which the eagles fling
To crag and cliff from dusky wing;
Such spoils her desperate step had sought,
Where scarce was footing for the goat.
The tartan plaid she first descried,
And shriek'd till all the rocks replied;
As loud she laugh'd when near they drew,
For then the Lowland garb she knew;
And then her hands she wildly wrung,
And then she wept, and then she sung —
She sung ! — the voice, in better time,
Perchance to harp or lute might chime;
And now, tho' strain'd and roughen'd,
    still
Rung wildly sweet to dale and hill : —

XXII.

SONG.

" They bid me sleep, they bid me pray,
    They say my brain is warp'd and
        wrung —
I cannot sleep on Highland brae,
    I cannot pray in Highland tongue.
But were I now where Allan * glides,
Or heard my native Devan's tides,
So sweetly would I rest, and pray
That Heaven would close my wintry day !

" 'Twas thus my hair they bade me braid,
    They made me to the church repair;
It was my bridal morn they said,
    And my true love would meet me there.
But woe betide the cruel guile,
That drown'd in blood the morning smile !
And woe betide the fairy dream !
I only waked to sob and scream."

XXIII.

" Who is this maid ? what means her lay ?
She hovers o'er the hollow way,
And flutters wide her mantle gray,
As the lone heron spreads his wing,
By twilight, o'er a haunted spring." —

* *Allan* and *Devan,* two rivers running through
Stirling Plain.

" 'Tis Blanche of Devan," Murdoch said,
" A crazed and captive Lowland maid,
Ta'en on the morn she was a bride,
When Roderick foray'd Devan-side.
The gay bridegroom resistance made,
And felt our Chief's unconquer'd blade.
I marvel she is now at large,
But oft she 'scapes from Maudlin's
    charge. —
Hence, brain-sick fool ! " — He raised
    his bow : —
" Now, if thou strikest her but one blow,
I'll pitch thee from the cliff as far
As ever peasant pitch'd a bar ! " —
" Thanks, champion, thanks ! " the Ma-
    niac cried,
And press'd her to Fitz-James's side.
" See the gray pennons I prepare,
To seek my true-love through the air;
I will not lend that savage groom,
To break his fall, one downy plume !
No ! — deep amid disjointed stones,
The wolves shall batten on his bones,
And then shall his detested plaid,
By bush and brier in mid air staid,
Wave forth a banner fair and free,
Meet signal for their revelry." —

XXIV.

" Hush thee, poor maiden, and be
    still ! " —
" O ! thou look'st kindly, and I will. —
Mine eye has dried and wasted been,
But still it loves the Lincoln green;
And, though mine ear is all unstrung,
Still, still it loves the Lowland tongue.

" For O my sweet William was forester
    true,
    He stole poor Blanche's heart away !
His coat it was all of the greenwood
    hue,
    And so blithely he trill'd the Low-
        land lay !

" It was not that I meant to tell,
But thou art wise and guessest well."
Then, in a low and broken tone,
And hurried note, the song went on.
Still on the Clansman, fearfully,
She fix'd her apprehensive eye;
Then turn'd it on the Knight, and then
Her look glanced wildly o'er the glen : —

XXV.

"The toils are pitch'd, and the stakes
    are set,
    Ever sing merrily, merrily;
The bows they bend, and the knives
    they whet,
    Hunters live so cheerily.

"It was a stag, a stag of ten,*
    Bearing its branches sturdily;
He came stately down the glen,
    Ever sing hardily, hardily.

"It was there he met with a wounded
    doe,
    She was bleeding deathfully;
She warn'd him of the toils below,
    O, so faithfully, faithfully!

"He had an eye, and he could heed,
    Ever sing warily, warily,
He had a foot, and he could speed —
    Hunters watch so narrowly."

XXVI.

Fitz-James's mind was passion-toss'd,
When Ellen's hints and fears were lost;
But Murdoch's shout suspicion wrought,
And Blanche's song conviction brought.
Not like a stag that spies the snare,
But lion of the hunt aware,
He waved at once his blade on high,
"Disclose thy treachery, or die!"
Forth at full speed the Clansman flew,
But in his race his bow he drew.
The shaft just grazed Fitz-James's crest,
And thrill'd in Blanche's faded breast. —
Murdoch of Alpine! prove thy speed,
For ne'er had Alpine's son such need!
With heart of fire, and foot of wind,
The fierce avenger is behind!
Fate judges of the rapid strife —
The forfeit death — the prize is life!
Thy kindred ambush lies before,
Close couch'd upon the heathery moor;
Them couldst thou reach! — It may not be,
Thine ambush'd kin thou ne'er shalt see,
The fiery Saxon gains on thee!
— Resistless speeds the deadly thrust,
As lightning strikes the pine to dust;

* Of ten branches to his antlers: a royal or
noble deer.

With foot and hand Fitz-James must
    strain,
Ere he can win his blade again.
Bent o'er the fallen, with falcon eye,
He grimly smiled to see him die;
Then slower wended back his way,
Where the poor maiden bleeding lay.

XXVII.

She sate beneath the birchen tree,
Her elbow resting on her knee;
She had withdrawn the fatal shaft,
And gazed on it, and feebly laugh'd;
Her wreath of broom and feathers gray,
Daggled with blood, beside her lay.
The Knight to stanch the life-stream tried.
"Stranger, it is in vain!" she cried.
"This hour of death has given me more
Of reason's power than years before;
For, as these ebbing veins decay,
My frenzied visions fade away.
A helpless injured wretch I die,
And something tells me in thine eye,
That thou wert mine avenger born. —
Seest thou this tress? — O! still I've worn
This little tress of yellow hair,
Through danger, frenzy, and despair!
It once was bright and clear as thine,
But blood and tears have dimm'd its shine.
I will not tell thee when 'twas shred,
Nor from what guiltless victim's head —
My brain would turn! — but it shall wave
Like plumage on thy helmet brave,
Till sun and wind shall bleach the stain,
And thou wilt bring it me again.
I waver still. — O God! more bright
Let reason beam her parting light! —
O! by thy knighthood's honor'd sign,
And for thy life preserved by mine,
When thou shalt see a darksome man,
Who boasts him Chief of Alpine's Clan,
With tartans broad and shadowy plume,
And hand of blood, and brow of gloom,
Be thy heart bold, thy weapon strong,
And wreak poor Blanche of Devan's
    wrong! —
They watch for thee by pass and fell . . .
Avoid the path . . . O God! . . . fare-
well."

XXVIII.

A kindly heart had brave Fitz-James;
Fast pour'd his eyes at pity's claims,

And now with mingled grief and ire,
He saw the murder'd maid expire.
' God, in my need, be my relief,
As I wreak this on yonder Chief ! "
A lock from Blanche's tresses fair
He blended with her bridegroom's hair;
The mingled braid in blood he dyed,
And placed it on his bonnet-side :
' By Him whose word is truth ! I swear,
No other favor will I wear,
Till this sad token I imbrue
In the best blood of Roderick Dhu !
— But hark ! what means yon faint hal-
loo ?
The chase is up, — but they shall know,
The stag at bay's a dangerous foe."
Barr'd from the known but guarded way,
Through copse and cliffs Fitz-James must
stray,
And oft must change his desperate track,
By stream and precipice turn'd back.
Heartless, fatigued, and faint, at length,
From lack of food and loss of strength,
He couch'd him in a thicket hoar,
And thought his toils and perils o'er :—
' Of all my rash adventures past,
This frantic feat must prove the last !
Who e'er so mad but might have guess'd,
That all this Highland hornet's nest
Would muster up in swarms so soon
As e'er they heard of bands at Doune ?—
Like bloodhounds now they search me out,
Hark to the whistle and the shout !—
If farther through the wilds I go,
I only fall upon the foe :
I'll couch me here till evening gray,
Then darkling try my dangerous way."

XXIX.

The shades of eve come slowly down,
The woods are wrapt in deeper brown,
The owl awakens from her dell,
The fox is heard upon the fell;
Enough remains of glimmering light
To guide the wanderer's steps aright.
Yet not enough from far to show
His figure to the watchful foe.
With cautious step, and ear awake,
He climbs the crag and threads the brake;
And not the summer solstice, there,
Temper'd the midnight mountain air,
But every breeze, that swept the wold,
Benumb'd his drenched limbs with cold.

In dread, in danger, and alone,
Famish'd and chill'd, through ways un-
known,
Tangled and steep, he journey'd on;
Till, as a rock's huge point he turn'd,
A watch-fire close before him burn'd.

XXX.

Beside its embers red and clear,
Bask'd, in his plaid, a mountaineer;
And up he sprung with sword in hand, —
" Thy name and purpose ! Saxon,
stand ! " —
" A stranger." — " What dost thou re-
quire ? "
" Rest and a guide, and food and fire.
My life's beset, my path is lost,
The gale has chill'd my limbs with frost."
" Art thou a friend to Roderick ? " —
" No." —
" Thou darest not call thyself a foe ? " —
" I dare ! to him and all the band
He brings to aid his murderous hand." —
" Bold words ! — but, though the beast
of game
The privilege of chase may claim,
Though space and law the stag we lend,
Ere hound we slip, or bow we bend,
Who ever reck'd, where, how, or when,
The prowling fox was trapp'd or slain ? [38]
Thus treacherous scouts,—yet sure they lie,
Who say thou camest a secret spy ! "
" They do, by Heaven ! — Come Roderick
Dhu,
And of his clan the boldest two,
And let me but till morning rest,
I write the falsehood on their crest." —
" If by the blaze I mark aright,
Thou bear'st the belt and spur of
Knight." —
" Then by these tokens mayest thou know
Each proud oppressor's mortal foe." —
" Enough, enough; sit down and share
A soldier's couch, a soldier's fare."

XXXI.

He gave him of his Highland cheer,
The harden'd flesh of mountain deer; [39]
Dry fuel on the fire he laid,
And bade the Saxon share his plaid.
He tended him like welcome guest,
Then thus his further speech address'd :—

" Stranger, I am to Roderick Dhu
A clansman born, a kinsman true;
Each word against his honor spoke,
Demands of me avenging stroke;
Yet more, — upon thy fate, 'tis said,
A mighty augury is laid.
It rests with me to wind my horn, —
Thou art with numbers overborne;
It rests with me, here, brand to brand,
Worn as thou art, to bid thee stand:
But, not for clan, nor kindred's cause,
Will I depart from honor's laws;
To assail a wearied man were shame,
And ' stranger ' is a holy name;
Guidance, and rest, and food, and fire,
In vain he never must require.
Then rest thee here till dawn of day;
Myself will guide thee on the way,
O'er stock and stone, through watch and
    ward,
Till past Clan-Alpine's outmost guard,
As far as Coilantogle's ford;
From thence thy warrant is thy sword." —
" I take thy courtesy, by Heaven,
As freely as 'tis nobly given ! "
" Well, rest thee; for the bittern's cry
Sings us the lake's wild lullaby."
With that he shook the gather'd heath,
And spread his plaid upon the wreath;
And the brave foemen, side by side,
Lay peaceful down like brothers tried,
And slept until the dawning beam
Purpled the mountain and the stream.

CANTO FIFTH.
THE COMBAT.
I.

FAIR as the earliest beam of eastern light,
    When first, by the bewilder'd pilgrim
        spied,
It smiles upon the dreary brow of night,
    And silvers o'er the torrent's foaming
        tide,
And lights the fearful path on mountain
        side; —
    Fair as that beam, although the fairest
        far,
Giving to horror grace, to danger pride,
    Shine martial Faith, and Courtesy's
        bright star,
Through all the wreckful storms that
    cloud the brow of War.

II.

That early beam, so fair and sheen,
Was twinkling through the hazel screen,
When, rousing at its glimmer red,
The warriors left their lowly bed,
Look'd out upon the dappled sky,
Mutter'd their soldier matins by,
And then awaked their fire, to steal,
As short and rude, their soldier meal.
That o'er, the Gael * around him threw
His graceful plaid of varied hue,
And, true to promise, led the way,
By thicket green and mountain gray.
A wildering path ! — they winded now
Along the precipice's brow,
Commanding the rich scenes beneath,
The windings of the Forth and Teith,
And all the vales beneath that lie,
Till Stirling's turrets melt in sky;
Then, sunk in copse, their farthest glance
Gain'd not the length of horseman's lance.
'Twas oft so steep, the foot was fain
Assistance from the hand to gain;
So tangled oft, that, bursting through,
Each hawthorn shed her showers of dew,
That diamond dew, so pure and clear,
It rivals all but Beauty's tear !

III.

At length they came where, stern and
        steep,
The hill sinks down upon the deep.
Here Vennachar in silver flows,
There, ridge on ridge, Benledi rose;
Ever the hollow path twined on,
Beneath steep bank and threatening
        stone;
A hundred men might hold the post
With hardihood against a host.
The rugged mountain's scanty cloak
Was dwarfish shrubs of birch and oak,
With shingles bare, and cliffs between,
And patches bright of bracken green,
And heather black, that waved so high,
It held the copse in rivalry.
But where the lake slept deep and still,
Dank osiers fringed the swamp and hill;
And oft both path and hill were torn,
Where wintry torrents down had borne,

* The Scottish Highlander calls himself *Gael*
or Gaul, and terms the Lowlanders *Sassenach,*
or Saxons.

And heap'd upon the cumber'd land
Its wreck of gravel, rocks, and sand
So toilsome was the road to trace,
The guide, abating of his pace,
Led slowly through the pass's jaws,
And ask'd Fitz-James, by what strange cause
He sought these wilds? traversed by few,
Without a pass from Roderick Dhu.

IV.

" Brave Gael, my pass in danger tried,
Hangs in my belt and by my side;
Yet, sooth to tell," the Saxon said,
" I dreamt not now to claim its aid.
When here, but three days since, I came,
Bewilder'd in pursuit of game,
All seem'd as peaceful and as still
As the mist slumbering on yon hill;
Thy dangerous Chief was then afar,
Nor soon expected back from war.
Thus said, at least, my mountain-guide,
Though deep, perchance, the villain lied."
" Yet why a second venture try?"
" A warrior thou, and ask me why! —
Moves our free course by such fix'd cause,
As gives the poor mechanic laws?
Enough, I sought to drive away
The lazy hours of peaceful day:
Slight cause will then suffice to guide
A Knight's free footsteps far and wide —
A falcon flown, a greyhound stray'd,
The merry glance of mountain maid;
Or, if a path be dangerous known,
The danger's self is lure alone."

V.

" Thy secret keep, I urge thee not: —
Yet, ere again ye sought this spot,
Say, heard ye naught of Lowland war,
Against Clan-Alpine, raised by Mar?"
—" No, by my word;—of bands prepared
To guard King James's sports I heard;
Nor doubt I aught, but, when they hear
This muster of the mountaineer,
Their pennons will abroad be flung,
Which else in Doune had peaceful hung."—
" Free be they flung! — for we were loth
Their silken folds should feast the moth.
Free be they flung! — as free shall wave
Clan-Alpine's pine in banner brave.

But, Stranger, peaceful since you came,
Bewilder'd in the mountain game,
Whence the bold boast by which you show
Vich-Alpine's vow'd and mortal foe?" —
" Warrior, but yester-morn, I knew
Naught of thy Chieftain, Roderick Dhu,
Save as an outlaw'd desperate man,
The chief of a rebellious clan,
Who, in the Regent's court and sight,
With ruffian dagger stabb'd a knight:
Yet this alone might from his part
Sever each true and loyal heart."

VI.

Wrathful at such arraignment foul,
Dark lower'd the clansman's sable scowl,
A space he paused, then sternly said: —
" And heard'st thou why he drew his blade?
Heard'st thou that shameful word and blow
Brought Roderick's vengeance on his foe?
What reck'd the Chieftain if he stood
On Highland heath, or Holy-Rood?
He rights such wrong where it is given,
If it were in the court of heaven." —
" Still was it outrage; —yet, 'tis true,
Not then claim'd sovereignty his due;
While Albany, with feeble hand,
Held borrow'd truncheon of command,[40]
The young King, mew'd in Stirling tower,
Was stranger to respect and power.
But then, thy Chieftain's robber life! —
Winning mean prey by causeless strife,
Wrenching from ruin'd Lowland swain
His herds and harvest rear'd in vain. —
Methinks a soul, like thine, should scorn
The spoils from such foul foray borne."

VII.

The Gael beheld him grim the while,
And answer'd with disdainful smile: —
" Saxon, from yonder mountain high,
I mark'd thee send delighted eye,
Far to the south and east, where lay,
Extended in succession gay,
Deep waving fields and pastures green,
With gentle slopes and groves between, —
These fertile plains, that soften'd vale,
Were once the birthright of the Gael;
The stranger came with iron hand,
And from our fathers reft the land.

Where dwell we now? See rudely swell
‸rag over crag, and fell o'er fell.
∿sk we this savage hill we tread,
For fatten'd steer or household bread:
Ask we for flocks these shingles dry,
And well the mountain might reply: —
' To you, as to your sires of yore,
Belong the target and claymore!
I give you shelter in my breast,
Your own good blades must win the rest.'
Pent in this fortress of the North,
Think'st thou we will not sally forth,
To spoil the spoiler as we may,
And from the robber rend the prey?
Ay, by my soul! — While on yon plain
The Saxon rears one shock of grain;
While, of ten thousand herds, there strays
But one along yon river's maze, —
The Gael, of plain and river heir,
Shall, with strong hand, redeem his share.
Where live the mountain chiefs who hold,
That plundering Lowland field and fold
Is aught but retribution true?
Seek other cause 'gainst Roderick Dhu.''

VIII.

Answer'd Fitz-James: — " And, if I
    sought,
Think'st thou no other could be brought?
What deem ye of my path waylaid?
My life given o'er to ambuscade? '' —
" As of a meed to rashness due:
Hadst thou sent warning fair and true, —
' I seek my hound, or falcon stray'd,
I seek, good faith, a Highland maid,'—
Free hadst thou been to come and go;
But secret path marks secret foe.
Nor yet, for this, even as a spy,
Hadst thou, unheard, been doom'd to die,
Save to fulfil an augury.'' —
" Well, let it pass; nor will I now
Fresh cause of enmity avow,
To chafe thy mood and cloud thy brow.
Enough, I am by promise tied
To match me with this man of pride:
Twice have I sought Clan-Alpine's glen
In peace; but when I come agen,
I come with banner, brand, and bow,
As leader seeks his mortal foe.
For love-lorn swain, in lady's bower,
Ne'er panted for the appointed hour,
As I, until before me stand
This rebel Chieftain and his band! '' —

IX.

" Have, then, thy wish! '' — He whistle
    shrill,
And he was answer'd from the hill;
Wild as the scream of the curlew,
From crag to crag the signal flew.
Instant, through copse and heᵃᵗ͏
    arose
Bonnets, and spears, and bended bows
On right, on left, above, below,
Sprung up at once the lurking foe;
From shingles gray their lances start,
The bracken bush sends forth the dart,
The rushes and the willow-wand
Are bristling into axe and brand,
And every tuft of broom gives life
To plaided warrior arm'd for strife.
That whistle garrison'd the glen
At once with full five hundred men,
As if the yawning hill to heaven
A subterranean host had given.
Watching their leader's beck and will,
All silent there they stood, and still.
Like the loose crags, whose threatenin
    mass
Lay tottering o'er the hollow pass,
As if an infant's touch could urge
Their headlong passage down the verge
With step and weapon forward flung,
Upon the mountain-side they hung.
The Mountaineer cast glance of pride
Along Benledi's living side,
Then fix'd his eye and sable brow
Full on Fitz-James: — " How say'st tho
    now?
These are Clan-Alpine's warriors true;
And, Saxon, — I am Roderick Dhu! ''

X.

Fitz-James was brave: — Though to hi
    heart
The life-blood thrill'd with sudden start
He mann'd himself with dauntless air,
Return'd the chief his haughty stare,
His back against a rock he bore,
And firmly placed his foot before: —
" Come one, come all! this rock shall fl
From its firm base as soon as I.''
Sir Roderick mark'd, — and in his eyes,
Respect was mingled with surprise,
And the stern joy which warriors feel
In foemen worthy of their steel.

ort space he stood; — then waved his
    hand:
own sunk the disappearing band;
ach warrior vanish'd where he stood,
broom or bracken, heath or wood;
unk brand, and spear, and bended bow,
osiers pale and copses low;
   seem'd as if their mother Earth
ad swallow'd up her warlike birth.
ne wind's last breath had toss'd in air,
ennon, and plaid, and plumage fair, —
he next but swept a lone hill-side,
There heath and fern were waving wide.
he sun's last glance was glinted back
rom spear and glaive, from targe and
    jack, —
he next, all unreflected shone
n bracken green and cold gray stone.

XI.

itz-James look'd round — yet scarce be-
    lieved
he witness that his sight received;
uch apparition well might seem
elusion of a dreadful dream.
r Roderick in suspense he eyed,
nd to his look the Chief replied: —
   Fear naught — nay, that I need not
    say —
ut — doubt not aught from mine array.
hou art my guest; — I pledged my word
s far as Coilantogle ford:
or would I call a clansman's brand
or aid against one valiant hand,
hough on our strife lay every vale
ent by the Saxon from the Gael.
o move we on; — I only meant
o show the reed on which you leant,
eeming this path you might pursue
Tithout a pass from Roderick Dhu." [41]
hey moved: — I said Fitz-James was
    brave,
s ever knight that belted glaive;
et dare not say, that now his blood
ept on its wont and temper'd flood,
s, following Roderick's stride, he drew
hat seeming lonesome pathway through,
Thich yet, by fearful proof, was rife
Tith lances, that, to take his life,
Taited but signal from a guide,
o late dishonor'd and defied.
ver, by stealth, his eye sought round
he vanish'd guardians of the ground,

And still, from copse and heather deep,
Fancy saw spear and broadsword peep,
And in the plover's shrilly strain,
The signal whistle heard again.
Nor breathed he free till far behind
The pass was left; for then they wind
Along a wide and level green,
Where neither tree nor tuft was seen,
Nor rush, nor bush of broom was near,
To hide a bonnet or a spear.

XII.

The Chief in silence strode before,
And reach'd that torrent's sounding shore,
Which, daughter of three mighty lakes,
From Vennachar in silver breaks,
Sweeps through the plain, and ceaseless
    mines
On Bochastle the mouldering lines,
Where Rome, the Empress of the world,
Of yore her eagle wings unfurl'd. [42]
And here his course the Chieftain staid,
Threw down his target and his plaid,
And to the Lowland warrior said: —
   "Bold Saxon! to his promise just,
Vich-Alpine has discharged his trust.
This murderous Chief, this ruthless man,
This head of a rebellious clan,
Hath led thee safe through watch and
    ward
Far past Clan-Alpine's outmost guard.
Now, man to man, and steel to steel,
A chieftain's vengeance thou shalt feel.
See here, all vantageless I stand,
Arm'd, like thyself, with single brand: [43]
For this is Coilantogle ford,
And thou must keep thee with thy sword."

XIII.

The Saxon paused: — "I ne'er delay'd,
When foeman bade me draw my blade;
Nay, more, brave Chief, I vow'd thy
    death;
Yet sure thy fair and generous faith,
And my deep debt for life preserved,
A better meed have well deserved:
Can naught but blood our feud atone?
Are there no means?" — "No, Stranger,
    none!
And hear, — to fire thy flagging zeal, —
The Saxon cause rests on thy steel;
For thus spoke Fate, by prophet bred
Between the living and the dead:

' Who spills the foremost foeman's life,
His party conquers in the strife.' ''—
" Then, by my word," the Saxon said,
" The riddle is already read.
Seek yonder brake beneath the cliff,—
There lies Red Murdoch, stark and stiff.
Thus Fate has solv'd her prophecy,
Then yield to Fate, and not to me.
To James, at Stirling, let us go,
When, if thou wilt be still his foe,
Or if the King shall not agree
To grant thee grace and favor free,
I plight mine honor, oath, and word,
That, to thy native strengths restored,
With each advantage shalt thou stand,
That aids thee now to guard thy land."

XIV.

Dark lightning flash'd from Roderick's
        eye:—
" Soars thy presumption, then, so high,
Because a wretched kern ye slew,
Homage to name to Roderick Dhu?
He yields not, he, to man nor Fate!
Thou add'st but fuel to my hate:—
My clansman's blood demands revenge.
Not yet prepared?—By heaven, I change
My thought, and hold thy valor light
As that of some vain carpet-knight,
Who ill-deserved my courteous care,
And whose best boast is but to wear
A braid of his fair lady's hair."—
" I thank thee, Roderick, for the word!
It nerves my heart, it steels my sword;
For I have sworn this braid to stain
In the best blood that warms thy vein.
Now, truce, farewell! and, ruth, be
        gone!—
Yet think not that by thee alone,
Proud Chief! can courtesy be shown!
Though not from copse, or heath, or
        cairn,
Start at my whistle clansmen stern,
Of this small horn one feeble blast
Would fearful odds against thee cast.
But fear not—doubt not—which thou
        wilt—
We try this quarrel hilt to hilt."—
Then each at once his falchion drew,
Each on the ground his scabbard threw,
Each look'd to sun, and stream, and
        plain,
As what they ne'er might see again;

Then foot, and point, and eye opposed,
In dubious strife they darkly closed.

XV.

I'll fared it then with Roderick Dhu,
That on the field his targe he threw,[44]
Whose brazen studs and tough bull-hide
Had death so often dash'd aside;
For, train'd abroad his arms to wield,
Fitz-James's blade was sword and shield
He practised every pass and ward,
To thrust, to strike, to feint, to guard;
While less expert, though stronger far,
The Gael maintain'd unequal war.
Three times in closing strife they stood
And thrice the Saxon's blade drank blood
No stinted draught, no scanty tide,
The gushing flood the tartans dyed.
Fierce Roderick felt the fatal drain,
And shower'd his blows like wintry rain
And, as firm rock, or castle-roof,
Against the winter shower is proof,
The foe, invulnerable still,
Foil'd his wild rage by steady skill:
Till, at advantage ta'en, his brand
Forced Roderick's weapon from his hand
And backward borne upon the lea,
Brought the proud chieftain to his knee

XVI.

" Now, yield thee, or by Him who mad
The world, thy heart's blood dyes m
        blade!''
" Thy threats, thy mercy, I defy!
Let recreant yield, who fears to die."
— Like adder darting from his coil,
Like wolf that dashes through the toil,
Like mountain-cat who guards her young
Full at Fitz-James's throat he sprung;
Received, but reck'd not of a wound,
And lock'd his arms his foeman round. —
Now, gallant Saxon, hold thine own!
No maiden's hand is round thee thrown
That desperate grasp thy frame might fee
Through bars of brass and triple steel!—
They tug, they strain! down, down the
        go,
The Gael above, Fitz-James below:
The Chieftain's gripe his throat com
        press'd,
His knee was planted on his breast;
His clotted locks he backward threw,
Across his brow his hand he drew,

'rom blood and mist to clear his sight,
'hen gleam'd aloft his dagger bright ! —
— But hate and fury ill supplied
'he stream of life's exhausted tide,
.nd all too late the advantage came,
'o turn the odds of deadly game;
'or, while the dagger gleam'd on high,
.eel'd soul and sense, reel'd brain and eye,
)own came the blow ! but in the heath
'he erring blade found bloodless sheath.
'he struggling foe may now unclasp
'he fainting Chief's relaxing grasp;
Inwounded from the dreadful close,
.ut breathless all, Fitz-James arose.

XVII.

Ie falter'd thanks to Heaven for life,
.edeem'd, unhoped, from desperate
     strife;
'ext on his foe his look he cast,
Vhose every gasp appear'd his last;
1 Roderick's gore he dipp'd the braid : —
Poor Blanche ! thy wrongs are dearly
     paid :
'et with thy foe must die or live,
he praise that Faith and Valor give. '
Vith that he blew a bugle-note,
'ndid the collar from his throat,
'nbonneted, and by the wave
ate down his brow and hands to lave.
'hen faint afar are heard the feet
*f rushing steeds in gallop fleet;
he sounds increase, and now are seen
our mounted squires in Lincoln green :
wo who bear lance, and two who lead,
y loosen'd rein, a saddled steed;
ach onward held his headlong course,
nd by Fitz-James rein'd up his horse, —
Vith wonder view'd the bloody spot. —
-" Exclaim not, gallants ! question not.
ou, Herbert and Luffness, alight,
nd bind the wounds of yonder knight;
et the gray palfrey bear his weight,
Ve destined for a fairer freight,
nd bring him on to Stirling straight :
will before at better speed,
o seek fresh horse and fitting weed.
he sun rides high ; — I must be boune,*
o see the archer-game at noon :
ut lightly Bayard clears the lea, —
e Vaux and Herries, follow me.

* Boune, prepared.

XVIII.

" Stand, Bayard, stand ! " — The steed
     obey'd,
With arching neck and bending head,
And glancing eye and quivering ear,
As if he loved his lord to hear.
No foot Fitz-James in stirrup staid,
No grasp upon the saddle laid,
But wreath'd his left hand in the mane,
And lightly bounded from the plain,
Turn'd on the horse his armed heel,
And stirr'd his courage with the steel.
Bounded the fiery steed in air,
The rider sate erect and fair,
Then like a bolt from steel crossbow
Forth launch'd, along the plain they go.
They dash'd that rapid torrent through,
And up Carhonie's hill they flew;
Still at the gallop prick'd the Knight,
His merry-men follow'd as they might.
Along thy banks, swift Teith ! they ride,
And in the race they mock thy tide;
Torry and Lendrick now are past,
And Deanstown lies behind them cast :
They rise, the banner'd towers of Doune,
They sink in distant woodland soon;
Blair-Drummond sees the hoof strike fire,
They sweep like breeze through Ochter-
     tyre;
They mark just glance and disappear
The lofty brow of ancient Kier;
They bathe their coursers' sweltering
     sides,
Dark Forth ! amid thy sluggish tides,
And on the opposing shore take ground,
With plash, with scramble, and with
     bound.
Right-hand they leave thy cliffs, Craig-
     Forth !
And soon the bulwark of the North,
Gray Stirling, with her towers and town,
Upon their fleet career look'd down.

XIX.

As up the flinty path they strain'd
Sudden his steed the leader rein'd;
A signal to his squire he flung,
Who instant to his stirrup sprung :—
" Seest thou, De Vaux, yon woodsman
     gray,
Who town-ward holds the rocky way,
Of stature tall and poor array?

Mark'st thou the firm, yet active stride,
With which he scales the mountain-side?
Know'st thou from whence he comes, or
        whom?''—
" No, by my word ; — a burly groom
He seems, who in the field or chase
A baron's train would nobly grace.'' —
" Out, out, De Vaux ! can fear supply,
And jealousy, no sharper eye?
Afar, ere to the hill he drew,
That stately form and step I knew;
Like form in Scotland is not seen,
Treads not such step on Scottish green.
'Tis James of Douglas, by Saint Serle !
The uncle of the banish'd Earl.
Away, away, to court, to show
The near approach of dreaded foe:
The King must stand upon his guard:
Douglas and he must meet prepared.''
Then right-hand wheel'd their steeds,
        and straight,
They won the castle's postern gate.

XX.

The Douglas, who had bent his way
From Cambuskenneth's abbey gray,
Now, as he climb'd the rocky shelf,
Held sad communion with himself: —
" Yes, all is true my fears could frame:
A prisoner lies the noble Græme,
And fiery Roderick soon will feel
The vengeance of the royal steel.
I, only I, can ward their fate,—
God grant the ransom come not late !
The Abbess hath her promise given,
My child shall be the bride of Heaven;—
— Be pardon'd one repining tear !
For He, who gave her, knows how
        dear,
How excellent ! but that is by,
And now my business is — to die.
— Ye towers ! within whose circuit dread
A Douglas by his sovereign bled;
And thou, O sad and fatal mound ! *
That oft hast heard the death-axe sound,
As on the noblest of the land
Fell the stern headsman's bloody hand,—
The dungeon, block, and nameless tomb
Prepare — for Douglas seeks his doom !
— But hark ! what blithe and jolly peal
Makes the Franciscan steeple reel?

* A mound on the north-east of Stirling Castle
where State criminals were executed.

And see ! upon the crowded street,
In motley groups what masquers meet !
Banner and pageant, pipe and drum,
And merry morrice-dancers come.
I guess, by all this quaint array,
The burghers hold their sports to-day.[45]
James will be there; he loves such show
Where the good yeoman bends his bow,
And the tough wrestler foils his foe,
As well as where, in proud career,
The high-borne tilter shivers spear.
I'll follow to the Castle-park,
And play my prize; — King James shall
        mark,
If age has tamed these sinews stark,
Whose force so oft, in happier days,
His boyish wonder loved to praise.''

XXI.

The castle gates were open flung,
The quivering drawbridge rock'd and
        rung,
And echo'd loud the flinty street
Beneath the coursers' clattering feet,
As slowly down the steep descent
Fair Scotland's King and nobles went,
While all along the crowded way
Was jubilee and loud huzza.
And ever James was bending low,
To his white jennet's saddle-bow,
Doffing his cap to city dame,
Who smiled and blush'd for pride and
        shame.
And well the simperer might be vain,—
He chose the fairest of the train.
Gravely he greets each city sire,
Commends each pageant's quaint attire,
Gives to the dancers thanks aloud,
And smiles and nods upon the crowd,
Who rend the heavens with their acclaims
" Long live the Commons' King, King
        James ! ''
Behind the King throng'd peer and knight,
And noble dame and damsel bright,
Whose fiery steeds ill brook'd the stay
Of the steep street and crowded way.
— But in the train you might discern
Dark lowering brow and visage stern;
There nobles mourn'd their pride re-
        strain'd,
And the mean burgher's joys disdain'd;
And chiefs, who, hostage for their clan,
Were each from home a banish'd man,

here thought upon their own gray tower,
heir waving woods, their feudal power,
nd deem'd themselves a shameful part
f pageant which they cursed in heart.

XXII.

ow, in the Castle-park, drew out
heir checker'd bands the joyous rout.
here morricers, with bell at heel,
nd blade in hand, their mazes wheel;
ɪt chief, beside the butts, there stand
ɔld Robin Hood [46] and all his band,—
riar Tuck with quarterstaff and cowl,
ld Scathelocke with his surly scowl,
aid Marion, fair as ivory bone,
arlet, and Mutch, and Little John;
ieir bugles challenge all that will,
 archery to prove their skill.
ie Douglas bent a bow of might, —
is first shaft centred in the white,
ɪd when in turn he shot again,
is second split the first in twain.
'om the King's hand must Douglas take
 silver dart, the archer's stake;
ɔndly he watch'd, with watery eye,
ɔme answering glance of sympathy, —
ɔ kind emotion made reply!
 different as to archer wight,
ie monarch gave the arrow bright.

XXIII.

ɔw, clear the ring! for, hand to hand,
ɪe manly wrestlers take their stand.
ʋo o'er the rest superior rose,
ɪd proud demanded mightier foes,
ɔr called in vain: for Douglas came.
 For life is Hugh of Larbert lame;
arce better John of Alloa's fare,
hom senseless home his comrades bear.
ize of the wrestling match, the King
 Douglas gave a golden ring,[47]
hile coldly glanced his eye of blue,
 frozen drop of wintry dew.
ɔuglas would speak, but in his breast
s struggling soul his words suppress'd;
dignant then he turn'd him where
eir arms the brawny yeomen bare,
 hurl the massive bar in air.
hen each his utmost strength had
 shown,
e Douglas rent an earth-fast stone
ɔm its deep bed, then heaved it high,
d sent the fragment through the sky,

A rood beyond the farthest mark;—
And still in Stirling's royal park,
The gray-hair'd sires, who know the past,
To strangers point the Douglas-cast,
And moralize on the decay
Of Scottish strength in modern day.

XXIV.

The vale with loud applauses rang,
The Ladies' Rock sent back the clang.
The King, with look unmoved, bestow'd
A purse well fill'd with pieces broad.
Indignant smiled the Douglas proud,
And threw the gold among the crowd,
Who now, with anxious wonder, scan,
And sharper glance, the dark gray man;
Till whispers rose among the throng,
That heart so free, and hand so strong,
Must to the Douglas blood belong;
The old men mark'd, and shook the head,
To see his hair with silver spread,
And wink'd aside, and told each son,
Of feats upon the English done,
Ere Douglas of the stalwart hand
Was exiled from his native land.
The women praised his stately form,
Though wreck'd by many a winter's
 storm!
The youth with awe and wonder saw
His strength surpassing Nature's law.
Thus judged, as is their wont, the crowd,
Till murmur rose to clamors loud.
But not a glance from that proud ring
Of peers who circled round the King,
With Douglas held communion kind,
Or call'd the banish'd man to mind;
No, not from those who, at the chase,
Once held his side the honor'd place,
Begirt his board, and, in the field,
Found safety underneath his shield;
For he, whom royal eyes disown,
When was his form to courtiers known!

XXV.

The Monarch saw the gambols flag,
And bade let loose a gallant stag,
Whose pride, the holiday to crown,
Two favorite greyhounds should pull
 down,
That venison free, and Bordeaux wine,
Might serve the archery to dine.
But Lufra, — whom from Douglas' side
Nor bribe nor threat could e'er divide,

The fleetest hound in all the North, —
Brave Lufra saw, and darted forth.
She left the royal hounds mid-way,
And dashing on the antler'd prey,
Sunk her sharp muzzle in his flank,
And deep the flowing life-blood drank.
The King's stout huntsman saw the sport
By strange intruder broken short,
Came up, and with his leash unbound,
In anger struck the noble hound.
— The Douglas had endured, that morn,
The King's cold look, the nobles' scorn,
And last, and worst to spirit proud,
Had borne the pity of the crowd;
But Lufra had been fondly bred,
To share his board, to watch his bed,
And oft would Ellen Lufra's neck
In maiden glee with garlands deck;
They were such playmates, that with name
Of Lufra, Ellen's image came.
His stifled wrath is brimming high,
In darken'd brow and flashing eye:
As waves before the bark divide,
The crowd gave way before his stride;
Needs but a buffet and no more,
The groom lies senseless in his gore.
Such blow no other hand could deal,
Though gauntleted in glove of steel.

XXVI.

Then clamor'd loud the royal train,
And brandish'd swords and staves amain.
But stern the Baron's warning : — "Back !
Back, on your lives, ye menial pack !
Beware the Douglas. — Yes ! behold,
King James ! the Douglas, doom'd of old,
And vainly sought for near and far,
A victim to atone the war,
A willing victim, now attends,
Nor craves thy grace but for his
 friends." —
"Thus is my clemency repaid?
Presumptuous Lord ! " the monarch said;
" Of thy misproud ambitious clan,
Thou, James of Bothwell, wert the man,
The only man, in whom a foe
My woman-mercy would not know :
But shall a Monarch's presence brook
Injurious blow, and haughty look? —
What ho ! the Captain of our Guard !
Give the offender fitting ward, —
Break off the sports ! " — for tumult rose,
And yeomen 'gan to bend their bows, —

" Break off the sports ! " he said, an
 frown'd,
" And bid our horsemen clear th
 ground."

XXVII.

Then uproar wild and misarray
Marr'd the fair form of festal day.
The horsemen prick'd among the crow
Repell'd by threats and insult loud;
To earth are borne the old and weak,
The timorous fly, the women shriek :
With flint, with shaft, with staff, with ba
The hardier urge tumultuous war.
At once round Douglas darkly sweep
The royal spears in circle deep,
And slowly scale the pathway steep;
While on the rear in thunder pour
The rabble with disorder'd roar.
With grief the noble Douglas saw
The Commons rise against the law,
And to the leading soldier said : —
" Sir John of Hyndford ! 'twas my bla
That knighthood on thy shoulder laid;
For that good deed, permit me then
A word with these misguided men : —

XXVIII.

" Hear, gentle friends ! ere yet for me
Ye break the bands of fealty.
My life, my honor, and my cause,
I tender free to Scotland's laws.
Are these so weak as must require
The aid of your misguided ire !
Or, if I suffer causeless wrong,
Is then my selfish rage so strong,
My sense of public weal so low,
That, for mean vengeance on a foe,
Those chords of love I should unbind,
Which knit my country and my kind?
Oh no ! Believe, in yonder tower
It will not sooth my captive hour,
To know those spears our foes shou
 dread,
For me in kindred gore are red;
To know, in fruitless brawl begun,
For me, that mother wails her son;
For me, that widow's mate expires;
For me, that orphans weep their sires;
That patriots mourn insulted laws,
And curse the Douglas for the cause.
O let your patience ward such ill,
And keep your right to love me still ! "

XXIX.

The crowd's wild fury sunk again
In tears, as tempests melt in rain.
With lifted hands and eyes, they pray'd
For blessings on his generous head,
Who for his country felt alone,
And prized her blood beyond his own.
Old men, upon the verge of life,
Bless'd him who staid the civil strife;
And mothers held their babes on high,
The self-devoted Chief to spy,
Triumphant over wrongs and ire,
To whom the prattlers owed a sire:
Even the rough soldier's heart was moved;
As if behind some bier beloved,
With trailing arms and drooping head,
The Douglas up the hill he led,
And at the Castle's battled verge
With sighs resign'd his honor'd charge.

XXX.

The offended Monarch rode apart,
With bitter thought and swelling heart,
And would not now vouchsafe again
Through Stirling streets to lead his train.
' O Lennox, who would wish to rule
This changeling crowd, this common fool?
Hear'st thou," he said, "the loud acclaim,
With which they shout the Douglas' name?
With like acclaim, the vulgar throat
Strain'd for King James their morning note;
With like acclaim they hail'd the day
When first I broke the Douglas' sway;
And like acclaim would Douglas greet,
If he could hurl me from my seat.
Who o'er the herd would wish to reign,
Fantastic, fickle, fierce, and vain!
Vain as the leaf upon the stream,
And fickle as a changeful dream;
Fantastic as a woman's mood,
And fierce as Frenzy's fever'd blood.
Thou many-headed monster-thing,
O who would wish to be thy king!

XXXI.

"But soft! what messenger of speed
Spurs hitherward his panting steed?
I guess his cognizance afar —
What from our cousin, John of Mar?"

" He prays, my liege, your sports keep bound
Within the safe and guarded ground:
For some foul purpose yet unknown, —
Most sure for evil to the throne, —
The outlaw'd Chieftain, Roderick Dhu,
Has summon'd his rebellious crew;
'Tis said, in James of Bothwell's aid
These loose banditti stand array'd.
The Earl of Mar, this morn, from Doune,
To break their muster march'd, and soon
Your grace will hear of battle fought;
But earnestly the Earl besought,
Till for such danger he provide,
With scanty train you will not ride." —

XXXII.

"Thou warn'st me I have done amiss, —
I should have earlier look'd to this:
I lost it in this bustling day.
— Retrace with speed thy former way;
Spare not for spoiling of thy steed,
The best of mine shall be thy meed.
Say to our faithful Lord of Mar,
We do forbid the intended war:
Roderick, this morn, in single fight,
Was made our prisoner by a knight;
And Douglas hath himself and cause
Submitted to our kingdom's laws.
The tidings of their leaders lost
Will soon dissolve the mountain host,
Nor would we that the vulgar feel,
For their Chief's crimes, avenging steel.
Bear Mar our message, Braco: fly!"
He turn'd his steed, — "My liege, I hie. —
Yet, ere I cross this lily lawn,
I fear the broadswords will be drawn."
The turf the flying courser spurn'd,
And to his towers the King return'd.

XXXIII.

Ill with King James's mood that day
Suited gay feast and minstrel lay;
Soon were dismiss'd the courtly throng,
And soon cut short the festal song.
Nor less upon the sadden'd town
The evening sunk in sorrow down.
The burghers spoke of civil jar,
Of rumor'd feuds and mountain war,
Of Moray, Mar, and Roderick Dhu,
All up in arms:— the Douglas too,

They mourn'd him pent within the hold,
"Where stout Earl William was of
  old," — *
And there his word the speaker staid,
And finger on his lip he laid,
Or pointed to his dagger blade.
But jaded horsemen, from the west,
At evening to the Castle press'd;
And busy talkers said they bore
Tidings of fight on Katrine's shore;
At noon the deadly fray begun,
And lasted till the set of sun.
Thus giddy rumor shook the town,
Till closed the Night her pennons brown.

CANTO SIXTH.

THE GUARD–ROOM.

I.

THE sun, awakening, through the smoky
    air
  Of the dark city casts a sullen glance,
Rousing each caitiff to his task of care,
  Of sinful man the sad inheritance;
Summoning revellers from the lagging
    dance,
  Scaring the prowling robber to his den;
Gilding on battled tower the warder's
    lance,
  And warning student pale to leave his
    pen,
And yield his drowsy eyes to the kind
    nurse of men.

What various scenes, and O ! what scenes
    of woe,
  Are witness'd by that red and struggling
    beam !
The fever'd patient from his pallet low,
  Through crowded hospital beholds it
    stream;
The ruin'd maiden trembles at its gleam,
  The debtor wakes to thought of gyve
    and jail,
The love-lorn wretch starts from torment-
    ing dream;
  The wakeful mother, by the glimmer-
    ing pale,
Trims her sick infant's couch, and soothes
    his feeble wail.

* He had been stabbed by James II. in Stirling Castle.

II.

At dawn the towers of Stirling rang
With soldier-step and weapon-clang,
While drums, with rolling note, foretel
Relief to weary sentinel.
Through narrow loop and casement barr'
The sunbeams sought the Court of Guar
And, struggling with the smoky air,
Deaden'd the torches' yellow glare.
In comfortless alliance shone
The lights through arch of blacken
    stone,
And show'd wild shapes in garb of war
Faces deform'd with beard and scar,
All haggard from the midnight watch,
And fever'd with the stern debauch;
For the oak table's massive board,
Flooded with wine, with fragments store
And beakers drain'd, and cups o'erthrow
Show'd in what sport the night h
    flown.
Some, weary, snored on floor and benc
Some labor'd still their thirst to quench
Some, chill'd with watching, spread th
    hands
O'er the huge chimney's dying brands,
While round them, or beside them flur
At every step their harness rung.

III.

These drew not for their fields the swor
Like tenants of a feudal lord,
Nor own'd the patriarchal claim
Of chieftain in their leader's name;
Adventurers they, from far who roved,
To live by battle which they loved.[48]
There the Italian's clouded face;
The swarthy Spaniard's there you trace
The mountain-loving Switzer there
More freely breathed in mountain air;
The Fleming there despised the soil,
That paid so ill the laborer's toil;
Their rolls showed French and Germ
    name;
And merry England's exiles came,
To share, with ill-concealed disdain,
Of Scotland's pay the scanty gain.
All brave in arms, well train'd to wield
The heavy halberd, brand, and shield;
In camps licentious, wild, and bold;
In pillage fierce and uncontroll'd;
And now, by holytide and feast,
From rules of discipline released.

IV.

hey held debate of bloody fray,
ought 'twixt Loch Katrine and Achray.
ierce was their speech, and, mid their
    words,
heir hands oft grappled to their swords;
Jor sunk their tone to spare the ear
Df wounded comrades groaning near,
Vhose mangled limbs, and bodies gored,
Bore token of the mountain sword.
hough, neighboring to the Court of
    Guard,
heir prayers and feverish wails were
    heard!
ad burden to the ruffian joke,
And savage oath by fury spoke!—
At length up started John of Brent,
A yeoman from the banks of Trent;
A stranger to respect or fear,
n peace a chaser of the deer,
n host a hardy mutineer,
But still the boldest of the crew,
Vhen deed of danger was to do.
He grieved, that day, their games cut
    short,
And marr'd the dicer's brawling sport,
And shouted loud:—" Renew the bowl!
And, while a merry catch I troll,
Let each the buxom chorus bear,
Like brethren of the brand and spear."

V.

SOLDIER'S SONG.

Dur vicar still preaches that Peter and
    Poule
Laid a swinging long curse on the bonny
    brown bowl,
That there's wrath and despair in the
    bonny black-jack,
And the seven deadly sins in a flagon of
    sack;
Yet whoop, Barnaby! off with thy liquor,
Drink upsees* out, and a fig for the vicar!

Dur vicar he calls it damnation to sip
The ripe ruddy dew of a woman's dear lip,
Says that Beelzebub lurks in her kerchief
    so sly,
And Apollyon shoots darts from her merry
    black eye.

* A Dutch health, or drinking word.

Yet whoop, Jack! kiss Gillian the quicker,
Till she bloom like a rose, and a fig for the
    vicar!

Our vicar thus preaches—and why should
    he not?
For the dues of his cure are the placket
    and pot;
And 'tis right of his office poor laymen
    to lurch,
Who infringe the domains of our good
    Mother Church.
Yet whoop, bully-boys! off with your
    liquor,
Sweet Marjorie's the word, and a fig for
    the vicar!

VI.

The warder's challenge, heard without,
Staid in mid-roar the merry shout.
A soldier to the portal went,—
" Here is old Bertram, sirs, of Ghent,
And,—beat for jubilee the drum!
A maid and minstrel with him come."
Bertram, a Fleming, gray and scarr'd,
Was entering now the Court of Guard,
A harper with him, and in plaid,
All muffled close, a mountain maid,
Who backward shrunk to 'scape the view
Of the loose scene and boisterous crew.
" What news?" they roar'd:—" I only
    know,
From noon till eve we fought with foe,
As wild and as untamable
As the rude mountains where they dwell;
On both sides store of blood is lost,
Nor much success can either boast."
" But whence thy captives, friend? such
    spoil
As theirs must needs reward thy toil.
Old dost thou wax, and wars grow sharp;
Thou now hast glee-maiden and harp!
Get thee an ape, and trudge the land,
The leader of a juggler band." [49]

VII.

" No, comrade;—no such fortune mine.
After the fight these sought our line,
That aged harper and the girl,
And, having audience of the Earl,
Mar bade I should purvey them steed,
And bring them hitherward with speed.

Forbear your mirth and rude alarm,
For none shall do them shame or harm."
"Hear ye his boast?" cried John of
       Brent,
Ever to strife and jangling bent;
"Shall he strike doe beside our lodge,
And yet the jealous niggard grudge
To pay the forester his fee?
I'll have my share, howe'er it be,
Despite of Moray, Mar, or thee."
Bertram his forward step withstood;
And, burning with his vengeful mood,
Old Allan, though unfit for strife,
Laid hand upon his dagger-knife;
But Ellen boldly stepp'd between,
And dropp'd at once the tartan screen:—
So, from his morning cloud, appears
The sun of May, through summer tears.
The savage soldiery, amazed,
As on descended angel gazed;
Even hardy Brent, abash'd and tamed,
Stood half admiring, half ashamed.

VIII.

Boldly she spoke:—"Soldiers, attend!
My father was the soldier's friend;
Cheer'd him in camps, in marches led,
And with him in the battle bled.
Not from the valiant, or the strong,
Should exile's daughter suffer wrong."—
Answer'd De Brent, most forward still
In every feat or good or ill:—
"I shame me of the part I play'd;
And thou an outlaw's child, poor maid!
An outlaw I by forest laws,
And merry Needwood knows the cause.
Poor Rose,—if Rose be living now,"—
He wiped his iron eye and brow,—
"Must bear such age, I think, as thou.—
Hear ye, my mates; I go to call
The Captain of our watch to hall:
There lies my halberd on the floor;
And he that steps my halberd o'er,
To do the maid injurious part,
My shaft shall quiver in his heart!—
Beware loose speech, or jesting rough:—
Ye all know John de Brent. Enough."

IX.

Their Captain came, a gallant young,—
(Of Tullibardine's house he sprung,)
Nor wore he yet the spurs of knight;
Gay was his mien, his humor light,

And, though by courtesy controll'd,
Forward his speech, his bearing bold.
The high-born maiden ill could brook
The scanning of his curious look
And dauntless eye;—and yet, in sooth,
Young Lewis was a generous youth;
But Ellen's lovely face and mien,
Ill suited to the garb and scene,
Might lightly bear construction strange,
And give loose fancy scope to range.
"Welcome to Stirling towers, fair maid!
Come ye to seek a champion's aid,
On palfrey white, with harper hoar,
Like errant damosel of yore?
Does thy high quest a knight require,
Or may the venture suit a squire?"
Her dark eye flash'd;—she paused and
        sigh'd:—
"O what have I to do with pride!
Through scenes of sorrow, shame, and
        strife,
A suppliant for a father's life,
I crave an audience of the King.
Behold, to back my suit, a ring,
The royal pledge of grateful claims,
Given by the Monarch to Fitz-James."

X.

The signet-ring young Lewis took,
With deep respect and alter'd look;
And said:— "This ring our duties own;
And pardon, if to worth unknown,
In semblance mean obscurely veil'd,
Lady, in aught my folly fail'd.
Soon as the day flings wide his gates,
The King shall know what suitor waits.
Please you, meanwhile, in fitting bower
Repose you till his waking hour;
Female attendance shall obey
Your hest, for service or array.
Permit I marshal you the way."
But, ere she follow'd, with the grace
And open bounty of her race,
She bade her slender purse be shared
Among the soldiers of the guard.
The rest with thanks their guerdon took;
But Brent, with shy and awkward look,
On the reluctant maiden's hold
Forced bluntly back the proffer'd gold:—
"Forgive a haughty English heart,
And O forget its ruder part!
The vacant purse shall be my share,
Which in my barret-cap I'll bear,

Perchance, in jeopardy of war,
Where gayer crests may keep afar.''
With thanks — 'twas all she could — the
    maid
His rugged courtesy repaid.

XI.

When Ellen forth with Lewis went,
Allan made suit to John of Brent:—
' My lady safe, O let your grace
Give me to see my master's face !
His minstrel I, — to share his doom
Bound from the cradle to the tomb.
Tenth in descent, since first my sires
Waked for his noble house their lyres,
Nor one of all the race was known
But prized its weal above their own.
With the Chief's birth begins our care;
Our harp must soothe the infant heir,
Teach the youth tales of fight, and
    grace
His earliest feat of field or chase;
In peace, in war, our rank we keep,
We cheer his board, we soothe his sleep,
Nor leave him till we pour our verse —
A doleful tribute ! — o'er his hearse.
Then let me share his captive lot;
It is my right — deny it not ! '' —
' Little we reck,'' said John of Brent,
' We Southern men, of long descent;
Nor wot we how a name — a word —
Makes clansmen vassals to a lord :
Yet kind my noble landlord's part, —
God bless the house of Beaudesert !
And, but I loved to drive the deer,
More than to guide the laboring steer,
    had not dwelt an outcast here.
Come, good old Minstrel, follow me;
Thy Lord and Chieftain shalt thou see.''

XII.

Then, from a rusted iron hook,
A bunch of ponderous keys he took,
Lighted a torch, and Allan led
Through grated arch and passage dread.
Portals they pass'd, where, deep within,
Spoke prisoner's moan, and fetters' din;
Through rugged vaults, where, loosely
    stored,
Lay wheel, and axe, and headsman's
    sword,
And many an hideous engine grim,
For wrenching joint, and crushing limb,
By artist form'd, who deem'd it shame
And sin to give their work a name.
They halted at a low-brow'd porch,
And Brent to Allan gave the torch,
While bolt and chain he backward roll'd,
And made the bar unhasp its hold.
They enter'd : — 'twas a prison-room
Of stern security and gloom,
Yet not a dungeon; for the day
Through lofty gratings found its way,
And rude and antique garniture
Deck'd the sad walls and oaken floor;
Such as the rugged days of old
Deem'd fit for captive noble's hold.
'' Here,'' said De Brent, ''thou mayst
    remain
Till the Leech visit him again.
Strict is his charge, the warders tell,
To tend the noble prisoner well.''
Retiring then, the bolt he drew,
And the lock's murmurs growl'd anew.
Roused at the sound, from lowly bed
A captive feebly raised his head;
The wondering Minstrel look'd, and
    knew —
Not his dear lord, but Roderick Dhu !
For, come from where Clan-Alpine
    fought,
They, erring, deem'd the Chief he sought.

XIII.

As the tall ship, whose lofty prore
Shall never stem the billows more,
Deserted by her gallant band,
Amid the breakers lies astrand, —
So, on his couch, lay Roderick Dhu !
And oft his fever'd limbs he threw
In toss abrupt, as when her sides
Lie rocking in the advancing tides,
That shake her frame with ceaseless
    beat,
Yet cannot heave her from her seat;—
O ! how unlike her course at sea !
Or his free step on hill and lea ! —
Soon as the Minstrel he could scan: —
'' What of thy lady? — of my clan? —
My mother ? — Douglas? — tell me all !
Have they been ruin'd in my fall?
Ah, yes ! or wherefore art thou here?
Yet speak, — speak boldly, — do not
    fear.''—
(For Allan, who his mood well knew,
Was choked with grief and terror too.) —

" Who fought — who fled? — Old man,
    be brief; —
Some might — for they had lost their
    Chief.
Who basely live?—who bravely died?"—
" O calm thee, Chief!" the Minstrel
    cried,
" Ellen is safe!" — " For that, thank
    Heaven!" —
" And hopes are for the Douglas given;—
The Lady Margaret, too, is well;
And, for thy clan, — on field or fell,
Has never harp of minstrel told,
Of combat fought so true and bold.
Thy stately Pine is yet unbent,
Though many a goodly bough is rent."

XIV.

The Chieftain rear'd his form on high,
And fever's fire was in his eye;
But ghastly, pale, and livid streaks
Checker'd his swarthy brow and cheeks.
— " Hark, Minstrel! I have heard thee
    play,
With measure bold, on festal day,
In yon lone isle, . . . again where ne'er
Shall harper play, or warrior hear! . . .
That stirring air that peals on high,
O'er Dermid's race our victory. —
Strike it![50] — and then, (for well thou
    canst,)
Free from thy minstrel-spirit glanced,
Fling me the picture of the fight,
When met my clan the Saxon might.
I'll listen, till my fancy hears
The clang of swords, the crash of spears!
These grates, these walls, shall vanish
    then,
For the fair field of fighting men,
And my free spirit burst away,
As if it soar'd from battle fray."
The trembling Bard with awe obey'd, —
Slow on the harp his hand he laid;
But soon remembrance of the sight
He witness'd from the mountain's height,
With what old Bertram told at night,
Awaken'd the full power of song,
And bore him in career along;—
As shallop launch'd on river's tide,
That slow and fearful leaves the side,
But, when it feels the middle stream,
Drives downward swift as lightning's
    beam.

XV.

BATTLE OF BEAL' AN DUINE.[51]

"The Minstrel came once more to view
The eastern ridge of Benvenue,
For, ere he parted, he would say
Farewell to lovely Loch Achray —
Where shall he find, in foreign land,
So lone a lake, so sweet a strand!
    There is no breeze upon the fern,
        Nor ripple on the lake,
    Upon her eyry nods the erne,
        The deer has sought the brake;
    The small birds will not sing aloud,
        The springing trout lies still,
    So darkly glooms yon thunder cloud,
    That swathes, as with a purple shroud,
        Benledi's distant hill.
    Is it the thunder's solemn sound
        That mutters deep and dread,
    Or echoes from the groaning ground
        The warrior's measured tread?
    Is it the lightning's quivering glance
        That on the thicket streams,
    Or do they flash on spear and lance
        The sun's retiring beams?
— I see the dagger-crest of Mar,
I see the Moray's silver star,
Wave o'er the cloud of Saxon war,
That up the lake comes winding far!
To hero boune for battle-strife,
    Or bard of martial lay,
'Twere worth ten years of peaceful life,
    One glance at their array!

XVI.

" Their light-arm'd archers far and
    near
    Survey'd the tangled ground,
Their centre ranks, with pike and
    spear,
    A twilight forest frown'd,
Their barded horsemen, in the rear,
    The stern battalia crown'd.
No cymbal clash'd, no clarion rang,
    Still were the pipe and drum;
Save heavy tread, and armor's clang,
    The sullen march was dumb.
There breathed no wind their crests to
    shake,
    Or wave their flags abroad;
Scarce the frail aspen seem'd to quake
    That shadow'd o'er their road.

Their vaward scouts no tidings bring,
　　Can rouse no lurking foe,
Nor spy a trace of living thing,
　　Save when they stirr'd the roe;
The host moves like a deep-sea wave,
Where rise no rocks its pride to brave,
　　High-swelling, dark, and slow.
The lake is pass'd, and now they gain
A narrow and a broken plain
　　Before the Trosachs' rugged jaws;
And here the horse and spearmen pause,
While to explore the dangerous glen,
Dive through the pass the archer-men.

XVII.

At once there rose so wild a yell
Within that dark and narrow dell,
As all the fiends, from heaven that fell,
Had peal'd the banner-cry of hell!
Forth from the pass in tumult driven,
Like chaff before the wind of heaven,
　　The archery appear;
For life! for life! their flight they ply —
And shriek, and shout, and battle-cry,
And plaids and bonnets waving high,
And broadswords flashing to the sky,
　　Are maddening in the rear.
Onward they drive, in dreadful race,
　　Pursuers and pursued;
Before that tide of flight and chase,
How shall it keep its rooted place,
　　The spearmen's twilight wood? —
'Down, down,' cried Mar, 'your
　　lances down!
Bear back both friend and foe!' —
Like reeds before the tempest's frown,
That serried grove of lances brown
　　At once lay levell'd low;
And closely shouldering side to side,
The bristling ranks the onset bide. —
'We'll quell the savage mountaineer,
　　As their Tinchel * cows the game!
They come as fleet as forest deer,
　　We'll drive them back as tame.' —

XVIII.

Bearing before them, in their course,
The relics of the archer force,

* A circle of sportsmen, who, by surrounding
great space, and gradually narrowing, brought
mense quantities of deer together, which
ually made desperate efforts to break through
e *Tinchel.*

Like wave with crest of sparkling foam,
Right onward did Clan-Alpine come.
　　Above the tide, each broadsword bright
　　Was brandishing like beam of light,
　　　　Each targe was dark below;
　　And with the ocean's mighty swing,
　　When heaving to the tempest's wing,
　　　　They hurl'd them on the foe.
I heard the lance's shivering crash,
As when the whirlwind rends the ash,
I heard the broadsword's deadly clang,
As if a hundred anvils rang!
　　But Moray wheel'd his rearward rank
　　Of horsemen on Clan-Alpine's flank,
　　— 'My banner-man, advance!
I see,' he cried, 'their column shake. —
　　Now, gallants! for your ladies' sake
　　Upon them with the lance!' —
　　The horsemen dash'd among the rout,
　　As deer break through the broom;
　　Their steeds are stout, their swords are
　　　　out,
　　　　They soon make lightsome room.
Clan-Alpine's best are backward borne:
Where, where was Roderick then!
One blast upon his bugle-horn
　　Were worth a thousand men!
And refluent through the pass of fear
　　The battle's tide was pour'd;
Vanish'd the Saxon's struggling spear,
　　Vanish'd the mountain-sword.
As Bracklinn's chasm, so black and steep
Receives her roaring linn,
As the dark caverns of the deep
　　Suck the wild whirlpool in,
So did the deep and darksome pass
Devour the battle's mingled mass:
None linger now upon the plain,
Save those who ne'er shall fight again.

XIX.

" Now westward rolls the battle's din,
That deep and doubling pass within.
—Minstrel, away, the work of fate
Is bearing on: its issue wait,
Where the rude Trosachs' dread defile
Opens on Katrine's lake and isle. —
Gray Benvenue I soon repass'd,
Loch Katrine lay beneath me cast.
　　The sun is set; — the clouds are met,
　　　　The lowering scowl of heaven
　　An inky hue of vivid blue
　　　　To the deep lake has given;

Strange gusts of wind from mountain-glen
Swept o'er the lake, then sunk agen.
I heeded not the eddying surge,
Mine eye but saw the Trosachs' gorge,
Mine ear but heard the sullen sound,
Which like an earthquake shook the
    ground,
And spoke the stern and desperate strife
That parts not but with parting life,
Seeming, to minstrel ear, to toll
The dirge of many a passing soul.
Nearer it comes — the dim-wood glen
The martial flood disgorged agen,
    But not in mingled tide;
The plaided warriors of the North
High on the mountain thunder forth
    And overhang its side;
While by the lake below appears
The dark'ning cloud of Saxon spears.
At weary bay each shatter'd band,
Eyeing their foemen, sternly stand;
Their banners stream like tatter'd sail,
That flings its fragments to the gale,
And broken arms and disarray
Mark'd the fell havoc of the day.

XX.

"Viewing the mountain's ridge askance,
The Saxon stood in sullen trance,
Till Moray pointed with his lance,
    And cried: — 'Behold yon isle! —
See! none are left to guard its strand,
But women weak, that wring the hand:
'Tis there of yore the robber band
    Their booty wont to pile;
My purse, with bonnet pieces store,
To him will swim a bow-shot o'er,
And loose a shallop from the shore.
Lightly we'll tame the war-wolf then,
Lords of his mate, and brood and den.''
Forth from the ranks a spearman sprung,
On earth his casque and corslet rung,
    He plunged him in the wave: —
All saw the deed — the purpose knew,
And to their clamors Benvenue
    A mingled echo gave;
The Saxons shout, their mate to cheer,
The helpless females scream for fear,
And yells for rage the mountaineer.
'Twas then, as by the outcry riven,
Pour'd down at once the lowering heaven;
A whirlwind swept Loch Katrine's breast,
Her billows rear'd their snowy crest.

Well for the swimmer swell'd they high,
To mar the Highland marksman's eye;
For round him shower'd, mid rain and
    hail,
The vengeful arrows of the Gael. —
In vain. — He nears the isle — and lo!
His hand is on a shallop's bow.
— Just then a flash of lightning came,
It tinged the waves and strand with flame
I mark'd Duncraggan's widow'd dame,
Behind an oak I saw her stand,
A naked dirk gleam'd in her hand:
It darken'd, — but amid the moan
Of waves, I heard a dying groan;
Another flash! — the spearman floats
A weltering corse beside the boats,
And the stern matron o'er him stood,
Her hand and dagger streaming blood.

XXI.

"'Revenge! revenge!' the Saxons
    cried,
The Gaels' exulting shout replied.
Despite the elemental rage,
Again they hurried to engage;
But, ere they closed in desperate fight,
Bloody with spurring came a knight,
Sprung from his horse, and, from a crag,
Waved 'twixt the hosts a milk-white flag
Clarion and trumpet by his side
Rung forth a truce-note high and wide,
While, in the Monarch's name, afar
A herald's voice forbade the war,
For Bothwell's lord, and Roderick bold
Were both, he said, in captive hold.''
— But here the lay made sudden stand!
The harp escaped the Minstrel's hand!
Oft had he stolen a glance, to spy
How Roderick brook'd his minstrelsy:
At first, the Chieftain, to the chime,
With lifted hand kept feeble time;
That motion ceased, — yet feeling strong
Varied his look as changed the song;
At length, no more his deafen'd ear
The minstrel melody can hear;
His face grows sharp, — his hands are
    clench'd,
As if some pang his heart-string
    wrench'd;
Set are his teeth, his fading eye
Is sternly fix'd on vacancy;
Thus motionless, and moanless, drew
His parting breath, stout Roderick Dhu

Old Allan-Bane look'd on aghast,
While grim and still his spirit pass'd:
But when he saw that life was fled,
He pour'd his wailing o'er the dead.

XXII.

LAMENT.

' And art thou cold and lowly laid,
Thy foeman's dread, thy people's aid,
Breadalbane's boast, Clan-Alpine's shade !
For thee shall none a requiem say?
—For thee,—who loved the minstrel's lay,
For thee, of Bothwell's house the stay,
The shelter of her exiled line,
E'en in this prison-house of thine,
I'll wail for Alpine's honor'd Pine !

" What groans shall yonder valleys fill !
What shrieks of grief shall rend yon hill !
What tears of burning rage shall thrill,
When mourns thy tribe thy battles done,
Thy fall before the race was won,
The sword ungirt ere set of sun !
There breathes not clansman of thy line,
But would have given his life for thine. —
O woe for Alpine's honor'd Pine ! —

" Sad was thy lot on mortal stage ! —
The captive thrush may brook the cage,
The prison'd eagle dies for rage.
Brave spirit, do not scorn my strain !
And, when its notes awake again,
Even she, so long beloved in vain,
Shall with my harp her voice combine,
And mix her woe and tears with mine,
To wail Clan-Alpine's honor'd Pine.''

XXIII.

Ellen, the while, with bursting heart,
Remain'd in lordly bower apart,
Where play'd with many-color'd gleams,
Through storied pane the rising beams.
In vain on gilded roof they fall,
And lighten'd up a tapestried wall,
And for her use a menial train
A rich collation spread in vain.
The banquet proud, the chamber gay,
Scarce drew one curious glance astray;
Or, if she look'd, 'twas but to say,
With better omen dawn'd the day
In that lone isle, where waved on high
The dun-deer's hide for canopy;
Where oft her noble father shared

The simple meal her care prepared,
While Lufra, crouching by her side,
Her station claim'd with jealous pride,
And Douglas, bent on woodland game,
Spoke of the chase to Malcolm Græme,
Whose answer, oft at random made,
The wandering of his thought betray'd. —
Those who such simple joys have known,
Are taught to prize them when they're
      gone.
But sudden, see, she lifts her head !
The window seeks with cautious tread.
What distant music has the power
To win her in this woeful hour !
'Twas from a turret that o'erhung
Her latticed bower, the strain was sung:

XXIV.

LAY OF THE IMPRISONED HUNTSMAN.

'' My hawk is tired of perch and hood,
My idle greyhound loathes his food,
My horse is weary of his stall,
And I am sick of captive thrall.
I wish I were, as I have been,
Hunting the hart in forest green,
With bended bow and bloodhound free,
For that's the life is meet for me.

I hate to learn the ebb of time,
From yon dull steeple's drowsy chime,
Or mark it as the sunbeams crawl,
Inch after inch along the wall.
The lark was wont my matins ring,
The sable rook my vespers sing,
These towers, although a king's they be,
Have not a hall of joy for me.

No more at dawning morn I rise,
And sun myself in Ellen's eyes,
Drive the fleet deer the forest through,
And homeward wend with evening dew;
A blithesome welcome blithely meet,
And lay my trophies at her feet,
While fled the eve on wing of glee, —
That life is lost to love and me ! ''

XXV.

The heart-sick lay was hardly said,
The list'ner had not turn'd her head,
It trickled still, the starting tear,
When light a footstep struck her ear,
And Snowdoun's graceful Knight was
      near.

She turn'd the hastier, lest again
The prisoner should renew his strain. —
"O welcome, brave Fitz-James!" she said.
" How may an almost orphan maid
Pay the deep debt " — " O say not so!
To me no gratitude you owe.
Not mine, alas! the boon to give,
And bid thy noble father live;
I can but be thy guide, sweet maid,
With Scotland's king thy suit to aid.
No tyrant he, though ire and pride
May lay his better mood aside.
Come, Ellen, come! 'tis more than time,
He holds his court at morning prime."
With beating heart, and bosom wrung,
As to a brother's arm she clung.
Gently he dried the falling tear,
And gently whisper'd hope and cheer;
Her faltering steps half led half staid,
Through gallery fair, and high arcade,
Till, at his touch, its wings of pride
A portal arch unfolded wide.

XXVI.

Within 'twas brilliant all and light,
A thronging scene of figures bright;
It glow'd on Ellen's dazzled sight,
As when the setting sun has given
Ten thousand hues to summer even,
And from their tissue, fancy frames
Aërial knights and fairy dames.
Still by Fitz-James her footing staid;
A few faint steps she forward made,
Then slow her drooping head she raised,
And fearful round the presence gazed
For him she sought, who own'd this state,
The dreaded prince whose will was fate.
She gazed on many a princely port,
Might well have ruled a royal court;
On many a splendid garb she gazed,
Then turn'd bewilder'd and amazed,
For all stood bare; and, in the room,
Fitz-James alone wore cap and plume.
To him each lady's look was lent;
On him each courtier's eye was bent;
Midst furs and silks, and jewels sheen,
He stood, in simple Lincoln green,
The centre of the glittering ring, —
And Snowdoun's Knight is Scotland's
King.[52]

XXVII.

As wreath of snow, on mountain-breast,
Slides from the rock that gave it rest,

Poor Ellen glided from her stay,
And at the Monarch's feet she lay;
No word her choking voice commands, —
She show'd the ring, she clasp'd her hands
O! not a moment could he brook,
The generous prince, that suppliant look
Gently he raised her; and, the while,
Check'd with a glance the circle's smile;
Graceful, but grave, her brow he kiss'd,
And bade her terrors be dismiss'd: —
" Yes, Fair: the wandering poor Fitz-
James
The fealty of Scotland claims.
To him thy woes, thy wishes, bring;
He will redeem his signet-ring.
Ask naught for Douglas; yester even,
His prince and he have much forgiven.
Wrong hath he had from slanderous
tongue,
I, from his rebel kinsmen, wrong.
We would not, to the vulgar crowd,
Yield what they craved with clamor loud;
Calmly we heard and judged his cause,
Our council aided, and our laws.
I stanch'd thy father's death-feud stern
With stout De Vaux and gray Glencairn;
And Bothwell's Lord henceforth we own
The friend and bulwark of our Throne.
But, lovely infidel, how now?
What clouds thy misbelieving brow?
Lord James of Douglas, lend thine aid;
Thou must confirm this doubting maid."

XXVIII.

Then forth the noble Douglas sprung,
And on his neck his daughter hung.
The Monarch drank, that happy hour,
The sweetest, holiest, draught of Power,—
When it can say, with godlike voice,
Arise, sad Virtue, and rejoice!
Yet would not James the general eye
On Nature's raptures long should pry,
He stepp'd between: — "Nay, Douglas,
nay,
Steal not my proselyte away!
The riddle 'tis my right to read,
That brought this happy chance to speed.
Yes, Ellen, when disguised I stray
In life's more low but happier way,
'Tis under name which veils my power,
Nor falsely veils — for Stirling's tower
Of yore the name of Snowdoun claims,[53]
And Normans call me James Fitz-James.

Thus watch I o'er insulted laws,
Thus learn to right the injured cause.'' —
Then, in a tone apart and low, —
' Ah, little traitress! none must know
What idle dream, what lighter thought,
What vanity full dearly bought,
Join'd to thine eye's dark witchcraft, drew
My spell-bound steps to Benvenue,
In dangerous hour, and all but gave
Thy Monarch's life to mountain glaive!''
Aloud he spoke: — '' Thou still dost hold
That little talisman of gold,
Pledge of my faith, Fitz-James's ring —
What seeks fair Ellen of the King?''

XXIX.

Full well the conscious maiden guess'd
He probed the weakness of her breast;
But, with that consciousness, there came
A lightening of her fears for Græme,
And more she deem'd the Monarch's ire
Kindled 'gainst him, who, for her sire,
Rebellious broadsword boldly drew;
And, to her generous feeling true,
She craved the grace of Roderick Dhu.
'' Forbear thy suit: — the King of Kings
Alone can stay life's parting wings.
I know his heart, I know his hand,
Have shared his cheer, and proved his
  brand: —
My fairest earldom would I give
To bid Clan-Alpine's Chieftain live!
Hast thou no other boon to crave?
No other captive friend to save?''
Blushing, she turn'd her from the King,
And to the Douglas gave the ring,
As if she wish'd her sire to speak
The suit that stain'd her glowing cheek.—
'' Nay, then, my pledge has lost its force,
And stubborn justice holds her course.
Malcolm, come forth!''—And, at the word,
Down kneel'd the Græme to Scotland's
  Lord.
'' For thee, rash youth, no suppliant sues,
From thee may Vengeance claim her dues,
Who, nurtured underneath our smile,
Hast paid our care by treacherous wile,
And sought amid thy faithful clan,
A refuge for an outlaw'd man,
Dishonoring thus thy loyal name. —
Fetters and warder for the Græme!''
His chain of gold the King unstrung,
The links o'er Malcolm's neck he flung,
Then gently drew the glittering band,
And laid the clasp on Ellen's hand.

HARP of the North, farewell!   The hills
  grow dark,
  On purple peaks a deeper shade de-
    scending;
In twilight copse the glow-worm lights
  her spark,
  The deer, half-seen, are to the covert
    wending.
Resume thy wizard elm! the fountain
  lending,
  And the wild breeze, thy wilder min-
    strelsy;
Thy numbers sweet with nature's vespers
  blending,
  With distant echo from the fold and lea,
And herd-boy's evening pipe, and hum
  of housing bee.

Yet, once again, farewell, thou Minstrel
  harp!
  Yet, once again, forgive my feeble sway,
  And little reck I of the censure sharp
    May idly cavil at an idle lay.
Much have I owed thy strains on life's
  long way,
  Through secret woes the world has
    never known,
When on the weary night dawn'd wearier
  day,
  And bitterer was the grief devour'd
    alone.
That I o'erlive such woes, Enchantress!
  is thine own.

Hark! as my lingering footsteps slow
  retire,
  Some Spirit of the Air has waked thy
    string!
'Tis now a seraph bold, with touch of fire,
  'Tis now the brush of Fairy's frolic wing.
Receding now, the dying numbers ring
  Fainter and fainter down the rugged
    dell,
And now the mountain breezes scarcely
  bring
  A wandering witch-note of the distant
    spell —
And now, 'tis silent all! — Enchantress,
  fare thee well!

THE
VISION OF DON RODERICK.

TO

JOHN WHITMORE, ESQ.

AND TO THE COMMITTEE OF SUBSCRIBERS FOR RELIEF OF THE PORTUGUESE
SUFFERERS IN WHICH HE PRESIDES,

THIS POEM

(THE VISION OF DON RODERICK),

COMPOSED FOR THE BENEFIT OF THE FUND UNDER THEIR MANAGEMENT,
IS RESPECTFULLY INSCRIBED BY

WALTER SCOTT.

PREFACE.

The following Poem is founded upon a Spanish Tradition, particularly detailed in the Notes ; but bearing, in general, that Don Roderick, the last Gothic King of Spain, when the Invasion of the Moors was impending, had the temerity to descend into an ancient vault near Toledo, the opening of which had been denounced as fatal to the Spanish Monarchy. The legend adds, that his rash curiosity was mortified by an emblematical representation of those Saracens who, in the year 714, defeated him in battle, and reduced Spain under their dominion. I have presumed to prolong the Vision of the Revolutions of Spain down to the present eventful crisis of the Peninsula ; and to divide it, by a supposed change of scene, into THREE PERIODS. *The* FIRST *of these represents the Invasion of the Moors, the Defeat and Death of Roderick, and closes with the peaceful occupation of the country by the Victors. The* SECOND PERIOD *embraces the state of the Peninsula, when the conquests of the Spaniards and Portuguese in the East and West Indies had raised to the highest pitch the renown of their arms ; sullied, however, by superstition and cruelty. An allusion to the inhumanities of the Inquisition terminates this picture. The* LAST PART *of the Poem opens with the state of Spain previous to the unparalleled treachery of* BUONAPARTE ; *gives a sketch of the usurpation attempted upon that unsuspicious and friendly kingdom, and terminates with the arrival of the British succors. It may be farther proper to mention, that the object of the Poem is less to commemorate or detail particular incidents, than to exhibit a general and impressive picture of the several periods brought upon the stage.*

EDINBURGH, *June* 24, 1811.

180

THE VISION OF DON RODERICK.

Quid dignum memorare tuis, Hispania, terris,
Vox humana valet! — CLAUDIAN.

INTRODUCTION.

I.

LIVES there a strain, whose sounds of
mounting fire
May rise distinguish'd o'er the din of
war;
Or died it with yon Master of the Lyre,
Who sung beleaguer'd Ilion's evil
star?
Such, WELLINGTON, might reach thee
from afar,
Wafting its descant wide o'er Ocean's
range;
Nor shouts, nor clashing arms, its mood
could mar,
All as it swell'd 'twixt each loud
trumpet-change,
That clangs to Britain victory, to Portugal
revenge!

II.

Yes! such a strain, with all o'er-pouring
measure,
Might melodize with each tumultuous
sound,
Each voice of fear or triumph, woe or
pleasure,
That rings Mondego's ravaged shores
around;
The thund'ring cry of hosts with conquest crown'd,
The female shriek, the ruin'd peasant's moan,
The shout of captives from their chains
unbound,
The foil'd oppressor's deep and
sullen groan,
A nation's choral hymn for tyranny o'erthrown.

III.

But we, weak minstrels of a laggard
day,
Skill'd but to imitate an elder
page,
Timid and raptureless, can we repay
The debt thou claim'st in this exhausted age?
Thou givest our lyres a theme, that
might engage
Those that could send thy name o'er
sea and land,
While sea and land shall last; for Homer's rage
A theme; a theme for Milton's
mighty hand —
How much unmeet for us, a faint degenerate band!

IV.

Ye mountains stern! within whose rugged breast
The friends of Scottish freedom found
repose;
Ye torrents! whose hoarse sounds have
soothed their rest,
Returning from the field of vanquish'd foes;
Say have ye lost each wild majestic
close,
That erst the choir of Bards or Druids
flung;
What time their hymn of victory
arose,
And Cattraeth's glens with voice of
triumph rung,
And mystic Merlin harp'd, and gray-
hair'd Llywarch sung! [1]

v.

O! if your wilds such minstrelsy retain,
    As sure your changeful gales seem
        oft to say,
When sweeping wild and sinking soft
        again,
    Like trumpet-jubilee, or harp's wild
        sway;
If ye can echo such triumphant lay,
    Then lend the note to him has loved
        you long!
Who pious gathered each tradition
        gray,
    That floats your solitary wastes along,
And with affection vain gave them new
        voice in song.

vi.

For not till now, how oft soe'er the task
    Of truant verse hath lighten'd graver
        care,
From Muse or Sylvan was he wont to
        ask,
    In phrase poetic, inspiration fair;
Careless he gave his numbers to the air,
    They came unsought for, if applauses
        came;
Nor for himself prefers he now the
        prayer;
    Let but his verse befit a hero's fame,
Immortal be the verse! — forgot the
        poet's name.

vii.

Hark, from yon misty cairn their answer
        tost:
    "Minstrel! the fame of whose ro-
        mantic lyre,
Capricious-swelling now, may soon be
        lost,
    Like the light flickering of a cottage
        fire;
If to such task presumptuous thou
        aspire,
    Seek not from us the meed to warrior
        due:
Age after age has gather'd son to
        sire,
    Since our gray cliffs the din of conflict
        knew,
Or, pealing through our vales, victorious
        bugles blew.

viii.

"Decay'd our old traditionary lore,
    Save where the lingering fays renew
        their ring,
By milk-maid seen beneath the haw-
        thorn hoar,
    Or round the marge of Minchmore's
        haunted spring: [2]
Save where their legends gray-hair'd
        shepherds sing,
    That now scarce win a listening ear
        but thine,
Of feuds obscure, and Border ravaging,
    And rugged deeds recount in rugged
        line,
Of moonlight foray made on Teviot,
        Tweed, or Tyne.

ix.

"No! search romantic lands, where
        the near Sun
    Gives with unstinted boon ethereal
        flame,
Where the rude villager, his labor
        done,
    In verse spontaneous [3] chants some
        favor'd name,
Whether Olalia's charms his tribute
        claim,
    Her eye of diamond, and her locks of
        jet;
Or whether, kindling at the deeds of
        Græme, [4]
    He sing, to wild Morisco measure
        set,
Old Albin's red claymore, green Erin's
        bayonet!

x.

"Explore those regions, where the
        flinty crest
    Of wild Nevada ever gleams with
        snows,
Where in the proud Alhambra's ruin'd
        breast
    Barbaric monuments of pomp repose;
Or where the banners of more ruthless
        foes
    Than the fierce Moor, float o'er To-
        ledo's fane,
From whose tall towers even now the
        patriot throws

An anxious glance, to spy upon the plain
The blended ranks of England, Portugal, and Spain.

XI.

" There, of Numantian fire a swarthy spark
　Still lightens in the sun-burnt native's eye;
The stately port, slow step, and visage dark,
　Still mark enduring pride and constancy.
And, if the glow of feudal chivalry
　Beam not, as once, thy nobles' dearest pride,
Iberia! oft thy crestless peasantry
　Have seen the plumed Hidalgo quit their side,
Have seen, yet dauntless stood — 'gainst fortune fought and died.

XII.

" And cherish'd still by that unchanging race,
　Are themes for minstrelsy more high than thine;
Of strange tradition many a mystic trace,
　Legend and vision, prophecy and sign:
Where wonders wild of Arabesque combine
With Gothic imagery of darker shade,
Forming a model meet for minstrel line.
　Go, seek such theme ! " — The Mountain Spirit said:
With filial awe I heard — I heard, and I obey'd.

I.

REARING their crests amid the cloudless skies,
　And darkly clustering in the pale moonlight,
Toledo's holy towers and spires arise,
　As from a trembling lake of silver white.

Their mingled shadows intercept the sight
　Of the broad burial-ground outstretch'd below,
And naught disturbs the silence of the night;
　All sleeps in sullen shade, or silver glow,
All save the heavy swell of Teio's ceaseless flow.

II.

All save the rushing swell of Teio's tide,
　Or, distant heard, a courser's neigh or tramp;
Their changing rounds as watchful horsemen ride,
　To guard the limits of King Roderick's camp.
For, through the river's night-fog rolling damp,
　Was many a proud pavilion dimly seen,
Which glimmer'd back against the moon's fair lamp,
　Tissues of silk and silver twisted sheen,
And standards proudly pitch'd, and warders arm'd between.

III.

But of their Monarch's person keeping ward,
　Since last the deep-mouth'd bell of vespers toll'd,
The chosen soldiers of the royal guard
　The post beneath the proud Cathedral hold;
A band unlike their Gothic sires of old,
　Who, for the cap of steel and iron mace,
Bear slender darts, and casques bedeck'd with gold,
　While silver-studded belts their shoulders grace,
Where ivory quivers ring in the broad falchion's place.

IV.

In the light language of an idle court,
　They murmur'd at their master's long delay,

And held his lengthen'd orisons in
    sport : —
" What ! will Don Roderick here till
    morning stay,
To wear in shrift and prayer the night
    away?
    And are his hours in such dull pen-
    ance past,
For fair Florinda's plunder'd charms
    to pay? " 5 —
    Then to the east their weary eyes
    they cast,
And wish'd the lingering dawn would
    glimmer forth at last.

v.

But, far within, Toledo's Prelate
    lent
An ear of fearful wonder to the King;
The silver lamp a fitful lustre sent,
    So long that sad confession witness-
    ing :
For Roderick told of many a hidden
    thing,
    Such as are lothly utter'd to the
    air,
When Fear, Remorse, and Shame the
    bosom wring,
    And Guilt his secret burden cannot
    bear,
And Conscience seeks in speech a respite
    from Despair.

vi.

Full on the Prelate's face, and silver
    hair,
    The stream of failing light was feebly
    roll'd :
But Roderick's visage, though his head
    was bare,
    Was shadow'd by his hand and man-
    tle's fold.
While of his hidden soul the sins he
    told,
    Proud Alaric's descendant could not
    brook,
That mortal man his bearing should
    behold,
    Or boast that he had seen, when
    Conscience shook,
Fear tame a monarch's brow, Remorse
    a warrior's look.

vii.

The old man's faded cheek wax'd ye
    more pale,
    As many a secret sad the King be
    wray'd;
As sign and glance eked out the unfin
    ish'd tale,
    When in the midst his falterin
    whisper staid. —
" Thus royal Witiza * was slain," —
    he said;
    " Yet, holy Father, deem not it wa
    I."
Thus still Ambition strives her crime
    to shade. —
    " Oh ! rather deem 'twas stern ne
    cessity !
Self-preservation bade, and I must kill o
    die.

viii.

" And if Florinda's shrieks alarm'd th
    air,
    If she invoked her absent sire in vain
And on her knees implored that I woul
    spare,
    Yet, reverend priest, thy sentenc
    rash refrain ! —
All is not as it seems — the female trai
    Know by their bearing to disguis
    their mood : " —
But Conscience here, as if in hig
    disdain,
    Sent to the Monarch's cheek th
    burning blood —
He stay'd his speech abrupt — and u
    the Prelate stood.

ix.

" O harden'd offspring of an iron race
    What of thy crimes, Don Roderick
    shall I say?
What alms, or prayers, or penance ca
    efface
    Murder's dark spot, wash treason'
    stain away !
For the foul ravisher how shall I pray
    Who, scarce repentant, makes hi
    crime his boast?

* Witiza was Roderick's predecessor on th
Spanish throne. He was slain by Roderick'
connivance.

How hope Almighty vengeance shall
delay,
   Unless in mercy to yon Christian
host,
He spare the shepherd, lest the guiltless
sheep be lost."

X.

Then kindled the dark Tyrant in his
mood,
   And to his brow return'd its dauntless
gloom;
" And welcome then," he cried, " be
blood for blood,
   For treason treachery, for dishonor
doom!
Yet will I know whence come they, or
by whom.
   Show, for thou canst — give forth
the fated key,
And guide me, Priest, to that mysterious room,
   Where, if aught true in old tradition
be,
His nation's future fates a Spanish King
shall see." —

XI.

" Ill-fated Prince! recall the desperate
word,
   Or pause ere yet the omen thou obey!
Bethink, yon spell-bound portal would
afford
   Never to former Monarch entrance-
way;
Nor shall it ever ope, old records say,
   Save to a King, the last of all his line,
What time his empire totters to decay,
   And treason digs, beneath, her fatal
mine,
And, high above, impends avenging wrath
divine." —

XII.

" Prelate! a Monarch's fate brooks no
delay;
   Lead on!" — The ponderous key
the old man took,
And held the winking lamp, and led
the way,
   By winding stair, dark aisle, and
secret nook,

Then on an ancient gateway bent his
look;
   And, as the key the desperate King
essay'd,
Low mutter'd thunders the Cathedral
shook,
   And twice he stopp'd, and twice new
effort made,
Till the huge bolts roll'd back, and the
loud hinges bray'd.

XIII.

Long, large, and lofty was that vaulted
hall;
   Roof, walls, and floor were all of
marble stone,
Of polished marble, black as funeral pall,
   Carved o'er with signs and charac-
ters unknown.
A paly light, as of the dawning, shone
   Through the sad bounds, but whence
they could not spy;
For window to the upper air was none;
   Yet, by that light, Don Roderick
could descry
Wonders that ne'er till then were seen by
mortal eye.

XIV.

Grim sentinels, against the upper wall,
   Of molten bronze, two Statues held
their place;
Massive their naked limbs, their stature
tall,
   Their frowning foreheads golden circles grace.
Moulded they seem'd for kings of giant
race,
   That liv'd and sinn'd before the
avenging flood;
This grasp'd a scythe, that rested on a
mace;
   This spread his wings for flight, that
pondering stood,
Each stubborn seem'd and stern, immu-
table of mood.

XV.

Fix'd was the right-hand Giant's brazen
look
   Upon his brother's glass of shifting
sand,

As if its ebb he measured by a book,
　　Whose iron volume loaded his huge
　　　　hand;
In which was wrote of many a fallen
　　　　land,
　　Of empires lost, and kings to exile
　　　　driven:
And o'er that pair their names in scroll
　　　　expand: —
　　" Lo, DESTINY and TIME ! to whom
　　　　by Heaven
The guidance of the earth is for a season
　　　　given." —

XVI.

Even while they read, the sand-glass
　　　　wastes away;
　　And, as the last and lagging grains
　　　　did creep,
That right-hand Giant 'gan his club up-
　　　　sway,
　　As one that startles from a heavy
　　　　sleep.
Full on the upper wall the mace's sweep
　　At once descended with the force of
　　　　thunder,
And hurtling down at once, in crumbled
　　　　heap,
　　The marble boundary was rent asun-
　　　　der,
And gave to Roderick's view new sights
　　　　of fear and wonder.

XVII.

For they might spy, beyond that mighty
　　　　breach,
　　Realms as of Spain in vision'd pros-
　　　　pect laid,
Castles and towers, in due proportion
　　　　each,
　　As by some skilful artist's hand por-
　　　　tray'd;
Here, crossed by many a wild Sierra's
　　　　shade,
　　And boundless plains that tire the
　　　　traveller's eye;
There, rich with vineyard and with
　　　　olive glade,
　　Or deep-embrown'd by forests huge
　　　　and high,
Or wash'd by mighty streams, that slowly
　　　　murmur'd by.

XVIII.

And here, as erst upon the antique
　　　　stage,
　　Pass'd forth the band of masquers
　　　　trimly led,
In various forms and various equipage,
　　While fitting strains the hearer's
　　　　fancy fed;
So, to sad Roderick's eye in order
　　　　spread,
　　Successive pageants fill'd that mystic
　　　　scene,
Showing the fate of battles ere they
　　　　bled,
　　And issue of events that had not
　　　　been;
And, ever and anon, strange sounds were
　　　　heard between.

XIX.

First shrill'd an unrepeated female
　　　　shriek ! —
　　It seem'd as if Don Roderick knew
　　　　the call,
For the bold blood was blanching in
　　　　his cheek. —
　　Then answer'd kettle-drum and ata-
　　　　bal,
Gong-peal and cymbal-clank the ear
　　　　appal,
　　The Tecbir war-cry, and the Lelie's
　　　　yell,[6]
Ring wildly dissonant along the hall.
　　Needs not to Roderick their dread
　　　　import tell —
" The Moor ! " he cried, " the Moor !
　　　　— ring out the Tocsin bell !

XX.

" They come ! they come ! I see the
　　　　groaning lands
　　White with the turbans of each Arab
　　　　horde;
Swart Zaarah joins her misbelieving
　　　　bands,
　　Alla and Mahomet their battle-word,
The choice they yield, the Koran or
　　　　the Sword —
　　See how the Christians rush to arms
　　　　amain ! —
In yonder shout the voice of conflict
　　　　roar'd,

The shadowy hosts are closing on the
plain —
Now, God and Saint Iago strike, for the
good cause of Spain !

XXI.

" By Heaven, the Moors prevail ! the
Christians yield !
Their coward leader gives for flight
the sign !
The sceptred craven mounts to quit the
field —
Is not yon steed Orelia? — Yes 'tis
mine ! [7]
But never was she turn'd from battle-
line :
Lo ! where the recreant spurs o'er
stock and stone !
Curses pursue the slave, and wrath .
divine !
Rivers ingulf him ! " — " Hush,"
in shuddering tone,
The Prelate said ; — " rash Prince, yon
vision'd form's thine own.".

XXII.

Just then, a torrent cross'd the flier's
course;
The dangerous ford the Kingly Likeness tried;
But the deep eddies whelm'd both man
and horse,
Swept like benighted peasant down
the tide;
And the proud Moslemah spread far
and wide,
As numerous as their native locust
band;
Berber and Ismael's sons the spoils
divide,
With naked cimeters mete out the
land,
And for the bondsmen base the freeborn
natives brand.

XXIII.

Then rose the grated Harem, to enclose
The loveliest maidens of the Chris-
tian line;
Then, menials, to their misbelieving foes,
Castile's young nobles held forbid-
den wine;

Then, too, the holy Cross, salvation's
sign,
By impious hands was from the altar
thrown,
And the deep aisles of the polluted
shrine
Echo'd, for holy hymn and organ-
tone,
The Santon's frantic dance, the Fakir s
gibbering moan.

XXIV.

How fares Don Roderick ? — E'en as
one who spies
Flames dart their glare o'er mid-
night's sable woof,
And hears around his children's pier-
cing cries,
And sees the pale assistants stand
aloof;
While cruel Conscience brings him bit-
ter proof,
His folly or his crime have caused
his grief;
And while above him nods the crum-
bling roof,
He curses earth and Heaven — him-
self in chief —
Desperate of earthly aid, despairing
Heaven's relief !

XXV.

That scythe-arm'd Giant turn'd his fatal
glass,
And twilight on the landscape closed
her wings;
Far to Asturian hills the war-sounds
pass,
And in their stead rebeck or timbrel
rings;
And to the sound the bell-deck'd dancer springs,
Bazaars resound as when their marts
are met,
In tourney light the Moor his jerrid *
flings,
And on the land as evening seem'd
to set,
The Imaum's chant was heard from
mosque or minaret.

---

* *Jerrid,* javelin.

XXVI.

So pass'd that pageant. Ere another
        came,
    The visionary scene was wrapp'd in
        smoke,
Whose sulph'rous wreaths were cross'd
    by sheets of flame;
    With every flash a bolt explosive
        broke,
Till Roderick deem'd the fiends had
    burst their yoke,
    And waved 'gainst heaven the infer-
        nal gonfalone? *
For War a new and dreadful language
        spoke,
    Never by ancient warrior heard or
        known;
Lightning and smoke her breath, and
    thunder was her tone.

XXVII.

From the dim landscape roll the clouds
        away —
    The Christians have regain'd their
        heritage;
Before the Cross has waned the Cres-
    cent's ray
    And many a monastery decks the
        stage,
And lofty church, and low-brow'd her-
    mitage.
    The land obeys a Hermit and a
        Knight, —
The Genii those of Spain for many an
        age;
    This clad in sackcloth, that in armor
        bright,
And that was VALOR named, this BIG-
    OTRY was hight.

XXVIII.

VALOR was harness'd like a Chief of old,
    Arm'd at all points, and prompt for
        knightly gest;
His sword was temper'd in the Ebro
    cold,
    Morena's eagle plume adorn'd his
        crest,
The spoils of Afric's lion bound his
    breast.

* *Gonfalone*, banner.

Fierce he stepp'd forward and flung
    down his gage;
As if of mortal kind to brave the
        best.
    Him follow'd his Companion, dark
        and sage,
As he, my Master, sung the dangerous
    Archimage.

XXIX.

Haughty of heart and brow the War-
    rior came,
    In look and language proud as proud
        might be,
Vaunting his lordship, lineage, fights,
    and fame:
    Yet was that barefoot monk more
        proud than he:
And as the ivy climbs the tallest tree,
    So round the loftiest soul his toils
        he wound,
And with his spells subdued the fierce
    and free,
    Till ermined Age and Youth in arms
        renown'd,
Honoring his scourge and hair-cloth,
    meekly kiss'd the ground.

XXX.

And thus it chanced that VALOR, peer-
    less knight,
    Who ne'er to King or Kaiser vail'd
        his crest,
Victorious still in bull-feast or in fight,
    Since first his limbs with mail he did
        invest,
Stoop'd ever to that Anchoret's be-
    hest:
    Nor reason'd of the right, nor of the
        wrong,
But at his bidding laid the lance in
    rest,
    And wrought fell deeds the troubled
        world along,
For he was fierce as brave, and pitiless
    as strong.

XXXI.

Oft his proud galleys sought some new-
    found world,
    That latest sees the sun, or first the
        morn;

Still at that Wizard's feet their spoils
   he hurl'd, —
  Ingots of ore from rich Potosi
   borne,
Crowns by Caciques,* aigrettes by
  Omrahs worn,
  Wrought of rare gems, but broken,
   rent, and foul;
Idols of gold from heathen temples
  torn,
  Bedabbled all with blood. — With
   grisly scowl
The Hermit mark'd the stains, and smiled
  beneath his cowl.

XXXII.

Then did he bless the offering, and
  bade make
  Tribute to Heaven of gratitude and
   praise:
And at his word the choral hymns
  awake,
  And many a hand the silver censer
   sways.
But with the incense-breath these censers raise,
  Mix steams from corpses smouldering in the fire;
The groans of prison'd victims mar
  the lays,
  And shrieks of agony confound the
   quire;
While mid the mingled sounds, the dark-
  en'd scenes expire.

XXXIII.

Preluding light, were strains of music
  heard,
  As once again revolved that measured sand;
Such sounds as when, for sylvan dance
  prepared,
  Gay Xeres summons forth her vin-
   tage band;
When for the light bolero ready
  stand
  The mozo blithe, with gay muchacha
   met,[8]
He conscious of his broider'd cap and
  band,

She of her netted locks and light
  corsette,
Each tiptoe perch'd to spring, and shake
  the castanet.

XXXIV.

And well such strains the opening scene
  became;
  For VALOR had relax'd his ardent
   look,
And at a lady's feet like lion tame,
  Lay stretch'd, full loth the weight
   of arms to brook;
And soften'd BIGOTRY, upon his book,
  Patter'd a task of little good or ill:
But the blithe peasant plied his prun-
  ing hook,
  Whistled the muleteer o'er vale and
   hill,
And rung from village-green the merry
  seguidille.

XXXV.

Gray Royalty, grown impotent of toil,
  Let the grave sceptre slip his lazy
   hold;
And, careless, saw his rule become the
  spoil
  Of a loose Female and her minion
   bold.
But peace was on the cottage and the
  fold,
  From court intrigue, from bickering
   faction far;
Beneath the chestnut-tree Love's tale
  was told,
  And to the tinkling of the light guitar,
Sweet stoop'd the western sun, sweet
  rose the evening star.

XXXVI.

As that sea-cloud, in size like human
  hand,
  When first from Carmel by the Tish-
   bite † seen,
Came slowly overshadowing Israel's
  land,
  A while, perchance, bedeck'd with
   colors sheen,

* *Caciques* and *Omrahs,* Peruvian and Mexi-
an chiefs or nobles.

† Elijah the Prophet. *See* 1 Kings, chap.
xviii., vs. 41-45.

While yet the sunbeams on its skirts
　　had been,
　　Limning with purple and with gold
　　　　its shroud,
Till darker folds obscured the blue serene,
　　And blotted heaven with one broad
　　　　sable cloud,
Then sheeted rain burst down, and whirl-
　　winds howl'd aloud: —

XXXVII.

Even so, upon that peaceful scene was
　　pour'd,
　　Like gathering clouds, full many a
　　　　foreign band,
And HE, their Leader, wore in sheath
　　his sword,
　　And offer'd peaceful front and open
　　　　hand,
Veiling the perjured treachery he
　　plann'd,
　　By friendship's zeal and honor's
　　　　specious guise,
Until he won the passes of the land;
　　Then burst were honor's oath and
　　　　friendship's ties!
He clutch'd his vulture-grasp, and call'd
　　fair Spain his prize.

XXXVIII.

An Iron Crown his anxious forehead bore;
　　And well such diadem his heart be-
　　　　came,
Who ne'er his purpose for remorse
　　gave o'er,
　　Or check'd his course for piety or
　　　　shame;
Who, train'd a soldier, deem'd a sol-
　　dier's fame
　　Might flourish in the wreath of bat-
　　　　tles won,
Though neither truth nor honor deck'd
　　his name;
　　Who, placed by fortune on a Mon-
　　　　arch's throne,
Reck'd not of Monarch's faith, or Mercy's
　　kingly tone.

XXXIX.

From a rude isle his ruder lineage came,
　　The spark, that, from a suburb-
　　　　hovel's hearth

Ascending, wraps some capital i
　　flame,
　　Hath not a meaner or more sordi
　　　　birth.
And for the soul that bade him wast
　　the earth —
　　The sable land-flood from som
　　　　swamp obscure,
That poisons the glad husband-fiel
　　with dearth,
　　And by destruction bids its fame er
　　　　dure,
Hath not a source more sullen, stagnan
　　and impure.*

XL.

Before that Leader strode a shadow
　　Form;
　　Her limbs like mist, her torch lik
　　　　meteor show'd,
With which she beckon'd him throug
　　fight and storm,
　　And all he crush'd that cross'd h
　　　　desperate road,
Nor thought, nor fear'd, nor look'd o
　　what he trode.
　　Realms could not glut his prid
　　　　blood could not slake,
So oft as e'er she shook her torc
　　abroad —
　　It was AMBITION bade her terro
　　　　wake,
Nor deign'd she, as of yore, a mild
　　form to take.

XLI.

No longer now she spurn'd at mea
　　revenge,
　　Or staid her hand for conquer'd fo
　　　　man's moan;
As when, the fates of aged Rome t
　　change,
　　By Cæsar's side she cross'd the Ru
　　　　bicon.
Nor joy'd she to bestow the spoils sh
　　won,
　　As when the banded powers
　　　　Greece were task'd
To war beneath the Youth of Mac
　　don:

* In historical truth, Napoleon I.'s family w
not plebeian.

No seemly veil her modern minion
    ask'd,
He saw her hideous face, and loved the
    fiend unmask'd.

XLII.

That Prelate mark'd his march — On
    banners blazed
  With battles won in many a distant
    land,
On eagle-standards and on arms he
    gazed;
  "And hopest thou then," he said,
    "thy power shall stand?
O, thou hast builded on the shifting
    sand,
  And thou hast temper'd it with
    slaughter's flood;
And know, fell scourge in the Al-
    mighty's hand,
  Gore-moisten'd trees shall perish in
    the bud,
And by a bloody death shall die the Man
    of Blood!"

XLIII.

The ruthless Leader beckon'd from
    his train
  A wan fraternal Shade, and bade
    him kneel,
And paled his temples with the crown
    of Spain,
  While trumpets rang, and heralds
    cried, "Castile!" [9]
Not that he loved him — No! — In no
    man's weal,
  Scarce in his own, e'er joy'd that
    sullen heart;
Yet round that throne he bade his war-
    riors wheel,
  That the poor puppet might perform
    his part,
And be a sceptred slave, at his stern beck
    to start.

XLIV.

But on the Natives of that Land misused,
  Not long the silence of amazement
    hung,
Nor brook'd they long their friendly
    faith abused;
  For, with a common shriek, the gen-
    eral tongue

Exclaim'd, "To arms!" and fast to
    arms they sprung.
  And VALOR woke, that Genius of
    the Land!
Pleasure, and ease, and sloth, aside he
    flung,
  As burst th' awakening Nazarite his
    band,
When 'gainst his treacherous foes he
    clench'd his dreadful hand.*

XLV.

That Mimic Monarch now cast anxious
    eye
  Upon the Satraps that begirt him
    round,
Now doff'd his royal robe in act to fly,
  And from his brow the diadem un-
    bound,
So oft, so near, the Patriot bugle
    wound,
  From Tarik's walls to Bilboa's moun-
    tains blown,
These martial satellites hard labor found
  To guard a while his substituted
    throne —
Light recking of his cause, but battling
    for their own.

XLVI.

From Alpuhara's peak that bugle rung,
  And it was echo'd from Corunna's
    wall;
Stately Seville responsive war-shot
    flung,
  Grenada caught it in her Moorish
    hall;
Galicia bade her children fight or fall,
  Wild Biscay shook his mountain
    coronet,
Valencia roused her at the battle-call,
  And, foremost still where Valor's
    sons are met,
First started to his gun each fiery
    Miquelet.

XLVII.

But unappall'd and burning for the
    fight,
  The Invaders march, of victory se-
    cure;

* Samson. *See* Judges, chap. xv. 9-16

Skilful their force to sever or unite,
  And train'd alike to vanquish or en-
    dure.
Nor skilful less, cheap conquest to
    ensure,
  Discord to breathe, and jealousy to
    sow,
To quell by boasting, and by bribes to
    lure;
  While naught against them bring
    the unpractised foe,
Save hearts for Freedom's cause, and
  hands for Freedom's blow.

XLVIII.

Proudly they march — but, O! they
    march not forth
  By one hot field to crown a brief
    campaign,
As when their Eagles, sweeping
    through the North,
  Destroy'd at every stoop an ancient
    reign!
Far other fate had Heaven decreed for
    Spain;
  In vain the steel, in vain the torch
    was plied,
New Patriot armies started from the
    slain,
  High blazed the war, and long, and
    far, and wide,[10]
And oft the God of Battles blest the
  righteous side.

XLIX.

Nor unatoned, where Freedom's foes
    prevail,
  Remain'd their savage waste. With
    blade and brand,
By day the Invaders ravaged hill and
    dale,
  But, with the darkness, the Guerilla
    band
Came like night's tempest, and avenged
    the land,
  And claim'd for blood the retribution
    due,
Probed the hard heart, and lopped the
    mur'drous hand;
  And Dawn, when o'er the scene her
    beams she threw,
Midst ruins they had made, the spoilers'
  corpses knew.

L.

What minstrel verse may sing, o
    tongue may tell,
  — Amid the vision'd strife from sea t
    sea,
How oft the Patriot banners rose o
    fell,
  Still honor'd in defeat as victory!
For that sad pageant of events to be
  Show'd every form of fight by fiel
    and flood;
Slaughter and Ruin, shouting fort
    their glee,
  Beheld, while riding on the tempe
    scud,
The waters choked with slain, the eart
  bedrench'd with blood!

LI.

Then Zaragoza — blighted be th
    tongue
  That names thy name without th
    honor due!
For never hath the harp of Minstr
    rung
  Of faith so felly proved, so firm
    true!
Mine, sap, and bomb, thy shatter
    ruins knew,
  Each art of war's extremity ha
    room,
Twice from thy half-sack'd streets th
    foe withdrew,
  And when at length stern fate d
    creed thy doom,
They won not Zaragoza, but her chi
  dren's bloody tomb.[11]

LII.

Yet raise thy head, sad city! Thoug
    in chains,
  Enthrall'd thou canst not be! Aris
    and claim
Reverence from every heart whe
    Freedom reigns,
  For what thou worshippest! — th
    sainted dame,
She of the Column, honor'd be h
    name,
  By all, whate'er their creed, wh
    honor love!
And like the sacred relics of the flam

That gave some martyr to the bless'd
    above,
To every loyal heart may thy sad embers
    prove !

LIII.

Nor thine alone such wreck.   Gerona
    fair !
    Faithful to death thy heroes shall be
      sung,
Manning the towers while o'er their
    heads the air
    Swart as the smoke from raging fur-
      nace hung;
Now thicker dark'ning where the mine
    was sprung,
    Now briefly lighten'd by the can-
      non's flare,
Now arch'd with fire-sparks as the
    bomb was flung,
    And redd'ning now with conflagra-
      tion's glare,
While by the fatal light the foes for storm
    prepare.

LIV.

While all around was danger, strife,
    and fear,
    While the earth shook, and darken'd
      was the sky,
And wide Destruction stunn'd the lis-
    tening ear,
    Appall'd the heart, and stupefied the
      eye, —
Afar was heard that thrice-repeated cry,
    In which old Albion's heart and
      tongue unite,
Whene'er her soul is up, and pulse
    beats high,
    Whether it hail the wine cup or the
      fight,
And bid each arm be strong, or bid each
    heart be light.

LV.

Don Roderick turn'd him as the shout
    grew loud —
    A varied scene the changeful vision
      show'd,
For, where the ocean mingled with the
    cloud,
    A gallant navy stemm'd the billows
      broad.

From mast and stern St. George's sym-
    bol flow'd,
    Blent with the silver cross to Scot-
      land dear;
Mottling the sea their landward barges
    row'd,
    And flash'd the sun on bayonet,
      brand, and spear,
And the wild beach return'd the seaman's
    jovial cheer.

LVI.

It was a dread, yet spirit-stirring sight !
    The billows foam'd beneath a thou-
      sand oars,
Fast as they land the red-cross ranks
    unite,
    Legions on legions bright'ning all
      the shores.
Then banners rise, and cannon-signal
    roars,
    Then peals the warlike thunder of
      the drum,
Thrills the loud fife, the trumpet-
    flourish pours,
    And patriot hopes awake, and doubts
      are dumb,
For, bold in Freedom's cause, the bands
    of Ocean come !

LVII.

A various host they come — whose
    ranks display
    Each mode in which the warrior
      meets the fight,
The deep battalion locks its firm array,
    And meditates his aim the marks-
      man light;
Far glance the light of sabres flashing
    bright,
    Where mounted squadrons shake the
      echoing mead,
Lacks not artillery breathing flame and
    night,
    Nor the fleet ordnance whirl'd by
      rapid steed,
That rivals lightning's flash in ruin and
    in speed.

LVIII.

A various host — from kindred realms
    they came,

Brethren in arms, but rivals in renown —
For yon fair bands shall merry England
claim,
    And with their deeds of valor deck
her crown.
Hers their bold port, and hers their
martial frown,
    And hers their scorn of death in
freedom's cause,
Their eyes of azure, and their locks of
brown,
    And the blunt speech that bursts
without a pause,
And freeborn thoughts, which league the
Soldier with the Laws.

LIX.

And, O! loved warriors of the Minstrel's land!
    Yonder your bonnets nod, your
tartans wave!
The rugged form may mark the mountain band,
    And harsher features, and a mien
more grave;
But ne'er in battle-field throbb'd heart
so brave,
    As that which beats beneath the
Scottish plaid;
And when the pibroch bids the battle
rave,
    And level for the charge your arms
are laid,
Where lives the desperate foe that for
such onset staid!

LX.

Hark! from yon stately ranks what
laughter rings,
    Mingling wild mirth with war's stern
minstrelsy,
His jest while each blithe comrade
round him flings,
    And moves to death with military
glee:
Boast, Erin, boast them! tameless,
frank, and free,
    In kindness warm, and fierce in
danger known,
Rough Nature's children, humorous as
she:

And HE, yon Chieftain — strike the
proudest tone
Of thy bold harp, green Isle!
    Hero is thine own.

LXI.

Now on the scene Vimeira * should be
shown,
On Talavera's fight should Roderick
gaze,
And hear Corunna wail her battle
won,
    And see Busaco's crest with light-
ning blaze : —
But shall fond fable mix with heroes'
praise?
    Hath Fiction's stage for Truth's long
triumphs room?
    And dare her wild-flowers mingle
with the bays,
    That claim a long eternity to bloom
Around the warrior's crest, and o'er the
warrior's tomb!

LXII.

Or may I give adventurous Fancy
scope,
    And stretch a bold hand to the awful
veil
That hides futurity from anxious hope,
    Bidding beyond it scenes of glory
hail,
And panting Europe rousing at the
tale
    Of Spain's invaders from her con-
fines hurl'd,
While kindling nations buckle on their
mail,
    And Fame, with clarion-blast and
wings unfurl'd,
To Freedom and Revenge awakes an injured World?

LXIII.

O vain, though anxious, is the glance
I cast,
    Since Fate has mark'd futurity her
own:

* The battle of Vimeira was fought August 21,
1808; Corunna, January 16, 1809: Talavera,
July 28, 1809; Busaco, September 27, 1810.

Yet fate resigns to worth the glorious
    past,
    The deeds recorded, and the laurels
    won.
Then, though the Vault of Destiny [12]
    be gone,
    King, Prelate, all the phantasms of
    my brain,
Melted away like mist-wreaths in the
    sun,
    Yet grant for faith, for valor, and
    for Spain,
ne note of pride and fire, a patriot's
    parting strain !

CONCLUSION.

I.

" Who shall command Estrella's moun-
    tain-tide
    Back to the source, when tempest-
    chafed, to hie?
Who, when Gascogne's vex'd gulf is
    raging wide,
    Shall hush it as a nurse her infant's
    cry?
His magic power let such vain boaster
    try,
    And when the torrent shall his voice
    obey,
And Biscay's whirlwinds list his lullaby,
    Let him stand forth and bar mine
    eagles' way,
nd they shall heed his voice, and at his
    bidding stay.

II.

" Else ne'er to stoop, till high on Lis-
    bon's towers,
    They close their wings, the symbol
    of our yoke,
And their own sea hath whelm'd yon
    red-cross Powers ! "
    Thus, on the summit of Alverca's
    rock,
To Marshal, Duke, and Peer, Gaul's
    Leader spoke.
    While downward on the land his
    legions press,
Before them it was rich with vine and
    flock,

And smiled like Eden in her summer
    dress;
Behind their wasteful march, a reeking
    wilderness.[13]

III.

And shall the boastful Chief maintain
    his word,
    Though Heaven hath heard the
    wailings of the land,
Though Lusitania whet her vengeful
    sword,
    Though Britons arm, and WELLING-
    TON command !
No ! grim Busaco's iron ridge shall
    stand
    An adamantine barrier to his force;
And from its base shall wheel his
    shatter'd band,
    As from the unshaken rock the tor-
    rent hoarse
Bears off its broken waves, and seeks a
    devious course.

IV.

Yet not because Alcoba's mountain-
    hawk
    Hath on his best and bravest made
    her food,
In numbers confident, yon Chief shall
    balk
    His Lord's imperial thirst for spoil
    and blood:
For full in view the promised conquest
    stood,
    And Lisbon's matrons from their
    walls might sum
The myriads that had half the world
    subdued,
    And hear the distant thunders of the
    drum,
That bids the bands of France to storm
    and havoc come.

V.

Four moons have heard these thunders
    idly roll'd,
    Have seen these wistful myriads eye
    their prey,
As famish'd wolves survey a guarded
    fold —
    But in the middle path a Lion lay !

At length they move — but not to battle-fray,
  Nor blaze yon fires where meets the manly fight;
Beacons of infamy, they light the way
Where cowardice and cruelty unite
To damn with double shame their ignominious flight!

VI.

O triumph for the Fiends of Lust and Wrath!
  Ne'er to be told, yet ne'er to be forgot,
What wanton horrors mark'd their wreckful path!
  The peasant butcher'd in his ruin'd cot,
The hoary priest even at the altar shot,
  Childhood and age given o'er to sword and flame,
Woman to infamy; — no crime forgot,
By which inventive demons might proclaim
Immortal hate to man, and scorn of God's great name!

VII.

The rudest sentinel, in Britain born,
  With horror paused to view the havoc done,
Gave his poor crust to feed some wretch forlorn,[14]
  Wiped his stern eye, then fiercer grasp'd his gun.
Nor with less zeal shall Britain's peaceful son
  Exult the debt of sympathy to pay;
Riches nor poverty the tax shall shun,
  Nor prince nor peer, the wealthy nor the gay,
Nor the poor peasant's mite, nor bard's more worthless lay.

VIII.

But thou — unfoughten wilt thou yield to Fate,
  Minion of Fortune, now miscall'd in vain!
Can vantage-ground no confidence create,
  Marcella's pass, nor Guarda's mountain-chain?

Vainglorious fugitive![15] yet tur[n] again!
  Behold, where, named by some prophetic Seer,
Flows Honor's Fountain,* and fore[] doom'd the stain
From thy dishonor'd name and arm[] to clear —
Fallen Child of Fortune, turn, redee[m] her favor here!

IX.

Yet, ere thou turn'st, collect each dis[] tant aid;
  Those chief that never heard th[e] lion roar!
Within whose souls lives not a trac[e] portray'd
  Of Talavera, or Mondego's shore!
Marshal each band thou hast, an[d] summon more;
  Of war's fell stratagems exhaust th[e] whole;
Rank upon rank, squadron on squadro[n] pour,
  Legion on Legion on thy foeme[n] roll,
And weary out his arm — thou canst n[ot] quell his soul.

X.

O vainly gleams with steel Agueda['s] shore,
  Vainly thy squadrons hide Assuava['s] plain,
And front the flying thunders as the[y] roar,
  With frantic charge and tenfold odds in vain![16]
And what avails thee that, for CAMERO[N] slain,[17]
  Wild from his plaided ranks th[e] yell was given —
Vengeance and grief gave mountain[] rage the reign,
  And, at the bloody spear-point head[] long driven,
Thy Despot's giant guards fled like th[e] rack of heaven.

* The literal translation of *Fuentes de He[]noro.*

XI.

Go, baffled boaster! teach thy haughty
mood
    To plead at thine imperious master's
    throne,
Say, thou hast left his legions in their
blood,
    Deceived his hopes, and frustrated
    thine own;
Say, that thine utmost skill and valor
shown,
    By British skill and valor were out-
    vied;
Last say, thy conqueror was WELLING-
TON!
    And if he chafe, be his own fortune
    tried —
od and our cause to friend, the venture
we'll abide.

XII.

But you, ye heroes of that well-fought
day,
    How shall a bard, unknowing and
    unknown,
His meed to each victorious leader
pay,
    Or bind on every brow the laurels
    won?
Yet fain my harp would wake its
boldest tone,
    O'er the wide sea to hail CADOGAN
    brave;
And he, perchance, the minstrel-note
might own,
    Mindful of meeting brief that For-
    tune gave
lid yon far western isles that hear the
Atlantic rave.

XIII.

Yes! hard the task, when Britons
wield the sword,
    To give each Chief and every field
    its fame:
Hark! Albuera thunders BERESFORD,
    And Red Barosa shouts for dauntless
    GRÆME!
O for a verse of tumult and of flame,
    Bold as the bursting of their cannon
    sound,
To bid the world re-echo to their fame!

For never, upon gory battle-ground,
With conquest's well-bought wreath were
    braver victors crown'd!

XIV.

O who shall grudge him Albuera's
bays,
    Who brought a race regenerate to
    the field,
Roused them to emulate their father's
praise,
    Temper'd their headlong rage, their
    courage steel'd,[18]
And raised fair Lusitania's fallen
shield,
    And gave new edge to Lusitania's
    sword,
And taught her sons forgotten arms to
wield —
    Shiver'd my harp, and burst its every
    chord,
If it forget thy worth, victorious BERES-
FORD!

XV.

Not on that bloody field of battle
won,
    Though Gaul's proud legions roll'd
    like mist away,
Was half his self-devoted valor
shown, —
    He gaged but life on that illustrious
    day;
But when he toil'd those squadrons to
array,
    Who fought like Britons in the
    bloody game,
Sharper than Polish pike or assagay,
    He braved the shafts of censure and
    of shame,
And, dearer far than life, he pledged a
soldier's fame.

XVI.

Nor be his praise o'erpast who strove
to hide
    Beneath the warrior's vest affection's
    wound,
Whose wish Héaven for his country's
weal denied;
    Danger and fate he sought, but
    glory found.

From clime to clime, where'er war's
trumpets sound,
The wanderer went; yet, Caledonia!
still
Thine was his thought in march and
tented ground;
He dream'd mid Alpine cliffs of
Athole's hill,
And heard in Ebro's roar his Lyndoch's
lovely rill.

XVII.

O hero of a race renown'd of old,
Whose war-cry oft has waked the
battle-swell,
Since first distinguish'd in the onset bold,
Wild sounding when the Roman
rampart fell!
By Wallace' side it rung the Southron's
knell,
Alderne, Kilsy the, and Tibber own'd
its fame,
Tummell's rude pass can of its terrors
tell,
But ne'er from prouder field arose the
name,
Than when wild Ronda learn'd the con-
quering shout of GRÆME! [19]

XVIII.

But all too long, through seas unknown
and dark,
(With Spenser's parable I close my
tale,)
By shoal and rock hath steer'd my venturous bark,
And landward now I drive before the
gale.
And now the blue and distant shore I
hail,
And nearer now I see the port expand,
And now I gladly furl my weary
sail,
And as the prow light touches on
the strand,
I strike my red-cross flag and bind my
skiff to land.

ROKEBY:

A POEM IN SIX CANTOS.

TO

JOHN B. S. MORRITT, ESQ.

THIS POEM, THE SCENE OF WHICH IS LAID IN HIS BEAUTIFUL DEMESNE OF
ROKEBY, IS INSCRIBED, IN TOKEN OF SINCERE FRIENDSHIP.

BY

WALTER SCOTT.

[DEC. 13, 1812.]

ADVERTISEMENT TO THE FIRST EDITION.

*The Scene of this Poem is laid at Rokeby, near Greta Bridge, in Yorkshire, and shifts
to the adjacent Fortress of Barnard Castle, and to other places in that Vicinity.*

*The Time occupied by the Action is a space of Five days, Three of which are supposed
to elapse between the end of the Fifth and the beginning of the Sixth Canto.*

*The date of the supposed events is immediately subsequent to the great Battle of Marston
Moor, 3d July, 1644. This period of public confusion has been chosen, without any purpose
of combining the Fable with the Military or Political Events of the Civil War, but only
as affording a degree of probability to the Fictitious narrative now presented to the Public.*

INTRODUCTION TO EDITION 1830.

BETWEEN the publication of " The Lady of the Lake," which was so eminently successful, and that of " Rokeby," in 1813, three years had intervened. I shall not, I believe, be accused of ever having attempted to usurp a superiority over many men of genius, my contemporaries : but, in point of popularity, not of actual talent, the caprice of the public had certainly given me such a temporary superiority over men, of whom, in regard to poetical fancy and feeling, I scarcely thought myself worthy to loose the shoe-latch. On the other hand, it would be absurd affectation in me to deny, that I conceived myself to understand, more perfectly than many of my contemporaries, the manner most likely to interest the great mass of mankind. Yet, even with this belief, I must truly and fairly say, that I always considered myself rather as one who held the bets, in time to be paid over to the winner, than as having any pretence to keep them in my own right.

In the mean time years crept on, and not without their usual depredations on the passing generation. My sons had arrived at the age when the paternal home was no longer their best abode, as both were destined to active life. The field-sports, to which I was peculiarly attached, had now less interest, and were replaced by other amusements of a more quiet character ; and the means and opportunity of pursuing these were to be sought for. I had, indeed, for some years attended to farming, a knowledge of which is, or at least was then, indispensable to the comfort of a family residing in a solitary country-house ; but although this was the favorite amusement of many of my friends, I have never been able to consider it as a source of pleasure. I never could think it a matter of passing importance, that my cattle, or crops, were better or more plentiful than those of my neighbors ; and nevertheless I began to feel the necessity of some more quiet out-door occupation, different from those I had hitherto pursued. I purchased a small farm of about one hundred acres, with the purpose of planting and improving it, to which property circumstances afterwards enabled me to make considerable additions ; and thus an era took place in my life, almost equal to the important one mentioned by the Vicar of Wakefield, when he removed from the Blue room to the Brown. In point of neighborhood, at least, the change of residence made little *more* difference. Abbotsford, to which we removed, was only six or seven miles down the Tweed, and lay on the same beautiful stream. It did not possess the romantic character of Ashestiel, my former residence ; but it had a stretch of meadow-land along the river, and possessed, in the phrase of the landscape-gardener, considerable capabilities. Above all, the land was my own, like Uncle Toby's Bowling-green, to do what I would with. It had been, though the gratification was long postponed, an early wish of mine to connect myself with my mother-earth, and prosecute those experiments by which a species of creative power is exercised over the face of nature. I can trace, even to childhood, a pleasure derived from Dodsley's account of Shenstone's Leasowes, and I envied the poet much more for the pleasure of accomplishing the objects detailed in his friend's sketch of his grounds, than for the possession of pipe, crook, flock, and Phillis to boot. My memory, also, tenacious of quaint expressions, still retained a phrase which it had gathered from an old almanac of Charles the Second's time (when everything down to almanacs affected to be smart), in which the reader, in the month of June, is advised, for health's sake, to walk a mile or two every day before breakfast, and, if he can possibly so manage, to let his exercise be taken upon his own land.

With the satisfaction of having attained the fulfilment of an early and long-cherished hope, I commenced my improvements, as delightful in their progress as those of the child who first makes a dress for a new doll. The nakedness of the land was in time hidden by woodlands of considerable extent — the smallest of possible cottages was progressively expanded into a sort of dream of a mansion-house, whimsical in the exterior, but convenient within. Nor did I forget what is the natural pleasure of every man who has been a reader, I mean the filling the shelves of a tolerably large library. All these objects I kept in view, to be executed as convenience should serve ; and although I knew many years must elapse before they could be attained, I was of a disposition to comfort myself with the Spanish proverb, " Time and I against any two."

The difficult and indispensable point, of finding a permanent subject of occupation, was now at length attained ; but there was annexed to it the necessity of becoming again a candidate for public favor ; for, as I was turned improver on the earth of the every-day world, it was under condition that the small tenement of Parnassus, which might be accessible to my labors, should not remain uncultivated.

I meditated, at first, a poem on the subject of Bruce, in which I made some progress, but afterwards judged it advisable to lay it aside, supposing that an English story might have more novelty ; in consequence, the precedence was given to " Rokeby."

If subject and scenery could have influenced the fate of a poem, that of " Rokeby " should have been eminently distinguished ; for the grounds belonged to a dear friend, with whom I had lived in habits of intimacy for many years, and the place itself united the romantic beauties of the wilds of Scotland with the rich and smiling aspect of the southern portion of the island. But the Cavaliers and Roundheads, whom I attempted to summon up to tenant this beautiful region, had for the public neither the novelty nor the peculiar interest of the primitive Highlanders. This, perhaps, was scarcely to be expected, considering that the general mind sympathizes readily and at once with the stamp which nature herself has affixed upon the manners of a people living in a simple and patriarchal state ; whereas it has more difficulty in understanding or interesting itself in manners founded upon those peculiar habits of thinking or acting, which are produced by the progress of society. We could read with pleasure the tale of the adventures of a Cossack or a Mongol Tartar, while we only wonder and stare over those of the lovers in the " Pleasing Chinese History," where the embarrassments turn upon difficulties arising out of unintelligible delicacies peculiar to the customs and manners of that affected people.

The cause of my failure had, however, a far deeper root. The manner, or style, which, by its novelty, attracted the public in an unusual degree, had now, after having been three times before them, exhausted the patience of the reader, and began in the fourth to lose its charms. The reviewers may be said to have apostrophized the author in the language of Parnell's Edwin : —

> " And here reverse the charm, he cries,
> And let it fairly now suffice,
> The gambol has been shown."

The licentious combination of rhymes, in a manner not perhaps very congenial to our language, had not been confined to the author. Indeed, in most similar cases, the inventors of such novelties have their reputation destroyed by their own imitators, as Actæon fell under the fury of his own dogs. The present author, like Bobadil, had taught his trick of fence to a hundred gentlemen (and ladies),[1] who could fence very nearly, or quite, as well as himself. For this there was no remedy ; the harmony became tiresome and ordinary, and both the original inventor and his invention must have fallen into contempt, if he had not found out another road to public favor. What has been said of the metre only, must be considered to apply equally to the structure of the Poem and of the style. The very best passages of any popular style are not, perhaps, susceptible of imitation, but they may be approached by men of talent ; and those who are less able to copy them, at least lay hold of their peculiar features, so as to produce a strong burlesque. In either way, the effect of the manner is rendered cheap and common ; and, in the latter case, ridiculous to boot. The evil consequences to an author's reputation are at least as fatal as those which come upon the musical composer, when his melody falls into the hands of the street ballad-singer.

Of the unfavorable species of imitation, the author's style gave room to a very large number, owing to an appearance of facility to which some of those who used the measure unquestionably leaned too far. The effect of the more favorable imitations, composed by persons of talent, was almost equally unfortunate to the original minstrel, by showing that they could overshoot him with his own bow. In short, the popularity which once attended the *School*, as it was called, was now fast decaying.

Besides all this, to have kept his ground at the crisis when " Rokeby " appeared, its author ought to have put forth his utmost strength, and to have possessed at least all his original advantages, for a mighty and unexpected rival was advancing on the stage — a rival not in poetical powers only, but in that art of attracting popularity, in which the present writer had hitherto preceded better men than himself. The reader will easily see that Byron is here meant, who, after a little velitation of no great promise, now appeared

---

[1] " Scott found peculiar favor and imitation among the fair sex. There was Miss Halford and Miss Mitford and Miss Francis ; but, with the greatest respect be it spoken, none of his imitators did much honor to the original, except Hogg, the Ettrick Shepherd, until the appearance of " The Bridal of Triermain " and " Harold the Dauntless," which, in the opinion of some, equalled if not surpassed him ; and lo! after three or four years, they turn out to be the Master's own composition." — *Byron.*

as a serious candidate, in the " First two Cantos of Childe Harold." [1]   I was astonished at the power evinced by that work, which neither the " Hours of Idleness," nor the " English Bards and Scotch Reviewers," had prepared me to expect from its author.   There was a depth in his thought, an eager abundance in his diction, which argued full confidence in the inexhaustible resources of which he felt himself possessed ; and there was some appearance of that labor of the file, which indicates that the author is conscious of the necessity of doing every justice to his work, that it may pass warrant.   Lord Byron was also a traveller, a man whose ideas were fired by having seen, in distant scenes of difficulty and danger, the places whose very names are recorded in our bosoms as the shrines of ancient poetry.   For his own misfortune, perhaps, but certainly to the high increase on his poetical character, nature had mixed in Lord Byron's system those passions which agitate the human heart with most violence, and which may be said to have hurried his bright career to an early close.   There would have been little wisdom in measuring my force with so formidable an antagonist ; and I was as likely to tire of playing the second fiddle in the concert, as my audience of hearing me.   Age also was advancing.   I was growing insensible to those subjects of excitation by which youth is agitated.   I had around me the most pleasant but least exciting of all society, that of kind friends and an affectionate family.   My circle of employments was a narrow one ; it occupied me constantly, and it became daily more difficult for me to interest myself in poetical composition : —

> " How happily the days of Thalaba went by ! "

Yet, though conscious that I must be, in the opinion of good judges, inferior to the place I had for four or five years held in letters, and feeling alike that the latter was one to which I had only a temporary right, I could not brook the idea of relinquishing literary occupation, which had been so long my chief diversion.   Neither was I disposed to choose the alternative of sinking into a mere editor and commentator, though that was a species of labor which I had practised, and to which I was attached.   But I could not endure to think that I might not, whether known or concealed, do something of more importance.   My inmost thoughts were those of the Trojan Captain in the galley race, —

> Non jam, prima peto Mnestheus, neque vincere certo :
> Quanquam O ! — sed superent, quibus hoc, Neptune, dedisti ;
> Extremos pudeat rediisse : hoc vincite, cives,
> Et prohibete nefas." [2] — Æn. lib. v. 194.

I had, indeed, some private reasons for my " Quanquam O !" which were not worse than those of Mnestheus.   I have already hinted that the materials were collected for a poem on the subject of Bruce, and fragments of it had been shown to some of my friends, and received with applause.   Notwithstanding, therefore, the eminent success of Byron, and the great chance of his taking the wind out of my sails, there was, I judged, a species of cowardice in desisting from the task which I had undertaken, and it was time enough to retreat when the battle should be more decidedly lost.   The sale of " Rokeby," excepting as compared with that of " The Lady of the Lake," was in the highest degree respectable ; and as it included fifteen hundred quartos [3] in those quarto-reading days, the trade had no reason to be dissatisfied.

ABBOTSFORD, *April*, 1830.

---

[1]   Published in London, March, 1812.

[2]   " I seek not now the foremost palm to gain :
     Though yet — but ah ! that haughty wish is vain !
     Let those enjoy it whom the gods ordain.
     But to be last, the lags of all the race ! —
     Redeem yourselves and me from that disgrace." — *Dryden.*

[3]   The quarto edition was published in January, 1813.

ROKEBY.

CANTO FIRST.

I.

THE Moon is in her summer glow,
But hoarse and high the breezes blow,
And, racking o'er her face, the cloud
Varies the tincture of her shroud;
On Barnard's towers, and Tees's stream,[1]
She changes as a guilty dream,
When Conscience, with remorse and fear,
Goads sleeping Fancy's wild career.
Her light seems now the blush of shame,
Seems now fierce anger's darker flame,
Shifting that shade, to come and go,
Like apprehension's hurried glow;
Then Sorrow's livery dims the air,
And dies in darkness, like despair.
Such varied hues the warder sees
Reflected from the woodland Tees,
Then from old Baliol's tower looks forth,
Sees the clouds mustering in the north,
Hears, upon turret-roof and wall,
By fits the plashing rain-drop fall,
Lists to the breeze's boding sound,
And wraps his shaggy mantle round.

II.

Those towers, which in the changeful gleam
Throw murky shadows on the stream,
Those towers of Barnard hold a guest,
The emotions of whose troubled breast,
In wild and strange confusion driven,
Rival the flitting rack of heaven.
Ere sleep stern OSWALD's senses tied,
Oft had he changed his weary side,
Composed his limbs, and vainly sought
By effort strong to banish thought.
Sleep came at length, but with a train
Of feelings true and fancies vain,
Mingling, in wild disorder cast,
The expected future with the past.
Conscience, anticipating time,
Already rues the enacted crime,
And calls her furies forth, to shake
The sounding scourge and hissing snake;
While her poor victim's outward throes
Bear witness to his mental woes,
And show what lesson may be read
Beside a sinner's restless bed.

III.

Thus Oswald's laboring feelings trace
Strange changes in his sleeping face,
Rapid and ominous as these
With which the moonbeams tinge the Tees.
There might be seen of shame the blush,
There anger's dark and fiercer flush,
While the perturbed sleeper's hand
Seem'd grasping dagger-knife, or brand.
Relax'd that grasp, the heavy sigh,
The tear in the half-opening eye,
The pallid cheek and brow, confess'd
That grief was busy in his breast;
Nor paused that mood — a sudden start
Impell'd the life-blood from the heart:
Features convulsed and mutterings dread
Show terror reigns in sorrow's stead.
That pang the painful slumber broke,
And Oswald with a start awoke.

IV.

He woke, and fear'd again to close
His eyelids in such dire repose;
He woke, — to watch the lamp, and tell
From hour to hour the castle-bell.

Or listen to the owlet's cry,
Or the sad breeze that whistles by,
Or catch, by fits, the tuneless rhyme
With which the warder cheats the time,
And envying think, how, when the sun
Bids the poor soldier's watch be done,
Couch'd on his straw, and fancy-free,
He sleeps like careless infancy.

V.

Far townward sounds a distant tread,
And Oswald, starting from his bed,
Hath caught it, though no human ear,[2]
Unsharpen'd by revenge and fear,
Could e'er distinguish horse's clank,
Until it reach'd the castle bank.
Now nigh and plain the sound appears,
The warder's challenge now he hears,
Then clanking chains and levers tell,
That o'er the moat the drawbridge fell,
And, in the castle court below,
Voices are heard, and torches glow,
As marshalling the stranger's way,
Straight for the room where Oswald lay;
The cry was: — "Tidings from the host,
Of weight — a messenger comes post."
Stifling the tumult of his breast,
His answer Oswald thus express'd: —
"Bring food and wine, and trim the fire,
Admit the stranger, and retire."

VI.

The stranger came with heavy stride,
The morion's plumes his visage hide,
And the buff-coat, an ample fold,
Mantles his form's gigantic mould.[3]
Full slender answer deigned he
To Oswald's anxious courtesy,
But mark'd, by a disdainful smile,
He saw and scorn'd the petty wile,
When Oswald changed the torch's place,
Anxious that on the soldier's face
Its partial lustre might be thrown,
To show his looks, yet hide his own.
His guest, the while, laid low aside
The ponderous cloak of tough bull's hide,
And to the torch glanced broad and clear
The corslet of a cuirassier:
Then from his brows the casque he drew,
And from the dank plume dash'd the dew,
From gloves of mail relieved his hands,
And spread them to the kindling brands;

And, turning to the genial board,
Without a health, or pledge, or word
Of meet and social reverence said,
Deeply he drank, and fiercely fed;
As free from ceremony's sway,
As famish'd wolf that tears his prey.

VII.

With deep impatience, tinged with fear,
His host beheld him gorge his cheer,
And quaff the full carouse, that lent
His brow a fiercer hardiment.
Now Oswald stood a space aside,
Now paced the room with hasty stride,
In feverish agony to learn
Tidings of deep and dread concern,
Cursing each moment that his guest
Protracted o'er his ruffian feast.
Yet, viewing with alarm, at last,
The end of that uncouth repast,
Almost he seem'd their haste to rue,
As, at his sign, his train withdrew,
And left him with the stranger, free
To question of his mystery.
Then did his silence long proclaim
A struggle between fear and shame.

VIII.

Much in the stranger's mien appears,
To justify suspicious fears.
On his dark face a scorching clime,[4]
And toil, had done the work of time,
Roughen'd the brow, the temples bared,
And sable hairs with silver shared,
Yet left — what age alone could tame —
The lip of pride, the eye of flame;
The full-drawn lip that upward curl'd,
The eye that seem'd to scorn the world.
That lip had terror never blench'd;
Ne'er in that eye had tear-drop quench'd
The flash severe of swarthy glow,
That mock'd at pain, and knew not woe.
Inured to danger's direst form,
Tornade and earthquake, flood and storm,
Death had he seen by sudden blow,
By wasting plague, by tortures slow,
By mine or breach, by steel or ball,
Knew all her shapes, and scorn'd them all.

IX.

But yet, though BERTRAM'S harden'd look,
Unmoved, could blood and danger brook,

Still worse than apathy had place
On his swart brow and callous face;
For evil passions, cherish'd long,
Had plough'd them with impressions
    strong.
All that gives gloss to sin, all gay
Light folly, past with youth away,
But rooted stood in manhood's hour,
The weeds of vice without their flower.
And yet the soil in which they grew,
Had it been tamed when life was new,
Had depth and vigor to bring forth
The hardier fruits of virtuous worth.
Not that, e'en then, his heart had known
The gentler feelings' kindly tone;
But lavish waste had been refined
To bounty in his chasten'd mind,
And lust of gold, that waste to feed,
Been lost in love of glory's meed,
And, frantic then no more, his pride
Had ta'en fair virtue for its guide.

X.

Even now, by conscience unrestrain'd,
Clogg'd by gross vice, by slaughter
    stain'd,
Still knew his daring soul to soar,
And mastery o'er the mind he bore;
For meaner guilt, or heart less hard,
Quail'd beneath Bertram's bold regard.
And this felt Oswald, while in vain
He strove, by many a winding train,
To lure his sullen guest to show,
Unask'd, the news he long'd to know,
While on far other subject hung
His heart, than falter'd from his tongue.
Yet naught for that his guest did deign
To note or spare his secret pain,
But still, in stern and stubborn sort,
Return'd him answer dark and short,
Or started from the theme, to range
In loose digression wild and strange,
And forced the embarrass'd host to buy,
By query close, direct reply.

XI.

A while he glozed upon the cause
Of Commons, Covenant, and Laws,
And Church Reform'd — but felt rebuke
Beneath grim Bertram's sneering look,
Then stammer'd — "Has a field been
    fought?
Has Bertram news of battle brought?

For sure a soldier, famed so far
In foreign fields for feats of war,
On eve of fight ne'er left the host,
Until the field were won and lost."
"Here, in your towers by circling Tees,
You, Oswald Wycliffe, rest at ease;
Why deem it strange that others come
To share such safe and easy home,
From fields where danger, death, and
    toil,
Are the reward of civil broil?" —
"Nay, mock not, friend! since well we
    know
The near advances of the foe,
To mar our northern army's work,
Encamp'd before beleaguer'd York;
Thy horse with valiant Fairfax lay,
And must have fought — how went the
    day?"

XII.

"Wouldst hear the tale? — On Marston
    heath [5]
Met, front to front, the ranks of death;
Flourish'd the trumpets fierce, and now
Fired was each eye, and flush'd each
    brow;
On either side loud clamors ring,
'God and the Cause!' — 'God and the
    King!'
Right English all, they rush'd to blows,
With naught to win, and all to lose.
I could have laugh'd — but lack'd the
    time —
To see, in phrenesy sublime,
How the fierce zealots fought and bled,
For king or state, as humor led;
Some for a dream of public good,
Some for church-tippet, gown, and hood,
Draining their veins, in death to claim
A patriot's or a martyr's name. —
Led Bertram Risingham the hearts,
That counter'd there on adverse parts,
No superstitious fool had I
Sought El Dorados in the sky!
Chili had heard me through her states,
And Lima oped her silver gates,
Rich Mexico I had march'd through,
And sack'd the splendors of Peru,
Till sunk Pizarro's daring name,
And, Cortez, thine, in Bertram's fame." —
"Still from the purpose wilt thou stray!
Good gentle friend, how went the day?

XIII.

" Good am I deem'd at trumpet-sound,
And good where goblets dance the round,
Though gentle ne'er was join'd, till now,
With rugged Bertram's breast and brow.
But I resume. The battle's rage
Was like the strife which currents wage
Where Orinoco, in his pride,
Rolls to the main no tribute tide,
But 'gainst broad ocean urges far
A rival sea of roaring war;
While, in ten thousand eddies driven,
The billows fling their foam to heaven,
And the pale pilot seeks in vain,
Where rolls the river, where the main.
Even thus upon the bloody field,
The eddying tides of conflict wheel'd
Ambiguous, till that heart of flame,
Hot Rupert, on our squadrons came,
Hurling against our spears a line
Of gallants, fiery as their wine;
Then ours, though stubborn in their zeal,
In zeal's despite began to reel.
What would'st thou more?—in tumult tost,
Our leaders fell, our ranks were lost.
A thousand men, who drew the sword
For both the Houses and the Word,
Preach'd forth from hamlet, grange, and
down,
To curb the crosier and the crown,
Now, stark and stiff, lie stretch'd in gore,
And ne'er shall rail at mitre more. —
Thus fared it, when I left the fight,
With the good Cause and Commons' right."

XIV.

" Disastrous news !" dark Wycliffe said;
Assumed despondence bent his head,
While troubled joy was in his eye,
The well-feign'd sorrow to belie. —
-'' Disastrous news — when needed most,
Told ye not that your chiefs were lost?
Complete the woeful tale and say,
Who fell upon that fatal day;
What leaders of repute and name
Bought by their death a deathless fame.
If such my direst foeman's doom,
My tears shall dew his honor'd tomb. —
No answer? — Friend, of all our host,
Thou know'st whom I should hate the
most,
Whom thou, too, once wert wont to hate,
Yet leavest me doubtful of his fate."

With look unmoved, — " Of friend or foe,
Aught," answer'd Bertram, " would'st
thou know,
Demand in simple terms and plain,
A soldier's answer shalt thou gain;—
For question dark, or riddle high,
I have nor judgment nor reply."

XV.

The wrath his art and fear suppress'd
Now blazed at once in Wycliffe's breast,
And brave, from man so meanly born,
Roused his hereditary scorn.
"Wretch ! hast thou paid thy bloody debt
PHILIP OF MORTHAM, lives he yet?
False to thy patron or thine oath,
Trait'rous or perjured, one or both.
Slave ! hast thou kept thy promise plight
To slay thy leader in the fight?"
Then from his seat the soldier sprung,
And Wycliffe's hand he strongly wrung;
His grasp, as hard as glove of mail,
Forced the red blood-drop from the nail —
"A health !" he cried; and, ere he quaff'd
Flung from him Wycliffe's hand, an'
laugh'd :
— " Now, Oswald Wycliffe, speaks th'
heart !
Now play'st thou well thy genuine part
Worthy, but for thy craven fear,
Like me to roam a buccaneer.
What reck'st thou of the Cause divine,
If Mortham's wealth and lands be thine
What carest thou for beleaguer'd York,
If this good hand have done its work?
Or what, though Fairfax and his best
Are reddening Marston's swarthy breast,
If Philip Mortham with them lie,
Lending his life-blood to the dye? —
Sit, then ! and as mid comrades free
Carousing after victory,
When tales are told of blood and fear,
That boys and women shrink to hear,
From point to point I frankly tell
The deed of death as it befell.

XVI.

" When purposed vengeance I forego,
Term me a wretch, nor deem me foe;
And when an insult I forgive,
Then brand me as a slave, and live ! —
Philip of Mortham is with those
Whom Bertram Risingham calls foes;

Or whom more sure revenge attends,
If number'd with ungrateful friends.
As was his wont, ere battle glow'd,
Along the marshall'd ranks he rode,
And wore his visor up the while.
I saw his melancholy smile,
When, full opposed in front, he knew
Where ROKEBY'S kindred banner flew.
'And thus,' he said, ' will friends divide !'
I heard, and thought how, side by side,
We two had turn'd the battle's tide,
In many a well-debated field,
Where Bertram's breast was Philip's
    shield.
I thought on Darien's deserts pale,
Where death bestrides the evening gale,
How o'er my friend my cloak I threw,
And fenceless faced the deadly dew;
I thought on Quariana's cliff,
Where, rescued from our foundering skiff,
Through the white breaker's wrath I bore
Exhausted Mortham to the shore;
And when his side an arrow found,
I suck'd the Indian's venom'd wound.
These thoughts like torrents rush'd along,
To sweep away my purpose strong.

XVII.

' Hearts are not flint, and flints are rent;
Hearts are not steel, and steel is bent.
When Mortham bade me, as of yore,
Be near him in the battle's roar,
I scarcely saw the spears laid low,
I scarcely heard the trumpets blow;
Lost was the war in inward strife,
Debating Mortham's death or life.
'Twas then I thought, how, lured to come,
As partner of his wealth and home,
Years of piratic wandering o'er,
With him I sought our native shore.
But Mortham's lord grew far estranged
From the bold heart with whom he ranged;
Doubts, horrors, superstitious fears,
Sadden'd and dimm'd descending years;
The wily priests their victim sought,
And damn'd each free-born deed and
    thought.
Then must I seek another home,
My license shook his sober dome;
If gold he gave, in one wild day
I revell'd thrice the sum away.
An idle outcast then I stray'd,
Unfit for tillage or for trade,

Deem'd, like the steel of rusted lance,
Useless and dangerous at once.
The women fear'd my hardy look,
At my approach the peaceful shook;
The merchant saw my glance of flame,
And lock'd his hoards when Bertram came !
Each child of coward peace kept far
From the neglected son of war.

XVIII.

" But civil discord gave the call,
And made my trade the trade of all.
By Mortham urged, I came again
His vassals to the fight to train.
What guerdon waited on my care?
I could not cant of creed or prayer;
Sour fanatics each trust obtain'd,
And I, dishonor'd and disdain'd,
Gain'd but the high and happy lot,
In these poor arms to front the shot ! —
All this thou know'st, thy gestures tell;
Yet hear it o'er and mark it well.
'Tis honor bids me now relate
Each circumstance of Mortham's fate.

XIX.

" Thoughts, from the tongue that slowly
    part,
Glance quick as lightning through the
    heart,
As my spur press'd my courser's side,
Philip of Mortham's cause was tried,
And, ere the charging squadrons mix'd,
His plea was cast, his doom was fix'd.
I watch'd him through the doubtful fray,
That chang'd as March's moody day,
Till, like a stream that bursts its bank,
Fierce Rupert thunder'd on our flank.
'Twas then, midst tumult, smoke, and strife,
Where each man fought for death or life,
'Twas then I fired my petronel,
And Mortham, steed and rider, fell.
One dying look he upward cast,
Of wrath and anguish — 'twas his last.
Think not that there I stopp'd to view
What of the battle should ensue;
But ere I clear'd that bloody press,
Our northern horse ran masterless;
Monckton and Mitton told the news,
How troops of roundheads choked the
    Ouse,
And many a bonny Scot, aghast,
Spurring his palfrey northward, past,

Cursing the day when zeal or meed
First lured their Lesley o'er the Tweed.[6]
Yet when I reach'd the banks of Swale,
Had rumor learn'd another tale;
With his barb'd horse, fresh tidings say,
Stout Cromwell has redeem'd the day:[7]
But whether false the news, or true,
Oswald, I reck as light as you."

XX.

Not then by Wycliffe might be shown,
How his pride startled at the tone
In which his complice, fierce and free,
Asserted guilt's equality.
In smoothest terms his speech he wove,
Of endless friendship, faith, and love;
Promised and vow'd in courteous sort,
But Bertram broke professions short:—
" Wycliffe, be sure not here I stay,
No, scarcely till the rising day;
Warn'd by the legends of my youth,
I trust not an associate's truth.
Do not my native dales prolong
Of Percy Rede the tragic song.
Train'd forward to his bloody fall,
By Girsonfield, that treacherous Hall?[8]
Oft, by the Pringle's haunted side,
The shepherd sees his spectre glide.
And near the spot that gave her name,
The moated mound of Risingham,
Where Reed upon her margin sees
Sweet Woodburne's cottages and trees,
Some ancient sculptor's art has shown
An outlaw's image on the stone; [9]
Unmatch'd in strength, a giant he,
With quiver'd back, and kirtled knee.
Ask how he died, that hunter bold,
The tameless monarch of the wold,
And age and infancy can tell,
By brother's treachery he fell.
Thus warn'd by legends of my youth,
I trust to no associate's truth.

XXI.

" When last we reason'd of this deed,
Naught, I bethink me, was agreed,
Or by what rule, or when, or where,
The wealth of Mortham we should
    share.
Then list, while I the portion name,
Our differing laws give each to claim.
Thou, vassal sworn to England's throne,
Her rules of heritage must own;

They deal thee, as to nearest heir,
Thy kinsman's lands and livings fair,
And these I yield: — do thou revere
The statutes of the Buccaneer.[10]
Friend to the sea, and foeman sworn
To all that on her waves are borne,
When falls a mate in battle broil,
His comrade heirs his portion'd spoil;
When dies in fight a daring foe,
He claims his wealth who struck the
    blow;
And either rule to me assigns
Those spoils of Indian seas and mines,
Hoarded in Mortham's caverns dark;
Ingot of gold and diamond spark,
Chalice and plate from churches borne,
And gems from shrieking beauty torn,
Each string of pearl, each silver bar,
And all the wealth of western war.
I go to search, where, dark and deep,
Those trans-Atlantic treasures sleep.
Thou must along — for, lacking thee,
The heir will scarce find entrance free;
And then farewell.   I haste to try
Each varied pleasure wealth can buy;
When cloy'd each wish, these wars afford
Fresh work for Bertram's restless sword."

XXII.

An undecided answer hung
On Oswald's hesitating tongue.
Despite his craft, he heard with awe
This ruffian stabber fix the law;
While his own troubled passions veer
Through hatred, joy, regret, and fear:—
Joy'd at the soul that Bertram flies,
He grudged the murderer's mighty prize,
Hated his pride's presumptuous tone,
And fear'd to wend with him alone.
At length, that middle course to steer,
To cowardice and craft so dear,
" His charge," he said; " would ill allow
His absence from the fortress now;
WILFRID on Bertram should attend,
His son should journey with his friend."

XXIII.

Contempt kept Bertram's anger down,
And wreathed to savage smile his frown.
" Wilfrid, or thou — 'tis one to me,
Whichever bears the golden key.
Yet think not but I mark, and smile
To mark, thy poor and selfish wile!

If injury from me you fear,
What, Oswald Wycliffe, shields thee
    here?
I've sprung from walls more high than
    these,
I've swam through deeper streams than
    Tees.
Might not I stab thee, ere one yell
Could rouse the distant sentinel?
Start not — it is not my design,
But, if it were, weak fence were thine:
And, trust me, that, in time of need,
This hand hath done more desperate deed.
Go, haste and rouse thy slumbering son;
Time calls, and I must needs be gone.''

XXIV.

Naught of his sire's ungenerous part
Polluted Wilfrid's gentle heart;
A heart too soft from early life
To hold with fortune needful strife.
His sire, while yet a hardier race
Of numerous sons were Wycliffe's grace,
On Wilfrid set contemptuous brand,
For feeble heart and forceless hand;
But a fond mother's care and joy
Were centred in her sickly boy.
No touch of childhood's frolic mood
Show'd the elastic spring of blood;
Hour after hour he loved to pore
On Shakspeare's rich and varied lore,
But turn'd from martial scenes and light,
From Falstaff's feast and Percy's fight,
To ponder Jaques' moral strain,
And muse with Hamlet, wise in vain;
And weep himself to soft repose
O'er gentle Desdemona's woes.

XXV.

In youth he sought not pleasures found
By youth in horse and hawk and hound,
But loved the quiet joys that wake
By lonely stream and silent lake;
In Deepdale's solitude to lie,
Where all is cliff and copse and sky;
To climb Catcastle's dizzy peak,
Or lone Pendragon's mound to seek.
Such was his wont; and there his dream
Soar'd on some wild fantastic theme,
Of faithful love, or ceaseless spring,
Till Contemplation's wearied wing
The enthusiast could no more sustain,
And sad he sunk to earth again.

XXVI.

He loved — as many a lay can tell,
Preserved in Stanmore's lonely dell;
For his was minstrel's skill, he caught
The art unteachable, untaught;
He loved — his soul did nature frame
For love, and fancy nursed the flame;
Vainly he loved — for seldom swain
Of such soft mould is loved again;
Silent he loved — in every gaze
Was passion, friendship in his phrase.
So mused his life away — till died
His brethren all, their father's pride.
Wilfrid is now the only heir
Of all his stratagems and care,
And destined, darkling, to pursue
Ambition's maze by Oswald's clue.

XXVII.

Wilfrid must love and woo the bright
Matilda, heir of Rokeby's knight.
To love her was an easy hest,
The secret empress of his breast;
To woo her was a harder task
To one that durst not hope or ask.
Yet all Matilda could, she gave
In pity to her gentle slave;
Friendship, esteem, and fair regard,
And praise, the poet's best reward!
She read the tales his taste approved,
And sung the lays he framed or loved;
Yet, loth to nurse the fatal flame
Of hopeless love in friendship's name,
In kind caprice she oft withdrew
The favoring glance to friendship due,
Then grieved to see her victim's pain,
And gave the dangerous smiles again.

XXVIII.

So did the suit of Wilfrid stand,
When war's loud summons waked the land
Three banners, floating o'er the Tees,
The woe-foreboding peasant sees;
In concert oft they braved of old
The bordering Scot's incursion bold;
Frowning defiance in their pride,
Their vassals now and lords divide.
From his fair hall on Greta banks,
The Knight of Rokeby led his ranks,
To aid the valiant northern Earls,
Who drew the sword for royal Charles.
Mortham, by marriage near allied, —
His sister had been Rokeby's bride,

Though long before the civil fray,
In peaceful grave the lady lay, —
Philip of Mortham raised his band,
And march'd at Fairfax's command;
While Wycliffe, bound by many a train
Of kindred art with wily Vane,
Less prompt to brave the bloody field,
Made Barnard's battlements his shield,
Secured them with his Lunedale powers,
And for the Commons held the towers.

XXIX.

The lovely heir of Rokeby's Knight
Waits in his halls the event of fight;
For England's war revered the claim
Of every unprotected name.
And spared, amid its fiercest rage,
Childhood and womanhood and age.
But Wilfrid, son to Rokeby's foe,
Must the dear privilege forego,
By Greta's side, in evening gray,
To steal upon Matilda's way,
Striving, with fond hypocrisy
For careless step and vacant eye;
Calming each anxious look and glance,
To give the meeting all to chance,
Or framing, as a fair excuse,
The book, the pencil, or the muse;
Something to give, to sing, to say,
Some modern tale, some ancient lay.
Then, while the long'd-for minutes last,—
Ah! minutes quickly over-past!
Recording each expression free,
Of kind or careless courtesy,
Each friendly look, each softer tone,
As food for fancy when alone.
All this is o'er — but still unseen,
Wilfrid may lurk in Eastwood green,
To watch Matilda's wonted round,
While springs his heart at every sound.
She comes! 'tis but a passing sight,
Yet serves to cheat his weary night;
She comes not — He will wait the
　　hour,
When her lamp lightens in the tower;
'Tis something yet, if, as she past,
Her shade is o'er the lattice cast.
"What is my life, my hope?" he said;
"Alas! a transitory shade."

XXX.

Thus wore his life, though reason strove
For mastery in vain with love,

Forcing upon his thoughts the sum
Of present woe and ills to come,
While still he turn'd impatient ear
From Truth's intrusive voice severe.
Gentle, indifferent, and subdued,
In all but this, unmoved he view'd
Each outward change of ill and good:
But Wilfrid, docile, soft, and mild,
Was Fancy's spoil'd and wayward child;
In her bright car she bade him ride,
With one fair form to grace his side,
Or, in some wild and lone retreat,
Flung her high spells around his seat,
Bathed in her dews his languid head,
Her fairy mantle o'er him spread,
For him her opiates gave to flow,
Which he who tastes can ne'er forego,
And placed him in her circle, free
From every stern reality,
Till, to the Visionary, seem
Her day-dreams truth, and truth a dream.

XXXI.

Woe to the youth whom Fancy gains,
Winning from Reason's hand the reins,
Pity and woe! for such a mind
Is soft, contemplative, and kind;
And woe to those who train such youth,
And spare to press the rights of truth,
The mind to strengthen and anneal,
While on the stithy glows the steel!
O teach him while your lessons last,
To judge the present by the past;
Remind him of each wish pursued,
How rich it glow'd with promised
　　good;
Remind him of each wish enjoy'd,
How soon his hopes possession cloy'd!
Tell him, we play unequal game,
Whene'er we shoot by Fancy's aim;
And, ere he strip him for her race,
Show the conditions of the chase.
Two sisters by the goal are set,
Cold Disappointment and Regret;
One disenchants the winner's eyes,
And strips of all its worth the prize.
While one augments its gaudy show,
More to enhance the loser's woe.
The victor sees his fairy gold,
Transform'd, when won, to drossy mold;
But still the vanquish'd mourns his
　　loss,
And rues, as gold, that glittering dross.

XXXII.

More wouldst thou know — yon tower
  survey,
Yon couch unpress'd since parting day,
Yon untrimm'd lamp, whose yellow gleam
Is mingling with the cold moonbeam,
And yon thin form! — the hectic red
On his pale cheek unequal spread;
The head reclin'd, the loosen'd hair,
The limbs relaxed, the mournful air. —
See, he looks up; a woeful smile
Lightens his woe-worn cheek a while, —
Tis Fancy wakes some idle thought,
To gild the ruin she has wrought;
For, like the bat of Indian brakes,
Her pinions fan the wound she makes,
And soothing thus the dreamer's pain,
She drinks his life-blood from the vein.
Now to the lattice turn his eyes,
Vain hope! to see the sun arise.
The moon with clouds is still o'ercast,
Still howls by fits the stormy blast;
Another hour must wear away,
Ere the East kindle into day,
And hark! to waste that weary hour, —
He tries the minstrel's magic power: —

XXXIII.

SONG.

To the Moon.

Hail to thy cold and clouded beam,
  Pale pilgrim of the troubled sky!
Hail, though the mists that o'er thee stream
  Lend to thy brow their sullen dye!
How should thy pure and peaceful eye
  Untroubled view our scenes below,
Or how a tearless beam supply
  To light a world of war and woe!

Fair Queen! I will not blame thee now,
  As once by Greta's fairy side
Each little cloud that dimm'd thy brow
  Did then an angel's beauty hide.
And of the shades I then could chide,
  Still are the thoughts to memory dear,
For, while a softer strain I tried,
  They hid my blush, and calm'd my fear.

Then did I swear thy ray serene
  Was form'd to light some lonely dell,
By two fond lovers only seen,
  Reflected from the crystal well,

Or sleeping on the mossy cell,
  Or quivering on the lattice bright,
Or glancing on their couch, to tell
  How swiftly wanes the summer night!

XXXIV.

He starts — a step at this lone hour!
A voice — his father seeks the tower,
With haggard look and troubled sense,
Fresh from his dreadful conference.
"Wilfrid — what, not to sleep address'd?
Thou hast no cares to chase thy rest.
Mortham has fall'n on Marston-moor;
Bertram brings warrant to secure
His treasures, bought by spoil and blood,
For the State's use and public good.
The menials will thy voice obey;
Let his commission have its way,
In every point, in every word." —
Then, in a whisper — "Take thy sword!
Bertram is — what I must not tell.
I hear his hasty step — farewell!"

CANTO SECOND.

I.

FAR in the chambers of the west,
The gale has sigh'd itself to rest;
The moon was cloudless now and clear,
But pale and soon to disappear.
The thin gray clouds wax dimly light
On Brusleton and Houghton height:
And the rich dale, that eastward lay,
Waited the wakening touch of day,
To give its woods and cultured plain
And towers and spires, to light again.
But, westward, Stanmore's shapeless
  swell,
And Lunedale wild, and Kelton-fell,
And rock-begirdled Gilmanscar,
And Arkingarth, lay dark afar,
While as a livelier twilight falls,
Emerge proud Barnard's banner'd walls,
High crown'd he sits, in dawning pale,
The sovereign of the lovely vale.

II.

What prospects, from his watch-tower
  high,
Gleam gradual on the warder's eye! —

Far sweeping to the east, he sees
Down his deep woods the course of
    Tees,[11]
And tracks his wanderings by the steam
Of summer vapors from the stream;
And ere he paced his destined hour
By Brackenbury's dungeon-tower,
These silver mists shall melt away,
And dew the woods with glittering spray,
Then in broad lustre shall be shown
That mighty trench of living stone,
And each huge trunk that, from the side,
Reclines him o'er the darksome tide,
Where Tees, full many a fathom low,
Wears with his rage no common foe;
For pebbly bank, nor sand-bed here,
Nor clay-mound, checks his fierce career,
Condemn'd to mine a channell'd way,
O'er solid sheets of marble gray.

III.

Nor Tees alone, in dawning bright,
Shall rush upon the ravish'd sight;
But many a tributary stream
Each from his own dark dell shall gleam;
Staindrop, who, from her sylvan bowers,
Salutes proud Raby's battled towers;
The rural brook of Egliston,
And Balder, named from Odin's son;
And Greta, to whose banks ere long
We lead the lovers of the song;
And silver Lune, from Stanmore wild,
And fairy Thorsgill's murmuring child,
And last and least, but loveliest still,
Romantic Deepdale's slender rill.
Who in that dim-wood glen hath stray'd,
Yet long'd for Roslin's magic glade?
Who, wandering there, hath sought to
    change,
Even for that vale so stern and strange,
Where Cartland's Crags,* fantastic rent,
Through her green copse like spires are
    sent?
Yet, Albin, yet the praise be thine,
Thy scenes and story to combine!
Thou bid'st him, who by Roslin strays,
List to the deeds of other days;
Mid Cartland's Crags thou show'st the
    cave,
The refuge of thy champion brave;

* Near Lanark : celebrated as among the favorite retreats of Sir William Wallace.

Giving each rock its storied tale,
Pouring a lay for every dale,
Knitting, as with a moral band,
Thy native legends with thy land,
To lend each scene the interest high
Which genius beams from Beauty's eye.

IV.

Bertram awaited not the sight
Which sun-rise shows from Barnard'
    height,
But from the towers, preventing day,
With Wilfrid took his early way,
While misty dawn, and moonbeam pale
Still mingled in the silent dale.
By Barnard's bridge of stately stone,
The southern bank of Tees they won;
Their winding path then eastward cast,
And Egliston's gray ruins pass'd;[12]
Each on his own deep visions bent,
Silent and sad they onward went.
Well may you think that Bertram's mood,
To Wilfrid savage seem'd and rude;
Well may you think bold Risingham
Held Wilfrid trivial, poor, and tame;
And small the intercourse, I ween,
Such uncongenial souls between.

V.

Stern Bertram shunn'd the nearer way,
Through Rokeby's park and chase that lay,
And, skirting high the valley's ridge,
They cross'd by Greta's ancient bridge,
Descending where her waters wind
Free for a space and unconfined,
As, 'scaped from Brignall's dark-wood
    glen,
She seeks wild Mortham's deeper den.
There, as his eye glanced o'er the mound,
Raised by that Legion [13] long renown'd,
Whose votive shrine asserts their claim,
Of pious, faithful, conquering fame,
"Stern sons of war!" sad Wilfrid sigh'd,
"Behold the boast of Roman pride!
What now of all your toils are known?
A grassy trench, a broken stone!" —
This to himself; for moral strain
To Bertram were address'd in vain.

VI.

Of different mood, a deeper sigh
Awoke, when Rokeby's turrets high [14]

Were northward in the dawning seen
To rear them o'er the thicket green.
O then, tho' Spenser's self had stray'd
Beside him through the lovely glade,
Lending his rich luxuriant glow
Of fancy, all its charms to show,
Pointing the stream rejoicing free,
As captive set at liberty,
Flashing her sparkling waves abroad,
And clamoring joyful on her road ;
Pointing where, up the sunny banks,
The trees retire in scatter'd ranks,
Save where, advanced before the rest,
On knoll or hillock rears his crest,
Lonely and huge, the giant Oak,
As champions, when their band is broke,
Stand forth to guard the rearward post,
The bulwark of the scatter'd host —
All this, and more, might Spenser say,
Yet waste in vain his magic lay,
While Wilfrid eyed the distant tower,
Whose lattice lights Matilda's bower.

VII.

The open vale is soon passed o'er,
Rokeby, though nigh, is seen no more;
Sinking mid Greta's thickets deep,
A wild and darker course they keep,
A stern and lone, yet lovely road,
As e'er the foot of Minstrel trode ! 15
Broad shadows o'er their passage fell,
Deeper and narrower grew the dell;
It seem'd some mountain, rent and riven,
A channel for the stream had given,
So high the cliffs of limestone gray
Hung beetling o'er the torrent's way,
Yielding, along their rugged base,
A flinty footpath's niggard space,
Where he, who winds 'twixt rock and
    wave,
May hear the headlong torrent rave,
And like a steed in frantic fit,
That flings the froth from curb and bit,
May view her chafe her waves to spray,
O'er every rock that bars her way,
Till foam-globes on her eddies ride,
Thick as the schemes of human pride
That down life's current drive amain,
As frail, as frothy, and as vain !

VIII.

The cliffs that rear their haughty head
High o'er the river's darksome bed,

Were now all naked, wild, and gray,
Now waving all with greenwood spray;
Here trees to every crevice clung,
And o'er the dell their branches hung;
And there, all splinter'd and uneven,
The shiver'd rocks ascend to heaven;
Oft, too, the ivy swath'd their breast,
And wreathed its garland round their
    crest.
Or from the spires bade loosely flare
Its tendrils in the middle air.
As pennons wont to wave of old
O'er the high feast of Baron bold,
When revell'd loud the feudal rout,
And the arch'd halls return'd their shout;
Such and more wild is Greta's roar,
And such the echoes from her shore.
And so the ivied banner's gleam,
Waved wildly o'er the brawling stream.

IX.

Now from the stream the rocks recede,
But leave between no sunny mead,
No, nor the spot of pebbly sand,
Oft found by such a mountain strand;
Forming such warm and dry retreat,
As fancy deems the lonely seat,
Where hermit wandering from his cell,
His rosary might love to tell.
But here, 'twixt rock and river, grew
A dismal grove of sable yew,
With whose sad tints were mingled seen
The blighted fir's sepulchral green.
Seem'd that the trees their shadows cast,
The earth that nourish'd them to blast;
For never knew that swarthy grove
The verdant hue that fairies love;
Nor wilding green, nor woodland flower,
Arose within its baleful bower:
The dank and sable earth receives
Its only carpet from the leaves,
That, from the withering branches cast,
Bestrew'd the ground with every blast.
Though now the sun was o'er the hill,
In this dark spot 'twas twilight still,
Save that on Greta's farther side
Some straggling beams through copse-
    wood glide;
And wild and savage contrast made
That dingle's deep and funeral shade,
With the bright tints of early day,
Which, glimmering through the ivy spray,
On the opposing summit lay.

x.

The lated peasant shunn'd the dell;
For Superstition wont to tell
Of many a grisly sound and sight,
Scaring its path at dead of night.
When Christmas logs blaze high and wide,
Such wonders speed the festal tide;
While Curiosity and Fear,
Pleasure and Pain, sit crouching near,
Till childhood's cheek no longer glows,
And village maidens lose the rose.
The thrilling interest rises higher,
The circle closes nigh and nigher,
And shuddering glance is cast behind,
As louder moans the wintry wind.
Believe, that fitting scene was laid
For such wild tales in Mortham glade;
For who had seen, on Greta's side,
By that dim light fierce Bertram stride,
In such a spot, at such an hour, —
If touch'd by Superstition's power,
Might well have deem'd that Hell had given
A murderer's ghost to upper heaven,
While Wilfrid's form had seem'd to glide
Like his pale victim by his side.

XI.

Nor think to village swains alone
Are these unearthly terrors known;
For not to rank nor sex confined
Is this vain ague of the mind:
Hearts firm as steel, as marble hard,
'Gainst faith and love and pity barr'd,
Have quaked, like aspen leaves in May,
Beneath its universal sway.
Bertram had listed many a tale
Of wonder in his native dale,
That in his secret soul retain'd
The credence they in childhood gain'd:
Nor less his wild adventurous youth
Believed in every legend's truth;
Learn'd when, beneath the tropic gale,
Full swell'd the vessel's steady sail,
And the broad Indian moon her light
Pour'd on the watch of middle night,
When seamen love to hear and tell
Of portent, prodigy, and spell:
What gales are sold on Lapland's shore,
How whistle rash bids tempests roar,[16]
Of witch, of mermaid, and of sprite,
Of Erick's cap and Elmo's light;[17]

Or of that Phantom Ship, whose form
Shoots like a meteor through the storm;
When the dark scud comes driving hard
And lower'd is every topsail-yard,
And canvas, wove in earthly looms,
No more to brave the storm presumes!
Then mid the war of sea and sky,
Top and top-gallant hoisted high,
Full spread and crowded every sail,
The Demon Frigate braves the gale;[18]
And well the doom'd spectators know
The harbinger of wreck and woe.

XII.

Then, too, were told, in stifled tone,
Marvels and omens all their own;
How, by some desert isle or key,[19]
Where Spaniards wrought their cruelty,
Or where the savage pirate's mood
Repaid it home in deeds of blood,
Strange nightly sounds of woe and fear
Appall'd the listening Buccaneer,
Whose light-arm'd shallop anchor'd lay
In ambush by the lonely bay.
The groan of grief, the shriek of pain,
Ring from the moonlight groves o'
  cane;
The fierce adventurer's heart they scare,
Who wearies memory for a prayer,
Curses the road-stead, and with gale
Of early morning lifts the sail,
To give, in thirst of blood and prey,
A legend for another bay.

XIII.

Thus, as a man, a youth, a child,
Train'd in the mystic and the wild,
With this on Bertram's soul at times
Rush'd a dark feeling of his crimes;
Such to his troubled soul their form,
As the pale Death-ship to the storm,
And such their omen dim and dread,
As shrieks and voices of the dead. —
That pang, whose transitory force
Hover'd 'twixt horror and remorse;
That pang, perchance, his bosom press'd,
As Wilfrid sudden he address'd: —
" Wilfrid, this glen is never trod
Until the sun rides high abroad;
Yet twice have I beheld to-day
A Form, that seem'd to dog our way;
Twice from my glance it seem'd to flee,
And shroud itself by cliff or tree.

low think'st thou?—Is our path waylaid?
Or hath thy sire my trust betrayed?
If so " — Ere, starting from his dream,
That turn'd upon a gentler theme,
Wilfrid had roused him to reply,
Bertram sprung forward, shouting high,
" Whate'er thou art, thou now shalt
    stand ! "
And forth he darted, sword in hand.

XIV.

As bursts the levin, in his wrath
He shot him down the sounding path;
Rock, wood, and stream, rang wildly out,
To his loud step and savage shout.
Seems that the object of his race
Hath scaled the cliffs; his frantic chase
Sidelong he turns, and now 'tis bent
Right up the rock's tall battlement;
Straining each sinew to ascend,
Foot, hand, and knee, their aid must lend.
Wilfrid, all dizzy with dismay,
Views from beneath his dreadful way:
Now to the oak's warp'd roots he clings,
Now trusts his weight to ivy strings;
Now, like the wild-goat, must he dare
An unsupported leap in air;
Hid in the shrubby rain-course now,
You mark him by the crashing bough,
And by his corslet's sullen clank,
And by the stones spurn'd from the bank,
And by the hawk scared from her nest,
And ravens croaking o'er their guest,
Who deem his forfeit limbs shall pay
The tribute of his bold essay.

XV.

See ! he emerges — desperate now
All farther course — Yon beetling brow
In cragged nakedness sublime,
What heart or foot shall dare to climb?
It bears no tendril for his clasp,
Presents no angle for his grasp:
Sole stay his foot may rest upon,
Is yon earth-bedded jetting stone.
Balanced on such precarious prop,
He strains his grasp to reach the top.
Just as the dangerous stretch he makes,
By Heaven, his faithless footstool shakes !
Beneath his tottering bulk it bends,
It sways . . . it loosens . . . it descends !
And downward holds its headlong way,
Crashing o'er rock and copsewood spray,

Loud thunders shake the echoing dell ! —
Fell it alone ? — alone it fell.
Just on the very verge of fate,
The hardy Bertram's falling weight
He trusted to his sinewy hands,
And on the top unharm'd he stands ! —

XVI.

Wilfrid a safer path pursued;
At intervals where, roughly hew'd,
Rude steps ascending from the dell
Render'd the cliffs accessible.
By circuit slow he thus attain'd
The height that Risingham had gain'd
And when he issued from the wood,
Before the gate of Mortham stood.[20]
'Twas a fair scene ! the sunbeam lay
On battled tower and portal gray :
And from the grassy slope he sees
The Greta flow to meet the Tees;
Where, issuing from her darksome bed,
She caught the morning's eastern red,
And through the softening vale below
Roll'd her bright waves in rosy glow,
All blushing to her bridal bed,
Like some shy maid in convent bred;
While linnet, lark, and blackbird gay,
Sing forth her nuptial roundelay.

XVII.

'Twas sweetly sung that roundelay;
That summer morn shone bright and
    gay;
But morning beam, and wild-bird's call,
Awaked not Mortham's silent hall.
No porter, by the low-brow'd gate,
Took in the wonted niche his seat;
To the paved court no peasant drew;
Waked to their toil no menial crew;
The maiden's carol was not heard,
As to her morning task she fared :
In the void offices around,
Rung not a hoof, nor bay'd a hound;
Nor eager steed, with shrilling neigh,
Accused the lagging groom's delay;
Untrimm'd, undress'd, neglected now,
Was alley'd walk and orchard bough;
All spoke the master's absent care,
All spoke neglect and disrepair.
South of the gate an arrow flight,
Two mighty elms their limbs unite,
As if a canopy to spread
O'er the lone dwelling of the dead;

For their huge boughs in arches bent
Above a massive monument,
Carv'd o'er in ancient Gothic wise,
With many a scutcheon and device;
There, spent with toil and sunk in gloom,
Bertram stood pondering by the tomb.

XVIII.

" It vanish'd, like a flitting ghost!
Behind this tomb," he said, "'twas lost —
This tomb, where oft I deem'd lies stored
Of Mortham's Indian wealth the hoard.
'Tis true, the aged servants said
Here his lamented wife is laid;
But weightier reasons may be guess'd
For their lord's strict and stern behest,
That none should on his steps intrude,
Whene'er he sought this solitude. —
An ancient mariner I knew,
What time I sail'd with Morgan's crew,
Who oft, mid our carousals, spake
Of Raleigh, Frobisher, and Drake;
Adventurous hearts! who barter'd bold,
Their English steel for Spanish gold.
Trust not, would say his experience say,
Captain or comrade with your prey;
But seek some charnel, when, at full,
The moon gilds skeleton and skull:
There dig, and tomb your precious heap,
And bid the dead your treasure keep; [21]
Sure stewards they, if fitting spell
Their service to the task compel.
Lacks there such charnel? — kill a slave,
Or prisoner, on the treasure-grave;
And bid his discontented ghost
Stalk nightly on his lonely post. —
Such was his tale. Its truth, I ween,
Is in my morning vision seen."

XIX.

Wilfrid, who scorn'd the legend wild,
In mingled mirth and pity smiled,
Much marvelling that a breast so bold
In such fond tale belief should hold;
But yet of Bertram sought to know
The apparition's form and show. —
The power within the guilty breast,
Oft vanquish'd, never quite suppress'd,
That unsubdued and lurking lies
To take the felon by surprise,
And force him, as by magic spell,
In his despite his guilt to tell, [22] —

That power in Bertram's breast awoke;
Scarce conscious he was heard, he spoke: —
" 'Twas Mortham's form, from foot to head!
His morion, with the plume of red,
His shape, his mien — 'twas Mortham right
As when I slew him in the fight." —
"Thou slay him? — thou?" — With conscious start
He heard, then mann'd his haughty heart
" I slew him? — I! — I had forgot
Thou, stripling, knew'st not of the plot
But it is spoken — nor will I
Deed done, or spoken word, deny.
I slew him; I! for thankless pride;
'Twas by this hand that Mortham died.'

XX.

Wilfrid, of gentle hand and heart,
Averse to every active part,
But most averse to martial broil,
From danger shrunk, and turn'd from toil;
Yet the meek lover of the lyre
Nursed one brave spark of noble fire,
Against injustice, fraud, or wrong,
His blood beat high, his hand wax'd strong.
Not his the nerves that could sustain,
Unshaken, danger, toil, and pain;
But, when that spark blazed forth to flame.
He rose superior to his frame.
And now it came, that generous mood:
And, in full current of his blood,
On Bertram he laid desperate hand,
Placed firm his foot, and drew his brand.
"Should every fiend, to whom thou'rt sold,
Rise in thine aid, I keep my hold.
Arouse there, ho! take spear and sword!
Attach the murderer of your Lord!"

XXI.

A moment, fix'd as by a spell,
Stood Bertram. — It seem'd miracle,
That one so feeble, soft, and tame
Set grasp on warlike Risingham.
But when he felt a feeble stroke,
The fiend within the ruffian woke!
To wrench the sword from Wilfrid's hand,
To dash him headlong on the sand,
Was but one moment's work, — one more

Had drench'd the blade in Wilfrid's gore;
But, in the instant it arose,
To end his life, his love, his woes,
A warlike form, that mark'd the scene,
Presents his rapier sheathed between,
Parries the fast-descending blow,
And steps 'twixt Wilfrid and his foe;
Nor then unscabbarded his brand,
But, sternly pointing with his hand,
With monarch's voice forbade the fight,
And motion'd Bertram from his sight.
"Go, and repent," he said, "while time
Is given thee; add not crime to crime."

XXII.

Mute and uncertain and amazed,
As on a vision Bertram gazed!
'Twas Mortham's bearing, bold and high,
His sinewy frame, his falcon eye,
His look and accent of command,
The martial gesture of his hand,
His stately form, spare-built and tall,
His war-bleach'd locks — 'twas Mortham all.
Through Bertram's dizzy brain career
A thousand thoughts, and all of fear;
His wavering faith received not quite
The form he saw as Mortham's sprite,
But more he fear'd it, if it stood
His lord, in living flesh and blood. —
What spectre can the charnel send,
So dreadful as an injured friend?
Then, too, the habit of command,
Used by the leader of the band,
When Risingham, for many a day,
Had march'd and fought beneath his sway,
Tamed him — and, with reverted face,
Backwards he bore his sullen pace;
Oft stopp'd, and oft on Mortham stared,
And dark as rated mastiff glared;
But when the tramp of steeds was heard,
Plunged in the glen, and disappear'd; —
Nor longer there the warrior stood,
Retiring eastward through the wood;
But first to Wilfrid warning gives,
"Tell thou to none that Mortham lives."

XXIII.

Still rung these words in Wilfrid's ear,
Hinting he knew not what of fear;
When nearer came the coursers' tread,
And, with his father at their head,
Of horsemen arm'd a gallant power
Rein'd up their steeds before the tower.
"Whence these pale looks, my son?"
he said:
"Where's Bertram? — Why that naked
blade?"
Wilfrid ambiguously replied,
(For Mortham's charge his honor tied,)
"Bertram is gone — the villain's word
Avouch'd him murderer of his lord!
Even now we fought — but, when your
tread
Announced you nigh, the felon fled."
In Wycliffe's conscious eye appear
A guilty hope, a guilty fear;
On his pale brow the dewdrop broke,
And his lip quiver'd as he spoke:—

XXIV.

"A murderer! — Philip Mortham died
Amid the battle's wildest tide.
Wilfrid! or Bertram raves, or you!
Yet, grant such strange confession true,
Pursuit were vain — let him fly far —
Justice must sleep in civil war."
A gallant Youth rode near his side,
Brave Rokeby's page, in battle tried;
That morn, an embassy of weight
He brought to Barnard's castle gate,
And follow'd now in Wycliffe's train,
An answer for his lord to gain.
His steed, whose arch'd and sable neck
A hundred wreaths of foam bedeck,
Chafed not against the curb more high
Than he at Oswald's cold reply;
He bit his lip, implored his saint,
(His the old faith) — then burst re-
straint : —

XXV.

"Yes! I beheld his bloody fall
By that base traitor's dastard ball,
Just when I thought to measure sword, —
Presumptuous hope! — with Mortham's
lord.
And shall the murderer 'scape, who slew
His leader, generous, brave, and true?
Escape, while on the dew you trace
The marks of his gigantic pace?
No! ere the sun that dew shall dry,
False Risingham shall yield or die. —
Ring out the castle 'larum bell!
Arouse the peasants with the knell!

Meantime disperse — ride, gallants, ride!
Beset the wood on every side.
But if among you one there be,
That honors Mortham's memory,
Let him dismount and follow me!
Else on your crests sit fear and shame,
And foul suspicion dog your name!"

XXVI.

Instant to earth young REDMOND sprung;
Instant on earth the harness rung
Of twenty men of Wycliffe's band,
Who waited not their lord's command.
Redmond his spurs from buskins drew,
His mantle from his shoulders threw,
His pistols in his belt he placed,
The green-wood gain'd, the footsteps
        traced,
Shouted like huntsman to his hounds,
"To cover, hark!" — and in he bounds.
Scarce heard was Oswald's anxious cry,
"Suspicion! yes — pursue him, fly —
But venture not, in useless strife,
On ruffian desperate of his life,
Whoever finds him, shoot him dead!
Five hundred nobles for his head!"

XXVII.

The horsemen gallop'd, to make good
Each path that issued from the wood.
Loud from the thickets rung the shout
Of Redmond and his eager rout!
With them was Wilfrid, stung with ire,
And envying Redmond's martial fire,
And emulous of fame. — But where
Is Oswald, noble Mortham's heir?
He, bound by honor, law, and faith,
Avenger of his kinsman's death? —
Leaning against the elmin tree,
With drooping head and slacken'd knee,
And clenched teeth, and close-clasp'd
        hands,
In agony of soul he stands!
His downcast eye on earth is bent,
His soul to every sound is lent;
For in each shout that cleaves the air,
May ring discovery and despair.

XXVIII.

What 'vail'd it him, that brightly play'd
The morning sun on Mortham's glade?
All seems in giddy round to ride,
Like objects on a stormy tide,

Seen eddying by the moonlight dim,
Imperfectly to sink and swim.
What 'vail'd it, that the fair domain,
Its battled mansion, hill, and plain,
On which the sun so brightly shone,
Envied so long, was now his own?
The lowest dungeon, in that hour,
Of Brackenbury's dismal tower,[23]
Had been his choice, could such
        doom
Have open'd Mortham's bloody tomb!
Forced, too, to turn unwilling ear
To each surmise of hope or fear,
Murmur'd among the rustics round,
Who gather'd at the 'larum sound;
He dared not turn his head away,
E'en to look up to heaven to pray,
Or call on hell in bitter mood,
For one sharp death-shot from the wood.

XXIX.

At length, o'erpast that dreadful space,
Back straggling came the scatter'd chase
Jaded and weary, horse and man,
Return'd the troopers one by one.
Wilfrid, the last, arrived to say,
All trace was lost of Bertram's way,
Though Redmond still, up Brignall wood
The hopeless quest in vain pursued. —
O, fatal doom of human race!
What tyrant passions passions chase!
Remorse from Oswald's brow is gone,
Avarice and pride resume their throne;
The pang of instant terror by,
They dictate thus their slave's reply:—

XXX.

"Ay — let him range like hasty hound
And if the grim wolf's lair be found,
Small is my care how goes the game
With Redmond or with Risingham. —
Nay, answer not, thou simple boy!
Thy fair Matilda, all so coy
To thee, is of another mood
To that bold youth of Erin's blood.
Thy ditties will she freely praise,
And pay thy pains with courtly phrase;
In a rough path will oft command —
Accept at least — thy friendly hand;
His she avoids, or, urged and pray'd,
Unwilling takes his proffer'd aid,
While conscious passion plainly speaks
In downcast look and blushing cheeks.

Whene'er he sings, will she glide nigh,
And all her soul is in her eye;
Yet doubts she still to tender free
The wonted words of courtesy.
These are strong signs! — yet wherefore sigh,
And wipe, effeminate, thine eye?
Thine shall she be, if thou attend
The counsels of thy sire and friend.

XXXI.

Scarce wert thou gone, when peep of light
Brought genuine news of Marston's fight.
Brave Cromwell turn'd the doubtful tide,
And conquest bless'd the rightful side;
Three thousand cavaliers lie dead,
Rupert and that bold Marquis fled;
Nobles and knights, so proud of late,
Must fine for freedom and estate.
Of these, committed to my charge,
Is Rokeby, prisoner at large;
Redmond, his page, arrived to say
He reaches Barnard's towers to-day.
Light heavy shall his ransom be,
Unless that maid compound with thee ! [24]
Go to her now — be bold of cheer,
While her soul floats 'twixt hope and fear;
It is the very change of tide,
When best the female heart is tried —
Pride, prejudice, and modesty
Are in the current swept to sea;
And the bold swain, who plies his oar,
May lightly row his bark to shore."

CANTO THIRD.

I.

THE hunting tribes of air and earth
Respect the brethren of their birth;
Nature, who loves the claim of kind,
Less cruel chase to each assign'd.
The falcon, poised on soaring wing,
Watches the wild-duck by the spring;
The slow-hound wakes the fox's lair;
The greyhound presses on the hare;
The eagle pounces on the lamb;
The wolf devours the fleecy dam:
Even tiger fell, and sullen bear,
Their likeness and their lineage spare;

Man, only, mars kind Nature's plan,
And turns the fierce pursuit on man:
Plying war's desultory trade,
Incursion, flight, and ambuscade,
Since Nimrod, Cush's mighty son,
At first the bloody game begun.

II.

The Indian, prowling for his prey,
Who hears the settlers track his way, [25]
And knows in distant forest far
Camp his red brethren of the war;
He, when each double and disguise
To baffle the pursuit he tries,
Low crouching now his head to hide,
Where swampy streams thro' rushes glide,
Now covering with the wither'd leaves
The foot-prints that the dew receives:
He, skill'd in every sylvan guile,
Knows not, nor tries such various wile,
As Risingham, when on the wind
Arose the loud pursuit behind.
In Redesdale his youth had heard
Each art her wily dalesmen dared,
When Rooken-edge, and Redswair high,
To bugle rung and blood-hound's cry, [26]
Announcing Jedwood-axe and spear,
And Lid'sdale riders in the rear;
And well his venturous life had proved
The lessons that his childhood loved.

III.

Oft had he shown in climes afar,
Each attribute of roving war;
The sharpen'd ear, the piercing eye,
The quick resolve in danger nigh;
The speed, that in the flight or chase,
Outstripp'd the Charib's rapid race;
The steady brain, the sinewy limb,
To leap, to climb, to dive, to swim;
The iron frame inured to bear
Each dire inclemency of air,
Nor less confirm'd to undergo
Fatigue's faint chill, and famine's throe.
These arts he proved, his life to save,
In peril oft by land and wave,
On Arawaca's desert shore,
Or where La Plata's billows roar,
When oft the sons of vengeful Spain
Track'd the marauder's steps in vain
These arts in Indian warfare tried,
Must save him now by Greta's side.

IV.

'Twas then, in hour of utmost need,
He proved his courage, art, and speed.
Now slow he stalk'd with stealthy
        pace,
Now started forth in rapid race,
Oft doubling back in mazy train,
To blind the trace the dews retain;
Now clomb the rocks projecting high,
To baffle the pursuer's eye;
Now sought the stream, whose brawling
        sound
The echo of his footsteps drown'd.
But if the forest verge he nears,
There trample steeds,and glimmer spears;
If deeper down the copse he drew,
He heard the rangers' loud halloo,
Beating each cover while they came,
As if to start the sylvan game.
'Twas then — like tiger close beset
At every pass with toil and net,
'Counter'd, where'er he turns his glare,
By clashing arms and torches' flare,
Who meditates, with furious bound,
To burst on hunter, horse, and hound, —
'Twas then that Bertram's soul arose,
Prompting to rush upon his foes:
But as that crouching tiger, cow'd
By brandish'd steel and shouting crowd,
Retreats beneath the jungle's shroud,
Bertram suspends his purpose stern,
And couches in the brake and fern,
Hiding his face, lest foemen spy
The sparkle of his swarthy eye.[27]

V.

Then Bertram might the bearing trace
Of the bold youth who led the chase;
Who paused to list for every sound,
Climb every height to look around,
Then rushing on with naked sword,
Each dingle's bosky depths explored.
'Twas Redmond — by the azure eye;
'Twas Redmond — by the locks that fly
Disorder'd from his glowing cheek;
Mien, face, and form, young Redmond
        speak.
A form more active, light, and strong,
Ne'er shot the ranks of war along;
The modest, yet the manly mien,
Might grace the court of maiden queen.
A face more fair you well might find,
For Redmond's knew the sun and wind,

Nor boasted, from their tinge when free
The charm of regularity;
But every feature had the power
To aid the expression of the hour:
Whether gay wit, and humor sly,
Danced laughing in his light-blue eye;
Or bended brow, and glance of fire,
And kindling cheek, spoke Erin's ire;
Or soft and sadden'd glances show
Her ready sympathy with woe;
Or in that wayward mood of mind,
When various feelings are combined,
When joy and sorrow mingle near,
And hope's bright wings are check'd b
        fear,
And rising doubts keep transport down,
And anger lends a short-lived frown;
In that strange mood which maids approv
Even when they dare not call it love;
With every change his features play'd,
As aspens show the light and shade.

VI.

Well Risingham young Redmond knew
And much he marvell'd that the crew,
Roused to revenge bold Mortham dead,
Were by that Mortham's foeman led;
For never felt his soul the woe,
That wails a generous foeman low,
Far less that sense of justice strong,
That wreaks a generous foeman's wrong
But small his leisure now to pause;
Redmond is first, where'er the cause:
And twice that Redmond came so near
Where Bertram couch'd like hunted deer
The very boughs his steps displace,
Rustled against the ruffian's face,
Who, desperate, twice prepared to start
And plunge his dagger in his heart !
But Redmond turn'd a different way,
And the bent boughs resumed their sway
And Bertram held it wise, unseen,
Deeper to plunge in coppice green.
Thus, circled in his coil, the snake,
When roving hunters beat the brake,
Watches with red and glistening eye,
Prepared, if heedless step draw nigh,
With forked tongue and venom'd fang
Instant to dart the deadly pang;
But if the intruders turn aside,
Away his coils unfolded glide,
And through the deep savannah wind,
Some undisturb'd retreat to find.

VII.

ut Bertram, as he backward drew,
nd heard the loud pursuit renew,
nd Redmond's hollo on the wind,
ft mutter'd in his savage mind: —
Redmond O'Neale! were thou and I
lone this day's event to try,
Vith not a second here to see,
ut the gray cliff and oaken tree, —
hat voice of thine that shouts so loud,
hould ne'er repeat its summons proud!
o! nor e'er try its melting power
gain in maiden's summer bower."
luded, now behind him die,
aint and more faint, each hostile cry;
Ie stands in Scargill wood alone,
or hears he now a harsher tone
han the hoarse cushat's plaintive cry,
r Greta's sound that murmurs by;
nd on the dale, so lone and wild,
he summer sun in quiet smiled.

VIII.

Ie listen'd long with anxious heart,
ar bent to hear, and foot to start,
nd, while his stretch'd attention glows,
efused his weary frame repose.
Twas silence all — he laid him down,
Vhere purple heath profusely strown,
nd throatwort, with its azure bell,
nd moss and thyme his cushion swell.
here, spent with toil, he listless eyed
he course of Greta's playful tide;
eneath her banks now eddying dun,
ow brightly gleaming to the sun,
s, dancing over rock and stone,
a yellow light her currents shone,
Tatching in hue the favorite gem
f Albin's mountain-diadem.
hen, tired to watch the current's play,
Le turn'd his weary eyes away,
o where the bank opposing show'd
s huge, square cliffs thro' shaggy wood.
ne, prominent above the rest,
ear'd to the sun his pale gray breast;
round its broken summit grew
he hazel rude and sable yew;
thousand varied lichens dyed
s waste and weather-beaten side,
nd round its rugged basis lay,
y time or thunder rent away,
ragments, that, from its frontlet torn,
Vere mantled now by verdant thorn.

Such was the scene's wild majesty,
That filled stern Bertram's gazing eye.

IX.

In sullen mood he lay reclined,
Revolving, in his stormy mind,
The felon deed, the fruitless guilt,
His patron's blood by treason spilt;
A crime, it seem'd, so dire and dread,
That it had power to wake the dead.
Then, pondering on his life betray'd
By Oswald's art to Redmond's blade,
In treacherous purpose to withhold,
So seem'd it, Mortham's promised gold,
A deep and full revenge he vow'd
On Redmond, forward, fierce, and proud;
Revenge on Wilfrid — on his sire
Redoubled vengeance, swift and dire!—
If, in such a mood (as legends say,
And well believed that simple day),
The Enemy of man has power
To profit by the evil hour,
Here stood a wretch, prepared to change
His soul's redemption for revenge! [28]
But though his vows, with such a fire
Of earnest and intense desire
For vengeance dark and fell, were made,
As well might reach hell's lowest shade,
No deeper clouds the grove embrown'd,
No nether thunders shook the ground;—
The demon knew his vassal's heart,
And spared temptation's needless art.

X.

Oft, mingled with the direful theme,
Came Mortham's form — Was it a dream?
Or had he seen, in vision true,
That very Mortham whom he slew?
Or had in living flesh appear'd
The only man on earth he fear'd? —
To try the mystic cause intent,
His eyes, that on the cliff were bent,
'Counter'd at once a dazzling glance,
Like sunbeam flash'd from sword or
lance.
At once he started as for fight,
But not a foeman was in sight;
He heard the cushat's murmur hoarse,
He heard the river's sounding course;
The solitary woodlands lay,
As slumbering in the summer ray.
He gazed, like lion roused, around,
Then sunk again upon the ground.

'Twas but, he thought, some fitful beam,
Glanced sudden from the sparkling
   stream;
Then plunged him from his gloomy train
Of ill-connected thoughts again,
Until a voice behind him cried :—
" Bertram ! well met on Greta side."

XI.

Instant his sword was in his hand,
As instant sunk the ready brand ;
Yet, dubious still, opposed he stood
To him that issued from the wood :
" Guy Denzil ! — is it thou ? " he said ;
" Do we two meet in Scargill shade ? —
Stand back a space ! — thy purpose show,
Whether thou comest as friend or foe.
Report hath said, that Denzil's name
From Rokeby's band was razed with
   shame." —
" A shame I owe that hot O'Neale,
Who told his knight, in peevish zeal,
Of my marauding on the clowns
Of Calverley and Bradford downs.[29]
I reck not. In a war to strive,
Where, save the leaders, none can thrive,
Suits ill my mood; and better game
Awaits us both, if thou'rt the same
Unscrupulous, bold Risingham,
Who watch'd with me in midnight dark,
To snatch a deer from Rokeby-park.
How think'st thou ? "—" Speak thy pur-
   pose out;
I love not mystery or doubt." —

XII.

" Then, list. — Not far there lurk a crew
Of trusty comrades stanch and true,
Glean'd from both factions — Round-
   heads freed
From cant of sermon and of creed;
And Cavaliers, whose souls, like mine,
Spurn at the bonds of discipline.
Wiser, we judge, by dale and wold,
A warfare of our own to hold,
Than breathe our last on battle-down,
For cloak or surplice, mace or crown.
Our schemes are laid, our purpose set,
A chief and leader lack we yet. —
Thou art a wanderer, it is said;
For Mortham's death, thy steps way-laid,
Thy head at price — so say our spies,
Who range the valley in disguise.

Join then with us :— tho' wild debate
And wrangling rend our infant state,
Each to an equal loth to bow,
Will yield to chief renown'd as thou." –

XIII.

" Even now," thought Bertram, passion
   stirr'd,
" I called on hell, and hell has heard !
What lack I, vengeance to command,
But of stanch comrades such a band?
This Denzil, vow'd to every evil,
Might read a lesson to the devil.
Well, be it so ! each knave and fool
Shall serve as my revenge's tool."—
Aloud, " I take thy proffer, Guy,
But tell me where thy comrades lie ? "
" Not far from hence," Guy Denzil said
" Descend, and cross the river's bed,
Where rises yonder cliff so gray."
" Do thou," said Bertram, " lead th
   way."
Then mutter'd, " It is best make sure;
Guy Denzil's faith was never pure."
He follow'd down the steep descent,
Then through the Greta's streams the
   went;
And, when they reach'd the farther shor
They stood the lonely cliff before.

XIV.

With wonder Bertram heard within
The flinty rock a murmur'd din;
But when Guy pull'd the wilding spray
And brambles, from its base away,
He saw, appearing to the air,
A little entrance, low and square,
Like opening cell of hermit lone,
Dark, winding through the living stone
Here enter'd Denzil, Bertram here;
And loud and louder on their ear,
As from the bowels of the earth,
Resounded shouts of boisterous mirth.
Of old, the cavern strait and rude,
In slaty rock the peasant hew'd:
And Brignall's woods, and Scargill's wav
E'en now, o'er many a sister cave,[30]
Where, far within the darksome rift,
The wedge and lever ply their thrift.
But war had silenced rural trade,
And the deserted mine was made
The banquet-hall and fortress too,
Of Denzil and his desperate crew.—

ιere Guilt his anxious revel kept;
ιere, on his sordid pallet, slept
ιιilt-born Excess, the goblet drain'd
ιill in his slumbering grasp retain'd;
εgret was there, his eye still cast
ith vain repining on the past;
ιmong the feasters waited near
ιrrow, and unrepentant Fear,
ιd Blasphemy, to frenzy driven,
ith his own crimes reproaching heaven;
hile Bertram show'd, amid the crew,
ιe Master-Fiend that Milton drew.

XV.

ιark ! the loud revel wakes again,
ι greet the leader of the train.
ιhold the group by the pale lamp,
ιat struggles with the earthy damp.
ι what strange features Vice hath known,
ι single out and mark her own !
ιet some there are, whose brows retain
ιess deeply stamp'd her brand and stain.
ιe yon pale stripling ! when a boy,
ι mother's pride, a father's joy !
ιow, 'gainst the vault's rude walls re-
        clined,
ι early image fills his mind :
ιhe cottage, once his sire's, he sees,
ιmbower'd upon the banks of Tees;
ιe views sweet Winston's woodland
        scene,
ιnd shares the dance on Gainford-green.
ι tear is springing — but the zest
ιf some wild tale or brutal jest,
ιath to loud laughter stirr'd the rest.
ιn him they call, the aptest mate
ιor jovial song and merry feat :
ιast flies his dream — with dauntless
        air
ιs one victorious o'er Despair,
ιe bids the ruby cup go round,
ιill sense and sorrow both are drown'd :
ιnd soon, in merry wassail, he,
ιhe life of all their revelry,
ιeals his loud song ! — The muse has
        found
ιer blossoms on the wildest ground,
ιid noxious weeds at random strew'd,
ιhemselves all profitless and rude. —
ιith desperate merriment he sung,
ιhe cavern to the chorus rung;
ιet mingled with his reckless glee
ιemorse's bitter agony.

XVI.

SONG.

O, Brignall banks are wild and fair,
    And Greta woods are green,
And you may gather garlands there,
    Would grace a summer queen.
And as I rode by Dalton-hall,
    Beneath the turrets high,
A Maiden on the castle wall
    Was singing merrily, —

CHORUS.

"O, Brignall banks are fresh and fair,
    And Greta woods are green;
I'd rather rove with Edmund there,
    Than reign our English queen." —

"If, Maiden, thou wouldst wend with me,
    To leave both tower and town,
Thou first must guess what life lead we,
    That dwell by dale and down?
And if thou canst that riddle read,
    As read full well you may,
Then to the greenwood shalt thou speed,
    As blithe as Queen of May." —

CHORUS.

Yet sung she, "Brignall banks are fair,
    And Greta woods are green;
I'd rather rove with Edmund there,
    Than reign our English queen.

XVII.

"I read you, by your bugle-horn,
    And by your palfrey good,
I read you for a ranger sworn,
    To keep the king's greenwood." —
"A Ranger, lady, winds his horn,
    And 'tis at peep of light;
His blast is heard at merry morn,
    And mine at dead of night." —

CHORUS.

Yet sung she, "Brignall banks are fair,
    And Greta woods are gay;
I would I were with Edmund there,
    To reign his Queen of May !

"With burnish'd brand and musketoon,
    So gallantly you come,
I read you for a bold Dragoon,
    That lists the tuck of drum." —

"I list no more the tuck of drum,
  No more the trumpet hear;
But when the beetle sounds his hum,
  My comrades take the spear.

CHORUS.

"And, O! tho' Brignall banks be fair,
  And Greta woods be gay,
Yet mickle must the maiden dare,
  Would reign my Queen of May!

XVIII.

"Maiden! a nameless life I lead,
  A nameless death I'll die!
The fiend, whose lantern lights the mead,
  Were better mate than I!
And when I'm with my comrades met,
  Beneath the greenwood bough,
What once we were we all forget,
  Nor think what we are now.

CHORUS.

"Yet Brignall banks are fresh and fair,
  And Greta woods are green,
And you may gather garlands there,
  Would grace a summer queen."

When Edmund ceased his simple song,
Was silence on the sullen throng,
Till waked some ruder mate their glee
With note of coarser minstrelsy.
But, far apart, in dark divan,
Denzil and Bertram many a plan
Of import foul and fierce design'd,
While still on Bertram's grasping mind
The wealth of murder'd Mortham hung;
Tho' half he fear'd his daring tongue,
When it should give his wishes birth,
Might raise a spectre from the earth!

XIX.

At length his wondrous tale he told:
When, scornful, smiled his comrade bold;
For, train'd in license of a court,
Religion's self was Denzil's sport;
Then judge in what contempt he held
The visionary tales of eld!
His awe for Bertram scarce repress'd
The unbeliever's sneering jest.
"'Twere hard," he said, "for sage or seer
To spell the subject of your fear;
Nor do I boast the art renown'd,
Vision and omen to expound.

Yet, faith, if I must needs afford
To spectre watching treasured hoard,
As bandog keeps his master's roof,
Bidding the plunderer stand aloof,
This doubt remains — thy goblin gaunt
Hath chosen ill his ghostly haunt;
For why his guard on Mortham hold,
When Rokeby castle hath the gold
Thy patron won on Indian soil,
By stealth, by piracy, and spoil?"

XX.

At this he paused — for angry shame
Lower'd on the brow of Risingham.
He blush'd to think that he should see
Assertor of an airy dream,
And gave his wrath another theme.
"Denzil," he says, "tho' lowly laid,
Wrong not the memory of the dead;
For, while he lived, at Mortham's look
Thy very soul, Guy Denzil, shook!
And when he tax'd thy breach of word
To yon fair Rose of Allenford,
I saw thee crouch like chasten'd hound
Whose back the huntsman's lash hath
    found.
Nor dare to call his foreign wealth
The spoil of piracy or stealth;
He won it bravely with his brand,
When Spain waged warfare with our
    land.[31]
Mark, too — I brook no idle jeer,
Nor couple Bertram's name with fear;
Mine is but half the demon's lot,
For I believe, but tremble not. —
Enough of this. — Say, why this hoard
Thou deem'st at Rokeby castle stored;
Or think'st that Mortham would bestow
His treasure with his faction's foe?"

XXI.

Soon quench'd was Denzil's ill-time
    mirth;
Rather he would have seen the earth
Give to ten thousand spectres birth,
Than venture to awake to flame
The deadly wrath of Risingham.
Submiss he answer'd:— "Mortham's
    mind,
Thou know'st, to joy was ill inclined.
In youth, 'tis said, a gallant free,
A lusty reveller was he;
But since return'd from over sea,

sullen and a silent mood
ath numb'd the current of his blood.
ence he refused each kindly call
o Rokeby's hospitable hall,
nd our stout knight, at dawn of morn
ho loved to hear the bugle horn,
or less, when eve his oaks embrown'd,
o see the ruddy cup go round,
ook umbrage that a friend so near
efused to share his chase and cheer;
hus did the kindred barons jar,
re they divided in the war.
et, trust me, friend, Matilda fair
f Mortham's wealth is destined heir." —

XXII.

Destined to her! to yon slight maid!
he prize my life had wellnigh paid,
hen 'gainst Laroche, by Cayo's wave,
fought, my patron's wealth to save! —
enzil, I knew him long, yet ne'er
new him that joyous cavalier,
hom youthful friends and early fame
all'd soul of gallantry and game.
moody man, he sought our crew,
esperate and dark, whom no one knew;
nd rose, as men with us must rise,
y scorning life and all its ties.
n each adventure rash he roved,
s danger for itself he loved;
n his sad brow nor mirth nor wine
ould e'er one wrinkled knot untwine;
l was the omen if he smiled,
or 'twas in peril stern and wild;
ut when he laugh'd, each luckless mate
ight hold our fortune desperate.
oremost he fought in every broil,
hen scornful turn'd him from the spoil;
ay, often strove to bar the way
etween his comrades and their prey;
reaching, even then, to such as we,
ot with our dear-bought victory,
f mercy and humanity.

XXIII.

I loved him well — His fearless part,
is gallant leading, won my heart.
nd after each victorious fight,
was I that wrangled for his right,
edeem'd his portion of the prey
hat greedier mates had torn away:
 field and storm thrice saved his life,
nd once amid our comrades' strife.[82] —

Yes, I have loved thee! Well have proved
My toil, my danger, how I loved!
Yet will I mourn no more thy fate,
Ingrate in life, in death ingrate.
Rise if thou canst!" he look'd around,
And sternly stamp'd upon the ground —
" Rise, with thy bearing proud and high,
Even as this morn it met mine eye,
And give me, if thou darest, the lie!"
He paused—then, calm and passion-freed,
Bade Denzil with his tale proceed.

XXIV.

" Bertram, to thee I need not tell,
What thou hast cause to wot so well,
How Superstition's nets were twined
Around the Lord of Mortham's mind!
But since he drove thee from his tower,
A maid he found in Greta's bower,
Whose speech, like David's harp, had
          sway,
To charm his evil fiend away.
I know not if her features moved
Remembrance of the wife he loved;
But he would gaze upon her eye,
Till his mood soften'd to a sigh.
He, whom no living mortal sought
To question of his secret thought,
Now every thought and care confess'd
To his fair niece's faithful breast;
Nor was there aught of rich and rare,
In earth, in ocean, or in air,
But it must deck Matilda's hair.
Her love still bound him unto life;
But then awoke the civil strife,
And menials bore, by his commands,
Three coffers, with their iron bands,
From Mortham's vault, at midnight deep,
To her lone bower in Rokeby-Keep,
Ponderous with gold and plate of pride,
His gift, if he in battle died." —

XXV.

" Then Denzil, as I guess, lays train,
These iron-banded chests to gain;
Else, wherefore should he hover here,
Where many a peril waits him near,
For all his feats of war and peace,
For plunder'd boors, and harts of greese?*
Since thro' the hamlets as he fared,
What hearth has Guy's marauding spared,

* Deer in season.

Or where the chase that hath not rung
With Denzil's bow, at midnight
   strung ? " —
" I hold my wont — my rangers go,
Even now, to track a milk-white doe.
By Rokeby-hall she takes her lair,
In Greta wood she harbors fair,
And when my huntsman marks her way,
What think'st thou, Bertram, of the prey?
Were Rokeby's daughter in our power,
We rate her ransom at her dower."

XXVI.

" 'Tis well! — there's vengeance in the
   thought:
Matilda is by Wilfrid sought;
And hot-brain'd Redmond, too, 'tis said,
Pays lover's homage to the maid.
Bertram she scorn'd. — If met by chance,
She turn'd from me her shuddering
   glance,
Like a nice dame, that will not brook
On what she hates and loathes to look;
She told to Mortham she could ne'er
Behold me without secret fear,
Foreboding evil. — She may rue
To find her prophecy fall true!
The war has weeded Rokeby's train,
Few followers in his halls remain:
If thy scheme miss, then, brief and bold,
We are enow to storm the hold;
Bear off the plunder, and the dame,
And leave the castle all in flame." —

XXVII.

" Still art thou Valor's venturous son!
Yet ponder first the risk to run:
The menials of the castle, true,
And stubborn to their charge, though
   few;
The wall to scale — the moat to cross —
The wicket-grate — the inner fosse." —
—"Fool! if we blench for toys like these,
On what fair guerdon can we seize?
Our hardiest venture, to explore
Some wretched peasant's fenceless door,
And the best prize we bear away,
The earnings of his sordid day." —
" A while thy hasty taunt forbear:
In sight of road more sure and fair,
Thou wouldst not choose, in blindfold
   wrath,
Or wantonness, a desperate path?

List, then; — for vantage or assault,
From gilded vane to dungeon-vault,
Each pass of Rokeby-house I know:
There is one postern, dark and low,
That issues at a secret spot,
By most neglected or forgot.
Now, could a spial of our train
On fair pretext admittance gain,
That sally-port might be unbarr'd:
Then, vain were battlement and ward!"-

XXVIII.

" Now speak'st thou well: — to me t]
   same,
If force or art shall urge the game;
Indifferent, if like fox I wind,
Or spring like tiger on the hind. —
But, hark! our merry men so gay
Troll forth another roundelay." —

SONG.

" A weary lot is thine, fair maid,
  A weary lot is thine!
To pull the thorn thy brow
   braid,
  And press the rue for wine!
A lightsome eye, a soldier's mien,
  A feather of the blue,
A doublet of the Lincoln green, —
  No more of me you knew,
            My love
No more of me you knew.

" This morn is merry June, I trow,
  The rose is budding fain;
But she shall bloom in winter snow,
  Ere we two meet again."
He turn'd his charger as he spake,
  Upon the river shore,
He gave his bridle-reins a shake,
  Said, " Adieu for evermore,
            My love
And adieu for evermore." — [33]

XXIX.

" What youth is this, your band amon
The best for minstrelsy and song?
In his wild notes seem aptly met
A strain of pleasure and regret." —
" Edmund of Winston is his name;
The hamlet sounded with the fame
Of early hopes his childhood gave, —
Now centr'd all in Brignall cave!

watch him well — his wayward course
shows oft a tincture of remorse.
Some early love-shaft grazed his heart,
And oft the scar will ache and smart.
Yet is he useful; — of the rest,
My fits, the darling and the jest,
His harp, his story, and his lay,
Oft aid the idle hours away.
When unemploy'd, each fiery mate
Is ripe for mutinous debate.
He tuned his strings e'en now — again
He wakes them with a blither strain."

XXX.

SONG.

Allen-a-Dale.

Allen-a-Dale has no fagot for burning,
Allen-a-Dale has no furrow for turning,
Allen-a-Dale has no fleece for the spin-
ing,
Yet Allen-a-Dale has red gold for the
winning.
Come, read me my riddle! come, hear-
ken my tale!
And tell me the craft of bold Allen-a-
Dale.

The Baron of Ravensworth * prances in
pride,
And he views his domains upon Arkin-
dale side,
The mere for his net, and the land for
his game,
The chase for the wild, and the park for
the tame,
Yet the fish of the lake, and the deer of
the vale,
Are less free to Lord Dacre than Allen-
a-Dale!

Allen-a-Dale was ne'er belted a knight,
Though his spur be as sharp, and his
blade be as bright;
Allen-a-Dale is no baron or lord,
Yet twenty tall yeomen will draw at his
word;

* The ruins of Ravensworth Castle stand in
the North Riding of Yorkshire, about three
miles from the town of Richmond, and adjoining to the waste called the Forest of Arkingarth. It belonged originally to the powerful
family of Fitz-Hugh, from whom it passed to
the Lords Dacre of the South.

And the best of our nobles his bonnet
will vail,
Who at Rere-cross [34] on Stanmore meets
Allen-a-Dale.

Allen-a-Dale to his wooing is come;
The mother, she ask'd of his household
and home:
" Tho' the castle of Richmond stand fair
on the hill,
My hall," quoth bold Allen, " shows
gallanter still;
'Tis the blue vault of heaven, with its
crescent so pale,
And with all its bright spangles!" said
Allen-a-Dale.

The father was steel, and the mother was
stone;
They lifted the latch, and they bade him
begone;
But loud, on the morrow, their wail and
their cry:
He had laugh'd on the lass with his
bonny black eye,
And she fled to the forest to hear a love-
tale,
And the youth it was told by was Allen-
a-Dale!

XXXI.

" Thou see'st that, whether sad or gay,
Love mingles ever in his lay.
But when his boyish wayward fit
Is o'er, he hath address and wit;
O! 'tis a brain of fire, can ape
Each dialect, each various shape."
" Nay, then, to aid thy project, Guy —
Soft! who comes here?"—"My trusty spy,
Speak, Hamlin! hast thou lodged our
deer?" — [35]
" I have — but two fair stags are near.
I watch'd her, as she slowly stray'd
From Egliston up Thorsgill glade;
But Wilfrid Wycliffe sought her side,
And then young Redmond, in his pride,
Shot down to meet them on their way:
Much, as it seem'd, was theirs to say
There's time to pitch both toil and net,
Before their path he homeward set."
A hurried and a whisper'd speech
Did Bertram's will to Denzil teach;
Who, turning to the robber band,
Bade four, the bravest, take the brand.

CANTO FOURTH.

I.

WHEN Denmark's raven soar'd on high,
Triumphant thro' Northumbrian sky,
Till, hovering near, her fatal croak
Bade Reged's Britons dread the yoke,[36]
And the broad shadow of her wing
Blacken'd each cataract and spring,
Where Tees in tumult leaves his source,
Thundering o'er Caldron and High-
 Force:
Beneath the shade the Northmen came,
Fix'd on each vale a Runic name,[37]
Rear'd high their altar's rugged stone,
And gave their Gods the land they won.
Then, Balder, one bleak garth was thine,
And one sweet brooklet's silver line,
And Woden's Croft did title gain
From the stern Father of the Slain;
But to the Monarch of the Mace,
That held in fight the foremost place,
To Odin's son, and Sifia's spouse,
Near Stratforth high they paid their vows,
Remember'd Thor's victorious fame,
And gave the dell the Thunderer's name.

II.

Yet Scald or Kemper err'd, I ween,
Who gave that soft and quiet scene,
With all its varied light and shade,
And every little sunny glade,
And the blithe brook that strolls along
Its pebbled bed with summer song,
To the grim God of blood and scar,
The grisly King of Northern War.
O, better were its banks assign'd
To spirits of a gentler kind!
For where the thicket-groups recede,
And the rath primrose decks the mead,
The velvet grass seems carpet meet
For the light fairies' lively feet.
Yon tufted knoll, with daisies strown,
Might make proud Oberon a throne,
While, hidden in the thicket nigh,
Puck should brood o'er his frolic sly;
And where profuse the wood-vetch clings
Round ash and elm, in verdant rings,
Its pale and azure-pencill'd flower
Should canopy Titania's bower.

III.

Here rise no cliffs the vale to shade;
But, skirting every sunny glade,
In fair variety of green
The woodland lends its sylvan screen.
Hoary, yet haughty, frowns the oak,
Its boughs by weight of ages broke;
And towers erect, in sable spire,
The pine-tree scathed by lightning fire;
The drooping ash and birch, between,
Hang their fair tresses o'er the green,
And all beneath, at random grow
Each coppice dwarf of varied show,
Or, round the stems profusely twined,
Fling summer odors on the wind.
Such varied group Urbino's hand
Round Him of Tarsus nobly plann'd,
What time he bade proud Athens own
On Mars's Mount the God unknown!
Then gray Philosophy stood nigh,
Tho' bent by age, in spirit high:
Then rose the scar-seam'd veteran's spear
There Grecian Beauty bent to hear,
While Childhood at her foot was placed
Or clung delighted to her waist.

IV.

"And rest we here," Matilda said,
And sat her in the varying shade.
"Chance-met, we well may steal an hour
To friendship due, from fortune's power
Thou, Wilfrid, ever kind, must lend
Thy counsel to thy sister-friend;
And, Redmond, thou, at my behest,
No farther urge thy desperate quest.
For to my care a charge is left,
Dangerous to one of aid bereft;
Wellnigh an orphan, and alone,
Captive her sire, her house o'erthrown.
Wilfrid, with wonted kindness graced,
Beside her on the turf she placed;
Then paused, with downcast look and ey
Nor bade young Redmond seat him nig
Her conscious diffidence he saw,
Drew backward, as in modest awe,
And sat a little space removed,
Unmark'd to gaze on her he loved.

V.

Wreathed in its dark-brown rings, h
 hair
Half hid Matilda's forehead fair,
Half hid and half reveal'd to view
Her full dark eye of hazel hue.
The rose, with faint and feeble streak,
So slightly tinged the maiden's cheek,

hat you had said her hue was pale;
ut if she faced the summer gale,
r spoke, or sung, or quicker moved,
r heard the praise of those she loved,
r when of interest was express'd
ught that waked feeling in her breast,
he mantling blood in ready play
ivall'd the blush of rising day.
here was a soft and pensive grace,
. cast of thought upon her face,
hat suited well the forehead high,
he eyelash dark, and downcast eye;
he mild expression spoke a mind
1 duty firm, composed, resign'd;
Tis that which Roman art has given
o mark their maiden Queen of Heaven.
n hours of sport, that mood gave way
o fancy's light and frolic play;
.nd when the dance, or tale, or song,
n harmless mirth sped time along,
ull oft her doting sire would call
Iis Maud the merriest of them all.
ut days of war and civil crime,
.llow'd but ill such festal time,
.nd her soft pensiveness of brow
Iad deepen'd into sadness now.
n Marston field her father ta'en,
Ier friends dispersed, brave Mortham
slain,
Vhile every ill her soul foretold,
rom Oswald's thirst of power and gold,
.nd boding thoughts that she must
part
Vith a soft vision of her heart,—
.ll lower'd around the lovely maid,
o darken her dejection's shade.

VI.

Vho has not heard — while Erin yet
trove 'gainst the Saxon's iron bit —
Vho has not heard how brave O'Neale
n English blood imbrued his steel,[38]
.gainst St. George's cross blazed high
he banners of his Tanistry,
o fiery Essex gave the foil,
.nd reign'd a prince on Ulster's soil?
3ut chief arose his victor pride,
Vhen that brave Marshal fought and
died,[39]
.nd Avon-Duff to ocean bore
-Iis billows red with Saxon gore.
Twas first in that disastrous fight,
Rokeby and Mortham proved their might.

There had they fallen 'mongst the rest,
But pity touch'd a chieftain's breast;
The Tanist he to great O'Neale;[40]
He check'd his followers' bloody zeal,
To quarter took the kinsmen bold,
And bore them to his mountain-hold,
Gave them each sylvan joy to know,
Slieve-Donard's cliffs and woods could
show,
Shared with them Erin's festal cheer,
Show'd them the chase of wolf and deer.
And, when a fitting time was come,
Safe and unransom'd sent them home,
Loaded with many a gift, to prove
A generous foe's respect and love.

VII.

Years speed away. On Rokeby's head
Some touch of early snow was shed;
Calm he enjoy'd, by Greta's wave,
The peace which James the Peaceful gave,
While Mortham, far beyond the main,
Waged his fierce wars on Indian Spain.—
It chanced upon a wintry night,
That whiten'd Stanmore's stormy height,
The chase was o'er, the stag was kill'd,
In Rokeby hall the cups were fill'd,
And by the huge stone chimney sate
The Knight in hospitable state.
Moonless the sky, the hour was late,
When a loud summons shook the gate,
And sore for entrance and for aid
A voice of foreign accent pray'd.
The porter answer'd to the call,
And instant rush'd into to the hall
A Man, whose aspect and attire
Startled the circle by the fire.

VIII.

His plaited hair in elf-locks spread
Around his bare and matted head;
On leg and thigh, close stretch'd and trim,
His vesture show'd the sinewy limb;
In saffron dyed, a linen vest
Was frequent folded round his breast:
A mantle long and loose he wore,
Shaggy with ice, and stain'd with gore.
He clasp'd a burden to his heart,
And, resting on a knotted dart,
The snow from hair and beard he shook,
And round him gazed with wilder'd look;
Then up the hall with staggering pace,
He hasten'd by the blaze to place,

Half lifeless from the bitter air,
His load, a Boy of beauty rare.
To Rokeby, next, he louted low,
Then stood erect his tale to show,
With wild majestic port and tone,
Like envoy of some barbarous throne.[41]
"Sir Richard, Lord of Rokeby, hear!
Turlough O'Neale salutes thee dear;
He graces thee, and to thy care
Young Redmond gives, his grandson
　　fair.
He bids thee breed him as thy son,
For Turlough's days of joy are done;
And other lords have seized his land,
And faint and feeble is his hand;
And all the glory of Tyrone
Is like a morning vapor flown.
To bind the duty on thy soul,
He bids thee think on Erin's bowl!
If any wrong the young O'Neale,
He bids thee think of Erin's steel.
To Mortham first this charge was due,
But, in his absence, honors you. —
Now is my master's message by,
And Ferraught will contented die."

IX.

His look grew fix'd, his cheek grew pale,
He sunk when he had told his tale;
For, hid beneath his mantle wide,
A mortal wound was in his side.
Vain was all aid — in terror wild,
And sorrow, scream'd the orphan Child.
Poor Ferraught raised his wistful eyes,
And faintly strove to soothe his cries;
All reckless of his dying pain,
He blest and blest him o'er again!
And kiss'd the little hands outspread,
And kiss'd and cross'd the infant head,
And, in his native tongue and phrase,
Pray'd to each Saint to watch his days;
Then all his strength together drew,
The charge to Rokeby to renew.
When half was falter'd from his breast,
And half by dying signs express'd,
"Bless the O'Neale!" he faintly said,
And thus the faithful spirit fled.

X.

'Twas long ere soothing might prevail
Upon the Child to end the tale;
And then he said, that from his home
His grandsire had been forced to roam,

Which had not been if Redmond's hand
Had but had strength to draw the brand
The brand of Lenauch More the Red,
That hung beside the gray wolf's head. —
'Twas from his broken phrase described
His foster-father was his guide,[42]
Who, in his charge, from Ulster bore
Letters and gifts a goodly store:
But ruffians met them in the wood,
Ferraught in battle boldly stood,
Till wounded and o'erpower'd at length
And stripp'd of all, his failing strength
Just bore him here — and then the child
Renew'd again his moaning wild.

XI.

The tear down childhood's cheek that
　　flows,
Is like the dewdrop on the rose;
When next the summer breeze comes by,
And waves the bush, the flower is dry.
Won by their care, the orphan Child
Soon on his new protector smiled,
With dimpled cheek and eye so fair,
Thro' his thick curls of flaxen hair,
But blithest laugh'd that cheek and eye,
When Rokeby's little maid was nigh;
'Twas his, with elder brother's pride,
Matilda's tottering steps to guide;
His native lays in Irish tongue,
To soothe her infant ear he sung,
And primrose twined with daisy fair,
To form a chaplet for her hair.
By lawn, by grove, by brooklet's strand
The children still were hand in hand,
And good Sir Richard smiling eyed
The early knot so kindly tied.

XII.

But summer months bring wilding shoots
From bud to bloom, from bloom to fruit,
And years draw on our human span,
From child to boy, from boy to man;
And soon in Rokeby's woods is seen
A gallant boy in hunter's green.
He loves to wake the felon boar,
In his dark haunt on Greta's shore,
And loves, against the deer so dun,
To draw the shaft, or lift the gun:
Yet more he loves, in autumn prime,
The hazel's spreading boughs to climb,
And down its cluster'd stores to hail,
Where young Matilda holds her veil.

nd she, whose veil receives the shower,
s alter'd too, and knows her power;
ssumes a monitress's pride,
Her Redmond's dangerous sports to chide,
et listens still to hear him tell
How the grim wild boar fought and fell,
How at his fall the bugle rung,
ill rock and greenwood answer flung;
hen blesses her, that man can find
pastime of such savage kind!

XIII.

ut Redmond knew to weave his tale
o well with praise of wood and dale,
nd knew so well each point to trace,
ives living interest to the chase,
nd knew so well o'er all to throw
His spirit's wild romantic glow,
hat, while she blamed, and while she
    fear'd,
he loved each venturous tale she heard.
ft, too, when drifted snow and rain
o bower and hall their steps restrain,
ogether they explored the page
f glowing bard or gifted sage:
ft, placed the evening fire beside,
he minstrel art alternate tried,
While gladsome harp and lively lay
ade winter-night flit fast away;
hus, from their childhood, blending still
heir sport, their study, and their skill,
n union of the soul they prove,
ut must not think that it was love.
ut tho' they dared not, envious Fame
oon dared to give that union name;
nd when so often, side by side,
rom year to year the pair she eyed,
he sometimes blamed the good old
    Knight,
s dull of ear and dim of sight,
ometimes his purpose would declare,
hat young O'Neale should wed his heir.

XIV.

he suit of Wilfrid rent disguise
nd bandage from the lovers' eyes;
Twas plain that Oswald, for his son,
Had Rokeby's favor wellnigh won.
ow must they meet with change of
    cheer,
With mutual looks of shame and fear;
ow must Matilda stray apart,
o school her disobedient heart:

And Redmond now alone must rue
The love he never can subdue.
But factions rose, and Rokeby sware
No rebel's son should wed his heir;
And Redmond, nurtured while a child
In many a bard's traditions wild,
Now sought the lonely wood or stream,
To cherish there a happier dream,
Of maiden won by sword or lance,
As in the regions of romance;
And count the heroes of his line,
Great Nial of the Pledges Nine,[43]
Shane-Dymas[44] wild, and Geraldine,[45]
And Connan-more, who vow'd his race
Forever to the fight and chase,
And cursed him, of his lineage born,
Should sheathe the sword to reap the
    corn,
Or leave the mountain and the wold,
To shroud himself in castled hold.
From such examples hope he drew,
And brighten'd as the trumpet blew.

XV.

If brides were won by heart and blade,
Redmond had both his cause to aid,
And all beside of nurture rare
That might beseem a baron's heir.
Turlough O'Neale, in Erin's strife,
On Rokeby's Lord bestow'd his life,
And well did Rokeby's generous Knight
Young Redmond for the deed requite.
Nor was his liberal care and cost
Upon the gallant stripling lost;
Seek the North-Riding broad and wide,
Like Redmond none could steed bestride;
From Tynemouth search to Cumberland,
Like Redmond none could wield a brand;
And then, of humor kind and free,
And bearing him to each degree
With frank and fearless courtesy,
There never youth was form'd to steal
Upon the heart like brave O'Neale.

XVI.

Sir Richard loved him as his son:
And when the days of peace were done,
And to the gales of war he gave
The banner of his sires to wave,
Redmond, distinguish'd by his care,
He chose that honor'd flag to bear,
And named his page, the next degree,
In that old time, to chivalry.[46]

In five pitch'd fields he well maintain'd
The honor'd place his worth obtain'd,
And high was Redmond's youthful name
Blazed in the roll of martial fame.
Had fortune smiled on Marston fight,
The eve had seen him dubb'd a knight;
Twice, mid the battle's doubtful strife,
Of Rokeby's Lord he saved the life.
But when he saw him prisoner made,
He kiss'd and then resign'd his blade,
And yielded him an easy prey
To those who led the Knight away;
Resolved Matilda's sire should prove
In prison, as in fight, his love.

XVII.

When lovers meet in adverse hour,
'Tis like a sun-glimpse through a shower,
A watery ray, an instant seen
The darkly closing clouds between.
As Redmond on the turf reclined,
The past and present fill'd his mind:
" It was not thus," Affection said,
" I dream'd of my return, dear maid!
Not thus, when from thy trembling hand,
I took the banner and the brand,
When round me, as the bugles blew,
Their blades three hundred warriors drew,
And, while the standard I unroll'd,
Clash'd their bright arms, with clamor
    bold.
Where is that banner now? — its pride
Lies 'whelm'd in Ouse's sullen tide!
Where now these warriors?—in theirgore,
They cumber Marston's dismal moor!
And what avails a useless brand,
Held by a captive's shackled hand,
That only would his life retain,
To aid thy sire to bear his chain!"
Thus Redmond to himself apart;
Nor lighter was his rival's heart;
For Wilfrid, while his generous soul
Disdain'd to profit by control,
By many a sign could mark too plain,
Save with such aid, his hopes were vain —
But now Matilda's accents stole
On the dark visions of their soul,
And bade their mournful musing fly,
Like mist before the zephyr's sigh.

XVIII.

" I need not to my friends recall,
How Mortham shunn'd my father's hall;

A man of silence and of woe,
Yet ever anxious to bestow
On my poor self whate'er could prove
A kinsman's confidence and love.
My feeble aid could sometimes chase
The clouds of sorrow for a space:
But oftener, fix'd beyond my power,
I mark'd his deep despondence lower.
One dismal cause, by all unguess'd,
His fearful confidence confess'd;
And twice it was my hap to see
Examples of that agony,
Which for a season can o'erstrain
And wreck the structure of the brain.
He had the awful power to know
The approaching mental overthrow,
And while his mind had courage yet
To struggle with the dreadful fit,
The victim writhed against its throes,
Like wretch beneath a murderer's blows
This malady, I well could mark,
Sprung from some direful cause and dark
But still he kept its source conceal'd,
Till arming for the civil field;
Then in my charge he bade me hold
A treasure huge of gems and gold,
With this disjointed dismal scroll,
That tells the secret of his soul,
In such wild words as oft betray,
A mind by anguish forced astray." —

XIX.

MORTHAM'S HISTORY.

" Matilda! thou hast seen me start,
As if a dagger thrill'd my heart,
When it has hap'd some casual phrase
Waked memory of my former days.
Believe, that few can backward cast
Their thoughts with pleasure on the past
But I! — my youth was rash and vain,
And blood and rage my manhood stain,
And my gray hairs must now descend
To my cold grave without a friend!
Even thou, Matilda, wilt disown
Thy kinsman, when his guilt is known.
And must I lift the bloody veil,
That hides my dark and fatal tale!
I must — I will — Pale phantom, cease
Leave me one little hour in peace!
Thus haunted, think'st thou I have skin
Thine own commission to fulfil?
Or, while thou point'st with gesture fierce
Thy blighted cheek, thy bloody hearse,

How can I paint thee as thou wert,
So fair in face, so warm in heart!

XX.

Yes, she was fair! — Matilda, thou
Hast a soft sadness on thy brow;
But hers was like the sunny glow,
That laughs on earth and all below!
We wedded secret — there was need —
Differing in country and in creed;
And, when to Mortham's tower she came,
We mention'd not her race and name,
Until thy sire, who fought afar,
Should turn him home from foreign war,
On whose kind influence we relied
To soothe her father's ire and pride.
Few months we lived retired, unknown,
To all but one dear friend alone,
One darling friend — I spare his shame,
I will not write the villain's name!
My trespasses I might forget,
And sue in vengeance for the debt
Due by a brother worm to me,
Ungrateful to God's clemency,
That spared me penitential time,
Nor cut me off amid my crime. —

XXI.

" A kindly smile to all she lent,
But on her husband's friend 'twas bent
So kind, that from its harmless glee,
The wretch misconstrued villany.
Repulsed in his presumptuous love,
A vengeful snare the traitor wove.
Alone we sat — the flask had flow'd,
My blood with heat unwonted glow'd,
When thro' the alley'd walk we spied
With hurried step my Edith glide,
Cowering beneath the verdant screen,
As one unwilling to be seen.
Words cannot paint the fiendish smile,
That curl'd the traitor's cheek the while!
Fiercely I question'd of the cause;
He made a cold and artful pause;
Then pray'd it might not chafe my
   mood —
There was a gallant in the wood ! '
We had been shooting at the deer;
My cross-bow (evil chance!) was near:
That ready weapon of my wrath
I caught, and, hasting up the path,
In the yew grove my wife I found,
A stranger's arms her neck had bound !

I mark'd his heart — the bow I drew —
I loosed the shaft — 'twas more than true !
I found my Edith's dying charms
Lock'd in her murder'd brother's arms !
He came in secret to inquire
Her state, and reconcile her sire.

XXII.

"All fled my rage — the villain first,
Whose craft my jealousy had nursed;
He sought in far and foreign clime
To 'scape the vengeance of his crime.
The manner of the slaughter done
Was known to few, my guilt to none;
Some tale my faithful steward framed —
I know not what — of shaft mis-aim'd;
And even from those the act who knew,
He hid the hand from which it flew.
Untouch'd by human laws I stood,
But GOD had heard the cry of blood !
There is a blank upon my mind,
A fearful vision ill-defined,
Of raving till my flesh was torn,
Of dungeon-bolts and fetters worn —
And when I waked to woe more mild,
And question'd of my infant child,
(Have I not written, that she bare
A boy, like summer morning fair?) —
With looks confused my menials tell
That armed men in Mortham dell
Beset the nurse's evening way,
And bore her, with her charge, away.
My faithless friend, and none but he,
Could profit by this villany;
Him, then, I sought, with purpose dread
Of treble vengeance on his head !
He 'scaped me — but my bosom's wound
Some faint relief from wandering found;
And over distant land and sea
I bore my load of misery.

XXIII.

" 'Twas then that fate my footsteps led
Among a daring crew and dread,
With whom full oft my hated life
I ventured in such desperate strife,
That even my fierce associates saw
My frantic deeds with doubt and awe.
Much then I learn'd, and much can show,
Of human guilt and human woe,
Yet ne'er have, in my wanderings, known
A wretch whose sorrows match'd my
   own ! —

It chanced, that after battle fray,
Upon the bloody field we lay;
The yellow moon her lustre shed
Upon the wounded and the dead,
While, sense in toil and wassail drown'd,
My ruffian comrades slept around,
There came a voice — its silver tone
Was soft, Matilda, as thine own:—
' Ah, wretch! ' it said, ' what makest
        thou here,
While unavenged my bloody bier,
While unprotected lives mine heir,
Without a father's name and care?'

XXIV.

"I heard—obey'd—and homeward drew.
The fiercest of our desperate crew
I brought at time of need to aid
My purposed vengeance, long delay'd.
But, humble be my thanks to Heaven,
That better hopes and thoughts has given,
And by our Lord's dear prayer has
        taught,
Mercy by mercy must be bought! —
Let me in misery rejoice —
I've seen his face — I've heard his voice—
I claim'd of him my only child —
As he disown'd the theft, he smiled!
That very calm and callous look,
That fiendish sneer his visage took,
As when he said, in scornful mood:—
' There is a gallant in the wood! '
I did not slay him as he stood —
All praise be to my Maker given!
Long sufferance is one path to Heaven."

XXV.

Thus far the woeful tale was heard,
When something in the thicket stirr'd.
Up Redmond sprung; the villain Guy
(For he it was that lurk'd so nigh),
Drew back — he durst not cross his steel
A moment's space with brave O'Neale
For all the treasured gold that rests
In Mortham's iron-banded chests.
Redmond resumed his seat;— he said,
Some roe was rustling in the shade.
Bertram laugh'd grimly when he saw
His timorous comrade backward draw;
" A trusty mate art thou, to fear
A single arm, and aid so near!
Yet have I seen thee mark a deer.
Give me thy carabine — I'll show,

An art that thou wilt gladly know,
How thou mayst safely quell a foe."

XXVI.

On hands and knees fierce Bertram dre
The spreading birch and hazels through
Till he had Redmond full in view;
The gun he levell'd. — Mark like this
Was Bertram never known to miss,
When fair opposed to aim there sate
An object of his mortal hate.
That day young Redmond's death ha
        seen,
But twice Matilda came between
The carabine and Redmond's breast,
Just ere the spring his finger press'd.
A deadly oath the ruffian swore,
But yet his fell design forebore.
" It ne'er," he mutter'd, " shall be said
That thus I scath'd thee, haughty maid !
Then moved to seek more open aim,
When to his side Guy Denzil came:
" Bertram, forbear ! — we are undone
Forever, if thou fire the gun.
By all the fiends, an armed force
Descends the dell, of foot and horse !
We perish if they hear a shot —
Madman ! we have a safer plot —
Nay, friend, be ruled, and bear the
        back !
Behold, down yonder hollow track,
The warlike leader of the band
Comes, with his broadsword in his hand.'
Bertram look'd up; he saw, he knew
That Denzil's fears had counsell'd true,
Then cursed his fortune and withdrew,
Threaded the woodlands undescried,
And gained the cave on Greta side.

XXVII.

They whom dark Bertram, in his wrath
Doom'd to captivity or death,
Their thoughts to one sad subject lent,
Saw not nor heard the ambushment.
Heedless and unconcern'd they sate,
While on the very verge of fate;
Heedless and unconcern'd remain'd,
When Heaven the murderer's arm re-
        strain'd;
As ships drift darkling down the tide,
Nor see the shelves o'er which they glide.
Uninterrupted thus they heard
What Mortham's closing tale declared.

He spoke of wealth as of a load,
By Fortune on a wretch bestow'd,
In bitter mockery of hate,
His cureless woes to aggravate;
But yet he pray'd Matilda's care
Might save that treasure for his heir —
His Edith's son — for still he raved
As confident his life was saved;
In frequent vision, he averr'd,
He saw his face, his voice he heard;
Then argued calm — had murder been,
The blood, the corpses, had been seen;
Some had pretended, too, to mark
On Windermere a stranger bark,
Whose crew, with jealous care, yet mild,
Guarded a female and a child.
While these faint proofs he told and press'd,
Hope seem'd to kindle in his breast;
Tho' inconsistent, vague, and vain,
It warp'd his judgment, and his brain.

XXVIII.

These solemn words his story close:—
' Heaven witness for me, that I chose
My part in this sad civil fight,
Moved by no cause but England's right.
My country's groans have bid me draw
My sword for Gospel and for law;—
These righted, I fling arms aside,
And seek my son thro' Europe wide.
My wealth, on which a kinsman nigh
Already casts a grasping eye,
With thee may unsuspected lie.
When of my death Matilda hears,
Let her retain her trust three years;
If none, from me, the treasure claim,
Perish'd is Mortham's race and name.
Then let it leave her generous hand,
And flow in bounty o'er the land;
Soften the wounded prisoner's lot,
Rebuild the peasant's ruin'd cot;
So spoils, acquired by fight afar,
Shall mitigate domestic war.''

XXIX.

The generous youths, who well had known
Of Mortham's mind the powerful tone,
To that high mind, by sorrow swerved,
Gave sympathy his woes deserved;
But Wilfrid chief, who saw reveal'd
Why Mortham wish'd his life conceal'd,
In secret, doubtless, to pursue
The schemes his wilder'd fancy drew.
Thoughtful he heard Matilda tell,
That she would share her father's cell,
His partner of captivity,
Where'er his prison-house should be;
Yet grieved to think that Rokeby hall,
Dismantled, and forsook by all,
Open to rapine and to stealth,
Had now no safe-guard for the wealth
Intrusted by her kinsman kind,
And for such noble use design'd.
" Was Barnard Castle then her choice,''
Wilfrid enquired with hasty voice,
" Since there the victor's laws ordain,
Her father must a space remain?''
A flutter'd hope his accent shook,
A flutter'd joy was in his look.
Matilda hasten'd to reply,
For anger flash'd in Redmond's eye;—
" Duty,'' she said, with gentle grace,
" Kind Wilfrid, has no choice of place;
Else had I for my sire assign'd
Prison less galling to his mind,
Than that his wild-wood haunts which sees
And hears the murmurs of the Tees,
Recalling thus, with every glance,
What captive's sorrow can enhance;
But where those woes are highest, there
Needs Rokeby most his daughter's care.''

XXX.

He felt the kindly check she gave,
And stood abash'd — then answer'd grave:
" I sought thy purpose, noble maid,
Thy doubts to clear, thy schemes to aid.
I have beneath mine own command,
So wills my sire, a gallant band,
And well could send some horseman wight
To bear the treasure forth by night,
And so bestow it as you deem
In these ill days may safest seem.'' —
" Thanks, gentle Wilfrid, thanks,'' she said:
" O, be it not one day delay'd!
And, more, thy sister-friend to aid,
Be thou thyself content to hold,
In thine own keeping, Mortham's gold,
Safest with thee.'' — While thus she spoke,
Arm'd soldiers on their converse broke,

The same of whose approach afraid,
The ruffians left their ambuscade.
Their chief to Wilfrid bended low,
Then look'd around as for a foe.
" What mean'st thou, friend," young
    Wycliffe said,
" Why thus in arms beset the glade ?'' —
" That would I gladly learn from you:
For up my squadron as I drew,
To exercise our martial game
Upon the moor of Barninghame,
A stranger told you were waylaid,
Surrounded, and to death betray'd.
He had a leader's voice, I ween,
A falcon glance, a warrior's mien.
He bade me bring you instant aid;
I doubted not, and I obey'd.''

XXXI.

Wilfrid changed color, and amazed,
Turn'd short, and on the speaker gazed;
While Redmond every thicket round
Track'd earnest as a questing hound,
And Denzil's carabine he found;
Sure evidence, by which they knew
The warning was as kind as true.
Wisest it seem'd, with cautious speed
To leave the dell.   It was agreed,
That Redmond, with Matilda fair,
And fitting guard, should home repair;
At nightfall Wilfrid should attend,
With a strong band, his sister-friend,
To bear with her from Rokeby's bowers
To Barnard Castle's lofty towers,
Secret and safe the banded chests,
In which the wealth of Mortham rests
This hasty purpose fix'd, they part,
Each with a grieved and anxious heart.

CANTO FIFTH.

I.

THE sultry summer day is done,
The western hills have hid the sun,
But mountain peak and village spire
Retain reflection of his fire.
Old Barnard's towers are purple still,
To those that gaze from Toller-hill;
Distant and high, the tower of Bowes
Like steel upon the anvil glows;
And Stanmore's ridge, behind that lay,
Rich with the spoils of parting day,

In crimson and in gold array'd,
Streaks yet a while the closing shade,
Then slow resigns to darkening heaven
The tints which brighter hours had
    given.
Thus aged men, full loth and slow,
The vanities of life forego,
And count their youthful follies o'er,
Till Memory lends her light no more.

II.

The eve, that slow on upland fades,
Has darker closed on Rokeby's glades,
Where, sunk within their banks profound
Her guardian streams to meeting wound.
The stately oaks, whose sombre frown
Of noontide made a twilight brown,
Impervious now to fainter light,
Of twilight make an early night.
Hoarse into middle air arose
The vespers of the roosting crows,
And with congenial murmurs seem
To wake the Genii of the stream;
For louder clamor'd Greta's tide,
And Tees in deeper voice replied,
And fitful waked the evening wind,
Fitful in sighs its breath resign'd.
Wilfrid, whose fancy-nurtured soul
Felt in the scene a soft control,
With lighter footstep press'd the ground,
And often paused to look around;
And, tho' his path was to his love,
Could not but linger in the grove,
To drink the thrilling interest dear,
Of awful pleasure check'd by fear.
Such inconsistent moods have we,
Even when our passions strike the key.

III.

Now, thro' the wood's dark mazes past,
The opening lawn he reach'd at last,
Where, silver'd by the moonlight ray,
The ancient Hall before him lay.
Those martial terrors long were fled,
That frown'd of old around its head:
The battlements, the turrets gray,
Seem'd half abandon'd to decay; [47]
On barbican and keep of stone
Stern Time the foeman's work had done.
Where banners the invader braved,
The harebell now and wallflower waved;
In the rude guard-room, where of yore
Their weary hours the warders wore,

Now, while the cheerful fagots blaze,
On the paved floor the spindle plays;
The flanking guns dismounted lie,
The moat is ruinous and dry,
The grim portcullis gone — and all
The fortress turn'd to peaceful Hall.

IV.

But yet precautions, lately ta'en,
Show'd danger's day revived again;
The court-yard wall show'd marks of care,
The fall'n defences to repair,
Lending such strength as might withstand
The insult of marauding band.
The beams once more were taught to bear
The trembling drawbridge into air,
And not, till question'd o'er and o'er,
For Wilfrid oped the jealous door,
And when he enter'd bolt and bar
Resumed their place with sullen jar;
Then, as he cross'd the vaulted porch,
The old gray porter raised his torch,
And view'd him o'er, from foot to head,
Ere to the hall his steps he led.
That huge old hall, of knightly state,
Dismantled seem'd and desolate.
The moon thro' transom-shafts of stone,
Which cross'd the latticed oriels, shone,
And by the mournful light she gave,
The Gothic vault seem'd funeral cave.
Pennon and banner waved no more
O'er beams of stag and tusks of boar,
Nor glimmering arms were marshall'd seen
To glance those sylvan spoils between.
Those arms, those ensigns, borne away,
Accomplish'd Rokeby's brave array,
But all were lost on Marston's day!
Yet here and there the moonbeams fall
Where armor yet adorns the wall,
Cumbrous of size, uncouth to sight,
And useless in the modern fight!
Like veteran relic of the wars,
Known only by neglected scars.

V.

Matilda soon to greet him came,
And bade them light the evening flame;
Said, all for parting was prepared,
And tarried but for Wilfrid's guard.
But then, reluctant to unfold
His father's avarice of gold,
He hinted, that lest jealous eye
Should on their precious burden pry,
He judged it best the castle gate
To enter when the night wore late;
And therefore he had left command
With those he trusted of his band,
That they should be at Rokeby met,
What time the midnight-watch was set.
Now Redmond came, whose anxious care
Till then was busied to prepare
All needful, meetly to arrange
The mansion for its mournful change.
With Wilfrid's care and kindness pleased,
His cold unready hand he seized,
And press'd it, till his kindly strain
The gentle youth return'd again.
Seem'd as between them this was said,
"A while let jealously be dead;
And let our contest be, whose care
Shall best assist this helpless fair."

VI.

There was no speech the truce to bind,
It was a compact of the mind, —
A generous thought, at once impress'd
On either rival's generous breast.
Matilda well the secret took,
From sudden change of mien and look;
And — for not small had been her fear
Of jealous ire and danger near —
Felt, even in her dejected state,
A joy beyond the reach of fate.
They closed beside the chimney's blaze,
And talk'd and hoped for happier days,
And lent their spirits' rising glow
A while to gild impending woe; —
High privilege of youthful time,
Worth all the pleasures of our prime!
The bickering fagot sparkled bright,
And gave the scene of love to sight,
Bade Wilfrid's check more lively glow,
Play'd on Matilda's neck of snow,
Her nut-brown curls and forehead high,
And laugh'd in Redmond's azure eye.
Two lovers by the maiden sate,
Without a glance of jealous hate;
The maid her lovers sat between,
With open brow and equal mien; —
It is a sight but rarely spied,
Thanks to man's wrath and woman's pride.

VII.

While thus in peaceful guise they sate,
A knock alarm'd the outer gate,
And ere the tardy porter stirr'd,
The tinkling of a harp was heard.
A manly voice of mellow swell,
Bore burden to the music well.

SONG.

" Summer eve is gone and past,
Summer dew is falling fast; —
I have wander'd all the day,
Do not bid me farther stray!
Gentle hearts, of gentle kin,
Take the wandering harper in!"

But the stern porter answer gave,
With " Get thee hence, thou strolling knave;
The king wants soldiers; war, I trow,
Were meeter trade for such as thou."
At this unkind reproof, again
Answer'd the ready Minstrel's strain.

SONG RESUMED.

" Bid not me, in battle-field,
Buckler lift, or broadsword wield!
All my strength and all my art
Is to touch the gentle heart,
With the wizard notes that ring
From the peaceful minstrel-string."

The porter, all unmoved, replied: —
" Depart in peace, with Heaven to guide;
If longer by the gate thou dwell,
Trust me, thou shalt not part so well."

VIII.

With somewhat of appealing look,
The harper's part young Wilfrid took:
" These notess so wild and ready thrill,
They show no vulgar minstrel's skill;
Hard were his task to seek a home
More distant, since the night is come,
And for his faith I dare engage —
Your Harpool's blood is sour'd by age.
His gate, once readily display'd,
To greet the friend, the poor to aid,
Now even to me, though known of old,
Did but reluctantly unfold."—
" O blame not, as poor Harpool's crime
An evil of this evil time.

He deems dependent on his care
The safety of his patron's heir,
Nor judges meet to ope the tower
To guest unknown at parting hour,
Urging his duty to excess
Of rough and stubborn faithfulness.
For this poor harper, I would fain
He may relax: — Hark to his strain!"—

IX.

SONG RESUMED.

" I have song of war for knight,
Lay of love for lady bright,
Fairy tale to lull the heir,
Goblin grim the maids to scare.
Dark the night, and long till day,
Do not bid me farther stray!

" Rokeby's lords of martial fame,
I can count them name by name;
Legends of their line there be,
Known to few, but known to me;
If you honor Rokeby's kin,
Take the wandering harper in!

" Rokeby's lords had fair regard
For the harp, and for the bard:
Baron's race throve never well,
Where the curse of minstrel fell.
If you love that noble kin,
Take the weary harper in!"—

" Hark! Harpool parleys — there is hope,"
Said Redmond, "that the gate will ope."—
— "For all thy brag and boast, I trow,
Naught know'st thou of the Felon Sow," [48]
Quoth Harpool, "nor how Greta-side
She roam'd, and Rokeby forest wide:
Nor how Ralph Rokeby gave the beast
To Richmond's friars to make a feast.
Of Gilbert Griffinson the tale
Goes, and of gallant Peter Dale,
That well could strike with sword amain,
And of the valiant son of Spain,
Friar Middleton, and blithe Sir Ralph:
There was a jest to make us laugh!
If thou canst tell it, in yon shed
Thou'st won thy supper and thy bed."

X.

atilda smiled; " Cold hope," said she,
From Harpool's love of minstrelsy!
ut, for this harper, may we dare,
edmond, to mend his couch and fare?"—
O, ask me not! — At minstrel-string
y heart from infancy would spring;
or can I hear its simplest strain,
ut it brings Erin's dream again,
/hen placed by Owen Lysagh's knee,
The Filea of O'Neale was he,[49]
blind and bearded man, whose eld
/as sacred as a prophet's held,)
ve seen a ring of rugged kerne,
/ith aspects shaggy, wild, and stern,
nchanted by the master's lay,
inger around the livelong day,
iift from wild rage to wilder glee,
o love, to grief, to ecstasy,
nd feel each varied change of soul
bedient to the bard's control. —
h, Clandeboy! thy friendly floor
ieve-Donard's oak shall light no more;[50]
or Owen's harp, beside the blaze,
ell maiden's love, or hero's praise!
he mantling brambles hide thy hearth,
entre of hospitable mirth;
ll undistinguish'd in the glade,
y sires' glad home is prostrate laid,
heir vassals wander wide and far,
erve foreign lords in distant war,
nd now the stranger's sons enjoy
he lovely woods of Clandeboy!"
e spoke, and proudly turn'd aside,
he starting tear to dry and hide.

XI.

[M]atilda's dark and soften'd eye
/as glistening ere O'Neale's was dry.
er hand upon his arm she laid,—
It is the will of Heaven," she said.
And think'st thou, Redmond, I can part
rom this loved home with lightsome
          heart,
eaving to wild neglect whate'er
ven from my infancy was dear?
or in this calm domestic bound
/ere all Matilda's pleasures found.
hat hearth, my sire was wont to grace,
ull soon may be a stranger's place;
his hall, in which a child I play'd,
ike thine, dear Redmond, lowly laid,
he bramble and the thorn may braid;

Or, passed for aye from me and mine,
It ne'er may shelter Rokeby's line.
Yet is this consolation given,
My Redmond — 'tis the will of Heaven."
Her word, her action, and her phrase,
Were kindly as in early days;
For cold reserve had lost its power,
In sorrow's sympathetic hour.
Young Redmond dared not trust his voice,
But rather had it been his choice
To share that melancholy hour,
Than, arm'd with all a chieftain's power,
In full possession to enjoy
Slieve-Donard wide, and Clandeboy.

XII.

The blood left Wilfrid's ashen cheek;
Matilda sees, and hastes to speak: —
" Happy in friendship's ready aid,
Let all my murmurs here be staid!
And Rokeby's Maiden will not part
From Rokeby's hall with moody heart.
This night at least, for Rokeby's fame,
The hospitable hearth shall flame,
And, ere its native heir retire,
Find for the wanderer rest and fire,
While this poor harper, by the blaze,
Recounts the tale of other days.
Bid Harpool ope the door with speed,
Admit him, and relieve each need. —
Meantime, kind Wycliffe, wilt thou try
Thy minstrel skill? — Nay, no reply —
And look not sad! — I guess thy thought,
Thy verse with laurels would be bought;
And poor Matilda, landless now,
Has not a garland for thy brow.
True, I must leave sweet Rokeby's glades,
Nor wander more in Greta's shades:
But sure, no rigid jailer, thou
Wilt a short prison-walk allow,
Where summer flowers grow wild at will,
On Marwood-chase and Toller Hill;[51]
Then holly green and lily gay
Shall twine in guerdon of thy lay."
The mournful youth, a space aside,
To tune Matilda's harp applied;
And then a low sad descant rung,
As prelude to the lay he sung:—

XIII.

THE CYPRESS WREATH.

O, Lady twine no wreath for me,
Or twine it of the cypress-tree!

Too lively glow the lilies light,
The varnish'd holly's all too bright,
The May-flower and the eglantine
May shade a brow less sad than mine;
But, Lady, weave no wreath for me,
Or weave it of the cypress-tree!

Let dimpled Mirth his temples twine
With tendrils of the laughing vine;
The manly oak, the pensive yew,
To patriot and to sage be due;
The myrtle bough bids lovers live,
But that Matilda will not give;
Then, Lady, twine no wreath for me,
Or twine it of the cypress-tree!

Let merry England proudly rear
Her blended roses, bought so dear;
Let Albin bind her bonnet blue
With heath and harebell dipp'd in dew;
On favor'd Erin's crest be seen
The flower she loves of emerald green —
But, Lady, twine no wreath for me,
Or twine it of the cypress-tree.

Strike the wild harp, while maids prepare
The ivy meet for minstrel's hair;
And, while his crown of laurel-leaves,
With bloody hand the victor weaves,
Let the loud trump his triumph tell;
But, when you hear the passing-bell,
Then, Lady, twine a wreath for me,
And twine it of the cypress-tree.

Yes! twine for me the cypress bough;
But, O Matilda, twine not now!
Stay till a few brief months are past,
And I have look'd and loved my last!
When villagers my shroud bestrew
With pansies, rosemary, and rue,—
Then, Lady, weave a wreath for me,
And weave it of the cypress-tree.

XIV.

O'Neale observed the starting tear,
And spoke with kind and blithesome
    cheer: —
"No, noble Wilfrid! ere the day
When mourns the land thy silent lay,
Shall many a wreath be freely wove
By hand of friendship and of love.
I would not wish that rigid Fate
Had doom'd thee to a captive's state,

Whose hands are bound by honor's law
Who wears a sword he must not draw;
But were it so, in Minstrel pride
The land togetner would we ride,
On prancing steeds, like harpers old,
Bound for the halls of barons bold,
Each lover of the lyre we'd seek,
From Michael's Mount to Skiddaw's Peak
Survey wild Albin's mountain strand,
And roam green Erin's lovely land,
While thou the gentler souls should mov
With lay of pity and of love,
And I, thy mate, in rougher strain,
Would sing of war and warriors slain.
Old England's bards were vanquish'
    then,
And Scotland's vaunted Hawthornden,
And, silenced on Iernian shore,
M'Curtin's harp should charm no more!"[5]
In lively mood he spoke, to wile
From Wilfrid's woe-worn cheek a smile

XV.

"But," said Matilda, "ere thy name,
Good Redmond, gain its destined fame,
Say, wilt thou kindly deign to call
Thy brother-minstrel to the hall?
Bid all the household, too, attend,
Each in his rank a humble friend;
I know their faithful hearts will grieve,
When their poor Mistress takes her leave
So let the horn and beaker flow
To mitigate their parting woe."
The harper came; — in youth's first prim
Himself; in mode of olden time
His garb was fashion'd, to express
The ancient English minstrel's dress,
A seemly gown of Kendal green,
With gorget closed of silver sheen;
His harp in silken scarf was slung,
And by his side an anlace hung.
It seem'd some masquer's quaint array,
For revel or for holiday.

XVI.

He made obeisance with a free
Yet studied air of courtesy.
Each look and accent, framed to please,
Seem'd to affect a playful ease;
His face was of that doubtful kind,
That wins the eye, but not the mind;
Yet harsh it seem'd to deem amiss
Of brow so young and smooth as this.

iis was the subtle look and sly,
hat, spying all, seemed naught to spy;
ound all the group his glances stole,
nmark'd themselves, to mark the whole.
et sunk beneath Matilda's look,
or could the eye of Redmond brook.
o the suspicious, or the old,
ubtile and dangerous and bold
iad seem'd this self-invited guest;
ut young our lovers, — and the rest,
Vrapt in their sorrow and their fear
t parting of their Mistress dear,
'ear-blinded to the Castle-hall
ame as to bear her funeral pall.

XVII.

ll that expression base was gone,
Vhen waked the guest his minstrel tone;
: fled at inspiration's call,
s erst the demon fled from Saul.
Iore noble glance he cast around,
Iore free-drawn breath inspired the
    sound,
Iis pulse beat bolder and more high,
n all the pride of minstrelsy!
las! too soon that pride was o'er,
unk with the lay that bade it soar!
Iis soul resumed, with habit's chain,
ts vices wild and follies vain,
nd gave the talent, with him born,
o be a common curse and scorn.
uch was the youth whom Rokeby's Maid,
Vith condescending kindness, pray'd
Iere to renew the strains she loved,
t distance heard and well approved.

XVIII.
SONG.
The Harp.

was a wild and wayward boy,
Iy childhood scorn'd each childish toy,
Retired from all, reserved and coy,
    To musing prone,
woo'd my solitary joy,
    My Harp alone.

Iy youth, with bold Ambition's mood,
Despised the humble stream and wood,
Vhere my poor father's cottage stood,
    To fame unknown; —
What should my soaring views make
    good?
    My Harp alone!

Love came with all his frantic fire,
And wild romance of vain desire:
The baron's daughter heard my lyre,
    And praised the tone; —
What could presumptuous hope inspire?
    My Harp alone!

At manhood's touch the bubble burst,
And manhood's pride the vision curst,
And all that had my folly nursed
    Love's sway to own;
Yet spared the spell that lull'd me first,
    My Harp alone!

Woe came with war, and want with woe;
And it was mine to undergo
Each outrage of the rebel foe: —
    Can aught atone
My fields laid waste, my cot laid low?
    My Harp alone!

Ambition's dreams I've seen depart,
Have rued of penury the smart,
Have felt of love the venom'd dart,
    When hope was flown;
Yet rests one solace to my heart, –
    My Harp alone!

Then over mountain, moor, and hill,
My faithful Harp, I'll bear thee still;
And when this life of want and ill
    Is wellnigh gone,
Thy strings mine elegy shall thrill,
    My Harp alone!

XIX.

" A pleasing lay! " Matilda said;
But Harpool shook his old gray head,
And took his baton and his torch,
To seek his guard-room in the porch.
Edmund observed, with sudden change,
Among the strings his fingers range,
Until they waked a bolder glee
Of military melody;
Then paused amid the martial sound,
And look'd with well-feign'd fear
    around; —
" None to this noble house belong,"
He said, " that would a Minstrel wrong,
Whose fate has been, through good and ill,
To love his Royal Master still;
And with your honor'd leave, would fain
Rejoice you with a loyal strain."

Then, as assured by sign and look,
The warlike tone again he took;
And Harpool stopp'd, and turn'd to
    hear
A ditty of the Cavalier.

XX.
SONG.
The Cavalier.

While the dawn on the mountain was
    misty and gray,
My true love has mounted his steed and
    away
Over hill, over valley, o'er dale, and o'er
    down:
Heaven shield the brave Gallant that
    fights for the Crown!

He has doff'd the silk doublet the breast-
    plate to bear,
He has placed the steel-cap o'er his long
    flowing hair,
From his belt to his stirrup his broad-
    sword hangs down, —
Heaven shield the brave Gallant that
    fights for the Crown!

For the rights of fair England that broad-
    sword he draws,
Her King is his leader, her Church is his
    cause;
His watchword is honor, his pay is re-
    nown, —
GOD strike with the Gallant that strikes
    for the Crown!

They may boast of their Fairfax, their
    Waller, and all
The round-headed rebels of Westminster
    Hall;
But tell these bold traitors of London's
    proud town,
That the spears of the North have en-
    circled the Crown.

There's Derby and Cavendish, dread of
    their foes;
There's Erin's High Ormond, and Scot-
    land's Montrose!
Would you match the base Skippon, and
    Massey, and Brown,
With the Barons of England, that fight
    for the Crown?

Now joy to the crest of the brave Cav
    alier!
Be his banner unconquer'd, resistless h
    spear,
Till in peace and in triumph his toils h
    may drown,
In a pledge to fair England, her Church
    and her Crown.

XXI.

" Alas ! " Matilda said, " that strain,
Good harper, now is heard in vain !
The time has been, at such a sound,
When Rokeby's vassals gather'd round,
A hundred manly hearts would bound;
But now the stirring verse we hear,
Like trump in dying soldier's ear!
Listless and sad the notes we own,
The power to answer them is flown.
Yet not without his meet applause,
Be he that sings the rightful cause,
Even when the crisis of its fate
To human eye seems desperate.
While Rokeby's Heir such power retains
Let this slight guerdon pay thy pains: —
And, lend thy harp; I fain would try,
If my poor skill can aught supply,
Ere yet I leave my father's hall,
To mourn the cause in which we fall."

XXII.

The harper, with a downcast look,
And trembling hand, her bounty took, ~
As yet, the conscious pride of art
Had steel'd him in his treacherous part;
A powerful spring of force unguess'd,
That hath each gentler mood suppress'd
And reign'd in many a human breast;
From his that plans the red campaign,
To his that wastes the woodland reign.
The failing wing, the blood-shot eye, —
The sportsman marks with apathy,
Each feeling of his victim's ill
Drown'd in his own successful skill.
The veteran, too, who now no more
Aspires to head the battle's roar,
Loves still the triumph of his art,
And traces on the pencill'd chart,
Some stern invader's destined way,
Through blood and ruin, to his prey;
Patriots to death, and towns to flame,
He dooms to raise another's name,
And shares the guilt, though not the fame.

What pays him for his span of time
Spent in premeditating crime?
What against pity arms his heart?—
t is the conscious pride of art.

XXIII.

But principles in Edmund's mind
Were baseless, vague, and undefined,
His soul, like bark with rudder lost,
On Passion's changeful tide was tost,
Nor Vice nor Virtue had the power
Beyond the impression of the hour;
And, O! when Passion rules, how
    rare
The hours that fall to Virtue's share!
Yet now she roused her — for the pride
That lack of sterner guilt supplied,
Could scarce support him when arose
The lay that mourned Matilda's woes.

SONG.

The Farewell.

The sound of Rokeby's woods I hear,
    They mingle with the song:
Dark Greta's voice is in mine ear,
    I must not hear them long.
From every loved and native haunt
    The native Heir must stray,
And, like a ghost whom sunbeams aunt,
    Must part before the day.

Soon from the halls my fathers rear'd
    Their scutcheons may descend.
A line so long beloved and fear'd
    May soon obscurely end.
No longer here Matilda's tone
    Shall bid those echoes swell;
Yet shall they hear her proudly own
    The cause in which we fell.

The Lady paused, and then again
Resumed the lay in loftier strain.

XXIV.

Let our halls and towers decay,
    Be our name and line forgot,
Lands and manors pass away, —
    We but share our Monarch's lot.
If no more our annals show
    Battles won and banners taken,
Still in death, defeat, and woe,
    Ours be loyalty unshaken!

Constant still in danger's hour,
    Princes own'd our fathers' aid;
Lands and honors, wealth and power,
    Well their loyalty repaid.
Perish wealth and power and pride!
    Mortal boons by mortals given;
But let constancy abide, —
    Constancy's the gift of Heaven.

XXV.

While thus Matilda's lay was heard,
A thousand thoughts in Edmund stirr'd.
In peasant life he might have known
As fair a face, as sweet a tone;
But village notes could ne'er supply
That rich and varied melody;
And ne'er in cottage-maid was seen
The easy dignity of mien,
Claiming respect, yet waiving state,
That marks the daughters of the great.
Yet not, perchance, had these alone
His scheme of purposed guilt o'erthrown;
But while her energy of mind
Superior rose to griefs combined,
Lending its kindling to her eye,
Giving her form new majesty, —
To Edmund's thought Matilda seem'd
The very object he had dream'd;
When, long ere guilt his soul had known,
In Winston bowers he mused alone,
Taxing his fancy to combine
The face, the air, the voice divine,
Of princess fair, by cruel fate
Reft of her honors, power, and state,
Till to her rightful realm restored
By destined hero's conquering sword.

XXVI.

" Such was my vision!" Edmund
    thought,
" And have I, then, the ruin wrought
Of such a maid, that fancy ne'er
In fairest vision form'd her peer?
Was it my hand that could unclose
The postern to her ruthless foes?
Foes, lost to honor, law, and faith,
Their kindest mercy sudden death!
Have I done this? I! who have swore,
That if the globe such angel bore,
I would have traced its circle broad,
To kiss the ground on which she trode! —
And now—O! would that earth would rive
And close upon me while alive! —

Is there no hope? Is all then lost? —
Bertram's already on his post!
Even now, beside the Hall's arch'd
    door,
I saw his shadow cross the floor!
He was to wait my signal strain —
A little respite thus we gain:
By what I heard the menials say,
Young Wycliffe's troop are on their
    way. —
Alarm precipitates the crime!
My harp must wear away the time." —
And then, in accents faint and low,
He falter'd forth a tale of woe.

XXVII.

BALLAD.

"And whither would you lead me
    then?"
    Quoth the Friar of orders gray;
And the Ruffians twain replied again,
    "By a dying woman to pray."

"I see," he said, "a lovely sight,
    A sight bodes little harm,
A lady as a lily bright,
    With an infant on her arm."

"Then do thine office, Friar gray,
    And see thou shrive her free?
Else shall the sprite, that parts to-night,
    Fling all its guilt on thee.

"Let mass be said, and trentals read,
    When thou'rt to convent gone,
And bid the bell of St. Benedict
    Toll out its deepest tone."

The shrift is done, the Friar has gone,
    Blindfolded as he came —
Next morning, all in Littlecot Hall [53]
    Were weeping for their dame.

Wild Darrel is an alter'd man,
    The village crones can tell;
He looks pale as clay, and strives to
    pray,
    If he hears the convent bell.

If prince or peer cross Darrel's way,
    He'll beard him in his pride —
If he meet a Friar of orders gray,
    He droops and turns aside.

XXVIII.

"Harper! methinks thy magic lays,"
Matilda said, "can goblins raise!
Well nigh my fancy can discern,
Near the dark porch, a visage stern;
E'en now, in yonder shadowy nook,
I see it! — Redmond, Wilfrid, look! —
A human form distinct and clear —
God for thy mercy! — It draws near!"
She saw too true. Stride after stride,
The centre of that chamber wide
Fierce Bertram gain'd; then made a
    stand,
And, proudly waving his hand,
Thunder'd: — "Be still, upon your lives!
He bleeds who speaks, he dies who
    strives."
Behind their chief, the robber crew
Forth from the darken'd portal drew
In silence — save that echo dread
Return'd their heavy measured tread.
The lamp's uncertain lustre gave
Their arms to gleam, their plumes to
    wave;
File after file in order pass,
Like forms on Banquo's mystic glass.
Then, halting at their leader's sign,
At once they form'd and curved their line,
Hemming within its crescent drear
Their victims like a herd of deer.
Another sign, and to the aim
Levell'd at once their muskets came,
As waiting but their chieftain's word,
To make their fatal volley heard.

XXIX.

Back in a heap the menials drew;
Yet, even in mortal terror, true,
Their pale and startled group oppose
Between Matilda and the foes.
"O, haste thee, Wilfrid!" Redmond
    cried;
"Undo that wicket by thy side!
Bear hence Matilda — gain the wood —
The pass may be a while made good —
Thy band, ere this, must sure be nigh —
O speak not — dally not — but fly!"
While yet the crowd their motions hide,
Through the low wicket door they glide.
Through vaulted passages they wind,
In Gothic intricacy twined;
Wilfrid half led, and half he bore,
Matilda to the postern-door,

And safe beneath the forest tree,
The Lady stands at liberty.
The moonbeams, the fresh gale's caress,
Renew'd suspended consciousness: —
" Where's Redmond? " eagerly she cries;
' Thou answer'st not — he dies! he dies!
And thou hast left him, all bereft
Of mortal aid — with murderers left!
I know it well — he would not yield
His sword to man — his doom is seal'd!
For my scorn'd life, which thou hast
    bought
At price of his, I thank thee not."

XXX.

The unjust reproach, the angry look,
The heart of Wilfrid could not brook.
' Lady," he said, " my band is near,
In safety thou mayest rest thee here.
For Redmond's death thou shalt not
    mourn,
If mine can buy his safe return."
He turn'd away — his heart throbb'd
    high,
The tear was bursting from his eye;
The sense of her injustice press'd
Upon the Maid's distracted breast: —
" Stay, Wilfrid, stay! all aid is vain!"
He heard, but turn'd him not again;
He reaches now the postern-door,
Now enters — and is seen no more.

XXXI.

With all the agony that e'er
Was gender'd 'twixt suspense and fear,
She watch'd the line of windows tall,
Whose Gothic lattice lights the Hall,
Distinguish'd by the paly red
The lamps in dim reflection shed,
While all beside in wan moonlight
Each grated casement glimmer'd white,
No sight of harm, no sound of ill,
It is a deep and midnight still.
Who look'd upon the scene had guess'd
All in the Castle were at rest;
When sudden on the window shone
A lightning flash, just seen and gone!
A shot is heard. — Again the flame
Flash'd thick and fast — a volley came!
Then echo'd wildly, from within,
Of shout and scream the mingled din,
And weapon-clash and maddening cry,
Of those who kill, and those who die! —

As fill'd the Hall with sulphurous smoke,
More red, more dark, the death-flash
    broke:
And forms were on the lattice cast,
That struck, or struggled, as they past.

XXXII.

What sounds upon the midnight wind
Approach so rapidly behind?
It is, it is, the tramp of steeds,
Matilda hears the sound, she speeds,
Seizes upon the leader's rein: —
" O, haste to aid, ere aid be vain!
Fly to the postern — gain the Hall! "
From saddle spring the troopers all;
Their gallant steeds, at liberty,
Run wild along the moonlight lea,
But, ere they burst upon the scene,
Full stubborn had the conflict been.
When Bertram mark'd Matilda's flight,
It gave the signal for the fight;
And Rokeby's veterans, seam'd with scars
Of Scotland's and of Erin's wars,
Their momentary panic o'er,
Stood to the arms which then they bore.
(For they were weapon'd, and prepared
Their mistress on her way to guard.)
Then cheer'd them to the fight O'Neale,
Then peal'd the shot, and clash'd the
    steel;
The war-smoke soon with sable breath
Darken'd the scene of blood and death,
While on the few defenders close
The Bandits, with redoubled blows,
And, twice driven back, yet fierce and fell
Renew the charge with frantic yell.

XXXIII.

Wilfrid has fall'n — but o'er him stood
Young Redmond, soil'd with smoke and
    blood,
Cheering his mates with heart and hand
Still to make good their desperate stand.
" Up, comrades, up! In Rokeby halls
Ne'er be it said our courage falls.
What! faint ye for their savage cry,
Or do the smoke-wreaths daunt your eye?
These rafters have return'd a shout
As loud at Rokeby's wassail rout,
As thick a smoke these hearths have given
At Hallow-tide or Christmas-even.[54]
Stand to it yet! renew the fight,
For Rokeby's and Matilda's right!

These slaves! they dare not, hand to hand,
Bide buffet from a true man's brand.''
Impetuous, active, fierce, and young,
Upon the advancing foes he sprung.
Woe to the wretch at whom is bent
His brandish'd falchion's sheer descent!
Backward they scatter'd as he came,
Like wolves before the levin flame,
When, mid their howling conclave driven,
Hath glanced the thunderbolt of heaven.
Bertram rush'd on — but Harpool clasp'd
His knees, although in death he gasp'd,
His falling corpse before him flung,
And round the trammell'd ruffian clung.
Just then, the soldiers filled the dome,
And, shouting, charged the felons home
So fiercely, that, in panic dread,
They broke, they yielded, fell, or fled.
Bertram's stern voice they heed no more,
Though heard above the battle's roar;
While, trampling down the dying man,
He strove, with volley'd threat and ban,
In scorn of odds, in fate's despite,
To rally up the desperate fight.

XXXIV.

Soon murkier clouds the Hall enfold
Than e'er from battle-thunders roll'd,
So dense, the combatants scarce know
To aim or to avoid the blow.
Smothering and blindfold grows the fight —
But soon shall dawn a dismal light!
Mid cries, and clashing arms, there came
The hollow sound of rushing flame;
New horrors on the tumult dire
Arise — the Castle is on fire!
Doubtful, if chance had cast the brand,
Or frantic Bertram's desperate hand.
Matilda saw — for frequent broke
From the dim casements gusts of smoke.
Yon tower, which late so clear defined
On the fair hemisphere reclined,
That, pencill'd on its azure pure,
The eye could count each embrazure,
Now, swathed within the sweeping cloud,
Seems giant-spectre in his shroud;
Till, from each loop-hole flashing light,
A spout of fire shines ruddy bright,
And, gathering to united glare,
Streams high into the midnight air;
A dismal beacon, far and wide
That waken'd Greta's slumbering side,

Soon all beneath, through gallery long,
And pendant arch, the fire flash'd strong
Snatching whatever could maintain,
Raise, or extend, its furious reign;
Startling, with closer cause of dread,
The females who the conflict fled,
And now rush'd forth upon the plain,
Filling the air with clamors vain.

XXXV.

But ceased not yet, the Hall within,
The shriek, the shout, the carnage-din,
Till bursting lattices give proof
The flames have caught the rafter'd roof
What! wait they till its beams amain
Crash on the slayers and the slain?
The alarm is caught—the drawbridge falls
The warriors hurry from the walls,
But, by the conflagration's light,
Upon the lawn renew the fight.
Each struggling felon down was hew'd,
Not one could gain the sheltering wood;
But forth the affrighted harper sprung,
And to Matilda's robe he clung.
Her shriek, entreaty, and command,
Stopp'd the pursuer's lifted hand.
Denzil and he alive were ta'en;
The rest, save Bertram, all are slain.

XXXVI.

And where is Bertram? — Soaring high,
The general flame ascends the sky;
In gather'd group the soldiers gaze
Upon the broad and roaring blaze,
When, like infernal demon sent,
Red from his penal element,
To plague and to pollute the air, —
His face all gore, on fire his hair,
Forth from the central mass of smoke
The giant form of Bertram broke!
His brandish'd sword on high he rears,
Then plunged among opposing spears;
Round his left arm his mantle truss'd,
Received and foil'd three lances' thrust;
Nor these his headlong course withstood,
Like reeds he snapp'd the tough ash-wood.
In vain his foes around him clung;
With matchless force aside he flung
Their boldest, — as the bull, at bay,
Tosses the ban-dogs from his way,
Through forty foes his path he made,
And safely gain'd the forest glade.

XXXVII.

Scarce was this final conflict o'er,
When from the postern Redmond bore
Wilfrid, who, as of life bereft,
Had in the fatal hall been left,
Deserted there by all his train:
But Redmond saw, and turn'd again. —
Beneath an oak he laid him down,
That in the blaze gleam'd ruddy brown,
And then his mantle's clasp undid;
Matilda held his drooping head,
Till, given to breathe the freer air,
Returning life repaid their care.
He gazed on them with heavy sigh:—
"I could have wish'd even thus to die ! "
No more he said — for now with speed
Each trooper had regain'd his steed:
The ready palfreys stood array'd,
For Redmond and for Rokeby's Maid;
Two Wilfred on his horse sustain,
One leads his charger by the rein.
But oft Matilda look'd behind,
As up the Vale of Tees they wind,
Where far the mansion of her sires
Beacon'd the dale with midnight fires.
In gloomy arch above them spread,
The clouded heaven lower'd bloody red;
Beneath, in sombre light, the flood
Appear'd to roll in waves of blood.
Then, one by one, was heard to fall
The Tower, the donjon-keep, the hall.
Each rushing down with thunder sound,
A space the conflagration drown'd;
Till, gathering strength, again it rose,
Announced its triumph in its close,
Shook wide its light the landscape o'er,
Then sunk, — and Rokeby was no more !

CANTO SIXTH.

I.

THE summer sun whose early power
Was wont to gild Matilda's bower,
And rouse her with his matin ray
Her duteous orisons to pay,
That morning sun had three times seen
The flowers unfold on Rokeby green,
But sees no more the slumbers fly
From fair Matilda's hazel eye;
That morning sun has three times broke
On Rokeby's glades of elm and oak,

But, rising from their sylvan screen,
Marks no gray turrets glance between.
A shapeless mass lie keep and tower,
That, hissing to the morning shower,
Can but with smouldering vapor pay
The early smile of summer day.
The peasant, to his labor bound,
Pauses to view the blacken'd mound,
Striving, amid the ruin'd space,
Each well-remember'd spot to trace.
That length of frail and fire-scorch'd wall
Once screen'd the hospitable hall;
When yonder broken arch was whole,
'T was there was dealt the weekly dole;
And where yon tottering columns nod,
The chapel sent the hymn to God. —
So flits the world's uncertain span !
Nor zeal for God, nor love for man,
Gives mortal monuments a date
Beyond the power of Time and Fate.
The towers must share the builder's
    doom;
Ruin is theirs, and his a tomb:
But better boon benignant Heaven
To Faith and Charity has given,
And bids the Christian hope sublime
Transcend the bounds of Fate and Time.

II.

Now the third night of summer came,
Since that which witness'd Rokeby's
    flame.
On Brignall cliffs and Scargill brake
The owlet's homilies awake,
The bittern scream'd from rush and flag,
The raven slumber'd on his crag,
Forth from his den the otter drew, —
Grayling and trout their tyrant knew,
As between reed and sedge he peers,
With fierce round snout and sharpen'd
    ears,
Or prowling by the moonbeam cool,
Watches the stream or swims the pool;—
Perch'd on his wonted eyrie high,
Sleep seal'd the tercelet's wearied eye,
That all the day had watch'd so well
The cushat dart across the dell.
In dubious beam reflected shone
That lofty cliff of pale gray stone,
Beside whose base the secret cave
To rapine late a refuge gave.
The crag's wild crest of copse and yew
On Greta's breast dark shadows threw;

Shadows that met or shunn'd the sight,
With every change of fitful light;
As hope and fear alternate chase
Our course through life's uncertain race.

III.

Gliding by crag and copsewood green,
A solitary form was seen
To trace with stealthy pace the wold,
Like fox that seeks the midnight fold,
And pauses oft, and cowers dismay'd,
At every breath that stirs the shade.
He passes now the ivy bush, —
The owl has seen him, and is hush;
He passes now the dodder'd oak, —
Ye heard the startled raven croak;
Lower and lower he descends,
Rustle the leaves, the brushwood bends;
The otter hears him tread the shore,
And dives, and is beheld no more;
And by the cliff of pale gray stone
The midnight wanderer stands alone.
Methinks that by the moon we trace
A well-remember'd form and face!
That stripling shape, that cheek so pale,
Combine to tell a rueful tale,
Of powers misused, of passion's force,
Of guilt, of grief, and of remorse!
'Tis Edmund's eye, at every sound
That flings that guilty glance around;
'Tis Edmund's trembling haste divides
The brushwood that the cavern hides;
And, when its narrow porch lies bare,
'Tis Edmund's form that enters there.

IV.

His flint and steel have sparkled bright,
A lamp hath lent the cavern light.
Fearful and quick his eye surveys
Each angle of the gloomy maze.
Since last he left that stern abode,
It seem'd as none its floor had trode;
Untouch'd appear'd the various spoil,
The purchase of his comrades' toil;
Masks and disguises grim'd with mud,
Arms broken and defiled with blood,
And all the nameless tools that aid
Night-felons in their lawless trade,
Upon the gloomy walls were hung,
Or lay in nooks obscurely flung.
Still on the sordid board appear
The relics of the noontide cheer;

Flagons and emptied flasks were there,
And bench o'erthrown, and shatter'd
　　chair;
And all around the semblance show'd,
As when the final revel glow'd,
When the red sun was setting fast,
And parting pledge Guy Denzil past.
"To Rokeby treasure-vaults!" they
　　quaff'd,
And shouted loud and wildly laugh'd,
Pour'd maddening from the rocky door,
And parted — to return no more!
They found in Rokeby vaults their doom,
A bloody death, a burning tomb!

V.

There his own peasant dress he spies,
Doff'd to assume that quaint disguise;
And, shuddering, thought upon his glee,
When prank'd in garb of minstrelsy.
"O, be the fatal art accurst,"
He cried, "that moved my folly first;
Till, bribed by bandits' base applause,
I burst through God's and Nature's laws!
Three summer days are scantly past
Since I have trod this cavern last,
A thoughtless wretch, and prompt to err —
But, O, as yet no murderer!
Even now I list my comrades' cheer,
That general laugh is in mine ear,
Which raised my pulse and steel'd my
　　heart,
As I rehearsed my treacherous part —
And would that all since then could seem
The phantom of a fever's dream!
But fatal Memory notes too well
The horrors of the dying yell
From my despairing mates that broke,
When flash'd the fire and roll'd the
　　smoke;
When the avengers shouting came,
And hemm'd us 'twixt the sword and
　　flame!
My frantic flight, — the lifted brand, —
That angel's interposing hand! ——
If, for my life from slaughter freed,
I yet could pay some grateful meed!
Perchance this object of my quest
May aid" — he turn'd, nor spoke the rest.

VI.

Due northward from the rugged hearth,
With paces five he metes the earth,

Then toil'd with mattock to explore
The entrails of the cabin floor,
Nor paused till, deep beneath the ground,
His search a small steel casket found.
Just as he stoop'd to loose its hasp,
His shoulder felt a giant grasp;
He started, and look'd up aghast,
Then shriek'd! — 'Twas Bertram held
    him fast.
' Fear not ! " he said; but who could hear
That deep stern voice, and cease to fear.
' Fear not ! — By Heaven, he shakes as
    much
As partridge in the falcon's clutch:" —
He raised him, and unloosed his hold,
While from the opening casket roll'd
A chain and reliquaire of gold.
Bertram beheld it with surprise,
Gazed on its fashion and device,
Then, cheering Edmund as he could,
Somewhat he smooth'd his rugged mood:
For still the youth's half-lifted eye
Quiver'd with terror's agony,
And sidelong glanced, as to explore,
In meditated flight, the door.
"Sit," Bertram said, "from danger free:
Thou canst not, and thou shalt not, flee.
Chance brings me hither; hill and plain
I've sought for refuge-place in vain.
And tell me now, thou aguish boy,
What makest thou here? what means
    this toy?
Denzil and thou, I mark'd, were ta'en;
What lucky chance unbound your chain?
I deem'd, long since on Baliol's tower,
Your heads were warp'd with sun and
    shower.
Tell me the whole — and, mark ! naught
    e'er
Chafes me like falsehood, or like fear."
Gathering his courage to his aid,
But trembling still, the youth obey'd: —

VII.

" Denzil and I two nights pass'd o'er
In fetters on the dungeon floor.
A guest the third sad morrow brought:
Our hold dark Oswald Wycliffe sought,
And eyed my comrade long askance,
With fix'd and penetrating glance.
' Guy Denzil art thou call'd?' — 'The
    same.' —
' At Court who served wild Buckinghame;

Thence banish'd, won a keeper's place,
So Villiers will'd, in Marwood-chase;
That lost — I need not tell thee why —
Thou madest thy wit thy wants supply,
Then fought for Rokeby: — Have I
    guess'd
My prisoner right?' — 'At thy behest.' —
He paused a while, and then went on
With low and confidential tone; —
Me, as I judge, not then he saw,
Close nestled in my couch of straw —
' List to me, Guy. Thou know'st the
    great
Have frequent need of what they hate;
Hence, in their favor oft we see
Unscrupled, useful men like thee.
Were I disposed to bid thee live,
What pledge of faith hast thou to give?'

VIII.

" The ready Fiend, who never yet
Hath failed to sharpen Denzil's wit,
Prompted his lie — ' His only child
Should rest his pledge.' — The Baron
    smiled,
And turn'd to me — ' Thou art his son?'
I bow'd — our fetters were undone,
And we were led to hear apart
A dreadful lesson of his art.
Wilfrid, he said, his heir and son,
Had fair Matilda's favor won;
And long since had their union been,
But for her father's bigot spleen,
Whose brute and blindfold party-rage
Would, force per force, her hand engage
To a base kern of Irish earth,
Unknown his lineage and his birth,
Save that a dying ruffian bore
The infant brat to Rokeby door.
Gentle restraint, he said, would lead
Old Rokeby to enlarge his creed;
But fair occasion he must find
For such restraint well-meant and kind,
The Knight being render'd to his charge
But as a prisoner at large.

IX.

" He school'd us in a well-forged tale,
Of scheme the Castle walls to scale,
To which was leagued each Cavalier
That dwells upon the Tyne and Wear;
That Rokeby, his parole forgot,
Had dealt with us to aid the plot.

Such was the charge, which Denzil's zeal
Of hate to Rokeby and O'Neale
Proffer'd as witness, to make good,
Even though the forfeit were their blood.
I scrupled, until o'er and o'er
His prisoner's safety Wycliffe swore;
And then — alas! what needs there more?
I knew I should not live to say
The proffer I refused that day;
Ashamed to live, yet loth to die,
I soil'd me with their infamy!''
" Poor youth," said Bertram, " wavering
          still,
Unfit alike for good or ill!
But what fell next?'' — " Soon as at large
Was scroll'd and sign'd our fatal charge,
There never yet, on tragic stage,
Was seen so well a painted rage
As Oswald's show'd! With loud alarm
He call'd his garrison to arm;
From tower to tower, from post to
          post,
He hurried as if all were lost;
Consign'd to dungeon and to chain
The good old Knight and all his train;
Warn'd each suspected Cavalier,
Within his limits, to appear
To-morrow, at the hour of noon,
In the high church at Egliston.'' —

X.

" Of Egliston! — Even now I pass'd,''
Said Bertram, " as the night closed fast;
Torches and cressets gleam'd around,
I heard the saw and hammer sound,
And I could mark they toil'd to raise
A scaffold, hung with sable baize,
Which the grim headsman's scene dis-
          play'd,
Block, axe, and sawdust ready laid.
Some evil deed will there be done,
Unless Matilda wed his son; —
She loves him not — 'tis shrewdly guess'd
That Redmond rules the damsel's breast.
This is of Oswald's skill;
But I may meet, and foil him still; —
How camest thou to thy freedom?'' —
          " There
Lies mystery more dark and rare.
In midst of Wycliffe's well-feign'd rage,
A scroll was offer'd by a page,
Who told, a muffled horseman late
Had left it at the Castle-gate.

He broke the seal — his cheek show'd
          change,
Sudden, portentous, wild and strange;
The mimic passion of his eye
Was turn'd to actual agony;
His hand like summer sapling shook,
Terror and guilt were in his look.
Denzil he judged, in time of need,
Fit counsellor for evil deed;
And thus apart his counsel broke,
While with a ghastly smile he spoke:

XI.

" ' As in the pageants of the stage,
The dead awake in this wild age,
Mortham—whom all men deem'd decreed
In his own deadly snare to bleed,
Slain by a bravo, whom, o'er sea,
He train'd to aid in murdering me, —
Mortham has 'scaped! The coward shot
The steed, but harm'd the rider not.' ''
Here, with an execration fell,
Bertram leap'd up, and paced the cell:
" Thine own gray head, or bosom dark,"
He utter'd, " may be surer mark! ''
Then sat, and sign'd to Edmund, pale
With terror, to resume his tale.
" Wycliffe went on: — ' Mark with what
          flights
Of wilder'd reverie he writes: —

THE LETTER.

" ' Ruler of Mortham's destiny!
Though dead, thy victim lives to thee.
Once had he all that binds to life,
A lovely child, a lovelier wife;
Wealth, fame, and friendship, were his
          own —
Thou gavest the word, and they are flown!
Mark how he pays thee: — To thy hand
He yields his honors and his land,
One boon premised; — Restore his child,
And, from his native land exiled,
Mortham no more returns to claim
His lands, his honors, or his name;
Refuse him this, and from the slain
Thou shalt see Mortham rise again.' —

XII.

" This billet while the Baron read,
His faltering accents show'd his dread;
He press'd his forehead with his palm,
Then took a scornful tone and calm:

Wild as the winds, as billows wild!
What wot I of his spouse or child?
Hither he brought a joyous dame,
Unknown her lineage or her name:
Her, in some frantic fit, he slew;
The nurse and child in fear withdrew.
Heaven be my witness! wist I where
To find this youth, my kinsman's heir, —
Unguerdon'd I would give with joy
The father's arms to fold his boy,
And Mortham's lands and towers resign
To the just heirs of Mortham's line.' —
Thou know'st that scarcely e'en his fear
Suppresses Denzil's cynic sneer: —
Then happy is thy vassal's part,'
He said, ' to ease his patron's heart!
In thine own jailer's watchful care
Lies Mortham's just and rightful heir;
Thy generous wish is fully won, —
Redmond O'Neale is Mortham's son.' —

XIII.

' Up starting with a frenzied look,
His clenched hand the Baron shook:
Is Hell at work? or dost thou rave,
Or darest thou palter with me, slave?
Perchance thou wot'st not, Barnard's towers
Have racks, of strange and ghastly powers.'
Denzil, who well his safety knew,
Firmly rejoin'd, ' I tell thee true.
Thy racks could give thee but to know
The proofs, which I, untortured, show. —
It chanced upon a winter night,
When early snow made Stanmore white,
That very night, when first of all
Redmond O'Neale saw Rokeby hall,
It was my goodly lot to gain
A reliquary and a chain,
Twisted and chased of massive gold.
— Demand not how the prize I hold!
It was not given, nor lent, nor sold. —
Gilt tablets to the chain were hung,
With letters in the Irish tongue.
I hid my spoil, for there was need
That I should leave the land with speed;
Nor then I deem'd it safe to bear
On mine own person gems so rare.
Small heed I of the tablets took,
But since have spell'd them by the book,
When some sojourn in Erin's land
Of their wild speech had given command.

But darkling was the sense; the phrase
And language those of other days,
Involved of purpose, as to foil
An interloper's prying toil.
The words, but not the sense, I knew,
Till fortune gave the guiding clue.

XIV.

" ' Three days since, was that clue re-
        veal'd
In Thorsgill as I lay conceal'd,
And heard at full when Rokeby's Maid
Her uncle's history display'd;
And now I can interpret well
Each syllable the tablets tell.
Mark, then: Fair Edith was the joy
Of old O'Neale of Clandeboy;
But from her sire and country fled,
In secret Mortham's Lord to wed.
O'Neale, his first resentment o'er,
Despatched his son to Greta's shore,
Enjoining he should make him known
(Until his farther will were shown)
To Edith, but to her alone.
What of their ill-starr'd meeting fell,
Lord Wycliffe knows, and none so well.

XV.

" ' O'Neale it was, who, in despair,
Robb'd Mortham of his infant heir;
He bred him in their nurture wild,
And call'd him murder'd Connel's child.
Soon died the nurse; the Clan believed
What from their Chieftain they received.
His purpose was, that ne'er again
The boy should cross the Irish main;
But, like his mountain sires, enjoy
The woods and wastes of Clandeboy.
Then on the land wild troubles came,
And stronger Chieftains urged a claim,
And wrested from the old man's hands
His native towers, his father's lands.
Unable then, amid the strife,
To guard young Redmond's rights or life,
Late and reluctant he restores
The infant to his native shores,
With goodly gifts and letters stored,
With many a deep conjuring word,
To Mortham and to Rokeby's Lord.
Naught knew the clod of Irish earth,
Who was the guide, of Redmond's birth:
But deem'd his Chief's commands were laid
On both, by both to be obey'd.

How he was wounded by the way,
I need not, and I list not say.' —

XVI.

" ' A wondrous tale ! and, grant it true,
What,' Wycliffe answer'd, ' might I do?
Heaven knows, as willingly as now
I raise the bonnet from my brow,
Would I my kinsman's manors fair
Restore to Mortham, or his heir;
But Mortham is distraught — O'Neale
Has drawn for tyranny his steel,
Malignant to our rightful cause,
And train'd in Rome's delusive laws.
Hark thee apart !'—They whisper'd long,
Till Denzil's voice grew bold and strong;—
' My proofs ! I never will,' he said,
' Show mortal man where they are laid.
Nor hope discovery to foreclose,
By giving me to feed the crows;
For I have mates at large, who know
Where I am wont such toys to stow.
Free me from peril and from band,
These tablets are at thy command:
Nor were it hard to form some train,
To wile old Mortham o'er the main.
Then, lunatic's nor papist's hand
Should wrest from thine the goodly land.'
— ' I like thy wit,' said Wycliffe, ' well;
But here in hostage shalt thou dwell.
Thy son, unless my purpose err,
May prove the trustier messenger.
A scroll to Mortham shall he bear
From me, and fetch these tokens rare.
Gold shalt thou have, and that good store,
And freedom, his commission o'er;
But if his faith should chance to fail,
The gibbet frees thee from the jail.' —

XVII.

" Mesh'd in the net himself had twined,
What subterfuge could Denzil find?
He told me, with reluctant sigh,
That hidden here the tokens lie;
Conjured my swift return and aid,
By all he scoff'd and disobey'd,
And look'd as if the noose were tied,
And I the priest who left his side.
This scroll for Mortham Wycliffe gave,
Whom I must seek by Greta's wave;
Or in the hut where chief he hides,
Where Thorsgill's forester resides.

(Then chanced it wandering in the glade
That he descried our ambuscade.)
I was dismiss'd as evening fell,
And reach'd but now this rocky cell. " —
" Give Oswald's letter." — Bertram
read,
And tore it fiercely shred by shred:—
" All lies and villany ! to blind
His noble kinsman's generous mind,
And train him on from day to day,
Till he can take his life away. —
And now declare thy purpose, youth,
Nor dare to answer, save the truth;
If aught I mark of Denzil's art,
I'll tear the secret from thy heart ! " —

XVIII.

" It needs not.   I renounce," he said,
" My tutor and his deadly trade.
Fix'd was my purpose to declare
To Mortham, Redmond is his heir;
To tell him in what risk he stands,
And yield these tokens to his hands.
Fix'd was my purpose to atone,
Far as I may, the evil done;
And fix'd it rests — if I survive
This night, and leave this cave alive."
" And Denzil? " — " Let them ply the
rack
Even till his joints and sinews crack !
If Oswald tear him limb from limb,
What ruth can Denzil claim from him,
Whose thoughtless youth he led astray,
And damn'd to this unhallow'd way?
He school'd me faith and vows were vain;
Now let my master reap his gain." —
" True," answer'd Bertram, " 'tis his
meed;
There's retribution in the deed.
But thou — thou art not for our course,
Hast fear, hast pity, hast remorse:
And he with us the gale who braves,
Must heave such cargo to the waves,
Or lag with overloaded prore,
While barks unburden'd reach the shore."

XIX.

He paused, and, stretching him at length,
Seem'd to repose his bulky strength.
Communing with his secret mind,
As half he sat, and half reclined,
One ample hand his forehead press'd,
And one was dropp'd across his breast.

he shaggy eyebrows deeper came
bove his eyes of swarthy flame;
is lip of pride a while forbore
he haughty curve till then it wore;
he unalter'd fierceness of his look
shade of darken'd sadness took, —
or dark and sad a presage press'd,
esistlessly on Bertram's breast, —
nd when he spoke, his wonted tone,
ɔ fierce, abrupt, and brief, was gone.
is voice was steady, low, and deep,
ike distant waves, when breezes sleep;
nd sorrow mix'd with Edmund's fear,
s low unbroken depth to hear.

XX.

Edmund, in thy sad tale I find
he woe that warp'd my patron's mind;
'would wake the fountains of the eye
ɪ other men, but mine are dry.
Iortham must never see the fool,
hat sold himself base Wycliffe's tool;
et less from thirst of sordid gain,
han to avenge supposed disdain.
ay, Bertram rues his fault; — a word,
ill now, from Bertram never heard:
ay, too, that Mortham's Lord he
     prays
'o think but on their former days;
ɔn Quariana's beach and rock,
ɔn Cayo's bursting battle-shock,
ɔn Darien's sands and deadly dew,
ɪnd on the dart Tlatzeca threw; —
'erchance my patron yet may hear
Iore that may grace his comrade's bier.
Iy soul hath felt a secret weight,
ɪ warning of approaching fate;
ɪs priest had said, ' Return, repent ! '
ɪs well to bid that rock be rent.
'irm as that flint I face mine end;
Iy heart may burst, but cannot bend.

XXI.

" The dawning of my youth, with awe
ɪnd prophecy, the Dalesmen saw;
'or over Redesdale it came,
ɪs bodeful as their beacon-flame.
Edmund, thy years were scarcely mine,
ʋhen, challenging the Clans of Tyne,
ɪo bring their best my brand to prove,
ɔ'er Hexham's altar hung my glove; 55
ɪut Tynedale, nor in tower nor town,
ɪeld champion meet to take it down.

My noontide, India may declare;
Like her fierce sun, I fired the air !
Like him, to wood and cave bade fly
Her natives, from mine angry eye.
Panama's maids shall long look pale
When Risingham inspires the tale;
Chili's dark matrons long shall tame
The froward child with Bertram's name.
And now, my race of terror run,
Mine be the eve of tropic sun !
No pale gradations quench his ray,
No twilight dews his wrath allay;
With disk like battle-target red,
He rushes to his burning bed,
Dyes the wide wave with bloody light,
Then sinks at once — and all is night. —

XXII.

"Now to thy mission, Edmund. Fly,
Seek Mortham out, and bid him hie
To Richmond, where his troops are laid,
And lead his force to Redmond's aid.
Say, till he reaches Egliston,
A friend will watch to guard his son.
Now, fare-thee-well ! for night draws on,
And I would rest me here alone."
Despite his ill-dissembled fear,
There swam in Edmund's eye a tear;
A tribute to the courage high,
That stoop'd not in extremity,
But strove, irregularly great,
To triumph o'er approaching fate !
Bertram beheld the dewdrop start,
It almost touch'd his iron heart: —
" I did not think there lived," he said,
"One, who would tear for Bertram
     shed."
He loosen'd then his baldric's hold,
A buckle broad of massive gold; —
" Of all the spoil that paid his pains,
But this with Risingham remains;
And this, dear Edmund, thou shalt take,
And wear it long for Bertram's sake.
Once more — to Mortham speed amain;
Farewell ! and turn thee not again."

XXIII.

The night has yielded to the morn,
And far the hours of prime are worn.
Oswald, who, since the dawn of day,
Had cursed his messenger's delay,
Impatient question'd now his train,
" Was Denzil's son return'd again ? "

It chanced there answer'd of the crew,
A menial, whom young Edmund knew:
" No son of Denzil this," — he said;
" A peasant boy from Winston glade,
For song and ministrelsy renown'd,
And knavish pranks, the hamlets round."
" Not Denzil's son! — From   Winston
      vale ! —
Then it was false, that specious tale:
Or, worse — he hath despatch'd the youth
To show to Mortham's Lord its truth.
Fool that I was ! — but 'tis too late : —
This is the very turn of fate ! —
The tale, or true or false, relies
On Denzil's evidence ! — He dies !
Ho ! Provost Marshal ! instantly
Lead Denzil to the gallows-tree !
Allow him not a parting word:
Short be the shrift, and sure the cord !
Then let his gory head appal
Marauders from the Castle-wall.
Lead forth thy guard, that duty done,
With best despatch to Egliston. —
— Basil, tell Wilfrid he must straight
Attend me at the Castle-gate."

XXIV.

" Alas ! " the old domestic said,
And shook his venerable head,
" Alas, my lord ! full ill to-day
May my young master brook the way !
The leech has spoke with grave alarm,
Of unseen hurt, of secret harm,
Of sorrow lurking at the heart,
That mars and lets his healing art." —
" Tush, tell not me ! — Romantic boys
Pine themselves sick for airy toys,
I will find cure for Wilfrid soon;
Bid him for Egliston be boune,
And quick ! — I hear the dull death-drum
Tell Denzil's hour of fate is come."
He paused with scornful smile, and then
Resumed his train of thought agen.
" Now comes my fortune's crisis near !
Entreaty boots not — instant fear,
Naught else, can bend Matilda's pride,
Or win her to be Wilfrid's bride.
But when she sees the scaffold placed,
With axe and block and headsman graced,
And when she deems, that to deny
Dooms Redmond and her sire to die,
She must give way.—Then, were the line
Of Rokeby once combined with mine,

I gain the weather-gage of fate '
If Mortham come, he comes too late,
While I, allied thus and prepared,
Bid him defiance to his beard. —
— If she prove stubborn, shall I dare
To drop the axe ! — Soft ! pause w
      there.
Mortham still lives — yon youth may tel
His tale — and Fairfax loves him well; —
Else, wherefore should I now delay
To sweep this Redmond from my way?
But she to piety perforce
Must yield. — Without there ! Sound t
      horse."

XXV.

'Twas bustle in the court below, —
" Mount, and march forward ! " — Fortl
      they go;
Steeds neigh and trample all around,
Steel rings, spears glimmer, trumpet
      sound. —
Just then was sung his parting hymn;
And Denzil turn'd his eyeballs dim,
And, scarcely conscious what he sees,
Follows the horsemen down the Tees;
And, scarcely conscious what he hears,
The trumpets tingle in his ears.
O'er the long bridge they're sweepin
      now,
The van is hid by greenwood bough;
But ere the rearward had passed o'er,
Guy Denzil heard and saw no more !
One stroke, upon the Castle bell,
To Oswald rung his dying knell.

XXVI.

O, for that pencil, erst profuse
Of chivalry's emblazon'd hues,
That traced of old, in Woodstock bower
The pageant of the Leaf and Flower,
And bodied forth the tourney high,
Held for the hand of Emily !
Then might I paint the tumult broad,
That to the crowded abbey flow'd,
And pour'd, as with an ocean's sound,
Into the church's ample bound !
Then might I show each varying mien,
Exulting, woeful, or serene;
Indifference, with his idiot stare,
And Sympathy, with anxious air;
Paint the dejected Cavalier,
Doubtful, disarm'd, and sad of cheer;

id his proud foe, whose formal eye
aim'd conquest now and mastery;
id the brute crowd, whose envious zeal
uzzas each turn of Fortune's wheel,
id loudest shouts when lowest lie
xalted worth and station high.
et what may such a wish avail?
is mine to tell an onward tale,
urrying, as best I can, along,
ie hearers and the hasty song; —
ke traveller when approaching home,
ho sees the shades of evening come,
nd must not now his course delay,
r choose the fair, but winding way;
ay, scarcely may his pace suspend,
here o'er his head the wildings bend,
o bless the breeze that cools his brow,
r snatch a blossom from the bough.

XXVII.

he reverend pile lay wild and waste,
rofaned, dishonor'd, and defaced.
hrough storied lattices no more
i soften'd light the sunbeams pour,
ilding the Gothic sculpture rich
if shrine, and monument, and niche.
he Civil fury of the time
Iade sport of sacrilegious crime;
'or dark Fanaticism rent
ltar and screen and ornament,
nd peasant hands the tombs o'erthrew
)f Bowes, of Rokeby, and Fitz-Hugh.
.nd now was seen, unwonted sight,
n holy walls a scaffold dight;
Vhere once the priest, of grace divine,
)ealt to his flock the mystic sign,
here stood the block display'd, and there
he headsman grim his hatchet bare;
.nd for the word of Hope and Faith,
Resounded loud a doom of death.
hrice the fierce trumpet's breath was
　　　heard,
.nd echo'd thrice the herald's word,
Dooming, for breach of martial laws,
And treason to the Commons' cause,
The Knight of Rokeby and O'Neale
To stoop their heads to block and steel.
The trumpets flourish'd high and shrill,
Then was a silence dead and still;
And silent prayers to heaven were cast,
And stifled sobs were bursting fast,
Till from the crowd begun to rise
Murmurs of sorrow or surprise,

And from the distant aisles there came
Deep-mutter'd threats, with Wycliffe's
　　　name.

XXVIII.

But Oswald, guarded by his band,
Powerful in evil, waved his hand,
And bade Sedition's voice be dead,
On peril of the murmurer's head.
Then first his glance sought Rokeby's
　　　Knight;
Who gazed on the tremendous sight,
As calm as if he came a guest
To kindred Baron's feudal feast,
As calm as if that trumpet-call
Were summons to the banner'd hall;
Firm in his loyalty he stood,
And prompt to seal it with his blood.
With downcast look drew Oswald nigh,—
He durst not cope with Rokeby's eye!
And said, with low and faltering breath,
"Thou know'st the terms of life and
　　　death."
The Knight then turn'd, and sternly
　　　smiled:—
'The maiden is mine only child,
Yet shall my blessings leave her head,
If with a traitor's son she wed."
Then Redmond spoke:—"The life of one
Might thy malignity atone,
On me be flung a double guilt!
Spare Rokeby's blood, let mine be spilt!"
Wycliffe had listen'd to his suit,
But dread prevail'd, and he was mute.

XXIX.

And now he pours his choice of fear
In secret on Matilda's ear;
"An union form'd with me and mine,
Ensures the faith of Rokeby's line.
Consent, and all this dread array,
Like morning dream shall pass away;
Refuse, and, by my duty press'd,
I give the word — thou know'st the rest."
Matilda, still and motionless,
With terror heard the dread address,
Pale as the sheeted maid who dies
To hopeless love a sacrifice;
Then wrung her hands in agony,
And round her cast bewilder'd eye.
Now on the scaffold glanced, and now
On Wycliffe's unrelenting brow.
She veil'd her face, and, with a voice
Scarce audible: — "I make my choice!

Spare but their lives!—for, aught beside,
Let Wilfrid's doom my fate decide.
He once was generous!" — as she spoke,
Dark Wycliffe's joy in triumph broke: —
"Wilfrid, where loiter'd ye so late?
Why upon Basil rest thy weight? —
Art spell-bound by enchanter's wand? —
Kneel, kneel, and take her yielded hand;
Thank her with raptures, simple boy!
Should tears and trembling speak thy
        joy?" —
" O hush, my sire!   To prayer and tear
Of mine thou hast refused thine ear;
But now the awful hour draws on,
When truth must speak in loftier tone."

XXX.

He took Matilda's hand:—" Dear maid,
Couldst thou so injure me," he said,
" Of thy poor friend so basely deem,
As blend with him this barbarous scheme?
Alas! my efforts, made in vain,
Might well have saved this added pain.
But now, bear witness earth and heaven,
That ne'er was hope to mortal given,
So twisted with the strings of life,
As this — to call Matilda wife!
I bid it now for ever part,
And with the effort bursts my heart!"
His feeble frame was worn so low,
With wounds, with watching, and with
        woe,
That nature could no more sustain
The agony of mental pain.
He kneel'd — his lip her hand had
        press'd, —
Just then he felt the stern arrest.
Lower and lower sunk his head. —
They raised him, — but the life was fled!
Then, first alarm'd, his sire and train
Tried every aid, but tried in vain.
The soul, too soft its ills to bear,
Had left our mortal hemisphere,
And sought in better world the meed,
To blameless life by Heaven decreed.

XXXI.

The wretched sire beheld, aghast,
With Wilfrid all his projects past,
All turn'd and centred on his son,
On Wilfrid all — and he was gone.
" And I am childless now," he said,
" Childless, through that relentless maid!

A lifetime's arts, in vain essay'd,
Are bursting on their artist's head!
Here lies my Wilfrid dead — and there
Comes hated Mortham for his heir,
Eager to knit in happy band
With Rokeby's heiress Redmond's hand
And shall their triumph soar o'er all
The schemes deep-laid to work their
        fall?
No! — deeds, which prudence might no
        dare,
Appal not vengeance and despair.
The murderess weeps upon his bier —
I'll change to real that feigned tear!
They all shall share destruction's shock;—
Ho! lead the captives to the block!"
But ill his Provost could divine
His feelings, and forbore the sign.
" Slave! to the block! — or I, or they,
Shall face the judgment-seat this day!"

XXXII.

The outmost crowd have heard a sound
Like horse's hoof on harden'd ground:
Nearer it came, and yet more near, —
The very death's-men paused to hear.
'Tis in the church-yard now — the tread
Hath waked the dwelling of the dead!
Fresh sod, and old sepulchral stone,
Return the tramp in varied tone.
All eyes upon the gateway hung,
When through the Gothic arch there
        sprung
A horseman arm'd, at headlong speed —
Sable his cloak, his plume, his steed.[56]
Fire from the flinty floor was spurn'd,
The vaults unwonted clang return'd! —
One instant's glance around he threw,
From saddlebow his pistol drew.
Grimly determined was his look!
His charger with the spurs he strook —
All scatter'd backward as he came,
For all knew Bertram Risingham!
Three bounds that noble courser gave;
The first has reach'd the central nave,
The second clear'd the chancel wide,
The third — he was at Wycliffe's side.
Full levell'd at the Baron's head,
Rung the report — the bullet sped —
And to his long account, and last,
Without a groan dark Oswald past!
All was so quick that it might seem
A flash of lightning or a dream.

XXXIII.

While yet the smoke the deed conceals,
Bertram his ready charger wheels;
But flounder'd on the pavement floor
The steed, and down the rider bore,
And, bursting in the headlong sway,
The faithless saddle-girths gave way.
'Twas while he toil'd him to be freed,
And with the rein to raise the steed,
That from amazement's iron trance
All Wycliffe's soldiers waked at once.
Sword, halbert, musket-butt, their blows
Hail'd upon Bertram as he rose;
A score of pikes, with each a wound,
Bore down and pinn'd him to the ground;
But still his struggling force he rears,
Gainst hacking brands and stabbing spears;
Thrice from assailants shook him free,
Once gain'd his feet, and twice his knee.
By tenfold odds oppress'd at length,
Despite his struggles and his strength,
He took a hundred mortal wounds,
As mute as fox 'mongst mangling hounds;
And when he died, his parting groan
Had more of laughter than of moan!
— They gazed, as when a lion dies,
And hunters scarcely trust their eyes,
But bend their weapons on the slain,
Lest the grim king should rouse again!
Then blow and insult some renew'd,
And from the trunk, the head had hew'd,
But Basil's voice the deed forbade;
A mantle o'er the corse he laid: —
"Fell as he was in act and mind,
He left no bolder heart behind:
Then give him, for a soldier meet,
A soldier's cloak for winding-sheet."

XXXIV.

No more of death and dying pang,
No more of trump and bugle clang,
Tho' thro' the sounding woods there come
Banner and bugle, trump and drum.
Arm'd with such powers as well had freed
Young Redmond at his utmost need,
And back'd with such a band of horse,
As might less ample powers enforce;
Possess'd of every proof and sign
That gave an heir to Mortham's line,
And yielded to a father's arms
An image of his Edith's charms, —
Mortham is come, to hear and see
Of this strange morn the history.
What saw he? — not the church's floor,
Cumber'd with dead and stain'd with gore;
What heard he? — not the clamorous crowd,
That shout their gratulations loud:
Redmond he saw and heard alone,
Clasp'd him, and sobb'd, "My son! my son!" —

XXXV.

This chanced upon a summer morn,
When yellow waved the heavy corn:
But when brown August o'er the land
Call'd forth the reaper's busy band,
A gladsome sight the sylvan road
From Egliston to Mortham show'd.
A while the hardy rustic leaves
The task to bind and pile the sheaves,
And maids their sickles fling aside,
To gaze on bridegroom and on bride,
And childhood's wondering group draws near,
And from the gleaner's hands the ear
Drops, while she folds them for a prayer
And blessing on the lovely pair.
'Twas then the Maid of Rokeby gave
Her plighted troth to Redmond brave;
And Teesdale can remember yet
How Fate to Virtue paid her debt,
And, for their troubles, bade them prove
A lengthen'd life of peace and love.

Time and Tide had thus their sway,
Yielding, like an April day,
Smiling noon for sullen morrow,
Years of joy for hours of sorrow!

THE

BRIDAL OF TRIERMAIN:

OR,

THE VALE OF ST. JOHN.

A LOVER'S TALE.

PREFACE TO FIRST EDITION.

IN the *Edinburgh Annual Register* for the year 1809, Three Fragments were inserted, written in imitation of Living Poets. It must have been apparent, that by these prolusions nothing burlesque, or disrespectful to the authors, was intended, but that they were offered to the public as serious, though certainly very imperfect, imitations of that style of composition, by which each of the writers is supposed to be distinguished. As these exercises attracted a greater degree of attention than the author anticipated, he has been induced to complete one of them, and present it as a separate publication.

It is not in this place that an examination of the works of the master * whom he has here adopted as his model, can, with propriety, be introduced; since his general acquiescence in the favorable suffrage of the public must necessarily be inferred from the attempt he has now made. He is induced, by the nature of his subject, to offer a few remarks on what has been called ROMANTIC POETRY; the popularity of which has been revived in the present day, under the auspices, and by the unparalleled success, of one individual.

The original purpose of poetry is either religious or historical, or, as must frequently happen, a mixture of both. To modern readers, the poems of Homer have many of the features of pure romance; but in the estimation of his contemporaries, they probably derived their chief value from their supposed historical authenticity. The same may be generally said of the poetry of all early ages. The marvels and miracles which the poet blends with his song, do not exceed in number or extravagance the figments of the historians of the same period of society; and, indeed, the difference betwixt poetry and prose, as the vehicles of historical truth, is always of late introduction. Poets, under various denominations of Bards, Scalds, Chroniclers, and so forth, are the first historians of all nations. Their intention is to relate the events they have witnessed, or the traditions that have reached them; and they clothe the relation in rhyme, merely as the means of rendering it more solemn in the narrative or more easily committed to memory. But as the poetical historian improves in the art of conveying information, the authenticity of his narrative unavoidably declines. He is tempted to dilate and dwell upon the events that are interesting to his imagination, and, conscious how indifferent his audience is to the naked truth of his poem, his history gradually becomes a romance.

It is in this situation that those epics are found, which have been generally regarded the standards of poetry; and it has happened somewhat strangely, that the moderns have pointed out as the characteristics and peculiar excellencies of narrative poetry, the very circumstances which the authors themselves adopted, only because their art involved the

---

* Scott himself. The poem was published anonymously, the author being desirous to entrap Jeffrey and his other critics. It was for some time supposed to be the work of William Erskine, Lord Kinnedder.

duties of the historian as well as the poet. It cannot be believed, for example, that Homer selected the siege of Troy as the most appropriate subject for poetry; his purpose was to write the early history of his country; the event he has chosen, though not very fruitful in varied incident, nor perfectly well adapted for poetry, was nevertheless combined with traditionary and genealogical anecdotes extremely interesting to those who were to listen to him; and this he has adorned by the exertions of a genius, which, if it has been equalled, has certainly been never surpassed. It was not till comparatively a late period that the general accuracy of his narrative, or his purpose in composing it, was brought into question. Δοκεῖ πρῶτος [ὁ Ἀναξαγόρας] (καθ' ἅ φησι Φαβορῖνος ἐν παντοδαπῇ Ἱστορίᾳ) τὴν Ὁμήρου ποίησιν ἀποφήνασθαι εἶναι περὶ ἀρετῆς καὶ δικαιοσύνης.* But whatever theories might be framed by speculative men, his work was of an historical, not of an allegorical nature. Ἐναντίλλετο μετὰ τοῦ Μέντεω καὶ ὅπου ἑκάστοτε ἀφίκοιτο, πάντα τὰ ἐπιχώρια διερωτᾶτο καὶ ἱστορέων ἐπυνθάνετο· εἰκὸς δέ μιν ἦν καὶ μνημόσυνα πάντων γράφεσθαι.† Instead of recommending the choice of a subject similar to that of Homer, it was to be expected that critics should have exhorted the poets of these latter days to adopt or invent a narrative in itself more susceptible of poetical ornament, and to avail themselves of that advantage in order to compensate, in some degree, the inferiority of genius. The contrary course has been inculcated by almost all the writers upon the *Epopœia;* with what success, the fate of Homer's numerous imitators may best show. The *ultimum supplicium* of criticism was inflicted on the author if he did not choose a subject which at once deprived him of all claim to originality, and placed him, if not in actual contest, at least in fatal comparison, with those giants in the land whom it was most his interest to avoid. The celebrated receipt for writing an epic poem, which appeared in *The Guardian,‡* was the first instance in which common sense was applied to this department of poetry; and, indeed, if the question be considered on its own merits, we must be satisfied that narrative poetry, if strictly confined to the great occurrences of history, would be deprived of the individual interest which it is so well calculated to excite.

Modern poets may therefore be pardoned in seeking simpler subjects of verse, more interesting in proportion to their simplicity. Two or three figures, well grouped, suit the artist better than a crowd, for whatever purpose assembled. For the same reason, a scene immediately presented to the imagination, and directly brought home to the feelings, though involving the fate of but one or two persons, is more favorable for poetry than the political struggles and convulsions which influence the fate of kingdoms. The former are within the reach and comprehension of all, and, if depicted with vigor, seldom fail to fix attention: The other, if more sublime, are more vague and distant, less capable of being distinctly understood, and infinitely less capable of exciting those sentiments which it is the very purpose of poetry to inspire. To generalize is always to destroy effect. We would, for example, be more interested in the fate of an individual soldier in combat, than in the grand event of a general action; with the happiness of two lovers raised from misery and anxiety to peace and union, than with the successful exertions of a whole nation. From what causes this may originate, is a separate and obviously an immaterial consideration. Before ascribing this peculiarity to causes decidedly and odiously selfish, it is proper to recollect, that while men see only a limited space, and while their affections and conduct are regulated, not by aspiring to a universal good, but by exerting their power of making themselves and others happy within the limited scale allotted to each individual, so long will individual history and individual virtue be the readier and more accessible road to general interest and attention; and, perhaps, we may add, that it is the more useful, as well as the more accessible, inasmuch as it affords an example capable of being easily imitated.

According to the author's idea of Romantic Poetry, as distinguished from Epic, the former comprehends a fictitious narrative, framed and combined at the pleasure of the writer; beginning and ending as he may judge best; which neither exacts nor refuses the use of supernatural machinery; which is free from the technical rules of the *Epée;* and is subject only to those which good sense, good taste, and good morals apply to every species of poetry without exception. The date may be in a remote age, or in the present; the story may detail the adventures of a prince or of a peasant. In a word, the author is absolute master of his country and its inhabitants, and everything is permitted to him,

---

* Diogenes Laertius: *lib. ii., Anax. Segm.* 11.

† *Homeri Vita*, in Herod, Henr. Steph. 1670, p. 356.

‡ Written by Alexander Pope.

excepting to be heavy or prosaic, from which, free and unembarrassed as he is, he has a manner of apology. Those, it is probable, will be found the peculiarities of this species of composition; and before joining the outcry against the vitiated taste that fosters and encourages it, the justice and grounds of it ought to be made perfectly apparent. If the want of sieges, and battles, and great military evolutions, in our poetry, is complained of, let us reflect, that the campaigns and heroes of our days are perpetuated in a record that neither requires nor admits of the aid of fiction; and if the complaint refers to the inferiority of our bards, let us pay a just tribute to their modesty, limiting them, as it does, to subjects which, however indifferently treated, have still the interest and charm of novelty, and which thus prevents them from adding insipidity to their other more insuperable defects.

THE BRIDAL OF TRIERMAIN.

INTRODUCTION.

I.

Come, Lucy! while 'tis morning hour,
  The woodland brook we needs must
      pass;
So, ere the sun assume his power,
We shelter in our poplar bower,
Where the dew lies long upon the flower,
  Though vanish'd from the velvet grass.
Curbing the stream, the stony ridge
May serve us for a sylvan bridge;
For here compell'd to disunite,
    Round petty isles the runnels glide,
And chafing off their puny spite,
The shallow murmurs waste their might,
  Yielding to footstep free and light
    A dry-shod pass from side to side.

II.

Say, why this hesitating pause?
And, Lucy, as thy step withdraws,
Why sidelong eye the streamlet's brim?
  Titania's foot without a slip,
Like thine, though timid, light, and slim,
  From stone to stone might safely trip,
  Nor risk the glow-worm clasp to dip
That binds her slipper's silken rim.
Or trust thy lover's strength: nor fear
That this same stalwart arm of mine,
Which could yon oak's prone trunk up-
      rear,
Shall shrink beneath the burden dear
  Of form so slender, light, and fine —
So, — now, the danger dared at last,
Look back, and smile at perils past!

III.

And now we reach the favorite glade,
  Paled in by copsewood, cliff, and stone,
Where never harsher sounds invade,
To break affection's whispering tone,
Than the deep breeze that waves the
      shade,
    Than the small brooklet's feeble
      moan.
Come! rest thee on thy wonted seat;
  Moss'd is the stone, the turf is green,
A place where lovers best may meet,
  Who would not that their love be
      seen.
The boughs, that dim the summer sky,
Shall hide us from each lurking spy,
    That fain would spread the invidious
      tale!
How Lucy of the lofty eye,
Noble in birth, in fortunes high,
She for whom lords and barons sigh,
  Meets her poor Arthur in the dale.

IV.

How deep that blush! — how deep that
      sigh!
And why does Lucy shun mine eye?
Is it because that crimson draws
Its color from some secret cause,
Some hidden movement of the breast
She would not that her Arthur guess'd?
O! quicker far is lover's ken
Than the dull glance of common men,
And, by strange sympathy, can spell
The thoughts the loved one will not
      tell?
And mine, in Lucy's blush, saw met
The hues of pleasure and regret;
    Pride mingled in the sigh her voice,
      And shared with Love the crimson
      glow;

Well pleased that thou art Arthur's
    choice,
  Yet shamed thine own is placed so
    low:
Thou turn'st thy self-confessing cheek,
    As if to meet the breeze's cooling;
Then, Lucy, hear thy tutor speak,
  For Love, too, has his hours of
    schooling.

v.

Too oft the anxious eye has spied
That secret grief thou fain wouldst hide,
The passing pang of humbled pride;
  Too oft, when through the splendid
    hall,
  The load-star of each heart and eye,
  My fair one leads the glittering ball,
Will her stol'n glance on Arthur fall
  With such a blush and such a sigh!
Thou would'st not yield, for wealth or
    rank,
  The heart thy worth and beauty won,
Nor leave me on this mossy bank,
  To meet a rival on a throne:
Why, then, should vain repinings rise,
That to thy lover fate denies
A nobler name, a wide domain,
A Baron's birth, a menial train,
Since Heaven assign'd him, for his
    part,
A lyre, a falchion, and a heart?

vi.

My sword — its master must be dumb;
  But, when a soldier names my name,
Approach, my Lucy! fearless come,
  Nor dread to hear of Arthur's shame.
My heart — mid all yon courtly crew,
  Of lordly rank and lofty line,
Is there to love and honor true,
  That boasts a pulse so warm as mine?
They praised thy diamonds' lustre rare —
  Match'd with thine eyes, I thought it
    faded;
They praised the pearls that bound thy
    hair —
  I only saw the locks they braided;
They talk of wealthy dower and land,
  And titles of high birth the token —
I thought of Lucy's heart and hand,
  Nor knew the sense of what was
    spoken.

And yet, if rank'd in Fortune's roll,
  I might have learn'd their choice u
    wise,
Who rate the dower above the soul,
  And Lucy's diamonds o'er her eyes.

vii.

My lyre — it is an idle toy,
  That borrows accents not its own,
Like warbler of Columbian sky,
  That sings but in a mimic tone.*
Ne'er did it sound o'er sainted well,
Nor boasts it aught of Border Spell;
  Its strings no feudal slogan pour,
  Its heroes draw no broad claymore;
  No shouting clans applauses raise,
  Because it sung their father's praise;
  On Scottish moor, or English down,
  It ne'er was graced by fair renown;
  Nor won, — best meed to minst
    true, —
  One favoring smile from fair Bu
    CLEUCH!
By one poor streamlet sounds its tor
And heard by one dear maid alone.

viii.

But, if thou bid'st, these tones sh
    tell
Of errant knight, and damozelle;
Of the dread knot a Wizard tied,
In punishment of maiden's pride,
In notes of marvel and of fear,
That best may charm romantic ear.
For Lucy loves, — like COLLINS, i
  star'd name!
Whose lay's requital was that tardy fam
Who bound no laurel round his livi
  head,
Should hang it o'er his monument wh
  dead, —
For Lucy loves to tread enchanted stran
And thread, like him, the maze of Fair
  land;
Of golden battlements, to view t
  gleam,
And slumber soft by some Elysian strean
Such lays she loves, — and such r
  Lucy's choice,
What other song can claim her Poe
  voice?

---

* The Mocking Bird.

CANTO FIRST.

I.

ﾍERE is the Maiden of mortal strain,
 at may match with the Baron of Triermain? [1]
: must be lovely, and constant, and
   kind,
ly and pure, and humble of mind,
:he of cheer, and gentle of mood,
 ﾚteous, and generous, and noble of
   blood —
vely as the sun's first ray,
ﾑen it breaks the clouds of an April
   day;
 ﾑstant and true as the widow'd dove,
 ﾑd as a minstrel that sings of love;
'e as the fountain in rocky cave,
ﾍere never sunbeam kiss'd the wave;
ﾑmble as maiden that loves in vain,
>ly as hermit's vesper strain;
ﾑtle as breeze that but whispers and
   dies,
 t blithe as the light leaves that dance
   in its sighs;
 ﾚteous as monarch the morn he is
   crown'd,
ﾑerous as spring-dews that bless the
   glad ground;
ﾑle her blood as the currents that met
 the veins of the noblest Plantagenet —
 ﾑh must her form be, her mood, and
   her strain,
 ﾑt shall match with Sir Roland of
   Triermain.

II.

 Roland de Vaux he hath laid him to
   sleep,
 s blood it was fever'd, his breathing
   was deep,
 had been pricking against the Scot,
 e foray was long, and the skirmish hot;
 s dinted helm and his buckler's plight
 ﾚe token of a stubborn fight.
   All in the castle must hold them still,
 ﾚpers must lull him to his rest,
 th the slow soft tunes he loves the best,
 l sleep sink down upon his breast,
   Like the dew on a summer hill.

III.

 was the dawn of an autumn day;
 ﾚe sun was struggling with frost-fog gray,

That like a silvery cape was spread
Round Skiddaw's dim and distant head,
And faintly gleam'd each painted pane
Of the lordly halls of Triermain,
   When that Baron bold awoke.
Starting he woke, and loudly did call,
Rousing his menials in bower and
   hall,
   While hastily he spoke: —

IV.

" Hearken, my minstrels!   Which of ye
   all
Touch'd his harp with that dying fall,
   So sweet, so soft, so faint,
It seem'd an angel's whisper'd call
   To an expiring saint?
And hearken, my merry-men!   What
   time or where
   Did she pass, that maid with her
   heavenly brow,
With her look so sweet and her eyes so
   fair,
And her graceful step and her angel air,
And the eagle plume in her dark-brown
   hair,
   That pass'd from my bower e'en
   now?"

V.

Answer'd him Richard de Bretville; he
Was chief of the Baron's minstrelsy, —
" Silent, noble chieftain, we
   Have sat since midnight close,
When such lulling sounds as the brooklet
   sings,
Murmur'd from our melting strings,
   And hush'd you to repose.
   Had a harp-note sounded here,
   It had caught my watchful ear,
Although it fell as faint and shy
As bashful maiden's half-form'd sigh,
   When she thinks her lover near." —
Answer'd Philip of Fasthwaite tall,
He kept guard in the outer-hall: —
" Since at eve our watch took post,
Not a foot has thy portal cross'd;
   Else had I heard the steps, though
   low
And light they fell, as when earth re-
   ceives,
In morn of frost, the wither'd leaves,
   That drop when no winds blow." —

VI.

" Then come thou hither, Henry my page,
Whom I saved from the sack of Hermit-
    age,
When that dark castle, tower, and spire,
Rose to the skies a pile of fire,
    And redden'd all the Nine-stane
      Hill,
And the shrieks of death, that wildly
    broke
Through devouring flame and smother-
    ing smoke,
    Made the warrior's heart-blood chill.
The trustiest thou of all my train,
My fleetest courser thou must rein,
    And ride to Lyulph's tower,
And from the Baron of Triermain
    Greet well that sage of power.
He is sprung from Druid sires,
And British bards that tuned their lyres
To Arthur's and Pendragon's praise,
And his who sleeps at Dunmailraise. *
Gifted like his gifted race,
He the characters can trace,
Graven deep in elder time
Upon Helvellyn's cliffs sublime;
Sign and sigil well doth he know,
And can bode of weal and woe,
Of kingdoms' fall and fate of wars,
From mystic dreams and course of stars.
He shall tell if middle earth
To that enchanting shape gave birth,
Or if 'twas but an airy thing,
Such as fantastic slumbers bring,
Framed from the rainbow's varying dyes,
Or fading tints of western skies.
For, by the blessed Rood I swear,
If that fair form breathe vital air,
No other maiden by my side
Shall ever rest De Vaux's bride ! "

VII.

The faithful Page he mounts his steed,
And soon he cross'd green Irthing's
    mead,
Dash'd o'er Kirkoswald's verdant plain,
And Eden barr'd his course in vain.
He pass'd red Penrith's Table Round,[2]
For feats of chivalry renown'd,

* Dunmailraise is one of the grand passes
from Cumberland into Westmoreland. There is
a cairn on it said to be the monument of Dunmail, the last King of Cumberland.

Left Mayburgh's mound [3] and stones
    power,
By Druids raised in magic hour,
And traced the Eamont's winding wa
Till Ulfo's † lake beneath him lay.

VII.

Onward he rode, the pathway still
Winding betwixt the lake and hill;
Till, on the fragment of a rock,
Struck from its base by lightning shoc
    He saw the hoary Sage:
The silver moss and lichen twined,
With fern and deer-hair check'd and lin
    A cushion fit for age;
And o'er him shook the aspen-tree,
A restless, rustling canopy.
Then sprung young Henry from his se
    And greeted Lyulph grave,
And then his master's tale did tell,
    And then for counsel crave.
The Man of Years mused long and de
Of time's lost treasures taking keep,
And then, as rousing from a sleep,
    His solemn answer gave:—

IX.

" That maid is born of middle earth,
    And may of man be won,
Though there have glided since her bi
    Five hundred years and one.
But where's the Knight in all the nor
That dare the adventure follow forth,
So perilous to knightly worth,
    In the valley of St. John?
Listen, youth, to what I tell,
And bind it on thy memory well;
Nor muse that I commence the rhyme
Far distant mid the wrecks of time.
The mystic tale, by bard and sage,
Is handed down from Merlin's age.

X.

LYULPH'S TALE.

" KING ARTHUR has ridden from me
    Carlisle
    When Pentecost was o'er:
He journey'd like errant-knight the wh
And sweetly the summer sun did smil
    On mountain, moss, and moor.

† Ulswater.

ove his solitary track
se Glaramara's ridgy back,
nid whose yawning gulfs the sun
st umber'd radiance red and dun,
ough never sunbeam could discern
e surface of that sable tarn,[4]
whose black mirror you may spy
e stars, while noontide lights the sky.
e gallant King he skirted still
e margin of that mighty hill;
ck upon rocks incumbent hung,
d torrents, down the gullies flung,
n'd the rude river that brawl'd on,
coiling now from crag and stone,
w diving deep from human ken,
d raving down its darksome glen.
e Monarch judged this desert wild,
th such romantic ruin piled,
as theatre by Nature's hand
r feat of high achievement plann'd.

XI.

O rather he chose, that Monarch bold,
  On vent'rous quest to ride,
plate and mail, by wood and wold,
an, with ermine trapp'd and cloth of
    gold,
  In princely bower to bide;
e bursting crash of a foeman's spear
  As it shiver'd against his mail,
as merrier music to his ear
  Than courtier's whisper'd tale;
d the clash of Caliburn* more dear,
  When on the hostile casque it rung,
    Than all the lays
    To their monarch's praise
  That the harpers of Reged sung.
e loved better to rest by wood or river,
an in bower of his bride, Dame
    Guenever,
r he left that lady, so lovely of cheer,
follow adventures of danger and fear;
d the frank-hearted Monarch full little
    did wot,
at she smiled, in his absence, on brave
    Lancelot.

XII.

He rode, till over down and dell
e shade more broad and deeper fell;

* King Arthur's sword, called by Tennyson
calibur.

And though around the mountain's head
Flow'd streams of purple, and gold,
  and red,
Dark at the base, unblest by beam,
Frown'd the black rocks, and roar'd the
  stream.
With toil the King his way pursued
By lonely Threlkeld's waste and wood,
Till on his course obliquely shone
The narrow valley of SAINT JOHN,
Down sloping to the western sky,
Where lingering sunbeams love to lie.
Right glad to feel those beams again,
The King drew up his charger's rein;
With gauntlet raised he screen'd his sight,
As dazzled with the level light,
And, from beneath his glove of mail,
Scann'd at his ease the lovely vale,
While 'gainst the sun his armor bright
Gleam'd ruddy like the beacon's light.

XIII.

"Paled in by many a lofty hill,
The narrow dale lay smooth and still,
And, down its verdant bosom led,
A winding brooklet found its bed.
But, midmost of the vale, a mound
Arose with airy turrets crown'd,
Buttress, and rampire's circling bound,
  And mighty keep and tower;
Seem'd some primeval giant's hand
The castle's massive walls had plann'd,
A ponderous bulwark to withstand
  Ambitious Nimrod's power.
Above the moated entrance slung,
The balanced drawbridge trembling hung,
  As jealous of a foe;
Wicket of oak, as iron hard,
Wfth iron studded, clench'd and barr'd,
And prong'd portcullis, join'd to guard
  The gloomy pass below.
But the gray walls no banners crown'd,
Upon the watch-tower's airy round
No warder stood his horn to sound,
No guard beside the bridge was found,
And where the Gothic gateway frown'd,
  Glanced neither bill nor bow.

XIV.

"Beneath the castle's gloomy pride
In ample round did Arthur ride
Three times; nor living thing he spied,
  Nor heard a living sound,

Save that, awakening from her dream,
The owlet now began to scream,
In concert with the rushing stream,
     That wash'd the battled mound.
He lighted from his goodly steed,
And he left him to graze on bank and mead;
And slowly he climb'd the narrow way,
That reach'd the entrance grim and gray,
And he stood the outward arch below,
And his bugle-horn prepared to blow,
     In summons blithe and bold,
Deeming to rouse from iron sleep
The guardian of this dismal Keep,
     Which well he guess'd the hold
Of wizard stern, or goblin grim,
Or pagan of gigantic limb,
     The tyrant of the wold.

XV.

" The ivory bugle's golden tip
Twice touch'd the monarch's manly lip,
     And twice his hand withdrew.
— Think not but Arthur's heart was good !
His shield was cross'd by the blessed rood,
Had a pagan host before him stood,
     He had charged them through and
         through;
Yet the silence of that ancient place
Sunk on his heart, and he paused a space
     Ere yet his horn he blew.
But, instant as its 'larum rung,
The castle gate was open flung,
Portcullis rose with crashing groan
Full harshly up its groove of stone;
The balance-beams obey'd the blast,
And down the trembling drawbridge cast;
The vaulted arch before him lay,
With naught to bar the gloomy way,
And onward Arthur paced, with hand
On Caliburn's resistless brand.

XVI.

" A hundred torches, flashing bright,
Dispell'd at once the gloomy night
     That lour'd along the walls,
And show'd the King's astonish'd sight
     The inmates of the halls.
Nor wizard stern, nor goblin grim,
Nor giant huge of form and limb,
     Nor heathen knight, was there:
But the cressets, which odors flung aloft,
Show'd by their yellow light and soft,
     A band of damsels fair.

Onward they came, like summer wav
     That dances to the shore;
A hundred voices welcome gave,
     And welcome o'er and o'er !
A hundred lovely hands assail
The bucklers of the monarch's mail,
And busy labor'd to unhasp
Rivet of steel and iron clasp.
One wrapp'd him in a mantle fair,
And one flung odors on his hair;
His short curl'd ringlets one smoot
     down,
One wreathed them with a myrtle cro
A bride upon her wedding-day,
Was tended ne'er by troop so gay.

XVII.

" Loud laugh'd they all, — the King
     vain,
With questions task'd the giddy train
Let him entreat, or crave, or call,
'Twas one reply — loud laugh'd they
Then o'er him mimic chains they flin
Framed of the fairest flowers of sprir
While some their gentle force unite,
Onward to drag the wondering knigh
Some, bolder, urge his pace with blo
Dealt with the lily or the rose.
Behind him were in triumph borne
The warlike arms he late had worn.
Four of the train combined to rear
The terrors of Tintadgel's spear;[5]
Two, laughing at their lack of strengt
Dragg'd Caliburn in cumbrous length
One, while she aped a martial stride,
Placed on her brows the helmet's pric
Then scream'd, 'twixt laughter and s
     prise,
To feel its depth o'erwhelm her eyes.
With revel-shout, and triumph-song,
Thus gayly march'd the giddy throng.

XVIII.

" Through many a gallery and hall
They led, I ween, their royal thrall;
At length, beneath a fair arcade
Their march and song at once they sta
The eldest maiden of the band,
     (The lovely maid was scarce ei
     teen,)
Raised, with imposing air her hand,
And reverent silence did command,
     On entrance of their Queen,

And they were mute. — But as a glance
They steal on Arthur's countenance,
　Bewilder'd with surprise,
Their smother'd mirth again 'gan speak,
In archly dimpled chin and cheek,
　And laughter-lighted eyes.

XIX.

" The attributes of those high days
Now only live in minstrel-lays;
For Nature, now exhausted, still
Was then profuse of good and ill.
Strength was gigantic, valor high,
And wisdom soar'd beyond the sky,
And beauty had such matchless beam
As lights not now a lover's dream.
Yet e'en in that romantic age,
　Ne'er were such charms by mortal
　　seen,
As Arthur's dazzled eyes engage,
When forth on that enchanted stage,
With glittering train of maid and page,
　Advanced the castle's Queen !
While up the hall she slowly pass'd,
Her dark eye on the King she cast,
　That flash'd expression strong;
The longer dwelt that lingering look,
Her cheek the livelier color took,
And scarce the shame-faced King could
　brook
　　The gaze that lasted long.
A sage, who had that look espied,
Where kindling passion strove with pride,
　Had whispered, ' Prince, beware !
From the chafed tiger rend the prey,
Rush on the lion when at bay,
Bar the fell dragon's blighted way,
　But shun that lovely snare ! ' —

XX.

At once that inward strife suppress'd,
The dame approach'd her warlike guest,
With greeting in that fair degree,
Where female pride and courtesy
Are blended with such passing art
As awes at once and charms the heart.
A courtly welcome first she gave,
Then of his goodness 'gan to crave
　Construction fair and true
Of her light maidens' idle mirth,
Who drew from lonely glens their birth,
For knew to pay to stranger worth
　And dignity their due;

And then she pray'd that he would rest
That night her castle's honor'd guest.
The Monarch meekly thanks express'd;
The banquet rose at her behest,
With lay and tale, and laugh and jest,
　Apace the evening flew.

XXI.

" The lady sate the Monarch by,
Now in her turn abash'd and shy,
And with indifference seem'd to hear
The toys he whisper'd in her ear.
Her bearing modest was and fair,
Yet shadows of constraint were there,
That show'd an over-cautious care
　Some inward thought to hide;
Oft did she pause in full reply,
And oft cast down her large dark eye,
Oft check'd the soft voluptuous sigh,
　That heaved her bosom's pride.
Slight symptoms these, but shepherds
　know
How hot the mid-day sun shall glow,
　From the mist of morning sky;
And so the wily Monarch guess'd,
That this assumed restraint express'd
More ardent passions in the breast,
　Than ventured to the eye.
Closer he press'd, while beakers rang,
While maidens laugh'd and minstrels sang
　Still closer to her ear —
But why pursue the common tale?
Or wherefore show how knights prevail
　When ladies dare to hear?
Or wherefore trace from what slight cause
Its source one tyrant passion draws,
　Till, mastering all within,
Where lives the men that has not tried,
How mirth can into folly glide,
　And folly into sin ?"

CANTO SECOND.

I.

LYULPH'S TALE, CONTINUED.

" ANOTHER day, another day,
And yet another glides away !
The Saxon stern, the pagan Dane,
Maraud on Britain's shores again.
Arthur, of Christendom the flower,
Lies loitering in a lady's bower;

The horn, that foemen wont to fear,
Sounds but to wake the Cumbrian deer,
And Caliburn, the British pride,
Hangs useless by a lover's side.

II.

"Another day, another day,
And yet another glides away!
Heroic plans in pleasure drown'd,
He thinks not of the Table Round;
In lawless love dissolved his life,
He thinks not of his beauteous wife:
Better he loves to snatch a flower
From bosom of his paramour,
Than from a Saxon knight to wrest
The honors of his heathen crest!
Better to wreathe, mid tresses brown,
The heron's plume her hawk struck down,
Than o'er the altar give to flow
The banners of a Paynim foe.
Thus, week by week, and day by day,
His life inglorious glides away:
But she, that soothes his dream, with fear
Beholds his hour of waking near!

III.

"Much force have mortal charms to stay
Our peace in Virtue's toilsome way;
But Guendolen's might far outshine
Each maid of merely mortal line.
Her mother was of human birth,
Her sire a Genie of the earth,
In days of old deem'd to preside
O'er lovers' wiles and beauty's pride,
By youths and virgins worshipp'd long,
With festive dance and choral song,
Till, when the cross to Britain came,
On heathen altars died the flame.
Now, deep in Wastdale solitude,
The downfall of his rights he rued,
And, born of his resentment heir,
He train'd to guile that lady fair,
To sink in slothful sin and shame
The champions of the Christian name.
Well skill'd to keep vain thoughts alive,
And all to promise, naught to give, —
The timid youth had hope in store,
The bold and pressing gain'd no more.
As wilder'd children leave their home,
After the rainbow's arch to roam,
Her lovers barter'd fair esteem,
Faith, fame, and honor, for a dream.

IV.

"Her sire's soft arts the soul to tame
She practised thus — till Arthur came;
Then, frail humanity had part,
And all the mother claim'd her heart.
Forgot each rule her father gave,
Sunk from a princess to a slave,
Too late must Guendolen deplore,
He, that has all, can hope no more!
Now must she see her lover strain
At every turn her feeble chain;
Watch, to new-bind each knot, and shrink
To view each fast-decaying link.
Art she invokes to Nature's aid,
Her vest to zone, her locks to braid;
Each varied pleasure heard her call,
The feast, the tourney, and the ball:
Her storied lore she next applies,
Taxing her mind to aid her eyes;
Now more than mortal wise, and then
In female softness sunk again:
Now, raptured, with each wish complying,
With feign'd reluctance now denying;
Each charm she varied, to retain
A varying heart — and all in vain!

V.

"Thus in the garden's narrow bound,
Flank'd by some castle's Gothic round,
Fain would the artist's skill provide,
The limits of his realms to hide.
The walks and labyrinths he twines,
Shade after shade with skill combines,
With many a varied flowery knot,
And copse, and arbor, decks the spot,
Tempting the hasty foot to stay,
And linger on the lovely way ——
Vain art! vain hope! 'tis fruitless all!
At length we reach the bounding wall,
And, sick of flower and trim-dress'd tree,
Long for rough glades and forest free.

VI.

"Three summer months had scant
        flown,
When Arthur, in embarrass'd tone,
Spoke of his liegemen and his throne;
Said, all too long had been his stay,
And duties, which a Monarch sway,
Duties, unknown to humbler men,
Must tear her knight from Guendolen.—
She listen'd silently the while,
Her mood express'd in bitter smile;

Beneath her eye must Arthur quail,
And oft resume the unfinish'd tale,
Confessing, by his downcast eye,
The wrong he sought to justify.
He ceased. A moment mute she gazed,
And then her looks to heaven she raised;
One palm her temples veil'd, to hide
The tear that sprung in spite of pride!
The other for an instant press'd
The foldings of her silken vest!

VII.

'At her reproachful sign and look,
The hint the Monarch's conscience
    took.
Eager he spoke: — 'No, lady, no!
Deem not of British Arthur so,
Nor think he can deserter prove
To the dear pledge of mutual love.
I swear by sceptre and by sword,
As belted knight and Britain's lord,
That if a boy shall claim my care,
That boy is born a kingdom's heir;
But, if a maiden Fate allows,
To choose that maid a fitting spouse,
A summer-day in lists shall strive
My knights, — the bravest knights alive, —
And he, the best and bravest tried,
Shall Arthur's daughter claim for bride.'—
He spoke, with voice resolved and high—
The lady deign'd him not reply.

VIII.

'At dawn of morn, ere on the brake
His matins did a warbler make,
Or stirr'd his wing to brush away
A single dew-drop from the spray,
Ere yet a sunbeam through the mist,
The castle-battlements had kiss'd,
The gates revolve, the drawbridge falls,
And Arthur sallies from the walls.
Doff'd his soft garb of Persia's loom,
And steel from spur to helmet-plume,
His Libyan steed full proudly trode,
And joyful neigh'd beneath his load.
The Monarch gave a passing sigh
To penitence and pleasures by,
When, lo! to his astonish'd ken
Appear'd the form of Guendolen.

IX.

'Beyond the outmost wall she stood,
Attir'd like huntress of the wood:

Sandall'd her feet, her ankles bare,
And eagle-plumage deck'd her hair;
Firm was her look, her bearing bold,
And in her hand a cup of gold.
'Thou goest,' she said, 'and ne'er again
Must we two meet, in joy or pain.
Full fain would I this hour delay,
Though weak the wish — yet wilt thou
    stay?
— No! thou look'st forward. Still
    attend, —
Part we like lover and like friend.'
She raised the cup — 'Not this the juice
The sluggish vines of earth produce;
Pledge we, at parting, in the draught
Which Genii love!'—she said, and quaff'd,
And strange unwonted lustres fly
From her flush'd cheek and sparkling eye.

X.

"The courteous Monarch bent him
    low,
And, stooping down from saddle-bow,
Lifted the cup, in act to drink.
A drop escaped the goblet's brink —
Intense as liquid fire from hell,
Upon the charger's neck it fell.
Screaming with agony and fright,
He bolted twenty feet upright!—
— The peasant still can show the dint,
Where his hoofs lighted on the flint. —
From Arthur's hand the goblet flew,
Scattering a shower of fiery dew,[6]
That burn'd and blighted where it fell!
The frantic steed rush'd up the dell,
As whistles from the bow the reed;
Nor bit nor reign could check his speed,
    Until he gain'd the hill;
Then breath and sinew fail'd apace,
And, reeling from the desperate race,
    He stood, exhausted, still.
The Monarch, breathless and amazed,
Back on the fatal castle gazed —
Nor tower nor donjon could he spy,
Darkening against the morning sky;[7]
But, on the spot where once they frown'd,
The lonely streamlet brawl'd around
A tufted knoll, where dimly shone
Fragments of rocks and rifted stone.
Musing on this strange hap the while,
The king wends back to fair Carlisle:
And cares, that cumber royal sway,
Wore memory of the past away.

XI.

" Full fifteen years, and more, were sped,
Each brought new wreaths to Arthur's
    head.
Twelve bloody fields, with glory fought,[8]
The Saxons to subjection brought:
Rython, the mighty giant, slain
By his good brand, relieved Bretagne:
The Pictish Gillamore in fight,
And Roman Lucius own'd his might;
And wide were through the world re-
    nown'd
The glories of his Table Round.
Each knight who sought adventurous
    fame,
To the bold court of Britain came,
And all who suffer'd causeless wrong,
From tyrant proud, or faitour strong,
Sought Arthur's presence to complain,
Nor there for aid implored in vain.

XII.

" For this the King, with pomp and pride,
Held solemn court at Whitsuntide,
    And summon'd Prince and Peer,
All who owed homage for their land,
Or who craved knighthood from his hand,
Or who had succor to demand,
    To come from far and near.
At such high tide were glee and game
Mingled with feats of martial fame,
For many a stranger champion came,
    In lists to break a spear;
And not a knight of Arthur's host,
Save that he trode some foreign coast,
But at this feast of Pentecost
    Before him must appear.
Ah, Minstrels! when the Table Round
Arose, with all its warriors crown'd,
There was a theme for bards to sound
    In triumph to their string!
Five hundred years are past and gone,
But time shall draw his dying groan,
Ere he behold the British throne
    Begirt with such a ring;

XIII.

" The heralds named the appointed spot,
As Caerlon or Camelot,
    Or Carlisle fair and free.
At Penrith, now, the feast was set,
And in fair Eamont's vale were met
    The flower of Chivalry.

There Galaad sate with manly grace,
Yet maiden meekness in his face;
There Morolt of the iron mace,
    And love-lorn Tristrem there;[9]
And Dinadam with lively glance,
And Lanval with the fairy lance,
And Mordred with his look askance,
    Brunor and Bevidere.
Why should I tell of members more?
Sir Cay, Sir Banier, and Sir Bore,
    Sir Carodac the keen,
The Gentle Gawain's courteous lore,
Hector de Mares and Pellinore,
And Lancelot, that evermore
Look'd stol'n-wise on the Queen.[10]

XIV.

" When wine and mirth did most abound,
And harpers play'd their blithest round,
A shrilly trumpet shook the ground,
    And marshals clear'd the ring;
A maiden, on a palfrey white,
Heading a band of damsels bright,
Paced through the circle, to alight
    And kneel before the King.
Arthur, with strong emotion, saw
Her graceful boldness check'd by awe,
Her dress, like huntress of the wold,
Her bow and baldric trapp'd with gold,
Her sandall'd feet, her ankles bare,
And the eagle-plume that deck'd her hair.
Graceful her veil she backward flung —
The King, as from his seat he sprung,
    Almost cried ' Guendolen ! '
But 'twas a face more frank and wild,
Betwixt the woman and the child,
Where less of magic beauty smiled
    Than of the race of men;
And in the forehead's haughty grace
The lines of Britain's royal race,
    Pendragon's you might ken.

XV.

" Faltering, yet gracefully, she said: —
' Great Prince ! behold an orphan maid,
In her departed mother's name,
A father's vow'd protection claim !
The vow was sworn in desert lone,
In the deep valley of St. John.'
At once the King the suppliant raised,
And kiss'd her brow, her beauty praised;
His vow, he said, should well be kept,
Ere in the sea the sun was dipp'd, —

Then, conscious, glanced upon his
　　queen;
But she, unruffled at the scene
Of human frailty, construed mild,
Look'd upon Lancelot and smiled.

XVI.

"'Up! up! each knight of gallant crest
　Take buckler, spear, and brand!
He that to-day shall bear him best,
　Shall win my Gyneth's hand.
And Arthur's daughter, when a bride,
　Shall bring a noble dower;
Both fair Strath-Clyde and Reged wide,
　And Carlisle town and tower.'
Then might you hear each valiant knight,
　To page and squire that cried,
Bring my armor bright, and my courser
　wight!
Tis not each day that a warrior's might
　May win a royal bride.'
Then cloaks and caps of maintenance
　In haste aside they fling;
The helmets glance, and gleams the lance,
　And the steel-weaved hauberks ring.
Small care had they of their peaceful
　array,
　They might gather it that wolde;
For brake and bramble glitter'd gay,
　With pearls and cloth of gold.

XVII.

"Within trumpet sound of the Table
　Round
　Were fifty champions free,
And they all arise to fight that prize, —
　They all arise but three.
For love's fond troth, nor wedlock's oath,
　One gallant could withhold,
For priests will allow of a broken vow,
　For penance or for gold.
But sigh and glance from ladies bright
　Among the troop were thrown,
To plead their right, and true-love plight,
　And plain of honor flown.
The knights they busied them so fast,
　With buckling spur and belt,
That sigh and look, by ladies cast,
　Were neither seen nor felt.
From pleading or upbraiding glance,
　Each gallant turns aside,
And only thought, ' If speeds my lance,
　A queen becomes my bride!

She has fair Strath-Clyde, and Reged
　wide,
　And Carlisle tower and town;
She is the loveliest maid, beside,
　That ever heir'd a crown.'
So in haste their coursers they bestride,
　And strike their visors down.

XVIII.

"The champions, arm'd in martial sort,
　Have throng'd into the list,
And but three knights of Arthur's court
　Are from the tourney miss'd.
And still these lovers' fame survives
　For faith so constant shown —
There were two who loved their neigh-
　bor's wives,
　And one who loved his own.[11]
The first was Lancelot de Lac,
　The second Tristrem bold,
The third was valiant Carodac,
　Who won the cup of gold,[12]
What time, of all King Arthur's crew,
　(Thereof came jeer and laugh,)
He, as the mate of lady true,
　Alone the cup could quaff.
Though envy's tongue would fain surmise,
　That but for very shame,
Sir Carodac, to fight that prize,
　Had given both cup and dame;
Yet, since but one of that fair court
　Was true to wedlock's shrine,
Brand him who will with base report, —
　He shall be free from mine.

XIX.

"Now caracoled the steeds in air,
　Now plumes and pennons wanton'd
　　fair,
As all around the lists so wide
In panoply the champions ride.
King Arthur saw with startled eye,
The flower of chivalry march by,
The bulwark of the Christian creed,
The kingdom's shield in hour of need.
Too late he thought him of the woe
Might from their civil conflict flow;
For well he knew they would not part
Till cold was many a gallant heart.
His hasty vow he 'gan to rue,
And Gyneth then apart he drew;
To her his leading-staff resign'd,
But added caution grave and kind: —

xx.

"'Thou seest, my child, as promise-
    bound,
I bid the trump for tourney sound.
Take thou my warder as the queen
And umpire of the martial scene;
But mark thou this: — as Beauty bright
Is polar star to valiant knight,
As at her word his sword he draws,
His fairest guerdon her applause,
So gentle maid should never ask
Of Knighthood vain and dangerous task;
And Beauty's eyes should ever be
Like the twin stars that soothe the sea,
And Beauty's breath should whisper peace,
And bid the storm of battle cease.
I tell thee this, lest all too far,
These knights urge tourney into war.
Blithe at the trumpet let them go,
And fairly counter blow for blow; —
No striplings these, who succor need
For a razed helm or falling steed.
But, Gyneth, when the strife grows warm,
And threatens death or deadly harm,
Thy sire entreats, thy king commands,
Thou drop the warder from thy hands.
Trust thou thy father with thy fate,
Doubt not he choose thee fitting mate;
Nor be it said, through Gyneth's pride
A rose of Arthur's chaplet died.''

xxi.

"A proud and discontented glow
O'ershadow'd Gyneth's brow of snow;
    She put the warder by: —
'Reserve thy boon, my liege,' she said,
'Thus chaffer'd down and limited,
Debased and narrow, for a maid
    Of less degree than I.
No petty chief but holds his heir
At a more honor'd price and rare
    Than Britain's King holds me!
Although the sun-burn'd maid, for dower,
Has but her father's rugged tower,
    His barren hill and lee.' —
King Arthur swore, 'By crown and sword,
As belted knight and Britain's lord,
That a whole summer's day should strive
His knights, the bravest knights alive!'
'Recall thine oath! and to her glen
Poor Gyneth can return agen!
Not on thy daughter will the stain,
That soils thy sword and crown remain.

But think not she will e'er be bride
Save to the bravest, proved and tried;
Pendragon's daughter will not fear
For clashing sword or splinter'd spear,
    Nor shrink though blood should flow;
And all too well sad Guendolen
Hath taught the faithlessness of men,
That child of hers should pity, when
    Their meed they undergo.' —

xxii.

"He frown'd and sigh'd, the Monarch
    bold: —
'I give — what I may not withhold;
For, not for danger, dread, or death,
Must British Arthur break his faith.
Too late I mark, thy mother's art
Hath taught thee this relentless part.
I blame her not, for she had wrong,
But not to these my faults belong.
Use, then, the warder as thou wilt;
But trust me, that if life be spilt,
In Arthur's love, in Arthur's grace,
Gyneth shall lose a daughter's place.'
With that he turn'd his head aside,
Nor brook'd to gaze upon her pride,
As, with the truncheon raised, she sate
The arbitress of mortal fate:
Nor brook'd to mark, in ranks disposed
How the bold champions stood opposed
For shrill the trumpet-flourish fell
Upon his ear like passing bell!
Then first from sight of martial fray
Did Britain's hero turn away.

xxiii.

"But Gyneth heard the clangor high,
As hears the hawk the partridge cry.
Oh, blame her not! the blood wa
    hers,
That at the trumpet's summons stirs! —
And e'en the gentlest female eye
Might the brave strife of chivalry
    A while untroubled view;
So well accomplish'd was each knight,
To strike and to defend in fight,
Their meeting was a goodly sight,
    While plate and mail held true.
The lists with painted plumes were strewn
Upon the wind at random thrown,
But helm and breastplate bloodless shone
It seem'd their feather'd crests alone
    Should this encounter rue.

And ever, as the combat grows,
The trumpet's cheery voice arose,
Like lark's shrill song the flourish flows,
Heard while the gale of April blows
 The merry greenwood through.

XXIV.

" But soon to earnest grew their game,
The spears drew blood, the swords struck
 flame,
And, horse and man, to ground there
 came
 Knights, who shall rise no more !
Gone was the pride the war that graced,
Gay shields were cleft, and crests defaced,
And steel coats riven, and helms unbraced,
 And pennons stream'd with gore.
Gone, too, were fence and fair array,
And desperate strength made deadly way
At random through the bloody fray,
And blows were dealt with headlong
 sway,
 Unheeding where they fell;
And now the trumpet's clamors seem
Like the shrill sea-bird's wailing scream,
Heard o'er the whirlpool's gulfing stream,
 The sinking seaman's knell !

XXV.

" Seem'd in this dismal hour, that Fate
Would Camlan's ruin antedate,
 And spare dark Mordred's crime;
Already gasping on the ground
Lie twenty of the Table Round,
 Of chivalry the prime.
Arthur, in anguish, tore away
From head and beard his tresses gray,
And she, proud Gyneth, felt dismay,
 And quaked with ruth and fear;
But still she deem'd her mother's shade
Hung o'er the tumult, and forbade
The sign that had the slaughter staid,
 And chid the rising tear.
Then Brunor, Taulas, Mador, fell,
Helias the White, and Lionel,
 And many a champion more;
Rochemont and Dinadam are down,
And Ferrand of the Forest Brown
 Lies gasping in his gore.
Vanoc, by mighty Morolt press'd
Even to the confines of the list,
Young Vanoc of the beardless face,
(Fame spoke the youth of Merlin's race,)

O'erpower'd at Gyneth's footstool bled,
His heart's-blood dyed her sandals red.
But then the sky was overcast,
Then howl'd at once a whirlwind's blast,
 And, rent by sudden throes,
Yawn'd in mid lists the quaking earth,
And from the gulf, — tremendous
 birth ! —
 The form of Merlin rose.

XXVI.

" Sternly the Wizard Prophet eyed
The dreary lists with slaughter dyed,
 And sternly raised his hand : —
' Madmen,' he said, ' your strife forbear;
And thou, fair cause of mischief, hear
 The doom thy fates demand !
 Long shall close in stony sleep
 Eyes for ruth that would not weep;
 Iron lethargy shall seal
 Heart that pity scorn'd to feel.
 Yet because thy mother's art
 Warp'd thine unsuspicious heart,
 And for love of Arthur's race,
 Punishment is blent with grace,
 Thou shall bear thy penance lone
 In the Valley of Saint John,
 And this weird * shall overtake thee;
 Sleep, until a knight shall wake thee,
 For feats or arms as far renown'd
 As warrior of the Table Round.
 Long endurance of thy slumber
 Well may teach the world to number
 All their woes from Gyneth's pride,
 When the Red Cross champions died.'

XXVII.

" As Merlin speaks, on Gyneth's eye
Slumber's load begins to lie;
Fear and anger vainly strive
Still to keep its light alive.
Twice, with effort and with pause,
O'er her brow her hand she draws;
Twice her strength in vain she tries,
From the fatal chair to rise;
Merlin's magic doom is spoken,
Vanoc's death must now be wroken.
Slow the dark-fringed eyelids fall,
Curtaining each azure ball,
Slowly as on summer eves
Violets fold their dusky leaves.

* Doom.

The weighty baton of command
Now bears down her sinking hand,
On her shoulder droops her head;
Net of pearl and golden thread,
Bursting, gave her locks to flow
O'er her arm and breast of snow.
And so lovely seem'd she there,
Spell-bound in her ivory chair,
That her angry sire, repenting,
Craved stern Merlin for relenting,
And the champions, for her sake,
Would again the contest wake;
Till, in necromantic night,
Gyneth vanish'd from their sight.

XXVIII.

" Still she bears her weird alone,
In the Valley of Saint John;
And her semblance oft will seem,
Mingling in a champion's dream,
Of her weary lot to 'plain,
And crave his aid to burst her chain.
While her wondrous tale was new,
Warriors to her rescue drew,
East and west, and south and north,
From the Liffy, Thames, and Forth.
Most have sought in vain the glen,
Tower nor castle could they ken;
Not at every time or tide,
Nor by every eye, descried.
Fast and vigil must be borne,
Many a night in watching worn,
Ere an eye of mortal powers
Can discern those magic towers.
Of the persevering few,
Some from hopeless task withdrew,
When they read the dismal threat
Graved upon the gloomy gate.
Few have braved the yawning door,
And those few return'd no more.
In the lapse of time forgot,
Wellnigh lost is Gyneth's lot;
Sound her sleep as in the tomb,
Till waken'd by the trump of doom."

END OF LYULPH'S TALE.

Here pause my tale; for all too soon,
My Lucy, comes the hour of noon.
Already from thy lofty dome
Its courtly inmates 'gin to roam,
And each, to kill the goodly day
That God has granted them, his way

Of lazy sauntering has sought;
　　Lordlings and witlings not a few,
Incapable of doing aught,
　　Yet ill at ease with naught to do.
Here is no longer place for me;
For, Lucy, thou wouldst blush to see
　　Some phantom, fashionably thin,
　　With limb of lath and kerchief'd chin,
　　And lounging gape, or sneering grin,
Steal sudden on our privacy.
And how should I, so humbly born,
Endure the graceful spectre's scorn?
Faith ! ill, I fear, while conjuring wand
Of English oak is hard at hand.

II.

Or grant the hour be all too soon
For Hessian boot and pantaloon,
And grant the lounger seldom strays
Beyond the smooth and gravell'd maze,
Laud we the gods, that Fashion's train
Holds hearts of more adventurous strain
Artists are hers, who scorn to trace
Their rules from Nature's boundless
　　grace,
But their right paramount assert
To limit her by pedant art,
Damning whate'er of vast and fair
Exceeds a canvas three feet square.
This thicket for their *gumption* fit,
May furnish such a happy *bit*.
Bards, too, are hers, wont to recite
Their own sweet lays by waxen light,
Half in the salver's tingle drown'd,
While the *chasse-café* glides around;
And such may hither secret stray,
To labor an extempore :
Or sportsman, with his boisterous hollo,
May here his wiser spaniel follow,
Or stage-struck Juliet may presume
To choose this bower for tiring-room;
And we alike must shun regard,
From painter, player, sportsman, bard.
Insects that skim in Fashion's sky,
Wasp, blue-bottle, or butterfly,
Lucy, have all alarms for us,
For all can hum and all can buzz.

III.

But oh, my Lucy, say how long
We still must dread this trifling throng,
And stoop to hide, with coward art,
The genuine feelings of the heart !

No parents thine whose just command
Should rule their child's obedient hand:
Thy guardians, with contending voice,
Press each his individual choice.
And which is Lucy's? — Can it be
That puny fop, trimm'd cap-a-pie,
Who loves in the saloon to show ·
The arms that never knew a foe;
Whose sabre trails along the ground,
Whose legs in shapeless boots are drown'd;
A new Achilles, sure, — the steel
Fled from his breast to fence his heel;
One, for the simple manly grace
That wont to deck our martial race,
　Who comes in foreign trashery
　　Of tinkling chain and spur,
　A walking haberdashery,
　　Of feathers, lace, and fur:
In Rowley's antiquated phrase,
Horse-milliner of modern days?

IV.

　Or is it he, the wordy youth,
　　So early train'd for statesman's part,
　Who talks of honor, faith, and truth,
　　As themes that he has got by heart;
Whose ethics Chesterfield can teach,
Whose logic is from Single-speech;[18]
Who scorns the meanest thought to
　vent,
Save in the phrase of Parliament;
Who, in a tale of cat and mouse,
Calls " order," and " divides the house,"
Who " craves permission to reply,"
Whose " noble friend is in his eye;"
Whose loving tender some have reckon'd
A *motion*, you should gladly *second ?*

V.

What, neither !　Can there be a third,
To such resistless swains preferr'd? —
O why, my Lucy, turn aside,
With that quick glance of injured pride?
Forgive me, love, I cannot bear
That alter'd and resentful air.
Were all the wealth of Russell mine,
And all the rank of Howard's line,
All would I give for leave to dry
That dewdrop trembling in thine eye.
Think not I fear such fops can wile
From Lucy more than careless smile;
But yet if wealth and high degree
Give gilded counters currency,

Must I not fear, when rank and birth
Stamp the pure ore of genuine worth?
Nobles there are, whose martial fires
Rival the fame that raised their sires,
And patriots, skill'd through storms of fate
To guide and guard the reeling state.
Such, such there are — if such should
　come,
Arthur must tremble and be dumb,
Self-exiled seek some distant shore,
And mourn till life and grief are o'er.

VI.

What sight, what signal of alarm,
That Lucy clings to Arthur's arm?
Or is it, that the rugged way
Makes Beauty lean on lover's stay?
Oh, no ! for on the vale and brake,
Nor sight nor sounds of danger wake,
And this trim sward of velvet green,
Were carpet for the Fairy Queen.
That pressure slight was but to tell,
That Lucy loves her Arthur well,
And fain would banish from his mind
Suspicious fear and doubt unkind.

VII.

But would'st thou bid the demons fly
Like mist before the dawning sky,
There is but one resistless spell —
Say, wilt thou guess, or must I tell?
'Twere hard to name, in minstrel phrase,
A landaulet and four blood-bays,
But bards agree this wizard band
Can but be bound in Northern land.
'Tis there—nay, draw not back thy hand !
'Tis there this slender finger round
Must golden amulet be bound,
Which, bless'd with many a holy prayer,
Can change to rapture lover's care,
And doubt and jealousy shall die,
And fears give place to ecstasy.

VIII.

Now, trust me, Lucy, all too long
Has been thy lover's tale and song.
O, why so silent, love, I pray?
Have I not spoke the livelong day?
And will not Lucy deign to say
　　One word her friend to bless?
I ask but one — a simple sound,
Within three little letters bound,
　　O, let the word be YES !

CANTO THIRD.

INTRODUCTION.

I.

Long loved, long woo'd, and lately won,
My life's best hope, and now mine
　　own !
Doth not this rude and Alpine glen
Recall our favorite haunts agen?
A wild resemblance we can trace,
Though reft of every softer grace,
As the rough warrior's brow may bear
A likeness to a sister fair.
Full well advised our Highland host,
That this wild pass on foot be cross'd,
While round Ben-Cruach's mighty base
Wheel the slow steed and lingering chaise.
The keen old carle, with Scottish pride,
He praised his glen and mountains wide;
An eye he bears for nature's face,
Ay, and for woman's lovely grace.
Even in such mean degree we find
The subtle Scot's observing mind;
For, nor the chariot nor the train
Could gape of vulgar wonder gain,
But when old Allan would expound
Of Beal-na-paish * the Celtic sound,
His bonnet doff'd, and bow, applied
His legend to my bonny bride;
While Lucy blush'd beneath his eye,
Courteous and cautious, shrewd and sly.

II.

Enough of him.— Now, ere we lose,
Plunged in the vale, the distant views,
Turn thee, my love ! look back once more
To the blue lake's retiring shore.
On its smooth breast the shadows seem
Like objects in a morning dream,
What time the slumberer is aware
He sleeps, and all the vision's air:
Even so, on yonder liquid lawn,
In hues of bright reflection drawn,
Distinct the shaggy mountains lie,
Distinct the rocks, distinct the sky;
The summer-clouds so plain we note,
That we might count each dappled spot:
We gaze and we admire, yet know
The scene is all delusive show.
Such dreams of bliss would Arthur draw,
When first his Lucy's form he saw;

* *Beal-na-paish*, in English the Vale of the
Bridal.

Yet sigh'd and sicken'd as he drew,
Despairing they could e'er prove true !

III.

But, Lucy, turn thee now, to view
　　Up the fair glen, our destine
　　　　way:
The fairy path that we pursue,
Distinguish'd but by greener hue,
　　Winds round the purple brae,
While Alpine flowers of varied dye
For carpet serve, or tapestry.
See how the little runnels leap,
In threads of silver, down the steep,
　　To swell the brooklet's moan !
Seems that the Highland Naiad grieves
Fantastic while her crown she weaves,
Of rowan, birch, and alder-leaves,
　　So lovely, and so lone.
There's no illusion there; these flowers
That wailing brook, these lovely bowers
　　Are, Lucy, all our own;
And, since thine Arthur call'd thee
　　wife,
Such seems the prospect of his life,
A lovely path, on-winding still,
By gurgling brook and sloping hill.
'Tis true, that mortals cannot tell
What waits them in the distant dell;
But be it hap, or be it harm,
We tread the pathway arm in arm.

IV.

And now, my Lucy, wot'st thou why
I could thy bidding twice deny,
When twice you pray'd I would again
Resume the legendary strain
Of the bold knight of Triermain?
At length yon peevish vow you swore,
That you would sue to me no more,
Until the minstrel fit drew near,
And made me prize a listening ear.
But, loveliest, when thou first didst
　　pray
Continuance of the knightly lay,
Was it not on the happy day
　　That made thy hand mine own?
When, dizzied with mine ecstasy,
Naught past, or present, or to be,
Could I or think on, hear, or see,
　　Save, Lucy, thee alone !
A giddy draught my rapture was,
As ever chemist's magic gas.

V.

ain the summons I denied
yon fair capital of Clyde:
y Harp — or let me rather choose
e good old classic form — my Muse,
'or Harp's an over-scutched phrase,
orn out by bards of modern days),
y Muse, then — seldom will she wake,
ve by dim wood and silent lake;
e is the wild and rustic Maid,
hose foot unsandall'd loves to tread
here the soft greensward is inlaid
    With varied moss and thyme;
d, lest the simple lily-braid,
at coronets her temples, fade,
e hides her still in greenwood shade,
    To meditate her rhyme.

VI.

d now she comes! The murmur dear
the wild brook hath caught her ear,
    The glades hath won her eye;
e longs to join with each blithe rill
at dances down the Highland hill,
    Her blither melody.
d now, my Lucy's way to cheer,
e bids Ben-Cruach's echoes hear
ow closed the tale, my love whilere
    Loved for its chivalry.
st how she tells, in notes of flame,
Child Roland to the dark tower came."

———

CANTO THIRD.

I.

EWCASTLE now must keep the Hold,
Speir-Adam's steeds must bide in stall,
Hartley-burn the bowmen bold
Must only shoot from battled wall,
nd Liddesdale may buckle spur,
And Teviot now may belt the brand,
rras and Ewes keep nightly stir,
And Eskdale foray Cumberland.
wasted fields and plunder'd flocks
The Borderers bootless may complain;
ey lack the sword of brave de Vaux,
There comes no aid from Triermain.
at lord, on high adventure bound,
Hath wander'd forth alone,
nd day and night keeps watchful round
In the valley of Saint John.

II.

When first began his vigil bold,
The moon twelve summer nights was old,
    And shone both fair and full;
High in the vault of cloudless hue,
O'er streamlet, dale, and rock she threw
    Her light composed and cool.
Stretch'd on the brown hill's heathy breast,
    Sir Roland eyed the vale;
Chief where, distinguish'd from the rest,
Those clustering rocks uprear'd their crest,
The dwelling of the fair distress'd,
    As told gray Lyulph's tale.
Thus as he lay, the lamp of night
Was quivering on his armor bright,
    In beams that rose and fell,
And danced upon his buckler's boss,
That lay beside him on the moss,
    As on a crystal well.

III.

Ever he watch'd, and oft he deem'd,
While on the mound the moonlight
        stream'd,
    It alter'd to his eyes;
Fain would he hope the rocks 'gan change
To buttress'd walls their shapeless range,
Fain think, by transmutation strange,
    He saw gray turrets rise.
But scarce his heart with hope throbb'd
        high,
Before the wild illusions fly,
    Which fancy had conceived,
Abetted by an anxious eye
    That long'd to be deceived.
It was a fond deception all,
Such as, in solitary hall,
    Beguiles the musing eye,
When, gazing on the sinking fire,
Bulwarks, and battlement, and spire,
    In the red gulf we spy.
For, seen by moon of middle night,
Or by the blaze of noontide bright,
Or by the dawn of morning light,
    Or evening's western flame,
In every tide, at every hour,
In mist, in sunshine, and in shower,
    The rocks remain'd the same.

IV.

Oft has he traced the charmed mound,
Oft climb'd its crest, or paced it round,
    Yet nothing might explore,

Save that the crags so rudely piled,
At distance seen, resemblance wild
　　To a rough fortress bore.
Yet still his watch the Warrior keeps,
Feeds hard and spare, and seldom sleeps,
　　And drinks but of the well;
Ever by day he walks the hill,
And when the evening gale is chill,
　　He seeks a rocky cell,
Like hermit poor to bid his bead,
And tell his Ave and his Creed,
Invoking every saint at need,
　　For aid to burst his spell.

v.

And now the moon her orb has hid,
And dwindled to a silver thread,
　　Dim seen in middle heaven,
While o'er its curve careering fast,
Before the fury of the blast
　　The midnight clouds are driven.
The brooklet raved, for on the hills,
The upland showers had swoln the rills,
　　And down the torrents came;
Mutter'd the distant thunder dread,
And frequent o'er the vale was spread
　　A sheet of lightning flame.
De Vaux, within his mountain cave,
(No human step the storm durst brave,)
To moody meditation gave
　　Each faculty of soul,
Till, lull'd by distant torrent sound,
And the sad winds that whistled round,
Upon his thoughts, in musing drown'd,
　　A broken slumber stole.

vi.

'Twas then was heard a heavy sound,
　　(Sound, strange and fearful there to hear,
'Mongst desert hills, where, leagues around,
　　Dwelt but the gor-cock and the deer:)
As, starting from his couch of fern,
Again he heard in clangor stern,
　　That deep and solemn swell, —
Twelve times, in measured tone, it spoke,
Like some proud minster's pealing clock,
　　Or city's larum-bell.
What thought was Roland's first when fell,
In that deep wilderness, the knell
　　Upon his startled ear?

To slander warrior were I loth,
Yet must I hold my minstrel troth, —
　　It was a thought of fear.

vii.

But lively was the mingled thrill
That chased that momentary chill,
　　For Love's keen wish was there,
And eager Hope, and Valor high,
And the proud glow of Chivalry,
　　That burn'd to do and dare,
Forth from the cave the Warri[or] rush'd,
Long ere the mountain-voice w[as] hush'd,
　　That answer'd to the knell;
For long and far the unwonted sound,
Eddying in echoes round and round,
　　Was toss'd from fell to fell;
And Glaramara answer flung,
And Grisdale-pike responsive rung,
And Legbert heights their echo[es] swung,
　　As far as Derwent's dell.

viii.

Forth upon trackless darkness gazed
The Knight, bedeafen'd and amazed,
　　Till all was hush'd and still,
Save the swoln torrent's sullen roar,
And the night-blast that wildly bore
　　Its course along the hill.
Then on the northern sky there came
A light, as of reflected flame,
　　And over Legbert-head,
As if by magic art controll'd,
A mighty meteor slowly roll'd
　　Its orb of fiery red;
Thou wouldst have thought some dem[on] dire
Came mounted on that car of fire,
　　To do his errand dread.
Far on the sloping valley's course,
On thicket, rock, and torrent hoarse,
Shingle and scrae,* and fell and force,†
　　A dusky light arose:
Display'd, yet alter'd was the scene;
Dark rock, and brook of silver sheen,
Even the gay thicket's summer green,
　　In bloody tincture glows.

* Bank of loose stones.
† Waterfall.

IX.

e Vaux had mark'd the sunbeams set,
t eve, upon the coronet
    Of that enchanted mound,
nd seen but crags at random flung,
hat, o'er the brawling torrent hung,
    In desolation frown'd.
hat sees he by that meteor's lour? —
banner'd Castle, keep, and tower,
    Return the lurid gleam,
ith battled walls and buttress fast,
nd barbican * and ballium † vast,
nd airy flanking towers, that cast
    Their shadows on the stream.
is no deceit! — distinctly clear
renell ‡ and parapet appear,
hile o'er the pile that meteor drear
    Makes momentary pause;
hen forth its solemn path it drew,
nd fainter yet and fainter grew
hose gloomy towers upon the view,
    As its wild light withdraws.

X.

orth from the cave did Roland rush,
'er crag and stream, through brier and
        bush;
    Yet far he had not sped,
re sunk was that portentous light
ehind the hills, and utter night
    Was on the valley spread.
e paused perforce, and blew his horn,
nd, on the mountain-echoes borne,
    Was heard an answering sound,
wild and lonely trumpet-note, —
middle air it seem'd to float
    High o'er the battled mound;
nd sounds were heard, as when a guard
f some proud castle, holding ward,
    Pace forth their nightly round.
he valiant Knight of Triermain
ung forth his challenge-blast again,
    But answer came there none;
nd mid the mingled wind and rain,
arkling he sought the vale in vain,
    Until the dawning shone;
nd when it dawn'd, that wondrous sight,
istinctly seen by meteor light,
    It all had pass'd away!

* The outer defence of a castle gate.
† A fortified court.
‡ Apertures for shooting arrows.

And that enchanted mount once more
A pile of granite fragments bore,
    As at the close of day.

XI.

Steel'd for the deed, De Vaux's heart
Scorn'd from his venturous quest to part,
    He walks the vale once more;
But only sees, by night or day,
That shatter'd pile of rocks so gray,
    Hears but the torrent's roar.
Till when, through hills of azure borne,
The moon renew'd her silver horn,
    Just at the time her waning ray
Had faded in the dawning day,
    A summer mist arose;
Adown the vale the vapors float,
And cloudy undulations moat
That tufted mound of mystic note,
    As round its base they close.
And higher now the fleecy tide
Ascends its stern and shaggy side,
    Until the airy billows hide
The rock's majestic isle;
It seem'd a veil of filmy lawn,
By some fantastic fairy drawn
    Around enchanted pile.

XII.

The breeze came softly down the brook,
    And, sighing as it blew,
The veil of silver mist it shook,
    And to De Vaux's eager look
    Renew'd that wondrous view.
For, though the loitering vapor braved
The gentle breeze, yet oft it waved
    Its mantle's dewy fold;
And still, when shook that filmy screen,
Were towers and bastions dimly seen,
And Gothic battlements between
    Their gloomy length unroll'd.
Speed, speed, De Vaux, ere on thine eye
Once more the fleeting vision die!
    — The gallant knight 'gan speed
As prompt and light as, when the hound
Is opening, and the horn is wound,
    Careers the hunter's steed.
Down the steep dell his course amain
    Hath rivall'd archer's shaft;
But ere the mound he could attain,
The rocks their shapeless form regain,
And, mocking loud his labor vain,
    The mountain spirits laugh'd.

Far up the echoing dell was borne
Their wild unearthly shout of scorn.

XIII.

Wroth wax'd the Warrior. — "Am I then
Fool'd by the enemies of men,
Like a poor hind, whose homeward way
Is haunted by malicious fay!
Is Triermain become your taunt,
De Vaux your scorn? False fiends, avaunt!"
A weighty curtal-axe he bare;
The baleful blade so bright and square,
And the tough shaft of heben wood,
Were oft in Scottish gore imbrued.
Backward his stately form he drew,
And at the rocks the weapon threw,
Just where one crag's projected crest
Hung proudly balanced o'er the rest.
Hurl'd with main force, the weapon's shock
Rent a huge fragment of the rock.
If by mere strength, 'twere hard to tell,
Or if the blow dissolved some spell,
But down the headlong ruin came,
With cloud of dust and flash of flame.
Down bank, o'er bush, its course was borne,
Crush'd lay the copse, the earth was torn,
Till staid at length, the ruin dread
Cumber'd the torrent's rocky bed,
And bade the water's high-swoln tide
Seek other passage for its pride.

XIV.

When ceased that thunder, Triermain
Survey'd the mound's rude front again;
And lo! the ruin had laid bare,
Hewn in the stone, a winding stair,
Whose moss'd and fractured steps might lend
The means the summit to ascend;
And by whose aid the brave De Vaux
Began to scale these magic rocks,
And soon a platform won,
Where, the wild witchery to close,
Within three lances' length arose
The Castle of Saint John.
No misty phantom of the air,
No meteor-blazon'd show was there;
In morning splendor, full and fair,
The massive fortress shone.

XV.

Embattled high and proudly tower'd,
Shaded by pond'rous flankers, lower'd
The portal's gloomy way.
Though for six hundred years and more
Its strength had brook'd the tempest roar,
The scutcheon'd emblems which it bore
Had suffer'd no decay:
But from the eastern battlement
A turret had made sheer descent,
And, down in recent ruin rent,
In the mid torrent lay.
Else, o'er the Castle's brow sublime,
Insults of violence or of time
Unfelt had pass'd away.
In shapeless characters of yore,
The gate this stern inscription bore:—

XVI.

INSCRIPTION.

" Patience waits the destined day,
Strength can clear the cumber'd way.
Warrior, who hast waited long,
Firm of soul, of sinew strong,
It is given to thee to gaze
On the pile of ancient days.
Never mortal builder's hand
This enduring fabric plann'd;
Sigh and sigil, word of power,
From the earth raised keep and tower.
View it o'er, and pace it round,
Rampart, turret, battled mound.
Dare no more! To cross the gate
Were to tamper with thy fate:
Strength and fortitude were vain,
View it o'er — and turn again."

XVII.

"That would I," said the Warrior bold,
"If that my frame were bent and old,
And my thin blood dropp'd slow and cold
As icicle in thaw;
But while my heart can feel it dance,
Blithe as the sparkling wine of France,
And this good arm wields sword or lance,
I mock these words of awe:"
He said! The wicket felt the sway
Of his strong hand, and straight gave way,
And, with rude crash and jarring bray,
The rusty bolts withdraw;
But o'er the threshold as he strode,
And forward took the vaulted road,

n unseen arm, with force amain,
he ponderous gate flung close again.
    And rusted bolt and bar
pontaneous took their place once more,
Vhile the deep arch with sullen roar
    Return'd their surly jar.
Now closed is the gin and the prey
        within
    By the rood of Lanercost!
ut he that would win the war-wolf's skin,
    May rue him of his boast.''
hus muttering, on the Warrior went,
y dubious light down deep descent.

XVIII.

nbarr'd, unlock'd, unwatch'd, a port
ed to the Castle's outer court:
here the main fortress, broad and tall,
pread its long range of bower and hall,
    And towers of varied size,
Vrought with each ornament extreme,
hat Gothic art, in wildest dream
    Of fancy, could devise;
ut full between the Warrior's way
nd the main portal arch, there lay
    An inner moat;
    Nor bridge nor boat
ffords De Vaux the means to cross
he clear, profound, and silent fosse.
lis arms aside in haste he flings,
uirass of steel and hauberk rings,
nd down falls helm, and down the shield,
.ough with the dints of many a field.
air was his manly form, and fair
lis keen dark eye, and close curl'd hair,
Vhen, all unarm'd, save that the brand
f well-proved metal graced his hand,
Vith naught to fence his dauntless breast
ut the close gipon's * under-vest,
Vhose sullied buff the sable stains
f hauberk and of mail retains, —
.oland De Vaux upon the brim
f the broad moat stood prompt to swim.

XIX.

.ccoutred thus he dared the tide,
.nd soon he reach'd the farther side,
    And enter'd soon the Hold,
.nd paced a hall, whose walls so wide
Vere blazon'd all with feats of pride,
    By warriors done of old.

* A sort of doublet, worn beneath the armor.

In middle lists they counter'd here,
    While trumpets seem'd to blow;
And there, in den or desert drear,
    They quelled gigantic foe,
Braved the fierce griffon in his ire,
Or faced the dragon's breath of fire.
Strange in their arms, and strange in face,
Heroes they seem'd of ancient race,
Whose deeds of arms, and race, and name,
Forgotten long by later fame,
    Were here depicted, to appal
Those of an age degenerate,
Whose bold intrusion braved their fate,
    In this enchanted hall.
For some short space the venturous Knight
With these high marvels fed his sight,
Then sought the chamber's upper end,
Where three broad easy steps ascend
    To an arch'd portal door,
In whose broad folding leaves of state
Was framed a wicket window-grate,
    And, ere he ventured more,
The gallant Knight took earnest view
The grated wicket-window through.

XX.

O, for his arms! Of martial weed
Had never mortal Knight such need!
He spied a stately gallery; all
Of snow-white marble was the wall,
    The vaulting, and the floor;
And, contrast strange, on either hand
There stood array'd in sable band
Four Maids whom Afric bore:
And each a Libyan tiger led,
Held by as bright and frail a thread
    As Lucy's golden hair, —
For the leash that bound these monsters
        dread
    Was but of gossamer.
Each Maiden's short barbaric vest
Left all unclosed the knee and breast,
    And limbs of shapely jet;
White was their vest and turban'd fold,
On arms and ankles rings of gold
    In savage pomp were set;
A quiver on their shoulders lay,
And in their hand an assagay.
Such and so silent stood they there,
    That Roland wellnigh hoped
He saw a band of statues rare,
Station'd the gazer's soul to scare;
    But when the wicket oped,

Each grisly beast 'gan upward draw,
Roll'd his grim eye, and spread his claw,
Scented the air, and lick'd his jaw;
While these weird maids, in Moorish
tongue,
A wild and dismal warning sung:—

XXI.

" Rash adventurer, bear thee back!
Dread the spell of Dahomay!
Fear the race of Zaharak,*
Daughters of the burning day!

" When the whirlwind's gusts are wheel-
ing,
Ours it is the dance to braid;
Zarah's sands in pillars reeling,
Join the measure that we tread,
When the moon has donn'd her cloak,
And the stars are red to see,
Shrill when pipes the sad Siroc,
Music meet for such as we.

" Where the shatter'd columns lie,
Showing Carthage once had been,
If the wandering Santon's eye
Our mysterious rites hath seen, —
Oft he cons the prayer of death,
To the nations preaches doom,
' Azrael's brand hath left the sheath!
Moslems, think upon the tomb!'

" Ours the scorpion, ours the snake,
Ours the hydra of the fen,
Ours the tiger of the brake,
All that plagues the sons of men.
Ours the tempest's midnight wrack,
Pestilence that wastes by day —
Dread the race of Zaharak!
Fear the spell of Dahomay!"

XXII.

Uncouth and strange the accents shrill
Rung those vaulted roofs among,
Long it was ere, faint and still,
Died the far resounding song.
While yet the distant echoes roll,
The Warrior communed with his soul:—
" When first I took this venturous quest,
I swore upon the rood,
Neither to stop, nor turn, nor rest,
For evil or for good.

* The Arab name of the great desert.

My forward path too well I ween,
Lies yonder fearful ranks between!
For man unarm'd, 'tis bootless hope
With tigers and with fiends to cope —
Yet, if I turn, what waits me there,
Save famine dire and fell despair? —
Other conclusion let me try,
Since, choose howe'er I list, I die.
Forward, lies faith and knightly fame;
Behind, are perjury and shame,
In life or death I hold my word!"
With that he drew his trusty sword,
Caught down a banner from the wall,
And enter'd thus the fearful hall.

XXIII.

On high each wayward Maiden threw
Her swarthy arm, with wild halloo!
On either side a tiger sprung —
Against the leftward foe he flung
The ready banner, to engage
With tangling folds the brutal rage;
The right-hand monster in mid-air
He struck so fiercely and so fair,
Through gullet and through spinal bone
The trenchant blade had sheerly gone.
His grisly brethren ramp'd and yell'd,
But the slight leash their rage withheld,
Whilst, 'twixt their ranks, the dangerou
road
Firmly, though swift, the champion strode
Safe to the gallery's bound he drew,
Safe pass'd an open portal through;
And when against pursuit he flung
The gate, judge if the echoes rung!
Onward his daring course he bore,
While mix'd with dying growl and roar
Wild jubilee and loud hurra
Pursued him on his venturous way.

XXIV.

" Hurra, hurra! Our watch is done!
We hail once more the tropic sun.
Pallid beams of northern day,
Farewell, farewell! Hurra, hurra!

" Five hundred years o'er this cold glen
Hath the pale sun come round agen;
Foot of man, till now, hath ne'er
Dared to cross the Hall of Fear.

" Warrior! thou, whose dauntless heart
Gives us from our ward to part,

as strong in future trial,
ere resistance is denial.

Now for Afric's glowing sky,
enga wide and Atlas high,
narak and Dahomay! —
unt the winds! Hurra, hurra!"

XXV.

e wizard song at distance died,
As if in ether borne astray,
ile through waste halls and chambers
  wide
The Knight pursued his steady way,
l to a lofty dome he came,
at flash'd with such a brilliant flame,
if the wealth of all the world
re there in rich confusion hurl'd.
here the gold, in sandy heaps,
th duller earth, incorporate, sleeps,
s there in ingots piled, and there
n'd badge of empery it bare:
nder, huge bars of silver lay,
nm'd by the diamond's neighboring
  ray,
e the pale moon in morning day;
d in the midst four Maidens stand,
e daughters of some distant land.
eir hue was of the dark-red dye,
at fringes oft a thunder sky;
eir hands palmetto baskets bare,
d cotton fillets bound their hair;
n was their form, their mien was
  shy,
earth they bent the humbled eye,
ded their arms, and suppliant kneel'd,
d thus their proffer'd gifts reveal'd.

XXVI.

CHORUS.

ee the treasures Merlin piled,
tion meet for Arthur's child.
he in Wealth's unbounded stream,
alth that Avarice ne'er could dream!"

FIRST MAIDEN.

ee these clots of virgin gold!
er'd from the sparry mould,
ure's mystic alchemy
the mine thus bade them lie;
d their orient smile can win
ngs to stoop, and saints to sin." —

SECOND MAIDEN.

" See these pearls, that long have slept;
These were tears by Naiads wept
For the loss of Marinel.
Tritons in the silver shell
Treasured them, till hard and white
As the teeth of Amphitrite." —

THIRD MAIDEN.

" Does a livelier hue delight?
Here are rubies blazing bright,
Here the emerald's fairy green,
And the topaz glows between;
Here their varied hues unite,
In the changeful chrysolite." —

FOURTH MAIDEN.

" Leave these gems of poorer shine,
Leave them all and look on mine!
While their glories I expand,
Shade thine eye-brows with thy hand.
Mid-day sun and diamond's blaze
Blind the rash beholder's gaze."

CHORUS.

" Warrior, seize the splendid store;
Would 'twere all our mountains bore!
We should ne'er in future story,
Read, Peru, thy perish'd glory!' "

XXVII.

Calmly and unconcern'd, the Knight
Waved aside the treasures bright: —
" Gentle Maidens, rise, I pray!
Bar not thus my destined way.
Let these boasted brilliant toys
Braid the hair of girls and boys!
Bid your streams of gold expand
O'er proud London's thirsty land.
De Vaux of wealth saw never need,
Save to purvey him arms and steed.
And all the ore he deign'd to hoard
Inlays his helm, and hilts his sword."
Thus gently parting from their hold,
He left, unmoved, the dome of gold.

XXVIII.

And now the morning sun was high,
De Vaux was weary, faint, and dry;
When, lo! a plashing sound he hears,
A gladsome signal that he nears
    Some frolic water-run;

And soon he reach'd a court-yard square;
Where, dancing in the sultry air,
Toss'd high aloft, a fountain fair
　　Was sparkling in the sun.
On right and left, a fair arcade,
In long perspective view display'd
Alleys and bowers, for sun or shade:
　　But, full in front, a door,
Low-brow'd and dark, seem'd as it led
To the lone dwelling of the dead,
　　Whose memory was no more.

XXIX.

Here stopp'd De Vaux an instant's space,
To bathe his parched lips and face,
　　And mark'd with well-pleased eye,
Refracted on the fountain stream,
In rainbow hues the dazzling beam
　　Of that gay summer sky.
His senses felt a mild control,
Like that which lulls the weary soul,
　　From contemplation high.
Relaxing, when the ear receives
The music that the greenwood leaves
　　Make to the breezes' sigh.

XXX.

And oft in such a dreamy mood,
　　The half-shut eye can frame
Fair apparitions in the wood,
As if the nymphs of field and flood
　　In gay procession came.
Are these of such fantastic mould,
　　Seen distant down the fair arcade,
These Maids enlink'd in sister-fold,
　　Who, late at bashful distance staid,
　　Now tripping from the greenwood
　　　shade,
Nearer the musing champion draw,
And, in a pause of seeming awe,
　　Again stand doubtful now? —
Ah, that sly pause of witching powers!
That seems to say, "To please be ours,
　　Be yours to tell us how."
Their hue was of the golden glow
That suns of Candahar bestow,
O'er which in slight suffusion flows
A frequent tinge of paly rose;
Their limbs were fashion'd fair and free,
In nature's justest symmetry;
And, wreath'd with flowers, with odors
　　graced,
Their raven ringlets reach'd the waist,

In eastern pomp, its gilding pale
The hennah lent each shapely nail,
And the dark sumah gave the eye
More liquid and more lustrous dye.
The spotless veil of misty lawn,
In studied disarrangement, drawn
　　The form and bosom o'er,
To win the eye, or tempt the touch,
For modesty show'd all too much —
　　Too much — yet promised more: -

XXXI.

" Gentle Knight, a while delay,"
Thus they sung, " thy toilsome way,
While we pay the duty due
To our Master and to you.
Over Avarice, over Fear,
Love triumphant led thee here;
Warrior, list to us, for we
Are slaves to Love, are friends to thee
Though no treasured gems have we,
To proffer on the bended knee,
Though we boast nor arm nor heart,
For the assagay or dart,
Swains allow each simple girl
Ruby lip and teeth of pearl;
Or, if dangers more you prize,
Flatterers find them in our eyes.

"Stay, then, gentle Warrior, stay,
Rest till evening steal on day;
Stay, O, stay! in yonder bowers
We will braid thy locks with flowers,
Spread the feast and fill the wine,
Charm thy ear with sounds divine,
Weave our dances till delight
Yield to languor, day to night.

"Then shall she you most approve,
Sing the lays that best you love,
Soft thy mossy couch shall spread,
Watch thy pillow, prop thy head,
Till the weary night be o'er —
Gentle Warrior, wouldst thou more?
Wouldst thou more, fair Warrior,
　　she
Is slave to Love, and slave to thee."

XXXII.

O, do not hold it for a crime
In the bold hero of my rhyme,
　　For Stoic look
　　And meet rebuke,

e lack'd the heart or time;
s round the band of sirens trip,
e kiss'd one damsel's laughing lip,
nd press'd another's proffer'd hand.
poke to them all in accents bland,
ut broke their magic circle through: —
" Kind Maids," he said, " adieu, adieu !
y fate, my fortune, forward lies."
e said, and vanish'd from their eyes;
ut, as he dared that darksome way,
till heard behind their lovely lay : —
" Fair Flower of Courtesy, depart !
o, where the feelings of the heart
Vith the warm pulse in concord move;
o, where Virtue sanctions Love ! "

XXXIII.

Downward De Vaux through darksome ways
    And ruin'd vaults has gone,
Till issue from their wilder'd maze,
   Or safe retreat, seem'd none,
And e'en the dismal path he strays
   Grew worse as he went on.
or cheerful sun, for living air,
oul vapors rise and mine-fires glare,
Vhose fearful light the dangers show'd,
hat dogg'd him on that dreadful road;
eep pits, and lakes of waters dun,
hey show'd, but show'd not how to
   shun.
hese scenes of desolate despair,
hese smothering clouds of poison'd
   air,
low gladly had De Vaux exchanged,
hough 'twere to face yon tigers ranged !
   Nay, soothful bards have said,
o perilous his state seem'd now
e wish'd him under arbor bough
   With Asia's willing maid.
Vhen, joyful sound ! at distance near,
trumpet flourish'd loud and clear,
nd as it ceased, a lofty lay
eem'd thus to chide his lagging way : —

XXXIV.

" Son of Honor, theme of story,
hink on the reward before ye !
anger, darkness, toil, despise;
Tis Ambition bids thee rise.

" He that would her heights ascend,
Many a weary step must wend?

Hand and foot and knee he tries;
   Thus Ambition's minions rise.

" Lag not now, though rough the way,
   Fortune's mood brooks no delay;
Grasp the boon that's spread before ye,
Monarch's power, and Conqueror's
   glory ! "

It ceased.   Advancing on the sound,
A steep ascent the Wanderer found,
   And then a turret stair :
Nor climb'd he far its steepy round
   Till fresher blew the air,
And next a welcome glimpse was given,
That cheer'd him with the light of heaven.
   At length his toil had won
A lofty hall with trophies dress'd,
Where, as to greet imperial guest,
Four Maidens stood, whose crimson vest
   Was bound with golden zone.

XXXV.

Of Europe seem'd the damsels all;
The first a nymph of lively Gaul,
Whose easy step and laughing eye
Her borrow'd air of awe belie;
   The next a maid of Spain,
Dark-eyed, dark-hair'd, sedate, yet bold :
White ivory skin and tress of gold,
Her shy and bashful comrade told
   For daughter of Almaine.
These maidens bore a royal robe,
With crown, with sceptre, and with
   globe,
   Emblems of empery;
The fourth a space behind them stood,
And leant upon a harp, in mood
   Of minstrel ecstasy.
Of merry England she, in dress
Like ancient British Druidess.
Her hair an azure fillet bound,
Her graceful vesture swept the ground,
   And, in her hand display'd,
A crown did that fourth Maiden hold,
But unadorn'd with gems and gold,
   Of glossy laurel made.

XXXVI.

At once to brave De Vaux knelt down
   These foremost Maidens three,
And proffer'd sceptre, robe, and crown,
   Liegedom and seignorie,

O'er many a region wide and fair,
Destined, they said, for Arthur's heir;
　But homage would he none: —
" Rather," he said, " De Vaux would
　　ride,
A Warden of the Border-side,
In plate and mail, than, robed in pride,
　A monarch's empire own;
Rather, far rather, would he be
A free-born knight of England free,
　Than sit on Despot's throne."
So pass'd he on, when that fourth Maid,
　As starting from a trance,
Upon the harp her finger laid;
Her magic touch the chords obey'd,
　Their soul awaked at once!

SONG OF THE FOURTH MAIDEN.

" Quake to your foundations deep,
Stately Towers, and Banner'd Keep,
Bid your vaulted echoes moan,
As the dreaded step they own.

" Fiends, that wait on Merlin's spell,
Hear the foot-fall! mark it well!
Spread your dusty wings abroad,
Boune ye for your homeward road!

" It is HIS, the first who e'er
Dared the dismal Hall of Fear;
HIS, who hath the snares defied
Spread by Pleasure, Wealth and Pride.

" Quake to your foundations deep,
Bastion huge, and Turret steep!
Tremble, Keep, and totter, Tower!
This is Gyneth's waking hour."

XXXVII.

Thus while she sung, the venturous
　　Knight
Has reach'd a bower, where milder light
　Through crimson curtains fell;
Such soften'd shade the hill receives,
Her purple veil when twilight leaves
　Upon its western swell.
That bower, the gazer to bewitch,
Hath wondrous store of rare and rich
　As e'er was seen with eye;
For there by magic skill, I wis,
Form of each thing that living is
　Was limn'd in proper dye.
All seem'd to sleep — the timid hare
On form, the stag upon his lair,

The eagle in her eyry fair
　Between the earth and sky.
But what of pictured rich and rare
Could　win　De　Vaux's　eye-glanc
　　where,
Deep slumbering in the fatal chair,
　He saw King Arthur's child!
Doubt, and anger, and dismay,
From her brow had pass'd away,
Forgot was that fell tourney-day,
　For, as she slept, she smiled!
It seem'd, that the repentant Seer
Her sleep of many a hundred year
　With gentle dreams beguiled.

XXXVIII.

That form of maiden loveliness,
　'Twixt childhood and 'twixt youth
That ivory chair, that sylvan dress,
The arms and ankles bare, express
　Of Lyulph's tale the truth.
Still upon her garment's hem
Vanoc's blood made purple gem,
And the warder of command
Cumber'd still her sleeping hand;
Still her dark locks dishevell'd flow
From net of pearl o'er breast of snow;
And so fair the slumberer seems,
That De Vaux impeach'd his dreams,
Vapid all and void of might,
Hiding half her charms from sight.
Motionless a while he stands,
Folds his arms and clasps his hands,
Trembling in his fitful joy,
Doubtful how he should destroy
　Long-enduring spell;
Doubtful, too, when slowly rise
Dark-fringed lids of Gyneth's eyes,
　What these eyes shall tell. —
" St. George! St. Mary! can it be,
That they will kindly look on me! "

XXXIX.

Gently, lo! the Warrior kneels,
Soft that lovely hand he steals,
Soft to kiss, and soft to clasp —
But the warder leaves her grasp;
　Lightning flashes, rolls the thunde
Gyneth startles from her sleep,　.
Totters Tower, and trembles Keep,
　Burst the Castle-walls asunder!
Fierce and frequent were the shocks,
　Melt the magic halls away;

——But beneath their mystic rocks,
In the arms of bold De Vaux,
　　Safe the princess lay;
Safe and free from magic power,
Blushing like the rose's flower
　　Opening to the day;
And round the champion's brows were
　　bound
The crown that Druidess had wound,
　　Of the green laurel-bay.
And this was what remain'd of all
The wealth of that enchanted hall,
　　The Garland and the Dame:
But where should Warrior seek the
　　meed,
Due to high worth for daring deed,
　　Except from LOVE and FAME!

CONCLUSION.

I.

My Lucy, when the maid is won,
The Minstrel's task, thou know'st, is done;
　　And to require of bard
That to his dregs the tale should run,
　　Were ordinance too hard.
Our lovers, briefly be it said,
Wedded as lovers wont to wed,
　　When tale or play is o'er;
Lived long and blest, loved fond and true,
And saw a numerous race renew
　　The honors that they bore.
Know, too, that when a pilgrim strays,
In morning mist or evening maze,
　　Along the mountain lone,
That fairy fortress often mocks
His gaze upon the castled rocks
　　Of the Valley of St. John;

But never man since brave De Vaux
　　The charmed portal won.
'Tis now a vain illusive show,
That melts whene'er the sunbeams glow
　　Or the fresh breeze hath blown.

II.

But see, my love, where far below
Our lingering wheels are moving slow,
　　The whiles, up-gazing still,
Our menials eye our steepy way,
Marvelling, perchance, what whim can
　　stay
Our steps, when eve is sinking gray,
　　On this gigantic hill.
So think the vulgar — Life and time
Ring all their joys in one dull chime
　　Of luxury and ease:
And, O! beside these simple knaves,
How many better born are slaves
　　To such coarse joys as these, —
Dead to the nobler sense that glows
When Nature's grander scenes unclose!
But, Lucy, we will love them yet,
The mountain's misty coronet,
　　The greenwood, and the wold;
And love the more, that of their maze
Adventure high of other days
　　By ancient bards is told,
Bringing, perchance, like my poor tale,
Some moral truth in fiction's veil:
Nor love them less, that o'er the hill
The evening breeze, as now, comes
　　chill; —
My love shall wrap her warm,
And, fearless of the slippery way,
While safe she trips the heathy brae,
　　Shall hang on Arthur's arm.

THE

LORD OF THE ISLES.

IN SIX CANTOS.

ADVERTISEMENT TO THE FIRST EDITION.

The scene of this poem lies, at first, in the Castle of Artornish, on the coast of Argyle-shire; and, afterwards, in the Islands of Skye and Arran, and upon the coast of Ayrshire. Finally, it is laid near Stirling. The story opens in the spring of the year 1307, *when Bruce, who had been driven out of Scotland by the English, and the Barons who adhered to that foreign interest, returned from the Island of Rachrin, on the coast of Ireland, again to assert his claims to the Scottish crown. Many of the personages and incidents intro-duced are of historical celebrity. The authorities used are chiefly those of the venerable Lord Hailes, as well entitled to be called the restorer of Scottish history, as Bruce the re-storer of Scottish monarchy; and of Archdeacon Barbour, a correct edition of whose Met-rical History* of Robert Bruce will soon, I trust, appear under the care of my learned friend, the Rev. Dr. Jamieson.*

ABBOTSFORD, 10*th December,* 1814.

INTRODUCTION TO EDITION 1830.

I COULD hardly have chosen a subject more popular in Scotland than anything con-nected with the Bruce's history, unless I had attempted that of Wallace. But I am decidedly of opinion, that a popular, or what is called a *taking* title, though well qualified to ensure the publishers against loss, and clear their shelves of the original impression, is rather apt to be hazardous than otherwise to the reputation of the author. He who attempts a subject of distinguished popularity, has not the privilege of awakening the enthusiasm of his audience; on the contrary, it is already awakened, and glows, it may be, more ardently than that of the author himself. In this case, the warmth of the author is inferior to that of the party whom he addresses, who has, therefore, little chance of being, in Bayes's phrase, "elevated and surprised" by what he has thought of with more enthusiasm than the writer. The sense of this risk, joined to the consciousness of striving against wind and tide, made the task of composing the proposed Poem somewhat heavy and hopeless;

* "The Bruce and Wallace." 2 vols., 4to, 1820.

but, like the prize-fighter in " As You Like It," I was to wrestle for my reputation, and not neglect any advantage. In a most agreeable pleasure-voyage, which I have tried to commemorate in the Introduction to the new edition of the " Pirate," I visited, in social and friendly company, the coasts and islands of Scotland, and made myself acquainted with the localities of which I meant to treat. But this voyage, which was in every other effect so delightful, was in its conclusion saddened by one of those strokes of fate which so often mingle themselves with our pleasures. The accomplished and excellent person * who had recommended to me the subject for " The Lay of the Last Minstrel," and to whom I proposed to inscribe what I already suspected might be the close of my poetical labors, was unexpectedly removed from the world, which she seemed only to have visited for purposes of kindness and benevolence. It is needless to say how the author's feelings, or the composition of his trifling work, were affected by a circumstance which occasioned so many tears and so much sorrow. True it is, that " The Lord of the Isles " was concluded, unwillingly and in haste, under the painful feeling of one who has a task which must be finished, rather than with the ardor of one who endeavors to perform that task well. Although the Poem cannot be said to have made a favorable impression on the public, the sale of fifteen thousand copies enabled the author to retreat from the field with the honors of war.

In the mean time, what was necessarily to be considered as a failure, was much reconciled to my feelings by the success attending my attempt in another species of composition. " Waverley " had, under strict incognito, taken its flight from the press, just before I set out upon the voyage already mentioned ; it had now made its way to popularity, and the success of that work, and the volumes which followed, was sufficient to have satisfied a greater appetite for applause than I have at any time possessed.†

I may as well add in this place, that, being much urged by my intimate friend, now un happily no more, William Erskine (a Scottish judge, by the title of Lord Kinnedder), I agreed to write the little romantic tale called the " Bridal of Triermain ; " but it was on the condition that he should make no serious effort to disown the composition, if report should lay it at his door. As he was more than suspected of a taste for poetry, and as I took care, in several places, to mix something which might resemble (as far as was in my power) my friend's feeling and manner, the train easily caught, and two large editions were sold. A third being called for, Lord Kinnedder became unwilling to aid any longer a deception which was going further than he expected or desired, and the real author's name was given. Upon another occasion, I sent up another of these trifles, which, like school-boys' kites, served to show how the wind of popular taste was setting. The manner was supposed to be that of a rude minstrel or Scald, in opposition to the " Bridal of Triermain," which was designed to belong rather to the Italian school.

This new fugitive piece was called " Harold the Dauntless ; " and I am still astonished at my having committed the gross error of selecting the very name which Lord Byron had made so famous. It encountered rather an odd fate. My ingenious friend, Mr. James Hogg, had published about the same time, a work called the " Poetic Mirror," containing imitations of the principal living poets. There was in it a very good imitation of my own style, which bore such a resemblance to " Harold the Dauntless," that there was no discovering the original from the imitation ; and I believe that many who took the trouble of thinking upon the subject, were rather of the opinion that my ingenious friend was the true, and not the fictitious Simon Pure. Since this period, which was in the year 1817, the author has not been an intruder on the public by any poetical work of importance.

ABBOTSFORD, *April,* 1830.   W. S.

---

* Harriet, Duchess of Buccleuch, died Aug. 24, 1814.
† The first edition of Waverley appeared in July, 1814.

THE LORD OF THE ISLES.

CANTO FIRST.

AUTUMN departs — but still his mantle's fold
Rests on the groves of noble Somerville,*
Beneath a shroud of russet dropp'd with gold
Tweed and his tributaries mingle still;
Hoarser the wind, and deeper sounds the rill,
Yet lingering notes of sylvan music swell,
The deep-toned cushat, and the redbreast shrill;
And yet some tints of summer splendor tell
When the broad sun sinks down on Ettrick's western fell.

Autumn departs — from Gala's fields †
no more
Come rural sounds our kindred banks to cheer;
Blent with the stream, and gale that wafts it o'er,
No more the distant reaper's mirth we hear.
The last blithe shout hath died upon our ear,
And harvest-home hath hush'd the clanging wain,
On the waste hill no forms of life appear,
Save where, sad laggard of the autumnal train,
Some age-struck wanderer gleans few ears of scatter'd grain.

Deem'st thou these sadden'd scenes have pleasure still,
Lovest thou through Autumn's fading realms to stray,
To see the heath-flower wither'd on the hill,
To listen to the wood's expiring lay,
To note the red leaf shivering on the spray,
To mark the last bright tints the mountain stain,
On the waste fields to trace the gleaner's way,
And moralize on mortal joy and pain? —
O! if such scenes thou lovest, scorn not the minstrel strain.

No! do not scorn, although its hoarser note
Scarce with the cushat's homely song can vie,
Though faint its beauties as the tints remote
That gleam through mist in autumn's evening sky,
And few as leaves that tremble, sear and dry,

---

* The Pavilion was a frequent residence of Lord Somerville, who was the intimate friend and almost daily companion of the poet. He died in 1819. It was situated on the Tweed, over against Melrose, and in sight of Abbotsford.

† The river Gala, famous in song, flows into the Tweed a few hundred yards below Abbotsford; but probably the word *Gala* here stands for the poet's neighbor and kinsman, John Scott, Esq., of Gala.

When wild November hath his bugle
    wound;
Nor mock my toil — a lonely gleaner I
Through fields time-wasted, on sad in-
    quest bound,
here happier bards of yore have richer
    harvest found.

So shalt thou list, and haply not un-
    moved,
To a wild tale of Albyn's warrior day;
In distant lands, by the rough West
    reproved,
Still lives some relics of the ancient lay.
For, when on Coolin's hills the lights
    decay,
With such the Seer of Skye the eve
    beguiles;
'Tis known amidst the pathless wastes
    of Reay,
In Harries known, and in Iona's piles,
here rest from mortal coil the Mighty
    of the Isles.

I.

Wake, Maid of Lorn!" the Minstrels
    sung.
y rugged halls, Artornish! rung,[1]
d the dark seas thy towers that lave,
aved on the beach a softer wave,
    mid the tuneful choir to keep
e diapason of the Deep.
ll'd were the winds of Inninmore,
d green Loch-Alline's woodland shore,
    if wild woods and waves had pleasure
listing to the lovely measure.
d ne'er to symphony more sweet
ve mountain echoes answer meet,
ice, met from mainland and from isle,
ss, Arran, Ilay, and Argyle,
ch minstrel's tributary lay
id homage to the festal day.
ll and dishonor'd were the bard,
orthless of guerdon and regard,
af to the hope of minstrel fame,
lady's smiles, his noblest aim,
ho on that morn's resistless call
ere silent in Artornish hall.

II.

Wake, Maid of Lorn!" 'twas thus they
    sung,
d yet more proud the descant rung,

"Wake, Maid of Lorn! high right is ours,
To charm dull sleep from Beauty's bowers.
Earth, Ocean, Air, have naught so shy
But owns the power of minstrelsy.
In Lettermore the timid deer
Will pause, the harp's wild chime to hear;
Rude Heiskar's seal through surges dark
Will long pursue the minstrel's bark;[2]
To list his notes, the eagle proud
Will poise him on Ben-Cailliach's cloud;
Then let not Maiden's ear disdain
The summons of the minstrel train,
But while our harps wild music make,
Edith of Lorn, awake, awake!

III.

"O wake, while Dawn, with dewy shine,
Wakes Nature's charms to vie with thine!
She bids the mottled thrush rejoice
To mate thy melody of voice;
The dew that on the violet lies
Mocks the dark lustre of thine eyes;
But, Edith, wake, and all we see
Of sweet and fair shall yield to thee!" —
"She comes not yet," gray Ferrand cried;
"Brethren, let softer spell be tried,
Those notes prolong'd, that soothing
    theme
Which best may mix with Beauty's dream,
And whisper, with their silvery tone,
The hope she loves, yet fears to own."
He spoke, and on the harp-strings died
The strains of flattery and of pride;
More soft, more low, more tender fell
The lay of love he bade them tell.

IV.

"Wake, Maid of Lorn! the moments fly,
    Which yet that maiden-name allow;
Wake, Maiden, wake! the hour is nigh
    When Love shall claim a plighted vow.
By Fear, thy bosom's fluttering guest,
    By Hope, that soon shall fears remove,
We bid thee break the bonds of rest,
    And wake thee at the call of Love!

"Wake, Edith, wake! in yonder bay
    Lies many a galley gayly mann'd,
We hear the merry pibrochs play,
    We see the streamers' silken band.
What Chieftain's praise these pibrochs
    swell,
    What crest is on these banners wove,

The harp, the minstrel, dare not tell —
The riddle must be read by Love.''

v.

Retired her maiden train among,
Edith of Lorn received the song,
But tamed the minstrel's pride had been
That had her cold demeanor seen;
For not upon her cheek awoke
The glow of pride when Flattery spoke,
Nor could their tenderest numbers bring
One sigh responsive to the string.
As vainly had her maidens vied
In skill to deck the princely bride.
Her locks, in dark-brown length array'd,
Cathleen of Ulne, 'twas thine to braid;
Young Eva with meet reverence drew
On the light foot the silken shoe,
While on the ankle's slender round
Those strings of pearl fair Bertha wound,
That, bleach'd Lochryan's depths within,
Seem'd dusky still on Edith's skin.
But Einion, of experience old,
Had weightiest task — the mantle's fold
In many an artful plait she tied,
To show the form it seem'd to hide,
Till on the floor descending roll'd
Its waves of crimson blent with gold.

vi.

O! lives there now so cold a maid,
Who thus in beauty's pomp array'd,
In beauty's proudest pitch of power,
And conquest won — the bridal hour —
With every charm that wins the heart,
By Nature given, enhanced by Art,
Could yet the fair reflection view,
In the bright mirror pictured true,
And not one dimple on her cheek
A tell-tale consciousness bespeak?
Lives still such maid?—Fair damsels, say,
For further vouches not my lay,
Save that such lived in Britain's isle,
When Lorn's bright Edith scorn'd to
smile.

vii.

But Morag, to whose fostering care
Proud Lorn had given his daughter fair,
Morag, who saw a mother's aid
By all a daughter's love repaid,
(Strict was that bond — most kind of all—
Inviolate in Highland hall) —

Gray Morag sate a space apart.
In Edith's eyes to read her heart.
In vain the attendants' fond appeal
To Morag's skill, to Morag's zeal;
She mark'd her child receive their care
Cold as the image sculptured fair,
(Form of some sainted patroness,)
Which cloister'd maids combine to dress
She mark'd — and knew her nursling
heart
In the vain pomp took little part.
Wistful a while she gazed — then press'
The maiden to her anxious breast
In finish'd loveliness — and led
To where a turret's airy head,
Slender and steep, and battled round,
O'erlook'd, dark Mull! thy might
Sound,[3]
Where thwarting tides,with mingled roa
Part thy swarth hills from Morven's shor

viii.

'' Daughter,'' she said, '' these seas b
hold,
Round twice a hundred islands roll'd,
From Hirt, that hears their norther
roar,
To the green Ilay's fertile shore;[*]
Or mainland turn, where many a towe
Owns thy bold brother's feudal power,
Each on its own dark cape reclined,
And listening to its own wild wind,
From where Mingarry, sternly placed,
O'erawes the woodland and the waste,
To where Dunstaffnage hears the ragin
Of Connal with his rocks engaging.
Think'st thou, amid this ample round,
A single brow but thine has frown'd,
To sadden this auspicious hour,
That bids the daughter of high Lorn
Impledge her spousal faith to wed
The heir of mighty Somerled![4]
Ronald, from many a hero sprung,
The fair, the valiant, and the young,
LORD OF THE ISLES, whose lofty nam
A thousand bards have given to fame,

[*] St. Kilda is the most northerly of the t
hundred or more Western Islands. It was
ciently called Hirth or Hirt, probably mean
Earth; being, in fact, the whole earth to its
habitants. Green Ilay is, if not the largest,
the most fertile and important, of the Hebrid
and was originally the principal abode of
Lords of the Isles.

he mate of monarchs, and allied
on equal terms with England's pride. —
rom chieftain's tower to bondsman's
        cot,
Who hears the tale, and triumphs not?
he damsel dons her best attire,
he shepherd lights his beltane fire,
y, joy! each warder's horn hath sung,
y, joy! each matin bell hath rung;
he holy priest says grateful mass,
ud shouts each hardy galla-glass,
o mountain den holds outcast boor,
f heart so dull, of soul so poor,
at he hath flung his task aside,
d claim'd this morn for holy-tide;
et, empress of this joyful day,
lith is sad while all are gay." —

IX.

oud Edith's soul came to her eye,
sentment check'd the struggling sigh,
er hurrying hand indignant dried
he burning tears of injured pride: —
Morag, forbear! or lend thy praise
o swell yon hireling harpers' lays;
ake to yon maids thy boast of power,
at they may waste a wondering hour,
lling of banners proudly borne,
pealing bell and bugle-horn,
, theme more dear, of robes of price,
ownlets and gauds of rare device.
at thou, experienced as thou art,
ink'st thou with these to cheat the heart,
at, bound in strong affection's chain,
oks for return and looks in vain?
o! sum thine Edith's wretched lot
these brief words — He loves her not!

X.

Debate it not — too long I strove
call his cold observance love,
blinded by the league that styled
ith of Lorn — while yet a child,
e tripp'd the heath by Morag's side, —
e brave Lord Ronald's destined bride.
e yet I saw him, while afar
s broadsword blazed in Scotland's war,
ain'd to believe our fates the same,
y bosom throbbed when Ronald's name
me gracing Fame's heroic tale,
e perfume on the summer gale.
hat pilgrim sought our halls, nor told
Ronald's deeds in battle bold?

Who touch'd the harp to heroes' praise,
But his achievements swell'd the lays?
Even Morag — not a tale of fame
Was hers but closed with Ronald's name.
He came! and all that had been told
Of his high worth seem'd poor and cold,
Tame, lifeless, void of energy,
Unjust to Ronald and to me!

XI.

"Since then, what thought had Edith's
        heart
And gave not plighted love its part! —
And what requital? cold delay —
Excuse that shunn'd the spousal day. —
It dawns, and Ronald is not here! —
Hunts he Bentalla's nimble deer,
Or loiters he in secret dell
To bid some lighter love farewell,
And swear, that though he may not scorn
A daughter of the House of Lorn,[6]
Yet, when these formal rites are o'er,
Again they meet, to part no more?"

XII.

— "Hush, daughter, hush? thy doubts
        remove,
More nobly think of Ronald's love.
Look, where beneath the castle gray
His fleet unmoor from Aros bay!
See'st not each galley's topmast bend,
As on the yards the sails ascend?
Hiding the dark-blue land, they rise
Like the white clouds on April skies;
The shouting vassals man the oars,
Behind them sink Mull's mountain shores,
Onward their merry course they keep,
Through whistling breeze and foaming
        deep.
And mark the headmost, seaward cast,
Stoop to the freshening gale her mast,
As if she veil'd its banner'd pride,
To greet afar her prince's bride!
Thy Ronald comes, and while in speed
His galley mates the flying steed,
He chides her sloth!" — Fair Edith
        sigh'd,
Blushed, sadly smiled, and thus replied: —

XIII.

"Sweet thought, but vain! — No, Morag,
        mark,
Type of his course, yon lonely bark,

That oft hath shifted helm and sail,
To win its way against the gale.
Since peep of morn, my vacant eyes
Have view'd by fits the course she tries;
Now, though the darkening scud comes on,
And dawn's fair promises be gone,
And though the weary crew may see
Our sheltering haven on their lee,
Still closer to the rising wind
They strive her shivering sail to bind,
Still nearer to the shelves' dread verge
At every tack their course they urge,
As if they fear'd Artonish more
Than adverse winds and breakers' roar.

XIV.

Sooth spoke the maid. — Amid the tide
　The skiff she mark'd lay tossing sore,
And shifted oft her stooping side,
　In weary tack from shore to shore.
Yet on her destined course no more
　She gain'd, of forward way,
Than what a minstrel may compare
To the poor meed which peasants share,
　Who toil the livelong day;
And such the risk her pilot braves,
　That oft, before she wore,
Her bowsprit kiss'd the broken waves,
Where in white foam the ocean raves
　Upon the shelving shore.
Yet, to their destined purpose true,
Undaunted toil'd her hardy crew,
　Nor look'd where shelter lay,
Nor for Artornish Castle drew,
　Nor steer'd for Aros bay.

XV.

Thus while they strove with wind and seas,
Borne onward by the willing breeze,
　Lord Ronald's fleet swept by,
Streamer'd with silk, and trick'd with
　gold,
Mann'd with the noble and the bold
　Of Island chivalry.
Around their prows the ocean roars,
And chafes beneath their thousand oars,
　Yet bears them on their way;
So chafes the war-horse in his might,
That fieldward bears some valiant knight,
Champs, till both bit and boss are white,
　But, foaming, must obey.
On each gay deck they might behold
Lances of steel and crests of gold,

And hauberks with their burnish'd fol
　That shimmer'd fair and free;
And each proud galley, as she pass'd,
To the wild cadence of the blast
　Gave wilder minstrelsy.
Full many a shrill triumphant note
Saline and Scallastle bade float
　Their misty shores around;
And Morven's echoes answer'd well,
And Duart heard the distant swell
　Come down the darksome Sound.

XVI.

So bore they on with mirth and pride
And if that laboring bark they spied,
　'Twas with such idle eye
As nobles cast on lowly boor,
When, toiling in his task obscure,
　They pass him careless by.
Let them sweep on with heedless eye
But, had they known what mighty p
　In that frail vessel lay,
The famish'd wolf, that prowls the w
Had scatheless passed the unguarded f
Ere, drifting by these galleys bold,
　Unchallenged were her way!
And thou, Lord Ronald, sweep
　on,
With mirth, and pride, and minstrel t
But hadst thou known who sail'
　nigh,
Far other glance were in thine eye!
Far other flush were on thy brow,
That, shaded by the bonnet, now
Assumes but ill the blithesome cheer
Of bridegroom when the bride is nea

XVII.

Yes, sweep they on! — We will not le
For them that triumph, those who gr
　With that armada gay
Be laughter loud and jocund shout,
And bards to cheer the wassail rout,
　With tale, romance, and lay;
And of wild mirth each clamorous a
Which, if it cannot cheer the heart,
May stupify and stun its smart,
　For one loud busy day.
Yes, sweep they on! — But with that
　Abides the minstrel tale,
Where there was dread of surge and
Labor that strained each sinew stiff,
　And one sad Maiden's wail.

XVIII.

ll day with fruitless strife they toil'd,
  /ith eve the ebbing currents boil'd
   More fierce from strait and lake;
nd midway through the channel met
  onflicting tides that foam and fret,
nd high their mingled billows jet,
  s spears, that, in the battle set,
   Spring upward as they break.
hen, too, the lights of eve were past,
nd louder sung the western blast
   On rocks of Inninmore;
ent was the sail, and strain'd the mast,
nd many a leak was gaping fast,
nd the pale steersman stood aghast,
   And gave the conflict o'er

XIX.

'was then that One, whose lofty looк
or labor dull'd nor terror shook,
  Thus to the Leader spoke:—
Brother, how hopest thou to abide
he fury of this wilder'd tide,
r how avoid the rock's rude side,
  Until the day has broke?
idst thou not mark the vessel reel,
/ith quivering planks, and groaning keel,
  At the last billow's shock?
et how of better ·counsel tell,
hough here thou see'st poor Isabel
  Half dead with want and fear;
or look on sea, or look on land,
n yon dark sky — on every hand
  Despair and death are near.
or her alone I grieve, — on me
anger sits light, by land and sea,
  I follow where thou wilt;
ither to bide the tempest's lour,
r wend to yon unfriendly tower,
r rush amid their naval power,
/ith war-cry wake their wassail-hour,
  And die with hand on hilt."

XX.

hat elder Leader's calm reply
  In steady voice was given:—
In man's most dark extremity
  Oft succor dawns from Heaven.
dward, trim thou the shatter'd sail,
he helm be mine, and down the gale
  Let our free course be driven;
ɔ shall we 'scape the western bay,
he hostile fleet, the unequal fray,

So safely hold our vessel's way
  Beneath the Castle wall;
For if a hope of safety rest,
'Tis on the sacred name of guest,
Who seeks for shelter, storm-distress d,
  Within a chieftain's hall.
If not — it best beseems our worth,
Our name, our right, our lofty birth,
  By noble hands to fall."

XXI.

The helm, to his strong arm consign'd,
Gave the reef'd sail to meet the wind,
  And on her alter'd way,
Fierce bounding, forward sprung the ship,
Like greyhound starting from the slip
  To seize his flying prey.
Awaked before the rushing prow,
The mimic fires of ocean glow,
  Those lightnings of the wave;[7]
Wild sparkles crest the broken tides,
And, flashing round, the vessel's sides
  With elvish lustre lave,
While, far behind, their livid light
To the dark billows of the night
  A gloomy splendor gave.
It seems as if old Ocean shakes
From his dark brow the lucid flakes
  In envious pageantry,
To match the meteor-light that streaks
  Grim Hecla's midnight sky.

XXII.

Nor lack'd they steadier light to keep
Their course upon the darken'd deep;—
Artornish, on her frowning steep
  'Twixt cloud and ocean hung,
Glanced with a thousand lights of glee,
And landward far, and far to sea,
  Her festal radiance flung.
By that blithe beacon-light they steer'd,
  Whose lustre mingled well
With the pale beam that now appear'd,
As the cold moon her head uprear'd
  Above the eastern fell.

XXIII.

Thus guided, on their course they bore,
Until they near'd the mainland shore,
When frequent on the hollow blast
Wild shouts of merriment were cast,
And wind and wave and sea-birds' cry
With wassail sounds in concert vie,

Like funeral shrieks with revelry,
　Or like the battle-shout
By peasants heard from cliffs on high,
When Triumph, Rage, and Agony,
　Madden the fight and rout.
Now nearer yet, through mist and storm
Dimly arose the Castle's form,
　And deepen'd shadow made,
Far lengthen'd on the main below,
Where, dancing in reflected glow,
　A hundred torches play'd,
Spangling the wave with lights as vain
As pleasures in this vale of pain,
　That dazzle as they fade.

XXIV.

Beneath the Castle's sheltering lee,
They staid their course in quiet sea.
Hewn in the rock, a passage there
Sought the dark fortress by a stair,
　So strait, so high, so steep,
With peasant's staff one valiant hand
Might well the dizzy pass have mann'd,
'Gainst hundreds arm'd with spear and
　　brand,
　And plunged them in the deep.
His bugle then the helmsman wound;
Loud answer'd every echo round,
　From turret, rock, and bay,
The postern's hinges crash and groan,
And soon the warder's cresset shone
On those rude steps of slippery stone,
　To light the upward way.
"Thrice welcome, holy Sire!" he said;
"Full long the spousal train have staid,
　And, vex'd at thy delay,
Fear'd lest, amidst these wildering seas,
The darksome night and freshening breeze
　Had driven thy bark astray."

XXV.

"Warder," the younger stranger said,
"Thine erring guess some mirth had made
In mirthful hour; but nights like these,
When the rough winds wake western seas,
Brook not of glee.　We crave some aid
And needful shelter for this maid
　Until the break of day;
For, to ourselves, the deck's rude plank
Is easy as the mossy bank
　That's breath'd upon by May.
And for our storm-toss'd skiff we seek
Short shelter in this leeward creek,

Prompt when the dawn the east sha'
　streak
　Again to bear away." —
Answer'd the Warder:— "In what nam
Assert ye hospitable claim?
　Whence come, or whither bound?
Hath Erin seen your parting sails?
Or come ye on Norweyan gales?
And seek ye England's fertile vales,
　Or Scotland's mountain ground?" —

XXVI.

"Warriors — for other title none
For some brief space we list to own,
Bound by a vow — warriors are we;
In strife by land, and storm by sea,
　We have been known to fame;
And these brief words have impo
　dear,
When sounded in a noble ear,
To harbor safe, and friendly cheer,
　That gives us rightful claim.
Grant us the trivial boon we seek,
And we in other realms will speak
　Fair of your courtesy;
Deny — and be your niggard Hold
Scorn'd by the noble and the bold,
Shunn'd by the pilgrim on the wold,
　And wanderer on the lea!" —

XXVII.

"Bold stranger, no — 'gainst claim li
　thine,
No bolt revolves by hand of mine,
Though urged in tone that more express
A monarch than a suppliant guest.
Be what ye will, Artornish Hall
On this glad eve is free to all.
Though ye had drawn a hostile sword
'Gainst our ally, great England's Lord
Or mail upon your shoulders borne,
To battle with the Lord of Lorn,
Or, outlaw'd, dwelt by greenwood tree
With the fierce Knight of Ellerslie,*
Or aided even the murderous strife,
When Comyn fell beneath the knife
Of that fell homicide The Bruce,†
This night had been a term of truce. –
Ho, vassals! give these guests your car
And show the narrow postern stair."

---

* Sir William Wallace.
† See Note 12.

XXVIII.

land these two bold brethren leapt,
The weary crew their vessel kept,)
nd, lighted by the torches' flare,
That seaward flung their smoky glare,
he younger knight that maiden bare
  Half lifeless up the rock;
n his strong shoulder lean'd her head,
nd down her long dark tresses shed,
s the wild vines in tendrils spread,
  Droops from the mountain oak.
im follow'd close that elder Lord,
nd in his hand a sheathed sword,
  Such as few arms could wield;
ut when he boun'd him to such task,
ell could it cleave the strongest casque,
  And rend the surest shield.

XXIX.

he raised portcullis' arch they pass,
he wicket with its bars of brass,
  The entrance long and low,
ank'd at each turn by loop-holes strait,
Where bowmen might in ambush wait,
f force or fraud should burst the gate,)
  To gall an entering foe.
ut every jealous post of ward
Was now defenceless and unbarr'd,
  And all the passage free
o one low-brow'd and vaulted room,
Where squire and yeoman, page and
    groom,
  Plied their loud revelry.

XXX.

nd "Rest ye here," the Warder
    bade,
Till to our Lord your suit is said. —
nd, comrades, gaze not on the maid,
nd on these men who ask our aid,
  As if ye ne'er had seen
damsel tired of midnight bark,
r wanderers of a moulding stark,
  And bearing martial mien."
ut not for Eachin's reproof
Vould page or vassal stand aloof,
  But crowded on to stare,
s men of courtesy untaught,
ill fiery Edward roughly caught,
  From one the foremost there,
is checker'd plaid, and in its shroud,
o hide her from the vulgar crowd,
  Involved his sister fair.

His brother, as the clansman bent
His sullen brow in discontent,
  Made brief and stern excuse: —
"Vassal, were thine the cloak of pall
That decks thy lord in bridal hall,
  'Twere honor'd by her use."

XXXI.

Proud was his tone, but calm; his eye
Had that compelling dignity,
His mien that bearing haught and high,
  Which common spirits fear!
Needed nor word nor signal more,
Nod, wink, and laughter, all were
    o'er;
Upon each other back they bore,
  And gazed like startled deer.
But now appear'd the Seneschal,
Commission'd by his Lord to call
The strangers to the Baron's hall,
  Where feasted fair and free
That Island Prince in nuptial tide,
With Edith there his lovely bride,
And her bold brother by her side,
And many a chief, the flower and pride
  Of Western land and sea.

Here pause we, gentles, for a space;
And if our tale hath won your grace,
Grant us brief patience, and again
We will renew the minstrel strain.

CANTO SECOND.

I.

FILL the bright goblet, spread the fes-
    tive board!
Summon the gay, the noble, and the
    fair!
Through the loud hall in joyous concert
    pour'd,
Let mirth and music sound the dirge of
    Care!
But ask thou not if Happiness be there,
If the loud laugh disguise convulsive
    throe,
Or if the brow the heart's true livery
    wear;
Lift not the festal mask! — enough to
    know,
No scene of mortal life but teems with
    mortal woe.

II.

With beakers' clang, with harpers' lay,
With all that olden time deem'd gay,
The Island Chieftain feasted high;
But there was in his troubled eye
A gloomy fire, and on his brow,
Now sudden flush'd, and faded now,
Emotions such as draw their birth
From deeper source than festal mirth.
By fits he paused, and harper's strain
And jester's tale went round in vain,
Or fell but on his idle ear
Like distant sounds which dreamers hear.
Then would he rouse him, and employ
Each art to aid the clamorous joy,
   And call for pledge and lay,
And, for brief space, of all the crowd,
As he was loudest of the loud,
   Seem gayest of the gay.

III.

Yet naught amiss the bridal throng
Mark'd in brief mirth, or musing long;
The vacant brow, the unlistening ear,
They gave to thoughts of raptures near,
And his fierce starts of sudden glee
Seem'd bursts of bridegroom's ecstasy.
Nor thus alone misjudged the crowd,
Since lofty Lorn, suspicious, proud,
And jealous of his honor'd line,
And that keen knight, De Argentine,[8]
(From England sent on errand high,
The western league more firm to tie,)
Both deem'd in Ronald's mood to find
A lover's transport-troubled mind.
But one sad heart, one tearful eye,
Pierced deeper through the mystery,
And watch'd, with agony and fear,
Her wayward bridegroom's varied cheer.

IV.

She watch'd — yet fear'd to meet his
   glance,
And he shunn'd hers; —till when by chance
They met, the point of foeman's lance
   Had given a milder pang!
Beneath the intolerable smart
He writhed;— then sternly mann'd his
   heart
To play his hard but destined part,
   And from the table sprang.
" Fill me the mighty cup! " he said,
" Erst own'd by royal Somerled: [9]

Fill it, till on the studded brim
In burning gold the bubbles swim,
And every gem of varied shine
Glow doubly bright in rosy wine !
   To you, brave lord, and brother min
     Of Lorn, this pledge I drink —
   The union of Our House with thine,
     By this fair bridal-link ! ''

V.

" Let it pass round !'' quoth he of Lcr
" And in good time : — that winded ho
   Must of the Abbot tell;
The laggard monk is come at last.''
Lord Ronald heard the bugle-blast,
And on the floor at random cast,
   The untasted goblet fell.
But when the warder in his ear
Tells other news, his blither cheer
   Returns like sun of May,
When through a thunder-cloud
   beams ! —
Lord of two hundred isles, he seems
   As glad of brief delay,
As some poor criminal might feel,
When, from the gibbet or the wheel,
   Respited for a day.

VI.

" Brother of Lorn," with hurried voic
He said, " and you, fair lords, rejoice
   Here, to augment our glee,
Come wandering knights from travel fa
Well proved, they say, in strife of war,
   And tempest on the sea. —
Ho ! give them at your board such plac
   As best their presences may grace,
     And bid them welcome free ! ''
With solemn step, and silver wand,
The Seneschal the presence scann'd
Of these strange guests; and well he kne
How to assign their rank its due;
   For though the costly furs
That erst had deck'd their caps were torn
And their gay robes were over-worn,
   And soil'd their gilded spurs,
Yet such a high commanding grace
Was in their mien and in their face,
As suited best the princely dais,*
   And royal canopy;

* Dais — the great hall-table — elevated a ste
or two above the rest of the room.

d there he marshall'd them their place,
First of that company.

VII.

en lords and ladies spake aside,
d angry looks the error chide,
at gave to guests unnamed, unknown,
place so near their prince's throne;
But Owen Erraught said: —
For forty years a seneschal,
marshal guests in bower and hall
Has been my honor'd trade.
rship and birth to me are known,
look, by bearing, and by tone,
t by furr'd robe or broider'd zone;
And 'gainst an oaken bough
gage my silver wand of state,
at these three strangers oft have sate
In higher place than now." —

VIII.

, too," the aged Ferrand said,
Am qualified by minstrel trade
Of rank and place to tell; —
rk'd ye the younger stranger's eye,
y mates, how quick, how keen, how high,
How fierce its flashes fell,
ancing among the noble rout
if to seek the noblest out,
cause the owner might not brook
a any save his peers to look?
And yet it moves me more,
at steady, calm, majestic brow,
ith which the elder chief even now
Scann'd the gay presence o'er,
ke being of superior kind,
whose high-toned impartial mind
grees of mortal rank and state
em objects of indifferent weight.
The lady too — though closely tied
The mantle veil both face and eye,
Her motion's grace it could not hide,
Nor cloud her form's fair symmetry."

IX.

spicious doubt and lordly scorn
ur'd on the haughty front of Lorn.
om underneath his brows of pride,
e stranger guests he sternly eyed,
d whisper'd closely what the ear
Argentine alone might hear;
Then question'd, high and brief,

If, in their voyage, aught they knew
Of the rebellious Scottish crew,
Who to Rath-Erin's shelter drew,
   With Carrick's outlaw'd Chief ! [10]
And if, their winter's exile o'er,
They harbor'd still by Ulster's shore,
Or launch'd their galleys on the main,
To vex their native land again?

X.

That younger stranger, fierce and high,
At once confronts the Chieftain's eye
   With look of equal scorn: —
" Of rebels have we naught to show;
But if of Royal Bruce thou'dst know,
   I warn thee he has sworn,
Ere thrice three days shall come and go,
His banner Scottish winds shall blow,
Despite each mean or mighty foe,
From England's every bill and bow,
   To Allaster of Lorn."
Kindled the mountain Chieftain's ire,
But Ronald quench'd the rising fire: —
" Brother, it better suits the time
To chase the night with Ferrand's rhyme,
Than wake, midst mirth and wine, the jars
That flow from these unhappy wars." —
" Content," said Lorn; and spoke apart
With Ferrand, master of his art,
   Then whisper'd Argentine: —
" The lay I named will carry smart
To these bold strangers' haughty heart,
   If right this guess of mine."
He ceased, and it was silence all,
Until the minstrel waked the hall.

XI.

THE BROOCH OF LORN.[11]

" Whence the brooch of burning gold,
That clasps the Chieftain's mantle-fold,
Wrought and chased with rare device,
Studded fair with gems of price,
On the varied tartans beaming,
As, through night's pale rainbow gleaming,
Fainter now, now seen afar,
Fitful shines the northern star?

" Gem ! ne'er wrought on Highland mountain,
Did the fairy of the fountain,
Or the mermaid of the wave,
Frame thee in some coral cave?

Did, in Iceland's darksome mine,
Dwarf's swart hands thy metal twine?
Or, mortal-moulded, comest thou here,
From England's love, or France's fear?

XII.

SONG CONTINUED.

" No! — thy splendors nothing tell
Foreign art or faëry spell,
Moulded thou for monarch's use,
By the overweening Bruce,
When the royal robe he tied
O'er a heart of wrath and pride;
Thence in triumph wert thou torn,
By the victor hand of Lorn!

" When the gem was won and lost,
Widely was the war-cry toss'd!
Rung aloud Bendourish Fell,
Answer'd Douchart's sounding dell,
Fled the deer from wild Teyndrum,
When the homicide, o'ercome,
Hardly 'scaped with scathe and scorn,
Left the pledge with conquering Lorn!

XIII.

SONG CONCLUED.

" Vain was then the Douglas' brand,*
Vain the Campbell's vaunted hand,
Vain Kirkpatrick's bloody dirk,
Making sure of murderer's work: 12
Barendown fled fast away,
Fled the fiery De la Haye,13
When this brooch, triumphant borne,
Beam'd upon the breast of Lorn.

" Farthest fled its former Lord,
Left his men to brand and cord,
Bloody brand of Highland steel,
English gibbet, axe, and wheel.
Let him fly from coast to coast,
Dogg'd by Comyn's vengeful ghost,
While his spoils, in triumph worn,
Long shall grace victorious Lorn! "

XIV.

As glares the tiger on his foes,
Hemm'd in by hunters, spears, and bows,

---

* Sir James, called the good Lord Douglas,
who was wounded at the battle of Dalry, and
Sir Nigel or Niel Campbell, who married Marjorie, sister to Robert Bruce, were among his
most faithful adherents.

And, ere he bounds upon the ring,
Selects the object of his spring, —
Now on the Bard, now on his Lord,
So Edward glared and grasp'd his sword—
But stern his brother spoke: — " Be sti
What! art thou yet so wild of will,
After high deeds and sufferings long,
To chafe thee for a menial's song?—
Well hast thou framed, Old Man, th
strains
To praise the hand that pays thy pains
Yet something might thy song have to
Of Lorn's three vassals, true and bold,
Who rent their Lord from Bruce's hol
As underneath his knee he lay,
And died to save him in the fray.
I've heard the Bruce's cloak and clasp
Was clench'd within their dying grasp,
What time a hundred foemen more
Rush'd in, and back the victor bore,
Long after Lorn had left the strife,
Full glad to 'scape with limb and life. —
Enough of this — And, Minstrel, hold,
As minstrel hire, this chain of gold,
For future lays a fair excuse,
To speak more nobly of the Bruce."

XV.

" Now, by Columba's shrine, I swear,
And every saint that's buried there,
'Tis he himself! " Lorn sternly cries,
" And for my kinsman's death he dies.
As loudly Ronald calls — " Forbear!
Not in my sight while brand I wear,
O'ermatched by odds, shall warri
fall,
Or blood of stranger stain my hall!
This ancient fortress of my race
Shall be misfortune's resting-place,
Shelter and shield of the distress'd,
No slaughter-house for shipwreck
guest." —
" Talk not to me," fierce Lorn replied
" Of odds or match! — when Comyn die
Three daggers clash'd within his side!
Talk not to me of sheltering hall,
The Church of God saw Comyn fall!
On God's own altar streamed his bloo
While o'er my prostrate kinsman stood
The ruthless murderer — e'en as now —
With armed hand and scornful brow! -
Up, all who love me! blow on blow!
And lay the outlaw'd felons low! "

XVI.

hen up sprang many a mainland Lord,
bedient to their Chieftain's word.
arcaldine's arm is high in air,
nd Kinloch-Alline's blade is bare,
lack Murthok's dirk has left its sheath,
nd clench'd is Dermid's hand of death.
neir mutter'd threats of vengeance swell
ato a wild and warlike yell;
nward they press with weapons high,
ne affrighted females shriek and fly,
nd, Scotland, then thy brightest ray
ad darken'd ere its noon of day, —
at every chief of birth and fame,
nat from the Isles of Ocean came,
t Ronald's side that hour withstood
erce Lorn's relentless thirst for blood.

XVII.

ave Torquil from Dunvegan high,
ord of the misty hills of Skye,
ac-Niel, wild Bara's ancient thane,
uart, of bold Clan-Gillian's strain,
ergus of Canna's castled bay,
ac-Duffith, Lord of Colonsay,
oon as they saw the broadswords glance,
ith ready weapons rose at once,
ore prompt, that many an ancient feud,
all oft suppress'd, full oft renew'd,
low'd 'twixt the chieftains of Argyle,
nd many a lord of ocean's isle.
ild was the scene—each sword was bare,
ack stream'd each chieftain's shaggy
         hair,
gloomy opposition set,
yes, hands, and brandish'd weapons
         met;
ue gleaming o'er the social board,
ash'd to the torches many a sword;
nd soon those bridal lights may shine
a purple blood for rosy wine.

XVIII.

hile thus for blows and death prepared,
ach heart was up, each weapon bared,
ach foot advanced, — a surly pause
ill reverenced hospitable laws.
l menaced violence, but alike
eluctant each the first to strike,
for aye accursed in minstrel line
he who brawls mid song and wine,)
nd, match'd in numbers and in might,
oubtful and desperate seem'd the fight.

Thus threat and murmur died away,
Till on the crowded hall there lay
Such silence, as the deadly still,
Ere bursts the thunder on the hill.
With blade advanced, each chieftain bold
Show'd like the Sworder's form of old,
As wanting still the torch of life,
To wake the marble into strife.

XIX.

That awful pause the stranger maid,
And Edith, seized to pray for aid.
As to De Argentine she clung,
Away her veil the stranger flung,
And, lovely mid her wild despair,
Fast stream'd her eyes, wide flow'd her
         hair: —
" O thou, of knighthood once the flower,
Sure refuge in distressful hour,
Thou, who in Judah well hast fought
For our dear faith, and oft hast sought
Renown in knightly exercise,
When this poor hand has dealt the prize.
Say, can thy soul of honor brook
On the unequal strife to look,
When, butcher'd thus in peaceful hall,
Those once thy friends, my brethren,
         fall ! "
To Argentine she turn'd her word,
But her eye sought the Island Lord.
A flush like evening's setting flame
Glow'd on his cheek; his hardy frame,
As with a brief convulsion, shook:
With hurried voice and eager look, —
" Fear not," he said, " my Isabel !
What said I, — Edith ! — all is well —
Nay, fear not — I will well provide
The safety of my lovely bride —
My bride ? " but there the accents clung
In tremor to his faltering tongue.

XX.

Now rose De Argentine, to claim
The prisoners in his sovereign's name,
To England's crown, who, vassals sworn,
'Gainst their liege lord had weapon
         borne —
(Such speech, I ween, was but to hide
His care their safety to provide;
For knight more true in thought and deed
Than Argentine ne'er spurr'd a steed) —
And Ronald, who his meaning guess'd,
Seem'd half to sanction the request.

This purpose fiery Torquil broke: —
" Somewhat we've heard of England's
　　yoke,"
He said, " and, in our islands, Fame
Hath whisper'd of a lawful claim,
That calls the Bruce fair Scotland's
　　Lord,
Though dispossess'd by foreign sword.
This craves reflection — but though right
And just the charge of England's Knight,
Let England's crown her rebels seize
Where she has power; — in towers like
　　these,
Midst Scottish Chieftains summon'd here
To bridal mirth and bridal cheer,
Be sure, with no consent of mine,
Shall either Lorn or Argentine
With chains or violence, in our sight,
Oppress a brave and banish'd Knight."

XXI.

Then waked the wild debate again,
With brawling threat and clamor vain.
Vassals and menials, thronging in,
Lent their brute rage to swell the din;
When, far and wide, a bugle-clang
From the dark ocean upward rang.
　　" The Abbot comes ! " they cry at once,
　　" The holy man, whose favor'd glance
　　Hath sainted visions known;
　　Angels have met him on the way,
　　Beside the blessed martyrs' bay,
　　　And by Columba's stone.
　　His monks have heard their hymnings
　　　high
　　Sound from the summit of Dun-Y,
　　　To cheer his penance lone,
When at each cross, on girth and wold,
(Their number thrice a hundred-fold,)
His prayer he made, his beads he told,
　　With Aves many a one —
He comes our feuds to reconcile,
A sainted man from sainted isle;
We will his holy doom abide,
The Abbot shall our strife decide."

XXII.

Scarcely this fair accord was o'er,
When through the wide revolving door
　　The black-stoled brethren wind;
Twelve sandall'd monks, who relics bore,
With many a torch-bearer before,
　　And many a cross behind,

Then sunk each fierce uplifted hand,
And dagger bright and flashing brand
　　Dropp'd swiftly at the sight;
They vanish'd from the Churchman's ey
As shooting stars, that glance and die,
　　Dart from the vault of night.

XXIII.

The Abbot on the threshold stood,
And in his hand the holy rood;
Back on his shoulders flow'd his hood,
　　The torch's glaring ray
Show'd, in its red and flashing light,
His wither'd cheek and amice white,
His blue eye glistening cold and brigh
　　His tresses scant and gray.
" Fair Lords," he said, " our Lady
　　love,
And peace be with you from above,
　　And Benedicite !
— But what means this ? no peace is her
Do dirks unsheathed suit bridal cheer
　　Or are these naked brands
A seemly show for Churchman's sight
When he comes summon'd to unite
　　Betrothed hearts and hands ? "

XXIV

Then cloaking hate with fiery zeal,
Proud Lorn first answer'd the appeal:
　　" Thou comest, O holy Man,
True sons of blessed Church to greet,
But little deeming here to meet
　　A wretch, beneath the ban
Of Pope and Church, for murder done
Even on the sacred altar-stone ! —
Well mayest thou wonder we should kn
Such miscreant here, nor lay him low,
Or dream of greeting, peace, or truce
With excommunicated Bruce !
Yet well I grant, to end debate,
The sainted voice decide his fate."

XXV.

Then Ronald pled the stranger's cause
And knighthood's oath and honor's law
And Isabel, on bended knee,
Brought pray'rs and tears to back
　　plea;
And Edith lent her generous aid,
And wept, and Lorn for mercy pray'd
Hence," he exclaim'd, "degenerate ma
Was't not enough to Ronald's bower

brought thee, like a paramour,[14]
r bond-maid at her master's gate,
is careless cold approach to wait? —
it the bold Lord of Cumberland,
ie gallant Clifford, seeks thy hand;
is it shall be — Nay, no reply!
ence! till those rebel eyes be dry."
'ith grief the Abbot heard and saw,
et naught relax'd his brow of awe.

XXVI.

ien Argentine, in England's name,
> highly urged his sovereign's claim,
e waked a spark, that, long suppress'd,
ad smoulder'd in Lord Ronald's breast;
nd now, as from the flint the fire,
ash'd forth at once his generous ire:—
Enough of noble blood," he said,
By English Edward had been shed,
nce matchless Wallace first had been
   mock'ry crown'd with wreaths of
      green,[15]
id done to death by felon hand,
>r guarding well his father's land.
here's Nigel Bruce? and De la Haye,
id valiant Seton — where are they?
here Somerville, the kind and free?
id Fraser, flower of chivalry?
ave they not been on gibbet bound,
ieir quarters flung to hawk and hound,
id hold we here a cold debate,
> yield more victims to their fate?
hat! can the English Leopard's mood
ver be gorged with northern blood?
as not the life of Athole shed,
> soothe the tyrant's sicken'd bed?[16]
id must his word, till dying day,
: naught but quarter, hang, and slay! —
iou frown'st, De Argentine, — My gage
prompt to prove the strife I wage." —

XXVII.

Nor deem," said stout Dunvegan's
   knight,
That thou shalt brave alone the fight!
/ saints of isle and mainland both,
/ Woden wild (my grandsire's oath),*
et Rome and England do their worst,
owe'er attainted or accursed,

* The Macleods and most other distinguished
ebridean families were of Scandinavian descent.
ie family names, Torquil, Thormod, etc., are
Norwegian.

If Bruce shall e'er find friends again,
Once more to brave a battle-plain,
If Douglas couch again his lance,
Or Randolph dare another chance,
Old Torquil will not be to lack,
With twice a thousand at his back. —
Nay, chafe not at my bearing bold,
Good Abbot! for thou know'st of old,
Torquil's rude thought and stubborn will
Smack of the wild Norwegian still:
Nor will I barter Freedom's cause
For England's wealth, or Rome's ap-
   plause."

XXVIII.

The Abbot seem'd with eye severe
The hardy Chieftain's speech to hear;
Then on King Robert turn'd the Monk,
But twice his courage came and sunk,
Confronted with the hero's look;
Twice fell his eye, his accents shook;
At length, resolved in tone and brow,
Sternly he question'd him:— "And thou,
Unhappy! what hast thou to plead,
Why I denounce not on thy deed
That awful doom which canons tell
Shuts paradise, and opens hell!
Anathema of power so dread,
It blends the living with the dead,
Bids each good angel soar away,
And every ill one claim his prey;
Expels thee from the Church's care,
And deafens Heaven against thy prayer;
Arms every hand against thy life,
Bans all who aid thee in the strife,
Nay, each whose succor, cold and scant,
With meanest alms relieves thy want;
Haunts thee while living—and, when dead,
Dwells on thy yet devoted head,
Rends Honor's scutcheon from thy
   hearse,
Stills o'er thy bier the holy verse,
And spurns thy corpse from hallow'd
   ground,
Flung like vile carrion to the hound;
Such is the dire and desperate doom
For sacrilege, decreed by Rome;
And such the well-deserved meed
Of thine unhallow'd, ruthless deed."

XXIX.

"Abbot!" the Bruce replied, "thy charge
It boots not to dispute at large.

This much, howe'er, I bid thee know,
No selfish vengeance dealt the blow,
For Comyn died his country's foe.
Nor blame I friends whose ill-timed speed
Fulfilled my soon-repented deed,
Nor censure those from whose stern tongue
The dire anathema has rung.
I only blame mine own wild ire,
By Scotland's wrongs incensed to fire.
Heaven knows my purpose to atone,
Far as I may, the evil done,
And hears a penitent's appeal
From papal curse and prelate's zeal.
My first and dearest task achieved,
Fair Scotland from her thrall relieved,
Shall many a priest in cope and stole
Say requiem for Red Comyn's soul,
While I the blessed cross advance,
And expiate this unhappy chance
In Palestine, with sword and lance.[17]
But, while content the church should
      know
My conscience owns the debt I owe,
Unto De Argentine and Lorn
The name of traitor I return,
Bid them defiance stern and high,
And give them in their throats the lie!
These brief words spoke, I speak no
      more,
Do what thou wilt; my shrift is o'er."

XXX.

Like man by prodigy amazed,
Upon the King the Abbot gazed;
Then o'er his pallid features glance
Convulsions of ecstatic trance.
His breathing came more thick and fast,
And from his pale blue eyes were cast
Strange rays of wild and wandering light;
Uprise his locks in silver white,
Flush'd is his brow, through every vein
In azure tide the currents strain,
And undistinguish'd accents broke
The awful stillness ere he spoke:—

XXXI.

" De Bruce! I rose with purpose dread
To speak my curse upon thy head,[18]
And give thee as an outcast o'er
To him who burns to shed thy gore;
But, like the Midianite of old,
Who stood on Zophim, heaven-con-
      troll'd,

I feel within mine aged breast
A power that will not be repress'd.
It prompts my voice, it swells my veins
It burns, it maddens, it constrains! —
De Bruce, thy sacrilegious blow
Hath at God's altar slain thy foe:
O'ermaster'd yet by high behest,
I bless thee, and thou shalt be bless'd.
He spoke, and o'er the astonish'd thron
Was silence, awful, deep, and long.

XXXII.

Again that light has fired his eye,
Again his form swells bold and high,
The broken voice of age is gone,
'Tis vigorous manhood's lofty tone:—
" Thrice vanquish'd on the battle-plair
Thy followers slaughter'd, fled, or ta'en
A hunted wanderer on the wild,
On foreign shores a man exiled,[19]
Disown'd, deserted, and distress'd,
I bless thee, and thou shalt be bless'd
Bless'd in the hall and in the field,
Under the mantle as the shield.
Avenger of thy country's shame,
Restorer of her injured fame,
Bless'd in thy sceptre and thy sword,
De Bruce, fair Scotland's rightful Lord
Bless'd in thy deeds and in thy fame,
What lengthen'd honors wait thy nam
In distant ages, sire to son
Shall tell thy tale of freedom won,
And teach his infants, in the use
Of earliest speech, to falter Bruce.
Go, then, triumphant! sweep along
Thy course, the theme of many a song
The Power, whose dictates swell r
      breast,
Hath bless'd thee, and thou shalt
      bless'd! —
Enough — my short-lived strength d
      cays,
And sinks the momentary blaze. —
Heaven hath our destined purpose brok
Not here must nuptial vow be spoke;
Brethren, our errand here is o'er,
Our task discharged. — Unmoor, u
      moor!"
His priests received the exhausted Mon
As breathless in their arms he sunk.
Punctual his orders to obey,
The train refused all longer stay,
Embark'd, raised sail, and bore away.

CANTO THIRD.

I.

HAST thou not mark'd, when o'er thy
　　startled head
Sudden and deep the thunder-peal has
　　roll'd,
How, when its echoes fell, a silence
　　dead
Sunk on the wood, the meadow, and
　　the wold?
The rye-grass shakes not on the sod-
　　built fold,
The rustling aspen's leaves are mute
　　and still,
The wall-flower waves not on the ruin'd
　　hold,
Till, murmuring distant first, then near
　　and shrill,
The savage whirlwind wakes, and sweeps
　　the groaning hill.

II.

rtornish! such a silence sunk
pon thy halls, when that gray Monk
　His prophet speech had spoke;
nd his obedient brethren's sail
Jas stretch'd to meet the southern gale
　Before a whisper woke.
hen murmuring sounds of doubt and
　　fear,
ʼose pour'd in many an anxious ear,
　The solemn stillness broke;
nd still they gazed with eager guess,
ʼhere, in an oriel's deep recess,
ʼe Island Prince seem'd bent to press
ʼhat Lorn, by his impatient cheer,
ʼnd gesture fierce, scarce deign'd to hear.

III.

ʼarting at length, with frowning look,
ʼis hand he clench'd, his head he shook,
　And sternly flung apart: —
ʼAnd deem'st thou me so mean of mood,
ʼs to forget the mortal feud,
ʼnd clasp the hand with blood imbrued
　From my dear Kinsman's heart?
ʼthis thy rede? — a due return
ʼor ancient league and friendship sworn!
ʼt well our mountain proverb shows
ʼe faith of Islesmen ebbs and flows.
ʼe it even so — believe, ere long,
ʼe that now bears shall wreak the
　　wrong. —

Call Edith — call the Maid of Lorn!
My sister, slaves! — for further scorn,
Be sure nor she nor I will stay. —
Away, De Argentine, away! —
We nor ally nor brother know,
In Bruce's friend, or England's foe."

IV.

But who the Chieftain's rage can tell,
When, sought from lowest dungeon cell
To highest tower the castle round,
No Lady Edith was there found!
He　shouted: — " Falsehood! — treach-
　　ery! —
Revenge and blood! — a lordly meed
To him that will avenge the deed!
A Baron's lands!" — His frantic mood
Was scarcely by the news withstood,
That Morag shared his sister's flight,
And that, in hurry of the night,
'Scaped noteless, and without remark,
Two strangers sought the Abbot's bark. —
" Man every galley! — fly — pursue!
The priest his treachery shall rue!
Ay, and the time shall quickly come,
When we shall hear the thanks that Rome
Will pay his feigned prophecy!"
Such was fierce Lorn's indignant cry;
And Cormac Doil in haste obey'd,
Hoisted his sail, his anchor weigh'd,
(For, glad of each pretext for spoil,
A pirate sworn was Cormac Doil.)
But others, lingering, spoke apart: —
" The Maid has given her maiden heart
　To Ronald of the Isles,
And, fearful lest her brother's word
Bestow her on that English Lord,
　She seeks Iona's piles,
And wisely deems it best to dwell
A votaress in the holy cell,
Until these feuds so fierce and fell
　The Abbot reconciles."

V.

As, impotent of ire, the hall
Echo'd to Lorn's impatient call,
" My horse, my mantle, and my train!
Let none who honors Lorn remain!" —
Courteous, but stern, a bold request
To Bruce De Argentine express'd: —
" Lord Earl," he said, — " I cannot
　　chuse
But yield such title to the Bruce,

Though name and earldom both are gone,
Since he braced rebel's armor on —
But, Earl or Serf—rude phrase was thine
Of late, and launch'd at Argentine;
Such as compels me to demand
Redress of honor at thy hand.
We need not to each other tell,
That both can wield their weapons well;
  Then do me but the soldier grace,
  This glove upon thy helm to place
    Where we may meet in fight;
  And I will say, as still I've said,
  Though by ambition far misled,
    Thou art a noble knight." —

VI.

" And I," the princely Bruce replied,
" Might term it stain on knighthood's
    pride
That the bright sword of Argentine
Should in a tyrant's quarrel shine;
  But, for your brave request,
Be sure the honor'd pledge you gave
In every battle-field shall wave
  Upon my helmet-crest:
Believe, that if my hasty tongue
Hath done thine honor causeless wrong,
  It shall be well redress'd.
Not dearer to my soul was glove,
Bestow'd in youth by lady's love,
  Than this which thou hast given!
Thus, then, my noble foe I greet;
Health and high fortune till we meet,
  And then — what pleases Heaven."

VII.

Thus parted they — for now, with sound
Like waves roll'd back from rocky
    ground,
  The friends of Lorn retire;
Each mainland chieftain, with his train,
Draws to his mountain towers again,
Pondering how mortal schemes prove
    vain,
  And mortal hopes expire.
But through the castle double guard,
By Ronald's charge, kept wakeful ward'
Wicket and gate were trebly barr'd,
  By beam and bolt and chain;
Then of the guests, in courteous sort,
He pray'd excuse for mirth broke short,
And bade them in Artonish fort
  In confidence remain.

Now torch and menial tendance led
Chieftain and knight to bower and bed
And beads were told, and Aves said,
  And soon they sunk away
Into such sleep, as wont to shed
Oblivion on the weary head,
  After a toilsome day.

VIII.

But soon uproused, the Monarch cried
To Edward slumbering by his side : —
  " Awake, or sleep for aye !
Even now there jarr'd a secret door —
A taper-light gleams on the floor —
  Up, Edward, up, I say !
Some one glides in like midnight ghost -
Nay, strike not ! 'tis our noble Host.'
Advancing then his taper's flame,
Ronald stept forth, and with him came
  Dunvegan's chief—each bent the kne
  To Bruce in sign of fealty,
    And proffer'd him his sword,
  And hail'd him in a monarch's style,
  As king of mainland and of isle,
    And Scotland's rightful lord.
" And O," said Ronald, " Own'd
    Heaven !
Say, is my erring youth forgiven,
By falsehood's arts from duty driven,
  Who rebel falchion drew,
Yet ever to thy deeds of fame,
Even while I strove against thy claim,
  Paid homage just and true ? " —
" Alas ! dear youth, the unhappy time
Answer'd the Bruce, " must bear th
  crime,
  Since, guiltier far than you,
Even I " — he paused; for Falkirk
  woes
Upon his conscious soul arose.[20]
The Chieftain to his breast he press'd,
And in a sigh conceal'd the rest.

IX.

They proffer'd aid, by arms and .ght,
To repossess him in his right;
But well their counsels must be weigh'
Ere banners raised and musters made,
For English hire and Lorn's intrigues
Bound many chiefs in southern leagues
In answer, Bruce his purpose bold
To his new vassals frankly told : —
  " The winter worn in exile o'er,

long'd for Carrick's kindred shore.
I thought upon my native Ayr,
And long'd to see the burly fare
That Clifford makes, whose lordly call
Now echoes through my father's hall.
At first my course to Arran led,
Where valiant Lennox gathers head,
And on the sea, by tempest toss'd,
Our barks dispersed, our purpose cross'd,
Mine own, a hostile sail to shun,
Far from her destined course had run,
When that wise will, which masters
    ours,
Compell'd us to your friendly towers."

X.

Then Torquil spoke: — "The time craves
    speed!
We must not linger in our deed,
But instant pray our Sovereign Liege,
To shun the perils of a siege.
The vengeful Lorn, with all his powers,
Lies but too near Artornish towers,
And England's light-arm'd vessels ride,
Not distant far, the waves of Clyde,
Prompt at these tidings to unmoor,
And sweep each strait, and guard each
    shore.
Then, till this fresh alarm pass by,
Secret and safe my Liege must lie
In the far bounds of friendly Skye,
Torquil thy pilot and thy guide." —
— Not so, brave Chieftain," Ronald cried;
"Myself will on my Sovereign wait,
And raise in arms the men of Sleate,
Whilst thou, renown'd where chiefs de-
    bate,
Shalt sway their souls by counsel sage,
And awe them by thy locks of age."
— "And if my words in weight shall fail,
His ponderous sword shall turn the scale."

XI.

The scheme," said Bruce, "contents
    me well;
Meantime, 'twere best that Isabel,
For safety, with my bark and crew,
Again to friendly Erin drew.
There Edward, too, shall with her wend,
To need to cheer her and defend,
And muster up each scatter'd friend." —
Here seem'd it as Lord Ronald's ear
Would other counsel gladlier hear;

But, all achieved as soon as plann'd,
Both barks, in secret arm'd and mann'd,
    From out the haven bore;
On different voyage forth they ply,
This for the coast of winged Skye,
    And that for Erin's shore.

XII.

With Bruce and Ronald bides the tale. —
To favoring winds they gave the sail,
Till Mull's dark headlands scarce they
    knew,
And Ardnamurchan's hills were blue.
But then the squalls blew close and hard,
And, fain to strike the galley's yard,
    And take them to the oar,
With these rude seas in weary plight,
They strove the livelong day and night,
Nor till the dawning had a sight
    Of Skye's romantic shore.
Where Coolin stoops him to the west,
They saw upon his shiver'd crest
    The sun's arising gleam;
But such the labor and delay,
Ere they were moor'd in Scavigh bay,
(For calmer heaven compell'd to stay,)
    He shot a western beam.
Then Ronald said: — "If true mine eye,
These are the savage wilds that lie
North of Strathnardill and Dunskye; [21]
    No human foot comes here,
And, since these adverse breezes blow,
If my good Liege love hunter's bow,
What hinders that on land we go,
    And strike a mountain-deer?
Allan, my page, shall with us wend;
A bow full deftly can he bend,
And, if we meet a herd, may send
    A shaft shall mend our cheer."
Then each took bow and bolts in hand,
Their row-boat launch'd and leapt to land,
    And left their skiff and train,
Where a wild stream, with headlong shock,
Came brawling down its bed of rock,
    To mingle with the main.

XIII.

A while their route they silent made,
    As men who stalk for mountain-deer,
Till the good Bruce to Ronald said: —
    " St. Mary! what a scene is here!
I've traversed many a mountain-strand,
    Abroad and in my native land,

And it has been my lot to tread
Where safety more than pleasure led;
Thus, many a waste I've wander'd o'er,
Clomb many a crag, cross'd many a
    moor,
    But, by my halidome,
A scene so rude, so wild as this,
Yet so sublime in barrenness,
Ne'er did my wandering footsteps press,
    Where'er I happ'd to roam.''

XIV.

No marvel thus the Monarch spake;
    For rarely human eye has known
A scene so stern as that dread lake,
    With its dark ledge of barren stone.
Seems that primeval earthquake's sway
Hath rent a strange and shatter'd way
    Through the rude bosom of the hill,
And that each naked precipice,
Sable ravine, and dark abyss,
    Tells of the outrage still.
The wildest glen, but this, can show
Some touch of Nature's genial glow;
On high Benmore green mosses grow,
And heath-bells bud in deep Glencroe,
    And copse on Cruchan-Ben;
But here, — above, around, below,
    On mountain or in glen,
Nor tree, nor shrub, nor plant, nor flower,
Nor aught of vegetative power,
    The weary eye may ken.
For all is rocks at random thrown,
Black waves, bare crags, and banks of
    stone;
    As if were here denied
The summer sun, the spring's sweet dew,
That clothe with many a varied hue
    The bleakest mountain-side.

XV.

And wilder, forward as they wound,
. Were the proud cliffs and lake profound.
Huge terraces of granite black
Afforded rude and cumber'd track;
    For from the mountain hoar,
Hurl'd headlong in some night of fear,
When yell'd the wolf and fled the deer,
    Loose crags had toppled o'er;
And some, chance-poised and balanced,
    lay,
So that a stripling arm might sway
    A mass no host could raise,

In Nature's rage at random thrown,
Yet trembling like the Druid's stone
    On its precarious base.
The evening mists, with ceaseless change
Now clothed the mountains' lofty range
    Now left their foreheads bare,
And round the skirts their mantle furl'd
Or on the sable waters curl'd,
Or on the eddying breezes whirl'd,
    Dispersed in middle air.
And oft, condensed, at once they lower
When, brief and fierce, the mountain
    shower
    Pours like a torrent down,
And when return the sun's glad beams,
Whiten'd with foam a thousand streams
    Leap from the mountain's crown.

XVI.

"This lake," said Bruce, " whose bar
    riers drear
Are precipices sharp and sheer,
Yielding no track for goat or deer,
    Save the black shelves we tread,
How term you its dark waves? and how
Yon northern mountain's pathless brow
    And yonder peak of dread,
That to the evening sun uplifts
The grisly gulfs and slaty rifts,
    Which seam its shiver'd head? '' —
" Coriskin call the dark lake's name,
Coolin the ridge, as bards proclaim,
From old Cuchullin, chief of fame.
But bards, familiar in our isles
Rather with Nature's frowns than smiles
Full oft their careless humors please
By sportive names from scenes like these
I would old Torquil were to show
His maidens with their breasts of snow
Or that my noble Liege were nigh
To hear his nurse sing lullaby !
(The Maids — tall cliffs with breaker
    white,
The Nurse — a torrent's roaring might,
Or that your eye could see the mood
Of Corryvrekin's whirlpool rude,
When dons the Hag her whiten'd hood—
'Tis thus our islesmen's fancy frames,
For scenes so stern, fantastic names.''

XVII.

Answer'd the Bruce:—''And musing min
Might here a graver moral find.

These mighty cliffs, that heave on high
Their naked brows to middle sky,
Indifferent to the sun or snow,
Where naught can fade, and naught can
    blow,
May they not mark a Monarch's fate, —
Raised high mid storms of strife and state,
Beyond life's lowlier pleasures placed,
His soul a rock, his heart a waste?
O'er hope and love and fear aloft
High rears his crowned head — But soft!
Look, underneath yon jutting crag
Are hunters and a slaughter'd stag.
Who may they be?   But late you said
No steps these desert regions tread.'' —

XVIII.

'' So said I — and believed in sooth,''
Ronald replied, '' I spoke the truth.
Yet now I spy, by yonder stone,
Five men — they mark us, and come on;
And by their badge on bonnet borne,
I guess them of the land of Lorn,
Foes to my Liege.'' — '' So let it be;
I've faced worse odds than five to three —
— But the poor page can little aid;
Then be our battle thus array'd,
If our free passage they contest;
Cope thou with two, I'll match the
    rest.'' —
'' Not so, my Liege — for, by my life,
This sword shall meet the treble strife;
My strength, my skill in arms, more
    small,
And less the loss should Ronald fall.
But islemen soon to soldiers grow,
Allan has sword as well as bow,
And were my Monarch's order given,
Two shafts should make our number
    even.'' —
'' No! not to save my life!'' he said;
'' Enough of blood rests on my head,
Too rashly spill'd — we soon shall know,
Whether they come as friend or foe.''

XIX.

Nigh came the strangers, and more
    nigh; —
Still less they pleased the Monarch's eye.
Men were they all of evil mien,
Down-look'd, unwilling to be seen;
They moved with half-resolved pace,
And bent on earth each gloomy face.

The foremost two were fair array'd,
With brogue and bonnet, trews and plaid,
And bore the arms of mountaineers,
Daggers and broadswords, bows and
    spears.
The three, that lagg'd small space behind,
Seem'd serfs of more degraded kind;
Goat-skins or deer-hides o'er them cast,
Made a rude fence against the blast;
Their arms and feet and heads were bare,
Matted their beards, unshorn their hair;
For arms, the caitiffs bore in hand,
A club, an axe, a rusty brand.

XX.

Onward, still mute, they kept the track; —
'' Tell who ye be, or else stand back,''
Said Bruce; '' in deserts when they meet,
Men pass not as in peaceful street.''
Still, at his stern command, they stood,
And proffer'd greeting brief and rude,
But acted courtesy so ill,
As seem'd of fear, and not of will.
'' Wanderers we are, as you may be;
Men hither driven by wind and sea,
Who, if you list to taste our cheer,
Will share with you this fallow deer.''—
'' If from the sea, where lies your
    bark?'' —
'' Ten fathom deep in ocean dark!
Wreck'd yesternight: but we are men,
Who little sense of peril ken.
The shades come down — the day is
    shut —
Will you go with us to our hut?'' —
'' Our vessel waits us in the bay;
Thanks for your proffer — have good-
    day.'' —
'' Was that your galley, then, which rode
Not far from shore when evening
    glow'd?'' —
'' It was.'' — '' Then spare your needless
    pain,
There she will now be sought in vain.
We saw her from the mountain-head,
When, with St. George's blazon red,
A southern vessel bore in sight,
And yours raised sail, and took to
    flight.'' —

XXI.

'' Now, by the rood, unwelcome news!''
Thus with Lord Ronald communed Bruce;

' Nor rests there light enough to show
If this their tale be true or no.
The men seem bred of churlish kind,
Yet mellow nuts have hardest rind;
We will go with them — food and fire
And sheltering roof our wants require.
Sure guard 'gainst treachery will we keep,
And watch by turns our comrades'
　　sleep. —
Good fellows, thanks; your guests we'll
　　be,
And well will pay the courtesy.
Come, lead us where your lodging lies, —
— Nay, soft, we mix not companies. —
Show us the path o'er crag and stone,
And we will follow you; — lead on."

XXII.

They reach'd the dreary cabin, made
Of sails against a rock display'd,
　　And there, on entering, found
A slender boy, whose form and mien
Ill suited with such savage scene,
In cap and cloak of velvet green,
　　Low seated on the ground.
His garb was such as minstrels wear,
Dark was his hue, and dark his hair,
His youthful cheek was marr'd by care,
　　His eyes in sorrow drown'd.
" Whence this poor boy?" — As Ron-
　　ald spoke,
The voice his trance of anguish broke;
As if awaked from ghastly dream,
He raised his head with start and scream,
　　And wildly gazed around;
Then to the wall his face he turn'd,
And his dark neck with blushes burn'd.

XXIII.

" Whose is the boy?" again he said. —
" By chance of war our captive made;
He may be yours, if you should hold
That music has more charms than gold;
For, though from earliest childhood
　　mute,
The lad can deftly touch the lute,
　　And on the rote and viol play,
　　And well can drive the time away
　　　For those who love such glee;
For me, the favoring breeze, when
　　loud
　　It pipes upon the galley's shroud,
　　Makes blither melody." —

"Hath he, then, sense of spoken sound?"
" Ay; so his mother bade us know,
A crone in our late shipwreck drown'd,
　　And hence the silly stripling's woe.
More of the youth I cannot say,
Our captive but since yesterday;
When wind and weather wax'd so grim,
We little listed think of him. —
But why waste time in idle words?
Sit to your cheer — unbelt your swords."
Sudden the captive turn'd his head,
And one quick glance to Ronald sped.
It was a keen and warning look,
And well the Chief the signal took.

XXIV.

" Kind host," he said, " our needs re-
　　quire
A separate board and separate fire;
For know, that on a pilgrimage
Wend I, my comrade, and this page.
And, sworn to vigil and to fast,
Long as this hallow'd task shall last,
We never doff the plaid or sword,
Or feast us at a stranger's board;
And never share one common sleep,
But one must still his vigil keep.
Thus, for our separate use, good friend,
We'll hold this hut's remoter end." —
" A churlish vow," the eldest said,
" And hard, methinks, to be obey'd.
How say you, if, to wreak the scorn
That pays our kindness harsh return,
We should refuse to share our meal?"
" Then say we, that our swords are steel!
And our vow binds us not to fast,
Where gold or force may buy repast." —
Their host's dark brow grew keen and
　　fell,
His teeth are clench'd, his features swell;
Yet sunk the felon's moody ire
Before Lord Ronald's glance of fire,
Nor could his craven courage brook
The Monarch's calm and dauntless look.
With laugh constrain'd, — " Let every
　　man
Follow the fashion of his clan.
Each to his separate quarters keep,
And feed or fast, or wake or sleep."

XXV.

Their fire at separate distance burns,
By turns they eat, keep guard by turns;

or evil seem'd that old man's eye,
dark and designing, fierce yet shy.
till he avoided forward look,
but slow and circumspectly took
a circling, never-ceasing glance,
by doubt and cunning mark'd at once,
Which shot a mischief-boding ray,
from under eyebrows shagg'd and gray.
The younger, too, who seemed his son,
Had that dark look the timid shun;
The half-clad serfs behind them sate,
And scowl'd a glare 'twixt fear and hate —
Till all, as darkness onward crept,
Couch'd down, and seem'd to sleep or slept.
For he, that boy, whose powerless tongue
Must trust his eyes to wail his wrong,
A longer watch of sorrow made,
But stretch'd his limbs to slumber laid.

XXVI.

Not in his dangerous host confides
The King, but wary watch provides.
Roland keeps ward till midnight past,
Then wakes the King, young Allan last;
Thus rank'd, to give the youthful page
The rest required by tender age.
What is Lord Ronald's wakeful thought,
To chase the languor toil had brought? —
For deem not that he deign'd to throw
Much care upon such coward foe,) —
He thinks of lovely Isabel,
When at her foeman's feet she fell,
Nor less when, placed in princely selle,
She glanced on him with favoring eyes,
At Woodstock when he won the prize,
Nor, fair in joy, in sorrow fair,
In pride of place as mid despair,
Must she alone engross his care.
His thoughts to his betrothed bride,
To Edith, turn. — O how decide,
When here his love and heart are given,
And there his faith stands plight to
      Heaven!
No drowsy ward 'tis his to keep,
For seldom lovers long for sleep.
Till sung his midnight hymn the owl,
Answer'd the dog-fox with his howl,
Then waked the King; — at his request,
Lord Ronald stretch'd himself to rest.

XXVII.

What spell was good King Robert's, say,
To drive the weary night away?

His was the patriot's burning thought,
Of Freedom's battle bravely fought,
Of castles storm'd, of cities freed,
Of deep design and daring deed,
Of England's roses reft and torn,
And Scotland's cross in triumph worn,
Of rout and rally, war and truce, —
As heroes think, so thought the Bruce.
No marvel, mid such musings high,
Sleep shunn'd the Monarch's thoughtful
      eye.
Now over Coolin's eastern head
The grayish light begins to spread,
The otter to his cavern drew,
And clamor'd shrill the wakening mew;
Then watch'd the page; — to needful rest
The King resign'd his anxious breast.

XXVIII.

To Allan's eyes was harder task,
The weary watch their safeties ask.
He trimm'd the fire, and gave to shine
With bickering light the splinter'd pine;
Then gazed awhile, where silent laid
Their hosts were shrouded by the plaid.
But little fear waked in his mind,
For he was bred of martial kind,
And, if to manhood he arrive,
May match the boldest knight alive.
Then thought he of his mother's tower,
His little sisters' greenwood bower,
How there the Easter-gambols pass,
And of Dan Joseph's lengthen'd mass.
But still before his weary eye
In rays prolong'd the blazes die. —
Again he roused him ; — on the lake
Look'd forth, where now the twilight
      flake
Of pale cold dawn began to wake.
On Coolin's cliffs the mists lay furl'd,
The morning breeze the lake had curl'd,
The short dark waves, heaved to the land,
With ceaseless splash kiss'd cliff or sand;
It was a slumbrous sound; — he turn'd
To tales at which his youth had burn'd,
Of pilgrim's path by demon cross'd,
Of sprightly elf or yelling ghost,
Of the wild witch's baneful cot,
And mermaid's alabaster grot,
Who bathes her limbs in sunless well
Deep in Strathaird's enchanted cell.[22]
Thither in fancy wrapt he flies,
And on his sight the vaults arise;

That hut's dark walls he sees no more,
His foot is on the marble floor,
And o'er his head the dazzling spars
Gleam like a firmament of stars!
— Hark! hears he not the sea-nymph
          speak
Her anger in that thrilling shriek! —
No! all too late, with Allan's dream
Mingled the captive's warning scream.
As from the ground he strives to start,
A ruffian's dagger finds his heart!
Upward he casts his dizzy eyes, . . .
Murmurs his master's name, . . . and
          dies!

XXIX.

Not so awoke the King! his hand
Snatch'd from the flame a knotted brand,
The nearest weapon of his wrath;
With this he cross'd the murderer's path,
          And venged young Allan well!
The spatter'd brain and bubbling blood
Hiss'd on the half-extinguish'd wood,
          The miscreant gasp'd and fell!
Nor rose in peace the Island Lord;
One caitiff died upon his sword,
And one beneath his grasp lies prone,
In mortal grapple overthrown.
But while Lord Ronald's dagger drank
The life-blood from his panting flank,
The Father-ruffian of the band
Behind him rears a coward hand!
— O for a moment's aid,
Till Bruce, who deals no double blow,
Dash to the earth another foe,
          Above his comrade laid! —
And it is gain'd — the captive sprung
On the raised arm, and closely clung,
          And, ere he shook him loose,
The master'd felon press'd the ground,
And gasp'd beneath the mortal wound,
          While o'er him stands the Bruce.

XXX.

"Miscreant! while lasts thy flitting
          spark,
Give me to know the purpose dark,
That arm'd thy hand with murderous
          knife,
Against offenceless stranger's life?"—
"No stranger thou!" with accent fell,
Murmur'd the wretch; "I know thee
          well;

And know thee for the foeman sworn
Of my high Chief, the mighty Lorn."—
"Speak yet again, and speak the truth
For thy soul's sake! — from whence thi
          youth?
His country, birth, and name declare,
And thus one evil deed repair."—
— "Vex me no more! . . . my bloo
          runs cold. . . .
No more I know than I have told.
We found him in a bark we sought
With different purpose . . . and
          thought" . . .
Fate cut him short; in blood and broil,
As he had lived, died Cormac Doil.

XXXI.

Then resting on his bloody blade,
The valiant Bruce to Roland said:—
"Now shame upon us both! — that boy
          Lifts his mute face to heaven,
And clasps his hands to testify
His gratitude to God on high,
          For strange deliverance given.
His speechless gesture thanks hath paid
Which our free tongues have left un-
          said!"
He raised the youth with kindly word,
But mark'd him shudder at the sword:
He cleansed it from its hue of death,
And plunged the weapon in its sheath.
"Alas, poor child! unfitting part
Fate doom'd, when with so soft a heart,
          And form so slight as thine,
She made thee first a pirate's slave,
Then, in his stead, a patron gave
          Of wayward lot like mine;
A landless prince, whose wandering life
Is but one scene of blood and strife —
Yet scant of friends the Bruce shall be,
But he'll find resting-place for thee.—
Come, noble Ronald! o'er the dead
Enough thy generous grief is paid,
And well has Allan's fate been wroke;
Come, wend we hence—the day has broke.
Seek we our bark — I trust the tale
Was false, that she had hoisted sail."

XXXII.

Yet, ere they left that charnel-cell,
The Island Lord bade sad farewell
To Allan: — "Who shall tell this tale,'
He said, "in halls of Donagaile!

Oh, who his widow'd mother tell,
That, ere his bloom, her fairest fell! —
Rest thee, poor youth! and trust my care
For mass and knell and funeral prayer;
While o'er those caitiffs, where they lie,
The wolf shall snarl, the raven cry!''
And now the eastern mountain's head
On the dark lake threw lustre red;
Bright gleams of gold and purple streak
Ravine and precipice and peak —
So earthly power at distance shows;
Reveals his splendor, hides his woes.)
O'er sheets of granite dark and broad,
Rent and unequal, lay the road.
In sad discourse the warriors wind,
And the mute captive moves behind.

CANTO FOURTH.

I.

STRANGER! if e'er thine ardent step hath traced
The northern realms of ancient Caledon,
Where the proud Queen of Wilderness hath placed,
By lake and cataract, her lonely throne;
Sublime but sad delight thy soul hath known,
Gazing on pathless glen and mountain high,
Listing where from the cliffs the torrents thrown
Mingle their echoes with the eagle's cry,
And with the sounding lake, and with the moaning sky.

Yes! 'twas sublime, but sad. — The loneliness
Loaded thy heart, the desert tired thine eye;
And strange and awful fears began to press
Thy bosom with a stern solemnity.
Then hast thou wish'd some woodman's cottage nigh,
Something that show'd of life, though low and mean:
Glad sight, its curling wreath of smoke to spy,
Glad sound, its cock's blithe carol would have been,
Or children whooping wild beneath the willows green.

Such are the scenes, where savage grandeur wakes
An awful thrill that softens into sighs;
Such feelings rouse them by dim Rannoch's lakes,
In dark Glencoe such gloomy raptures rise;
Or farther, where, beneath the northern skies,
Chides wild Loch-Eribol his caverns hoar —
But, be the minstrel judge, they yield the prize
Of desert dignity to that dread shore,
That sees grim Coolin rise, and hears Coriskin roar.

II.

Through such wild scenes the champion pass'd,
When bold halloo and bugle blast
Upon the breeze came loud and fast.
"There," said the Bruce, "rung Edward's horn!
What can have caused such brief return?
And see, brave Ronald, — see him dart
O'er stock and stone like hunted hart,
Precipitate, as is the use,
In war or sport, of Edward Bruce.
— He marks us, and his eager cry
Will tell his news ere he be nigh.''

III.

Loud Edward shouts: — "What make ye here,
Warring upon the mountain-deer,
When Scotland wants her king?
A bark from Lennox cross'd our track,
With her in speed I hurried back,
These joyful news to bring —
The Stuart stirs in Teviotdale,
And Douglas wakes his native vale;
Thy storm-toss'd fleet hath won its way
With little loss to Brodick-Bay,
And Lennox, with a gallant band,
Waits but thy coming and command
To waft them o'er to Carrick strand.

There are blithe news! — but mark the
          close!
Edward, the deadliest of our foes,
As with his host he northward pass'd,
Hath on the Borders breathed his last.''

IV.

Still stood the Bruce — his steady cheek
Was little wont his joy to speak,
     But then his color rose:—
" Now, Scotland! shortly shalt thou see,
With God's high will, thy children free,
     And vengeance on thy foes!
Yet to no sense of selfish wrongs,
Bear witness with me, Heaven, belongs
My joy o'er Edward's bier;[23]
I took my knighthood at his hand,
And lordship held of him, and land,
     And well may vouch it here,
That, blot the story from his page,
Of Scotland ruin'd in his rage,
You read a monarch brave and sage,
     And to his people dear."—
" Let London's burghers mourn her
          Lord,
And Croydon monks his praise record,''
     The eager Edward said:—
" Eternal as his own, my hate
Surmounts the bounds of mortal fate,
     And dies not with the dead!
Such hate was his on Solway's strand,
When vengeance clench'd his palsied
          hand,
That pointed yet to Scotland's land,
     As his last accents pray'd
Disgrace and curse upon his heir,
If he one Scottish head should spare,
Till stretch'd upon the bloody lair
     Each rebel corpse was laid!
Such hate was his, when his last breath
Renounced the peaceful house of death,
And bade his bones to Scotland's coast
Be borne by his remorseless host,
As if his dead and stony eye
Could still enjoy her misery!
Such hate was his — dark, deadly, long!
Mine, — as enduring, deep, and strong!''

V.

" Let women, Edward, war with words,
With curses monks, but men with swords:
Nor doubt of living foes, to sate
Deepest revenge and deadliest hate.

Now, to the sea! behold the beach,
And see the galleys' pendants stretch
Their fluttering length down favoring gale
Aboard, aboard! and hoist the sail.
Hold we our way for Arran first,
Where meet in arms our friends dispersed
Lennox the loyal, De la Haye,
And Boyd the bold in battle fray.
I long the hardy band to head,
And see once more my standard spread.—
Does noble Ronald share our course,
Or stay to raise his island force?"—
"Come weal, come woe, by Bruce's side,'
Replied the Chief, " will Ronald bide.
And since two galleys yonder ride,
Be mine, so please my liege, dismiss'd
To wake to arms the clans of Uist,
And all who hear the Minch's roar,
On the Long Island's lonely shore.
The nearer Isles, with slight delay,
Ourselves may summon in our way;
And soon on Arran's shore shall meet,
With Torquil's aid, a gallant fleet,
If aught avails their Chieftain's hest
Among the islesmen of the west.''

VI.

Thus was their venturous council said.
But, ere their sails the galleys spread,
Coriskin dark and Coolin high
Echoed the dirge's doleful cry.
Along that sable lake pass'd slow, —
Fit scene for such a sight of woe,
The sorrowing islesmen, as they bore
The murder'd Allan to the shore.
At every pause, with dismal shout,
Their coronach of grief rung out.
And ever, when they moved again,
The pipes resumed their clamorous strain
And, with the pibroch's shrilling wail,
Mourn'd the young heir of Donagaile.
Round and around, from cliff and cave,
His answer stern old Coolin gave,
Till high upon his misty side
Languish'd the mournful notes, and died;
For never sounds, by mortal made,
Attain'd his high and haggard head,
That echoes but the tempest's moan,
Or the deep thunder's rending groan.

VII.

Merrily, merrily bounds the bark,
     She bounds before the gale.

The mountain breeze from Ben-na-darch
  Is joyous in her sail!
With fluttering sound like laughter hoarse,
  The cords and canvas strain,
The waves, divided by her force,
In rippling eddies chased her course,
  As if they laugh'd again.
Not down the breeze more blithely
    flew,
Skimming the wave, the light sea-mew,
  Than the gay galley bore
Her course upon that favoring wind,
And Coolin's crest has sunk behind,
  And Slapin's cavern'd shore.
Twas then that warlike signals wake
Dunscaith's dark towers and Eisord's
    lake,
And soon, from Cavilgarrigh's head,
Thick wreaths of eddying smoke were
    spread;
A summons these of war and wrath
To the brave clans of Sleat and Strath.
  And, ready at the sight,
Each warrior to his weapons sprung,
And targe upon his shoulder flung,
  Impatient for the fight.
Mac-Kinnon's chief, in warfare gray,
Had charge to muster their array,
And guide their barks to Brodick-Bay.

VIII.

Signal of Ronald's high command,
A beacon gleam'd o'er sea and land,
From Canna's tower, that, steep and
    gray,
Like falcon-nest o'erhangs the bay.
Seek not the giddy crag to climb,
To view the turret scathed by time;
It is a task of doubt and fear
To aught but goat or mountain-deer.
  But rest thee on the silver beach,
  And let the aged herdsman teach
    His tale of former day;
  His cur's wild clamor he shall chide,
  And for thy seat by ocean's side,
    His varied plaid display;
  Then tell, how with their Chieftain
    came,
  In ancient times a foreign dame
    To yonder turret gray.
Stern was her Lord's suspicious mind,
Who in so rude a jail confined
  So soft and fair a thrall!

And oft, when moon on ocean slept,
That lovely lady sate and wept
  Upon the castle wall,
And turn'd her eye to southern climes,
And thought perchance of happier times,
And touch'd her lute by fits, and sung
Wild ditties in her native tongue.
And still, when on the cliff and bay,
Placid and pale the moonbeams play,
  And every breeze is mute,
Upon the lone Hebridean's ear
Steals a strange pleasure mix'd with fear,
While from that cliff he seems to hear
  The murmur of a lute,
And sounds, as of a captive lone,
That mourns her woes in tongue un-
    known. —
Strange is the tale — but all too long
Already hath it staid the song —
  Yet who may pass them by,
That crag and tower in ruins gray,
Nor to their hapless tenant pay
  The tribute of a sigh!

IX.

Merily, merrily bounds the bark
  O'er the broad ocean driven,
Her path by Ronin's mountains dark
  The steersman's hand hath given.
And Ronin's mountains dark have sent
  Their hunters to the shore,[24]
And each his ashen bow unbent,
  And gave his pastime o'er,
And at the Island Lord's command,
For hunting spear took warrior's brand.
On Scooreigg next a warning light
Summon'd her warriors to the fight;
A numerous race, ere stern MacLeod
O'er their bleak shores in vengeance
    strode,[25]
When all in vain the ocean-cave
Its refuge to his victims gave.
The Chief, relentless in his wrath,
With blazing heath blockades the path;
In dense and stifling volumes roll'd,
The vapor fill'd the cavern'd hold!
The warrior-threat, the infant's plain,
The mother's screams, were heard in vain!
The vengeful Chief maintains his fires,
Till in the vault a tribe expires!
The bones which strew that cavern's
    gloom
Too well attest their dismal doom.

X.

Merrily, merrily goes the bark
　On a breeze from the northward free,
So shoots through the morning sky the
　　lark,
　Or the swan through the summer sea.
The shores of Mull on the eastward lay,
And Ulva dark and Colonsay,
And all the group of islets gay
　That guard famed Staffa round.
Then all unknown its columns rose,
Where dark and undisturb'd repose
　The cormorant had found,
And the shy seal had quiet home,
And welter'd in that wondrous dome,
Where, as to shame the temples deck'd
By skill of earthly architect,
Nature herself, it seem'd, would raise
A Minster to her Maker's praise!
Not for a meaner use ascend
Her columns, or her arches bend;
Nor of a theme less solemn tells
That mighty surge that ebbs and swells,
And still, between each awful pause,
From the high vault an answer draws,
In varied tone prolong'd and high,
That mocks the organ's melody.
Nor doth its entrance front in vain
To old Iona's holy fane,
That Nature's voice might seem to say :—
" Well hast thou done, frail child of clay !
Thy humble powers that stately shrine
Task'd high and hard — but witness
　　mine ! ''

XI.

Merrily, merrily goes the bark,
　Before the gale she bounds;
So darts the dolphin from the shark,
　Or the deer before the hounds.
They left Loch-Tua on their lee,
And they waken'd the men of the wild
　　Tiree,
　And the Chief of the sandy Coll;
They paused not at Columba's isle,
Though peal'd the bells from the holy
　　pile
With long and measured toll;
No time for matin or for mass,
And the sounds of the holy summons pass
　Away in the billows' roll.
Lochbuie's fierce and warlike Lord
Their signal saw, and grasp'd his sword,

And verdant Islay call'd her host,
And the clans of Jura's rugged coast
　Lord Ronald's call obey,
And Scarba's isle, whose tortured shore
Still rings to Corrievreken's roar,
　And lonely Colonsay;
—Scenes sung by him who sings no
　　more ! [26]
His bright and brief career is o'er,
　And mute his tuneful strains;
Quench'd is his lamp of varied lore,
That loved the light of song to pour;
A distant and a deadly shore
　Has LEYDEN'S cold remains !

XII.

Ever the breeze blows merrily,
But the galley ploughs no more the sea.
Lest, rounding wild Cantire, they meet
The southern foemen's watchful fleet,
　They held unwonted way;—
Up Tarbat's western lake they bore,
Then dragg'd their bark the isthmus
　　o'er, [27]
As far as Kilmaconnel's shore,
　Upon the eastern bay.
It was a wondrous sight to see
Topmast and pennon glitter free,
High raised above the greenwood tree,
As on dry land the galley moves,
By cliff and copse and alder groves.
Deep import from that selcouth sign,
Did many a mountain Seer divine,
For ancient legends told the Gael,
That when a royal bark should sail
　O'er Kilmaconnel moss,
Old Albyn should in fight prevail,
And every foe should faint and quail
　Before her silver Cross.

XIII.

Now launch'd once more, the inland
　　sea
They furrow with fair augury,
　And steer for Arran's isle;
The sun, ere yet he sunk behind
Ben-Ghoil, "the Mountain of the Wind,''
Gave his grim peaks a greeting kind,
　And bade Loch Ranza smile. [28]
Thither their destined course they drew;
It seem'd the isle her monarch knew,
So brilliant was the landward view,
　The ocean so serene;

Each puny wave in diamonds roll'd
O'er the calm deep, where hues of gold
    With azure strove and green.
The hill, the vale, the tree, the tower,
Glow'd with the tint of evening's hour,
    The beach was silver sheen,
The wind breathed soft as lover's sigh,
And, oft renew'd, seem'd oft to die,
    With breathless pause between.
O who, with speech of war and woes,
Would wish to break the soft repose
    Of such enchanting scene!

XIV.

Is it of war Lord Ronald speaks?
The blush that dyes his manly cheeks,
The timid look and downcast eye,
And faltering voice the theme deny.
    And good King Robert's brow express'd,
    He ponder'd o'er some high request,
        As doubtful to approve;
    Yet in his eye and lip the while,
    Dwelt the half-pitying glance and smile,
    Which manhood's graver mood beguile,
        When lovers talk of love.
Anxious his suit Lord Ronald pled:—
"And for my bride betrothed," he
        said,
" My Liege has heard the rumor spread,
Of Edith from Artornish fled.
Too hard her fate— I claim no right
To blame her for her hasty flight;
Be joy and happiness her lot!—
But she hath fled the bridal knot,
And Lorn recall'd his promised plight,
In the assembled chieftains' sight.—
    When, to fulfil our fathers' band,
    I proffer'd all I could— my hand—
        I was repulsed with scorn;
    Mine honor I should ill assert,
    And worse the feelings of my heart,
    If I should play a suitor's part
        Again, to pleasure Lorn."

XV.

" Young Lord," the royal Bruce replied,
" That question must the Church decide;
Yet seems it hard, since rumors state
Edith takes Clifford for her mate,
The very tie, which she hath broke,
To thee should still be binding yoke.
But, for my sister Isabel—
The mood of woman who can tell?

I guess the Champion of the Rock,
Victorious in the tourney shock,
That knight unknown, to whom the prize
She dealt,— had favor in her eyes;
But since our brother Nigel's fate,
Our ruin'd house and hapless state,
From worldly joys and hopes estranged,
Much is the hapless mourner changed.
Perchance," here smiled the noble King,
" This tale may other musings bring.
Soon shall we know— yon mountains hide
The little convent of Saint Bride;
There, sent by Edward, she must stay,
Till fate shall give more prosperous day;
And thither will I bear thy suit,
Nor will thine advocate be mute."

XVI.

As thus they talk'd in earnest mood,
That speechless boy beside them stood.
He stoop'd his head against the mast,
And bitter sobs came thick and fast,
A grief that would not be repress'd,
But seem'd to burst his youthful breast.
His hands, against his forehead held,
As if by force his tears repell'd,
But through his fingers, long and slight,
Fast trill'd the drops of crystal bright.
Edward, who walk'd the deck apart,
First spied this conflict of the heart.
Thoughtless as brave, with bluntness kind
He sought to cheer the sorrower's mind;
By force the slender hand he drew
From those poor eyes that stream'd with
        dew.
As in his hold the stripling strove,—
('Twas a rough grasp, though meant in
        love,)
Away his tears the warrior swept,
And bade shame on him that he wept:—
" I would to Heaven, thy helpless tongue
Could tell me who hath wrought thee
        wrong!
For, were he of our crew the best,
The insult went not unredress'd.
Come, cheer thee; thou art now of age
To be a warrior's gallant page;
Thou shalt be mine!— a palfrey fair
O'er hill and holt my boy shall bear,
To hold my bow in hunting grove,
Or speed on errand to my love;
For well I wot thou wilt not tell
The temple where my wishes dwell."

XVII.

Bruce interposed:— "Gay Edward, no,
This is no youth to hold thy bow,
To fill thy goblet, or to bear
Thy message light to lighter fair.
Thou art a patron all too wild
And thoughtless, for this orphan child.
See'st thou not how apart he steals,
Keeps lonely couch, and lonely meals?
Fitter by far in yon calm cell
To tend our sister Isabel,
With Father Augustin to share
The peaceful change of convent prayer,
Than wander wild adventures through,
With such a reckless guide as you."—
"Thanks, brother!" Edward answer'd
        gay,
"For the high laud thy words convey!
But we may learn some future day,
If thou or I can this poor boy
Protect the best, or best employ.
Meanwhile, our vessel nears the strand;
Launch we the boat and seek the land."

XVIII.

To land King Robert lightly sprung,
And thrice aloud his bugle rung
With note prolong'd and varied strain,
Till bold Ben Ghoil replied again.
Good Douglas then, and De la Haye,
Had in a glen a hart at bay,
And Lennox cheer'd the laggard hounds,
When waked that horn the greenwood
        bounds.
"It is the foe!" cried Boyd, who came
In breathless haste with eye of flame, —
"It is the foe!— Each valiant lord
Fling by his bow, and grasp his sword!"—
"Not so," replied the good Lord James,
"That blast no English bugle claims.
Oft have I heard it fire the fight,
Cheer the pursuit, or stop the flight.
Dead were my heart, and deaf mine
        ear,
If Bruce should call, nor Douglas hear!
Each to Loch Ranza's margin spring;
That blast was winded by the King!" [29]

XIX.

Fast to their mates the tidings spread,
And fast to shore the warriors sped.
Bursting from glen and greenwood tree,
High waked their loyal jubilee!

Around the royal Bruce they crowd,
And clasp'd his hands, and wept aloud.
Veterans of early fields were there,
Whose helmets press'd their hoary hair,
Whose swords and axes bore a stain
From life-blood of the red-hair'd Dane;
And boys, whose hands scarce brook'd
        to wield
The heavy sword or bossy shield.
Men too were there, that bore the scars
Impress'd in Albyn's woeful wars,
At Falkirk's fierce and fatal fight,
Teyndrum's dread rout, and Methven's
        flight;
The might of Douglas there was seen,
There Lennox with his graceful mien;
Kirkpatrick, Closeburn's dreaded Knight;
The Lindsay, fiery, fierce, and light;
The Heir of murder'd De la Haye,
And Boyd the grave, and Seton gay.
Around their King regain'd they press'd,
Wept, shouted, clasp'd him to their breast,
And young and old, and serf and lord,
And he who ne'er unsheathed a sword,
And he in many a peril tried,
Alike resolved the brunt to bide,
And live or die by Bruce's side!

XX.

Oh, War! thou hast thy fierce delight,
Thy gleams of joy, intensely bright!
Such gleams, as from thy polish'd shield
Fly dazzling o'er the battle-field!
Such transports wake, severe and high,
Amid the pealing conquest-cry;
Scarce less, when, after battle lost,
Muster the remnants of a host,
And as each comrade's name they tell,
Who in the well-fought conflict fell,
Knitting stern brow o'er flashing eye,
Vow to avenge them or to die! —
Warriors!—and where are warriors found,
If not on martial Britain's ground?
And who, when waked with note of fire,
Love more than they the British lyre? —
Know ye not, — hearts to honor dear!
That joy, deep-thrilling, stern, severe,
At which the heart-strings vibrate high,
And wake the fountains of the eye?
And blame ye, then, the Bruce, if trace
Of tear is on his manly face,
When, scanty relics of the train
That hail'd at Scone his early reign,

his patriot band around him hung,
nd to his knees and bosom clung? —
ame ye the Bruce? — his brother
  blamed,
it shared the weakness, while ashamed,
'ith haughty laugh his head he turn'd,
nd dash'd away the tear he scorn'd.[30]

XXI.

'is morning, and the Convent bell
ong time had ceased its matin knell,
  Within thy walls, Saint Bride!
n aged Sister sought the cell
ssign'd to Lady Isabel,
  And hurriedly she cried: —
Haste, gentle Lady, haste — there waits
  noble stranger at the gates;
aint Bride's poor vot'ress ne'er has seen
  Knight of such a princely mien;
is errand, as he bade me tell,
s with the Lady Isabel."
he princess rose, — for on her knee
ow bent she told her rosary: —
  Let him by thee his purpose teach;
may not give a stranger speech." —
Saint Bride forefend, thou royal Maid!"
he portress cross'd herself, and said: —
  Not to be prioress might I
ebate his will, his suit deny." —
  Has earthly show then, simple fool,
ower o'er a sister of thy rule?
nd art thou, like the worldly train,
bdued by splendors light and vain?" —

XXII.

No, Lady! in old eyes like mine,
auds have no glitter, gems no shine;
or grace his rank attendants vain,
ne youthful page is all his train.
is the form, the eye, the word,
he bearing of that stranger Lord;
is stature, manly, bold, and tall,
uilt like a castle's battled wall,
et moulded in such just degrees,
is giant strength seems lightsome ease.
lose as the tendrils of the vine
is locks upon his forehead twine,
et-black, save where some touch of gray
as ta'en the youthful hue away.
Weather and war their rougher trace
ave left on that majestic face; —
ut 'tis his dignity of eye!
here, if a suppliant, would I fly,

Secure mid danger, wrongs, and grief,
Of sympathy, redress, relief —
That glance, if guilty, would I dread
More than the doom that spoke me
  dead!" —
" Enough, enough," the princess cried,
' 'Tis Scotland's hope, her joy, her pride!
To meaner front was ne'er assign'd
Such mastery o'er the common mind —
Bestow'd thy high designs to aid,
How long, O Heaven! how long de-
  lay'd! —
Haste, Mona, haste, to introduce
My darling brother, royal Bruce!"

XXIII.

They met like friends who part in pain,
And meet in doubtful hope again.
But when subdued that fitful swell,
The Bruce survey'd the humble cell: —
" And this is thine, poor Isabel! —
That pallet-couch, and naked wall,
For room of state, and bed of pall;
For costly robes and jewels rare,
A string of beads and zone of hair;
And for the trumpet's sprightly call
To sport or banquet, grove or hall,
The bell's grim voice divide thy care,
'Twixt hours of penitence and prayer! —
O ill for thee, my royal claim
From the First David's sainted name!
O woe for thee, that while he sought
His right, thy brother feebly fought!" —

XXIV.

" Now lay these vain regrets aside,
And be the unshaken Bruce!" she cried.
" For more I glory to have shared
The woes thy venturous spirit dared,
When raising first thy valiant band
In rescue of thy native land,
Than had fair Fortune set me down
The partner of an empire's crown.
And grieve not that on Pleasure's stream
No more I drive in giddy dream,
For Heaven the erring pilot knew,
And from the gulf the vessel drew,
Tried me with judgments stern and great,
My house's ruin, thy defeat,
Poor Nigel's death, till, tamed, I own,
My hopes are fix'd on Heaven alone;
Nor e'er shall earthy prospects win
My heart to this vain world of sin." —

XXV.

" Nay, Isabel, for such stern choice,
First wilt thou wait thy brother's voice;
Then ponder if in convent scene
No softer thoughts might intervene —
Say they were of that unknown Knight,
Victor in Woodstock's tourney-fight —
Nay, if his name such blush you owe,
Victorious o'er a fairer foe ! ''
Truly his penetrating eye
Hath caught that blush's passing dye, —
Like the last beam of evening thrown
On a white cloud, — just seen and gone.
Soon with calm cheek and steady eye,
The princess made composed reply : —
" I guess my brother's meaning well;
For not so silent is the cell,
But we have heard the islesmen all
Arm in thy cause at Ronald's call,
And mine eyes prove that Knight un-
        known
And the brave Island Lord are one. —
Had then his suit been earlier made,
In his own name, with thee to aid,
(But that his plighted faith forbade,)
I know not. . . . But thy page so near ?—
This is no tale for menial's ear.''

XXVI.

Still stood that page, as far apart
    As the small cell would space afford;
With dizzy eye and bursting heart,
    He leant his weight on Bruce's sword;
The monarch's mantle too he bore,
And drew the fold his visage o'er.
"Fear not for him :— in murderous strife,"
Said Bruce, " his warning saved my
        life;
Full seldom parts he from my side,
And in his silence I confide,
Since he can tell no tale again.
He is a boy of gentle strain,
And I have purposed he shall dwell
In Augustin the chaplain's cell,
And wait on thee, my Isabel. —
Mind not his tears; I've seen them flow,
As in the thaw dissolves the snow.
'Tis a kind youth, but fanciful,
Unfit against the tide to pull,
And those that with the Bruce would sail,
Must learn to strive with stream and gale.
But forward, gentle Isabel —
My answer for Lord Ronald tell.'' —

XXVII.

" This answer be to Ronald given —
The heart he asks is fix'd on heaven.
My love was like a summer flower,
That wither'd in the wintry hour,
Born but of vanity and pride,
And with these sunny visions died.
If further press his suit — then say,
He should his plighted troth obey,
Troth plighted both with ring and word
And sworn on crucifix and sword. —
Oh, shame thee, Robert ! I have seen
Thou hast a woman's guardian been !
Even in extremity's dread hour,
When press'd on thee the Southern power
And safety, to all human sight,
Was only found in rapid flight,
Thou heard'st a wretched female plain
In agony of travail-pain,
And thou didst bid thy little band
Upon the instant turn and stand,
And dare the worst the foe might do,
Rather than, like a knight untrue,
Leave to pursuers merciless
A woman in her last distress.[31]
And wilt thou now deny thine aid
To an oppress'd and injured maid,
Even plead for Ronald's perfidy,
And press his fickle faith on me ? —
So witness Heaven, as true I vow,
Had I those earthly feelings now,
Which could my former bosom move
Ere taught to set its hopes above,
I'd spurn each proffer he could bring,
Till at my feet he laid the ring,
The ring and spousal contract both,
And fair acquittal of his oath,
By her who brooks his perjured scorn,
The ill-requited Maid of Lorn ! ''

XXVIII.

With sudden impulse forward sprung
The page, and on her neck he hung;
Then, recollected instantly,
His head he stoop'd, and bent his knee,
Kiss'd twice the hand of Isabel,
Arose, and sudden left the cell. —
The princess, loosen'd from his hold,
Blushed angry at his bearing bold;
    But good King Robert cried :—
" Chafe not—by signs he speaks his mind
He heard the plan my care design'd,
    Nor could his transports hide. —

t, sister, now bethink thee well;
easy choice the convent cell!
ust, I shall play no tyrant part,
ther to force thy hand or heart,
suffer that Lord Ronald scorn,
wrong for thee, the Maid of Lorn.
at think, — not long the time has been,
at thou wert wont to sigh unseen,
d wouldst the ditties best approve,
at told some lay of hapless love.
w are thy wishes in thy power,
d thou art bent on cloister bower!
if our Edward knew the change,
ow would his busy satire range,
ith many a sarcasm varied still
woman's wish, and woman's will!'"—

XXIX.

Brother, I well believe," she said,
Even so would Edward's part be play'd.
indly in heart, in word severe,
foe to thought, and grief, and fear,
e holds his humor uncontroll'd;
t thou art of another mould.
y then to Ronald, as I say,
nless before my feet he lay
he ring which bound the faith he swore,
y Edith freely yielded o'er,
e moves his suit to me no more.
or do I promise, even if now
e stood absolved of spousal vow,
hat I would change my purpose made
o shelter me in holy shade.—
rother, for little space, farewell!
o other duties warns the bell!'"—

XXX.

Lost to the world," King Robert said,
When he had left the royal maid,
Lost to the world by lot severe,
what a gem lies buried here,
ipp'd by misfortune's cruel frost,
he buds of fair affection lost!
ut what have I with love to do?
ar sterner cares my lot pursue.
- Pent in this isle we may not lie,
or would it long our wants supply.
ight opposite, the mainland towers
f my own Turnberry court our powers.
- Might not my father's beadsman hoar,
uthbert, who dwells upon the shore,
indle a signal-flame, to show
he time propitious for the blow?

It shall be so — some friend shall bear
Our mandate with despatch and care;
— Edward shall find the messenger.
That fortress ours, the island fleet
May on the coast of Carrick meet. —
O Scotland! shall it e'er be mine
To wreak thy wrongs in battle-line,
To raise my victor-head, and see
Thy hills, thy dales, thy people free, —
That glance of bliss is all I crave!
Betwixt my labors and my grave!'"
Then down the hill he slowly went,
Oft pausing on the steep descent,
And reach'd the spot where his bold train
Held rustic camp upon the plain.

CANTO FIFTH.

I.

On fair Loch-Ranza stream'd the early day,
Thin wreaths of cottage smoke are upward curl'd
From the lone hamlet, which her inland bay
And circling mountains sever from the world.
And there the fisherman his sail unfurl'd,
The goat-herd drove his kids to steep Ben-Ghoil,
Before the hut the dame her spindle twirl'd,
Courting the sunbeam as she plied her toil, —
For, wake where'er he may, Man wakes to care and coil.

But other duties call'd each convent maid,
Roused by the summons of the moss-grown bell;
Sung were the matins, and the mass was said,
And every sister sought her separate cell,
Such was the rule, — her rosary to tell.
And Isabel has knelt in lonely prayer;
The sunbeam, through the narrow lattice, fell
Upon the snowy neck and long dark hair,
As stoop'd her gentle head in meek devotion there.

II.

She raised her eyes, that duty done,
When glanced upon the pavement-stone,
Gemm'd and enchased, a golden ring,
Bound to a scroll with silken string,
With few brief words inscribed to tell,
" This for the Lady Isabel."
Within, the writing further bore : —
" 'Twas with this ring his plight he swore,
With this his promise I restore;
To her who can the heart command,
Well may I yield the plighted hand.
And O ! for better fortune born,
Grudge not a passing sigh to mourn
Her who was Edith once of Lorn ! "
One single flash of glad surprise
Just glanced from Isabel's dark eyes,
But vanish'd in the blush of shame,
That, as its penance, instant came.
" O thought unworthy of my race !
Selfish, ungenerous, mean, and base,
A moment's throb of joy to own,
That rose upon her hopes o'erthrown ! —
Thou pledge of vows too well believed,
Of man ingrate and maid deceived,
Think not thy lustre here shall gain
Another heart to hope in vain !
For thou shalt rest, thou tempting gaud,
Where worldly thoughts are overawed,
And worldly splendors sink debased."—
Then by the cross the ring she placed.

III.

Next rose the thought, — its owner far,
How came it here through bolt and bar ? —
But the dim lattice is ajar. —
She looks abroad, the morning dew
A light short step had brush'd anew,
   And there were foot-prints seen
On the carved buttress rising still,
Till on the mossy window-sill,
   Their track effaced the green.
The ivy twigs were torn and fray'd,
As if some climber's steps to aid. —
But who the hardy messenger,
Whose venturous path these signs infer ?—
" Strange doubts are mine ! — Mona,
   draw nigh;
—Naught 'scapes old Mona's curious eye—
What strangers, gentle mother, say,
Have sought these holy walls to-day?"—
" None, Lady, none of note or name:
Only your brother's foot-page came,

At peep of dawn — I pray'd him pass
To chapel where they said the mass;
But like an arrow he shot by,
And tears seem'd bursting from his eye

IV.

The truth at once on Isabel,
As darted by a sunbeam, fell :—
" 'Tis Edith's self ! — her speechless wo
Her form, her looks, the secret show !
— Instant, good Mona, to the bay,
And to my royal brother say,
I do conjure him seek my cell,
With that mute page he loves so well."
"What ! know'st thou not his warlike ho
At break of day has left our coast ?
My old eyes saw them from the tower.
At eve they couch'd in greenwood bowe
At dawn a bugle signal, made
By their bold Lord, their ranks array'
Up sprung the spears through bush an
   tree,
No time for benedicite !
Like deer, that, rousing from their lair
Just shake the dewdrops from their ha
And toss their armed crests aloft,
Such matins theirs ! " — " Good mothe
   soft —
Where does my brother bend his way?
" As I have heard, for Brodick-Bay.
Across the isle — of barks a score
Lie there, 'tis said, to waft them o'er,
On sudden news, to Carrick-shore."—
" If such their purpose, deep the need
Said anxious Isabel, " of speed !
Call Father Augustin, good dame."
The nun obey'd, the Father came.

V.

" Kind Father, hie without delay,
Across the hills to Brodick-Bay.
This message to the Bruce be given :—
I pray him, by his hopes of Heaven,
That, till he speak with me, he stay ! —
Or, if his haste brook no delay,
That he deliver, on my suit,
Into thy charge that stripling mute.
Thus prays his sister Isabel,
For causes more than she may tell—
Away, good father ! and take heed,
That life and death are on thy speed."
His cowl the good old priest did on,
Took his piked staff and sandall'd shoo

And, like a palmer bent by eld,
O'er moss and moor his journey held.

VI.

Heavy and dull the foot of age,
And rugged was the pilgrimage;
But none was there beside, whose care
Might such important message bear.
Through birchen copse he wander'd slow,
Stunted and sapless, thin and low;
By many a mountain stream he pass'd,
From the tall cliffs in tumult cast,
Dashing to foam their waters dun,
And sparkling in the summer sun.
Round his gray head the wild curlew
In many a fearless circle flew.
O'er chasms he pass'd where fractures
    wide
Craved wary eye and ample stride; [32]
He cross'd his brow beside the stone
Where Druids erst heard victims groan,
And at the cairns upon the wild,
O'er many a heathen hero piled,
He breathed a timid prayer for those
Who died ere Shiloh's sun arose.
Beside Macfarlane's Cross he staid,
There told his hours within the shade,
And at the stream his thirst allay'd.
Thence onward journeying, slowly still,
As evening closed he reach'd the hill,
Where, rising through the woodland green,
Old Brodick's gothic towers were seen,
From Hastings, late their English lord,
Douglas had won them by the sword. [33]
The sun that sunk behind the isle,
Now tinged them with a parting smile.

VII.

But though the beams of light decay,
'Twas bustle all in Brodick-Bay.
The Bruce's followers crowd the shore,
And boats and barges some unmoor,
Some raise the sail, some seize the oar;
Their eyes oft turn'd where glimmer'd far
What might have seem'd an early star
On heaven's blue arch, save that its light
Was all too flickering, fierce, and bright.
    Far distant in the south, the ray
    Shone pale amid retiring day,
        But as, on Carrick shore,
    Dim seen in outline faintly blue,
    The shades of evening closer drew,
        It kindled more and more.

The monk's slow steps now press the
    sands,
And now amid a scene he stands,
    Full strange to churchman's eye;
Warriors, who, arming for the fight,
Rivet and clasp their harness light,
And twinkling spears, and axes bright,
    And helmets flashing high.
Oft, too, with unaccustom'd ears,
    A language much unmeet he hears, [34]
        While, hastening all on board,
    As stormy as the swelling surge
    That mix'd its roar, the leaders urge
    Their followers to the ocean verge,
        With many a haughty word.

VIII.

Through that wild throng the Father
    pass'd,
And reach'd the Royal Bruce at last.
He leant against a stranded boat,
That the approaching tide must float,
And counted every rippling wave,
As higher yet her sides they lave,
And oft the distant fire he eyed,
And closer yet his hauberk tied,
And loosen'd in its sheath his brand.
Edward and Lennox were at hand,
Douglas and Ronald had the care
The soldiers to the barks to share. —
The Monk approach'd and homage paid;
"And art thou come," King Robert said,
"So far to bless us ere we part?" —
— "My Liege, and with a loyal heart!—
But other charge I have to tell," —
And spoke the hest of Isabel.
— "Now by Saint Giles," the monarch
    cried,
"This moves me much! this morning
    tide,
I sent the stripling to Saint Bride,
With my commandment there to bide."
— "Thither he came the portress show'd,
But there, my Liege, made brief abode."

IX.

"'Twas I," said Edward, "found em-
    ploy
Of nobler import for the boy.
Deep pondering in my anxious mind,
A fitting messenger to find,
To bear my written mandate o'er
To Cuthbert on the Carrick shore,

I chanced, at early dawn, to pass
The chapel gate to snatch a mass.
I found the stripling on a tomb
Low-seated, weeping for the doom
That gave his youth to convent gloom.
I told my purpose, and his eyes
Flashed joyful at the glad surprise.
He bounded to the skiff, the sail
Was spread before a prosperous gale,
And well my charge he hath obey'd;
For, see! the ruddy signal made,
That Clifford, with his merry-men all,
Guards carelessly our father's hall." —

X.

" O wild of thought, and hard of heart!"
Answered the Monarch, " on a part
Of such deep danger to employ
A mute, an orphan, and a boy
Unfit for flight, unfit for strife,
Without a tongue to plead for life!
Now, were my right restored by Heaven,
Edward, my crown I would have given,
Ere, thrust on such adventure wild,
I perill'd thus the helpless child." —
— Offended half, and half submiss: —
" Brother and Liege, of blame like this,"
Edward replied, " I little dream'd.
A stranger messenger, I deemed,
Might safest seek the beadsman's cell,
Where all thy squires are known so well.
Noteless his presence, sharp his sense,
His imperfection his defence.
If seen, none can his errand guess;
If ta'en, his words no tale express —
Methinks, too, yonder beacon's shine
Might expiate greater fault than mine."—
" Rash," said King Robert, " was the deed —
But it is done — Embark with speed! —
Good Father, say to Isabel
How this unhappy chance befell;
If well we thrive on yonder shore,
Soon shall my care her page restore.
Our greeting to our sister bear,
And think of us in mass and prayer."

XI.

" Ay!" said the Priest, " while this poor hand　.
Can chalice raise or cross command,
While my old voice has accents' use,
Can Augustin forget the Bruce!"

Then to his side Lord Ronald press'd,
And whisper'd: — " Bear thou this request,
That when by Bruce's side I fight,
For Scotland's crown and freedom' right,
The princess grace her knight to bear
Some token of her favoring care;
It shall be shown where England's best
May shrink to see it on my crest.
And for the boy — since weightier care
For royal Bruce the times prepare,
The helpless youth is Ronald's charge,
His couch my plaid, his fence my targe."
He ceased; for many an eager hand
Had urged the barges from the strand.
Their number was a score and ten,
They bore thrice threescore chosen men
With such small force did Bruce at last
The die for death or empire cast!

XII.

Now on the darkening main afloat,
Ready and mann'd, rocks every boat;
Beneath their oars the ocean's might
Was dash'd to sparks of glimmering light
Faint and more faint, as off they bore,
Their armor glanced against the shore,
And, mingled with the dashing tide,
Their murmuring voices distant died. —
" God speed them!" said the Priest, a dark
On distant billows glides each bark;
" O Heaven! when swords for freedom shine,
And monarch's right, the cause is thine
Edge doubly every patriot blow!
Beat down the banners of the foe!
And be it to the nations known,
That Victory is from God alone!"
As up the hill his path he drew,
He turn'd his blessings to renew,
Oft turn'd, till on the darken'd coast
All traces of their course were lost;
Then slowly bent to Brodick tower,
To shelter for the evening hour.

XIII.

In night the fairy prospects sink,
Where Cumray's isles with verdant link
Close the fair entrance of the Clyde;
The woods of Bute, no more descried,
Are gone — and on the placid sea
The rowers ply their task with glee,

While hands that knightly lances bore
Impatient aid the laboring oar.
The half-faced moon shone dim and pale,
And glanced against the whiten'd sail;
But on that ruddy beacon-light
Each steersman kept the helm aright,
And oft, for such the King's command,
That all at once might reach the strand,
From boat to boat loud shout and hail
Warn'd them to crowd or slacken sail.
South and by west the armada bore,
And near at length the Carrick shore.
As less and less the distance grows,
High and more high the beacon rose;
The light, that seem'd a twinkling star,
Now blazed portentous, fierce, and far.
Dark-red the heaven above it glow'd,
Dark-red the sea beneath it flow'd,
Red rose the rocks on ocean's brim,
In blood-red light her islets swim;
Wild scream the dazzled sea-fowl gave,
Dropp'd from their crags on plashing wave.
The deer to distant covert drew,
The black-cock deem'd it day, and crew.
Like some tall castle given to flame,
O'er half the land the lustre came.
Now, good my Liege, and brother sage,
What think ye of mine elfin page?" —
"Row on!" the noble King replied,
"We'll learn the truth whate'er betide;
Yet sure the beadsman and the child
Could ne'er have waked that beacon wild."

XIV.

With that the boats approach'd the land,
But Edward's grounded on the sand;
The eager Knight leap'd in the sea
Waist-deep, and first on shore was he,
Though every barge's hardy band
Contended which should gain the land,
When that strange light, which, seen afar,
Seem'd steady as the polar star,
Now, like a prophet's fiery chair,
Seem'd travelling the realms of air.
Wide o'er the sky the splendor glows,
As that portentous meteor rose;
Helm, ax, and falchion glitter'd bright,
And in the red and dusky light
His comrade's face each warrior saw,
Nor marvell'd it was pale with awe,
Then high in air the beams were lost,
And darkness sunk upon the coast. —

Ronald to Heaven a prayer address'd,
And Douglas cross'd his dauntless breast;
"Saint James protect us!" Lennox cried,
But reckless Edward spoke aside: —
"Deem'st thou, Kirkpatrick, in that flame,
Red Comyn's angry spirit came,
Or would thy dauntless heart endure
Once more to make assurance sure?"
"Hush!" said the Bruce, "we soon
    shall know
If this be sorcerer's empty show,
Or stratagem of southern foe.
The moon shines out — upon the sand
Let every leader rank his band."

XV.

Faintly the moon's pale beams supply
That ruddy light's unnatural dye;
The dubious cold reflection lay
On the wet sands and quiet bay.
Beneath the rocks King Robert drew
His scatter'd files to order due,
Till shield compact and serried spear
In the cool light shone blue and clear.
Then down a path that sought the tide,
That speechless page was seen to glide;
He knelt him lowly on the sand,
And gave a scroll to Robert's hand.
"A torch," the Monarch cried, "What
    ho!
Now shall we Cuthbert's tidings know."
But evil news the letters bare,
The Clifford's force was strong and ware,
Augmented, too, that very morn,
By mountaineers who came with Lorn.
Long harrow'd by oppressor's hand,
Courage and faith had fled the land,
And over Carrick, dark and deep,
Had sunk dejection's iron sleep. —
Cuthbert had seen that beacon-flame,
Unwitting from what source it came.
Doubtful of perilous event,
Edward's mute messenger he sent,
If Bruce deceived should venture o'er,
To warn him from the fatal shore.

XVI.

As round the torch the leaders crowd,
Bruce read these chilling news aloud.
"What counsel, nobles, have we now? —
To ambush us in greenwood bough,
And take the chance which fate may send
To bring our enterprise to end,

Or shall we turn us to the main
As exiles, and embark again?" —
Answer'd fierce Edward: — "Hap what
may,
In Carrick, Carrick's Lord must stay.
I would not minstrels told the tale,
Wildfire or meteor made us quail." —
Answer'd the Douglas: — "If my Liege
May win yon walls by storm or siege,
Then were each brave and patriot heart
Kindled of new for loyal part." —
Answer'd Lord Ronald: — "Not for
shame
Would I that aged Torquil came,
And found, for all our empty boast,
Without a blow we fled the coast.
I will not credit that this land,
So famed for warlike heart and hand,
The nurse of Wallace and of Bruce,
Will long with tyrants hold a truce." —
"Prove we our fate — the brunt we'll
bide!"
So Boyd and Haye and Lennox cried;
So said, so vow'd, the leaders all;
So Bruce resolved: — "And in my hall
Since the Bold Southern make their home,
The hour of payment soon shall come,
When with a rough and rugged host
Clifford may reckon to his cost.
Meantime, through well-known bosk and
dell,
I'll lead where we may shelter well."

XVII.

Now ask you whence that wondrous light,
Whose fairy glow beguiled their sight? —
It ne'er was known [35] — yet gray-hair'd
eld
A superstitious credence held,
That never did a mortal hand
Wake its broad glare on Carrick strand;
Nay, and that on the self-same night
When Bruce cross'd o'er, still gleams the
light.
Yearly it gleams o'er mount and moor,
And glittering wave and crimson'd
shore —
But whether beam celestial lent
By Heaven to aid the King's descent,
Or fire hell-kindled from beneath,
To lure him to defeat and death,
Or were it but some meteor strange,
Of such a oft through midnight range,

Startling the traveller late and lone,
I know not — and it ne'er was known.

XVIII.

Now up the rocky pass they drew,
And Ronald, to his promise true,
Still made his arm the stripling's stay,
To aid him on the rugged way.
"Now cheer thee, simple Amadine!
Why throbs that silly heart of thine?"
— That name the pirates to their slave
(In Gaelic 'tis the Changeling) gave —
"Dost thou not rest thee on my arm?
Do not my plaid-folds hold thee warm
Hath not the wild bull's treble hide
This targe for thee and me supplied?
Is not Clan-Colla's sword of steel?
And, trembler, canst thou terror feel!
Cheer thee, and still that throbbing heart
From Ronald's guard thou shalt
part."
— O! many a shaft, at random sent,
Finds mark the archer little meant!
And many a word, at random spoken,
May soothe or wound a heart that
broken!
Half soothed, half grieved, half terrifie
Close drew the page to Ronald's side;
A wild delirious thrill of joy
Was in that hour of agony,
As up the steepy pass he strove,
Fear, toil, and sorrow, lost in love!

XIX.

The barrier of that iron shore,
The rock's steep ledge, is now climb'd o'e
And from the castle's distant wall,
From tower to tower the warders call
The sound swings over land and sea,
And marks a watchful enemy. —
They gain'd the Chase, a wide domain
Left for the Castle's sylvan reign,
(Seek not the scene — the ax, the ploug
The boor's dull fence have marr'd
now,)
But then, soft swept in velvet green
The plain with many a glade between
Whose tangled alleys far invade
The depth of the brown forest shade.
Here the tall fern obscured the lawn,
Fair shelter for the sportive fawn,
There, tufted close with copsewood gre
Was many a swelling hillock seen;

And all around was verdure meet
For pressure of the fairies' feet.
The glossy holly loved the park,
The yew-tree lent its shadow dark,
And many an old oak, worn and bare,
With all its shiver'd boughs, was there.
Lovely between, the moonbeams fell
On lawn and hillock, glade and dell.
The gallant Monarch sigh'd to see
These glades so loved in childhood free,
Bethinking that, as outlaw now,
He ranged beneath the forest bough.

XX.

Fast o'er the moonlight Chase they sped.
Well knew the band that measured tread,
When, in retreat or in advance,
The serried warriors move at once;
And evil were the luck, if dawn
Descried them on the open lawn.
Copses they traverse, brooks they cross,
Strain up the bank and o'er the moss.
From the exhausted page's brow
Cold drops of toil are streaming now:
With effort faint and lengthen'd pause,
His weary step the stripling draws,
" Nay, droop not yet ! " the warrior said;
" Come, let me give thee ease and aid !
Strong are mine arms, and little care
A weight so slight as thine to bear. —
What ! wilt thou not? — capricious boy !
Then thine own limbs and strength employ.
Pass but this night, and pass thy care,
I'll place thee with a lady fair,
Where thou shalt tune thy lute to tell
How Ronald loves fair Isabel ! "
Worn out, dishearten'd, and dismay'd,
Here Amadine let go the plaid:
His trembling limbs their aid refuse,
He sunk among the midnight dews !

XXI.

What may be done? — the night is gone —
The Bruce's band moves swiftly on —
Eternal shame, if at the brunt
Lord Ronald grace not battle's front !
" See yonder oak, within whose trunk
Decay a darken'd cell hath sunk;
Enter and rest thee there a space,
Wrap in my plaid thy limbs, thy face.
I will not be, believe me, far;
But must not quit the ranks of war.

Well will I mark the bosky bourne,
And soon, to guard thee hence, return. —
Nay, weep not so, thou simple boy !
But sleep in peace, and wake in joy."
In sylvan lodging close bestow'd,
He placed the page, and onward strode
With strength put forth, o'er moss and brook,
And soon the marching band o'ertook.

XXII.

Thus strangely left, long sobb'd and wept
The page, till, wearied out, he slept —
A rough voice waked his dream:—" Nay, here,
Here by this thicket, pass'd the deer —
Beneath that oak old Ryno staid —
What have we here ? — A Scottish plaid,
And in its folds a stripling laid? —
Come forth ! thy name and business tell !—
What, silent? — Then I guess thee well,
The spy that sought old Cuthbert's cell,
Wafted from Arran yester morn —
Come, comrades, we will straight return.
Our Lord may choose the rack should teach
To this young lurcher use of speech.
Thy bow-string till I bind him fast." —
" Nay, but he weeps and stands aghast;
Unbound we'll lead him, fear it not;
'Tis a fair stripling, though a Scot."
The hunters to the castle sped,
And there the hapless captive led.

XXIII.

Stout Clifford in the castle-court
Prepared him for the morning sport;
And now with Lorn held deep discourse,
Now gave command for hound and horse.
War-steeds and palfreys paw'd the ground,
And many a deer-dog howl'd around.
To Amadine, Lorn's well-known word
Replying to that Southern Lord,
Mix'd with this clanging din might seem
The phantasm of a fever'd dream.
The tone upon his ringing ears
Came like the sound which fancy hears,
When in rude waves or roaring winds
Some words of woe the muser finds,
Until more loudly and more near,
Their speech arrests the page's ear.

XXIV.

"And was she thus," said Clifford, "lost?
The priest should rue it to his cost!
What says the monk?" — "The holy Sire
Owns, that in masquer's quaint attire
She sought his skiff, disguised, unknown
To all except to him alone.
But, says the priest, a bark from Lorn
Laid them aboard that very morn,
And pirates seized her for their prey.
He proffer'd ransom-gold to pay,
And they agreed; — but ere told o'er,
The winds blow loud, the billows roar;
They sever'd, and they met no more.
He deems — such tempest vex'd the coast —
Ship, crew, and fugitive were lost.
So let it be, with the disgrace
And scandal of her lofty race!
Thrice better she had ne'er been born,
Than brought her infamy on Lorn!"

XXV.

Lord Clifford now the captive spied: —
"Whom, Herbert, hast thou there?" he
        cried.
"A spy we seized within the Chase,
A hollow oak his lurking-place." —
"What tidings can the youth afford?" —
"He plays the mute." — "Then noose a
        cord —
Unless brave Lorn reverse the doom
For his plaid's sake." — "Clan-Colla's
        loom,"
Said Lorn, whose careless glances trace
Rather the vesture than the face,
"Clan-Colla's dames such tartans twine;
Wearer nor plaid claims care of mine.
Give him, if my advice you crave,
His own scathed oak; and let him wave
In air, unless, by terror wrung,
A frank confession find his tongue. —
Nor shall he die without his rite;
— Thou, Angus Roy, attend the sight,
And give Clan-Colla's dirge thy breath,
As they convey him to his death." —
"O brother! cruel to the last!"
Through the poor captive's bosom pass'd
The thought, but, to his purpose true,
He said not, though he sigh'd, "Adieu!"

XXVI.

And will he keep his purpose still,
In sight of that last closing ill,
When one poor breath, one single word,
May freedom, safety, life afford?
Can he resist the instinctive call,
For life that bids us barter all? —
Love, strong as death, his heart hat
        steel'd,
His nerves hath strung — he will not yield
Since that poor breath, that little word,
May yield Lord Ronald to the sword. —
Clan-Colla's dirge is pealing wide,
The grisly headsman's by his side;
Along the greenwood Chase they bend,
And now their march has ghastly end!
That old and shatter'd oak beneath,
They destine for the place of death.
— What thoughts are his, while all i
        vain
His eye for aid explores the plain?
What thoughts, while, with a dizzy ear,
He hears the death-prayer mutter'd near,
And must he die such death accurst,
Or will that bosom-secret burst?
Cold on his brow breaks terror's dew,
His trembling lips are livid blue;
The agony of parting life
Has naught to match that moment's strife

XXVII.

But other witnesses are nigh,
Who mock at fear, and death defy!
Soon as the dire lament was play'd,
It waked the lurking ambuscade.
The Island Lord look'd forth, and spied
The cause, and loud in fury cried: —
"By Heaven, they lead the page to die
And mock me in his agony!
They shall abye it!" — On his arm
Bruce laid strong grasp: — "They sha
        not harm
A ringlet of the stripling's hair;
But, till I give the word, forbear.
— Douglas, lead fifty of our force
Up yonder hollow water-course,
And couch thee midway on the wold,
Between the flyers and their hold:
A spear above the copse display'd,
Be signal of the ambush made.
— Edward, with forty spearmen, straig
Through yonder copse approach the gat
And, when thou hear'st the battle-din,
Rush forward, and the passage win,
Secure the drawbridge — storm the por
And man and guard the castle-court. —

The rest move slowly forth with me,
In shelter of the forest-tree,
Till Douglas at his post I see."

XXVIII.

Like war-dogs eager to rush on,
Compell'd to wait the signal blown,
Hid, and scarce hid, by greenwood bough,
Trembling with rage, stands Ronald now,
And in his grasp his sword gleams blue,
Soon to be dyed with deadlier hue. —
Meanwhile the Bruce, with steady eye,
Sees the dark death-train moving by,
And, heedful, measures oft the space
The Douglas and his band must trace,
Ere they can reach their destined ground.
Now sinks the dirge's wailing sound,
Now cluster round the direful tree
That slow and solemn company,
While hymnmistuned and mutter'd prayer
The victim for his fate prepare. —
What glances o'er the greenwood shade?
The spear that marks the ambuscade!
' Now, noble Chief! I leave thee loose;
Upon them, Ronald ! " said the Bruce.

XXIX.

" The Bruce, the Bruce ! " to well-known
       cry
His native rocks and woods reply.
' The Bruce, the Bruce ! " in that dread
       word
The knell of hundred deaths was heard.
The astonish'd Southern gazed at first,
Where the wild tempest was to burst,
That waked in that presaging name.
Before, behind, around it came !
Half-arm'd, surprised, on every side
Hemm'd in, hew'd down, they bled and
       died.
Deep in the ring the Bruce engaged,
And fierce Clan-Colla's broadsword
       raged !
Full soon the few who fought were sped,
Nor better was their lot who fled,
And met, mid terror's wild career,
The Douglas's redoubted spear !
Two hundred yeomen on that morn
The castle left, and none returned.

XXX.

Not on their flight press'd Ronald's brand,
A gentler duty claim'd his hand.

He raised the page, where on the plain
His fear had sunk him with the slain;
And twice, that morn, surprise well
       near
Betray'd the secret kept by fear;
Once, when, with life returning, came
To the boy's lip Lord Ronald's name,
And hardly recollection drown'd
The accents in a murmuring sound;
And once, when scarce he could resist
The Chieftain's care to loose the vest,
Drawn tightly o'er his laboring breast,
But then the Bruce's bugle blew,
For martial work was yet to do.

XXXI.

A harder task fierce Edward waits.
Ere signal given, the castle gates
       His fury had assail'd;
Such was his wonted reckless mood,
Yet desperate valor oft made good,
Even by its daring, venture rude,
       Where prudence might have fail'd.
Upon the bridge his strength he threw,
And struck the iron chain in two,
       By which its planks arose;
The warder next his ax's edge
Struck down upon the threshold ledge,
'Twixt door and post a ghastly wedge !
       The gate they may not close.
Well fought the Southern in the fray,
Clifford and Lorn fought well that day,
But stubborn Edward forced his way
       Against a hundred foes.
Loud came the cry, " The Bruce, the
       Bruce ! "
No hope or in defence or truce,
       Fresh combatants pour in;
Mad with success, and drunk with
       gore,
They drive the struggling foe before,
       And ward on ward they win.
Unsparing was the vengeful sword,
And limbs were lopp'd and life-blood
       pour'd,
The cry of death and conflict roar'd,
       And fearful was the din !
The startling horses plunged and flung,
Clamor'd the dogs till turrets rung,
       Nor sunk the fearful cry,
Till not a foeman was there found
Alive, save those who on the ground
       Groan'd in their agony !

XXXII.

The valiant Clifford is no more:
On Ronald's broadsword stream'd his
    gore,
But better hap had he of Lorn,
Who, by the foeman backward borne,
Yet gain'd with slender train the port,
Where lay his bark beneath the fort,
    And cut the cable loose.
Short were his shrift in that debate,
That hour of fury and of fate,
    If Lorn encounter'd Bruce!
Then long and loud the victor shout
From turret and from tower rung out,
    The rugged vaults replied;
And from the donjon tower on high,
The men of Carrick may descry
Saint Andrew's cross, in blazonry
    Of silver, waving wide!

XXXIII.

The Bruce hath won his father's hall! [36]
— "Welcome, brave friends and com-
    rades all,
    Welcome to mirth and joy!
The first, the last, is welcome here,
From lord and chieftain, prince and peer,
    To this poor speechless boy.
Great God! once more my sire's abode
Is mine — behold the floor I trode
    In tottering infancy!
And there the vaulted arch, whose sound
Echoed my joyous shout and bound
In boyhood, and that rung around
    To youth's unthinking glee!
O first, to thee, all gracious Heaven,
Then to my friends, my thanks be
    given!" —
He paused a space, his brow he cross'd —
Then on the board his sword he toss'd,
Yet steaming hot; with Southern gore
From hilt to point 'twas crimson'd o'er.

XXXIV.

"Bring here," he said, "the mazers
    four,*
My noble fathers loved of yore.
Thrice let them circle round the board,
The pledge, fair Scotland's rights re-
    stored!

* *The mazers four*, large drinking cups, or
goblets.

And he whose lips shall touch the wine
Without a vow as true as mine,
To hold both lands and life at naught,
Until her freedom shall be bought, —
Be brand of a disloyal Scot,
And lasting infamy his lot!
Sit, gentle friends! our hour of glee
Is brief, we'll spend it joyously!
Blithest of all the sun's bright beams,
When betwixt storm and storm he
    gleams.
Well is our country's work begun,
But more, far more, must yet be done.
Speed messengers the country through;
Arouse old friends, and gather new;
Warn Lanark's knights to gird their
    mail,
Rouse the brave sons of Teviotdale,
Let Ettrick's archers sharp their darts,
The fairest forms, the truest hearts!
Call all, call all! from Reedswair-Path
To the wild confines of Cape Wrath;
Wide let the news through Scotland
    ring, —
The Northern Eagle claps his wing!"

CANTO SIXTH.

I.

O who, that shared them, ever shall
    forget
The emotions of the spirit-rousing
    time,
When breathless in the mart the
    couriers met,
Early and late, at evening and at
    prime;
When the loud cannon and the merry
    chime
Hail'd news on news, as field on field
    was won!
When Hope, long doubtful, soar'd at
    length sublime,
And our glad eyes, awake as day be-
    gun,
Watch'd Joy's broad banner rise, to meet
    the rising sun!

O these were hours, when thrilling
    joy repaid
A long, long course of darkness, doubts,
    and fears!

The heart-sick faintness of the hope
  delay'd,
The waste, the woe, the bloodshed,
  and the tears,
That track'd with terror twenty rolling
  years,
All was forgot in that blithe jubilee !
Her downcast eye even pale Affliction
  rears,
To sigh a thankful prayer, amid the
  glee,
hat hail'd the Despot's fall, and peace
  and liberty !

Such news o'er Scotland's hills tri-
  umphant rode,
When 'gainst the invaders turn'd the
  battle's scale,
When Bruce's banner had victorious
  flow'd
O'er Loudoun's mountain, and in
  Ury's vale; [37]
When English blood oft deluged
  Douglasdale, [38]
And fiery Edward routed stout St.
  John, [39]
When Randolph's war-cry swell'd the
  Southern gale, [40]
And many a fortress, town, and tower,
  was won,
nd Fame still sounded forth fresh deeds
  of glory done.

II.

lithe tidings flew from baron's tower,
o peasant's cot, to forest bower,
nd waked the solitary cell,
/here lone St. Bride's recluses dwell.
rincess no more, fair Isabel,
  A vot'ress of the order now,
ay, did the rule that bid thee wear
im veil and woollen scapulaire,
nd reft thy locks of dark-brown hair,
  That stern and rigid vow,
)id it condemn the transport high,
/hich glisten'd in thy watery eye,
/hen minstrel or when palmer told
ach fresh exploit of Bruce the bold? —
.nd whose the lovely form, that shares
hy anxious hopes, thy fears, thy prayers?
Jo sister she of convent shade !
o say these locks in lengthen'd braid,
o say the blushes and the sighs,
he tremors that unbidden rise,

When, mingled with the Bruce's fame,
The brave Lord Ronald's praises came.

III.

Believe, his father's castle won,
And his bold enterprise begun,
That Bruce's earliest cares restore
The speechless page to Arran's shore:
Nor think that long the quaint disguise
Conceal'd her from her sister's eyes;
And sister-like in love they dwell
In that lone convent's silent cell.
There Bruce's slow assent allows
Fair Isabel the veil and vows;
And there, her sex's dress regain'd,
The lovely Maid of Lorn remained,
Unnamed, unknown, while Scotland
  far
Resounded with the din of war;
And many a month, and many a day,
In calm seclusion wore away.

IV.

These days, these months, to years had
  worn,
When tidings of high weight were borne
  To that lone island's shore;
Of all the Scottish conquests made
By the First Edward's ruthless blade,
  His son retain'd no more,
Northward of Tweed, but Stirling's
  towers,
Beleaguer'd by King Robert's powers;
  And they took term of truce, [41]
If England's King should not relieve
The siege ere John the Baptist's eve,
  To yield them to the Bruce.
England was roused — on every side
Courier and post and herald hied,
  To summon prince and peer,
At Berwick-bounds to meet their Liege,
Prepared to raise fair Stirling's siege,
  With buckler, brand, and spear.
The term was nigh — they muster'd fast,
By beacon and by bugle-blast
  Forth marshall'd for the field;
There rode each knight of noble name,
There England's hardy archers came,
The land they trode seem'd all on flame,
  With banner, blade, and shield !
And not famed England's powers alone
Renown'd in arms, the summons own;
  For Neustria's knights obeyd,

Gascogne hath lent her horsemen good,
And Cambria, but of late subdued,
Sent forth her mountain multitude,[42]
And Connoght pour'd from waste and
    wood
Her hundred tribes, whose sceptre rude
    Dark Eth O'Connor sway'd.[43]

V.

Right to devoted Caledon
The storm of war rolls slowly on,
    With menace deep and dread;
So the dark clouds, with gathering power,
Suspend awhile the threaten'd shower,
Till every peak and summit lower
    Round the pale pilgrim's head.
Not with such pilgrim's startled eye
King Robert mark'd the tempest nigh!
    Resolved the brunt to bide,
His royal summons warn'd the land,
That all who own'd their King's command
Should instant take the spear and brand,
    To combat at his side.
O who may tell the sons of fame,
That at King Robert's bidding came,
    To battle for the right!
From Cheviot to the shores of Ross,
From Solway-Sands to Marshal's-Moss,
    All boun'd them for the fight.
Such news the royal courier tells,
Who came to rouse dark Arran's dells;
But farther tidings must the ear
    Of Isabel in secret hear.
These in her cloister walk, next morn,
Thus shared she with the Maid of Lorn:—

VI.

" My Edith, can I tell how dear
Our intercourse of hearts sincere
    Hath been to Isabel? —
Judge then the sorrow of my heart,
When I must say the words, We part!
    The cheerless convent-cell
Was not, sweet maiden, made for thee;
Go thou where thy vocation free
    On happier fortunes fell.
Nor, Edith, judge thyself betray'd,
Though Robert knows that Lorn's high
    Maid
And his poor silent page were one.
Versed in the fickle heart of man,
Earnest and anxious hath he look'd
How Ronald's heart the message brook'd

That gave him, with her last farewell,
The charge of Sister Isabel,
To think upon thy better right,
And keep the faith his promise plight.
Forgive him for thy sister's sake,
At first if vain repinings wake —
    Long since that mood is gone;
Now dwells he on thy juster claims,
And oft his breach of faith he blames —
    Forgive him for thine own! "

VII.

" No! never to Lord Ronald's bower
Will I again as paramour " ——
" Nay, hush thee, too impatient maid,
Until my final tale be said! —
The good King Robert would engage
Edith once more his elfin page,
By her own heart, and her own eye,
Her lover's penitence to try —
Safe in his royal charge, and free,
Should such thy final purpose be,
Again unknown to seek the cell,
And live and die with Isabel."
Thus spoke the maid. — King Robert's
    eye
Might have some glance of policy;
Dunstaffnage had the monarch ta'en,
And Lorn had own'd King Robert's reign,
Her brother had to England fled,
And there in banishment was dead;
Ample, through exile, death, and flight,
O'er tower and land was Edith's right;
This ample right o'er tower and land
Were safe in Ronald's faithful hand.

VIII.

Embarrass'd eye and blushing cheek
Pleasure, and shame, and fear bespeak,
Yet much the reasoning Edith made: —
' Her sister's faith she must upbraid,
Who gave such secret, dark and dear,
In counsel to another's ear.
Why should she leave the peaceful cell?—
How should she part with Isabel? —
How wear that strange attire agen? —
How risk herself midst martial men? —
And how be guarded on the way? —
At least she might entreat delay.'
Kind Isabel, with secret smile,
Saw and forgave the maiden's wile,
Reluctant to be thought to move
At the first call of truant love.

IX.

Oh, blame her not! — when zephyrs wake,
The aspen's trembling leaves must shake;
When beams the sun through April's shower
It needs must bloom, the violet flower;
And Love, howe'er the maiden strive,
Must with reviving hope revive!
A thousand soft excuses came,
To plead his cause 'gainst virgin shame.
Pledged by their sires in earliest youth,
He had her plighted faith and truth —
Then, 'twas her Liege's strict command,
And she, beneath his royal hand,
A ward in person and in land: —
And, last, she was resolved to stay
Only brief space — one little day —
Close hidden in her safe disguise
From all, but most from Ronald's eyes —
But once to see him more! nor blame
Her wish — to hear him name her name! —
Then, to bear back to solitude
The thought he had his falsehood rued!
But Isabel, who long had seen
Her pallid cheek and pensive mien,
And well herself the cause might know,
Though innocent, of Edith's woe,
Joy'd, generous, that revolving time
Gave means to expiate the crime.
High glow'd her bosom as she said: —
'Well shall her sufferings be repaid!'
Now came the parting hour — a band
From Arran's mountains left the land;
Their chief, Fitz-Louis, had the care
The speechless Amadine to bear
To Bruce, with honor, as behoved
To page the monarch dearly loved.

X.

The King had deem'd the maiden bright
Should reach him long before the fight,
But storms and fate her course delay:
It was on eve of battle-day,
When o'er the Gillie's-hill she rode,
The landscape like a furnace glow'd,
And far as e'er the eye was borne,
The lances waved like autumn-corn.
In battles four beneath their eye,
The forces of King Robert lie.
And one below the hill was laid,
Reserved for rescue and for aid;
And three, advanced, form'd vaward-line,
'Twixt Bannock's brook and Ninian's
    shrine.

Detach'd was each, yet each so nigh
As well might mutual aid supply.
Beyond, the Southern host appears,
A boundless wilderness of spears,
Whose verge or rear the anxious eye
Strove far, but strove in vain, to spy.
Thick flashing in the evening beam,
Glaives, lances, bills, and banners gleam;
And where the heaven join'd with the hill
Was distant armor flashing still,
So wide, so far, the boundless host
Seem'd in the blue horizon lost.

XI.

Down from the hill the maiden pass'd,
At the wild show of war aghast;
And traversed first the rearward host,
Reserved for aid where needed most.
The men of Carrick and of Ayr,
Lennox and Lanark, too, were there,
    And all the western land;
With these the valiant of the Isles
Beneath their chieftains rank'd their files,
    In many a plaided band.
There, in the centre, proudly raised,
The Bruce's royal standard blazed,
And there Lord Ronald's banner bore
A galley driven by sail and oar.
A wild, yet pleasing contrast, made
Warriors in mail and plate array'd,
With the plumed bonnet and the plaid
    By these Hebrideans worn;
But O! unseen for three long years,
Dear was the garb of mountaineers
    To the fair Maid of Lorn!
For one she look'd — but he was far
Busied amid the ranks of war —
Yet with affection's troubled eye
She mark'd his banner boldly fly,
Gave on the countless foe a glance,
And thought on battle's desperate chance.

XII.

To centre of the vaward-line
Fitz-Louis guided Amadine.
Arm'd all on foot, that host appears
A serried mass of glimmering spears.
There stood the Marchers' warlike band,
The warriors there of Lodon's land;
Ettrick and Liddell bent the yew,
A band of archers fierce, though few;
The men of Nith and Annan's vale,
And the bold Spears of Teviotdale; —

The dauntless Douglas these obey,
And the young Stuart's gentle sway.
North-eastward by Saint Ninian's shrine,
Beneath fierce Randolph's charge, combine
The warriors whom the hardy North
From Tay to Sutherland sent forth.
The rest of Scotland's war-array
With Edward Bruce to westward lay,
Where Bannock, with his broken bank
And deep ravine, protects their flank.
Behind them, screen'd by sheltering wood,
The gallant Keith, Lord Marshal, stood:
His men-at-arms bear mace and lance,
And plumes that wave, and helms that
        glance.
Thus fair divided by the King,
Centre, and right, and left-ward wing,
Composed his front; nor distant far
Was strong reserve to aid the war.
And 'twas to front of this array,
Her guide and Edith made their way.

XIII.

Here must they pause: for, in advance
As far as one might pitch a lance,
The monarch rode along the van,[44]
The foe's approaching force to scan,
His line to marshal and to range,
And ranks to square and fronts to change.
Alone he rode — from head to heel
Sheathed in his ready arms of steel;
Nor mounted yet on war-horse wight,
But, till more near the shock of fight,
Reining a palfrey low and light.
A diadem of gold was set
Above his bright steel basinet,
And clasp'd within its glittering twine
Was seen the glove of Argentine;
Truncheon or leading staff he lacks,
Bearing, instead, a battle-ax.
He ranged his soldiers for the fight,
Accoutred thus, in open sight
Of either host. — Three bowshots far,
Paused the deep front of England's war,
And rested on their arms awhile,
To close and rank their warlike file,
And hold high council, if that night
Should view the strife, or dawning light.

XIV.

O gay, yet fearful to behold,
Flashing with steel and rough with gold,
    And bristled o'er with bills and spears,

With plumes and pennons waving fair,
Was that bright battle-front! for there
    Rode England's King and peers:
And who, that saw that monarch ride,
His kingdom battled by his side,
Could then his direful doom foretell! —
Fair was his seat in kingly selle,
And in his sprightly eye was set
Some spark of the Plantagenet.
Though light and wandering was h.
        glance,
It flash'd at sight of shield and lance.
" Know'st thou," he said, " De Argen
        tine,
Yon knight who marshals thus the:
        line?" —
" The tokens on his helmet tell
The Bruce, my Liege: I know him well.
" And shall the audacious traitor brave
The presence where our banners wave?
" So please, my Liege," said Argentine
" Were he but horsed on steed like mine
To give him fair and knightly chance,
I would adventure forth my lance." —
" In battle-day," the King replied,
" Nice tourney rules are set aside.
— Still must the rebel dare our wrath?
Set on him — sweep him from ou
        path!" —
And, at King Edward's signal, soon
Dash'd from the ranks Sir Henry Boune

XV

Of Hereford's high blood he came,
A race renown'd for knightly fame.
He burn'd before his Monarch's eye
To do some deed of chivalry.
He spurr'd his steed, he couch'd hi
        lance,
And darted on the Bruce at once.
— As motionless as rocks, that bide
The wrath of the advancing tide,
The Bruce stood fast. — Each breast bea
        high,
And dazzled was each gazing eye —
The heart had hardly time to think,
The eyelid scarce had time to wink,
While on the King, like flash of flame,
Spurr'd to full speed the war-horse came
The partridge may the falcon mock,
If that slight palfrey stand the shock —
But, swerving from the knight's career,
Just as they met, Bruce shunn'd the spear

Onward the baffled warrior bore
His course—but soon his course was o'er !
High in his stirrups stood the King,
And gave his battle-ax the swing,
Right on De Boune, the whiles he pass'd,
Fell that stern dint — the first — the last ! —
Such strength upon the blow was put,
The helmet crash'd like hazel-nut;
The ax-shaft, with its brazen clasp,
Was shiver'd to the gauntlet grasp.
Springs from the blow the startled horse,
Drops to the plain the lifeless corse;
— First of that fatal field, how soon,
How sudden, fell the fierce De Boune !

XVI.

One pitying glance the Monarch sped,
Where on the field his foe lay dead;
Then gently turn'd his palfrey's head,
And, pacing back his sober way,
Slowly he gain'd his own array.
There round their King the leaders crowd,
And blame his recklessness aloud,
That risk'd 'gainst each adventurous spear
A life so valued and so dear.
His broken weapon's shaft survey'd
The King, and careless answer made:—
" My loss may pay my folly's tax;
I've broke my trusty battle-ax."
'Twas then Fitz-Louis, bending low,
Did Isabel's commission show;
Edith, disguised, at distance stands,
And hides her blushes with her hands.
The Monarch's brow has changed its hue,
Away the gory ax he threw,
While to the seeming page he drew,
Clearing war's terrors from his eye.
Her hand with gentle ease he took,
With such a kind protecting look,
As to a weak and timid boy
Might speak, that elder brother's care
And elder brother's love was there.

XVII.

" Fear not," he said, " young Amadine !"
Then whisper'd: — " Still that name be thine.
Fate plays her wonted fantasy,
Kind Amadine, with thee and me,
And sends thee here in doubtful hour.
But soon we are beyond her power;
For on this chosen battle-plain,
Victor or vanquish'd, I remain.
Do thou to yonder hill repair;
The followers of our host are there,
And all who may not weapons bare. —
Fitz-Louis, have him in thy care. —
Joyful we meet, if all go well;
If not, in Arran's holy cell
Thou must take part with Isabel;
For brave Lord Ronald, too, hath sworn,
Not to regain the Maid of Lorn,
(The bliss on earth he covets most,)
Would he forsake his battle-post,
Or shun the fortune that may fall
To Bruce, to Scotland, and to all. —
But, hark ! some news these trumpets tell;
Forgive my haste — farewell ! — farewell !" —
And in a lower voice he said:—
" Be of good cheer — farewell, sweet maid !" —

XVIII.

" What train of dust, with trumpet-sound
And glimmering spear, is wheeling round
Our leftward flank ?"— the Monarch cried,
To Moray's Earl who rode beside.
" Lo ! round thy station pass the foes !
Randolph, thy wreath has lost a rose; "
The Earl his visor closed, and said,
" My wreath shall bloom, or life shall fade. —
Follow, my household !" — And they go
Like lightning on the advancing foe.
" My Liege," said noble Douglas then,
" Earl Randolph has but one to ten:
Let me go forth his band to aid ! " —
— " Stir not.   The error he hath made,
Let him amend it as he may;
I will not weaken mine array."
Then loudly rose the conflict-cry,
And Douglas's brave heart swell'd high:—
" My Liege," he said, " with patient ear
I must not Moray's death-knell hear ! "—
" Then go — but speed thee back again."
Forth sprang the Douglas with his train,
But, when they won a rising hill,
He bade his followers stand them still. —
" See, see ! the routed Southern fly !
The Earl hath won the victory.
Lo ! where yon steeds run masterless,
His banner towers above the press.

Rein up; our presence would impair
The fame we come too late to share."
Back to the host the Douglas rode,
And soon glad tidings are abroad,
That, Dayncourt by stout Randolph slain,
His followers fled with loosen'd rein. —
That skirmish closed the busy day,
And couch'd in battle's prompt array,
Each army on their weapons lay.

XIX.

It was a night of lovely June,
High rode in cloudless blue the moon,
  Demayet smiled beneath her ray;
Old Stirling's towers arose in light,
And twined in links of silver bright,
  Her winding river lay.
Ah, gentle planet! other sight
Shall greet thee next returning night,
Of broken arms and banners tore,
And marshes dark with human gore,
And piles of slaughter'd men and horse,
And Forth that floats the frequent corse,
And many a wounded wretch to plain
Beneath thy silver light in vain!
But now, from England's host, the cry
Thou hear'st of wassail revelry,
While from the Scottish legions pass
The murmur'd prayer, the early mass! —
Here, numbers had presumption given;
There, bands o'ermatched sought aid from
    Heaven.

XX.

On Gillie's-hill, whose height commands
The battle-field, fair Edith stands,
With serf and page unfit for war,
To eye the conflict from afar.
O! with what doubtful agony
She sees the dawning tint the sky! —
Now on the Ochils gleams the sun,
And glistens now Demayet dun;
  Is it the lark that carols shrill?
  Is it the bittern's early hum?
No! — distant, but increasing still,
  The trumpet's sound swells up the hill,
  With the deep murmur of the drum.
Responsive from the Scottish host,
Pipe-clang and bugle sound were toss'd,[45]
His breast and brow each soldier cross'd,
  And started from the ground;
Arm'd and array'd for instant fight,
Rose archer, spearman, squire, and knight,

And in the pomp of battle bright
  The dread battalia frown'd.

XXI.

Now onward, and in open view,
The countless ranks of England drew,
Dark rolling like the ocean-tide,
When the rough west hath chafed his pride,
And his deep roar sends challenge wide
  To all that bars his way!
In front the gallant archers trode,
The men-at-arms behind them rode,
And midmost of the phalanx broad
  The Monarch held his sway.
Beside him many a war-horse fumes,
Around him waves a sea of plumes,
Where many a knight in battle known,
And some who spurs had first braced on,
And deem'd that fight should see them
    won,
  King Edward's hests obey.
De Argentine attends his side,
With stout De Valence, Pembroke's
    pride,
Selected champions from the train,
To wait upon his bridle-rein.
Upon the Scottish foe he gazed —
— At once before his sight amazed,
  Sunk banner, spear, and shield;
Each weapon-point is downward sent,
Each warrior to the ground is bent.
" The rebels, Argentine, repent!
  For pardon they have kneel'd " —
" Ay! — but they bend to other powers,
And other pardon sue than ours!
See where yon bare-foot Abbot stands,
And blesses them with lifted hands![46]
Upon the spot where they have kneel'd,
These men will die or win the field." —
— " Then prove we if they die or win!
Bid Gloster's Earl the fight begin."

XXII.

Earl Gilbert waved his truncheon high,
  Just as the Northern ranks arose,
Signal for England's archery
  To halt and bend their bows.
Then stepp'd each yeoman forth a pace,
Glanced at the intervening space,
  And raised his left hand high;
To the right ear the cords they bring —
— At once ten thousand bow-strings ring,
  Ten thousand arrows fly!

Nor paused on the devoted Scot
The ceaseless fury of their shot;
   As fiercely and as fast,
Forth whistling came the gray-goose wing
As the wild hailstones pelt and ring
   Adown December's blast.
Nor mountain targe of tough bull-hide,
Nor lowland mail, that storm may bide;
Woe, woe to Scotland's banner'd pride,
   If the fell shower may last!
Upon the right, behind the wood,
Each by his steed dismounted, stood
   The Scottish chivalry;—
With foot in stirrup, hand on mane,
Fierce Edward Bruce can scarce restrain
His own keen heart, his eager train,
Until the archers gain'd the plain:
   Then "Mount, ye gallants free!"
He cried; and vaulting from the ground,
His saddle every horseman found.
On high their glittering crests they toss,
As springs the wild-fire from the moss;
The shield hangs down on every breast,
Each ready lance is in the rest,
   And loud shouts Edward Bruce:—
"Forth, Marshal! on the peasant foe!
We'll tame the terrors of their bow,
   And cut the bow-string loose!" [47]

XXIII.

Then spurs were dash'd in chargers'
      flanks,
They rush'd among the archer ranks.
No spears were there the shock to let,
No stakes to turn the charge were set,
And how shall yeoman's armor slight,
Stand the long lance and mace of might?
Or what may their short swords avail,
'Gainst barbed horse and shirt of mail?
Amid their ranks the chargers sprung,
High o'er their heads the weapons swung,
And shriek and groan and vengeful shout
Give note of triumph and of rout!
Awhile, with stubborn hardihood,
Their English hearts the strife made good.
Borne down at length on every side,
Compell'd to flight, they scatter wide.—
Let stags of Sherwood leap for glee,
And bound the deer of Dallom-Lee!
The broken bows of Bannock's shore
Shall in the greenwood ring no more!
Round Wakefield's merry May-pole now,
The maids may twine the summer bough,

May northward look with longing glance,
For those that wont to lead the dance,
For the blithe archers look in vain!
Broken, dispersed, in flight o'erta'en,
Pierced through, trode down, by thou-
      sands slain,
They cumber Bannock's bloody plain.

XXIV.

The King with scorn beheld their flight.
"Are these," he said, "our yeoman
      wight?
Each braggart churl could boast before,
Twelve Scottish lives his baldric bore! [48]
Fitter to plunder chase or park,
Than make a manly foe their mark. —
Forward, each gentleman and knight!
Let gentle blood show generous might,
And chivalry redeem the fight!"
To rightward of the wild affray,
The field show'd fair and level way;
   But, in mid-space, the Bruce's care
Had bored the ground with many a pit,
With turf and brushwood hidden yet,
   That form'd a ghastly snare.
Rushing, ten thousand horsemen came,
With spears in rest, and hearts on flame,
   That panted for the shock!
With blazing crests and banners spread,
And trumpet-clang and clamor dread,
The wide plain thunder'd to their tread,
   As far as Stirling rock.
Down! down! in headlong overthrow,
Horsemen and horse, the foremost go, [49]
   Wild floundering on the field!
The first are in destruction's gorge,
Their followers wildly o'er them urge:—
   The knightly helm and shield,
The mail, the acton, and the spear,
Strong hand, high heart, are useless
      here!
Loud from the mass confused the cry
Of dying warriors swells on high,
And steeds that shriek in agony! [50]
They came like mountain-torrent red,
That thunders o'er its rocky bed;
They broke like that same torrent's
      wave
When swallow'd by a darksome cave.
Billows on billows burst and boil,
Maintaining still the stern turmoil,
And to their wild and tortured groan
Each adds new terrors of his own!

XXV.

Too strong in courage and in might
Was England yet, to yield the fight.
　Her noblest all are here;
Names that to fear were never known,
Bold Norfolk's Earl De Brotherton,
　And Oxford's famed De Vere.
There Gloster plied the bloody sword,
And Berkley, Grey, and Hereford,
　Bottetourt and Sanzavere,
Ross, Montague, and Mauley, came,
And Courtenay's pride, and Percy's
　fame —
Names known too well in Scotland's war,
At Falkirk, Methven, and Dunbar,
Blazed broader yet in after years,
At Cressy red and fell Poitiers.
Pembroke with these, and Argentine,
Brought up the rearward battle-line.
With caution o'er the ground they tread,
Slippery with blood and piled with dead,
Till hand to hand in battle set,
The bills with spears and axes met,
And, closing dark on every side,
Raged the full contest far and wide.
Then was the strength of Douglas tried,
Then proved was Randolph's generous
　pride,
And well did Stewart's actions grace
The sire of Scotland's royal race!
　Firmly they kept their ground;
As firmly England onward press'd,
And down went many a noble crest,
And rent was many a valiant breast,
　And Slaughter revell'd round.

XXVI.

Unflinching foot 'gainst foot was set,
Unceasing blow by blow was met:
　The groans of those who fell
Were drown'd amid the shriller clang
That from the blades and harness rang,
　And in the battle-yell.
Yet fast they fell, unheard, forgot,
Both Southern fierce and hardy Scot;
And O! amid that waste of life,
What various motives fired the strife!
The aspiring Noble bled for fame,
The Patriot for his country's claim;
This Knight his youthful strength to prove,
And that to win his lady's love;
Some fought from ruffian thirst of blood,
From habit some, or hardihood.

But ruffian stern, and soldier good,
　The noble and the slave,
From various cause the same wild road,
On the same bloody morning, trode,
　To that dark inn, the grave!

XXVII

The tug of strife to flag begins,
Though neither loses yet nor wins.
High rides the sun, thick rolls the dust,
And feebler speeds the blow and thrust.
Douglas leans on his war-sword now,
And Randolph wipes his bloody brow;
Nor less had toil'd each Southern knight,
From morn till mid-day in the fight.
Strong Egremont for air must gasp,
Beauchamp undoes his visor-clasp,
And Montague must quit his spear,
And sinks thy falchion, bold De Vere!
The blows of Berkley fall less fast,
And gallant Pembroke's bugle-blast
　Hath lost its lively tone;
Sinks, Argentine, thy battle-word,
And Percy's shout was fainter heard,
　" My merry-men, fight on!"

XXVIII.

Bruce, with the pilot's wary eye,
The slackening of the storm could spy.
　" One effort more, and Scotland's free!
　Lord of the Isles, my trust in thee
　Is firm as Ailsa Rock;[51]
　Rush on with Highland sword and targe,
　I with my Carrick spearman charge;
　　Now, forward to the shock!"
At once the spears were forward
　thrown,
Against the sun the broadswords shone;
The pibroch lent its maddening tone,
And loud King Robert's voice was
　known:—
"Carrick, press on—they fail, they fail!
Press on, brave sons of Innisgail,
　The foe is fainting fast!
Each strike for parent, child, and wife,
For Scotland, liberty, and life,—
　The battle cannot last!"

XXIX.

The fresh and desperate onset bore
The foes three furlongs back and more,
Leaving their noblest in their gore.
　Alone, De Argentine

Yet bears on high his red-cross shield,
Gathers the relics of the field,
Renews the ranks where they have reel'd,
   And still makes good the line.
Brief strife, but fierce,— his efforts raise
A bright, but momentary blaze.
Fair Edith heard the Southern shout,
Beheld them turning from the rout,
Heard the wild call their trumpets sent,
In notes 'twixt triumph and lament.
That rallying force, combined anew,
Appear'd in her distracted view,
   To hem the Islesmen round:—
" O God! the combat they renew,
   And is no rescue found!
And ye that look thus tamely on,
And see your native land o'erthrown,
O! are your hearts of flesh or stone?"

XXX.

The multitude that watch'd afar,
Rejected from the ranks of war,
Had not unmoved beheld the fight,
When strove the Bruce for Scotland's
   right;
Each heart had caught the patriot spark,
Old man and stripling, priest and clerk,
Bondsman and serf; even female hand
Stretch'd to the hatchet or the brand;
   But, when mute Amadine they heard
   Give to their zeal his signal-word,
     A frenzy fired the throng:—
" Portents and miracles impeach
Our sloth—the dumb our duties teach—
And he that gives the mute his speech,
   Can bid the weak be strong.
To us, as to our lords, are given
A native earth, a promised heaven;
To us, as to our lords, belongs
The vengeance for our nation's wrongs;
The choice, 'twixt death or freedom,
   warms
Our breasts as theirs—To arms, to arms!"
To arms they flew,—ax, club, or spear,—
And mimic ensigns high they rear,[52]
And, like a banner'd host afar,
Bear down on England's wearied war.

XXXI.

Already scatter'd o'er the plain,
Reproof, command, and counsel vain,
The rearward squadrons fled amain,
   Or made but doubtful stay;

But when they mark'd the seeming show
Of fresh and fierce and marshall'd foe,
   The boldest broke array.
O give their hapless prince his due!
In vain the royal Edward threw
   His person mid the spears,
Cried, " Fight!" to terror and despair,
Menaced, and wept, and tore his hair,
   And cursed their caitiff fears!
Till Pembroke turn'd his bridle rein,
And forced him from the fatal plain.
With them rode Argentine, until
They gain'd the summit of the hill,
   But quitted there the train:—
" In yonder field a gage I left,—
I must not live of fame bereft;
   I needs must turn again.
Speed hence, my Liege, for on your trace
The fiery Douglas takes the chase,
   I know his banner well.
God send my Sovereign joy and bliss,
And many a happier field than this!—
   Once more, my Liege, farewell."

XXXII.

Again he faced the battle-field,—
Wildly they fly, are slain, or yield.
" Now then," he said, and couch'd his
   spear,
" My course is run, the goal is near;
One effort more, one brave career,
   Must close this race of mine."
Then in his stirrups rising high,
He shouted loud his battle-cry:—
   " Saint James for Argentine!"
And, of the bold pursuers, four
The gallant knight from saddle bore;
But not unharm'd—a lance's point
Has found his breastplate's loosen'd joint,
   An ax has razed his crest;
Yet still on Colonsay's fierce lord,
Who press'd the chase with gory sword,
   He rode with spear in rest,
And through his bloody tartans bored,
   And through his gallant breast.
Nail'd to the earth, the mountaineer
Yet writhed him up against the spear,
   And swung his broadsword round!
— Stirrup, steel-boot, and cuish gave way,
Beneath that blow's tremendous sway,
   The blood gush'd from the wound;
And the grim Lord of Colonsay
   Hath turn'd him on the ground,

And laugh'd in death-pang, that his blade
The mortal thrust so well repaid.

XXXIII.

Now toil'd the Bruce, the battle done,
To use his conquest boldly won;
And gave command for horse and spear
To press the Southern's scatter'd rear,
Nor let his broken force combine,
— When the war-cry of Argentine
  Fell faintly on his ear;
" Save, save his life," he cried, " O save
The kind, the noble, and the brave ! "
The squadrons round free passage gave,
  The wounded knight drew near;
He raised his red-cross shield no more,
Helm, cuish, and breastplate, stream'd
    with gore,
Yet, as he saw the King advance,
He strove even then to couch his lance —
  The effort was in vain !
The spur-stroke fail'd to rouse the horse;
Wounded and weary, in mid course   .
  He stumbled on the plain.
Then foremost was the generous Bruce
To raise his head, his helm to loose: —
" Lord Earl, the day is thine !
My Sovereign's charge, and adverse fate,
Have made our meeting all too late:
  Yet this may Argentine,
As boon from ancient comrade, crave, —
A Christian's mass, a soldier's grave."

XXXIV.

Bruce press'd his dying hand — its grasp
Kindly replied; but, in his clasp,
  It stiffen'd and grew cold —
" And, O farewell ! " the victor cried,
" Of chivalry the flower and pride,
  The arm in battle bold,
The courteous mien, the noble race,
The stainless faith, the manly face ! —
Bid Ninian's convent light their shrine,
For late-wake of De Argentine.
O'er better knight on death-bier laid,
Torch never gleam'd nor mass was said ! "

XXXV.

Nor for De Argentine alone,
Through Ninian's church these torches
    shone,
And rose the death-prayer's awful tone.

That yellow lustre glimmer'd pale,
On broken plate and bloodied mail,
Rent crest and shatter'd coronet,
Of Baron, Earl, and Banneret;
And the best names that England knew
Claim'd in the death-prayer dismal due.
  Yet mourn not, Land of Fame !
Though ne'er the Leopards on thy shield
Retreated from so sad a field,
  Since Norman William came.
Oft may thine annals justly boast
Of battles stern by Scotland lost;
  Grudge not her victory,
When for her freeborn rights she strove;
Rights dear to all who freedom love,
  To none so dear as thee !

XXXVI.

Turn we to Bruce, whose curious ear
Must from Fitz-Louis tidings hear:
With him a hundred voices tell
Of prodigy and miracle,
  " For the mute page had spoke." —
" Page ! " said Fitz-Louis, " rather say,
An angel sent from realms of day,
  To burst the English yoke.
I saw his plume and bonnet drop,
When hurrying from the mountain-top;
A lovely brow, dark locks that wave,
To his bright eyes new lustre gave;
A step as light upon the green,
As if his pinions waved unseen !" —
" Spoke he with none ? " — " With none
    — one word
Burst when he saw the Island Lord,
Returning from the battle-field." —
" What answer made the Chief? " —
    " He kneel'd,
Durst not look up, but mutter'd low,
Some mingled sounds that none might
    know,
And greeted him 'twixt joy and fear,
As being of superior sphere."

XXXVII.

Even upon Bannock's bloody plain,
Heap'd then with thousands of the slain,
Mid victor monarch's musings high,
Mirth laugh'd in good King Robert's eye:
" And bore he such angelic air,
Such noble front, such waving hair?
Hath Ronald kneel'd to him?" he said,
" Then must we call the church to aid —

r will be to the Abbot known,
e these strange news are wider blown.
 Cambuskenneth straight ye pass,
d deck the church for solemn mass,
 pay for high deliverance given,
nation's thanks to gracious Heaven.
t him array, besides, such state,
 should on princes' nuptials wait.
rself the cause, through fortune's
 spite,
at once broke short that spousal rite,
rself will grace, with early morn,
e bridal of the Maid of Lorn."

CONCLUSION.

Go forth, my Song, upon thy venturous way;
Go boldly forth; nor yet thy master
 blame,
Who chose no patron for his humble
 lay,
And graced thy numbers with no
 friendly name,
Whose partial zeal might smooth thy
 path to fame.

There was — and O! how many sorrows crowd
Into these two brief words !—*there was*
 a claim
By generous friendship given — had
 fate allow'd,
It well had bid thee rank the proudest of
 the proud !

All angel now — yet little less than all,
While still a pilgrim in our world
 below !
What 'vails it us that patience to
 recall,
Which hid its own to soothe all other
 woe;
What 'vails to tell, how Virtue's pur-
 est glow
Shone yet more lovely in a form so fair,
And, least of all, what 'vails the
 world should know,
That one poor garland, twined to deck
 thy hair,
Is hung upon thy hearse to droop and
 wither there !

THE

FIELD OF WATERLOO.

A POEM.

TO HER GRACE THE

DUCHESS OF WELLINGTON,

PRINCESS OF WATERLOO, Etc., Etc.

THE FOLLOWING VERSES ARE MOST RESPECTFULLY INSCRIBED BY

THE AUTHOR.

ADVERTISEMENT.

t may be some apology for the imperfections of this poem, that it was composed hastily, during a short tour upon the Continent, when the Author's labors were liable to fre- t interruption; but its best apology is. that it was written for the purpose of assist- the Waterloo Subscription.

BBOTSFORD, 1815.

THE FIELD OF WATERLOO.

Though Valois braved young Edward's gentle hand,
And Albert rush'd on Henry's way-worn band,
With Europe's chosen sons, in arms renown'd,
Yet not on Vere's bold archers long they look'd,
Nor Audley's squires, nor Mowbray's yeomen brook'd, —
They saw their standard fall, and left their monarch bound. — AKENSIDE.

I.

AIR Brussels, thou art far behind,
Though, lingering on the morning wind,
We yet may hear the hour
Peal'd over orchard and canal,
With voice prolong'd and measured
    fall,
From proud St. Michael's tower;
By wood, dark Soignies, holds us now,*
Where the tall beeches' glossy bough,
For many a league around,
With birch and darksome oak between,
Spreads deep and far a pathless screen,
Of tangled forest ground.
Stems planted close by stems defy
The adventurous foot; — the curious eye
For access seeks in vain;
And the brown tapestry of leaves,
Strew'd on the blighted ground, receives
Nor sun, nor air, nor rain.
No opening glade dawns on our way,
No streamlet, glancing to the ray,
Our woodland path has cross'd;
And the straight causeway which we
    tread
Prolongs a line of dull arcade,
Unvarying through the unvaried shade
Until in distance lost.

* The wood of Soignies is a remnant of the forest of Ardennes, the scene of the charming and romantic incidents of Shakespeare's "As you Like It."

II.

A brighter, livelier scene succeeds;
In groups the scattering wood recedes,
Hedge-rows, and huts, and sunny
    meads,
    And corn-fields, glance between;
The peasant at his labor blithe,
Plies the hook'd staff and shorten'd
    scythe : [1] —
But when these ears were green,
Placed close within destruction's scope,
Full little was that rustic's hope
    Their ripening to have seen !
And, lo, a hamlet and its fane : —
Let not the gazer with disdain
    Their architecture view;
For yonder rude ungraceful shrine,†
And disproportion'd spire, are thine,
    Immortal WATERLOO !

III.

Fear not the heat, though full and
    high,
The sun has scorch'd the autumn sky,
And scarce a forest straggler now
To shade us spreads a greenwood bough;
These fields have seen a hotter day
Than e'er was fired by sunny ray.

† The chapel, or "votive fane," built by the Marquis of Castanaza, in the hope that his sovereign, Carlos II. of Spain, might be blest with an heir.

343

Yet one mile on — yon shatter'd hedge
Crests the soft hill whose long smooth
    ridge
Looks on the field below,
And sinks so gently on the dale,
That not the folds of Beauty's veil
In easier curves can flow.
Brief space from thence, the ground again
Ascending slowly from the plane,
    Forms an opposing screen,
Which, with its crest of upland ground,
Shuts the horizon all around.
    The soften'd veil between
Slopes smooth and fair for courser's tread;
Not the most timid maid need dread
To give her snow-white palfrey head
    On that wide stubble ground;
Nor wood, nor tree, nor bush, are there,
Her course to intercept or scare,
    Nor fosse nor fence are found,
Save where, from out her shatter'd bow-
    ers,
Rise Hougomont's dismantled towers.

IV.

Now, see'st thou aught in this lone
    scene
Can tell of that which late hath been? —
    A stranger might reply: —
" The bare extent of stubble-plain
Seems lately lighten'd of its grain ;
And yonder sable tracks remain
Marks of the peasant's ponderous wain,
    When harvest-home was nigh.
On these broad spots of trampled ground,
Perchance the rustics danced such round
    As Teniers loved to draw ;
And where the earth seems scorch'd by
    flame,
To dress the homely feast they came,
And toil'd the kerchief'd village dame
    Around her fire of straw."

V.

So deem'st thou — so each mortal deems,
Of that which is from that which seems. —
    But other harvest here,
Than that which peasant's scythe de-
    mands,
Was gather'd in by sterner hands,
    With bayonet, blade, and spear.
No vulgar crop was theirs to reap;
No stinted harvest thin and cheap!

Heroes before each fatal sweep
    Fell thick as ripen'd grain;
And ere the darkening of the day,
Piled high as autumn shocks, there la'
The ghastly harvest of the fray,
    The corpses of the slain.

VI.

Ay, look again — that line, so black
And trampled, marks the bivouac,
Yon deep-graved ruts the artillery's tra
    So often lost and won;
And close beside, the harden'd mud
Still shows where, fetlock deep in blo
The fierce dragoon, through battle's flo
    Dash'd the hot war-horse on.
These spots of excavation tell
The ravage of the bursting shell —
And feel'st thou not the tainted steam
That reeks against the sultry beam,
    From yonder trenched mound?
The pestilential fumes declare
That Carnage has replenish'd there
    Her garner-house profound.

VII.

Far other harvest-home and feast,
Than claims the boor from scythe releas
    On these scorch'd fields were know
Death hover'd o'er the maddening rou
And, in the thrilling battle-shout,
Sent for the bloody banquet out
    A summons of his own.
Through rolling smoke the Demon's
Could well each destined guest espy,
Well could his ear in ecstasy
    Distinguish every tone
That fill'd the chorus of the fray —
From cannon-roar and trumpet-bray,
From charging squadrons' wild hurra,
From the wild clang that mark'd their wa
    Down to the dying groan,
And the last sob of life's decay,
    When breath was all but flown.

VIII.

Feast on, stern foe of mortal life,
Feast on ! but think not that a strife,
With such promiscuous carnage rife,
    Protracted space may last;
The deadly tug of war at length
Must limits find in human strength,
    And cease when these are past.

n hope !—That morn's o'erclouded sun
ird the wild shout of fight begun
Cre he attain'd his height,
l through the war-smoke, volumed
    high,
l peals that unremitted cry,
'hough now he stoops to night.

ten long hours of doubt and dread,
sh succors from the extended head
either hill the contest fed;
till down the slope they drew,
e charge of columns paused not,
· ceased the storm of shell and shot;
'or all that war could do
skill and force was proved that day,
l turn'd not yet the doubtful fray
On bloody Waterloo.

IX.

e Brussels ! then what thoughts were
    thine,[2]
en ceaseless from the distant line
Continued thunders came !
ch burgher held his breath, to hear,
·se forerunners of havoc near,
Of rapine and of flame.
at ghastly sights were thine to meet,
en rolling through thy stately street,
e wounded show'd their mangled plight
·oken of the unfinish'd fight,
l from each anguish-laden wain
e blood-drops laid thy dust like rain !
w often in the distant drum
ard'st thou the fell Invader come,
ile Ruin, shouting to his band,
·ok high her torch and gory brand !—
·er thee, fair City ! From yon stand,
·atient, still his outstretch'd hand
·oints to his prey in vain,
ile maddening in his eager mood,
l all unwont to be withstood,
Ie fires the fight again.

X.

·n ! On ! " was still his stern exclaim;[3]
·onfront the battery's jaws of flame !
Rush on the levell'd gun !
steel-clad cuirassiers, advance !
ch Uhlan forward with his lance,
Guard, my Chosen, charge forFrance,
'rance and Napoleon ! "
·d answer'd their acclaiming shout,
·eting the mandate which sent out

Their bravest and their best to dare
The fate their leader shunn'd to share.[4]
But HE, his country's sword and shield,
Still in the battle-front reveal'd,
Where danger fiercest swept the field,
    Came like a beam of light,
In action prompt, in sentence brief —
"Soldiers, stand firm," exclaim'd the
    Chief,
    " England shall tell the fight ! " [5]

XI.

On came the whirlwind — like the last
But fiercest sweep of tempest-blast —
On came the whirlwind — steel-gleams
    broke
Like lightning through the rolling smoke;
    The war was waked anew,
Three hundred cannon-mouths roar'd
    loud,
And from their throats, with flash and
    cloud,
    Their showers of iron threw.
Beneath their fire, in full career,
Rush'd on the ponderous cuirassier,
The lancer couch'd his ruthless spear,
And hurrying as to havoc near,
    The cohorts' eagles flew.
In one dark torrent, broad and strong,
The advancing onset roll'd along,
Forth harbinger'd by fierce acclaim,
That, from the shroud of smoke and
    flame,
Peal'd widely the imperial name.

XII.

But on the British heart were lost
The terrors of the charging host;
For not an eye the storm that view'd
Changed its proud glance of fortitude,
Nor was one forward footstep staid,
As dropp'd the dying and the dead.
Fast as their ranks the thunders tear,
Fast they renew'd each serried square;
And on the wounded and the slain
Closed their diminish'd files again,
Till from their line scarce spear's lengths
    three,
Emerging from the smoke they see
Helmet, and plume, and panoply, —
    Then waked their fire at once !
Each musketeer's revolving knell,
As fast, as regularly fell,

As when they practise to display
Their discipline on festal day.
　Then down went helm and lance,
Down were the eagle banners sent,
Down reeling steeds and riders went,
Corslets were pierced, and pennons rent;
　And, to augment the fray,
Wheel'd full against their staggering
　　flanks,
The English horsemen's foaming ranks
　Forced their resistless way.
Then to the musket-knell succeeds
The clash of swords—the neigh of steeds—
As plies the smith his clanging trade,[6]
Against the cuirass rang the blade;
And while amid their close array
The well-served cannon rent their way,
And while amid their scatter'd band
Raged the fierce rider's bloody brand,
Recoil'd in common rout and fear,
Lancer and guard and cuirassier,
Horsemen and foot—a mingled host,
Their leaders fall'n, their standards lost.

XIII.

Then, WELLINGTON! thy piercing eye
This crisis caught of destiny—
　The British host had stood
That morn 'gainst charge of sword and
　　lance *
As their own ocean-rocks hold stance,
But when thy voice had said, "Advance!"
　They were their ocean's flood.—
O Thou, whose inauspicious aim
Hath wrought thy host this hour of shame,
Think'st thou thy broken bands will bide
The terrors of yon rushing tide?
Or will thy chosen brook to feel
The British shock of levell'd steel,[7]
　Or dost thou turn thine eye
Where coming squadrons gleam afar,
And fresher thunders wake the war,
　And other standards fly?—
Think not that in yon columns, file
Thy conquering troops from distant
　　Dyle—
　Is Blucher yet unknown?

* "The British square stood unmoved, and never gave fire until the cavalry were within ten yards, when men rolled one way, horses galloped another, and the cuirassiers were in every instance driven back."—*Life of Bonaparte*, vol. ix. p. 12.

Or dwells not in thy memory still,
(Heard frequent in thine hour of ill,)
What notes of hate and vengeance th
　In Prussia's trumpet tone?—
What yet remains?—shall it be thin
To head the relics of thy line
　In one dread effort more?—
The Roman lore thy leisure loved,
And thou canst tell what fortune pro
　That Chieftain, who, of yore,
Ambition's dizzy paths essay'd,
And with the gladiators' aid
　For empire enterprised—
He stood the cast his rashness play'd,
Left not the victims he had made,
Dug his red grave with his own blade
And on the field he lost was laid,
　Abhorr'd—but not despised.

XIV.

But if revolves thy fainter thought
On safety—howsoever bought,—
Then turn thy fearful rein and ride,
Though twice ten thousand men h
　　died
　On this eventful day,
To gild the military fame
Which thou, for life, in traffic tame
　Wilt barter thus away.
Shall future ages tell this tale
Of inconsistence faint and frail?
And art thou He of Lodi's bridge,
Marengo's field, and Wagram's ridge
　Or is thy soul like mountain-tide,
That, swell'd by winter storm and show
Rolls down in turbulence of power,
　A torrent fierce and wide;
Reft of these aids, a rill obscure,
Shrinking unnoticed, mean and poor,
　Whose channel shows display'd
The wrecks of its impetuous course,
But not one symptom of the force
　By which these wrecks were made

XV.

Spur on thy way!—since now thine
Has brook'd thy veterans' wish to he
　Who, as thy flight they eyed,
Exclaim'd,—while tears of angu
　　came,
Wrung forth by pride, and rage, and
　　shame:—
　"O, that he had but died!"

t yet, to sum this hour of ill,
ook, ere thou leavest the fatal hill,
 Back on yon broken ranks —
oon whose wild confusion gleams
e moon, as on the troubled streams
 When rivers break their banks,
d, to the ruin'd peasant's eye,
jects half seen roll swiftly by,
 Down the dread current hurl'd —
 mingle banner, wain, and gun,
here the tumultuous fight rolls on
 warriors, who, when morn begun,
Defied a banded world.

XVI.

st — frequent to the hurrying rout,
e stern pursuers' vengeful shout
lls, that upon their broken rear
ges the Prussian's bloody spear.
So fell a shriek was none,
nen Beresina's icy flood
dden'd and thaw'd with flame and
 blood,
d, pressing on thy desperate way,
ised oft and long their wild hurra,
The children of the Don.
ine ear no yell of horror cleft
 ominous, when all bereft
 aid, the valiant Polack left * —
, left by thee — found soldier's grave
 Leipsic's corpse-encumber'd wave.
te, in those various perils past,
served thee still some future cast;
 the dread die thou now hast thrown,
ngs not a single field alone,
r one campaign — thy martial fame,
y empire, dynasty, and name,
Have felt the final stroke;
d now, o'er thy devoted head
e last stern vial's wrath is shed,
The last dread seal is broke.

XVII.

ce live thou wilt — refuse not now
fore these demagogues to bow,
e objects of thy scorn and hate,
no shall thy once imperial fate
ke wordly theme of vain debate. —
 shall we say, thou stoop'st less low
 seeking refuge from the foe,

Against whose heart, in prosperous life,
Thine hand hath ever held the knife?
 Such homage hath been paid
By Roman and by Grecian voice,
And there were honor in the choice,
 If it were freely made.
Then safely come, — in one so low —
So lost, — we cannot own a foe;
Though dear experience bid us end,
In thee we ne'er can hail a friend. —
Come, howsoe'er — but do not hide
Close in thy heart that germ of pride,
 Erewhile, by gifted bard espied,
 That " yet imperial hope; " †
Think not that for a fresh rebound,
To raise ambition from the ground,
 We yield thee means or scope.
In safety come — but ne'er again
Hold type of independent reign;
 No islet calls thee lord,
We leave thee no confederate band,
No symbol of thy lost command,
To be a dagger in the hand
 From which we wrench'd the sword.

XVIII.

Yet, even in yon sequester'd spot,
May worthier conquest be thy lot
 Than yet thy life has known;
Conquest, unbought by blood or harm,
That needs nor foreign aid nor arm,
 A triumph all thine own.
Such waits thee when thou shalt control
Those passions wild, that stubborn soul,
 That marr'd thy prosperous scene:
Hear this — from no unmoved heart,
Which sighs, comparing what THOU ART
 With what thou MIGHT'ST HAVE BEEN !

XIX.

Thou, too, whose deeds of fame renew'd
Bankrupt a nation's gratitude,
To thine own noble heart must owe
More than the meed she can bestow.
For not a people's just acclaim,
Not the full hail of Europe's fame,
Thy Prince's smiles, thy State's decree,
The ducal rank, the garter'd knee,
Not these such pure delight afford
As that, when hanging up thy sword,

* For an account of the death of Poniatowski
eipsic, see Sir Walter Scott's *Life of Bona-*
te, vol. vii. p. 401.

† See Byron's " Ode to Napoleon."

Well may'st thou think : — " This honest
    steel
Was ever drawn for public weal;
And, such was rightful Heaven's decree,
Ne'er sheathed unless with victory ! "

XX.

Look forth, once more, with soften'd
    heart,
Ere from the field of fame we part;
Triumph and Sorrow border near,
And joy oft melts into a tear.
Alas ! what links of love that morn
Has War's rude hand asunder torn !
For ne'er was field so sternly fought,
And ne'er was conquest dearer bought.
Here piled in common slaughter sleep
Those whom affection long shall weep :
Here rests the sire, that ne'er shall strain
His orphans to his heart again;
The son, whom, on his native shore,
The parent's voice shall bless no more;
The bridegroom, who has hardly press'd
His blushing consort to his breast :
The husband, whom through many a year
Long love and mutual faith endear.
Thou canst not name one tender tie,
But here dissolved its relics lie !
O ! when thou see'st some mourner's veil
Shroud her thin form and visage pale,
Or mark'st the Matron's bursting tears
Stream when the stricken drum she hears;
Or see'st how manlier grief, suppress'd,
Is laboring in a father's breast, —
With no inquiry vain pursue
The cause, but think on Waterloo !

XXI.

Period of honor as of woes,
What bright careers 'twas thine to close ! [8]
Mark'd on thy roll of blood what names
To Briton's memory, and to Fame's,
Laid there their last immortal claims !
Thou saw'st in seas of gore expire
Redoubted PICTON'S soul of fire —
Saw'st in the mingled carnage lie
All that of PONSONBY could die —
DE LANCEY change Love's bridal wreath,
For laurels from the hand of Death [9] —
Saw'st gallant MILLER'S failing eye [10]
Still bent where Albion's banners fly,
And CAMERON, [11] in the shock of steel,
Die like the offspring of Lochiel;

And generous GORDON, [12] mid the strife
Fall, while he watch'd his leader's life. —
Ah ! though her guardian angel's shield
Fenced Britain's hero through the field,
Fate not the less her power made known
Through his friends' hearts to pierce his
    own ! *

XXII.

Forgive, brave Dead, the imperfect lay
Who may your names, your numbers say
What high-strung harp, what lofty line
To each the dear-earn'd praise assign,
From high-born chiefs of martial fame
To the poor soldier's lowlier name?
Lightly ye rose that dawning day,
From your cold couch of swamp and clay,
To fill, before the sun was low,
The bed that morning cannot know. —
Oft may the tear the green sod steep,
And sacred be the heroes' sleep,
    Till time shall cease to run;
And ne'er beside their noble grave,
May Briton pass and fail to crave
A blessing on the fallen brave
    Who fought with Wellington !

XXIII.

Farewell, sad Field ! whose blighted
    face
Wears desolation's withering trace;
Long shall my memory retain
Thy shatter'd huts and trampled grain,
With every mark of martial wrong,
That scathe thy towers, fair Hougomont !
Yet though thy garden's green arcade
The marksman's fatal post was made,
Though on thy shatter'd beeches fell
The blended rage of shot and shell,
Though from thy blacken'd portals torn
Their fall thy blighted fruit-trees mourn,
Has not such havoc bought a name
Immortal in the rolls of fame?
Yes — Agincourt may be forgot,
And Cressy be an unknown spot,
    And Blenheim's name be new;
But still in story and in song,
For many an age remembered long,
Shall live the towers of Hougomont,
    And Field of Waterloo.

* The grief of the victor for the fate of his
friends is touchingly described by those who witnessed it.

CONCLUSION.

Stern tide of human Time! that
　know'st not rest,
But sweeping from the cradle to the tomb,
Bear'st ever downward on thy dusky
　breast,
Successive generations to their doom;
While thy capacious stream has equal
　room
For the gay bark where Pleasure's
　streamers sport,
And for the prison-ship of guilt and
　gloom,
The fisher-skiff, and barge that bears a
　court,
All wafting onward all to one dark silent
　port; —

Stern tide of Time! through what
　mysterious change
Of hope and fear have our frail barks
　been driven!
For ne'er, before, vicissitude so
　strange
Was to one race of Adam's offspring
　given.
And sure such varied change of sea
　and heaven,
Such unexpected bursts of joy and woe,
Such fearful strife as that where we
　have striven,
Succeeding ages ne'er again shall know,
Until the awful term when Thou shalt
　cease to flow!

Well hast thou stood, my Country! —
　the brave fight
Hast well maintain'd through good
　report and ill;
In thy just cause and in thy native
　might,
And in Heaven's grace and justice
　constant still;
Whether the banded prowess, strength,
　and skill
Of half the world against thee stood
　array'd,
Or when, with better views and freer
　will,
Beside thee Europe's noblest drew the
　blade,
Each emulous in arms the Ocean Queen
　to aid.

Well art thou now repaid — though
　slowly rose,
And struggled long with mists thy blaze
　of fame,
While like the dawn that in the orient
　glows
On the broad wave its earlier lustre
　came;
Then eastern Egypt saw the growing
　flame,
And Maida's myrtles gleam'd beneath
　its ray,
Where first the soldier, stung with
　generous shame,
Rivall'd the heroes of the wat'ry
　way,
And wash'd in foeman's gore unjust
　reproach away.

Now, Island Empress, wave thy crest
　on high,
And bid the banner of thy Patron
　flow,
Gallant St. George, the flower of
　Chivalry,
For thou hast faced, like him, a dragon
　foe,
And rescued innocence from over-
　throw,
And trampled down, like him, tyrannic
　might,
And to the gazing world mayst proudly
　show
The chosen emblem of thy sainted
　Knight,
Who quell'd devouring pride, and vindi-
　cated right.

Yet mid the confidence of just renown,
Renown dear-bought, but dearer thus
　acquired,
Write, Britain, write the moral lesson
　down:
'Tis not alone the heart with valor
　fired,
The discipline so dreaded and admired,
In many a field of bloody conquest
　known;
— Such may by fame be lured, by gold
　be hired —
'Tis constancy in thy good cause alone,
Best justifies the meed thy valiant sons
　have won.

HAROLD THE DAUNTLESS.

A POEM IN SIX CANTOS.

INTRODUCTION.

THERE is a mood of mind, we all have known
On drowsy eve, or dark and lowering day,
When the tired spirits lose their sprightly tone,
And naught can chase the lingering hours away.
Dull on our soul falls Fancy's dazzling ray,
And Wisdom holds his steadier torch in vain,
Obscured the painting seems, mistuned the lay,
Nor dare we of our listless load complain,
For who for sympathy may seek that cannot tell of pain?

The jolly sportsman knows such dreari-hood,
When bursts in deluge the autumnal rain,
Clouding that morn which threats the heath-cock's brood;
Of such, in summer's drought, the anglers plain,
Who hope the soft mild southern shower in vain:
But, more than all, the discontented fair,
Whom father stern, and sterner aunt, restrain
From country-ball, or race occurring rare,
While all her friends around their vestments gay prepare.

Ennui! — or, as our mothers call thee, Spleen!
To thee we owe full many a ra[ ] device;
Thine is the sheaf of painted cards ween,
The rolling billiard-ball, the rattli[ ] dice;
The turning-lathe for framing gimcra[ ] nice;
The amateur's blotch'd pallet th[ ] mayst claim,
Retort, and air-pump, threatening fro[ ] and mice,
(Murders disguised by philosoph[ ] name,)
And much of trifling grave, and much buxom game.

Then of the books, to catch thy drow[ ] glance
Compiled, what bard the catalog[ ] may quote!
Plays, poems, novels, never read b[ ] once; —
But not of such the tale fair Edgewor[ ] wrote,
That bears thy name, and is thine a[ ] tidote;
And not of such the strain my Tho[ ] son sung,
Delicious dreams inspiring by his not[ ]
What time to Indolence his harp [ ] strung; —
Oh! might my lay be ranked that happi[ ] list among!

350

Each hath his refuge whom thy cares
 assail.
For me, I love my study-fire to trim,
And con right vacantly some idle tale,
Displaying on the couch each listless
 limb,
Till on the drowsy page the lights
 grow dim,
And doubtful slumber half supplies the
 theme;
While antique shapes of knight and
 giant grim,
Damsel and dwarf, in long procession
 gleam,
d the Romancer's tale becomes the
 Reader's dream.

'Tis thus my malady I well may
 bear,
Albeit outstretched, like Pope's own
 Paridel,*
Upon the rack of a too-easy chair;
And find, to cheat the time, a power-
 ful spell
In old romaunts of errantry that
 tell,
Or later legends of the fairy-folk,
Or Oriental tale of Afrite fell,
Of Genii, Talisman, and broad-wing'd
 Roc,
ough taste may blush and frown, and
 sober reason mock.

Oft at such season, too, will rhymes
 unsought
Arrange themselves in some romantic
 lay; —
The which, as things unfitting graver
 thought,
Are burnt or blotted on some wiser
 day. —
These few survive — and proudly let
 me say,
Court not the critic's smile, nor dread
 his frown;
They well may serve to while an hour
 away,
Nor does the volume ask for more
 renown,
han Ennui's yawning smile, what time
 she drops it down.

* "The Dunciad," Book IV. l. 341.

CANTO FIRST.

I.

LIST to the valorous deeds that were done
By Harold the Dauntless, Count Witi-
 kind's son !
Count Witikind came of a regal strain,
And roved with his Norsemen the land
 and the main.
Woe to the realms which he coasted !
 for there
Was shedding of blood and rending of hair,
Rape of maiden, and slaughter of priest,
Gathering of ravens and wolves to the
 feast :
When he hoisted his standard black,
Before him was battle, behind him wrack,
And he burn'd the churches, that heathen
 Dane,
To light his band to their barks again.

II.

On Erin's shores was his outrage known,
The winds of France had his banners
 blown;
Little was there to plunder, yet still
His pirates had foray'd on Scottish hill :
But upon merry England's coast
More frequent he sail'd, for he won the
 most.
So wide and so far his ravage they knew,
If a sail but gleam'd white 'gainst the
 welkin blue,
Trumpet and bugle to arms did call,
Burghers hasten'd to man the wall,
Peasants fled inland his fury to 'scape,
Beacons were lighted on headland and
 cape,
Bells were toll'd out, and aye as they rung,
Fearful and faintly the gray brothers
 sung : —
" Bless us, St. Mary, from flood and from
 fire,
From famine and pest, and Count Witi-
 kind's ire ! "

III.

He liked the wealth of fair England so
 well,
That he sought in her bosom as native to
 dwell.
He enter'd the Humber in fearful hour,
And disembark'd with his Danish power.

Three Earls came against him with all
    their train, —
Two hath he taken, and one hath he
    slain.
Count Witikind left the Humber's rich
    strand,
And he wasted and warr'd in Northum-
    berland.
But the Saxon King was a sire in age,
Weak in battle, in council sage;
Peace of that heathen leader he sought,
Gifts he gave, and quiet he bought;
And the Count took upon him the peace-
    able style
Of a vassal and liegeman of Britain's
    broad isle.

IV.

Time will rust the sharpest sword,
Time will consume the strongest cord;
That which moulders hemp and steel,
Mortal arm and nerve must feel.
Of the Danish band, whom Count Witi-
    kind led,
Many wax'd aged, and many were dead;
Himself found his armor full weighty to
    bear,
Wrinkled his brows grew, and hoary his
    hair.
He lean'd on a staff, when his step went
    abroad,
And patient his palfrey, when steed he
    bestrode.
As he grew feebler, his wildness ceased,
He made himself peace with prelate and
    priest;
Made his peace, and, stooping his head,
Patiently listed the counsel they said.
Saint Cuthbert's Bishop was holy and
    grave,
Wise and good was the counsel he gave:—

V.

"Thou hast murder'd, robb'd, and spoil'd,
Time it is thy poor soul were assoil'd;
Priests didst thou slay, and churches burn,
Time it is now to repentance to turn;
Fiends hast thou worshipp'd, with fiend-
    ish rite,
Leave now the darkness, and wend into
    light:
O! while life and space are given,
Turn thee yet, and think of Heaven!"

That stern old heathen his head he rais
And on the good prelate he steadfas
    gazed: —
"Give me broad lands on the Wear a
    the Tyne,
My faith I will leave, and I'll clea
    unto thine."

VI.

Broad lands he gave him on Tyne a
    Wear,
To be held of the Church by bridle a
    spear;
Part of Monkwearmouth, of Tyned
    part,
To better his will, and to soften his hea
Count Witikind was a joyful man,
Less for the faith than the lands that
    wan.
The high church of Durham is dres
    for the day,
The clergy are rank'd in their sole
    array;
There came the Count, in a bear-s
    warm,
Leaning on Hilda his concubine's arn
He kneel'd before Saint Cuthbert's shri
With patience unwonted at rites divin
He abjured the gods of heathen race,
And he bent his head at the font of gra
But such was the grisly old proselyt
    look,
That the priest who baptized him gr
    pale and shook;
And the old monks mutter'd bene
    their hood: —
"Of a stem so stubborn can never spri
    good!"

VII.

Up then arose that grim convertite,
Homeward he hied him when ended
    rite;
The Prelate in honor will with him ri
And feast in his castle on Tyne's fair si
Banners and banderols danced in
    wind,
Monks rode before them, and spearm
    behind;
Onward they pass'd till fairly did shin
Pennon and cross on the bosom of Tyn
And full in front did that fortress low
In darksome strength with its buttr
    and tower;

the castle gate was young Harold there,
ount Witikind's only offspring and heir.

VIII.

oung Harold was fear'd for his hardihood,
s strength of frame, and his fury of
mood.
ude he was and wild to behold,
ore neither collar nor bracelet of gold,
ap of vair nor rich array,
uch as should grace that festal day:
is doublet of bull's hide was all unbraced,
ncover'd his head, and his sandal unlaced:
is shaggy black lock on his brow hung
low,
nd his eyes glanced through them a
swarthy glow;
Danish club in his hand he bore,
he spikes were clotted with recent gore;
t his back a she-wolf, and her wolf-
cubs twain,
the dangerous chase that morning
slain.
ude was the greeting his father he made,
one to the Bishop, — while thus he
said: —

IX.

What priest-led hypocrite art thou,
ith thy humble look and thy monkish
brow.
ike a shaveling who studies to cheat his
vow?
anst thou be Witikind the Waster
known,
oyal Eric's fearless son,
aughty Gunhilda's haughtier lord,
Who won his bride by the axe and sword;
rom the shrine of St. Peter the chalice
who tore,
nd melted to bracelets for Freya and
Thor;
Vith one blow of his gauntlet who burst
the skull,
efore Odin's stone, of the Mountain
Bull?
hen ye worshipp'd with rites that to
war-gods belong,
Vith the deed of the brave, and the blow
of the strong;

And now, in thine age to dotage sunk,
Wilt thou patter thy crimes to a shaven
monk, —
Lay down thy mail-shirt for clothing of
hair, —
Fasting and scourge, like a slave, wilt
thou bear?
Or, at best, be admitted in slothful
bower
To batten with priest and with paramour?
Oh! out upon thine endless shame!
Each Scald's high harp shall blast thy
fame,
And thy son will refuse thee a father's
name!''

X.

Ireful wax'd old Witikind's look,
His faltering voice with fury shook: —
'' Hear me, Harold of harden'd heart!
Stubborn and wilful ever thou wert.
Thine outrage insane I command thee
cease,
Fear my wrath and remain at peace: —
Just is the debt of repentance I've paid,
Richly the Church has a recompense
made,
And the truth of her doctrines I prove
with my blade,
But reckoning to none of my actions I
owe,
And least to my son such accounting will
show.
Why speak I to thee of repentance or
truth,
Who ne'er from thy childhood knew
reason or ruth?
Hence! to the wolf and the bear in her
den;
These are thy mates, and not rational
men.''

XI.

Grimly smiled Harold, and coldly replied:
'' We must honor our sires, if we fear
when they chide.
For me, I am yet what thy lessons have
made,
I was rock'd in a buckler and fed from a
blade;
An infant, was taught to clasp hands and
to shout
From the roof of the tower when the
flame had broke out;

In the blood of slain foemen my finger
   to dip,
And tinge with its purple my cheek and
   my lip, —
'Tis thou know'st not truth, that has
   barter'd in eld,
For a price, the brave faith that thine
   ancestors held.
When this wolf,'' — and the carcass he
   flung on the plain, —
" Shall wake and give food to her nurse-
   lings again,
The face of his father will Harold review;
Till then, aged Heathen, young Christian,
   adieu ! ''

XII.

Priest, monk, and prelate, stood aghast,
As through the pageant the heathen
   pass'd.
A cross-bearer out of his saddle he flung,
Laid his hand on the pommel, and into
   it sprung.
Loud was the shriek and deep the groan,
When the holy sign on the earth was
   thrown !
The fierce old Count unsheathed his
   brand,
But the calmer prelate stay'd his hand: —
" Let him pass free ! — Heaven knows
   its hour, —
But he must own repentance's power,
Pray and weep, and penance bear,
Ere he hold land by the Tyne and the
   Wear.''
Thus in scorn and in wrath from his
   father is gone
Young Harold the Dauntless, Count
   Witikind's son.

XIII.

High was the feasting in Witikind's
   hall,
Revell'd priests, soldiers, and pagans,
   and all;
And e'en the good Bishop was fain to
   endure
The scandal, which time and instruction
   might cure:
It were dangerous, he deem'd, at the
   first to restrain,
In his wine and his wassail, a half-chris-
   ten'd Dane.

The mead flow'd around, and the ale w
   drain'd dry,
Wild was the laughter, the song, and t
   cry;
With Kyrie Eleison, came clamorou
   in
The war-songs of Danesmen, Norwey
   and Finn.
Till man after man the contention g
   o'er,
Outstretch'd on the rushes that strew
   the hall floor;
And the tempest within, having ceas
   its wild rout,
Gave place to the tempest that thunde
   without.

XIV.

Apart from the wassail, in turret alone
Lay flaxen-hair'd Gunnar, old Erme
   garde's son;
In the train of Lord Harold that Pa
   was the first,
For Harold in childhood had Erme
   garde nursed;
And grieved was young Gunnar his m
   ter should roam,
Unhoused and unfriended, an exile fr
   home.
He heard the deep thunder, the plashi
   of rain,
He saw the red lightning through sh
   hole and pane;
" And oh ! '' said the Page, " on t
   shelterless wold
Lord Harold is wandering in darkn
   and cold !
What though he was stubborn, and w
   ward, and wild,
He endured me because I was Erme
   garde's child, —
And often from dawn till the set of t
   sun,
In the chase, by his stirrup, unbidden
   run;
I would I were older, and knighthoo
   could bear,
I would soon quit the banks of the Ty
   and the Wear;
For my mother's command, with her l
   parting breath,.
Bade me follow her nursling in life a
   to death.

XV.

It pours and it thunders, it lightens amain,
s if Lok, the Destroyer, had burst from his chain!
ccursed by the Church and expell'd by his sire,
or Christian nor Dane give him shelter or fire,
nd this tempest what mortal may house-less endure?
naided, unmantled, he dies on the moor!
hate'er comes of Gunnar, he tarries not here.''
e leapt from his couch and he grasp'd to his spear;
ught the hall of the feast.   Undisturb'd by his tread,
ie wassailers slept fast as the sleep of the dead:
Ungrateful and bestial!'' his anger broke forth,
To forget mid your goblets the pride of the North!
id you, ye cowl'd priests, who have plenty in store,
ust give Gunnar for ransom a palfrey and ore.''

XVI.

ien, heeding full little of ban or of curse,
e has seized on the Prior of Jorvaulx's purse:
int Meneholt's Abbot next morning has miss'd
is mantle, deep furr'd from the cape to the wrist.
ie Seneschal's keys from his belt he has ta'en
/ell drench'd on that eve was old Hildebrand's brain).
» the stable-yard he made his way,
id mounted the Bishop's palfrey gay,
.stle and hamlet behind him has cast,
id right on his way to the moorland has pass'd.
re snorted the palfrey, unused to face
weather so wild at so rash a pace;
long he snorted, so loud he neigh'd,
iere answer'd a steed that was bound beside,

And the red flash of lightning show'd where there lay
His master, Lord Harold, outstretch'd on the clay.

XVII.

Up he started, and thunder'd out:—
"Stand!"
And raised the club in his deadly hand.
The flaxen-hair'd Gunnar his purpose told,
Show'd the palfrey and profferr'd the gold.
"Back, back, and home, thou simple boy!
Thou canst not share my grief or joy:
Have I not mark'd thee wail and cry
When thou hast seen a sparrow die?
And canst thou, as my follower should,
Wade ankle-deep through foeman's blood,
Dare mortal and immortal foe,
The gods above, the fiends below,
And man on earth, more hateful still,
The very fountain-head of ill?
Desperate of life, and careless of death,
Lover of bloodshed, and slaughter, and scathe,
Such must thou be with me to roam,
And such thou canst not be — back, and home!''

XVIII.

Young Gunnar shook like an aspen bough,
As he heard the harsh voice and beheld the dark brow,
And half he repented his purpose and vow.
But now to draw back were bootless shame,
And he loved his master, so urged his claim:—
"Alas! if my arm and my courage be weak,
Bear with me awhile for old Ermengarde's sake;
Nor deem so lightly of Gunnar's faith,
As to fear he would break it for peril of death.
Have I not risk'd it to fetch thee this gold,
This surcoat and mantle to fence thee from cold?
And, did I bear a baser mind,
What lot remains if I stay behind?
The priests' revenge, thy father's wrath,
A dungeon, and a shameful death.''

XIX.

With gentler look Lord Harold eyed
The Page, then turn'd his head aside;
And either a tear did his eyelash stain,
Or it caught a drop of the passing rain.
" Art thou an outcast, then?" quoth he;
" The meeter page to follow me."
'Twere bootless to tell what climes they
    sought,
Ventures achieved, and battles fought;
How oft with few, how oft alone,
Fierce Harold's arm the field hath won.
Men swore his eye, that flash'd so red
When each other glance was quenched
    with dread,
Bore oft a light of deadly flame,
That ne'er from mortal courage came.
Those limbs so strong, that mood so stern,
That loved the couch of heath and fern,
Afar from hamlet, tower, and town,
More than to rest on driven down;
That stubborn frame, that sullen mood,
Men deem'd must come of aught but
    good;
And they whisper'd, the great Master
    Fiend was at one
With Harold the Dauntless, Count Witi-
    kind's son.

XX.

Years after years had gone and fled,
The good old Prelate lies lapp'd in lead;
In the chapel still is shown
His sculptured form on a marble stone,
With staff and ring and scapulaire,
And folded hands in the act of prayer.
Saint Cuthbert's mitre is resting now
On the haughty Saxon, bold Aldingar's
    brow;
The power of his crozier he loved to ex-
    tend
O'er whatever would break, or whatever
    would bend;
And now hath he clothed him in cope and
    in pall,
And the Chapter of Durham has met at
    his call.
" And hear ye not, brethren," the proud
    Bishop said,
" That our vassal, the Danish Count
    Witikind's dead?
All his gold and his goods hath he given
To holy Church for the love of Heaven,

And had founded a chantry with stipen
    and dole,
That priests and that beadsmen may pra
    for his soul:
Harold his son is wandering abroad,
Dreaded by man and abhorr'd by God;
Meet it is not, that such should heir
The lands of the Church on the Tyne an
    the Wear,
And at her pleasure her hallow'd hands
May now resume these wealthy lands.

XXI.

Answer'd good Eustace, a canon old:—
" Harold is tameless, and furious, an
    bold;
Ever Renown blows a note of fame,
And a note of fear, when she sounds h
    name;
Much of bloodshed and much of scathe
Have been their lot who have waked h
    wrath.
Leave him these lands and lordshi
    still;
Heaven in its hour may change his wil
But if reft of gold, and of living bare,
An evil counsellor is despair."
More had he said, but the Prelate frown'
And murmur'd his brethren who sa
    around,
And with one consent have they give
    their doom,
That the Church should the lands of Sai
    Cuthbert resume.
So will'd the Prelate: and canon and dea
Gave to his judgment their loud amen.

CANTO SECOND.

I.

'Tis merry in greenwood — thus runs th
    old lay,—
In the gladsome month of lively May,
When the wild birds' song on stem an
    spray
    Invites to forest bower;
Then rears the ash his airy crest,
Then shines the birch in silver vest,
And the beech in glistening leaves is dres
And dark between shows the oak's prou
    breast,
    Like a chieftain's frowning tower;

ough a thousand branches join their
 screen,
et the broken sunbeams glance between,
d tip the leaves with lighter green,
 With brighter tints the flower;
ill is the heart that loves not then
e deep recess of the wildwood glen,
here roe and red-deer find sheltering
 den,
 When the sun is in his power.

II.

ess merry, perchance, is the fading leaf
at follows so soon on the gather'd
 sheaf,
 When the greenwood loses the name;
ent is then the forest bound,
ve the redbreast's note, and the rustling
 sound
frost-nipt leaves that are dropping
 round,
the deep-mouth'd cry of the distant
 hound
 That opens on his game:
et then, too, I love the forest wide,
hether the sun in splendor ride,
d gild its many-color'd side;
whether the soft or silvery haze,
vapory folds o'er the landscape strays,
d half involves the woodland maze,
 Like an early widow's veil,
here wimpling tissue from the gaze
e form half hides, and half betrays,
Of beauty wan and pale.

III.

ir Metelill was a woodland maid,
er father a rover of greenwood shade,
forest statutes undismay'd,
 Who lived by bow and quiver;
ell known was Wulfstane's archery,
merry Tyne both on moor and lea,
rough wooded Weardale's glens so free,
ell beside Stanhope's wildwood tree,
And well on Ganlesse river.
t free though he trespass'd on woodland game,
ore known and more fear'd was the
 wizard fame
Jutta of Rookhope, the Outlaw's dame;
ar'd when she frown'd was her eye of
 flame,
More fear'd when in wrath she laugh'd;

For, then, 'twas said, more fatal true
To its dread aim her spell-glance flew,
Than when from Wulfstane's bended yew
 Sprung forth the gray-goose shaft.

IV.

Yet had this fierce and dreaded pair,
So Heaven decreed, a daughter fair;
 None brighter crown'd the bed,
In Britain's bounds, of peer or prince,
Nor hath, perchance, a lovelier since,
 In this fair isle been bred.
And naught of fraud, or ire, or ill,
Was known to gentle Metelill, —
 A simple maiden she;
The spells in dimpled smile that lie,
And a downcast blush, and the darts that fly
With the sidelong glance of a hazel eye,
 Were her arms and witchery.
So young, so simple was she yet,
She scarce could childhood's joys forget,
 And still she loved, in secret set
 Beneath the greenwood tree,
To plait the rushy coronet,
And braid with flowers her locks of jet,
 As when in infancy; —
Yet could that heart, so simple, prove
The early dawn of stealing love:
 Ah! gentle maid, beware!
The power who, now so mild a guest,
Gives dangerous yet delicious zest
To the calm pleasures of thy breast,
Will soon, a tyrant o'er the rest,
 Let none his empire share.

V.

One morn in kirtle green array'd,
Deep in the wood the maiden stray'd,
 And, where a fountain sprung,
She sate her down, unseen, to thread
The scarlet berry's mimic braid,
 And while the beads she strung,
Like the blithe lark, whose carol gay
Gives a good-morrow to the day,
 So lightsomely she sung: —

VI.
SONG.

"LORD WILLIAM was born in gilded
 bower,
The heir of Wilton's lofty tower;
Yet better loves Lord William now
To roam beneath wild Rookhope's brow;

And William has lived where ladies fair
With gawds and jewels deck their hair,
Yet better loves the dewdrops still
That pearl the locks of Metelill.

" The pious Palmer loves, I wis,
Saint Cuthbert's hallow'd beads to kiss,
But I, though simple girl I be,
Might have such homage paid to me;
For did Lord William see me suit
This necklace of the bramble's fruit,
He fain — but must not have his will —
Would kiss the beads of Metelill.

" My nurse has told me many a tale,
How vows of love are weak and frail;
My mother says that courtly youth
By rustic maid means seldom sooth,
What should they mean? it cannot be,
That such a warning's meant for me,
For naught — oh ! naught of fraud or ill
Can William mean to Metelill ! "

VII.

Sudden she stops — and starts to feel
A weighty hand, a glove of steel,
Upon her shrinking shoulders laid;
Fearful she turn'd, and saw, dismay'd,
A Knight in plate and mail array'd,
His crest and bearing worn and fray'd,
    His surcoat soil'd and riven,
Form'd like that giant race of yore,
Whose long-continued crimes outwore
    The sufferance of Heaven.
Stern accents made his pleasure known,
Though then he used his gentlest tone : —
" Maiden," he said, " sing forth thy
    glee,
Start not — sing on — it pleases me."

VIII.

Secured within his powerful hold,
To bend her knee, her hands to fold,
    Was all the maiden might;
And " Oh ! forgive," she faintly said,
" The terrors of a simple maid,
    If thou art mortal wight?
But if — of such strange tales are told —
Unearthly warrior of the wold,
Thou comest to chide mine accents bold,
My mother, Jutta, knows the spell,
At noon and midnight pleasing well
    The disembodied ear.

Oh ! let her powerful charms atone
For aught my rashness may have done,
    And cease thy grasp of fear."
Then laugh'd the Knight — his laughter
    sound
Half in the hollow helmet drown'd;
His barred visor then he raised,
And steady on the maiden gazed.
He smooth'd his brows, as best he might
To the dread calm of autumn night,
    When sinks the tempest roar;
Yet still the cautious fishers eye
The clouds, and fear the gloomy sky,
    And haul their barks on shore.

IX.

" Damsel," he said, " be wise and learn
Matters of weight and deep concern :
    From distant realms I come,
And, wanderer long, at length have
    plann'd
In this my native Northern land
    To seek myself a home.
Nor that alone — a mate I seek;
She must be gentle, soft, and meek, —
    No lordly dame for me;
Myself am something rough of mood,
And feel the fire of royal blood,
    And therefore do not hold it good
    To match in my degree.
Then, since coy maidens say my face
Is harsh, my form devoid of grace,
For a fair lineage to provide,
'Tis meet that my selected bride
In lineaments be fair;
I love thine well — till now I ne'er
Look'd patient on a face of fear,
But now that tremulous sob and tear
    Become thy beauty rare.
One kiss — nay, damsel, coy it not ! —
And now go seek thy parents' cot,
And say, a bridegroom soon I come,
To woo my love, and bear her home."

X.

Home sprung the maid without a pause
As leveret 'scaped from greyhound's jaws
But still she lock'd, howe'er distress'd,
The secret in her boding breast;
Dreading her sire, who oft forbade
Her steps should stray to distant glade.
Night came — to her accustom'd nook
Her distaff aged Jutta took,

And by the lamp's imperfect glow,
Rough Wulfstane trimm'd his shafts and
    bow.
Sudden and clamorous, from the ground
Upstarted slumbering brach and hound;
Loud knocking next the lodge alarms,
And Wulfstane snatches at his arms,
When open flew the yielding door,
And that grim Warrior press'd the floor : —

XI.

"All peace be here. — What ! none re-
    plies?
Dismiss your fears, and your surprise.
'Tis I — that Maid hath told my tale, —
Or, trembler, did thy courage fail?
It recks not — It is I demand
Fair Metelill in marriage band;
Harold the Dauntless I, whose name
Is brave men's boast and caitiff's shame."
The parents sought each other's eyes,
With awe, resentment, and surprise :
Wulfstane, to quarrel prompt, began
The stranger's size and thews to scan;
But as he scann'd his courage sunk,
And from unequal strife he shrunk,
Then forth, to blight and blemish, flies
The harmful curse from Jutta's eyes;
Yet, fatal howsoe'er, the spell
On Harold innocently fell !
And disappointment and amaze
Were in the witch's wilder'd gaze.

XII.

But soon the wit of woman woke,
And to the Warrior mild she spoke : —
Her child was all too young."—"A toy,
The refuge of a maiden coy." —
Again, "A powerful baron's heir
Claims in her heart an interest fair." —
A trifle — whisper in his ear,
That Harold is a suitor here ! " —
Baffled at length she sought delay :
Would not the knight till morning stay?
Late was the hour — he there might rest
Till morn, their lodge's honor'd guest."
Such were her words — her craft might
    cast,
Her honor'd guest should sleep his last :
No, not to-night — but soon," he swore,
He would return, nor leave them more."
The threshold then his huge stride crost,
And soon he was in darkness lost.

XIII.

Appall'd a while the parents stood,
Then changed their fear to angry mood,
And foremost fell their words of ill
On unresisting Metelill;
Was she not caution'd and forbid,
Forewarn'd, implored, accused, and chid,
And must she still to greenwood roam,
To marshal such misfortune home?
"Hence, minion—to thy chamber hence—
There prudence learn and penitence."
She went — her lonely couch to steep
In tears which absent lovers weep;
Or if she gain'd a troubled sleep,
Fierce Harold's suit was still the theme
And terror of her feverish dream.

XIV.

Scarce was she gone, her dame and sire
Upon each other bent their ire : —
" A woodsman thou, and hast a spear,
And couldst thou such an insult bear?"
Sullen he said : — " A man contends
With men, a witch with sprites and fiends;
Not to mere mortal wight belong
Yon gloomy brow and frame so strong;
But thou — is this thy promise fair,
That your Lord William, wealthy heir
To Ulrick, Baron of Witton-le-Wear,
Should Metelill to altar bear?
Do all the spells thou boast'st as thine
Serve but to slay some peasant's kine,
His grain in autumn's storms to steep,
Or thorough fog and fen to sweep,
And hag-ride some poor rustic's sleep?
Is such mean mischief worth the fame
Of sorceress and witch's name?
Fame, which with all men's wish con-
    spires,
With thy deserts and my desires,
To damn thy corpse to penal fires?
Out on thee, witch ! aroint ! aroint !
What now shall put thy schemes in joint?
What save this trusty arrow's point,
From the dark dingle when it flies,
And he who meets it gasps and dies."

XV.

Stern she replied : — " I will not wage
War with thy folly or thy rage;
But ere the morrow's sun be low,
Wulfstane of Rookhope, thou shalt know,
If I can venge me on a foe.

Believe the while, that whatsoe'er
I spoke, in ire, of bow and spear,
It is not Harold's destiny
The death of pilfer'd deer to die.
But he, and thou, and yon pale moon,
(That shall be yet more pallid soon,
Before she sink behind the dell,)
Thou, she, and Harold too, shall tell
What Jutta knows of charm or spell."
Thus muttering, to the door she bent
Her wayward steps, and forth she went,
And left alone the moody sire,
To cherish or to slake his ire.

XVI.

Far faster than belong'd to age
Has Jutta made her pilgrimage.
A priest has met her as she pass'd,
And cross'd himself and stood aghast.
She traced a hamlet — not a cur
His throat would ope, his foot would stir;
By crouch, by trembling, and by groan,
They made her hated presence known!
But when she trode the sable fell,
Were wilder sounds her way to tell, —
For far was heard the fox's yell,
The black-cock waked and faintly crew,
Scream'd o'er the moss the scared curlew;
Where o'er the cataract the oak
Lay slant, was heard the raven's croak;
The mountain-cat, which sought his prey,
Glared, scream'd, and started from her
            way.
Such music cheer'd her journey lone
To the deep dell and rocking stone;
There, with unhallow'd hymn of praise,
She called a God of heathen days.

XVII.

INVOCATION.

" From thy Pomeranian throne,
Hewn in rock of living stone,
Where, to thy godhead faithful yet,
Bend Esthonian, Finn, and Lett,
And their swords in vengeance whet,
That shall make thine altars wet,
Wet and red for ages more
With the Christians' hated gore, —
Hear me! Sovereign of the Rock,
Hear me! mighty Zernebock! *

* *Zernebock, Cherny Bog,* Slavonic for Black
God.

" Mightiest of the mighty known,
Here thy wonders have been shown;
Hundred tribes in various tongue
Oft have here thy praises sung;
Down that stone with Runic seam'd,
Hundred victims' blood hath stream'd!
Now one woman comes alone,
And but wets it with her own,
The last, the feeblest of thy flock, —
Hear — and be present, Zernebock!

" Hark! he comes! the night-blast cold
Wilder sweeps along the wold;
The cloudless moon grows dark and dim,
And bristling hair and quaking limb
Proclaim the Master Demon nigh, —
Those who view his form shall die!
Lo! I stoop and veil my head;
Thou who ridest the tempest dread,
Shaking hill and rending oak —
Spare me! spare me! Zernebock.

" He comes not yet! shall cold delay
Thy votaress at her need repay?
Thou — shall I call thee god or fiend?—
Let others on thy mood attend
With prayer and ritual — Jutta's arms
Are necromantic words and charms;
Mine is the spell, that, utter'd once,
Shall wake Thy Master from his trance
Shake his red mansion-house of pain,
And burst his seven-times-twisted
            chain! —
So! com'st thou ere the spell is spoke?
I own thy presence, Zernebock." —

XVIII.

" Daughter of dust," the Deep Voice
            said,
— Shook while it spoke the vale for
            dread,
Rock'd on the base that massive stone,
The Evil Deity to own, —
" Daughter of dust! not mine the power
Thou seek'st on Harold's fatal hour.
'Twixt heaven and hell there is a strife
Waged for his soul and for his life,
And fain would we the combat win,
And snatch him in his hour of sin.
There is a star now rising red,
That threats him with an influence dread
Woman, thine arts of malice whet,
To use the space before it set.

nvolve him with the Church in strife,
ush on adventurous chance his life;
>urself will in the hour of need,
s best we may thy counsels speed.''
o ceased the Voice; for seven leagues
  round
Cach hamlet started at the sound;
3ut slept again, as slowly died
ts thunders on the hill's brown side.

XIX.

5 And is this all,'' said Jutta stern,
5 That thou canst teach and I can learn?
Ience! to the land of fog and waste,
'here fittest is thine influence placed,
'hou powerless, sluggish deity!
3ut ne'er shall Briton bend the knee
\gain before so poor a god.''
>he struck the altar with her rod:
>light was the touch, as when at need
\ damsel stirs her tardy steed;
3ut to the blow the stone gave place,
And, starting from its balanced base,
Roll'd thundering down the moonlight
  dell, —
Re-echo'd moorland, rock, and fell;
nto the moonlight tarn it dash'd,
Their shores the sounding surges lash'd,
  And there was ripple, rage, and foam;
3ut on that lake, so dark and lone,
*lacid and pale the moonbeam shone
  As Jutta hied her home.

CANTO THIRD.

I.

GRAY towers of Durham! there was
  once a time
I view'd your battlements with such
  vague hope,
As brightens life in its first dawning
  prime;
Not that e'en then came within fancy's
  scope
A vision vain of mitre, throne, or cope;
Yet, gazing on the venerable hall,
Her flattering dreams would in per-
  spective ope
Some reverend room, some preben-
  dary's stall, —
And thus Hope me deceived as she de-
  ceiveth all.

Well yet I love thy mix'd and massive
  piles,
Half church of God, half castle 'gainst
  the Scot,
And long to roam these venerable
  aisles,
With records stored of deeds long
  since forgot;
There might I share my Surtees'* happier lot,
Who leaves at will his patrimonial field
To ransack every crypt and hallow'd
  spot,
And from oblivion rend the spoils they
  yield,
Restoring priestly chant and clang of
  knightly shield.

Vain is the wish — since other cares
  demand
Each vacant hour, and in another
  clime;
But still that northern harp invites my
  hand,
Which tells the wonder of thine earlier
  time;
And fain its numbers would I now
  command
To paint the beauties of that dawning
  fair,
When Harold, gazing from its lofty
  stand,
Upon the western heights of Beaure-
  paire,
Saw Saxon Eadmer's towers begirt by
  winding Wear.

II.

Fair on the half-seen stream the sun-
  beams danced,
Betraying it beneath the woodland
  bank,
And fair between the Gothic turrets
  glanced
Broad lights, and shadows fell on front
  and flank,
And girdled in the massive donjon
  Keep,
And from their circuit peal'd o'er bush
  and bank

---

* Robert Surtees of Mainsforth, F.S.A., author
of "The History and Antiquities of the County
Palatine of Durham."

The matin bell with summons long and
   deep,
And echo answer'd still with long-re-
   sounding sweep.

III.

The morning mists rose from the ground,
Each merry bird awaken'd round,
   As if in revelry;
Afar the bugles' clanging sound
Call'd to the chase the lagging hound;
   The gale breathed soft and free,
And seem'd to linger on its way
To catch fresh odors from the spray,
And waved it in its wanton play
   So light and gamesomely.
The scenes which morning beams reveal,
Its sounds to hear, its gales to feel
In all their fragrance round him steal,
It melted Harold's heart of steel,
   And, hardly wotting why,
He doff'd his helmet's gloomy pride,
And hung it on a tree beside,
   Laid mace and falchion by,
And on the greensward sate him down,
And from his dark habitual frown
   Relax'd his rugged brow —
Whoever hath the doubtful task
From that stern Dane a boon to ask,
   Were wise to ask it now.

IV.

His place beside young Gunnar took,
And mark'd his master's softening
   look,
And in his eye's dark mirror spied
The gloom of stormy thoughts subside,
And cautious watch'd the fittest tide
   To speak a warning word.
So when the torrent's billows shrink,
The timid pilgrim on the brink
Waits long to see them wave and
   sink,
   Ere he dare brave the ford,
And often after doubtful pause,
His step advances or withdraws:
Fearful to move the slumbering ire
Of his stern lord thus stood the squire,
   Till Harold raised his eye,
That glanced as when athwart the
   shroud
Of the dispersing tempest-cloud
   The bursting sunbeams fly:—

V.

" Arouse thee, son of Ermengarde,
Offspring of prophetess and bard !
Take harp and greet this lovely prime
With some high strain of Runic rhyme,
Strong, deep, and powerful ! Peal it roun
Like that loud bell's sonorous sound,
Yet wild by fits, as when the lay
Of bird and bugle hail the day.
Such was my grandsire Eric's sport,
When dawn gleam'd on his martial court
Heymar the Scald, with harp's high
   sound,
Summon'd the chiefs who slept around;
Couch'd on the spoils of wolf and bear
They roused like lions from their lair,
Then rush'd in emulation forth
To enhance the glories of the North. —
Proud Eric, mightiest of thy race,
Where is thy shadowy resting place?
In wild Valhalla hast thou quaff'd
From foeman's skull metheglin draught
Or wanderest where thy cairn was piled
To frown o'er oceans wide and wild?
Or have the milder Christians given
Thy refuge in their peaceful heaven?
Where'er thou art, to thee are known
Our toils endured, our trophies won,
Our wars, our wanderings, and our woes."
He ceased, and Gunnar's song arose:—

VI.

SONG.

" Hawk and osprey screamed for joy
O'er the beetling cliffs of Hoy,
Crimson foam the beach o'erspread,
The heath was dyed with darker red,
When o'er Eric, Inguar's son,
Dane and Northman piled the stone;
Singing wild the war-song stern:—
' Rest thee, Dweller of the Cairn ! '

" Where eddying currents foam and boi
By Bersa's burgh and Græmsay's isle,
The seaman sees a martial form
Half-mingled with the mist and storm.
In anxious awe he bears away
To moor his bark in Stromna's bay,
And murmurs from the bounding stern :—
' Rest thee, Dweller of the Cairn ! '

" What cares disturb the mighty dead?
Each honor'd rite was duly paid;

o daring hand thy helm unlaced,
ηy sword, thy shield, were near thee
   placed, —
ηy flinty couch no tear profaned,
'ithout, with hostile blood 'twas stain'd;
'ithin, 'twas lined with moss and fern; —
hen rest thee, Dweller of the Cairn ! "

He may not rest: from realms afar
omes voice of battle and of war,
f conquest wrought with bloody hand
n Carmel's cliffs and Jordan's strand,
Vhen Odin's warlike son could daunt
he turban'd race of Termagaunt." —

VII.

Peace," said the Knight, " the noble
   Scald
ur warlike fathers' deeds recall'd,
ut never strove to soothe the son
Vith tales of what himself had done.
t Odin's board the bard sits high
Vhose harp ne'er stoop'd to flattery;
ut highest he whose daring lay
.ath dared unwelcome truths to say."
Vith doubtful smile young Gunnar eyed
Iis master's looks, and naught replied —
ut well that smile his master led
o construe what he left unsaid : —
Is it to me, thou timid youth,
hou fear'st to speak unwelcome truth?
Iy soul no more thy censure grieves
han frosts rob laurels of their leaves.
ay on — and yet — beware the rude
.nd wild distemper of my blood;
oth were I that mine ire should wrong
he youth that bore my shield so long,
.nd who in service constant still,
'hough weak in frame, art strong in
   will." —
Oh ! " quoth the page, " even there depends
Iy counsel — there my warning tends —
ft seems as of my master's breast
ome demon were the sudden guest;
'hen at the first misconstrued word
Iis hands is on the mace and sword,
rom her firm seat his wisdom driven,
Iis life to countless dangers given. —
) ! would that Gunnar could suffice
'o be the fiend's last sacrifice,
o that, when glutted with my gore,
Ie fled and tempted thee no more ! "

VIII.

Then waved his hand, and shook his head
The impatient Dane, while thus he
   said : —
" Profane not, youth — it is not thine
To judge the spirit of our line —
The bold Berserkar's rage divine,
Through whose inspiring, deeds are
   wrought
Past human strength and human thought.
When full upon his gloomy soul
The champion feels the influence roll,
He swims the lake, he leaps the wall —
Heeds not the depth, nor plumbs the
   fall —
Unshielded, mail-less, on he goes
Singly against a host of foes;
Their spears he holds like wither'd reeds.
Their mail like maiden's silken weeds;
One 'gainst a hundred will he strive,
Take countless wounds and yet survive.
Then rush the eagles to his cry
Of slaughter and of victory, —
And blood he quaffs like Odin's bowl,
Deep drinks his sword, — deep drinks his
   soul;
And all that meet him in his ire
He gives to ruin, rout, and fire;
Then, like gorged lion, seeks some den,
And couches till he's man agen. —
Thou know'st the signs of look and limb,
When 'gins that rage to overbrim —
Thou know'st when I am moved, and
   why;
And when thou seest me roll mine eye,
Set my teeth thus, and stamp my foot,
Regard thy safety and be mute;
But else speak boldly out whate'er
Is fitting that a knight should hear.
I love thee, youth. Thy lay has power
Upon my dark and sullen hour; —
So Christian monks are wont to say
Demons of old were charmed away;
Then fear not I will rashly deem
Ill of thy speech, whate'er the theme."

IX.

As down some strait in doubt and dread
The watchful pilot drops the lead,
And, cautious in the midst to steer,
The shoaling channel sounds with fear;
So, lest on dangerous ground he swerved,
The Page his master's brow observed,

Pausing at intervals to fling
His hand o'er the melodious string,
And to his moody breast apply
The soothing charm of harmony,
While hinted half, and half exprest,
This warning song convey'd the rest:—

SONG.

I.

" Ill fares the bark with tackle riven,
And ill when on the breakers driven,—
Ill when the storm-sprite shrieks in air,
And the scared mermaid tears her hair;
But worse when on her helm the hand
Of some false traitor holds command.

2.

" Ill fares the fainting Palmer, placed
Mid Hebron's rocks or Rana's waste,—
Ill when the scorching sun is high,
And the expected font is dry,—
Worse when his guide o'er sand and heath,
The barbarous Copt, has plann'd his
    death.

3.

" Ill fares the Knight with buckler cleft,
And ill when of his helm bereft,—
Ill when his steed to earth is flung,
Or from his grasp his falchion wrung;
But worse, if instant ruin token,
When he lists rede by woman spoken." —

X.

" How now, fond boy? — Canst thou
    think ill,"
Said Harold, " of fair Metelill?" —
" She may be fair," the Page replied,
    As through the strings he ranged,—
" She may be fair; but yet," he cried,
    And then the strain he changed,—

SONG.

I.

" She may be fair," he sang, " but yet
    Far fairer have I seen
Than she, for all her locks of jet,
    And eyes so dark and sheen.
Were I a Danish knight in arms,
    As one day I may be,
My heart should own no foreign
    charms,—
A Danish maid for me.

2.

" I love my father's northern land,
    Where the dark pine-trees grow,
And the bold Baltic's echoing strand
    Looks o'er each grassy oe.*
I love to mark the lingering sun,
    From Denmark loth to go,
And leaving on the billows bright,
To cheer the short-lived summer night,
    A path of ruddy glow.

3.

" But most   northern maid I love,
    With breast like Denmark's snow,
And form as fair as Denmark's pine,
Who loves with purple heath to twine
    Her locks of sunny glow;
And sweetly blends that shade of gold
    With the cheek's rosy hue,
And faith might for her mirror hold
    That eye of matchless blue.

4.

" 'Tis hers the manly sports to love
    That southern maidens fear,
To bend the bow by stream and grove,
    And lift the hunter's spear.
She can her chosen champion's flight
    With eye undazzled see,
Clasp him victorious from the strife,
Or on his corpse yield up her life,—
    A Danish maid for me ! "

XI.

Then smiled the Dane : — " Thou canst
    so well
The virtues of our maidens tell,
Half could I wish my choice had been
Blue eyes, and hair of golden sheen,
And lofty soul; — yet what of ill
Hast thou to charge on Metelill?" —
" Nothing on her," young Gunnar said,
" But her base sire's ignoble trade.
Her mother, too — the general fame
Hath given to Jutta evil name,
And in her gray eye is a flame
Art cannot hide, nor fear can tame. —
That sordid woodman's peasant cot
Twice have thine honor'd footsteps sought
And twice return'd with such ill rede
As sent thee on some desperate deed." —

* *Oe*, island.

XII.

Thou errest; Jutta wisely said,
e that comes suitor to a maid,
e link'd in marriage, should provide
nds and a dwelling for his bride —
y father's, by the Tyne and Wear,
ave reclaim'd." — " O, all too dear,
d all too dangerous the prize,
en were it won," young Gunnar
cries; —
And then this Jutta's fresh device,
at thou shouldst seek, a heathen Dane,
om Durham's priests a boon to gain,
hen thou hast left their vassals slain
their own halls ! " — Flush'd Harold's
eye,
under'd his voice : — " False Page,
you lie !
e castle, hall and tower, is mine,
ilt by old Witikind on Tyne.
e wild-cat will defend his den,
ghts for her nest the timid wren;
d think'st thou I'll forego my right
r dread of monk or monkish knight?
) and away, that deepening bell
oth of the Bishop's conclave tell.
ither will I, in manner due,
 Jutta bade, my claim to sue;
d, if to right me they are loth,
en woe to church and chapter both ! "
ow shift the scene, and let the curtain
fall,
d our next entry be Saint Cuthbert's
hall.

CANTO FOURTH.

I.

FULL many a bard hath sung the solemn
gloom
Of the long Gothic aisle and stone-
ribb'd roof,
O'er-canopying shrine, and gorgeous
tomb,
Carved screen, and altar glimmering far
aloof,
And blending with the shade, — a
matchless proof
Of high devotion, which hath now
wax'd cold;
Yet legends say, that Luxury's brute
hoof

Intruded oft within such sacred fold,
Like step of Bel's false priest, track'd in
his fame of old.

Well pleased am I, howe'er, that when
the rout
Of our rude neighbors whilome deign'd
to come,
Uncall'd, and eke unwelcome, to sweep
out
And cleanse our chancel from the rags
of Rome,
They spoke not on our ancient fame
the doom
To which their bigot zeal gave o'er
their own,
But spared the martyr'd saint and
storied tomb,
Tho' papal miracles had graced the
stone,
And tho' the aisles still loved the organ's
swelling tone.

And deem not, tho' 'tis now my part
to paint
A Prelate sway'd by love of power and
gold,
That all who wore the mitre of our Saint
Like to ambitious Aldingar I hold;
Since both in modern times and days of
old
It sate on those whose virtues might
atone
Their predecessors' frailties trebly told;
Matthew and Morton we as such may
own —
And such (if fame speak truth) the
honor'd Barrington.

II.

But now to earlier and to ruder times,
As subject meet, I tune my rugged
rhymes,
Telling how fairly the chapter was met,
And rood and books in seemly order
set;
Huge brass-clasp'd volumes, which the
hand
Of studious priest but rarely scann'd,
Now on fair carved desk display'd,
'Twas theirs the solemn scene to aid.
O'erhead with many a scutcheon graced,
And quaint devices interlaced,

A labyrinth of crossing rows,
The roof in lessening arches shows;
Beneath its shade placed proud and
  high,
With footstool and with canopy,
Sate Aldingar, — and prelate ne'er
More haughty graced Saint Cuthbert's
  chair;
Canons and deacons were placed below,
In due degree and lengthen'd row.
Unmoved and silent each sat there,
Like image, in his oaken chair;
Nor head, nor hand, nor foot they
  stirr'd,
Nor lock of hair, nor tress of beard;
And of their eyes severe alone
The twinkle show'd they were not
  stone.

III.

The Prelate was to speech address'd,
Each head sunk reverent on each
  breast;
But ere his voice was heard — without
Arose a wild tumultuous shout,
Offspring of wonder mix'd with fear,
Such as in crowded streets we hear
Hailing the flames, that, bursting out,
Attract yet scare the rabble rout.
Ere it had ceased, a giant hand
Shook oaken door and iron band,
Till oak and iron both gave way,
Clash'd the long bolts, the hinges bray,
And, ere upon angel or saint they can
  call,
Stands Harold the Dauntless in midst of
  the hall.

IV.

"Now save ye, my masters, both rochet
  and rood,
From Bishop with mitre to Deacon with
  hood!
For here stands Count Harold, old Witikind's son,
Come to sue for the lands which his ancestors won."
The Prelate look'd round him with sore
  troubled eye,
Unwilling to grant, yet afraid to deny;
While each Canon and Deacon who heard
  the Dane speak,
To be safely at home would have fasted
  a week

Then Aldingar roused him, and answer'd
  again: —
"Thou suest for a boon which thou can
  not obtain;
The Church hath no fiefs for an unchri
  ten'd Dane.
Thy father was wise, and his treasure ha
  given,
That the priests of a chantry might hym
  him to heaven;
And the fiefs which whilome he possess'
  as his due,
Have lapsed to the Church, and bee
  granted anew
To Anthony Conyers and Alberic Vere
For the service Saint Cuthbert's blest ban
  ner to bear,
When the bands of the North come to fora
  the Wear;
Then disturb not our conclave with wran
  gling or blame,
But in peace and in patience pass hence
  as ye came."

V.

Loud laugh'd the stern Pagan: — "They'
  free from the care
Of fief and of service, both Conyers an
  Vere, —
Six feet of your chancel is all they wi
  need,
A buckler of stone and a corslet of lead.-
Ho, Gunnar! — the tokens;" — and
  sever'd anew,
A head and a hand on the altar h
  threw.
Then shudder'd with terror both Cano
  and Monk,
They knew the glazed eye and the coun
  tenance shrunk,
And of Anthony Conyers the half-grizzle
  hair,
And the scar on the hand of Sir Alber
  Vere.
There was not a churchman or priest th
  was there,
But grew pale at the sight, and betoc
  him to prayer.

VI.

Count Harold laugh'd at their looks
  fear: —
"Was this the hand should your bann
  bear?

as that the head should wear the
　　casque
battle at the Church's task?
'as it to such you gave the place
Harold with the heavy mace?
nd me between the Wear and Tyne
knight will wield this club of mine, —
ive him my fiefs, and I will say
here's wit beneath the cowl of gray.''
e raised it, rough with many a stain,
aught from crush'd skull and spouting
　　brain !
e wheel'd it that it shrilly sung,
nd the aisles echo'd as it swung,
hen dash'd it down with sheer descent,
nd split King Osric's monument. —
How like ye this music ! How trow ye
　　the hand
hat can wield such a mace may be reft
　　of its land?
o answer? — I spare ye a space to
　　agree,
nd Saint Cuthbert inspire you, a saint if
　　he be.
en strides through your chancel, ten
　　strokes on your bell,
nd again I am with you — grave fathers,
　　farewell.''

VII.

e turn'd from their presence, he clash'd
　　the oak door,
nd the clang of his stride died away on
　　the floor;
nd his head from his bosom the Prelate
　　uprears
/ith a ghost-seer's look when the ghost
　　disappears.
Ye priests of Saint Cuthbert, now give
　　me your rede,
or never of counsel had Bishop more
　　need !
/ere the arch-fiend incarnate in flesh and
　　in bone,
he language, the look, and the laugh
　　were his own.
n the bounds of Saint Cuthbert there is
　　not a knight
are confront in our quarrel yon goblin
　　in fight;
hen rede me aright to his claim to
　　reply,
'is unlawful to grant, and 'tis death to
　　deny.''

VIII.

On venison and malmsie that morning
　　had fed
The Cellarer Vinsauf — 'twas thus that
　　he said : —
" Delay till to-morrow the Chapter's
　　reply;
Let the feast be spread fair, and the wine
　　be pour'd high:
If he's mortal he drinks, — if he drinks,
　　he is ours —
His bracelets of iron, — his bed in our
　　towers.''
This man had a laughing eye,
Trust not, friends, when such you spy;
A beaker's depth he well could drain,
Revel, sport, and jest amain —
The haunch of the deer and the grape's
　　bright dye
Never bard loved them better than I;
But sooner than Vinsauf fill'd me my
　　wine,
Pass'd me his jest, and laugh'd at mine,
Though the buck were of Bearpark, of
　　Bordeaux the vine,
With the dullest hermit I'd rather dine
On an oaken cake and a draught of the
　　Tyne.

IX.

Walwayn the leech spoke next. He
　　knew
Each plant that loves the sun and dew,
But special those whose juice can gain
Dominion o'er the blood and brain;
The peasant who saw him by pale moon-
　　beam
Gathering such herbs by bank and stream,
Deem'd his thin form and soundless tread
Were those of wanderer from the dead. —
" Vinsauf, thy wine,'' he said, " hath
　　power,
Our gyves are heavy, strong our tower;
Yet three drops from this flask of mine,
More strong than dungeons, gyves, or
　　wine,
Shall give him prison under ground
More dark, more narrow, more profound.
Short rede, good rede, let Harold have —
A dog's death, and a heathen's grave.''
I have lain on a sick man's bed,
Watching for hours for the leech's tread,
As if I deem'd that his presence alone
Were of power to bid my pain begone;

I have listed his words of comfort
  given,
As if to oracles from heaven;
I have counted his steps from my chamber door,
And bless'd them when they were heard
  no more;—
But sooner than Walwayn my sick couch
  should nigh,
My choice were, by leech-craft unaided,
  to die.

X.

" Such service done in fervent zeal
The Church may pardon and conceal,"
The doubtful Prelate said, " but ne'er
The counsel ere the act should hear.—
Anselm of Jarrow, advise us now,
The stamp of wisdom is on thy brow;
Thy days, thy nights, in cloister pent,
Are still to mystic learning lent;—
Anselm of Jarrow, in thee is my hope,
Thou well mayst give counsel to Prelate
  or Pope."

XI.

Answer'd the Prior:—" 'Tis wisdom's
  use
Still to delay what we dare not refuse:
Ere granting the boon he comes hither to
  ask,
Shape for the giant gigantic task;
Let us see how a step so sounding can
  tread
In paths of darkness, danger, and dread;
He may not, he will not, impugn our
  decree,
That calls but for proof of his chivalry;
And were Guy to return, or Sir Bevis the
  Strong,
Our wilds have adventure might cumber
  them long—
The Castle of Seven Shields "—" Kind
  Anselm, no more!
The step of the Pagan approaches the
  door."
The churchmen were hush'd. In his
  mantle of skin,
With his mace on his shoulder, Count
  Harold strode in.
There was foam on his lips, there was fire
  in his eye,
For, chafed by attendance, his fury was
  nigh.

" Ho ! Bishop," he said, " dost thou gra...
  me my claim?
Or must I assert it by falchion and flame...

XII.

"On thy suit, gallant Harold," the Bish...
  replied,
In accents which trembled, " we may r...
  decide,
Until proof of your strength and yo...
  valor we saw—
'Tis not that we doubt them, but such...
  the law."—
" And would you, Sir Prelate, have H...
  old make sport
For the cowls and the shavelings that he...
  in thy court?
Say what shall he do?— From the shri...
  shall he tear
The lead bier of thy patron, and heave...
  in air,
And thro' the long chancel make Cu...
  bert take wing,
With the speed of a bullet dismiss'd fr...
  the sling? "—
" Nay, spare such probation," the C...
  larer said,
" From the mouth of our minstrels t...
  task shall be read.
While the wine sparkles high in the go...
  let of gold,
And the revel is loudest, thy task sh...
  be told;
And thyself, gallant Harold, shall, he...
  ing it, tell
That the Bishop, his cowls, and his shav...
  lings, meant well."

XIII.

Loud revell'd the guests, and the gobl...
  loud rang,
But louder the minstrel, Hugh Menevil...
  sang;
And Harold, the hurry and pride of who...
  soul,
E'en when verging to fury, own'd musi...
  control,
Still bent on the harper his broad sable ey...
And often untasted the goblet pass'd b...
Than wine, or than wassail, to him w...
  more dear
The minstrel's high tale of enchantme...
  to hear;

And the Bishop that day might of Vinsauf
 complain
That his art had but wasted his wine-
 casks in vain.

XIV.
THE CASTLE OF THE SEVEN SHIELDS.
A Ballad.

The Druid Urien had daughters seven,
Their skill could call the moon from
 heaven:
So fair their forms and so high their
 fame,
That seven proud kings for their suitors
 came.

King Mador and Rhys came from Powis
 and Wales,
Unshorn were their hair, and unpruned
 were their nails;
From Strath-Clwyde was Ewain, and
 Ewain was lame,
And the red-bearded Donald from Gallo-
 way came.

Lot, King of Lodon, was hunchback'd
 from youth;
Dunmail of Cumbria had never a tooth;
But Adolf of Bambrough, Northumberland's heir,
Was gay and was gallant, was young and
 was fair.

There was strife 'mongst the sisters, for
 each one would have
For husband King Adolf, the gallant and
 brave;
And envy bred hate, and hate urged them
 to blows,
When the firm earth was cleft, and the
 Arch-fiend arose!

He swore to the maidens their wish to
 fulfil —
They swore to the foe they would work
 by his will.
A spindle and distaff to each hath he given,
" Now hearken my spell," said the Outcast of Heaven.

" Ye shall ply these spindles at midnight
 hour,
And for every spindle shall rise a tower,

Where the right shall be feeble, the wrong
 shall have power,
And there shall ye dwell with your paramour."

Beneath the pale moonlight they sate on
 the wold,
And the rhymes which they chanted must
 never be told;
And as the black wool from the distaff
 they sped,
With blood from their bosom they mois-
 ten'd the thread.

As light danced the spindles beneath the
 cold gleam,
The castle arose like the birth of a
 dream—
The seven towers ascended like mist from
 the ground,
Seven portals defend them, seven ditches
 surround.

Within that dread castle seven monarchs
 were wed,
But six of the seven ere the morning lay
 dead;
With their eyes all on fire, and their
 daggers all red,
Seven damsels surround the Northumbrian's bed.

" Six kingly bridegrooms to death we
 have done,
Six gallant kingdoms King Adolf hath
 won.
Six lovely brides all his pleasures to do,
Or the bed of the seventh will be hus-
 bandless too."

Well chanced it that Adolf the night when
 he wed,
Had confess'd and had sain'd him ere
 boune to his bed;
He sprung from the couch and the broadsword he drew,
And there the seven daughters of Urien
 he slew.

The gate of the castle he bolted and
 seal'd,
And hung o'er each arch-stone a crown
 and a shield !

To the cells of Saint Dunstan then wended
   his way,
And died in his cloister an anchorite
   gray.

Seven monarchs' wealth in that castle lie
   stow'd,
The foul fiends brood o'er them like raven
   and toad.

Whoever shall guesten these chambers
   within,
From curfew to matins, that treasure
   shall win.

But manhood grows faint as the world
   waxes old!
There lives not in Britain a champion so
   bold,
So dauntless of heart, and so prudent of
   brain,
As to dare the adventure that treasure to
   gain.

The waste ridge of Cheviot shall wave
   with the rye,
Before the rude Scots shall Northumberland fly,
And the flint cliffs of Bambro' shall melt
   in the sun,
Before that adventure be perill'd and won.

XV.

" And is this my probation?" wild Har-
   old he said,
" Within a lone castle to press a lone
   bed? —
Good even, my Lord Bishop, — Saint
   Cuthbert to borrow,
The Castle of Seven Shields receives me
   to-morrow."

CANTO FIFTH.

I.

DENMARK's sage courtier to her
   princely youth,
Granting his cloud an ouzel or a whale,
Spoke, though unwittingly, a partial
   truth;
For Fantasy embroiders Nature's veil.
The tints of ruddy eve, or dawning
   pale,

Of the swart thunder-cloud, or silve
   haze,
Are but the ground-work of the ric
   detail,
Which Fantasy with pencil wild por
   trays,
Blending what seems and is, in the rap
   muser's gaze.

Nor are the stubborn forms of earth
   and stone
Less to the Sorceress's empire given;
For not with unsubstantial hues alone
Caught from the varying surge, o
   vacant heaven,
From bursting sunbeam or from flash
   ing levin,
She limns her pictures: on the earth
   as air,
Arise her castles, and her car is driven;
And never gazed the eye on scene so fair
But of its boasted charms gave Fancy
   half the share.

II.

Up a wild pass went Harold, bent to
   prove,
Hugh Meneville, the adventure of thy
   lay;
Gunnar pursued his steps in faith and
   love, .
Ever companion of his master's way.
Midward their path, a rock of granite
   gray
From the adjoining cliff had made de
   scent, —
A barren mass — yet with her drooping spray
Had a young birch-tree crown'd its
   battlement,
Twisting her fibrous roots through cranny,
   flaw, and rent.

This rock and tree could Gunnar's
   thought engage
Till Fancy brought the tear-drop to his
   eye,
And at his master ask'd the timid
   Page; —
" What is the emblem that a bard
   should spy
In that rude rock and its green can-
   opy?"

And Harold said : — " Like to the helmet brave
Of warrior slain in fight it seems to lie,
And these same drooping boughs do
   o'er it wave
ot all unlike the plume his lady's favor
   gave." —

" Ah, no ! " replied the Page; " the
   ill-starr'd love
Of some poor maid is in the emblem
   shown,
Whose fates are with some hero's in-
   terwove,
And rooted on a heart to love unknown:
And as the gentle dews of heaven
   alone
Nourish these drooping boughs, and as
   the scathe
Of the red lightning rends both tree
   and stone,
So fares it with her unrequited faith, —
er sole relief is tears — her only refuge
   death." —

III.

Thou art a fond fantastic boy,"
arold replied, " to females coy,
   Yet prating still of love;
ven so amid the clash of war
know thou lovest to keep afar,
hough destined by thy evil star
   With one like me to rove,
hose business and whose joys are found
pon the bloody battle-ground.
et, foolish trembler as thou art,
hou hast a nook of my rude heart,
nd thou and I will never part; —
arold would wrap the world in flame
re injury on Gunnar came ! "

IV.

he grateful Page made no reply,
ut turn'd to Heaven his gentle eye,
nd clasp'd his hands, as one who said :—
My toils — my wanderings are o'erpaid ! "
hen in a gayer, lighter strain,
ompell'd himself to speech again;
   And, as they flow'd along,
is words took cadence soft and slow
nd liquid, like dissolving snow,
   They melted into song : —

V.

" What tho' thro' fields of carnage wide
I may not follow Harold's stride,
   Yet who with faithful Gunnar's pride
     Lord Harold's feats can see?
And dearer than the couch of pride
He loves the bed of gray wolf's hide,
When slumbering by Lord Harold's side
     In forest, field, or lea." —

VI.

" Break off ! " said Harold, in a tone
Where hurry and surprise were shown,
   With some slight touch of fear, —
" Break off ! we are not here alone;
A Palmer form comes slowly on !
By cowl, and staff, and mantle known,
   My monitor is near.
Now mark him, Gunnar, heedfully,
He pauses by the blighted tree —
Dost see him, youth ? —Thou couldst not
   see
When in the vale of Galilee
   I first beheld his form,
Nor when we met that other while
In Cephalonia's rocky isle,
   Before the fearful storm, —
Dost see him now ? " The Page, distraught
With terror, answer'd : — " I see naught,
   And there is naught to see,
Save that the oak's scathed boughs fling
   down
Upon the path a shadow brown,
That, like a pilgrim's dusky gown,
   Waves with the waving tree."

VII.

Count Harold gazed upon the oak
As if his eyestrings would have broke,
   And then resolvedly said : —
" Be what it will yon phantom gray —
Nor heaven nor hell shall ever say
That for their shadows from his way
   Count Harold turn'd dismay'd;
I'll speak him, tho' his accents fill
My heart with that unwonted thrill
   Which vulgar minds call fear.
I will subdue it ! " — Forth he strode,
Paused where the blighted oak-tree
   show'd
Its sable shadow on the road,
And, folding on his bosom broad
   His arms, said : — " Speak — I hear."

VIII.

The Deep Voice said: — "O wild of will,
Furious thy purpose to fulfill —
Heart-sear'd and unrepentant still,
How long, O Harold, shall thy tread
Disturb the slumbers of the dead?
Each step in thy wild way thou makest,
The ashes of the dead thou wakest;
And shout in triumph o'er thy path
The fiends of bloodshed and of wrath.
In this thine hour, yet turn and hear!
For life is brief and judgment near."

IX.

Then ceased The Voice. — The Dane re-
    plied
In tones where awe and inborn pride
For mastery strove: — "In vain ye chide
The wolf for ravaging the flock,
Or with its hardness taunt the rock, —
I am as they — my Danish strain
Sends streams of fire through every vein.
Amid thy realms of ghoul and ghost,
Say, is the fame of Eric lost,
Or Witikind's the Waster, known
Where fame or spoil was to be won;
    Whose galleys ne'er bore off a shore
    They left not black with flame? —
He was my sire, — and, sprung of him,
That rover merciless and grim,
    Can I be soft and tame?
Part hence, and with my crimes no more
    upbraid me,
I am that Waster's son, and am but
    what he made me."

X.

The Phantom groan'd; — the mountain
    shook around,
The fawn and wild doe started at the
    sound,
The gorse and fern did wildly round
    them wave,
As if some sudden storm the impulse
    gave.
"All thou hast said is truth. — Yet on
    the head
Of that bad sire let not the charge be laid,
That he, like thee, with unrelenting pace,
From grave to cradle ran the evil race: —
Relentless in his avarice and ire,
Churches and towns he gave to sword
    and fire;

Shed blood like water, wasted eve
    land,
Like the destroying angel's burni
    brand;
Fulfill'd whate'er of ill might be i
    vented,
Yes — all these things he did — he di
    but he REPENTED!
Perchance it is part of his punishme
    still,
That his offspring pursues his examp
    of ill.
But thou, when thy tempest of wra
    shall next shake thee,
Gird thy loins for resistance, my son, a
    awake thee;
If thou yield'st to thy fury, how tempt
    soever,
The gate of repentance shall ope for th
    NEVER!"

XI.

"He is gone," said Lord Harold, a
    gazed as he spoke;
"There is naught on the path but t
    shade of the oak.
He is gone, whose strange presence r
    feeling oppress'd,
Like the night-hag that sits on the slu
    berer's breast.
My heart beats as thick as a fugitiv
    tread,
And cold dews drop from my brow a
    my head. —
Ho! Gunnar, the flasket yon almor
    gave;
He said that three drops would rec
    from the grave.
For the first time Count Harold ow
    leechcraft has power,
Or, his courage to aid, lacks the juice
    a flower!"
The page gave the flasket, which W
    wayn had fill'd
With the juice of wild roots that his
    had distill'd —
So baneful their influence on all that h
    breath,
One drop had been frenzy, and two h
    been death.
Harold took it, but drank not; for ju
    lee shrill,
And music and clamor were heard on t
    hill,

And down the steep pathway, o'er stock
   and o'er stone,
The train of a bridal came blithesomely
   on;
There was song, there was pipe, there
   was timbrel, and still
The burden was: " Joy to the fair
   Metelill!"

XII.

Harold might see from his high stance,
Himself unseen, that train advance
   With mirth and melody; —
On horse and foot a mingled throng
Measuring their steps to bridal song
   And bridal minstrelsy;
And ever when the blithesome rout
Lent to the song their choral shout,
Redoubling echoes roll'd about,
While echoing cave and cliffs sent out
   The answering symphony
Of all those mimic notes which dwell
In hollow rock and sounding dell.

XIII.

Joy shook his torch above the band,
By many a various passion fann'd; —
As elemental sparks can feed
On essence pure and coarsest weed,
Gentle, or stormy, or refined,
Joy takes the colors of the mind.
Lightsome and pure, but unrepress'd,
He fired the bridegroom's gallant breast;
More feebly strove with maiden fear,
Yet still joy glimmer'd through the tear
On the bride's blushing cheek, that shows
Like dewdrop on the budding rose;
While Wulfstane's gloomy smile declared
The glee that selfish avarice shared,
And pleased revenge and malice high
Joy's semblance took in Jutta's eye.
On dangerous adventure sped,
The witch deem'd Harold with the dead,
For thus that morn her Demon said: —
" If, ere the set of sun, be tied
The knot 'twixt bridegroom and his
   bride,
The Dane shall have no power of ill
O'er William and o'er Metelill."
And the pleased witch made answer: —
   " Then
Must Harold have pass'd from the paths
   of men!

Evil repose may his spirit have, —
May hemlock and mandrake find root in
   his grave, —
May his death-sleep be dogged by dreams
   of dismay,
And his waking be worse at the answering day."

XIV.

Such was their various mood of glee
Blent in one shout of ecstasy.
But still when Joy is brimming highest,
Of Sorrow and Misfortune nighest,
Of Terror with her ague cheek,
And lurking Danger, sages speak: —
These haunt each path, but chief they
   lay
Their snares beside the primrose way. —
Thus found that bridal band their path
Beset by Harold in his wrath.
Trembling beneath his maddening mood,
High on a rock the giant stood;
His shout was like the doom of death
Spoke o'er their heads that pass'd beneath.
His destined victims might not spy
The reddening terrors of his eye, —
The frown of rage that writhed his face,—
The lip that foam'd like boar's in chase;
But all could see — and, seeing, all
Bore back to shun the threaten'd fall —
The fragment which their giant foe
Rent from the cliff and heaved to throw.

XV.

Backward they bore; — yet are there two
   For battle who prepare:
No pause of dread Lord William knew
   Ere his good blade was bare;
And Wulfstane bent his fatal yew,
But ere the silken cord he drew,
As hurl'd from Hecla's thunder, flew
   That ruin through the air!
Full on the outlaw's front it came,
And all that late had human name,
And human face, and human frame,
That lived, and moved, and had free will
To choose the path of good or ill,
   Is to its reckoning gone;
And naught of Wulfstane rests behind,
   Save that beneath that stone,
Half-buried in the dinted clay,
A red and shapeless mass there lay
   Of mingled flesh and bone!

XVI.

As from the bosom of the sky
　The eagle darts amain,
Three bounds from yonder summit high
　Placed Harold on the plain.
As the scared wild-fowl scream and fly,
　So fled the bridal train;
As 'gainst the eagle's peerless might
The noble falcon dares the fight,
　But dares the fight in vain,
So fought the bridegroom; from his hand
The Dane's rude mace has struck his brand,
Its glittering fragments strew the sand,
　Its lord lies on the plain.
Now, Heaven! take noble William's
　part,
And melt that yet unmelted heart,
Or, ere his bridal hour depart,
　The hapless bridegroom's slain!

XVII.

Count Harold's frenzied rage is high,
There is a death-fire in his eye,
Deep furrows on his brow are trench'd,
His teeth are set, his hand is clench'd,
The foam upon his lip is white,
His deadly arm is up to smite!
But as the mace aloft he swung,
To stop the blow young Gunnar sprung,
Around his master's knees he clung,
　And cried: — " In mercy spare!
O, think upon the words of fear
Spoke by that visionary Seer,
The crisis he foretold is here, —
　Grant mercy — or despair!"
This word suspended Harold's mood,
Yet still with arm upraised he stood,
And visage like the headsman's rude
　That pauses for the sign.
" O mark thee with the blessed rood,"
The page implored; "speak word of
　good,
Resist the fiend, or be subdued!"
　He sign'd the cross divine —
Instant his eye hath human light,
Less red, less keen, less fiercely bright;
His brow relax'd the obdurate frown,
The fatal mace sinks gently down,
　He turns and strides away;
Yet oft, like revellers who leave
Unfinish'd feast, looks back to grieve,
As if repenting the reprieve
　He granted to his prey.

Yet still of forbearance one sign hath he
　given,
And fierce Witikind's son made one step
　towards heaven.

XVIII.

But tho' his dreaded footsteps part,
Death is behind and shakes his dart;
Lord William on the plain is lying,
Beside him Metelill seems dying!
Bring odors — essences in haste —
And lo! a flasket richly chased, —
But Jutta the elixir proves
Ere pouring it for those she loves. —
Then Walwayn's potion was not wasted,
For when three drops the hag had tasted
　So dismal was her yell,
Each bird of evil omen woke,
The raven gave his fatal croak,
And shriek'd the night-crow from the oak
The screech-owl from the thicket broke
　And flutter'd down the dell!
So fearful was the sound and stern,
The slumbers of the full-gorged erne
Were startled, and from furze and fern
　Of forest and of fell,
The fox and famish'd wolf replied,
(For wolves then prowl'd the Cheviot side,)
From mountain head to mountain head
The unhallow'd sounds around were sped;
But when their latest echo fled,
The sorceress on the ground lay dead.

XIX.

Such was the scene of blood and woes,
With which the bridal morn arose
　Of William and of Metelill;
But oft, when dawning 'gins to spread,
The summer morn peeps dim and red
　Above the eastern hill,
Ere, bright and fair, upon his road
The King of Splendor walks abroad;
So when this cloud had pass'd away,
Bright was the noontide of their day,
And all serene its setting ray.

CANTO SIXTH.

I.

WELL do I hope that this my minstrel
　tale
Will tempt no traveller from southern
　fields,

Whether in tilbury, barouche, or mail,
To view the Castle of these Seven Proud
    Shields.
Small confirmation its condition yields
To Meneville's high lay. — No towers
    are seen
On the wild heath, but those that Fancy
    builds,
And, save a fosse that tracks the moor
    with green,
Is naught remains to tell of what may
    there have been.

And yet grave authors, with the no
    small waste
Of their grave time, have dignified the
    spot
By theories, to prove the fortress placed
By Roman bands, to curb the invading
    Scot.
Hutchinson, Horsley, Camden, I might
    quote,
But rather choose the theory less civil
Of boors, who, origin of things for-
    got,
Refer still to the origin of evil,
And for their master-mason choose that
    master-fiend the Devil.

II.

Therefore, I say, it was on fiend-built
    towers
That stout Count Harold bent his won-
    dering gaze,
When evening dew was on the heather
    flowers,
And the last sunbeams made the moun-
    tain blaze,
And tinged the battlements of other
    days
With the bright level light ere sinking
    down. —
Illumined thus, the Dauntless Dane
    surveys
The Seven Proud Shields that o'er the
    portal frown,
And on their blazons traced high marks
    of old renown.

A wolf North Wales-had on his armor-
    coat,
And Rhys of Powis-land a couchant
    stag;

Strath-Clwyde's strange emblem was
    a stranded boat,
Donald of Galloway's a trotting nag;
A corn-sheaf gilt was fertile Lodon's
    brag;
A dudgeon-dagger was by Dunmail
    worn;
Northumbrian Adolf gave a sea-beat
    crag
Surmounted by a cross — such signs
    were borne
Upon these antique shields, all wasted
    now and worn.

III.

These scann'd, Count Harold sought
    the castle door,
Whose ponderous bolts were rusted to
    decay;
Yet till that hour adventurous knight
    forbore
The unobstructed passage to essay.
More strong than armed warders in
    array,
And obstacle more sure than bolt or
    bar,
Sate in the portal Terror and Dis-
    may,
While Superstition, who forbade to
    war
With foes of other mould than mortal
    clay,
Cast spells across the gate, and barr'd
    the onward way.

Vain now these spells; for soon with
    heavy clank
The feebly-fasten'd gate was inward
    push'd,
And, as it oped. thro' that emblazon'd
    rank
Of antique shields, the wind of even-
    ing rush'd
With sound most like a groan, and
    then was hush'd.
Is none who on such spot such sounds
    could hear
But to his heart the blood had faster
    rush'd;
Yet to bold Harold's breast that throb
    was dear —
It spoke of danger nigh, but had no
    touch of fear.

IV.

Yet Harold and his Page no signs have
  traced
Within the castle, that of danger
  show'd,
For still the hills and courts were wild
  and waste,
As thro' their precincts the adventurers
  trode.
The seven huge towers rose stately,
  tall, and broad,
Each tower presenting to their scrutiny
A hall in which a king might make
  abode,
And fast beside, garnish'd both proud
  and high,
Was placed a bower for rest in which a
  king might lie.

As if a bridal there of late had been,
Deck'd stood the table in each gor-
  geous hall;
And yet it was two hundred years, I
  ween,
Since date of that unhallow'd festival.
Flagons, and ewers, and standing cups
  were all
Of tarnished gold, or silver nothing
  clear,
With throne begilt, and canopy of
  pall,
And tapestry clothed the walls with
  fragments sear —
Frail as the spider's mesh did that rich
  woof appear.

V.

In every bower, as round a hearse,
  was hung
A dusky crimson curtain o'er the
  bed,
And on each couch in ghastly wise
  were flung
The wasted relics of a monarch dead;
Barbaric ornaments around were spread,
Vests twined with gold, and chains of
  precious stone,
And golden circlets, meet for monarch's
  head;
While grinn'd, as if in scorn amongst
  them thrown,
The wearer's fleshless skull, alike with
  dust bestrown.

For these were they who, drunken
  with delight,
On pleasure's opiate pillow laid their
  head,
For whom the bride's shy footsteps,
  slow and light,
Was changed ere morning to the murderer's tread.
For human bliss and woe in the frail
  thread
Of human life are all so closely twined,
That till the shears of Fate the texture
  shred,
The close succession cannot be dis-
  join'd,
Nor dare we, from one hour, judge that
  which comes behind.

VI.

But where the work of vengeance had
  been done,
In that seventh chamber, was a sterner
  sight;
There of the witch-brides lay each
  skeleton,
Still in the posture as to death when dight,
For this lay prone, by one blow slain
  outright;
And that, as one who struggled long
  in dying;
One bony hand held knife, as if to
  smite;
One bent on fleshless knees, as mercy
  crying;
One lay across the door, as kill'd in act
  of flying.

The stern Dane smiled this charnel-
  house to see, —
For his chafed thought return'd to
  Metelill; —
And "Well," he said, "hath woman's
  perfidy,
Empty as air, as water volatile,
Been here avenged. — The origin of ill
Thro' woman rose, the Christian doc-
  trine saith:
Nor deem I, Gunnar, that thy minstrel
  skill
Can show example where a woman's
  breath
Hath made a true-love vow, and
  tempted, kept her faith."

VII.

ae minstrel-boy half smiled, half sigh'd,
ad his half-filling eyes he dried,
adsaid: "The theme I should but wrong,
aless it were my dying song,
Dur Scalds have said, in dying hour
ae northern harp has treble power,)
se could I tell of woman's faith,
efying danger, scorn, and death.
rm was that faith, — as diamond stone
are and unflaw'd, — her love unknown,
ad unrequited; — firm and pure,
er stainless faith could all endure;
'om clime to clime, from place to place,
arough want, and danger, and disgrace,
wanderer's wayward steps could trace.
ll this she did, and guerdon none
equired, save that her burial-stone
aould make at length the secret known,
Thus hath a faithful woman done.' —
ot in each breast such truth is laid,
at Eivir was a Danish maid." —

VIII.

Thou art a wild enthusiast," said
ount Harold, "for thy Danish maid;
ad yet, young Gunnar, I will own
ers were a faith to rest upon.
at Eivir sleeps beneath her stone,
ad all resembling her are gone.
That maid e'er show'd such constancy
a plighted faith, like thine to me?
at couch thee, boy; the darksome shade
alls thickly round, nor be dismay'd
Because the dead are by.
hey were as we; our little day
'erspent, and we shall be as they.
et near me, Gunnar, be thou laid,
hy couch upon my mantle made,
nat thou mayst think, should fear invade,
Thy master slumbers nigh."
aus conch'd they in that dread abode,
ntil the beams of dawning glow'd.

IX.

n alter'd man Lord Harold rose,
When he beheld that dawn unclose —
There's trouble in his eyes,
nd traces on his brow and cheek
f mingled awe and wonder speak:
"My page," he said, "arise; —
eave we this place, my page."—No more
e utter'd till the castle door

They cross'd, but there he paused and
said: —
"My wildness hath awaked the dead —
Disturb'd the sacred tomb!
Methought this night I stood on high,
Where Hecla roars in middle sky,
And in her cavern'd gulfs could spy
The central place of doom;
And there before my mortal eye
Souls of the dead came flitting by,
Whom fiends, with many a fiendish cry,
Bore to that evil den!
My eyes grew dizzy, and my brain
Was wilder'd, as the elvish train,
With shriek and howl, dragg'd on amain
Those who had late been men.

X.

"With haggard eyes and streaming hair,
Jutta the Sorceress was there,
And there pass'd Wulfstane, lately slain,
All crush'd and foul with bloody stain. —
More had I seen, but that uprose
A whirlwind wild, and swept the snows;
And with such sound as when at need
A champion spurs his horse to speed,
Three armed knights rush on, who lead
Caparison'd a sable steed.
Sable their harness, and there came
Thro' their closed visors sparks of flame.
The first proclaimed, in sounds of fear: —
'Harold the Dauntless, welcome here'. '
The next cried: — 'Jubilee! we've won
Count Witikind the Waster's son!'
And the third rider sternly spoke: —
'Mount, in the name of Zernebock! —
From us, O Harold, were thy powers, —
Thy strength, thy dauntlessness are ours;
Nor think, a vassal thou of hell,
With hell canst strive.' The fiend spoke
true!
My inmost soul the summons knew,
As captives know the knell
That says the headsman's sword is bare,
And, with an accent of despair,
Commands them quit their cell.
I felt resistance was in vain,
My foot had that fell stirrup ta'en,
My hand was on the fatal mane,
When to my rescue sped
That Palmer's visionary form,
And — like the passing of a storm —
The demons yell'd and fled!

XI.

" His sable cowl flung back, reveal'd
The features it before conceal'd;
    And, Gunnar, I could find
In him whose counsels strove to stay
So oft my course on wilful way,
    My father Witikind !
Doom'd for his sins, and doom'd for mine,
A wanderer upon earth to pine
Until his son shall turn to grace,
And smooth for him a resting-place. —
Gunnar, he must not haunt in vain
This world of wretchedness and pain;
I'll tame my wilful heart to live
In peace — to pity and forgive —
And thou, for so the Vision said,
Must in thy Lord's repentance aid.
Thy mother was a prophetess,
He said, who by her skill could guess
How close the fatal textures join
Which knit thy thread of life with mine;
Then, dark, he hinted of disguise
She framed to cheat too curious eyes,
That not a moment might divide
Thy fated footsteps from my side.
Methought while thus my sire did teach,
I caught the meaning of his speech,
Yet seems its purport doubtful now."
His hand then sought his thoughtful brow,
Then first he mark'd that in the tower
His glove was left at waking hour.

XII.

Trembling at first, and deadly pale,
Had Gunnar heard the vision'd tale;
But when he learn'd the dubious close,
He blush'd like any opening rose.
And, glad to hide his tell-tale cheek,
Hied back that glove of mail to seek;
When soon a shriek of deadly dread
Summon'd his master to his aid.

XIII.

What sees Count Harold in that bower,
    So late his resting-place? —
The semblance of the Evil Power,
    Adored by all his race !
Odin in living form stood there,
His cloak the spoils of Polar bear;
For plumy crest a meteor shed
Its gloomy radiance o'er his head,
Yet veil'd its haggard majesty
To the wild lightnings of his eye.

Such height was his, as when in stone
O'er Upsal's giant altar shown :
    So flow'd his hoary beard;
Such was his lance of mountain-pine,
So did his sevenfold buckler shine; —
    But when his voice he rear'd,
Deep, without harshness, slow and strong
The powerful accents roll'd along,
And, while he spoke, his hand was laid
On Captive Gunnar's shrinking head.

XIV.

" Harold," he said, " what rage is thine
To quit the worship of thy line,
    To leave thy Warrior-God ? —
With me is glory or disgrace,
Mine is the onset and the chase,
Embattled hosts before my face
    Are wither'd by a nod.
Wilt thou then forfeit that high seat
Deserved by many a dauntless feat,
Among the heroes of thy line,
Eric and fiery Thorarine ? —
Thou wilt not. Only can I give
The joys for which the valiant live,
Victory and vengeance — only I
Can give the joys for which they die,
The immortal tilt — the banquet full,
The brimming draught from foeman's skull
Mine art thou, witness this thy glove,
The faithful pledge of vassal's love."

XV.

" Tempter," said Harold, firm of heart,
" I charge thee, hence ! whate'er thou art
I do defy thee — and resist
The kindling frenzy of my breast,
Waked by thy words; and of my mail,
Nor glove, nor buckler, splent, nor nail
Shall rest with thee — that youth release
And God, or Demon, part in peace." —
" Eivir," the Shape replied, " is mine,
Mark'd in the birth-hour with my sign.
Think'st thou that priest with drops of
    spray
Could wash that blood-red mark away ?
Or that a borrow'd sex and name
Can abrogate a Godhead's claim ? "
Thrill'd this strange speech thro' Harold'
    brain,
He clenched his teeth in high disdain,
For not his new-born faith subdued
Some tokens of his ancient mood :—

Now, by the hope so lately given
Of better trust and purer heaven,
  will assail thee, fiend ! ''— Then rose
His mace, and with a storm of blows
The mortal and the Demon close.

XVI.

moke roll'd above, fire flash'd around,
Darken'd the sky and shook the ground;
  But not the artillery of hell,
The bickering lightning, nor the rock
Of turrets to the earthquake's shock,
  Could Harold's courage quell.
ternly the Dane his purpose kept,
And blows on blows resistless heap'd,
  Till quail'd that Demon Form,
And — for his power to hurt or kill
Was bounded by a higher will —
  Evanish'd in the storm.
For paused the Champion of the North,
But raised and bore his Eivir forth,
From that wild scene of fiendish strife,
To light, to liberty, and life !

XVII.

He placed her on a bank of moss,
  A silver runnel bubbled by,
And new-born thoughts his soul engross,
And tremors yet unknown across
  His stubborn sinews fly,
The while with timid hand the dew
Upon her brow and neck he threw,
And mark'd how life with rosy hue
On her pale cheek revived anew,
  And glimmer'd in her eye.
nly he said : — " That silken tress, —
What blindness mine that could not
  guess !
Or how could page's rugged dress
  That bosom's pride belie?
, dull of heart, thro' wild and wave
In search of blood and death to rave,
  With such a partner nigh ! ''

XVIII.

hen in a mirror'd pool he peer'd,
Blamed his rough locks and shaggy beard,
The stains of recent conflict clear'd, —
  And thus the Champion proved,
That he fears now who never fear'd,
  And loves who never loved.

And Eivir — life is on her cheek,
And yet she will not move or speak,
  Nor will her eyelid fully ope;
Perchance it loves, that half-shut eye,
Through its long fringe, reserved and
  shy,
Affection's opening dawn to spy;
And the deep blush, which bids its dye
O'er cheek, and brow, and bosom fly,
  Speaks shame-facedness and hope.

XIX.

But vainly seems the Dane to seek
For terms his new-born love to speak,—
For words, save those of wrath and
  wrong,
Till now were strangers to his tongue;
So, when he raised the blushing maid,
In blunt and honest terms he said,
('Twere well that maids, when lovers
  woo,
Heard none more soft, were all as true):—
" Eivir ! since thou for many a day
Hast follow'd Harold's wayward way,
It is but meet that in the line
Of after-life I follow thine.
To-morrow is Saint Cuthbert's tide,
And we will grace his altar's side,
A Christian knight and Christian bride;
And of Witikind's son shall the marvel
  be said,
That on the same morn he was christen'd
  and wed.''

CONCLUSION.

And now, Ennui, what ails thee, weary
  maid?
And why these listless looks of yawn-
  ing sorrow?
No need to turn the page, as if 'twere
  lead,
Or fling aside the volume till to-morrow.
Be cheer'd — 'tis ended — and I will
  not borrow,
To try thy patience more, one anecdote
From Bartholine, or Perinskiöld, or
  Snorro.
Then pardon thou thy minstrel, who
  hath wrote
A Tale six cantos long, yet scorn'd to add
  a note.

CONTRIBUTIONS to MINSTRELSY

OF THE

SCOTTISH BORDER.

IMITATIONS OF THE ANCIENT BALLAD.

THOMAS THE RHYMER.

IN THREE PARTS.

PART FIRST. — ANCIENT.

FEW personages are so renowned in tradition as Thomas of Ercildoune, known by the appellation of *The Rhymer*. Uniting, or supposing to unite, in his person the powers of poetical composition and of vaticination, his memory, even after the lapse of five hundred years, is regarded with veneration by his countrymen. To give anything like a certain history of this remarkable man would be indeed difficult; but the curious may derive some satisfaction from the particulars here brought together.

It is agreed on all hands, that the residence, and probably the birthplace, of this ancient bard was Ercildoune, a village situated upon the Leader, two miles above its junction with the Tweed. The ruins of an ancient tower are still pointed out as the Rhymer's castle. The uniform tradition bears, that his surname was Lermont, or Learmont; and that the appellation of *The Rhymer* was conferred on him in consequence of his poetical compositions. There remains, nevertheless, some doubt upon the subject.

We are better able to ascertain the period at which Thomas of Ercildoune lived, being the latter end of the thirteenth century. I am inclined to place his death a little farther back than Mr. Pinkerton, who supposes that he was alive in 1300. — (*List of Scottish Poets.*)

It cannot be doubted that Thomas of Ercildoune was a remarkable and important person in his own time, since, very shortly after his death, we find him celebrated as a prophet and as a poet. Whether he himself made any pretensions to the first of these characters, or whether it was gratuitously conferred upon him by the credulity of posterity, it seems difficult to decide. If we may believe Mackenzie, Learmont only versified the prophecies delivered by Eliza, an inspired nun of a convent at Haddington. But of this there seems not to be the most distant proof. On the contrary, all ancient authors, who quote th Rhymer's prophecies, uniformly suppose them to have been emitted by himself.

The popular tale bears, that Thomas was carried off, at an early age, to the Fairy Lan where he acquired all the knowledge which made him afterwards so famous. After seve years' residence, he was permitted to return to the earth, to enlighten and astonish his countr men by his prophetic powers; still, however, remaining bound to return to his royal mi tress, when she should intimate her pleasure. Accordingly, while Thomas was makin merry with his friends in the Tower of Ercildoune, a person came running in, and tol with marks of fear and astonishment, that a hart and hind had left the neighboring fores and were, composedly and slowly, parading the street of the village. The prophet instant arose, left his habitation, and followed the wonderful animals to the forest, whence he wa never seen to return. According to the popular belief, he still "drees his weird" in Fai Land, and is one day expected to revisit earth. In the mean while, his memory is held i the most profound respect. The Eildon Tree, from beneath the shade of which he delivere his prophecies, now no longer exists; but the spot is marked by a large stone, called Eildo Tree Stone. A neighboring rivulet takes the name of the Bogle Burn (Goblin Brook) fro the Rhymer's supernatural visitants.

It seemed to the Editor unpardonable to dismiss a person so important in Border trad tions as the Rhymer, without some further notice than a simple commentary upon th following ballad. It is given from a copy, obtained from a lady residing not far from E cildoune, corrected and enlarged by one in Mrs. Brown's MSS. The former copy, howeve as might be expected, is far more minute as to local description. To this old tale the Edito has ventured to add a Second Part, consisting of a kind of canto, from the printed prop ecies vulgarly ascribed to the Rhymer; and a Third Part, entirely modern, founded upo the tradition of his having returned with the hart and the hind to the Land of Faëry. T make his peace with the more severe antiquaries, the Editor has prefixed to the Secon Part some remarks on Learmont's prophecies.

True Thomas lay on Huntlie bank;*
  A ferlie † he spied wi' his ee;
And there he saw a ladye bright,
  Come riding down by the Eildon Tree.

Her shirt was o' the grass-green silk,
  Her mantle o' the velvet fyne;
At ilka ‡ tett of her horse's mane,
  Hung fifty siller bells and nine.

True Thomas he pull'd aff his cap,
  And louted § low down to his knee:—
"All hail, thou mighty Queen of Heaven!
  For thy peer on earth I never did see."—

"O no, O no, Thomas," she said,
  "That name does not belang to me;
I am but the Queen of fair Elfland,
  That am hither come to visit thee.

"Harp and carp, Thomas," she said;
  "Harp and carp along wi' me;
And if ye dare to kiss my lips,
  Sure of your bodie I will be."-

"Betide me weal, betide me woe,
  That weird ‖ shall never daunto me."—
Syne he has kiss'd her rosy lips,
  All underneath the Eildon Tree.

"Now, ye maun go wi' me," she said;
  "True Thomas, ye maun go wi' me;
And ye maun serve me seven years,
  Thro' weal or woe as may chance t be."

She mounted on her milk-white steed;
  She's ta'en true Thomas up behind:
And aye, whene'er her bridle rung,
  The steed flew swifter than the wind.

O they rade on, and farther on;
  The steed gaed swifter than the wind
Until they reach'd a desert wide,
  And living land was left behind.

---

* Huntley Bank and the adjoining ravine, called from immemorial tradition *The Rhymer's Glen*, were ultimately included in the domain of Abbotsford. The scenery of this glen forms the background of Edwin Landseer's portrait of Sir Walter Scott, painted in 1833.

† Wonder

‡ Each.

§ Bowed.

‖ Destiny shall not alarm me.

Light down, light down, now true Thomas,
And lean your head upon my knee;
Bide and rest a little space,
And I will shew you ferlies three.

O see ye not yon narrow road,
So thick beset with thorns and briers?
That is the path of righteousness,
Though after it but few enquires.

And see ye not that braid braid road,
That lies across that lily leven?
That is the path of wickedness,
Though some call it the road to heaven.

And see not ye that bonny road,
That winds about the fernie brae?
That is the road to fair Elfland,
Where thou and I this night maun gae.

But, Thomas, ye maun hold your tongue,
Whatever ye may hear or see;
For, if ye speak word in Elflyn land,
Ye'll ne'er get back to your ain coun-
trie."

they rade on, and farther on,
And they waded through rivers aboon
the knee,
And they saw neither sun nor moon,
But they heard the roaring of the sea.

It was mirk mirk night, and there was
nae stern light,*
And they waded through red blude to
the knee,
For a' the blude that's shed on earth
Rins through the springs o' that coun-
trie.

Syne they came on to a garden green,
And she pu'd an apple frae a tree †—
"Take this for thy wages, true Thomas;
It will give thee the tongue that can
never lie."—

"My tongue is mine ain," true Thomas
said;
"A gudely gift ye wad gie to me!
I neither dought to buy nor sell,
At fair or tryst where I may be.

"I dought neither speak to prince or
peer,
Nor ask of grace from fair ladye."—
"Now hold thy peace!" the lady said,
"For as I say, so must it be."—

He has gotten a coat of the even cloth,
And a pair of shoes of velvet green;
And till seven years were gane and
past,
True Thomas on earth was never seen.

PART SECOND. — ALTERED FROM ANCIENT PROPHECIES.

THE prophecies, ascribed to Thomas of Ercildoune, have been the principal means of securing to him remembrance "amongst the sons of his people." The author of *Sir Tristrem* would long ago have joined, in the vale of oblivion, "Clerk of Tranent, who wrote the adventure of *Schir Gawain*," if, by good hap, the same current of ideas respecting antiquity, which causes Virgil to be regarded as a magician by the Lazzaroni of Naples, had not exalted the Bard of Ercildoune to the prophetic character. Perhaps, indeed, he himself affected it during his life. We know, at least, for certain, that a belief in his supernatural knowledge was current soon after his death. His prophecies are alluded to by Barbour, by Wintown, and by Henry the Minstrel, or *Blind Harry*, as he is usually termed. None of these authors, however, give the words of any of the Rhymer's vaticinations, but merely narrate, historically, his having predicted the events of which they speak. The earliest of the prophecies ascribed to him, which is now extant, is quoted by Mr. Pinkerton from a MS. It is supposed to be a response from Thomas of Ercildoune to a question from the heroic Countess of March, renowned for the defence of the Castle of Dunbar against the English, and termed, in the familiar dialect of her time, *Black Agnes* of Dunbar. This prophecy is

---

* Star light.

† The traditional commentary upon this ballad informs us, that the apple was the produce of the fatal Tree of Knowledge, and that the garden was the terrestrial paradise. The repugnance of Thomas to be debarred the use of falsehood, when he might find it convenient, has a comic effect.

remarkable, in so far as it bears very little resemblance to any verses published in the printe copy of the Rhymer's supposed prophecies.

Corspatrick (Comes Patrick) Earl of March, but more commonly taking his title fro his castle of Dunbar, acted a noted part during the wars of Edward I. in Scotland. A Thomas of Ercildoune is said to have delivered to him his famous prophecy of King Ale ander's death, the Editor has chosen to introduce him into the following ballad. All th prophetic verses are selected from Hart's publication. *

WHEN seven years were come and gane,
  The sun blinked fair on pool and
    stream;
And Thomas lay on Huntlie Bank,
  Like one awaken'd from a dream.

He heard the trampling of a steed,
  He saw the flash of armor flee,
And he beheld a gallant knight
  Come riding down by the Eildon-tree.

He was a stalwart knight, and strong;
  Of giant make he 'pear'd to be:
He stirr'd his horse, as he were wode,
  Wi' gilded spurs, of faushion free.

Says — "Well met, well met, true
    Thomas!
  Some uncouth ferlies show to me."—
Says — "Christ thee save, Corspatrick
    brave!
  Thrice welcume, good Dunbar, to me!

"Light down, light down, Corspatrick
    brave!
  And I will show thee curses three,
Shall gar fair Scotland greet and grane,
  And change the green to the black
    livery.

"A storm shall roar this very hour,
  From Ross's hill to Solway sea."—
"Ye lied, ye lied, ye warlock hoar,
  For the sun shines sweet on fauld and
    lea."

He put his hand on the Earlie's head;
  He show'd him a rock beside the sea,

Where a king lay stiff beneath his steed
  And steel-dight nobles wiped their e

"The neist curse lights on Branxt
    hills:
  By Flodden's high and heathery side
Shall wave a banner red as blude,
  And chieftains throng wi' meikle pric

"A Scottish king shall come full keen
  The ruddy lion beareth he;
A feather'd arrow sharp, I ween
  Shall make him wink and warre to se

"When he is bloody, and all to bledd
  Thus to his men he still shall say:—
'For God's sake, turn ye back again,
  And give yon southern folk a fray!
Why should I lose the right is mine?
  My doom is not to die this day.' ‡

"Yet turn ye to the eastern hand,
  And woe and wonder ye sall see;
How forty thousand spearmen stand,
  Where yon rank river meets t
    sea."

"There shall the lion lose the gylte,
  And the libbards § bear it clean awa
At Pinkyn Cleuch there shall be spilt
  Much gentil bluid that day."—

"Enough, enough, of curse and ban;
  Some blessings show thou now to me
Or, by the faith o' my bodie," Corspatri
    said,
  "Ye shall rue the day ye e'er sa
    me!"—

* Prophecies supposed to have been delivered by True Thomas, Bede, Merlin, etc., publishe by Andro Hart, 1615. An exact reprint of Hart's volume, from the copy in the library at Abbot ford, under the care of the learned antiquary Mr. David Laing of Edinburgh, was announced in 18 as soon to appear.

† King Alexander III., killed by a fall from his horse near Kinghorn.

‡ The uncertainty which long prevailed in Scotland, concerning the fate of James IV., well known.

§ Leopards of Plantagenet. The Scottish banner is a lion on a field *gules;* the Englis banner then was the three leopards.

The first of blessings I shall thee show,
Is by a burn, that's call'd of bread;[*]
here Saxon men shall tine the bow,
And find their arrows lack the head.

Beside that brigg, out ower that burn,
Where the water bickereth bright and
    sheen,
all many a fallen courser spurn,
And knights shall die in battle keen.

Beside a headless cross of stone,
The libbards there shall lose the gree:
e raven shall come, the erne shall go,
And drink the Saxon bluid sae free.
e cross of stone they shall not know,
So thick the corses there shall be."—

"But tell me, now," said brave Dunbar,
    "True Thomas, tell now unto me,
What man shall rule the isle Britain,
    Even from the north to the southern
        sea?"—

"A French Queen shall bear the son,[†]
    Shall rule all Britain to the sea;
He of the Bruce's blood shall come,
    As near as in the ninth degree.

"The waters worship shall his race;
    Likewise the waves of the farthest
        sea;
For they shall ride over ocean wide,
    With hempen bridles, and horse of
        tree."

PART THIRD. — MODERN.

THOMAS THE RHYMER was renowned among his contemporaries, as the author of the cele-
ated romance of *Sir Tristrem*. Of this once-admired poem only one copy is now known
exist, which is in the Advocates' Library. The Editor, in 1804, published a small edition
this curious work; which, if it does not revive the reputation of the Bard of Ercildoune,
at least the earliest specimen of Scottish poetry hitherto published. Some account of
is romance has already been given to the world in Mr. ELLIS'S *Specimens of Ancient
oetry*, vol. i. p. 165; iii., p. 410; a work to which our predecessors and our posterity are
ike obliged; the former, for the preservation of the best-selected examples of their poetical
ste; and the latter, for a history of the English language, which will only cease to be in-
resting with the existence of our mother-tongue, and all that genius and learning have
corded in it. It is sufficient here to mention, that so great was the reputation of the
mance of *Sir Tristrem*, that few were thought capable of reciting it after the manner of
e author.
The following attempt to commemorate the Rhymer's poetical fame, and the traditional
count of his marvellous return to Fairy Land, being entirely modern, would have been
aced with greater propriety among the class of Modern Ballads, had it not been for its
mediate connection with the first and second parts of the same story.

HEN seven years more were come and
    gone,
Was war through Scotland spread,
d Ruberslaw show'd high Dunyon [‡]
His beacon blazing red.

en all by bonny Coldingknow §
Pitched pallilouns ‖ took their room,

And crested helms, and spears a-rowe,
    Glanced gayly through the broom.

The Leader, rolling to the Tweed,
    Resounds the ensenzie; ¶
They roused the deer from Caddenhead,
    To distant Torwoodlee.**

[*] *Bannock*, or *Breed* Burn. One of Thomas's
mes preserved by tradition runs thus : —

> The burn of breid
> Shall run fou reid.

e bannock is the name given by the Scots to a
ck round cake of unleavened bread.

[†] James VI., son of Mary Queen of *France
d Scotland.

[‡] Hills near Jedburgh.   ‖ Tents.

§ An ancient tower near Ercildoune, belonging

to a family of the name of Home. One of
Thomas's prophecies is said to have run thus : —

"Vengeance! vengeance! when and where?
On the hour of Coldingknow now and ever
    mair!"

The spot is rendered classical by its having
given its name to the beautiful melody, *The
Broom of the Cowdenknows*.

¶ *Ensenzie* — War-cry, or gathering word.

** Places in Selkirkshire.

The feast was spread in Ercildoune,
  In Learmont's high and ancient hall;
And there were knights of great renown,
  And ladies, laced in pall.

Nor lacked they, while they sat at dine,
  The music nor the tale,
Nor goblets of the blood-red wine,
  Nor mantling quaighs * of ale.

True Thomas rose, with harp in hand,
  When as the feast was done:
(In minstrel strife, in Fairy Land,
  The elfin harp he won.)

Hushed were the throng, both limb and tongue,
  And harpers for envy pale;
And armed lords lean'd on their swords,
  And hearken'd to the tale.

In numbers high, the witching tale
  The prophet poured along;
No after bard might e'er avail
  Those numbers to prolong.

Yet fragments of the lofty strain
  Float down the tide of years,
As, buoyant on the stormy main,
  A parted wreck appears.

He sung King Arthur's Table Round:
  The Warrior of the Lake;
How courteous Gawaine met the wound,
  And bled for ladies' sake.

But chief, in gentle Tristrem's praise,
  The notes melodious swell;
Was none excelled in Arthur's days,
  The knight of Lionelle.

For Marke, his cowardly uncle's right,
  A venom'd wound he bore;
When fierce Morholde he slew in fight,
  Upon the Irish shore.

No art the poison might withstand;
  No medicine could be found,
Till lovely Isolde's lily hand
  Had probed the rankling wound.

* *Quaighs* — Wooden cups, composed of staves hooped together.

With gentle hand and soothing tongue
  She bore the leech's part;
And, while she o'er his sick-bed hung,
  He paid her with his heart.

O fatal was the gift, I ween!
  For, doomed in evil tide,
The maid must be rude Cornwall's quee[n]
  His cowardly uncle's bride.

Their loves, their woes, the gifted bar[d]
  In fairy tissue wove;
Where lords, and knights, and ladi[es]
    bright,
  In gay confusion strove.

The Garde Joyeuse, amid the tale,
  High reared its glittering head;
And Avalon's enchanted vale
  In all its wonders spread.

Brangwain was there, and Segramore,
  And fiend-born Merlin's gramarye;
Of that famed wizard's mighty lore,
  O who could sing but he?

Through many a maze the winning son[g]
  In changeful passion led,
Till bent at length the listening throng
  O'er Tristrem's dying bed.

His ancient wounds their scars expand,
  With agony his heart is wrung;
O where is Isolde's lilye hand,
  And where her soothing tongue?

She comes! she comes!—like flash of flam[e]
  Can lovers' footsteps fly:
She comes! she comes! — she only can[e]
  To see her Tristrem die.

She saw him die; her latest sigh
  Joined in a kiss his parting breath,
The gentlest pair that Britain bare,
  United are in death.

There paused the harp: its lingering soun[d]
  Died slowly on the ear;
The silent guests still bent around,
  For still they seemed to hear.

Then woe broke forth in murmurs weak[,]
  Nor ladies heaved alone the sigh;

But half ashamed, the rugged cheek
  Did many a gauntlet dry.

On Leader's stream and Learmont's tower,
  The mists of evening close;
In camp, in castle, or in bower,
  Each warrior sought repose.

Lord Douglas, in his lofty tent,
  Dreamed o'er the woeful tale;
When footsteps light, across the bent,
  The warrior's ear assail.

He starts, he wakes: — " What, Richard, ho !
  Arise, my page, arise !
What venturous wight, at dead of night,
  Dare step where Douglas lies? " —

Then forth they rushed : by Leader's tide,
  A selcouth * sight they see —
A hart and hind pace side by side,
  As white as snow on Fairnalie.†

Beneath the moon, with gesture proud,
  They stately move and slow;
Nor scare they at the gathering crowd,
  Who marvel as they go.

To Learmont's tower a message sped,
  As fast as page might run;
And Thomas started from his bed,
  And soon his clothes did on.

First he woxe pale, and then woxe red;
  Never a word he spake but three : —
My sand is run; my thread is spun;
  This sign regardeth me."

The elfin harp his neck around,
  In minstrel guise, he hung;

* Wondrous.
† An ancient seat upon the Tweed in Selkirkshire.

And on the wind, in doleful sound,
  Its dying accents rung.

Then forth he went; yet turned him oft
  To view his ancient hall :
On the gray tower, in lustre soft,
  The autumn moonbeams fall.

And Leader's waves, like silver sheen,
  Danced shimmering in the ray;
In deepening mass, at distance seen,
  Broad Soltra's mountains lay.

" Farewell, my fathers' ancient tower !
  A long farewell," said he :
" The scene of pleasure, pomp, or power,
  Thou never more shalt be.

" To Learmont's name no foot of earth
  Shall here again belong,
And, on thy hospitable hearth,
  The hare shall leave her young.

" Adieu ! adieu ! " again he cried,
  All as he turn'd him roun' —
" Farewell to Leader's silver tide !
  Farewell to Ercildoune ! "

The hart and hind approached the place,
  As lingering yet he stood;
And there, before Lord Douglas' face,
  With them he crossed the flood.

Lord Douglas leaped on his berry-brown steed,
  And spurred him the Leader o'er;
But, though he rode with lightning speed,
  He never saw them more.

Some said to hill, and some to glen,
  Their wondrous course had been;
But ne'er in haunts of living men
  Again was Thomas seen.

GLENFINLAS; OR, LORD RONALD'S CORONACH.*

THE simple tradition, upon which the following stanzas are founded, runs thus: Whil two Highland hunters were passing the night in a solitary *bothy* (a hut built for the pu pose of hunting), and making merry over their venison and whiskey, one of them expresse a wish that they had pretty lasses to complete their party. The words were scarcely u tered, when two beautiful young women, habited in green, entered the hut, dancing an singing. One of the hunters was seduced by the siren who attached herself particularly t him, to leave the hut: the other remained, and, suspicious of the fair seducers, continue to play upon a trump, or Jew's harp, some strain, consecrated to the Virgin Mary. Da at length came, and the temptress vanished. Searching in the forest, he found the bone of his unfortunate friend, who had been torn to pieces and devoured by the fiend into whos toils he had fallen. The place was from thence called the Glen of the Green Women.

Glenfinlas is a tract of forest-ground, lying in the Highlands of Perthshire, not fro Callender in Menteith. It was formerly a royal forest, and now belongs to the Earl c Moray. This country, as well as the adjacent district of Balquidder, was, in times c yore, chiefly inhabited by the Macgregors. To the west of the Forest of Glenfinlas lie Loch Katrine, and its romantic avenue, called the Trosachs. Benledi, Benmore, and Be voirlich, are mountains in the same district, and at no great distance from Glenfinla The river Teith passes Callender and the Castle of Doune, and joins the Forth near Sti ling. The Pass of Lenny is immediately above Callender, and is the principal access t the Highlands, from that town. Glenartney is a forest, near Benvoirlich. The who forms a sublime tract of alpine scenery.

This ballad first appeared in the *Tales of Wonder*, by Lewis.

> For them the viewless forms of air obey,
> Their bidding heed, and at their beck repair;
> They know what spirit brews the stormful day,
> And heartless oft, like moody madness, stare,
> To see the phantom-train their secret work prepare.—COLLINS.

O HONE a rie'! O hone a rie'! †
The pride of Albin's line is o'er,
And fall'n Glenartney's stateliest tree;
  We ne'er shall see Lord Ronald
  more!—

O, sprung from great Macgillianore,
  The chief that never fear'd a foe,
How matchless was thy broad claymore,
  How deadly thine unerring bow!

Well can the Saxon widows tell, ‡
  How, on the Teith's resounding shore,
The boldest Lowland warriors fell,
  As down from Lenny's pass you bore.

But o'er his hills, in festal day,
  How blazed Lord Ronald's beltane-
  tree,[1]
While youths and maids the light strath-
  spey
  So nimbly danced with Highland glee!

Cheer'd by the strength of Ronald's shel
  E'en age forgot his tresses hoar;
But now the loud lament we swell,
  O ne'er to see Lord Ronald more!

From distant isles a chieftain came,
  The joys of Ronald's halls to find,
And chase with him the dark-brown gam
  That bounds o'er Albin's hills of win

'Twas Moy; whom in Columba's isle
  The Seer's prophetic spirit found,[2]
As, with a minstrel's fire the while,
  He waked his harp's harmonioussoun

Full many a spell to him was known,
  Which wandering spirits shrink to hea
And many a lay of potent tone,
  Was never meant for mortal ear.

For there, 'tis said, in mystic mood,
  High converse with the dead they hol

---

* *Coronach*—is the lamentation for a deceased warrior, sung by the aged of the clan.

† *O hone a rie'*—"Alas for the chief!"

‡ The term Sassenach, or Saxon, is applied by the Highlanders to their Low Country neighbor

nd oft espy the fated shroud,
That shall the future corpse enfold.

so it fell, that on a day,
To rouse the red deer from their den,
ιe Chiefs have ta'en their distant way,
And scour'd the deep Glenfinlas glen.

ɔ vassals wait their sports to aid,
To watch their safety, deck their board;
ιeir simple dress, the Highland plaid,
Their trusty guard, the Highland sword.

ιree summer days, through brake and
    dell,
Their whistling shafts successful flew;
ιd still, when dewy evening fell,
The quarry to their hut they drew.

gray Glenfinlas' deepest nook
The solitary cabin stood,
ιst by Moneira's sullen brook,
Which murmurs through that lonely
    wood.

ɔft fell the night, the sky was calm,
When three successive days had flown;
ιd summer mist in dewy balm
Steep'd heathy bank and mossy stone.

ιe moon, half-hid in silvery flake,
Afar her dubious radiance shed,
ιivering on Katrine's distant lakes
And resting on Benledi's head.

ɔw in their hut, in social guise,
Their sylvan fare the Chiefs enjoy;
ιd pleasure laughs in Ronald's eyes,
As many a pledge he quaffs to Moy.

What lack we here to crown our bliss,
While thus the pulse of joy beats high?
hat, but fair woman's yielding kiss,
Her panting breath and melting eye?

To chase the deer of yonder shades,
This morning left their father's pile
ιe fairest of our mountain maids,
The daughters of the proud Glengyle.

Long have I sought sweet Mary's heart,
And dropp'd the tear, and heaved the
    sigh;
ιt vain the lover's wily art,
Beneath a sister's watchful eye.

"But thou mayst teach that guardian fair,
    While far with Mary I am flown,
Of other hearts to cease her care,
    And find it hard to guard her own.

"Touch but thy harp, thou soon shalt see
    The lovely Flora of Glengyle,
Unmindful of her charge and me,
    Hang on thy notes, 'twixt tear and smile.

"Or, if she choose a melting tale,
    All underneath the greenwood bough,
Will good St. Oran's rule prevail,[3]
    Stern huntsman of the rigid brow!" —

"Since Enrick's fight, since Morna's
    death,
    No more on me shall rapture rise,
Responsive to the panting breath,
    Or yielding kiss, or melting eyes.

"E'en then, when o'er the heath of woe,
    Where sunk my hopes of love and fame,
I bade my harp's wild wailings flow,
    On me the Seer's sad spirit came.

"The last dread curse of angry heaven,
    With ghastly sights and sounds of woe,
To dash each glimpse of joy was given —
    The gift, the future ill to know.

"The bark thou saw'st, yon summer
    morn,
    So gayly part from Oban's bay,
My eye beheld her dash'd and torn,
    Far on the rocky Colonsay.

"Thy Fergus too — thy sister's son,
    Thou saw'st, with pride, the gallant's
    power,
As marching 'gainst the Lord of Downe,
    He left the skirts of huge Benmore.

"Thou only saw'st their tartans * wave,
    As down Benvoirlich's side they
    wound,
Heard'st but the pibroch,† answering
    brave
    To many a target clanking round.

* *Tartans* — the full Highland dress, made of
the checkered stuff so termed.

† *Pibroch* — a piece of martial music, adapted
to the Highland bagpipe.

"I heard the groans, I mark'd the tears,
　I saw the wound his bosom bore,
When on the serried Saxon spears
　He pour'd his clan's resistless roar.

"And thou, who bidst me think of bliss,
　And bidst my heart awake to glee,
And court, like thee, the wanton kiss —
　That heart, O Ronald, bleeds for thee!

"I see the death-damps chill thy brow,
　I hear thy Warning Spirit cry;
The corpse-lights dance — they're gone,
　　and now. . . .
　No more is given to gifted eye!" —

"Alone enjoy thy dreary dreams,
　Sad prophet of the evil hour!
Say, should we scorn joy's transient
　　beams,
　Because to-morrow's storm may lour?

"Or false, or sooth, thy words of woe,
　Clangillian's Chieftain ne'er shall fear;
His blood shall bound at rapture's glow,
　Though doom'd to stain the Saxon
　　spear.

"E'en now, to meet me in yon dell
　My Mary's buskins brush the dew."
He spoke, nor bade the Chief farewell,
　But call'd his dogs, and gay withdrew.

Within an hour return'd each hound;
　In rush'd the rousers of the deer;
They howl'd in melancholy sound,
　Then closely couch'd beside the Seer.

No Ronald yet, though midnight came;
　And sad were Moy's prophetic dreams,
As, bending o'er the dying flame,
　He fed the watch-fire's quivering
　　gleams.

Sudden the hounds erect their ears,
　And sudden cease their moaning howl;
Close press'd to Moy, they mark their fears
　By shivering limbs and stifled growl.

Untouch'd, the harp began to ring,
　As softly, slowly, oped the door;
And shook responsive every string,
　As light a footstep press'd the floor.

And by the watch-fire's glimmering light
　Close by the minstrel's side was seen
A huntress maid, in beauty bright,
　All dropping wet her robes of green.

All dropping wet her garments seem;
　Chill'd was her cheek, her bosom bare
As, bending o'er the dying gleam,
　She wrung the moisture from her hair.

With maiden blush, she softly said: —
　"O gentle huntsman, hast thou seen
In deep Glenfinlas' moonlight glade,
　A lovely maid in vest of green;

"With her a Chief in Highland pride,
　His shoulders bear the hunter's bow,
The mountain dirk adorns his side,
　Far on the wind his tartans flow?" —

"And who art thou? and who are they?"
　All ghastly gazing, Moy replied:
"'And why, beneath the moon's pale ray
　Dare ye thus roam Glenfinlas' side?"—

"Where wild Loch Katrine pours her tide
　Blue, dark, and deep, round many a
　　isle,
Our father's towers o'erhang her side,
　The castle of the bold Glengyle.

"To chase the dun Glenfinlas deer,
　Our woodland course this morn we bore
And haply met, while wandering here,
　The son of great Macgillianore.

"O aid me, then, to seek the pair,
　Whom, loitering in the woods, I lost
Alone, I dare not venture there,
　Where walks, they say, the shrieking
　　ghost." —

"Yes, many a shrieking ghost walks
　　there;
　Then, first, my own sad vow to keep
Here will I pour my midnight prayer,
　Which still must rise when mortals
　　sleep."—

"O first, for pity's gentle sake,
　Guide a lone wanderer on her way!
For I must cross the haunted brake,
　And reach my father's towers ere day

First, three times tell each Ave-bead,
And thrice a Pater-noster say;
Then kiss with me the holy rede;
So shall we safely wend our way."—

O shame to knighthood, strange and
foul!
Go, doff the bonnet from thy brow,
And shroud thee in the monkish cowl,
Which best befits thy sullen vow.

Not so, by high Dunlathmon's fire,
Thy heart was froze to love and joy,
When gayly rung thy raptured lyre
To wanton Morna's melting eye."

Wild stared the minstrel's eyes of flame,
And high his sable locks arose,
And quick his color went and came,
As fear and rage alternate rose.

And thou! when by the blazing oak
I lay, to her and love resign'd,
Say, rode ye on the eddying smoke,
Or sail'd ye on the midnight wind?

Not thine a race of mortal blood,
Nor old Glengyle's pretended line;
Thy dame, the Lady of the Flood—
Thy sire, the Monarch of the Mine."

He mutter'd thrice St. Oran's rhyme,
And thrice St. Fillan's powerful
prayer; [4]
Then turn'd him to the eastern clime,
And sternly shook his coal-black hair.

And, bending o'er the harp, he flung
His wildest witch-notes on the wind;
And 'loud, and high, and strange, they
rung
As many a magic change they find.

Tall wax'd the Spirit's altering form,
Till to the roof her stature grew:
Then, mingling with the rising storm,
With one wild yell away she flew.

Rain beats, hail rattles, whirlwinds tear:
The slender hut in fragments flew;
But not a lock of Moy's loose hair
Was waved by wind, or wet by dew.

Wild mingling with the howling gale,
Loud bursts of ghastly laughter rise;
High o'er the minstrel's head they sail,
And die amid the northern skies.

The voice of thunder shook the wood,
As ceased the more than mortal yell;
And, spattering foul, a shower of blood
Upon the hissing firebrands fell.

Next dropp'd from high a mangled
arm;
The fingers strain'd a half-drawn blade;
And last, the life-blood streaming warm,
Torn from the trunk, a gasping head.

Oft o'er that head, in battling field,
Stream'd the proud crest of high Ben-
more;
That arm the broad claymore could wield,
Which dyed the Teith with Saxon
gore.

Woe to Moneira's sullen rills!
Woe to Glenfinlas' dreary glen!
There never son of Albin's hills
Shall draw the hunter's shaft agen.

E'en the tired pilgrim's burning feet
At noon shall shun that sheltering den,
Lest, journeying in their rage, he meet
The wayward Ladies of the Glen.

And we—behind the Chieftain's shield,
No more shall we in safety dwell;
None leads the people to the field—
And we the loud lament must swell.

O hone a rie'! O hone a rie'!
The pride of Albin's line is o'er!
And fall'n Glenartney's stateliest tree;
We ne'er shall see Lord Ronald more!

Lewis's collection produced also what Scott
justly calls his "first serious attempts in verse;"
and of these the earliest appears to have been the
Glenfinlas. Here the scene is laid in the most
favorite district of his favorite Perthshire Highlands; and the Gaelic tradition on which it is
founded was far more likely to draw out the
secret strength of his genius, as well as to arrest
the feelings of his countrymen, than any subject with which the stores of German *diablerie*
could have supplied him.— *Life of Scott*, vol.
ii., p. 25.

THE EVE OF ST. JOHN.

SMAYLHO'ME, or Smallholm Tower, the scene of the following ballad, is situated on th northern boundary of Roxburghshire, among a cluster of wild rocks, called Sandiknow Crags, the property of Hugh Scott, Esq., of Harden [Lord Polwarth]. The tower is a high square building, surrounded by an outer wall, now ruinous. The circuit of the oute court, being defended on three sides by a precipice and morass, is accessible only from th west, by a steep and rocky path. The apartments, as is usual in a Border keep, or fortress are placed one above another, and communicate by a narrow stair ; on the roof are tw bartizans, or platforms, for defence or pleasure. The inner door of the tower is wood, th outer an iron gate ; the distance between them being nine feet, the thickness, namely, o the wall. From the elevated situation of Smaylho'me Tower, it is seen many miles i every direction. Among the crags by which it is surrounded, one, more eminent, is calle the *Watchfold*, and is said to have been the station of a beacon, in the times of war wit England. Without the tower-court is a ruined chapel. Brotherstone is a heath, in th neighborhood of Smaylho'me Tower.

This ballad was first printed in Mr. LEWIS's *Tales of Wonder*. It is here publishe with some additional illustrations, particularly an account of the battle of Ancram Moor which seemed proper in a work upon Border antiquities. The catastrophe of the tale i founded upon a well-known Irish tradition. The ancient fortress and its vicinity forme the scene of the Editor's infancy, and seemed to claim from him this attempt to celebrat them in a Border tale.

THE Baron of Smaylho'me rose with day,
   He spurr'd his courser on,
Without stop or stay down the rocky way,
   That leads to Brotherstone.

He went not with the bold Buccleuch,
   His banner broad to rear;
He went not 'gainst the English yew,
   To lift the Scottish spear.

Yet his plate-jack * was braced, and his
   helmet was laced,
   And his vaunt-brace of proof he wore :
At his saddle-gerthe was a good steel
   sperthe,
   Full ten pound weight and more.

The Baron return'd in three days' space,
   And his looks were sad and sour;
And weary was his courser's pace,
   As he reach'd his rocky tower.

He came not from where Ancram Moor [1]
   Ran red with English blood;
Where the Douglas true, and the bold
   Buccleuch,
   'Gainst keen Lord Evers stood.

* The plate-jack is coat-armor ; the vaunt-brace or wam-brace, armor for the body ; the sperthe, a battle-ax.

Yet was his helmet hack'd and hew'd,
   His acton pierced and tore,
His axe and his dagger with blood im
   brued, —
   But it was not English gore.

He lighted at the Chapellage,
   He held him close and still;
And he whistled thrice for his little foot
   page;
   His name was English Will.

"Come thou hither, my little foot-page,
   Come hither to my knee;
Though thou art young and tender o
   age,
   I think thou art true to me.

"Come, tell me all that thou hast seen,
   And look thou tell me true !
Since I from Smaylho'me tower hav
   been,
   What did thy lady do ? " —

"My lady, each night, sought the lonel
   light,
   That burns on the wild Watchfold;
For, from height to height, the beacon
   bright
   Of the English foemen told.

The bittern clamor'd from the moss,
The wind blew loud and shrill;
Yet the craggy pathway she did cross
To the eiry Beacon Hill.

I watch'd her steps, and silent came
Where she sat her on a stone; —
No watchman stood by the dreary flame,
It burned all alone.

The second night I kept her in sight,
Till to the fire she came,
And, by Mary's might! an Armed Knight
Stood by the lonely flame.

And many a word that warlike lord
Did speak to my lady there;
But the rain fell fast, and loud blew the
blast,
And I heard not what they were.

The third night there the sky was fair,
And the mountain-blast was still,
As again I watch'd the secret pair,
On the lonesome Beacon Hill.

And I heard her name the midnight hour,
And name this holy eve;
And say, ' Come this night to thy lady's
bower,
Ask no bold Baron's leave.

' He lifts his spear with the bold Buc-
cleuch;
His lady is all alone;
The door she'll undo, to her knight so
true,
On the eve of good St. John.' —

' I cannot come; I must not come:
I dare not come to thee;
On the eve of St. John I must wander
alone:
In thy bower I may not be.' —

' Now, out on thee, fainthearted knight!
Thou shouldst not say me nay;
For the eve is sweet, and when lovers meet,
Is worth the whole summer's day.

' And I'll chain the blood-hound, and
the warder shall not sound,
And rushes shall be strew'd on the stair:

So, by the black-rood stone,* and by holy
St. John,
I conjure thee, my love, to be there!'

" ' Though the blood-hound be mute, and
the rush beneath my foot,
And the warder his bugle should not
blow,
Yet there sleepeth a priest in a chamber
to the east,
And my footstep he would know.' —

" ' O fear not the priest, who sleepeth
to the east!
For to Dryburgh † the way he has
ta'en;
And there to say mass, till three days do
pass,
For the soul of a knight that is slayne.'

" He turn'd him around, and grimly he
frown'd;
Then he laugh'd right scornfully —
' He who says the mass-rite for the soul
of that knight,
May as well say mass for me!

" ' At the lone midnight hour, when bad
spirits have power,
In thy chamber will I be.'
With that he was gone, and my lady left
alone,
And no more did I see."

Then changed, I trow, was that bold
Baron's brow,
From the dark to the blood-red high;
" Now, tell me the mien of the knight
thou hast seen,
For, by Mary, he shall die!" —

" His arms shone full bright, in the bea-
con's red light:
His plume it was scarlet and blue;
On his shield was a hound, in a silver
leash bound,
And his crest was a branch of the yew.'

---

* The black-rood of Melrose was a crucifix of
black marble, and of superior sanctity.

† Dryburgh Abbey stands on the banks of the
Tweed. After its dissolution, it became the
property of the Haliburtons of Newmains, and
afterwards the seat of the Earls of Buchan.

"Thou liest, thou liest, thou little foot-
page,
    Loud dost thou lie to me!
For that knight is cold, and low laid in
    the mould,
    All under the Eildon-tree." * —

"Yet hear but my word, my noble lord!
    For I heard her name his name;
And that lady bright she called the knight
    Sir Richard of Coldinghame!"

The bold Baron's brow then changed, I
    trow,
    From high blood-red to pale —
"The grave is deep and dark — and the
    corpse is stiff and stark —
    So I may not trust thy tale.

"Where fair Tweed flows round holy
    Melrose,
    And Eildon slopes to the plain,
Full three nights ago, by some secret
    foe,
    That gay gallant was slain.

"The varying light deceived thy sight,
    And the wild winds drown'd the name;
For the Dryburgh bells ring, and the
    white monks do sing,
    For Sir Richard of Coldinghame!"

He pass'd the court-gate, and he oped
    the tower-gate,
    And he mounted the narrow stair,
To the bartizan-seat, where, with maids
    that on her wait,
    He found his lady fair.

That lady sat in mournful mood;
    Look'd over hill and vale;
Over Tweed's fair flood, and Mertoun's
    wood,
    And all down Teviotdale.

"Now hail, now hail, thou lady
    bright!" —
    "Now hail, thou Baron true!

* Eildon is a high hill, terminating in three
conical summits, immediately above the town of
Melrose, where are the admired ruins of a magnificent monastery. Eildon-tree is said to be
the spot where Thomas the Rhymer uttered
prophecies.

What news, what news, from Ancram
    fight?
What news from the bold Buc-
    cleuch?" —

"The Ancram moor is red with gore,
    For many a Southron fell;
And Buccleuch has charged us, evermore
    To watch our beacons well." —

The lady blush'd red, but nothing sh
    said:
    Nor added the Baron a word:
Then she stepp'd down the stair to her
    chamber fair,
    And so did her moody lord.

In sleep the lady mourn'd, and the Baro
    toss'd and turn'd,
    And oft to himself he said: —
"The worms around him creep, and hi
    bloody grave is deep. * * *
    It cannot give up the dead!" —

It was near the ringing of matin-bell,
    The night was well-nigh done,
When a heavy sleep on that baron fell,
    On the eve of good St. John.

The lady look'd through the chambe
    fair,
    By the light of a dying flame;
And she was aware of a knight stoo
    there —
    Sir Richard of Coldinghame!

"Alas! away! away!" she cried,
    "For the holy Virgin's sake!" —
"Lady, I know who sleeps by thy side,
    But, lady, he will not awake.

"By Eildon-tree, for long nights three,
    In bloody grave have I lain;
The mass and the death-prayer are sai
    for me,
    But, lady, they are said in vain.

"By the Baron's brand, near Tweed'
    fair strand,
    Most foully slain, I fell;
And my restless sprite, on the beacon
    height,
    For a space is doom'd to dwell,

At our trysting-place, for a certain space,
I must wander to and fro:
…t I had not had power to come to thy
    bower,
Hadst thou not conjured me so."

…ve master'd fear—her brow she cross'd;
" How, Richard, hast thou sped?
…d art thou saved, or art thou lost?" —
The vision shook his head!

…Who spilleth life, shall forfeit life;
    So bid thy lord believe:
…at lawless love is guilt above,
    This awful sign receive.

…e laid his left palm on an oaken beam:
    His right upon her hand;

The lady shrunk, and fainting sunk,
    For it scorch'd like a fiery brand.

The sable score, of fingers four,
    Remains on that board impress'd;
And for evermore that lady wore
    A covering on her wrist.[2]

There is a nun in Dryburgh bower,
    Ne'er looks upon the sun;
There is a monk in Melrose tower,
    He speaketh word to none.

That nun, who ne'er beholds the day,[3]
    That monk, who speaks to none —
That nun was Smaylho'me's Lady
    gay,
    That monk the bold Baron.

CADYOW CASTLE.

THE ruins of Cadyow or Cadzow Castle, the ancient baronial residence of the family of …amilton, are situated upon the precipitous banks of the river Evan, about two miles above …s junction with the Clyde. It was dismantled, in the conclusion of the Civil Wars, during …e reign of the unfortunate Mary, to whose cause the house of Hamilton devoted them-…lves with a generous zeal, which occasioned their temporary obscurity, and very nearly …eir total ruin. The situation of the ruins, embosomed in wood, darkened by ivy and …eeping shrubs, and overhanging the brawling torrent, is romantic in the highest degree. … the immediate vicinity of Cadyow is a grove of immense oaks, the remains of the Cale-…nian Forest, which anciently extended through the south of Scotland, from the eastern … the Atlantic Ocean. Some of these trees measure twenty-five feet and upwards, in cir-…mference; and the state of decay, in which they now appear, shows that they may have …itnessed the rites of the Druids. The whole scenery is included in the magnificent and …tensive park of the Duke of Hamilton. There was long preserved in this forest the breed … the Scottish wild cattle, until their ferocity occasioned their being extirpated, about forty …ars ago.* Their appearance was beautiful, being milk-white, with black muzzles, horns, …d hoofs. The bulls are described by ancient authors as having white manes; but those … latter days had lost that peculiarity, perhaps by intermixture with the tame breed.†

In detailing the death of the Regent Murray, which is made the subject of the following …llad, it would be injustice to my readers to use other words than those of Dr. Robertson, …hose account of that memorable event forms a beautiful piece of historical painting.

" Hamilton of Bothwellhaugh was the person who committed this barbarous action. He …d been condemned to death soon after the battle of Langside, as we have already related. …d owed his life to the Regent's clemency. But part of his estate had been bestowed upon …e of the Regent's favorites,‡ who seized his house, and turned out his wife, naked, in a …ld night, into the open fields, where, before next morning, she became furiously mad. This …jury made a deeper impression on him than the benefit he had received, and from that …oment he vowed to be revenged of the Regent. Party rage strengthened and inflamed

---

* The editor of the edition of 1833 says that a magnificent herd of these cattle still remained till …out that time in Cadyow Forest.

† They were formerly kept in the park of Drumlanrig, and are still to be seen at Chillingham …stle in Northumberland.

‡ This was Sir James Bellenden, Lord Justice-Clerk, whose shameful and inhuman rapacity …casioned the catastrophe in the text. — SPOTTISWOODE.

his private resentment. His kinsmen, the Hamiltons, applauded the enterprise. Th maxim of that age justified the most desperate course he could take to obtain vengeanc He followed the Regent for some time, and watched for an opportunity to strike the blov He resolved at last to wait till his enemy should arrive at Linlithgow, through which l was to pass in his way from Stirling to Edinburgh. He took his stand in a wooden ga lery, * which had a window towards the street; spread a feather-bed on the floor, to hinde the noise of his feet from being heard, hung up a black cloth behind him, that his shado might not be observed from without, and, after all this preparation, calmly expected th Regent's approach, who had lodged, during the night, in a house not far distant. Son indistinct information of the danger which threatened him had been conveyed to the Regen and he paid so much regard to it that he resolved to return by the same gate through whic he had entered, and to fetch a compass round the town. But, as the crowd about the gat was great, and he himself unacquainted with fear, he proceeded directly along the street and the throng of people obliging him to move very slowly, gave the assassin time to tak so true an aim, that he shot him, with a single bullet, through the lower part of his bell and killed the horse of a gentleman who rode on his other side. His followers instantl endeavored to break into the house whence the blow had come; but they found the doc strongly barricaded, and, before it could be forced open, Hamilton had mounted a flee horse,† which stood ready for him at a back passage, and was got far beyond their reach The Regent died the same night of his wound." — *History of Scotland*, book v.

Bothwellhaugh rode straight to Hamilton, where he was received in triumph; for th ashes of the houses in Clydesdale, which had been burned by Murray's army, were ye smoking; and party prejudice, the habits of the age, and the enormity of the provocation seemed to his kinsmen to justify the deed. After a short abode at Hamilton, this fierc and determined man left Scotland, and served in France, under the patronage of the famil of Guise, to whom he was doubtless recommended by having avenged the cause of the niece, Queen Mary, upon her ungrateful brother. De Thou has recorded that an attemp was made to engage him to assassinate Gaspar de Coligni, the famous admiral of Franc and the buckler of the Huguenot cause. But the character of Bothwellhaugh was mistake He was no mercenary trader in blood, and rejected the offer with contempt and indignatio He had no authority, he said, from Scotland to commit murders in France; he had avenge his own just quarrel, but he would neither for price nor prayer avenge that of another mar — *Thuanus*, chap. 46.

The Regent's death happened 23rd January, 1569. It is applauded or stigmatized, b contemporary historians, according to their religious or party prejudices. The triump of Blackwood is unbounded. He not only extols the pious feat of Bothwellhaugh, " who he observes, "satisfied with a single ounce of lead, him whose sacrilegious avarice ha stripped the metropolitan church of St. Andrews of its covering:" but he ascribes it to im mediate divine inspiration, and the escape of Hamilton to little less than the miraculou interference of the Deity. — JEBB, vol. ii. p. 263. With equal injustice, it was, by other made the ground of a general national reflection; for, when Mather urged Berney to assa sinate Burleigh, and quoted the example of Poltrot and Bothwellhaugh, the other conspir tor answered "that neyther Poltrot nor Hambleton did attempt their enterpryse withou some reason or consideration to lead them to it; as the one, by hyre, and promise of prefe ment or rewarde; the other, upon desperate mind of revenge, for a lyttle wrong done unt him, as the report goethe, according to the vyle trayterous disposysyon of the hoole natyo of the Scottes." — MURDIN's *State Papers*, vol. i. p. 197.

Addressed to the Right Honorable Lady Anne Hamilton.‡

WHEN princely Hamilton's abode
Ennobled Cadyow's Gothic towers,
The song went round, the goblet flow'd,
And revel sped the laughing hours.

Then, thrilling to the harp's gay sound,
So sweetly rung each vaulted wall,
And echoed light the dancer's bound,
As mirth and music cheer'd the hall.

---

* The house to which this projecting gallery was attached was the property of the Archbishop St. Andrews, a natural brother to the Duke of Châtelherault, and uncle to Bothwellhaugh. Thi among many other circumstances, seems to evince the aid which Bothwellhaugh received from h clan in effecting his purpose.

† The gift of Lord John Hamilton, Commendator of Arbroath.

‡ Eldest daughter of Archibald, 9th Duke of Hamilton.

But Cadyow's towers, in ruin laid,
  And vaults, by ivy mantled o'er,
Thrill to the music of the shade,
  Or echo Evan's hoarser roar.

Yet still, of Cadyow's faded fame,
  You bid me tell a minstrel tale,
And tune my harp, of Border frame,
  On the wild banks of Evandale.

For thou, from scenes of courtly pride,
  From pleasure's lighter scenes, canst turn,
To draw oblivion's pall aside,
  And mark the long-forgotten urn.

Then, noble maid! at thy command,
  Again the crumbled halls shall rise.
Lo! as on Evan's banks we stand,
  The past returns — the present flies.

Where, with the rock's wood-cover'd side,
  Were blended late the ruins green,
Rise turrets in fantastic pride,
  And feudal banners flaunt between:

There the rude torrent's brawling course,
  Was shagg'd with thorn and tangling sloe,
The ashler buttress braves its force,
  And ramparts frown in battled row.

'Tis night — the shade of keep and spire
  Obscurely dance on Evan's stream;
And on the wave the warder's fire
  Is checkering the moonlight beam.

Fades slow their light; the east is gray;
  The weary warder leaves his tower;
Steeds snort, uncoupled stag-hounds bay,
  And merry hunters quit the bower.

The drawbridge falls — they hurry out —
  Clatters each plank and swinging chain,
As, dashing o'er, the jovial rout
  Urge the shy steed, and slack the rein.

First of his troop, the Chief rode on;*
  His shouting merry-men throng behind;

The steed of princely Hamilton
  Was fleeter than the mountain wind.

From the thick copse the roebucks bound,
  The startled red-deer scuds the plain,
For the hoarse bugle's warrior-sound
  Has roused the mountain haunts again.

Through the huge oaks of Evandale,
  Whose limbs a thousand years have worn,
What sullen roar comes down the gale,
  And drowns the hunter's pealing horn?

Mightiest of all the beasts of chase,
  That roam in woody Caledon,
Crashing the forest in his race,
  The Mountain Bull comes thundering on.

Fierce, on the hunter's quiver'd band,
  He rolls his eyes of swarthy glow,
Spurns, with black hoof and horn, the sand,
  And tosses high his mane of snow.

Aim'd well, the Chieftain's lance has flown;
  Struggling in blood the savage lies;
His roar is sunk in hollow groan —
  Sound, merry huntsman! sound the *pryse!* [1]

'Tis noon — against the knotted oak
  The hunters rest the idle spear;
Curls through the trees the slender smoke,
  Where yeoman dight the woodland cheer.

Proudly the Chieftain mark'd his clan,
  On greenwood lap all careless thrown,
Yet miss'd his eye the boldest man
  That bore the name of Hamilton.

"Why fills not Bothwellhaugh his place,
  Still wont our weal and woe to share?
Why comes he not our sport to grace?
  Why shares he not our hunter's fare!" —

---

* The head of the family of Hamilton, at this period, was James, Earl of Arran, Duke of Châtel-

herault, in France, and first peer of the Scottish realm. In 1569 he was appointed by Queen Mary her lieutenant-general in Scotland, under the singular title of her adopted father.

Stern Claud replied,[2] with darkening
   face,
(Gray Paisley's haughty lord was he,)
" At merry feast, or buxom chase,
   No more the warrior wilt thou see.

" Few suns have set since Woodhouselee[3]
   Saw Bothwellhaugh's bright goblets
   foam,
When to his hearths, in social glee,
   The war-worn soldier turn'd him
   home.

" There, wan from her maternal throes,
   His Margaret, beautiful and mild,
Sate in her bower, a pallid rose,
   And peaceful nursed her new-born
   child.

" O change accursed! past are those
   days;
   False Murray's ruthless spoilers came,
And, for the heart's domestic blaze,
   Ascends destruction's volumed flame.

" What sheeted phantom wanders wild,
   Where mountain Eske through wood-
   land flows,
Her arms enfold a shadowy child —
   Oh! is it she, the pallid rose?

" The wilder'd traveller sees her glide,
   And hears her feeble voice with awe —
' Revenge,' she cries, ' on Murray's pride!
   And woe for injured Bothwellhaugh!'"

He ceased — and cries of rage and grief
   Burst mingling from the kindred band,
And half arose the kindling Chief,
   And half unsheathed his Arran brand.

But who, o'er bush, o'er stream and
   rock,
   Rides headlong with resistless speed,
Whose bloody poniard's frantic stroke
   Drives to the leap his jaded steed;[4]

Whose cheek is pale, whose eyeballs
   glare,
   As one some vision'd sight that saw,
Whose hands are bloody, loose his
   hair? —
   'Tis he! 'tis he! 'tis Bothwellhaugh.

From gory selle,* and reeling steed,
   Sprung the fierce horseman with
   bound,
And, reeking from the recent deed,
   He dash'd his carbine on the ground.

Sternly he spoke: — " ' Tis sweet t
   hear
In good greenwood the bugle blown,
But sweeter to Revenge's ear,
   To drink a tyrant's dying groan.

" Your slaughter'd quarry proudly trode
   At dawning morn, o'er dale and down
But prouder base-born Murray rode
   Through old Linlithgow's crowde
   town.

" From the wild Border's humbled side,
   In haughty triumph marched he,
While Knox relax'd his bigot pride,
   And smiled, the traitorous pomp t
   see.

" But can stern Power, with all his vaun
   Or Pomp, with all her courtly glare,
The settled heart of Vengeance daunt,
   Or change the purpose of Despair!

" With hackbut bent,[6] my secret stand
   Dark as the purposed deed, I chose,
And mark'd, where, mingling in h
   band,
   Troop'd Scottish pikes and Englis
   bows.

" Dark Morton,† girt with many a spea
   Murder's foul minion, led the van;
And clash'd their broadswords in th
   rear
   The wild Macfarlanes' plaided clan.[7]

" Glencairn and stout Parkhead[8] wer
   nigh,
Obsequious at their Regent's rein,
And haggard Lindesay's iron eye,
   That saw fair Mary weep in vain.[9]

* _Selle_ — saddle. A word used by Spens
and other ancient authors.

† Of this noted person, it is enough to sa
that he was active in the murder of David Rizzi
and at least privy to that of Darnley.

" Mid pennon'd spears, a steely grove,
 Proud Murray's plumage floated high;
Scarce could his trampling charger move,
 So close the minions crowded nigh.[10]

" From the raised visor's shade, his eye,
 Dark-rolling, glanced the ranks along,
And his steel truncheon, waved on high,
 Seem'd marshalling the iron throng.

" But yet his sadden'd brow confessed
 A passing shade of doubt and awe;
Some fiend was whispering in his breast,
 ' Beware of injured Bothwellhaugh!'

" The death-shot parts — the charger
  springs —
 Wild rises tumult's startling roar!
And Murray's plumy helmet rings —
 — Rings on the ground, to rise no
  more.

" What joy the raptured youth can feel,
 To hear her love the loved one tell —
Or he, who broaches on his steel
 The wolf, by whom his infant fell!

" But dearer to my injured eye
 To see in dust proud Murray roll,
And mine was ten times trebled joy,
 To hear him groan his felon soul,

" My Margaret's spectre glided near,
 With pride her bleeding victim saw;

And shriek'd in his death-deafen'd ear,
 ' Remember injured Bothwellhaugh!'

" Then speed thee, noble Châtlerault!
 Spread to the wind thy banner'd tree! *
Each warrior bend his Clydesdale bow!—
 Murray is fall'n, and Scotland free!"

Vaults every warrior to his steed;
 Loud bugles join their wild acclaim:—
" Murray is fall'n, and Scotland freed!
 Couch, Arran! couch thy spear of
  flame!"

But, see! the minstrel vision fails —
 The glimmering spears are seen no
  more,
The shouts of war die on the gales,
 Or sink in Evan's lonely roar.

For the loud bugle, pealing high,
 The blackbird whistles down the
And sunk in ivied ruins lie
 The banner'd towers of Evandale.

For chiefs, intent on bloody deed,
 And vengeance shouting o'er the slain,
Lo! high-born Beauty rules the steed,
 Or graceful guides the silken rein.

And long may Peace and Plenty own
 The maids who list the minstrel's tale;
Nor e'er a ruder guest be known
 On the fair banks of Evandale!

THE GRAY BROTHER.

A FRAGMENT.

THE imperfect state of this ballad, which was written several years ago, is not a cir-cumstance affected for the purpose of giving it that peculiar interest which is often found to arise from ungratified curiosity. On the contrary, it was the Editor's intention to have completed the tale, if he had found himself able to succeed to his own satisfaction. Yield-ing to the opinion of persons, whose judgment, if not biased by the partiality of friendship, is entitled to deference, he has preferred inserting these verses as a fragment, to his inten-tion of entirely suppressing them.

The tradition upon which the tale is founded, regards a house upon the barony of Gil-merton, near Lasswade, in Mid-Lothian. This building, now called Gilmerton Grange, was originally named Burndale, from the following tragic adventure. The barony of Gil-merton belonged, of yore, to a gentleman named Heron, who had one beautiful daughter.

---

* An oak, half-sawn, with the motto *through*, is an ancient cognizance of the family of Hamilton.

This young lady was seduced by the Abbot of Newbattle, a richly endowed abbey, upo the banks of the South Esk, now a seat of the Marquis of Lothian. Heron came to th knowledge of this circumstance, and learned also that the lovers carried on their guilt intercourse by the connivance of the lady's nurse, who lived at this house of Gilmerto Grange, or Burndale. He formed a resolution of bloody vengeance, undeterred by th supposed sanctity of the clerical character, or by the stronger claims of natural affection Choosing, therefore, a dark and windy night, when the objects of his vengeance wer engaged in a stolen interview, he set fire to a stack of dried thorns and other combustibles which he had caused to be piled against the house, and reduced to a pile of glowing ashe the dwelling, with all its inmates.*

The scene with which the ballad opens, was suggested by the following curious passage extracted from the life of Alexander Peden, one of the wandering and persecuted teacher of the sect of Cameronians, during the reign of Charles II. and his successor, James. Thi person was supposed by his followers, and, perhaps, really believed himself, to be pos sessed of supernatural gifts; for the wild scenes which they frequented, and the constan dangers which were incurred through their proscription, deepened upon their minds th gloom of superstition, so general in that age: —

" About the same time he [Peden] came to Andrew Normand's house, in the parish o Alloway, in the shire of Ayr, being to preach at night in his barn. After he came in, he halted a little, leaning upon a chair-back, with his face covered; when he lifted up hi head, he said, ' They are in this house that I have not one word of salvation unto;' he halted a little again, saying, 'This is strange, that the devil will not go out, that we may begin our work.' Then there was a woman went out, ill-looked upon almost all her life and to her dying hour, for a witch, with many presumptions of the same. It escaped me in the former passages, what John Murhead (whom I have often mentioned) told me, tha when he came from Ireland to Galloway, he was at family-worship, and giving some notes of the Scripture read, when a very ill-looking man came, and sat down within the door, a the back of the *hallan* [partition of the cottage]: immediately he halted and said, ' There is some unhappy body just now come into this house. I charge him to go out, and no stop my mouth!' This person went out, and he *insisted* (went on), yet he saw him neither come in nor go out." — *The Life and Prophecies of Mr. Alexander Peden, late Minister of the Gospel at New Glenluce, in Galloway,* part ii., § 26.

A friendly correspondent remarks, " that the incapacity of proceeding in the perform ance of a religious duty, when a contaminated person is present, is of much higher antiq uity than the era of the Rev. Mr. Alexander Peden." — *Vide Hygini Fabulas,* cap. 26. " *Medea Corintho exul, Athenas, ad Ægeum Pandionis filium devenit in hospitium, eique nupsit.*

———— " *Postea sacerdos Dianæ Medeam exagitare cæpit, regique negabat sacra caste facere posse, eo quod in ea civitate esset mulier venefica et scelerata; tunc exulatur.*"

THE Pope he was saying the high, high
  mass,
  All on St. Peter's day,
With the power to him given, by the
  saints in heaven,
  To wash men's sins away.

The Pope he was saying the blessed mass,
  And the people kneel'd around,
And from each man's soul his sins did
  pass,
  As he kissed the holy ground.

And all, among the crowded throng,
  Was still both limb and tongue,

While through vaulted roof and aisles aloof
  The holy accents rung.

At the holiest word he quiver'd for fear
  And falter'd in the sound —
And when he would the chalice rear,
  He dropp'd it to the ground.

" The breath of one of evil deed
  Pollutes our sacred day;
He has no portion in our creed,
  No part in what I say.

" A being, whom no blessed word
  To ghostly peace can bring;

* This tradition was communicated to me by John Clerk, Esq., of Eldin, author of an " Essay upon Naval Tactics," who will be remembered by posterity as having taught the genius of Britain to concentrate her thunders, and to launch them against her foes with an unerring aim.

wretch, at whose approach abhorr'd,
  Recoils each holy thing.

Up, up, unhappy! haste, arise!
  My adjuration fear!
charge thee not to stop my voice,
  Nor longer tarry here!"

mid them all a pilgrim kneel'd,
  In gown of sackcloth gray;
ar journeying from his native field,
  He first saw Rome that day.

or forty days and nights so drear,
  I ween he had not spoke,
nd, save with bread and water clear,
  His fast he ne'er had broke.

mid the penitential flock,
  Seem'd none more bent to pray;
But, when the Holy Father spoke,
  He rose and went his way.

Again unto his native land
  His weary course he drew;
To Lothian's fair and fertile strand,
  And Pentland's mountains blue.

His unblest feet his native seat,
  Mid Esk's fair woods, regain;
Through woods more fair no stream more
    sweet
  Rolls to the eastern main.

And lords to meet the pilgrim came,
  And vassals bent the knee;
For all mid Scotland's chiefs of fame,
Was none more famed than he.

And boldly for his country, still,
  In battle he had stood,
Ay, even when on the banks of Till
  Her noblest pour'd their blood.

Sweet are the paths, O passing sweet!
  By Esk's fair streams that run,
O'er airy steep, through copsewood deep,
  Impervious to the sun.

There the rapt poet's step may rove,
  And yield the muse the day;
There Beauty, led by timid Love,
  May shun the tell-tale ray;

From that fair dome, where suit is paid
  By blast of bugle free,[1]
To Auchendinny's hazel glade,[2]
  And haunted Woodhouselee.

Who knows not Melville's beechy grove,[3]
  And Roslin's rocky glen,[4]
Dalkeith, which all the virtues love,[5]
  And classic Hawthornden?[6]

Yet never a path, from day to day,
  The pilgrim's footsteps range,
Save but the solitary way
  To Burndale's ruin'd grange.

A woeful place was that, I ween,
  As sorrow could desire;
For nodding to the fall was each crum-
    bling wall,
  And the roof was scathed with fire.

It fell upon a summer's eve,
  While, on Carnethy's head,
The last faint gleams of the sun's low
    beams
  Had streak'd the gray with red;

And the convent bell did vespers tell,
  Newbattle's oaks among,
And mingled with the solemn knell
  Our Ladye's evening song;

The heavy knell, the choir's faint swell,
  Came slowly down the wind,
And on the pilgrim's ear they fell,
  As his wonted path he did find.

Deep sunk in thought, I ween, he was,
  Nor ever raised his eye,
Until he came to that dreary place,
  Which did all in ruins lie.

He gazed on the walls, so scathed with
    fire,
  With many a bitter groan —
And there was aware of a Gray Friar,
  Resting him on a stone.

"Now, Christ thee save!" said the Gray
    Brother;
  "Some pilgrim thou seemest to be."
But in sore amaze did Lord Albert gaze,
  Nor answer again made he.

"O come ye from east, or come ye from
    west,
  Or bring reliques from over the sea;
Or come ye from the shrine of St. James
    the divine,
  Or St. John of Beverley?"

"I come not from the shrine of St. James
    the divine,
  Nor bring reliques from over the sea;
I bring but a curse from our father, the
    Pope,
  Which forever will cling to me." —

"Now, woeful pilgrim, say not so!
  But kneel thee down to me,
And shrive thee so clean of thy deadly sin,
  That absolved thou mayst be." —

"And who art thou, thou Gra
    Brother,
  That I should shrive to thee,
When He, to whom are given the ke
    of earth and heaven,
  Has no power to pardon me?" —

"Oh I am sent from a distant clime,
  Five thousand miles away,
And all to absolve a foul, foul crime,
  Done *here* 'twixt night and day."

The pilgrim kneel'd him on the sand,
  And thus began his saye —
When on his neck an ice-cold hand
  Did that Gray Brother laye.

    *   *   *   *

BALLADS

(TRANSLATED OR IMITATED)

FROM THE GERMAN, Etc.

WILLIAM AND HELEN.

[1796.]

IMITATED FROM THE "LENORE" OF BÜRGER.

I.

FROM heavy dreams fair Helen rose,
  And eyed the dawning red: —
"Alas, my love, thou tarriest long!
  O art thou false or dead?"

II.

With gallant Frederick's princely power
  He sought the bold Crusade;
But not a word from Judah's wars
  Told Helen how he sped.

III.

With Paynim and with Saracen
  At length a truce was made,
And every knight return'd to dry
  The tears his love had shed.

IV.

Our gallant host was homeward bound
  With many a song of joy;
Green waved the laurel in each plume,
  The badge of victory.

V.

And old and young, and sire and son,
  To meet them crowd the way,

With shouts, and mirth, and melody,
  The debt of love to pay.

VI.

Full many a maid her true-love met,
  And sobb'd in his embrace,
And fluttering joy in tears and smiles
  Array'd full many a face.

VII

Nor joy nor smile for Helen sad;
  She sought the host in vain;
For none could tell her William's fate,
  If faithless, or if slain.

VIII.

The martial band is past and gone;
  She rends her raven hair,
And in distraction's bitter mood
  She weeps with wild despair.

IX.

"O rise, my child," her mother said,
  "Nor sorrow thus in vain;
A perjured lover's fleeting heart,
  No tears recall again." —

X.

" O mother, what is gone, is gone,
　　What's lost for ever lorn:
Death, death alone can comfort me;
　　O had I ne'er been born!

XI.

" O break, my heart, — O break at once!
　　Drink my life-blood, Despair!
No joy remains on earth for me,
　　For me in Heaven no share." —

XII.

" O enter not in judgment, Lord! "
　　The pious mother prays;
" Impute not guilt to thy frail child!
　　She knows not what she says.

XIII.

" O say thy pater noster, child!
　　O turn to God and grace!
His will, that turn'd thy bliss to bale,
　　Can change thy bale to bliss." —

XIV.

" O mother, mother, what is bliss?
　　O mother, what is bale?
My William's love was Heaven on earth,
　　Without it earth is Hell.

XV.

" Why should I pray to ruthless Heaven,
　　Since my loved William's slain?
I only pray'd for William's sake,
　　And all my prayers were vain." —

XVI.

" O take the sacrament, my child,
　　And check these tears that flow;
By resignation's humble prayer,
　　O hallow'd be thy woe!" —

XVII.

" No sacrament can quench this fire,
　　Or slake this scorching pain;
No sacrament can bid the dead
　　Arise and live again.

XVIII.

" O break, my heart, — O break at once!
　　Be thou my god, Despair!

Heaven's heaviest blow has fallen on me
　　And vain each fruitless prayer." —

XIX.

" O enter not in judgment, Lord,
　　With thy frail child of clay!
She knows not what her tongue has spoke
　　Impute it not, I pray!

XX.

" Forbear, my child, this desperate woe
　　And turn to God and grace;
Well can devotion's heavenly glow
　　Convert thy bale to bliss." —

XXI.

" O mother, mother, what is bliss?
　　O mother, what is bale?
Without my William what were Heaven
　　Or with him what were Hell?" —

XXII.

Wild she arraigns the eternal doom,
　　Upbraids each sacred power,
Till, spent, she sought her silent room,
　　All in the lonely tower.

XXIII.

She beat her breast, she wrung her hand
　　Till sun and day were o'er,
And through the glimmering lattice shone
　　The twinkling of the star.

XXIV.

Then, crash! the heavy drawbridge fell
　　That o'er the moat was hung;
And, clatter! clatter! on its boards
　　The hoof of courser rung.

XXV.

The clank of echoing steel was heard,
　　As off the rider bounded;
And slowly on the winding stair
　　A heavy footstep sounded.

XXVI.

And hark! and hark! a knock — Tap!
　　tap!
A rustling stifled noise; —
Door-latch and tinkling staples ring; —
At length a whispering voice: —

XXVII.

Awake, awake, arise, my love!
How, Helen, dost thou fare?
Wakest thou, or sleep'st? laugh'st thou,
    or weep'st?
Hast thought on me, my fair?"—

XXVIII.

My love! my love!—so late by night!
I waked, I wept for thee:
Much have I borne since dawn of morn;
Where William, could'st thou be!"—

XXIX.

We saddle late—from Hungary
I rode since darkness fell;
And to its bourne we both return
Before the matin-bell."

XXX.

O rest this night within my arms,
And warm thee in their fold!
Hill howls through hawthorn bush the
    wind:—
My love is deadly cold"—

XXXI.

Let the wind howl thro' hawthorn bush!
This night we must away;
The steed is wight, the spur is bright;
I cannot stay till day.

XXXII.

Busk, busk, and boune!* Thou
    mount'st behind
Upon my black barb steed.
O'er stock and stile, a hundred miles,
We haste to bridal bed."—

XXXIII.

To-night—to-night a hundred miles!—
O dearest William stay!
The bell strikes twelve—dark, dismal hour!
O wait, my love, till day!"—

XXXIV.

Look here, look here—the moon
    shines clear—
Full fast I ween we ride;

Busk — to dress. *Boune* — to prepare one's
  for a journey.

Mount and away! for ere the day
We reach our bridal bed.

XXXV.

"The black barb snorts, the bridle rings;
Haste, busk, and boune, and seat
    thee!
The feast is made, the chamber spread,
The bridal guests await thee."—

XXXVI.

Strong love prevail'd: She busks, she
    bounes,
She mounts the barb behind,
And round her darling William's waist
Her lily arms she twined.

XXXVII.

And, hurry! hurry! off they rode,
As fast as fast might be;
Spurn'd from the courser's thundering
    heels
The flashing pebbles flee.

XXXVIII.

And on the right, and on the left,
Ere they could snatch a view,
Fast, fast each mountain, mead, and
    plain,
And cot, and castle, flew.

XXXIX.

"Sit fast—dost fear?—The moon
    shines clear—
Fleet goes my barb—keep hold!
Fear'st thou?"—"O no!" she faintly
    said;
"But why so stern and cold?

XL.

"What yonder rings? what yonder sings?
Why shrieks the owlet gray?"
"'Tis death-bells' clang, 'tis funeral
    song,
The body to the clay.

XLI.

"With song and clang, at morrow's
    dawn,
Ye may inter the dead:
To-night I ride with my young bride,
To deck our bridal bed.

XLII.

"Come with thy choir, thou coffin'd
    guest,
    To swell our nuptial song!
Come, priest, to bless our marriage feast!
    Come all, come all along!"—

XLIII.

Ceased clang and song; down sunk the
    bier;
    The shrouded corpse arose:
And, hurry! hurry! all the train
    The thundering steed pursues.

XLIV.

And, forward! forward! on they go;
    High snorts the straining steed;
Thick pants the rider's laboring breath,
    As headlong on they speed.

XLV.

"O William, why this savage haste?
    And where thy bridal bed?"—
"'Tis distant far, low, damp, and chill,
    And narrow, trustless maid."—

XLVI.

"No room for me?"— "Enough for
    both;—
    Speed, speed, my barb, thy course!"
O'er thundering bridge, through boiling
    surge,
    He drove the furious horse.

XLVII.

Tramp! tramp! along the land they
    rode,*
    Splash! splash! along the sea;
The scourge is wight, the spur is bright,
    The flashing pebbles flee.

* In the preface to the edition of "William
and Helen," published anonymously in 1796, Sir
Walter Scott says:— "The first two lines of the
forty-seventh stanza, descriptive of the speed of
the lovers, may perhaps bring to the recollection
of many a passage extremely similar in a translation of " Lenore," which first appeared in the
Monthly Magazine. In justice to himself, the
translator thinks it his duty to acknowledge that
his curiosity was first attracted to this truly
romantic story by a gentleman, who having
heard " Lenore " once read in manuscript, could
only recollect the general outlines, and a part of
a couplet which, from the singularity of its

XLVIII.

Fled past on right and left how fast
    Each forest, grove, and bower!
On right and left fled past how fast
    Each city, town, and tower!

XLIX.

"Dost fear? dost fear? The moon shin
    clear,
    Dost fear to ride with me?—
Hurrah! hurrah! the dead can ride!"
    "O William, let them be!—

L.

"See there, see there! What yond
    swings
    And creaks mid whistling rain?"—
"Gibbet and steel, th' accursed whee
    A murderer in his chain.—

LI.

"Hollo! thou felon, follow here:
    To bridal bed we ride;
And thou shalt prance a fetter dance
    Before me and my bride."

LII.

And, hurry! hurry! clash, clash, clas
    The wasted form descends;
And fleet as wind through hazel bush
    The wild career attends.

LIII.

Tramp! tramp! along the land they ro
    Splash! splash! along the sea;
The scourge is red, the spur drops bloo
    The flashing pebbles flee.

LIV.

How fled what moonshine faint
    show'd!
    How fled what darkness hid!
How fled the earth beneath their feet,
    The heaven above their head!

structure and frequent recurrence, had remain
impressed upon his memory. If, from desp
of rendering the passage so happily, the prope
of another has been invaded, the transla
makes the only atonement now in his pow
by restoring it thus publicly to the righ
owner.

LV.

*Dost fear? dost fear? The moon
    shines clear,
And well the dead can ride;
Does faithful Helen fear for them?"—
    "O leave in peace the dead!"—

LVI.

' Barb! barb! methinks I hear the cock;
    The sand will soon be run:
Barb! Barb! I smell the morning air;
    The race is wellnigh done."—

LVII.

Tramp! tramp! along the land they rode;
    Splash! splash! along the sea;
The scourge is red, the spur drops blood,
    The flashing pebbles flee.

LVIII.

' Hurrah! hurrah! well ride the dead;
    The bride, the bride is come;
And soon we reach the bridal bed,
    For, Helen, here's my home."—

LIX.

Reluctant on its rusty hinge
    Revolved an iron door,
And by the pale moon's setting beam
    Were seen a church and tower.

LX.

With many a shriek and cry whiz round
    The birds of midnight, scared;
And rustling like autumnal leaves
    Unhallowed ghosts were heard.

LXI.

O'er many a tomb and tombstone pale
    He spurr'd the fiery horse,
Till sudden at an open grave
    He check'd the wondrous course.

LXII.

The falling gauntlet quits the rein,
    Down drops the casque of steel,
The cuirass leaves his shrinking side,
    The spur his gory heel.

LXIII.

The eyes desert the naked skull,
    The mould'ring flesh the bone,
Till Helen's lily arms entwine
    A ghastly skeleton.

LXIV.

The furious barb snorts fire and foam,
    And, with a tearful bound,
Dissolves at once in empty air,
    And leaves her on the ground.

LXV.

Half seen by fits, by fits half heard,
    Pale spectres flit along,
Wheel round the maid in dismal dance,
    And howl the funeral song:

LXVI

" E'en when the heart's with anguish
    cleft,
    Revere the doom of Heaven,
Her soul is from her body reft:
    Her spirit is forgiven!"

THE WILD HUNTSMAN.*

[1796.]

This is a translation, or rather an imitation, of the *Wilde Jäger* of the German poet Bürger. The tradition upon which it is founded bears, that formerly a Wildgrave, or keeper of a royal forest, named Falkenburg, was so much addicted to the pleasures of the chase, and otherwise so extremely profligate and cruel, that he not only followed this unhallowed amusement on the Sabbath, and other days consecrated to religious duty, but accompanied it with the most unheard-of oppression upon the poor peasants who were under his vassal-

* Published (1796) with " William and Helen," entitled " THE CHASE."

age. When this second Nimrod died, the people adopted a superstition, founded probably on the many various uncouth sounds heard in the depth of a German forest during the silence of the night. They conceived they still heard the cry of the Wildgrave's hounds; and the well known cheer of the deceased hunter, the sounds of his horse's feet, and the rustling of the branches before the game, the pack, and the sportsmen, are also distinctly discriminated; but the phantoms are rarely, if ever, visible. Once, as a benighted *Chasseur* heard this infernal chase pass by him, at the sound of the halloo, with which the Spectre Huntsman cheered his hounds, he could not refrain from crying " *Glück zu Falkenburg!* " [Good sport to ye, Falkenburg!] " Dost thou wish me good sport? " answered a hoarse voice; " thou shalt share the game; " and there was thrown at him what seemed to be a huge piece of foul carrion. The daring *Chasseur* lost two of his best horses soon after, and never perfectly recovered the personal effects of this ghostly greeting. This tale, though told with some variations, is universally believed all over Germany.

The French had a similar tradition concerning an aërial hunter, who infested the forest of Fontainebleau.

THE Wildgrave winds his bugle horn,
  To horse, to horse! halloo, halloo!
His fiery courser snuffs the morn,
  And thronging serfs their lord pursue.

The eager pack, from couples freed,
  Dash through the brush, the brier, the brake;
While answering hound, and horn, and steed,
  The mountain echoes startling wake.

The beams of God's own hallow'd day
  Had painted yonder spire with gold,
And, calling sinful man to pray,
  Loud, long, and deep the bell had toll'd:

But still the Wildgrave onward rides;
  Halloo, halloo! and, hark again!
When spurring from opposing sides,
  Two Stranger Horsemen join the train.

Who was each Stranger, left and right,
  Well may I guess, but dare not tell;
The right-hand steed was silver white,
  The left, the swarthy hue of Hell.

The right-hand Horseman young and fair,
  His smile was like the morn of May;
The left, from eye of tawny glare,
  Shot midnight lightning's lurid ray.

He waved his huntsman's cap on high,
  Cried: " Welcome, welcome, noble lord!
What sport can earth, or sea, or sky,
  To match the princely chase, afford? "

" Cease thy loud bugle's clanging knell,'
  Cried the fair youth, with silver voice;
" And for devotion's choral swell
  Exchange the rude unhallow'd noise.

" To-day the ill-omen'd chase forbear,
  Yon bell yet summons to the fane;
To-day the Warning Spirit hear,
  To-morrow thou mayst mourn in vain." —

" Away, and sweep the glades along! "
  The Sable Hunter hoarse replies;
" To muttering monks leave matin-song,
  And bells, and books, and mysteries."

The Wildgrave spurr'd his ardent steed,
  And, launching forward with a bound,
" Who, for thy drowsy priestlike rede,
  Would leave the jovial horn and hound?

" Hence, if our manly sport offend!
  With pious fools go chant and pray: —
Well hast thou spoke, my dark-brow'd friend;
  Halloo, halloo! and, hark away! "

The Wildgrave spurr'd his courser light,
  O'er moss and moor, o'er holt and hill;
And on the left and on the right,
  Each stranger Horseman follow'd still.

Up springs, from yonder tangled thorn,
  A stag more white than mountain snow,
And louder rung the Wildgrave's horn,
  " Hark forward, forward! holla, ho! "

A heedless wretch has cross'd the way;
  He gasps the thundering hoofs below;

ut, live who can, or die who may,
Still, "Forward, forward!" on they go.

ee, where yon simple fences meet,
A field with Autumn's blessings
crown'd;
ee, prostrate at the Wildgrave's feet,
A husbandman with toil embrown'd:

O mercy, mercy, noble lord!
Spare the poor's pittance," was his cry,
Earn'd by the sweat these brows have
pour'd,
In scorching hour of fierce July." —

arnest the right-hand Stranger pleads,
The left still cheering to the prey;
he impetuous Earl no warning heeds,
But furious holds the onward way.

Away, thou hound! so basely born,
Or dread the scourge's echoing
blow!" —
hen loudly rung his bugle horn,
"Hark forward, forward, holla, ho!"

o said, so done: — A single bound
Clears the poor laborer's humble pale,
Wild follows man, and horse, and hound,
Like dark December's stormy gale.

nd man and horse, and hound and horn,
Destructive sweep the field along;
While, joying o'er the wasted corn,
Fell Famine marks the maddening
throng.

gain uproused, the timorous prey
Scours moss and moor, and holt and
hill;
Hard run, he feels his strength decay,
And trusts for life his simple skill.

oo dangerous solitude appear'd;
He seeks the shelter of the crowd;
mid the flock's domestic herd
His harmless head he hopes to shroud.

'er moss and moor, and holt and hill,
His track the steady blood-hounds
trace;
'er moss and moor, unwearied still,
The furious Earl pursues the chase.

Full lowly did the herdsman fall: —
"O spare, thou noble Baron, spare
These herds, a widow's little all;
These flocks, an orphan's fleecy
care!" —

Earnest the right-hand Stranger pleads,
The left still cheering to the prey;
The Earl nor prayer nor pity heeds,
But furious keeps the onward way.

"Unmanner'd dog! To stop my sport,
Vain were thy cant and beggar whine,
Though human spirits, of thy sort,
Were tenants of these carrion kine!"

Again he winds his bugle-horn,
"Hark forward, forward, holla, ho!"
And through the herd, in ruthless scorn,
He cheers his furious hounds to go.

In heaps the throttled victims fall;
Down sinks their mangled herdsman
near;
The murderous cries the stag appal, —
Again he starts, new-nerved by fear.

With blood besmear'd, and white with
foam,
While big the tears of anguish pour,
He seeks, amid the forest's gloom,
The humble hermit's hallow'd bower,

But man and horse, and horn and hound,
Fast rattling on his traces go;
The sacred chapel rung around
With, "Hark away! and, holla, ho!"

All mild, amid the rout profane,
The holy hermit pour'd his prayer: —
"Forbear with blood God's house to stain;
Revere his altar, and forbear!

"The meanest brute has rights to plead,
Which, wrong'd by cruelty, or pride,
Draw vengeance on the ruthless head: —
Be warn'd at length, and turn aside."

Still the Fair Horseman anxious pleads;
The Black, wild whooping, points the
prey: —
Alas! the Earl no warning heeds,
But frantic keeps the forward way.

" Holy or not, or right or wrong,
  Thy altar, and its rites, I spurn;
Not sainted martyrs' sacred song,
  Not God himself, shall make me turn ! "

He spurs his horse, he winds his horn,
  " Hark forward, forward, holla, ho ! "
But off, on whirlwind's pinion borne,
  The stag, the hut, the hermit, go.

And horse and man, and horn and
    hound,
  And clamor of the chase, was gone;
For hoofs, and howls, and bugle-sound,
  A deadly silence reign'd alone.

Wild gazed the affrighted Earl around;
  He strove in vain to wake his horn,
In vain to call; for not a sound
  Could from his anxious lips be borne.

He listens for his trusty hounds;
  No distant baying reach'd his ears:
His courser, rooted to the ground,
  The quickening spur unmindful bears.

Still dark and darker frown the shades,
  Dark as the darkness of the grave;
And not a sound the still invades,
  Save what a distant torrent gave.

High o'er the sinner's humbled head
  At length the solemn silence broke;
And, from a cloud of swarthy red,
  The awful voice of thunder spoke: —

" Oppressor of creation fair !
  Apostate Spirits' harden'd tool !
Scorner of God ! Scourge of the poor !
  The measure of thy cup is full.

" Be chased forever through the wood;
  Forever roam the affrighted wild;
And let thy fate instruct the proud,
  God's meanest creature is his child."

'Twas hush'd: One flash, of sombre glare
  With yellow tinged the forests brown
Uprose the Wildgrave's bristling hair,
  And horror chill'd each nerve and bone.

Cold pour'd the sweat in freezing rill;
  A rising wind began to sing;
And louder, louder, louder still,
  Brought storm and tempest on its wing.

Earth heard the call; — her entrails rend
  From yawning rifts, with many a yell
Mix'd with sulphureous flames, ascend
  The misbegotten dogs of hell.

What ghastly Huntsman next arose,
  Well may I guess, but dare not tell;
His eye like midnight lightning glows,
  His steed the swarthy hue of hell.

The Wildgrave flies o'er bush and thorn
  With many a shriek of helpless woe;
Behind him hound, and horse, and horn
  And, " Hark away, and holla, ho ! "

With wild despair's reverted eye,
  Close, close behind he marks the
    throng,
With bloody fangs and eager cry;
  In frantic fear he scours along.

Still, still shall last the dreadful chase,
  Till time itself shall have an end;
By day, they scour earth's cavern'd space
  At midnight's witching hour, ascend.

This is the horn, and hound, and horse,
  That oft the lated peasant hears;
Appall'd, he signs the frequent cross,
  When the wild din invades his ears.

The wakeful priest oft drops a tear
  For human pride, for human woe,
When, at his midnight mass he hears
  The infernal cry of, " Holla, ho ! "

THE FIRE-KING.

"The blessings of the evil Genii, which are curses, were upon him." — *Eastern Tale.*

[1801.]

THIS ballad was written at the request of MR. LEWIS, to be inserted in his *Tales of Wonder.** It is the third in a series of four ballads, on the subject of Elementary Spirits. The story is, however, partly historical; for it is recorded, that during the struggles of the Latin kingdom of Jerusalem, a Knight-Templar, called Saint Alban, deserted to the Saracens, and defeated the Christians in many combats, till he was finally routed and slain, in conflict with King Baldwin under the walls of Jerusalem.

OLD knights and fair dames, to my harp
    give an ear,
Of love, and of war, and of wonder to
    hear,
And you haply may sigh, in the midst of
    your glee,
At the tale of Count Albert, and fair
    Rosalie.

O see you that castle, so strong and so
    high?
And see you that lady, the tear in her eye?
And see you that palmer, from Palestine's
    land,
The shell on his hat, and the staff in his
    hand? —

"Now palmer, gray palmer, O tell unto
    me,
What news bring you home from the Holy
    Countrie?
And how goes the warfare by Galilee's
    strand?
And how fare our nobles, the flower of
    the land?" —

"O well goes the warfare by Galilee's
    wave,
For Gilead, and Nablous, and Ramah we
    have;
And well fare our nobles by Mount Leba-
    non,
For the Heathen have lost, and the Chris-
    tians have won."

A fair chain of gold mid her ringlets there
    hung;
Over the palmer's gray locks the fair chain
    has she flung:

"O palmer, gray palmer, this chain be
    thy fee,
For the news thou hast brought from the
    Holy Countrie.

"And, palmer, good palmer, by Galilee's
    wave,
O saw ye Count Albert, the gentle and
    brave?
When the Crescent went back, and the
    Red-cross rush'd on,
O saw ye him foremost on Mount Leba-
    non?" —

"O lady, fair lady, the tree green it
    grows;
O lady, fair lady, the stream pure it flows;
Your castle stands strong, and your hopes
    soar on high;
But, lady, fair lady, all blossoms to die.

"The green boughs they wither, the thun-
    derbolt falls,
It leaves of your castle but levin-scorch'd
    walls;
The pure stream runs muddy; the gay
    hope is gone;
Count Albert is prisoner on Mount Leba-
    non."

O she's ta'en a horse, should be fleet at
    her speed;
And she's ta'en a sword, should be sharp
    at her need;
And she has ta'en shipping for Palestine's
    land,
To ransom Count Albert from Soldanrie's
    hand.

* Published in 1801.

Small thought had Count Albert on fair Rosalie,
Small thought on his faith, or his knighthood, had he:
A heathenish damsel his light heart had won,
The Soldan's fair daughter of Mount Lebanon.

" O Christian, brave Christian, my love wouldst thou be,
Three things must thou do ere I hearken to thee;
Our laws and our worship on thee shalt thou take,
And this thou shalt first do for Zulema's sake.

" And, next, in the cavern, where burns evermore
The mystical flame which the Curdmans adore,
Alone, and in silence, three nights shalt thou wake,
And this thou shalt next do for Zulema's sake.

" And, last, thou shalt aid us with counsel and hand,
To drive the Frank robber from Palestine's land;
For my lord and my love then Count Albert I'll take,
When all this is accomplish'd for Zulema's sake."

He has thrown by his helmet, and cross-handled sword,
Renouncing his knighthood, denying his Lord;
He has ta'en the green caftan, and turban put on,
For the love of the maiden of fair Lebanon.

And in the dread cavern, deep, deep under ground,
Which fifty steel gates and steel portals surround,
He has watch'd until daybreak, but sight saw he none,
Save the flame burning bright on its altar of stone.

Amazed was the Princess, the Sold[an] amazed,
Sore murmur'd the priests as on Alb[ert] they gazed;
They search'd all his garments, an[d] under his weeds,
They found, and took from him, his ros[ary] beads.

Again in the cavern, deep, deep und[er] ground,
He watch'd the lone night, while [the] winds whistled round;
Far off was their murmur, it came n[ot] more nigh,
The flame burn'd unmoved, and naug[ht] else did he spy.

Loud murmur'd the priests, and amaz[ed] was the King,
While many dark spells of their wit[ch]craft they sing;
They search'd Albert's body, and, lo! his breast
Was the sign of the Cross, by his fat[her] impress'd.

The priests they erase it with care a[nd] with pain,
And the recreant return'd to the cav[ern] again;
But, as he descended, a whisper th[ere] fell:
It was his good angel, who bade h[im] farewell!

High bristled his hair, his heart flutte[r'd] and beat,
And he turn'd him five steps, half solved to retreat;
But his heart it was harden'd, his p[ur]pose was gone,
When he thought of the Maiden of Lebanon.

Scarce pass'd he the archway, the thre[shold] old scarce trode,
When the winds from the four points [of] heaven were abroad;
They made each steel portal to rattle a[nd] ring,
And, borne on the blast, came the dr[ead] Fire-King.

ull sore rock'd the cavern whene'er he
    drew nigh,
he fire on the altar blazed bickering and
    high;
a volcanic explosions the mountains pro-
    claim
he dreadful approach of the Monarch
    of Flame.

nmeasured in height, undistinguish'd
    in form,
is breath it was lightning, his voice it
    was storm;
ween the stout heart of Count Albert
    was tame,
hen he saw in his terrors the Monarch
    of Flame.

a his hand a broad falchion blue-glim-
    mer'd through smoke,
nd Mount Lebanon shook as the mon-
    arch he spoke : —
With this brand shalt thou conquer,
    thus long, and no more,
ill thou bend to the Cross, and the Vir-
    gin adore.''

he cloud-shrouded Arm gives the wea-
    pon; and see!
he recreant receives the charm'd gift
    on his knee;
he thunders growl distant, and faint
    gleam the fires,
s, borne on the whirlwind, the phan-
    tom retires.

ount Albert has arm'd him the Paynim
    among,
hough his heart it was false, yet his
    arm it was strong;
nd the Red-cross wax'd faint, and the
    Crescent came on,
rom the day he commanded on Mount
    Lebanon.

rom Lebanon's Forests to Galilee's
    wave,
he sands of Samaar drank the blood of
    the brave;
'ill the Knights of the Temple and
    Knights of Saint John,
Vith Salem's King Baldwin, against him
    came on.

The war-cymbals clatter'd, the trumpets
    replied,
The lances were couch'd, and they closed
    on each side;
And horsemen and horses Count Albert
    o'erthrew,
Till he pierced the thick tumult King
    Baldwin unto.

Against the charm'd blade which Count
    Albert did wield,
The fence had been vain of the King's
    Red-cross shield;
But a Page thrust him forward the mon-
    arch before,
And cleft the proud turban the renegade
    wore.

So fell was the dint, that Count Albert
    stoop'd low
Before the cross'd shield, to his steel
    saddle-bow;
And scarce had he bent to the Red-cross
    his head, —
" *Bonne Grace, Notre Dame!* '' he un-
    wittingly said.

Sore sigh'd the charm'd sword, for its
    virtue was o'er,
It sprung from his grasp, and was never
    seen more;
But true men have said, that the light-
    ning's red-wing
Did waft back the brand to the dread
    Fire-King.

He clench'd his set teeth, and his gaunt-
    leted hand;
He stretch'd, with one buffet, that Page
    on the strand;
As back from the stripling the broken
    casque roll'd,
You might see the blue eyes, and the
    ringlets of gold.

Short time had Count Albert in horror
    to stare
On those death-swimming eyeballs and
    blood-clotted hair;
For down came the Templars, like Ce-
    dron in flood,
And dyed their long lances in Saracen
    blood.

The Saracens, Curdmans, and Ishmaelites yield
To the scallop, the saltier, and crossleted shield;
And the eagles were gorged with the infidel dead,
From Bethsaida's fountains to Naphthali's head.

The Battle is over on Bethsaida's plain.—
Oh, who is yon Paynim lies stretch'd mid the slain?
And who is yon Page lying cold at his knee?
Oh, who but Count Albert and fair Rosalie! —

The Lady was buried in Salem's bless
bound,
The Count he was left to the vulture an
hound:
Her soul to high mercy Our Lady d
bring;
His went on the blast to the dread Fir
King.

Yet many a minstrel, in harping, can te
How the Red-cross it conquer'd, t
Crescent it fell:
And lords and gay ladies have sigh'
mid their glee,
At the tale of Count Albert and fa
Rosalie.

FREDERICK AND ALICE.

[1801.]

THIS tale is imitated rather than translated, from a fragment introduced in Goethe
"Claudina von Villa Bella," where it is sung by a member of a gang of banditti, to engag
the attention of the family, while his companions break into the castle. It owes any littl
merit it may possess to my friend MR. LEWIS, to whom it was sent in an extremel
rude state, and who, after some material improvements, published it in his *Tales o
Wonder.*

FREDERICK leaves the land of France,
  Homeward hastes his steps to measure,
Careless casts the parting glance
  On the scene of former pleasure.

Joying in his prancing steed,
  Keen to prove his untried blade,
Hope's gay dreams the soldier lead
  Over mountain, moor, and glade.

Helpless, ruin'd, left forlorn,
  Lovely Alice wept alone;
Mourn'd o'er love's fond contract torn,
  Hope, and peace, and honor flown.

Mark her breast's convulsive throbs,
  See, the tear of anguish flows! —
Mingling soon with bursting sobs,
  Loud the laugh of frenzy rose.

Wild she cursed, and wild she pray'd;
  Seven long days and nights are o'er;

Death and pity brought his aid,
  As the village bell struck four.

Far from her, and far from France,
  Faithless Frederick onward rides;
Marking, blithe, the morning's glance
  Mantling o'er the mountain's sides.

Heard ye not the boding sound,
  As the tongue of yonder tower,
Slowly, to the hills around,
  Told the fourth, the fated hour?

Starts the steed, and snuffs the air,
  Yet no cause of dread appears;
Bristles high the rider's hair,
  Struck with strange, mysterious fear

Desperate as his terrors rise,
  In the steed the spur he hides;
From himself in vain he flies;
  Anxious, restless, on he rides.

even long days, and seven long nights,
  Wild he wander'd, woe the while!
easeless care, and causeless fright,
  Urge his footsteps many a mile.

ark the seventh sad night descends;
  Rivers swell and rain-streams pour,
While the deafening thunder lends
  All the terrors of its roar.

Weary, wet, and spent with toil,
  Where his head shall Frederick hide?
There, but in yon ruin'd aisle,
  By the lightning's flash descried.

o the portal, dank and low,
  Fast his steed the wanderer bound:
own a ruin'd staircase slow,
  Next his darkling way he wound.

ong drear vaults before him lie!
  Glimmering lights are seen to glide!—
Blessed Mary, hear my cry!
  Deign a sinner's steps to guide!"

ften lost their quivering beam,
  Still the lights move slow before,
ill they rest their ghastly gleam
  Right against an iron door.

hundering voices from within,
  Mix'd with peals of laughter, rose;

As they fell, a solemn strain
  Lent its wild and wondrous close!

Midst the din, he seem'd to hear
  Voice of friends, by din removed;—
Well he knew that solemn air,
  'Twas the lay that Alice loved. —

Hark! for now a solemn knell,
  Four times on the still night broke;
Four times, at its deaden'd swell,
  Echoes from the ruins spoke.

As the lengthened clangors die,
  Slowly opes the iron door!
Straight a banquet met his eye,
  But a funeral's form it wore!

Coffins for the seats extend;
  All with black the board was spread;
Girt by parent, brother, friend,
  Long since numbered with the dead!

Alice, in her grave-clothes bound,
  Ghastly, smiling, points a seat;
All arose, with thundering sound;
  All the expected stranger greet.

High their meagre arms they wave,
  Wild their notes of welcome swell:—
" Welcome, traitor, to the grave!
  Perjured, bid the light farewell!"

THE BATTLE OF SEMPACH.*

[1818.]

THESE verses are a literal translation of an ancient Swiss ballad upon the battle of Sempach, fought 9th July, 1386, being the victory by which the Swiss cantons established their dependence: the author, Albert Tchudi, denominated the Souter, from his profession of shoemaker. He was a citizen of Lucerne, esteemed highly among his countrymen, both or his powers as a *Meister-Singer*, or minstrel, and his courage as a soldier.

The circumstance of their being written by a poet returning from the well-fought field e describes, and in which his country's fortune was secured, may confer on Tchudi's verses a interest which they are not entitled to claim from their poetical merit. But ballad petry, the more literally it is translated, the more it loses its simplicity, without acquiring ther grace or strength; and therefore, some of the faults of the verses must be imputed to ne translator's feeling it a duty to keep as closely as possible to his original. The vari-1s puns, rude attempts at pleasantry, and disproportioned episodes must be set down Tchudi's account, or to the taste of his age.

* First published in *Blackwood*, Feb. 1818.

The military antiquary will derive some amusement from the minute particulars whic the martial poet has recorded. The mode in which the Austrian men-at-arms received th charge of the Swiss, was by forming a phalanx, which they defended with their long lance. The gallant Winkelried, who sacrificed his own life by rushing among the spears, claspin in his arms as many as he could grasp, and thus opening a gap in those iron battalions, celebrated in Swiss history. When fairly mingled together, the unwieldy length of the weapons, and cumbrous weight of their defensive armor, rendered the Austrian men-a arms a very unequal match for the light-armed mountaineers. The victories obtained b the Swiss over the German chivalry, hitherto deemed as formidable on foot as on hors back, led to important changes in the art of war. The poet describes the Austrian knight and squires as cutting the peaks from their boots ere they could act upon foot, in allusio to an inconvenient piece of foppery, often mentioned in the Middle Ages. Leopold III Archduke of Austria, called "the handsome man-at-arms," was slain in the battle of Sem pach, with the flower of his chivalry.

'TWAS when among our linden-trees
  The bees had housed in swarms,
(And gray-hair'd peasants say that these
  Betoken foreign arms,)

Then look'd we down to Willisow,
  The land was all in flame;
We knew the Archduke Leopold
  With all his army came.

The Austrian nobles made their vow,
  So hot their heart and bold: —
"On Switzer carles we'll trample now,
  And slay both young and old."

With clarion loud, and banner proud,
  From Zurich on the lake,
In martial pomp and fair array,
  Their onward march they make.

"Now list, ye lowland nobles all —
  Ye seek the mountain strand,
Nor wot ye what shall be your lot
  In such a dangerous land.

"I rede ye, shrive ye of your sins,
  Before ye farther go,
A skirmish in Helvetian hills
  May send your souls to woe." —

"But where now shall we find a priest
  Our shrift that he may hear?"
"The Switzer priest * has ta'en the field,
  He deals a penance drear.

"Right heavily upon your head
  He'll lay his hand of steel;

* All the Swiss priests able to bear arms
fought in this strife for their native land.

And with his trusty partisan
  Your absolution deal." —

'Twas on a Monday morning then;
  The corn was steep'd in dew,
And merry maids had sickles ta'en,
  When the host to Sempach drew.

The stalwart men of fair Lucerne
  Together have they join'd;
The pith and core of manhood stern,
  Was none cast looks behind.

It was the Lord of Hare-castle,
  And to the Duke he said: —
"Yon little band of brethren true
  Will meet us undismay'd." —

"O Hare castle,† thou heart of hare!"
  Fierce Oxenstern replied. —
"Shalt see then how the game will fare,"
  The taunted knight replied.

There was lacing then of helmets brigh
  And closing ranks amain;
The peaks they hew'd from their boo
    points,
  Might well-nigh load a wain.‡

And thus they to each other said: —
  "Yon handful down to hew
Will be no boastful tale to tell,
  The peasants are so few."

† Hasen-stein in the original: literally Har stone.

‡ The boots of this period had long points the toes; so long that in the time of Richard I they were chained up to the knees. Of cour they greatly impeded the wearer's movements foot.

gallant Swiss Confederates there
They pray'd to God aloud,
he display'd his rainbow fair
Against a swarthy cloud.

n heart and pulse throbb'd more and
    more
With courage firm and high,
down the good Confederates bore
On the Austrian chivalry.

Austrian Lion* 'gan to growl,
And toss his mane and tail;
ball, and shaft, and crossbow bolt,
Went whistling forth like hail.

ace, pike, and halbert mingled there,
The game was nothing sweet;
boughs of many a stately tree
Lay shiver'd at their feet.

Austrian men-at-arms stood fast,
So close their spears they laid;
chafed the gallant Winkelried,
Who to his comrades said: —

have a virtuous wife at home,
A wife and infant son;
ave them to my country's care, —
This field shall soon be won.

These nobles lay their spears right
    thick,
And keep full firm array,
shall my charge their order break,
And make my brethren way."

rush'd against the Austrian band,
n desperate career,
d with his body, breast, and hand,
Bore down each hostile spear.

ur lances splinter'd on his crest,
Six shiver'd in his side;
l on the serried files he press'd —
He broke their ranks, and died.

is patriot's self-devoted deed
First tamed the Lion's mood,
d the four forest cantons freed
From thraldom by his blood.

* A pun on the Archduke's name, Leo-pold.

Right where his charge had made a
    lane
His valiant comrades burst,
With sword, and ax, and partisan,
    And hack, and stab, and thrust.

The daunted Lion 'gan to whine,
    And granted ground amain,
The Mountain Bull † he bent his brows,
    And gored his sides again.

Then lost was banner, spear, and shield,
    At Sempach in the flight,
The cloister vaults at König's-field
    Hold many an Austrian knight.

It was the Archduke Leopold,
    So lordly would he ride,
But he came against the Switzer churls,
    And they slew him in his pride.

The heifer said unto the bull:
    "And shall I not complain?
There came a foreign nobleman
    To milk me on the plain.

"One thrust of thine outrageous horn
    Has gall'd the knight so sore,
That to the churchyard he is borne
    To range our glens no more."

An Austrian noble left the stour,
    And fast the flight 'gan take;
And he arrived in luckless hour
    At Sempach on the lake.

He and his squire a fisher call'd,
    (His name was Hans von Rot,)
"For love, or meed, or charity,
    Receive us in thy boat!"

Their anxious call the fisher heard,
    And, glad the meed to win,
His shallop to the shore he steer'd,
    And took the flyers in.

And while against the tide and wind
    Hans stoutly rowed his way,
The noble to his follower sign'd
    He should the boatman slay.

† A pun on the Urus, or wild-bull, which gave
name to the Canton of Uri.

The fisher's back was to them turn'd,
　The squire his dagger drew,
Hans saw his shadow in the lake,
　The boat he overthrew.

He 'whelm'd the boat, and as they strove,
　He stunn'd them with his oar: —
" Now, drink ye deep, my gentle sirs,
　You'll ne'er stab boatman more.

" Two gilded fishes in the lake
　This morning have I caught,
Their silver scales may much avail,
　Their carrion flesh is naught."

It was a messenger of woe
　Has sought the Austrian land: —

" Ah! gracious lady, evil news!
　My lord lies on the strand.

" At Sempach, on the battle-field,
　His bloody corpse lies there." —
" Ah, gracious God!" the lady cried,
　" What tidings of despair! "

Now would you know the minstrel wig
　Who sings of strife so stern,
Albert the Souter is he hight,
　A burgher of Lucerne.

A merry man was he, I wot,
　The night he made the lay,
Returning from the bloody spot,
　Where God had judged the day.

THE NOBLE MORINGER.*

AN ANCIENT BALLAD.

[1819.]

THE original of these verses occurs in a collection of German popular songs entitl
" Sammlung Deutschen Volkslieder," Berlin, 1807. The legend turns on an incident n
peculiar to Germany, and which, perhaps, was not unlikely to happen when crusade
abode long in the Holy Land, and their disconsolate dames received no tidings of the
fate.

I.

O, WILL you hear a knightly tale of old
　Bohemian day?
It was the noble Moringer in wedlock bed
　he lay;
He halsed and kiss'd his dearest dame,
　that was as sweet as May,
And said, " Now, lady of my heart,
　attend the words I say.

II.

" 'Tis I have vow'd a pilgrimage unto a
　distant shrine,
And I must seek Saint Thomas-land, and
　leave the land that's mine;
Here shalt thou dwell the while in state,
　so thou wilt pledge thy fay,
That thou for my return wilt wait seven
　twelve-months and a day."

III.

Then out and spoke that Lady brig
　sore troubled in her cheer: —
" Now tell me true, thou noble knig
　what order takest thou here;
And who shall lead thy vassal band, a
　hold thy lordly sway,
And be thy lady's guardian true wh
　thou art far away?"

IV.

Out spoke the noble Moringer: — "
　that have thou no care,
There's many a valiant gentleman of
　holds living fair;
The trustiest shall rule my land, my v
　sals and my state,
And be a guardian tried and true to th
　my lovely mate.

* Composed during Sir Walter Scott's severe and alarming illness of April, 1819, and dictated
the intervals of exquisite pain to his daughter Sophia and his friend William Laidlaw. It was pu
lished in the *Edinburgh Annual Register*, 1819.

V.

As Christian-man, I needs must keep
the vow which I have plight,
hen I am far in foreign land, remember
thy true knight;
d cease, my dearest dame, to grieve, for
vain were sorrow now,
t grant thy Moringer his leave, since
God hath heard his vow."

VI.

was the noble Moringer from bed he
made him boune,
d met him there his Chamberlain, with
ewer and with gown;
flung his mantle on his back, 'twas
furr'd with miniver,
dipp'd his hand in water cold and
bathed his forehead fair.

VII.

Now hear," he said, " Sir Chamberlain,
true vassal art thou mine,
d such the trust that I repose in that
proved worth of thine,
r seven years shalt thou rule my towers,
and lead my vassal train,
d pledge thee for my lady's faith till
I return again."

VIII.

e Chamberlain was blunt and true, and
sturdily said he: —
bide, my lord, and rule your own, and
take this rede from me:
at woman's faith's a brittle trust. —
Seven twelve-months didst thou say ?
pledge me for no lady's truth beyond
the seventh fair day."

IX.

e noble Baron turn'd him round, his
heart was full of care;
gallant Esquire stood him nigh, he
was Marstetten's heir,
whom he spoke right anxiously: —
" Thou trusty squire to me,
t thou receive this weighty trust when
I am o'er the sea?

X.

"To watch and ward my castle strong,
and to protect my land,
And to the hunting or the host to lead my
vassal band;
And pledge thee for my lady's faith till
seven long years are gone,
And guard her as Our Lady dear was
guarded by Saint John."

XI.

Marstetten's heir was kind and true, but
fiery, hot, and young,
And readily he answer made with too
presumptuous tongue:—
" My noble lord, cast care away, and on
your journey wend,
And trust this charge to me until your
pilgrimage have end.

XII.

" Rely upon my plighted faith, which
shall be truly tried,
To guard your lands, and ward your
towers, and with your vassals ride;
And for your lovely Lady's faith, so virtuous and so dear,
I'll gage my head it knows no change,
be absent thirty year."

XIII.

The noble Moringer took cheer when
thus he heard him speak,
And doubt forsook his troubled brow,
and sorrow left his cheek;
A long adieu he bids to all — hoists top-
sails, and away,
And wanders in Saint Thomas-land seven
twelve-months and a day.

XIV.

It was the noble Moringer within an or-
chard slept,
When on the Baron's slumbering sense a
boding vision crept;
And whisper'd in his ear a voice: —
" 'Tis time, Sir Knight, to wake,
Thy lady and thy heritage another mas-
ter take.

XV.

"Thy tower another banner knows, thy
   steeds another rein,
And stoop them to another's will thy
   gallant vassal train ;
And she, the Lady of thy love, so faithful once and fair,
This night within thy father's hall she
   weds Marstetten's heir."

XVI.

It is the noble Moringer starts up and
   tears his beard : —
"O would that I had ne'er been born !
   what tidings have I heard ?
To lose my lordship and my lands the
   less would be my care,
But, God ! that e'er a squire untrue
   should wed my Lady fair.

XVII.

"O good Saint Thomas, hear," he pray'd,
   "my patron Saint art thou,
A traitor robs me of my land even while
   I pay my vow !
My wife he brings to infamy that was so
   pure of name,
And I am far in foreign land, and must
   endure the shame."

XVIII.

It was the good Saint Thomas, then, who
   heard his pilgrim's prayer,
And sent a sleep so deep and dead that
   it o'erpower'd his care;
He waked in fair Bohemian land outstretch'd beside a rill,
High on the right a castle stood, low on
   the left a mill.

XIX.

The Moringer he started up as one from
   spell unbound,
And dizzy with surprise and joy gazed
   wildly all around:—
"I know my fathers' ancient towers, the
   mill, the stream I know,
Now blessed be my patron Saint who
   cheer'd his pilgrim's woe ! "

XX.

He leant upon his pilgrim staff, and
   the mill he drew,
So alter'd was his goodly form that n⟨o⟩
   their master knew;
The Baron to the miller said : — "G⟨o⟩
   friend, for charity,
Tell a poor palmer in your land w⟨h⟩
   tidings may there be ? "

XXI.

The miller answer'd him again : — " ⟨I⟩
   knew of little news,
Save that the Lady of the land did a n⟨ew⟩
   bridegroom choose;
Her husband died in distant land, su⟨ch⟩
   is the constant word,
His death sits heavy on our souls, he w⟨as⟩
   a worthy Lord.

XXII.

"Of him I held the little mill which w⟨ins⟩
   me living free,
God rest the Baron in his grave, he s⟨o⟩
   was kind to me !
And when Saint Martin's tide co⟨mes⟩
   round, and millers take their toll
The priest that prays for Moringer sh⟨all⟩
   have both cope and stole."

XXIII.

It was the noble Moringer to climb
   hill began,
And stood before the bolted gate a w⟨eary⟩
   and weary man : —
"Now help me, every saint in hea⟨ven⟩
   that can compassion take,
To gain the entrance of my hall this w⟨oe⟩
   ful match to break."

XXIV.

His very knock it sounded sad, his ⟨step⟩
   was sad and slow,
For heart and head, and voice and ha⟨nd⟩
   were heavy all with woe;
And to the warder thus he spoke⟨:⟩
   "Friend to thy Lady say,
A pilgrim from Saint Thomas-land cra⟨ves⟩
   harbor for a day.

XXV.

" I've wander'd many a weary step, my
strength is well-nigh done,
And if she turn me from her gate I'll
see no morrow's sun;
I pray, for sweet Saint Thomas' sake, a
pilgrim's bed and dole,
And for the sake of Moringer's, her
once-loved husband's soul."

XXVI.

It was the stalwart warder then he came
his dame before: —
" A pilgrim, worn and travel-toil'd,
stands at the castle-door;
And prays, for sweet Saint Thomas' sake,
for harbor and for dole,
And for the sake of Moringer thy noble
husband's soul."

XXVII.

The Lady's gentle heart was moved: —
" Do up the gate," she said,
" And bid the wanderer welcome be to
banquet and to bed;
And since he names my husband's name,
so that he lists to stay,
These towers shall be his harborage a
twelvemonth and a day."

XXVIII.

It was the stalwart warder then undid the
portal broad;
It was the noble Moringer that o'er the
threshold strode: —
" And have thou thanks, kind Heaven,"
he said, " though from a man of sin,
That the true lord stands here once more
his castle-gate within."

XXIX.

Then up the halls paced Moringer, his
step was sad and slow;
It sat full heavy on his heart, none
seem'd their Lord to know;
He sat him on a lowly bench, oppress'd
with woe and wrong,
Short space he sat, but ne'er to him
seem'd little space so long.

XXX.

Now spent was day, and feasting o'er,
and come was evening hour,
The time was nigh when new-made brides
retire to nuptial bower;
" Our castle's wont," a brides-man said,
" hath been both firm and long,
No guest to harbor in our halls till he
shall chant a song."

XXXI.

Then spoke the youthful bridegroom
there, as he sat by the bride: —
" My merry minstrel folk," quoth he,
" lay shalm and harp aside;
Our pilgrim guest must sing a lay, the
castle's rule to hold,
And well his guerdon will I pay with
garment and with gold." —

XXXII.

" Chill flows the lay of frozen age,"
'twas thus the pilgrim sung,
" Nor golden meed nor garment gay un-
locks his heavy tongue;
Once did I sit, thou bridegroom gay, at
board as rich as thine,
And by my side as fair a bride with all
her charms was mine.

XXXIII.

" But time traced furrows on my face, and
I grew silver-hair'd,
For locks of brown, and cheeks of youth,
she left this brow and beard;
Once rich, but now a palmer poor, I
tread life's latest stage,
And mingle with your bridal mirth the
lay of frozen age."

XXXIV.

It was the noble Lady there this woeful
lay that hears,
And for the aged pilgrim's grief her eye
was dimm'd with tears;
She bade her gallant cupbearer a golden
beaker take,
And bear it to the palmer poor to quaff
it for her sake.

XXXV.

It was the noble Moringer that dropp'd
    amid the wine
A bridal ring of burning gold so costly
    and so fine:
Now listen, gentles, to my song; it tells
    you but the sooth,
'Twas with that very ring of gold he
    pledged his bridal truth.

XXXVI.

Then to the cupbearer he said: — "Do
    me one kindly deed,
And should my better days return, full
    rich shall be thy meed;
Bear back the golden cup again to yonder
    bride so gay,
And crave her of her courtesy to pledge
    the palmer gray."

XXXVII.

The cupbearer was courtly bred, nor was
    the boon denied;
The golden cup he took again, and bore
    it to the bride: —
"Lady," he said, "your reverend guest
    sends this, and bids me pray,
That, in thy noble courtesy, thou pledge
    the palmer gray."

XXXVIII.

The ring hath caught the Lady's eye, she
    views it close and near;
Then might you hear her shriek aloud: —
    "The Moringer is here!"
Then might you see her start from seat,
    while tears in torrents fell,
But whether 'twas for joy or woe, the
    ladies best can tell.

XXXIX.

But loud she utter'd thanks to Heaven,
    and every saintly power,
That had return'd the Moringer before
    the midnight hour;

And loud she utter'd vow on vow, tha[t]
    never was there bride,
That had like her preserved her troth, o[r]
    been so sorely tried.

XL.

"Yes, here I claim the praise," she sai[d]
    "to constant matrons due,
Who keep the troth that they have pligh[t]
    so steadfastly and true;
For count the term howe'er you will, s[o]
    that you count aright,
Seven twelve-months and a day are ou[t]
    when bells toll twelve to-night."

XLI.

It was Marstetten then rose up, his fa[l]
    chion there he drew;
He kneel'd before the Moringer, an[d]
    down his weapon threw: —
"My oath and knightly faith are broke[,]
    these were the words he said,
"Then take, my liege, thy vassal's swor[d]
    and take thy vassal's head."

XLII.

The noble Moringer he smiled, and the[n]
    aloud did say: —
"He gathers wisdom that hath roam[ed]
    seven twelve-months and a day;
My daughter now hath fifteen years, fa[ir]
    speaks her sweet and fair,
I give her for the bride you lose, and nam[e]
    her for my heir.

XLIII.

"The young bridegroom hath youth[ful]
    bride, the old bridegroom the old[,]
Whose faith was kept till term and ti[me]
    so punctually were told;
But blessings on the warder kind th[at]
    oped my castle gate,
For had I come at morrow tide, I cam[e]
    a day too late."

THE ERL-KING.

FROM THE GERMAN OF GOETHE.

The Erl-King—Erlen-König, or Alder-King—is a goblin that haunts the Black Forest in Thuringia.—
'o be read by a candle particularly long in the snuff.

, WHO rides by night thro' the woodland
　　so wild?
t is the fond father embracing his
　　child;
nd close the boy nestles within his loved
　　arm,
o hold himself fast, and to keep himself
　　warm.

O father, see yonder! see yonder!" he
　　says; —
My boy, upon what dost thou fearfully
　　gaze?" —
O, 'tis the Erl-King with his crown and
　　his shroud."
No, my son, it is but a dark wreath of
　　the cloud."

(THE ERL-KING SPEAKS.)

O come and go with me, thou loveliest
　　child;
y many a gay sport shall thy time be
　　beguiled;
y mother keeps for thee full many a
　　fair toy,
nd many a fine flower shall she pluck
　　for my boy."

O father, my father, and did you not
　　hear
he Erl-King whisper so low in my
　　ear?" —
Be still, my heart's darling — my child,
　　be at ease;
was but the wild blast as it sung thro'
　　the trees."

ERL-KING.

" O wilt thou go with me, thou loveliest
　　boy?
My daughter shall tend thee with care
　　and with joy;
She shall bear thee so lightly thro' wet
　　and thro' wild,
And press thee, and kiss thee, and sing
　　to my child."

" O father, my father, and saw you not
　　plain,
The Erl-King's pale daughter glide past
　　thro' the rain?" —
" O yes, my loved treasure, I knew it
　　full soon;
It was the gray willow that danced to the
　　moon."

ERL-KING.

O come and go with me, no longer delay,
Or else, silly child, I will drag thee away."
" O father! O father! now, now keep
　　your hold,
The Erl-King has seized me — his grasp
　　is so cold!" —

Sore trembled the father; he spurr'd
　　thro' the wild,
Clasping close to his bosom his shudder-
　　ing child;
He reaches his dwelling in doubt and in
　　dread,
But, clasp'd to his bosom, the infant was
　　dead!"

MISCELLANEOUS POEMS.

JUVENILE LINES.
FROM VIRGIL.

1782. — ÆTAT. 11.

"SCOTT's autobiography tells us that his translations in verse from Horace and Virgil were often approved by Dr. Adams [Rector of the High School, Edinburgh]. One of these little pieces, written in a weak, boyish scrawl, within pencilled marks still visible, had been carefully preserved by his mother; it was found folded up in a cover, inscribed by the old lady, — "*My Walter's first lines*, 1782." — Lockhart, *Life of Scott*, vol. i. p. 129.

IN awful ruins Ætna thunders nigh,
And sends in pitchy whirlwinds to the sky
Black clouds of smoke, which still as
    they aspire,
From their dark sides there bursts the
    glowing fire;
At other times huge balls of fire are
    toss'd,
That lick the stars, and in the smoke are
    lost;
Sometimes the mount, with vast convul-
    sions torn,
Emits huge rocks, which instantly are
    borne
With loud explosions to the starry skies,
The stones made liquid as the huge mass
    flies,
Then back again with greater weight
    recoils,
While Ætna thundering from the bottom
    boils.

ON A THUNDER STORM
1783. — Æt. 12.

"IN Scott's Introduction to the Lay, he alludes to an original effusion of these 'school boy days,' prompted by a thunder-storm, which he says 'was much approved of, until a malevolent critic sprung up in the shape of an apothecary's blue-buskined wife,' etc. These lines and another short piece, 'On the Setting Sun,' were lately found wrapped up in a cover, inscribed by Dr. Adams, 'Walter Scott, July 1783.'"

LOUD o'er my head though awful thunder
    roll,
And vivid lightnings flash from pole to
    pole,
Yet 'tis thy voice, my God, that bids them
    fly,
Thy arm directs those lightnings through
    the sky.
Then let the good thy mighty name revere,
And harden'd sinners thy just vengeance
    fear.

ON THE SETTING SUN.
1783.

THOSE evening clouds, that setting ray,
And beauteous tints, serve to display
   Their great Creator's praise;
Then let the short-lived thing call'd man,
Whose life's comprised within a span,
   To Him his homage raise.

We often praise the evening clouds,
   And tints so gay and bold,
But seldom think upon our God,
   Who tinged these clouds with gold.

THE VIOLET.

THESE lines were first published in the English Minstrelsy, 1810. They were written in 1797, on occasion of the poet's disappointment in love. — See *Life of Scott*, vol. i. p. 333.

THE violet in her green-wood bower,
Where birchen boughs with hazels
mingle,
May boast itself the fairest flower
In glen, or copse, or forest dingle.

Though fair her gems of azure hue,
Beneath the dew-drop's weight reclin-
ing,
I've seen an eye of lovelier hue,
More sweet through wat'ry lustre shin-
ing.

The summer sun that dew shall dry,
Ere yet the day be past its morrow;
Nor longer in my false love's eye
Remain'd the tear of parting sorrow.

TO A LADY.

WITH FLOWERS FROM A ROMAN WALL.

WRITTEN in 1797, on an excursion from Gills-land, in Cumberland. See *Life*, vol. i. p. 365.

TAKE these flowers which, purple waving,
On the ruin'd rampart grew,
Where, the sons of freedom braving,
Rome's imperial standards flew.

Warriors from the breach of danger
Pluck no longer laurels there;
They but yield the passing stranger
Wild-flower wreaths for Beauty's hair.

WAR–SONG.

OF THE ROYAL EDINBURGH LIGHT DRAGOONS.*

1797.

To horse! to horse! the standard flies,
The bugles sound the call;
The Gallic navy stems the seas,
The voice of battle's on the breeze,
Arouse ye, one and all!

From high Dunedin's towers we come,
A band of brothers true;
Our casques the leopard's spoils surround,
With Scotland's hardy thistle crown'd;
We boast the red and blue.†

Though tamely couch'd to Gallia's frown
Dull Holland's tardy train;
Their ravish'd toys tho' Romans mourn;
Tho' gallant Switzers vainly spurn,
And, foaming, gnaw the chain;

Oh! had they mark'd the avenging call
Their brethren's murder gave, ‡
Disunion ne'er their ranks had mown,
Nor patriot valor, desperate grown,
Sought freedom in the grave!

Shall we, too, bend the stubborn head,
In Freedom's temple born,
Dress our pale cheek in timid smile
To hail a master in our isle,
Or brook a victor's scorn?

No! though destruction o'er the land
Come pouring as a flood,
The sun, that sees our falling day,
Shall mark our sabres' deadly sway,
And set that night in blood.

For gold let Gallia's legions fight,
Or plunder's bloody gain;
Unbribed, unbought, our swords we
draw,
To guard our king, to fence our law,
Nor shall their edge be vain.

If ever breath of British gale
Shall fan the tri-color,
Or footstep of invader rude,
With rapine foul, and red with blood,
Pollute our happy shore, —

Then farewell home! and farewell friends!
Adieu each tender tie!
Resolved, we mingle in the tide,
Where charging squadrons furious ride,
To conquer or to die.

---

* Written during the apprehension of an inva-sion, this song appeared originally in the *Scott's Magazine* in 1802. Sir Walter was then Quarter-master of the Edinburgh Light Cavalry.

† The royal colors.
‡ The allusion is to the massacre of the Swiss Guards on the fatal 10th of August, 1792.

To horse! to horse! the sabres gleam;
  High sounds our bugle-call;
Combined by honor's sacred tie,
Our word is *Laws and Liberty!*
March forward, one and all!

THE BARD'S INCANTATION.

WRITTEN UNDER THE THREAT OF INVA-
SION IN THE AUTUMN OF 1804.

THE forest of Glenmore is drear,
  It is all of black pine and the dark oak-
    tree;
And the midnight wind, to the mountain
    deer,
  Is whistling the forest lullaby;
The moon looks thro' the drifting storm,
But the troubled lake reflects not her form,
For the waves roll whitening to the land,
And dash against the shelvy strand.
There is a voice among the trees,
  That mingles with the groaning oak —
That mingles with the stormy breeze,
  And the lake-waves dashing against the
    rock; —
There is a voice within the wood,
The voice of the bard in fitful mood,
His song was louder than the blast,
As the bard of Glenmore thro' the forest
    past: —

"Wake ye from your sleep of death,
  Minstrels and bards of other days!
For the midnight wind is on the heath,
  And the midnight meteors dimly blaze:
The Spectre with his Bloody Hand,*
Is wandering through the wild woodland:
The owl and the raven are mute for dread,
And the time is meet to awake the dead!

"Souls of the mighty, wake and say,
  To what high strain your harps were
    strung,
When Lochlin plow'd her billowy way,
  And on your shores her Norsemen flung?
Her Norsemen train'd to spoil and blood,
Skill'd to prepare the raven's food,
All, by your harpings, doom'd to die
On bloody Largs and Loncarty.†

* The forest of Glenmore is haunted by a
spirit called Lhamdearg, or Red-hand.

† Where the Norwegian invader of Scotland
received two bloody defeats.

"Mute are ye all? No murmurs strang
  Upon the midnight breeze sail by;
Nor through the pines, with whistlin
    change
  Mimic the harp's wild harmony?
Mute are ye now? — Ye ne'er were mut
When Murder with his bloody foot,
And Rapine with his iron hand,
Were hovering near yon mountain stran

"O yet awake the strain to tell,
  By every deed in song enroll'd,
By every chief who fought or fell,
  For Albion's weal in battle bold: —
From Coilgach, ‡ first who roll'd his ca
Thro' the deep ranks of Roman war,
To him, of veteran memory dear,
Who victor died on Aboukir.

"By all their swords, by all their scars
  By all their names, a mighty spell,
By all their wounds, by all their wars,
  Arise, the mighty strain to tell!
For fiercer than fierce Hengist's strain,
More impious han the heathen Dane,
More grasping han all-grasping Rome
Gaul's ravening legions hither come!"—

The wind is hush'd, and still the lake: -
  Strange murmurs fill my tingling ear
Bristles my hair, my sinews quake,
  At the dread voice of other years: —
"When targets clash'd, and bugles run,
And blades round warriors' heads we
    flung,
The foremost of the band were we,
And hymn'd the joys of Liberty!"

HELVELLYN.
1805.

IN the spring of 1805, a young gentleman
talents, and of a most amiable disposition, perish
by losing his way on the mountain Helvelly
His remains were not discovered till three mont
afterwards, when they were found guarded by
faithful terrier-bitch, his constant attendant du
ing frequent solitary rambles through the wil
of Cumberland and Westmoreland.

I CLIMB'D the dark brow of the migh
    Helvellyn,
  Lakes and mountains beneath m
    gleam'd misty and wide;

‡ The Galgacus of Tacitus.

ll was still, save by fits, when the eagle
  was yelling,
  And starting around me the echoes replied.
n the right, Striden-edge round the Red-
  tarn was bending,
  nd Catchedicam its left verge was defending.
ne huge nameless rock in the front was
  ascending,
  When I mark'd the sad spot where the
  wanderer had died.

ark green was that spot mid the brown
  mountain-heather,
  Where the Pilgrim of Nature lay
  stretch'd in decay,
ke the corpse of an outcast abandon'd
  to weather,
  Till the mountain winds wasted the
  tenantless clay.
or yet quite deserted, tho' lonely extended,
  r, faithful in death, his mute favorite
  attended,
ne much-loved remains of her master
  defended,
  And chased the hill-fox and the raven
  away.

ow long didst thou think that his silence
  was slumber?
  When the wind waved his garment,
  how oft didst thou start?
ow many long days and long weeks
  didst thou number,
  Ere he faded before thee, the friend of
  thy heart?
nd, oh! was it meet, that — no requiem
  read o'er him —
  mother to weep, and no friend to deplore him,
  nd thou, little guardian, alone stretch'd
  before him —
  Unhonor'd the Pilgrim from life should
  depart?

hen a Prince to the fate of the Peasant
  has yielded,
  The tapestry waves dark round the dim-
  lighted hall;
  ith scutcheons of silver the coffin is
  shielded,
  And pages stand mute by the canopied
  pall;

Thro' the courts, at deep midnight, the
  torches are gleaming;
In the proudly-arch'd chapel the banners
  are beaming,
Far adown the long aisle sacred music is
  streaming,   [fall.
  Lamenting a Chief of the people should

But meeter for thee, gentle lover of
  nature,
  To lay down thy head like the meek
  mountain lamb,
When, wilder'd, he drops from some cliff
  huge in stature,
  And draws his last sob by the side of
  his dam.
And more stately thy couch by this desert
  lake lying,
Thy obsequies sung by the gray plover
  flying,
With one faithful friend but to witness
  thy dying,
  In the arms of Helvellyn and Catchedicam.

THE DYING BARD.

1806.

AIR — *Daffydz Gangwen.*

THE Welsh tradition bears, that a Bard, on
his death-bed, demanded his harp, and played
the air to which these verses are adapted; requesting that it might be performed at his
funeral.

I.

DINAS EMLINN, lament; for the moment
  is nigh,
When mute in the woodlands thine echoes
  shall die:
No more by sweet Teivi Cadwallon shall
  rave,
And mix his wild notes with the wild dashing wave.

II.

In spring and in autumn thy glories of
  shade
Unhonor'd shall flourish, unhonor'd shall
  fade;
For soon shall be lifeless the eye and the
  tongue,
That view'd them with rapture, with
  rapture that sung.

III.

Thy sons, Dinas Emlinn, may march in
their pride,
And chase the proud Saxon from Presta-
tyn's side;
But where is the harp shall give life to
their name?
And where is the bard shall give heroes
their fame?

IV.

And oh, Dinas Emlinn, thy daughters so
fair,
Who heave the white bosom, and wave
the dark hair;
What tuneful enthusiast shall worship
their eye,
When half of their charms with Cadwallon
shall die?

V.

Then adieu, silver Teivi! I quit thy loved
scene,
To join the dim choir of the bards who
have been;
With Lewarch, and Meilor, and Merlin
the Old,
And sage Taliessin, high harping to hold.

VI.

And adieu, Dinas Emlinn! still green be
thy shades,
Unconquer'd thy warriors, and matchless
thy maids!
And thou, whose faint warblings my weakness can tell,
Farewell, my loved Harp, my last treasure, farewell!

THE NORMAN HORSE-SHOE.
1806.

A:R — *The War-Song of the Men of Glamorgan.*

THE Welsh, inhabiting a mountainous country,
and possessing only an inferior breed of horses,
were usually unable to encounter the shock of
the Anglo-Norman cavalry. Occasionally, however, they were successful in repelling the invaders; and the following verses are supposed
to celebrate a defeat of CLARE, Earl of Striguil
and Pembroke, and of NEVILLE, Baron of

Chepstow, Lords-Marchers of Monmouthshir
Rymny is a stream which divides the counti
of Monmouth and Glamorgan: Caerphili, th
scene of the supposed battle, is a vale upon i
banks, dignified by the ruins of a very ancie
castle.

I.

RED glows the forge in Striguil's bound
And hammers din, and anvil sounds,
And armorers, with iron toil,
Barb many a steed for battle's broil.
Foul fall the hand which bends th
steel
Around the courser's thundering heel,
That e'er shall dint a sable wound
On fair Glamorgan's velvet ground!

II.

From Chepstow's towers, ere dawn
morn,
Was heard afar the bugle horn;
And forth in banded pomp and pride,
Stout Clare and fiery Neville ride.
They swore their banners broad shoul
gleam,
In crimson light, on Rymny's stream;
They vow'd, Caerphili's sod should fee
The Norman charger's spurning heel.

III.

And sooth they swore — the sun arose,
And Rymny's wave with crimson glows
For Clare's red banner, floating wide,
Roll'd down the stream to Severn
tide!
And sooth they vow'd — the trample
green
Show'd where hot Neville's charge ha
been:
In every sable hoof-tramp stood
A Norman horseman's curdling blood!

IV.

Old Chepstow's brides may curse the toi
That arm'd stout Clare for Cambria
broil;
Their orphans long the art may rue,
For Neville's war-horse forged the sho
No more the stamp of armed steed
Shall dint Glamorgan's velvet mead;
Nor trace be there, in early spring,
Save of the Fairies' emerald ring.

THE MAID OF TORO.

1806.

Low shone the sun on the fair lake of
Toro,
And weak were the whispers that waved
the dark wood,
I as a fair maiden, bewilder'd in sorrow,
Sorely sigh'd to the breezes, and wept
to the flood: —
O saints! from the mansions of bliss
lowly bending;
Sweet Virgin! who hearest the suppliant's cry,
w grant my petition, in anguish ascending:
My Henry restore, or let Eleanor die!"

I distant and faint were the sounds of
the battle,
With the breezes they rise, with the
breezes they fail,
l the shout, and the groan, and the
conflict's dread rattle,
And the chase's wild clamor, came
loading the gale.
eathless she gazed on the woodlands so
dreary;
Slowly approaching a warrior was
seen;
e's ebbing tide mark'd his footsteps so
weary,
Cleft was his helmet, and woe was his
mien.

O save thee, fair maid, for our armies
are flying!
O save thee, fair maid, for thy guardian
is low!
adly cold on yon heath thy brave Henry
is lying,
And fast through the woodland approaches the foe."
arce could he falter the tidings of sorrow,
And scarce could she hear them, benumb'd with despair:
d when the sun sank on the sweet lake
of Toro,
Forever he set to the Brave and the Fair.

THE PALMER.

1806.

"O OPEN the door, some pity to show,
Keen blows the northern wind!
The glen is white with the drifted snow,
And the path is hard to find.

"No outlaw seeks your castle gate,
From chasing the King's deer,
Though even an outlaw's wretched state
Might claim compassion here.

"A weary Palmer, worn and weak,
I wander for my sin;
O open, for Our Lady's sake!
A pilgrim's blessing win!

"I'll give you pardons from the Pope,
And reliques from o'er the sea;
Or if for these you will not ope,
Yet open for charity.

"The hare is crouching in her form,
The hart beside the hind;
An aged man, amid the storm,
No shelter can I find.

"You hear the Ettrick's sullen roar,
Dark, deep, and strong is he,
And I must ford the Ettrick o'er
Unless you pity me.

"The iron gate is bolted hard,
At which I knock in vain;
The owner's heart is closer barr'd,
Who hears me thus complain.

"Farewell, farewell! and Mary grant,
When old and frail you be,
You never may the shelter want,
That's now denied to me."

The Ranger on his couch lay warm,
And heard him plead in vain;
But oft amid December's storm,
He'll hear that voice again:

For lo, when through the vapors dark,
Morn shone on Ettrick fair,
A corpse amid the elders rank,
The Palmer welter'd there.

THE MAID OF NEIDPATH.

1806.

THERE is a tradition in Tweeddale, that, when Neidpath Castle, near Peebles, was inhabited by the Earls of March, a mutual passion subsisted between a daughter of that noble family, and a son of the Laird of Tushielaw, in Ettrick Forest. As the alliance was thought unsuitable by her parents, the young man went abroad. During his absence, the lady fell into a consumption ; and at length, as the only means of saving her life, her father consented that her lover should be recalled. On the day when he was expected to pass through Peebles, on the road to Tushielaw, the young lady, though much exhausted, caused herself to be carried to the balcony of a house in Peebles, belonging to the family, that she might see him as he rode past. Her anxiety and eagerness gave such force to her organs, that she is said to have distinguished his horse's footsteps at an incredible distance. But Tushielaw, unprepared for the change in her appearance, and not expecting to see her in that place, rode on without recognizing her, or even slackening his pace. The lady was unable to support the shock ; and, after a short struggle, died in the arms of her attendants. There is an incident similar to this traditional tale in Count Hamilton's " Fleur d'Épine."

O LOVERS' eyes are sharp to see,
    And lovers' ears in hearing;
And love, in life's extremity,
    Can lend an hour of cheering.
Disease had been in Mary's bower,
    And slow decay from mourning,
Though now she sits on Neidpath's tower,
    To watch her love's returning.

All sunk and dim her eyes so bright,
    Her form decay'd by pining,
Till through her wasted hand, at night,
    You saw the taper shining;
By fits, a sultry hectic hue,
    Across her cheek was flying;
By fits, so ashy pale she grew,
    Her maidens thought her dying.

Yet keenest powers to see and hear,
    Seem'd in her frame residing;
Before the watch-dog prick'd his ear,
    She heard her lover's riding;
Ere scarce a distant form was kenn'd,
    She knew, and waved to greet him;
And o'er the battlement did bend,
    As on the wing to meet him.

He came — he pass'd — a heedless gaze,
    As o'er some stranger glancing;
Her welcome, spoke in faltering phras
    Lost in his courser's prancing —
The castle arch, whose hollow tone
    Returns each whisper spoken,
Could scarcely catch the feeble moan,
    Which told her heart was broken.

WANDERING WILLIE.

1806.

ALL joy was bereft me the day that y
    left me,
    And climb'd the tall vessel to sail y
    wide sea;
O weary betide it ! I wander beside it,
    And bann'd it for parting my Wil
    and me.

Far o'er the wave hast thou follow'd t
    fortune,
    Oft fought the squadrons of France a
    of Spain;
Ae kiss of welcome's worth twenty
    parting,
    Now I hae gotten my Willie again.

When the sky it was mirk, and the wir
    they were wailing,
    I sat on the beach wi' the tear in my
And thought o' the bark where
    Willie was sailing,
    And wish'd that the tempest could
    blaw on me.

Now that thy gallant ship rides at
    mooring,
    Now that my wanderer's in safety
    hame,
Music to me were the wildest wind's roar
    That e'er o'er Inch-Keith drove
    dark ocean faem.

When the lights they did blaze, and
    guns they did rattle,
    And blithe was each heart for the gr
    victory,
In secret I wept for the dangers of bat
    And thy glory itself was scarce com
    to me.

But now shalt thou tell, while I eag
    listen,
    Of each bold adventure, and ev
    brave scar;

d trust me, I'll smile, though my een
they may glisten;
For sweet after danger's the tale of the
war.

d oh, how we doubt when there's distance 'tween lovers,
When there's naething to speak to the
heart thro' the ee;
ow often the kindest and warmest prove
rovers,
And the love of the faithfullest ebbs
like the sea.

ll, at times — could I help it? — I pined
and I ponder'd
If love could change notes like the bird
on the tree —
w I'll ne'er ask if thine eyes may hae
wander'd,
Enough, thy leal heart has been constant to me.

elcome from sweeping o'er sea and
through channel,
Hardships and danger despising for fame,
rnishing story for glory's bright annal,
Welcome, my wanderer, to Jeanie and
hame;

ough, now thy story in annals of glory
Has humbled the pride of France, Holland, and Spain;
o more shalt thou grieve me, no more
shalt thou leave me,
I never will part with my Willie again.

HUNTING SONG.*
1808.

AKEN, lords and ladies gay,
n the mountain dawns the day;
l the jolly chase is here,
ith hawk, and horse, and hunting-spear!
ounds are in their couples yelling,
awks are whistling, horns are knelling,
errily, merrily, mingle they: —
Waken, lords and ladies gay."

aken, lords and ladies gay,
e mist has left the mountain gray,

* Published in the continuation of Strutt's cu-
us romance called "Queenhoo Hall," 1808.

Springlets in the dawn are steaming,
Diamonds on the brake are gleaming;
And foresters have busy been,
To track the buck in thickets green;
Now we come to chant our lay: —
"Waken, lords and ladies gay."

Waken, lords and ladies gay,
To the green-wood haste away;
We can show you where he lies,
Fleet of foot, and tall of size;
We can show the marks he made
When, 'gainst the oak his antlers fray'd:
You shall see him brought to bay: —
"Waken, lords and ladies gay."

Louder, louder chant the lay,
Waken, lords and ladies gay!
Tell them youth, and mirth, and glee,
Run a course as well as we;
Time, stern huntsman! who can baulk,
Staunch as hound, and fleet as hawk:
Think of this, and rise with day,
Gentle lords and ladies gay.

HEALTH TO LORD MELVILLE. †
1806.
AIR — *Carrickfergus.*

SINCE here we are set in array round the
table,
Five hundred good fellows well met in
a hall,
Come listen, brave boys, and I'll sing as
I'm able,
How innocence triumph'd, and pride
got a fall.
But push round the claret —
Come, stewards, don't spare it —
With rapture you'll drink to the toast
that I give:
Here, boys,
Off with it merrily —
MELVILLE forever, and long may he live!

What were the Whigs doing, when boldly
pursuing,
PITT banish'd Rebellion, gave Treason
a string?

† A Broadside printed at the time of Lord
Melville's acquittal.

Why, they swore on their honor, for
  ARTHUR O'CONNOR,
And fought hard for DESPARD against
  country and king.
    Well, then, we knew, boys,
      PITT and MELVILLE were true
      boys,
And the tempest was raised by the friends
  of Reform.
    Ah, woe!
    Weep to his memory;
Low lies the Pilot that weather'd the
  storm!

And pray, don't you mind when the
  Blues first were raising,
  And we scarcely could think the house
  safe o'er our heads?
When villains and coxcombs, French
  politics praising,
  Drove peace from our tables and sleep
  from our beds?
    Our hearts they grew bolder
    When, musket on shoulder,
Stepp'd forth our old Statesman example
  to give.
    Come, boys, never fear,
    Drink the Blue Grenadier —
Here's to old HARRY, and long may he
  live!

They would turn us adrift; though rely,
  sir, upon it —
  Our own faithful chronicles warrant us
  that
The free mountaineer and his bonny blue
  bonnet
  Have oft gone as far as the regular's hat.
    We laugh at their taunting,
    For all we are wanting
Is license our life for our country to give.
    Off with it merrily,
    Horse, foot, and artillery,
Each loyal Volunteer, long may he live!

'Tis not us alone, boys—the Army and Navy
  Have each got a slap mid their politic
  pranks;
CORNWALLIS cashier'd, that watch'd winters to save ye,
  And the Cape call'd a bauble, unworthy
  of thanks.
    But vain is their taunt;
    No soldier shall want

The thanks that his country to valor can giv
    Come, boys,
    Drink it off merrily, —
SIR DAVID and POPHAM, and long ma
  they live!

And then our revenue — Lord knows ho
  they view'd it,
  While each petty statesman talke
  lofty and big;
But the beer-tax was weak, as if Whi
  bread had brew'd it,
  And the pig-iron duty a shame to a pi
    In vain is their vaunting;
    Too surely there's wanting
What judgment, experience, and stead
  ness give:
    Come, boys,
    Drink it off merrily, —
Health to sage MELVILLE, and long ma
  he live!

Our King, too — our princess — I da
  not say more, sir,—
  May Providence watch them with mer
  and might!
While there's one Scottish hand that ca
  wag a claymore, sir,
  They shall ne'er want a friend to stan
  up for their right.
    Be damn'd he that dare not, —
    For my part, I'll spare not
To beauty afflicted a tribute to give:
    Fill it up steadily,
    Drink it off readily —
Here's to the Princess, and long ma
  she live!

And since we must not set Auld Reek
  in glory,
  And make her brown visage as light
   her heart;*
Till each man illumine his own upper stor
  Nor law-book nor lawyer shall for
  us to part.
    In GRENVILLE and SPENCER,
    And some few good men, sir,
High talents we honor, slight differen
  forgive;
    But the Brewer we'll hoax,
    Tallyho to the Fox,
And drink MELVILLE forever, as long
  we live!

* The Edinburgh magistrates refused to pe
mit illuminations.

EPITAPH.

1808.

Designed for a monument in Lichfield Cathedral, at the burial-place of the family of Miss Seward.

AMID these aisles, where once his precepts show'd
The Heavenward pathway which in life he trod,
This simple tablet marks a Father's bier,
And those he loved in life, in death are near;
For him, for them, a Daughter bade it rise,
Memorial of domestic charities.
Still wouldst thou know why, o'er the marble spread,
In female grace the willow droops her head;
Why on her branches, silent and unstrung,
The minstrel harp is emblematic hung;
What poet's voice is smothered here in dust,
Till waked to join the chorus of the just,—
Lo! one brief line an answer sad supplies,
Honor'd, beloved, and mourn'd, here SEWARD lies,
Her worth, her warmth of heart, let friendship say, —
Go seek her genius in her living lay.

THE RESOLVE.

IN IMITATION OF AN OLD ENGLISH POEM.

Published in the "Edinburgh Annual Register."

1808.

MY wayward fate I needs must plain,
Though bootless be the theme.
I loved, and was beloved again,
Yet all was but a dream;
For, as her love was quickly got,
So it was quickly gone;
No more I'll bask in flame so hot,
But coldly dwell alone.

Not maid more bright than maid was e'er
My fancy shall beguile,
By flattering word or feigned tear,
By gesture, look, or smile·

No more I'll call the shaft fair shot,
Till it has fairly flown,
Nor scorch me at a flame so hot; —
I'll rather freeze alone.

Each ambush'd Cupid I'll defy,
In cheek, or chin, or brow,
And deem the glance of woman's eye
As weak as woman's vow:
I'll lightly hold the lady's heart,
That is but lightly won;
I'll steel my breast to beauty's art,
And learn to live alone.

The flaunting torch soon blazes out,
The diamond's ray abides;
The flame its glory hurls about,
The gem its lustre hides:
Such gem I fondly deem'd was mine,
And glow'd a diamond stone,
But, since each eye may see it shine,
I'll darkling dwell alone.

No waking dream shall tinge my thought
With eyes so bright and vain;
No silken net, so lightly wrought,
Shall tangle me again:
No more I'll pay so dear for wit,
I'll live upon mine own;
Nor shall wild passion trouble it, —
I'll rather dwell alone.

And thus I'll hush my heart to rest: —
"Thy loving labor's lost;
Thou shalt no more be wildly blest,
To be so strangely crost:
The widow'd turtles mateless die,
The phœnix is but one;
They seek no loves — no more will I —
I'll rather dwell alone."

PROLOGUE.

TO MISS BAILLIE'S PLAY OF "THE FAMILY LEGEND."

1809.

'TIS sweet to hear expiring Summer's sigh,
Thro' forests tinged with russet, wail and die;
'Tis sweet and sad the latest notes to hear
Of distant music, dying on the ear;

But far more sadly sweet, on foreign strand
We list the legends of our native land,
Link'd as they come with every tender tie,
Memorials dear of youth and infancy.

Chief, thy wild tales, romantic Caledon,
Wake keen remembrance in each hardy
    son.
Whether on India's burning coasts he toil,
Or till Acadia's * winter-fetter'd soil,
He hears with throbbing heart and mois-
    ten'd eyes,
And, as he hears, what dear illusions rise !
It opens on his soul his native dell,
The woods' wild waving, and the water's
    swell;
Tradition's theme, the tower that threats
    the plain,
The mossy cairn that hides the hero slain;
The cot, beneath whose simple porch were
    told,
By gray-hair'd patriarch, the tales of old,
The infant group, that hush'd their sports
    the while,
And the dear maid who listen'd with a
    smile.
The wanderer, while the vision warms his
    brain,
Is denizen of Scotland once again.

    Are such keen feelings to the crowd
        confined,
And sleep they in the Poet's gifted mind?
Oh no ! For She, within whose mighty page
Each tyrant Passion shows his woe and rage,
Has felt the wizard influence they inspire,
And to your own traditions tuned her lyre.
Yourselves shall judge — whoe'er has
    raised the sail
By Mull's dark coast, has heard this even-
    ing's tale.
The plaided boatman, resting on his oar,
Points to the fatal rock amid the roar
Of whitening waves, and tells whate'er
    to-night
Our humble stage shall offer to your sight;
Proudly preferr'd that first our efforts give
Scenes glowing from her pen to breathe
    and live;
More proudly yet, should Caledon approve
The filial token of a Daughter's love.

* Acadia, or Nova Scotia.

THE POACHER.

*Written in imitation of Crabbe, and
published in the Edinburgh Annual
Register of 1809.*

WELCOME, grave Stranger, to our green
    retreats,
Where health with exercise and freedom
    meets !
Thrice welcome, Sage, whose philosophic
    plan
By Nature's limits metes the rights of
    man !
Generous as he, who now for freedom
    bawls,
Now gives full value for true Indian
    shawls:
O'er court, o'er custom-house, his shoe
    who flings,
Now bilks excisemen, and now bullies
    kings !
Like his, I ween, thy comprehensive mind
Holds laws as mouse-traps baited for man-
    kind;
Thine eye, applausive, each sly vermin
    sees,
That balks the snare, yet battens on the
    cheese;
Thine ear has heard, with scorn instead
    of awe,
Our buck-skinn'd justices expound the
    law,
Wire-draw the acts that fix for wires the
    pain,
And for the netted partridge noose the
    swain;
And thy vindictive arm would fain have
    broke
The last light fetter of the feudal yoke,
To give the denizens of wood and wild,
Nature's free race, to each her free-born
    child.
Hence hast thou mark'd, with grief, fair
    London's race
Mock'd with the boon of one poor Easter
    chase,
And long'd to send them forth as free as
    when
Pour'd o'er Chantilly the Parisian train,
When musket, pistol, blunderbuss, com-
    bined,
And scarce the field-pieces were left be-
    hind !

A squadron's charge each leveret's heart dismay'd,
On every covey fired a bold brigade;
La douce Humanité approved the sport,
For great the alarm indeed, yet small the hurt;
Shouts patriotic solemnized the day,
And Seine re-echo'd Vive la Liberté!
But mad Citoyen, meek Monsieur again,
With some few added links resumes his chain.
Then, since such scenes to France no more are known,
Come, view with me a hero of thine own!
One, whose free actions vindicate the cause
Of sylvan liberty o'er feudal laws.

Seek we yon glades, where the proud oak o'ertops
Wide-waving seas of birch and hazel copse,
Leaving between deserted isles of land,
Where stunted heath is patch'd with ruddy sand,
And lonely on the waste the yew is seen,
Or straggling hollies spread a brighter green.
Here, little worn, and winding dark and steep,
Our scarce-mark'd path descends yon dingle deep:
Hollow — but heedful, cautious of a trip, —
In earthly mire philosophy may slip.
Step slow and wary o'er that swampy steam,
Still, guided by the charcoal's smothering steam,
We reach the frail yet barricaded door
Of hovel form'd for poorest of the poor;
To hearthe the fire, no vent the smoke receives,
The walls are wattles, and the covering leaves;
For, if such hut, our forest statutes say,
Rise in the progress of one night and day
Tho' placed where still the Conqueror's hests o'erawe,
And his son's stirrup shines the badge of law),*

* In the forest courts the presiding judge used to wear as a badge of officer an antique stirrup, said to have been that of William Rufus.

The builder claims the unenviable boon,
To tenant dwelling, framed as slight and soon
As wigwam wild, that shrouds the native frore
On the bleak coast of frost-barr'd Labrador.†

Approach, and through the unlatticed window peep —
Nay, shrink not back, the inmate is asleep;
Sunk mid yon sordid blankets, till the sun
Stoop to the west, the plunderer's toils are done.
Loaded and primed, and prompt for desperate hand,
Rifle and fowling-piece beside him stand;
While round the hut are in disorder laid
The tools and booty of his lawless trade;
For force or fraud, resistance or escape,
The crow, the saw, the bludgeon, and the crape.
His pilfer'd powder in yon nook he hoards,
And the filch'd lead the church's roof affords —
(Hence shall the rector's congregation fret,
That while his sermon's dry his walls are wet.)
The fish-spear barb'd, the sweeping nets are there,
Doe-hides, and pheasant plumes, and skins of hare,
Cordage for toils, and wiring for the snare.
Barter'd for game from chase or warren won,
Yon cask holds moonlight,‡ run when moon was none;
And late-snatch'd spoils lie stow'd in hutch apart,
To wait the associate higgler's evening cart.

Look on his pallet foul, and mark his rest:
What scenes perturb'd are acting in his breast!

† The New Forest, Hampshire, is now disforested, and its laws, etc., are become things of the past.

‡ A cant term for smuggled spirits.

His sable brow is wet and wrung with
    pain,
And his dilated nostril toils in vain;
For short and scant the breath each effort
    draws,
And 'twixt each effort Nature claims a
    pause.
Beyond the loose and sable neckcloth
    stretch'd,
His sinewy throat seems by convulsion
    twitch'd,
While the tongue falters, as to utterance
    loth,
Sounds of dire import, — watchword,
    threat, and oath.
Tho' stupefied by toil, and drugg'd with
    gin,
The body sleep, the restless guest within
Now plies on wood and wold his lawless
    trade,
Now in the fangs of justice wakes dis-
    may'd. —

" Was that wild start of terror and
    despair,
Those bursting eyeballs, and that wilder'd
    air,
Signs of compunction for a murder'd
    hare?
Do the locks bristle and the eyebrows
    arch,
For grouse or partridge massacred in
    March?"

No, scoffer, no! Attend, and mark with
    awe,
There is no wicket in the gate of law!
He, that would e'er so lightly set ajar
That awful portal, must undo each bar:
Tempting occasion, habit, passion, pride,
Will join to storm the breach, and force
    the barrier wide.

That ruffian, whom true men avoid and
    dread,
Whom bruisers, poachers, smugglers,
    call Black Ned,
Was Edward Mansell once; — the light-
    est heart
That ever play'd on holiday his part!
The leader he in every Christmas game,
The harvest-feast grew blither when he
    came,

And liveliest on the chords the bow di
    glance,
When Edward named the tune and le
    the dance.
Kind was his heart, his passions quic
    and strong,
Hearty his laugh, and jovial wa, his song
And if he loved a gun, his father swore:—
" 'Twas but a trick of youth would soo
    be o'er,
Himself had done the same some thirt
    years before."

But he whose humors spurn law's awf
    yoke,
Must herd with those by whom law
    bonds are broke.
The common dread of justice soon allie
The clown, who robs the warren, or excise
With sterner felons train'd to act mor
    dread,
Even with the wretch by whom his fello
    bled.
Then, — as in plagues the foul conta
    gions pass,
Leavening and festering the corrupte
    mass, —
Guilt leagues with guilt, while mutua
    motives draw,
Their hope impunity, their fear the law
Their foes, their friends, their rendezvou
    the same,
Till the revenue balk'd, or pilfer'd game
Flesh the young culprit, and example lead
To darker villany, and direr deeds.

Wild howl'd the wind the forest glade
    along,
And oft the owl renew'd her dismal song
Around the spot where erst he felt th
    wound,
Red William's spectre walk'd his mid
    night round.
When o'er the swamp he cast his bligh
    ing look,
From the green marshes of the stagnar
    brook
The bittern's sullen shout the sedge
    shook!
The waning moon, with storm-presagin
    gleam,
Now gave and now withheld her doub
    ful beam;

The old Oak stoop'd his arms, then flung
    them high,
Bellowing and groaning to the troubled
    sky —
'Twas then, that, couch'd amid the brush-
    wood sere,
In Malwood-walk young Mansell watch'd
    the deer:
The fattest buck received his deadly
    shot —
The watchful keeper heard, and sought
    the spot.
Stout were their hearts, and stubborn
    was their strife,
O'erpower'd at length the Outlaw drew
    his knife!
Next morn a corpse was found upon the
    fell —
The rest his waking agony may tell!

SONG.

OH, say not, my love, with that mortified
    air,
    That your spring-time of pleasure is
        flown,
Nor bid me to maids that are younger
    repair,
    For those raptures that still are thine
        own.

Though April his temples may wreathe
    with the vine,
    Its tendrils in infancy curl'd,
'Tis the ardor of August matures us the
    wine,
    Whose life-blood enlivens the world.

Though thy form, that was fashion'd as
    light as a fay's,
    Has assumed a proportion more round,
And thy glance, that was bright as a fal-
    con's at gaze,
    Looks soberly now on the ground, —

Enough, after absence to meet me
    again,
    Thy steps still with ecstasy move;
Enough, that those dear sober glances
    retain
    For me the kind language of love.

THE BOLD DRAGOON;

OR, THE PLAIN OF BADAJOZ.

1812.

'TWAS a Maréchal of France, and he fain
    would honor gain,
And he long'd to take a passing glance
    at Portugal from Spain;
    With his flying guns this gallant gay,
    And boasted *corps d'armée* —
O he fear'd not our dragoons, with their
    long swords, boldly riding,
    Whack, fal de ral, etc.

To Campo Mayor come, he had quietly
    sat down,
Just a fricassee to pick, while his soldiers
    sack'd the town,
    When, 'twas *peste! morbleu! mon
        Général,*
    Hear the English bugle-call!
And behold the light dragoons, with their
    long swords, boldly riding,
    Whack, fal de ral, etc.

Right about went horse and foot, artillery
    and all,
And, as the devil leaves a house, they
    tumbled through the wall;*
    They took no time to seek the door,
    But, best foot set before —
O they ran from our dragoons, with their
    long swords, boldly riding,
    Whack, fal de ral, etc.

Those valiant men of France they had
    scarcely fled a mile,
When on their flank there soused at once
    the British rank and file:
    For Long, De Grey, and Otway, then
    Ne'er minded one to ten,
But came on like light dragoons, with
    their long swords, boldly riding,
    Whack, fal de ral, etc.

Three hundred British lads they made
    three thousand reel,
Their hearts were made of English oak,
    their swords of Sheffield steel,

* In their hasty evacuation of Campo Mayor
the French pulled down a part of the rampart,
and marched out on the glacis.

Their horses were in Yorkshire bred,
And Beresford them led;
So huzza for brave dragoons, with their
    long swords, boldly riding,
Whack, fal de ral, etc.

Then here's a health to Wellington, to
    Beresford, to Long,
And a single word of Bonaparte before
    I close my song:
The eagles that to fight he brings
Should serve his men with wings,
When they meet the bold dragoons, with
    their long swords, boldly riding,
Whack, fal de ral, etc.

ON THE MASSACRE OF GLENCOE.

1814.

"IN the beginning of the year 1692, an action of unexampled barbarity disgraced the government of King William III. in Scotland. In the August preceding, a proclamation had been issued offering an indemnity to such insurgents as should take the oaths to the King and Queen, on or before the last day of December; and the chiefs of such tribes as had been in arms for James, soon after took advantage of the proclamation. But Macdonald of Glencoe was prevented by accident, rather than by design, from tendering his submission within the limited time. In the end of December he went to Colonel Hill, who commanded the garrison in Fort William, to take the oaths of allegiance to the government; and the latter having furnished him with a letter to Sir Colin Campbell, sheriff of the county of Argyle, directed him to repair immediately to Inverary, to make his submission in a legal manner before that magistrate. But the way to Inverary lay through almost impassable mountains, the season was extremely rigorous, and the whole country was covered with a deep snow. So eager, however, was Macdonald to take the oaths before the limited time should expire, that, though the road lay within half a mile of his own house, he stopped not to visit his family, and, after various obstructions, arrived at Inverary. The time had elapsed, and the sheriff hesitated to receive his submission; but Macdonald prevailed by his importunities, and even tears, in inducing that functionary to administer to him the oath of allegiance, and to certify the cause of his delay. At this time Sir John Dalrymple, afterwards Earl of Stair, being in attendance upon William as Secretary of State for Scotland, took advantage of Macdonald's neglecting to take the oath within the time prescribed, and procured from the King a warrant of military execution against that chief and his whole clan. This was done at the instigation of the Earl of Breadalbane, whose lands the Glencoe men had plundered, and whose treachery to government in negotiating with the Highland clans, Macdonald himself had exposed. The King was accordingly persuaded that Glencoe was the main obstacle to the pacification of the Highlands; and the fact of the unfortunate chief's submission having been concealed, the sanguinary orders for proceeding to military execution against his clan were in consequence obtained. The warrant was both signed and countersigned by the King's own hand, and the Secretary urged the officers who commanded in the Highlands to execute their orders with the utmost rigor. Campbell of Glenlyon, a captain in Argyle's regiment, and two subalterns, were ordered to repair to Glencoe on the first of February with a hundred and twenty men. Campbell, being uncle to young Macdonald's wife, was received by the father with all manner of friendship and hospitality. The men were lodged at free quarters in the houses of his tenants, and received the kindest entertainment. Till the 13th of the month the troops lived in the utmost harmony and familiarity with the people; and on the very night of the massacre the officers passed the evening at cards in Macdonald's house. In the night, Lieutenant Lindsay, with a party of soldiers, called in a friendly manner at his door, and was instantly admitted. Macdonald, while in the act of rising to receive his guest, was shot dead through the back with two bullets. His wife had already dressed; but she was stripped naked by the soldiers, who tore the rings off her fingers with their teeth. The slaughter now became general, and neither age nor infirmity was spared. Some women, in defending their children, were killed; boys imploring mercy were shot dead by officers on whose knees they hung. In one place nine persons, as they sat enjoying themselves at table, were butchered by the soldiers. In Inverriggon, Campbell's own quarters, nine men were first bound by the soldiers, and then shot at intervals one by one. Nearly forty persons were massacred by the troops; and several who fled to the mountains perished by famine and the inclemency of the season. Those who escaped owed their lives to a tempestuous night. Lieutenant-Colonel Hamilton, who had received the charge of the execution from Dalrymple, was on his march with four hundred men, to guard all the passes from the valley of Glencoe; but he was obliged to stop by the severity of the weather, which proved the safety of the unfortunate clan. Next day he entered the valley, laid the houses in ashes, and carried away the cattle and spoil, which were divided among the officers and soldiers." — *Article* "BRITAIN;" *Encyc. Britannica.* — *New Edition.*

"O TELL me, Harper, wherefore flow
Thy wayward notes of wail and woe,
Far down the desert of Glencoe,
    Where none may list their melody?
Say, harp'st thou to the mists that fly,
Or to the dun-deer glancing by,
Or to the eagle, that from high
    Screams chorus to thy minstrelsy?" —

'No, not to these, for they have rest, —
The mist-wreath has the mountain-crest,
The stag his lair, the erne her nest,
  Abode of lone security.
But those for whom I pour the lay,
Not wild-wood deep, nor mountain
    gray,
Not this deep dell, that shrouds from
    day,
  Could screen from treacherous cruelty.

"Their flag was furl'd, and mute their
    drum,
The very household dogs were dumb,
Unwont to bay at guests that come
  In guise of hospitality.
His blithest notes the piper plied,
Her gayest snood the maiden tied,
The dame her distaff flung aside,
  To tend her kindly housewifery.

"The hand that mingled in the meal,
At midnight drew the felon steel,
And gave the host's kind breast to feel
  Meed for his hospitality!
The friendly hearth which warm'd that
    hand,
At midnight arm'd it with the brand,
That bade destruction's flames expand
  Their red and fearful blazonry.

"Then woman's shriek was heard in
    vain,
Nor infancy's unpitied plain,
More than the warrior's groan, could
    gain   .
  Respite from ruthless butchery!
The winter wind that whistled shrill,
The snows that night that cloaked the
    hill,
Though wild and pitiless, had still
  Far more than Southern clemency.

" Long have my harp's best notes been
    gone,
Few are its strings, and faint their tone,
They can but sound in desert lone
  Their gray-hair'd master's misery.
Were each gray hair a minstrel string,
Each chord should imprecations fling,
Till startled Scotland loud should ring: —
  ' Revenge for blood and treachery!' "

FOR A' THAT AN' A' THAT.*

A NEW SONG TO AN OLD TUNE.

1814.

THOUGH right be aft put down by strength,
  As mony a day we saw that,
The true and leilfu' cause at length
  Shall bear the grie for a' that.
For a' that an' a' that,
  Guns, guillotines, and a' that,
The Fleur-de-lis, that lost her right,
  Is queen again for a' that!

We'll twine her in a friendly knot
  With England's Rose, and a' that;
The Shamrock shall not be forgot,
  For Wellington made braw that.
The Thistle, though her leaf be rude,
  Yet faith we'll no misca' that,
She shelter'd in her solitude
  The Fleur-de-lis, for a' that.

The Austrian vine, the Prussian Pine
  (For Blucher's sake, hurra that),
The Spanish Olive, too, shall join,
  And bloom in peace for a' that.
Stout Russia's Hemp, so surely twined
  Around our wreath we'll draw that,
And he that would the cord unbind,
  Shall have it for his gra-vat!

Or, if to choke sae puir a sot,
  Your pity scorn to thraw that,
The Devil's elbow be his lot,
  Where he may sit and claw that.
In spite of slight, in spite of might,
  In spite of brags, an' a' that,
The lads that battled for the right,
  Have won the day, an' a' that!

There's ae bit spot I had forgot,
  America they ca' that;
A coward plot her rats had got
  Their father's flag to gnaw that;
Now see it fly top-gallant high,
  Atlantic winds shall blaw that,
And Yankee loon, beware your croun,
  There's kames in hand to claw that!

* Sung at the first meeting of the Pitt Club of
Scotland.

For on the land, or on the sea,
　Where'er the breezes blaw that,
The British flag shall bear the grie
　And win the day for a' that!

SONG.

FOR THE ANNIVERSARY MEETING OF THE PITT CLUB OF SCOTLAND.

1814.

O, DREAD was the time, and more dread-
　　ful the omen,
　When the brave on Marengo lay
　　slaughter'd in vain,
And beholding broad Europe bow'd down
　　by her foemen,
　PITT closed in his anguish the map of
　　her reign!
Not the fate of broad Europe could bend
　　his brave spirit
To take for his country the safety of shame,
O, then in her triumph remember his merit,
　And hallow the goblet that flows to his
　　name.

Round the husbandman's head, while he
　　traces the furrow,
　The mists of the winter may mingle
　　with rain,
He may plough it with labor, and sow it
　　in sorrow,
　And sigh while he fears he has sow'd
　　it in vain;
He may die ere his children shall reap in
　　their gladness,
　But the blithe harvest-home shall re-
　　member his claim;
And their jubilee-shout shall be soften'd
　　with sadness,
　While they hallow the goblet that flows
　　to his name.

Though anxious and timeless, his life was
　　expended,
　In toils for our country preserved by
　　his care,
Though he died ere one ray o'er the
　　nations ascended,
　To light the long darkness of doubt
　　and despair;
The storms he endured in our Britain's
　　December,
　The perils his wisdom foresaw and o'er-
　　came,

In her glory's rich harvest shall Britain
　　remember,
　And hallow the goblet that flows to his
　　name.

Nor forget HIS gray head, who, all dark
　　in affliction,
　Is deaf to the tales of our victories won,
And to sounds the most dear to paternal
　　affection,
　The shout of his people applauding his
　　SON;
By his firmness unmoved in success and
　　disaster,
　By his long reign of virtue, remember
　　his claim!
With our tribute to PITT join the praise
　　of his Master,
　Though a tear stain the goblet that
　　flows to his name.

Yet again fill the wine-cup, and change
　　the sad measure,
　The rites of our grief and our gratitude
　　paid,
To our Prince, to our Heroes, devote the
　　bright treasure,
　The wisdom that plann'd, and the zeal
　　that obey'd;
Fill WELLINGTON'S cup till it beam like
　　his glory,
　Forget not our own brave DALHOUSIE
　　and GRÆME;
A thousand years hence hearts shall bound
　　at their story,
　And hallow the goblet that flows to
　　their fame.

LINES.

ADDRESSED TO RANALD MACDONALD, ESQ., OF STAFFA.*

1814.

STAFFA, sprung from high Macdonald,
Worthy branch of old Clan-Ranald!
Staffa! king of all kind fellows!
Well befall thy hills and valleys,

---

* Afterwards Sir Reginald Macdonald Stewart Seton, of Staffa, Allanton, and Touch, Baronet. He died 16th April, 1838, in his 61st year. The reader will find a warm tribute to Staffa's char- acter as a Highland landlord, in Scott's article on Sir John Carr's Caledonian Sketches. — *Mis- cellaneous Prose Works*, vol. xix.

akes and inlets, deeps and shallows,
liffs of darkness, caves of wonder,
choing the Atlantic thunder;
ountains which the gray mist covers,
Vhere the Chieftain spirit hovers,
ausing while his pinions quiver,
tretch'd to quit our land forever !
ach kind influence reign above thee !
Varmer heart 'twixt this and Staffa,
eats not, than in heart of Staffa !

PHAROS LOQUITUR.*

AR in the bosom of the deep,
'er these wild shelves my watch I keep;
ruddy gem of changeful light,
ound on the dusky brow of night,
he seaman bids my lustre hail,
nd scorns to strike his timorous sail.

LETTER IN VERSE.

N THE VOYAGE WITH THE COMMISSION-
ERS OF NORTHERN LIGHTS.

"OF the letters which Scott wrote to his
iends during those happy six weeks, I have
covered only one, and it is, thanks to the
isure of the yacht, in verse. The strong
id easy heroics of the first section prove, I
iink, that Mr. Canning did not err when he
old him that if he chose he might emulate
ven Dryden's command of that noble measure;
id the dancing anapæsts of the second, show
iat he could with equal facility have rivalled
ie gay graces of Cotton, Anstey, or Moore." —
ockhart, *Life*, vol. iv., p. 372.

O HIS GRACE THE DUKE OF BUCCLEUCH,
ETC.

Lighthouse Yacht, in the sound of Lerwick
Zetland, 8th August, 1814.

HEALTH to the chieftain from his clansman true !
rom her true minstrel, health to fair
Buccleuch !

* "On the 30th of July, 1814, Mr. Hamilton,
Ir. Erskine, and Mr. Duff, Commissioners,
long with Mr. (now Sir) Walter Scott, and
ie writer, visited the Lighthouse; the Com-
iissioners being then on one of their voyages
f Inspection, noticed in the Introduction.
'hey breakfasted in the Library, when Sir
Valter, at the entreaty of the party, upon in-
cribing his name in the Album, added these
iteresting lines." — *Stevenson's Account of the
ell-Rock Lighthouse.* 1824. Scott's Diary
f the Voyage is now published in the 4th
olume on his *Life*.

Health from the isles, where dewy Morn-
ing weaves
Her chaplet with the tints that Twilight
leaves;
Where late the sun scarce vanish'd from
the sight,
And his bright pathway graced the short-
lived night,
Though darker now as autumn's shades
extend,
The north winds whistle and the mists
ascend !
Health from the land where eddying
whirlwinds toss
The storm-rock'd *cradle* of the Cape of
Noss !
On outstretch'd cords the giddy engine
slides,
His own strong arm the bold adventurer
guides,
And he that lists such desperate feat to
try,
May, like the sea-mew, skim 'twixt earth
and sky,
And feel the mid-air gales around him
blow,
And see the billows rage five hundred feet
below.

Here, by each stormy peak and desert
shore,
The hardy islesman tugs the daring oar,
Practised alike his venturous course to
keep,
Through the white breakers of the path-
less deep,
By ceaseless peril and by toil to gain
A wretched pittance from the niggard
main;
And when the worn-out drudge old ocean
leaves,
What comfort greets him, and what hut re-
ceives?
Lady ! the worst your presence ere has
cheer'd
(When want and sorrow fled as you ap-
pear'd)
Were to a Zetlander as the high dome
Of proud Drumlanrig to my humble home.
Here rise no groves, and here no gardens
blow,
Here even the hardy heath scarce dares
to grow;

But rocks on rocks, in mist and storm
    array'd,
Stretch far to sea their giant colonnade,
With many a cavern seam'd, the dreary
    haunt
Of the dun seal and swarthy cormorant.
Wild round their rifted brows, with fre-
    quent cry
As of lament, the gulls and gannets fly,
And from their sable base, with sullen
    sound,
In sheets of whitening foam the waves
    rebound.

Yet even these coasts a touch of envy gain
From those whose land has known op-
    pression's chain;
For here the industrious Dutchman comes
    once more
To moor his fishing craft by Bressey's
    shore;
Greets every former mate and brother tar,
Marvels how Lerwick 'scaped the rage of
    war,
Tells many a tale of Gallic outrage done,
And ends by blessing God and Wel-
    lington.
Here too the Greenland tar, a fiercer guest,
Claims a brief hour of riot, not of rest:
Proves each wild frolic that in wine has
    birth,
And wakes the land with brawls and
    boisterous mirth.
A sadder sight on yon poor vessel's prow
The captive Norseman sits in silent woe,
And eyes the flags of Britain as they flow.
Hard fate of war, which bade her terrors
    sway
His destined course, and seize so mean a
    prey;
A bark with planks so warp'd and seams
    so riven,
She scarce might face the gentlest air of
    heaven;
Pensive he sits, and questions oft if none
Can list his speech, and understand his
    moan;
In vain — no Islesman now can use the
    tongue
Of the bold Norse, from whom their lin-
    eage sprung.
Not thus of old the Norseman hither came,
Won by the love of danger or of fame;

On every storm-beat cape a shapeless
    tower
Tells of their wars, their conquests, and
    their power;
For ne'er for Grecia's vales, or Latian land
Was fiercer strife than for this barren
    strand;
A race severe — the isle and ocean lords
Loved for its own delight the strife of
    swords;
With scornful laugh the mortal pang
    defied,
And blest their gods that they in battle
    died.

Such were the sires of Zetland's simple
    race,
And still the eye may faint resemblance
    trace
In the blue eye, tall form, proportion fair,
The limbs athletic, and the long light
    hair —
(Such was the mien, as Scald and Min-
    strel sings,
Of fair-hair'd Harold, first of Norway's
    Kings);
But their high deeds to scale these crags
    confined,
Their only warfare is with waves and wind.

Why should I talk of Mousa's castled
    coast?
Why of the horrors of the Sumburgh
    Rost?
May not these bald disjointed lines suffice
Penn'd while my comrades whirl the rat-
    tling dice —
While down the cabin skylight lessening
    shine
The rays, and eve is chased with mirth
    and wine?
Imagined, while down Mousa's desert bay
Our well-trimm'd vessel urged her nimble
    way,
While to the freshening breeze she lean'd
    her side,
And bade her bowsprit kiss the foamy tide?

Such are the lays that Zetland isles
    supply;
Drench'd with the drizzly spray and drop-
    ping sky,
Weary and wet, a sea-sick minstrel I —

POSTSCRIPTUM.

Kirkwall, Orkney, Aug. 13, 1814.

In respect that your Grace has com-
    mission'd a Kraken,
You will please be inform'd that they
    seldom are taken;
It is January two years, the Zetland folks
    say,
Since they saw the last Kraken in Scallo-
    way bay;
He lay in the offing a fortnight or more,
But the devil a Zetlander put from the
    shore,
Though bold in the seas of the North to
    assail
The morse and the sea-horse, the gram-
    pus and whale.
If your Grace thinks I'm writing the thing
    that is not,
You may ask at a namesake of ours, Mr.
    Scott —
He's not from our clan, though his
    merits deserve it,
But springs, I'm inform'd, from the Scotts
    of Scotstarvet);*
He question'd the folks who beheld it
    with eyes,
But they differ'd confoundedly as to the
    size.
For instance, the modest and diffident
    swore
That it seem'd like the keel of a ship, and
    no more —
Those of eyesight more clear, or of fancy
    more high,
Said it rose like an island 'twixt ocean
    and sky —
But all of the hulk had a steady opinion
That 'twas sure a *live* subject of Neptune's
    dominion —
And I think, my Lord Duke, your Grace
    hardly would wish,
To cumber your house, such a kettle of
    fish.
Had your order related to night-caps or
    hose,
Or mittens of worsted, there's plenty of
    those.

* The Scotts of Scotstarvet, and other families
  the same in Fife and elsewhere, claim no kin-
  red with the great clan of the Border — and
  car armorial bearings are different.

Or would you be pleased but to fancy a
    whale?
And direct me to send it — by sea or by
    mail?
The season, I'm told, is nigh over, but still
I could get you one fit for the lake at
    Bow-hill.
Indeed, as to whales, there's no need to
    be thrifty,
Since one day last fortnight two hundred
    and fifty,
Pursued by seven Orkneymen's boats and
    no more,
Betwixt Truffness and Luffness were
    drawn on the shore!
You'd ask if I saw this same wonderful
    sight;
I own that I did not, but easily might —
For this mighty shoal of leviathans lay
On our lee-beam a mile, in the loop of
    the bay,
And the islesmen of Sanda were all at
    the spoil.
And *flinching*, (so term it) the blubber
    to boil;
(Ye spirits of lavender, drown the re-
    flection
That awakes at the thought of this odor-
    ous dissection.)
To see this huge marvel full fain would
    we go,
But Wilson, the wind, and the current,
    said no.
We have now got to Kirkwall, and needs
    I must stare
When I think that in verse I have once
    call'd it *fair ;*
'Tis a base little borough, both dirty and
    mean —
There's nothing to hear, and there's
    naught to be seen,
Save a church, where, of old times, a
    prelate harangued,
And a palace that's built by an earl that
    was hang'd.
But, farewell to Kirkwall — aboard we
    are going,
The anchor's a-peak, and the breezes are
    blowing;
Our commodore calls all his band to
    their places,
And 'tis time to release you — good night
    to your Graces!

BRIDAL SONG.

To the tune of "I have been a Fiddler,"
etc.
1814.

"The following song, which has been since borrowed by the worshipful author of the famous 'History of Fryar Bacon,' has been with difficulty deciphered. It seems to have been sung on occasions of carrying home the bride."

And did you not hear of a mirth befell
The morrow after a wedding day,
And carrying a bride at home to dwell?
And away to Tewin, away, away.

The quintain was set, and the garlands
were made,
'Tis pity old customs should ever decay;
And woe be to him that was horsed on a
jade,
For he carried no credit away, away.

We met a concert of fiddle-de-dees;
We set them a-cockhorse, and made
them play
The winning of Bullen, and Upsey-frees,
And away to Tewin, away, away!

There was ne'er a lad in all the parish
That would go to the plough that day;
But on his fore-horse his wench he carries,
And away to Tewin, away, away!

The butler was quick, and the ale he did tap,
The maidens did make the chamber
full gay;
The servants did give me a fuddling cup,
And I did carry't away, away.

The smith of the town his liquor so took,
That he was persuaded that the ground
look'd blue;
And I dare boldly be sworn on a book,
Such smith as he there's but a few.

A posset was made, and the women did
sip,
And simpering said, they could eat no
more;
Full many a maiden was laid on the lip.—
I'll say no more, but give o'er, give o'er.

Waverley: Appendix to the General
Preface.

LINES BY EDWARD WAVERLEY

1814.

"On receiving intelligence of his commissio
as captain of a troop of horse in Colonel Gardi
ner's regiment, his tutor, Mr. Pembroke, picke
up about Edward's room some fragments of i
regular verse, which he appeared to have com
posed under the influences of the agitating feeling
occasioned by this sudden page being turned u
to him in the book of life."

Late, when the Autumn evening fell
On Mirkwood-Mere's romantic dell,
The lake return'd in chasten'd gleam,
The purple cloud, the golden beam:
Reflected in the crystal pool,
Headland and bank lay fair and cool;
The weather-tinted rock and tower,
Each drooping tree, each fairy flower,
So true, so soft, the mirror gave,
As if there lay beneath the wave,
Secure from trouble, toil, and care,
A world than earthly world more fair.

But distant winds began to wake,
And roused the Genius of the Lake!
He heard the groaning of the oak,
And donn'd at once his sable cloak,
As warrior, at the battle cry,
Invests him with his panoply;
Then, as the whirlwind nearer prest,
He 'gan to shake his foamy crest
O'er furrow'd brow and blacken'd
cheek,
And bade his surge in thunder speak.
In wild and broken eddies whirl'd,
Flitted that fond ideal world;
And, to the shore in tumult tost,
The realms of fairy bliss were lost.

Yet, with a stern delight and strange,
I saw the spirit-stirring change.
As warr'd the wind with wave an
wood,
Upon the ruin'd tower I stood,
And felt my heart more strongly bound
Responsive to the lofty sound,
While, joying in the mighty roar,
I mourn'd that tranquil scene no more.

So, on the idle dreams of youth
Breaks the loud trumpet call of Truth,
Bids each fair vision pass away,
Like landscape on the lake that lay,

s fair, as flitting, and as frail,
s that which fled the Autumn gale —
orever dead to Fancy's eye
e each gay form that glided by,
While dreams of love and lady's charms
ive place to honor and to arms!
Waverley, chap. v.

DAVIE GELLATLEY'S SONGS.

1814.

" He [Daft Davie Gellatley] sung with great
earnestness, and not without some taste, a
agment of an old Scotch ditty."

ALSE love, and hast thou play'd me this
In summer among the flowers?
will repay thee back again
In winter among the showers.
nless again, again, my love,
Unless you turn again;
s you with other maidens rove,
I'll smile on other men.*

HE Knight's to the mountain
His bugle to wind;
he Lady's to greenwood
Her garland to bind.
he bower of Burd Ellen
Has moss on the floor,
hat the step of Lord William
Be silent and sure.
Waverley, chap. ix.

"The stamping of horses was now heard in
e court, and Davie Gellatley's voice singing to
e two large deer greyhounds."

IE away, hie away,
ver bank and over brae,
Where the copsewood is the greenest,
Where the fountains glisten sheenest,
Where the lady-fern grows strongest,
Where the morning dew lies longest,
Where the black-cock sweetest sips it,
Where the fairy latest trips it:
Hie to haunts right seldom seen,
Lovely, lonesome, cool, and green,
ver bank and over brae,
Hie away, hie away.
Waverley, chap. xii.

* This is a genuine ancient fragment, with
ome alteration in the last two lines.

YOUNG men will love thee more fair and
more fast;
Heard ye so merry the little bird sing?
Old men's love the longest will last,
*And the throstle-cock's head is under
his wing.*

The young man's wrath is like light straw
on fire;
Heard ye so merry the little bird sing?
But like red-hot steel is the old man's ire,
*And the throstle-cock's head is under
his wing.*

The young man may brawl at the evening
board;
Heard ye so merry the little bird sing?
But the old man will draw at the dawning
the sword,
*And the throstle-cock's head is under
his wing.*
Waverley, chap. xiv.

ST. SWITHIN'S CHAIR.

1814.

ON Hallow-Mass Eve, ere you boune ye
to rest,
Ever beware that your couch be bless'd;
Sign it with cross, and sain it with bead,
Sing the Ave, and say the Creed.

For on Hallow-Mass Eve the Night-Hag
will ride,
And all her nine-fold sweeping on by
her side,
Whether the wind sing lowly or loud,
Sailing through moonshine or swathed in
the cloud.

The Lady she sat in St. Swithin's Chair,
The dew of the night has damp'd her hair:
Her cheek was pale—but resolved and high
Was the word of her lip and the glance
of her eye.

She mutter'd the spell of Swithin bold,
When his naked foot traced the midnight
wold,
When he stopp'd the Hag as she rode
the night,
And bade her descend, and her promise
plight.

He that dare sit on St. Swithin's Chair,
When the Night-Hag wings the troubled
    air,
Questions three, when he speaks the spell,
He may ask, and she must tell.

The Baron has been with King Robert
    his liege
These three long years in battle and siege;
News are there none of his weal or his
    woe,
And fain the Lady his fate would know.

She shudders and stops as the charm she
    speaks: —
Is it the moody owl that shrieks?
Or is that sound, betwixt laughter and
    scream,
The voice of the Demon who haunts the
    stream?

The moan of the wind sunk silent and
    low,
And the roaring torrent had ceased to
    flow;
The calm was more dreadful than raging
    storm,
When the cold gray mist brought the
    ghastly form!

.   .   .   .   .   .

Waverley, chap. xiii.

FLORA MACIVOR'S SONG.

1814.

THERE is mist on the mountain, and night
    on the vale,
But more dark is the sleep of the sons of
    the Gael.
A stranger commanded — it sunk on the
    land,
It has frozen each heart and benumb'd
    every hand!

The dirk and the target lie sordid with
    dust,
The bloodless claymore is but redden'd
    with rust;
On the hill or the glen if a gun should
    appear,
It is only to war with the heath-cock or
    deer.

The deeds of our sires if our bards shou[ld]
    rehearse,
Let a blush or a blow be the meed [of]
    their verse!
Be mute every string, and be hush'd ever[y]
    tone,
That shall bid us remember the fame th[at]
    is flown.

But the dark hours of night and of slumb[er]
    are past,
The morn on our mountains is dawnin[g]
    at last!
Glenaladale's peaks are illumed with th[e]
    rays,
And the streams of Glenfinnan leap brig[ht]
    in the blaze.

O high-minded Moray! — the exiled —
    the dear! —
In the blush of the dawning the STANDAR[D]
    uprear!
Wide, wide on the winds of the north l[et]
    it fly,
Like the sun's latest flash when the tem[-]
    pest is nigh!

Ye sons of the strong, when that dawnin[g]
    shall break,
Need the harp of the aged remind yo[u]
    to wake?
That dawn never beam'd on your fore[-]
    fathers' eye,
But it roused each high chieftain to van[-]
    quish or die.

O sprung from the Kings who in Isla[y]
    kept state,
Proud chiefs of Clan-Ranald, Glengarry[,]
    and Sleat!
Combine like three streams from on[e]
    mountain of snow,
And resistless in union rush down on th[e]
    foe.

True son of Sir Evan, undaunted Loch[-]
    iel,
Place thy targe on thy shoulder and bur[-]
    nish thy steel!
Rough Keppoch, give breath to th[y]
    bugle's bold swell,
Till far Coryarrick resound to th[e]
    knell!

tern son of Lord Kenneth, high chief
of Kintail,
et the stag in thy standard bound wild
in the gale!
lay the race of Clan-Gillian, the fearless and free,
Lemember Glenlivat, Harlaw, and Dundee!

et the clan of Gray Fingon, whose offspring has given
uch heroes to earth, and such martyrs to
heaven,
nite with the race of renown'd Rorri
More,
o launch the long galley and stretch to
the oar!

low Mac-Shimei will joy when their
chief shall display
he yew-crested bonnet o'er tresses of
gray!
low the race of wrong'd Alpine and murder'd Glencoe
hall shout for revenge when they pour
on the foe!

e sons of brown Dermid, who slew the
wild boar,
esume the pure faith of the great
Callum-More!
lac-Niel of the Islands, and Moy of the
Lake,
or honor, for freedom, for vengeance
awake!

wake on your hills, on your islands
awake!
rave sons of the mountain, the fritn,
and the lake!
'is the bugle — but not for the chase is
the call;
'is the pibroch's shrill summons — but
not to the hall.

'is the summons of heroes for conquest
or death,
Vhen the banners are blazing on mountain and heath;
hey call to the dirk, the claymore, and
the targe,
o the march and the muster, the line
and the charge.

Be the brand of each chieftain like Fin's
in his ire!
May the blood through his veins flow
like currents of fire!
Burst the base foreign yoke as your sires
did of yore!
Or die, like your sires, and endure it no
more!

Waverley, chap. xxii.

TO AN OAK TREE.

1814.

*In the Churchyard of ——, in the High-
lands of Scotland, said to mark the grave
of Captain Wogan, killed in 1649.*

EMBLEM of England's ancient faith,
    Full proudly may thy branches wave,
Where loyalty lies low in death,
    And valor fills a timeless grave.

And thou, brave tenant of the tomb!
    Repine not if our clime deny,
Above thine honor'd sod to bloom,
    The flowrets of a milder sky.

These owe their birth to genial May;
    Beneath a fiercer sun they pine,
Before the winter storm decay —
    And can their worth be type of thine?

No! for mid storms of Fate opposing,
    Still higher swell'd thy dauntless heart,
And while Despair the scene was closing,
    Commenced thy brief but brilliant part.

'Twas then thou sought'st on Albyn's
    hill
(When England's sons the strife re-
    sign'd),
A rugged race resisting still,
    And unsubdued though unrefined.

Thy death's hour heard no kindred wail,
    No holy knell thy requiem rung!
Thy mourners were the plaided Gael,
    Thy dirge the clamorous pibroch sung.

Yet who, in Fortune's summer-shine
    To waste life's longest term away,
Would change that glorious dawn of thine,
    Though darken'd ere its noontide day?

Be thine the Tree whose dauntless boughs
  Brave summer's drought and winter's
    gloom!
Rome bound with oak her patriots' brows,
  As Albyn shadows Wogan's tomb.
          Waverley, chap. xxix.

FOLLOW, FOLLOW ME.

1814.

BUT follow, follow me,
While glow-worms light the lea,
I'll show ye where the dead should be —
Each in his shroud,
While the winds pipe loud,
And the red moon peeps dim thro' the cloud.

Follow, follow me!
Brave should he be
That treads by night the dead man's lea!
          Waverley, chap. lxiii.

FAREWELL TO MACKENZIE,

HIGH CHIEF OF KINTAIL.

From the Gaelic.

1815.

THE original verses are arranged to a beautiful Gaelic air, of which the chorus is adapted to the double pull upon the oars of a galley, and which is therefore distinct from the ordinary jorrams, or boat-songs. They were composed by the Family Bard upon the departure of the Earl of Seaforth, who was obliged to take refuge in Spain, after an unsuccessful effort at insurrection in favor of the Stuart family, in the year 1718.

FAREWELL to Mackenneth, great Earl of
  the North,
The Lord of Lochcarron, Glenshiel, and
  Seaforth;
To the Chieftain this morning his course
  who began,
Launching forth on the billows his bark
  like a swan.
For a far foreign land he has hoisted his
  sail:
Farewell to Mackenzie, High Chief of
  Kintail!

O swift be the galley, and hardy her crew,
May her captain be skilful, her mariners
  true,

In danger undaunted, unwearied by toi
Tho' the whirlwind should rise, and th
  ocean should boil:
On the brave vessel's gunnel I drank h
  bonail,*
And farewell to Mackenzie, High Chie
  of Kintail!

Awake in thy chamber, thou sweet sout
  land gale!
Like the sighs of his people, breathe so
  on his sail:
Be prolong'd as regret, that his vassa
  must know,
Be fair as their faith, and sincere as the
  woe:
Be so soft, and so fair, and so faithfu
  sweet gale,
Wafting onward Mackenzie, High Chi
  of Kintail!

Be his pilot experienced, and trusty, an
  wise,
To measure the seas and to study th
  skies:
May he hoist all his canvas from stream
  to deck,
But O! crowd it higher when wafting hi
  back —
Till the cliffs of Skooroora, and Conar
  glad vale,
Shall welcome Mackenzie, High Chief
  Kintail!

IMITATION OF THE PRECEDING SONC

So sung the old Bard, in the grief of l
  heart,
When he saw his lov'd Lord from l
  people depart.
Now mute on thy mountains, O Alby
  are heard
Nor the voice of the song, nor the ha
  of the bard;
Or its strings are but waked by the ste
  winter gale,
As they mourn for Mackenzie, last Ch
  of Kintail†.

* Bonail, or Bonallez, the old Scottish phra
for a feast at parting with a friend.

† (These verses were written shortly after t
death of Lord Seaforth, the last male represen
tive of his illustrious house.)

rom the far Southland Border a Minstrel came forth,
nd he waited the hour that some Bard
 of the north
lis hand on the harp of the ancient
 should cast,
nd bid its wild numbers mix high with
 the blast;
ut no bard was there left in the land of
 the Gael
o lament for Mackenzie, last Chief of
 Kintail.

nd shalt thou then sleep, did the Minstrel exclaim,
ike the son of the lowly, unnoticed by
 fame?
o, son of Fitzgerald! in accents of woe,
he song thou hast loved o'er thy coffin
 shall flow,
nd teach thy wild mountains to join in
 the wail
hat laments for Mackenzie, last Chief
 of Kintail.

n vain the bright course of thy talents to
 wrong,
ate deadened thine ear and imprison'd
 thy tongue;
or brighter o'er all her obstructions arose
he glow of the genius they could not
 oppose;
nd who in the land of the Saxon or Gael
ight match with Mackenzie, High Chief
 of Kintail?

hy sons rose around thee in light and in
 love,
ll a father could hope, all a friend could
 approve;
What 'vails it the tale of thy sorrows to tell,
n the spring-time of youth and of promise they fell!
f the line of Fitzgerald remains not a male
o bear the proud name of the Chief of
 Kintail.

nd thou, gentle Dame,† who must bear,
 to thy grief,
or thy clan and thy country the cares
 of a Chief,

Whom brief rolling moons in six changes
 have left,
Of thy husband, and father, and brethren
 bereft;
To thine ear of affection, how sad is the
 hail
That salutes thee the Heir of the line of
 Kintail!

WAR–SONG OF LACHLAN,

HIGH CHIEF OF MACLEAN.

From the Gaelic.

1815.

THIS song appears to be imperfect, or, at
least, like many of the early Gaelic poems,
makes a rapid transition from one subject to
another, from the situation, namely, of one
of the daughters of the clan, who opens the
song by lamenting the absence of her lover, to
an eulogium over the military glories of the
Chieftain. The translator has endeavored to
imitate the abrupt style of the original.

A WEARY month has wander'd o'er
Since last we parted on the shore;
Heaven! that I saw thee, Love, once more,
 Safe on that shore again! —
'Twas valiant Lachlan gave the word:
Lachlan, of many a galley lord:
He call'd his kindred bands on board,
 And launch'd them on the main.

Clan-Gillian is to ocean gone,
Clan-Gillian fierce in foray known;
Rejoicing in the glory won
 In many a bloody broil:
For wide is heard the thundering fray,
The rout, the ruin, the dismay,
When from the twilight glens away
 Clan-Gillian drives the spoil.

Woe to the hills that shall rebound
Our banner'd bag-pipes' maddening
 sound;
Clan-Gillian's onset echoing round,
 Shall shake their inmost cell.
Woe to the bark whose crew shall gaze,
Where Lachlan's silken streamer plays!
The fools might face the lightning's blaze
 As wisely and as well!

Samuel Hood, afterwards Mrs. Stewart Mackenzie of Seaforth and Glasserton.

* The Honorable Lady Hood, daughter of
e last Lord Seaforth, widow of Admiral Sir

SAINT CLOUD.

Paris, 5th September, 1815.

SOFT spread the southern summer night
  Her veil of darksome blue;
Ten thousand stars combined to light
  The terrace of Saint Cloud.

The evening breezes gently sigh'd,
  Like breath of lover true,
Bewailing the deserted pride
  And wreck of sweet Saint Cloud.

The drum's deep roll was heard afar,
  The bugle wildly blew
Good-night to Hulan and Hussar,
  That garrison Saint Cloud.

The startled Naiads from the shade
  With broken urns withdrew,
And silenced was that proud cascade,
  The glory of Saint Cloud.

We sate upon its steps of stone,
  Nor could its silence rue,
When waked to music of our own,
  The echoes of Saint Cloud.

Slow Seine might hear each lovely note
  Fall light as summer dew,
While through the moonless air they float,
  Prolong'd from fair Saint Cloud.

And sure a melody more sweet
  His waters never knew,
Though music's self was wont to meet
  With Princes at Saint Cloud.

Nor then, with more delighted ear,
  The circle round her drew,
Than ours, when gather'd round to hear
  Our songstress at Saint Cloud.

Few happy hours poor mortals pass, —
  Then give those hours their due,
And rank among the foremost class
  Our evenings at Saint Cloud.

THE DANCE OF DEATH.
1815.
I.

NIGHT and morning were at meeting
  Over Waterloo;
Cocks had sung their earliest greeting;
  Faint and low they crew;
For no paly beam yet shone
On the heights of Mount Saint John;
Tempest-clouds prolong'd the sway
Of timeless darkness over day;
Whirlwind, thunder-clap, and shower,
Mark'd it a predestined hour.
Broad and frequent through the night
Flashed the sheets of levin-light;
Muskets, glancing lightnings back,
Show'd the dreary bivouac
  Where the soldier lay,
Chill and stiff, and drench'd with rain,
Wishing dawn of morn again,
  Though death should come with day.

II.

'Tis at such a tide and hour,
Wizard, witch, and fiend have power,
And ghastly forms thro' mist and shower
  Gleam on the gifted ken;
And then the affrighted prophet's ear
Drinks whispers strange of fate and fear
Presaging death and ruin near
  Among the sons of men; —
Apart from Albyn's war-array,
'Twas then gray Allan sleepless lay;
Gray Allan, who, for many a day,
  Had follow'd stout and stern,
Where, thro' battle's rout and reel,
Storm of shot and hedge of steel,
Led the grandson of Lochiel,
  Valiant Fassiefern.
Thro' steel and shot he leads no more,
Low laid mid friends' and foemen's gore
But long his native lake's wild shore,
And Sunart rough, and high Ardgower,
  And Morven long shall tell,
And proud Bennevis hear with awe,
How, upon bloody Quatre-Bras,
Brave Cameron heard the wild hurra
  Of conquest as he fell.

III.

Lone on the outskirts of the host,
The weary sentinel held post,
And heard, through darkness far aloof,
The frequent clang of courser's hoof,
Where held the cloak'd patrol the
  course,
And spurr'd 'gainst storm the swerving
  horse;
But there are sounds in Allan's ear,
Patrol nor sentinel may hear.

d sights before his eye aghast
visible to them have past,
When down the destined plain,
wixt Britain and the bands of France,
ild as marsh-born meteor's glance,
ange phantoms wheel'd a revel dance,
And doom'd the future slain. —
ch forms were seen, such sounds were
   heard,
hen Scotland's James his march prepared
For Flodden's fatal plain;
ch, when he drew his ruthless sword,
Choosers of the Slain, adored
The yet unchristen'd Dane.
a indistinct and phantom band,
ey wheel'd their ring-dance hand in
   hand,
With gestures wild and dread;
e Seer, who watch'd them ride the
   storm,
w thro' their faint and shadowy form
The lightning's flash more red;
   And still their ghastly roundelay
   Was of the coming battle-fray,
     And of the destined dead.

IV.
SONG.

Wheel the wild dance
While lightnings glance,
   And thunders rattle loud,
And call the brave
To bloody grave,
   To sleep without a shroud.

Our airy feet,
So light and fleet,
   They do not bend the rye
That sinks its head when whirlwinds
   rave,
And swells again in eddying wave,
   As each wild gust blows by;
But still the corn,
At dawn of morn,
   Our fatal steps that bore,
At eve lies waste,
A trampled paste
   Of blackening mud and gore.

V.

Wheel the wild dance
While lightnings glance,
   And thunders rattle loud,
And call the brave
To bloody grave,
   To sleep without a shroud.

Wheel the wild dance!
Brave sons of France,
   For you our ring makes room;
Make space full wide
For martial pride,
   For banner, spear, and plume.
Approach, draw near,
Proud cuirassier!
   Room for the men of steel!
Thro' crest and plate
The broadsword's weight
   Both head and heart shall feel.

VI.

Wheel the wild dance
While lightnings glance,
   And thunders rattle loud,
And call the brave
To bloody grave,
   To sleep without a shroud.

Sons of the spear!
You feel us near
   In many a ghastly dream;
With fancy's eye
Our forms you spy,
   And hear our fatal scream.
With clearer sight
Ere falls the night,
   Just when to weal or woe
Your disembodied souls take flight
On trembling wing — each startled
   sprite
Our choir of death shall know.

VII.

Wheel the wild dance
While lightnings glance,
   And thunders rattle loud,
And call the brave
To bloody grave,
   To sleep without a shroud.

Burst, ye clouds, in tempest showers,
Redder rain shall soon be ours —
   See the east grows wan —
Yield we place to sterner game,
Ere deadlier bolts and direr flame

Shall the welkin's thunders shame:
Elemental rage is tame
  To the wrath of man.

VIII.

At morn, gray Allan's mates with awe
Heard of the vision'd sights he saw,
  The legend heard him say;
But the Seer's gifted eye was dim,
Deafen'd his ear, and stark his limb,
Ere closed that bloody day —
He sleeps far from his Highland heath, —
But often of the Dance of Death
  His comrades tell the tale,
On picket-post, when ebbs the night,
And waning watch-fires glow less bright,
  And dawn is glimmering pale.

ROMANCE OF DUNOIS.*

FROM THE FRENCH.

1815.

THE original of this little Romance makes
part of a manuscript collection of French Songs
(probably compiled by some young officer), which
was found on the field of Waterloo, so much
stained with clay and blood, as sufficiently to indicate what had been the fate of its late owner.
The song is popular in France, and is rather a
good specimen of the style of composition to
which it belongs. The translation is strictly
literal.

IT was Dunois, the young and brave, was
  bound for Palestine;
But first he made his orisons before Saint
  Mary's shrine:
"And grant, immortal Queen of Heaven,"
  was still the Soldier's prayer,
"That I may prove the bravest knight,
  and love the fairest fair."

His oath of honor on the shrine he graved
  it with his sword,
And follow'd to the Holy Land the banner of his Lord;
Where, faithful to his noble vow, his war-
  cry fill'd the air,
"Be honor'd aye the bravest knight,
  beloved the fairest fair."

* "Partant pour la Syrie" was written and
set to music by Queen Hortense of Holland, the
daughter of Josephine, and the mother of Napoleon III. It has become the national air of
France.

They owed the conquest to his arm, an[d]
  then his Liege-Lord said, —
"The heart that has for honor beat b[y]
  bliss must be repaid. —
My daughter Isabel and thou shall be
  wedded pair,
For thou art bravest of the brave, sh[e]
  fairest of the fair."

And then they bound the holy knot befor[e]
  Saint Mary's shrine,
That makes a paradise on earth, if hear[t]
  and hands combine;
And every lord and lady bright, that we[re]
  in chapel there,
Cried "Honor'd be the bravest knigh[t]
  beloved the fairest fair."

THE TROUBADOUR.

FROM THE SAME COLLECTION.

Also Written and Composed by Que[en]
Hortense.

1815.

GLOWING with love, on fire for fame,
  A Troubadour that hated sorrow,
Beneath his Lady's window came,
  And thus he sung his last good-m[or]-
    row: —
"My arm it is my country's right,
  My heart is in my true-love's bower[;]
Gayly for love and fame to fight
  Befits the gallant Troubadour."

And while he march'd with helm on he[ad]
  And harp in hand, the descant rung[,]
As, faithful to his favorite maid,
  The minstrel-burden still he sung: —
"My arm it is my country's right,
  My heart is in my lady's bower;
Resolved for love and fame to fight,
  I come a gallant Troubadour."

Even when the battle-roar was deep,
  With dauntless heart he hew'd his w[ay]
Mid splintering lance and falchion-swe[ep,]
  And still was heard his warrior-lay: —
"My life it is my country's right,
  My heart is in my lady's bower;
For love to die, for fame to fight,
  Becomes the valiant Troubadour."

Alas! upon the bloody field
  He fell beneath the foeman's glaive,
But still reclining on his shield,
  Expiring sung the exulting stave: —
' My life it is my country's right,
  My heart is in my lady's bower;
For love and fame to fall in fight
  Becomes the valiant Troubadour."

FROM THE FRENCH.*

1815.

T chanced that Cupid on a season,
  By Fancy urged, resolved to wed,
But could not settle whether Reason
  Or Folly should partake his bed.

What does he then? — Upon my life,
  'Twas bad example for a deity —
He takes me Reason for a wife,
  And Folly for his hours of gayety.

Though thus he dealt in petty treason,
  He loved them both in equal measure;
Fidelity was born of Reason,
  And Folly brought to bed of Pleasure.

SONG.

*On the lifting of the banner of the House
of Buccleuch, at a great foot-ball match
on Carterhaugh.†*

1815.

From the brown crest of Newark its sum-
    mons extending,
  Our signal is waving in smoke and in
    flame;
And each forester blithe, from his moun-
    tain descending,
  Bounds light o'er the heather to join in
    the game.

CHORUS.

*Then up with the Banner, let forest winds
    fan her,
  She has blazed over Ettrick eight ages
    and more;*

*In sport we'll attend her, in battle defend
    her,
  With heart and with hand, like our
    fathers before.*

When the Southern invader spread waste
    and disorder,
  At the glance of her crescents he paused
    and withdrew,
For around them were marshall'd the
    pride of the Border,
  The Flowers of the Forest, the bands
    of BUCCLEUCH.
      Then up with the Banner, etc.

A Stripling's weak hand to our revel has
    borne her,‡
  No mail-glove has grasp'd her, no
    spearmen surround;
But ere a bold foeman should scathe or
    should scorn her,
  A thousand true hearts would be cold
    on the ground.
      Then up with the Banner, etc.

We forget each contention of civil dissen-
    sion,
  And hail, like our brethren, HOME,
    DOUGLAS, and CAR:
And ELLIOT and PRINGLE in pastime
    shall mingle,
  As welcome in peace as their fathers
    in war.
      Then up with the Banner, etc.

Then strip, lads, and to it, tho' sharp be
    the weather,
  And if, by mischance, you should hap-
    pen to fall,
There are worse things in life than a
    tumble on heather,
  And life is itself but a game at foot-ball.
      Then up with the Banner, etc.

And when it is over, we'll drink a blithe
    measure
  To each Laird and each Lady that
    witness'd our fun,
And to every blithe heart that took part
    in our pleasure,
  To the lads that have lost and the lads
    that have won.
      Then up with the Banner, etc.

* From the same collection as the two preceding songs.

† The foot-ball match took place Dec. 5, 1815,
and was also celebrated by the Ettrick Shepherd.

‡ The bearer of the standard was the author's
eldest son.

May the Forest still flourish, both Borough
    and Landward,
    From the hall of the Peer to the Herd's
      ingle-nook;
And huzza! my brave hearts, for BUC-
    CLEUCH and his standard,
    For the King and the Country, the
      Clan and the Duke!

Then up with the Banner, let forest winds
    fan her,
    She has blazed over Ettrick eight ages
    and more;
In sport we'll attend her, in battle defend
    her,
    With heart and with hand, like our
    fathers before.

LULLABY OF AN INFANT CHIEF.

AIR — *Cadul gu lo.**

1815.

I.

O HUSH thee, my baby, thy sire was a
    knight,
Thy mother a lady, both lovely and bright;
The woods and the glens, from the towers
    which we see,
They are all belonging, dear baby, to thee.
    O ho ro, i ri ri, cadul gu lo,
    O ho ro, i ri ri, etc.

II.

O, fear not the bugle, though loudly it
    blows,
It calls but the warders that guard thy
    repose;
Their bows would be bended, their blades
    would be red,
Ere the step of a foeman draws near to
    thy bed.
    O ho ro, i ri ri, etc.

III.

O, hush thee, my baby, the time soon
    will come,
When thy sleep shall be broken by trum-
    pet and drum;

* Sleep till day.

Then hush thee, my darling, take rest
    while you may,
For strife comes with manhood, and wak-
    ing with day.
    O ho ro, i ri ri, etc.

SONGS OF MEG MERRILIES.

1815.

I.

"TWIST YE, TWINE YE."

TWIST ye, twine ye! even so,
Mingle shades of joy and woe,
Hope, and fear, and peace, and strife,
In the thread of human life.

While the mystic twist is spinning,
And the infant's life beginning,
Dimly seen through twilight bending,
Lo, what varied shapes attending!

Passions wild, and follies vain,
Pleasures soon exchanged for pain;
Doubt, and jealousy, and fear,
In the magic dance appear.

Now they wax, and now they dwindle,
Whirling with the whirling spindle.
Twist ye, twine ye! even so,
Mingle human bliss and woe.

    Guy Mannering, chap. iii.

II.

THE DYING GYPSY'S DIRGE.

WASTED, weary, wherefore stay,
Wrestling thus with earth and clay?
From the body pass away; —
    Hark! the mass is singing.

From thee doff thy mortal weed,
Mary Mother be thy speed,
Saints to help thee at thy need; —
    Hark! the knell is ringing.

Fear not snow-drift driving fast,
Sleet, or hail, or levin blast;
Soon the shroud shall lap thee fast,
And the sleep be on thee cast
    That shall ne'er know waking.

Haste thee, haste thee, to be gone,
Earth flits fast, and time draws on, —
Gasp thy gasp, and groan thy groan,
        Day is near the breaking.
    Guy Mannering, chap. xxvii.

THE RETURN TO ULSTER.
1816.

Once again, — but how changed since
    my wand'rings began, —
I have heard the deep voice of the Lagan
    and Bann,
And the pines of Clanbrassi resound to
    the roar
That wearies the echoes of fair Tullamore.
Alas! my poor bosom, and why shouldst
    thou burn?
With the scenes of my youth can its rap-
    tures return?
Can I live the dear life of delusion again,
That flow'd when these echoes first mix'd
    with my strain?

It was then that around me, tho' poor
    and unknown,
High spells of mysterious enchantment
    were thrown;
The streams were of silver, of diamond
    the dew,
The land was an Eden, for fancy was new.
I had heard of our bards, and my soul
    was on fire
At the rush of their verse, and the sweep
    of their lyre:
To me 'twas not legend, nor tale to the ear,
But a vision of noontide, distinguish'd
    and clear.

Ultonia's old heroes awoke at the call,
And renew'd the wild pomp of the chase
    and the hall;
And the standard of Fion * flash'd fierce
    from on high,
Like a burst of the sun when the tempest
    is nigh.
It seem'd that the harp of green Erin
    once more
Could renew all the glories she boasted
    of yore. —

* The Standard of Fion or Fingal was called
by the Irish bards the *Sun-burst*, rendered *Sunbeam* by Macpherson.

Yet why at remembrance, fond heart,
    should'st thou burn?
They were days of delusion and cannot
    return.

But was she, too, a phantom, the Maid
    who stood by,
And listed my lay, while she turn'd from
    mine eye?
Was she, too, a vision, just glancing to
    view,
Then dispersed in the sunbeam, or melted
    to dew?
Oh! would it had been so, — Oh! would
    that her eye
Had been but a star-glance that shot thro'
    the sky,
And her voice that was moulded to mel-
    ody's thrill,
Had been but a zephyr, that sigh'd and
    was still!

Oh! would it had been so, — not then
    this poor heart
Had learn'd the sad lesson, to love and
    to part;
To bear, unassisted, its burden of care,
While I toil'd for the wealth I had no
    one to share.
Not then had I said, when life's summer
    was done,
And the hours of her autumn were fast
    speeding on: —
"Take the fame and the riches ye brought
    in your train,
And restore me the dream of my spring-
    tide again."

JOCK OF HAZELDEAN.
Air — *A Border Melody.*
1816.

The first stanza of this ballad is ancient. The
others were written for Mr. Campbell's Albyn's
Anthology.

I.

"Why weep ye by the tide, ladie?
    Why weep ye by the tide?
I'll wed ye to my youngest son,
    And ye sall be his bride.
And ye sall be his bride, ladie,
    Sae comely to be seen " —
But aye she loot the tears down fa'
    For Jock of Hazeldean.

II.

"Now let this wilfu' grief be done,
  And dry that cheek so pale;
Young Frank is chief of Errington,
  And lord of Langley-dale;
His step is first in peaceful ha',
  His sword in battle keen" —
But aye she loot the tears down fa'
  For Jock of Hazeldean.

III.

"A chain of gold ye sall not lack,
  Nor braid to bind your hair;
Nor mettled hound, nor managed hawk,
  Nor palfrey fresh and fair;
And you, the foremost o' them a',
  Shall ride our forest queen" —
But aye she loot the tears down fa'
  For Jock of Hazeldean.

IV.

The kirk was deck'd at morning-tide,
  The tapers glimmer'd fair;
The priest and bridegroom wait the bride,
  And dame and knight are there.
They sought her baith by bower and ha';
  The ladie was not seen!
She's o'er the Border, and awa'
  Wi' Jock of Hazeldean.

PIBROCH OF DONALD DHU.*

Air —"*Piobair of Donuil Dhuidh.*"

1816.

This is a very ancient pibroch belonging to
Clan Macdonald, and supposed to refer to the
expedition of Donald Balloch, who, in 1431,
launched from the Isles with a considerable
force, invaded Lochaber, and at Inverlochy defeated and put to flight the Earls of Mar and
Caithness, though at the head of an army superior to his own. The words of the set, theme, or
melody, to which the pipe variations are applied,
run thus in Gaelic : —

Piobaireachd Dhonuil Dhuidh, piobaireachd
  Dhonuil
Piobaireachd Dhonuil Dhuidh, piobaireachd
  Dhonuil;
Piobaireachd Dhonuil Dhuidh, piobaireachd
  Dhonuil;
Piob agus bratach air faiche Inverlochi.

The pipe-summons of Donald the Black,
The pipe-summons of Donald the Black,
The war-pipe and the pennon are on the gathering
  place at Inverlochy.

* *Dhu* — the Black.

Pibroch of Donuil Dhu,
  Pibroch of Donuil,
Wake thy wild voice anew,
  Summon Clan-Conuil.
Come away, come away,
  Hark to the summons!
Come in your war array,
  Gentles and commons.

Come from deep glen and
  From mountain so rocky,
The war-pipe and pennon
  Are at Inverlochy.
Come every hill-plaid and
  True heart that wears one,
Come every steel blade and
  Strong hand that bears one.

Leave untended the herd,
  The flock without shelter;
Leave the corpse uninterr'd,
  The bride at the altar;
Leave the deer, leave the steer,
  Leave nets and barges:
Come with your fighting-gear,
  Broadswords and targes.

Come as the winds come, when
  Forests are rended,
Come as the waves come, when
  Navies are stranded:
Faster come, faster come,
  Faster and faster,
Chief, vassal, page, and groom,
  Tenant and master.

Fast they come, fast they come;
  See how they gather!
Wide waves the eagle plume,
  Blended with heather.
Cast your plaids, draw your blades,
  Forward each man set!
Pibroch of Donuil Dhu,
  Knell for the onset!

NORA'S VOW.

Air — *Cha teid mis a chaoidh.**
Written for Albyn's Anthology.

1816.

In the original Gaelic, the lady makes protestations that she will not go with the Red Earl's
son, until the swan should build in the cliff, and

* "I will never go with him."

ne eagle in the lake — until one mountain should change place with another, and so forth. It is but fair to add, that there is no authority for supposing that she altered her mind — except the vehemence of her protestation.

I.

HEAR what Highland Nora said: -
" The Earlie's son I will not wed,
Should all the race of nature die,
And none be left but he and I.
For all the gold, for all the gear,
And all the lands both far and near,
That ever valor lost or won,
I would not wed the Earlie's son.''

II.

" A maiden's vows,'' old Callum spoke,
" Are lightly made and lightly broke;
The heather on the mountain's height
Begins to bloom in purple light;
The frost-wind soon shall sweep away
That lustre deep from glen and brae;
Yet Nora, ere its bloom be gone,
May blithely wed the Earlie's son.'' —

III.

" The swan,'' she said, " the lake's clear breast
May barter for the eagle's nest;
The Awe's fierce stream may backward turn,
Ben-Cruaichan fall, and crush Kilchurn;
Our kilted clans, when blood is high,
Before their foes may turn and fly;
But I, were all these marvels done,
Would never wed the Earlie's son.''

IV.

Still in the water-lily's shade.
Her wonted nest the wild-swan made;
Ben-Cruaichan stands as fast as ever,
Still downward foams the Awe's fierce river;
To shun the clash of foeman's steel,
No Highland brogue has turn'd the heel;
But Nora's heart is lost and won,
— She's wedded to the Earlie's son !

MACGREGOR'S GATHERING.
AIR— *Thain' a Grigalach.**
WRITTEN FOR ALBYN'S ANTHOLOGY.
1816.

THESE verses are adapted to a very wild yet lively gathering-tune, used by the MacGregors.

* " The MacGregor is come.''

The severe treatment of this clan, their outlawry, and the proscription of their very name, are alluded to in the Ballad.

THE moon's on the lake, and the mist's on the brae,
And the Clan has a name that is nameless by day;
  Then gather, gather, gather, Grigalach !
  Gather, gather, gather, etc.

Our signal for fight, that from monarchs we drew,
Must be heard but by night in our vengeful haloo !
  Then haloo, Grigalach ! haloo, Grigalach !
  Haloo, haloo, haloo, Grigalach, etc.

Glen Orchy's proud mountains, Coalchuirn and her towers,
Glenstrae and Glenlyon no longer are ours;
  We're landless, landless, landless, Grigalach !
  Landless, landless, landless, etc.

But doom'd and devoted by vassal and lord,
MacGregor has still both his heart and his sword !
  Then courage, courage, courage, Grigalach !
  Courage, courage, courage, etc.

If they rob us of name, and pursue us with beagles,
Give their roofs to the flame, and their flesh to the eagles !
  Then vengeance, vengeance, vengeance, Grigalach !
  Vengeance, vengeance, vengeance, etc.

While there's leaves in the forest, and foam on the river,
MacGregor, despite them, shall flourish forever !
  Come then, Grigalach ! come then, Grigalach !
  Come then, come then, come then, etc.

Through the depths of Loch Katrine the steed shall career,
O'er the peak of Ben-Lomond the galley shall steer,

And the rocks of Craig-Royston like
   icicles melt,
Ere our wrongs be forgot, or our ven-
   geance unfelt!
   Then gather, gather, gather, Griga-
     lach!
   Gather, gather, gather, etc.

VERSES.

COMPOSED FOR THE OCCASION, ADAPTED
TO HAYDN'S AIR,

" *God Save the Emperor Francis*,"

AND SUNG BY A SELECT BAND AFTER
THE DINNER GIVEN BY THE LORD
PROVOST OF EDINBURGH TO THE

GRAND-DUKE NICHOLAS OF
RUSSIA AND HIS SUITE.

19TH DECEMBER, 1816.

GOD protect brave ALEXANDER,
   Heaven defend the noble Tsar,
Mighty Russia's high Commander,
   First in Europe's banded war!
For the realms he did deliver
   From the tyrant overthrown,
Thou, of every good the Giver,
   Grant him long to bless his own!
Bless him, mid his land's disaster,
   For her rights who battled brave,
Of the land of foemen master,
   Bless him who their wrongs forgave!

O'er his just resentment victor,
   Victor over Europe's foes,
Late and long supreme director,
   Grant in peace his reign may close!
Hail! then, hail! illustrious Stranger!
   Welcome to our mountain strand!
Mutual interests, hopes, and danger,
   Link us with thy native land.
Freemen's force, or false beguiling,
   Shall that union ne'er divide,
Hand in hand while peace is smiling,
   And in battle side by side.

TIME.
1816.

" WHY sit'st thou by that ruin'd hall,
   Thou aged carle so stern and gray?

Dost thou its former pride recall,
   Or ponder how it pass'd away!" —

" Know'st thou not me!" the Deep
   Voice cried;
   " So long enjoy'd, so oft misused —
Alternate, in thy fickle pride,
   Desired, neglected, and accused!

" Before my breath, like blazing flax,
   Man and his marvels pass away!
And changing empires wane and wax,
   Are founded, flourish, and decay.

" Redeem mine hours — the space is brief—
   While in my glass the sand-grain
     shiver,
And measureless thy joy or grief,
   When TIME, and thou shalt part for
     ever!"
          The Antiquary, chap. x.

ELSPETH'S BALLAD.
1816.

THE herring loves the merry moon-light,
   The mackerel loves the wind,
But the oyster loves the dredging sang,
   For they come of a gentle kind.

Now haud your tongue, baith wife and
   carle,
   And listen great and sma',
And I will sing of Glenallan's Earl
   That fought on the red Harlaw.

The cronach's cried on Bennachie,
   And doun the Don and a',
And hieland and lawland may mournfu'be
   For the sair field of Harlaw. —

They saddled a hundred milk-white steeds,
   They hae bridled a hundred black,
With a chafron of steel on each horse's
   head,
   And a good knight upon his back.

They hadna ridden a mile, a mile,
   A mile but barely ten,
When Donald came branking down the
   brae
   Wi' twenty thousand men.

Their tartans they were waving wide,
  Their glaives were glancing clear,
The pibrochs rung frae side to side,
  Would deafen ye to hear.

The great Earl in his stirrup stood,
  That Highland host to see:
" Now here a knight that's stout and
      good
  May prove a jeopardie:

' What would'st thou do, my squire so
      gay,
  That rides beside my reyne. —
Were ye Glenallan's Earl the day,
  And I were Roland Cheyne?

' To turn the rein were sin and shame,
  To fight were wondrous peril, —
What would ye do now, Roland Cheyne,
  Were ye Glenallan's Earl ! " —

' Were I Glenallan's Earl this tide,
  And ye were Roland Cheyne,
The spur should be in my horse's side,
  And the bridle upon his mane.

' If they hae twenty thousand blades,
  And we twice ten times ten,
Yet they hae but their tartan plaids,
  And we are mail-clad men.

' My horse shall ride through ranks sae
      rude,
  As through the moorland fern, —
Then ne'er let the gentle Norman blude
  Grow cauld for Highland kerne."

     *   *   *   *   *   *

He turn'd him right and round again,
  Said, Scorn na at my mither;
Light loves I may get mony a ane,
  But minnie ne'er anither.
                The Antiquary, chap. xl.

MOTTOES.

FROM "THE ANTIQUARY."

I KNEW Anselmo. He was shrewd and
      prudent,
Wisdom and cunning had their shares of
      him;

But he was shrewish as a wayward child,
And pleased again by toys which child-
      hood please;
As — book of fables graced with print of
      wood,
Or else the jingling of a rusty medal,
Or the rare melody of some old ditty,
That first was sung to please King Pepin's
      cradle.

CHAP. IX.

" Be brave," she cried, " you yet may
      be our guest,
Our haunted room was ever held the best:
If, then, your valor can the fight sustain
Of rustling curtains, and the clinking
      chain;
If your courageous tongue have powers
      to talk,
When round your bed the horrid ghost
      shall walk,
If you dare ask it why it leaves its tomb,
I'll see your sheets well air'd, and show
      the room.
                          True Story.

CHAP. XXI.

— The Lord Abbot had a soul
Subtile and quick, and searching as the
      fire:
By magic stairs he went as deep as hell,
And if in devils' possession gold be kept,
He brought some sure from thence — 'tis
      hid in caves,
Known, save to me, to none.
              The Wonder of a Kingdome.

CHAP. XXX.

Who is he? — One that for the lack of
      land
Shall fight upon the water — he hath chal-
      lenged
Formerly the grand whale; and by his
      titles
Of Leviathan, Behemoth, and so forth.
He tilted with a sword-fish — Marry, sir,
Th' aquatic had the best — the argument
Still galls our champion's breech.
                          Old Play.

CHAP. XXXI.

Tell me not of it, friend — when the
      young weep,
Their tears are lukewarm brine; — from
      our old eyes

Sorrow falls down like hail-drops of the
North,
Chilling the furrows of our wither'd cheeks,
Cold as our hopes, and harden'd as our
feeling —
Theirs, as they fall, sink sightless — ours
recoil,
Heap the fair plain, and bleaken all be-
fore us.

Old Play.

CHAP. XXXIII.

Remorse — she ne'er forsakes us!
A bloodhound stanch — she tracks our
rapid step
Through the wild labyrinth of youthful
frenzy,
Unheard, perchance, until old age hath
tamed us;
Then in our lair, when Time hath chill'd
our joints,
And maim'd our hope of combat, or of
flight,
We hear her deep-mouth'd bay, announcing all
Of wrath and woe and punishment that
bides us.

Old Play.

CHAP. XXXIV.

Still in his dead hand clench'd remain
the strings
That thrill his father's heart — e'en as
the limb,
Lopp'd off and laid in grave, retains, they
tell us,
Strange commerce with the mutilated
stump,
Whose nerves are twinging still in
maim'd existence.

Old Play.

CHAP. XXXV.

—— Life, with you,
Glows in the brain and dances in the
arteries;
'Tis like the wine some joyous guest hath
quaff'd,
That glads the heart and elevates the
fancy: —
Mine is the poor residuum of the cup,
Vapid, and dull, and tasteless, only
soiling
With its base dregs the vessel that con-
tains it.

Old Play.

CHAP. XXXVII.

Yes! I love Justice well — as well as you
do —
But, since the good dame's blind, she
shall excuse me,
If, time and reason fitting, I prove dumb;
The breath I utter now shall be no means
To take away from me my breath in
future.

Old Play.

CHAP. XXXVIII.

Well, well, at worst, 'tis neither theft nor
coinage,
Granting I knew all that you charge me
with.
What, tho' the tomb hath borne a second
birth,
And given the wealth to one that knew
not on't,
Yet fair exchange was never robbery,
Far less pure bounty.

Old Play.

CHAP. XL.

Life ebbs from such old age, unmark'd
and silent,
As the slow neap-tide leaves yon stranded
galley.
Late she rock'd merrily at the least
impulse
That wind or wave could give; but now
her keel
Is settling on the sand, her mast has ta'en
An angle with the sky, from which it
shifts not.
Each wave receding shakes her less and
less,
Till, bedded on the strand, she shall
remain
Useless as motionless.

Old Play.

CHAP. XLI.

So, while the Goose, of whom the fable
told,
Incumbent, brooded o'er her eggs of gold,
With hand outstretch'd, impatient to
destroy,
Stole on her secret nest the cruel Boy,
Whose gripe rapacious changed her splen-
did dream,
For wings vain fluttering, and for dying
scream.

The Loves of the Sea-Weeds.

CHAP. XLII.

Let those go see who will — I like it not—
For say he was a slave to rank and pomp,
And all the nothings he is now divorced
    from
By the hard doom of stern necessity;
Yet is it sad to mark his alter'd brow,
Where vanity adjusts her flimsy veil
O'er the deep wrinkles of repentant An-
    guish.

Old Play.

CHAP. XLIII.

Fortune, you say, flies from us — She but
    circles,
Like the fleet sea-bird round the fowler's
    skiff, —
Lost in the mist one moment, and the
    next
Brushing the white sail with her whiter
    wing,
As if to court the aim. — Experience
    watches,
And has her on the wheel.

Old Play.

CHAP. XLIV.

Nay, if she love me not, I care not for
    her;
Shall I look pale because the maiden
    blooms?
Or sigh because she smiles — and smiles
    on others?
Not I, by Heaven! — I hold my peace
    too dear,
To let it, like the plume upon her cap,
Shake at each nod that her caprice shall
    dictate.

Old Play.

MOTTO FROM "THE BLACK DWARF."

1816.

CHAP. XVI.

— 'Twas time and griefs
That framed him thus: Time, with his
    fairer hand,
Offering the fortunes of his former days,
The former man may make him — Bring
    us to him,
And chance it as it may.

Old Play.

MAJOR BELLENDEN'S SONG.

1816.

And what tho' winter will pinch severe
    Thro' locks of gray and a cloak that's
    old,
Yet keep up thy heart, bold cavalier,
    For a cup of sack shall fence the cold.
For time will rust the brightest blade,
    And years will break the strongest
    bow;
Was never wight so starkly made,
    But time and years would overthrow!

Old Mortality, chap. xix.

VERSES FOUND IN BOTHWELL'S POCKET-BOOK.*

1816.

Thy hue, dear pledge, is pure and bright,
As in that well-remember'd night,
When first thy mystic braid was wove,
And first my Agnes whisper'd love.

Since then how often hast thou press'd
The torrid zone of this wild breast,
Whose wrath and hate have sworn to
    dwell
With the first sin which peopled hell.
A breast whose blood's a troubled ocean,
Each throb the earthquake's wild com-
    motion! —
O, if such clime thou canst endure,
Yet keep thy hue unstain'd and pure,
What conquest o'er each erring thought
Of that fierce realm had Agnes wrought!
I had not wander'd wild and wide,
With such an angel for my guide;
Nor heaven nor earth could then reprove
    me,
If she had lived, and lived to love me.

Not then this world's wild joys had been
To me one savage hunting scene,
My sole delight the headlong race,
And frantic hurry of the chase;

* "With these letters was a lock of hair
wrapped in a copy of verses, written obviously
with a feeling which atoned, in Morton's opinion,
for the roughness of the poetry, and the conceits
with which it abounded, according to the taste of
the period."

To start, pursue, and bring to bay,
Rush in, drag down, and rend my prey,
Then — from the carcass turn away!
Mine ireful mood had sweetness tamed,
And soothed each wound which pride
    inflamed!
Yes, God and man might now approve me,
If thou hadst lived, and lived to love me.
    Old Mortality, chap. xxiii.

MOTTOES.

FROM "OLD MORTALITY."

CHAP. XIV.

MY hounds may a' rin masterless,
    My hawks may fly frae tree to tree,
My lord may grip my vassal lands,
    For there again maun I never be!
        Old Ballad.

CHAP. XXXIV.

Sound, sound the clarion, fill the fife!
    To all the sensual world proclaim,
One crowded hour of glorious life
    Is worth an age without a name.
        Anonymous.

THE SEARCH AFTER HAPPINESS;

OR, THE QUEST OF SULTAUN SOLIMAUN.

1817.

I.

OH for a glance of that gay Muse's eye,
That lighten'd on Bandello's laughing
    tale,
And twinkled with a lustre shrewd and
    sly,
When Giam Battista* bade her vision
    hail! —
Yet fear not, ladies, the naïve detail
Given by the natives of that land ca-
    norous;
Italian license loves to leap the pale,
We Britons have the fear of shame
    before us,
And, if not wise in mirth, at least must
    be decorous.

* The hint of the following tale is taken from
"La Camiscia Magica," a novel by Giam Battista
Casti.

II.

In the far eastern clime, no great while
    since,
Lived Sultaun Solimaun, a mighty prince,
Whose eyes, as oft as they perform'd their
    round,
Beheld all others fix'd upon the ground:
Whose ears received the same unvaried
    phrase: —
" Sultaun! thy vassal hears, and he
    obeys!"
All have their tastes — this may the fancy
    strike
Of such grave folks as pomp and grand-
    eur like;
For me, I love the honest heart and warm
Of Monarch who can amble round his farm,
Or, when the toil of state no more annoys,
In chimney-corner seek domestic joys —
I love a prince will bid the bottle pass,
Exchanging with his subjects glance and
    glass;
In fitting time, can, gayest of the gay,
Keep up the jest, and mingle in the lay —
Such Monarchs best our free-born hu-
    mors suit,
But Despots must be stately, stern, and
    mute.

III.

This Solimaun, Serendib had in sway —
And where's Serendib? may some critic
    say. —
Good lack, mine honest friend, consul
    the chart,
Scare not my Pegasus before I start!
If Rennell has it not, you'll find, mayhap
The isle laid down in Captain Sinbad's
    map, —
Famed mariner! whose merciless narra-
    tions
Drove every friend and kinsman out of
    patience,
Till, fain to find a guest who thought
    them shorter,
He deign'd to tell them over to a porter —
The last edition see, by Long & Co.,
Rees, Hurst, and Orme, our fathers in
    the Row.

IV.

Serendib found, deem not my tale a fic-
    tion —
This Sultaun, whether lacking contradic-
    tion —

(A sort of stimulant which hath its uses,
To raise the spirits and reform the juices,
— Sovereign specific for all sorts of cures
In my wife's practice, and perhaps in
    yours),
The Sultaun lacking this same wholesome
    bitter,
Or cordial smooth for prince's palate
    fitter —
Or if some Mollah had hag-rid his dreams
With Degial, Ginnistan, and such wild
    themes
Belonging to the Mollah's subtle craft,
I wot not — but the Sultaun never laugh'd,
Scarce ate or drank, and took a melancholy,
That scorn'd all remedy—profane or holy;
In his long list of melancholies, mad,
Or mazed, or dumb, hath Burton none
    so bad.*

V.

Physicians soon arrived, sage, ware, and
    tried,
    As e'er scrawl'd jargon in a darken'd
      room;
With heedful glance the Sultaun's tongue
    they eyed,
Peep'd in his bath, and God knows where
    beside,
    And then in solemn accent spoke their
      doom: —
'His Majesty is very far from well."
Then each to work with his specific fell:
The Hakim Ibrahim *instanter* brought
His unguent Mahazzim al Zerdukkaut,
While Roompot, a practitioner more wily,
Relied on his Munaskif al fillfily.†
More and yet more in deep array appear,
And some the front assail, and some the
    rear;
Their remedies to reinforce and vary,
Came surgeon eke, and eke apothecary;
Till the tired Monarch, tho' of words
    grown chary,
Yet dropt, to recompense their fruitless
    labor,
Some hint about a bowstring or a sabre.
There lack'd, I promise you, no longer
    speeches
To rid the palace of those learned leeches.

VI.

Then was the council call'd—by their advice
(They deem'd the matter ticklish all, and
    nice,
    And sought to shift it off from their
      own shoulders),
Tartars and couriers in all speed were
    sent,
To call a sort of Eastern Parliament
    Of feudatory chieftains and freehold-
      ers —
Such have the Persians at this very day,
My gallant Malcolm calls them *cou-
    roultai;* ‡ —
I'm not prepared to show in this slight
    song
That to Serendib the same forms belong,
E'en let the learn'd go search, and tell
    me if I'm wrong.

VII.

The Omrahs, each with hand on cimetar,
Gave, like Sempronius, still their voice
    for war: —
" The sabre of the Sultaun in its sheath,
Too long has slept, nor own'd the work
    of death;
Let the Tambourgi bid his signal rattle,
Bang the loud gong, and raise the shout
    of battle !
This dreary cloud that dims our sove-
    reign's day,
Shall from his kindled bosom flit away,
When the bold Lootie wheels his courser
    round,
And the arm'd elephant shall shake the
    ground.
Each noble pants to own the glorious
    summons —
And for the charges — Lo ! your faithful
    Commons ! "
The Riots who attended in their places
    (Serendib language calls a farmer Riot)
Look'd ruefully in one another's faces,
    From this oration auguring much dis-
    quiet,
Double assessment, forage, and free
    quarters;
And fearing these as Chinamen the Tar-
    tars,

---

* See Burton, *Anatomy of Melancholy.*

† See D'Herbelot, or the " Recipes of Avi-
cenna."

‡ See Sir John Malcolm's " History of
Persia."

Or as the whisker'd vermin fear the
　mousers,
Each fumbled in the pocket of his
　trowsers.

VIII.

And next came forth the reverend Con-
　vocation,
　Bald heads, white beards, and many a
　　turban green,
Imaum and Mollah there of every station,
　Santon, Fakir, and Calendar were seen.
　Their votes were various — some advised
　　a Mosque
With fitting revenues should be erected,
　With seemly gardens and with gay
　　Kiosque,
　To recreate a band of priests selected;
Others opined that through the realms a
　dole
　Be made to holy men, whose prayers
　　might profit
The Sultaun's weal in body and in soul.
　But their long-headed Chief, the Sheik
　　Ul-Sofit,
More closely touch'd the point: — "Thy
　studious mood,"
Quoth he, "O Prince! hath thicken'd
　all thy blood,
And dull'd thy brain with labor beyond
　measure;
Wherefore relax a space and take thy
　pleasure,
And toy with beauty, or tell o'er thy
　treasure;
From all the cares of state, my Liege,
　enlarge thee,
And leave the burden to thy faithful
　clergy."

IX.

These counsels sage availed not a whit,
　And so the patient (as is not uncommon
Where grave physicians lose their time
　and wit)
　Resolved to take advice of an old
　　woman;
His mother she, a dame who once was
　beauteous,
And still was call'd so by each subject
　duteous.
Now, whether Fatima was witch in ear-
　nest,
　Or only made believe, I cannot say —

But she profess'd to cure disease the
　sternest,
　By dint of magic amulet or lay;
And, when all other skill in vain was
　shown,
She deem'd it fitting time to use her own.

X.

" *Sympathia magica* hath wonders done "
　(Thus did old Fatima bespeak her son),
" It works upon the fibres and the pores,
And thus, insensibly, our health restores,
And it must help us here. — Thou must
　endure
The ill, my son, or travel for the cure.
Search land and sea, and get where'er
　you can,
The inmost vesture of a happy man,
I mean his SHIRT, my son; which, taken
　warm
And fresh from off his back, shall chase
　your harm,
Bid every current of your veins rejoice,
And your dull heart leap light as shep-
　herd-boy's."
Such was the counsel from his mother
　came; —
I know not if she had some under-game,
As Doctors have, who bid their patients
　roam
And live abroad, when sure to die at home:
Or if she thought, that, somehow or
　another,
Queen-Regent sounded better than Queen-
　Mother;
But, says the Chronicle (who will, go
　look it),
That such was her advice — the Sultaun
　took it.

XI.

All are on board — the Sultaun and his
　train,
In gilded galley prompt to plough the
　main.
　The old Rais * was the first who ques-
　　tion'd, " Whither? "
They paused — " Arabia," thought the
　pensive Prince,
"Was call'd the Happy many ages since —
For Mokha, Rais." — And they came
　safely thither.

* Sea captain.

But not in Araby, with all her balm,
Not where Judea weeps beneath her palm,
Not in rich Egypt, not in Nubian waste,
Could there the step of happiness be
  traced,
One Copt alone profess'd to have seen
  her smile,
When Bruce his goblet fill'd at infant
  Nile:
She bless'd the dauntless traveller as he
  quaff'd,
But vanish'd from him with the ended
  draught.

XII.

" Enough of turbans," said the weary
  King,
" These dolimans of ours are not the
  thing;
Try we the Giaours, these men of coat
  and cap, I
Incline to think some of them must be
  happy;
At least, they have as fair a cause as any
  can,
They drink good wine and keep no Ram-
  azan.
Then northward, ho!" — The vessel cuts
  the sea,
And fair Italia lies upon her lee. —
But fair Italia, she who once unfurl'd
Her eagle banners o'er a conquer'd world,
Long from her throne of domination
  tumbled,
Lay, by her quondam vassals, sorely
  humbled;
The Pope himself look'd pensive, pale,
  and lean,
And was not half the man he once had
  been.
" While these the priest and those the
  noble fleeces,
Our poor old boot," they said, "is torn
  to pieces.
Its tops the vengeful claws of Austria feel,
And the Great Devil is rending toe and
  heel.*
If happiness you seek, to tell you truly,
We think she dwells with one Giovanni
  Bulli;

* The "boot" is Italy: Florence, Venice
and the Northern Cities are called the "tops;"
the "toe and heel" are the Calarias, then infested with freebooters, one of the leaders being
known as Fra Diavolo.

A tramontane, a heretic, — the buck,
Poffaredio! still has all the luck;
By land or ocean never strikes his flag —
And then — a perfect walking money-
  bag."
Off set our prince to seek John Bull's
  abode,
But first took France — it lay upon the
  road.

XIII.

Monsieur Baboon, after much late com-
  motion,
Was agitated like a settling ocean,
Quite out of sorts, and could not tell what
  ail'd him,
Only the glory of his house had fail'd
  him;
Besides some tumors on his noddle
  biding,
Gave indication of a recent hiding.
Our Prince, though Sultauns of such things
  are heedless,
Thought it a thing indelicate and needless
To ask, if at that moment he was happy.
And Monsieur, seeing that he was *comme
  il faut*, a
Loud voice muster'd up, for " *Vive le
  Roi !* "
  Then whisper'd, " 'Ave you any news
    of Nappy?"
The Sultaun answer'd him with a cross
  question: —
  " Pray, can you tell me aught of one
    John Bull,
  That dwells somewhere beyond your
    herring-pool?"
The query seem'd of difficult digestion,
The party shrugg'd, and grinn'd, and
  took his snuff,
And found his whole good-breeding scarce
  enough.

XIV.

Twitching his visage into as many puckers
As damsels wont to put into their tuckers
(Ere liberal Fashion damn'd both lace
  and lawn,
And bade the veil of modesty be drawn),
Replied the Frenchman, after a brief
  pause: —
  " Jean Bool! — I vas not known him —
    Yes, I vas —
  I vas remember dat, von year or two,
  I saw him at von place call'd Vaterloo —

Ma foi! il s'est très joliment battu,
Dat is for Englishman,—m'entendez-vous?
But den he had wit him one damn son-
gun,
Rogue I no like — dey call him Velling-
ton."
Monsieur's politeness could not hide his
fret,
So Solimaun took leave, and cross'd the
strait.

XV.

John Bull was in his very worst of moods,
Raving of sterile farms and unsold goods;
His sugar-loaves and bales about he threw,
And on his counter beat the devil's tattoo.
His wars were ended, and the victory won,
But then, 'twas reckoning-day with honest
John;
And authors vouch, 'twas still this
Worthy's way,
"Never to grumble till he came to pay;
And then he always thinks, his temper's
such,
The work too little and the pay too
much."
Yet, grumbler as he is, so kind and
hearty,
That when his mortal foe was on the floor,
And past the power to harm his quiet
more,
Poor John had well nigh wept for
Bonaparte!
Such was the wight whom Solimaun
salam'd, —
"And who are you," John answer'd,
"and be damn'd!"

XVI.

"A stranger, come to see the happiest
man, —
So, signior, all avouch, — in Frangistan."
"Happy? my tenants breaking on my
hand;
Unstock'd my pastures, and untill'd my
land;
Sugar and rum a drug, and mice and
moths
The sole consumers of my good broad-
cloths —
Happy? — Why, cursed war and racking tax
Have left us scarcely raiment to our
backs." —

"In that case, signior, I may take my leave
I came to ask a favor — but I grieve " -
"Favor?" said John, and eyed the Su
taun hard,
"It's my belief you come to break th
yard! —
But, stay, you look like some poor foreig
sinner, —
Take that to buy yourself a shirt an
dinner." —
With that he chuck'd a guinea at his head
But, with due dignity, the Sultaun said : -
"Permit me, sir, your bounty to decline
A *shirt* indeed I seek, but none of thine
Signior, I kiss your hands, so fare yo
well." —
"Kiss and be damn'd," quoth John
"and go to hell!"

XVII.

Next door to John there dwelt his siste
Peg,
Once a wild lass as ever shook a leg
When the blithe bagpipe blew — bu
soberer now,
She *doucely* span her flax and milk'd he
cow.
And whereas erst she was a needy slatter
Nor now of wealth or cleanliness a patter
Yet once a-month her house was partl
swept,
And once a-week a plenteous board sh
kept,
And whereas, eke, the vixen used he
claws
And teeth, of yore, on slender provoca
tion,
She now was grown amenable to laws,
A quiet soul as any in the nation;
The sole remembrance of her warlike joy
Was in old songs she sang to please he
boys.
John Bull, whom, in their years of earl
strife,
She wont to lead a cat-and-doggish life,
Now found the woman, as he said,
neighbor,
Who look'd to the main chance, decline
no labor,
Loved a long grace, and spoke a norther
jargon,
And was damn'd close in making of a
bargain.

XVIII.

The Sultaun enter'd, and he made his leg,
And with decorum curtsy'd sister Peg.
(She loved a book, and knew a thing or
    two,
And guess'd at once with whom she had
    to do.)
She bade him "Sit into the fire," and took
Her dram, her cake, her kebbuck from
    the nook;
Ask'd him " about the news from Eastern
    parts;
And of her absent bairns, puir Highland
    hearts !
If peace brought down the price of tea
    and pepper,
And if the *nitmugs* were grown *ony*
    cheaper; —
Were there nae *speerings* of our Mungo
    Park —
Ye'll be the gentleman that wants the
    sark?
If ye wad buy a web o' auld wife's
    spinnin',
I'll warrant ye it's a weel-wearing linen."

XIX.

Then up got Peg, and round the house
    'gan scuttle
In search of goods her customer to nail,
Until the Sultaun strain'd his princely
    throttle,
    And hollo'd: — " Ma'am that is not
    what I ail.
Pray, are you happy, ma'am, in this snug
    glen?"
" Happy?" said Peg; " What for d'ye
    want to ken?
Besides, just think upon this by-gane
    year,
    Grain wadna pay the yoking of the
    pleugh." —
" What say you to the present?" —
    " Meal's sae dear,
    To mak' their *brose* my bairns have
    scarce aneugh." —
" The devil take the shirt," said Soli-
    maun,
" I think my quest will end as it began. —
Farewell, ma'am; nay, no ceremony, I
    beg." —
" Ye'll no be for the linen then?" said
Peg.

XX.

Now, for the land of verdant Erin,
The Sultaun's royal bark is steering,
The Emerald Isle, where honest Paddy
    dwells,
The cousin of John Bull, as story tells.
For a long space had John, with words
    of thunder,
Hard looks, and harder knocks, kept
    Paddy under,
Till the poor lad, like boy that's flogg'd
    unduly,
Had gotten somewhat restive and unruly.
Hard was his lot and lodging, you'll allow,
A wigwam that would hardly serve a sow;
His landlord, and of middle-men two brace,
Had screw'd his rent up to the starving-
    place;
His garment was a topcoat, and an old one,
His meal was a potato, and a cold one;
But still for fun or frolic, and all that,
In the round world was not the match of
    Pat.

XXI.

The Sultaun saw him on a holiday,
Which is with Paddy still a jolly day;
When mass is ended, and his load of sins
Confess'd, and Mother Church hath from
    her binns
Dealt forth a bonus of imputed merit,
Then is Pat's time for fancy, whim, and
    spirit !
To jest, to sing, to caper fair and free,
And dance as light as leaf upon the tree.
" By Mahomet," said Sultaun Solimaun,
" That ragged fellow is our very man !
Rush in and seize him, do not do him hurt,
But, will he nill he, let me have his
    shirt." —

XXII.

Shilela their plan was well-nigh after
    baulking
(Much less provocation will set it a walk-
    ing),
But the odds that foil'd Hercules foil'd
    Paddy Whack;
They seiz'd and they floor'd and they
    stripp'd him — Alack !
Up-bubboo ! Paddy had not —— a shirt
    to his back ! ! !
And the King, disappointed, with sorrow
    and shame,
Went back to Serendib as sad as he came.

THE SUN UPON THE WEIRDLAW HILL.

AIR — *Rimhin aluin 'stu mo run.*

1817.

THE sun upon the Weirdlaw Hill,
  In Ettrick's vale is sinking sweet;
The westland wind is hush and still,
  The lake lies sleeping at my feet.
Yet not the landscape to mine eye
  Bears those bright hues that once it bore;
Though evening, with her richest dye,
  Flames o'er the hills of Ettrick's shore.

With listless look along the plain,
  I see Tweed's silver current glide,
And coldly mark the holy fane,
  Of Melrose rise in ruin'd pride.
The quiet lake, the balmy air,
  The hill, the stream, the tower, the tree,
Are they still such as once they were?
  Or is the dreary change in me?

Alas, the warp'd and broken board,
  How can it bear the painter's dye!
The harp of strain'd and tuneless chord,
  How to the minstrel's skill reply!
To aching eyes each landscape lowers,
  To feverish pulse each gale blows chill;
And Araby's or Eden's bowers
  Were barren as this moorland hill.

THE MONKS OF BANGOR'S MARCH.

AIR — "*Ymdaith Mionge.*"

WRITTEN FOR MR. GEORGE THOMSON'S WELSH MELODIES.

1817.

ÆTHELFRID or OLFRID, King of Northumberland, having besieged Chester in 613, and BROCKMAEL, a British Prince, advancing to relieve it, the religious of the neighboring Monastery of Bangor marched in procession to pray for the success of their countrymen. But the British being totally defeated, the heathen victor put the monks to the sword, and destroyed their monastery. The tune to which these verses are adapted is called the Monks' March, and is supposed to have been played at their ill-omened procession.

WHEN the heathen trumpet's clang
Round beleaguer'd Chester rang,
Veiled nun and friar gray
March'd from Bangor's fair Abbaye:

High their holy anthem sounds,
Cestria's vale the hymn rebounds,
Floating down the sylvan Dee,
  O miserere, Domine!

On the long procession goes,
Glory round their crosses glows,
And the Virgin-mother mild,
In their peaceful banner smiled:
Who could think such saintly band
Doom'd to feel unhallow'd hand?
Such was the Divine decree,
  O miserere, Domine!

Bands that masses only sung,
Hands that censers only swung,
Met the northern bow and bill,
Heard the war-cry wild and shrill:
Woe to Brockmael's feeble hand,
Woe to Olfrid's bloody brand,
Woe to Saxon cruelty,
  O miserere, Domine!

Weltering amid warriors slain,
Spurn'd by steeds with bloody mane,
Slaughter'd down by heathen blade,
Bangor's peaceful monks are laid;
Word of parting rest unspoke,
Mass unsung, and bread unbroke;
For their souls for charity,
  Sing, O miserere, Domine!

Bangor! o'er the murder wail!
Long thy ruins told the tale;
Shatter'd tower and broken arch
Long recall'd the woeful march;*
On thy shrine no tapers burn,
Never shall thy priests return;
The pilgrim sighs, and sings for thee:
  O miserere, Domine!

MR. KEMBLE'S FAREWELL ADDRESS,

ON TAKING LEAVE OF THE EDINBURGH STAGE.

1817.

As the worn war-horse, at the trumpet's sound,
Erects his mane, and neighs, and paws the ground —

* In William of Malmsbury's time the ruins of Bangor still attested the cruelty of the Northumbrians.

isdains the ease his generous lord
  assigns,
nd longs to rush on the embattled lines,
I, your plaudits ringing on mine ear,
n scarce sustain to think our parting
  near;
think my scenic hour forever past,
nd that these valued plaudits are my
  last.
hy should we part, while still some
  powers remain,
at in your service strive not yet in
  vain?
nnot high zeal the strength of youth
  supply,
nd sense of duty fire the fading eye;
d all the wrongs of age remain subdued
neath the burning glow of gratitude?
no! — the taper, wearing to its close,
t for a space in fitful lustre glows;
t all too soon the transient gleam is
  past —
cannot be renew'd, and will not last;
en duty, zeal, and gratitude, can wage
t short-lived conflict with the frosts of
  age.
s! it were poor, remembering what I
  was,
live a pensioner on your applause,
drain the dregs of your endurance
  dry,
d take, as alms, the praise I once could
  buy;
l every sneering youth around inquires: —
s this the man who once could please
  our sires?"
d scorn assumes compassion's doubtful
  mien,
warn me off from the encumber'd
  scene.
is must not be; and higher duties crave
me space between the theatre and the
  grave,
at, like the Roman in the Capitol,
nay adjust my mantle ere I fall:
y life's brief act in public service flown,
e last the closing scene, must be my
  own.

Here, then, adieu! while yet some
  well-graced parts
ay fix an ancient favorite in your hearts,

Not quite to be forgotten, even when
You look on better actors, younger men:
And if your bosoms own this kindly debt
Of old remembrance, how shall mine
  forget —
O, how forget! — how oft I hither came
In anxious hope, how oft return'd with
  fame!
How oft around your circle this weak hand
Has waved immortal Shakspeare's magic
  wand,
Till the full burst of inspiration came,
And I have felt, and you have fann'd the
  flame!
By memory treasured, while her reign
  endures,
Those hours must live — and all their
  charms are yours.
  O favor'd Land, renown'd for arts and
  arms,
For manly talent, and for female charms,
Could this full bosom prompt the sinking
  line,
What fervent benedictions now were
  thine!
But my last part is play'd, my knell is
  rung,
When e'en your praise falls faltering from
  my tongue;
And all that you can hear, or I can tell,
Is — Friends and Patrons, hail! and
  FARE YOU WELL!

LINES.

WRITTEN FOR MISS SMITH.*

1817.

WHEN the lone pilgrim views afar
The shrine that is his guiding star,
With awe his footsteps print the road
Which the loved saint of yore has trod.
As near he draws, and yet more near,
His dim eye sparkles with a tear;
The Gothic fane's unwonted show,
The choral hymn, the taper's glow,
Oppress his soul; while they delight
And chasten rapture with affright.

* Written for recitation by the distinguished actress, Miss Smith, afterwards Mrs. Bartley, on the night of her benefit at the Edinburgh Theatre, 1817, but they reached her too late for her purpose.

No longer dare he think his toil
Can merit aught his patron's smile;
Too light appears the distant way,
The chilly eve, the sultry day —
All these endured no favor claim,
But murmuring forth the sainted name,
He lays his little offering down,
And only deprecates a frown.

We, too, who ply the Thespian art,
Oft feel such bodings of the heart,
And, when our utmost powers are strain'd,
Dare hardly hope your favor gain'd.
She, who from sister climes has sought
The ancient land where Wallace fought —
Land long renown'd for arms and arts,
And conquering eyes and dauntless
    hearts —
She, as the flutterings *here* avow,
Feels all the pilgrim's terror *now;*
Yet sure on Caledonian plain
The stranger never sued in vain.
'Tis yours the hospitable task
To give the applause she dare not ask;
And they who bid the pilgrim speed,
The pilgrim's blessing be their meed.

———

LETTER

TO HIS GRACE THE DUKE OF BUCCLEUCH, DRUMLANRIG CASTLE.

Sanquhar, 2 o'clock, July 30, 1817.

FROM Ross, where the clouds on Benlo-
    mond are sleeping —
From Greenock, where Clyde to the
    Ocean is sweeping —
From Largs, where the Scotch gave the
    Northmen a drilling —
From Ardrossan, whose harbor cost many
    a shilling —
From old Cumnock where beds are as
    hard as a plank, sir —
From a chop and green pease, and a
    chicken in Sanquhar,
This eve, please the fates, at Drumlanrig
    we anchor.

                W. S.

[Sir Walter's companion on this excursion
was Captain, now Sir Adam Ferguson. — See
Life, vol. v., p. 234.]

TO THE MEMORY OF EDWAR THE BLACK PRINCE.

1817.

" A BLOTTED piece of paper dropped out of t
book, and being taken up by my father, he i
terrupted a hint from Owen, on the proprie
of securing loose memoranda with a little pas
by exclaiming, 'To the memory of Edward t
Black Prince — What's all this? — verses! —
Heaven, Frank, you are a greater blockhe
than I supposed you!'"

O FOR the voice of that wild horn,
On Fontarabian echoes borne,
    The dying hero's call,
That told imperial Charlemagne,
How Paynim sons of swarthy Spain
    Had wrought his champion's fa

"'*Fontarabian echoes!*' continued my fath
interrupting himself; 'the Fontarabian F
would have been more to the purpose. — P
nim? — What's Paynim? — Could you not s
Pagan as well, and write English, at least, if y
must needs write nonsense.'"

Sad over earth and ocean sounding,
And England's distant cliffs astoun
    ing,
    Such are the notes should say
How Britain's hope, and France's fe
Victor of Cressy and Poitier,
    In Bordeaux dying lay.

"'Poitiers, by the way, is always spelled w
an *s*, and I know no reason why orthograp
should give place to rhyme.'"

" Raise my faint head, my squires
    he said,
"And let the casement be display'd
    That I may see once more
The splendor of the setting sun
Gleam on thy mirror'd wave, Garonr
    And Blaye's empurpled shore.'

"'*Garonne* and *sun* is a bad rhyme. W
Frank, you do not even understand the begga
trade you have chosen.'"

" Like me, he sinks to Glory's slee
His fall the dews of evening steep,
    As if in sorrow shed.
So soft shall fall the trickling tear,
When England's maids and matrons he
    Of their Black Edward dead.

" And though my sun of glory set,
Nor France nor England shall forget
    The terror of my name;
nd oft shall Britain's heroes rise,
ew planets in these southern skies,
    Thro' clouds of blood and flame."

" ' A cloud of flame is something new. — Good-
orrow, my masters all, and a merry Christmas
you! — Why, the bellman writes better lines." '

Rob Roy, chap. ii.

RANSLATION FROM ARIOSTO.*
1817.

" SHE [Miss Vernon] proceeded to read the
st stanza, which was nearly to the following
rpose : " —

ADIES and knights, and arms, and love's
    fair flame,
Deeds of emprize and courtesy, I sing;
That time the Moors from sultry Afric
    came,
Led on by Agramant, their youthful king,
e whom revenge and hasty ire did bring
O'er the broad wave, in France to
    waste and war;
ich ills from old Trojano's death did
    spring,
Which to avenge he came from realms
    afar,
And menaced Christian Charles, the
    Roman Emperor.
f dauntless Ronald, too, my strain shall
    sound,
In import never known in prose and
    rhyme.
ow He, the chief of judgment deem'd
    profound,
For luckless love was crazed upon a
    time —

" ' There is a great deal of it,' said she, glan-
g along the paper, and interrupting the sweetest
unds which mortal ears can drink in : those of
youthful poet's verses, namely, read by the lips
ich are dearest to them."

Rob Roy, chap. xvi.

MOTTOES

FROM "ROB ROY."

CHAP. X.

the wide pile, by others heeded not,
ers was one sacred solitary spot,

* The *Orlando Furioso.*

Whose gloomy isles and bending shelves
    contain,
For moral hunger food, and cures for
    moral pain.

Anonymous.

CHAP. XIII.

Dire was his thought, who first in poison
    steep'd
The weapon form'd for slaughter — direr
    his,
And worthier of damnation, who in-
    still'd
The mortal venom in the social cup,
To fill the veins with death instead of
    life.

Anonymous.

CHAP. XXII.

Look round thee, young Astolpho : Here's
    the place
Which men (for being poor) are sent to
    starve in, —
Rude remedy, I trow, for sore disease.
Within these walls, stifled by damp and
    stench,
Doth Hope's fair torch expire : and at
    the snuff,
Ere yet 'tis quite extinct, rude, wild, and
    wayward,
The desperate revelries of wild despair,
Kindling their hell-born cressets, light to
    deeds
That the poor captive would have died
    ere practised,
Till bondage sunk his soul to his condi-
    tion.

The Prison, scene iii. act i.

CHAP. XXVII.

Far as the eye could reach no tree was
    seen,
Earth, clad in russet, scorn'd the lively
    green;
No birds, except as birds of passage,
    flew;
No bee was heard to hum, no dove to
    coo;
No streams, as amber smooth, as amber
    clear,
Were seen to glide, or heard to warble
    here.

Prophecy of Famine.

CHAP. XXXI.

"Woe to the vanquish'd!" was stern
 Brenno's word,
When sunk proud Rome beneath the
 Gallic sword —
"Woe to the vanquish'd!" when his
 massive blade
Bore down the scale against her ransom
 weigh'd,
And on the field of foughten battle still,
Woe knows no limit save the victor's
 will.

The Gaulliad.

CHAP. XXXII.

And be he safe restored ere evening set,
Or, if there's vengeance in an injured
 heart,
And power to wreck it in an armed hand,
Your land shall ache for 't.

Old Play.

CHAP. XXXVI.

Farewell to the land where the clouds
 love to rest,
Like the shroud of the dead on the mountain's cold breast;
To the cataract's roar where the eagles
 reply,
And the lake her lone bosom expands to
 the sky.

EPILOGUE TO "THE APPEAL."*

SPOKEN BY MRS. HENRY SIDDONS.

FEB. 16, 1818.

A CAT of yore (or else old Æsop lied)
Was changed into a fair and blooming
 bride,
But spied a mouse upon her marriage-day,
Forgot her spouse, and seized upon her
 prey;
Even thus my bridegroom lawyer, as you
 saw,
Threw off poor me, and pounced upon
 papa.
His neck from Hymen's mystic knot made
 loose,
He twisted round my sire's the literal
 noose.

* "The Appeal," a tragedy by John Galt.

Such are the fruits of our dramatic lab
Since the New Jail became our next-do
 neighbor.

Yes, times *are* changed; for, in yo
 father's age,
The lawyers were the patrons of the stag
However high advanced by future fate,
There stands the bench (*points to the Pi*
 that first received their weight.
The future legal sage, 'twas ours to see
Doom though unwigg'd and plead wit
 out a fee.

But now, astounding each poor mimic el
Instead of lawyers comes the Law hersel
Tremendous neighbor on our right s
 dwells,
Builds high her towers and excavates h
 cells;
While on the left she agitates the town
With the tempestuous question, Up
 down?
'Twixt Scylla and Charybdis thus stand w
Law's final end, and law's uncertainty.
But soft! who lives at Rome the Po
 must flatter,
And jails and lawsuits are no jesting matte
Then — just farewell! We wait wi
 serious awe
Till your applause or censure gives t
 law.
Trusting our humble efforts may assure y
We hold you Court and Counsel, Jud
 and Jury.

MACKRIMMON'S LAMENT.

1818.

AIR — "*Cha till mi tuille.*"*

MACKRIMMON, hereditary piper to the Lai
of Macleod, is said to have composed this Lame
when the Clan was about to depart upon a d
tant and dangerous expedition. The Minst
was impressed with a belief, which the eve
verified, that he was to be slain in the approac
ing feud; and hence the Gaelic words, "*Cha*
*mi tuille; ged thillis Macleod, cha till Mac
rimmon,*" "I shall never return; althou
Macleod returns, yet Mackrimmon shall ne
return!" The piece is but too well known, fr
its being the strain with which the emigran
from the West Highlands and Isles usually ta
leave of their native shore.

* "We return no more."

Macleod's wizard flag from the gray
    castle sallies,
The rowers are seated, unmoor'd are the
    galleys:
Gleam war-ax and broadsword, clang tar-
    get and quiver,
As Mackrimmon sings, "Farewell to
    Dunvegan forever!
Farewell to each cliff, on which breakers
    are foaming;
Farewell each dark glen, in which red-
    deer are roaming;
Farewell, lonely Skye, to lake, mountain,
    and river;
Macleod may return, but Mackrimmon
    shall never!

'Farewell the bright clouds that on
    Quillan are sleeping;
Farewell the bright eyes in the Dun that
    are weeping;
To each minstrel delusion, farewell!—
    and forever—
Mackrimmon departs to return to you never.
The *Banshee's* wild voice sings the death-
    lirge before me,
The pall of the dead for a mantle hangs
    o'er me;
But my heart shall not flag, and my nerves
    shall not shiver,
Though devoted I go, to return again never.

'Too oft shall the notes of Mackrim-
    mon's bewailing
Be heard when the Gael on their exile
    are sailing;
Dear land! to the shores, whence unwill-
    ing we sever,
Return—return—return shall we never!
Cha till, cha till, cha till sin tuille!
Cha till, cha till, cha till sin tuille,
Cha till, cha till, cha till sin tuille,
Ged thillis Macleod, cha till Mackrim-
    mon!"

DONALD CAIRD'S COME AGAIN.

Air—"*Malcolm Caird's* * *come again.*"
1818.

CHORUS.

Donald Caird's *come again!*
Donald Caird's come again!

* Caird signifies tinker.

Tell the news in brugh and glen,
Donald Caird's come again.

Donald Caird can lilt and sing,
Blithely dance the Highland fling,
Drink till the gudeman be blind,
Fleech till the gudewife be kind;
Hoop a leglin, clout a pan,
Or crack a pow wi' ony man;
Tell the news in brugh and glen,
Donald Caird's come again.

    Donald Caird's come again!
    Donald Caird's come again!
    Tell the news in brugh and glen,
    Donald Caird's come again.

Donald Caird can wire a maukin,
Kens the wiles o' dun-deer staukin',
Leisters kipper, makes a shift
To shoot a muir-fowl in the drift;
Water-bailiffs, rangers, keepers,
He can wauk when they are sleepers;
Not for bountith or reward
Dare ye mell wi' Donald Caird.

    Donald Caird's come again!
    Donald Caird's come again!
    Gar the bagpipes hum amain,
    Donald Caird's come again.

Donald Caird can drink a gill
Fast as hostler-wife can fill;
Ilka ane that sells gude liquor
Kens how Donald bends a bicker;
When he's fou he's stout and saucy,
Keeps the cantle o' the cawsey;
Hieland chief and Lawland laird
Maun gie room to Donald Caird!

    Donald Caird's come again!
    Donald Caird's come again!
    Tell the news in brugh and glen,
    Donald Caird's come again.

Steek the amrie, lock the kist,
Else some gear may weel be misst:
Donald Caird finds orra things
Where Allan Gregor fand the tings;
Dunts of Kebbuck, taits o' woo,
Whiles a hen and whiles a sow,
Webs or duds frae hedge or yard—
'Ware the wuddie, Donald Caird!

Donald Caird's come again !
Donald Caird's come again !
Dinna let the Shirra ken
Donald Caird's come again.

On Donald Caird the doom was stern,
Craig to tether, legs to airn,
But Donald Caird, wi' mickle study,
Caught the gift to cheat the wuddie;
Rings of airn, and bolts of steel,
Fell like ice frae hand and heel !
Watch the sheep in fauld and glen,
Donald Caird's come again !

Donald Caird's come again !
Donald Caird's come again !
Dinna let the Justice ken
Donald Caird's come again.

EFFIE DEAN'S SONGS.
1818.

THE elfin knight sate on the brae,
  The broom grows bonny, the broom
    grows fair;
And by there came lilting a lady so gay,
  And we daurna gang down to the broom
    nae mair.

Thro' the kirkyard
I met wi' the Laird;
  The silly puir body he said me nae
    harm;
But just ere 'twas dark
I met wi' the clerk —
Heart of Mid Lothian, chap. x.

MADGE WILDFIRE'S SONGS.
1818.

WHEN the gledd's in the blue cloud,
  The lavrock lies still;
When the hound's in the green-wood,
  The hind keeps the hill.

O sleep ye sound, Sir James, she said,
  When ye suld rise and ride?
There's twenty men, wi' bow and blade,
  Are seeking where ye hide.
Heart of Mid Lothian, chap. xv.

Hey for cavaliers, ho for cavaliers,
  Dub a dub, dub a dub;
  Have at old Beelzebub, —
  Oliver's running for fear. —

I glance like the wildfire thro' country
    and town;
I'm seen on the causeway — I'm seen on
    the down;
The lightning that flashes so bright and
    so free,
Is scarcely so blithe or so bonny as me.

What did ye wi' the bridal ring — bridal
    ring — bridal ring?
What did ye wi' your wedding ring, ye
    little cutty quean, O?
I gied it till a sodger, a sodger, a sodger,
I gied it till a sodger, an auld true love
    of mine, O.
Heart of Mid Lothian, chap. xvi.

Good even, good fair moon, good even
    to thee;
I prithee, dear moon, now show to me
The form and the features, the speech
    and degree,
Of the man that true lover of mine shall be.

It is the bonny butcher lad,
  That wears the sleeves of blue;
He sells the flesh on Saturday,
  On Friday that he slew.

There's a bloodhound ranging Tinwald
    Wood,
  There's harness glancing sheen;
There's a maiden sits on Tinwald brae,
  And she sings loud between.
    O sleep ye sound, etc.
Heart of Mid Lothian, chap. xviii.

Up in the air,
On my bonnie gray mare,
And I see, and I see, and I see her yet
Heart of Mid Lothian, chap. xix.

In the bonnie cells of Bedlam,
  Ere I was ane and twenty,
I had hempen bracelets strong,
  And merry whips, ding-dong,
    And prayers and fasting plenty.

My banes are buried in yon kirk-yard
  Sae far ayont the sea,
And it is but my blithesome ghaist
  That's speaking now to thee.
Heart of Mid Lothian, chap. xxix.

------

m Madge of the country, I'm Madge
    of the town,
nd I'm Madge of the lad I am blithest
    to own —
he Lady of Beever in diamonds may
    shine,
ut has not a heart half so lightsome as
    mine.
am Queen of the Wake, and I'm Lady
    of May,
nd I lead the blithe ring round the
    May-pole to-day;
he wild-fire that flashes so fair and so free
Jas never so bright or so bonnie as me.
Heart of Mid Lothian, chap. xxxi.

------

ur work is over — over now;
he goodman wipes his weary brow,
he last long wain wends slow away,
nd we are free to sport and play.

he night comes on when sets the sun,
nd labor ends when day is done.
Vhen Autumn's gone, and Winter's come,
Ve hold our jovial harvest-home.

Vhen the fight of grace is fought, —
Vhen the marriage vest is wrought, —
Vhen Faith has chased cold Doubt away,
nd hope but sickens at delay, —

Vhen Charity, imprison'd here,
ongs for a more expanded sphere;
)off thy robe of sin and clay;
Christian, rise, and come away.

Cauld is my bed, Lord Archibald,
  And sad my sleep of sorrow:

But thine sall be as sad and cauld,
  My fause true-love! to-morrow.

And weep ye not, my maidens free,
  Though death your mistress borrow,
For he for whom I die to-day
  Shall die for me to-morrow.

Proud Maisie is in the wood,
  Walking so early;
Sweet Robin sits on the bush,
  Singing so rarely.

"Tell me, thou bonny bird,
  When shall I marry me!" —
"When six braw gentlemen
  Kirkward shall carry ye."

"Who makes the bridal bed,
  Birdie, say truly?" —
"The gray-headed sexton
  That delves the grave duly.

"The glow-worm o'er grave and stone
  Shall light thee steady.
The owl from the steeple sing,
  'Welcome, proud lady.'"

MOTTOES.

FROM "THE HEART OF MID LOTHIAN."

CHAP. VIII.

ARTHUR's Seat shall be my bed,
  The sheets shall ne'er be prest by me;
St. Anton's well shall be my drink,
  Sin' my true love's forsaken me.
Old Song.

CHAP. XII.

Then she stretch'd out her lily hand,
  And for to do her best,
Hae back thy faith and troth, Willie,
  God gie thy soul good rest.
Old Ballad.

CHAP. XIV.

Dark and eerie was the night,
  And lonely was the way,
As Janet wi' her green mantill
  To Miles' Cross she did gae.
Old Ballad.

EPITAPH ON MRS. ERSKINE.*

1819.

PLAIN, as her native dignity of mind,
Arise the tomb of her we have resign'd;
Unflaw'd and stainless be the marble
　　scroll,
Emblem of lovely form and candid soul.
But, oh! what symbol may avail, to tell
The kindness, wit, and sense, we loved
　　so well!
What sculpture show the broken ties of life,
Here buried with the parent, friend, and
　　wife!
Or on the tablet stamp each title dear,
By which thine urn, EUPHEMIA, claims
　　the tear!
Yet taught, by thy meek sufferance, to
　　assume
Patience in anguish, hope beyond the
　　tomb,
Resign'd, though sad, this votive verse
　　shall flow,
And brief, alas! as thy brief span below.

LUCY ASHTON'S SONG.

1819.

LOOK not thou on beauty's charming, —
Sit thou still when kings are arming, —
Taste not when the wine-cup glistens, —
Speak not when the people listens, —
Stop thine ear against the singer, —
From the red gold keep thy finger, —
Vacant heart, and hand, and eye,
Easy live and quiet die.
The Bride of Lammermoor, chap. iii.

NORMAN THE FORESTER'S SONG.

1819.

THE monk must arise when the matins
　　ring,
　The abbot may sleep to their chime;
But the yeoman must start when the
　　bugles sing,
　'Tis time, my hearts, 'tis time.

* Mrs. Euphemia Robison, wife of William Erskine (afterwards Lord Kinedder), died September, 1819.

There's bucks and raes on Billhope brae
　There's a herd on Shortwood Shaw;
But a lily white doe in the garden goes
　She's fairly worth them a'.
The Bride of Lammermoor, chap. iii.

MOTTOES.

FROM "THE BRIDE OF LAMMERMOOR."

CHAP. VII.

Now, Billy Bewick, keep good heart,
　And of thy talking let me be;
But if thou art a man, as I am sure thou
　　art,
　Come over the dyke and fight with me.
　　　　　　　　　Old Ballad.

CHAP. VIII.

The hearth in hall was black and dead,
　No board was dight in bower within,
Nor merry bowl nor welcome bed;
　"Here's sorry cheer," quoth the Heir
　　of Lynne.
　　　　　　　　　Old Ballad.†

CHAP. XIV.

As, to the Autumn breeze's bugle-sound,
Various and vague the dry leaves dance
　　their round;
Or, from the garner-door, on ether borne,
The chaff flies devious from the winnow'd
　　corn;
So vague, so devious, at the breath of
　　heaven,
From their fix'd aim are mortal counsels
　　driven.
　　　　　　　　　Anonymous.

CHAP. XVII.

—— Here is a father now,
Will truck his daughter for a foreign ven-
　　ture,
Make her a stop-gap to some canker'd
　　feud,
Or fling her o'er, like Jonah, to the
　　fishes,
To appease the sea at highest.
　　　　　　　　　Anonymous.

† The first three lines are believed to be
Scott's.

CHAP. XXVII.

Why, now I have Dame Fortune by the
forelock,
And if she 'scapes my grasp, the fault is
mine;
He that hath buffeted with stern adversity,
Best knows to shape his course to favoring breezes.

Old Play.

ANNOT LYLE'S SONGS.
1819.

I.

Birds of omen dark and foul,
Night-crow, raven, bat, and owl,
Leave the sick man to his dream —
All night long he heard your scream;
Haste to cave and ruin'd tower,
Ivy tod, or dingled-bower,
There to wink and mope; for, hark!
In the mid air sings the lark.

II.

Hie to moorish gills and rocks,
Prowling wolf and wily fox, —
Hie ye fast, nor turn your view,
Though the lamb bleats to the ewe.
Couch your trains and speed your flight,
Safety parts with parting night;
And on distant echo borne,
Comes the hunter's early horn.

III.

The moon's wan crescent scarcely gleams,
Ghost-like she fades in morning beams;
Hence, each peevish imp and fay
That scare the pilgrim on his way. —
Quench, kelpy! quench, in fog and fen,
Thy torch, that cheats benighted men;
Thy dance is o'er, thy reign is done,
For Benyieglo hath seen the sun.

IV.

Wild thoughts, that, sinful, dark, and deep,
O'erpower the passive mind in sleep,
Pass from the slumberer's soul away,
Like night-mists from the brow of day:
Foul hag, whose blasted visage grim
Smothers the pulse, unnerves the limb,
Spur thy dark palfrey, and begone!
Thou darest not face the godlike sun.

The Legend of Montrose, chap. vi.

GAZE NOT UPON THE STARS.
1819.

Gaze not upon the stars, fond sage,
In them no influence lies;
To read the fate of youth or age
Look on my Helen's eyes.

Yet, rash astrologer, refrain!
Too dearly would be won
The prescience of another's pain
If purchased by thine own.

The Legend of Montrose, chap. vi.

THE ORPHAN MAID.
1819.

November's hail-cloud drifts away,
November's sunbeam wan
Looks coldly on the castle gray,
When forth comes Lady Anne.

The orphan by the oak was set,
Her arms, her feet, were bare;
The hail-drops had not melted yet,
Amid her raven hair.

" And dame," she said, " by all the ties
That child and mother know,
Aid one who never knew these joys,
Relieve an orphan's woe."

The lady said: — " An orphan's state
Is hard and sad to bear;
Yet worse the widow'd mother's fate,
Who mourns both lord and heir.

" Twelve times the rolling year has sped,
Since, while from vengeance wild
Of fierce Strathallan's chief I fled,
Forth's eddies whelm'd my child." —

" Twelve times the year its course has
borne,"
The wandering maid replied,
" Since fishers on St. Bridget's morn
Drew nets on Campsie side.

" St. Bridget sent no scaly spoil;
An infant, well-nigh dead,
They saved, and rear'd in want and toil,
To beg from you her bread."

That orphan maid the lady kiss'd : —
  " My husband's looks you bear;
Saint Bridget and her morn be blest !
  You are his widow's heir."

They've robed that maid, so poor and
    pale,
  In silk and sendals rare,
And pearls, for drops of frozen hail,
  Are glistening in her hair.
  The Legend of Montrose, chap. ix.

"WERT THOU LIKE ME."
1819.

WERT thou like me in life's low vale,
  With thee how blest that life I'd share;
With thee I'd fly wherever gale
  Could waft or bounding galley bear.
But parted by severe decree,
  Far different must our fortunes prove,
May thine be joy — enough for me
  To weep and pray for him I love.

The pangs this foolish heart must feel
  When hope shall be forever flown,
No sullen murmurs shall reveal,
  No selfish murmurs ever own.
Nor will I thro' life's weary years
  Like a pale drooping mourner move,
While I can think my secret tears
  May wound the heart of him I love.
  The Legend of Montrose, chap. xxi.

THE CRUSADER'S RETURN.
1819.
I.

HIGH deeds achieved of knightly fame,
From Palestine the champion came;
The cross upon his shoulders borne,
Battle and blast had dimm'd and torn.
Each dint upon his batter'd shield
Was token of a foughten field;
And thus, beneath his lady's bower,
He sung, as fell the twilight hour : —

II.

" Joy to the fair ! — thy knight behold,
Return'd from yonder land of gold;

No wealth he brings, no wealth can need,
Save his good arms and battle-steed;
His spurs to dash against a foe,
His lance and sword to lay him low;
Such all the trophies of his toil,
Such — and the hope of Tekla's smile !

III.

" Joy to the fair ! whose constant knig[
Her favor fired to feats of might !
Unnoted shall she not remain
Where meet the bright and noble train
Minstrel shall sing, and herald tell —
' Mark yonder maid of beauty well;
'Tis she for whose bright eyes was won
The listed field of Ascalon !

IV.

" ' Note well her smile ! it edged the bla[
Which fifty wives to widows made,
When, vain his strength and Mahound[
    spell,
Iconium's turban'd Soldan fell.
See'st thou her locks, whose sunny glo[
Half shows, half shades, her neck of snow[
Twines not of them one golden thread
But for its sake a Paynim bled.'

V.

" Joy to the fair ! — my name unknow[
Each deed, and all its praise, thine ow[
Then, oh ! unbar this churlish gate,
The night-dew falls, the hour is late.
Inured to Syria's glowing breath,
I feel the north breeze chill as death;
Let grateful love quell maiden shame,
And grant him bliss who brings th[
    fame."
  Ivanhoe, chap. xviii.

THE BAREFOOTED FRIAR.
1819.
I.

I'LL give thee, good fellow, a twel[
    month or twain,
To search Europe thro' from Byzanti[
    to Spain !
But ne'er shall you find, should y[
    search till you tire,
So happy a man as the Barefooted Fri[

II.

Your knight for his lady pricks forth in
career,
And is brought home at even-song prick'd
through with a spear;
I confess him in haste — for his lady de-
sires
No comfort on earth save the Barefooted
Friar's.

III.

Your monarch! — Pshaw! many a prince
has been known
To barter his robes for our cowl and our
gown;
But which of us e'er felt the idle desire
To exchange for a crown the gray hood
of a Friar?

IV.

The Friar has walked out, and where'er
he has gone,
The land and its fatness is mark'd for his
own;
He can roam where he lists, he can stop
where he tires,
For every man's house is the Barefooted
Friar's.

V.

He's expected at noon, and no wight,
till he comes,
May profane the great chair, or the por-
ridge of plums;
For the best of the cheer, and the seat
by the fire,
The undenied right of the Barefooted
Friar.

VI.

He's expected at night, and the pasty's
made hot;
They broach the brown ale, and they fill
the black pot;
And the good-wife would wish the good-
man in the mire,
Ere he lack'd a soft pillow, the Barefooted
Friar.

VII.

Long flourish the sandal, the cord, and
the cope,
The dread of the devil and trust of the
Pope!

For to gather life's roses unscathed by
the brier
Is granted alone to the Barefooted Friar.

Ivanhoe, chap. xviii.

SAXON WAR-SONG.
1819.

"THE fire was spreading rapidly through all
parts of the castle, when Ulrica, who had first
kindled it, appeared on a turret, in the guise of
one of the ancient furies, yelling forth a war-song,
such as was of yore chanted on the field of battle
by the yet heathen Saxons. . . . Tradition has
preserved some wild strophes of the barbarous
hymn which she chanted wildly amid that scene
of fire and slaughter."

I.

WHET the bright steel,
Sons of the White Dragon!
Kindle the torch,
Daughter of Hengist!
The steel glimmers not for the carving
of the banquet,
It is hard, broad, and sharply pointed;
The torch goeth not to the bridal chamber,
It steams and glitters blue with sulphur.
Whet the steel, the raven croaks!
Light the torch, Zernebock is yelling!
Whet the steel, sons of the Dragon!
Kindle the torch, daughter of Hengist!

II.

The black cloud is low over the thane's
castle;
The eagle screams—he rides on its bosom.
Scream not, gray rider of the sable cloud,
Thy banquet is prepared!
The maidens of Valhalla look forth,
The race of Hengist will send them
guests.
Shake your black tresses, maidens of
Valhalla!
And strike your loud timbrels for joy!
Many a haughty step bends to your halls,
Many a helmed head.

III.

Dark sits the evening upon the thane's
castle,
The black clouds gather round;
Soon shall they be red as the blood of
the valiant!

The destroyer of forests shall shake his
    red crest against them;
He, the bright consumer of palaces,
Broad waves he his blazing banner,
Red, wide, and dusky,
Over the strife of the valiant;
His joy is in the clashing swords and
    broken bucklers;
He loves to lick the hissing blood as it
    bursts warm from the wound!

IV.

All must perish!
The sword cleaveth the helmet;
The strong armor is pierced by the lance,
Fire devoureth the dwelling of princes,
Engines break down the fences of battle.
All must perish!
The race of Hengist is gone —
The name of Horsa is no more!
Shrink not then from your doom, sons of
    the sword!
Let your blades drink blood like wine;
Feast ye in the banquet of slaughter,
By the light of the blazing halls!
Strong be your swords while your blood
    is warm,
And spare neither for pity nor fear,
For vengeance hath but an hour;
Strong hate itself shall expire!
I also must perish.*

REBECCA'S HYMN.

WHEN Israel, of the Lord beloved,
    Out from the land of bondage came,
Her fathers' God before her moved,
    An awful guide in smoke and flame.
By day, along the astonish'd lands
    The clouded pillar glided slow;

* "It will readily occur to the antiquary,
that these verses are intended to imitate the antique poetry of the Scalds — the minstrels of the
old Scandinavians — the race, as the Laureate
[Southey] so happily terms them, —
  "'Stern to inflict, and stubborn to endure,
  Who smiled in death.'
  "The poetry of the Anglo-Saxons, after their
civilization and conversion, was of a different
and softer character; but in the circumstances
of Ulrica, she may be not unnaturally supposed
to return to the wild strains which animated her
forefathers during the times of Paganism and
untamed ferocity."
                   Ivanhoe, chap. xxxi.

By night Arabia's crimson'd sands
    Return'd the fiery column's glow.

There rose the choral hymn of praise,
    And trump and timbrel answer'd keen
And Zion's daughters pour'd their lays.
    With priest's and warrior's voice be-
      tween.
No portents now our foes amaze,
    Forsaken Israel wanders lone:
Our fathers would not know THY ways
    And THOU hast left them to their own

But present still, though now unseen!
    When brightly shines the prosperous day
Be thoughts of THEE a cloudy screen
    To temper the deceitful ray.
And oh, when stoops on Judah's path
    In shade and storm the frequent night
Be THOU, long-suffering, slow to wrath
    A burning and a shining light!

Our harps we left by Babel's streams,
    The tyrant's jest, the Gentile's scorn
No censer round our altar beams,
    And mute are timbrel, harp, and horn
But THOU hast said, The blood of goat
    The flesh of rams, I will not prize;
A contrite heart, a humble thought,
    Are mine accepted sacrifice.

                Ivanhoe, chap. xxxix.

A VIRELAI.

1819.

THE BLACK KNIGHT.

ANNA-MARIE, love, up is the sun,
Anna-Marie, love, morn is begun;
Mists are dispersing, love, birds singing
    free,
Up in the morning, love, Anna-Marie.
Anna-Marie, love, up in the morn,
The hunter is winding blithe sounds
    his horn,
The echo rings merry from rock and free
    tree.
'Tis time to arouse thee, love, Anna-
    Marie.

WAMBA.

O Tybalt, love, Tybalt, awake me not yet
Around my soft pillow while softer dreams
    flit;

or what are the joys that in waking we
    prove,
ompared with these visions, O Tybalt,
    my love?
et the birds to the rise of the mist carol
    shrill;
et the hunter blow out his loud horn on
    the hill,
ofter sounds, softer pleasures, in slumber
    I prove,
ut think not I dream'd of thee, Tybalt,
    my love.

          Ivanhoe, chap. xl.

*Duet between the Knight of the Fetterlock
    and the Jester.*

1819.

KNIGHT AND WAMBA.

HERE came three merry men from south,
    west, and north,
  Ever more sing the roundelay;
o win the Widow of Wycombe forth,
  And where was the widow might say
    them nay?

he first was a knight, and from Tynedale
    he came,
  Ever more sing the roundelay;
nd his fathers, God save us, were men
    of great fame,
  And where was the widow might say
    him nay?

f his father the laird, of his uncle the
    squire,
  He boasted in rhyme and in roundelay;
he bade him go bask by his sea-coal fire,
  For she was the widow would say him
    nay.

WAMBA.

he next that came forth, swore by blood
    and by nails,
  Merrily sing the roundelay;
ur's a gentleman, God wot, and Hur's
    lineage was of Wales,
  And where was the widow might say
    him nay?

r David ap Morgan ap Griffith ap Hugh
  Ap Tudor ap Rhice, quoth his rounde-
    lay;

She said that one widow for so many was
    too few,
  And she bade the Welshman wend his
    way.

But then next came a yeoman, a yeoman
    of Kent,
  Jollily singing his roundelay;
He spoke to the widow of living and rent,
  And where was a widow could say him
    nay?

BOTH.

So the knight and the squire were both
    left in the mire,
  There for to sing their roundelay;
For a yeoman of Kent, with his yearly rent,
  There ne'er was a widow could say him
    nay.

          Ivanhoe, chap. xl.

FUNERAL HYMN.

1819.

DUST unto dust,
To this all must;
  The tenant has resign'd
The faded form
To waste and worm —
  Corruption claims her kind.

Thro' paths unknown
Thy soul hath flown,
  To seek the realms of woe,
Where fiery pain
Shall urge the stain
  Of actions done below.

In that sad place,
By Mary's grace,
  Brief may thy dwelling be;
Till prayers and alms,
And holy psalms,
  Shall set the captive free.

       Ivanhoe, Chap. xlii.

MOTTOES.

FROM "IVANHOE."

CHAP. XXVI.

THE hottest horse will oft be cool,
  The dullest will show fire;

The friar will often play the fool,
　The fool will play the friar.

CHAP. XXX.

Approach the chamber, look upon his bed,
His is the passing of no peaceful ghost,
Which, as the lark arises to the sky,
Mid morning's sweetest breeze and softest
　dew,
Is wing'd to heaven by good men's sighs
　and tears!
Anselm parts otherwise.

Old Play.

CHAP. XXXIII.

Trust me, each state must have its poli-
　cies:
Kingdoms have edicts, cities have their
　charters;
Even the wild outlaw, in his forest-walk,
Keeps yet some touch of civil discipline.
For not since Adam wore his verdant
　apron,
Hath man with man in social union dwelt,
But laws were made to draw that union
　closer.

Old Play.

CHAP. XXXVI.

Arouse the tiger of Hyrcanian deserts,
Strive with the half-starved lion for his
　prey;
Lesser the risk, than rouse the slumbering
　fire
Of wild Fanaticism.

Anonymous.

CHAP. XXXVII.

Say not my art is fraud — all live by
　seeming.
The beggar begs with it, and the gay
　courtier
Gains land and title, rank and rule, by
　seeming:
The clergy scorn it not, and the bold
　soldier
Will eke with it his service. — All admit
　it,
All practise it; and he who is content
With showing what he is, shall have
　small credit
In church, or camp, or state. — So wags
　the world.

Old Play.

CHAP. XXXVIII.

Stern was the law which bade its votaries
　leave
At human woes with human hearts to
　grieve;
Stern was the law which at the winning
　wile
Of frank and harmless mirth forbade to
　smile;
But sterner still, when high the iron rod
Of tyrant power she shook, and call'd
　that power of God.

The Middle Ages.

CHAP. XLII.

I found them winding of Marcello's corpse
And there was such a solemn melody,
'Twixt doleful songs, tears, and sad
　elegies,
Such as old grandames watching by the
　dead
Are wont to outwear the night with.

Old Play.

SONGS OF THE WHITE LADY OF AVENEL.

1820.

(1.) — ON TWEED RIVER.

I.

MERRILY swim we, the moon shines
　bright,
Both current and ripple are dancing in
　light.
We have roused the night raven, I heard
　him croak,
As we plashed along beneath the oak
That flings its broad branches so far and
　so wide,
Their shadows are dancing in midst of
　the tide.
"Who wakens my nestlings?" the raven
　he said,
"My beak shall ere morn in his blood
　be red!
For a blue swollen corpse is a dainty meal,
And I'll have my share with the pike and
　the eel."

II.

Merrily swim we, the moon shines bright,
There's a golden gleam on the distant
　height:

here's a silver shower on the alders dank,
and the drooping willows that wave on
    the bank.
see the Abbey, both turret and tower,
it is all astir for the vesper hour;
he Monks for the chapel are leaving
    each cell,
but where's Father Philip should toll the
    bell?

III.

Merrily swim we, the moon shines bright,
Downward we drift through shadow and
    light;
Under yon rock the eddies sleep,
Calm and silent, dark and deep.
The Kelpy has risen from the fathomless
    pool,
He has lighted his candle of death and
    of dool;
Look, Father, look, and you'll laugh to
    see
How he gapes and glares with his eyes
    on thee!

IV.

Good luck to your fishing, whom watch
    ye to-night?
A man of mean or a man of might?
Is it layman or priest that must float in
    your cóve,
Or lover who crosses to visit his love?
Hark! heard ye the Kelpy reply as we
    past: —
God's blessing on the warder, he lock'd
    the bridge fast!
All that come to my cove are sunk,
Priest or layman, lover or monk."

. . . . . .

landed — landed! the black book hath
    won,
Else had you seen Berwick with morning
    sun!
Sain ye, and save ye, and blithe mot ye be,
For seldom they land that go swimming
    with me.
        The Monastery, chap. v.

(2.)—TO THE SUB-PRIOR.

GOOD evening, Sir Priest, and so late as
    you ride,
With your mule so fair, and your mantle
    so wide;

But ride you thro' valley, or ride you o'er
    hill,
There is one that has warrant to wait on
    you still.
        Back, back,
           The volume black!
I have a warrant to carry it back.

What, ho! Sub-Prior, and came you but
    here
To conjure a book from a dead woman's
    bier?
Sain you, and save you, be wary and wise,
Ride back with the book, or you'll pay
    for your prize.
        Back, back,
           There's death in the track!
In the name of my master, I bid thee
    bear back.

"In the name of MY Master," said the astonished Monk, "that name before which all things
created tremble, I conjure thee to say what thou
art that hauntest me thus?"

The same voice replied: —

That which is neither ill nor well,
That which belongs not to heaven nor to
    hell,
A wreath of the mist, a bubble of the
    stream,
'Twixt a waking thought and a sleeping
    dream;
        A form that men spy
        With the half-shut eye
In the beams of the setting sun, am I.

Vainly, Sir Prior, wouldst thou bar me
    my right!
Like the star when it shoots, I can dart
    thro' the night;
I can dance on the torrent, and ride on
    the air,
And travel the world with the bonny
    night-mare.
        Again, again,
        At the crook of the glen,
Where bickers the burnie, I'll meet thee
    again.

Men of good are bold as sackless,*
Men of rude are wild and reckless.

        * *Sackless* — Innocent.

Lie thou still
  In the nook of the hill,
For those be before thee, that wish thee
  ill.

The Monastery, chap. ix.

HALBERT'S INCANTATION.

THRICE to the holly brake —
  Thrice to the well: —
I bid thee awake,
  White Maid of Avenel!

Noon gleams on the Lake —
  Noon glows on the Fell —
Wake thee, O wake,
  White Maid of Avenel.

The Monastery, chap. xi.

---

(3) — THE WHITE LADY'S ANSWER.

YOUTH of the dark eye, wherefore didst
  thou call me?
Wherefore art thou here, if terrors can
  appal thee?
He that seeks to deal with us must know
  nor fear nor failing;
To coward and churl our speech is dark,
  our gifts are unavailing.
The breeze that brought me hither now
  must sweep Egyptian ground,
The fleecy cloud on which I ride for
  Araby is bound,
The fleecy cloud is drifting by, the breeze
  sighs for my stay,
For I must sail a thousand miles before
  the close of day.
What I am I must not show —
What I am thou couldst not know —
Something betwixt heaven and hell —
Something that neither stood nor fell —
Something that thro' thy wit or will
May work thee good — may work thee ill.
Neither substance quite, nor shadow,
Haunting lonely moors and meadow,
Dancing by the haunted spring,
Riding on the whirlwind's wing;
Aping in fantastic fashion
Every change of human passion,
While o'er our frozen minds they pass,
Like shadows from the mirror'd glass.
Wayward, fickle, is our mood,
Hovering betwixt bad and good,

Happier than brief-dated man,
Living ten times o'er his span;
Far less happy, for we have
Help nor hope beyond the grave!
Man awakes to joy or sorrow;
Ours the sleep that knows no morrow.
This is all that I can show —
This is all that thou may'st know.

Ay! and I taught thee the word and th
  spell,
To waken me here by the Fairies' Well.
But thou hast loved the heron and hawk
  More than to seek my haunted walk;
And thou hast loved the lance and th
  sword,
More than good text and holy word;
And thou hast loved the deer to track,
More than the lines and the letters black
And thou art a ranger of moss and wood
And scornest the nurture of gentle bloo

Thy craven fear my truth accused,
Thine idlehood my trust abused;
He that draws to harbor late,
Must sleep without, or burst the gate.
There is a star for thee which burn'd;
Its influence wanes, its course is turn'd
Valor and constancy alone
Can bring thee back the chance that
  flown.

Within that awful volume lies
The mystery of mysteries!
Happiest they of human race,
To whom God has granted grace
To read, to fear, to hope, to pray,
To lift the latch, and force the way;
And better had they ne'er been born
Who read to doubt, or read to scorn

Many a fathom dark and deep
I have laid the book to sleep;
Ethereal fires around it glowing —
Ethereal music ever flowing —
  The sacred pledge of Heaven
All things revere,
Each in his sphere,
  Save man for whom 'twas given:
Lend thy hand, and thou shalt spy
Things ne'er seen by mortal eye.

Fearest thou to go with me?
Still it is free to thee
  A peasant to dwell;
Thou may'st drive the dull steer,
And chase the king's deer,
But never more come near
  This haunted well.

___

ere lies the volume thou boldly hast sought;
uch it, and take it, 'twill dearly be bought.

___

    Rash thy deed,
    Mortal weed
To immortal flames applying;
    Rasher trust
    Has thing of dust,
On his own weak worth relying:
rip thee of such fences vain,
rip, and prove thy luck again.

___

ortal warp and mortal woof
nnot break this charmed roof;
l that mortal art hath wrought
our cell returns to naught.
e molten gold returns to clay,
e polish'd diamond melts away:
l is alter'd, all is flown,
ught stands fast but truth alone.
t for that thy quest give o'er:
urage! prove thy chance once more.

___

as! alas!
t ours the grace
ese holy characters to trace;
dle forms of painted air,
Not to us is given to share
e boon bestow'd on Adam's race.
With patience bide,
Heaven will provide
e fitting time, the fitting guide.
        The Monastery, chap. xii.

___

SONGS.

HALBERT'S SECOND INTERVIEW WITH
  THE WHITE LADY OF AVENEL.

is is the day when the fairy kind
weeping alone for their hopeless lot,

And the wood-maiden sighs to the sighing wind,
And the mermaiden weeps in her crystal grot;
For this is a day that the deed was wrought,
In which we have neither part nor share;
For the children of clay was salvation bought,
But not for the forms of sea or air!
And ever the mortal is most forlorn,
Who meeteth our race on the Friday morn.

___

Daring youth! for thee it is well,
Here calling me in haunted dell,
That thy heart has not quail'd,
Nor thy courage fail'd,
And that thou couldst brook
The angry look
Of her of Avenel.
Did one limb shiver,
Or an eyelid quiver,
Thou wert lost forever.
Though I am form'd from the ether blue,
And my blood is of the unfallen dew,
And thou art framed of mud and dust,
'Tis thine to speak, reply I must.

___

A mightier wizard far than I
  Wields o'er the universe his power;
Him owns the eagle in the sky,
  The turtle in the bower.

___

Changeful in shape, yet mightiest still,
He wields the heart of man at will,
From ill to good, from good to ill,
  In cot and castle-tower.

___

Ask thy heart, whose secret cell
Is fill'd with Mary Avenel!
Ask thy pride, why scornful look
In Mary's view it will not brook?
Ask it, why thou seek'st to rise
Among the mighty and the wise, —
Why thou spurn'st thy lowly lot, —
Why thy pastimes are forgot, —
Why thou wouldst in bloody strife
Mend thy luck or lose thy life?
Ask thy heart, and it shall tell,
Sighing from its secret cell,
'Tis for Mary Avenel.

Do not ask me;
On doubts like these thou canst not task
   me.
We only see the passing show
Of human passions' ebb and flow;
And view the pageant's idle glance,
As mortals eye the northern dance,
When thousand streamers, flashing bright,
Career it o'er the brow of night,
And gazers mark their changeful gleams,
But feel no influence from their beams.

By ties mysterious link'd, our fated race
Holds strange connection with the sons
   of men.
The star that rose upon the House of
   Avenel,
When Norman Ulric first assumed the
   name,
That star, when culminating in its orbit,
Shot from its sphere a drop of diamond
   dew,
And this bright font received it — and a
   Spirit
Rose from the fountain, and her date of
   life
Hath co-existence with the House of
   Avenel,
And with the star that rules it.

Look on my girdle — on this thread of
   gold —
'Tis fine as web of lightest gossamer,
And, but there is a spell on't, would not
   bind,
Light as they are, the folds of my thin robe.
But when 'twas donn'd, it was a massive
   chain,
Such as might bind the champion of the
   Jews,
Even when his locks were longest — it
   hath dwindled,
Hath minished in its substance and its
   strength,
As sank the greatness of the House of
   Avenel.
When this frail thread gives way, I to
   the elements
Resign the principles of life they lent me.
Ask me no more of this ! — the stars for-
   bid it.

Dim burns the once bright star of Avene
Dim as the beacon when the morn is nig
And the o'er-wearied warder leaves t
   lighthouse;
There is an influence sorrowful and fea
   ful,
That dogs its downward course. Disa
   trous passion,
Fierce hate and rivalry, are in the aspe
That lowers upon its fortunes.

Complain not of me, child of clay,
If to thy harm I yield the way.
We, who soar thy sphere above,
Know not aught of hate or love;
As will or wisdom rules thy mood,
My gifts to evil turn or good.
When Piercie Shafton boasteth high,
Let this token meet his eye,
The Sun is westering from the dell,
Thy wish is granted, fare thee well.

      The Monastery, chap. xvii.

THE WHITE LADY TO MARY AVENEL.

1820.

MAIDEN, whose sorrows wail the Liv
   Dead,
   Whose eyes shall commune with
     Dead Alive,
Maiden, attend ! Beneath my foot lies
   The Word, the Law, the Path wh
     thou dost strive
To find, and canst not find. — Co
   Spirits shed
   Tears for their lot, it were my lot
     weep,
Showing the road which I shall ne
   tread,
   Though my foot points it. — Sle
     eternal sleep,
Dark, long, and cold forgetfulness
   lot ! —
   But do not thou at human ills repin
Secure there lies full guerdon in this s
   For all the woes that wait frail Ada
     line —
Stoop then and make it yours. — I r
   not make it mine !

      The Monastery, chap. xxx

THE WHITE LADY TO EDWARD GLENDENNING.

1820.

THOU who seek'st my fountain lone,
With thoughts and hopes thou dar'st not
own;
Whose heart within leap'd wildly glad,
When most his brow seem'd dark and
sad;
Hie thee back, thou find'st not here
Corpse or coffin, grave or bier;
The Dead Alive is gone and fled —
Go thou, and join the Living Dead!

The Living Dead, whose sober brow
Oft shrouds such thoughts as thou hast
now,
Whose hearts within are seldom cured
Of passions by their vows abjured;
Where, under sad and solemn show,
Vain hopes are nursed, wild wishes
glow.
Seek the convent's vaulted room,
Prayer and vigil be thy doom;
Doff the green, and don the gray,
To the cloister hence away!

The Monastery, chap. xxxii.

THE WHITE LADY'S FAREWELL.

1820.

FARE THEE WELL, thou Holly green!
Thou shalt seldom now be seen,
With all thy glittering garlands bend-
ing,
As to greet my slow descending,
Startling the bewilder'd hind,
Who sees thee wave without a wind.

Farewell, Fountain! now not long
Shalt thou murmur to my song,
While thy crystal bubbles glancing,
Keep the time in mystic dancing,
Rise and swell, are burst and lost,
Like mortal schemes by fortune cross'd.

The knot of fate at length is tied,
The Churl is Lord, the Maid is Bride!
Vainly did my magic sleight
Send the lover from her sight;

Wither bush, and perish well,
Fall'n is lofty Avenel!

The Monastery, chap. xxxvii.

BORDER BALLAD.

1820.

I.

MARCH, march, Ettrick and Teviotdale,
  Why the deil dinna ye march forward
  in order?
March, march, Eskdale and Liddisdale,
  All the Blue Bonnets are bound for
  the Border.
    Many a banner spread,
    Flutters above your head,
  Many a crest that is famous in story.
    Mount and make ready then,
    Sons of the mountain glen,
  Fight for the Queen and our old Scot-
  tish glory.

II.

Come from the hills where your hirsels
  are grazing,
  Come from the glen of the buck and
  the roe;
Come to the crag where the beacon is
  blazing,
  Come with the buckler, the lance, and
  the bow.
    Trumpets are sounding,
    War-steeds are bounding,
  Stand to your arms, and march in good
  order;
    England shall many a day
    Tell of the bloody fray,
  When the Blue Bonnets came over the
  Border.

The Monastery, chap. xxv.

PARAPHRASE FROM HORACE.

Ne sit ancillae tibi amor pudori.

  TAKE thou no scorn
  Of fiction born
Fair Fiction's muse to woo.
  Old Homer's theme
  Was but a dream —
Himself a fiction too.

The Monastery, Introduction.

MOTTOES.

FROM "THE MONASTERY."

1820.

CHAP. I.

O AY! the Monks, the Monks, they did
 the mischief!
Theirs all the grossness, all the superstition
Of a most gross and superstitious age. —
May HE be praised that sent the healthful
 tempest,
And scatter'd all these pestilential vapors;
But that we owed them *all* to yonder
 Harlot,
Throned on the seven hills with her cup
 of gold,
I will as soon believe, with kind Sir Roger,
That old Moll White took wing with cat
 and broomstick,
And raised the last night's thunder.
Old Play.

CHAP. II.

In yon lone vale his early youth was bred.
Not solitary then — the bugle-horn
Of fell Alecto often waked its windings,
From where the brook joins the majestic
 river,
To the wild northern bog, the curlew's
 haunt,
Where oozes forth its first and feeble
 streamlet.
Old Play.

CHAP. V.

A priest, ye cry, a priest! Lame Shep-
 herds they,
How shall they gather in the straggling
 flock?
Dumb dogs which bark not — how shall
 they compel
The loitering vagrants to the Master's
 fold?
Fitter to bask before the blazing fire,
And snuff the mess neat-handed Phyllis
 dresses,
Than on the snow-wreath battle with the
 wolf.
The Reformation.

CHAP. VI.

Now let us sit in conclave. That these
 weeds
Be rooted from the vineyard of the church.

That these foul tares he severed from th[e]
 wheat,
We are, I trust, agreed. Yet how to [do]
 this,
Nor hurt the wholesome crop and tend[er]
 vine plants,
Craves good advisement.
The Reformation.

CHAP. VIII.

Nay, dally not with time, the wise man'[s]
 treasure,
Though fools are lavish on't; — the fat[e]
 Fisher
Hooks souls, while we waste moments.
Old Play.

CHAP. XI.

You call this education, do you not?
Why 'tis the forced march of a herd o[f]
 bullocks
Before a shouting drover. The glad va[le]
Move on at ease, and pause a while t[o]
 snatch
A passing morsel from the dewy gree[n]
 sward;
While all the blows, the oaths, the indi[g]
 nation,
Fall on the croupe of the ill-fated lagga[rd]
That cripples in the rear.
Old Play.

CHAP. XII.

There's something in that ancient supe[r]
 stition,
Which, erring as it is, our fancy loves.
The spring that, with its thousand cryst[al]
 bubbles,
Bursts from the bosom of some desert roc[k]
In secret solitude, may well be deem'd
The haunt of something purer, more re[-]
 fined,
And mightier than ourselves.
Old Play.

CHAP. XIV.

Nay, let me have the friends who eat m[y]
 victuals,
As various as my dishes. The feast'[s]
 naught,
Where one huge plate predominates. —
 John Plaintext,
He shall be mighty beef, our Englis[h]
 staple:
The worthy Alderman, a butter'd dump[-]
 ling;

Yon pair of whisker'd Cornets, ruffs and
  rees;
Their friend the Dandy, a green goose in
  sippets.
And so the board is spread at once and
  fill'd
On the same principle — Variety.
New Play.

CHAP. XV.

He strikes no coin, 'tis true, but coins
  new phrases,
And vends them forth as knaves vend
  gilded counters,
Which wise men scorn, and fools accept
  in payment.
Old Play.

CHAP. XIX.

Now choose thee, gallant, betwixt wealth
  and honor;
There lies the pelf, in sum to bear thee
  through
The dance of youth, and the turmoil of
  manhood,
Yet leave enough for age's chimney-
  corner;
But an thou grasp to it, farewell, Ambi-
  tion!
Farewell each hope of bettering thy con-
  dition,
And raising thy low rank above the churls
That till the earth for bread!
Old Play.

CHAP. XXI.

Indifferent, but indifferent — pshaw! he
  doth it not
Like one who is his craft's master — ne'er-
  theless
I have seen a clown confer a bloody cox-
  comb
On one who was a master of defence.
Old Play.

CHAP. XXII.

Yes, life hath left him — every busy
  thought,
Each fiery passion, every strong affection,
The sense of outward ill and inward sor-
  row,
Are fled at once from the pale trunk be-
  fore me;
And I have given that which spoke and
  moved,
Thought, acted, suffer'd, as a living man,

To be a ghastly form of bloody clay,
Soon the foul food for reptiles.
Old Play.

CHAP. XXIII.

'Tis when the wound is stiffening with
  the cold,
The warrior first feels pain — 'tis when
  the heat
And fiery fever of his soul is past,
The sinner feels remorse.
Old Play.

CHAP. XXIV.

I'll walk on tiptoe; arm my eye with
  caution,
My heart with courage, and my hand
  with weapon,
Like him who ventures on a lion's den.
Old Play.

CHAP. XXVII.

Now, by Our Lady, Sheriff, 'tis hard
  reckoning,
That I, with every odds of birth and
  barony,
Should be detain'd here for the casual
  death
Of a wild forester, whose utmost having
Is but the brazen buckle of the belt
In which he sticks his hedge-knife.
Old Play.

CHAP. XXX.

You call it an ill angel — it may be so;
But sure I am, among the ranks which
  fell,
'Tis the first fiend e'er counsell'd man to
  rise,
And win the bliss the sprite himself had
  forfeited.
Old Play.

CHAP. XXXI.

At school I knew him — a sharp-witted
  youth,
Grave, thoughtful, and reserved among
  his mates,
Turning the hours of sport and food to
  labor,
Starving his body to inform his mind.
Old Play.

CHAP. XXXII.

Then in my gown of sober gray
  Along the mountain path I'll wander,
And wind my solitary way
  To the sad shrine that courts me yonder.

There in the calm monastic shade
  All injuries may be forgiven,
And there for thee, obdurate maid,
  My orisons shall rise to Heaven.
    The Cruel Lady of the Mountain.

CHAP. XXXIII.

Now on my faith this gear is all entangled,
Like to the yarn-clew of the drowsy
    knitter,
Dragg'd by the frolic kitten thro' the
    cabin,
While the good dame sits nodding o'er
    the fire —
Masters, attend; 'twill crave some skill
    to clear it !
    Old Play.

CHAP. XXXIV.

It is not texts will do it. Church artillery
Are silenced soon by real ordnance,
And canons are but vain opposed to
    cannon.
Go, coin your crosier, melt your church
    plate down,
Bid the starved soldiers banquet in your
    halls,
And quaff your long-saved hogsheads. —
    Turn them out
Thus primed with your good cheer, to
    guard your wall,
And they will venture for 't.
    Old Play.

MOTTOES
FROM "THE ABBOT."
1820.

CHAP. V.

—— In the wild storm,
The seaman hews his mast down, and the
    merchant
Heaves to the billows wares he once
    deem'd precious;
So prince and peer, mid popular con-
    tentions,
Cast off their favorites.
    Old Play.

CHAP. VI.

Thou hast each secret of the household,
    Francis;
I dare be sworn thou hast been in the
    buttery

Steeping thy curious humor in fat ale,
And in the butler's tattle — ay, or chatting
With the glib waiting-woman o'er he
    comfits —
These bear the key to each domestie
    mystery.
    Old Play.

CHAP. VII.

When I hae a saxpence under my thumb
Then I get credit in ilka town;
But when I am poor, they bid me gae by
O, poverty parts good company.
    Old Song.

CHAP. VIII.

The sacred tapers' lights are gone,
Gray moss has clad the altar stone,
The holy image is o'erthrown,
  The bell has ceased to toll.
The long-ribb'd aisles are burst and
    shrunk,
The holy shrines to ruin sunk,
Departed is the pious monk,
  God's blessing on his soul !
    Rediviva.

CHAP. IX.

Kneel with me — swear it — 'tis not ir
    words I trust,
Save when they're fenced with an appea
    to Heaven.
    Old Play.

CHAP. XI.

Life hath its May, and all is mirthful then
The woods are vocal, and the flowers al
    odor;
Its very blast has mirth in't, — and the
    maidens,
The while they don their cloaks to screer
    their kirtles,
Laugh at the rain that wets them.
    Old Play.

CHAP. XII.

Nay, hear me, brother—I am elder, wiser
And holier than thou; and age, and wis
    dom,
And holiness, have peremptory claims,
And will be listen'd to.
    Old Play.

CHAP. XVI.

Youth ! thou wear'st to manhood now,
Darker lip and darker brow,
Statelier step, more pensive mien,
In thy face and gait are seen;

Thou must now brook midnight watches,
Take thy food and sport by snatches!
For the gambol and the jest,
Thou wert wont to love the best,
Graver follies must thou follow,
But as senseless, false, and hollow.

Life, a Poem.

CHAP. XVIII.

—— The sky is clouded, Gaspard,
And the vext ocean sleeps a troubled sleep
Beneath a lurid gleam of parting sunshine.
Such slumber hangs o'er discontented
    lands,
While factions doubt, as yet if they have
    strength
To front the open battle.

Albion, a Poem.

CHAP. XIX.

It is and is not—'tis the thing I sought for,
Have kneel'd for, pray'd for, risk'd my
    fame and life for,
And yet it is not — no more than the
    shadow
Upon the hard, cold, flat, and polish'd
    mirror,
Is the warm, graceful, rounded, living
    substance
Which it presents in form and lineament.

Old Play.

CHAP. XX.

Now have you reft me from my staff, my
    guide,
Who taught my youth as men teach un-
    tamed falcons
To use my strength discreetly — I am reft
Of comrade and of counsel!

Old Play.

CHAP. XXIII.

Give me a morsel on the greensward
    rather,
Coarse as you will the cooking. — Let
    the fresh spring
Bubble beside my napkin — and the free
    birds,
Twittering and chirping, hop from bough
    to bough,
To claim the crumbs I leave for per-
    quisites —
Your prison-feasts I like not.

The Woodman, a Drama.

CHAP. XXIV.

'Tis a weary life this ——
Vaults overhead, and grates and bars
    around me,
And my sad hours spent with as sad com-
    panions,
Whose thoughts are brooding o'er their
    own mischances,
Far, far too deeply to take part in mine.

The Woodsman.

CHAP. XXV.

And when Love's torch hath set the
    heart in flame,
Comes Seignor Reason with his saws and
    cautions,
Giving such aid as the old gray-beard
    Sexton,
Who from the church-vault drags his
    crazy engine,
To ply its dribbling ineffectual stream-
    let
Against a conflagration.

Old Play.

CHAP. XXVIII.

Yes, it is she whose eyes looked on thy
    childhood,
And watch'd with trembling hope thy
    dawn of youth,
That now with these same eye-balls,
    dimm'd with age,
And dimmer yet with tears, sees thy dis-
    honor.

Old Play.

CHAP. XXX.

In some breasts passion lies conceal'd and
    silent,
Like war's swart powder in a castle vault,
Until occasion, like the linstock, lights
    it:
Then comes at once the lightning and
    the thunder,
And distant echoes tell that all is rent
    asunder.

Old Play.

CHAP. XXXVI.

He mounted himself on a coal black steed,
    And her on a freckled gray,
With a buglet horn hung down from his
    side,
    And roundly they rode away.

Old Ballad.

GOLDTHRED'S SONG.

1821.

OF all the birds on bush or tree,
  Commend me to the owl,
Since he may best ensample be
  To those the cup that trowl.
For when the sun hath left the west,
He chooses the tree that he loves the best,
And he whoops out his song, and he
    laughs at his jest.
Then, tho' hours be late, and weather
    foul,
We'll drink to the health of the bonny,
    bonny owl.

The lark is but a bumpkin fowl,
  He sleeps in his nest till morn;
But my blessing upon the jolly owl,
  That all night blows his horn.
Then up with your cup till you stagger
    in speech,
And match me this scratch, till you swag-
    ger and screech,
And drink till you wink, my merry men
    each;
For, tho' hours be late, and weather be
    foul,
We'll drink to the health of the bonny,
    bonny owl.

Kenilworth, chap. ii.

SPEECH OF THE PORTER.*

1821.

WHAT stir, what turmoil have we for the
    nones?
Stand back, my masters, or beware your
    bones!
Sirs, I'm a warder, and no man of straw;
My voice keeps order, and my club gives
    law.

Yet soft — nay, stay — what vision have
    we here?
What dainty darling's this? — what peer-
    less peer?
What loveliest face, that loving ranks
    enfold
Like brightest diamond chased in purest
    gold?

* Imitated from Gascoigne.

Dazzled and blind, mine office I forsake
My club, my key, my knee, my homage
    take!
Bright paragon, pass on in joy and bliss; —
Beshrew the gate that opes not wide a
    such a sight as this!

Kenilworth, chap. xxx.

MOTTOES

FROM "KENILWORTH."

1821.

CHAP. III.

NAY, I'll hold touch: — the game sha
    be played out,
It ne'er shall stop for me, this merr
    wager;
That which I say when gamesome, I'
    avouch
In my most sober mood, ne'er trust m
    else.

The Hazard Table.

CHAP. IV.

Not serve two masters? — Here's a yout
    will try it —
Would fain serve God, yet give the dev
    his due;
Says grace before he doth a deed of vil
    lany,
And returns his thanks devoutly whe
    'tis acted.

Old Play.

CHAP. V.

—— He was a man
Versed in the world as pilot in his com
    pass.
The needle pointed ever to that interest
Which was his lodestar, and he sprea
    his sails
With vantage to the gale of others' pas
    sions.

The Deceiver, a Tragedy.

CHAP. VII.

—— This is He
Who rides on the court-gale; controls it
    tides;
Knows all their secret shoals and fata
    eddies;
Whose frown abases, and whose smil
    exalts.

e shines like any rainbow — and, perchance,
is colors are as transient.

Old Play.

CHAP. XIV.

his is rare news thou tell'st me, my good
fellow;
nere are two bulls fierce battling on the
green
or one fair heifer — if the one goes down,
he dale will be more peaceful, and the
herd,
hich have small interest in their brul-
ziement,
ay pasture there in peace.

Old Play.

CHAP. XVII.

'ell, then, our course is chosen; spread
the sail,
eave aft the lead, and mark the sound-
ings well;
ok to the helm, good master — many
a shoal
arks this stern coast, and rocks where
sits the Siren,
ho, like Ambition, lures men to their ruin.

The Shipwreck.

CHAP. XXV.

ark! the bells summon, and the bugle
calls,
it she the fairest answers not; the tide
nobles and of ladies throngs the halls,
it she the loveliest must in secret hide.
hat eyes were thine, proud Prince,
which in the gleam
yon gay meteors lost that better sense,
at o'er the glow-worm doth the star
esteem,
ad merit's modest blush o'er courtly
insolence.

The Glass Slipper.

CHAP. XXVIII.

hat, man, ne'er lack a draught, when
the full can
ands at thine elbow, and craves empty-
ing! —
ay, fear not me, for I have no delight
watch men's vices, since I have myself
virtue naught to boast of. — I'm a
striker,

Would have the world strike with me,
pell-mell, all.

Pandæmonium.

CHAP. XXX.

Now bid the steeple rock — she comes,
she comes! —
Speak for us, bells — speak for us, shrill-
tongued tuckets!
Stand to thy linstock, gunner; let the
cannon
Play such a peal, as if a paynim foe
Came stretch'd in turban'd ranks to storm
the ramparts;
We will have pageants too — but that
craves wit,
And I'm a rough-hewn soldier.

The Virgin-Queen, A Tragi-Comedy.

CHAP. XXXII.

The wisest sovereigns err like private men,
And royal hand has sometimes laid the
sword
Of chivalry upon a worthless shoulder,
Which better had been branded by the
hangman.
What then? Kings do their best, — and
they and we
Must answer for the intent, and not the
event.

Old Play.

CHAP. XXXIII.

Here stands the victim; — there the proud
betrayer, —
E'en as the hind pull'd down by strangling dogs,
Lies at the hunter's feet — who courteous proffers
To some high dame, the Dian of the
chase,
To whom he looks for guerdon, his sharp
blade,
To gash the sobbing throat.

The Woodsman.

CHAP. XL.

High o'er the eastern steep the sun is
beaming,
And darkness flies with her deceitful
shadows;
So truth prevails o'er falsehood.

Old Play.

THE SONG OF THE TEMPEST.*

1821.

I.

STERN eagle of the far north-west,
Thou that bearest in thy grasp the thun-
derbolt,
Thou whose rushing pinions stir ocean to
madness,
Thou the destroyer of herds, thou the
scatterer of navies,
Amidst the scream of thy rage,
Amidst the rushing of thy onward wings,
Tho' thy scream be loud as the cry of a
perishing nation,
Tho' the rushing of thy wings be like the
roar of ten thousand waves,
Yet hear, in thine ire and thy haste,
Hear thou the voice of the Reim-kennar.

II.

Thou hast met the pine-trees of Dront-
heim,
Their dark green heads lie prostrate be-
side their uprooted stems;
Thou hast met the rider of the ocean,
The tall, the strong bark of the fearless
rover,
And she has struck to thee the topsail
That she had not vail'd to a royal armada.
Thou hast met the tower that bears its
crest among the clouds,
The battled massive tower of the jarl of
former days,
And the cope-stone of the turret
Is lying upon its hospitable hearth;
But thou too shalt stoop, proud compel-
ler of clouds,
When thou hearest the voice of the
Reim-kennar.

III.

There are verses that can stop the stag
in the forest,
Ay, when the dark-color'd dog is opening on his track;
There are verses can make the wild hawk
pause on the wing,

Like the falcon that wears the hood a[n]
jesses,
And who knows the shrill whistle of t[h]
fowler.
Thou who canst mock at the scream [of]
the drowning mariner,
And the crash of the ravaged forest,
And the groan of the overwhelm[ed]
crowds,
When the church hath fallen in the m[o]
ment of prayer;
There are sounds which thou also must lis[t]
When they are chanted by the voice [of]
the Reim-kennar.

IV.

Enough of woe hast thou wrought [on]
the ocean,
The widows wring their hands on t[h]
beach;
Enough of woe hast thou wrought on t[he]
land,
The husbandman folds his arms in d[e]
spair.
Cease thou the waving of thy pinions;
Let the ocean repose in her dark strengt[h]
Cease thou the flashing of thine eye;
Let the thunderbolt sleep in the armo[ry]
of Odin.
Be thou still at my bidding, viewle[ss]
racer of the north-western heaven,
Sleep thou at the voice of Norna t[he]
Reim-kennar.

"A long silence followed the last verse, u[ntil]
Norna resumed her chant, but with a chang[e]
and more soothing modulation of voice and tun[e.]

V.

Eagle of the far north-western waters,
Thou hast heard the voice of the Rei[m-]
kennar,
Thou hast closed thy wide sails at h[er]
bidding,
And folded them in peace by thy side.
My blessing be on thy retiring path;
When thou stoopest from thy place [on]
high,
Soft be thy slumbers in the caverns [of]
the unknown ocean,
Rest till destiny shall again awaken the[e,]
Eagle of the north-west, thou hast hea[rd]
the voice of the Reim-kennar.

The Pirate, chap. vi.

* A Norwegian invocation, still preserved in
the island of Uist under the name of the Song of
the "Reim-kennar," tho' some call it the "Song
of the Tempest."

CLAUD HALCRO'S SONG: "MARY."

1821.

FAREWELL to Northmaven,
  Gray Hillswicke, farewell!
To the calms of thy haven,
  The storms on thy fell —
To each breeze that can vary
  The mood of thy main,
And to thee, bonny Mary!
  We meet not again!

Farewell the wild ferry,
  Which Hacon could brave,
When the peaks of the Skerry
  Were white in the wave.
There's a maid may look over
  These wild waves in vain, —
For the skiff of her lover —
  He comes not again!

The vows thou hast broke,
  On the wild currents fling them;
On the quicksand and rock
  Let the mermaidens sing them.
New sweetness they'll give her
  Bewildering strain;
But there's one who will never
  Believe them again.

O were there an island,
  Tho' ever so wild,
Where woman could smile, and
  No man be beguiled —
Too tempting a snare
  To poor mortals were given;
And the hope would fix there,
  That should anchor in heaven.

The Pirate, chap. xii.

THE SONG OF HAROLD HARFAGER.*

1821.

HE sun is rising dimly red,
he wind is wailing low and dread;
rom his cliff the eagle sallies,
eaves the wolf his darksome valleys;

* "THE bard [Halcro] chanted to a low, wild,
monotonous air, varied only by the efforts of the
nger to give interest and emphasis to particu-
r passages, the following imitation of a northern
ar-song."

In the midst the ravens hover,
Peep the wild dogs from the cover,
Screaming, croaking, baying, yelling,
Each in his wild accents telling: —
" Soon we feast on dead and dying,
Fair-hair'd Harold's flag is flying."

Many a crest on air is streaming,
Many a helmet darkly gleaming,
Many an arm the ax uprears,
Doom'd to hew the wood of spears.
All along the crowded ranks
Horses neigh and armor clanks;
Chiefs are shouting, clarions ringing,
Louder still the bard is singing: —
" Gather footmen, gather horsemen,
To the field, ye valiant Norsemen!

" Halt ye not for food or slumber,
View not vantage, count not number:
Jolly reapers, forward still,
Grow the crop on vale or hill,
Thick or scatter'd, stiff or lithe,
It shall down before the scythe.
Forward with your sickles bright,
Reap the harvest of the fight. —
Onward footmen, onward horsemen,
To the charge, ye gallant Norsemen!

" Fatal Choosers † of the Slaughter,
O'er you hovers Odin's daughter;
Hear the choice she spreads before ye, —
Victory, and wealth, and glory;
Or old Valhalla's roaring hail,
Her ever-circling mead and ale,
Where for eternity unite
The joys of wassail and of fight.
Headlong forward, foot and horsemen,
Charge and fight, and die like Norse-
  men!" —

The Pirate, chap. xv.

SONG OF THE MERMAIDS AND MERMEN.

1821.

MERMAID.

FATHOMS deep beneath the wave,
  Stringing beads of glistering pearl,
Singing the achievements brave
  Of many an old Norwegian earl;

† The Valkyriur.

Dwelling where the tempest's raving
   Falls as light upon our ear,
As the sigh of lover, craving
   Pity from his lady dear,
Children of wild Thule, we,
From the deep caves of the sea,
As the lark springs from the lea,
Hither come, to share your glee.

MERMAN.

From reining of the water-horse,
   That bounded till the waves were foam-
      ing,
Watching the infant tempest's course,
   Chasing the sea-snake in his roaming;
From winding charge-notes on the shell,
   When the huge whale and swordfish
      duel,
Or tolling shroudless seamen's knell,
   When the winds and waves are cruel;
Children of wild Thule, we
Have plough'd such furrows on the sea,
As the steer draws on the lea,
And hither we come to share your glee.

MERMAIDS AND MERMEN.

We heard you in our twilight caves,
   A hundred fathom deep below,
For notes of joy can pierce the waves,
   That drown each sound of war and woe.
Those who dwell beneath the sea
   Love the sons of Thule well;
Thus, to aid your mirth bring we
   Dance, and song, and sounding shell.
Children of dark Thule, know,
Those who dwell by haaf and voe,
Where your daring shallops row
Come to share the festal show.
          The Pirate, chap. xvi.

NORNA'S SONG.
1821.

For leagues along the watery way,
   Thro' gulf and stream my course has
      been;
The billows know my Runic lay,
   And smooth their crests to silent green.

The billows know my Runic lay, —
   The gulf grows smooth, the stream is
      still,

But human hearts, more wild than they
   Know but the rule of wayward will.

One hour is mine, in all the year,
   To tell my woes, — and one alone;
When gleams this magic lamp 'tis
   here, —
   When dies the mystic light, 'tis gone.

Daughters of northern Magnus, hail!
   The lamp is lit, the flame is clear, —
To you I come to tell my tale,
   Awake, arise, my tale to hear!
          The Pirate, chap. xix.

NORNA AND TROLD.
1821.
NORNA.

Dwellers of the mountain, rise,
Trold the powerful, Haims the wise!
Ye who taught weak woman's tongue
Words that sway the weak and strong, —
Ye who taught weak woman's hand
How to wield the magic wand,
And wake the gales on Foulah's steep,
Or lull wild Sumburgh's waves to
   sleep!
Still are ye yet? Not yours the power
Ye knew in Odin's mightier hour.
What are ye now but empty names,
Powerful Trold, sagacious Haims,
That lightly spoken, lightly heard,
Float on the ear like thistle's beard?

TROLD THE DWARF.

A thousand winters dark have flown
Since o'er the threshold of my stone
A votaress past, my power to own.
   Visitor bold
Of the mansion of Trold,
   Maiden haughty of heart,
Who hast hither presumed
Ungifted, undoom'd
   Thou shalt not depart: —
The power thou dost covet
   O'er tempest and wave,
Shall be thine, thou proud maiden,
   By beach and by cave, —
By stack and by skerry, by noup and
   by voe,

By air and by wick, and by helyer and
gio *
And by every wild shore which the
northern winds know
And the northern tides lave.
But tho' this shall be given thee, thou
desperately brave,
doom thee that never
The gift thou shalt have
Till thou reave thy life's giver
Of the gift which he gave.

NORNA.

Dark are thy words and severe,
Thou dweller in the stone;
But trembling and fear
To her are unknown,
Who hath sought thee here
In thy dwelling lone.
Come what comes soever,
The worst I can endure;
Life is but a short fever,
And death is the cure.

The Pirate, chap. xix.

CLAUD HALCRO AND NORNA.
1821.
CLAUD HALCRO.

MOTHER darksome, Mother dread,
Dweller on the Fitful Head,
Thou canst see what deeds are done
Under the never-setting sun.
Look thro' sleet, and look thro' frost,
Look to Greenland's caves and coast, —
By the ice-berg is a sail
Chasing of the swarthy whale;
Mother doubtful, Mother dread,
Tell us, has the good ship sped?

NORNA.

The thought of the aged is ever on gear, —
On his fishing, his furrow, his flock, and
his steer;
But thrive may his fishing, flock, furrow,
and herd,
While the aged for anguish shall tear his
gray beard.

* *Stack*, an insulated precipitous rock;
skerry, a bare rocky islet; *noup*, a precipitous
headland, sloping gently inland; *voe*, a salt inland lake; *air*, open sea beach; *helyer*, a cavern
into which the sea flows; *gio*, a deep ravine.

The ship, well-laden as bark need be,
Lies deep in the furrow of the Iceland
sea; —
The breeze for Zetland blows fair and
soft,
And gayly the garland is fluttering aloft;
Seven good fishes have spouted their last,
And their jaw-bones are hanging to yard
and mast;
Two are for Lerwick, and two for Kirk-
wall, —
Three for Burgh-Westra, the choicest of
all.

CLAUD HALCRO.

Mother doubtful, Mother dread!
Dweller of the Fitful Head,
Thou hast conn'd full many a rhyme,
That lives upon the surge of time:
Tell me, shall my lays be sung,
Like Hacon's of the Golden Tongue,
Long after Halcro's dead and gone?
Or, shall Hialtland's minstrel own
One note to rival glorious John?

NORNA.

The infant loves the rattle's noise;
Age, double childhood, hath its toys;
But different far the descant rings,
As strikes a different hand the strings.
The eagle mounts the polar sky —
The imber-goose, unskill'd to fly,
Must be content to glide along,
Where seal and sea-dog list his song.

CLAUD HALCRO.

Be mine the imber-goose to play,
And haunt lone cave and silent bay;
The archer's aim so shall I shun —
So shall I 'scape the levell'd gun —
Content my verses' tuneless jingle
With Thule's sounding tides to mingle,
While, to the ear of wondering wight,
Upon the distant headland's height,
Soften'd by murmur of the sea,
The rude sounds seem like harmony !

* * * * * *

Mother doubtful, Mother dread,
Dweller of the Fitful Head,
A gallant bark from far abroad,
Saint Magnus hath her in his road,
With guns and firelocks not a few —
A silken and a scarlet crew,

Deep stored with precious merchandise,
Of gold and goods of rare device —
What interest hath our comrade bold
In bark and crew, in goods and gold?

NORNA.

Gold is ruddy, fair, and free,
Blood is crimson, and dark to see;
I look'd out on Saint Magnus Bay,
And I saw a falcon that struck her prey,
A gobbet of flesh in her beak she bore,
And talons and singles are dripping with
    gore; —
Let him that asks after them look on his
    hand,
And if there is blood on't, he's one of
    their band.

CLAUD HALCRO.

Mother doubtful, Mother dread,
Dweller of the Fitful Head,
Well thou know'st it is thy task
To tell what Beauty will not ask; —
Then steep thy words in wine and milk,
And weave a doom of gold and silk; —
For we would know, shall Brenda prove
In love, and happy in her love?

NORNA.

Untouch'd by love, the maiden's breast
Is like the snow on Rona's crest,
High seated in the middle sky,
In bright and barren purity;
But by the sunbeam gently kiss'd,
Scarce by the gazing eye 'tis miss'd,
Ere down the lonely valley stealing,
Fresh grass and growth its course reveal-
    ing,
It cheers the flock, revives the flower,
And decks some happy shepherd's bower.

MAGNUS TROIL.

Mother, speak, and do not tarry,
Here's a maiden fain would marry;
Shall she marry, ay or not?
If she marry, what's her lot?

NORNA.

Untouch'd by love, the maiden's breast
Is like the snow on Rona's crest;
So pure, so free from earthly dye,
It seems, whilst leaning on the sky,
Part of the heaven to which 'tis nigh;

But passion, like the wild March rain,
May soil the wreath with many a stain.
We gaze — the lovely vision's gone —
A torrent fills the bed of stone,
That hurrying to destruction's shock,
Leaps headlong from the lofty rock.

The Pirate, chap. xxi.

SONG OF THE ZETLAND FISHERMEN.

1821.

FAREWELL, merry maidens, to song and
    to laugh,
For the brave lads of Westra are bound
    to the haaf;
And we must have labor, and hunger, and
    pain,
Ere we dance with the maids of Dunross-
    ness again.

For now, in our trim boats of Noroway
    deal,
We must dance on the waves, with the
    porpoise and seal!
The breeze it shall pipe, so it pipe not
    too high,
And the gull be our songstress whene'er
    she flits by.

Sing on, my brave bird, while we follow,
    like thee,
By bank, shoal, and quicksand, the
    swarms of the sea;
And when twenty score fishes are strain-
    ing our line,
Sing louder, brave bird, for their spoils
    shall be thine.

We'll sing while we bait, and we'll sing
    while we haul,
For the deeps of the haaf have enough
    for us all:
There is torsk for the gentle, and skate
    for the carle,
And there's wealth for bold Magnus, the
    son of the earl.

Huzza! my brave comrades, give way for
    the haaf,
We shall sooner come back to the dance
    and the laugh;

'or life without mirth is a lamp without
  oil;
'hen mirth and long life to the bold
  Magnus Troil!

The Pirate, chap. xxii.

CLEVELAND'S SERENADE.

1821.

LOVE wakes and weeps
  While Beauty sleeps!
) for Music's softest numbers
  To prompt a theme,
  For Beauty's dream,
oft as the pillow of her slumbers!

Thro' groves of palm
  Sigh gales of balm,
'ire-flies on the air are wheeling;
  While thro' the gloom
  Comes soft perfume,
'he distant beds of flowers revealing.

O wake and live!
  No dream can give
A shadow'd bliss, the real excelling;
  No longer sleep,
  From lattice peep,
And list the tale that Love is telling!

" HER lover, as if determined upon gaining her
ar by music of another strain, sung the following
ragment of a sea-ditty: " —

'AREWELL! farewell! the voice you
  hear
Has left its last soft tone with you, —
'ts next must join the seaward cheer,
  And shout among the shouting crew.

'he accents which I scarce could form
  Beneath your frown's controlling
    check,
Just give the word above the storm,
  To cut the mast and clear the wreck.

'he timid eye I dared not raise, —
  The hand, that shook when press'd to
    thine,
Just point the guns upon the chase —
  Must bid the deadly cutlass shine.

To all I love, or hope, or fear,
  Honor, or own, a long adieu!
To all that life has soft and dear,
  Farewell! save memory of you!

The Pirate, chap. xxiii.

CLAUD HALCRO'S VERSES.

1821.

" A SCRAP of an old Norse ditty which might
run thus in English: " —

AND you shall deal the funeral dole;
  Ay, deal it, mother mine,
To weary body, and to heavy soul,
  The white bread and the wine.

And you shall deal my horses of pride;
  Ay, deal them, mother mine;
And you shall deal my lands so wide,
  And deal my castles nine.

But deal not vengeance for the deed,
  And deal not for the crime;
Thy body to its place, and the soul to
  Heaven's grace,
  And the rest in God's own time.

The Pirate, chap. xxiii.

CLAUD HALCRO'S INVOCATION.

1821.

" HALCRO began to conjure her in an ancient
rhyme which occurred to him as suited to the
occasion, and which had in its gibberish a wild
and unearthly sound which may be lost in the
ensuing translation: " —

ST. MAGNUS control thee, that martyr of
  treason;
St. Ronan rebuke thee with rhyme and
  with reason;
By the mass of St. Martin, the might of
  St. Mary,
Be thou gone, or thy weird shall be worse
  if thou tarry!
  If of good, go hence and hallow thee;
  If of ill, let the earth swallow thee;
  If thou'rt of air, let the gray mist fold
    thee;
  If of earth, let the swart mine hold thee.
  If a pixie, seek thy ring;
  If a nixie, seek thy spring:

If on middle earth thou'st been
Slave of sorrow, shame, and sin,
Hast eat the bread of toil and strife,
And dree'd the lot which men call life,
Begone to thy stone! for thy coffin is
   scant of thee;
The worm, thy playfellow, wails for the
   want of thee.
Hence, houseless ghost! let the earth hide
   thee;
Till Michael shall blow the blast see that
   there thou bide thee!
Phantom, fly hence! take the Cross f― a
   token,
Hence pass till Hallow-mass! — my spell
   is spoken!

Where corpse-light
Dances bright,
Be it day or night,
Be it by light or dark
There shall corpse lie stiff and stark.

Menseful maiden ne'er should rise
Till the first beam tinge the skies;
Silk-fringed eyelids still should close,
Till the sun hast kiss'd the rose;
Maiden's foot we should not view
Mark'd with tiny print on dew,
Till the opening flowerets spread
Carpet meet for beauty's tread.

The Pirate, chap. xxiii.

NORNA'S RUNIC RHYME.

1821.

Champion, famed for warlike toil,
Art thou silent, Ribolt Troil?
Sand, and dust, and pebbly stones,
Are leaving bare thy giant bones.
Who dared touch the wild bear's skin
Ye slumber'd on, while life was in? —
A woman now, or babe, may come
And cast the covering from thy tomb.

Yet be not wrathful, Chief, nor blight
Mine eyes or ears with sound or sight!
I come not, with unhallow'd tread,
To wake the slumbers of the dead,
Or lay thy giant relics bare;
But what I seek thou well canst spare.

Be it to my hand allow'd
To shear a merk's weight from thy shroud
Yet leave thee sheeted lead enough
To shield thy bones from weather rough

See, I draw my magic knife —
Never, while thou wert in life,
Laid'st thou still for sloth or fear,
When point and edge were glittering near
See, the cerements now I sever —
Waken now, or sleep forever!
Thou wilt not wake?—the deed is done!—
The prize I sought is fairly won.

Thanks, Ribolt, thanks, — for this the se
Shall smooth its ruffled crest for thee —
And while afar its billows foam,
Subside to peace near Ribolt's tomb.
Thanks, Ribolt, thanks—for this the migh
Of wild winds raging at their height,
When to thy place of slumber nigh,
Shall soften to a lullaby.

She, the dame of doubt and dread,
Norna of the Fitful Head,
Mighty in her own despite, —
Miserable in her might;
In despair and frenzy great,
In her greatness desolate;
Wisest, wickedest who lives, —
Well can keep the word she gives.

The Pirate, chap. xxv.

NORNA'S SPELLS.

1821.

"Muttering that the elemental spirit must b
thanked [Norna], recited, in her usual monote
nous, yet wild mode of chanting, the followin
verses:" —

Thou, so needful, yet so dread,
With cloudy crest, and wing of red —
Thou, without whose genial breath
The North would sleep the sleep of death
Who deign'st to warm the cottage hearth
Yet hurl'st proud palaces to earth, —
Brightest, keenest, of the Powers,
Which form and rule this world of ours
With my rhyme of Runic, I
Thank thee for thy agency.

"She then severed a portion from the sma
mass of sheet lead which lay upon the table and

placing it in the crucible, subjected it to the action of the lighted charcoal, and, as it melted, she sung:" —

Old Reim-kennar, to thy art
Mother Hertha sends her part;
She, whose gracious bounty gives
Needful food for all that lives.
From the deep mine of the North
Came the mystic metal forth,
Doom'd amidst disjointed stones,
Long to cere a champion's bones,
Disinhumed my charms to aid —
Mother Earth, my thanks are paid.

"She then poured out some water from the jar into a large cup or goblet, and sung once more, as she slowly stirred it round with the end of her staff:" —

Girdle of our islands dear,
Element of Water, hear!
Thou whose power can overwhelm
Broken mounds and ruin'd realm
　　On the lowly Belgian strand;
All thy fiercest range can never
Of our soil a furlong sever
　　From our rock-defended land;
Play then gently thou thy part,
To assist old Norna's art.

"She then, with a pair of pincers removed the crucible from the chafing-dish, and poured the lead, now entirely melted, into the bowl of water, repeating at the same time:" —

Elements, each other greeting,
Gifts and power attend your meeting:

TO THE SPIRIT OF THE WINDS.

Thou, that over billows dark,
Safely send'st the fisher's bark,
Giving him a path and motion
Thro' the wilderness of ocean;
Thou, that when the billows brave ye,
O'er the shelves canst drive the navy, —
Didst thou chafe as one neglected,
While thy brethren were respected?
To appease thee, see, I tear
This full grasp of grizzled hair.
Oft thy breath hath thro' it sung,
Softening to my magic tongue, —
Now, 'tis thine to bid it fly
Thro' the wide expanse of sky,
Mid the countless swarms to sail
Of wild-fowl wheeling on thy gale;
Take thy portion and rejoice, —
Spirit, thou hast heard my voice!

"She selected from the fused metal a piece about the size of a small nut, bearing in shape a close resemblance to that of the human heart, and approaching Minna, again spoke in song:" — .

She who sits by haunted well,
Is subject to the Nixie's spell;
She who walks on lonely beach,
To the Mermaid's charmed speech;
She who walks round ring of green,
Offends the peevish fairy Queen;
And she who takes rest in the Dwarfie's cave,
A weary weird of woe shall have.

By ring, by spring, by cave, by shore,
Minna Troil has braved all this and more;
And yet hath the root of her sorrow and ill,
A source that's more deep and more mystical still. —

Thou art within a demon's hold,
More wise than Haims, more strong than Trold.
No siren sings so sweet as he, —
No fay springs lighter on the lea;
No elfin power hath half the art,
To soothe, to move, to wring the heart, —
Life-blood from the cheek to drain,
Drench the eye and dry the vein.
Maiden, ere we farther go,
Dost thou note me, ay or no?

MINNA.

I mark thee, my mother, both word, look, and sign;
Speak on with thy riddle — to read it be mine.

NORNA.

Mark me! for the word I speak
Shall bring the color to thy cheek.
This laden heart, so light of cost,
The symbol of a treasure lost,
Thou shalt wear in hope and in peace,
That the cause of your sickness and sorrow may cease,
When crimson foot meets crimson hand
I. the Martyr's Aisle, and in Orkney land.

"She knotted the leaden heart to a chain of gold and hung it around Minna's neck, singing, as she performed that last branch of the spell:" —

Be patient, be patient; for Patience hath power
To ward us in danger, like mantle in shower;

A fairy gift you best may hold
In a chain of fairy gold; —
The chain and the gift are each a true
    token,
That not without warrant old Norna has
    spoken;
But thy nearest and dearest must never
    behold them,
Till time shall accomplish the truths I
    have told them.

                    The Pirate, chap. xxviii.

BRYCE SNAILSFOOT'S SIGN.

1821.

"THE sign bore on the opposite side an emblematic device, resembling our first parents in
their vegetable garments, with this legend:" —

POOR sinners whom the snake deceives
Are fain to cover them with leaves.
Zetland hath no leaves, 'tis true,
Because that trees are none or few;
But we have flax and taits of woo'*
For linen cloth and wadmaal† blue;
And we have many of foreign knacks
Of finer waft than woo' or flax.
Ye gallanty Lambmas lads, appear,
And bring your Lambmas sisters here;
Bryce Snailsfoot spares not cost or care
To pleasure every gentle pair.

                    The Pirate, chap. xxxii.

FRAGMENT OF A SEA-DITTY.

1821.

ROBIN Rover
    Said to his crew: —
"Up with the black flag,
    Down with the blue!
Fire on the main-top,
    Fire on the bow,
Fire on the gun-deck,
    Fire down below!"

                    The Pirate, chap. xxxii.

-----

* Tufts of wool.
† Wadmaal, vadmel; homespun woollen cloth
of which the Norwegian peasantry make their
clothes.

DICK FLETCHER'S DITTY.

1821.

IT was a ship, and a ship of fame,
Launch'd off the stocks, bound for the
    main,
With a hundred and fifty brisk young men,
All pick'd and chosen every one.

Captain Glen was our Captain's name,
A very gallant and brisk young man,
As bold a sailor as e'er went to sea;
And we were bound for high Barbary!

                    The Pirate, chap, xxxvi.

MOTTOES.

FROM "THE PIRATE."

CHAP. II.

'TIS not alone the scene — the man, An-
    selmo,
The man finds sympathies in these wild
    wastes,
And roughly tumbling seas, which fairer
    views
And smoother waves deny him.

                    Ancient Drama.

CHAP. III.

O, Bessy Bell and Mary Gray,
    They were twa bonnie lassies;
They biggit a house on yon burn-brae,
    And theekit ower wi' rashes.

Fair Bessy Bell I looed yestreen,
    And thought I ne'er could alter;
But Mary Gray's twa pawky een
    Have garr'd my fancy falter.

                    Scots Song.

CHAP. IV.

This is no pilgrim's morning — yon gray
    mist
Lies upon hill and dale, and field and
    forest,
Like the dun wimple of a new-made
    widow:
And by my faith, although my heart be
    soft,
I'd rather hear that widow weep and sigh,
And tell the virtues of the dear departed,

Than, when the tempest sends his voice
    abroad,
Be subject to its fury.

The Double Nuptials.

CHAP. V.

The wind blew keen frae north and east;
    It blew upon the floor.
Quo' our good man to our good wife: —
    " Get up and bar the door."

" My hand is in my housewifeskep,
    Good man, as ye may see;
If it shouldna be barr'd this hundred
    years
    It's no be barr'd for me."

Old Song.

CHAP. VII.

She does no work by halves, yon raving
    ocean;
Engulfing those she strangles, her wild
    womb
Affords the mariners whom she hath dealt
    on,
Their death at once, and sepulchre.

Old Play.

CHAP. IX.

This is a gentle trader, and a prudent; —
He's no Autolycus, to blear your eye
With quips of worldly gauds and game-
    someness;
But seasons all his glittering merchandise
With wholesome doctrine suited to the use,
As men sauce goose with sage and rose-
    mary.

Old Play.

CHAP XI.

———— All your ancient customs
And long-descended usages, I'll change.
Ye shall not eat, nor drink, nor speak,
    nor move,
Think, look, or walk, as ye were wont to
    do.
Even your marriage-beds shall know mu-
    tation;
The bride shall have the stock, the groom
    the wall;
For all old practice will I turn and
    change,
And call it reformation — marry will I !

'Tis Even that we're at Odds.

CHAP. XIV.

We'll keep our customs ; — what is law
    itself,
But old establish'd custom? What religion
(I mean, with one-half of the men that
    use it),
Save the good use and wont that carries
    them
To worship how and where their fathers
    worshipp'd?
All things resolve in custom; — we'll
    keep ours.

Old Play.

CHAP XXIII.

There was shaking of hands, and sorrow
    of heart,
For the hour was approaching when merry
    folks must part;
So we called for our horses, and asked
    for our way,
While the jolly old landlord said, "Noth-
    ing's to pay."

Lilliput, a Poem.

CHAP. XXIX.

See yonder woman, whom our swains
    revere,
And dread in secret, while they take her
    counsel
When sweetheart shall be kind, or when
    cross dame shall die;
Where lurks the thief who stole the silver
    tankard,
And how the pestilent murrain may be
    cured.
This sage adviser's mad, stark mad, my
    friend;
Yet, in her madness hath the art and
    cunning
To wring fools' secrets from their inmost
    bosoms,
And pay inquirers with the coin they gave
    her.

Old Play.

CHAP. XXX.

What ho, my jovial mates! come on !
    we'll frolic it
Like fairies frisking in the merry moon-
    shine,
Seen by the curtal friar, who, from some
    christening,
Or some blithe bridal, hies belated cell-
    ward; —

He starts, and changes his bold bottle
        swagger
To churchman's pace professional, — and,
        ransacking
His treacherous memory for some holy
        hymn,
Finds but the roundel of the midnight
        catch.

                                    Old Play.

CHAP. XXXII.

I strive like the vessel in the tide-way,
Which, lacking favoring breeze, hath not
        the power
To stem the powerful current. — Even
        so,
Resolving daily to forsake my vices,
Habits, strong circumstance, renewed
        temptation,
Sweep me to sea again. — O heavenly
        breath,
Fill thou my sails, and aid the feeble ves-
        sel,
Which ne'er can reach the blessed port
        without thee!

            'Tis Odds when Evens meet.

CHAP. XXXIII.

Parental love, my friend, has power o'er
        wisdom,
And is the charm, which, like the fal-
        coner's lure,
Can bring from heaven the highest soaring
        spirits.
So, when famed Prosper doff'd his magic
        robe,
It was Miranda pluck'd it from his shoul-
        ders.

                                    Old Play.

CHAP. XXXIV.

Hark to the insult loud, the bitter sneer,
The fierce threat answering to the brutal
        jeer;
Oaths fly like pistol shots, and vengeful
        words
Clash with each other like conflicting
        swords.
The robbers' quarrel by such sounds is
        shown,
And true men have some chance to gain
        their own.

                            Captivity, a Poem.

CHAP. XXXVII.

Over the mountains, and under the waves,
Over the fountains, and under the graves,
        Under floods that are deepest,
            Which Neptune obey,
        Over rocks that are steepest,
            Love will find out the way

                                    Old Song.

ON ETTRICK FOREST'S MOUN-
TAINS DUN. *
1822.

On Ettrick Forest's mountains dun,
'Tis blithe to hear the sportsman's gun,
And seek the heath-frequenting brood
Far through the noonday solitude;
By many a cairn and trenched mound,
Where chiefs of yore sleep lone and sound,
And springs, where gray-hair'd shepherds
        tell,
That still the fairies love to dwell.

Along the silver streams of Tweed,
'Tis blithe the mimic fly to lead,
When to the hook the salmon springs,
And the line whistles thro' the rings;
The boiling eddy see him try,
Then dashing from the current high,
Till watchful eye and cautious hand
Have led his wasted strength to land.

'Tis blithe along the midnight tide,
With stalwart arm the boat to guide;
On high the dazzling blaze to rear,
And heedful plunge the barbed spear;
Rock, wood, and scaur, emerging bright,
Fling on the stream their ruddy light,
And from the bank our band appears
Like Genii, arm'd with fiery spears.

'Tis blithe at eve to tell the tale,
How we succeed and how we fail,
Whether at Alwyn's † lordly meal,
Or lowlier board of Ashestiel;
While the gay tapers cheerly shine,
Bickers the fire, and flows the wine —
Days free from thought, and nights from
        care,
My blessing on the Forest fair!

* Written after the poet had been engaged in
a week's shooting and fishing with friends

† *Alywn,* the seat of the Lord Somerville.

FAREWELL TO THE MUSE.*

1822.

ENCHANTRESS, farewell, who so oft hast
decoy'd me,
At the close of the evening thro' woodlands to roam,
Where the forester, lated, with wonder
espied me
Explore the wild scenes he was quitting
for home.

Farewell, and take with thee thy numbers
wild speaking
The language alternate of rapture and
woe:
Ah! none but some lover whose heart-
strings are breaking,
The pang that I feel at our parting can
know.

Each joy thou couldst double, and when
there came sorrow,
Or pale disappointment, to darken my
way,
What voice was like thine, that could
sing of to-morrow,
Till forgot in the strain was the grief
of to-day!

But when friends drop around us in life's
weary waning,
The grief, Queen of Numbers, thou
canst not assuage;
Nor the gradual estrangement of those
yet remaining,
The languor of pain, and the chillness
of age.

'Twas thou that once taught me, in
accents bewailing,
To sing how a warrior lay stretch'd on
the plain,
And a maiden hung o'er him with aid unavailing,
And held to his lips the cold goblet in vain.

As vain thy enchantments, O Queen of
wild Numbers,
To a bard when the reign of his fancy
is o'er,
And the quick pulse of feeling in apathy
slumbers —
Farewell, then, Enchantress! I meet
thee no more!

* Written during illness for Mr. George
Thomson's Scottish Collection.

THE MAID OF ISLA.

AIR — *The Maid of Isla.*

WRITTEN FOR MR. GEORGE THOMSON'S
SCOTTISH MELODIES.

1822.

OH, Maid of Isla, from the cliff,
That looks on troubled wave and sky,
Dost thou not see yon little skiff
Contend with ocean gallantly?

Now beating 'gainst the breeze and surge,
And steep'd her leeward deck in foam,
Why does she war unequal urge? —
Oh, Isla's maid, she seeks her home.

Oh, Isla's Maid, yon sea-bird mark,
Her white wing gleams thro' mist and
spray,
Against the storm-cloud, lowering dark,
As to the rock she wheels away; —
Where clouds are dark, and billows rave,
Why to the shelter should she come
Of cliff, exposed to wind and wave? —
Oh, Maid of Isla, 'tis her home!

As breeze and tide to yonder skiff,
Thou'rt adverse to the suit I bring,
And cold as is yon wintry cliff,
Where sea-birds close their wearied
wing.
Yet cold as rock, unkind as wave,
Still, Isla's Maid, to thee I come;
For in thy love, or in his grave,
Must Allan Vourich find his home.

CARLE, NOW THE KING'S COME. †

BEING NEW WORDS TO AN AULD SPRING.

1822.

THE news has flown frae mouth to mouth,
The North for ance has bang'd the South;
The deil a Scotsman's die o' drouth,
Carle, now the King's come!

CHORUS.

Carle, now the King's come!
Carle, now the King's come!
Thou shalt dance, and I will sing
Carle, now the King's come!

† An imitation of an old Jacobite ditty,
written on the arrival of George IV. in Scotland, August, 1822, and printed as a broadside.

Auld England held him lang and fast;
And Ireland had a joyfu' cast;
But Scotland's turn is come at last —
　　　Carle, now the King's come!

Auld Reekie, in her rokelay gray,
Thought never to have seen the day;
He's been a weary time away —
　　　But, Carle, now the King's come!

She's skirling frae the castle-hill;
The Carline's voice is grown sae shrill,
Ye'll hear her at the Canon-mill —
　　　Carle, now the King's come!

"Up, bairns!" she cries, "baith grit
　　　and sma',
And busk ye for the weapon-shaw!
Stand by me, and we'll bang them a' —
　　　Carle, now the King's come!

"Come from Newbattle's ancient spires,
Bauld Lothian, with your knights and
　　　squires,
And match the metal of your sires —
　　　Carle, now the King's come!

"You're welcome hame, my Montagu!*
Bring in your hand the young Buccleuch;
I'm missing some that I may rue —
　　　Carle, now the King's come!

"Come, Haddington, the kind and gay,
You've graced my causeway mony a
　　　day;
I'll weep the cause if you should stay —
　　　Carle, now the King's come!

"Come, premier Duke,† and carry doun
Frae yonder craig his ancient croun;
It's had a lang sleep an' a soun' —
　　　But, Carle, now the King's come!

"Come, Athole, from the hill and wood,
Bring down your clansmen like a cloud;
Come, Morton, show the Douglas'
　　　blood, —
　　　Carle, now the King's come!

"Come, Tweeddale, true as sword
　　　sheath,
Come, Hopetoun, fear'd on fields
　　　death;
Come, Clerk, ‡ and give your bug
　　　breath;
　　　Carle, now the King's come!

"Come, Wemyss, who modest mer
　　　aids,
Come, Roseberry, from Dalmeny shade
Breadalbane, bring your belted plaids,
　　　Carle, now the King's come!

"Come, stately Niddrie, auld and true,
Girt with the sword that Minden knew;
We have o'er few such lairds as you —
　　　Carle, now the King's come!

"King Arthur's grown a common crier
He's heard in Fife and far Cantire, —
'Fie, lads, behold my crest of fire!'
　　　Carle, now the King's come!

"Saint Abb roars out: 'I see hir
　　　pass,
Between Tantallon and the Bass!'
Calton, get out your keeking-glass —
　　　Carle, now the King's come!"

The Carline stopp'd; and, sure I am,
For very glee had ta'en a dwam,
But Oman § help'd her to a dram. —
　　　Cogie, now the Kings come!

　　　Cogie, now the King's come!
　　　Cogie, now the King's come!
I'se be fou and ye's be toom, ‖
　　　Cogie, now the King's come!

PART SECOND.

A Hawick gill of mountain dew,
Heised up Auld Reekie's heart, I trow.

cient royal crown of Scotland on horseback i
King George's procession from Holyrood to th
castle. "Yonder craig" is the castle.

　‡ The Baron of Pennycuik, bound by hi
tenure to meet the sovereign whenever he o
she visits Edinburgh at the Harestone (in whic
the standard of James IV. was erected when hi
army encamped on the Borough muir), and ther
blow three blasts on a horn.

　§ The landlord of the Waterloo Hotel.
　‖ Empty.

---

　* Lord Montagu, uncle and guardian to the
young Duke of Buccleuch, placed His Grace's
residence of Dalkeith at his Majesty's disposal
during his visit to Scotland.

　† The Duke of Hamilton, Earl of Angus, the
premier duke of Scotland. He carried the an-

t minded her of Waterloo —
    Carle, now the King's come!

gain I heard her summons swell,
or, sic a dirdum and a yell,
t drown'd Saint Giles's jowing bell —
    Carle, now the King's come!

" My trusty Provost, tried and tight,
tand forward for the Good Town's right,
here's waur than you been made
    knight * —
    Carle, now the King's come!

" My reverend Clergy, look ye say
he best of thanksgivings ye ha'e,
nd warstle for a sunny day —
    Carle, now the King's come!

" My Doctors, look that you agree,
ure a' the town without a fee;
ly Lawyers, dinna pike a plea, —
    Carle, now the King's come!

" Come forth each sturdy Burgher's bairn,
hat dints on wood or clanks on airn,
hat fires the o'en, or winds the pirn —
    Carle, now the King's come!

" Come forward with the Blanket Blue,†
our sires were loyal men and true,
s Scotland's foemen oft might rue —
    Carle, now the King's come!

" Scots downa loup, and rin and rave,
Ve're steady folks and something grave,
Ve'll keep the causeway firm and brave,
    Carle, now the King's come!

" Sir Thomas, ‡ thunder from your rock,
ill Pentland dinnles wi' the shock,
nd lace wi' fire my snood o' smoke —
    Carle, now the King's come!

" Melville, bring out your bands of blue,
,' Louden lads, baith stout and true,

With Elcho, Hope, and Cockburn, too —
    Carle, now the King's come! §

" And you, who on yon bluidy braes
Compell'd the vanquish'd Despot's praise,
Rank out — rank out — my gallant
    Greys ‖ —
    Carle, now the King's come!

" Cock o' the North, my Huntly bra',
Where are you with the Forty-twa?
Ah! wae's my heart that ye're awa' —
    Carle, now the King's come!

" But yonder come my canty Celts,
With durk and pistols at their belts;
Thank God, we've still some plaids and
    kilts —
    Carle, now the King's come!

"Lord, how the pibrochs groan and
    yell!
Macdonnel's ta'en the field himsel',
Macleod comes branking o'er the fell —
    Carle, how the King's come!

" Bend up your bow each Archer spark,
For you're to guard him light and
    dark;
Faith, lads, for ance ye've hit the mark —
    Carle, now the King's come!

"Young Errol, ¶ take the sword of state,
The sceptre, Panie-Morarchate; **
Knight Mareschal, see ye clear the gate
    Carle, now the King's come!

"Kind cummer, Leith, ye've been mis-set,
But dinna be upon the fret —
Ye'se hae the handsel of him yet,
    Carle, now the King's come!

* The Lord Provost had the agreeable sur-
ise of hearing his health proposed, at the civic
anquet given to George IV. in the Parliament
ouse, as "Sir William Arbuthnot, Bart."

† A Blue Blanket is the standard of the in-
orporated trades of Edinburgh.

‡ Sir Thomas Bradford, then commander of
e forces in Scotland.

§ Lord Melville, Colonel of the Mid-Lothian
Yeomanry Cavalry; Sir John Hope of Pinkie,
Bart., major; Robert Cockburn, Esq., and Lord
Elcho, captain in the same corps in which Sir
Walter Scott had formerly been quarter-master.

‖ The Scots Greys, of whom General Sir
James Stewart of Coltness, Bart, was commander.
Napoleon said of them at Waterloo: *Ces beaux
chevaux gris, comme ils travaillent!*

¶ The Earl of Errol is hereditary Lord High
Constable of Scotland.

** In more correct Gaelic autography, Benam-
horar-chat, Female Lord of the Chatte, or Great
Lady of the Cat, the Keltic title of the Countess
of Sutherland, whose cognizance was a wild cat.

"My daughters, come with een sae
    blue,
Your garlands weave, your blossoms
    strew,
He ne'er saw fairer flowers than you —
    Carle, now the King's come!

"What shall we do for the propine —
We used to offer something fine,
But ne'er a groat's in pouch of mine —
    Carle, now the King's come!

"Deil care — for that I'se never start,
We'll welcome him with Highland heart;
Whate'er we have he's get a part —
    Carle, now the King's come!

"I'll show him mason-work this day —
Nane of your bricks of Babel clay,
But towers shall stand till Time's away —
    Carle, now the King's come!

"I'll show him wit, I'll show him lair,
And gallant lads and lasses fair,
And what wad kind heart wish for mair?
    Carle, now the King's come!

"Step out, Sir John,* of projects rife,
Come win the thanks of an auld wife,
And bring him health and length of
    life —
    Carle, now the King's come!"

* * *

RHYMES OF ALSATIA.

1822.

I.

THE CLAIMING OF PRIVILEGE.

YOUR supplicant, by name
    Nigel Graham,
In fear of mishap
From a shoulder-tap,
And dreading a claw
From the talons of law,
    That are sharper than briars,
His freedom to sue
And rescue by you,

Thro' weapon and wit,
From warrant and writ,
From bailiff's hand,
From tip staff's wand
    Is come hither to Whitefriars.

II.

THE OATH.

By spigot and barrel,
    By bilboe and buff,
Thou art sworn to the quarrel
    Of the blades of the huff.
For Whitefriars and its claims
    To be champion or martyr,
And to fight for its Dames
    Like a Knight of the Garter.

III.

THE PRIVILEGE OF SANCTUARY.

From the touch of the tip,
    From the blight of the warrant,
From the watchmen who skip
    On the harman-beck's errand;†
From the Bailiff's cramp speech
    That makes man a thrall,
I charm thee from each
    And I charm thee from all
Thy freedom's complete
    As a blade of the huff,
To be cheated and cheat,
    To be cuff'd and to cuff;
To stride, swear, and swagger,
    To drink till you stagger,
To stare and to stab,
    And to brandish your dagger
    In the cause of your drab;
To walk wool-ward in winter,
    Drink brandy, and smoke,
And go fresco in summer
    For want of a cloak;
To eke out your living
    By the wag of your elbow,
By falham and gourd
    And by baring of bilboe;
To live by your shifts
    And to swear by your honor
Are the freedom and gifts
    Of which I am the donor.

The Fortunes of Nigel, chap. xvii.

* Sir John Sinclair, Bart., author of "The
Code of Health and Longevity," and father of
the celebrated writer, Catherine Sinclair.

† Constable.

MOTTOES.

1822.

CHAP. I.

Now Scott and English are agreed,
And Saunders hastes to cross the Tweed,
Where, such the splendors that attend him,
His very mother scarce had kenned him.
His metamorphosis behold,
From Glasgow frieze to cloth of gold,
His backsword with the iron hilt,
To rapier fairly hatched and gilt;
Was ever seen a gallant braver?
His very bonnet's grown a beaver.

The Reformation.

CHAP. II.

This, Sir, is one among the Seignory,
Has wealth at will, and will to use his wealth,
And wit to increase it.   Marry, his worst folly
Lies in a thriftless sort of charity,
That goes a-gadding sometimes after objects
Which wise men will not see when thrust upon them.

The Old Couple.

CHAP. IV.

Ay, sir, the clouted shoe hath ofttimes craft in't,
As says the rustic proverb: and your citizen,
In's grogram suit, gold chain, and well-blacked shoes,
Bears under his flat cap ofttimes a brain
Wiser than burns beneath the cap and feather,
Or seethes within the statesman's velvet nightcap.

Read me my Riddle.

CHAP. V.

Wherefore come ye not to court?
Certain 'tis the rarest sport;
There are silks and jewels glistening,
Prattling fools and wise men listening,
Bullies among brave men justling,
Beggars amongst nobles bustling;
Low-breathed talkers, minion lispers,
Cutting honest throats by whispers;
Wherefore come ye not to court?
Skelton swears 'tis glorious sport.

Skelton Skeltonizeth.

CHAP. VI.

O, I do know him, 'tis the mouldy lemon
Which our court wits will wet their lips withal,
When they would sauce their honied conversation
With somewhat sharper flavor. — Marry, sir,
That virtue's well-nigh left him — all the juice
That was so sharp and poignant, is squeezed out;
While the poor rind, although as sour as ever,
Must season soon the draff we give our grunters,
For two-legged things are weary on't.

The Chamberlain, a Comedy.

CHAP. VII.

Things needful we have thought on; but the thing
Of all most needful — that which Scripture terms,
As if alone it merited regard,
The ONE thing needful — that's yet unconsidered.

The Chamberlain.

CHAP. VIII.

Ay! mark the matron well; and laugh not, Harry,
At her old steeple-hat and velvet guard.
I've call'd her like the ear of Dionysius;
I mean that ear-form'd vault, built on his dungeon
To catch the groan and discontented murmurs
Of his poor bondsmen. — Even so doth Martha
Drink up, for her own purpose, all that passes,
Or is supposed to pass, in this wide city —
She can retail it too, if that her profit
Shall call on her to do so; and retail it
For your advantage, so that you can make
Your profit jump with hers.

The Conspiracy.

CHAP. XII.

—— This is the very barnyard,
Where muster daily the prime cocks o’
  the game,
Ruffle their pinions, crow till they are
  hoarse,
And spar about a barleycorn. Here, too,
  chickens,
The callow, unfledged brood of forward
  folly,
Learn first to rear the crest, and aim the
  spur,
And tune their note like full-plumed
  Chanticleer.

The Bear Garden.

CHAP. XIII.

Let the proud salmon gorge the feathered
  hook,
Then strike, and then you have him. —
  He will wince;
Spin out your line that it shall whistle
  from you
Some twenty yards or so, yet you shall
  have him —
Marry! you must have patience. — The
  stout rock
Which is his trust, hath edges something
  sharp;
And the deep pool hath ooze and sludge
  enough
To mar your fishing — ’less you are more
  careful.

Albion, or the Double Kings.

CHAP. XIV.

Bingo, why, Bingo! hey, boy, — here,
  sir, here —
He’s gone and off, but he’ll be home
  before us; —
’Tis the most wayward cur e’er mumbled
  bone,
Or dogged a master’s footsteps. — Bingo
  loves me
Better than beggar ever loved his
  alms;
Yet when he takes such humor, you may
  coax
Sweet Mistress Fantasy, your worship’s
  mistress,
Out of her sullen moods, as soon as Bingo.

The Dominie and his Dog.

CHAP. XV.

’Twas when fleet Snowball’s head was
  woxen gray,
A luckless leveret met him on his way, —
Who knows not Snowball — he whose
  race renowned
Is still victorious on each coursing ground;
Swaffham, Newmarket, and the Roman
  camp
Have seen them victors o’er each meaner
  stamp. —
In vain the youngling sought with doub-
  ling wile
The hedge, the hill, the thicket, or the
  stile.
Experience sage the lack of speed sup-
  plied,
And in the gap he sought, the victim died
So was I once, in thy fair street, Saint
  James,
Through walking cavaliers, and car-borne
  dames,
Descried, pursued, turned o’er again and
  o’er,
Coursed, coted, mouthed by an unfeeling
  bore.

Etc., etc., etc.

CHAP. XVI.

Give way — give way — I must and will
  have justice!
And tell me not of privilege and place;
Where I am injured, there I’ll sue redress
Look to it, every one who bars my access;
I have a heart to feel the injury,
A hand to right myself, and, by my honor,
That hand shall grasp what gray-beard
  Law denies me.

The Chamberlain.

CHAP. XVII.

Come hither, young one — Mark me!
  Thou art now
’Mongst men o’ the sword, that live by
  reputation
More than by constant income. — Single-
  suited
They are, I grant you; yet each single
  suit
Maintains, on the rough guess, a thousand
  followers —
And they be men, who, hazarding their all,

Needful apparel, necessary income,
And human body, and immortal soul,
Do in the very deed but hazard nothing —
So strictly is that ALL bound in reversion;
Clothes to the broker, income to the
  ursurer, —
And body to disease, and soul to the foul
  fiend;
Who laughs to see soldadoes and foola-
  does,
Play better than himself his game on earth.

The Mohocks.

CHAP. XIX.

By this good light, a wench of matchless
  mettle !
This were a leaguer-lass to love a soldier,
To bind his wounds, and kiss his bloody
  brow,
And sing a roundel as she help'd to arm
  him,
Though the rough foeman's drums were
  beat so nigh,
They seem'd to bear the burden.

Old Play.

CHAP. XX.

Credit me, friend, it hath been ever thus,
Since the ark rested on Mt. Ararat, —
False men hath sworn, and woman hath
  believed,
Repented, and reproach'd, and then be-
  lieved once more.

The New World.

CHAP. XXI.

Rove not from pole to pole; the man
  lives here
Whose razor's edge's only equal'd by his
  beer;
And where in either sense the Cockney-
  put
May, if he pleases, get confounded *cut.*

*On the Sign of an Ale-House
  kept by a Barber.*

CHAP. XXII.

Chance will not do the work. — Chance
  sends the breeze;
But if the pilot slumber at the helm,
The very wind that wafts us towards the
  port

May dash us on the shelves. — The steersman's part is vigilance,
Blow it or rough or smooth.

Old Play.

CHAP. XXIII.

SWASH–BUCKLER. Bilboe's the word.
PIERROT. It hath been spoke too
  often,
The spell hath lost its charm; — I tell
  thee, friend,
The meanest cur that walks the streets
  will turn
And snarl against your proffer'd basti-
  nado.
SWASH–BUCKLER. 'Tis art shall do it,
  then. I will dose the mongrels,
Or in plain terms, I'll use the private
  knife
'Stead of the brandish'd falchion.

Old Play.

CHAP. XXIV.

This is the time — heaven's maiden-sen-
  tinel
Hath quitted her high watch — the lesser
  spangles
Are paling one by one; give me the
  ladder
And the short lever ; — bid Anthony
Keep with his carabine the wicket-gate;
And do thou bare thy knife and follow me,
For we will in and do it. Darkness like
  this
Is dawning of our fortunes.

Old Play.

CHAP. XXV.

Death finds us mid our playthings —
  snatches us,
As a cross nurse might do a wayward
  child,
From all our toys and baubles. His
  rough call
Unlooses all our favorite ties on earth;
And well if they are such as may be answer'd
In yonder world, where all is judged of
  truly.

Old Play.

CHAP. XXVI.

Give us good voyage, gentle stream —
  we stun not
Thy sober ear with sounds of revelry;

Wake not the slumbering echoes of thy
　　banks
With voice of flute and horn; — we do
　　not seek
On the broad pathway of thy swelling
　　bosom
To glide in silent safety.
　　　　　　　The Double Bridal.

CHAP. XXVII.

This way lie safety and a sure retreat,
Yonder lie danger, shame, and punish-
　　ment.
Most welcome danger, then.　Nay, let
　　me say,
Tho' spoke with swelling heart, — wel-
　　come e'en shame,
And welcome punishment; for, call me
　　guilty,
I do but pay the tax that's due to justice;
And call me guiltless, then that punish-
　　ment
Is shame to those alone who do inflict it.
　　　　　　　The Tribunal.

CHAP. XXIX.

How fares the man on whom good men
　　would look
With eyes where scorn and censure com-
　　bated,
But that kind Christian love hath taught
　　the lesson —
That they who merit most contempt and
　　hate,
Do most deserve our pity.
　　　　　　　Old Play.

CHAP. XXXI.

Marry, come up, sir, with your gentle
　　blood !
Here's a red stream beneath his coarse
　　blue doublet,
That warms the heart as kindly as if
　　drawn
From the far source of old Assyrian kings,
Who first made mankind subject to their
　　sway.
　　　　　　　Old Play.

CHAP. XXXV.

We are not worse at once — the course
　　of evil
Begins so slowly, and from such slight
　　source,

An infant's hand might stem its breach
　　with clay;
But let the stream get deeper, and phi-
　　losophy —
Ay, and religion too — shall strive in vain
To turn the headlong torrent.
　　　　　　　Old Play.

THE BANNATYNE CLUB.*
1823.
I.

ASSIST me, ye friends of Old Books and
　　Old Wine,
To sing in the praises of sage Bannatyne,
Who left such a treasure of old Scottish lore
As enables each age to print one volume
　　more.
　　One volume more, my friends, one vol-
　　　ume more,
　　We'll ransack old Banny for one vol-
　　　ume more.

II.

And first, Allan Ramsay was eager to glean
From Bannatyne's *Hortus* his bright
　　Evergreen;
Two light little volumes (intended for four)
Still leave us the task to print one volume
　　more.
　　　　　　One volume more, etc.

III.

His ways were not ours, for he cared not
　　a pin
How much he left out, or how much he
　　put in;
The truth of the reading he thought was
　　a bore,
So this accurate age calls for one volume
　　more.
　　　　　　One volume more, etc.

IV.

Correct and sagacious, then came my
　　Lord Hailes,
And weigh'd every letter in critical scales,

* This Club was founded in 1822 for the publication or reprint of rare and curious works connected with the history and antiquities of Scotland.
Sir Walter Scott was its first president, and wrote
these verses for the anniversary dinner of March,
1823.

ut left out some brief words, which the
prudish abhor,
nd castrated Banny in one volume more.
One volume more, my friends, one
volume more,
We'll restore Banny's manhood in one
volume more.

v.

ohn Pinkerton next, and I'm truly concern'd
can't call that worthy so candid as
learn'd;
e rail'd at the plaid and blasphemed the
Claymore,
nd set Scots by the ears in his one volume more.
One volume more, my friends, one
volume more,
Kelt and Goth shall be pleased with
one volume more.

vi.

s bitter as gall, and as sharp as a razor,
nd feeding on herbs as a Nebuchad-
nezzar;
is diet too acid, his temper too sour,
ittle Ritson came out with his two volumes more.
But one volume more, my friends, one
volume more,
We'll dine on roast beef and print one
volume more.

vii.

he stout Gothic yeditur next on the roll,
ith his beard like a brush and as black
as a coal,
nd honest Graysteel that was true to
the core,*
ent their hearts, and their hands each
to one volume more.
One volume more, etc.

viii.

nce by these single champions what
wonders were done,
hat may not be achieved by our Thirty
and One;

* "The stout Gothic yeditur" was James
bold; the nickname was bestowed upon him
Lord Eldin, then Mr. John Clerk. David
rd, editor of "Songs and Historical Ballads,"
s called Graysteel from having been long in
successful quest of the romance of that name.

Law, Gospel, and Commerce we count
in our corps,
And the Trade and the Press join for one
volume more.
One volume more, etc.

IX.

Ancient libels and contraband books I
assure ye,
We'll print as secure from Exchequer or
Jury;
Then hear your Committee and let them
count o'er
The Chiels they intend in their three
volumes more.
Three volumes more, etc.

X.

They'll produce you King Jamie the
sapient and Sext,
And the Rob of Dumblane and her Bishops
come next;
One tome miscellaneous they'll add to
your store,
Resolving next year to print four volumes
more.
Four volumes more, my friends, four
volumes more;
Pay down your subscriptions for four
volumes more.

MOTTOES.

FROM "PEVERIL OF THE PEAK."

1823.

CHAP. II.

WHY, then, we will have bellowing of
beeves,
Broaching of barrels, brandishing of
spigots;
Blood shall flow freely, but it shall be gore
Of herds and flocks, and venison and
poultry,
Join'd to the brave heart's-blood of John-
a-Barley-corn!
Old Play.

CHAP. III.

Here's neither want of appetite nor
mouths;
Pray Heaven we be not scant of meat or
mirth!
Old Play.

CHAP. IV.

No, sir, — I will not pledge ; — I'm one
　of those
Who think good wine needs neither bush
　nor preface
To make it welcome. If you doubt my
　word,
Fill the quart-cup, and see if I will choke
　on't.

Old Play.

CHAP. VI.

You shall have no worse prison than my
　chamber,
Nor jailer than myself.

The Captain.

CHAP. IX.

BESSUS. 'Tis a challenge, Sir, is it not?
GENTLEMAN. 'Tis an inviting to the
　field.

King and No King.

CHAP. XVI.

ASCASTO. Can she not speak?
OSWALD. If speech be only in accented
　sounds,
Framed by the tongue and lips, the
　maiden's dumb;
But if by quick and apprehensive look,
By motion, sign, and glance, to give
　each meaning,
Express as clothed in language, be term'd
　speech,
She hath that wondrous faculty; for her
　eyes,
Like the bright stars of heaven, can
　hold discourse,
Though it be mute and soundless.

Old Play.

CHAP. XVII.

This is a love meeting? See, the maiden
　mourns,
And the sad suitor bends his looks on
　earth.
There's more hath pass'd between them
　than belongs
To Love's sweet sorrows.

Old Play.

CHAP. XIX.

Now, hoist the anchor, mates, and let
　the sails

Give their broad bosom to the buxom
　wind,
Like lass that wooes a lover.

Anonymous.

CHAP. XXII.

He was a fellow in a peasant's garb;
Yet one could censure you a woodcock
　carving
Like any courtier at the ordinary.

The Ordinary.

CHAP. XXIII.

The Gordon then his bugle blew,
　And said : — "Awa, awa !
The House of Rhodes is all on flame,
　I hauld it time to ga' ! "

Old Ballad.

CHAP. XXIV.

We meet, as men see phantoms in a dream,
Which glide and sigh, and sign, and move
　their lips,
But make no sound; or, if they utter voice,
'Tis but a low and undistinguished moan-
　ing,
Which has nor word nor sense of utter'd
　sound.

The Chieftain.

CHAP. XXV.

The course of human life is changeful still
As is the fickle wind and wandering rill,
Or, like the light dance which the wild
　breeze weaves
Amidst the faded race of fallen leaves;
Which now its breath bears down, now
　tosses high,
Beats to the earth, or wafts to middle sky,
Such, and so varied, the precarious play
Of fate with man, frail tenant of a day.

Anonymous.

CHAP. XXVI.

Necessity — thou best of peacemakers,
As well as surest prompter of invention —
Help us to composition !

Anonymous.

CHAP. XXVII.

—— This is some creature of the element,
Most like your sea-gull. He can whistle
　and whistle
His screaming song, e'en when the storm
　is loudest.

...ke for his sheeted couch the restless
  foam
. the wild wave-crest, slumber in the
  calm,
.d dally with the storm. Yet 'tis a gull,
. arrant gull, with all this.
                    The Chieftain.

CHAP. XXXI.

.fear the devil worst when gown and
  cassock,
., in the lack of them, old Calvin's cloak,
.nceals his cloven hoof.
                    Anonymous.

CHAP. XXXIII.

.is the black ban-dog of our jail. Pray
  look on him,
.t at a wary distance; rouse him not;
. bays not till he worries.
            The Black Dog of Newgate.

CHAP. XXXVIII.

.Speak not of niceness when there's
  chance of wreck,"
.e captain said, as ladies writhed their
  neck
. see the dying dolphin flap the deck;
. If we go down, on us these gentry sup;
. e dine upon them, if we haul them up.
.ise men applaud us when we eat the
  eaters,
. the devil laughs when the keen folks
  cheat the cheaters."
                    The Sea Voyage.

CHAP. XLIV.

.d some for safety took the dreadful
  leap;
.me for the voice of Heaven seemed
  calling on them;
.me for advancement, or for lucre's
  sake —
.eaped in frolic.   *The Dream.*

CHAP. XLV.

.igh feasting was there there—the gilded
  roofs
.ung to the wassail-health — the dancer's
  step
.rung to the chord responsive — the gay
  gamester
. fate's disposal flung his heap of gold,

And laughed alike when it increased or
  lessened;
Such virtue hath court-air to teach us
  patience
Which schoolmen preach in vain.
            Why come ye not to Court?

COUNTY GUY.

1823.

AH ! County Guy, the hour is nigh,
  The sun has left the lea,
The orange flower perfumes the bower,
  The breeze is on the sea.
The lark, his lay who thrill'd all day,
  Sits hush'd his partner nigh;
Breeze, bird, and flower, confess the hour,
  But where is County Guy?

The village maid steals thro' the shade,
  Her shepherd's suit to hear;
To beauty shy, by lattice high,
  Sings high-born Cavalier.
The star of Love, all stars above,
  Now reigns o'er earth and sky;
And high and low the influence know —
  But where is County Guy?
            Quentin Durward, chap. iv.

PARAPHRASE FROM "ORLANDO FURIOSO."

1823.

SOME better bard shall sing in feudal state
How Braquemont's Castle oped its Gothic
  gate,
When on the wandering Scot its lovely
  heir
Bestow'd her beauty and 'an earldom fair
            Quentin Durward, chap. xxxvii.

MOTTOES.

FROM "QUENTIN DURWARD."

CHAP. III.

FULL in the midst a mighty pile arose,
Where iron-grated gates their strength
  oppose

To each invading step, and strong and steep
The battled walls arose, the fosse sunk
  deep.
'Slow round the fortress rolled the sluggish stream,
And high in middle air the warder's turrets gleam.
                          Anonymous.

CHAP. VII.

Justice of Peace. Here, hand me down
  the statute — read the articles —
Swear, kiss the book — subscribe, and be
  a hero;
Drawing a portion from the public stock
For deeds of valor to be done hereafter —
Sixpence per day, subsistence and arrears.
                The Recruiting Officer.

CHAP. XI.

Painters show Cupid blind — Hath Hy-
  men eyes?
Or is his sight warped by those spectacles
Which parents, guardians, and advisers
  lend him,
That he may look through them on lands
  and mansions,
On jewels, gold, and all such rich dota-
  tions,
And see their value ten times magnified?—
Methinks 'twill brook a question.
        The Miseries of Enforced Marriage.

CHAP. XII

This is a lecturer so skill'd in policy,
That (no disparagement to Satan's cun-
  ning)
He well might read a lesson to the devil,
And teach the old seducer new tempta-
  tions.
                          Old Play.

CHAP. XIV.

I see thee yet, fair France — thou favor'd
  land
Of art and nature — thou art still before me :
Thy sons, to whom their labor is a sport,
So well thy grateful soil returns its tribute;
Thy sun-burnt daughters, with their laugh-
  ing eyes
And glossy raven-locks. But, favor'd
  France,
Thou hast had many a tale of woe to tell,
In ancient times as now.
                          Anonymous.

CHAP. XV.

He was a son of Egypt, as he told me,
And one descended from those drea
  magicians,
Who waged rash war, when Israel dwe
  in Goshen,
With Israel and her Prophet — matchir
  rod
With his the sons of Levi's — and e
  countering
Jehovah's miracles with incantations,
Till upon Egypt came the avenging Ange
And those proud sages wept for the
  first-born,
As wept the unletter'd peasant.
                          Anonymous.

CHAP. XVI.

I am as free as Nature first made man,
Ere the base laws of servitude began,
When wild in woods the noble sava
  ran.
            The Conquest of Granada. *

CHAP. XXIV.

Rescue or none, Sir Knight, I am yo
  captive;
Deal with me what your nobleness su
  gests —
Thinking the chance of war may one d
  place you
Where I must now be reckon'd — i' the r
Of melancholy prisoners.
                          Anonymous.

CHAP. XXV.

No human quality is so well wove
In warp and woof, but there's some fla
  in it;
I've known a brave man fly a shepher
  cur,
A wise man so demean him, drivelli
  idiocy
Had well-nigh been ashamed on't. F
  your crafty,
Your worldly-wise man, he, above the re
Weaves his own snares so fine, he's off
  caught in them.
                          Old Play.

---

* It will be remembered that when Scott v
about fifteen he wrote a poem in four books,
titled, " The Conquest of Granada," but imme
ately burned it. The lines may be a remi
cence of the lost poem.

CHAP. XXVI.

When Princes meet, astrologers may
mark it
In ominous conjunction, full of boding,
Like that of Mars with Saturn.

Old Play.

CHAP. XXIX.

Thy time is not yet out — the devil thou
servest
Has not as yet deserted thee.   He aids
The friends who drudge for him, as the
blind man
Was aided by the guide, who lent his
shoulder
O'er rough and smooth, until he reach'd
the brink
Of the fell precipice — then hurl'd him
downward.

Old Play.

CHAP. XXX.

Our counsels waver like the unsteady bark,
That reels amid the strife of meeting currents.

Old Play.

CHAP. XXXI.

Hold fast thy truth, young soldier. —
Gentle maiden,
Keep you your promise plight — leave
age its subtleties,
And gray-hair'd policy its maze of false-
hood;
But be you candid as the morning sky,
Ere the high sun sucks vapors up to stain
it.

The Trial.

MOTTOES.

FROM "ST. RONAN'S WELL."

1823.

CHAP. III.

THERE must be government in all society:
Bees have their Queen, and stag-herds
have their leader;
Rome had her consuls, Athens had her
archons,
And we, sir, have our Managing Committee.

The Album of St. Ronan's.

CHAP. IX.

We meet as shadows in the land of dreams
Which speak not but in signs.

Anonymous.

CHAP. X.

Come, let me have thy counsel, for I
need it;
Thou art of those, who better help their
friends
With sage advice, than usurers with gold,
Or brawlers with their swords — I'll trust
to thee,
For I ask only from thee words, not deeds.

The Devil hath met his Match.

CHAP. XI.

Nearest of blood should still be next in
love ;
And when I see these happy children
playing,
While William gathers flowers for Ellen's
ringlets,
And Ellen dresses flies for William's angle,
I scarce can think, that in advancing life,
Coldness, unkindness, interest, or sus-
picion,
Will e'er divide that unity so sacred,
Which Nature bound at birth.

Anonymous.

CHAP. XXIII.

Oh! you would be a vestal maid, I war-
rant,
The bride of Heaven — Come — we may
shake your purpose:
For here I bring in hand a jolly suitor
Hath ta'en degrees in the seven sciences
The ladies love best — He is young and
noble,
Handsome and valiant, gay and rich, and
liberal.

The Nun.

CHAP. XXXII.

It comes — it wrings me in my parting
hour,
The long-hid crime — the well-disguised
guilt.
Bring me some holy priest to lay the
spectre !

Old Play.

CHAP. XXXIII.

On the lee-beam lies the land, boys,
  See all clear to reef each course;
Let the fore-sheet go, don't mind, boys,
  Though the weather should be worse.

The Storm.

CHAP. XXXVIII.

What sheeted ghost is wandering through
  the storm?
For never did a maid of middle earth
Choose such a time or spot to vent her
  sorrows.

Old Play.

CHAP. XXXIX.

Here come we to our close — for that
  which follows
Is but the tale of dull, unvaried misery.
Steep crags and headlong linns may court
  the pencil
Like sudden haps, dark plots, and strange
  adventures;
But who would paint the dull and fog-
  wrapt moor,
In its long tract of sterile desolation?

Old Play.

EPILOGUE.

TO THE DRAMA FOUNDED ON "ST. RONAN'S WELL."

1824.

"AFTER the play, the following humorous
address (ascribed to an eminent literary character) was spoken with infinite effect by Mr.
Mackay in the character of MEG DODS." —
Edinburgh Weekly Journal, 9th June, 1824.

Enter MEG DODS, *encircled by a crowd
of unruly boys, whom a Town's Officer is driving off.*

THAT'S right, friend — drive the gaitlings
  back,
And lend yon muckle ane a whack;
Your Embro' bairns are grown a pack
    Sae proud and saucy,
They scarce will let an auld wife walk
    Upon your causey.

I've seen the day they would been scaur'd
Wi' the Tolbooth, or wi' the Guard,
Or maybe wud hae some regard
    For Jamie Laing * —

* James Laing, head of the Edinburgh Police
at that time, and a constant terror to evil-doers.

The Water-hole † was right well wared
    On sic a gang.

But whar's the gude Tolbooth ‡ gane now
Whar's the auld Claught,§ wi' red and blue
Whar's Jamie Laing? and whar's John
  Doo? ‖
    And whar's the Weigh-house
Deil hae't I see but what is new,
    Except the Playhouse.

Yoursells are changed frae head to heel
There's some that gar the causeway reel
With clashing hufe and rattling wheel,
    And horses canterin',
Wha's fathers daunder'd hame as weel
    Wi' lass and lantern.

Mysell being in the public line,
I look for howfs I kenn'd lang syne,
Whar gentles used to drink gude wine,
    And eat cheap dinners;
But deil a soul gangs there to dine,
    Of saunts or sinners!

Fortune's ¶ and Hunter's gane, alas!
And Bayle's is lost in empty space;
And now, if folk would splice a brace,
    Or crack a bottle,
They gang to a new-fangled place
    They ca' a Hottle.

The deevil hottle them for Meg.
They are sae greedy and sae gleg,
That if ye're served but wi' an egg,
    (And that's puir pickin',)
In comes a chiel, and makes a leg,
    And charges chicken!

"And wha may ye be," gin ye speer,
"That brings your auld-warld claver
  here!"
Troth, if there's onybody near
    That kens the roads,
I'll haud ye Burgundy to beer,
    He kens Meg Dods.

† Watch-hole.

‡ The Tolbooth was the great Edinburgh Ja[il]
pulled down in 1817.

§ The Claught was the old Town Guard.

‖ John Doo, or Dhu, one of the Guard
Police.

¶ Fortune's, Hunter's, and Bayle's were ta[verns].
erns.

came a piece frae west o' Currie;
And, since I see you're in a hurry,
Your patience I'll nae langer worry,
　　But be sae crouse
As speak a word for ane Will Murray,
　　That keeps this house.*

Plays are auld-fashion'd things in truth,
And ye've seen wonders mair uncouth;
Yet actors shouldna suffer drouth,
　　Or want of dramock,
Although they speak but wi' their mouth,
　　Not with their stamock.

But ye take care of a' folk's pantry;
And surely to hae stooden sentry
Ower this big house (that's far frae rent
　　free),
　　For a lone sister,
's claim as gude's to be a ventri† —
　　How'st ca'd — loquister.

Weel, sirs, gude-e'en, and have a care
The bairns make fun o' Meg nae
　　mair;
For gin they do, she tells you fair,
　　And without failzie,
As sure as ever ye sit there,
　　She'll tell the Bailie.

COWLEY'S CATCH AMPLIFIED.

1824.

For all our men were very very merry,
　　And all our men were drinking;
There were two men of mine,
Three men of thine,
And three that belong'd to old Sir Thom
　　o' Lyne; —

As they went to the ferry
They were very very merry,
　　And all our men were drinking.

Jack look'd at the sun and cried " Fire !
　　fire ! fire ! "
Tom startled his Keffel in Birkendale
　　mire;

* The Edinburgh Theatre.
† An allusion to the recent performances of
Alexandre, the ventriloquist.

Jem started a calf and halloo'd for a stag;
Will mounted a gate-port instead of his
　　nag; —

For all of our men were very very merry,
　　And all our men were drinking;

There were three men of mine,
Three men of thine,
And three that belong'd to old Sir Thom
　　o' Lyne; —

As they went to the ferry
They were very very merry,
　　For all our men were drinking.
　　　　　　　Red Gauntlet, Letter x.

CONSOLATION.

1824.

As lords their laborers' hire delay,
　　Fate quits our toil with hopes to come,
Which, if far short of present pay,
　　Still owns a debt and names a sum.

Quit not the pledge, frail sufferer, then,
　　Although a distant date be given;
Despair is treason towards man,
　　And blasphemy to Heaven.
　　　　　　　Redgauntlet, chap. ix.

TO J. G. LOCKHART, ESQ.

ON THE COMPOSITION OF MAIDA'S EPITAPH.

1824.

" Maidæ Marmorea dormis sub imagine Maida !
　Ad januam domini sit tibi terra levis."
　　　　　　　See *Life of Scott*.

" DEAR JOHN, — I some time ago wrote
　　to inform his
Fat Worship of *jaces*, misprinted for *dor-
　mis ;*
But that several Southrons assured me
　　the *januam*
Was a twitch to both ears of Ass Pris-
　cian's cranium.
You, perhaps, may observe that one
　　Lionel Berguer,
In defence of our blunder appears a
　　stout arguer;

But at length I have settled, I hope, all
  these clatters,
By a *rowt* in the papers — fine place for
  such matters.
I have, therefore, to make it for once
  my command, sir,
That my gudeson shall leave the whole
  thing in my hand, sir,
And by no means accomplish what James
  says you threaten,
Some banter in Blackwood to claim your
  dog-Latin.
I have various reasons of weight, on my
  word, sir,
For pronouncing a step of this sort were
  absurd, sir. —
Firstly, erudite sir, 'twas against your
  advising
I adopted the lines this monstrosity lies in;
For you modestly hinted my English
  translation
Would become better far such a digni-
  fied station.
Second — how, in God's name, would my
  bacon be saved,
By not having writ what I clearly en-
  graved?
On the contrary, I, on the whole, think
  it better
To be whipped as the thief, than his
  lousy resetter.
Thirdly — don't you perceive that I
  don't care a boodle,
Although fifty false metres were flung at
  my noodle,
For my back is as broad and as hard as
  Benlomon's,
And I treat as I please both the Greeks
  and the Romans;
Whereas the said heathens might rather
  look serious
At a kick on their drum from the scribe
  of Valerius.
And, fourthly and lastly — it is my good
  pleasure
To remain the sole source of that mur-
  derous measure.
So *stet pro ratione voluntas* — be tractile.
Invade not, I say, my own dear little dactyl,
If you do, you'll occasion a breach in
  our intercourse.
To-morrow will see me in town for the
  winter-course,

But not at your door, at the usual hour, sir,
My own pye-house daughter's good pro
  to devour, sir.
Ergo — peace! — on your duty, you
  squeamishness throttle,
And we'll soothe Priscian's spleen wit
  a canny third bottle.
A fig for all dactyls, a fig for all spondees
A fig for all dunces and dominie Grundys
A fig for dry thrapples, south, north
  east, and west, sir,
Speates and raxes * ere five for a famish
  ing guest, sir;
And as Fatsman † and I have some topic
  for haver, he'll
Be invited, I hope, to meet me an
  Dame Peveril,
Upon whom, to say nothing of Oury an
  Anne, you a
Dog shall be deemed if you fasten you
  Janua.

LINES.

ADDRESSED TO

MONSIEUR ALEXANDRE, ‡

THE CELEBRATED VENTRILOQUIST.

1824.

Of yore, in old England, it was no
  thought good
To carry two visages under one hood;
What should folk say to *you?* who hav
  faces such plenty,
That from under one hood you last nigh
  show'd us twenty!
Stand forth, arch deceiver, and tell us i
  truth,
Are you handsome or ugly, in age or i
  youth!

* See *Scott's Essays.*

† A nickname for James Ballantyne.

‡ " When Monsieur Alexandre, the cele
brated ventriloquist, was in Scotland, in 182
he paid a visit to Abbotsford, where he ente
tained his distinguished host and the oth
visitors with his unrivalled imitations. Ne
morning, when he was about to depart, S
Walter felt a good deal embarrassed as to th
sort of acknowledgment he should offer; but a
length, resolving that it would probably be mo
agreeable to the young foreigner to be paid i
professional coin, if in any, he stepped aside fo
a few minutes, and, on returning, presented hi
with this epigram." The lines were publishe
in the *Edinburgh Annual Register* for 1824.

Man, woman, or child—a dog or a mouse?
Or are you at once, each live thing in
    the house?
Each live thing did I ask? — each dead
    implement, too,
A workshop in your person, — saw,
    chisel, and screw!
Above all, are you one individual? I
    know
You must be at least Alexandre and Co.
But I think you're a troop — an assem-
    blage — a mob,
And that I, as the Sheriff, should take
    up the job;
And instead of rehearsing your wonders
    in verse,
Must read you the Riot Act, and bid you
    disperse.

LIFE OF NAPOLEON.

June, 1825.

" THE rapid accumulation of books and MSS.
or the life of Napoleon was at once flattering
and alarming ; and one of his notes to me, about
the middle of June, had these rhymes by way of
postscript : — "

WHEN with Poetry dealing
Room enough in a shieling;
Neither cabin nor hovel
Too small for a novel:
Tho' my back I should rub
On Diogenes' tub,
How my fancy could prance
In a dance of romance !
But my house I must swap
With some Brobdignag chap,
Ere I grapple, God bless me ! with Em-
    peror Nap.
            LOCKHART'S *Life of Scott.*

SOLDIER, WAKE.

1825.

I.

SOLDIER, wake — the day is peeping,
Honor ne'er was won in sleeping,
Never when the sunbeams still
Lay unreflected on the hill:
'Tis when they are glinted back
From ax and armor, spear and jack,

That they promise future story
Many a page of deathless glory.
Shields that are the foeman's terror,
Ever are the morning's mirror.

II.

Arm and up — the morning beam
Hath call'd the rustic to his team,
Hath call'd the falconer to the lake,
Hath call'd the huntsman to the brake;
The early student ponders o'er
His dusty tomes of ancient lore.
Soldier, wake — thy harvest, fame;
Thy study, conquest; war, thy game.
Shield, that would be foeman's terror,
Still should gleam the morning's mirror.

III.

Poor hire repays the rustic's pain;
More paltry still the sportsman's gain;
Vainest of all, the student's theme
Ends in some metaphysic dream:
Yet each is up, and each has toil'd
Since first the peep of dawn has smiled;
And each is eagerer in his aim
Than he who barters life for fame.
Up, up, and arm thee, son of terror !
Be thy bright shield the morning's
    mirror.
            The Betrothed, chap. xiv.

SONGS FROM " THE BETROTHED."

THE TRUTH OF WOMAN.

1825.

I.

WOMAN's faith, and woman's trust —
Write the characters in dust;
Stamp them on the running stream,
Print them on the moon's pale beam,
And each evanescent letter
Shall be clearer, firmer, better,
And more permanent, I ween,
Than the thing those letters mean.

II.

I have strain'd the spider's thread
'Gainst the promise of a maid; .
I have weigh'd a grain of sand
'Gainst her plight of heart and hand;

I told my true love of the token,
How her faith proved light, and her word
    was broken:
Again her word and truth she plight,
And I believed them again ere night.

                The Betrothed, chap. xx.

A WELSH LAY.

1825.

I asked of my harp, "Who hath injured
    thy cords?"
And she replied, "The crooked finger,
    which I mocked in my tune."
A blade of silver may be bended — a
    blade of steel abideth —
Kindness fadeth away, but vengeance
    endureth.

The sweet taste of mead passeth from
    the lips,
But they are long corroded by the juice
    of wormwood:
The lamb is brought to the shambles, but
    the wolf rangeth the mountain;
Kindness fadeth away, but vengeance
    endureth.

I asked the red-hot iron, when it glim-
    mered on the anvil,
"Wherefore glowest thou longer than
    the fire-brand?" —
"I was born in the dark mine, and the
    brand in the pleasant greenwood."
Kindness fadeth away, but vengeance
    endureth.

I asked the green oak of the assembly,
    "Wherefore its boughs were dry and
    seared like the horns of the stag?"
And it showed me that a small worm had
    gnawed its roots.
The boy who remembered the scourge,
    undid the wicket of the castle at mid-
    night.
Kindness fadeth away, but vengeance
    endureth.

Lightning destroyeth temples, though their
    spires pierce the clouds;

Storms destroy armadas, though the
    sails intercept the gale.
He that is in his glory falleth, and tha
    by a contemptible enemy.
Kindness fadeth away, but vengeanc
    endureth.

                The Betrothed, chap, xxxi.

MOTTOES.
FROM "THE BETROTHED."

CHAP. II.

IN Madoc's tent the clarion sounds,
    With rapid clangor hurried far;
Each hill and dale the note rebounds,
    But when return the sons of war!
Thou, born of stern Necessity,
Dull Peace! the valley yields to thee,
And owns thy melancholy sway.

                Welsh Poem.

CHAP. VII.

O, sadly shines the morning sun
    On leagur'd castle wall,
When bastion, tower, and battlement,
    Seem nodding to their fall.

                Old Ballad.

CHAP. XII.

Now all ye ladies of fair Scotland,
    And ladies of England that happ
    would prove,
Marry never for houses, nor marry for lan
    Nor marry for nothing but only love.

                Family Quarrels.

CHAP. XIII.

Too much rest is rust,
    There's ever cheer in changing;
We tyne by too much trust,
    So we'll be up and ranging.

                Old Song.

CHAP. XVII.

Ring out the merry bell, the bride ap
    proaches;
The blush upon her cheek has shame
    the morning,
For that is dawning palely.   Grant, goc
    saints,
These clouds betoken naught of evil omen

                Old Play.

CHAP. XX.

The king call'd down his merry men all
  By one and by two and three;
Earl Marshal was wont to be the foremost
  one,
  But the hindermost man was he.
            Old Ballad.

CHAP. XXVII.

Julia.   ———— Gentle sir,
You are our captive — but we'll use you so,
That you shall think your prison joys may
  match
Whate'er your liberty hath known of
  pleasure.
  Roderick.   No, fairest, we have trifled
  here too long;
And, lingering to see your roses blossom,
I've let my laurels wither.
            Old Play.

CHAP. XXXI.

Oh, fear not, fear not, good Lord John,
  That I would you betray,
Or sue requital for a debt,
  Which Nature cannot pay.

Bear witness, all ye sacred powers,
  Ye lights that 'gin to shine
This night shall prove the sacred tie
  That binds your faith and mine.

———

AHRIMAN.

1825.

DARK Ahriman, whom Irak still
Holds origin of woe and ill!
  When bending at thy shrine,
We view the world with troubled eye,
Where see we 'neath the extended sky,
  An empire matching thine?

If the Benigner Power can yield
A fountain in the desert field,
  Where weary pilgrims drink;
Thine are the waves that lash the rock,
Thine the tornado's deadly shock,
  Where countless navies sink!

Or, if He bid the soil dispense
Balsams to cheer the sinking sense,
  How few can they deliver

From lingering pains, or pang intense,
Red Fever, spotted Pestilence,
  The arrows of thy quiver!

Chief in Man's bosom sits thy sway,
And frequent, while in words we pray
  Before another throne,
Whate'er of specious form be there,
The secret meaning of the prayer
  Is, Ahriman, thine own.

Say, hast thou feeling, sense, and form,
Thunder thy voice, thy garments storm,
  As Eastern Magi say;
With sentient soul of hate and wrath,
And wings to sweep thy deadly path,
  And fangs to tear thy prey?

Or art thou mixt in Nature's source,
An ever operating force,
  Converting good to ill;
An evil principle innate
Contending with our better fate,
  And, oh! victorious still?

Howe'er it be, dispute is vain,
On all without thou hold'st thy reign,
  Nor less on all within;
Each mortal passion's fierce career,
Love, hate, ambition, joy, and fear,
  Thou goadest into sin.

Whene'er a sunny gleam appears,
To brighten up our vale of tears,
  Thou art not distant far;
Mid such brief solace of our lives,
Thou whett'st our very banquet-knives
  To tools of death and war. —

Thus, from the moment of our birth,
Long as we linger on the earth,
  Thou rul'st the fate of men;
Thine are the pangs of life's last hour,
And — who dare answer? — is thy power.
  Dark Spirit! ended THEN?
            The Talisman, chap. iii.

———

TO THE ARCH-DUKE OF AUSTRIA.

1825.

WHAT brave chief shall head the forces,
Where the red-cross legions gather?

Best of horsemen, best of horses,
  Highest head and fairest feather.
          Hoch lebe Herzog Leopold!

Ask not Austria why mid princes
  Still her banner rises highest;
Ask as well the strong-wing'd eagle
  Why to heaven he soars the nighest!
          The Talisman, chap. xi.

SONG OF BLONDEL. — THE BLOODY VEST.

1825.

'TWAS near the fair city of Benevent,
When the sun was setting on bough and bent,
And knights were preparing in bower and tent,
On the eve of the Baptist's tournament;
When in Lincoln green a stripling gent,
Well seeming a page by a princess sent,
Wander'd the camp, and, still as he went,
Enquired for the Englishman, Thomas à Kent.

Far hath he fared, and farther must fare,
Till he finds his pavilion nor stately nor rare, —
Little save iron and steel was there;
And, as lacking the coin to pay armorer's care,
With his sinewy arms to the shoulders bare,
The good knight with hammer and file did repair
The mail that to-morrow must see him wear,
For the honor of Saint John and his lady fair.

" Thus speaks my lady," the page said he,
And the knight bent lowly both head and knee,
" She is Benevent's Princess so high in degree,
And thou art as lowly as knight may well be —
He that would climb so lofty a tree,
Or spring such a gulf as divides her from thee,

Must dare some high deed, by which all men may see
His ambition is back'd by his high chivalrie.

" Therefore thus speaks my lady," the fair page he said,
And the knight lowly louted with hand and with head,
" Fling aside the good armor in which thou art clad,
And don thou this weed of her nightgear instead,
For a hauberk of steel, a kirtle of thread:
And charge, thus attired, in the tournament dread,
And fight as thy wont is where most blood is shed,
And bring honor away, or remain with the dead."

Untroubled in his look, and untroubled in his breast,
The knight the weed hath taken, and reverently hath kiss'd;
" Now blest be the moment, the messenger be blest!
Much honor'd do I hold me in my lady's high behest;
And say unto my lady, in this dear nightweed drest,
To the best arm'd champion I will not vail my crest;
But if I live and bear me well 'tis her turn to take the test."
Here, gentles, ends the foremost fytte of the Lay of the bloody Vest.

FYTTE SECOND.

The Baptist's fair morrow beheld gallant feats —
There was winning of honor, and losing of seats —
There was hewing with falchions, and splintering of staves,
The victors won glory, the vanquish'd won graves.
O, many a knight there fought bravely and well,
Yet one was accounted his peers to excel;

And 'twas he whose sole armor on body
and breast,
Seem'd the weed of a damsel when boune
for her rest.

There were some dealt him wounds that
were bloody and sore,
But others respected his plight, and forbore.
' It is some oath of honor," they said,
" and I trow
'Twere unknightly to slay him achieving
his vow."
Then the Prince, for his sake, bade the
tournament cease,
He flung down his warder, the trumpets
sung peace;
And the judges declare, and competitors
yield,
That the Knight of the Night-gear was
first in the field.

The feast it was nigh, and the mass it
was nigher,
When before the fair Princess low louted
a squire,
And deliver'd a garment unseemly to
view,
With sword-cut and spear-thrust, all
hack'd and pierced through;
All rent and all tatter'd, all clotted with
blood,
With foam of the horses, with dust, and
with mud,
Not the point of that lady's small finger,
I ween,
Could have rested on spot was unsullied
and clean.

" This token my master, Sir Thomas à
Kent,
Restores to the Princess of fair Benevent.
He that climbs the tall tree has won right
to the fruit,
He that leaps the wide gulf should pre-
vail in his suit;
Thro' life's utmost peril the prize I have
won,
And now must the faith of my mistress
be shown:
For she who prompts knight on such
danger to run,
Much avouch his true service in front of
the sun.

" ' I restore,' says my master, ' the garment I've worn,
And I claim of the Princess to don it in
turn;
For its stains and its rents she should
prize it the more,
Since by shame 'tis unsullied, tho' crimson'd with gore.' "
Then deep blush'd the Princess — yet
kiss'd she and prest
The blood-spotted robe to her lips and
her breast.
" Go tell my true knight, church and
chamber shall show,
If I value the blood on this garment or
no. "

And when it was time for the nobles to
pass
In solemn procession to minster and mass,
The first walk'd the Princess in purple
and pall,
But the blood-besmear'd night-robe she
wore over all;
And eke, in the hall, where they all sat
at dine,
When she knelt to her father and proffer'd the wine,
Over all her rich robes and state jewels
she wore,
That wimple unseemly bedabbled with
gore.

Then lords whisper'd ladies, as well you
may think,
And ladies replied, with nod, titter, and
wink;
And the Prince, who in anger and shame
had look'd down,
Turn'd at length to his daughter, and
spoke with a frown: —
" Now since thou hast publish'd thy folly
and guilt,
E'en atone with thy hand for the blood
thou has spilt:
Yet sore for thy boldness you both will
repent,
When you wander as exiles from fair
Benevent."

Then out spoke stout Thomas, in hall
where he stood,
Exhausted and feeble, but dauntless of
mood: —

" The blood that I lost for this daughter
        of thine,
I pour'd forth as freely as flask gives its
        wine;
And if for my sake she brooks penance
        and blame,
Do not doubt I will save her from suffer-
        ing and shame;
And light will she reck of thy princedom
        and rent,
When I hail her, in England, the Countess
        of Kent."

The Talisman, chap. xxvi.

MOTTOES.

FROM " THE TALISMAN."

CHAP. VI.

Now change the scene and let the trum-
        pets sound,
For we must rouse the lion from his lair.

Old Play.

CHAP. IX.

THIS is the Prince of Leeches; fever,
        plague,
Cold rheum, and hot podagra, do but look
        on him,
And quit their grasp upon the tortured
        sinews.

Anonymous.

CHAP. XIII.

You talk of Gayety and Innocence!
The moment when the fatal fruit was
        eaten,
They parted ne'er to meet again; and
        Malice
Has ever since been playmate to light
        Gayety,
From the first moment when the smiling
        infant
Destroys the flower or butterfly he toys
        with,
To the last chuckle of the dying miser,
Who on his deathbed laughs his last to hear
His wealthy neighbor has become a bank-
        rupt.

Old Play.

CHAP. XVI.

'Tis not her sense — for sure, in that
There's nothing more than common;

And all her wit is only chat,
        Like any other woman.

Song.

CHAP. XVII.

Were every hair upon his head a life,
And every life were to be supplicated
By numbers equal to those hairs quad-
        rupled,
Life after life should out like waning stars
Before the daybreak — or as festive lamps,
Which have lent lustre to the midnight
        revel,
Each after each are quench'd when guests
        depart.

Old Play.

CHAP. XIX.

Must we then sheath our still victorious
        sword;
Turn back our forward step which ever
        trode
O'er foemen's necks the onward path of
        glory;
Unclasp the mail, which with a solemn
        vow,
In God's own house we hung upon our
        shoulders;
That vow, as unaccomplish'd as the
        promise
Which village nurses make to still their
        children,
And after think no more of? —

The Crusade, a Tragedy.

CHAP. XX.

When beauty leads the lion in her toils,
Such are her charms, he dare not raise his
        mane,
Far less expand the terror of his fangs.
So great Alcides made his club a distaff,
And spun to please fair Omphale.

Anonymous.

CHAP. XXIII.

MID these wild scenes Enchantment
        waves her hand,
To change the face of the mysterious land,
Till the bewildering scenes around us seem
The vain productions of a feverish dream.

Astolpho, a Romance.

CHAP. XXIV.

—— A grain of dust
Soiling our cup, will make our sense reject

Fastidiously the draught which we did
   thirst for;
A rusted nail placed near the faithful
   compass,
Will sway it from the truth, and wreck
   the argosy.
Even this small cause of anger and disgust
Will break the bonds of amity 'mongst
   princes,
And wreck their noblest purposes.

                 The Crusade.

CHAP. XXVI.

The tears I shed must ever fall!
   I weep not for an absent swain,
For time may happier hours recall,
   And parted lovers meet again.

I weep not for the silent dead,
   Their pains are past, their sorrows o'er,
And those that loved their steps must
   tread
   When death shall join to part no more.

But worse than absence, worse than death,
   She wept her lover's sullied fame,
And, fired with all the pride of birth,
   She wept a soldier's injured name.

                 Ballad.*

OBEY THE DOOM.
1826.

By pathless march, by greenwood tree,
It is thy weird to follow me —
To follow me thro' the ghastly moon-
   light —
To follow me thro' the shadows of
   night —
To follow me, comrade, still art thou
   bound:
I conjure thee by the unstanch'd
   wound —
I conjure thee by the last words I spoke,
When the body slept and the spirit awoke
In the very last pangs of the deadly
   stroke.

        Woodstock, chap. xiv.

* The last four lines of this ballad were written by Scott; the eight preceding are from "The
Song of Genius," by Helen D'Arcy Cranstoun,
afterwards Mrs. Dugald Stewart.

GLEE FOR KING CHARLES.
1826.

Bring the bowl which you boast,
   Fill it up to the brim;
'Tis to him we love most,
   And to all who love him.
Brave gallants, stand up,
   And avaunt, ye base carles!
Were there death in the cup,
   Here's a health to King Charles!

Tho' he wanders thro' dangers,
   Unaided, unknown,
Dependent on strangers,
   Estranged from his own;
Tho' 'tis under our breath,
   Amidst forfeits and perils,
Here's to honor and faith,
   And a health to King Charles!

Let such honors abound
   As the time can afford,
The knee on the ground,
   And the hand on the sword;
But the time shall come round,
   When mid Lords, Dukes, and Earls,
The loud trumpets shall sound,
   Here's a health to King Charles!

        Woodstock, chap. xx.

ONE HOUR WITH THEE.†
1826.

An hour with thee! — When earliest day
Dapples with gold the eastern gray,
Oh, what can frame my mind to bear
The toil and turmoil, cark and care,
New griefs, which coming hours unfold,
And sad remembrance of the old?
        One hour with thee!

One hour with thee!—When burning June
Waves his red flag at pitch of noon;
What shall repay the faithful swain,
His labor on the sultry plain;
And more than cave or sheltering bough,
Cool feverish blood, and throbbing brow?
        One hour with thee!

† "He sung, but with more taste than execution, the air of a French rondelai, to which some
of the wits or sonnetteers in his gay and roving
train had adapted English verses."

One hour with thee!— When sun is set,
O, what can teach me to forget
The thankless labors of the day;
The hopes, the wishes, flung away;
The increasing wants and lessening gains,
The master's pride, who scorns my
pains?

One hour with thee!
Woodstock, chap. xxvi.

WILDRAKE'S TOAST.

1826.

SON of a witch,
Mayst thou die in a ditch
  With the butchers who backed thy
    quarrels;
And rot above ground,
While the world shall resound
  A welcome to Royal King Charles.

Woodstock, chap. xxx.

MOTTOES.

FROM "WOODSTOCK."

CHAP. II.

COME forth, old man—Thy daughter's side
  Is now the fitting place for thee;
When time hath quell'd the oak's bold pride,
The youthful tendril yet may hide
  The ruins of the parent tree.

CHAP. IV.

Yon path of greensward
Winds round by sparry grot and gay pa-
  vilion;
There is no flint to gall thy tender foot;
There's ready shelter from each breeze or
  shower. —
But Duty guides not that way — see her
  stand,
With wand entwined with amaranth, near
  yon cliffs.
Oft where she leads, thy blood must mark
  thy footsteps,
Oft where she leads, thy head must bear
  the storm,
And thy shrunk form endure heat, cold,
  and hunger;
But she will guide thee up to noble
  heights,

Which he who gains seems native of the
  sky,
While earthly things lie stretch'd beneath
  his feet,
Diminish'd, shrunk, and valueless.

Anonymous.

CHAP. V.

My tongue pads slowly under this new
  language,
And starts and stumbles at these uncouth
  phrases.
They may be great in worth and weight,
  but hang
Upon the native glibness of my language
Like Saul's plate-armor on the shepherd
  boy,
Encumbering and not arming him.

J. B.

CHAP. X.

Here we have one head
Upon two bodies — your two-headed bul-
  lock
Is but an ass to such a prodigy.
These two have but one meaning,
  thought, and counsel;
And when the single noddle has spoke out
The four legs scrape assent to it.

Old Play.

CHAP. XIV.

Deeds are done on earth
Which have their punishment ere the
  earth closes
Upon the perpetrators. Be it the working
Of the remorse-stirr'd fancy, or the vision
Distinct and real, of unearthly being,
All ages witness, that beside the couch
Of the fell homicide oft stalks the ghost
Of him he slew, and shows the shadowy
  wound.

Old Play.

CHAP. XVII.

We do that in our zeal,
Our calmer moments are afraid to answer.

Anonymous.

CHAP. XXIV.

The deadliest snakes are those which
  twined 'mongst flowers,
Blend their bright coloring with the varied
  blossoms,
Their fierce eyes glittering like the spangled dewdrops,

In all so like what nature has most harmless,
That sportive innocence, which dreads
   no danger,
Is poison'd unawares.
                  Old Play.

VERSES FROM SCOTT'S JOURNAL.

1826.

PARODY ON MOORE'S "MINSTREL BOY."

O LAND of Cakes! said the Northern
   Bard,
  Tho' all the world betrays thee,
One faithful pen thy rights shall guard,
  One faithful harp shall praise thee.

ON HIS PROCRASTINATION.

HEIGHHO,
  I can't say no,
But this piece of task-work off I can
  stave, O,
For Malachi's * posting into an octavo;
To correct the proof sheets only this
  night I have, O,
So, Madame Conscience, you've gotten
  as good as you gave, O;
But to-morrow's a new day, and we'll
  better behave, O,
So I lay down the pen, and your pardon
  I crave, O.

A SWIFTIANISM.

I LOLL in my chair,
  And around me I stare
With a critical air,
  Like a calf at a fair;
And, say I, Mrs. Duty,
  Good-morrow to your beauty;
I kiss your sweet shoe-tie,
  And hope I can suit ye.

ON LEAVING MRS. BROWN'S LODGINGS.

So goodbye, Mrs. Brown,
I am going out of town,
Over dale, over down,

* The "Epistles of Malachi Malagrowther,
Esq.," for writing which Scott neglected "Woodstock."

Where bugs bite not,
Where lodgers fight not,
Where below you chairmen drink not,
Where beside you gutters stink not;
But all is fresh and clean and gay,
And merry lambkins sport and play,
And they toss with rakes uncommonly
  short hay,
Which looks as if it had been sown only
  the other day,
And where oats are at twenty-five shillings a boll they say;
But all's one for that, since I must and
  will away.

ON A DAY'S STINT.

AND long ere dinner-time I have
  Full eight close pages wrote.
What, Duty, hast thou now to crave?
  Well done, Sir Walter Scott!

ON HIS SON'S QUARTERS.

LOUGHREA is a blackguard place,
  To Gort I give my curse;
Athlone itself is bad enough,
  But Ballinrobe is worse.
I cannot tell which is the worst,
  They're all so very bad;
But of all towns I ever saw,
  Bad luck to Kinnegad.

ON A PROVOCATION FROM JOSEPH HUME.

I'M not a King nor nae sic thing;
  My word it may not stand;
But Joseph may a buffet bide,
  Come he beneath my brand.

ON HIGH PRICES.

AND so 'twill be when I am gone,
The increasing charge will still go on,
And other bards shall climb these hills,
And curse your charge, *dear* evening bills!

FAREWELL TO THE OLD YEAR.

IT's useless to murmur and pout,
  There's no good in making ado;
'Tis well the old year is out,
  And time to begin a new!

MOTTO FROM "THE HIGHLAND WIDOW."

1827.

CHAP. II.

O, I'M come to the Low Country,
  Och, och, ohonochie,
Without a penny in my pouch
  To buy a meal for me.
I was the proudest of my clan,
  Long, long, may I repine;
And Donald was the bravest man,
  And Donald he was mine.

          Old Song.

MOTTO FROM "THE TWO DROVERS."

1827.

CHAP. II.

WERE ever two such loving friends! —
  How could they disagree?
O thus it was, he loved him dear,
  And thought how to requite him;
And having no friend left but he,
  He did resolve to fight him.

        Duke upon Duke.

VERSES FROM SCOTT'S JOURNAL.

1827.

ON HIS WORK.

HE walk'd and wrought, poor soul!
  What then?
Why, then he walk'd and wrought again.

AFTER MORNING VISITORS.

I GROW vaporish and odd,
And would not do the least right thing,
Neither for goddess nor for god,
Nor paint nor jest nor laugh nor sing.

THE DEATH OF KEELDAR.

These stanzas were written for Hood's "Gem," 1828, and accompanied an engraving from Cooper's painting of the Death of Keeldar.

UP rose the sun o'er moor and mead;
Up with the sun rose Percy Rede;
Brave Keeldar, from his couples freed,
  Career'd along the lea;
The palfrey sprung with sprightly bound,
As if to match the gamesome hound;
His horn the gallant huntsman wound:
  They were a jovial three!

Man, hound, or horse, of higher fame,
To wake the wild deer never came,
Since Alnwick's Earl pursued the game
  On Cheviot's rueful day;
Keeldar was matchless in his speed,
Than Tarras, ne'er was stauncher steed,
A peerless archer, Percy Rede,
  And right dear friends were they.

The chase engross'd their joys and woes,
Together at the dawn they rose,
Together shared the noon's repose,
  By fountain or by stream;
And oft, when evening skies were red,
The heather was their common bed,
Where each, as wildering fancy led,
  Still hunted in his dream.

Now is the thrilling moment near,
Of sylvan hope, and sylvan fear,
Yon thicket holds the harbor'd deer,
  The signs the hunters know; —
With eyes of flame, and quivering ears,
The brake sagacious Keeldar nears;
The restless palfrey paws and rears;
  The archer strings his bow.

The game's afoot! — Halloo! Halloo!
Hunter, and horse, and hound pursue: —
But woe the shaft that erring flew —
  That e'er it left the string!
And ill betide the faithless yew!
The stag bounds scathless o'er the dew,
And gallant Keeldar's life-blood true
  Has drench'd the gray goose wing.

The noble hound — he dies, he dies,
Death, death has glazed his fixed eyes,
Stiff on the bloody heath he lies,
  Without a groan or quiver.
Now day may break and bugle sound,
And whoop and halloo ring around,
And o'er his couch the stag may bound,
  But Keeldar sleeps forever.

Dilated nostrils, staring eyes,
Mark the poor palfrey's mute surprise,
He knows not that his comrade dies,
    Nor what is death — but still
His aspect hath expression drear
Of grief and wonder, mix'd with fear,
Like startled children when they hear
    Some mystic tale of ill.

But he that bent the fatal bow,
Can well the sun of evil know,
And o'er his favorite, bending low,
    In speechless grief recline;
Can think he hears the senseless clay
In unreproachful accents say : —
" The hand that took my life away,
    Dear master, was it thine?

" And if it be, the shaft be blest,
Which sure some erring aim addrest,
Since in your service prized, carest
    I in your service die;
And you may have a fleeter hound,
To match the dun-deer's merry bound,
But by your couch wilt ne'er be found
    So true a guard as I."

And to his last stout Percy rued
The fatal chance; for when he stood
'Gainst fearful odds in deadly feud,
    And fell amid the fray,
E'en with his dying voice he cried,
" Had Keeldar but been at my side,
Your treacherous ambush had been spied,
    I had not died to-day ! "

Remembrance of the erring bow
Long since had joined the tides which flow,
Conveying human bliss and woe
    Down dark oblivion's river;
But Art can Time's stern doom arrest,
And snatch his spoil from Lethe's breast,
And, in her Cooper's colors drest,
    The scene shall live forever.

MOTTO FROM "MY AUNT MARGARET'S MIRROR."

1828.

THERE are times
When Fancy plays her gambols, in despite
Even of our watchful senses, when in sooth
Substance seems shadow, shadow sub-
    stance seems,
When the broad, palpable, and mark'd
    partition,
'Twixt that which is and is not, seems
    dissolved,
As if the mental eye gain'd power to
    gaze
Beyond the limits of the existing world.
Such hours of shadowy dreams I better
    love
Than all the gross realities of life.

Anonymous.

MOTTOES.

FROM "THE FAIR MAID OF PERTH."

1828.

CHAP. I.

" BEHOLD the Tiber ! " the vain Roman
    cried,
Viewing the ample Tay from Baiglie's side;
But where's the Scot that would the
    vaunt repay,
And hail the puny Tiber for the Tay?

Anonymous.

CHAP. VIII.

Within the bounds of Annandale,
    The gentle Johnstones ride;
They have been there a thousand years,
    A thousand more they'll bide.

Old Ballad.

CHAP. XI.

Fair is the damsel, passing fair, —
    Sunny at distance gleams her smile;
Approach — the cloud of woeful care
    Hangs trembling in her eye the while.

Lucinda, a Ballad.

CHAP. XXXIII.

The hour is nigh: now hearts beat high;
    Each sword is sharpened well;
And who dares die, who stoops to fly,
    To-morrow's light shall tell.

Sir Edwald.

THE LAY OF POOR LOUISE.

1828.

AH, poor Louise ! The livelong day
She roams from cot to castle gay;
And still her voice and viol say,
Ah, maids, beware the woodland way,
    Think on Louise !

Ah, poor Louise! The sun was high,
It smirch'd her cheek, it dimm'd her eye.
The woodland walk was cool and nigh,
Where birds with chiming streamlets vie
        To cheer Louise.

Ah, poor Louise! The savage bear
Made ne'er that lovely grove his lair;
The wolves molest not paths so fair —
But better far had such been there
        For poor Louise.

Ah, poor Louise! In woody wold
She met a huntsman fair and bold;
His baldric was of silk and gold,
And many a witching tale he told
        To poor Louise.

Ah, poor Louise! Small cause to pine
Hast thou for treasures of the mine;
For peace of mind, that gift divine,
And spotless innocence, were thine,
        Ah, poor Louise!

Ah, poor Louise! Thy treasure's reft!
I know not if by force or theft,
Or part by violence, part by gift;
But misery is all that's left
        To poor Louise.

Let poor Louise some succor have!
She will not long your bounty crave,
Or tire the gay with warning stave —
For Heaven has grace, and earth a grave
        For poor Louise.
Fair Maid of Perth, chap. x.

OLIVER PROUDFUTE'S GLEE.
1828.

My dog and I we have a trick
To visit maids when they are sick;
When they are sick and like to die,
O thither do come my dog and I!

And when I die, as needs must hap,
Then bury me under the good ale-tap;
With folded hands there let me lie,
Cheek for jowl, my dog and I.
Fair Maid of Perth, chap. xvi.

CHANT OVER THE DEAD.
1828.

Viewless Essence, thin and bare,
Well-nigh melted into air;
Still with fondness hovering near
The earthly form thou once didst wear.

Pause upon thy pinion's flight,
Be thy course to left or right;
Be thou doom'd to soar or sink,
Pause upon the awful brink.

To avenge the deed expelling
Thee untimely from thy dwelling,
Mystic force thou shalt retain
O'er the blood and o'er the brain.

When the form thou shalt espy
That darken'd on thy closing eye,
When the footstep thou shalt hear,
That thrill'd upon thy dying ear;

Then strange sympathies shall wake,
The flesh shall thrill, the nerves shall
    quake;
The wounds renew their clotter'd flood,
And every drop cry blood for blood.
Fair Maid of Perth, chap. xxii.

A DIRGE.
1828.

Yes, thou mayst sigh,
And look once more at all around,
At stream and bank, and sky and ground.
Thy life its final course has found,
    And thou must die.

Yes, lay thee down,
And while thy struggling pulses flutter,
Bid the gray monk his soul mass mutter,
And the deep bell its death-tone utter —
    Thy life is gone.

Be not afraid.
'Tis but a pang, and then a thrill,
A fever fit, and then a chill;
And then an end of human ill,
    For thou art dead.
Fair Maid of Perth, chap. xxx.

VERSE FROM SCOTT'S JOURNAL.

1828.

ON THE COLNE.

For the Colne
Is black and swollen.
 Snake-like he winds his way,
Unlike the burns
From Highland urns
 That dance by crag and brae.

GLENGARRY'S DEATH–SONG.*

1828.

Land of the Gael, thy glory has flown!
For the star of the North from its orbit
 is thrown;
Dark, dark is thy sorrow, and hopeless
 thy pain,
For no star e'er shall beam with its lustre
 again.
 Glengarry — Glengarry is gone evermore,
 Glengarry — Glengarry we'll ever deplore.

O tell of the warrior who never did yield,
O tell of the chief who was falchion and
 shield,
O think of the patriot, most ardent and
 kind;
Then sigh for Glengarry, in whom all
 were joined.

The chieftains may gather — the combatants call,
One champion is absent — that champion
 was all;
The bright eye of genius and valor may
 flame,
But who now shall light it to honor and
 fame.

* Miss Macdonell wrote from
 "Mavis Bank, Rothesay,
   on the *17th of April,* 1893: —
 "My father died in January, 1828, and my
mother came to Merchiston Castle, Edinburgh,
where she lived from May, 1828, to May, 1830.
It was there I first saw the "Death-Song," and
was told by mother that Sir Walter Scott had
written it and sent it to her. I believe she got it
soon after we all came South in May 1828, and
has always been in whatever houses we lived
ever since."

See the light bark how toss'd! she's
 wreck'd on the wave!
See dauntless Glengarry on the verge of
 the grave!
See his leap — see that gash, and that eye
 now so dim!
And thy heart must be steel'd, if it bleed
 not for him.

Arise, thou young branch of so noble a
 stem,
Obscurity marks not the worth of a gem;
O hear the last wish of thy father for thee:
" Be all to thy country, Glengarry should
 be."

Why sounds the loud pibroch, why tolls
 the death bell,
Why crowd our bold clansmen to Garry's
 green vale?
'Tis to mourn for their chief — for Glengarry the brave,
Tis to tell that a hero is laid in his grave.

O! heard ye that anthem, slow, pealing
 on high!
The shades of the valiant are come from
 the sky,
And the Genii of Gaeldoch are first in
 the throng,
O list to the theme of their aerial song.

It's " Welcome Glengarry, thy clansmen's fast friend."
It's " Welcome to joys that shall nc'er
 have an end,
The halls of great Odin are open to thee,
O welcome Glengarry, the gallant and
 free."

THE SECRET TRIBUNAL.

1829.

The Initiated.

Measurers of good and evil,
Bring the square, the line, the level, —
Rear the altar, dig the trench,
Blood both stone and ditch shall drench
Cubits six, from end to end,
Must the fatal bench extend, —
Cubits six, from side to side,
Judge and culprit must divide.

On the east the Court assembles,
On the west the Accused trembles —
Answer, brethren, all and one,
Is the ritual rightly done?

Answer.

On life and soul, on blood and bone,
One for all, and all for one,
We warrant this is rightly done.

Judges.

How wears the night? — Doth morning shine
In early radiance on the Rhine?
What music floats upon his tide?
Do birds the tardy morning chide?
Brethren, look out from hill and height,
And answer true, How wears the night?

Answer.

The night is old; on Rhine's broad breast
Glance drowsy stars which long to rest.
    No beams are twinkling in the east.
There is a voice upon the flood,
The stern still call of blood for blood:
    'Tis time we listen the behest.

Chorus.

Up, then, up! When day's at rest,
    'Tis time that such as we are watchers:
Rise to judgment, brethren, rise!
Vengeance knows not sleepy eyes,
    He and night are matchers.
        Anne of Geierstein, chap. xx.

MOTTOES.

FROM ANNE OF GEIERSTEIN.

1829.

CHAP. V.

I WAS one
Who loved the greenwood bank and lowing herd,
The russet prize, the lowly peasant's life,
Season'd with sweet content, more than the halls
Where revellers feast to fever-height. Believe me,
There ne'er was poison mixt in maple bowl.
            Anonymous.

CHAP. VIII.

They saw that city welcoming the Rhine
As from his mountain heritage he burst
As purposed proud Orgetorix of yore,
Leaving the desert region of the hills,
To lord it o'er the fertile plains of Gaul.
            Helvetia.

CHAP. X.

We know not when we sleep nor when we wake.
Visions distinct and perfect cross our eye
Which to the slumberer seem realities;
And while they waked, some men have seen such sights
As set at naught the evidence of sense,
And left them well persuaded they were dreaming.
            Anonymous.

CHAP. XI.

These be the adept's doctrines — every element
Is peopled with its separate race of spirits.
The airy Sylphs on the blue ether float,
Deep in the earthy cavern skulks the Gnome;
The sea-green Naiad skims the ocean billow,
And the fierce fire is yet a friendly home
To its peculiar sprite — the Salamander.
            Anonymous.

CHAP. XXII.

Tell me not of it — I could ne'er abide
The mummery of all that forced civility.
" Pray, seat yourself, my lord," with cringing hams
The speech is spoken, and, with bended knee,
Heard by the smiling courtier. — " Before you, sir?
It must be on the earth then." Hang them all!
The pride which cloaks itself in such poor fashion
Is scarcely fit to swell a beggar's bosom.
            Old Play.

CHAP. XXIX.

A mirthful man he was — the snows of age
Fell, but they did not chill him. Gaiety
Even in life's closing, touched his teeming brain

With such wild visions as the setting sun
Raises in front of some hoar glacier,
Painting the bleak ice with a thousand
    hues.
Old Play.

CHAP. XXX.

Ay, this is he who wears the wreath of bays
Wove by Apollo and the Sisters Nine,
Which Jove's dread lightning scathes not.
    He hath doft
The cumbrous helm of steel, and flung
    aside
The yet more galling diadem of gold:
While, with a leafy circlet round his brows,
He reigns the King of Lovers and of Poets.

CHAP. XXXI.

————— Want you a man
Experienced in the world and its affairs?
Here he is for your purpose. He's a monk.
He hath forsworn the world and all its
    work —
The rather that he knows it passing well,
Special the worst of it; for he's a monk.
Old Play.

CHAP. XXXIII.

Toll, toll the bell!
    Greatness is o'er,
The heart has broke,
    To ache no more;
An unsubstantial pageant all —
Drop o'er the scene the funeral pall.
Old Poem.

CHAP. XXXV.

————— Here's a weapon now,
Shall shake a conquering general in his
    tent,
A monarch on his throne, or reach a
    prelate,
However holy be his offices,
E'en while he serves the altar.
Old Play.

VERSES FROM SCOTT'S
JOURNAL.

1829.

LATE FRIENDSHIP.

No after friendships e'er can raise
The endearments of our early days.

ON THE CATASTROPHE TO "ANNE OF GEIERSTEIN."

It sticks like a pistol half out of its holster,
Or rather indeed like an obstinate bolster,
Which I think I have seen you attempt-
    ing, my dear,
In vain to cram into a small pillow-beer.

JOY AND WEALTH.

Give me the joy that sickens not the heart,
Give me the wealth that has no wings to fly.

A MORAL.

So there ends the tale
  With a hey, with a hoy,
So there ends the tale
    With a ho!
There is a moral. If you fail
  To seize it by the tale,
Its import will exhale,
    You must know.

ON FAILING TO HEAR MADAME CA-RADORI SING JOCK OF HAZELDEAN.

However, Madame Caradori,
To miss you I am very sorry;
I should have taken it for glory
To have heard you sing my Border story.

LOCALITIES AT BLAIR-ADAM.

Lochornie and Lochornie Moss,
The Louting Stane and Dodgell's Cross,
Craigen Cat and Craigen Crow,
Craiggaveral, the King's Cross, and Dun-
    glow.

INSCRIPTION

FOR THE MONUMENT OF THE REV.
GEORGE SCOTT.

1830.

To youth, to age, alike, this tablet pale
Tells the brief moral of its tragic tale.
Art thou a parent? — Reverence this bier —
The parents' fondest hopes lie buried here.

Art thou a youth, prepared on life to start,
With opening talents and a generous heart,
Fair hopes and flattering prospects all
  thine own?
Lo! here their end — a monumental stone!
But let submission tame each sorrowing
  thought,
Heaven crown'd its champion ere the
  fight was fought.

THE FORAY.

1830.

The last of our steers on our board has
  been spread,
And the last flask of wine in our goblet
  is red;
Up! up, my brave kinsmen! belt swords,
  and begone! —
There are dangers to dare, and there's
  spoil to be won.

The eyes, that so lately mixt glances with
  ours,
For a space must be dim, as they gaze
  from the towers,
And strive to distinguish, thro' tempest
  and gloom,
The prance of the steed, and the toss of
  the plume.

The rain is descending, the wind rises
  loud,
And the moon her red beacon has veil'd
  with a cloud;
'Tis the better, my mates! for the warder's
  dull eye
Shall in confidence slumber, nor dream
  we are nigh.

Our steeds are impatient! I hear my
  blithe Gray!
There is life in his hoof-clang, and hope
  in his neigh;
Like the flash of a meteor, the glance of
  his mane
Shall marshal your march thro' the darkness and rain.

The drawbridge has dropped, the bugle
  has blown;
One pledge is to quaff yet — then mount
  and begone! —

To their honor and peace, that shall res
  with the slain!
To their health and their glee, that se
  Teviot again!

MOTTOES.

FROM "COUNT ROBERT OF PARIS."

1831.

CHAP. II.

Othus. —— This superb successor
Of the earth's mistress, as thou vainly
  speakest,
Stands midst these ages as, on the wide
  ocean,
The last spared fragment of a spacious
  land,
That in some grand and awful ministration
Of mighty nature has engulfed been,
Doth lift aloft its dark and rocky cliffs
O'er the wild waste around, and sadly
  frowns
In lonely majesty.

  Constantine Paleologus, scene i.

CHAP. III.

Here, youth, thy foot unbrace,
  Here, youth, thy brow unbraid,
Each tribute that may grace
  The threshold here be paid.
Walk with the stealthy pace
  Which Nature teaches deer,
When, echoing in the chase,
  The hunter's horn they hear.

  The Court.

CHAP. V.

The storm increases — 'tis no sunny
  shower,
Fostered in the moist breast of March o
  April,
Or such as parched Summer cools his lip
  with;
Heaven's windows are flung wide; the
  inmost deeps
Call in hoarse greeting one upon another;
On comes the flood in all its foaming
  horrors,
And where's the dike shall stop it?

  The Deluge, a Poem.

CHAP. VI.

Vain man, thou may'st esteem thy love
    as fair
As fond hyperboles suffice to raise.
She may be all that's matchless in her
    person,
And all-divine in soul to match her body;
But take this from me — thou shalt never
    call her
Superior to her sex, while *one* survives,
And I am her true votary.

Old Play.

CHAP. IX.

Between the foaming jaws of the white
    torrent,
The skilful artist draws a sudden mound;
By level long he subdivides their strength,
Stealing the waters from their rocky
    bed,
First to diminish what he means to con-
    quer;
Then, for the residue he forms a road,
Easy to keep, and painful to desert,
And guiding to the end the planner aim'd
    at.

The Engineer.

CHAP. X.

These were wild times — the antipodes
    of ours:
Ladies were there, who oftener saw them-
    selves
In the broad lustre of a foeman's shield
Than in a mirror, and who rather sought
To match themselves in battle than in
    dalliance
To meet a lover's onset. — But though
    Nature
Was outraged thus, she was not over-
    come.

Feudal Times.

CHAP. XI.

Without a ruin, broken, tangled, cum-
    brous,
Within it was a little paradise,
Where Taste had made her dwelling
    Statuary,
First-born of human art, moulded her
    images,
And bade men mark and worship.

Anonymous.

CHAP. XII.

The parties met.   The wily, wordy Greek,
Weighing each word, and canvassing each
    syllable;
Evading, arguing, equivocating.
And the stern Frank came with his two-
    hand sword,
Watching to see which way the balance
    sways,
That he may throw it in, and turn the
    scales.

Palestine.

CHAP. XVI.

Strange ape of man! who loathes thee
    while he scorns thee;
Half a reproach to us and half a jest.
What fancies can be ours ere we have
    pleasure
In viewing our own form, our pride and
    passions,
Reflected in a shape grotesque as thine!

Anonymous.

CHAP. XVII.

'Tis strange that, in the dark sulphureous
    mine,
Where wild ambition piles its ripening
    stores
Of slumbering thunder, Love will inter-
    pose
His tiny torch, and cause the stern ex-
    plosion
To burst, when the deviser's least aware.

Anonymous.

CHAP. XX.

She comes! she comes! in all the charms
    of youth,
Unequall'd love, and unsuspected truth.

CHAP. XXIV.

All is prepared — the chambers of the
    mine
Are crammed with the combustible,
    which, harmless
While yet unkindled, as the sable sand,
Needs but a spark to change its nature so,
That he who wakes it from its slumbrous
    mood,
Dreads scarce the explosion less than he
    who knows
That 'tis his towers which meet its fury.

Anonymous.

CHAP. XXV.

Heaven knows its time; the bullet has
    its billet,
Arrow and javelin each its destined pur-
    pose;
The fated beasts of Nature's lower strain
Have each their separate task.
Old Play.

CHAP. XXVI.

Will you hear of a Spanish Lady,
    How she woo'd an Englishman?
Garments gay, as rich as may be,
    Deck'd with jewels, she had on.
Of a comely countenance and grace was
    she,
And birth and parentage of high degree.
Old Ballad.

MOTTOES.

FROM "CASTLE DANGEROUS."

1831.

CHAP. V.

A TALE of sorrow, for your eyes may weep;
A tale of horror, for your flesh may tingle;
A tale of wonder, for the eyebrows arch,
And the flesh curdles if you read it rightly.
Old Play.

CHAP. XI.

Where is he? Has the deep earth swal-
    lowed him?
Or hath he melted like some airy phantom
That shuns the approach of morn and the
    young sun?
Or hath he wrapped him in Cimmerian
    darkness,
And pass'd beyond the circuit of the sight
With things of the night's shadows?
Anonymous.

CHAP. XIV.

The way is long, my children, long an
    rough —
The moors are dreary, and the woods ar
    dark;
But he that creeps from cradle on t
    grave,
Unskill'd save in the velvet course o
    fortune,
Hath missed the discipline of nobl
    hearts.
Old Play.

CHAP. XVIII.

His talk was of another world — his bode
    ments
Strange, doubtful, and mysterious; thos
    who heard him
Listen'd as to a man in feverish dreams
Who speaks of other objects than th
    present,
And mutters like to him who sees
    vision.
Old Play.

CHAP. XX.

Cry the wild war-note, let the champior
    pass,
Do bravely each, and God defend th
    right;
Upon Saint Andrew thrice can they thu
    cry,
And thrice they shout on height,
And then marked them on the English
    men,
As I have told you right.
Saint George the bright, our ladies' knigh
To name they were full fain;
Our Englishmen they cried on height,
And thrice they shout again.
Old Ballad.

FRAGMENTS.

OF VERY EARLY DATE.

BOTHWELL CASTLE.

1799.

WHEN fruitful Clydesdale's apple bowers
  Are mellowing in the noon;
When sighs round Pembroke's ruin'd towers
  The sultry breath of June;

When Clyde, despite his sheltering wood,
  Must leave his channel dry;
And vainly o'er the limpid flood
  The angler guides his fly;

If chance by Bothwell's lovely braes
  A wanderer thou hast been,
Or hid thee from the summer's blaze
  In Blantyre's bowers of green,

Full where the copsewood opens wild
  Thy pilgrim step hath staid,
Where Bothwell's towers, in ruin piled,
  O'erlook the verdant glade;

And many a tale of love and fear
  Hath mingled with the scene —
Of Bothwell's banks that bloom'd so dear,
  And Bothwell's bonny Jean.

O, if with rugged minstrel lays
  Unsated be thy ear,
And thou of deeds of other days
  Another tale wilt hear, —

Then all beneath the spreading beech,
  Flung careless on the lea,
The Gothic muse the tale shall teach
  Of Bothwell's sisters three.

Wight Wallace stood on Deckmont head,
  He blew his bugle round,
Till the wild bull in Cadyow wood
  Has started at the sound.

St. George's cross, o'er Bothwell hung,
  Was waving far and wide,
And from the lofty turret flung
  Its crimson blaze on Clyde;

And rising at the bugle blast
  That mark'd the Scottish foe,
Old England's yeomen muster'd fast,
  And bent the Norman bow.

Tall in the midst Sir Aylmer rose,
  Proud Pembroke's Earl was he —
While —— * * * * * * * *

THE SHEPHERD'S TALE.

1799.

* * * * * * *

AND ne'er but once, my son, he says,
  Was yon sad cavern trod,
In persecution's iron days,
  When the land was left by God.

From Bewlie bog, with slaughter red,
  A wanderer hither drew,
And oft he stopt and turn'd his head,
  As by fits the night wind blew;

For trampling round by Cheviot edge
  Were heard the troopers keen,
And frequent from the Whitelaw ridge
  The death-shot flash'd between.

The moonbeams thro' the misty shower
　　On yon dark cavern fell;
Thro' the cloudy night the snow gleam'd
　　white,
　　Which sunbeam ne'er could quell.

" Yon cavern dark is rough and rude,
　　And cold its jaws of snow;
But more rough and rude are the men of
　　blood,
　　That hunt my life below.

" Yon spell-bound den, as the aged tell,
　　Was hewn by demon's hands;
But I had lourd * melle with the fiends
　　of hell,
　　Than with Clavers and his band."

He heard the deep-mouth'd bloodhound
　　bark,
　　He heard the horse's neigh,
He plunged him in the cavern dark,
　　And downward sped his way.

Now faintly down the winding path
　　Came the cry of the faulting hound,
And the mutter'd oath of balked wrath
　　Was lost in hollow sound.

He threw him on the flinted floor,
　　And held his breath for fear;
He rose and bitter cursed his foes,
　　As the sounds died on his ear: —

" O bare thine arm, thou battling Lord,
　　For Scotland's wandering band;
Dash from the oppressor's grasp the
　　sword,
　　And sweep him from the land !

" Forget not thou thy people's groans
　　From dark Dunnotter's tower,
Mixt with the sea-fowl's shrilly moans,
　　And ocean's bursting roar !

" O, in fell Clavers' hour of pride,
　　Even in his mightiest day,
As bold he strides through conquest's tide,
　　O stretch him on the clay !

" His widow and his little ones,
　　O may their tower of trust

* *Lourd: i.e.,* liefer — rather.

Remove its strong foundation stones,
　　And crush them in the dust ! " —

" Sweet prayers to me," a voice replied
　　" Thrice welcome guest of mine ! "
And glimmering on the cavern side,
　　A light was seen to shine.

An aged man, in amice brown,
　　Stood by the wanderer's side,
By powerful charm, a dead man's arm
　　The torch's light supplied.

From each stiff finger, stretch'd upright
　　Arose a ghastly flame,
That waved not in the blast of light
　　Which thro' the cavern came.

O, deadly blue was that taper's hue,
　　That flamed the cavern o'er;
But more deadly blue was the ghastly hue
　　Of his eyes who the taper bore.

He laid on his head a hand like lead,
　　As heavy, pale, and cold: —
" Vengeance be thine, thou guest of mine
　　If thy heart be firm and bold.

" But if faint thy heart, and caitiff fear
　　Thy recreant sinews know,
The mountain erne thy heart shall tear,
　　Thy nerves the hooded crow."

The wanderer raised him undismay'd: —
　　" My soul, by dangers steel'd,
Is stubborn as my border blade,
　　Which never knew to yield.

" And if thy power can speed the hour
　　Of vengeance on my foes,
Theirs be the fate, from bridge and gate
　　To feed the hooded crows."

The Brownie looked him in the face,
　　And his color fled with speed: —
" I fear me," quoth he, " uneath it will
　　be
　　To match thy word and deed.

" In ancient days when English bands
　　Sore ravaged Scotland fair,
The sword and shield of Scottish land
　　Was valiant Halbert Kerr.

' A warlock loved the warrior well,
  Sir Michael Scott by name,
And he sought for his sake a spell to make,
  Should the Southern foemen tame.

' ' Look, thou,' he said, ' from Cessford
    head,
  As the July sun sinks low,
And when glimmering white on Cheviot's
    height
  Thou shalt spy a wreath of snow,
The spell is complete which shall bring
    to thy feet
  The haughty Saxon foe.'

' For many a year wrought the wizard here,
  In Cheviot's bosom low,
Till the spell was complete, and in July's
    heat
  Appeared December's snow;
But Cessford's Halbert never came
  The wondrous cause to know.

' For years before in Bowden aisle
  The warrior's bones had lain,
And after short while, by female guile,
  Sir Michael Scott was slain.

' But me and my brethren in this cell
  His mighty charms retain, —
And he that can quell the powerful spell
  Shall o'er broad Scotland reign.''

He led him thro' an iron door
  And up a winding stair,
And in wild amaze did the wanderer gaze
  On the sight which opened there.

Thro' the gloomy night flashed ruddy light,
  A thousand torches glow;
The cave rose high, like the vaulted sky,
  O'er stalls in double row.

In every stall of that endless hall
  Stood a steed in barbing bright;
At the foot of each steed, all arm'd save
    the head,
  Lay stretch'd a stalwart knight.

In each mail'd hand was a naked brand;
  As they lay on the black bull's hide,
Each visage stern did upwards turn,
  With eyeballs fixt and wide.

A launcegay strong, full twelve ells long,
  By every warrior hung;
At each pommel there, for battle yare,
  A Jedwood ax was slung.

The casque hung near each cavalier;
  The plumes waved mournfully
At every tread which the wanderer made
  Thro' the hall of gramarye.

The ruddy beam of the torches' gleam
  That glared the warriors on,
Reflected light from armor bright,
  In noontide splendor shone.

And onward seen in lustre sheen,
  Still lengthening on the sight,
Thro' the boundless hall stood steeds in
    stall,
  And by each lay a sable knight.

Still as the dead lay each horseman dread,
  And moved nor limb nor tongue;
Each steed stood stiff as an earthfast cliff,
  Nor hoof nor bridle rung.

No sounds thro' all the spacious hall
  The deadly still divide,
Save where echoes aloof from the vaulted
    roof
  To the wanderer's step replied.

At length before his wondering eyes,
  On an iron column borne,
Of antique shape, and giant size,
  Appear'd a sword and horn.

" Now choose thee here," quoth his leader,
  " Thy venturous fortune try;
Thy woe and weal, thy boot and bale,
  In yon brand and bugle lie.''

To the fatal brand he mounted his hand,
  But his soul did quiver and quail:
The life-blood did start to his shuddering
    heart,
  And left him wan and pale.

The brand he forsook, and the horn he
    took
  To 'say a gentle sound;
But so wild a blast from the bugle brast,
  That the Cheviot rock'd around.

From Forth to Tees, from seas to seas,
  The awful bugle rung;
On Carlisle wall, and Berwick withal,
  To arms the warders sprung.

With clank and clang the cavern rang,
  The steeds did stamp and neigh;
And loud was the yell as each warrior fell
  Sterte up with whoop and cry.

" Woe, woe," they cried, " thou caitiff
    coward,
  That ever thou wert born !
Why drew ye not the knightly sword
  Before ye blew the horn ? "

The morning on the mountain shone,
  And on the bloody ground,
Hurl'd from the cave with shiver'd bone,
  The mangled wretch was found.

And still beneath the cavern dread,
  Among the glidders gray,
A shapeless stone with lichens spread,
  Marks where the wanderer lay.

*   *   *   *   *   *

CHEVIOT.
1799.

*   *   *   *   *   *

Go sit old Cheviot's crest below,
And pensive mark the lingering snow
  In all his scaurs abide,
And slow dissolving from the hill
In many a sightless, soundless rill,
  Feed sparkling Bowmont's tide.

Fair shines the stream by bank and lea,
As wimpling to the eastern sea
  She seeks Till's sullen bed,
Indenting deep the fatal plain,
Where Scotland's noblest, brave in vain,
  Around their monarch bled.

And westward hills on hills you see,
Even as old Ocean's mightiest sea
  Heaves high her waves of foam,
Dark and snow-ridged from Cutsfeld's
    wold
To the proud foot of Cheviot roll'd,
  Earth's mountain billows come.

*   *   *   *   *   *

THE PAGE'S SONG.
1799.

IT was a little naughty page,
    Ha ! ha !
Would catch a bird was clos'd in cage,
    Sa ! sa !
    Ha ! ha !
    Sa ! sa !

He seiz'd the cage, the latch did draw,
    Ha ! ha !
And in he thrust his knavish paw,
    Sa ! sa !
    Ha ! ha !
    Sa ! sa !

The bird dash'd out and gain'd the thorn,
    Ha ! ha !
And laugh'd the silly fool to scorn,
    Sa ! sa !
    Ha ! ha !
    Sa ! sa !

Goetz of Berlichingen, act iii. sc. xix.

THE REIVER'S WEDDING.
1802.

O WILL ye hear a myrthful bourd ?
  Or will ye hear of courtesie ?
Or will ye hear how a gallant lord
  Was wedded to a gay ladye ?

" Ca' out the kye," quo' the village herd
  As he stood on the knowe,
" Ca' this ane's nine and that ane's ten,
  And bauld Lord William's cow." —

" Ah ! by my sooth," quoth William then
  " And stands it that way now,
When knave and churl have nine and ten,
  That the lord has but his cow ?

" I swear by the light of the Michaelmas
    moon,
  And the might of Mary high,
And by the edge of my braidsword brown,
  They shall soon say Harden's kye."

He took a bugle frae his side,
  With names carv'd o'er and o'er —

Full many a chief of meikle pride
  That Border bugle bore —

He blew a note baith sharp and hie,
  Till rock and water rang around —
Threescore of moss-troopers and three
  Have mounted at that bugle sound.

The Michaelmas moon had enter'd then,
  And ere she wan the full,
We might see by her light in Harden
    Glen
  A bow o' kye and a bassen'd bull.

And loud and loud in Harden tower
  The quaigh gaed round wi' meikle glee;
For the English beef was brought in
    bower,
  And the English ale flow'd merrilie.

And mony a guest from Teviotside
  And Yarrow's Braes was there;
Was never a lord in Scotland wide
  That made more dainty fare.

They ate, they laugh'd, they sang, and
    quaff'd,
  Till naught on board was seen,
When knight and squire were boune to
    dine,
  But a spur of silver sheen.

Lord William has ta'en his berry brown
    steed —
  A sore shent man was he;
"Wait ye, my guests, a little speed —
  Weel feasted ye shall be."

He rode him down by Falsehope burn,
  His cousin dear to see,
With him to take a riding turn —
  Wat-draw-the-sword was he.

And when he came to Falsehope glen
  Beneath the trysting-tree,
On the smooth green was carved plain,
  "To Lochwood bound are we."

"O, if they be gane to dark Lochwood
  To drive the Warden's gear,
Betwixt our names, I ween, there's
    feud;
  I'll go and have my share:

"For little reck I for Johnstone's feud,
  The Warden though he be."
So Lord William is away to dark Loch-
    wood,
  With riders barely three.

The Warden's daughters in Lochwood
    sate,
  Were all both fair and gay,
All save the Lady Margaret,
  And she was wan and wae.

The sister, Jean, had a full fair skin,
  And Grace was bauld and braw;
But the leal-fast heart her breast within,
  It weel was worth them a'.

Her father's pranked her sisters twa
  With meikle joy and pride;
But Margaret maun seek Dundrennan's
    wa' —
  She ne'er can be a bride.

On spear and casque by gallants gent
  Her sisters' scarfs were borne,
But never at tilt or tournament
  Were Margaret's colors worn.

Her sisters rode to Thirlstane bower,
  But she was left at hame
To wander round the gloomy tower,
  And sigh young Harden's name.

"Of all the knights, the knight most fair,
  From Yarrow to the Tyne,"
Soft sigh'd the maid, "is Harden's heir,
  But ne'er can he be mine;

"Of all the maids, the foulest maid
  From Teviot to the Dee,
Ah!" sighing sad, that lady said,
  "Can ne'er young Harden's be."

She looked up the briery glen,
  And up the mossy brae,
And she saw a score of her father's men
  Yclad in the Johnstone gray.

O fast and fast they downwards sped
  The moss and briers among,
And in the midst the troopers led
  A shackled knight along.

*   *   *   *   *   *

DRAMATIC PIECES.

HALIDON HILL;

A DRAMATIC SKETCH FROM SCOTTISH HISTORY.

PREFACE.

THE subject is to be found in Scottish history; but not to overload so slight a publication with antiquarian research, or quotations from obscure chronicles, it may be sufficient to refer the reader to PINKERTON'S *History of Scotland*, vol. i. p. 72.

The Regent of the sketch is a character purely imaginary. The tradition of the Swinton family, which still survives in a lineal descent, and to which the author has the honor to be related, avers that the Swinton who fell at Homildon had slain Gordon's father; which seems sufficient ground for adopting that circumstance into the following dramatic sketch though it is rendered improbable by other authorities.

If any reader will take the trouble of looking at Froissart, Fordun, or other historians of the period, he will find that the character of the Lord of Swinton, for strength, courage and conduct, is by no means exaggerated.

ABBOTSFORD, 1822.   W. S.

DRAMATIS PERSONÆ.

SCOTTISH.

THE REGENT OF SCOTLAND.

GORDON,
SWINTON,
LENNOX,
SUTHERLAND,   *Scottish chiefs and*
ROSS,   *Nobles.*
MAXWELL,
JOHNSTON,
LINDESAY,

ADAM DE VIPONT, *a Knight Templar.*
THE PRIOR OF MAISON–DIEU.
REYNALD, *Swinton's Squire.*
HOB HATTELY, *a Border Moss-Trooper.*
Heralds.

ENGLISH.

KING EDWARD III.

CHANDOS,   *English and Norman*
PERCY,   *Nobles.*
RIBAUMONT,

THE ABBOT OF WALTHAMSTOW.

ACT I. — SCENE I.

The northern side of the eminence of Halidon. The back Scene represents the summit of the ascent, occupied by the Rear-guard of the Scottish army. Bodies of armed Men appear as advancing from different points, to join the main Body.

Enter DE VIPONT *and the* PRIOR OF MAISON–DIEU.

VIP.   No farther, Father — here I need no guidance —
I have already brought your peaceful step
Too near the verge of battle.
    PRI.   Fain would I see you join some Baron's banner,

544

Before I say farewell. The honor'd sword
That fought so well in Syria, should not
    wave
Amid the ignoble crowd.

Vip. Each spot is noble in a pitched
    field,
So that a man has room to fight and fall
    on't.
But I shall find out friends. 'Tis scarce
    twelve years
Since I left Scotland for the wars of Pa-
    lestine,
And then the flower of all the Scottish
    nobles
Were known to me; and I, in my degree,
Not all unknown to them.

Pri. Alas! there have been changes
    since that time!
The Royal Bruce, with Randolph, Doug-
    las, Grahame,
Then shook in field the banners which
    now moulder
Over their graves i' the chancel.

Vip. And thence comes it,
That while I look'd on many a well-known
    crest
And blazon'd shield, as hitherward we
    came,
The faces of the Barons who display'd
    them
Were all unknown to me. Brave youths
    they seem'd;
Yet, surely, fitter to adorn the tilt-yard,
Than to be leaders of a war. Their fol-
    lowers,
Young like themselves, seem like them-
    selves unpractised —
Look at their battle-rank.

Pri. I cannot gaze on't with undazzled
    eye,
So thick the rays dart back from shield
    and helmet,
And sword and battle-ax, and spear and
    pennon.
Sure, 'tis a gallant show! The Bruce
    himself
Hath often conquer'd at the head of
    fewer
And worse appointed followers.

Vip. Ay, but 'twas Bruce that led
    them. Reverend Father,
'Tis not the falchion's weight decides a
    combat;

It is the strong and skilful hand that
    wields it.
Ill fate, that we should lack the noble
    King,
And all his champions now! Time call'd
    them not,
For when I parted hence for Palestine,
The brows of most were free from grizzl'd
    hair.

Pri. Too true, alas! But well you
    know, in Scotland
Few hairs are silver'd underneath the
    helmet;
'Tis cowls like mine which hide them.
    'Mongst the laity,
War's the rash reaper, who thrusts in his
    sickle
Before the grain is white. In threescore
    years
And ten, which I have seen, I have out-
    lived
Well-nigh two generations of our nobles.
The race which holds yon summit is the
    third.

Vip. Thou mayst outlive them also.

Pri.   Heaven forfend!
My prayer shall be, that Heaven will
    close my eyes,
Before they look upon the wrath to come.

Vip. Retire, retire, good Father! —
    Pray for Scotland —
Think not on me. Here comes an ancient
    friend,
Brother in arms, with whom to-day I'll
    join me.
Back to your choir, assemble all your
    brotherhood,
And weary Heaven with prayers for
    victory.

Pri. Heaven's blessing rest with thee,
Champion of Heaven, and of thy suffer-
    ing country!

    [*Exit* Prior. Vipont *draws a
    little aside and lets down the
    beaver of his helmet.*

Enter Swinton, *followed by* Reynald
*and others, to whom he speaks as he
enters.*

Swi. Halt here, and plant my pennon,
    till the Regent
Assign our band its station in the host.

Rey. That must be by the Standard.

We have had
That right since good Saint David's reign
at least.
Fain would I see the Marcher would dispute it.

Swi. Peace, Reynald! Where the
general plants the soldier,
There is his place of honor, and there only
His valor can win worship. Thou'rt of
those
Who would have war's deep art bear the
wild semblance
Of some disorder'd hunting, where, pell
mell,
Each trusting to the swiftness of his horse,
Gallants press on to see the quarry fall.
Yon steel-clad Southrons, Reynald, are
no deer;
And England's Edward is no stag at bay.

Vip. (*advancing*). There needed not,
to blazon forth the Swinton,
His ancient burgonet, the sable Boar
Chain'd to the gnarled oak, *— nor his
proud step,
Nor giant stature, nor the pondrous mace,
Which only he, of Scotland's realm, can
wield;
His discipline and wisdom mark the
leader,
As doth his frame the champion. Hail,
brave Swinton!

Swi. Brave Templar, thanks! Such
your cross'd shoulder speaks you;
But the closed visor, which conceals your
features,
Forbids more knowledge. Umfraville,
perhaps —

Vip. (*unclosing his helmet*). No; one
less worthy of our sacred Order.
Yet, unless Syrian suns have scorch'd
my features
Swart as my sable visor, Alan Swinton
Will welcome Symon Vipont.

Swi. (*embracing him*). As the blithe
reaper
Welcomes a practised mate, when the
ripe harvest

* "The armorial bearings of the ancient family
of Swinton are *sable*, a chevron, *or* between
three boars' heads erased *argent*. Crest, a boar
chained to a tree, and above, on a scroll, *J'espère*.
Supporters — two boars standing on a compart-
ment whereon are the words *Je pense*." — *Douglas's Baronage.*

Lies deep before him, and the sun is high
Thou'lt follow yon old pennon, wilt thou
not?
'Tis tatter'd since thou saw'st it, and the
Boar-heads
Look as if brought from off some Christ-
mas board,
Where knives had notch'd them deeply.

Vip. Have with them, ne'ertheless
The Stuart's Chequer,
The bloody Heart of Douglas, Ross's
Lymphads,
Sutherland's Wild-cats, nor the royal
Lion,
Rampant in golden treasure, wins me
from them.
We'll back the Boar-heads bravely. I
see round them
A chosen band of lances — some well
known to me.
Where's the main body of thy followers?

Swi. Symon de Vipont, thou dost
see them all
That Swinton's bugle-horn can call to
battle,
However loud it rings. There's not a
boy
Left in my halls, whose arm has strength
enough
To bear a sword — there's not a man
behind,
However old, who moves without a staff.
Striplings and graybeards, every one is
here,
And here all should be — Scotland needs
them all,
And more and better men, were each a
Hercules,
And yonder handful centupled.

Vip. A thousand followers — such
with friends and kinsmen,
Allies and vassals, thou wert wont to
lead —
A thousand followers shrunk to sixty
lances
In twelve years' space? — And thy brave
sons, Sir Alan?
Alas! I fear to ask.

Swi. All slain, De Vipont. In my
empty home
A puny babe lisps to a widow'd mother: —
"Where is my grandsire? wherefore do
you weep?"

But for that prattler, Lyulph's house is
heirless.
I'm an old oak, from which the foresters
Have hew'd four goodly boughs, and
left beside me
Only a sapling which the fawn may crush
As he springs over it.

Vip. All slain? — alas!

Swi. Ay, all, De Vipont. And their
attributes,
John with the Long Spear — Archibald
with the Ax —
Richard the Ready — and my youngest
darling,
My Fair-hair'd William — do but now
survive
In measures which the gray-hair'd minstrels sing
When they make maidens weep.

Vip. These wars with England they
have rooted out
The flowers of Christendom. Knights,
who might win
The sepulchre of Christ from the rude
heathen,
Fall in unholy warfare!

Swi. Unholy warfare? ay, well hast
thou named it;
But not with England — would her cloth-
yard shafts
Had bored their cuirasses! Their lives
had been
Lost like their grandsire's, in the bold
defence
Of their dear country; — but in private feud
With the proud Gordon, fell my Long-
spear'd John,
He with the Ax, and he men call'd the
Ready,
Ay, and my fair-hair'd Will — the Gor-
don's wrath
Devour'd my gallant issue.

Vip. Since thou dost weep, their death
is unavenged?

Swi. Templar, what think'st thou me?
— See yonder rock,
From which the fountain gushes — is it less
Compact of adamant, tho' waters flow
from it?
Firm hearts have moister eyes. — They
are avenged;
Wept not till they were — till the proud
Gordon

Had with his life-blood dyed my father's
sword,
In guerdon that he thinn'd my father's
lineage,
And then I wept my sons; and, as the
Gordon
Lay at my feet, there was a tear for him,
Which mingled with the rest. We had
been friends,
Had shared the banquet and the chase
together,
Fought side by side, — and our first cause
of strife,
Woe to the pride of both, was but a light
one!

Vip. You are at feud, then, with the
mighty Gordon?

Swi. At deadly feud. Here in this
Borderland,
Where the sire's quarrels descend upon
the son,
As due a part of his inheritance,
As the strong castle and the ancient blazon,
Where private Vengeance holds the scales
of justice,   [lously
Weighing each drop of blood as scrupu-
As Jews or Lombards balance silver pence,
Not in this land, 'twixt Solway and Saint
Abb's,
Rages a bitterer feud than mine and theirs,
The Swinton and the Gordon.

Vip. You, with some threescore lances
— and the Gordon
Leading a thousand followers.

Swi. You rate him far too low. Since
you sought Palestine,
He hath had grants of baronies and lord-
ships
In the far-distant North. A thousand horse
His southern friends and vassals always
number'd.
Add Badenoch kerne, and horse from
Dey and Spey,
He'll count a thousand more. — And
now, De Vipont,
If the Boar-heads seem in your eyes less
worthy
For lack of followers — seek yonder stand-
ard —
The bounding Stag, with a brave host
around it;
There the young Gordon makes his earli-
est field.

And pants to win his spurs.   His father's
    friend,
As well as mine, thou wert — go, join his
    pennon,
And grace him with thy presence.
    VIP.   When you were friends, I was the
    friend of both,
And now I can be enemy to neither;
But my poor person, tho' but slight the
    aid,
Joins on this field the banner of the two
Which hath the smallest following.
    SWI.   Spoke like the generous Knight,
    who gave up all,
Leading and lordship, in a heathen land
To fight, a Christian soldier!   Yet, in
    earnest,
I pray, De Vipont, you would join the
    Gordon
In this high battle.   'Tis a noble youth, —
So fame doth vouch him, — amorous,
    quick, and valiant;
Takes knighthood, too, this day, and
    well may use
His spurs too rashly in the wish to win
    them.
A friend like thee beside him in the fight,
Were worth a hundred spears, to rein his
    valor
And temper it with prudence: — 'tis the
    aged eagle
Teaches his brood to gaze upon the sun,
With eye undazzled.
    VIP.   Alas! brave Swinton!   Would'st
    thou train the hunter
That soon must bring thee to the bay?
    Your custom,
Your most unchristian, savage, fiend-like
    custom,
Binds Gordon to avenge his father's
    death.
    SWI.   Why, be it so!   I look for noth-
    ing else;
My part was acted when I slew his father,
Avenging my four sons. — Young Gor-
    don's sword,
If it should find my heart, can ne'er
    inflict there
A pang so poignant as his father's did.
But I would perish by a noble hand,
And such will his be if he bear him
    nobly,
Nobly and wisely on this field of Halidon.

Enter a PURSUIVANT.

    PUR.   Sir Knights, to council! — 'ti
    the Regent's order,
That knights and men of leading mee
    him instantly
Before the royal standard.   Edward's arm
Is seen from the hill summit.
    SWI.   Say to the Regent, we obey hi
    orders.   [*Exit* PURSUIVANT
    [*To* REYNALD.]   Hold thou my casque
    and furl my pennon up
Close to the staff.   I will not show m
    crest,
Nor standard, till the common foe sha
    challenge them.
I'll wake no civil strife, nor tempt th
    Gordon
With aught that's like defiance.
    VIP.   Will he not know your features
    SWI.   He never saw me.   In the di
    tant North,
Against his will, 'tis said, his friends de
    tain'd him
During his nurture — caring not, belike
To trust a pledge so precious near th
    Boar-tusks.
It was a natural but needless caution;
I wage no war with children, for I thin
Too deeply on mine own.
    VIP.   I have thought on it, and will se
    the Gordon
As we go hence to council.   I do bear
A cross, which binds me to be Christia
    priest
As well as Christian champion.   Go
    may grant
That I, at once his father's friend an
    yours,
May make some peace betwixt you.
    SWI.   When that your priestly zeal an
    knightly valor
Shall force the grave to render up t
    dead.   [*Exeunt several*

SCENE II.

The summit of Halidon Hill, before
   Regent's tent.   The royal standard
   Scotland is seen in the backgroun
   with the Pennons and Banners of
   principal Nobles around it.
Council of Scottish Nobles and Chie
   SUTHERLAND, ROSS, LENNOX, MA
   WELL, *and other nobles of the high*

rank, are close to the REGENT'S *person, and in the act of keen debate.* VIPONT *with* GORDON *and others remain grouped at some distance on the right hand of the Stage. On the left, standing also apart, is* SWINTON, *alone and bareheaded. The Nobles are dressed in Highland or Lowland habits, as historical costume requires. Trumpets, Heralds, etc., are in attendance.*

LEN. Nay, Lordings, put no shame
  upon my counsels.
I did but say, if we retired a little,
We should have fairer field and better
  vantage.
I've seen King Robert — ay, the Bruce
  himself —
Retreat six leagues in length, and think
  no shame on't.
  REG. Ay, but King Edward sent a
  haughty message,
Defying us to battle on this field,
This very hill of Halidon; if we leave
  it
Unfought withal, it squares not with our
  honor.
  SWI. (*apart*). A perilous honor that
  allows the enemy,
And such an enemy as this same Edward,
To choose our field of battle! He knows
  how
To make our Scottish pride betray its
  master
Into the pitfall.

[*During this speech the debate among
the Nobles is continued.*]

  SUTH. (*aloud*). We will not back one
  furlong — not one yard,
No, nor one inch; where'er we find the
  foe,
Or where the foe finds us, there will we
  fight him.
Retreat will dull the spirit of our followers,
Who now stand prompt for battle.
  ROSS. My Lords, methinks great Morarchat * has doubts,
That, if his Northern clans once turn the
  seam

Of their check'd hose behind, it will be
  hard
To halt and rally them.
  SUTH. Say'st thou, MacDonnell? —
  Add another falsehood,
And name when Morarchat was coward
  or traitor?
Thine island race, as chronicles can tell,
Were oft affianced to the Southron cause;
Loving the weight and temper of their
  gold,
More than the weight and temper of their
  steel.
  REG. Peace, my lords, ho.
  ROSS (*throwing down his glove*). Mac-
  Donnell will not peace! There lies my
  pledge,
Proud Morarchat, to witness thee a liar.
  MAX. Brought I all Nithsdale from the
  Western Border;
Left I my towers exposed to foraying
  England,
And thieving Annandale, to see such
  misrule?
  JOHNSTONE. Who speaks of Annan-
  dale?
Dare Maxwell slander
The gentle House of Lochwood? †
  REG. Peace, Lordings, once again.
  We represent
The Majesty of Scotland — in our presence
Brawling is treason.
  SUTH. Were it in presence of the King
  himself,
What should prevent my saying ——

Enter LINDESAY.

  LIN. You must determine quickly.
  Scarce a mile
Parts our vanguard from Edward's. On
  the plain
Bright gleams of armor flash thro' clouds
  of dust,
Like stars thro' frost-mist — steeds neigh,
  and weapons clash —
And arrows soon will whistle — the worst
  sound
That waits on English war. — You must
  determine.
  REG. We are determined. We will
  spare proud Edward

* Morarchate in the ancient Gaelic designa-
tion of the Earls of Sutherland.

† Lochwood Castle was the ancient seat of the
Johnstones, Lords of Annandale.

Half of the ground that parts us. — On-
ward, Lords;
Saint Andrew strike for Scotland! We
will lead
The middle ward ourselves, the Royal
Standard
Display'd beside us; and beneath its
shadow
Shall the young gallants, whom we knight
this day,
Fight for their golden spurs. — Lennox,
thou'rt wise,
And wilt obey command — lead thou the
rear.

   LEN. The rear? — why I the rear?
The van were fitter
For him who fought abreast with Robert
Bruce.

   SWI. (*apart*). Discretion hath for-
saken Lennox too!
The wisdom he was forty years in gathering
Has left him in an instant. 'Tis con-
tagious
Even to witness frenzy.

   SUTH. The Regent hath determined
well. The rear
Suits him the best who counsell'd our retreat.

   LEN. Proud Northern Thane, the van
were soon the rear,
Were thy disorder'd followers planted
there.

   SUTH. Then, for that very word I
make a vow,
By my broad Earldom and my father's
soul,
That, if I have not leading of the van,
I will not fight to-day!

   ROSS. Morarchat! thou the leading of
the van!
Not whilst MacDonnell lives.

   SWI. (*apart*). Nay, then a stone would
speak.
[*Addresses the* REGENT.] May't please
your Grace,
And you, great Lords, to hear an old
man's counsel,
That hath seen fights enow. These open
bickerings
Dishearten all our host. If that your
Grace
With these great Earls and Lords must
needs debate,

Let the closed tent conceal your disagree-
ment;
Else 'twill be said, ill fares it with the
flock,
If shepherds wrangle when the wolf is
nigh.

   REG. The old Knight counsels well
Let every Lord
Or Chief, who leads five hundred men
or more,
Follow to council — others are excluded—
We'll have no vulgar censurers of our
conduct — [*Looking at* SWINTON
Young Gordon, your high rank and nu-
merous following
Give you a seat with us, tho' yet un-
knighted.

   GORDON. I pray you, pardon me. My
youth's unfit
To sit in council, when that Knight's gray
hairs
And wisdom wait without.

   REG. Do as you will; we deign no
bid you twice.

[*The* REGENT, ROSS, SUTHERLAND,
LENNOX, MAXWELL, *etc.*, *enter t*
Tent. The rest remain groupe
about the Stage.

   GOR. (*observing* SWI). That helme
less old Knight, his giant stature,
His awful accents of rebuke and wisdom
Have caught my fancy strangely. He
doth seem
Like to some vision'd form which I hav
dream'd of,
But never saw with waking eyes till now
I will accost him.

   VIP. Pray you, do not so;
Anon I'll give you reason why you shou
not.
There's other work in hand ——

   GOR. I will but ask his name. There
in his presence
Something that works upon me like
spell,
Or like the feeling made my childish e
Dote upon tales of superstitious dread
Attracting while they chill'd my hea
with fear.
Now, born the Gordon, I do feel right w
I'm bound to fear naught earthly — a
I fear naught.

I'll know who this man is ——
[*Accosts* SWINTON.
Sir Knight, I pray you, of your gentle
courtesy,
To tell your honor'd name. I am ashamed,
Being unknown in arms, to say that mine
Is Adam Gordon.

SWINTON (*shows emotion, but instantly
subdues it*). It is a name that sound-
eth in my ear
Like to a death-knell — ay, and like the
call
Of the shrill trumpet to the mortal lists;
Yet, 'tis a name which ne'er hath been
dishonor'd.
And never will, I trust — most surely never
By such a youth as thou.

GOR. There's a mysterious courtesy in
this,
And yet it yields no answer to my question.
I trust you hold the Gordon not unworthy
To know the name he asks?

SWI. Worthy of all that openness and
honor
May show to friend or foe — but, for my
name,
Vipont will show it you; and, if it sounds
Harsh in your ear, remember that it
knells there
But at your own request. This day, at
least,
Tho' seldom wont to keep it in conceal-
ment,
As there's no cause I should, *you* had
not heard it.

GOR. This strange —

VIP. The mystery is needful. Follow
me. [*They retire behind the side
scene.*]

SWI. (*looking after them*). 'Tis a brave
youth. How blush'd his noble cheek,
While youthful modesty, and the embar-
rassment
Of curiosity, combined with wonder,
And half suspicion of some slight intended,
All mingled in the flush; but soon 'twill
deepen
Into revenge's glow. How slow is Vipont!
I wait the issue, as I've seen spectators
Suspend the motion even of the eyelids,
When the slow gunner, with his lighted
match,
Approach'd the charged cannon, in the act

To waken its dread slumbers. — Now 'tis
out;
He draws his sword, and rushes towards
me,
Who will not seek nor shun him.

Enter GORDON, *withheld by* VIPONT.

VIP. Hold, for the sake of Heaven! —
O, for the sake
Of your dear country, hold! — Has Swin-
ton slain your father,
And must you, therefore, be yourself a
parricide,
And stand recorded as the selfish traitor,
Who in her hour of need, his country's
cause
Deserts, that he may wreak a private
wrong?
Look to yon banner — that is Scotland's
standard;
Look to the Regent — he is Scotland's
general;
Look to the English — they are Scotland's
foemen!
Bethink thee, then, thou art a son of
Scotland,
And think on naught beside.

GOR. He hath come here to brave me
— Off! unhand me! —
Thou canst not be my father's ancient friend,
That stand'st 'twixt me and him who slew
my father.

VIP. You know not Swinton. Scarce
one passing thought
Of his high mind was with you; now, his
soul
Is fix'd on this day's battle. You might
slay him
At unawares, before he saw your blade
drawn, —
Stand still, and watch him close.

Enter MAXWELL *from the tent.*

SWI. How go our councils, Maxwell,
may I ask?

MAX. As wild, as if the very wind
and sea
With every breeze and every billow battled
For their precedence.

SWI. Most sure they are possess'd!
Some evil spirit,
To mock their valor, robs them of dis-
cretion.

Fie, fie upon 't!— O, that Dunfermline's
tomb
Could render up The Bruce! that Spain's
red shore
Could give us back the good Lord James
of Douglas!
Or that fierce Randolph, with his voice
of terror,
Were here, to awe these brawlers to submission!

Vip. (_to_ Gor). Thou hast perused him
at more leisure now.

Gor. I see the giant form which all
men speak of,
The stately port— but not the sullen eye,
Not the bloodthirsty look, that should
belong
To him that made me orphan. I shall
need
To name my father twice ere I can strike
At such gray hairs, and face of such com-
mand;
Yet my hand clenches on my falchion hilt,
In token he shall die.

Vip. Need I again remind you, that
the place
Permits not private quarrel?

Gor. I'm calm. I will not seek —
nay, I will shun it —
And yet methinks that such debate's the
fashion.
You've heard how taunts, reproaches,
and the lie,
The lie itself, have flown from mouth to
mouth;
As if a band of peasants were disputing
About a foot-ball match, rather than
Chiefs
Were ordering a battle. I am young,
And lack experience; tell me, brave De
Vipont,
Is such the fashion of your wars in Pales-
tine?

Vip. Such it at times hath been; and
then the Cross
Hath sunk before the Crescent. Heaven's
cause
Won us not victory where wisdom was
not. —
Behold yon English host come slowly on,
With equal front, rank marshall'd upon
rank,
As if one spirit ruled one moving body;

The leaders, in their places, each prepared
To charge, support, and rally, as the
fortune
Of changeful battle needs; then look on
ours,
Broken, disjointed, as the tumbling surges
Which the winds wake at random. Look
on both,
And dread the issue; yet there might be
succor.

Gor. We're fearfully o'ermatched in
discipline;
So even my inexperienced eye can judge.
What succor save in Heaven?

Vip. Heaven acts by human means.
The artist's skill
Supplies in war, as in mechanic crafts,
Deficiency of tools. There's courage,
wisdom,
And skill enough, live in one leader here,
As, flung into the balance, might avail
To counterpoise the odds 'twixt that ruled
host
And our wild multitude. — I must not
name him.

Gor. I guess, but dare not ask. —
What band is yonder,
Arranged as closely as the English dis-
cipline
Hath marshall'd their best files?

Vip. Know'st thou not the pennon?
One day, perhaps, thou'lt see it all too
closely; —
It is Sir Alan Swinton's.

Gor. These, then, are his, — the relics
of his power;
Yet worth an host of ordinary men. —
And I must slay my country's sagest
leader,
And crush by numbers that determined
handful,
When most my country needs their prac-
tised aid,
Or men will say, "There goes degenerate
Gordon;
His father's blood is on the Swinton's
sword,
And his is in his scabbard!" [_Muses._

Vip. (_apart_). High blood and mettle
Sparkle in this brave youth. If he surviv
This evil-omen'd day, I pawn my word
That, in the ruin which I now forebode

Scotland has treasure left. — How close
   he eyes
Each look and step of Swinton! Is it
   hate,
Or is it admiration, or are both
Commingled strangely in that steady gaze?

[Swinton *and* Maxwell *return
from the bottom of the stage.*

  Max. The storm is laid at length
   amongst these counsellors;
See, they come forth.
  Swi. And it is more than time;
For I can mark the vanguard archery
Handling their quivers — bending up their
   bows.

Enter the Regent *and Scottish Lords.*

  Reg. Thus shall it be, then, since we
   may no better;
And, since no Lord will yield one jot of
   way
To this high urgency, or give the vanguard
Up to another's guidance, we will abide
   them
Even on this bent; and as our troops are
   rank'd,
So shall they meet the foe. Chief, nor
   Thane,
Nor Noble, can complain of the preced-
   ence
Which chance has thus assign'd him.
  Swi. (*apart*). O, sage discipline,
That leaves to chance the marshalling of
   a battle !
  Gor. Move him to speech, De Vipont.
  Vip. Move *him !* — Move whom?
  Gor. Even him, whom, but brief space
   since,
My hand did burn to put to utter silence.
  Vip. I'll move it to him. — Swinton,
   speak to them,
They lack thy counsel sorely.
  Swi. Had I the thousand spears which
   once I led,
Had not thus been silent. But men's
   wisdom
Is rated by their means. From the poor
   leader
Of sixty lances, who seeks words of weight !
  Gor. (*steps forward*). Swinton, there's
   that of wisdom on thy brow,
And valor in thine eye, and that of peril

In this most urgent hour, that bids me
   say, —
Bids me, thy mortal foe, say, — Swinton,
   speak,
For King and Country's sake.
  Swi. Nay, if that voice commands me,
   speak I will;
It sounds as if the dead lays charge on me.
  Reg. (*to* Lennox, *with whom he has
   been consulting*). 'Tis better than
   you think. This broad hillside
Affords fair compass for our power's dis-
   play,
Rank above rank rising in seemly tiers;
So that the rearward stands as fair and
   open —
  Swi. As e'er stood mark before an
   English archer.
  Reg. Who dares to say so ? — Who
   is't dare impeach
Our rule of discipline ?
  Swi. A poor Knight of these Marches,
   good my Lord;
Alan of Swinton, who hath kept a house
   here,
He and his ancestry, since the old days
Of Malcolm, called the Maiden.
  Reg. You have brought here, even
   to this pitched field,
In which the Royal Banner is display'd,
I think some sixty spears, Sir Knight of
   Swinton;
Our musters name no more.
  Swi. I brought each man I had; and
   Chief, or Earl,
Thane, Duke, or dignitary, brings no
   more :
And with them brought I what may here
   be useful —
An aged eye; which, what in England,
   Scotland,
Spain, France, and Flanders, hath seen
   fifty battles,
And ta'en some judgment of them; a
   stark hand too,
Which plays as with a straw with this
   same mace, —
Which if a young arm here can wield
   more lightly,
I never more will offer word of counsel.
  Len. Hear him, my Lord; it is the
   noble Swinton —
He hath had high experience.

MAX.   He is noted
The wisest warrior 'twixt the Tweed and
    Solway, —
I do beseech you, hear him.
    JOHNSTONE. Ay, hear the Swinton —
    hear stout old Sir Alan;
Maxwell and Johnstone both agree for
    once.
    REG. Where's your impatience now?
Late you were all for battle, would not
    hear
Ourself pronounce a word — and now
    you gaze
On yon old warrior, in his antique armor,
As if he were arisen from the dead,
To bring us Bruce's counsel for the battle.
    SWI. 'Tis a proud word to speak; but
    he who fought
Long under Robert Bruce, may something
    guess,
Without communication with the dead,
At what he would have cousell'd. —
    Bruce had bidden ye
Review your battle-order, marshall'd
    broadly
Here on the bare hillside, and bidden
    you mark
Yon clouds of Southron archers, bearing
    down
To the green meadow-lands which stretch
    beneath; —
The Bruce had warn'd you, not a shaft
    to-day
But shall find mark within a Scottish
    bosom,
If thus our field be order'd. The callow
    boys,
Who draw but four-foot bows, shall gall
    our front,
While on our mainward, and upon the
    rear,
The cloth-yard shafts shall fall like death's
    own darts,
And, tho' blind men discharge them, find
    a mark.
Thus shall we die the death of slaughter'd
    deer,
Which, driven into the toils, are shot at
    ease
By boys and women, while they toss
    aloft
All idly and in vain their branchy horns,
As we shall shake our unavailing spears.

    REG. Tush, tell not me! if their shot
    fall like hail,
Our men have Milan coats to bear it out.
    SWI. Never did armorer temper steel
    on stithy
That made sure fence against an English
    arrow;
A cobweb gossamer were guard as good
Against a wasp-sting.
    REG. Who fears a wasp-sting ?
    SWI.   I, my Lord, fear none;
Yet should a wise man brush the insect
    off,
Or he may smart for it.
    REG. We'll keep the hill; it is the
    vantage ground
When the main battle joins.
    SWI. It ne'er will join, while their
    light archery
Can foil our spearmen and our barbed
    horse.
To hope Plantagenet would seek close
    combat
When he can conquer riskless, is to deem
Sagacious Edward simpler than a babe
In battle knowledge. Keep the hill, my
    Lord,
With the main body, if it is your pleasure;
But let a body of your chosen horse
Make execution on yon waspish archers
I've done such work before, and love it
    well;
If 'tis your pleasure to give me the leading
The dames of Sherwood, Inglewood, and
    Weardale,
Shall sit in widowhood and long for veni
    son,
And long in vain. Whoe'er remember
    Bannockburn, —
And when shall Scotsman, till the las
    loud trumpet,
Forget that stirring word ! — knows tha
    great battle
Even thus was fought and won.
    LEN. This is the shortest road t
    bandy blows;
For when the bills step forth and bow
    go back,
Then is the moment that our hardy spear
    men,
With their strong bodies, and their stub
    born hearts,
And limbs well knit by mountain exercise

At the close tug shall foil the short-
breath'd Southron.

Swi. I do not say the field will thus
be won;
The English host is numerous, brave, and
loyal;
Their Monarch most accomplish'd in war's
art,
Skill'd, resolute, and wary —

Reg. And if your scheme secure not
victory,
What does it promise us?

Swi.   This much at least, —
Darkling we shall not die: the peasant's
shaft,
Loosen'd perchance without an aim or
purpose,
Shall not drink up the life-blood we derive
From those famed ancestors, who made
their breasts
This frontier's barrier for a thousand
years.
We'll meet these Southron bravely hand
to hand,
And eye to eye, and weapon against
weapon;
Each man who falls shall see the foe who
strikes him.
While our good blades are faithful to the
hilts,
And our good hands to these good blades
are faithful,
Blow shall meet blow, and none fall un-
avenged
We shall not bleed alone.

Reg.   And this is all
Your wisdom hath devised ?

Swi. Not all; for I would pray you,
noble Lords,
(If one, among the guilty guiltiest,
might,)
For this one day to charm to ten hours'
rest
The never-dying worm of deadly feud,
The gnaws our vexed hearts — think no
one foe
Save Edward and his host : — days will
remain,
Ay, days by far too many will remain,
To avenge old feuds or struggle for pre-
cedence; —
Let this one day be Scotland's. — For
myself,

If there is any here may claim from me
(As well may chance) a debt of blood
and hatred,
My life is his to-morrow unresisting,
So he to-day will let me do the best
That my old arm may achieve for the
dear country
That's mother to us both.

> [Gordon *shows much emotion
> during this and the preceding
> speech of* Swinton.

Reg. It is a dream — a vision ! — if
one troop
Rush down upon the archers, all will
follow,
And order is destroy'd — we'll keep the
battle-rank
Our fathers wont to do.   No more on't.
— Ho !
Where be those youths seek knighthood
from our sword?

Her. Here are the Gordon, Somerville, and Hay,
And Hepburn, with a score of gallants
more.

Reg. Gordon, stand forth.

Gor.   I pray your Grace forgive me.

Reg. How ! seek you not for knighthood?

Gor.   I do thirst for't.
But, pardon me — 'tis from another sword.

Reg. It is your Sovereign's — seek you
for a worthier?

Gor. Who would drink purely, seeks
the secret fountain,
How small soever — not the general
stream,
Tho' it be deep and wide.   My lord, I seek
The boon of knighthood from the honor'd
weapon
Of the best knight, and of the sagest
leader,
That ever graced a ring of chivalry.
— Therefore, I beg the boon on bended
knee,
Even from Sir Alan Swinton.   [*Kneels.*

Reg. Degenerate boy !   Abject at once
and insolent ! —
See, Lords, he kneels to him that slew
his father !

Gor. (*starting up*). Shame be on him
who speaks such shameful word !

Shame be on him, whose tongue would
    sow dissension,
When most the time demands that native
    Scotsmen
Forget each private wrong!
    SWI. (*interrupting him*). Youth, since
      you crave me
To be your sire in chivalry, I remind you
War has its duties, Office has its reverence;
Who governs in the Sovereign's name is
    Sovereign;
Crave the Lord Regent's pardon.
    GOR. You task me justly, and I crave
      his pardon.   [*Bows to the* REGENT.
His and these noble Lords'; and pray
    them all
Bear witness to my words. — Ye noble
    presence,
Here I remit unto the Knight of Swin-
    ton
All bitter memory of my father's slaughter,
All thoughts of malice, hatred, and re-
    venge;
By no base fear or composition moved,
But by the thought, that in our country's
    battle
All hearts should be as one.   I do for-
    give him
As freely as I pray to be forgiven.
And once more kneel to him to sue for
    knighthood.
    SWI. (*affected and drawing his sword*).
Alas! brave youth, 'tis I should kneel to
    you,
And, tendering thee the hilt of the fell
    sword
That made thee fatherless, bid thee use
    the point
After thine own discretion.   For thy
    boon —
Trumpets, be ready— in the Holiest name
And in our Lady's and Saint Andrew's
    name,
    [*Touching his shoulder with his sword.*
I dub thee knight! — Arise, Sir Adam
    Gordon!
Be faithful, brave, and O, be fortunate,
Should this ill hour permit!

    [*The trumpets sound; the Heralds
      cry* "Largesse," *and the attend-
      ants shout* "A Gordon! A Gor-
      don!"

    REG. Beggars and flatterers!   Peace,
      peace, I say!
We'll to the Standard; knights shall there
    be made
Who will with better reason crave your
    clamor.
    LEN. What of Swinton's counsel?
Here's Maxwell and myself think it worth
    noting.
    REG. (*with concentrated indignation*).
Let the best knight, and let the sagest
    leader —
So Gordon quotes the man who slew his
    father, —
With his old pedigree and heavy mace,
Essay the adventure if it pleases him,
With his fair threescore horse.   As for
    ourselves,
We will not peril aught upon the measure.
    GOR. Lord Regent, you mistake; for
      if Sir Alan
Shall venture such attack, each man who
    calls
The Gordon Chief, and hopes or fears
    from him
Or good or evil, follows Swinton's banner
In this achievement.
    REG. Why, God ha' mercy!   This is
    of a piece.
Let young and old e'en follow their own
    counsel,
Since none will list to mine.
    ROSS. The Border cockerel fain would
    be on horseback;
'Tis safe to be prepared for fight or flight.
And this comes of it to give Northern
    lands
To the false Norman blood.
    GOR. Hearken, proud Chief of Isles!
      Within my stalls
I have two hundred horse; two hundred
    riders
Mount guard upon my castle, who would
    tread
Into the dust a thousand of your Red
    shanks,
Nor count it a day's service.
    SWI.   Hear I this
From thee, young man, and on the day
    of battle?
And to the brave MacDonnell?
    GOR. 'Twas he that urged me; but
    am rebuked.

REG. He crouches like a leash-hound
  to his master ! *

SWI. Each hound must do so that
  would head the deer —
'Tis mongrel curs that snatch at mate or
  master.

REG. Too much of this. Sirs, to the
  Royal Standard !
I bid you, in the name of good King
  David.
Sound trumpets — sound for Scotland and
  King David !

[*The* REGENT *and the rest go off,
  and the Scene closes. Manent*
  GORDON, SWINTON, *and* VI-
  PONT, *with* REYNALD *and followers.* LENNOX *follows the*
  REGENT; *but returns, and addresses* SWINTON.

LEN. O, were my western horsemen
  but come up,
I would take part with you !

SWI.   Better that you remain;
They lack discretion; such gray head as
  yours
May best supply that want.

Lennox, mine ancient friend, and honor'd
  lord,
Farewell, I think, forever !

LEN. Farewell, brave friend ! — and
  farewell, noble Gordon,
Whose sun will be eclipsed even as it
  rises ! —
The Regent will not aid you.

SWI. We will so bear us, that as soon
  the bloodhound
Shall halt, and take no part, what time
  his comrade
Is grappling with the deer, as he stand still,
And see us overmatch'd.

LEN. Alas ! thou dost not know how
  mean his pride is,
How strong his envy.

SWI. Then we will die, and leave the
  shame with him.   [*Exit* LENNOX.

VIP. (*to* GORDON). What ails thee,
  noble youth? What means this
  pause ?
Thou dost not rue thy generosity?

* The laws of chivalry demanded this submission to a father in chivalry.

GOR. I have been hurried on by strong
  impulse,
Like to a bark that scuds before the storm,
Till driven upon some strange and distant
  coast,
Which never pilot dream'd of. — Have
  I not forgiven?
And am I not still fatherless?

SWI.   Gordon, no;
For while we live I am a father to thee.

GOR. Thou, Swinton? — no ! — that
  cannot, cannot be.

SWI. Then change the phrase, and say,
  that while we live,
Gordon shall be my son. If thou art
  fatherless,
Am I not childless too? Bethink thee,
  Gordon,
Our death-feud was not like the house-
  hold fire,
Which the poor peasant hides among its
  embers,
To smoulder on, and wait a time for wak-
  ing.
Ours was the conflagration of the forest,
Which, in its fury, spares nor sprout nor
  stem,
Hoar oak, nor sapling — not to be extin-
  guish'd,
Till Heaven, in mercy, sends down all
  her waters;
But, once subdued, its flame is quench'd
  forever;
And spring shall hide the tract of devas-
  tation,
With foliage and with flowers. — Give
  me thy hand.

GOR. My hand and heart ! — And freely
  now ! — to fight !

VIP. How will you act? [*To* SWIN-
  TON.] The Gordon's band and thine
Are in the rearward left, I think, in
  scorn —
Ill post for them who wish to charge the
  foremost :

SWI. We'll turn the scorn to vantage,
  and descend
Sidelong the hill — some winding path
  there must be —
O, for a well-skill'd guide !

[HOB HATTELY *starts up from
  a thicket.*

Hob. So here he stands. — An ancient friend, Sir Alan.

Hob Hattely, or, if you like it better,
Hob of the Heron Plume, here stands your guide.

Swi. An ancient friend? — a most notorious knave,
Whose throat I've destin'd to the dodder'd oak
Before my castle, these ten months and more.
Was it not you who drove from Simprim-mains,
And Swinton-quarter, sixty head of cattle?

Hob. What then, if now I lead your sixty lances
Upon the English flank, where they'll find spoil
Is worth six hundred beeves?

Swi. Why, thou canst do it, knave.
I would not trust thee
With one poor bullock; yet would risk my life,
And all my followers, on thine honest guidance.

Hob. There is a dingle, and a most discreet one
(I've trod each step by starlight), that sweeps round
The rearward of this hill, and opens secretly
Upon the archers' flank. — Will not that serve
Your present turn, Sir Alan?

Swi.   Bravely, bravely!

Gor. Mount, sirs, and cry my slogan:
Let all who love the Gordon follow me!

Swi. Ay, let all follow — but in silence follow,
Scare not the hare that's couchant on her form —
The cushat from her nest — brush not, if possible,
The dew-drop from the spray —
Let no one whisper, until I cry, "Havoc!"
Then shout as loud's ye will. — On, on, brave Hob;
On, thou false thief, but yet most faithful Scotsman!

                                    [*Exeunt.*

ACT II. — Scene I.

A rising Ground immediately in front of the Position of the English Main Body. Percy, Chandos, Ribaumont, *and other English and Norman Nobles, are grouped on the Stage.*

Per. The Scots still keep the hill — the sun grows high;
Would that the charge would sound.

Cha. Thou scent'st the slaughter, Percy. — Who comes here?

(*Enter the* Abbot of Walthamstow.)

Now, by my life, the holy priest of Walthamstow,
Like to a lamb among a herd of wolves!
See, he's about to bleat.

Ab. The King, methinks, delays the onset long.

Cha. Your general, Father, like your rat-catcher,
Pauses to bait his traps, and set his snares.

Ab. The metaphor is decent.

Cha.   Reverend sir,
I will uphold it just. Our good King Edward
Will presently come to this battle-field,
And speak to you of the last tilting match,
Or of some feat he did a twenty years since;
But not a word of the day's work before him.
Even as the artist, sir, whose name offends you,
Sits prosing o'er his can, until the trap fall,
Announcing that the vermin are secured,
And then 'tis up, and on them.

Per. Chandos, you give your tongue too bold a license.

Cha. Percy, I am a necessary evil.
King Edward would not want me, if he could,
And could not, if he would. I know my value.
My heavy hand excuses my light tongue
So men wear weighty swords in their defence,
Although they may offend the tender shin
When the steel-boot is doff'd.

Ab.   My Lord of Chandos
This is but idle speech on brink of battle

When Christian men should think upon
  their sins;
For as the tree falls, so the trunk must
  lie,
Be it for good or evil. Lord, bethink
  thee,
Thou hast witheld from our most reverend
  house
The tithes of Everingham and Settleton;
Wilt thou make satisfaction to the Church,
Before her thunders strike thee? I do
  warn thee
In most paternal sort.
  CHA. I thank you, Father, filially;
Though but a truant son of Holy Church,
I would not choose to undergo her cen-
  sures,
When Scottish blades are waving at my
  throat.
I'll make fair composition.
  AB. No composition; I'll have all, or
  none.
  CHA. None, then — 'tis soonest spoke.
  I'll take my chance,
And trust my sinful soul to Heaven's
  mercy,
Rather than risk my worldly goods with
  thee —
My hour may not be come.
  AB. Impious — impenitent —
  PER. Hush! — the King — the King!

Enter KING EDWARD, *attended by*
  BALIOL *and others.*

  KING (*apart to* CHA.). Hark hither,
  Chandos! — Have the Yorkshire
  archers
Yet join'd the vanguard?
  CHA.   They are marching thither.
  K. ED. Bid them make haste, for
  shame — send a quick rider.
The loitering knaves! were it to steal my
  venison,
Their steps were light enough. — How
  now, Sir Abbot?
Say, is your reverence come to study
  with us
The princely art of war?
  AB. I've had a lecture from my Lord
  of Chandos,
In which he term'd your Grace a rat-
  catcher.
  K. ED. Chandos, how's this?

  CHA. O, I will prove it, Sir! — These
  skipping Scots
Have changed a dozen times 'twixt Bruce
  and Baliol,
Quitting each House when it began to
  totter;
They're fierce and cunning, treacherous,
  too, as rats,
And we, as such, will smoke them in
  their fastnesses.
  K. ED. These rats have seen your
  back, my Lord of Chandos,
And noble Percy's too.
  PER. Ay; but the mass which now lies
  weltering
On yon hill-side, like a Leviathan
That's stranded on the shallows, then
  had soul in't,
Order and discipline, and power of action.
Now 'tis a heedless corpse, which only
  shows,
By wild convulsions, that some life re-
  mains in't.
  K. ED. True, they had once a head;
  and 'twas a wise,
Altho' a rebel head.
  AB. (*bowing to the* KING). Would he
  were here! we should find one to
  match him.
  K. ED. There's something in that wish
  which wakes an echo
Within my bosom. Yet it is as well,
Or better, that the Bruce is in his grave.
We have enough of powerful foes on earth,
No need to summon them from other
  worlds.
  PER. Your Grace ne'er met the Bruce?
  K. ED. Never himself; but in my
  earliest field
I did encounter with his famous captains,
Douglas and Randolph. Faith! they
  press'd me hard.
  AB. My Liege, if I might urge you
  with a question,
Will the Scots fight to-day?
  K. ED. (*sharply*). Go look your bre-
  viary.
  CHA. (*apart*). The Abbot has it —
  Edward will not answer
On that nice point. We must observe
  his humor. — [*Addresses the* KING.]
Your first campaign, my Liege? — That
  was in Weardale,

When Douglas gave our camp yon mid-
    night ruffle,
And turn'd men's beds to biers.

    K. Ed. Ay, by Saint Edward! — I
escaped right nearly.
I was a soldier then for holidays,
And slept not in mine armor; my safe rest
Was startled by the cry of "Douglas!
    Douglas!"
And by my couch, a grisly chamberlain,
Stood Alan Swinton, with his bloody
    mace;
It was a churchman saved me — my stout
    chaplain,
Heaven quit his spirit! caught a weapon
    up,
And grappled with the giant. — How
    now, Louis!

Enter an Officer, who whispers the King.

    K. Ed. Say to him, — thus — and
thus —
                [*Whispers.*

    Ab. That Swinton's dead. A monk
of ours reported,
Bound homeward from St. Ninian's pil-
    grimage,
The Lord of Gordon slew him.

    Per. Father, and if your house stood
on our borders,
You might have cause to know that Swin-
    ton lives,
And is on horseback yet.

    Cha.   He slew the Gordon,
That's all the difference — a very trifle.

    Ab. Trifling to those who wage a war
more noble
Than with the arm of flesh.

    Cha. (*apart*). The Abbot's vex'd,
I'll rub the sore for him. —
(*Aloud*). I have seen priests that used
    that arm of flesh,
And used it sturdily. — Most reverend
    Father,
What say you to the chaplain's deed of
    arms
In the King's tent at Weardale?

    Ab. It was most sinful, being against
the canon
Prohibiting all churchmen to bear wea-
    pons;
And as he fell in that unseemly guise,
Perchance his soul may rue it.

    K. Ed. (*overhearing the last words*).
    Who may rue?
And what is to be rued?

    Cha. (*apart*). I'll match his Rever-
    ence for the tithes of Everingham.
— The Abbot says, my Liege, the deed
    was sinful,
By which your chaplain, wielding secular
    weapons,
Secured your Grace's life and liberty,
And that he suffers for 't in purgatory.

    K. Ed. (*to the* Abbot). Say'st thou
my chaplain is in purgatory?

    Ab. It is the canon speaks it, good my
Liege.

    K. Ed. In purgatory! thou shalt pray
him out on 't.
Or I will make thee wish thyself beside
    him.

    Ab. My Lord, perchance his soul is
past the aid
Of all the Church may do; — there is a
    place
From which there's no redemption.

    K. Ed. And if I thought my faithful
chaplain there,
Thou shouldst there join him, priest! —
    Go, watch, fast, pray.
And let me have such prayers as will
    storm Heaven —
None of your maim'd and mutter'd hunt-
    ing masses.

    Ab. (*apart to* Cha.). For God's sake
take him off.

    Cha. Wilt thou compound, then,
The tithes of Everingham?

    K. Ed. I tell thee, if thou bear'st the
keys of Heaven,
Abbot, thou shalt not turn a bolt with
    them
'Gainst any well-deserving English sub-
    ject.

    Ab. (*to* Cha.). We will compound and
grant thee, too, a share
I' the next indulgence. Thou dost need
    it much,
And greatly 'twill avail thee.

    Cha. Enough — we're friends, and
when occasion serves,
I will strike in. ——
        [*Looks as if towards the Scottish Army.*

    K. Ed. Answer, proud Abbot; is my
chaplain's soul,

If thou knowest aught on't, in the evil
  place?

CHA. My Liege, the Yorkshire men
  have gain'd the meadow.

I see the pennon green of merry Sherwood.

K. ED. Then give the signal instant!
  We have lost

But too much time already.

AB. My Liege, your holy chaplain's
  blessed soul —

K. ED. To hell with it and thee! Is
  this a time

To speak of monks and chaplains?

  [*Flourish of Trumpets answered
  by a distant sound of Bugles.*

See, Chandos, Percy— Ha, Saint George!
  Saint Edward!

See it descending now, the fatal hail-
  shower,

The storm of England's wrath — sure,
  swift, resistless,

Which no mail-coat can brook. — Brave
  English hearts!

How close they shoot together! — as one
  eye

Had aim'd five thousands shafts — as if
  one hand

Had loosed five thousand bow-strings!

PER.   The thick volley

Darkens the air, and hides the sun from
  us.

K. ED. It falls on those shall see the
  sun no more.

The winged, the resistless plague is with
  them.

How their vex'd host is reeling to and
  fro,

Like the chafed whale with fifty lances
  in him,

They do not see, and cannot shun the
  wound.

The storm is viewless as death's sable
  wing,

Unerring as his scythe.

PER. Horses and riders are going down
  together.

'Tis almost pity to see nobles fall,

And by a peasant's arrow.

BAL.   I could weep them,

Altho' they are my rebels.

CHA. (*aside to* PER.). His conquerors,
  he means, who cast him out

From his usurped kingdom. — (*Aloud.*)
  'Tis the worst of it,

That knights can claim small honor in
  the field

Which archers win, unaided by our
  lances.

K. ED. The battle is not ended.

  [*Looks towards the field.*

Not ended? — scarce begun! What
  horse are these,

Rush from the thicket underneath the hill?

PER. They're Hainaulters, the follow-
  lowers of Queen Isabel.

K. ED. (*hastily*). Hainaulters! — thou
  art blind — wear Hainaulters

Saint Andrew's silver cross? — or would
  they charge

Full on our archers, and make havoc of
  them? —

Bruce is alive again — ho, rescue!
  rescue! —

Who was't survey'd the ground?

RIBA. Most loyal Liege —

K. ED. A rose hath fallen from thy
  chaplet,* Ribaumont.

RIBA. I'll win it back, or lay my head
  beside it.   [*Exit.*

K. ED. Saint George! Saint Edward!
  Gentlemen, to horse,

And to the rescue! — Percy, lead the
  billmen;

Chandos, do thou bring up the men-at-
  arms. —

If yonder numerous host should now bear
  down

Bold as their vanguard (*to the* ABBOT),
  thou mayst pray for us,

We may need good men's prayers. —
  To the rescue,

Lords, to the rescue! ha, Saint George!
  Saint Edward!   [*Exeunt.*

SCENE II.

*A part of the Field of Battle betwixt the
  two Main Armies. Tumults behind
  the scenes; alarums, and cries of
  "Gordon! a Gordon!" "Swinton!"
  etc.*

---

* The well-known expression by which Robert
Bruce censured the negligence of Randolph, for
permitting an English body of cavalry to pass
his flank on the day preceding the battle of
Bannockburn.

*Enter, as victorious over the English van-
guard,* VIPONT, REYNALD, *and others.*

VIP. 'Tis sweet to hear these war-cries
sound together, —
Gordon and Swinton.
REY. 'Tis passing pleasant, yet 'tis
strange withal.
Faith, when at first I heard the Gordon's
slogan
Sounded so near me, I had nigh struck
down
The knave who cried it.

Enter SWINTON *and* GORDON.

SWI. Pitch down my pennon in yon
holly bush.
GOR. Mine in the thorn beside it; let
them wave,
As fought this morn their masters, side
by side.
SWI. Let the men rally, and restore
their ranks
Here in this vantage-ground — disorder'd
chase
Leads to disorder'd flight; we have done
our part,
And if we're succor'd now, Plantagenet
Must turn his bridle southward. —
Reynald, spur to the Regent with the
basnet
Of stout De Grey, the leader of their van-
guard;
Say, that in battle-front the Gordon slew
him,
And by that token bid him send us suc-
cor.
GOR. And tell him that when Selby's
headlong charge
Had well-nigh borne me down, Sir Alan
smote him.
I cannot send his helmet, never nutshell
Went to so many shivers. — Harkye,
grooms! [*To those behind the scenes.*
Why do you let my noble steed stand
stiffening
After so hot a course?
SWI. Ay, breathe your horses, they'll
have work anon,
For Edward's men-at-arms will soon be
on us,
The flower of England, Gascony, and
Flanders;

But with swift succor we will bide them
bravely. —
De Vipont, thou look'st sad.
VIP. It is because I hold a Templar's
sword
Wet to the crossed hilt with Christian
blood.
SWI. The blood of English archers —
what can gild
A Scottish blade more bravely?
VIP. Even therefore grieve I for those
gallant yeomen,
England's peculiar and appropriate sons,
Known in no other land. Each boasts
his hearth
And field as free as the best lord his
barony,
Owing subjection to no human vassalage,
Save to their King and law. Hence are
they resolute,
Leading the van on every day of battle,
As men who know the blessings they
defend.
Hence are they frank and generous in
peace,
As men who have their portion in its
plenty.
No other kingdom shows such worth and
happiness
Veil'd in such low estate — therefore I
mourn them.
SWI. I'll keep my sorrow for our native
Scots,
Who, spite of hardship, poverty, oppres-
sion,
Still follow to the field their Chieftain's
banner,
And die in the defence on't.
GOR. And if I live and see my halls
again,
They shall have portion in the good they
fight for.
Each hardy follower shall have his field,
His household hearth and sod-built home
as free
As ever Southron had. They shall be
happy! —
And my Elizabeth shall smile to see it!
I have betray'd myself.
SWI. Do not believe it. —
Vipont, do thou look out from yonder
height,
And see what motion in the Scottish host,

And in King Edward's. [*Exit* VIPONT.
  Now will I counsel thee;
The Templar's ear is for no tale of love,
Being wedded to his Order.   But I tell
    thee,
The brave young knight that hath no
    lady-love
Is like a lamp unlighted; his brave deeds,
And its rich painting, do seem then most
    glorious,
When the pure ray gleams through
    them. —
Hath thy Elizabeth no other name?
  GOR.   Múst I then speak of her to you,
    Sir Alan?
The thought of thee, and of thy matchless
    strength,
Hath conjured phantoms up amongst her
    dreams.
The name of Swinton hath been spell
    sufficient
To chase the rich blood from her lovely
    cheek,
And wouldst thou know hers?
  SWI.   I would, nay must.
Thy father in the paths of chivalry,
Should know the load-star thou dost rule
    thy course by.
  GOR.   Nay, then, her name is — hark —
                        [*Whispers.*
  SWI.   I know it well, that ancient
    northern house.
  GOR.   O, thou shalt see its fairest grace
    and honor
In my Elizabeth.   And if music touch
    thee —
  SWI.   It did, before disasters had un-
    tuned me.
  GOR.   O, her notes
Shall hush each sad remembrance to ob-
    livion,
Or melt them to such gentleness of feel-
    ing
That grief shall have its sweetness. Who,
    but she,
Knows the wild harpings of our native
    land?
Whether they lull the shepherd on his
    hill,
Or wake the knight to battle; rouse to
    merriment,
Or soothe to sadness; she can touch each
    mood.

Princes and statesmen, chiefs renown'd
    in arms,
And gray-hair'd bards, contend which
    shall the first
And choicest homage render to the en-
    chantress.
  SWI.   You speak her talent bravely.
  GOR.   Tho' you smile,
I do not speak it half.   Her gift creative,
New measures adds to every air she
    wakes;
Varying and gracing it with liquid sweet-
    ness,
Like the wild modulation of the lark;
Now leaving, now returning to the strain !
To listen to her, is to seem to wander
In some enchanted labyrinth of romance,
Whence nothing but the lovely fairy's
    will,
Who wove the spell, can extricate the
    wanderer.
Methinks I hear her now ! —
  SWI.   Bless'd privilege
Of youth !   There's scarce three minutes
    to decide
'Twixt death and life, 'twixt triumph and
    defeat,
Yet all his thoughts are in his lady's
    bower,
List'ning her harping ! [*Enter* VIPONT.
  Where are thine, De Vipont?
  VIP.   On death — on judgment — on
    eternity !
For time is over with us.
  SWI.   There moves not, then, one pen-
    non to our aid,
Of all that flutter yonder !
  VIP.   From the main English host come
    rushing forward
Pennons enow — ay, and their Royal
    Standard.
But ours stand rooted, as for crows to
    roost on.
  SWI. (*to himself*).   I'll rescue him at
    least. — Young Lord of Gordon,
Spur to the Regent — show the instant
    need ——
  GOR.   I penetrate thy purpose; but I
    go not.
  SWI.   Not at my bidding?   I thy sire
    in chivalry?
Thy leader in the battle? — I command
    thee !

Gor. No, thou wilt not command me
    seek my safety —
For such is thy kind meaning — at the
    expense
Of the last hope which Heaven reserves
    for Scotland.
While I abide no follower of mine
Will turn his rein for life; but were I
    gone,
What power can stay them? and, our
    band dispersed,
What sword shall for an instant stem yon
    host,
And save the latest chance for victory?
    Vip. The noble youth speaks truth;
    and were he gone,
There will not twenty spears be left with
    us.
    Gor. No, bravely as we have begun
    the field,
So let us fight it out.   The Regent's eyes,
More certain than a thousand messages,
Shall see us stand, the barrier of his host
Against yon blustering storm.   If not for
    honor,
If not for warlike rule, for shame at least
He must bear down to aid us.
    Swi.   Must it be so?
And I am forced to yield the sad consent,
Devoting thy young life?   O, Gordon,
    Gordon!
I do it as the patriarch doom'd his issue:
I at my country's, he at Heaven's com-
    mand;
But I seek vainly some atoning sacrifice,
Rather than such a victim! —(*Trumpets.*)
    Hark, they come!
That music sounds not like thy lady's lute.
    Gor. Yet shall my lady's name mix
    with it gayly. —
Mount, vassals, couch your lances, and
    cry, " Gordon!
Gordon for Scotland and Elizabeth! "
                    [*Exeunt.   Loud Alarums.*

SCENE III.

*Another part of the Field of Battle, adja-
cent to the former Scene.*

Alarums.   Enter SWINTON, *followed
by* HOB HATTELY.

    Swi.   Stand to it yet!   The man who
flies to-day,

May bastards warm them at his household
    hearth!
    Hob. That ne'er shall be my curse.
    My Magdalen
Is trusty as my broadsword.
    Swi.   Ha, thou knave,
Art thou dismounted too?
    Hob.   I know, Sir Alan,
You want no homeward guide; so threw
    my reins
Upon my palfrey's neck, and let him
    loose.
Within an hour he stands before my gate;
And Magdalen will need no other token
To bid the Melrose Monks say masses
    for me.
    Swi. Thou art resolved to cheat the
    halter, then?
    Hob.   It is my purpose,
Having lived a thief, to die a brave man's
    death,
And never had I a more glorious chance
    for't.
    Swi. Here lies the way to it, knave. —
    Make in, make in,
And aid young Gordon!

        [*Exeunt.   Loud and long Alar-
        ums.   After which the back
        Scene rises, and discovers* SWIN-
        TON *on the ground,* GORDON
        *supporting him, both much
        wounded.*

    Swi. All are cut down — the reapers
    have pass'd o'er us,
And hie to distant harvest. — My toil's
    over;
There lies my sickle.   (*Dropping his
    sword.*)   Hand of mine again
Shall never, never wield it!
    Gor. O valiant leader, is thy light ex-
    tinguish'd?
That only beacon-flame which promised
    safety
In this day's deadly wrack!
    Swi. My lamp hath long been dim!
    But thine, young Gordon,
Just kindled, to be quench'd so suddenly,
Ere Scotland saw its splendor! —
    Gor. Five thousand horse hung idly
    on yon hill,
Saw us o'erpowered, and no one stirr'd
    to aid us!

Swi. It was the Regent's envy. —
Out! — alas!
Why blame I him! — It was our civil
discord,
Our selfish vanity, our jealous hatred,
Which framed this day of dole for our
poor country. —
Had thy brave father held yon leading
staff,
As well his rank and valor might have
claim'd it,
We had not fall'n unaided. — How, O
how
Is he to answer it, whose deed pre-
vented —
Gor. Alas! alas! the author of the
death-feud,
He has his reckoning too! for had your
sons
And num'rous vassals lived, we had lack'd
no aid.
Swi. May God assoil the dead, and
him who follows!
We've drank the poison'd beverage which
we brew'd!
Have sown the wind, and reap'd the
tenfold whirlwind! —
But thou, brave youth, whose nobleness
of heart
Pour'd oil upon the wounds our hate in-
flicted;
Thou, who hast done no wrong, need'st
no forgiveness, —
Why should'st thou share our punish-
ment?
Gor. All need forgiveness — (*distant
alarums.*) — Hark, in yonder shout,
Did the main battles counter!
Swi. Look on the field, brave Gordon,
if thou canst,
And tell me how the day goes. — But I
guess,
Too surely do I guess —
Gor. All's lost! all's lost! — Of the
main Scottish host,
Some wildly fly, and some rush wildly
forward;
And some there are who seem to turn
their spears
Against their countrymen.
Swi. Rashness, and cowardice, and
secret treason
Combine to ruin us; and our hot valor,

Devoid of discipline, is madmen's
strength,
More fatal unto friends than enemies!
I'm glad that these dim eyes shall see no
more on't. —
Let thy hands close them, Gordon — I
will dream
My fair-hair'd William renders me that
office!   [*Dies.*
Gor. And, Swinton, I will think I do
that duty
To my dead father.

Enter De Vipont.

Vip. Fly, fly, brave youth! — A hand-
ful of thy followers,
The scatter'd gleaning of this desperate
day,
Still hover yonder to essay thy rescue —
O linger not! — I'll be your guide to
them.
Gor. Look there, and bid me fly! —
The oak has fall'n;
And the young ivy bush, which learn'd
to climb
By its support, must needs partake its
fall.
Vip. Swinton? Alas! the best, the
bravest, strongest,
And sagest of our Scottish chivalry!
Forgive one moment, if to save the
living,
My tongue should wrong the dead. —
Gordon, bethink thee,
Thou dost but stay to perish with the
corpse
Of him who slew thy father.
Gor. Ay, but he was my sire in
chivalry!
He taught my youth to soar above the
promptings
Of mean and selfish vengeance; gave my
youth
A name that shall not die even on this
death-spot.
Records shall tell this field had not been
lost,
Had all men fought like Swinton and
like Gordon.   [*Trumpets.*
Save thee, De Vipont. — Hark! the
Southron trumpets.
Vip. Nay, without thee I stir not.

Enter EDWARD, CHANDOS, PERCY, BALIOL, *&c.*

GOR. Ay, they come on — The Tyrant and the traitor,
Workman and tool, Plantagenet and Baliol. —
O for a moment's strength in this poor arm,
To do one glorious deed!

[*He rushes on the English, but is made prisoner with* VIPONT.

K. ED. Disarm them — harm them not; though it was they
Made havoc on the archers of our vanguard,
They and that bulky champion. Where is he?

CHA. Here lies the giant! Say his name, young Knight?

GOR. Let it suffice, he was a man this morning.

CHA. I question'd thee in sport. I do not need
Thy information, youth. Who that has fought
Thro' all these Scottish wars, but knows his crest?
The sable boar chained to the leafy oak,
And that huge mace still seen where war was wildest!

K. ED. 'Tis Alan Swinton!
Grim Chamberlain, who in my tent at Weardale,
Stood by my startled couch with torch and mace,
When the Black Douglas' war-cry waked my camp.

GOR. (*sinking down*). If thus thou know'st him,
Thou wilt respect his corpse.

K. ED. As belted Knight and crowned King, I will.

GOR. And let mine

Sleep at his side, in token that our death
Ended the feud of Swinton and of Gordon.

K. ED. It is the Gordon! — Is there aught beside
Edward can do to honor bravery,
Even in an enemy?

GOR. Nothing but this;
Let not base Baliol, with his touch or look,
Profane my corpse or Swinton's. I've some breath still,
Enough to say — Scotland — Elizabeth!
[*Dies.*

CHA. Baliol, I would not brook such dying looks,
To buy the crown you aim at.

K. ED. (*to* VIP.). Vipont, thy crossed shield shows ill in warfare
Against a Christian King.

VIP. That Christian King is warring upon Scotland.
I was a Scotsman ere I was a Templar,
Sworn to my country ere I knew my Order.

K. ED. I will but know thee as a Christian champion,
And set thee free unransom'd.

Enter ABBOT OF WALTHAMSTOW.

AB. Heaven grant your Majesty
Many such glorious days as this has been!

K. ED. It is a day of much and high advantage;
Glorious it might have been, had all our foes
Fought like these two brave champions.
— Strike the drums,
Sound trumpets, and pursue the fugitives,
Till the Tweed's eddies whelm them Berwick's render'd —
These wars, I trust, will soon find lasting close.

MACDUFF'S CROSS.

INTRODUCTION.

THESE few scenes had the honor to be included in a Miscellany, published in the year 1823, by Mrs. Joanna Baillie, and are here reprinted, to unite them with the trifles of the same kind which owe their birth to the author. The singular history of the Cross and Law of Clan MacDuff is given, at length enough to satisfy the keenest antiquary, in *The Minstrelsy of the Scottish Border*. It is here only necessary to state, that the Cross was a place of refuge to any person related to MacDuff, within the ninth degree, who, having committed homicide in sudden quarrel, should reach this place, prove his descent from the Thane of Fife, and pay a certain penalty.

The shaft of the Cross was destroyed at the Reformation. The huge block of stone which served for its pedestal is still in existence near the town of Newburgh, on a kind of pass which commands the county of Fife to the southward, and to the north the windings of the magnificent Tay and fertile country of Angusshire. The Cross bore an inscription, which is transmitted to us in an unintelligible form by Sir Robert Sibbald.

ABBOTSFORD, *January*, 1830.

TO

MRS. JOANNA BAILLIE,

AUTHORESS OF

'THE PLAYS ON THE PASSIONS.''

PRELUDE.

NAY, smile not, Lady, when I speak of witchcraft,
And say that still there lurks amongst our glens
Some touch of strange enchantment. — Mark that fragment,
I mean that rough-hewn block of massive stone,
Placed on the summit of this mountain pass,
Commanding prospect wide o'er field and fell,
And peopled village and extended moorland,
And the wide ocean and majestic Tay,
To the far distant Grampians. — Do not deem it
A loosen'd portion of the neighboring rock,
Detach'd by storm and thunder, — 'twas the pedestal

On which, in ancient times, a Cross was rear'd,
Carved o'er with words which foil'd philologists;
And the events it did commemorate
Were dark, remote, and undistinguishable,
As were the mystic characters it bore.
But, mark, — a wizard, born on Avon's bank,
Tuned but his harp to this wild northern theme,
And, lo! the scene is hallow'd. None shall pass,
Now, or in after days, beside that stone,
But he shall have strange visions; thoughts and words,
That shake, or rouse, or thrill the human heart,
Shall rush upon his memory when he hears
The spirit-stirring name of this rude symbol; —

567

Oblivious ages, at that simple spell,
Shall render back their terrors with their woes,
Alas! and with their crimes — and the proud phantoms
Shall move with step familiar to his eye,
And accents which, once heard, the ear forgets not,
Though ne'er again to list them. Siddons, thine,
Thou matchless Siddons! thrill upon our ear;
And on our eye thy lofty Brother's form
Rises as Scotland's monarch. — But, to thee,

Joanna, why to thee speak of such visions?
Thine own wild wand can raise them.

Yet since thou wilt an idle tale of mine,
Take one which scarcely is of worth enough
To give or to withhold. — Our time creeps on,
Fancy grows colder as the silvery hair
Tells the advancing winter of our life.
But if it be of worth enough to please,
That work it owes to her who set the task;
If otherwise, the fault rests with the author.

DRAMATIS PERSONÆ.

NINIAN,
WALDHAVE, } *Monks of Lindores.*

LINDESAY,
MAURICE BERKELEY, } *Scottish Barons.*

SCENE.

The summit of a Rocky Pass near to Newburgh, about two miles from the ancient Abbey of Lindores, in Fife. In the centre is MacDuff's Cross, an antique Monument; and at a small distance, on one side, a Chapel with a lamp burning.

Enter, as having ascended the Pass, NINIAN *and* WALDHAVE, *Monks of Lindores.* NINIAN *crosses himself, and seems to recite his devotions.* WALDHAVE *stands gazing on the prospect, as if in deep contemplation.*

NIN. Here stands the Cross, good brother, consecrated
By the bold Thane unto his patron saint
Magridius, once a brother of our house.
Canst thou not spare an ave or a creed?
Or hath the steep ascent exhausted you?
You trode it stoutly, tho' 'twas rough and toilsome.
WAL. I have trode a rougher.
NIN. On the Highland hills —
Scarcely within our sea-girt province here,
Unless upon the Lomonds or Bennarty.

WAL. I spoke not of the literal path, good father,
But of the road of life which I have travell'd,
Ere I assumed this habit; it was bounded,
Hedged in, and limited by earthly prospects,
As ours beneath was closed by dell and thicket.
Here we see wide and far, and the broad sky,
With wide horizon, opens full around,
While earthly objects dwindle. Brother Ninian,
Fain would I hope that mental elevation
Could raise me equally o'er worldly thoughts,
And place me nearer heaven.
NIN. 'Tis good morality. — But yet forget not,
That tho' we look on heaven from this high eminence,
Yet doth the Prince of all the airy space,
Arch-foe of man, possess the realms between.
WAL. Most true, good brother; and men may be farther

From the bright heaven they aim at, even
 because
They deem themselves secure on't.
NIN. (*after a pause*). You do gaze —
Strangers are wont to do so — on the pros-
 pect.
Yon is the Tay roll'd down from Highland
 hills,
That rests his waves, after so rude a race,
In the fair plains of Gowrie; — farther
 westward,
Proud Stirling rises; — yonder to the east,
Dundee, the gift of God, and fair Mont-
 rose,
And still more northward lie the ancient
 towers —
WAL. Of Edzell.
NIN.   How? know you the
 towers of Edzell?
WAL. I've heard of them.
NIN.   Then have you
 heard a tale,
Which when he tells, the peasant shakes
 his head,
And shuns the mouldering and deserted
 walls?
WAL. Why, and by whom deserted?
NIN.   Long the tale —
Enough to say that the last Lord of
 Edzell,
Bold Louis Lindesay, had a wife, and
 found ——
WAL. Enough is said, indeed — since
 a weak woman,
Ay, and a tempting fiend, lost Paradise,
When man was innocent.
NIN.   They fell at strife,
Men say, on slight occasion: that fierce
 Lindesay
Did bend his sword against De Berkeley's
 breast,
And that the lady threw herself between:
That then De Berkeley dealt the Baron's
 death-wound.
Enough, that from that time De Berkeley
 bore
A spear in foreign wars. But, it is said,
He hath return'd of late; and, therefore,
 brother,
The Prior hath ordain'd our vigil here,
To watch the privilege of the sanctuary,
And rights of Clan MacDuff.
WAL.   What rights are these?

NIN. Most true; you are but newly
 come from Rome,
And do not know our ancient usages.
Know, then, when fell Macbeth beneath
 the arm
Of the predestined knight, unborn of
 woman,
Three boons the victor ask'd, and thrice
 did Malcolm,
Stooping the sceptre by the Thane re-
 stored,
Assent to his request. And hence the rule,
That first when Scotland's King assumes
 the crown,
MacDuff's descendant rings his brow
 with it:
And hence, when Scotland's King calls
 forth his host,
MacDuff's descendant leads the van in
 battle:
And last, in guerdon of the crown re-
 stored,
Red with the blood of the usurping
 tyrant,
The right was granted in succeeding
 time,
That if a kinsman of the Thane of Fife
Commit a slaughter on a sudden impulse,
And fly for refuge to this Cross MacDuff,
For the Thane's sake he shall find sanc-
 tuary;
For here must the avenger's step be
 staid,
And here the panting homicide find safety.
WAL. And here a brother of your order
 watches,
To see the custom of your place observed?
NIN. Even so; — such is our convent's
 holy right,
Since Saint Magridius — blessed be his
 memory! —
Did by a vision warn the Abbot Eadmir. —
And chief we watch, when there is bicker-
 ing
Among the neighboring nobles, now most
 likely
From this return of Berkeley from abroad,
Having the Lindesay's blood upon his
 hand.
WAL. The Lindesay, then, was loved
 among his friends?
NIN. Honor'd and fear'd he was —
 but little loved;

For even his bounty bore a show of
  sternness;
And when his passion waked, he was a
  Sathan
Of wrath and injury.

    WAL. How now, Sir Priest! (*fiercely*)
— Forgive me — (*recollecting him-
self*) — I was dreaming
Of an old baron who did bear about him
Some touch of your Lord Reynold.

    NIN. Lindesay's name, my brother,
Indeed was Reynold; — and methinks,
  moreover,
That, as you spoke even now, he would
  have spoken.
I brought him a petition from our convent;
He granted straight, but in such tone and
  manner,
By my good saint! I thought myself scarce
  safe
Till Tay roll'd broad between us. I must
  now
Unto the chapel — meanwhile the watch
  is thine:
And, at thy word, the hurrying fugitive,
Should such arrive, must here find sanc-
  tuary;
And, at thy word, the fiery-paced avenger
Must stop his bloody course — e'en as
  swoln Jordan
Controll'd his waves, soon as they touch'd
  the feet
Of those who bore the ark.

    WAL.   Is this my charge?

    NIN. Even so; and I am near, should
  chance require me.
At midnight I relieve you on your watch,
When we may taste together some refresh-
  ment:
I have cared for it; and for a flask of
  wine; —
There is no sin, so that we drink it not
Until the midnight hour, when lauds have
  toll'd.
Farewell a while, and peaceful watch be
  with you!
             [*Exit towards the Chapel.*

    WAL. It is not with me, and alas!
  alas!
I know not where to seek it. This
  monk's mind
Is with his cloister match'd, nor lacks
  more room.

Its petty duties, formal ritual,
Its humble pleasures and its paltry troubles,
Fill up his round of life; even as some
  reptiles,
They say, are moulded to the very shape,
And all the angles of the rocky crevice,
In which they live and die. But for my-
  self,
Retired in passion to the narrow cell,
Couching my tired limbs in its recesses,
So ill-adapted am I to its limits,
That every attitude is agony. ——
How now! what brings him back? ——
             [*Re-enter* NINIAN.

    NIN. Look to your watch, my brother,
— horsemen come;
I heard their tread when kneeling in the
  chapel.

    WAL. (*looking to a distance*). My
  thoughts have wrapt me more then
  thy devotion,
Else had I heard the tread of distant
  horses
Farther than thou couldst hear the sacring
  bell;
But now in truth they come : — flight and
  pursuit
Are sights I've been long strange to.

    NIN. See how they gallop down the
  opposing hill!
Yon gray steed bounding down the head-
  long path,
As on the level meadow, while the black
Urged by the rider with his naked sword
Stoops on his prey, as I have seen th
  falcon
Lashing upon the heron. — Thou dos
  frown
And clench thy hand, as if it grasp'd
  weapon?

    WAL. 'Tis but for shame to see a man
  fly thus
While only one pursues him. Coward
  turn! —
Turn thee, I say! thou art as stout as he
And well mayst match thy single swor
  with his —
Shame, that a man should rein a steee
  like thee,
Yet fear to turn his front against a foe! —
I am ashamed to look on them.

    NIN. Yet look again; they quit thei
  horses now,

Unfit for the rough path : the fugitive
Keeps the advantage still.   They strain
    toward us.
    WAL. I'll not believe that ever the
    bold Thane
Rear'd up his Cross to be a sanctuary
To the base coward who shunn'd an
    equal combat. —
How 's this ? — that look, that mien —
    mine eyes grow dizzy !
    NIN. He comes ! — thou art a novice
    on this watch, —
Brother, I'll take the word and speak to
    him.
Pluck down thy cowl : know that we
    spiritual champions
Have honor to maintain, and must not
    seem
To quail before the laity.
    [WALDHAVE *lets down his cowl,
        and steps back.*

Enter MAURICE BERKELEY.

    NIN. Who art thou, stranger ! speak
    thy name and purpose.
    BER. I claim the privilege of Clan
    MacDuff.
My name is Maurice Berkeley, and my
    lineage
Allies me nearly with thy Thane of Fife.
    NIN. Give us to know the cause of
    sanctuary ?
    BER.   Let him show it,
Against whose violence I claim the
    privilege.

Enter LINDESAY *with his sword drawn.
He rushes at* BERKELEY : NINIAN *in-
terposes.*

    NIN. Peace, in the name of Saint Ma-
    gridius !
Peace, in our Prior's name, and in the
    name
Of that dear symbol, which did purchase
    peace
And good-will towards man !   I do com-
    mand thee
To sheathe thy sword, and stir no contest
    here.
    LIN. One charm I'll try first,
To lure the craven from the enchanted
    circle
Which he hath harbor'd in. — Hear you,
    De Berkeley,

This is my brother's sword — the hand it
    arms
Is weapon'd to avenge a brother's death :
If thou hast heart to step a furlong off,
And change three blows, — even for so
    short a space
As these good men may say an ave-
    marie, —
So, Heaven be good to me !   I will for-
    give thee
Thy deed and all its consequences.
    BER. Were not my right hand fetter'd
    by the thought
That slaying thee were but a double guilt
In which to steep my soul, no bridegroom
    ever
Stept forth to trip a measure with his
    bride
More joyfully than I, young man, would
    rush
To meet thy challenge.
    LIN. He quails, and shuns to look
    upon my weapon,
Yet boasts himself a Berkeley !
    BER. Lindesay, and if there were no
    deeper cause
For shunning thee than terror of thy
    weapon,
That rock-hewn Cross as soon should
    start and stir,
Because a shepherd-boy blew horn be-
    neath it,
As I for brag of thine.
    NIN. I charge you both, and in the
    name of Heaven,
Breathe no defiance on this sacred spot,
Where Christian men must bear them
    peacefully,
On pain of the Church thunders.   Calmly
    tell
Your cause of difference ; and, Lord Linde-
    say, thou
Be first to speak them.
    LIN. Ask the blue welkin — ask the
    silver Tay,
The Northern Grampians — all things
    know my wrongs ;
But ask not me to tell them, while the
    villain,
Who wrought them, stands and listens
    with a smile.
    NIN. It is said —
Since you refer us thus to general fame —

That Berkeley slew thy brother, the Lord
Louis,
In his own halls at Edzell —
   LIN. Ay, in his halls —
In his own halls, good father, that's the
word.
In his own house he slew him, while the
wine
Pass'd on the board between! The gal-
lant Thane
Who wreak'd Macbeth's inhospitable
murder,
Rear'd not yon Cross to sanction deeds
like these.
   BER. Thou say'st I came a guest! — I
came a victim —
A destined victim, train'd on to the doom
His frantic jealousy prepared for me.
He fix'd a quarrel on me, and we fought.
Can I forget the form that came between
us,
And perish'd by his sword? 'Twas then
I fought
For vengeance, — until then I guarded
life,
But then I sought to take it, and prevail'd.
   LIN. Wretch! thou didst first dishonor
to thy victim,
And then didst slay him!
   BER. There is a busy fiend tugs at my
heart,
But I will struggle with it! — Youthful
knight,
My heart is sick of war, my hand of
slaughter;
I come not to my lordships, or my land,
But just to seek a spot in some cold
cloister,
Which I may kneel on living, and, when
dead,
Which may suffice to cover me.
Forgive me that I caused your brother's
death;
And I forgive thee the injurious terms
With which thou taxest me.
   LIN. Take worse and blacker — Mur-
derer! adulterer!
Art thou not moved yet?
   BER.   Do not press me further.
The hunted stag, even when he seeks the
thicket,
Compell'd to stand at bay, grows dan-
gerous!

Most true thy brother perish'd by my
hand,
And if you term it murder — I must bear
it.
Thus far my patience can; but if thou
brand
The purity of yonder martyr'd saint,
Whom then my sword but poorly did
avenge,
With one injurious word, come to the
valley,
And I will show thee how it shall be
answer'd!
   NIN. This heat, Lord Berkeley, doth
but ill accord
With thy late pious patience.
   BER. Father, forgive, and let me stand
excused
To Heaven and thee, if patience brooks
no more.
I loved this lady — fondly, truly loved —
Loved her, and was beloved, ere yet her
father
Conferr'd her on another. While she
lived,
Each thought of her was to my soul as
hallow'd
As those I send to Heaven; and on her
grave,
Her bloody, early grave, while this poor
hand
Can hold a sword, shall no one cast a
scorn.
   LIN. Follow me. Thou shalt hear me
call the adulteress
By her right name. I'm glad there is yet
a spur
Can rouse thy sluggard mettle.
   BER. Make then obeisance to the
blessed Cross,
For it shall be on earth thy last devotion.
                    [*They are going off.*
   WAL. (*rushing forward*). Madmen,
stand! —
Stay but one second — answer but one
question. —
There, Maurice Berkeley, canst thou look
upon
That blessed sign, and swear thou'st
spoken truth?
   BER. I swear by Heaven,
And by the memory of that murder'd
innocent,

Each seeming charge against her was as
     false
As our blest Lady 's spotless ! — Hear,
     each saint !
Hear me, thou holy rood ! — hear me
     from heaven,
Thou martyr'd excellence ! — hear me
     from penal fire,
(For sure not yet thy guilt is expiated) !
Stern ghost of her destroyer ! —
   WAL. (*throws back his cowl*). He
     hears ! he hears ! thy spell hath raised
     the dead.
   LIN. My brother ! and alive ! —
   WAL. Alive, — but yet, my Richard,
     dead to thee,
No tie of kindred binds me to the world;
All were renounced, when, with reviving
     life,
Came the desire to seek the sacred
     cloister.
Alas, in vain ! for to that last retreat,
Like to a pack of bloodhounds in full
     chase,
My passion and my wrongs have follow'd
     me,

Wrath and remorse — and, to fill up the
     cry,
Thou hast brought vengeance hither.
   LIN.   I but sought
To do the act and duty of a brother.
   WAL. I ceased to be so when I left the
     world;
But if he can forgive as I forgive,
God sends me here a brother in my
     enemy,
To pray for me and with me. If thou
     canst,
De Berkeley, give thine hand, —
   BER. (*gives his hand*).   It is the will
Of Heaven, made manifest in thy pres-
     ervation,
To inhibit farther bloodshed; for De
     Berkeley,
The votary Maurice lays the title down.
Go to his halls, Lord Richard, where a
     maiden,
Kin to his blood, and daughter in
     affection,
Heirs his broad lands; — If thou canst
     love her, Lindesay,
Woo her, and be successful.

THE DOOM OF DEVORGOIL.

PREFACE.

THE first of these dramatic pieces was long since written, for the purpose of obliging
the late Mr. Terry,* then manager of the Adelphi Theatre, for whom the Author had a
particular regard. The manner in which the mimic goblins of Devorgoil are intermixed
with the supernatural machinery, was found to be objectionable, and the production had
other faults, which rendered it unfit for representation. I have called the piece a Melo-
drama, for want of a better name; but, as I learn from the unquestionable authority of
Mr. Colman's " Random Records," that one species of the drama is termed an *extravaganza*, I am sorry I was not sooner aware of a more appropriate name than that which I
had selected for " Devorgoil."

The Author's Publishers thought it desirable, that the scenes, long condemned to
oblivion, should be united to similar attempts of the same kind; and as he felt indifferent
on the subject, they are printed in the same volume with Halidon Hill and Macduff's Cross,
and thrown off in a separate form, for the convenience of those who possess former editions
of the Author's Poetical Works.

The general story of the Doom of Devorgoil is founded on an old Scottish tradition,
the scene of which lies in Galloway. The crime supposed to have occasioned the misfor

* Mr. Daniel Terry, the Comedian, died June 22, 1829.

tunes of this devoted house, is similar to that of a Lord Herries of Hoddam Castle, who is the principal personage of Mr. Charles Kirkpatrick Sharpe's interesting ballad in the "Minstrelsy of the Scottish Border," vol. iv. p. 307. In remorse for his crime, he built the singular monument called the Tower of Repentance. In many cases the Scottish superstitions allude to the fairies, or those who, for sins of a milder description, are permitted to wander with the "rout that never rest," as they were termed by Dr. Leyden. They imitate human labor and human amusements, but their toil is useless, and without any advantageous result ; and their gayety is unsubstantial and hollow. The phantom of Lord Erick is supposed to be a spectre of this character.

The story of the Ghostly Barber is told in many countries ; but the best narrative founded on the passage, is the tale called *Stumme Liebe,* among the legends of Musæus. I think it has been introduced upon the English stage in some pantomime, which was one objection to bringing it upon the scene a second time.

ABBOTSFORD, *April,* 1830.

DRAMATIS PERSONÆ.

OSWALD OF DEVORGOIL, *a decayed Scottish Baron.*
LEONARD, *a Ranger.*
DURWARD, *a Palmer.*
LANCELOT BLACKTHORN, *a Companion of Leonard, in love with Katleen.*
GULLCRAMMER, *a conceited Student.*
OWLSPIEGLE and } *Maskers, represented by Blackthorn and Flora.*
COCKLEDEMOY, }
SPIRIT OF LORD ERICK OF DEVORGOIL.
Peasants, Shepherds, and Vassals of inferior rank.
ELEANOR, *Wife of Oswald, descended of obscure Parentage.*
FLORA, *Daughter of Oswald.*
KATLEEN, *Niece of Eleanor.*

ACT I. — SCENE I.

The Scene represents a wild and hilly, but not a mountainous Country in a frontier district of Scotland. The flat scene exhibits the Castle of Devorgoil, decayed, and partly ruinous, situated upon a Lake, and connected with the land by a Drawbridge, which is lowered. Time — Sunset.

FLORA *enters from the Castle, looks timidly around, then comes forward and speaks.*

HE is not here — those pleasures are not ours
Which placid evening brings to all things else.

SONG.

The sun upon the lake is low,
  The wild birds hush their song,
The hills have evening's deepest glow,
  Yet Leonard tarries long.
Now all whom varied toil and care
  From home and love divide,
In the calm sunset may repair
  Each to the loved one's side.

The noble dame, on turret high,
  Who waits her gallant knight,
Looks to the western beam to spy
  The flash of armor bright.
The village maid, with hand on brow,
  The level ray to shade,
Upon the footpath watches now
  For Colin's darkening plaid.

Now to their mates the wild swans row,
  By day they swam apart : —
And to the thicket wanders slow
  The hind beside the hart.
The woodlark at his partner's side,
  Twitters his closing song —
All meet whom day and care divide,
  But Leonard tarries long.

[KATLEEN *has come out of the Castle while* FLORA *was singing, and speaks when the song is ended.*

KAT. Ah, my dear coz ! — if that your mother's niece
May so presume to call your father's daughter —
All these fond things have got some home of comfort

To tempt the rovers back — the lady's
    bower,
The shepherdess's hut, the wild swan's
    couch
Among the rushes, even the lark's low
    nest,
Has that of promise which lures home a
    lover, —
But we have naught of this.

    FLO. How call you, then, this castle of
    my sire,
The towers of Devorgoil?

    KAT. Dungeons for men, and palaces
    for owls;
Yet no wise owl would change a farmer's
    barn
For yonder hungry hall — our latest
    mouse,
Our last of mice, I tell you, has been found
Starved in the pantry; and the reverend
    spider,
Sole living tenant of the Baron's halls,
Who, train'd to abstinence, lived a whole
    summer
Upon a single fly, he's famish'd, too;
The cat is in the kitchen-chimney, seated
Upon our last of fagots, destined soon
To dress our last of suppers, and, poor
    soul,
Is starved with cold, and mewling mad
    with hunger.

    FLO. D'ye mock our misery, Katleen?
    KAT. No, but I am hysteric on the
    subject,
So I must laugh or cry, and laughing's
    lightest.
    FLO. Why stay you with us, then, my
    merry cousin?
From you my sire can ask no filial duty.
    KAT. No, thanks to Heaven!
No noble in wide Scotland, rich or poor,
Can claim an interest in the vulgar blood
That dances in my veins; and I might wed
A forester to-morrow, nothing fearing
The wrath of high-born kindred, and far
    less
That the dry bones of lead-lapp'd an-
    cestors
Would clatter in their cerements at the
    tidings.
    FLO. My mother, too, would gladly
    see you placed
Beyond the verge of our unhappiness,

Which, like a witch's circle, blights and
    taints
Whatever comes within it.
    KAT.   Ah! my good aunt!
She is a careful kinswoman, and prudent,
In all but marrying a ruin'd baron,
When she could take her choice of honest
    yeomen;
And now, to balance this ambitious error,
She presses on her daughter's love the suit
Of one who hath no touch of nobleness
In manners, birth, or mind, to recommend
    him, —
Sage Master Gullcrammer, the new-
    dubb'd preacher.
    FLO. Do not name him, Katleen!
    KAT. Ay, but I must, and with some
    gratitude.
I said but now, I saw our last of fagots
Destined to dress our last of meals, but
    said not
That the repast consisted of choice
    dainties,
Sent to our larder by that liberal suitor,
The kind Melchisedek.
    FLO.   Were famishing the word
I'd famish ere I tasted them — the fop,
The fool, the low-born, low-bred, pedant
    coxcomb!
    KAT. There spoke the blood of long-
    descended sires!
My cottage wisdom ought to echo back, —
O the snug parsonage! the well-paid
    stipend!
The yew-hedged garden! bee-hive, pigs,
    and poultry!
But, to speak honestly, the peasant Kat-
    leen,
Valuing these good things justly, still
    would scorn
To wed, for such, the paltry Gullcrammer,
As much as Lady Flora.
    FLO. Mock me not with a title, gentle
    cousin,
Which poverty has made ridiculous. —
                 [*Trumpets far off.*
Hark! they have broken up the weapon-
    shawing;
The vassals are dismiss'd, and marching
    homeward.
    KAT. Comes your sire back to-night?
    FLO.   He did propose
To tarry for the banquet. This day only,

Summon'd as a king's tenant, he resumes
The right of rank his birth assigns to him,
And mingles with the proudest.

KAT.   To return
To his domestic wretchedness to-mor-
    row —
I envy not the privilege.   Let us go
To yonder height, and see the marksmen
    practise;
They shoot their match down in the dale
    beyond,
Betwixt the Lowland and the Forest dis-
    trict,
By ancient custom, for a tun of wine.
Let us go and see which wins.

FLO.   That were too forward.

KAT. Why, you may drop the screen
    before your face,
Which some chance breeze may happily
    blow aside
Just when a youth of special note takes
    aim.
It chanced even so that memorable morn-
    ing,
When, nutting in the woods, we met
    young Leonard; —
And in good time here comes his sturdy
    comrade,
The rough Lance Blackthorn.

Enter LANCELOT BLACKTHORN, *a
Forester, with the Carcass of a Deer
on his back, and a Gun in his hand.*

BLA.   Save you, damsels!

KAT. Godden, good yeoman. — Come
    you from the Weaponshaw?

BLA. Not I, indeed; there lies the
    mark I shot at.
                          [*Lays down the Deer.*
The time has been I had not miss'd the
    sport,
Altho' Lord Nithsdale's self had wanted
    venison;
But this same mate of mine, young
    Leonard Dacre,
Makes me do what he lists; — he'll win
    the prize, tho':
The Forest district will not lose its honor,
And that is all I care for — (*some shots
    are heard*).   Hark! they're at it.
I'll go see the issue.

FLO.   Leave not here
The produce of your hunting.

BLA.   But I must tho'.
This is his lair to-night, for Leonard
    Dacre
Charged me to leave the stag at Devor-
    goil;
Then show me quickly where to stow the
    quarry,
And let me to the sports — (*more shots*).
    Come, hasten damsels!

FLO. It is impossible — we dare not
    take it.

BLA. There let it lie, then, and I'll
    wind my bugle,
That all within these tottering walls may
    know
That here lies venison, whoso likes to
    lift it.   [*About to blow.*

KAT. (*to* FLO.) He will alarm your
    mother; and, besides,
Our Forest proverb teaches, that no
    question
Should ask where venison comes from.
Your careful mother, with her wonted
    prudence,
Will hold its presence plead its own
    apology. —
Come, Blackthorn, I will show you where
to stow it.

    [*Exeunt* KATLEEN *and* BLACK-
    THORN *into the Castle — more
    shooting — then a distant shout
    — Stragglers, armed in different
    ways, pass over the stage, as if
    from the Weaponshaw.*

FLO. The prize is won; that general
    shout proclaim'd it.
The marksmen and the vassals are dis-
    persing.   [*She draws back.*

FIRST VASSAL (*a peasant*). Ay, ay,
    — 'tis lost and won, — the Forest
    have it.
'Tis they have all the luck on't.

SECOND VAS'. (*a shepherd*). Luck
    say'st thou, man? 'Tis patience,
    skill, and cunning.

THIRD VAS. 'Tis no such thing. — I
    had hit the mark precisely,
But for this cursed flint; and as I fired,
A swallow cross'd mine eye too. — Will
    you tell me
That that was but a chance, mine honest
    shepherd?

First Vas. Ay, and last year, when
Lancelot Blackthorn won it,
Because my powder happen'd to be damp,
Was there no luck in that? — The worse
luck mine.

Sec. Vas. Still I say, 'twas not chance;
it might be witchcraft.

First Vas. Faith, not unlikely, neigh-
bors; for these foresters
Do not often haunt about this ruin'd
castle,
I've seen myself this spark, — young
Leonard Dacre, —
Come stealing like a ghost ere break of
day,
And after sunset, too, along this path;
And well you know the haunted towers
of Devorgoil
Have no good reputation in the land.

Shep. That have they not. I've heard
my father say,
Ghosts dance as lightly in its moonlight
halls,
As ever maiden did at Midsummer
Upon the village-green.

First Vas. Those that frequent such
spirit-haunted ruins
Must needs know more than simple
Christians do. —
See, Lance this blessed moment leaves
the castle,
And comes to triumph o'er us.

[Blackthorn *enters from the
Castle, and comes forward while
they speak.*

Third Vas. A mighty triumph! What
is't after all,
Except the driving of a piece of lead,
As learned Master Gullcrammer defined it,
Just thro' the middle of a painted board?

Black. And if he so define it, by your
leave,
Your learned Master Gullcrammer's an
ass.

Third Vas. (*angrily*). He is a
preacher, huntsman, under favor.

Sec. Vas. No quarrelling, neighbors,
you may both be right.

Enter a Fourth Vassal, *with a gallon
stoup of wine.*

Fourth Vas. Why stand you brawling here? Young Leonard Dacre

Has set abroach the tun of wine he gain'd
That all may drink who list. Blackthorn,
I sought you;
Your comrade prays you will bestow this
flagon
Where you have left the deer you kill'd
this morning,

Black. And that I will; but first we
will take toll
To see if it's worth carriage. Shepherd,
thy horn.
There must be due allowance made for
leakage,
And that will come about a draught
apiece.
Skink it about, and, when our throats are
liquor'd,
We'll merrily trowl our song of Weapon-
shaw.

[*They drink about out of the*
Shepherd's *horn, and then
sing.*

SONG.

We love the shrill trumpet, we love the
drum's rattle,
They call us to sport, and they call us to
battle;
And old Scotland shall laugh at the
threats of a stranger,
While our comrades in pastime are comrades in danger.

If there's mirth in our house, 'tis our
neighbor that shares it —
If peril approach, 'tis our neighbor that
dares it;
And when we lead off to the pipe and the
tabor,
The fair hand we press is the hand of a
neighbor.

Then close your ranks, comrades — the
bands that combine them,
Faith, friendship, and brotherhood, join'd
to entwine them;
And we'll laugh at the threats of each insolent stranger,
While our comrades in sport are our
comrades in danger.

Black. Well, I must do mine errand.
Master flagon [*Shaking it.*

Is too consumptive for another bleeding.

SHEP. I must to my fold.

THIRD VAS. I'll to the butt of wine,
And see if that has given up the ghost
yet.

FIRST VAS. Have with you, neighbor,

[*BLACKTHORN enters the Castle, the rest exeunt severally.
MELCHISEDEK GULLCRAMMER
watches them off the stage, and
then enters from the side-scene.
His costume is a Geneva cloak
and band, with a high-crowned
hat; the rest of his dress in the
fashion of James the First's
time. He looks to the windows
of the Castle, then draws back
as if to escape observation,
while he brushes his cloak,
drives the white threads from
his waistcoat with his wetted
thumb, and dusts his shoes, all
with the air of one who would
not willingly be observed engaged in these offices. He then
adjusts his collar and band,
comes forward, and speaks.*

GULL. Right comely is thy garb, Mel-
chisedek;
As well beseemeth one, whom good Saint
Mungo,
The patron of our land and university,
Hath graced with license both to teach
and preach —
Who dare opine thou hither plod'st on
foot?
Trim sits thy cloak, unruffled is thy band,
And not a speck upon thine outward man
Bewrays the labors of thy weary sole.

[*Touches his shoe, and smiles
complacently.*

Quaint was that jest and pleasant! —
Now will I
Approach and hail the dwellers of this
fort;
But specially sweet Flora Devorgoil,
Ere her proud sire return. He loves me
not,
Mocketh my lineage, flouts at mine ad-
vancement —
Sour as the fruit the crab-tree furnishes,
And hard as is the cudgel it supplies;

But Flora — she's a lily on the lake,
And I must reach her, tho' I risk a duck-
ing.

[*As GULLCRAMMER moves towards the drawbridge, BAUL-
DIE DURWARD enters, and in-
terposes himself betwixt him
and the Castle. GULLCRAM-
MER stops and speaks.*

Whom have we here! — that ancient for-
tune-teller,
Papist and sorcerer, and sturdy beggar,
Old Bauldie Durward! Would I were
well past him!

[*DURWARD advances, partly in
the dress of a palmer, partly
in that of an old Scottish mendicant, having coarse blue cloak
and badge, white beard, etc.*

DUR. The blessing of the evening on
your worship,
And on your taff'ty doublet. Much I
marvel
Your wisdom chooseth such grim garb,
when tempests
Are gathering to the bursting.

[*GULLCRAMMER (looks to his dress,
and then to the sky, with some apprehension). Surely, Bauldie,*
Thou dost belie the evening; — in the west
The light sinks down as lovely as this band
Drops o'er this mantle. — Tush, man,
'twill be fair.

DUR. Ay, but the storm I bode is big
with blows,
Horsewhips for hailstones, clubs for
thunderbolts;
And for the wailing of the midnight wind
The unpitied howling of a cudgell'd cox-
comb.
Come, come, I know thou seek'st fair
Flora Devorgoil.

GUL. And if I did, I do the damsel
grace.
Her mother thinks so, and she has accepted
At these poor hands gifts of some consequence,
And curious dainties for the evening
cheer,
To which I am invited — she respects me.

DUR. But not so doth her father, haughty Oswald.
Bethink thee, he's a baron ——
  GUL.   And a bare one;
Construe me that, old man! — The crofts of Mucklewhame —
Destined for mine so soon as heaven and earth
Have shared my uncle's soul and bones between them —
The crofts of Mucklewhame, old man, which nourish
Three scores of sheep, three cows, with each her follower,
A female palfrey eke — I will be candid,
She is of that meek tribe whom, in derision,
Our wealthy southern neighbors nickname donkeys ——
  DUR. She hath her follower too, — when thou art there.
  GUL. I say to thee, these crofts of Mucklewhame,
In the mere tything of their stock and produce,
Outvie whatever patch of land remains
To this old rugged castle and its owner.
Well, therefore, may Melchisedek Gull-crammer,
Younger of Mucklewhame, for such I write me,
Master of Arts, by grace of good Saint Andrew,
Preacher, in brief expectance of a kirk,
Endow'd with ten score Scottish pounds per annum,
Being eight pounds, seventeen eight in sterling coin —
Well then, I say, may this Melchisedek,
Thus highly graced by fortune — and by nature
E'en gifted as thou seest — aspire to woo
The daughter of the beggar'd Devorgoil.
  DUR. Credit an old man's word, kind Master Gullcrammer,
You will not find it so. — Come, Sir, I've known
The hospitality of Mucklewhame;
It reach'd not to profuseness — yet, in gratitude
For the pure water of its living well,
And for the Barley loaves of its fair fields,

Wherein chopp'd straw contended with the grain
Which best should satisfy the appetite,
I would not see the hopeful heir of Mucklewhame
Thus fling himself in danger.
  GUL. Danger! what danger!—Know'st thou not old Oswald
This day attends the muster of the shire,
Where the crown-vassals meet to show their arms,
And their best horse of service? — 'Twas good sport
(And if a man had dared but laugh at it)
To see old Oswald with his rusty morion,
And huge two-handed sword, that might have seen
The field of Bannockburn or Chevy-Chase,
Without a squire or vassal, page or groom,
Or e'en a single pikeman at his heels,
Mix with the proudest nobles of the county,
And claim precedence for his tatter'd person
O'er armors double gilt and ostrich-plumage.
  DUR. Ay! 'twas the jest at which fools laugh the loudest,
The downfall of our old nobility —
Which may forerun the ruin of a kingdom.
I've seen an idiot clap his hands, and shout
To see a tower like yon (*points to a part of the Castle*) stoop to its base
In headlong ruin; while the wise look'd round,
And fearful sought a distant stance to watch
What fragment of the fabric next should follow;
For when the turrets fall, the walls are tottering.
  GUL. (*after pondering*). If that means aught, it means that thou saw'st old Oswald
Expell'd from the assembly.
  DUR.   Thy sharp wit
Hath glanced unwittingly right nigh the truth.
Expell'd he was not, but, his claim denied

At some contested point of ceremony,
He left the Weaponshaw in high dis-
pleasure,
And hither comes — his wonted bitter
temper
Scarce sweeten'd by the chances of the
day.
'Twere much like rashness should you
wait his coming.
And thither tends my counsel.

GUL. And I'll take it;
Good Bauldie Durward, I will take thy
counsel,
And will requite it with this minted
farthing,
That bears our sovereign's head in purest
copper.

DUR. Thanks to thy bounty! Haste
thee, good young master;
Oswald, besides the old two-handed
sword,
Bears in his hand a staff of potency,
To charm intruders from his castle pur-
lieus.

GUL. I do abhor all charms, nor will
abide
To hear or see, far less to feel their use.
Behold, I have departed. [*Exit hastily.*

Manet DURWARD.

DUR. Thus do I play the idle part of
one
Who seeks to save the moth from scorching him
In the bright taper's flame — and Flora's
beauty
Must, not unlike that taper, waste
away,
Gilding the rugged walls that saw it
kindled.
This was a shard-born beetle, heavy,
drossy,
Though boasting his dull drone and
gilded wing.
Here comes a flutterer of another stamp,
Whom the same ray is charming to his
ruin.

Enter LEONARD, *dressed as a huntsman;
he pauses before the Tower, and whistles a note or two at intervals — drawing back, as if fearful of observation —
yet waiting as if expecting some reply
—* DURWARD, *whom he had not observed, moves around, so as to fron*
LEONARD *unexpectedly.*

LEON. I am too late — it was no eas
task
To rid myself from yonder noisy revel
lers.
Flora! — I fear she's angry — Flora —
Flora!

SONG.

Admire not that I gain'd the prize
From all the village crew;
How could I fail with hand or eyes,
When heart and faith were true!

And when in floods of rosy wine
My comrades drown'd their cares,
I thought but that thy heart was mine
My own leapt light as theirs.

My brief delay then do not blame,
Nor deem your swain untrue;
My form but linger'd at the game,
My soul was still with you.

She hears not!

DUR. But a friend hath heard — Leo
ard, I pity thee.

LEON. (*starts, but recovers himself*
Pity, good father, is for those
want,
In age, in sorrow, in distress of mind,
Or agony of body. I'm in health —
Can match my limbs against the stag
chase,
Have means enough to meet my simp
wants,
And am so free of soul that I can carol
To woodland and to wild in notes
lively
As are my jolly bugle's.

DUR. Even therefore dost thou nee
my pity, Leonard,
And therefore I bestow it, praying the
Before thou feel'st the need, my mite
pity.
Leonard, thou lovest; and in that litt
word
There lies enough to claim the sympat
Of men who wear such hoary locks
mine,
And know what misplaced love is sure
end in.

LEON. Good father, thou art old, and
    even thy youth,
As thou hast told me, spent in cloister'd
    cells,
Fits thee but ill to judge the passions
Which are the joy and charm of social
    life.
Press me no farther, then, nor waste those
    moments
Whose worth thou canst not estimate.
             [*As turning from him.*
DUR. (*detains him*). Stay, young
    man!
Tis seldom that a beggar claims a debt;
Yet I bethink me of a gay young stripling,
That owes to these white locks and hoary
    beard
Something of reverence and of gratitude
More than he wills to pay.
    LEON. Forgive me, father. Often hast
    thou told me,
That in the ruin of my father's house
You saved the orphan Leonard in his
    cradle;
And well I know, that to thy care alone —
Care seconded by means beyond thy
    seeming —
owe whate'er of nurture I can boast.
    DUR. Then for thy life preserved,
And for the means of knowledge I have
    furnish'd
Which lacking, man is levell'd with the
    brutes),
Grant me this boon: — Avoid these fated
    walls!
A curse is on them, bitter, deep, and
    heavy,
Of power to split the massiest tower they
    boast
From pinnacle to dungeon vault. It rose
Upon the gay horizon of proud Devorgoil
As unregarded as the fleecy cloud,
The first forerunner of the hurricane,
Scarce seen amid the welkin's shadeless
    blue;
Dark grew it, and more dark, and still
    the fortunes
Of this doom'd family have darken'd
    with it.
It hid their sovereign's favor, and ob-
    scured
The lustre of their service, gender'd hate
Betwixt them and the mighty of the land;

Till by degrees the waxing tempest rose,
And stripp'd the goodly tree of fruit and
    flowers,
And buds, and boughs, and branches.
    There remains
A rugged trunk, dismember'd and un-
    sightly,
Waiting the bursting of the final bolt
To splinter it to shivers. Now, go pluck
Its single tendril to enwreath thy brow,
And rest beneath its shade — to share the
    ruin!
    LEON. This anathema,
Whence should it come?— How merited?
    and when?
    DUR. 'Twas in the days
Of Oswald's grandsire, — mid Galwegian
    chiefs
The fellest foe, the fiercest champion.
His blood-red pennons scared the Cum-
    brian coasts,
And wasted towns and manors mark'd
    his progress.
His galleys stored with treasure, and their
    decks
Crowded with English captives, who be-
    held,
With weeping eyes, their native shores
    retire,
He bore him homeward; but a tempest
    rose ——
    LEON. So far I've heard the tale,
And spare thee the recital: — The grim
    chief,
Marking his vessels labor on the sea,
And loth to lose his treasure, gave com-
    mand
To plunge his captives in the raging deep.
    DUR. There sunk the lineage of a noble
    name,
And the wild waves boom'd over sire and
    son,
Mother and nursling, of the House of
    Aglionby,
Leaving but one frail tendril. — Hence
    the fate
That hovers o'er these turrets, — hence
    the peasant,
Belated, hieing homewards, dreads to
    cast
A glance upon that portal, lest he see
The unshrouded spectres of the murder'd
    dead;

Or the avenging Angel, with his sword,
Waving destruction; or the grisly phantom
Of that fell Chief, the doer of the deed,
Which still, they say, roams thro' his empty halls,
And mourns their wasteness and their lonelihood.
    LEON. Such is the dotage
Of superstition, father; — ay, and the cant
Of hoodwink'd prejudice. — Not for atonement
Of some foul deed done in the ancient warfare,
When war was butchery, and men were wolves,
Doth Heaven consign the innocent to suffering.
I tell thee, Flora's virtues might atone
For all the massacres her sires have done
Since first the Pictish race their stained limbs
Array'd in wolf's skin.
    DUR. Leonard, ere yet this beggar's scrip and cloak
Supplied the place of mitre and of crosier,
Which in these alter'd lands must not be worn,
I was superior of a brotherhood
Of holy men, — the Prior of Lanercost.
Nobles then sought my footstool many a league,
There to unload their sins — questions of conscience
Of deepest import were not deem'd too nice
For my decision, youth. — But not even then,
With mitre on my brow, and all the voice
Which Rome gives to a father of her church,
Dared I pronounce so boldly on the ways
Of hidden Providence, as thou, young man,
Whose chiefest knowledge is to track a stag,
Or wind a bugle, hast presumed to do.
    LEON. Nay, I pray forgive me.
Father; thou know'st I meant not to presume ——
    DUR. Can I refuse thee pardon? —
Thou art all

That war and change have left to th[e]
    poor Durward.
Thy father, too, who lost his life an[d]
    fortune
Defending Lanercost, when its fair aisle[s]
Were spoil'd by sacrilege — I blest hi[s]
    banner,
And yet it prosper'd not. But — all [I]
    could —
Thee from the wreck I saved, and fo[r]
    thy sake
Have still dragg'd on my life of pilgrimag[e]
And penitence upon the hated shores
I else had left forever. Come with me
And I will teach thee there is healing i[n]
The wounds which friendship gives.
                                    [*Exeun[t.*

SCENE II.

*The Scene changes to the Interior of th[e]
Castle. An apartment is discovered
in which there is much appearance o[f]
present poverty, mixed with some reli[cs]
of former grandeur. On the wa[ll]
hangs, amongst other things, a suit [of]
ancient armor : by the table is a co[v]*
*ered basket ; behind, and concealed b[y]
it, the carcass of a roe-deer. There [is]
a small latticed window, which, ap*
*pearing to perforate a wall of gre[at]
thickness, is supposed to look out towar[d]
the drawbridge. It is in the shape o[f]
a loop-hole for musketry ; and, as is n[ot]
unusual in old buildings, is placed [so]
high up in the wall, that it is only a[p]
proached by five or six narrow ston[e]
steps.*

ELEANOR, *the wife of* OSWALD *of* DEVO[R]
GOIL, FLORA *and* KATLEEN, *he[r]
Daughter and Niece, are discovered [at]
work. The former spins, the latter a[re]
embroidering.* ELEANOR *quits her ou[n]
labor to examine the manner in whi[ch]
FLORA is executing her task, and shak[es]
her head as if dissatisfied.*

    ELE. Fy on it, Flora ! — this botch
        work of thine
Shows that thy mind is distant from th[e]
        task.
The finest tracery of our old cathedral
Had not a richer, freer, bolder pattern,
Than Flora once could trace. Th[y]
        thoughts are wandering.

FLO. They're with my father. Broad
upon the lake
The evening sun sunk down; huge piles
of clouds,
Crimson and sable, rose upon his disk,
And quench'd him ere his setting, like
some champion
In his last conflict, losing all his glory.
Sure signals those of storm. And if my
father
Be on his homeward road —

ELE.   But that he will not.
Baron of Devorgoil, this day at least
He banquets with the nobles — who, the
next,
Would scarce vouchsafe an alms to save
his household
From want or famine. Thanks to a kind
friend,
For one brief space we shall not need
their aid.

FLO. (*joyfully*). What! knew you
then his gift?
How silly I that would, yet durst not
tell it?
I fear my father will condemn us both,
That easily accepted such a present.

KAT. Now, here's the game a by-
stander sees better
Than those who play it. — My good aunt
is pondering
On the good cheer which Gullcrammer
has sent us,
And Flora thinks upon the forest venison.
                                        [*Aside.*

ELE. (*to* FLO.). Thy father need not
know on't — 'tis a boon
Comes timely, when frugality, nay, absti-
nence,
Might scarce avail us longer. I had
hoped
Ere now a visit from the youthful donor,
That we might thank his bounty; and
perhaps
My Flora thought the same, when Sun-
day's kerchief
And the best kirtle were sought out, and
donn'd
To grace a work-day evening.

FLO. Nay, mother, that is judging all
too close!
My work-day gown was torn — my kerchief sullied;

And thus — But, think you, will the gallant come?

ELE. He will, for with these dainties
came a message
From gentle Master Gullcrammer, to intimate —

FLO. (*greatly disappointed*). Gullcrammer?

KAT. There burst the bubble — down
fell house of cards,
And cousin's like to cry for 't!   [*Aside.*

ELE. Gullcrammer! ay, Gullcrammer; thou scorn'st not at him?
'Twere something short of wisdom in a
maiden,
Who, like the poor bat in the Grecian
fable,
Hovers betwixt two classes in the world,
And is disclaim'd by both the mouse and
.   bird.

KAT.   I am the poor mouse,
And may go creep into what hole I list,
And no one heed me — Yet I'll waste a
word
Of counsel on my betters.—Kind my aunt,
And you, my gentle cousin, were't not
better
We thought of dressing this same gear
for supper,
Than quarrelling about the worthless
donor?

ELE. Peace, minx!

FLO. Thou hast no feeling, cousin
Katleen.

KAT. So! I have brought them both
on my poor shoulders:
So meddling peace-makers are still rewarded:
E'en let them to 't again, and fight it out.

FLO. Mother, were I disclaim'd of
every class,
I would not therefore so disclaim myself,
As even a passing thought of scorn to
waste
On cloddish Gullcrammer.

ELE. List to me, love, and let adversity
Incline thine ear to wisdom. Look
around thee —
Of the gay youths who boast a noble name,
Which will incline to wed a dowerless
damsel?
And of the yeomanry, who, think'st thou,
Flora,

Would ask to share the labors of his farm
An high-born beggar? — This young man
is modest ——
 FLO. Silly, good mother; sheepish, if
you will it.
 ELE. E'en call it what you list — the
softer temper,
The fitter to endure the bitter sallies
Of one whose wit is all too sharp for mine.
 FLO. Mother, you cannot mean it as
you say;
You cannot bid me prize conceited folly?
 ELE. Content thee, child! — Each lot
has its own blessings.
This youth, with his plain-dealing honest
suit,
Proffers thee quiet, peace, and compe-
tence,
Redemption from a home, o'er which fell
Fate
Stoops like a falcon. — Oh! if thou
couldst choose
(As no such choice is given) 'twixt such
a mat
And some proud noble! — Who, in sober
judgment,
Would like to navigate the heady river,
Dashing in fury from its parent mountain,
More than the waters of the quiet lake?
 KAT. Now can I hold no longer —
Lake, good aunt?
Nay, in the name of truth, say mill-pond,
horse-pond;
Or if there be a pond more miry,
More sluggish, mean-derived, and base
than either,
Be such Gullcrammer's emblem — and his
portion!
 FLO. I would that he or I were in our
grave,
Rather than thus his suit should goad me!
— Mother,
Flora of Devorgoil, tho' low in fortunes,
Is still too high in mind to join her name
With such a base-born churl as Gullcram-
mer.
 ELE. You are trim maidens both!
(*To* FLORA.) Have you forgotten,
Or did you mean to call to *my* remem-
brance
Thy father chose a wife of peasant blood?
 FLO. Will you speak thus to me, or
think the stream

Can mock the fountain it derives it
source from?
My venerated mother! — in that name
Lies all on earth a child should chiefes
honor;
And with that name to mix reproach o
taunt,
Were only short of blasphemy to Heaven
 ELE. Then listen, Flora, to tha
mother's counsel,
Or rather profit by that mother's fate.
Your father's fortunes were but bent, no
broken,
Until he listen'd to his rash affection.
Means were afforded to redeem his house
Ample and large — the hand of a ricl
heiress
Awaited, almost courted, his acceptance
He saw my beauty — such it then was
call'd,
Or such at least he thought it — the
wither'd bush,
Whate'er it now may seem, had blossom
then, —
And he forsook the proud and wealthy
heiress,
To wed with me and ruin —
 KAT. (*aside*). The more fool
Say I, apart, the peasant maiden then,
Who might have chose a mate from hei
own hamlet.
 ELE. Friends fell off,
And to his own resources, his own coun-
sels,
Abandon'd, as they said, the thoughtless
prodigal,
Who had exchanged rank, riches, pomp,
and honor,
For the mean beauties of a cottage maid.
 FLO. It was done like my father,
Who scorn'd to sell what wealth car
never buy —
True love and free affections. And he
loves you!
If you have suffer'd in a weary world,
Your sorrows have been jointly borne,
and love
Has made the load sit lighter.
 ELE. Ay, but a misplaced match hath
that deep curse in't,
That can embitter e'en the purest streams
Of true affection. Thou hast seen me
seek,

With the strict caution early habits taught
    me,
To match our wants and means — hast
    seen thy father,
With aristocracy's high brow of scorn,
Spurn at economy, the cottage virtue,
As best befitting her whose sires were
    peasants:
Nor can I, when I see my lineage scorn'd,
Always conceal in what contempt I hold
The fancied claims of rank he clings to
    fondly.

FLO. Why will you do so — well you
    know it chafes him.

ELE. Flora, thy mother is but mortal
    woman,
Nor can at all times check an eager tongue.

KAT. (*aside*). That's no new tidings
    to her niece and daughter.

ELE. O may'st thou never know the
    spited feelings
That gender discord in adversity
Betwixt the dearest friends and truest
    lovers!
In the chill damping gale of poverty,
If Love's lamp go not out, it gleams but
    palely,
And twinkles in the socket.

FLO. But tenderness can screen it with
    her veil,
Till it revive again.   By gentleness, good
    mother,
How oft I've seen you soothe my father's
    mood!

KAT. Now there speak youthful hope
    and fantasy!   [*Aside.*

ELE. That is an easier task in youth
    than age;
Our temper hardens, and our charms decay,
And both are needed in that art of
    soothing.

KAT. And there speaks sad experience.
                                [*Aside.*

ELE. Besides, since that our state was
    utter desperate,
Darker his brow, more dangerous grow
    his words:
Fain would I snatch thee from the woe
    and wrath
Which darken'd long my life, and soon
    must end it.

    [*A knocking without*; ELEANOR
        shows alarm.

It was thy father's knock, — haste to the
    gate.
        [*Exeunt* FLORA *and* KATLEEN.
What can have happen'd? — he thought
    to stay the night.
This gear must not be seen.

    [*As she is about to remove the bas-
        ket, she sees the body of the roe-
        deer.*

What have we here? a roe-deer! — as I
    fear it,
This was the gift of which poor Flora
    thought.
The young and handsome hunter ——But
    time presses.

    [*She removes the basket and the roe
        into a closet.   As she has done* —

Enter OSWALD *of* DEVORGOIL, FLORA,
        and KATLEEN.

    [*He is dressed in a scarlet cloak,
        which should seem worn and old
        — a head-piece, and old-fashioned
        sword — the rest of his dress that
        of a peasant.   His countenance
        and manner should express the
        moody and irritable haughtiness
        of a proud man involved in
        calamity, and who has been ex-
        posed to recent insult.*

OSW. (*addressing his wife*). —
The sun hath set — why is the drawbridge
    lower'd?

ELE. The counterpoise has fail'd, and
    Flora's strength,
Katleen's, and mine united, could not
    raise it.

OSW. Flora and thou! a goodly gar-
    rison
To hold a castle, which, if fame says true,
Once foiled the King of Norse and all his
    rovers.

ELE. It might be so in ancient times,
    but now ——

OSW. A herd of deer might storm proud
    Devorgoil.

KAT. (*aside to* FLO.) You, Flora,
    know full well, one deer already
Has enter'd at the breach; and, what is
    worse,
The escort is not yet march'd off, for
    Blackthorn
Is still within the castle.

FLO. In heaven's name, rid him out
on't ere my father
Discovers he is here! Why went he not
before?
KAT. Because I staid him on some
little business;
I had a plan to scare poor paltry Gull-
crammer
Out of his paltry wits.
FLO. Well, haste ye now,
And try to get him off.
KAT. I will not promise that.
I would not turn an honest hunter's dog,
So well I love the woodcraft, out of shelter
In such a night as this, far less his master:
But I'll do this, — I'll try to hide him
for you.

OSW. (*whom his wife has assisted to
take off his cloak and feathered
cap*) —

Ay, take them off, and bring my peas-
ant's bonnet
And peasant's plaid — I'll oble it no
further.
Let them erase my name from honor's
lists,
And drag my scutcheon at their horses'
heels;
I have deserved it all, for I am poor,
And poverty hath neither right of birth,
Nor rank, relation, claim, nor privilege,
To match a new-coin'd viscount, whose
good-grandsire,
The lord be with him, was a careful
skipper,
And steer'd his paltry skiff 'twixt Leith
and Campvere —
Marry, sir, he could buy Geneva cheap,
And knew the coast by moonlight.
FLO. Mean you the Viscount Ellon-
dale, my father?
What strife has been between you?
OSW. O, a trifle!
Not worth a wise man's thinking twice
about; —
Precedence is a toy — a superstition
About a table's end, joint-stool, and
trencher.
Something was once thought due to long
descent,
And something to Galwegia's oldest
baron, —

But let that pass — a dream of the old
time.
ELE. It is indeed a dream.

OSW. (*turning upon her rather
quickly*) —

Ha! said ye? — let me hear these words
more plain.
ELE. Alas! they are but echoes of
your own.
Match'd with the real woes that hover
o'er us,
What are the idle visions of precedence,
But, as you term them, dreams, and toys,
and trifles,
Not worth a wise man's thinking twice
upon?
OSW. Ay, 'twas for you I framed that
consolation,
The true philosophy of clouted shoe
And linsey-woolsey kirtle. I know, that
minds
Of nobler stamp receive no dearer motive
Than what is linked with honor. Rib-
bons, tassels,
Which are but shreds of silk and spangled
tinsel —
The right of place, which in itself is mo-
mentary —
A word, which is but air — may in them-
selves,
And to the nobler file, be steep'd so
richly
In that elixir, honor, that the lack
Of things so very trivial in themselves
Shall be misfortune. One shall seek for
them
O'er the wild waves — one in the deadly
breach
And battle's headlong front — one in
the paths
Of midnight study, — and, in gaining these
Emblems of honor, each will hold him-
self
Repaid for all his labors, deeds, and
dangers.
What then should he think, knowing
them his own,
Who sees what warriors and what sages
toil for,
The formal and establish'd marks of
honor,
Usurp'd from him by upstart insolence?

Ele. (*who has listened to the last speech with some impatience*) —

This is but empty declamation, Oswald.
The fragments left at yonder full-spread banquet,
Nay, even the poorest crust swept from the table,
Ought to be far more precious to a father,
Whose family lacks food, than the vain boast,
He sate at the board-head.

Osw. Thou'lt drive me frantic! — I will tell thee, woman —
Yet why to thee?   There is another ear
Which that tale better suits, and he shall hear it.

[*Looks at his sword, which he has unbuckled, and addresses the rest of the speech to it.*

Yes, trusty friend, my father knew thy worth,
And often proved it—often told me of it.
Tho' thou and I be now held lightly of,
And want the gilded hatchments of the time,
I think we both may prove true metal still.
'Tis thou shalt tell this story, right this wrong:
Rest thou till time is fitting.

[*Hangs up the sword.*
[*The Women look at each other with anxiety during this speech, which they partly overhear. They both approach* Oswald.

Ele. Oswald, my dearest husband!
Flo.   My dear father!
Osw. Peace, both! — we speak no more of this.   I go
To heave the drawbridge up.   [*Exit.*

Katleen *mounts the steps towards the loop-hole, looks out, and speaks.*

Kat. The storm is gathering fast; broad, heavy drops
Fall plashing on the bosom of the lake,
And dash its inky surface into circles;
The distant hills are hid in wreaths of darkness.
'Twill be a fearful night.

Oswald *re-enters, and throws himself into a seat.*

Ele.   More dark and dreadful
Than is our destiny, it cannot be.

Osw. (*to* Flo.) Such is Heaven's will
— it is our part to bear it.
We're warranted, my child, from ancient story
And blessed writ, to say, that song assuages
The gloomy cares that prey upon our reason,
And wake a strife betwixt our better feelings
And the fierce dictates of the headlong passions.
Sing, then, my love; for if a voice have influence
To mediate peace betwixt me and my destiny,
Flora, it must be thine.
Flo.   My best to please you!

SONG.

When the tempest's at the loudest,
  On its gale the eagle rides;
When the ocean rolls the proudest,
  Thro' the foam the sea-bird glides —
All the range of wind and sea
Is subdued by constancy.

Gnawing want and sickness pining,
  All the ills that men endure;
Each their various pangs combining,
  Constancy can find a cure —
Pain, and Fear, and Poverty,
Are subdued by constancy.

Bar me from each wonted pleasure,
  Make me abject, mean, and poor;
Heap on insults without measure,
  Chain me to a dungeon floor —
I'll be happy, rich, and free,
If endow'd with constancy.

ACT II. — Scene I.

A Chamber in a distant part of the Castle. A large Window in the flat scene, supposed to look on the Lake, which is occasionally illuminated by lightning. There is a couch-bed in the room, and an antique cabinet.

Enter Katleen, *introducing* Black-
THORN.

Kat. This was the destined scene of action, Blackthorn,

And here our properties. But all in vain,
For of Gullcrammer we'll see naught to-
night,
Except the dainties that I told you of.

BLA. O, if he's left that same hog's
face and sausages,
He will try back upon them, never fear it.
The cur will open on the trail of bacon,
Like my old brach-hound.

KAT. And should that hap, we'll play
our comedy,
Shall we not, Blackthorn? Thou shalt
be Owlspiegle ——

BLA. And who may that hard-named
person be?

KAT. I've told you nine times over.

BLA. Yes, pretty Katleen, but my eyes
were busy
In looking at you all the time you were
talking;
And so I lost the tale.

KAT. Then shut your eyes, and let
your good ears
Do their good office.

BLA. That were too hard penance.
Tell but thy tale once more, and I will
hearken
As if I were thrown out, and listening
for
My blood-hound's distant bay.

KAT. A civil simile!
Then, for the tenth time, and the last, —
be told,
Owlspiegle was of old the wicked barber
To Erick, wicked Lord of Devorgoil.

BLA. The chief who drown'd his captives in the Solway?
We all have heard of him.

KAT. A hermit hoar, a venerable
man —
So goes the legend — came to wake re-
pentance
In the fierce lord, and tax'd him with his
guilt;
But he, heart-harden'd, turn'd into deris-
ion
The man of heaven, and, as his dignity
Consisted much in a long reverend beard,
Which reach'd his girdle, Erick caused
his barber,
This same Owlspiegle, violate its honors
With sacrilegious razor, and clip his hair
After the fashion of a roguish fool.

BLA. This was reversing of our ancient
proverb,
And shaving for the devil's, not for
God's sake.

KAT. True, most grave Blackthorn;
and in punishment
Of this foul act of scorn, the barber's
ghost
Is said to have no resting after death,
But haunts these halls, and chiefly this
same chamber,
Where the profanity was acted, trimming
And clipping all such guests as sleep
within it.
Such is at least the tale our elders tell,
With many others, of this haunted castle.

BLA. And you would have me take
this shape of Owlspiegle,
And trim the wise Melchisedek! — I
wonnot.

KAT. You will not!

BLA. No — unless you bear
a part.

KAT. What! can you not alone play
such a farce?

BLA. Not I — I'm dull. Besides, we
foresters
Still hunt our game in couples. Look
you, Katleen,
We danced at Shrovetide — then you
were my partner;
We sung at Christmas — you kept time
with me;
And if we go a mumming in this business,
By heaven, you must be one, or Master
Gullcrammer
Is like to rest unshaven ——

KAT. Why, you fool,
What end can this serve?

BLA. Nay, I know not, I.
But if we keep this wont of being partners,
Why, use makes perfect — who knows
what may happen?

KAT. Thou art a foolish patch — But
sing our carol,
As I have alter'd it, with some few words
To suit the characters, and I will bear —
                    [*Gives a paper.*

BLA. Part in the gambol. I'll go
study quickly.
Is there no other ghost, then, haunts the
castle,

But this same barber shave-a-penny gob-
    lin?
I thought they glanced in every beam of
    moonshine,
As frequent as a bat.
    KAT. I've heard my aunt's high hus-
    band tell of prophecies,
And fates impending o'er the house of
    Devorgoil;
Legends first coin'd by ancient supersti-
    tion,
And render'd current by credulity
And pride of lineage.   Five years have
    I dwelt,
And ne'er saw anything more mischievous
Than what I am myself.
    BLA. And that is quite enough, I war-
    rant you.
But, stay, where shall I find a dress
To play this — what d'ye call him —
    Owlspiegle?
    KAT. (*takes dresses out of the cabinet.*)
    Why, there are his own clothes,
Preserved with other trumpery of the sort,
For we've kept naught but what is good
    for naught.

[*She drops a cap as she draws out
    the clothes.   Blackthorn lifts it,
    and gives it to her.*

Nay, keep it for thy pains — it is a cox-
    comb, —
So call'd in ancient times, in ours a fool's
    cap, —
For you must know they kept a Fool at
    Devorgoil
In former days; but now are well con-
    tented
To play the fool themselves, to save ex-
    penses.
Yet give it me, I'll find a worthy use
    for 't.
I'll take this page's dress, to play the
    page
Cockledemoy, who waits on ghostly Owl-
    spiegle;
And yet 'tis needless, too, for Gullcram-
    mer
Will scarce be here to-night.
    BLA. I tell you that he will — I will
    uphold
His plighted faith and true allegiance
Unto a sows'd sow's face and sausages,

And such the dainties that you say he
    sent you,
Against all other likings whatsoever,
Except a certain sneaking of affection,
Which makes some folks I know of play
    the fool,
To please some other folks.
    KAT. Well, I do hope he'll come.
    There's first a chance
He will be cudgell'd by my noble uncle —
I cry his mercy — by my good aunt's
    husband,
Who did vow vengeance, knowing naught
    of him
But by report, and by a limping sonnet
Which he had fashion'd to my cousin's
    glory,
And forwarded by blind Tom Long the
    carrier;
So there's the chance, first of a hearty
    beating,
Which failing, we've this after-plot of
    vengeance.
    BLA. Kind damsel, how considerate
    and merciful!
But how shall we get off, our parts being
    play'd?
    KAT. For that we are well fitted: —
    here's a trap-door
Sinks with a counterpoise; — you shall
    go that way.
I'll make my exit yonder — 'neath the
    window,
A balcony communicates with the tower
That overhangs the lake.
    BLA. 'Twere a rare place, this house
    of Devorgoil,
To play at hide-and-seek in — shall we
One day, my pretty Katleen?
    KAT. Hands off, rude ranger!   I'm
    no managed hawk
To stoop to lure of yours. — But bear
    you gallantly;
This Gullcrammer hath vex'd my cousin
    much, —
I fain would have some vengeance.
    BLA. I'll bear my part with glee; —
    he spoke irreverently
Of practice at a mark!
    KAT.   That cries for vengeance.
But I must go — I hear my aunt's shrill
    voice!
My cousin and her father will scream next.

ELE. (*at a distance*). Katleen! Katleen!

BLA. Hark to old Sweetlips.
Away with you before the full cry open —
But stay, what have you there?

KAT. (*with a bundle she has taken from the wardrobe*) —
My dress, my page's dress — let it alone.

BLA. Your tiring-room is not, I hope, far distant;
You're inexperienced in these new habiliments —
I am most ready to assist your toilet.

KAT. Out, you great ass! was ever such a fool! [*Runs off.*

BLA. (*sings*).

O, Robin Hood was a bowman good,
　And a bowman good was he,
And he met with a maiden in merry Sherwood,
　All under the greenwood tree.

Now give me a kiss, quoth bold Robin Hood,
　Now give me a kiss, said he,
For there never came maid into merry Sherwood,
　But she paid the forester's fee.

I've coursed this twelvemonth this sly puss, young Katleen,
And she has dodged me, turn'd beneath my nose,
And flung me out a score of yards at once:
If this same gear fadge right, I'll cote and mouth her,
And then! whoop! dead! dead! dead! She is the metal
To make a woodman's wife of! —
　　　　　　[*Pauses a moment.*
Well — I can find a hare upon her form
With any man in Nithsdale—stalk a deer,
Run Reynard to the earth for all his doubles,
Reclaim a haggard hawk that's wild and wayward,
Can bait a wild cat, — sure the devil's in't
But I can match a woman — I'll to study.
　[*Sits down on the couch to examine the paper.*

SCENE II.

Scene changes to the inhabited apartment of the Castle, as in the last Scene of the preceding Act. A fire is kindled, by which OSWALD *sits in an attitude of deep and melancholy thought, without paying attention to what passes around him.* ELEANOR *is busy in covering a table;* FLORA *goes out and re-enters, as if busied in the kitchen. There should be some by-play — the Women whispering together, and watching the state of* OSWALD; *then separating and seeking to avoid his observation, when he casually raises his head and drops it again. This must be left to taste and management. The Women, in the first part of the scene, talk apart, and as if fearful of being overheard; the by-play of stopping occasionally, and attending to* OSWALD'S *movements, will give liveliness to the Scene.*

ELE. Is all prepared?
FLO. 　　　　Ay: but I doubt the issue
Will give my sire less pleasure than you hope for.
　ELE. Tush, maid — I know thy father's humor better.
He was high-bred in gentle luxuries;
And when our griefs began, I've wept apart,
While lordly cheer and high-fill'd cups of wine
Were blinding him against the woe to come.
He has turn'd his back upon a princely banquet;
We will not spread his board — this night at least,
Since chance hath better furnish'd — with dry bread,
And water from the well.

Enter KATLEEN, *and hears the last speech.*

KAT. (*aside*). Considerate aunt! she deems that a good supper
Were not a thing indifferent even to him
Who is to hang to-morrow. Since she thinks so,
We must take care the venison has due honor —
So much I owe the sturdy knave, Lance Blackthorn.

FLO. Mother, alas! when Grief turns reveller,
Despair is cup-bearer. What shall hap to-morrow?
ELE. I have learn'd carelessness from fruitless care.
Too long I've watch'd to-morrow; let it come
And cater for itself—Thou hear'st the thunder. [*Low and distant thunder*.
This is a gloomy night — within, alas!
          [*Looking at her husband*.
Still gloomier and more threatening. —
Let us use
Whatever means we have to drive it o'er,
And leave to Heaven to-morrow. Trust me, Flora,
'Tis the philosophy of desperate want
To match itself but with the present evil,
And face one grief at once.
Away! I wish thine aid, and not thy counsel.

          [*As* FLORA *is about to go off*,
          GULLCRAMMER'S *voice is heard
          behind the flat scene, as if from
          the drawbridge*.

GUL. (*behind*). Hillo — hillo — hilloa
          — hoa — hoa!

          [OSWALD *raises himself and lis-
          tens*; ELEANOR *goes up the steps
          and opens the window at the
          loop-hole*: GULLCRAMMER'S *voice
          is then heard more distinctly*.

GUL. Kind Lady Devorgoil — sweet Mistress Flora! —
The night grows fearful, I have lost my way,
And wander'd till the road turn'd round with me,
And brought me back. For Heaven's sake, give me shelter!
KAT. (*aside*). Now, as I live, the voice of Gullcrammer!
Now shall our gambol be played off with spirit;
I'll swear I am the only one to whom
That screech-owl whoop was e'er accept-
          able.
OSW. What bawling knave is this, that takes our dwelling
For some hedge-inn, the haunt of lated drunkards?

ELE. What shall I say? — Go, Kat-
leen, speak to him.
KAT. (*aside*). The game is in my hands — I will say something
Will fret the Baron's pride — and then he enters.
(*She speaks from the window*) — Good sir, be patient!
We are poor folks — it is but six Scotch miles
To the next borough town, where your Reverence
May be accommodated to your wants;
We are poor folks, an't please your Rev-
erence,
And keep a narrow household — there's no track
To lead your steps astray —
GUL. Nor none to lead them right. —
You kill me, lady,
If you deny me harbor. To budge from hence,
And in my weary plight, were sudden death,
Interment, funeral-sermon, tombstone, epitaph.
OSW. Who's he that is thus clamorous without?
(*To* ELE.) Thou know'st him?
ELE. (*confused*). I know him? — No
— yes — 'tis a worthy clergyman,
Benighted on his way; — but think not of him.
KAT. The morn will rise when that the tempest's past,
And if he miss the marsh, and can avoid
The crags upon the left, the road is plain.
OSW. Then this is all your piety! —
to leave
One whom the holy duties of his office
Have summon'd over moor and wilder-
ness,
To pray beside some dying wretch's bed,
Who (erring mortal) still would cleave to life, —
Or wake some stubborn sinner to repent-
ance, —
To leave him, after offices like these,
To choose his way in darkness 'twixt the marsh
And dizzy precipice?
ELE.   What can I do?

Osw. Do what thou canst—the wealth-
iest do no more;
And if so much, 'tis well. These crum-
bling walls,
While yet they bear a roof, shall now, as
ever,
Give shelter to the wanderer. — Have
we food?
He shall partake it. — Have we none?
the fast
Shall be accounted with the good man's
merits
And our misfortunes ——

*[He goes to the loop-hole while he
speaks, and places himself there
in room of his Wife, who comes
down with reluctance.*

Gul. (*without*). Hillo — hoa — hoa!
By my good faith, I cannot plod it
farther;
The attempt were death.
Osw. (*speaks from the window*) — Patience, my friend, I come to lower
the drawbridge. (*Descends, and exit.*
Ele. O that the screaming bittern had
his couch
Where he deserves it, in the deepest
marsh!
Kat. I would not give this sport for
all the rent
Of Devorgoil, when Devorgoil was rich-
est!
(*To* Ele.) But now you chided me, my
dearest aunt,
For wishing him a horse-pond for his
portion?
Ele. Yes, saucy girl; but, an it please
you, then
He was not fretting me. If he had sense
enough,
And skill to bear him as some casual
stranger, —
But he is dull as earth, and every hint
Is lost on him, as hail-shot on the cormo-
rant,
Whose hide is proof except to musket-
bulets!
Flo. (*apart*). And yet to such a one
would my kind mother,
Whose chiefest fault is loving me too
fondly,
Wed her poor daughter?

Enter Gullcrammer, *his dress damaged
by the storm ;* Eleanor *runs to meet
him, in order to explain to him that she
wished him to behave as a stranger.*
Gullcrammer, *mistaking her approach for an invitation to familiarity,
advances with the air of pedantic
conceit belonging to his character, when*
Oswald *enters, —* Eleanor *recovers
herself, and assumes an air of distance
—* Gullcrammer *is confounded, and
does not know what to make of it.*

Osw. The counterpoise has clean given
way; the bridge
Must e'en remain unraised, and leave us
open,
For this night's course at least, to passing visitants. —
What have we here? — is this the reverend man?

*[He takes up the candle, and sur-
veys* Gullcrammer, *who strives
to sustain the inspection with
confidence, while fear obviously
contends with conceit and desire to show himself to the best
advantage.*

Gul. Kind sir — or, good my lord, —
my band is ruffled,
But yet 'twas fresh this morning. This
fell shower
Hath somewhat smirch'd my cloak, but
you may note
It rates five marks per yard; my doublet
Hath fairly 'scaped — 'tis three-piled taffeta.

*[Opens his cloak, and displays his
doublet.*

Osw. A goodly inventory — Art thou
a preacher?
Gul. Yea — I laud Heaven and good
Saint Mungo for it.
Osw. 'Tis the time's plague, when
those that should weed follies
Out of the common field, have their own
minds
O'errun with foppery. — Envoys 'twixt
heaven and earth,
Example should with precept join, to
show us
How we may scorn the world with all its
vanities.

GUL. Nay, the high heavens forefend
   that I were vain !
When our learn'd Principal such sound-
   ing laud
Gave to mine Essay on the hidden quali-
   ties
Of the sulphuric mineral, I disclaim'd
All self-exaltment. And (*turning to the
   women*) when at the dance,
The lovely Saccharissa Kirkencroft,
Daughter to Kirkencroft of Kirkencroft,
Graced me with her soft hand, credit me,
   ladies,
That still I felt myself a mortal man,
Though beauty smiled on me.
   OSW. Come, sir, enough of this.
That you're our guest to-night, thank the
   rough heavens,
And all our worser fortunes; be conform-
   able
Unto my rules; these are no Saccharissas
To gild with compliments. There's in
   your profession,
As the best grain will have its piles of
   chaff,
A certain whiffler, who hath dared to bait
A noble maiden with love tales and son-
   nets;
And if I meet him, his Geneva cap
May scarce be proof to save his ass's ears.
   KAT. (*aside*). Umph — I am strongly
   tempted;
And yet I think I will be generous,
And give his brains a chance to save his
   bones.
Then there's more humor in our goblin
   plot,
Than in a simple drubbing.
   ELE. (*apart to* FLO.). What shall we
   do? If he discover him,
He'll fling him out at window.
   FLO. My father's hint to keep himself
   unknown
Is all too broad, I think, to be neglected.
   ELE. But yet the fool, if we produce
   his bounty,
May claim the merit of presenting it;
And then we're but lost women for ac-
   cepting
A gift our needs made timely.
   KAT.   Do not produce them.
E'en let the fop go supperless to bed,
And keep his bones whole.

OSW. (*to his Wife*) — Hast thou aught
To place before him ere he seek repose?
   ELE. Alas! too well you know our
   needful fare
Is of the narrowest now, and knows no
   surplus.
   OSW. Shame us not with thy niggard
   housekeeping:
He is a stranger — were it our last crust,
And he the veriest coxcomb e'er wore
   taffeta,
A pitch he's little short of — he must
   share it,
Tho' all should want to-morrow.

   GUL. (*partly overhearing what passes
   between them*) —

Nay, I am no lover of your sauced
   dainties —
Plain food and plenty is my motto still.
Your mountain air is bleak, and brings
   an appetite:
A soused sow's face, now, to my modest
   thinking,
Has ne'er a fellow. What think these
   fair ladies
Of a sow's face and sausages?
                [*Makes signs to* ELEANOR.
   FLO. Plague on the vulgar hind, and
   on his courtesies !
The whole truth will come out !
   OSW. What should they think, but
   that you're like to lack
Your favorite dishes, sir, unless perchance
You bring such dainties with you.
   GUL. No, not *with* me; not, indeed,
Directly *with* me; but — Aha ! fair ladies !
                [*Makes signs again.*
   KAT. He'll draw the beating down —
   Were that the worst,
Heaven's will be done !   [*Aside.*
   OSW. (*apart*). What can he mean? —
   this is the veriest dog-whelp —
Still he's a stranger, and the latest act
Of hospitality in this old mansion
Shall not be sullied.
   GUL. Troth, sir, I think, under the
   ladies' favor,
Without pretending skill in second-sight,
Those of my cloth being seldom con-
   jurers ——
   OSW. I'll take my Bible-oath that thou
   art none.   [*Aside.*

Gul. I do opine, still with the ladies'
   favor,
That I could guess the nature of our
   supper:
I do not say in such and such precedence
The dishes will be placed — housewives,
   as you know,
On such forms have their fancies; but, I
   say still,
That a sow's face and sausages ——
   Osw.   Peace, sir!
O'er-driven jests (if this be one) are in-
   solent.

   Flo. (*apart, seeing her mother uneasy.*)
The old saw still holds true — a churl's
   benefits,
Sauced with his lack of feeling, sense,
   and courtesy,
Savor like injuries.

       [*A horn is winded without ; then
       a loud knocking at the gate.*

   Leo. (*without*). Ope, for the sake of
   love and charity!

       [Oswald *goes to the loop-hole.*

   Gul. Heaven's mercy! should there
   come another stranger,
And he half-starved with wandering on
   the wolds,
The sow's face boasts no substance, nor
   the sausages,
To stand our reinforced attack! I judge,
   too,
By this starved Baron's language, there's
   no hope
Of a reserve of victuals.

   Flo. Go to the casement, cousin.
   Kat.   Go yourself,
And bid the gallant, who that bugle
   winded,
Sleep in the storm-swept waste; as meet
   for him
As for Lance Blackthorn. — Come, I'll
   not distress you;
I'll get admittance for this second suitor,
And we'll play out this gambol at cross
   purposes.
But see, your father has prevented me.

   Osw. (*seems to have spoken with those
    without, and answers*) —

Well, I will ope the door; one guest
   already,

Driven by the storm, has claim'd m[
   hospitality,
And you, if you were fiends, were scarc[
   less welcome
To this my mouldering roof, than empt[
   ignorance
And rank conceit. I hasten to admi[
   you.   [*Exit*
   Ele. (*to* Flo.). The tempest thickens[
   By that winded bugle,
I guess the guest that next will honor us[
Little deceiver, that didst mock m[
   troubles,
'Tis now thy turn to fear!

   Flo. Mother, if I knew less or mor[
   of this
Unthought-of and most perilous visita[
   tion,
I would your wishes were fulfill'd on me[
And I were wedded to a thing like yon.
   Gul. (*approaching*). Come, ladies[
   now you see the jest is threadbare.
And you must own that same sow's face
   and sausages ——

Re-enter Oswald *with* Leonard, *supporting* Bauldie Durward. Oswald
   takes a view of them, as formerly o[
   Gullcrammer, then speaks —

   Osw. (*to* Leo.). By thy green cassock[
   hunting-spear, and bugle,
I guess thou art a huntsman?

   Leo. (*bowing with respect*) —

A ranger of the neighboring royal forest[
Under the good Lord Nithsdale; hunts-
   man, therefore,
In time of peace; and when the land has[
   war,
To my best powers a soldier.
   Osw. Welcome, as either. I have[
   loved the chase,
And was a soldier once. — This aged[
   man,
What may he be?

   Dur. (*recovering his breath*) —

Is but a beggar, sir, a humble mendicant,
Who feels it passing strange, that from
   this roof,
Above all others, he should now crave
   shelter.
   Osw. Why so? You're welcome both
   — only the word

Warrants more courtesy than our present
    means
Permit us to bestow.   A huntsman and
    a soldier
May be a prince's comrade, much more
    mine;
And for a beggar — friend, there little
    lacks,
Save that blue gown and badge, and
    clouted pouches,
To make us comrades too; then welcome
    both,
And to a beggar's feast.   I fear, brown
    bread,
And water from the spring, will be the
    best on't;
For we had cast to wend abroad this
    evening,
And left our larder empty.
    GUL.   Yet, if some kindly fairy,
In our behalf, would search its hid
    recesses. —
(*Apart.*) We'll not go supperless now —
    we're three to one. —
Still do I say, that a soused face and
    sausages ——

    OSW. (*looks sternly at him, then at his
    wife*) —

There's something under this, but that
    the present
Is not a time to question. — (*To* ELE.)
    Wife, my mood
Is at such height of tide, that a turn'd
    feather
Would make me frantic now, with mirth
    or fury!
Tempt me no more — but if thou hast
    the things
This carrion crow so croaks for, bring
    them forth;
For, by my father's beard, if I stand
    caterer,
'Twill be a fearful banquet!
    ELE. Your pleasure be obey'd — Come
    aid me, Flora.   [*Exeunt.*

    [*During the following speeches, the
    Women place dishes on the table.*

    OSW. (*to* DUR.). How did you lose
    your path?
    DUR. E'en when we thought to find
    it a wild meteor

Danced in the moss, and led our feet
    astray. —
I give small credence to the tales of
    old,
Of Friar's-lantern told, and Will-o'-Wisp,
Else would I say, that some malicious
    demon
Guided us in a round; for to the moat,
Which we had pass'd two hours since
    were we led,
And there the gleam flicker'd and disap-
    pear'd,
Even on your drawbridge. I was so worn
    down,
So broke with laboring thro' marsh and
    moor,
That, wold I nold I, here my young con-
    ductor
Would needs implore for entrance; else,
    believe me,
I had not troubled you.
    OSW. And why not, father? — have
    you e'er heard aught,
Or of my house or me, that wanderers,
Whom or their roving trade or sudden
    circumstance
Oblige to seek a shelter, should avoid
The House of Devorgoil?
    DUR.   Sir, I am English born —
Native of Cumberland.   Enough is said
Why I should shun those towers, whose
    lords were hostile
To English blood, and unto Cumberland
Most hostile and most fatal.
    OSW. Ay, father.   Once my grandsire
    plough'd and harrow'd,
And sow'd with salt, the streets of your
    fair towns:
But what of that? — you have the 'vant-
    age now.
    DUR. True, Lord of Devorgoil, and
    well believe I,
That not in vain we sought these towers
    to-night,
So strangely guided, to behold their
    state.
    OSW. Ay, thou wouldst say, 'twas fit
    a Cumbrian beggar
Should sit an equal guest in his proud
    halls,
Whose fathers beggar'd Cumberland —
    Graybeard, let it be so,
I'll not dispute it with thee.

(*To* LEONARD, *who was speaking
to* FLORA, *but, on being surprised,
occupied himself with the suit of
armor*) —

    What makest thou
there, young man?

LEO. I marvell'd at this harness; it is
larger

Than arms of modern days. How richly
carved

With gold inlaid on steel — how close
the rivets —

How justly fit the joints! I think the
gauntlet

Would swallow twice my hand.

  [*He is about to take down some
part of the armor ;* OSWALD
interferes.

OSW.   Do not displace it.
My grandsire, Erick, doubled human
strength,

And almost human size —- and human
knowledge,

And human vice, and human virtue also,

As storm or sunshine chanced to occupy

His mental hemisphere. After a fatal
deed,

He hung his armor on the wall, forbidding

It e'er should be ta'en down. There is
a prophecy,

That of itself 'twill fall, upon the night

When, in the fiftieth year from his decease,

Devorgoil's feast is full. This is the era;

But, as too well you see, no meet occasion

Will do the downfall of the armor justice,

Or grace it with a feast. There let it
bide,

Trying its strength with the old walls it
hangs on,

Which shall fall soonest.

DUR. (*looking at the trophy with a
mixture of feeling*) —

Then since stern Erick's harness hangs
untouch'd,

Since his last fatal raid on Cumberland !

OSW. Ay, waste and want, and recklessness — a comrade

Still yoked with waste and want — have
stripp'd these walls

Of every other trophy. Antler'd skulls,

Whose branches vouch'd the tales old
vassals told

Of desperate chases — partisans and
spears —

Knights' barred helms and shields — the
shafts and bows,

Axes and breastplates, of the hardy yeomanry —

The banners of the vanquish'd — signs
these arms

Were not assumed in vain, have disappear'd;

Yes, one by one they all have disappear'd; —

And now Lord Erick's harness hangs
alone,

Midst implements of vulgar husbandry

And mean economy; as some old warrior,

Whom want hath made an inmate of
an almshouse,

Shows, mid the beggar'd spendthrifts,
base mechanics,

And bankrupt pedlers, with whom fate
has mix'd him.

DUR. Or rather like a pirate, whom
the prison-house,

Prime leveller next the grave, hath for
the first time

Mingled with peaceful captives, low in
fortunes,

But fair in innocence.

OSW. (*looking at* DURWARD *with surprise*) — Friend, thou art bitter !

DUR. Plain truth, sir, like the vulgar
copper coinage,

Despised amongst the gentry, still finds
value

And currency with beggars.

OSW.   Be it so.
I will not trench on the immunities

I soon may claim to share. Thy features,
too,

Tho' weather-beaten, and thy strain of
language,

Relish of better days. Come hither,
friend,

    [*They speak apart.*

And let me ask thee of thine occupation.

  [LEONARD *looks round, and, see-
ing* OSWALD *engaged with* DUR-
WARD, *and* GULLCRAMMER *with*
ELEANOR, *approaches towards*

FLORA, *who must give him an opportunity of doing so, with obvious attention on her part to give it the air of chance. The by-play here will rest with the Lady, who must engage the attention of the audience by playing off a little female hypocrisy and simple coquetry.*

LEO.   Flora ——

FLO.   Ay, gallant huntsman, may she deign to question
Why Leonard came not at the appointed hour;
Or why he came at midnight?

LEO.   Love has no certain lodestar, gentle Flora,
And oft gives up the helm to wayward pilotage.
To say the sooth — A beggar forced me hence,
And Will-o'-Wisp did guide us back again.

FLO.   Ay, ay, your beggar was the faded spectre
Of Poverty, that sits upon the threshold
Of these our ruin'd walls.   I've been unwise,
Leonard, to let you speak so oft with me;
And you a fool to say what you have said.
E'en let us here break short; and, wise at length,
Hold each our separate way thro' life's wide ocean.

LEO.   Nay, let us rather join our course together,
And share the breeze or tempest, doubling joys,
Relieving sorrows, warding evils off
With mutual effort, or enduring them
With mutual patience.

FLO.   This is but flattering counsel —
sweet and baneful;
But mine had wholesome bitter in't.

KAT.   Ay, ay; but like the sly apothecary,
You'll be the last to take the bitter drug
That you prescribe to others.

[*They whisper.* ELEANOR *advances to interrupt them, followed by* GULLCRAMMER.

ELE.   What, maid, no household cares?
Leave to your elders

The task of filling passing strangers' ears
With the due notes of welcome.

GUL.   Be it thine,
O, Mistress Flora, the more useful talent
Of filling strangers' stomachs with substantials;
That is to say, — for learned commentators
Do so expound substantials in some places, —
With a soused bacon-face and sausages.

FLO. (*apart*). Would thou wert soused, intolerable pedant,
Base, greedy, perverse, interrupting coxcomb!

KAT.   Hush, coz, for we'll be well avenged on him,
And ere this night goes o'er, else woman's wit
Cannot o'ertake her wishes.

[*She proceeds to arrange seats.* OSWALD *and* DURWARD *come forward in conversation.*

OSW.   I like thine humor well. — So all men beg ——

DUR.   Yes — I can make it good by proof.   Your soldier
Begs for a leaf of laurel, and a line
In the Gazette; — he brandishes his sword
To back his suit, and is a sturdy beggar.—
The courtier begs a ribbon or a star,
And, like our gentler mumpers, is provided
With false certificates of health and fortune
Lost in the public service. — For your lover
Who begs a sigh, a smile, a lock of hair,
A buskin-point, he maunds upon the pad,
With the true cant of pure mendicity.
" The smallest trifle to relieve a Christian,
And if it like your ladyship ! "
                [*In a begging tone*
KAT. (*apart*). This is a cunning knave, and feeds the humor
Of my aunt's husband, for I must not say
Mine honor'd uncle.   I will try a question. —
Your man of merit tho', who serves the commonwealth,
Nor asks for a requital? ——
                        [*To* DURWARD.

DUR.   Is a dumb beggar,
And lets his actions speak like signs for
     him,
Challenging double guerdon. — Now, I'll
     show
How your true beggar has the fair advan-
     tage
O'er all the tribes of cloak'd mendicity
I have told over to you. — The soldier's
     laurel,
The statesman's ribbon, and the lady's
     favor,
Once won and gain'd, are not held worth
     a farthing
By such as longest, loudest, canted for
     them;
Whereas your charitable halfpenny,
Which is the scope of a true beggar's suit,
Is worth *two* farthings, and, in times of
     plenty,
Will buy a crust of bread.

FLO. (*interrupting him, and addressing her father*) —

Sir, let me be a beggar with the time,
And pray you come to supper.

ELE. (*to* OSWALD, *apart*). Must *he*
     sit with us? [*Looking at* DURWARD.

OSW. Ay, ay, what else — since we
     are beggars all?
When cloaks are ragged, sure their worth
     is equal,
Whether at first they were of silk or
     woollen.

ELE. Thou art scarce consistent.
This day thou didst refuse a princely ban-
     quet,
Because a new-made lord was placed
     above thee;
And now ——

OSW. Wife, I have seen, at public exe-
     cutions,
A wretch that could not brook the hand
     of violence
Should push him from the scaffold, pluck
     up courage,
And, with a desperate sort of cheerfulness,
Take the fell plunge himself —
Welcome then, beggars, to a beggar's
     feast!

GUL. (*who has in the meanwhile seated
himself*) —

But this is more.—A better countenance,

Fair fall the hands that soused it! — tha
     this hog's,
Or prettier provender than these sam
     sausages,
(By what good friend sent hither, sha
     be nameless —
Doubtless some youth whom love hat
     made profuse,)

     [*Smiling significantly at* ELEANO
        and FLORA.]

No prince need wish to peck at. Long
     I ween,
Since that the nostrils of this house (b
     metaphor,
I mean the chimneys) smell'd a steam s
     grateful. —
By your good leave I cannot dally longe
        [*Helps himsel*

OSW. (*places* DURWARD *above* GULL
     CRAMMER). Meanwhile, sir,
Please it your youthful learning to giv
     place
To gray hairs and to wisdom; and, more
     over,
If you had tarried for the benediction——

GUL. (*somewhat abashed*). I said grac
     to myself.

OSW. (*not minding him*) — And waite
     for the company of others,
It had been better fashion. Time ha
     been,
I should have told a guest at Devorgoil
Bearing himself thus forward, he wa
     saucy.

     [*He seats himself, and helps the com
        pany and himself in dumb-show.
        There should be a contrast be
        twixt the precision of his aris
        tocratic civility and the rud
        underbreeding of* GULLCRAM
        MER.

OSW. (*having tasted the dish next him*
     — Why, this is venison, Eleanor!

GUL. Eh! What! Let's see — (*Pushe
     across* OSWALD *and helps himself.*
     It may be venison —
I'm sure 'tis not beef, veal, mutton, lamb,
     or pork;
Eke am I sure, that be it what it will,
It is not half so good as sausages,
Or as a sow's face soused.

OSW. Eleanor, whence all this? ——

ELE.   Wait till to-morrow,
You shall know all. It was a happy
chance
That furnish'd us to meet so many guests
—(*Fills wine*).
Try if your cup be not as richly garnish'd
As is your trencher.*

KAT. (*apart*). My aunt adheres to the
good cautious maxim
Of " Eat your pudding, friend, and hold
your tongue."

OSW. (*tastes the wine*). It is the grape
of Bordeaux.
Such dainties, once familiar to my board,
Have been estranged from 't long.

[*He again fills his glass, and continues to speak as he holds it up.*

Fill round, my friends — here is a
treacherous friend, now,
Smiles in your face, yet seeks to steal the
jewel,
Which is distinction between man and
brute —
I mean our reason; this he does, and
smiles.
But are not all friends treacherous? One
shall cross you
Even in your dearest interests — one shall
slander you —
This steal your daughter, that defraud
your purse;
But this gay flask of Bordeaux will but
borrow
Your sense of mortal sorrows for a season,
And leave, instead, a gay delirium.
Methinks my brain, unused to such gay
visitants,
The influence feels already! — we will
revel! —
Our banquet shall be loud! — it is our
last.
Katleen, thy song.

KAT. Not now, my lord — I mean to
sing to-night
For this same moderate, grave, and reverend clergyman:
I'll keep my voice till then.

ELE. Your round refusal shows but
cottage breeding.

* Wooden trenchers should be used, and the
quaigh, a Scottish drinking cup: whence our
word quaff.

KAT. Ay, my good aunt, for I was
cottage-nurtured,
And taught, I think, to prize my own
wild will
Above all sacrifice to compliment.
Here is a huntsman — in his eyes I read
it,
He sings the martial song my uncle
loves,
What time fierce Claver'se with his Cava-
liers,
Abjuring the new change of government,
Forcing his fearless way thro' timorous
friends,
And enemies as timorous, left the capi-
tal
To rouse in James's cause the distant
Highlands.
Have you ne'er heard the song, my noble
uncle?

OSW. Have I not heard, wench? — It
was I rode next him —
'Tis thirty summers since — rode by his
rein;
We marched on thro' the alarmed city,
As sweeps the osprey thro' a flock of
gulls,   •
Who scream and flutter, but dare no resistance
Against the bold sea-empress. They did
murmur,
The crowds before us, in their sullen
wrath,
And those whom we had pass'd, gathering fresh courage,
Cried havoc in the rear — we minded
them
E'en as the brave bark minds the bursting billows,
Which, yielding to her bows, burst on
her sides,
And ripple in her wake. — Sing me that
strain, (*To* LEO.)
And thou shalt have a meed I seldom
tender,
Because they're all I have to give — my
thanks.

LEO. Nay, if you'll bear with what I
cannot help,
A voice that's rough with hollowing to
the hounds,
I'll sing the song even as old Rowland
taught me.

SONG.

AIR, — " *The Bonnets of Bonny Dundee.*"

To the Lords of Convention 'twas Claver'se who spoke,
" Ere the King's crown shall fall, there are crowns to be broke:
So let each Cavalier who loves honor and me,
Come follow the bonnet of Bonny Dundee.

 Come fill up my cup, come fill up my can,
 Come saddle your horses, and call up your men;
 Come open the West Port, and let me gang free,
 And it's room for the bonnets of bonny Dundee ! "

Dundee he is mounted, he rides up the street,
The bells are rung backward, the drums they are beat:
But the Provost, douce man, said, " Just e'en let him be,
The Gude Town is weel quit of that Deil of Dundee."

 Come fill up my cup, etc.

As he rode down the sanctified bends of the Bow,
Ilk carline was flyting and shaking her pow;
But the young plants of grace they look'd couthie and slee,
Thinking, luck to thy bonnet, thou Bonny Dundee !

 Come fill up my cup, etc.

With sour-featured Whigs the Grassmarket was cramm'd,*
As if half the West had set tryst to be hang'd;
There was spite in each look, there was fear in each e'e,
As they watch'd for the bonnets of Bonny Dundee.

 Come fill up my cup, etc.

* Previous to 1784 the Grassmarket was the common place of execution at Edinburgh.

These cowls of Kilmarnock had spits and had spears,
And lang-hafted gullies to kill Cavaliers;
But they shrunk to close-heads, and the causeway was free,
At the toss of the bonnet of Bonny Dundee.

 Come fill up my cup, etc.

He spurr'd to the foot of the proud Castle rock,
And with the gay Gordon he gallantly spoke: —
" Let Mons Meg and her marrows speak twa words or three,
For the love of the bonnet of Bonny Dundee."

 Come fill up my cup, etc.

The Gordon demands of him which way he goes: —
" Where'er shall direct me the shade of Montrose !
Your Grace in short space shall hear tidings of me,
Or that low lies the bonnet of Bonny Dundee.

 Come fill up my cup, etc.

" There are hills beyond Pentland, and lands beyond Forth,
If there's lords in the Lowlands, there's chiefs in the North;
There are wild Duniewassals three thousand times three,
Will cry *hoigh !* for the bonnet of Bonny Dundee.

 Come fill up my cup, etc.

" There's brass on the target of barken'd bull-hide;
There's steel in the scabbard that dangles beside;
The brass shall be burnish'd, the steel shall flash free,
At a toss of the bonnet of Bonny Dundee.

 Come fill up my cup, etc.

" Away to the hills, to the caves, to the rocks ! —
Ere I own an usurper, I'll couch with the fox ! —

And tremble, false Whigs, in the midst
of your glee,
You have not seen the last of my bonnet
and me ! "

 Come fill up my cup, etc.

He waved his proud hand, and the trum-
pets were blown,
The kettle-drums clashed, and the horse-
men rode on,
Till on Ravelston's cliffs and on Clermis-
ton's lee,
Died away the wild war-notes of Bonny
Dundee.

 Come fill up my cup, come fill up
  my can,
 Come saddle the horses, and call
  up the men,
 Come open your gates, and let me
  gae free,
 For it's up with the bonnets of
  Bonny Dundee !

ELE. Katleen, do thou sing now. Thy
 uncle's cheerful;
We must not let his humor ebb again.
 KAT. But I'll do better, aunt, than if
 I sung,
For Flora can sing blithe; so can this
 huntsman,
As he has shown e'en now; let them duet
 it.
 OSW. Well, huntsman, we must give
 to freakish maiden
The freedom of her fancy. — Raise the
 carol,
And Flora, if she can, will join the
 measure.

   SONG.

When friends are met o'er merry cheer,
And lovely eyes are laughing near,
And in the goblet's bosom clear
 The cares of day are drown'd;

When puns are made, and bumpers
 quaff'd,
And wild Wit shoots his roving shaft,
And Mirth his jovial laugh has laugh'd,
 Then is our banquet crown'd,
  Ah gay,
 Then is our banquet crown'd.

When glees are sung, and catches troll'd,
And bashfulness grows bright and bold,
And beauty is no longer cold,
 And age no longer dull;
When chimes are brief, and cocks do crow,
To tell us it is time to go,
Yet how to part we do not know,
 Then is our feast at full,
  Ah gay,
 Then is our feast at full.

 OSW. (*rises with his cup in his hand*)—
Devorgoil's feast is full — Drink to the
 pledge !

 [*A tremendous burst of thunder follows these words of the Song ;
 and the Lightning should seem
 to strike the suit of black Armor,
 which falls with a crash. All
 rise in surprise and fear except
 *GULLCRAMMER, *who tumbles
 over backwards and lies still.*

 OSW. That sounded like the judgment
 peal — the roof
Still trembles with the volley.
 DUR.   Happy those,
Who are prepared to meet such fearful
 summons.
Leonard, what dost thou there?
 LEO. (*supporting* FLO.) The duty of
 a man —
Supporting innocence. Were it the final
 call,
I were not misemploy'd.
 OSW. The armor of my grandsire hath
 fall'n down,
And old saws have spoke truth. — (*Mus-
 ing.*) The fiftieth year —
Devorgoil's feast at fullest ! What to
 think of it —
 LEO. (*lifting a scroll which had fallen
 with the armor*) —
This may inform us. — (*Attempts to read
 the manuscript, shakes his head and
 gives it to* OSWALD) —
But not to eyes unlearn'd it tells its tidings.
 OSW. Hawks, hounds, and revelling
 consumed the hours
I should have given to study. (*Looks at
 the manuscript.*)
These characters I spell not more than
 thou.

They are not of our day, and, as I think,
Not of our language. — Where's our
　　scholar now,
So forward at the banquet? Is he laggard
Upon a point of learning?
　　LEO. Here is the man of letter'd dig-
nity,
E'en in a piteous case. (*Drags* GULL-
　　CRAMMER *forward.*)
　　OSW. Art waking, craven? Canst thou
　　read this scroll?
Or art thou only learn'd in sousing swine's
　　flesh,
And prompt in eating it?
　　GULL. Eh — ah! — oh — ho! — Have
you no better time
To tax a man with riddles, than the
　　moment
When he scarce knows whether he's
　　dead or living?
　　OSW. Confound the pedant?—Can you
　　read the scroll,
Or can you not, sir? If you *can*, pronounce
Its meaning speedily.
　　GUL. 　　*Can* I read it, quotha?
When at our learned University,
I gain'd first premium for Hebrew learn-
　　ing, —
Which was a pound of high-dried Scot-
　　tish snuff,
And half a peck of onions, with a bushel
Of curious oatmeal, — our learned Prin-
　　cipal
Did say, "Melchisedek, thou canst do
　　anything!"
Now comes he with his paltry scroll of
　　parchment,
And, "*Can* you read it?" — After such
　　affront,
The point is, if I *will.*
　　OSW. 　　A point soon solved,
Unless you choose to sleep among the
　　frogs;
For look you, sir, there is the chamber
　　window, —
Beneath it lies the lake.
　　ELE. Kind master Gullcrammer, be-
　　ware my husband.
He brooks no contradiction —'tis his fault,
And in his wrath he's dangerous.
　　GULL. (*looks at the scroll, and mutters
　　as if reading*) —
Hashgaboth hotch-potch —

A simple matter this to make a rout of —
*Ten rashersen bacon, mish-mash venison,
Sausagian soused-face* — 'Tis a simple
　　catalogue
Of our small supper — made by the grave
　　sage
Whose prescience knew this night that
　　we should feast
On venison, hash'd sow's face, and sau-
　　sages,
And hung his steel coat for a supper bell.
E'en let us to our provender again,
For it is written we shall finish it,
And bless our stars the lightning left it us.
　　OSW. This must be impudence or ig-
　　norance!
The spirit of rough Erick stirs within me,
And I will knock thy brains out if thou
　　falterest!
Expound the scroll to me!
　　GUL. 　　You're over-hasty;
And yet you may be right too — 'Tis
　　Samaritan,
Now I look closer on't, and I did take it
For simple Hebrew.
　　DUR. 'Tis Hebrew to a simpleton,
That we see plainly, friend — Give me
　　the scroll.
　　GUL. Alas, good friend! what would
　　you do with it?
　　DUR. (*takes it from him.*)
My best to read it, sir — The character
　　is Saxon,
Used at no distant date within this dis-
　　trict;
And thus the tenor runs — not in Samari-
　　tan,
Nor simple Hebrew, but in wholesome
　　English: —

　　　"Devorgoil, thy bright moon waneth,
　　And the rust thy harness staineth;
　　Servile guests the banquet soil
　　Of the once proud Devorgoil.
　　But should Black Erick's armor fall,
　　Look for guests shall scare you all!
　　They shall come ere peep of day, —
　　Wake and watch, and hope and pray."

　　KAT. (*to* FLO.) Here is fine foolery?
　　An old wall shakes
At a loud thunder-clap — down comes a
　　suit
Of ancient armor, when its wasted braces

Were all too rotten to sustain its weight —
A beggar cries out, Miracle ! — and your father,
Weighing the importance of his name and lineage,
Must needs believe the dotard !

FLO. Mock not, I pray you; this may be too serious.

KAT. And if I live till morning, I will have
The power to tell a better tale of wonder
Wrought on wise Gullcrammer. I'll go prepare me.   *[Exit.*

FLO. I have not Katleen's spirit, yet I hate
This Gullcrammer too heartily to stop
Any disgrace that's hasting towards him.

OSW. (*to whom the Beggar has been again reading the scroll*).

'Tis a strange prophecy ! — The silver moon,
Now waning sorely, is our ancient bearing —
Strange and unfitting guests —

GUL. (*interrupting him*). Ay, ay, the matter
Is, as you say, all moonshine in the water.

OSW. How mean you, sir? (*threatening.*)

GUL.   To show that I can rhyme
With yonder bluegown. Give me breath and time,
I will maintain, in spite of his pretense,
Mine exposition had the better sense —
It spoke good victuals and increase of cheer;
And his, more guests to eat what we have here —
An increment right needless.

OSW.   Get thee gone !
To kennel, hound !

GUL. The hound will have his bone.

[Takes up the platter of meat and a flask.

OSW. Flora, show him his chamber — take him hence,
Or, by the name I bear, I'll see his brains !

GUL. Ladies, good-night ! — I spare you, sir, the pains.

[Exit, lighted by FLORA *with a lamp.*

OSW. The owl is fled. — I'll not to bed to-night:
There is some change impending o'er this house,
For good or ill. I would some holy man
Were here, to counsel us what we should do.
Yon witless thin-faced gull is but a cassock
Stuff'd out with chaff and straw.

DUR. (*assuming an air of dignity*).
I have been wont,
In other days, to point to erring mortals
The rock which they should anchor on.

[He holds up a Cross — the rest take a posture of devotion, and the Scene closes.

ACT III. — SCENE I.

A ruinous Anteroom in the Castle.

Enter KATLEEN, *fantastically dressed to play the character of Cockledemoy, with the visor in her hand.*

KAT. I've scarce had time to glance at my sweet person,
Yet this much could I see, with half a glance,
My elfish dress becomes me — I'll not mask me
Till I have seen Lance Blackthorn. Lance, I say !   *[Calls.*
Blackthorn, make haste !

Enter BLACKTHORN, *half dressed as Owlspiegle.*

BLA. Here am I — Blackthorn in the upper half,
Much at your service; but my nether parts
Are goblinized and Owlspiegled. I had much ado
To get these trankums on. I judge Lord Erick
Kept no good house, and starved his quondam barber.

KAT. Peace, ass, and hide you — Gullcrammer is coming;
He left the hall before, but then took fright,
And e'en sneak'd back. The Lady Flora lights him —
Trim occupation for her ladyship !

Had you seen Leonard, when she left
　the hall
On such fine errand!

BLA. This Gullcrammer shall have a
　bob extraordinary
For my good comrade's sake. — But tell
me, Katleen,
What dress is this of yours?

KAT.　　　　　　　A page's, fool!

BLA. I am accounted no great scholar,
But 'tis a page that I would fain peruse
A little closer.　　　　[*Approaches her.*

KAT.　　　Put on your spectacles,
And try if you can read it at this distance,
For you shall come no nearer.

BLA. But is there nothing, then, save
　rank imposture,
In all these tales of goblinry at Devor-
　goil?

KAT. My aunt's grave lord thinks other-
　wise, supposing
That his great name so interests the
　Heavens,
That miracles must needs bespeak its fall.
I would that I were in a lowly cottage,
Beneath the greenwood, on its walls no
　armor
To court the levin-bolt ——

BLA. And a kind husband, Katleen,
To ward such dangers as must needs come
　nigh. —
My father's cottage stands so low and
　lone,
That you would think it solitude itself;
The greenwood shields it from the north-
　ern blast,
And, in the woodbine round its latticed
　casement,
The linnet's sure to build the earliest nest
In all the forest.

KAT. Peace, you fool, — they come.
　　　[FLORA *lights* GULLCRAMMER
　　　　across the Stage.

KAT. (*when they have passed*) — Away
　with you!
On with your cloak — be ready at the
　signal.

BLA. And shall we talk of that same
　cottage, Katleen,
At better leisure? I have much to say
In favor of my cottage.

KAT.　　　　If you will be talking,
You know I can't prevent you.

BLA.　　　　　　That's enough.
(*Aside.*) I shall have leave, I see, to
　spell the page
A little closer, when the due time comes.

SCENE II.

Scene changes to GULLCRAMMER'S *sleeping Apartment. He enters, ushered in
by* FLORA, *who sets on the table a flask,
with the lamp.*

FLO. A flask, in case your Reverence
　be athirsty;
A light, in case your Reverence be
　afear'd; —
And so, sweet slumber to your Rever-
　ence.

GUL. Kind Mistress Flora, will you? —
　eh! eh! eh!

FLO. Will I what?

GUL. Tarry a little?

FLO. (*smiling*). Kind Master Gull-
　crammer,
How can you ask me aught so unbecom-
　ing?

GUL. Oh, fie, fie, fie! — Believe me,
　Mistress Flora,
'Tis not for that — but being guided
　through
Such dreary galleries, stairs, and suites
　of rooms,
To this same cubicle, I'm somewhat loth
To bid adieu to pleasant company.

FLO. A flattering compliment! — In
　plain truth, you are frighten'd.

GUL. What! frighten'd? — I — I
　am not timorous.

FLO. Perhaps you've heard this is our
　haunted chamber?
But then it is our best. — Your Rever-
　ence knows,
That in all tales which turn upon a ghost,
Your traveller belated has the luck
To enjoy the haunted room — it is a
　rule: —
To some it were a hardship, but to you,
Who are a scholar, and not timorous ——

GUL. I did not say I was not timorous,
I said I was not temerarious. —
I'll to the hall again.

FLO.　　　　　You'll do your pleasure,
But you have somehow moved my father's
　anger,

And you had better meet our playful
    Owlspiegle —
So is our goblin call'd — than face Lord
    Oswald.
    GUL. Owlspiegle? —
It is an uncouth and outlandish name,
And in mine ears sounds fiendish.
    FLO. Hush, hush, hush!
Perhaps he hears us now — (*in an under-
    tone*) — A merry spirit;
None of your elves that pinch folks black
    and blue,
For lack of cleanliness.
    GUL. As for that, Mistress Flora,
My taffeta doublet hath been duly brush'd,
My shirt hebdomadal put on this morn-
    ing.
    FLO. Why, you need fear no goblins.
But this Owlspiegle
Is of another class; — yet has his frolics;
Cuts hair, trims beards, and plays amid
    his antics
The office of a sinful mortal barber.
Such is at least the rumor.
    GUL. He will not cut my clothes, or
    scar my face,
Or draw my blood?
    FLO.   Enormities like these
Were never charged against him.
    GUL. And, Mistress Flora, would you
    smile on me,
If, prick'd by the fond hope of your ap-
    proval,
Should endure this venture?
    FLO.   I do hope
    shall have cause to smile.
    GUL.   Well! in that hope
    will embrace the achievement for thy
    sake.   [*She is going.*
Yet, stay, stay, stay! — on second
    thoughts I will not —
've thought on it, and will the mortal
    cudgel
Rather endure than face the ghostly
    razor !
Your crab-tree's tough, but blunt, — your
    razor's polish'd,
But, as the proverb goes, 'tis cruel sharp.
'll to thy father, and unto his pleasure
Submit these destined shoulders.
    FLO.   But you shall not —
Believe me, sir, you shall not; he is
    desperate,

And better far be trimm'd by ghost or
    goblin,
Than by my sire in anger; — there are
    stores
Of hidden treasure, too, and Heaven
    knows what,
Buried among these ruins — you shall
    stay.
(*Apart.*) And if indeed there be such
    sprite as Owlspiegle,
And, lacking him, that thy fear plague
    thee not
Worse than a goblin, I have miss'd my
    purpose,
Which else stands good in either case. —
    Good-night, sir.
            [*Exit, and double locks the door.*
    GUL. Nay, hold ye, hold ! Nay, gentle
    Mistress Flora,
Wherefore this ceremony? — She has
    lock'd me in,
And left me to the goblin ! — (*Listening.*)
    So, so, so !
I hear her light foot trip to such a dis-
    tance,
That I believe the castle's breadth divides
    me
From human company. — I'm ill at
    ease —
But if this citadel (*laying his hand on
    his stomach*) were better victual'd,
It would be better mann'd.
            [*Sits down and drinks.*
She has a footstep light, and taper ankle.
            [*Chuckles.*
Aha ! that ankle ! yet, confound it too,
But for those charms Melchisedek had
    been
Snug in his bed at Mucklewhame — I say,
Confound her footstep, and her instep
    too,
To use a cobbler's phrase. — There I was
    quaint.
Now, what to do in this vile circumstance,
To watch or go to bed, I can't deter-
    mine;
Were I a-bed, the ghost might catch me
    napping,
And if I watch, my terrors will increase
As ghostly hours approach. I'll to my
    bed
E'en in my taffeta doublet, shrink my
    head

Beneath the clothes — leave the lamp
burning there,

        [Sets it on the table.
And trust to fate the issue.

    *[He lays aside his cloak, and
    brushes it, as from habit, start-
    ing at every moment ; ties a
    napkin over his head; then
    shrinks beneath the bed-clothes.
    He starts once or twice, and at
    length seems to go to sleep. A
    bell tolls* ONE. *He leaps up in
    his bed.*

GUL. I had just coax'd myself to sweet
    forgetfulness,
And that confounded bell, I hate all bells,
Except a dinner-bell — and yet I lie, too,—
I love the bell that soon shall tell the parish
Of Gabblegoose, Melchisedek's incum-
    bent —
And shall the future minister of Gabble-
    goose,
Whom his parishioners will soon require
To exorcise their ghosts, detect their
    witches,
Lie shivering in his bed for a pert goblin,
Whom, be he switch'd or cocktail'd,
    horn'd or poll'd,
A few tight Hebrew words will soon send
    packing?
Tush ! I will rouse the parson up within me,
And bid defiance —— (*A distant noise.*)
    In the name of Heaven,
What sounds are these? — O Lord ! this
    comes of rashness !

    *[Draws his head down under the
    bed-clothes.*

Duet without, between OWLSPIEGLE *and*
    COCKLEDEMOY.

OWLS.   Cockledemoy,
        My boy, my boy,
COCKL.   Here, father, here.
OWLS. Now the pole-star's red and burning,
    And the witch's spindle turning,
        Appear, appear !

    GUL. (*who has again raised himself,
    and listened with great terror to
    the Duet*) —

I have heard of the devil's dam before,
But never of his child. Now Heaven
    deliver me.

The Papists have the better of us there, —
They have their Latin prayers, cut and
    dried,
And pat for such occasion. — I can think
On naught but the vernacular.

OWLS.   Cockledemoy !
        My boy, my boy,
            We'll sport us here —
COCKL.   Our gambols play,
        Like elve and fay;
OWLS.   And domineer,
BOTH.   Laugh, frolic, and frisk, till the
        morning appear.
COCKL.   Lift latch — open clasp —
        Shoot bolt —and burst hasp

    *[The door opens with violence.
    Enter* BLACKTHORN *as* OWL-
    SPIEGLE, *fantastically dressed
    as a Spanish Barber, tall, thin,
    emaciated, and ghostly ;* KAT-
    LEEN, *as* COCKLEDEMOY, *at-
    tends as his page. All their
    manners, tones, and motions
    are fantastic, as those of Gob-
    lins. They make two or three
    times the circuit of the Room,
    without seeming to see* GULL-
    CRAMMER. *They then resume
    their Chant, or Recitative.*

OWLS.   Cockledemoy !
        My boy, my boy,
    What wilt thou do that will give
        thee joy?
    Wilt thou ride on the midnight
        owl?
COCKL.   No; for the weather is stormy
        and foul.
OWLS.   Cockledemoy !
        My boy, my boy,
    What wilt thou do that can give
        thee joy?
    With a needle for a sword, and
        a thimble for a hat,
    Wilt thou fight a traverse with
        the castle cat?
COCKL.   Oh no ! she has claws, and I
        like not that.

    GUL. I see the devil is a doting father,
And spoils his children — 'tis the surest
    way
To make curst imps of them. They see
    me not —

What will they think on next? It must
be own'd,
They have a dainty choice of occupations.

Owls. Cockledemoy!
   My boy, my boy,
   What shall we do that can give
      thee joy?
   Shall we go seek for a cuckoo's
      nest?

Cockl. That's best, that's best!

Both. About, about,
   Like an elvish scout,
   The cuckoo's a gull, and we'll
      soon find him out.

[*They search the room with mops
and mows. At length* Cockledemoy *jumps on the bed.* Gullcrammer *raises himself half up,
supporting himself by his hands.*
Cockledemoy *does the same,
and grins at him, then skips
from the bed, and runs to* Owlspiegle.

Cockl.   I've found the nest,
   And in it a guest,
   With a sable cloak and a taffeta
      vest;
   He must be wash'd, and trimm'd,
      and drest,
   To please the eyes he loves the
      best.

Owls. That's best, that's best.

Both. He must be shaved, and trimm'd
      and drest,
   To please the eyes he loves the
      best.

[*They arrange shaving things on
the table, and sing as they prepare them.*

Both. Know that all of the humbug, the
      bite, and the buz,
   Of the make-believe world, be-
      comes forfeit to us.

Owls. (*sharpening his razor*) —
   The sword this is made of was
      lost in a fray
   By a fop, who first bullied and
      then ran away;
   And the strap, from the hide of
      a lame racer, sold
   By Lord Match, to his friend,
      for some hundreds in gold.

Both. For all of the humbug, the bite,
      and the buz,
   Of the make-believe world, be-
      comes forfeit to us.

Cockl. (*placing the napkin*) —
   And this cambric napkin, so
      white and so fair,
   At an usurer's funeral I stole
      from the heir.

[*Drops something from a vial,
as going to make suds.*

   This dewdrop I caught from one
      eye of his mother,
   Which wept, while she ogled the
      parson with t'other.

Both. For all of the humbug, the bite,
      and the buz,
   Of the make-believe world, be-
      comes forfeit to us

Owls. (*arranging the lather and the
basin*) —
   My soap-ball is of the mild al-
      kali made,
   Which the soft dedicator em-
      ploys in his trade;
   And it froths with the pith of a
      promise, that's sworn
   By a lover at night, and forgot
      on the morn.

Both. For all of the humbug, the bite,
      and the buz,
   Of the make-believe world, be-
      comes forfeit to us.
   Halloo, halloo,
   The blackcock crew,
   Thrice shriek'd hath the owl,
      thrice croak'd hath the
      raven,
   Here ho! Master Gullcrammer,
      rise and be shaven?

Da capo.

Gul. (*who has been observing them*).
I'll pluck a spirit up, they're merry gob-
   lins,
And will deal mildly.   I will soothe their
   humor;
Besides, my beard lacks trimming.

[*He rises from his bed, and advances with great symptoms of
trepidation, but affecting an air*

of composure.   The Goblins re-
ceive him with fantastic cere-
mony.

Gentlemen, 'tis your will I should be
 trimm'd —
E'en do your pleasure.
          [*They point to a seat — he sits.*
          Think, howsoe'er,
Of me as one who hates to see his blood;
Therefore I do beseech you, signior,
Be gentle in your craft.   I know those
 barbers,
One would have harrows driven across
 his visnomy,
Rather than they should touch it with a
 razor.

OWLSPIEGLE *shaves* GULLCRAMMER *while*
          COCKLEDEMOY *sings.*

Father never started hair,
 Shaved too close, or left too bare —
Father's razor slips as glib
 As from courtly tongue a fib.
Whiskers, mustache, he can trim in
 Fashion meet to please the women;
Sharp's his blade, perfumed his lather !
 Happy those are trimm'd by father !

GUL. That's a good boy.   I love to
 hear a child
Stand for his father, if he were the devil.
          [*He motions to rise.*
Craving your pardon, sir. — What ! sit
 again ?
My hair lacks not your scissors.
          [OWLSPIEGLE *insists on his sitting.*
Nay, if you're peremptory, I'll ne'er dis-
 pute it,
Nor eat the cow and choke upon the tail —
E'en trim me to your fashion.

          [OWLSPIEGLE *cuts his hair, and*
          shaves his head ridiculously.

COCKLEDEMOY (*sings as before*).

Hair-breadth 'scapes, and hair-breadth
 snares,
Hair-brain'd follies, ventures, cares,
Part when father clips your hairs.
If there is a hero frantic,
Or a lover too romantic; —
If threescore seeks second spouse,
Or fourteen lists lover's vows,
Bring them here — for a Scotch boddle,
Owlspiegle shall trim their noddle.

[*They take the napkin from abou*
 GULLCRAMMER'S *neck.   He*
 makes bows of acknowledgment
 which they return fantastically
 and sing—

Thrice crow'd hath the blackcock, thrice
 croak'd hath the raven,
And Master Melchisedek Gullcrammer's
 shaven !
  GUL. My friends, you are too musical
 for me,
But though I cannot cope with you in
 song,
I would, in humble prose, inquire of you,
If that you will permit me to acquit
Even with the barber's pence the barber's
 service ?
          [*They shake their heads.*
Or if there is aught else that I can do for
 you,
Sweet Master Owlspiegle, or your loving
 child,
The hopeful Cockle'moy ?
COCKL. Sir, you have been trimm'd of
 late;
Smooth's your chin, and bald your pate;
Lest cold rheums should work you harm,
Here's a cap to keep you warm.
  GUL. Welcome, as Fortunatus' wish-
 ing cap,
For 'twas a cap that I was wishing for.
(There I was quaint in spite of mortal
 terror.)

          [*As he puts on the cap, a pair of*
          ass's ears disengage themselves.

Upon my faith, it is a dainty head-dress,
And might become an alderman ! —
 Thanks, sweet Monsieur,
Thou'rt a considerate youth.

          [*Both Goblins bow with ceremony*
          to GULLCRAMMER, *who returns*
          their salutation. OWLSPIEGLE
          descends by the trap-door.
          COCKLEDEMOY *springs out at*
          window.

          SONG (*without*).

OWL. Cockledemoy, my hope, my care,
 Where art thou now, O tell me where?
COCKL.   Up in the sky,
          On the bonny dragonfly,

Come, father, come you too —
She has four wings and strength enow,
And her long body has room for two.

GUL. Cockledemoy now is a naughty
  brat —
Would have the poor old stiff-rump'd
  devil, his father,
Peril his fiendish neck.   All boys are
  thoughtless.

SONG.

OWL. Which way didst thou take?
COCKL. I have fallen in the lake —
    Help, father, for Beelzebub's sake.

GUL. The imp is drown'd — a strange
  death for a devil!
O, may all boys take warning, and be
  civil;
Respect their loving sires, endure a chiding,
Nor roam by night on dragonflies a-riding!

COCKL. (*sings*). Now merrily, merrily,
    row I to shore,
    My bark is a bean-shell, a straw for
      an oar.
OWL. (*sings*). My life, my joy,
    My Cockledemoy!

GUL. I can bear this no longer — thus
  children are spoil'd.
(*Strikes into the tune.*) — Master Owl-
  spiegle, hoy!
He deserves to be whipp'd, little Cockle-
  demoy!
[*Their voices are heard as if dying away.*
GUL. They're gone! — Now, am I
  scared, or am I not?
I think the very desperate ecstasy
Of fear has given me courage.   This is
  strange, now!
When they were here I was not half so
  frighten'd
As now they are gone — they were a sort
  of company.
What a strange thing is use! — A horn,
  a claw,
The tip of a fiend's tail, was wont to
  scare me; —
Now am I with the devil hand and glove;
His soap has lather'd, and his razor shaved
  me;
I've joined him in a catch, kept time and
  tune,

Could dine with him, nor ask for a long
  spoon;
And if I keep not better company,
What will become of me when I shall die?
[*Exit.*

SCENE III.

*A Gothic Hall, waste and ruinous.   The
  moonlight is at times seen through the
  shafted windows.   Enter* KATLEEN
  and BLACKTHORN — *They have thrown
  off the more ludicrous parts of their disguise.*

KAT. This way — this way.   Was ever
  fool so gull'd!
BLA. I play'd the barber better than I
  thought for.
Well, I've an occupation in reserve,
When the long bow and merry musket
  fail me. —
But hark ye, pretty Katleen.
KAT.   What should I hearken to?
BLA. Art thou not afraid,
In these wild halls while playing feigned
  goblins,
That we may meet with real ones?
KAT.   Not a jot.
My spirit is too light, my heart too bold,
To fear a visit from the other world.
BLA. But is not this the place, the very
  hall
In which men say that Oswald's grand-
  father,
The black Lord Erick, walks his penance
  round?
Credit me, Katleen, these half-moulder'd
  columns
Have in their ruin something very fiendish,
And, if you'll take an honest friend's
  advice,
The sooner that you change their shat-
  ter'd splendor
For the snug cottage that I told you of,
Believe me, it will prove the blither
  dwelling.
KAT. If I e'er see that cottage, honest
  Blackthorn,
Believe me, it shall be from other motive
Than fear of Erick's spectre.
          [*A rustling sound is heard.*
BLA.   I heard a rustling sound —
Upon my life, there's something in the
  hall.

Katleen, besides us two!

KAT.   A yeoman thou,
A forester, and frighten'd! I am sorry
I gave the fool's-cap to poor Gullcrammer,
And let thy head go bare.

  [*The same rushing sound is repeated.*
BLA. Why, are you mad, or hear you
    not the sound?

KAT. And if I do, I take small heed
    of it.
Will you allow a maiden to be bolder
Than you, with beard on chin and sword
    at girdle?

BLA. Nay, if I had my sword, I would
    not care;
Tho' I ne'er heard of master of defence,
So active at his weapon as to brave
The devil, or a ghost — See! see! see
    yonder!

  [*A Figure is imperfectly seen be-*
    tween two of the pillars.

KAT. There's something moves, that's
    certain, and the moonlight,
Chased by the flitting gale, is too imperfect
To show its form; but, in the name of
    God,
I'll venture on it boldly.

BLA.   Wilt thou so?
Were I alone, now, I were strongly
    tempted
To trust my heels for safety; but with
    thee,
Be it fiend or fairy, Ill take risk to meet it.

KAT. It stands full in our path, and
    we must pass it,
Or tarry here all night.

BLA.   In its vile company?

  [*As they advance towards the*
    Figure, it is more plainly distin-
    guished, which might, I think,
    be contrived by raising successive
    screens of crape. The Figure is
    wrapped in a long robe, like the
    mantle of a Hermit, or Palmer.

PALMER. Ho! ye who thread by night
    these wildering scenes,
In garb of those who long have slept in
    death,
Fear ye the company of those you imitate?

BLA. This is the devil, Katleen, let us
    fly!   [*Runs off.*

KAT. I will not fly — why should I
    My nerves shake
To look on this strange vision, but my
    heart
Partakes not the alarm. — If thou dos
    come in Heaven's name,
In Heaven's name art thou welcome!

PAL. I come, by Heaven permitted
    Quit this castle:
There is a fate on't — if for good or evil
Brief space shall soon determine. I
    that fate,
If good, by lineage thou canst nothing
    claim,
If evil, much may'st suffer. — Leave these
    precincts.

KAT. Whate'er thou art, be answer'd
    — Know, I will not
Desert the kinswoman who train'd my
    youth;
Know, that I will not quit my friend, my
    Flora;
Know, that I will not leave the aged ma
Whose roof has shelter'd me. This i
    my resolve —
If evil come, I aid my friends to bear it
If good, my part shall be to see then
    prosper,
A portion in their happiness from which
No fiend can bar me.

PAL.   Maid, before thy courage
Firm built on innocence, even beings o
    nature,
More powerful far than thine, give place
    and way;
Take then this key, and wait the even
    with courage.

  [*He drops the key. — He disappear*
    gradually — the moonlight fail
    ing at the same time.

KAT. (*after a pause*). Whate'er it was
    'tis gone! My head turns round —
The blood that lately fortified my heart
Now eddies in full torrent to my brain,
And makes wild work with reason.
    will haste,
If that my steps can bear me so far safe
To living company. What if I meet it
Again in the long aisle, or vaulted pas
    sage?
And if I do, the strong support that bor
    me

Thro' this appalling interview, again
Shall strengthen and uphold me.

[*As she steps forward, she stumbles
over the key.*

What's this? The key? — there may be
mystery in't.
I'll to my kinswoman, when this dizzy fit
Will to give me leave to choose my way
aright.

[*She sits down exhausted.*

Re-enter BLACKTHORN, *with a drawn
sword and torch.*

BLA. Katleen! — what, Katleen! —
What a wretch was I
To leave her! — Katleen! — I am
weapon'd now,
And fear nor dog nor devil, — She re-
plies not!
Beast that I was! — nay, worse than
beast! The stag,
As timorous as he is, fights for his hind.
What's to be done? — I'll search this
cursed castle
From dungeon to the battlements; if I
find her not,
I'll fling me from the highest pinnacle —

KATLEEN (*who has somewhat gathered
her spirits in consequence of his entrance, comes behind and touches him :
he starts*).   Brave sir !
I'll spare you that rash leap — You're a
bold woodsman !
Surely I hope that from this night hence-
forward
You'll never kill a hare, since you're akin
to them.
O I could laugh — but that my head's so
dizzy.

BLA. Lean on me, Katleen — By my
honest word
I thought you close behind — I was surprised,
Not a jot frightened.

KAT. Thou art a fool to ask me to thy
cottage,
And then to show me at what slight expense
Of manhood I might master thee and it.

BLA. I'll take the risk of that — This
goblin business
Came rather unexpectedly; the best horse

Will start at sudden sights. Try me
again,
And if I prove not true to bonny Katleen,
Hang me in mine own bowstring.

[*Exeunt.*

SCENE IV.

*The Scene returns to the Apartment at the
beginning of Act Second.* OSWALD
and DURWARD *are discovered with*
ELEANOR, FLORA, *and* LEONARD —
DURWARD *shuts a Prayer-book, which
he seems to have been reading.*

DUR. 'Tis true — the difference betwixt
the churches,
Which zealots love to dwell on, to the
wise
Of either flock are of far less importance
Than those great truths to which all
Christian men
Subscribe with equal reverence.

OSW. We thank thee, father, for the
holy office,
Still best performed when the pastor's
tongue
Is echo to his breast: of jarring creeds
It ill beseems a layman's tongue to
speak —
Where have you stow'd yon prater?

[*To* FLORA.

FLO. Safe in the goblin-chamber.

ELE.   The goblin-chamber !
Maiden, wert thou frantic? — if his Rev-
erence
Have suffer'd harm by waspish Owl-
spiegle,
Be sure thou shalt abye it.

                Here he comes.
Can answer for himself !

Enter GULLCRAMMER *in the fashion in
which* OWLSPIEGLE *had put him ; having the fool's-cap on his head, and towel
about his neck, etc. His manner
through the scene is wild and extravagant, as if the fright had a little affected his brain.*

DUR. A goodly spectacle ! — Is there
such a goblin?
(*To* OSW.) Or has sheer terror made him
such a figure ?

OSW. There is a sort of wavering tradition

Of a malicious imp who teased all
    strangers;
My father wont to call him Owlspiegle.
    GUL. Who talks of Owlspiegle?
He is an honest fellow for a devil.
So is his son, the hopeful Cockle'moy.

(*Sings.*) " My hope, my joy,
                My Cockledemoy ! "

    LEO. The fool's bewitch'd — the gob-
lin hath furnish'd him
A cap which well befits his reverend wis-
    dom.
    FLO. If I could think he had lost his
    slender wits,
I should be sorry for the trick they play'd
    him.
    LEO. O fear him not; it were a foul
    reflection
On any fiend of sense and reputation,
To filch such petty wares as his poor
    brains.
    DUR. What saw'st thou, sir? — what
    heard'st thou?
    GUL. What was't I saw and heard?
That which old graybeards,
Who conjure Hebrew into Anglo-Saxon,
To cheat starved barons with, can little
    guess at.
    FLO. If he begin so roundly with my
    father,
His madness is not like to save his bones.
    GUL. Sirs, midnight came, and with it
    came the goblin.
I had reposed me after some brief study;
But as the soldier, sleeping in the trench,
Keeps sword and musket by him, so I
    had
My little Hebrew manual prompt for ser-
    vice.
    FLO. *Sausagian soused-face ;* that much
    of your Hebrew
Even I can bear in memory.
    GUL.   We counter'd,
The goblin and myself, even in mid-
    chamber,
And each stept back a pace, as 'twere to
    study
The foe he had to deal with ! — I be-
    thought me,
Ghosts ne'er have the first word, and so
    I took it,
And fired a volley of round Greek at him.

He stood his ground, and answer'd in
    the Syriac;
I flank'd my Greek with Hebrew, and
    compell'd him —   [*A noise heard.*
    OSW. Peace, idle prater ! — Hark —
    what sounds are these?
Amid the growling of the storm without,
I hear strange notes of music, and the
    clash
Of coursers' trampling feet.

    VOICES (*without*). We come, dark
        riders of the night,
    And flit before the dawning light;
    Hill and valley, far aloof,
    Shake to hear our chargers' hoof;
    But not a foot-stamp on the green
    At morn shall show where we have
        been.

    OSW. These must be revellers be-
    lated —
Let them pass on; the ruin'd halls of
    Devorgoil
Open to no such guests. —

    [*Flourish of trumpets at a distance,
        then nearer.*

                    They sound a summons;
What can they lack at this dead hour of
    night?
Look out, and see their number, and
    their bearing.
    LEO. (*goes up to the window*) —
'Tis strange — one single shadowy form
    alone
Is hovering on the drawbridge — far apart
Flit thro' the tempest banners, horse, and
    riders,
In darkness lost, or dimly seen by light-
    ning. —
Hither the figure moves -- the bolts re-
    volve —
The gate uncloses to him.
    ELE.   Heaven protect us

The PALMER *enters* — GULLCRAMMER
        runs off.

    OSW. Whence, and what art thou? —
    for what end come hither?
    PAL. I come from a far land, where
    the storm howls not,
And the sun sets not, to pronounce to
    thee,
Oswald of Devorgoil, thy house's fate.

DUR. I charge thee, in the name we
late have kneel'd to ——

PAL. Abbot of Lanercost, I bid thee
peace!

ninterrupted let me do mine errand:
aron of Devorgoil, son of the bold, the
proud,
he warlike and the mighty, wherefore
wear'st thou
he habit of a peasant? Tell me, wherefore
re thy fair halls thus waste — thy chambers bare? ——
Where are the tapestries, where the conquer'd banners,
rophies, and gilded arms, that deck'd
the walls
f once proud Devorgoil?

*[He advances, and places himself
where the Armor hung, so as to
be nearly in the centre of the
Scene.*

DUR. Whoe'er thou art — if thou dost
know so much,
eeds must thou know ——

OSW. Peace! I will answer here; to
me he spoke —
Iysterious stranger, briefly I reply:
peasant's dress befits a peasant's fortune;
nd 'twere vain mockery to array these
walls
trophies, of whose memory naught remains,
ave that the cruelty outvied the valor
f those who wore them.

PAL. Degenerate as thou art,
now'st thou to whom thou say'st this?

*[He drops his mantle, and is dis-
covered armed as nearly as may
be to the suit which hung on the
wall; all express terror.*

OSW. It is himself — the spirit of mine
Ancestor!

ERI. Tremble not, son, but hear me!

*[He strikes the wall; it opens, and
discovers the Treasure-Cham-
ber.*

There lies piled
he wealth I brought from wasted Cumberland,

Enough to reinstate thy ruin'd for-
tunes. ——
Cast from thine high-born brows that
peasant bonnet,
Throw from thy noble grasp the peas-
ant's staff —
O'er all, withdraw thine hand from that
mean mate,
Whom in an hour of reckless despera-
tion
Thy fortunes cast thee on. This do,
And be as great as e'er was Devorgoil,
When Devorgoil was richest!

DUR. Lord Oswald, thou art tempted
by a fiend,
Who doth assail thee on thy weakest
side, —
Thy pride of lineage, and thy love of
grandeur.
Stand fast — resist — contemn his fatal
offers!

ELE. Urge him not, father; if the
sacrifice
Of such a wasted woe-worm wretch as I
am
Can save him from the abyss of misery,
Upon whose verge he's tottering, let me
wander
An unacknowledged outcast from his
castle,
Even to the humble cottage I was born
in.

OSW. No, Ellen, no — it is not thus
they part,
Whose hearts and souls, disasters borne
in common
Have knit together, close as summer
saplings
Are twined in union by the eddying tem-
pest. ——
Spirit of Erick, while thou bear'st his
shape,
I'll answer with no ruder conjuration
Thy impious counsel, other than with
these words,
Depart, and tempt me not!

ERI. Then Fate will have her course. ——
Fall, massive grate,
Yield them the tempting view of these
rich treasures,
But bar them from possession! (*A portcullis falls before the door of the Treas-
ure-Chamber.*) Mortals, hear!

No hand may ope that gate, except the
   heir
Of plunder'd Aglionby, whose mighty
   wealth,
Ravish'd in evil hour, lies yonder piled;
And not his hand prevails without the
   key
Of Black Lord Erick. Brief space is
   given
To save proud Devorgoil — so wills high
   Heaven. [*Thunder; he disappears.*
  DUR. Gaze not so wildly; you have
   stood the trial
That his commission bore, and Heaven
   designs,
If I may spell his will, to rescue Devor-
   goil
Even by the Heir of Aglionby — Behold
   him
In that young forester, unto whose hand
Those bars shall yield the treasures of
   his house,
Destined to ransom yours. — Advance,
   young Leonard,
And prove the adventure.
  LEO. (*advances, and attempts the
   grate*). It is fast
As is the tower, rock-seated.
  OSW. We will fetch other means, and
   prove its strength,
Nor starve in poverty, with wealth before
   us.
  DUR. Think what the vision spoke;
The key — the fated key ——

Enter GULLCRAMMER

  GUL. A key? — I say a quay is what
   we want,
Thus by the learn'd orthographized —
   Q, u, a, y.
The lake is overflow'd! — a quay, a boat,
Oars, punt, or sculler, is all one to me ! —
We shall be drown'd, good people ! ! !

Enter KATLEEN *and* BLACKTHORN.

  KAT.   Deliver us!
Haste, save yourselves — the lake is ris-
   ing fast.
  BLA. 'T has risen my bow's height in
   the last five minutes,
And still is swelling strangely.
  GUL. (*who has stood astonished upon
   seeing them*) —

We shall be drown'd without your kin
   assistance.
Sweet Master Owlspiegle, your dragor
   fly —
Your straw, your bean-stalk, gent
   Cockle'moy !
  LEO. (*looking from the shot-hole*).
'Tis true, by all that's fearful. The prou
   lake
Peers, like ambitious tyrant, o'er hi
   bounds,
And soon will whelm the castle — eve
   the drawbridge
Is under water now.
  KAT. Let us escape ! Why stand yo
   gazing there?
  DUR. Upon the opening of that fat
   grate
Depends the fearful spell that now er
   traps us.
The key of Black Lord Erick — ere w
   find it,
The castle will be whelm'd beneath th
   waves,
And we shall perish in it !
  KAT. (*giving the key*). Here, prov
   this:
A chance most strange and fearful gav
   it me.

    [OSWALD *puts it into the lock, an
      attempts to turn it — a loud cla
      of thunder.*

  FLO. The lake still rises faster. — Leon
   ard, Leonard,
Canst thou not save us !

    [LEONARD *tries the lock -- it open
      with a violent noise, and th
      Portcullis rises. A loud strai
      of wild music. — There may
      a Chorus here.*

    [OSWALD *enters the apartmen
      and brings out a scroll.*

  LEO. The lake is ebbing with as won
   drous haste
As late it rose — the drawbridge is le
   dry !
  OSW. This may explain the cause —
(GULLCRAMMER *offers to take it.*) Bu
   soft you, sir,
We'll not disturb your learning for th
   matter;

Yet, since you've borne a part in this
  strange drama,
You shall not go unguerdon'd. Wise or
  learn'd,
Modest or gentle, Heaven alone can make
  thee,
Being so much otherwise; but from this
  abundance
Thou shalt have that shall gild thine
  ignorance,
Exalt thy base descent, make thy presumption
Seem modest confidence, and find thee
  hundreds
Ready to swear that same fool's cap of
  thine
Is reverend as a mitre.

GULL. Thanks, mighty baron, now no
  more a bare one!
I will be quaint with him, for all his
  quips. [*Aside.*
Osw. Nor shall kind Katleen lack
Her portion in our happiness.

KAT. Thanks, my good lord, but Katleen's fate is fix'd —
There is a certain valiant forester,
Too much afear'd of ghosts to sleep
  anights
In his lone cottage, without one to guard
  him. —

LEO. If I forget my comrade's faithful
  friendship,
May I be lost to fortune, hope, and love!
DUR. Peace, all! and hear the blessing which this scroll
Speaks unto faith, and constancy, and
  virtue: —

  "No more this castle's troubled guest,
  Dark Erick's spirit hath found rest.
  The storms of angry Fate are past,
  For Constancy defies their blast.
  Of Devorgoil the daughter free
  Shall wed the heir of Aglionby;
  Nor ever more dishonor soil
  The rescued house of Devorgoil!"

AUCHINDRANE; OR, THE AYRSHIRE TRAGEDY.

Cur aliquid vidi? cur noxia lumina feci!
Cur imprudenti cognita culpa mihi est?
Ovidii Tristium, Liber Secundus.

PREFACE.

THERE is not perhaps, upon record, a tale of horror which gives us a more perfect picture than is afforded by the present, of the violence of our ancestors, or the complicated
crimes into which they were hurried, by what their wise, but ill-enforced, laws termed the
heathenish and accursed practice of Deadly Feud. The author has tried to extract some
dramatic scenes out of it; but he is conscious no exertions of his can increase the horror
of that which is in itself so iniquitous. Yet, if we look at modern events, we must not
too hastily venture to conclude that our own times have so much the superiority over
former days as we might at first be tempted to infer. Our great object has been obtained.
The power of the laws extends over the country universally, and if criminals at present
sometimes escape punishment, this can only be by eluding justice, — not, as of old, by
defying it.

But the motives which influence modern ruffians to commit actions at which we pause
with wonder and horror, arise, in a great measure, from the thirst of gain. For the hope
of lucre, we have seen a wretch seduced to his fate, under the pretext that he was to share
in amusement and conviviality; and, for gold, we have seen the meanest of wretches
deprived of life, and their miserable remains cheated of the grave.

The loftier, if equally cruel, feelings of pride, ambition, and love of vengeance, were the idols of our forefathers, while the caitiffs of our city bend to Mammon, the meanest of the spirits who fell. The criminals, therefore, of former times, drew their hellish inspiration from a loftier source than is known to modern villains. The fever of unsated ambition, the frenzy of ungratified revenge, the *perfervidum ingenium Scotorum*, stigmatized by our jurists and our legislators, held life but as passing breath; and such enormities as now sound like the acts of a madman, were then the familiar deeds of every offended noble. With these observations we proceed to our story.

John Muir, or Mure, of Auchindrane, the contriver and executor of the following cruelties, was a gentleman of an ancient family and a good estate in the west of Scotland; bold, ambitious, treacherous to the last degree, and utterly unconscientious, — a Richard the Third in private life, inaccessible alike to pity and remorse. His view was to raise the power and extend the grandeur of his own family. This gentleman had married the daughter of Sir Thomas Kennedy of Barganie, who was, excepting the Earl of Cassilis, the most important person in all Carrick, the district of Ayrshire which he inhabited, and where the name of Kennedy held so great a sway as to give rise to the popular rhyme: —

> " 'Twixt Wigton and the town of Air,
> Portpatrick and the Cruives of Cree,
> No man need think for to bide there,
> Unless he court Saint Kennedie."

Now, Mure of Auchindrane, who had promised himself high advancement by means of his father-in-law, Barganie, saw, with envy and resentment, that his influence remained second and inferior to the House of Cassilis, chief of all the Kennedys. The Earl was indeed a minor, but his authority was maintained, and his affairs well managed, by his uncle, Sir Thomas Kennedy of Cullayne, the brother of the deceased Earl, and tutor and guardian to the present. This worthy gentleman supported his nephew's dignity and the credit of the house so effectually, that Barganie's consequence was much thrown into the shade, and the ambitious Auchindrane, his son-in-law, saw no better remedy than to remove so formidable a rival as Cullayne by violent means.

For this purpose, in the year of God 1597, he came with a party of followers to the town of Maybole (where Sir Thomas Kennedy of Cullayne then resided), and lay in ambush in an orchard, through which he knew his destined victim was to pass, in returning homewards from a house where he was engaged to sup. Sir Thomas Kennedy came alone, and unattended, when he was suddenly fired upon by Auchindrane and his accomplices, who, having missed their aim, drew their swords, and rushed upon him to slay him. But the party thus assailed at disadvantage, had the good fortune to hide himself for that time in a ruinous house, where he lay concealed till the inhabitants of the place came to his assistance.

Sir Thomas Kennedy prosecuted Mure for this assault, who, finding himself in danger from the law, made a sort of apology and agreement with the Lord of Cullayne, to whose daughter he united his eldest son, in testimony of the closest friendship in the future. This agreement was sincere on the part of Kennedy, who, after it had been entered into, showed himself Auchindrane's friend and assistant on all occasions. But it was most false and treacherous on that of Mure, who continued to nourish the purpose of murdering his new friend and ally on the first opportunity.

Auchindrane's first attempt to effect this was by means of the young Gilbert Kennedy of Barganie (the old Barganie, Auchindrane's father-in-law, was dead), whom he persuaded to brave the Earl of Cassilis, as one who usurped an undue influence over the rest of the name. Accordingly, the hot-headed youth, at the instigation of Auchindrane. rode past the gate of the Earl of Cassilis, without waiting on his chief, or sending him any message of civility. This led to mutual defiance, being regarded by the Earl, according to the ideas of the time, as a personal insult. Both parties took the field with their followers, at the head of about two hundred and fifty men on each side. Barganie, with the rashness of headlong courage, and Auchindrane, fired by deadly enmity to the House of Cassilis, made a precipitate attack on the Earl, whose men were strongly posted, and under cover. They were received by a heavy fire. Barganie was slain. Mure of Auchindrane, severely wounded in the thigh, became unable to sit his horse, and, the leaders thus slain or disabled, their party drew off without continuing the action. It must be particularly observed, that Sir Thomas Kennedy remained neuter in this quarrel, considering his con nection with Auchindrane as too intimate to be broken even by his desire to assist his nephew.

For this temperate and honorable conduct he met a vile reward; for Auchindrane, in resentment of the loss of his relative Barganie, and the downfall of his ambitious hopes, continued his practices against the life of Sir Thomas of Cullayne, though totally innocent of contributing to either. Chance favored his wicked purpose.

The Knight of Cullayne, finding himself obliged to go to Edinburgh on a particular day, sent a message by a servant to Mure, in which he told him, in the most unsuspecting confidence, the purpose of his journey, and named the road which he proposed to take, inviting Mure to meet him at Duppill, to the west of the town of Ayr, a place appointed, for the purpose of giving him any commissions which he might have for Edinburgh, and assuring his treacherous ally he would attend to any business which he might have in the Scottish metropolis as anxiously as to his own. Sir Thomas Kennedy's message was carried to the town of Maybole, where his messenger, for some trivial reason, had the impost committed to writing by a schoolmaster in that town, and despatched it to its destination by means of a poor student, named Dalrymple, instead of carrying it to the house of Auchindrane in person.

This suggested to Mure a diabolical plot. Having thus received tidings of Sir Thomas Kennedy's motions, he conceived the infernal purpose of having the confiding friend who sent the information, waylaid and murdered at the place appointed to meet with him, not only in friendship, but for the purpose of rendering him service. He dismissed the messenger Dalrymple, cautioning the lad to carry back the letter to Maybole, and to say that he had not found him, Auchindrane, in his house. Having taken this precaution, he proceeded to instigate the brother of the slain Gilbert of Barganie, Thomas Kennedy of Drumurghie by name, and Walter Mure of Cloncaird, a kinsman of his own, to take this opportunity of revenging Barganie's death. The fiery young men were easily induced to undertake the crime. They waylaid the unsuspecting Sir Thomas of Cullayne at the place appointed to meet the traitor Auchindrane, and the murderers having in company five or six servants, well mounted and armed, assaulted and cruelly murdered him with many wounds. They then plundered the dead corpse of his purse, containing a thousand merks in gold, cut off the gold buttons which he wore on his coat, and despoiled the body of some valuable rings and jewels.

The revenge due for his uncle's murder was keenly pursued by the Earl of Cassilis. As the murderers fled from trial, they were declared outlaws; which doom, being pronounced by three blasts of a horn, was called " being put to the horn, and declared the king's rebel." Mure of Auchindrane was strongly suspected of having been the instigator of the crime. But he conceived there could be no evidence to prove his guilt if he could keep the boy Dalrymple out of the way, who delivered the letter which made him acquainted with Cullayne's journey, and the place at which he meant to halt. On the contrary, he saw, that if the lad could be produced at the trial, it would afford ground of fatal presumption, since it could be then proved that persons so nearly connected with him as Kennedy and Cloncaird had left his house, and committed the murder at the very spot which Cullayne had fixed for their meeting.

To avoid this imminent danger, Mure brought Dalrymple to his house, and detained him there for several weeks. But the youth tiring of this confinement, Mure sent him to reside with a friend, Montgomery of Skellmorly, who maintained him under a borrowed name, amid the desert regions of the then almost savage island of Arran. Being confident in the absence of this material witness, Auchindrane, instead of flying, like his agents Drumurghie and Cloncaird, presented himself boldly at the bar, demanded a fair trial, and offered his person in combat to the death against any of Lord Cassilis's friends who might impugn his innocence. This audacity was successful, and he was dismissed without trial.

Still, however, Mure did not consider himself safe, so long as Dalrymple was within the realm of Scotland; and the danger grew more pressing when he learned that the lad had become impatient of the restraint which he sustained in the island of Arran, and returned to some of his friends in Ayrshire. Mure no sooner heard of this than he again obtained possession of the boy's person, and a second time concealed him at Auchindrane, until he found an opportunity to transport him to the Low Countries, where he contrived to have him enlisted in Buccleuch's regiment, trusting, doubtless, that some one of the numerous chances of war might destroy the poor young man whose life was so dangerous to him.

But after five or six years' uncertain safety, bought at the expense of so much violence and cunning, Auchindrane's fears were exasperated into frenzy, when he found this dangerous witness, having escaped from all the perils of climate and battle, had left, or been discharged from, the Legion of Borderers, and had again accomplished his return to Ayrshire. There is ground to suspect that Dalrymple knew the nature of the hold which he possessed over Auchindrane, and was desirous of extorting from his fears some better provision than he had found either in Arran or the Netherlands. But if so, it was a fatal experiment to tamper with the fears of such a man as Auchindrane, who determined to rid himself effectually of this unhappy young man.

Mure now lodged him in a house of his own, called Chapeldonan, tenanted by a vassal and connection of his, called James Bannatyne. This man he commissioned to meet him at ten o'clock at night on the sea-sands near Girvan, and bring with him the unfortunate Dalrymple, the object of his fear and dread. The victim seems to have come with Bannatyne without the least suspicion, though such might have been raised by the time and place appointed for the meeting. When Bannatyne and Dalrymple came to the appointed spot, Auchindrane met them, accompanied by his eldest son, James. Old Auchindrane, having taken Bannatyne aside, imparted his bloody purpose of ridding himself of Dalrymple forever, by murdering him on the spot. His own life and honor were, he said, endangered by the manner in which this inconvenient witness repeatedly thrust himself back into Ayrshire, and nothing could secure his safety but taking the lad's life, in which action he requested James Bannatyne's assistance. Bannatyne felt some compunction, and remonstrated against the cruel expedient, saying, it would be better to transport Dalrymple to Ireland, and take precautions against his return. While old Auchindrane seemed disposed to listen to this proposal, his son concluded that the time was come for accomplishing the purpose of their meeting, and without waiting the termination of his father's conference with Bannatyne, he rushed suddenly on Dalrymple, beat him to the ground, and, kneeling down on him, with his father's assistance accomplished the crime by strangling the unhappy object of their fear and jealousy. Bannatyne, the witness, and partly the accomplice, of the murder, assisted them in their attempt to make a hole in the sand, with a spade which they had brought on purpose, in order to conceal the dead body. But as the tide was coming in, the hole which they made filled with water before they could get the body buried, and the ground seemed to their terrified consciences to refuse to be accessory to concealing their crime. Despairing of hiding the corpse in the manner they proposed, the murderers carried it out into the sea as deep as they dared wade, and there abandoned it to the billows, trusting that a wind, which was blowing off the shore, would drive these remains of their crime out to sea, where they would never more be heard of. But the sea, as well as the land, seemed unwilling to conceal their cruelty. After floating for some hours, or days, the dead body was, by the wind and tide, again driven on shore, near the very spot where the murder had been committed.

This attracted general attention, and when the corpse was known to be that of the same William Dalrymple whom Auchindrane had so often spirited out of the country, or concealed when he was in it, a strong and general suspicion arose, that this young person had met with foul play from the bold, bad man who had shown himself so much interested in his absence. It was always said or supposed, that the dead body had bled at the approach of a grandchild of Mure of Auchindrane, a girl who, from curiosity, had come to look at a sight which others crowded to see. The bleeding of the murdered corpse at the touch of the murderer, was a thing at that time so much believed, that it was admitted as a proof of guilt ; but I know no case, save that of Auchindrane, in which the phenomenon was supposed to be extended to the approach of the innocent kindred ; nor do I think that the fact itself, though mentioned by ancient lawyers, was ever admitted to proof in the proceedings against Auchindrane.

It is certain, however, that Auchindrane found himself so much the object of suspicion from this new crime, that he resolved to fly from justice, and suffer himself to be declared a rebel and outlaw rather than face a trial. But his conduct in preparing to cover his flight with another motive than the real one, is a curious picture of the men and manners of the times. He knew well that if he were to shun his trial for the murder of Dalrymple, the whole country would consider him as a man guilty of a mean and disgraceful crime in putting to death an obscure lad, against whom he had no personal quarrel. He knew, besides, that his powerful friends, who would have interceded for him had his offence been merely burning a house, or killing a neighbor, would not plead for or stand by him in so pitiful a concern as the slaughter of this wretched wanderer

Accordingly, Mure sought to provide himself with some ostensible cause for avoiding law, with which the feelings of his kindred and friends might sympathize; and none occurred to him so natural as an assault upon some friend and adherent of the Earl of Cassilis. Should he kill such a one, it would be indeed an unlawful action, but so far from being infamous, would be accounted the natural consequence of the avowed quarrel between the families. With this purpose, Mure, with the assistance of a relative, of whom he seems always to have had some ready to execute his worst purposes, beset Hugh Kennedy of Garriehorne, a follower of the Earl's, against whom they had especial ill-will, fired their pistols at him, and used other means to put him to death. But Garriehorne, a stouthearted man, and well armed, defended himself in a very different manner from the unfortunate Knight of Cullayne, and beat off the assailants, wounding young Auchindrane in the right hand, so that he well-nigh lost the use of it.

But though Auchindrane's purpose did not entirely succeed, he availed himself of it to circulate a report, that if he could obtain a pardon for firing upon a feudal enemy with pistols, weapons declared unlawful by Act of Parliament, he would willingly stand his trial for the death of Dalrymple, respecting which he protested his total innocence. The King, however, was decidedly of opinion that the Mures, both father and son, were alike guilty of both crimes, and used intercession with the Earl of Abercorn, as a person of power in those western counties, as well as in Ireland, to arrest and transmit them prisoners to Edinburgh. In consequence of the Earl's exertions, old Auchindrane was made prisoner, and lodged in the tolbooth of Edinburgh.

Young Auchindrane no sooner heard that his father was in custody, than he became as apprehensive of Bannatyne (the accomplice of Dalrymple's murder) telling tales, as ever his father had been of Dalrymple. He therefore hastened to him, and prevailed on him to pass over for a while to the neighboring coast of Ireland, finding him money and means to accomplish the voyage, and engaging in the mean time to take care of his affairs in Scotland. Secure, as they thought, in this precaution, old Auchindrane persisted in his innocence, and his son found security to stand his trial. Both appeared with the same confidence at the day appointed, and braved the public justice, hoping to be put to a formal trial, in which Auchindrane reckoned upon an acquittal for want of the evidence which he had removed. The trial was, however, postponed, and Mure the elder was dismissed, under high security to return when called for.

But King James, being convinced of the guilt of the accused, ordered young Auchindrane, instead of being sent to trial, to be examined under the force of torture, in order to compel him to tell whatever he knew of the things charged against him. He was accordingly severely tortured; but the result only served to show that such examinations are as useless as they are cruel. A man of weak resolution, or of a nervous habit, would probably have assented to any confession, however false, rather than have endured the extremity of fear and pain to which Mure was subjected. But young Auchindrane, a strong and determined ruffian, endured the torture with the utmost firmness, and by the constant audacity with which, in spite of the intolerable pain, he continued to assert his innocence, he spread so favorable an opinion of his case, that the detaining him in prison, instead of bringing him to open trial, was censured as severe and oppressive. James, however, remained firmly persuaded of his guilt, and by an exertion of authority quite inconsistent with our present laws, commanded young Auchindrane to be still detained in close custody till further light could be thrown on these dark proceedings. He was detained accordingly by the King's express personal command, and against the opinion even of his privy councilors. This exertion of authority was much murmured against.

In the meanwhile, old Auchindrane, being, as we have seen, at liberty on pledges, skulked about in the west feeling how little security he had gained by Dalrymple's murder, and that he had placed himself by that crime in the power of Bannatyne, whose evidence concerning the death of Dalrymple could not be less fatal than what Dalrymple might have told concerning Auchindrane's accession to the conspiracy against Sir Thomas Kennedy of Cullayne. But though the event had shown the error of his wicked policy, Auchindrane could think of no better mode in this case than that which had failed in relation to Dalrymple. When any man's life became inconsistent with his own safety, no idea seems to have occurred to this inveterate ruffian, save to murder the person by whom he might himself be in any way endangered. He therefore attempted the life of James Bannatyne by more agents than one. Nay, he had nearly ripened a plan by which one Pennycuke was to be employed to slay Bannatyne, while, after the deed was done, it was devised that Mure of Auchnull, a connection of Bannatyne, should be instigated to slay Pennycuke; and thus close up the train of murders by one, which, flowing in the ordinary course of deadly feud, should have nothing in it so particular as to attract much attention.

But the justice of Heaven would bear this complicated train of iniquity no longer. Bannatyne, knowing with what sort of men he had to deal, kept on his guard, and by his caution disconcerted more than one attempt to take his life, while another miscarried by the remorse of Pennycuke, the agent whom Mure employed. At length Bannatyne, tiring of this state of insecurity, and in despair of escaping such repeated plots, and also feeling remorse for the crime to which he had been 'accessory, resolved rather to submit himself to the severity of the law, than remain the object of the principal criminal's practices. He surrendered himself to the Earl of Abercorn, and was transported to Edinburgh, where he confessed before the King and council all the particulars of the murder of Dalrymple, and the attempt to hide his body by committing it to the sea.

When Bannatyne was confronted with the two Mures before the Privy Council, they denied with vehemence every part of the evidence he had given, and affirmed that the witness had been bribed to destroy them by a false tale. Bannatyne's behavior seemed sincere and simple, that of Auchindrane more resolute and crafty. The wretched accomplice fell upon his knees, invoking God to witness that all the land in Scotland could not have bribed him to bring a false accusation against a master whom he had served, loved, and followed in so many dangers, and calling upon Auchindrane to honor God by confessing the crime he had committed. Mure the elder, on the other hand, boldly replied, that he hoped God would not so far forsake him as to permit him to confess a crime of which he was innocent, and exhorted Bannatyne in his turn to confess the practices by which he had been induced to devise such falsehood against him.

The two Mures, father and son, were therefore put upon their solemn trial along with Bannatyne, in 1611, and, after a great deal of evidence had been brought in support of Bannatyne's confession, all these were found guilty. The elder Auchindrane was convicted of counselling and directing the murder of Sir Thomas Kennedy of Cullayne, and also of the actual murder of the lad Dalrymple. Bannatyne and the young Mure were found guilty of the latter crime, and all three were sentenced to be beheaded. Bannatyne, however, the accomplice, received the King's pardon, in consequence of his voluntary surrender and confession. The two Mures were both executed. The younger was affected by the remonstrances of the clergy who attended him, and he confessed the guilt of which he was accused. The father, also, was at length brought to avow the fact, but in other respects died as impenitent as he had lived;—and so ended this dark and extraordinary tragedy.

The Lord Advocate of the day, Sir Thomas Hamilton, afterwards successively Earl of Melrose and of Haddington, seems to have busied himself much in drawing up a statement of this foul transaction, for the purpose of vindicating to the people of Scotland the severe course of justice observed by King James VI. He assumes the task in a high tone of prerogative law, and on the whole, seems at a loss whether to attribute to Providence, or to his most sacred Majesty, the greatest share in bringing to light these mysterious villanies, but rather inclines to the latter opinion. There is, I believe, no printed copy of the intended tract, which seems never to have been published; but the curious will be enabled to judge of it, as it appears in the next *fasciculus* of Mr. Robert Pitcairn's very interesting publications from the Scottish Criminal Record.

The family of Auchindrane did not become extinct on the death of the two homicides. The last descendant existed in the eighteenth century, a poor and distressed man. The following anecdote shows that he had a strong feeling of his situation :—

There was in front of the old castle a huge ash-tree, called the Dule-tree (*mourning-tree*) of Auchindrane, probably because it was the place where the baron executed the criminals who fell under his jurisdiction. It is described as having been the finest tree in the neighborhood. This last representative of the family of Auchindrane had the misfortune to be arrested for payment of a small debt: and, unable to discharge it, was preparing to accompany the messenger (bailiff) to the jail of Ayr. The servant of the law had compassion for his prisoner, and offered to accept of this remarkable tree as of value adequate to the discharge of the debt. "What," said the debtor, "sell the Dule-tree of Auchindrane. I will sooner die in the worst dungeon of your prison." In this luckless character the line of Auchindrane ended. The family, blackened with the crimes of its predecessors, became extinct, and the estate passed into other hands.

DRAMATIS PERSONÆ.

JOHN MURE OF AUCHINDRANE, *an Ayrshire Baron. He has been a follower of the Regent, Earl of Morton, during the Civil Wars, and hides an oppressive, ferocious, and unscrupulous disposition, under some pretences to strictness of life and doctrine, which, however, never influence his conduct. He is in danger from the law, owing to his having been formerly active in the assassination of the Earl of Cassilis.*

PHILIP MURE, *his Son, a wild, debauched profligate, professing and practising a contempt for his father's hypocrisy, while he is as fierce and licentious as Auchindrane himself.*

GIFFORD, *their Relation, a Courtier.*

QUENTIN BLANE, *a Youth, educated for a clergyman, but sent by* AUCHINDRANE *to serve in a Band of Auxiliaries in the wars of the Netherlands, and lately employed as Clerk or Comptroller to the Regiment — disbanded, however, and on his return to his native Country. He is of a mild, gentle, and rather feeble character, liable to be influenced by any person of stronger mind who will take the trouble to direct him. He is somewhat of a nervous temperament, varying from sadness to gayety, according to the impulse of the moment ; an amiable hypochondriac.*

HILDEBRAND, *a stout old Englishman, who, by feats of courage, has raised himself to the rank of Sergeant-Major (then of greater consequence than at present). He, too, has been disbanded, but cannot bring himself to believe that he has lost his command over his Regiment.*

ABRAHAM,
WILLIAMS,
JENKINS,
And Others.
} *Privates dismissed from the same Regiment in which* QUENTIN *and* HILDEBRAND *had served. These are mutinous, and are much disposed to remember former quarrels with their late officers.*

NEIL MACLELLAN, *Keeper of Auchindrane Forest and Game.*

EARL OF DUNBAR, *commanding an Army as Lieutenant of James I., for execution of Justice on Offenders.*

Guards, Attendants, etc., etc.

MARION, *Wife of* NEIL MACLELLAN.
ISABEL, *their daughter, a Girl of six years old.*
Other Children and Peasant Women.

ACT I. — SCENE I.

A rocky Bay on the Coast of Carrick, in Ayrshire, not far from the Point of Turnberry. The sea comes in upon a bold, rocky Shore. The remains of a small half-ruined Tower are seen on the right hand, overhanging the sea. There is a Vessel at a distance in the offing. A Boat at the bottom of the Stage lands eight or ten persons, dressed like disbanded, and in one or two cases like disabled, Soldiers. They come straggling forward with their knapsacks and bundles. HILDEBRAND, *the Sergeant belonging to the party, a stout elderly man, stands by the boat, as if superintending the disembarkation.* QUENTIN *remains apart.*

ABRAHAM. Farewell the flats of Holland, and right welcome
The cliffs of Scotland! Fare thee well, black beer
And Schiedam gin! and welcome twopenny
Oatcakes and usquebaugh.

WILLIAMS (*who wants an arm*). Farewell the gallant field, and "Forward, pikemen!"
For the bridge-end, the suburb, and the lane —
And, "Bless your honor, noble gentleman,
Remember a poor soldier!"

ABR. My tongue shall never need to smooth itself
To such poor sounds, while it can boldly say,
"Stand and deliver!"

WIL. Hush! the sergeant hears you.

ABR. And let him hear; he makes a bustle yonder,
And dreams of his authority, forgetting
We are disbanded men, o'er whom his halberd
Has not such influence as the beadle's baton.
We are no soldiers now, but every one
The lord of his own person.

WIL. A wretched lordship — and our freedom such
As that of the old cart-horse, when the owner
Turns him upon the common. I for one
Will still continue to respect the sergeant,
And the comptroller, too, — while the cash lasts.

ABR. I scorn them both. I am too stout a Scotsman
To bear a Southron's rule an instant longer
Than discipline obliges; and for Quentin,
Quentin, the quillman, Quentin, the comptroller,
We have no regiment now; or, if we had,
Quentin's no longer clerk to it.

WIL. For shame! for shame! — What,
shall old comrades jar thus,
And on the verge of parting, and forever? —
Nay, keep thy temper, Abraham, tho' a bad one. —
Good Master Quentin, let thy song last night
Give us once more our welcome to old Scotland.

ABR. Ay, they sing light whose task is telling money,
When dollars clink for chorus.

QUE. I've done with counting silver, honest Abraham,
As thou, I fear, with pouching thy small share on't.
But lend your voices, lads, and I will sing
As blithely yet as if a town were won;
As if upon a field of battle gain'd,
Our banners waved victorious. — (*He
sings, and the rest bear chorus.*)

SONG.

Hither we come,
Once slaves to the drum,

But no longer we list to its rattle;
  Adieu to the wars,
  With their slashes and scars,
The march, and the storm, and the battle

  There are some of us maim'd,
  And some that are lamed,
And some of old aches are complaining
  But we'll take up the tools,
  Which we flung by like fools,
'Gainst Don Spaniard to go a-campaigning.

  Dick Hawthorn doth vow
  To return to the plough,
Jack Steele to his anvil and hammer;
  The weaver shall find room
  At the wight-wapping loom,
And your clerk shall teach writing and grammar.

ABR. And this is all that thou canst do, gay Quentin?
To swagger o'er a herd of parish brats,
Cut cheese or dibble onions with the poniard,
And turn the sheath into a ferula?

QUE. I am the prodigal in holy writ
I cannot work — to beg I am ashamed.
Besides, good mates, I care not who may know it,
I'm e'en as fairly tired of this same fighting,
As the poor cur that's worried in the shambles
By all the mastiff dogs of all the butchers
Wherefore, farewell sword, poniard, petronel,
And welcome poverty, and peaceful labor

ABR. Clerk Quentin, if of fighting thou art tired,
By my good word, thou'rt quickly satisfied,
For thou'st seen but little on't.

WIL. Thou dost belie him — I have seen him fight
Bravely enough for one in his condition

ABR. What! he? that counter-casting smock-faced boy?
What was he but the colonel's scribbling drudge,
With men of straw to stuff the regiment roll;

With cipherings unjust to cheat his com-
rades,
And cloak false musters for our noble
captain?
He bid farewell to sword and petronel!
He should have said, farewell my pen
and standish.
These, with the rosin used to hide era-
sures,
Were the best friends he left in camp
behind him.
    QUE. The sword you scoff at is not
far, but scorns
The threats of an unmanner'd mutineer.
    SER. (*interposes*). We'll have no brawl-
ing. — Shall it e'er be said,
That being comrades six long years to-
gether,
While gulping down the frowsy fogs of
Holland,
We tilted at each other's throats so soon
As the first draught of native air re-
fresh'd them?
No! by Saint Dunstan, I forbid the com-
bat.
You all, methinks, do know this trusty
halberd;
For I opine, that every back amongst you
Hath felt the weight of the tough ashen
staff,
Endlong or overthwart. Who is it wishes
A remembrancer now? (*Raises his hal-
berd.*)
    ABR. Comrades, have you ears
To hear the old man bully? — eyes to see
His staff rear'd o'er your heads, as o'er
the hounds
The huntsman cracks his whip?
    WIL. Well said!— stout Abraham has
the right on't.—
I tell thee, sergeant, we do reverence thee,
And pardon the rash humors thou hast
caught,
Like wiser men, from thy authority.
'Tis ended, howsoe'er, and we'll not suffer
A word of sergeantry, or halberd-staff,
Nor the most petty threat of discipline.
If thou wilt lay aside thy pride of office,
And drop thy wont of swaggering and
commanding,
Thou art our comrade still for good or evil.
Else take thy course apart, or with the
clerk there —

A sergeant thou, and he being all thy regi-
ment.
    SER. Is't come to this, false knaves?
And think you not,
That if you bear a name o'er other sol-
diers,
It was because you follow'd to the charge
One that had zeal and skill enough to
lead you
Where fame was won by danger?
    WIL. We grant thy skill in leading,
noble sergeant,
Witness some empty boots and sleeves
amongst us,
Which else had still been tenanted with
limbs
In the full quantity; and for the arguments
With which you used to back our resolu-
tion,
Our shoulders do record them. At a word,
Will you conform, or must we part our
company?
    SER. Conform to you? Base dogs! I
would not lead you
A bolt-flight farther to be made a general.
Mean mutineers! when you swill'd off
the dregs
Of my poor sea-stores, it was: — " Noble
Sergeant! —
Heaven bless old Hildebrand! — we'll
follow him,
At least, until we safely see him lodged
Within the merry bounds of his own Eng-
land!"
    WIL. Ay, truly, sir; but, mark, the ale
was mighty,
And the Geneva potent. Such stout liquor
Makes violent protestations. Skink it
round,
If you have any left, to the same tune,
And we may find a chorus for it still.
    ABR. We lose our time. Tell us at
once, old man,
If thou wilt march with us, or stay with
Quentin?
    SER. Out, mutineers! Dishonor dog
your heels!
    ABR. Wilful will have his way. Adieu,
stout Hildebrand!
    [*The Soldiers go off laughing,
    and taking leave, with mockery,
    of the* SERGEANT *and* QUENTIN,
    who remain on the stage.]

SER. (*after a pause*). Fly you not
　with the rest ! — fail you to follow
Yon goodly friendship and fair example?
Come, take your wild-goose flight. I
　know you Scots,
Like your own sea-fowl, seek your course
　together.
　QUE. Faith, a poor heron I, who wing
　my flight
In loneliness, or with a single partner;
And right it is that I should seek for soli-
　tude,
Bringing but evil luck on them I herd with.
　SER. Thou'rt thankless. Had we
　landed on the coast,
Where our course bore us, thou wert far
　from home;
But the fierce wind that drove us round
　the island,
Barring each port and inlet that we aim'd
　at,
Hath wafted thee to harbor; for I judge
This is thy native land we disembark on.
　QUE. True, worthy friend. Each rock,
　each stream I look on,
Each bosky wood, and every frowning
　tower,
Awakens some young dream of infancy.
Yet such is my hard hap, I might more
　safely
Have look'd on Indian cliffs, or Afric's
　desert,
Than on my native shores. I'm like a
　babe
Doom'd to draw poison from my nurse's
　bosom.
　SER. Thou dream'st, young man. Un-
　real terrors haunt,
As I have noted, giddy brains like thine—
Flighty, poetic, and imaginative —
To whom a minstrel whim gives idle rap-
　ture,
And, when it fades, fantastic misery.
　QUE. But mine is not fantastic. I can
　tell thee,
Since I have known thee still my faithful
　friend,
In part at least the dangerous plight I stand
　in.
　SER. And I will hear thee willingly, the
　rather,
That I would let these vagabonds march
　on,

Nor join their troop again. Besides, goo
　sooth,
I'm wearied with the toil of yesterday,
And revel of last night. — And I may ai
　thee;
Yes, I may aid thee, comrade, and per
　chance
Thou may'st advantage me.
　QUE. May it prove well for both !—Bu
　note, my friend,
I can but intimate my mystic story.
Some of it lies so secret,—even the wind
That whistle round us must not know th
　whole —
An oath ! — an oath ! —
　SER. That must be kept, of course.
I ask but that which thou may'st freely
　tell.
　QUE. I was an orphan boy, and first saw
　light
Not far from where we stand — my lin
　eage low,
But honest in its poverty. A lord,
The master of the soil for many a mile,
Dreaded and powerful, took a kindl
　charge
For my advance in letters, and the qualitie
Of the poor orphan lad drew some ap
　plause.
The knight was proud of me, and, in hi
　halls,
I had such kind of welcome as the great
Give to the humble, whom they love to
　point to
As objects not unworthy their protection
Whose progress is some honor to thei
　patron —
A cure was spoken of, which I migh
　serve,
My manners, doctrine, and acquirements
　fitting.
　SER. Hitherto thy luck
Was of the best, good friend. Few lords
　had cared
If thou couldst read thy grammar or thy
　psalter :
Thou hadst been valued couldst thou scour
　a harness,
And dress a steed distinctly.
　QUE.　　　　　　My old master
Held different doctrine, at least it seem'd
　so —
But he was mix'd in many a deadly feud—

And here my tale grows mystic. I became
Unwitting and unwilling, the depositary,
Of a dread secret, and the knowledge on't
Has wreck'd my peace forever. It be-
came
My patron's will, that I, as one who knew
More than I should, must leave the realm
of Scotland,
And live or die within a distant land.

SER. Ah! thou hast done a fault in some
wild raid,
As you wild Scotsmen call them.

QUE.   Comrade, nay;
Mine was a peaceful part, and happ'd by
chance.
I must not tell you more. Enough, my
presence
Brought danger to my benefactor's house.
Tower after tower conceal'd me, willing
still
To hide my ill-omen'd face with owls and
ravens,
And let my patron's safety be the purchase
Of my severe and desolate captivity.
So thought I, when dark Arran, with its
walls
Of native rock, enclosed me. There I
lurk'd,
A peaceful stranger amid armed clans,
Without a friend to love or to defend me,
Where all beside were link'd by close alli-
ances.
At length I made my option to take service
In that same legion of auxiliaries
In which we lately served the Belgian.
Our leader, stout Montgomery, hath been
kind
Thro' full six years of warfare, and as-
sign'd me
More peaceful tasks than the rough front
of war,
For which my education little suited me.

SER. Ay, therein was Montgomery kind
indeed;
Nay, kinder than you think, my simple
Quentin.
The letters which you brought to the
Montgomery,
Pointed to thrust thee on some desperate
service,
Which should most likely end thee.

QUE. Bore I such letters? — Surely,
comrade, no.

Full deeply was the writer bound to aid me.
Perchance he only meant to prove my
mettle;
And it was but a trick of my bad fortune
That gave his letters ill interpretation.

SER. Ay, but thy better angel wrought
for good,
Whatever ill thy evil fate design'd thee.
Montgomery pitied thee, and changed thy
service
In the rough field for labor in the tent.
More fit for thy green years and peaceful
habits.

QUE. Even there his well-meant kind-
ness injured me.
My comrades hated, undervalued me,
And whatsoe'er of service I could do them,
They guerdon'd with ingratitude and
envy —
Such my strange doom, that if I serve a
man
At deepest risk, he is my foe forever!

SER. Hast thou worse fate than others
if it were so?
Worse even than me, thy friend, thine
officer, —
Whom yon ungrateful slaves have pitch'd
ashore,
As wild waves heap the sea-weed on the
beach,
And left him here, as if he had the pest
Or leprosy, and death were in his company?

QUE. They think at least you have the
worst of plagues,
The worst of leprosies, — they think you
poor.

SER. They think like lying villains
then; — I'm rich,
And they too might have felt it. I've a
thought —
But stay — what plans your wisdom for
yourself?

QUE. My thoughts are well-nigh des-
perate. But I purpose
Return to my stern patron — there to tell
him
That wars, and winds, and waves, have
cross'd his pleasure,
And cast me on the shore from whence he
banish'd me;
Then let him do his will and destine for me
A dungeon or a grave.

SER. Now, by the rood, thou art a
simple fool!
I can do better for thee. Mark me,
Quentin.
I took my license from the noble regiment,
Partly that I was worn with age and war-
fare,
Partly that an estate of yeomanry,
Of no great purchase, but enough to live
on,
Has call'd me owner since a kinsman's
death.
It lies in merry Yorkshire, where the
wealth
Of fold and furrow, proper to Old Eng-
land,
Stretches by streams which walk no slug-
gish pace,
But dance as light as yours. Now, good
friend Quentin,
This copyhold can keep two quiet inmates,
And I am childless. Wilt thou be my son?
QUE. Nay, you can only jest, my
worthy friend!
What claim have I to be a burden to you?
SER. The claim of him that wants, and
is in danger,
On him that has, and can afford protec-
tion.
Thou wouldst not fear a foeman in my
cottage,
Where a stout mastiff slumber'd on the
hearth,
And this good halberd hung above the
chimney?
But come—I have it—thou shalt earn thy
bread
Duly, and honorably, and usefully.
Our village schoolmaster hath left the
parish,
Forsook the ancient school-house with its
yew-trees,
That lurk'd beside a church two centuries
older, —
So long devotion took the lead of knowl-
edge;
And since his little flock are shepherdless,
'Tis thou shalt be promoted in his room;
And rather than thou wantest scholars,
man,
Myself will enter pupil. Better late,
Our proverb says, than never to do well.
And look you, on the holydays I'd tell,

To all the wondering boors and gaping
children,
Strange tales of what the regiment did
in Flanders,
And thou shouldst say Amen, and be my
warrant
That I speak truth to them.
QUE. Would I might take thy offer!
But, alas!
Thou art the hermit who compell'd a pil-
grim,
In name of heaven and heavenly charity,
To share his roof and meal, but found
too late
That he had drawn a curse on him and his,
By sheltering a wretch foredoom'd of
heaven!
SER. Thou talk'st in riddles to me.
QUE. If I do,
'Tis that I am a riddle to myself.
Thou know'st I am by nature born a
friend
To glee and merriment, can make wild
verses;
The jest or laugh has never stopp'd with
me,
When once 'twas set a rolling.
SER. I have known thee
A blithe companion still, and wonder now
Thou shouldst become thus crestfallen.
QUE. Does the lark sing her descant
when the falcon
Scales the blue vault with bolder wing
than hers,
And meditates a stoop? The mirth thou'st
noted
Was all deception, fraud. — Hated enough
For other causes, I did veil my feelings
Beneath the mask of mirth, — laugh'd,
sung, and caroll'd,
To gain some interest in my comrades'
bosoms,
Although mine own was bursting.
SER. Thou'rt a hypocrite
Of a new order.
QUE. But harmless as the innoxious
snake,
Which bears the adder's form, lurks in
his haunts,
Yet neither hath his fang-teeth nor his
poison.
Look you, kind Hildebrand, I would seem
merry,

est other men should, tiring of my sadness,
xpel me from them, as the hunted wether
s driven from the flock.

SER. Faith, thou hast borne it bravely
out.
Had I been ask'd to name the merriest
fellow
f all our muster-roll — that man wert
thou.

QUE. See'st thou, my friend, yon brook
dance down the valley,
and sing blithe carols over broken rock
and tiny waterfall, kissing each shrub
and each gay flower it nurses in its passage, —
Where, thinkst thou, is its source, the
bonny brook? —
t flows from forth a cavern, black and
gloomy,
ullen and sunless, like this heart of
mine,
Which others see in a false glare of gayety,
Which I have laid before you in its sadness.

SER. If such wild fancies dog thee,
wherefore leave
The trade where thou wert safe midst
others' dangers,
And venture to thy native land, where fate
Lies on the watch for thee? Had old
Montgomery
Been with the regiment, thou hadst had
no congé.

QUE. No, 'tis most likely. — But I had
a hope,
A poor, vain hope, that I might live obscurely
In some far corner of my native Scotland,
Which, of all others, splinter'd into districts,
Differing in manners, families, even language,
Seem'd a safe refuge for the humble
wretch
Whose highest hope was to remain unheard of.
But fate has baffled me — the winds and
waves,
With force resistless, have impell'd me
hither —
Have driven me to the clime most dangerous to me:

And I obey the call, like the hurt deer,
Which seeks instinctively his native lair,
Tho' his heart tells him it is but to die
there.

SER. 'Tis false, by Heaven, young
man! This same despair,
Tho' showing resignation in its banner,
Is but a kind of covert cowardice.
Wise men have said, that tho' our stars
incline,
They cannot force us. — Wisdom is the
pilot,
And if he cannot cross, he may evade
them.
You lend an ear to idle auguries,
The fruits of our last revels — still most
sad
Under the gloom that follows boisterous
mirth,
As earth looks blackest after brilliant
sunshine.

QUE. No, by my honest word. I join'd
the revel,
And aided it with laugh and song and
shout,
But my heart revell'd not; and, when
the mirth
Was at the loudest, on yon galliot's prow
I stood unmarked, and gazed upon the
land,
My native land — each cape and cliff I
knew.
"Behold me now," I said, "your des-
tined victim!"
So greets the sentenced criminal the head-
man,
Who slow approaches with his lifted axe.
"Hither I come," I said, "ye kindred
hills,
Whose darksome outline in a distant land
Haunted my slumbers; here I stand, thou
ocean,
Whose hoarse voice, murmuring in my
dreams, required me;
See me now here, ye winds, whose plain-
tive wail,
On yonder distant shores, appear'd to call
me —
Summon'd, behold me." And the winds
and waves,
And the deep echoes of the distant moun-
tain,
Made answer:— "Come and die!"

Ser. Fantastic all! Poor boy, thou art distracted
With the vain terrors of some feudal tyrant,
Whose frown hath been from infancy thy bugbear.
Why seek his presence?

Que. Wherefore does the moth
Fly to the scorching taper? — why the bird,
Dazzled by lights at midnight, seek the net? —
Why does the prey, which feels the fascination
Of the snake's glaring eye, drop in his jaws?

Ser. Such wild examples but refute themselves.
Let bird, let moth, let the coil'd adder's prey,
Resist the fascination and be safe.
Thou goest not near this Baron — if thou goest,
I will go with thee. Known in many a field,
Which he in a whole life of petty feud
Has never dream'd of, I will teach the knight
To rule him in this matter — be thy warrant,
That far from him, and from his petty lordship,
You shall henceforth tread English land, and never
Thy presence shall alarm his conscience more.

Que. 'Twere desperate risk for both.
I will far rather
Hastily guide thee thro' this dangerous province,
And seek thy school, thy yew-trees, and thy churchyard; —
The last, perchance, will be the first I find.

Ser. I would rather face him,
Like a bold Englishman that knows his right,
And will stand by his friend. And yet 'tis folly —
Fancies like these are not to be resisted;
'Tis better to escape them. Many a presage,
Too rashly braved, becomes its own accomplishment.

Then let us go — But whither? My old head
As little knows where it shall lie to-night
As yonder mutineers that left their officer;
As reckless of his quarters as these billows,
That leave the wither'd sea-weed on the beach,
And care not where they pile it.

Que. Think not for that, good friend.
We are in Scotland,
And if it is not varied from its wont,
Each cot, that sends a curl of smoke to heaven,
Will yield a stranger quarters for the night,
Simply because he needs them.

Ser. But are there none within an easy walk
Give lodgings here for hire? for I have left
Some of the Don's piastres (tho' I kept
The secret from yon gulls), and I had rather
Pay the fair reckoning I can well afford,
And my host takes with pleasure, than I'd cumber
Some poor man's roof with me and all my wants,
And tax his charity beyond discretion.

Que. Some six miles hence there is a town and hostelry.
But you are wayworn, and it is most likely
Our comrades must have fill'd it.

Ser. Out upon them! —
Were there a friendly mastiff who would lend me
Half of his supper, half of his poor kennel,
I would help Honesty to pick his bones,
And share his straw, far rather than I'd sup
On jolly fare with these base varlets!

Que. We'll manage better; for our Scottish dogs,
Tho' stout and trusty, are but ill-instructed
In hospitable rights. — Here is a maiden,
A little maid, will tell us of the country,
And sorely it is changed since I left it,
If we should fail to find a harborage.

Enter Isabel MacLellan, *a girl of about six years old, bearing a milk-pail on her head; she stops on seeing the* Sergeant *and* Quentin.

QUE. There's something in her look
　　that doth remind me —
But 'tis not wonder I find recollections
In all that here I look on.—Pretty maid —
　SER. You're slow, and hesitate. I will
　　be spokesman. —
Good even, my pretty maiden—canst thou
　　tell us,
Is there a Christian house would render
　　strangers,
For love or guerdon, a night's meal and
　　lodging?
　ISA. Full surely, sir; we dwell in yon
　　old house
Upon the cliff — they call it Chapeldonan.

　　　　(*Points to the building.*)

Our house is large enough, and if our
　　supper
Chance to be scant, you shall have half
　　of mine,
For, as I think, sir, you have been a
　　soldier.
Up yonder lies our house; I'll trip before,
And tell my mother she has guests
　　a-coming;
The path is something steep, but you shall
　　see
I'll be there first. I must chain up the
　　dogs, too;
Nimrod and Bloodylass are cross to
　　strangers,
But gentle when you know them.

　　[*Exit, and is seen partially ascend-
　　　ing to the Castle.*

　SER.　　　　　You have spoke
Your country folk aright, both for the
　　dogs
And for the people. We had luck to light
On one too young for cunning and for
　　selfishness. —
He's in a reverie — a deep one sure,
Since the gibe on his country wakes him
　　not. —
Bestir thee, Quentin !
　QUE.　　'Twas a wondrous likeness !
　SER. Likeness ! of whom? I'll warrant
　　thee of one
Whom thou hast loved and lost. Such
　　fantasies
Live long in brains like thine, which fash-
　　ion visions

Of woe and death when they are cross'd
　　in love,
As most men are or have been.
　QUE. The guess has touch'd me, tho'
　　it is but slightly,
'Mongst other woes: I knew in former
　　days,
A maid that view'd me with some glance
　　of favor;
But my fate carried me to other shores,
And she has since been wedded. I did
　　think on't
But as a bubble burst, a rainbow vanish'd;
It adds no deeper shade to the dark gloom
Which chills the springs of hope and life
　　within me.
Our guide hath got a trick of voice and
　　feature
Like to the maid I spoke of — that is all.
　SER. She bounds before us like a game-
　　some doe,
Or rather as the rock-bred eaglet soars
Up to her nest, as if she rose by will,
Without an effort. Now a Netherlander,
One of our Frogland friends, viewing the
　　scene,
Would take his oath that tower, and rock,
　　and maiden,
Were forms too light and lofty to be real,
And only some delusion of the fancy,
Such as men dream at sunset. I myself
Have kept the level ground so many
　　years,
I have well-nigh forgot the art to climb,
Unless assisted by thy younger arm.

　　[*They go off as if to ascend to the
　　　Tower, the* SERGEANT *leaning
　　　upon* QUENTIN.

　　　　　SCENE II.

Scene changes to the Front of the Old Tower.
　ISABEL *comes forward with her Mother,*
　—MARION *speaking as they advance.*

　MAR. I blame thee not, my child, for
　　bidding wanderers
Come share our food and shelter, if thy
　　father
Were here to welcome them; but, Isabel,
He waits upon his lord at Auchindrane,
And comes not home to-night.
　ISA.　　　What then, my mother?
The travellers do not ask to see my father;

Food, shelter, rest, is all the poor men
    want,
And we can give them these without my
    father.

  MAR. Thou canst not understand, nor
    I explain,
Why a lone female asks not visitants
What time her husband's absent. —
    (*Apart.*) My poor child,
And if thou'rt wedded to a jealous hus-
    band,
Thou'lt know too soon the cause.

  ISA. (*partly overhearing what her
    mother says*) —
Ay, but I know already — Jealousy
Is when my father chides, and you sit
    weeping.

  MAR. Out, little spy! thy father never
    chides;
Or, if he does, 'tis when his wife deserves it.
But to our strangers; they are old men,
    Isabel,
That seek this shelter, are they not?

  ISA.   One is old —
Old as this tower of ours, and worn like
    that,
Bearing deep marks of battles long since
    fought.

  MAR. Some remnant of the wars; he's
    welcome, surely,
Bringing no quality along with him
Which can alarm suspicion. — Well, the
    other?

  ISA. A young man, gentle-voiced and
    gentle-eyed,
Who looks and speaks like one the world
    has frown'd on;
But smiles when you smile, seeming that
    he feels
Joy in your joy, tho' he himself is sad.
Brown hair, and downcast looks.

  MAR. (*alarmed*). 'Tis but an idle
    thought — it cannot be!
(*Listens.*) I hear his accents — It is all
    too true —
My terrors were prophetic! —   I'll com-
    pose myself,
And then accost him firmly. Thus it must
    be.

    [*She retires hastily into the Tower.
    — The voices of the* SERGEANT
    and QUENTIN *are heard ascend-
    ing behind the Scenes.*

  QUE. One effort more — we stand upon
    the level.
I've seen thee work thee up glacis and
    cavalier
Steeper than this ascent, when cannon,
    culverine,
Musket, and hackbut, shower'd their shot
    upon thee,
And form'd, with ceaseless blaze, a fiery
    garland
Round the defences of the post you
    storm'd.

    [*They come on the Stage, and at
    the same time* MARION *re-enters
    from the Tower.*

  SER. Truly thou speak'st. I am the
    tardier
That I, in climbing hither, miss the fire,
Which wont to tell me there was death in
    loitering. —
Here stands, methinks, our hostess.

    [*He goes forward to address* MAR-
    ION. QUENTIN, *struck on see-
    ing her, keeps back.*

  SER. Kind dame, yon little lass hath
    brought you strangers,
Willing to be a trouble, not a charge to
    you.
We are disbanded soldiers, but have
    means
Ample enough to pay our journey home-
    ward.

  MAR. We keep no house of general
    entertainment,
But know our duty, sir, to locks like
    yours,
Whiten'd and thinn'd by many a long
    campaign.
Ill chances that my husband should be
    absent —
(*Apart.*) — Courage alone can make me
    struggle thro' it —
For in your comrade, tho' he hath forgot
    me,
I spy a friend whom I have known in
    school-days,
And whom I think MacLellan well re-
    members. —
(*She goes up to* QUENTIN.) You see a
    woman's memory
Is faithfuller than yours: for Quentin
    Blane

Hath not a greeting left for Marion
Harkness.

Que. (*with effort*). I seek, indeed, my
native land, good Marion,
But seek it like a stranger. All is changed,
And thou, thyself —

Mar. You left a giddy maiden,
And find, on your return, a wife and
mother.
Thine old acquaintance, Quentin, is my
mate —
Stout Niel MacLellan, ranger to our lord,
The Knight of Auchindrane. He's ab-
sent now,
But will rejoice to see his former com-
rade,
If, as I trust, you tarry his return.
(*Apart.*) Heaven grant he understand
my words by contraries !
He must remember Niel and he were
rivals ;
He must remember Niel and he were
foes ;
He must remember Niel is warm of tem-
per,
And think, instead of welcome, I would
blithely
Bid him, God speed you. But he is as
simple
And void of guile as ever.

Que. Marion, I gladly rest within your
cottage,
And gladly wait return of Niel MacLellan,
To clasp his hand, and wish him happi-
ness.
Some rising feelings might perhaps pre-
vent this —
But 'tis a peevish part to grudge our friends
Their share of fortune because we have
miss'd it ;
I can wish others joy and happiness,
Though I must ne'er partake them.

Mar. But if it grieve you —

Que. No ! do not fear. The brightest
gleams of hope
That shine on me are such as are reflected
From those which shine on others.

[*The* Sergeant *and* Quentin *enter the Tower with the little girl.*

Mar. (*comes forward, and speaks in
agitation*) —
Even so ! the simple youth has miss'd my
meaning :

I shame to make it plainer, or to say,
In one brief word, Pass on. — Heaven
guide the bark,
For we are on the breakers !

[*Exit into the Tower.*

ACT II. — Scene I.

*A Withdrawing Apartment in the Castle
of Auchindrane. Servants place a
Table, with a Flask of Wine and
Drinking-Cups.*

Enter Mure *of* Auchindrane, *with*
Albert Gifford, *his Relation and
Visitor. They place themselves by the
Table, after some complimentary cere-
mony. At some distance is heard the
noise of revelling.*

Auch. We're better placed for confidential talk,
Than in the hall fill'd with disbanded
soldiers,
And fools and fiddlers gather'd on the
highway, —
The worthy guests whom Philip crowds
my hall with,
And with them spends his evening.

Gif. But think you not, my friend, that
your son Philip
Should be participant of these our coun-
sels,
Being so deeply mingled in the danger —
Your house's only heir — your only son ?

Auch. Kind cousin Gifford, if thou
lack'st good counsel
At race, at cockpit, or at gambling table,
Or any freak by which men cheat them-
selves
As well of life as of the means to live,
Call for assistance upon Philip Mure ;
But in all serious parley spare invoking
him.

Gif. You speak too lightly of my cousin
Philip ;
All name him brave in arms.

Auch. A second Bevis ;
But I, my youth bred up in graver fashions,
Mourn o'er the mode of life in which he
spends,
Or rather dissipates, his time and sub-
stance.
No vagabond escapes his search — The
soldier

Spurn'd from the service, henceforth to
  be ruffian
Upon his own account, is Philip's com-
  rade;
The fiddler, whose crack'd crowd has still
  three strings on't;
The balladeer, whose voice has still two
  notes left;
Whate'er is roguish, and whate'er is
  vile,
Are welcome to the board of Auchin-
  drane,
And Philip will return them shout for
  shout,
And pledge for jovial pledge, and song
  for song,
Until the shame-faced sun peep at our
  windows,
And ask: "What have we here?"
  GIF. You take such revel deeply;—
    we are Scotsmen,
Far known for rustic hospitality,
That mind not birth or titles in our
  guests:
The harper has his seat beside our
  hearth,
The wanderer must find comfort at our
  board,
His name unask'd, his pedigree unknown;
So did our ancestors, and so must we.
  AUCH. All this is freely granted, worthy
    kinsman;
And prithee do not think me churl enough
To count how many sit beneath my salt.
I've wealth enough to fill my father's hall
Each day at noon, and feed the guests
  who crowd it;
I am near mate with those whom men
  call Lord,
Tho' a rude western knight. But mark
  me, cousin,
Altho' I feed wayfaring vagabonds,
I make them not my comrades. Such as I,
Who have advanced the fortunes of my
  line,
And swell'd a baron's turret to a palace,
Have oft the curse awaiting on our thrift,
To see, while yet we live, the things which
  must be
At our decease — the downfall of our
  family,
The loss of land and lordship, name and
  knighthood,

The wreck of the fair fabric we have built,
By a degenerate heir.   Philip has that
Of inborn meanness in him, that he loves
  not
The company of betters nor of equals ;
Never at ease, unless he bears the bell,
And crows the loudest in the company.
He's mesh'd, too, in the snares of every
  female
Who deigns to cast a passing glance on
  him —
Licentious, disrespectful, rash, and prof-
  ligate.
  GIF. Come, my good coz, think we too
    have been young,
And I will swear that in your father's
  lifetime
You have yourself been trapp'd by toys
  like these.
  AUCH. A fool I may have been — but
    not a madman;
I never play'd the rake among my fol-
  lowers,
Pursuing this man's sister, that man's
  wife:
And therefore never saw I man of mine,
When summon'd to obey my hest, grow
  restive,
Talk of his honor, of his peace destroy'd,
And, while obeying, mutter threats of
  vengeance.
But now the humor of an idle youth,
Disgusting trusted followers, sworn de-
  pendants,
Plays football with his honor and my
  safety.
  GIF. I'm sorry to find discord in your
    house,
For I had hoped, while bringing you cold
  news,
To find you arm'd in union 'gainst the
  danger.
  AUCH. What can man speak that I
    would shrink to hear,
And where the danger I would deign
  to shun?   (He rises.)
What should appal a man inured to perils,
Like the bold climber on the crags of
  Ailsa?
Winds whistle past him, billows rage be-
  low,
The sea-fowl sweep around, with shriek
  and clang,

ne single slip, one unadvised pace,
ne qualm of giddiness — and peace be
     with him!
ut he whose grasp is sure, whose step
     is firm,
Vhose brain is constant — he makes one
     proud rock
'he means to scale another, till he stand
'riumphant on the peak.

GIF.   And so I trust
'hou wilt surmount the danger now ap-
     proaching,
Vhich scarcely can I frame my tongue
     to tell you,
'hough I rode here on purpose.

AUCH.   Cousin, I think thy heart was
     never coward,
And strange it seems thy tongue should
     take such semblance.
've heard of many a loud-mouth'd, noisy
     braggart,
Vhose hand gave feeble sanction to his
     tongue;
But thou art one whose heart can think
     bold things,
Vhose hand can act them — but who
     shrinks to speak them!

GIF.   And if I speak them not, 'tis that
     I shame
To tell thee of the calumnies that load
     thee.
Things loudly spoken at the city Cross —
Things closely whisper'd in our Sover-
     eign's ear —
Things which the plumed lord and flat-
     capp'd citizen
Do circulate amid their different ranks —
Things false, no doubt; but, falsehoods
     while I deem them,
Still honoring thee, I shun the odious
     topic.

AUCH.   Shun it not, cousin; 'tis a
     friend's best office
To bring the news we hear unwillingly.
The sentinel, who tells the foe's approach,
And wakes the sleeping camp, does but
     his duty:
Be thou as bold in telling me of danger,
As I shall be in facing danger told of.

GIF.   I need not bid thee recollect the
     death-feud
That raged so long betwixt thy house and
     Cassilis;

I need not bid thee recollect the league,
When royal James himself stood mediator
Between thee and Earl Gilbert.

AUCH.   Call you these news? — You
     might as well have told me
That old King Coil is dead, and graved
     at Kylesfeld,
I'll help thee out — King James com-
     manded us
Henceforth to live in peace, made us clasp
     hands too.
O, sir, when such an union hath been
     made,
In heart and hand conjoining mortal foes,
Under a monarch's royal mediation,
The league is not forgotten.   And with
     this
What is there to be told?   The King
     commanded —
" Be friends."   No doubt we were so —
     Who dares doubt it?

GIF.   You speak but half the tale.

AUCH.   By good Saint Trimon, but I'll
     tell the whole!
There is no terror in the tale for me —
Go speak of ghosts to children! — This
     Earl Gilbert
(God sain him) loved Heaven's peace
     as well as I did,
And we were wondrous friends whene'er
     we met
At church or market, or in burrows town.
Midst this, our good Lord Gilbert, Earl
     of Cassilis,
Takes purpose he would journey forth to
     Edinburgh.
The King was doling gifts of abbey-lands,
Good things that thrifty house was wont
     to fish for.
Our mighty Earl forsakes his sea-wash'd
     castle,
Passes our borders some four miles from
     hence;
And, holding it unwholesome to be fast-
     ers
Long after sunrise, lo! the Earl and
     train
Dismount, to rest their nags and eat their
     breakfast.
The morning rose, the small birds caroll'd
     sweetly —
The corks were drawn, the pasty brooks
     incision —

His lordship jests, his train are choked
   with laughter;
When, — wondrous change of cheer, and
   most unlook'd for,
Strange epilogue to bottle and to baked
   meat ! —
Flash'd from the greenwood half a score
   of carabines;
And the good Earl of Cassilis, in his
   breakfast,
Had nooning, dinner, supper, all at once,
Even in the morning that he closed his
   journey;
And the grim sexton, for his chamberlain,
Made him the bed which rests the head
   forever.

   GIF. Told with much spirit, cousin —
   some there are
Would add, and in a tone resembling
   triumph,
And would that with these long establish'd facts
My tale began and ended ! I must tell
   you,
That evil-deeming censures of the events,
Both at the time and now, throw blame
   on thee —
Time, place, and circumstance, they say,
   proclaim thee,
Alike, the author of that morning's ambush.

   AUCH. Ay, 'tis an old belief in Carrick
   here,
Where natives do not always die in bed,
That if a Kennedy shall not attain
Methuselah's last span, a Mure has slain
   him;
Such is the general creed of all their clan.
Thank Heaven, that they are bound to
   prove the charge
They are so prompt in making. They
   have clamor'd
Enough of this before, to show their
   malice.
But what said these coward pickthanks
   when I came
Before the King, before the Justicers,
Rebutting all their calumnies, and daring
   them
To show that I knew aught of Cassilis'
   journey —
Which way he meant to travel — where
   to halt —

Without which knowledge I possess'd r
   means
To dress an ambush for him? Did I ne
Defy the assembled clan of Kennedys,
To show, by proof direct or inferential,
Wherefore they slander'd me with th
   foul charge?
My gauntlet rung before them in th
   court,
And I did dare the best of them to lift i
And prove such charge a true one — Di
   I not?

   GIF. I saw your gauntlet lie before th
   Kennedys,
Who looked on it as men do on an adde
Longing to crush, and yet afraid to gras
   it.
Not an eye sparkled — not a foot ad
   vanced —
No arm was stretch'd to lift the fatal sym
   bol.

   AUCH. Then, wherefore do the hilding
   murmur now?
Wish they to see again, how one bold Mur
Can baffle and defy their assembled valor

   GIF. No; but they speak of evidenc
   suppress'd.

   AUCH. Suppress'd ! — what evidence
   — by whom suppress'd?
What Will-o'-Wisp — what idiot of a wit
   ness,
Is he to whom they trace an empty voice
But cannot show his person?

   GIF.   They pretend,
With the King's leave, to bring it to a
   trial;
Averring that a lad named Quentin Blane
Brought thee a letter from the murder'd
   Earl,
With friendly greetings, telling of his
   journey,
The hour which he set forth, the place he
   halted at, —
Affording thee the means to form the am-
   bush,
Of which your hatred made the applica-
   tion.

   AUCH. A prudent Earl, indeed, if such
   his practice,
When dealing with a recent enemy !
And what should he propose by such
   strange confidence
In one who sought it not?

GIF. His purposes were kindly, say the
   Kennedys —
Desiring you would meet him where he
   halted,
Offering to undertake whate'er commis-
   sions
You listed trust him with, for court or
   city:
And, thus apprised of Cassilis' purposed
   journey,
And of his halting-place, you placed the
   ambush,
Prepared the homicides ——

  AUCH. They're free to say their pleas-
   ure. They are men
Of the new court — and I am but a frag-
   ment
Of stout old Morton's faction. It is rea-
   son
That such as I be rooted from the
   earth,
That they may have full room to spread
   their branches.
No doubt, 'tis easy to find strolling va-
   grants
To prove whate'er they prompt. This
   Quentin Blane —
Did you not call him so? — why comes
   he now?
And wherefore not before? This must
   be answer'd —
(*Abruptly.*) — Where is he now?

  GIF. Abroad — they say — kidnapp'd.
By you kidnapp'd, that he might die in
   Flanders.
But orders have been sent for his dis-
   charge,
And his transmission hither.

  AUCH. (*assuming an air of com-
   posure*). —
When they produce such witness, cousin
   Gifford,
We'll be prepared to meet it. In the
   meanwhile,
The King doth ill to throw his royal
   sceptre
In the accuser's scale, ere he can know
How justice shall incline it.

  GIF.   Our sage prince
Resents, it may be, less the death of Cassilis,
Than he is angry that the feud should
   burn,

After his royal voice had said, " Be
   quench'd: "
Thus urging prosecution less for slaughter,
Than that, being done against the King's
   command,
Treason is mix'd with homicide.

  AUCH. Ha! ha! most true, my cousin.
Why, well consider'd, 'tis a crime so
   great
To slay one's enemy, the King forbidding
   it,
Like parricide, it should be held impos-
   sible.
'Tis just as if a wretch retain'd the evil,
When the King's touch had bid the sores
   be heal'd;
And such a crime merits the stake at
   least.
What! can there be within a Scottish
   bosom
A feud so deadly, that it kept its ground
When the King said, " Be friends! " It
   is not credible.
Were I King James, I never would be-
   lieve it;
I'd rather think the story all a dream,
And that there was no friendship, feud,
   nor journey,
No halt, no ambush, and no Earl of Cas-
   silis,
Than dream anointed Majesty has
   wrong !—

  GIF. Speak within door, coz.

  AUCH.   O, true. — (*Aside.*) — I
   shall betray myself
Even to this half-bred fool. — I must
   have room,
Room for an instant, or I suffocate. —
Cousin, I prithee call our Philip hither —
Forgive me; 'twere more meet I sum-
   mon'd him
Myself; but then the sight of yonder
   revel
Would chafe my blood, and I have need
   of coolness.

  GIF. I understand thee — I will bring
   him straight.   [*Exit.*

  AUCH. And if thou dost, he's lost his
   ancient trick
To fathom, as he wont, his five-pint
   flagons. —
This space is mine — O for the power to
   fill it,

Instead of senseless rage and empty curses,
With the dark spell which witches learn
　　from fiends,
That smites the object of their hate afar,
Nor leaves a token of its mystic action,
Stealing the soul from out the unscathed
　　body,
As lightning melts the blade, nor harms
　　the scabbard !
— 'Tis vain to wish for it — Each curse
　　of mine
Falls to the ground as harmless as the
　　arrows
Which children shoot at stars ! The time
　　for thought,
If thought could aught avail me, melts
　　away,
Like to a snowball in a schoolboy's hand,
That melts the faster the more close he
　　grasps it ! —
If I had time, this Scottish Solomon,
Whom some call son of David the Musi-
　　cian,*
Might find it perilous work to march to
　　Carrick.
There's many a feud still slumbering in
　　its ashes,
Whose embers are yet red.　Nobles we
　　have,
Stout as old Graysteel, and as hot as
　　Bothwell;
Here too are castles look from crags as
　　high
On seas as wide as Logan's.　So the
　　King —
Pshaw ! He is here again —

Enter GIFFORD.

　　Gif.　　　　　　　　I heard you name
The King, my kinsman; know, he comes
　　not hither.
　　Auch. (*affecting indifference*).　Nay,
　　then we need not broach our barrels,
　　cousin,
Nor purchase us new jerkins. — Comes
　　not Philip?
　　Gif.　Yes, sir.　He tarries but to drink
　　a service
To his good friends at parting.
　　Auch.　Friends for the beadle or the
　　sheriff-officer.

---

* An allusion to the calumnious report that
James VI. was son to Queen Mary by Rizzio.

Well, let it pass.　Who comes, and how
　　attended,
Since James designs not westward?
　　Gif.　O you shall have, instead, his
　　fiery functionary,
George Home that was, but now Dun-
　　bar's great Earl;
He leads a royal host, and comes to
　　show you
How he distributes justice on the Border,
Where judge and hangman oft revers
　　their office,
And the noose does its work before th
　　sentence.
But I have said my tidings best and worst
None but yourself can know what course
　　the time
And peril may demand.　To lift your
　　banner,
If I might be a judge, were desperat
　　game:
Ireland and Galloway offer you conven
　　ience
For flight, if flight be thought the bette
　　remedy;
To face the court requires the conscious
　　ness
And confidence of innocence.　You alone
Can judge if you possess these attributes

(*A noise behind the scenes.*)

　　Auch.　Philip, I think, has broken up
　　his revels;
His ragged regiment are dispersing them.
Well liquor'd doubtless.　They're dis-
　　banded soldiers,
Or some such vagabonds. — Here comes
　　the gallant.

Enter PHILIP.　*He has a buff-coat and
head-piece, wears a sword and dagger,
with pistols at his girdle.　He appears
to be affected by liquor, but to be by no
means intoxicated.*

　　Auch.　You scarce have been made
　　known to one another,
Altho' you sate together at the board. —
Son Philip, know and prize our cousin
　　Gifford.
　　Phi. (*tastes the wine on the table*). —
If you had praised him, sir, you had
　　been loth
To have welcomed him in bastard Alicant.

I'll make amends, by pledging his good
    journey
In glorious Burgundy. — The stirrup-cup,
    ho!
And bring my cousin's horses to the court.
    AUCH. (*draws him aside*). —
The stirrup-cup! He doth not ride to-
    night —
Shame on such churlish conduct to a
    kinsman!
    PHI. (*aside to his father*). I've news
    of pressing import.
Send the fool off. — Stay, I will start
    him for you.
(*To* GIF.) Yes, my kind cousin, Bur-
    gundy is better,
On a night-ride, to those who thread our
    moors,
And we may deal it freely to our friends,
For we came freely by it. Yonder ocean
Rolls many a purple cask upon our shore
Rough with embossed shells and shagged
    sea-weed,
When the good skipper and his careful
    crew
Have had their latest earthly draught of
    brine,
And gone to quench, or to endure their
    thirst,
Where nectar's plenty, or even water's
    scarce,
And filter'd to the parched crew by drops-
    ful.
    AUCH. Thou'rt mad, son Philip! Gif-
    ford's no intruder,
That we should rid him hence by such
    wild rants:
My kinsman hither rode at his own dan-
    ger,
To tell us that Dunbar is hasting to us,
With a strong force, and with the King's
    commission,
To enforce against our house a hateful
    charge,
With every measure of extremity.
    PHI. And is this all that our good
    cousin tells us?
I can say more, thanks to the ragged
    regiment,
With whose good company you have up-
    braided me,
On whose authority, I tell thee, cousin,
Dunbar is here already.

    GIF.   Already?
    PHI. Yes, gentle coz. And you, my
    sire, be hasty
In what you think to do.
    AUCH. I think thou darest not jest on
    such a subject.
Where hadst thou these fair tidings?
    PHI. Where you, too, might have
    heard them, noble father,
Save that your ears, nail'd to our kins-
    man's lips,
Would list no coarser accents. O, my
    soldiers,
My merry crew of vagabonds, forever!
Scum of the Netherlands, and wash'd
    ashore
Upon this coast like unregarded sea-weed,
They had not been two hours on Scottish
    land,
When, lo! they met a military friend,
An ancient fourier, known to them of
    old,
Who, warm'd by certain stoups of search-
    ing wine,
Inform'd his old companions that Dunbar
Left Glasgow yesterday, comes here to-
    morrow;
Himself, he said, was sent a spy before,
To view what preparations we were
    making.
    AUCH. (*to* GIF.). If this be sooth, good
    kinsman, thou must claim
To take a part with us for life and death,
Or speed from hence, and leave us to
    our fortune.
    GIF. In such dilemma,
Believe me, friend, I'd choose upon the
    instant —
But I lack harness, and a steed to charge
    on,
For mine is overtired, and, save my page,
There's not a man to back me. But I'll
    hie
To Kyle, and raise my vassals to your aid.
    PHI. 'Twill be when the rats,
That on these tidings fly this house of
    ours,
Come back to pay their rents. — (*Apart.*)
    AUCH.   Courage, cousin!
Thou goest not hence ill mounted for thy
    need;
Full forty coursers feed in my wide
    stalls —

The best of them is yours to speed your
journey.

PHI. Stand not on ceremony, good our
cousin,
When safety signs, to shorten courtesy.

GIF. (*to* AUCH.). Farewell, then,
cousin; for my tarrying here
Were ruin to myself, small aid to you;
Yet loving well your name and family,
I'd fain —

PHI. Be gone? — that is our object,
too —
Kinsman, adieu.

[*Exit* GIFFORD, PHILIP *calls
after him.*

You Yeoman of the stable,
Give Master Gifford there my fleetest
steed,
Yon cut-tail'd roan, that trembles at a
spear. —

(*Trampling of the horse heard
going off.*)

Hark! he departs. How swift the dastard rides,
To shun the neighborhood of jeopardy!

(*He lays aside the appearance of
levity which he has hitherto
worn, and says very seri-
ously*) —

And, now, my father —

AUCH. And now, my son — thou'st
ta'en a perilous game
Into thine hands, rejecting elder counsel, —
How dost thou mean to play it?

PHI. Sir, good gamesters play not
Till they review the cards which fate has
dealt them,
Computing thus the chances of the game,
And woefully they seem to weigh against
us.

AUCH. Exile's a passing ill, and may
be borne;
And when Dunbar and all his myrmidons
Are eastward turn'd, we'll seize our own
again.

PHI. Would that were all the risk we
had to stand to!
But more and worse, — a doom of treason, forfeiture,
Death to ourselves, dishonor to our
house,

Is what the stern Justiciary menaces;
And, fatally for us, he hath the means
To make his threatenings good.

AUCH. It cannot be. I tell thee,
there's no force
In Scottish law to raze a house like mine,
Coeval with the time the Lords of Gal-
loway
Submitted them unto the Scottish sceptre,
Renouncing rights of Tanistry and Bre-
hon.
Some dreams they have of evidence —
some suspicion;
But old Montgomery knows my purpose
well,
And long before their mandate reach the
camp
To crave the presence of this mighty wit-
ness,
He will be fitted with an answer to it.

PHI. Father, what we call great, is
often ruin'd
By means so ludicrously disproportion'd,
They make me think upon the gunner's
linstock,
Which, yielding forth a light about the
size
And semblance of the glowworm, yet
applied
To powder, blew a palace into atoms,
Sent a young King — a young Queen's
mate, at least —
Into the air, as high as e'er flew night-
hawk,
And made such wild work in the realm
of Scotland,
As they can tell who heard, — and you
were one
Who saw, perhaps, the night-flight which
began it.

AUCH. If thou hast naught to speak
but drunken folly,
I cannot listen longer.

PHI. I will speak brief and sudden. —
There is one
Whose tongue to us has the same peril-
ous force
Which Bothwell's powder had to Kirk
of Field;
One whose least tones, and those but
peasant accents,
Could rend the roof off our fathers' castle,
Level its tallest turret with its base;

And he that doth possess this wondrous power
Sleeps this same night not five miles distant from us.

AUCH. *(who had looked on* PHILIP *with much appearance of astonishment and doubt, exclaims).* —
Then thou art mad indeed! Ha! ha! I'm glad on't.
I'd purchase an escape from what I dread,
Even by the frenzy of my only son.

PHI. I thank you, but agree not to the bargain.
You rest on what yon civet cat has said:
Yon silken doublet, stuff'd with rotten straw,
Told you but half the truth, and knew no more.
But my good vagrants had a perfect tale.
They told me, little judging the importance,
That Quentin Blane had been discharged with them.
They told me, that a quarrel happ'd at landing,
And that the youngster and an ancient sergeant
Had left their company, and taken refuge
In Chapeldonan, where our ranger dwells;
They saw him scale the cliff on which it stands,
Ere they were out of sight; the old man with him,
And therefore laugh no more at me as mad;
But laugh, if thou hast list for merriment,
To think he stands on the same land with us,
Whose absence thou wouldst deem were cheaply purchased
With thy soul's ransom and thy body's danger.

AUCH. 'Tis then a fatal truth. Thou art no yelper
To open rashly on so wild a scent;
Thou'rt the young bloodhound, which careers and springs,
Frolics and fawns, as if the friend of man,
But seizes on his victim like a tiger.

PHI. No matter what I am — I'm as you bred me;

So let that pass till there be time to mend me,
And let us speak like men, and to the purpose.
This object of our fear and of our dread,
Since such our pride must own him, sleeps to-night
Within our power: — to-morrow in Dunbar's,
And we are then his victims.

AUCH. He is *ours* to-night.

PHI. He is. I'll answer that Mac-Lellan's trusty.

AUCH. Yet he replied to you to-day full rudely.

PHI. Yes! the poor knave has got a handsome wife,
And is gone mad with jealousy.

AUCH. Fool! — when we need the utmost faith, allegiance,
Obedience, and attachment in our vassals,
Thy wild intrigues pour gall into their hearts,
And turn their love to hatred!

PHI. Most reverend sire, you talk of ancient morals,
Preach'd on by Knox, and practised by Glencairn.*
Respectable, indeed, but somewhat musty
In these our modern nostrils. In our days
If a young baron chance to leave his vassal
The sole possessor of a handsome wife,
'Tis sign he loves his follower; and if not,
He loves his follower's wife, which often proves
The surer bond of patronage. Take either case,
Favor flows in of course, and vassals rise.

AUCH. Philip, this is infamous,
And what is worse, impolitic. Take example:
Break not God's laws or man's for each temptation

---

* Alexander, Fifth Earl of Glencairn, called "The Good Earl," concurred in the Reformation, asisting the Reformers with pen and sword. He had a chief command in the army raised against Queen Mary in June, 1567 and demolished the altar, broke the images, tore down the pictures and committed other acts of iconoclastic vandalism in the Chapel royal of Holyrood-house after the Queen was conducted to Lochleven. He was the author of a satirical poem against the Roman Catholics called "The Hermit of Allareit" (Loretto). He died in 1574.

That youth and blood suggest.   I am a
man —
A weak and erring man; — full well thou
know'st
That I may hardly term myself a pattern
Even to my son; yet thus far will I say,
I never swerved from my integrity,
Save at the voice of strong necessity,
Or such o'erpowering view of high ad-
vantage
As wise men liken to necesssity,
In strength and force compulsive.   No
one saw me
Exchange my reputation for my pleasure,
Or do the devil's work without his wages.
I practised prudence, and paid tax to vir-
tue,
By following her behests, save where
strong reason
Compell'd a deviation.   Then, if preach-
ers
At times look'd sour, or elders shook their
heads,
They could not term my walk irregular;
For I stood up still for the worthier cause,
A pillar, tho' a flaw'd one, of the altar,
Kept a strict walk, and led three hundred
horse.
    PHI. Ah, these three hundred horse in
such rough times
Were better commendation to a party
Than all your efforts at hypocrisy,
Betray'd so oft by avarice and ambition,
And dragg'd to open shame.   But, right-
eous father,
When sire and son unite in mutual crime,
And join their efforts to the same enormity,
It is no time to measure other's faults,
Or fix the amount of each.   Most moral
father,
Think if it be a moment to weigh
The vices of the Heir of Auchindrane,
Or take precaution that the ancient house
Shall have another heir than the sly cour-
tier
That's gaping for the forfeiture.
    AUCH. We'll disappoint him, Philip, —
We'll disappoint him yet.   It is a folly,
A wilful cheat, to cast our eyes behind,
When time, and the fast flitting oppor-
tunity,
Call loudly — nay, compel us to look for-
ward:

Why are we not already at MacLellan's,
Since there the victim sleeps?
    PHI.   Nay, soft, I pray thee.
I had not made your piety my confessor,
Nor enter'd in debate on these sage coun-
sels,
Which you're more like to give than I to
profit by,
Could I have used the time more use-
fully;
But first an interval must pass between
The fate of Quentin and the little artifice
That shall detach him from his comrade,
The stout old soldier that I told you of.
    AUCH. How work a point so difficult
— so dangerous?
    PHI. 'Tis cared for.   Mark, my father,
the convenience
Arising from mean company.   My agents
Are at my hand, like a good workman's
tools,
And if I mean a mischief, ten to one
That they anticipate the deed and guilt.
Well knowing this, when first the va-
grants' tattle
Gave me the hint that Quentin was so
near us,
Instant I sent MacLellan, with strong
charges
To stop him for the night, and bring me
word,
Like an accomplish'd spy, how all things
stood,
Lulling the enemy into security.
    AUCH. There was a prudent general !
    PHI. MacLellan went and came within
the hour.
The jealous bee, which buzzes in his night-
cap,
Has humm'd to him, this fellow, Quentin
Blane,
Had been in schoolboy days an humble
lover
Of his own pretty wife —
    AUCH.   Most fortunate !
The knave will be more prompt to serve
our purpose.
    PHI. No doubt on't.   Mid the tidings
he brought back,
Was one of some importance.   The old man
Is flush of dollars; this I caused him tell
Among his comrades, who became as
eager

To have him in their company, as e'er
They had been wild to part with him. And
    in brief space,
A letter's framed by an old hand amongst
    them,
Familiar with such feats. It bore the
    name
And character of old Montgomery,
Whom he might well suppose at no great
    distance,
Commanding his old Sergeant Hildebrand,
By all the ties of late authority,
Conjuring him by ancient soldiership,
To hasten to his mansion instantly,
On business of high import, with a charge
To come alone —

AUCH. Well, he sets out, I doubt it
    not: what follows?

PHI. I am not curious into others' prac-
    tices, —
So far I'm an economist in guilt,
As you, my sire, advise. But on the road
To old Montgomery's he meets his com-
    rades;
They nourish grudge against him and his
    dollars,
And things may hap, which counsel,
    learn'd in law,
Call Robbery and Murder. Should he
    live,
He has seen naught that we would hide
    from him.

AUCH. Who carries the forged letter to
    the veteran?

PHI. Why, Niel MacLellan, who re-
    turn'd again
To his own tower, as if to pass the night
    there.
They pass'd on him, or tried to pass, a
    story,
As if they wish'd the sergeant's company,
Without the young comptroller's — that
    is Quentin's,
And he became an agent of their plot,
That he might better carry on our own.

AUCH. There's life in it — yes, there is
    life in 't;
And we will have a mounted party ready
To scour the moors in quest of the banditti
That kill'd the poor old man — they shall
    die instantly.
Dunbar shall see us use sharp justice here
As well as he in Teviotdale. You are sure

You gave no hint nor impulse to their
    purpose?

PHI. It needed not. The whole pack
    oped at once
Upon the scent of dollars. — But time
    comes
When I must seek the tower, and act with
    Niel
What farther's to be done.

AUCH. Alone with him thou goest not.
    He bears grudge —
Thou art my only son, and on a night
When such wild passions are so free
    abroad,
When such wild deeds are doing, 'tis but
    natural
I guarantee thy safety. — I'll ride with
    thee.

PHI. E'en as you will, my lord. But
    — pardon me —
If you will come, let us not have a word
Of conscience, and of pity, and of forgive-
    ness;
Fine words to-morrow, out of place to-
    night.
Take counsel, then — leave all this work
    to me;
Call up your household, make fit prepara-
    tion,
In love and peace, to welcome this Earl
    Justiciar,
As one that's free of guilt. Go, deck the
    castle
As for an honor'd guest. Hallow the
    chapel
(If they have power to hallow it) with
    thy prayers.
Let me ride forth alone, and ere the sun
Comes o'er the eastern hill, thou shalt
    accost him :
"Now do thy worst, thou oft-returning
    spy,
Here's naught thou canst discover."

AUCH. Yet goest thou not alone with
    that MacLellan !
He deems thou bearest will to injure him,
And seek'st occasion suiting to such will.
Philip, thou art irreverent, fierce, ill-
    nurtured,
Stain'd with low vices, which disgust a
    father;
Yet ridest thou not alone with yonder
    man, —

Come weal, come woe, myself will go
   with thee.
  [*Exit, and calls to horse behind the
   scene.*

PHI. (*alone*). Now would I give my
   fleetest horse to know
What sudden thought roused this pater-
   nal care,
And if 'tis on his own account or mine;
'Tis true, he hath the deepest share in all
That's likely now to hap, or which has
   happen'd.
Yet strong thro' Nature's universal reign,
The link which binds the parent to the
   offspring:
The she-wolf knows it, and the tigress
   owns it.
So that dark man, who, shunning what is
   vicious,
Ne'er turned aside from an atrocity,
Hath still some care left for his hapless
   offspring.
Therefore 'tis meet, tho' wayward, light,
   and stubborn,
That I should do for him all that a son
Can do for sire — and his dark wisdom
   join'd
To influence my bold courses, 'twill be
   hard
To break our mutual purpose. — Horses
   there!   [*Exit.*

ACT III. — SCENE I.

*It is Moonlight. The Scene is the Beach
beneath the Tower which was exhibited
in the first scene, — the Vessel is gone
from her anchorage.* AUCHINDRANE
and PHILIP, *as if dismounted from
their horses, come forward cautiously.*

PHI. The nags are safely stow'd.
   Their noise might scare him;
Let them be safe, and ready when we
   need them.
The business is but short. We'll call
   MacLellan,
To wake him, and in quiet bring him forth,
If he be so disposed; for here are waters
Enough to drown, and sand enough to
   cover him.
But if he hesitate, or fear to meet us,
By heaven I'll deal on him in Chapeldo-
   nan

With my own hand! —
    AUCH. Too furious boy! — alarm o
   noise undoes us:
Our practice must be silent as 'tis sudden
Bethink thee that conviction of thi
   slaughter
Confirms the very worst of accusations
Our foes can bring against us. Where
   fore should we,
Who by birth and fortune mate with
   nobles,
And are allied with them, take this lad's
   life, —
His peasant life, — unless to quash his
   evidence,
Taking such pains to rid him from the
   world,
Who would, if spared, have fix'd a crime
   upon us.
    PHI. Well, I do own me one of those
   wise folks,
Who think that when a deed of fate is
   plann'd
The execution cannot be too rapid.
But do we still keep purpose? Is't deter-
   mined
He sails for Ireland — and without a
   wherry?
Salt water is his passport — is it not so?
    AUCH. I would it could be otherwise!
Might he not go there while in life and
   limb,
And breathe his span out in another air?
Many seek Ulster never to return —
Why might this wretched youth not harbor
   there?
    PHI. With all my heart. It is small
   honor to me
To be the agent in a work like this. —
Yet this poor caitiff, having thrust himself
Into the secrets of a noble house,
And twined himself so closely with our
   safety,
That we must perish, or that he must die,
I'll hesitate as little on the action,
As I would do to slay the animal
Whose flesh supplies my dinner. 'Tis as
   harmless,
That deer or steer, as is this Quentin
   Blane,
And not more necessary is its death
To our accommodation — so we slay it
Without a moment's pause or hesitation.

AUCH. 'Tis not, my son, the feeling call'd remorse,
That now lies tugging at this heart of mine,
Engendering thoughts that stop the lifted hand.
Have I not heard John Knox pour forth his thunders
Against the oppressor and the man of blood
In accents of a minister of vengeance?
Were not his fiery eyeballs turned on me,
As if he said expressly: "Thou'rt the man?"
Yet did my solid purpose, as I listen'd,
Remain unshaken as that massive rock.
    PHI. Well, then, I'll understand 'tis not remorse, —
As 'tis a foible little known to thee, —
That interrupts thy purpose. What, then, is it?
Is't scorn, or is't compassion? One thing's certain, —
Either the feeling must have free indulgence,
Or fully be subjected to your reason —
There is no room for these same treacherous courses,
Which men call moderate measures.
We must confide in Quentin, or must slay him.
    AUCH. In Ireland he might live afar from us.
    PHI. Among Queen Mary's faithful partisans,
Your ancient enemies, the haughty Hamiltons,
The stern MacDonnells, and resentful Græmes —
With these around him, and with Cassilis' death
Exasperating them against you, think, my father,
What chance of Quentin's silence.
    AUCH. Too true — too true. He is a silly youth, too,
Who had not wit to shift for his own living —
A bashful lover, whom his rivals laugh'd at —
Of pliant temper, which companions played on —
A moonlight waker, and a noontide dreamer —

A torturer of phrases into sonnets,
Whom all might lead that chose to praise his rhymes.
    PHI. I marvel that your memory has room
To hold so much on such a worthless subject.
    AUCH. Base in himself, and yet so strangely link'd
With me and with my fortunes, that I've studied
To read him thro' and thro', as I would read
Some paltry rhyme of vulgar prophecy,
Said to contain the fortunes of my house;
And let me speak him truly: — He is grateful,
Kind, tractable, obedient — a child
Might lead him by a thread — He shall not die!
    PHI. Indeed! — then have we had our midnight ride
To wondrous little purpose.
    AUCH. By the blue heaven,
Thou shalt not murder him, cold, selfish sensualist!
Yon pure vault speaks it — yonder summer moon,
With its ten million sparklers, cries, Forbear!
The deep earth sighs it forth — Thou shalt not murder!
Thou shalt not mar the image of thy maker!
Thou shalt not from thy brother take the life,
The gracious gift which God alone can give!
    PHI. Here is a worthy guerdon now, for stuffing
His memory with old saws and holy sayings!
They come upon him in the very crisis,
And when his resolution should be firmest,
They shake it like a palsy. — Let it be,
He'll end at last by yielding to temptation,
Consenting to the thing which must be done,
With more remorse the more he hesitates. —
(*To his Father, who has stood fixed after his last speech.*) —
Well, sir, 'tis fitting you resolve at last,

How the young clerk should be disposed
    upon;
Unless you would ride home to Auchin-
    drane,
And bid them rear the Maiden in the
    court-yard,
That when Dunbar comes, he have naught
    to do
But bid us kiss the cushion and the heads-
    man.
    AUCH. It is too true. — There is no
    safety for us,
Consistent with the unhappy wretch's life!
In Ireland he is sure to find my enemies.
Arran I've proved — the Netherlands
    I've tried,
But wilds and wars return him on my
    hands.
    PHI. Yet fear not, father, we'll make
    surer work;
The land has caves, the sea has whirlpools,
Where that which they suck in returns no
    more.
    AUCH. I will know naught of it, hard-
    hearted boy!
    PHI. Hard-hearted! Why — my heart
    is soft as yours;
But then they must not feel remorse at
    once —
We can't afford such wasteful tenderness:
I can mouth forth remorse as well as you.
Be executioner, and I'll be chaplain,
And say as mild and moving things as
    you can;
But one of us must keep his steely temper.
    AUCH. Do thou the deed — I cannot
    look on it.
    PHI. So be it. Walk with me — Mac-
    Lellan brings him.
The boat lies moor'd within that reach of
    rock,
And 'twill require our greatest strength
    combined
To launch it from the beach. Meantime,
    MacLellan
Brings our man hither. — See the twink-
    ling light
That glances in the tower.
    AUCH. Let us withdraw — for should
    he spy us suddenly,
He may suspect us, and alarm the family.
    PHI. Fear not — MacLellan has his
    trust and confidence,

Bought with a few sweet words and wel
    comes home.
    AUCH. But think you that the Ranger
    may be trusted?
    PHI. I'll answer for him, — Let's go
    float the shallop.

    [*They go off, and as they leave the*
    Stage, MACLELLAN *is seen de-*
    scending from the Tower with
    QUENTIN. *The former bears a*
    dark lantern. They come upon
    the Stage.

    MAC. (*showing the light*). —
So — bravely done — that's the last ledge
    of rocks,
And we are on the sands. — I have broke
    your slumbers
Somewhat untimely.
    QUE.   Do not think so, friend.
These six years past I have been used to
    stir
When the reveillé rung; and that, believe
    me,
Chooses the hours for rousing me at ran-
    dom,
And, having given it summons, yields no
    license
To indulge a second slumber. Nay more,
    I'll tell thee,
That, like a pleased child, I was e'en too
    happy
For sound repose.
    MAC.   The greater fool were you.
Men should enjoy the moments given to
    slumber;
For who can tell how soon may be the
    waking,
Or where we shall have leave to sleep
    again?
    QUE. The God of Slumber comes not
    at command.
Last night the blood danced merry thro'
    my veins:
Instead of finding this our land of Carrick
The dreary waste my fears had appre-
    hended,
I saw thy wife, MacLellan, and thy
    daughter,
And had a brother's welcome; saw thee
    too,
Renew'd my early friendship with you
    both,

And felt once more that I had friends and
country.
So keen the joy that tingled thro' my sys-
tem,
Join'd with the searching powers of yon-
der wine,
That I am glad to leave my feverish lair,
Altho' my hostess smooth'd my couch
herself,
To cool my brow upon this moonlight
beach,
Gaze on the moonlight dancing on the
waves.
Such scenes are wont to soothe me into
melancholy;
But such the hurry of my spirits now,
That everything I look on makes me
laugh.
   MAC. I've seen but few so gamesome,
Master Quentin,
Being roused from sleep so suddenly as
you were.
   QUE. Why, there's the jest on't. Your
old castle's haunted.
In vain the host — in vain the lovely
hostess,
In kind addition to all means of rest,
Add their best wishes for our sound re-
pose,
When some hobgoblin brings a pressing
message: —
Montgomery presently must see his ser-
geant,
And up gets Hildebrand, and off he
trudges.
I can't but laugh to think upon the grin
With which he doff'd the kerchief he had
twisted
Around his brows, and put his morion
on —
Ha! ha! ha! ha!
   MAC. I'm glad to see you merry,
Quentin.
   QUE. Why, faith, my spirits are but
transitory,
And you may live with me a month or
more,
And never see me smile. Then some
such trifle
As yonder little maid of yours would
laugh at,
Will serve me for a theme of merriment —
Even now, I scarce can keep my gravity;

We were so snugly settled in our quarters,
With full intent to let the sun be high
Ere we should leave our beds — and first
the one
And then the other's summon'd briefly
forth
To the old tune, " Black Bandsmen, up
and march ! ''
   MAC. Well, you shall sleep anon —
rely upon it —
And make up time misspent. Meantime,
methinks,
You are so merry on your broken slum-
bers,
You ask'd not why I call'd you.
   QUE.   I can guess.
You lack my aid to search the weir for
seals,
You lack my company to stalk a deer.
Think you I have forgot your sylvan tasks,
Which oft you have permitted me to
share,
Till days that we were rivals?
   MAC.   You have memory
Of that too ! —
   QUE.   Like the memory of a dream,
Delusion far too exquisite to last.
   MAC. You guess not then for what I
call you forth?
It was to meet a friend —
   QUE. What friend? Thyself excepted,
The good old man who's gone to see
Montgomery,
And one to whom I once gave dearer title,
I know not in wide Scotland man or
woman
Whom I could name a friend.
   MAC.   Thou art mistaken.
There is a Baron, and a powerful one —
   QUE. There flies my fit of mirth. You
have a grave
And alter'd man before you.
   MAC. Compose yourself, there is no
cause for fear, —
He will and must speak with you.
   QUE. Spare me the meeting, Niel, —
I cannot see him.
Say, I'm just landed on my native earth;
Say, that I will not cumber it a day;
Say, that my wretched thread of poor ex-
istence
Shall be drawn out in solitude and exile,
Where never memory of so mean a thing

Again shall cross his path — but do not
  ask me
To seek or speak again with that dark
  man !
MAC. Your fears are now as foolish as
  your mirth —
What should the powerful knight of
  Auchindrane
In common have with such a man as thou ?
  QUE. No matter what — Enough, I will
    not see him.
  MAC. He is thy master, and he claims
    obedience.
  QUE. My master ? Ay, my task-mas-
    ter — Ever since
I could write man, his hand hath been
  upon me;
No step I've made but cumber'd with his
  chain,
And I am weary on't — I will not see him.
  MAC. You must and shall — there is
    no remedy.
  QUE. Take heed that you compel me
    not to find one.
I've seen the wars since we had strife to-
  gether;
To put my late experience to the test
Were something dangerous — Ha ! I am
  betray'd !

[*While the latter part of this dialogue is passing,* AUCHINDRANE
and PHILIP *enter on the Stage
from behind and suddenly present themselves.*

AUCH. What says the runagate ?
QUE. (*laying aside all appearance of
resistance*). —
Nothing. You are my fate;
And in a shape more fearfully resistless
My evil angel could not stand before me.
  AUCH. And so you scruple, slave, at
  my command,
To meet me when I deign to ask thy pres-
  ence ?
  QUE. No, sir; I had forgot — I am
  your bond-slave;
But sure a passing thought of indepen-
  dence,
For which I've seen whole nations doing
  battle,
Was not, in one who has so long enjoyed
  it,

A crime beyond forgiveness.
  AUCH.   We shall see:
Thou wert my vassal, born upon my land,
Bred by my bounty. — It concern'd me
  highly,
Thou know'st it did — and yet, against
  my charge,
Again I find thy worthlessness in Scotland.
  QUE. Alas ! the wealthy and the power-
  ful know not
How very dear to those who have least
  share in't
Is that sweet word of country ! The poor
  exile
Feels, in each action of the varied day,
His doom of banishment. The very air
Cools not his brow as in his native land;
The scene is strange, the food is loathly
  to him;
The language — nay, the music jars his
  ear.
Why should I, guiltless of the slightest
  crime,
Suffer a punishment which, sparing life,
Deprives that life of all which men hold
  dear ?
  AUCH. Hear ye the serf I bred begin
  to reckon
Upon his rights and pleasures ! Who
  am I —
Thou abject, who am I, whose will thou
  thwartest ?
  PHI. Well spoke, my pious sire. There
  goes remorse !
Let once thy precious pride take fire, and
  then,
MacLellan, you and I may have small
  trouble.
  QUE. Your words are deadly, and your
  power resistless;
I'm in your hands — but, surely, less than
  life
May give you the security you seek,
Without commission of a mortal crime.
  AUCH. Who is't would deign to think
  upon thy life ?
I but require of thee to speed to Ireland
Where thou may'st sojourn for some little
  space,
Having due means of living dealt to thee
And, when it suits the changes of the
  times,
Permission to return.

Que.   Noble my lord,
I am too weak to combat with your pleas-
    ure;
Yet O, for mercy's sake, and for the sake
Of that dear land which is our common
    mother,
Let me not part in darkness from my
    country!
Pass but an hour or two, and every cape,
Headland, and bay, shall gleam with new-
    born light,
And I'll take boat as gayly as the bird
That soars to meet the morning.
Grant me but this — to show no darker
    thoughts
Are on your heart than those your speech
    expresses!
    Phi. A modest favor, friend, is this you
    ask!
Are we to pace the beach like watermen,
Waiting your worship's pleasure to take
    boat?
No, by my faith! you go upon the instant.
The boat lies ready, and the ship receives
    you
Near to the Point of Turnberry. — Come,
    we wait you;
Bestir you!
    Que. I obey. Then farewell, Scotland!
And Heaven forgive my sins, and grant
    that mercy
Which mortal man deserves not!
    Auch. (*speaks aside to his Son*). —
    What signal
Shall let me know 'tis done?
    Phi.   When the light is quench'd,
Your fears for Quentin Blane are at an
    end —
(*To* Que.) Come, comrade, come, we
    must begin our voyage.
    Que. But when — O when to end it!

[*He goes off reluctantly with* Philip
and MacLellan. Auchin-
drane *stands looking after
them. The Moon becomes over-
clouded, and the Stage dark.*
Auchindrane, *who has gazed
fixedly and eagerly after those
who have left the Stage, becomes
animated, and speaks.*

    Auch. It is no fallacy! — The night is
dark,
The moon has sunk before the deepening
    clouds;
I cannot on the murky beach distinguish
The shallop from the rocks which lie be-
    side it;
I cannot see tall Philip's floating plume,
Nor trace the sullen brow of Niel Mac-
    Lellan;
Yet still that caitiff's visage is before me.
With chattering teeth, mazed look, and
    bristling hair,
As he stood here this moment! — Have I
    changed
My human eyes for those of some night
    prowler,
The wolf's, the tiger-cat's, or the hoarse
    bird's
That spies its prey at midnight? I can
    see him —
Yes, I can see him, seeing no one else, —
And well it is I do so. In his absence,
Strange thoughts of pity mingled with my
    purpose,
And moved remorse within me. — But
    they vanish'd
Whene'er he stood a living man before
    me;
Then my antipathy awaked within me,
Seeing its object close within my reach,
Till I could scarce forbear him. — How
    they linger!
The boat's not yet to sea! — I ask myself,
What has the poor wretch done to wake
    my hatred —
Docile, obedient, and in sufferance pa-
    tient! —
As well demand what evil has the hare
Done to the hound that courses her in
    sport.
Instinct infallible supplies the reason —
And that must plead my cause. — The
    vision's gone!
Their boat now walks the waves; a single
    gleam,
Now seen, now lost, is all that marks her
    course;
That soon shall vanish too — then all is
    over! —
Would it were over, for in this moment lies
The agony of ages; — Now, 'tis gone —
And all is acted! No — she breasts again
The opposing wave, and bears the tiny
    sparkle

Upon her crest — (*A faint cry heard as from seaward.*)

Ah! there was fatal evidence,
All's over now, indeed! — The light is quench'd —
And Quentin, source of all my fear, exists not.
The morning tide shall sweep his corpse to sea,
And hide all memory of this stern night's work.

[*He walks in a slow and deeply meditative manner towards the side of the Stage, and suddenly meets* MARION, *the wife of* MAC-LELLAN, *who has descended from the Castle.*

Now, how to meet Dunbar — Heaven guard my senses!
Stand! who goes there? — Do spirits walk the earth
Ere yet they've left the body?
    MAR.   Is it you,
My lord, on this wild beach at such an hour?
    AUCH. It is MacLellan's wife, in search of him,
Or of her lover — of the murderer,
Or of the murder'd man. — Go to, Dame Marion;
Men have their hunting-gear to give an eye to,
Their snares and trackings for their game. But women
Should shun the night air. A young wife also,
Still more a handsome one, should keep her pillow
Till the sun gives example for her wakening.
Come, Dame, go back — back to your bed again.
    MAR. Hear me, my lord! there have been sights and sounds
That terrified my child and me — Groans, screams,
As if of dying seamen, came from ocean —
A corpse-light danced upon the crested waves
For several minutes' space, then sunk at once.
When we retired to rest we had two guests,

Besides my husband Niel — I'll tell your lordship
Who the men were ——
    AUCH. Pshaw, woman, can you think
That I have any interest in your gossips?
Please your own husband, and that you may please him,
Get thee to bed, and shut up doors, good dame.
Were I MacLellan, I should scarce be satisfied
To find thee wandering here in mist and moonlight,
When silence should be in thy habitation,
And sleep upon thy pillow.
    MAR.   Good my lord,
This is a holyday. — By an ancient custom
Our children seek the shore at break of day,
And gather shells, and dance, and play, and sport them
In honor of the Ocean. Old men say
The custom is derived from heathen times. Our Isabel
Is mistress of the feast, and you may think
She is awake already, and impatient
To be the first shall stand upon the beach,
And bid the sun good-morrow.
    AUCH.   Ay, indeed?
Linger such dregs of heathendom among you?
And hath Knox preach'd, and Wishart died, in vain?
Take notice, I forbid these sinful practices,
And will not have my followers mingle in them.
    MAR. If such your honor's pleasure, I must go
And lock the door on Isabel; she is wilful,
And voice of mine will have small force to keep her
From the amusement she so long has dream'd of.
But I must tell your honor, the old people,
That were survivors of the former race,
Prophesied evil if this day should pass
Without due homage to the mighty Ocean.
    AUCH. Folly and Papistry. — Perhaps the Ocean
Hath had his morning sacrifice already;
Or can you think the dreadful element,

Whose frown is death, whose roar the
  dirge of navies,
Will miss the idle pageant you prepare?
I've business for you, too — the dawn ad-
  vances —
I'd have thee lock thy little child in
  safety,
And get to Auchindrane before the sun
  rise;
Tell them to get a royal banquet ready,
As if a king were coming there to feast
  him.
  MAR. I will obey your pleasure. But
    my husband —
  AUCH. I wait him on the beach, and
    bring him in
To share the banquet.
  MAR.   But he has a friend,
Whom it would ill become him to intrude
Upon your hospitality.
  AUCH. Fear not; his friend shall be
    made welcome too,
Should he return with Niel.
  MAR. He must — he will return — he
    has no option.
  AUCH. (*apart*). Thus rashly do we
    deem of other's destiny —
He has indeed no option — but he comes
  not.
Begone on thy commission — I go this
  way
To meet thy husband.

> [MARION *goes to her Tower, and
> after entering it, is seen to come
> out, lock the door, and leave the
> stage, as if to execute* AUCHIN-
> DRANE'S *commission. He, ap-
> parently going off in a different
> direction, has watched her from
> the side of the stage, and on her
> departure speaks.*

  AUCH. Fare thee well, fond woman,
Most dangerous of spies — thou prying,
  prating,
Spying and telling woman! I've cut short
Thy dangerous testimony — Hated word!
What other evidence have we cut short,
And by what fated means, this dreary
  morning! —
Bright lances here and helmets! — I must
  shift
To join the others.   [*Exit.*

> *Enter from the other side the* SERGEANT,
> *accompanied with an Officer and two
> Pikemen.*

  SER. 'Twas in good time you came; a
    minute later
The knaves had ta'en my dollars and my
  life.
  OFF. You fought most stoutly. Two
    of them were down
Ere we came to your aid.
  SER.   Gramercy, halberd!
And well it happens, since your leader
  seeks
This Quentin Blane, that you have fall'n
  on me;
None else can surely tell you where he
  hides,
Being in some fear, and bent to quit this
  province.
  OFF. 'Twill do our Earl good service.
    He has sent
Despatches into Holland for this Quentin.
  SER. I left him two hours since in yon-
    der tower,
Under the guard of one who smoothly
  spoke,
Altho' he look'd but roughly — I will
  chide him
For bidding me go forth with yonder trai-
  tor.
  OFF. Assure yourself 'twas a concerted
    stratagem.
Montgomery's been at Holyrood for
  months,
And can have sent no letter — 'twas a plan
On you and on your dollars, and a base
  one,
To which this Ranger was most likely
  privy.
Such men as he hang on our fiercer barons,
The ready agents of their lawless will;
Boys of the belt, who aid their master's
  pleasures,
And in his moods ne'er scruple his in-
  junctions.
But haste, for now we must unkennel
  Quentin;
I've strictest charge concerning him.
  SER. Go up, then, to the tower.
You've younger limbs than mine; there
  shall you find him
Lounging and snoring, like a lazy cur
Before a stable door; it is his practice.

[*The* OFFICER *goes up to the Tower,
and after knocking without receiving an answer, turns the key
which* MARION *had left in the
lock, and enters;* ISABEL, *dressed
as if for her dance, runs out and
descends to the Stage; the* OFFI-
CER *follows.*

OFF. There's no one in the house, this
little maid
Excepted —

ISA. And for me, I'm there no longer,
And will not be again for three hours
good;
I'm going to join my playmates on the
sands.

OFF. (*detaining her*). You shall, when
you have told to me distinctly
Where are the guests who slept up there
last night.

ISA. Why, there is the old man, he
stands beside you,
The merry old man with the glistening
hair;
He left the tower at midnight, for my
father
Brought him a letter.

SER.   In ill hour I left you.
I wish to Heaven that I had stay'd with
you !
There is a nameless horror that comes
o'er me. —
Speak, pretty maiden, tell us what
chanced next,
And thou shalt have thy freedom.

ISA. After you went last night, my
father
Grew moody, and refused to doff his
clothes,
Or go to bed, as sometimes he will do
When there is aught to chafe him.   Until
past midnight,
He wander'd to and fro, then call'd the
stranger,
The gay young man, that sung such merry
songs,
Yet ever look'd most sadly whilst he sung
them;
And forth they went together.

OFF.   And you've seen
Or heard naught of them since ?

ISA. Seen surely nothing, and I cannot
think

That they have lot or share in what I
heard.
I heard my mother praying, for the corpse-
lights
Were dancing on the waves; and at one
o'clock,
Just as the Abbey steeple toll'd the knell,
There was a heavy plunge upon the
waters,
And some one cried aloud for mercy ! —
mercy !
It was the water-spirit, sure, which prom-
ised
Mercy to boat and fishermen, if we
Perform'd to-day's rites duly.   Let me
go —
I am to lead the ring.

OFF. (*to* SER.).   Detain her not.   She
cannot tell us more;
To give her liberty is the sure way
To lure her parents homeward. —
Strahan, take two men,
And should the father or the mother come,
Arrest them both, or either.   Auchindrane
May come upon the beach; arrest him
also,
But do not state a cause.   I'll back again,
And take directions from my Lord Dun-
bar.
Keep you upon the beach, and have an
eye
To all that passes there.
                           [*Exeunt separately.*

SCENE II.

*Scene changes to a remote and rocky part
of the Seabeach.*

Enter AUCHINDRANE, *meeting* PHILIP.

AUCH. The devil's brought his legions
to this beach,
That wont to be so lonely ;   morions,
lances,
Show in the morning beam as thick as
glowworms
At summer midnight.

PHI.   I'm right glad to see them,
Be they whoe'er they may, so they are
mortal;
For I've contended with a lifeless foe,
And I have lost the battle.   I would give
A thousand crowns to hear a mortal steel
Ring on a mortal harness.

AUCH. How now! art mad? or hast
    thou done the turn —
The turn we came for, and must live or
    die by?
PHI. 'Tis done, if man can do it; but
    I doubt
If this unhappy wretch have Heaven's
    permission
To die by mortal hands.
AUCH. Where is he? — where's Mac-
    Lellan?
PHI.   In the deep —
Both in the deep, and what's immortal
    of them
Gone to the judgment seat, where we
    must meet them.
UCH. MacLellan dead, and Quentin
    too? — So be it
To all that menace ill to Auchindrane,
Or have the power to injure! —Thy words
Are full of comfort, but thine eye and
    look
Have in this pallid gloom a ghastliness,
Which contradicts the tidings of thy
    tongue.
PHI. Hear me, old man — There *is* a
    heaven above us,
As you have heard old Knox and Wishart
    preach,
Tho' little to your boot. The dreaded
    witness
Is slain, and silent. But his misused body
Comes right ashore as if to cry for ven-
    geance;
It rides the waters like a living thing,
Erect, as if he trode the waves which bear
    him.
AUCH. Thou speakest frenzy, when
    sense is most required.
PHI. Hear me yet more! — I say I
    did the deed
With all the coolness of a practiced hunter
When dealing with a stag. I struck him
    overboard,
And with MacLellan's aid I held his head
Under the waters, while the Ranger tied
The weights we had provided to his feet.
We cast him loose when life and body
    parted,
And bade him speed for Ireland. But even
    then,
As in defiance of the words we spoke,
The body rose upright behind our stern,

One half in ocean, and one half in air,
And tided after as in chase of us.
AUCH. It was enchantment! — Did
    you strike at it?
PHI. Once and again. But blows
    avail'd no more
Than on a wreath of smoke, where they
    may break
The column for a moment, which unites
And is entire again. Thus the dead body
Sunk down before my oar, but rose un-
    harm'd,
And dogg'd us closer still, as in defiance.
AUCH. 'Twas Hell's own work! —
PHI. MacLellan then grew restive,
And, desperate in his fear, blasphemed
    aloud,
Cursing us both as authors of his ruin.
Myself was well-nigh frantic while per-
    sued
By this dread shape, upon whose ghastly
    features
The changeful moonbeam spread a grisly
    light,
And, baited thus, I took the nearest way
To ensure his silence, and to quell his
    noise;
I used my dagger, and I flung him over-
    board,
And half-expected his dead carcass also
Would join the chase — but he sank down
    at once.
AUCH. He had enough of mortal sin
    about him
To sink an argosy.
PHI. But now resolve you what defence
    to make,
If Quentin's body shall be recognized;
For 'tis ashore already; and he bears
Marks of my handiwork — so does Mac-
    Lellan.
AUCH. The concourse thickens still —
    Away, away!
We must avoid the multitude.
               [*They rush out.*

SCENE III.

*Scene changes to another part of the
Beach, Children are seen dancing, and
Villagers looking on.* ISABEL *seems
to take the management of the Dance.*

VIL. WOM. How well she queens it,
    the brave little maiden!

VIL. Ay, they all queen it from their very cradle,
These willing slaves of haughty Auchindrane.
But now I hear the old man's reign is ended; —
'Tis well — he has been tyrant long enough.

SECOND VIL. Finlay, speak low — you interrupt the sports.

THIRD VIL. Look out to sea! — There's something coming yonder,
Bound for the beach, will scare us from our mirth.

FOURTH VIL. Pshaw! it is but a seagull on the wing,
Between the wave and sky.

THIRD VIL.   Thou art a fool,
Standing on solid land — 'tis a dead body.

SECOND VIL. And if it be, he bears him like a live one,
Not prone and weltering, like a drowned corpse,
But bolt erect, as if he trode the waters,
And used them as his path.

FOURTH VIL.   It is a merman,
And nothing of this earth, alive or dead.

[*By degrees all the Dancers break off from their sport, and stand gazing to seaward, while an object, imperfectly seen, drifts towards the Beach, and at length arrives among the rocks which border the tide.*

THIRD VIL. Perhaps it is some wretch who needs assistance;
Jasper, make in and see.

SECOND VIL. Not I, my friend;
E'en take the risk yourself, you'd put on others.

[HILDEBRAND *has entered, and heard the two last words.*

SER. What, are you men?
Fear ye to look on what you must be one day?
I, who have seen a thousand dead and dying
Within a flight-shot square, will teach you how in war
We look upon the corpse when life has left it.

[*He goes to the back scene, and seems attempting to turn the body, which has come ashore with its face downward.*

Will none of you come aid to turn the body?

ISA. You're cowards all. — I'll help thee, good old man.

[*She goes to aid the* SERGEANT *with the body, and presently gives a cry, and faints.* HILDEBRAND *comes forward. All crowd round him; he speaks with an expression of horror.*

SER. 'Tis Quentin Blane! Poor youth, his gloomy bodings
Have been the prologue to an act of darkness;
His feet are manacled, his bosom stabb'd,
And he is foully murder'd.   The proud Knight
And his dark Ranger must have done this deed,
For which no common ruffian could have motive.

A PEASANT. Caution were best, old man — Thou art a stranger,
The Knight is great and powerful.

SER.   Let it be so.
Call'd on by Heaven to stand forth an avenger,
I will not blench for fear of mortal man.
Have I not seen that when that innocent
Had placed her hands upon the murder'd body,
His gaping wounds, that erst were soak'd with brine,
Burst forth with blood as ruddy as the cloud
Which now the sun does rise on!

PEASANT.   What of that?

SER. Nothing that can affect the innocent child;
But murder's guilt attaching to her father,
Since the blood musters in the victim's veins
At the approach of what holds lease from him
Of all that parents can transmit to children.
And here comes one to whom I'll vouch the circumstance.

The EARL OF DUNBAR *enters with Soldiers and others, having* AUCHIN-
DRANE *and* PHILIP *prisoners.*

DUN. Fetter the young ruffian and his
trait'rous father!

[*They are made secure.*

AUCH. 'Twas a lord spoke it — I have
known a knight,
Sir George of Home, who had not dared
to say so.
DUN. 'Tis Heaven, not I, decides upon
your guilt.
A harmless youth is traced within your
power,
Sleeps in your Ranger's house — his friend
at midnight
Is spirited away. Then lights are seen,
And groans are heard, and corpses come
ashore
Mangled with daggers, while (*to* PHI.)
your dagger wears
The sanguine livery of recent slaughter:
Here, too, the body of a murder'd victim
(Whom none but you had interest to re-
move)
Bleeds on a child's approach, because
the daughter
Of one the abettor of the wicked deed; —
All this, and other proofs corroborative,
Call on us briefly to pronounce the doom
We have in charge to utter.
AUCH. If my house perish, Heaven's
will be done!
I wish not to survive it; but, O Philip,
Would one could pay the ransom for us
both!
PHI. Father, 'tis fitter that we both
should die,
Leaving no heir behind. — The piety
Of a bless'd saint, the morals of an
anchorite,
Could not atone thy dark hypocrisy,
Or the wild profligacy I have practised.
Ruin'd our house, and shattered be our
towers,
And with them end the curse our sins
have merited!

THE HOUSE OF ASPEN.
A TRAGEDY.

ADVERTISEMENT.

THIS attempt at dramatic composition was executed nearly thirty years since, when the magnificent works of Goethe and Schiller were for the first time made known to the British public, and received, as many now alive must remember, with universal enthusiasm. What we admire we usually attempt to imitate; and the author, not trusting to his own efforts, borrowed the substance of the story and a part of the diction from a dramatic romance called " Der heilige Vehme " (The Secret Tribunal), which fills the sixth volume of the " Sagen der Vorzeit " (Tales of Antiquity), by Beit Weber. The drama must be termed rather a *rifacimento* of the original than a translation, since the whole is compressed, and the incidents and dialogue are occasionally much varied. The imitator is ignorant of the real name of his ingenious contemporary, and has been informed that of Beit Weber is fictitious.*

The late Mr. John Kemble at one time had some desire to bring out the play at Drury-Lane, then adorned by himself and his matchless sister, who were to have supported the characters of the unhappy son and mother; but great objections appeared to this proposal. There was danger that the mainspring of the story, — the binding engagements formed by members of the secret tribunal, — might not be sufficiently felt by an English audience, to whom the nature of that singularly mysterious institution was unknown from early associa-tion. There was also, according to Mr. Kemble's experienced opinion, too much blood, too

* George Wachter, who published various **works** under the pseudonym of *Veit Weber*, was born in 1763, and died in 1837. — *Ed.*

much of the dire catastrophe of Tom Thumb, when all die on the stage. It was, besides, esteemed perilous to place the fifth act and the parade and show of the secret conclave at the mercy of underlings and scene-shifters, who, by a ridiculous motion, gesture, or accent, might turn what should be grave into farce.

The author, or rather the translator, willingly acquiesced in this reasoning, and never afterwards made any attempt to gain the honor of the buskin. The German taste, also, caricatured by a number of imitators, who, incapable of copying the sublimity of the great masters of the school, supplied its place by extravagance and bombast, fell into disrepute, and received a *coup de grace* from the joint efforts of the late lamented Mr. Canning and Mr. Frere. The effect of their singularly happy piece of ridicule called "The Rovers," a mock play which appeared in *The Anti-Jacobin*, was, that the German school, with its beauties and its defects, passed completely out of fashion, and the following scenes were consigned to neglect and obscurity. Very lately, however, the writer chanced to look them over with feelings very different from those of the adventurous period of his literary life during which they had been written, and yet with such as perhaps a reformed libertine might regard the illegitimate production of an early amour. There is something to be ashamed of, certainly; but, after all, paternal vanity whispers that the child has a resemblance to the father.

To this it need only be added, that there are in existence so many manuscript copies of the following play, that if it should not find its way to the public sooner, it is certain to do so when the author can no more have any opportunity of correcting the press, and consequently at greater disadvantage than at present. Being of too small a size or consequence for a separate publication, the piece is sent as a contribution to *The Keepsake*, where the demerits may be hidden amid the beauties of more valuable articles.

ABBOTSFORD, *1st April*, 1829.

DRAMATIS PERSONÆ.

MEN.

RUDIGER, *Baron of Aspen, an old German warrior.*
GEORGE OF ASPEN, } *Sons to Rudiger.*
HENRY OF ASPEN, }
RODERIC, *Count of Maltingen, chief of a department of the Invisible Tribunal, and the hereditary enemy of the family of Aspen.*
WILLIAM, *Baron of Wolfstein, ally of Count Roderic.*
BERTRAM OF EBERSDORF, *brother to the former husband of the Baroness of Aspen, disguised as a Minstrel.*
DUKE OF BAVARIA.
WICKERD, } *Followers of the House of Aspen.*
REYNOLD, }
CONRAD, *Page of Honor to Henry of Aspen.*
MARTIN, *Squire to George of Aspen.*
HUGO, *Squire to Count Roderic.*
PETER, *an ancient domestic of Rudiger.*
FATHER LUDOVIC, *Chaplain to Rudiger.*

WOMEN.

ISABELLA, *formerly married to Arnolf of Ebersdorf, now wife of Rudiger.*
GERTRUDE, *Isabella's niece, betrothed to Henry.*
Soldiers, Judges of the Invisible Tribunal, etc.
SCENE.— *The Castle of Ebersdorf in Bavaria, the ruins of Griefenhaus, and the adjacent country.*

ACT I.—SCENE I.

An ancient Gothic chamber in the castle of Ebersdorf. Spears, crossbows, and arms, with the horns of buffaloes and of deer, are hung round the wall. An antique buffet with beakers and stone bottles.

RUDIGER, *Baron of Aspen, and his lady,* ISABELLA, *are discovered sitting at a large oaken table.*

RUD. A plague upon that roan horse! Had he not stumbled with me at the ford after our last skirmish, I had been now with my sons. And yonder the boys are, hardly three miles off, battling with Count Roderic, and their father must lie here like a worm-eaten manuscript in a convent library! Out upon it! Out upon it! Is it not hard that a warrior, who has travelled so many leagues to display the cross on the walls of Zion, should be now unable to lift a spear before his own castle gate?

ISA. Dear husband, your anxiety retards your recovery.

RUD. Maybe so; but not less than your silence and melancholy! Here have I sat this month, and more, since that cursed fall! Neither hunting nor feasting, nor lance-breaking for me! And my sons — George enters cold and reserved, as if he had the weight of the empire on his shoulders, utters by syllables a cold " How is it with you? " and shuts himself up for days in his solitary chamber — Henry, my cheerful Henry —

ISA. Surely, he at least —

RUD. Even he forsakes me, and skips up the tower staircase like lightning to join your fair ward, Gertrude, on the battlements. I cannot blame him: for, by my knightly faith, were I in his place, I think even these bruised bones would hardly keep me from her side. Still, however, here I must sit alone.

ISA. Not alone, dear husband. Heaven knows what I would do to soften your confinement.

RUD. Tell me not of that, lady. When I first knew thee, Isabella, the fair maid of Arnheim was the joy of her companions, and breathed life wherever she came. Thy father married thee to Arnolf of Ebersdorf — not much with thy will, 'tis true — (*She hides her face.*) Nay — forgive me, Isabella — but that is over — he died, and the ties between us, which thy marriage had broken, were renewed — but the sunshine of my Isabella's light heart returned no more.

ISA. (*weeping*). Beloved Rudiger, you search my very soul! Why will you recall past times — days of spring that can never return? Do I not love thee more than ever wife loved husband?

RUD. (*stretches out his arms — she embraces him*). And therefore art thou ever my beloved Isabella. But still, is it not true? Has not thy cheerfulness vanished since thou hast become Lady of Aspen? Dost thou repent of thy love to Rudiger?

ISA. Alas! no! never! never!

RUD. Then why dost thou herd with monks and priests, and leave thy old knight alone, when, for the first time in his stormy life, he has rested for weeks within the walls of his castle? Hast thou committed a crime from which Rudiger's love cannot absolve thee?

ISA. O many! many!

RUD. Then be this kiss thy penance. And tell me, Isabella, hast thou not founded a convent, and endowed it with the best of thy late husband's lands? Ay, and with a vineyard which I could have prized as well as the sleek monks. Dost thou not daily distribute alms to twenty pilgrims? Dost thou not cause ten masses to be sung each night for the repose of thy late husband's soul?

ISA. It will not know repose.

RUD. Well, well — God's peace be with Arnolf of Ebersdorf; the mention of him makes thee ever sad, though so many years have passed since his death.

ISA. But at present, dear husband, have I not the most just cause for anxiety? Are not Henry and George — our beloved sons, at this very moment perhaps engaged in doubtful contest with our hereditary foe, Count Roderic of Maltingen?

RUD. Now, there lies the difference; you sorrow that they are in danger. I that I cannot share it with them — Hark! I hear horses' feet on the drawbridge. Go to the window, Isabella.

ISA. (*at the window*). It is Wickerd, your squire.

RUD. Then shall we have tidings of George and Henry. (*Enter* WICKERD.) How now, Wickerd? Have you come to blows yet?

WIC. Not yet, noble sir.

RUD. Not yet? — shame on the boys' dallying — what wait they for?

WIC. The foe is strongly posted, sir knight, upon the Wolfshill, near the ruins of Griefenhaus: therefore your noble son, George of Aspen, greets you well, and requests twenty more men-at-arms, and, after they have joined him, he hopes, with the aid of St. Theodore, to send you news of victory.

RUD. (*attempts to rise hastily*). Saddle my black barb; I will head them myself. (*Sits down.*) A murrain on that stumbling roan! I had forgot my dislocated bones. Call Reynold, Wickerd, and bid him take all whom he can spare from defence of the castle — (WICKERD *is going*) — and ho! Wickerd, carry with you my black barb, and bid George charge upon him. (*Exit* WICKERD.) Now see, Isabella, if I disregard the boy's safety; I send him the best horse ever knight bestrode. When we lay before Ascalon, indeed, I had a bright bay Persian — Thou dost not heed me.

ISA. Forgive me, dear husband: are not our sons in danger? Will not our sins be visited upon them? Is not their present situation —

RUD. Situation? I know it well: as fair a field for open fight as I ever hunted over: see here — (*makes lines on the table*) — here is the ancient castle of Griefenhaus in ruins, here the Wolfshill; and here the marsh on the right.

ISA. The marsh of Griefenhaus?

RUD. Yes; by that the boys must pass.

ISA. Pass there! (*Apart.*) Avenging Heaven! thy hand is upon us!

[*Exit hastily.*

RUD. Whither now? Whither now? She is gone. Thus it goes. Peter! Peter! (*Enter* PETER.) Help me to the gallery, that I may see them on horseback.

[*Exit, leaning on* PETER.

Scene II.

The inner court of the castle of Ebersdorf; a quadrangle, surrounded with Gothic buildings; troopers, followers of RUDI-GER, *pass and re-pass in haste, as if preparing for an excursion.*

WICKERD *comes forward.*

WIC. What, ho! Reynold! Reynold! By our Lady, the spirit of the Seven Sleepers is upon him — So ho! not mounted yet! Reynold!

Enter REYNOLD.

REY. Here! Here! A devil choke thy bawling! thinkst thou old Reynold is not as ready for a skirmish as thou?

WIC. Nay, nay: I did but jest; but, by my sooth, it were a shame should our youngsters have yoked with Count Roderic before we graybeards come.

REY. Heaven forfend! Our troopers are but saddling their horses; five minutes more, and we are in our stirrups, and then let Count Roderic sit fast.

WIC. A plague on him! he has ever lain hard on the skirts of our noble master.

REY. Especially since he was refused the hand of our Lady's niece, the pretty Lady Gertrude.

WIC. Ay, marry! would nothing less serve the fox of Maltingen than the lovely lamb of our young Baron Henry! By my sooth, Reynold, when I look upon these two lovers, they make me full twenty years younger; and when I meet the man that would divide them — I say nothing — but let him look to it.

REY. And how fare our young lords?

WIC. Each well in his humor — Baron George stern and cold, according to his wont, and his brother as cheerful as ever.

REY. Well! — Baron Henry for me.

WIC. Yet George saved thy life.

REY. True — with as much indifference as if he had been snatching a chestnut out of the fire. Now, Baron Henry wept for my danger and my wounds. Therefore George shall ever command my life, but Henry my love.

WIC. Nay, Baron George shows his gloomy spirit even by the choice of a favorite.

REY. Ay — Martin, formerly the squire of Arnolf of Ebersdorf, his mother's first husband. — I marvel he could not have fitted himself with an attendant from among the faithful followers of his worthy father, whom Arnolf and his adherents used to hate as the Devil hates holy water. But Martin is a good soldier, and has stood toughly by George in many a hard brunt.

WIC. The knave is sturdy enough, but so sulky withal. — I have seen, brother Reynold, that when Martin showed his moody visage at the banquet, our noble mistress has dropped the wine she was raising to her lips, and exchanged her smiles for a ghastly frown, as if sorrow went by sympathy, as kissing goes by favor.

REY. His appearance reminds her of her first husband, and thou hast well seen *that* makes her ever sad.

WIC. Dost thou marvel at that? She was married to Arnolf by a species of force, and they say that before his death he compelled her to swear never to espouse Rudiger. The priests will not absolve her for the breach of that vow, and therefore she is troubled in mind. For, d'ye mark me, Reynold ——

[*Bugle sounds.*

REY. A truce to your preaching! To horse! and a blessing on your arms!

WIC. St. George grant it! [*Exeunt.*

Scene III.

The gallery of the castle, terminating in a large balcony commanding a distant prospect. — Voices, bugle-horns, kettle-drums, trampling of horses, etc., are heard without.

RUDIGER, *leaning on* PETER, *looks from the balcony.* GERTRUDE *and* ISABELLA *are near him.*

RUD. There they go at length — look, Isabella! look, my pretty Gertrude — these are the iron-handed warriors who shall tell Roderic what it will cost him to force thee from my protection — (*Flourish without. Rudiger stretches his arms from the balcony.*) Go, my children, and God's blessing with you. Look at my black barb, Gertrude. That horse shall let daylight in through a phalanx, were it twenty pikes deep. Shame on it that I cannot mount him! Seest thou how fierce old Reynold looks?

GER. I can hardly know my friends in their armor.

[*The bugles and kettle-drums are heard as at a greater distance.*

RUD. Now I could tell every one of their names, even at this distance; ay, and were they covered, as I have seen them, with dust and blood. He on the dapple gray is Wickerd — a hardy fellow, but somewhat given to prating. That is young Conrad who gallops so fast, page to thy Henry, my girl.

[*Bugles, etc., at a greater distance still.*

GER. Heaven guard them! Alas! the voice of war that calls the blood into your cheeks, chills and freezes mine.

RUD. Say not so. It is glorious, my girl, glorious! See how their armor glistens as they wind round yon hill! how their spears glimmer amid the long train of dust. Hark! you can still hear the faint notes of their trumpets — (*Bugles very faint.*) — And Rudiger, old Rudiger with the iron arm, as the crusaders used to call me, must remain behind with the priests and the women. Well! well! — (*Sings.*)

" It was a knight to battle rode,
    And as his war-horse he bestrode" —

Fill me a bowl of wine, Gertrude; and do thou, Peter, call the minstrel who came last night. — (*Sings.*)

" Off rode the horseman, dash, sa, sa!
    And stroked his whiskers, tra, la la." —

(PETER *goes out.* — RUDIGER *sits down, and* GERTRUDE *helps him with wine.*) Thanks, my love. It tastes ever best from thy hand. Isabella, here is glory and victory to our boys — (*Drinks.*) — Wilt thou not pledge me?

ISA. To their safety, and God grant it! — (*Drinks.*)

Enter BERTRAM *as a minstrel, with a boy bearing his harp. — Also* PETER.

RUD. Thy name, minstrel?

BER. Minhold, so please you.

RUD. Art thou a German?

BER. Yes, noble sir; and of this province.

RUD. Sing me a song of battle.

[BERTRAM *sings to the harp.*

RUD. Thanks, minstrel: well sung, and lustily. What sayst thou, Isabella?

ISA. I marked him not.

RUD. Nay, in sooth you are too anxious. Cheer up. And thou, too, my lovely Gertrude: in a few hours thy Henry shall return, and twine his laurels into a garland for thy hair. He fights for thee, and he must conquer.

GER. Alas! must blood be spilled for a silly maiden?

RUD. Surely; for what should knights break lances but for honor and ladies' love — ha, minstrel?

BER. So please you — also to punish crimes.

RUD. Out upon it! wouldst have us executioners, minstrel? Such work would disgrace our blades. We leave malefactors to the Secret Tribunal.

ISA. Merciful God! Thou hast spoken a word, Rudiger, of dreadful import.

GER. They say, that unknown and invisible themselves, these awful judges are ever present with the guilty; that the past and the present misdeeds, the secrets of the confessional, nay, the very thoughts of the heart, are before them; that their doom is as sure as that of fate, the means and executioners unknown.

RUD. They say true — the secrets of that association, and the names of those who compose it, are as inscrutable as the grave: we only know that it has taken deep root, and spread its branches wide. I sit down each day in my hall, nor know how many of these secret judges may surround me, all bound by the most solemn vow to avenge guilt. Once, and but once, a knight, at the earnest request and inquiries of the emperor, hinted that he belonged to the society: the next morning he was found slain in a forest: the poniard was left in the wound, and bore this label — "Thus do the invisible judges punish treachery."

GER. Gracious! aunt, you grow pale.

ISA. A slight indisposition only.

RUD. And what of it all? We know our hearts are open to our Creator: shall we fear any earthly inspection? Come to the battlements; there we shall soonest descry the return of our warriors.

[*Exit* RUDIGER, *with* GERTRUDE *and* PETER.

ISA. Minstrel, send the chaplain hither. (*Exit* BERTRAM.) Gracious Heaven! the guileless innocence of my niece, the manly honesty of my upright-hearted Rudiger, become daily tortures to me. While he was engaged in active and stormy exploits, fear for his safety, joy when he returned to his castle, enabled me to disguise my inward anguish from others. But from myself — Judges of blood, that lie concealed in noontide as in midnight, who boast to avenge the hidden guilt, and to penetrate the recesses of the human breast, how blind is your penetration, how vain your dagger, and your cord, compared to the conscience of the sinner!

Enter FATHER LUDOVIC.

LUD. Peace be with you, lady!

ISA. It is not with me: it is thy office to bring it.

LUD. And the cause is the absence of the young knights?

ISA. Their absence and their danger.

LUD. Daughter, thy hand has been stretched out in bounty to the sick and to the needy. Thou hast not denied a shelter to the weary, nor a tear to the afflicted. Trust in their prayers, and in those of the holy convent thou hast founded: peradventure they will bring back thy children to thy bosom.

ISA. Thy brethren cannot pray for me or mine. Their vow binds them to pray night and day for another — to supplicate, without ceasing, the Eternal Mercy for the soul of one who — Oh, only Heaven knows how much he needs their prayer!

LUD. Unbounded is the mercy of Heaven. The soul of thy former husband ——

ISA. I charge thee, priest, mention not the word. (*Apart.*) Wretch that I am, the meanest menial in my train has power to goad me to madness!

LUD. Hearken to me, daughter; thy crime against Arnolf of Ebersdorf cannot bear in the eye of Heaven so deep a dye of guilt.

Isa. Repeat that once more; say once again that it cannot — cannot bear so deep a dye. Prove to me that ages of the bitterest penance, that tears of the dearest blood, can erase such guilt. Prove but *that* to me, and I will build thee an abbey which shall put to shame the fairest fane in Christendom.

Lud. Nay, nay, daughter, your conscience is over tender. Supposing that, under dread of the stern Arnolf, you swore never to marry your present husband, still the exacting such an oath was unlawful, and the breach of it venial.

Isa. (*resuming her composure*). Be it so, good father: I yield to thy better reasons. And now tell me, has thy pious care achieved the task I intrusted to thee?

Lud. Of superintending the erection of the new hospital for pilgrims? I have, noble lady: and last night the minstrel now in the castle lodged there.

Isa. Wherefore came he then to the castle?

Lud. Reynold brought the commands of the Baron.

Isa. Whence comes he, and what is his tale? When he sung before Rudiger, I thought that long before I had heard such tones — seen such a face.

Lud. It is possible you may have seen him, lady, for he boasts to have been known to Arnolf of Ebersdorf, and to have lived formerly in this castle. He inquires much after *Martin*, Arnolf's squire.

Isa. Go, Ludovic — go quick, good father, seek him out, give him this purse, and bid him leave the castle, and speed him on his way.

Lud. May I ask why, noble lady?

Isa. Thou art inquisitive, priest; I honor the servants of God, but I foster not the prying spirit of a monk. Begone!

Lud. But the Baron, lady, will expect a reason why I dismiss his guest?

Isa. True, true (*recollecting herself*); pardon my warmth, good father, I was thinking of the cuckoo that grows too big for the nest of the sparrow, and

strangles its foster-mother. Do no such birds roost in convent-walls?

Lud. Lady, I understand you not.

Isa. Well, then, say to the Baron, that I have dismissed long ago all the attendants of the man of whom thou hast spoken, and that I wish to have none of them beneath my roof.

Lud. (*inquisitively*). Except Martin?

Isa. (*sharply*). Except Martin! who saved the life of my son George! Do as I command thee. [*Exit.*

Manet Ludovic.

Lud. Ever the same — stern and peremptory to others as rigorous to herself; haughty even to me, to whom, in another mood, she has knelt for absolution, and whose knees she has bathed in tears. I cannot fathom her. The unnatural zeal with which she performs her dreadful penances cannot be religion, for shrewdly I guess she believes not in their blessed efficacy. Well for her that she is the foundress of our convent, otherwise we might not have erred in denouncing her as a heretic! [*Exit.*

ACT II. — SCENE I.

A woodland prospect. — Through a long avenue, half-grown up by brambles, are discerned in the background the ruins of the ancient Castle of Griefenhaus. — The distant noise of battle is heard during this scene.

Enter GEORGE OF ASPEN, *armed with a battle-axe in his hand, as from horseback. He supports* MARTIN, *and brings him forward.*

Geo. Lay thee down here, old friend. The enemy's horsemen will hardly take their way among these branches, through which I have dragged thee.

Mar. Oh, do not leave me! leave me not an instant! My moments are now but few, and I would profit by them.

Geo. Martin, you forget yourself and me — I must back to the field.

Mar. (*attempts to rise*). Then drag me back thither also; I cannot die but in your presence — I dare not be alone. Stay, to give peace to my parting soul.

GEO. I am no priest, Martin. (*Going.*)

MAR. (*raising himself with great pain*). Baron George of Aspen, I saved thy life in battle: for that good deed, hear me but one moment.

GEO. I hear thee, my poor friend. (*Returning.*)

MAR. But come close — very close. See'st thou, sir knight — this wound I bore for thee — and this — and this — dost thou not remember?

GEO. I do.

MAR. I have served thee since thou wast a child; served thee faithfully — was never from thy side.

GEO. Thou hast.

MAR. And now I die in thy service.

GEO. Thou may'st recover.

MAR. I cannot. By my long service — by my scars — by this mortal gash, and by the death that I am to die — oh, do not hate me for what I am now to unfold!

GEO. Be assured I can never hate thee.

MAR. Ah, thou little knowest. — Swear to me thou wilt speak a word of comfort to my parting soul.

GEO. (*takes his hand*). I swear I will. (*Alarum and shouting.*) But be brief — thou knowest my haste.

MAR. Hear me, then. I was the squire, the beloved and favorite attendant, of Arnolf of Ebersdorf. Arnolf was savage as the mountain bear. He loved the Lady Isabel, but she requited not his passion. She loved thy father; but her sire, old Arnheim, was the friend of Arnolf, and she was forced to marry him. By midnight, in the chapel of Ebersdorf, the ill-omened rites were performed; her resistance, her screams were in vain. These arms detained her at the altar till the nuptial benediction was pronounced. Canst thou forgive me?

GEO. I do forgive thee. Thy obedience to thy savage master has been obliterated by a long train of service to his widow.

MAR. Services! ay, bloody services! for they commenced — do not quit my hand — they commenced with the murder of my master. (GEORGE *quits his hand,*

and stands aghast in speechless horror.) Trample on me! pursue me with your dagger! I aided your mother to poison her first husband! I thank Heaven, it is said.

GEO. My mother? Sacred Heaven! Martin, thou ravest — the fever of thy wound has distracted thee.

MAR. No! I am not mad! Would to God I were! Try me! Yonder is the Wolfshill — yonder the old castle of Griefenhaus — and yonder is the hemlock marsh (*in a whisper*) where I gathered the deadly plant that drugged Arnolf's cup of death. (GEORGE *traverses the stage in the utmost agitation, and sometimes stands over* MARTIN *with his hands clasped together.*) Oh, had you seen him when the potion took effect! Had you heard his ravings, and seen the contortions of his ghastly visage! — He died furious and impenitent, as he lived; and went — where I am shortly to go. You do not speak?

GEO. (*with exertion*). Miserable wretch! how can I?

MAR. Can you not forgive me?

GEO. May God pardon thee — I cannot!

MAR. I saved thy life —

GEO. For that, take my curse! (*He snatches up his battle-axe, and rushes out to the side from which the noise is heard.*)

MAR. Hear me! yet more — more horror! (*Attempts to rise, and falls heavily. A loud alarum.*)

Enter WICKERD, *hastily.*

WIC. In the name of God, Martin, lend me thy brand!

MAR. Take it.

WIC. Where is it?

MAR. (*looks wildly at him*). In the chapel at Ebersdorf, or buried in the hemlock marsh.

WIC. The old grumbler is crazy with his wounds. Martin, if thou hast a spark of reason in thee, give me thy sword. The day goes sore against us.

MAR. There it lies. Bury it in the heart of thy master George, thou wilt do him a good office — the office of a faithful servant.

Enter CONRAD.

CON. Away, Wickerd! to horse, and pursue! Baron George has turned the day; he fights more like a fiend than a man: he has unhorsed Roderic, and slain six of his troopers—they are in headlong fight—the hemlock marsh is red with their gore! (MARTIN *gives a deep groan, and faints.*) Away! away! (*They hurry off, as to the pursuit.*)

Enter RODERIC OF MALTINGEN, *without his helmet, his arms disordered and broken, holding the truncheon of a spear in his hand ; with him,* BARON WOLFSTEIN.

ROD. A curse on fortune, and a double curse upon George of Aspen! Never, never will I forgive him my disgrace — overthrown like a rotten trunk before a whirlwind!

WOLF. Be comforted, Count Roderic; it is well we have escaped being prisoners. See how the troopers of Aspen pour along the plain, like the billows of the Rhine! It is good we are shrouded by the thicket.

ROD. Why took he not my life, when he robbed me of my honor and my love? Why did his spear not pierce my heart, when mine shivered on his arms like a frail bulrush? (*Throws down the broken spear.*) Bear witness, heaven and earth, I outlive this disgrace only to avenge!

WOLF. Be comforted; the knights of Aspen have not gained a bloodless victory. And see, there lies one of George's followers — (*Seeing* MARTIN.)

ROD. His squire Martin; if he be not dead, we will secure him: he is the depository of the secrets of his master. Arouse thee, trusty follower of the house of Aspen!

MAR. (*reviving.*) Leave me not! leave me not! Baron George! my eyes are darkened with agony! I have not yet told all.

WOLF. The old man takes you for his master.

ROD. What wouldst thou tell?

MAR. Oh, I would tell all the temptations by which I was urged to the murder of Ebersdorf!

ROD. Murder! — this is worth marking. Proceed.

MAR. I loved a maiden, daughter of Arnolf's steward; my master seduced her — she became an outcast, and died in misery — I vowed vengeance — and I did avenge her.

ROD. Hadst thou accomplices?

MAR. None, but thy mother.

ROD. The Lady Isabella!

MAR. Ay; she hated her husband: he knew her love to Rudiger, and when she heard that thy father was returned from Palestine, her life was endangered by the transports of his jealousy — thus prepared for evil, the fiend tempted us, and we fell.

ROD. (*breaks into a transport*). Fortune! thou hast repaid me all! Love and vengeance are my own! — Wolfstein, recall our followers! quick, sound thy bugle — (WOLFSTEIN *sounds.*)

MAR. (*stares wildly round*). That was no note of Aspen — Count Roderic of Maltingen — Heavens! what have I said!

ROD. What thou canst not recall.

MAR. Then is my fate decreed! 'Tis as it should be! in this very place was the poison gather'd — 'tis retribution!

Enter three or four soldiers of RODERIC.

ROD. Secure this wounded trooper; bind his wounds and guard him well: carry him to the ruins of Griefenhaus, and conceal him till the troopers of Aspen have retired from the pursuit; — look to him, as you love your lives.

MAR. (*led off by soldiers*). Ministers of vengeance! my hour is come! [*Exeunt.*

ROD. Hope, joy, and triumph, once again are ye mine! Welcome to my heart, long-absent visitants! One lucky chance has thrown dominion into the scale of the house of Maltingen, and Aspen kicks the beam.

WOLF. I foresee, indeed, dishonor to the family of Aspen, should this wounded squire make good his tale.

ROD. And how thinkest thou this disgrace will fall on them?

WOLF. Surely by the public punishment of Lady Isabella.

ROD. And is that all?

WOLF. What more?

ROD. Shortsighted that thou art, is not George of Aspen, as well as thou, a member of the holy and invisible circle, over which I preside.

WOLF. Speak lower, for God's sake! these are things not to be mentioned before the sun.

ROD. True; but stands he not bound by the most solemn oath religion can devise, to discover to the tribunal whatever concealed iniquity shall come to his knowledge, be the Perpetrator whom he may — ay, were that perpetrator his own father — or mother; and can you doubt that he has heard Martin's confession?

WOLF. True; but, blessed Virgin! do you think he will accuse his own mother before the invisible judges?

ROD. If not, he becomes foresworn, and, by our law, must die. Either way my vengeance is complete — perjured or parricide, I care not; but, as the one or the other shall I crush the haughty George of Aspen.

WOLF. Thy vengeance strikes deep.

ROD. Deep as the wounds I have borne from this proud family. Rudiger slew my father in battle —George has twice baffled and dishonored my arms, and Henry has stolen the heart of my beloved: but no longer can Gertrude now remain under the care of the murderous dam of this brood of wolves; far less can she wed the smooth-cheeked boy, when this scene of villany shall be disclosed. [*Bugle.*

WOLF. Hark! they sound a retreat: let us go deeper into the wood.

ROD. The victors approach! I shall dash their triumph! — Issue the private summons for convoking the members this very evening; I will direct the other measures.

WOLF. What place?

ROD. The old chapel in the ruins of Griefenhaus, as usual. [*Exeunt.*

SCENE II.

Enter GEORGE OF ASPEN, as from the pursuit.

GEO. (*comes slowly forward*). How many wretches have sunk under my arm this day, to whom life was sweet, though the wretched bondsmen of Count Roderic! And I — I who sought death beneath every lifted battle-axe, and offered my breast to every arrow — I am cursed with victory and safety. Here I left the wretch —— Martin! — Martin! — what, ho! Martin! — Mother of God! he is gone! — Should he repeat the dreadful tale to any other — Martin! — He answers not. Perhaps he has crept into the thicket, and died there — were it so, the horrible secret is only mine.

Enter HENRY OF ASPEN, with WICKERD, REYNOLD, and followers.

HEN. Joy to thee, brother! though, by St. Francis, I would not gain another field at the price of seeing thee fight with such reckless desperation. Thy safety is little less than miraculous.

REY. By'r Lady, when Baron George struck, I think he must have forgot that his foes were God's creatures. Such furious doings I never saw, and I have been a trooper these forty-two years come St. Barnaby—

GEO. Peace! Saw any of you Martin?

WIC. Noble sir, I left him here not long since.

GEO. Alive or dead?

WIC. Alive, noble sir, but sorely wounded. I think he must be prisoner, for he could not have budged else from hence.

GEO. Heedless slave! Why didst thou leave him?

HEN. Dear brother, Wickerd acted for the best; he came to our assistance and the aid of his companions.

GEO. I tell thee, Henry, Martin's safety was of more importance than the lives of any ten that stand here.

WIC. (*muttering*). Here's much to do about an old crazy trencher-shifter.

GEO. What mutterest thou?

WIC. Only, sir knight, that Martin seemed out of his senses when I left him, and has perhaps wandered into the marsh, and perished there.

GEO. How — out of his senses? Did he speak to thee? — (*Apprehensively.*)

WIC. Yes, noble sir.

GEO. Dear Henry, step for an instant to yon tree — thou wilt see from thence if the foe rally upon the Wolfshill. (HENRY *retires*.) And do you stand back (*to the soldiers*).

[*He brings* WICKERD *forward*.

GEO. (*with marked apprehension*). What did Martin say to thee, Wickerd? — tell me, on thy allegiance.

WIC. Mere ravings, sir knight — offered me his sword to kill you.

GEO. Said he aught of killing any one else?

WIC. No; the pain of his wound seemed to have brought on a fever.

GEO. (*clasps his hands together*). I breathe again — I spy comfort. Why could I not see as well as this fellow, that the wounded wretch may have been distracted? Let me at least think so till proof shall show the truth. (*Aside.*) Wickerd, think not on what I said — the heat of the battle had chafed my blood. Thou hast wished for the Netherfarm at Ebersdorf — it shall be thine.

WIC. Thanks, my noble lord.

Re-enter HENRY.

HEN. No — they do not rally — they have had enough of it — but Wickerd and Conrad shall remain, with twenty troopers and a score of crossbowmen, and scour the woods towards Griefenhaus, to prevent the fugitives from making head. We will, with the rest, to Ebersdorf. What say you, brother?

GEO. Well ordered. Wickerd, look thou search everywhere for Martin; bring him to me dead or alive; leave not a nook of the wood unsought.

WIC. I warrant you, noble sir, I shall find him, could he clew himself up like a dormouse.

HEN. I think he must be prisoner.

GEO. Heaven forfend! Take a trumpet, Eustace (*to an attendant*), ride to the castle of Maltingen, and demand a parley. If Martin is prisoner, offer any ransom; offer ten — twenty — all our prisoners in exchange.

EUS. It shall be done, sir knight.

HEN. Ere we go, sound trumpets — strike up the song of victory.

SONG.

Joy to the victors! the sons of old Aspen!
 Joy to the race of the battle and scar!
Glory's proud garland triumphantly grasping;
 Generous in peace, and victorious in war.

Honor acquiring,
Valor inspiring,
Bursting resistless, through foemen they go:
War-axes wielding,
Broken ranks yielding,
Till from the battle proud Roderic retiring,
Yields in wild rout the fair palm to his foe.

Joy to each warrior, true follower of Aspen!
 Joy to the heroes that gain'd the bold day!
Health to our wounded, in agony gasping;
 Peace to our brethren that fell in the fray!

Boldly this morning,
Roderic's power scorning,
Well for their chieftain their blades did they wield;
Joy blest them dying,
As Maltingen flying,
Low laid his banners, our conquest adorning,
Their death-clouded eyeballs descried on the field!

Now to our home, the proud mansion of Aspen,
 Bend we, gay victors, triumphant away:
There each fond damsel, her gallant youth clasping,
 Shall wipe from his forehead the stains of the fray.

Listening the prancing
Of horses advancing;
E'en now on the turrets our maidens appear.
Love our hearts warming,
Songs the night charming,
Round goes the grape in the goblet gay dancing;
Love, wine, and song, our blithe evening shall cheer!

Hen. Now spread our banners, and to Ebersdorf in triumph. We carry relief to the anxious, joy to the heart of the aged, brother George. (*Going off.*)

Geo. Or treble misery and death.

[*Apart, and following slowly. The music sounds, and the followers of Aspen begin to file across the stage. The curtain falls.*

ACT III.—Scene I.
Castle of Ebersdorf.

Rudiger, Isabella, *and* Gertrude.

Rud. I prithee, dear wife, be merry. It must be over by this time, and happily, otherwise the bad news had reached us.

Isa. Should we not, then, have heard the tidings of the good?

Rud. Oh! these fly slower by half. Besides, I warrant all of them engaged in the pursuit. Oh! not a page would leave the skirts of the fugitives till they were fairly beaten into their holds; but had the boys lost the day, the stragglers had made for the castle. Go to the window, Gertrude: seest thou anything?

Ger. I think I see a horseman.

Isa. A single rider? then I fear me much.

Ger. It is only Father Ludovic.

Rud. A plague on thee! didst thou take a fat friar on a mule for a trooper of the house of Aspen?

Ger. But yonder is a cloud of dust.

Rud. (*eagerly*). Indeed!

Ger. It is only the wine sledges going to my aunt's convent.

Rud. The devil confound the wine sledges, and the mules, and the monks! Come from the window, and torment me no longer, thou seer of strange sights.

Ger. Dear uncle, what can I do to amuse you? Shall I tell you what I dreamed this morning?

Rud. Nonsense: but say on; anything is better than silence.

Ger. I thought I was in the chapel, and they were burying my Aunt Isabella alive. And who do you think, aunt, were the gravediggers who shovelled in the earth upon you? Even Baron George and old Martin,

Isa. (*appears shocked.*) Heaven! what an idea!

Ger. Do but think of my terror — and Minhold the minstrel played all the while to drown your screams.

Rud. And old Father Ludovic danced a saraband, with the steeple of the new convent upon his thick skull by way of mitre. A truce to this nonsense. Give us a song, my love, and leave thy dreams and visions.

Ger. What shall I sing to you?

Rud. Sing to me of war.

Ger. I cannot sing of battle; but I will sing you the Lament of Eleanor of Toro, when her lover was slain in the war.

Isa. Oh, no laments, Gertrude.

Rud. Then sing a song of mirth

Isa. Dear husband, is this a time for mirth?

Rud. Is it neither a time to sing of mirth nor of sorrow? Isabella would rather hear Father Ludovic chant the " De profundis."

Ger. Dear uncle, be not angry. At present, I can only sing the lay of poor Eleanor. It comes to my heart at this moment as if the sorrowful mourner had been my own sister.

SONG.*

Sweet shone the sun on the fair lake of Toro,
　Weak were the whispers that waved the dark wood,
As a fair maiden, bewilder'd in sorrow,
　Sigh'd to the breezes and wept to the flood: —
" Saints, from the mansion of bliss lowly bending,
　Virgin, that hear'st the poor suppliant's cry,
Grant my petition, in anguish ascending,
　My Frederick restore, or let Eleanor die.

Distant and faint were the sounds of the battle;
　With the breezes they rise, with the breezes they fail,

* Compare with "The Maid of Toro," *ante*, p. 429.

Till the shout, and the groan, and the
    conflict's dread rattle,
And the chase's wild clamor came load-
    ing the gale.
Breathless she gazed through the wood-
    land so dreary,
Slowly approaching, a warrior was
    seen;
Life's ebbing tide marked his footsteps so
    weary,
Cleft was his helmet, and woe was his
    mien.

" Save thee, fair maid, for our armies are
    flying;
Save thee, fair maid, for thy guardian
    is low;
Cold on yon heath thy bold Frederick is
    lying,
Fast thro' the woodland approaches
    the foe.''

[*The voice of* GERTRUDE *sinks by
degrees, till she bursts into tears.*

RUD. How now, Gertrude?
GER. Alas! may not the fate of poor
Eleanor at this moment be mine?
RUD. Never, my girl, never! (*Military
music is heard*). Hark! hark! to the
sounds that tell thee so.
    [*All rise and run to the window.*
RUD. Joy! joy! they come, and come
victorious. (*The chorus of the war-song
is heard without.*) Welcome! welcome!
once more have my old eyes seen the
banners of the house of Maltingen
trampled in the dust. — Isabella, broach
our oldest casks; wine is sweet after
war.

Enter HENRY, *followed by* REYNOLD
and troopers.

RUD. Joy to thee, my boy, let me press
thee to this old heart.
ISA. Bless thee, my son — (*Embraces
him.*) Oh, how many hours of bitter-
ness are compensated by this embrace !
Bless thee, my Henry! where hast thou
left thy brother?
HEN. Hard at hand: by this he is crossing the drawbridge. Hast thou no greetings for me, Gertrude? (*Goes to her.*)
GER. I joy not in battles.

RUD. But she had tears for thy danger.
HEN. Thanks, my gentle Gertrude.
See, I have brought back thy scarf from
no inglorious field.
GER. It is bloody ! — (*Shocked.*)
RUD. Dost start at that, my girl?
Were it his own blood, as it is that of
his foes, thou shouldst glory in it. — Go,
Reynold, make good cheer with thy
fellows.
    [*Exit* REYNOLD *and Soldiers.*

Enter GEORGE, *pensively.*

GEO. (*goes straight to* RUDIGER).
Father, thy blessing.
RUD. Thou hast it, boy.
ISA. (*rushes to embrace him — he
avoids her*). How? art thou wounded?
GEO. No.
RUD. Thou lookest deadly pale.
GEO. It is nothing.
ISA. Heaven's blessings on my gallant
George.
GEO. (*aside*). Dares she bestow a
blessing? Oh, Martin's tale was frenzy !
ISA. Smile upon us for once, my son;
darken not thy brow on this day of
gladness — few are our moments of joy
— should not my sons share in them?
GEO. (*aside*). She has moments of
joy — it *was* frenzy, then !
ISA. Gertrude, my love, assist me to
disarm the knight. (*She loosens and
takes off his casque.*)
GER. There is one, two, three hacks,
and none has pierced the steel.
RUD. Let me see. Let me see. A
trusty casque !
GER. Else hadst thou gone.
ISA. I will reward the armorer with
its weight in gold.
GEO. (*aside*). She *must* be innocent.
GER. And Henry's shield is hacked,
too. Let me show it to you, uncle.
(*She carries* HENRY'S *to* RUDIGER.)
RUD. Do, my love; and come hither,
Henry, thou shalt tell me how the day
went.
    [HENRY *and* GERTRUDE *converse
    apart with* RUDIGER; GEORGE
    comes forward; ISABELLA *comes
    to him.*

ISA. Surely, George, some evil has

befallen thee. Grave thou art ever, but so dreadfully gloomy —

Geo. *Evil*, indeed. — (*Aside.*) Now for the trial.

Isa. Has your loss been great?

Geo. No! — Yes! — (*Apart.*) I cannot do it.

Isa. Perhaps some friend lost?

Geo. It must be. — *Martin is dead.* — (*He regards her with apprehension, but steadily, as he pronounces these words.*)

Isa. (*starts, then shows a ghastly expression of joy*). Dead!

Geo. (*almost overcome by his feelings*). Guilty! Guilty! — (*Apart.*)

Isa. (*without observing his emotion*). Didst thou say dead?

Geo. Did I — no — I only said mortally wounded.

Isa. Wounded? only wounded? Where is he? Let me fly to him. — (*Going.*)

Geo. (*sternly*). Hold, lady! — Speak not so loud! — Thou canst not see him! — He is a prisoner.

Isa. A prisoner and wounded? Fly to his deliverance! — Offer wealth, lands, castles, — all our possessions for his ransom. Never shall I know peace till these walls, or till the grave secures him.

Geo. (*apart*). Guilty! Guilty!

Enter Peter.

Pet. Hugo, squire to the Count of Maltingen, has arrived with a message.

Rud. I will receive him in the hall.

[*Exit, leaning on* Gertrude *and* Henry.

Isa. Go, George — see after Martin.

Geo. (*firmly*). No, I have a task to perform; and though the earth should open and devour me alive — I will accomplish it. But first — but first — Nature, take thy tribute. — (*He falls on his mother's neck, and weeps bitterly.*)

Isa. George! my son! for Heaven's sake, what dreadful frenzy!

Geo. (*walks two turns across the stage and composes himself*). Listen, mother — I knew a knight in Hungary, gallant in battle, hospitable and generous in peace. The king gave him his friend-

ship, and the administration of a province; that province was infested by thieves and murderers. You mark me? —

Isa. Most heedfully.

Geo. The knight was sworn — bound by an oath the most dreadful that can be taken by man — to deal among offenders, evenhanded, stern and impartial justice. Was it not a dreadful vow?

Isa. (*with an affectation of composure*). Solemn, doubtless, as the oath of every magistrate.

Geo. And inviolable?

Isa. Surely — inviolable.

Geo. Well! it happened, that when he rode out against the banditti, he made a prisoner. And who, think you, that prisoner was?

Isa. I know not (*with increasing terror*).

Geo. (*trembling, but proceeding rapidly.*) His own twin-brother, who sucked the same breasts with him, and lay in the bosom of the same mother — his brother, whom he loved as his own soul — what should that knight have done unto his brother?

Isa. (*almost speechless*). Alas! what did he do?

Geo. He did (*turning his head from her, and with clasped hands*) what I can never do: — he did his duty.

Isa. My son! my son! — Mercy! Mercy! (*Clings to him.*)

Geo. Is it then true?

Isa. What?

Geo. What Martin said. (Isabella *hides her face.*) It is true!

Isa. (*looks up with an air of dignity.*) Hear, Framer of the laws of Nature! the mother is judged by the child — (*Turns towards him.*) Yes, it is true — true that, fearful of my own life, I secured it by the murder of my tyrant. Mistaken coward! I little knew on what terrors I ran, to avoid one moment's agony. — Thou hast the secret!

Geo. Knowest thou to whom thou hast told it?

Isa. To my son.

Geo. No! No! To an executioner!

Isa. Be it so — go, proclaim my crime, and forget not my punishment. Forget not that the murderess of her husband has dragged out years of hidden remorse, to be brought at last to the scaffold by her own cherished son — thou art silent.

GEO. The language of Nature is no more. How shall I learn another?

ISA. Look upon me, George. Should the executioner be abashed before the criminal — look upon me, my son. From my soul do I forgive thee.

GEO. Forgive me what?

ISA. What thou dost meditate — be vengeance heavy, but let it be secret — add not the death of a father to that of the sinner! Oh! Rudiger! Rudiger! innocent cause of all my guilt and all my woe, how wilt thou tear thy silver locks when thou shalt hear her guilt whom thou hast so often clasped to thy bosom — hear her infamy proclaimed by the son of thy fondest hopes — (*Weeps.*)

GEO. (*struggling for breath*). Nature will have utterance, mother, dearest mother, I will save you or perish! (*Throws himself into her arms.*) Thus fall my vows.

ISA. Man thyself! I ask not safety from thee. Never shall it be said that Isabella of Aspen turned her son from the path of duty, though his footsteps must pass over her mangled corpse. Man thyself.

GEO. No! No! The ties of Nature were knit by God himself. Cursed be the stoic pride that would rend them asunder, and call it virtue!

ISA. My son! My son! How shall I behold thee hereafter?

[*Three knocks are heard upon the door of the apartment.*]

GEO. Hark! One — two — three. Roderic, thou art speedy! (*Apart.*)

ISA. (*opens the door*). A parchment stuck to the door with a poniard! (*Opens it.*) Heaven and earth! — a summons from the invisible judges! — (*Drops the parchment.*)

GEO. (*reads with emotion.*) "Isabella of Aspen, accused of murder by poison, we conjure thee, by the cord and by the steel, to appear this night before the avengers of blood, who judge in secret and avenge in secret, like the Deity. As thou art innocent or guilty, so be thy deliverance." — Martin, Martin, thou hast played false!

ISA. Alas! whither shall I fly?

GEO. Thou canst not fly; instant death would follow the attempt: a hundred thousand arms would be raised against thy life; every morsel thou didst taste, every drop which thou didst drink, the very breeze of heaven that fanned thee, would come loaded with destruction. One chance of safety is open, — obey the summons.

ISA. And perish? Yet why should I still fear death? Be it so.

GEO. No — I have sworn to save you. I will not do the work by halves. Does any one save Martin know of the dreadful deed?

ISA. None.

GEO. Then go — assert your innocence, and leave the rest to me.

ISA. Wretch that I am! How can I support the task you would impose?

GEO. Think on my father. Live for him; he will need all the comfort thou canst bestow. Let the thought that his destruction is involved in thine, carry thee through the dreadful trial.

ISA. Be it so. — For Rudiger I have lived, for him I will continue to bear the burden of existence; but the instant that my guilt comes to his knowledge shall be the last of my life. Ere I would bear from him one glance of hatred or of scorn, this dagger should drink my blood. (*Puts the poniard into her bosom.*)

GEO. Fear not. He can never know. No evidence shall appear against you.

ISA. How shall I obey the summons, and where find the terrible judgment seat?

GEO. Leave that to the judges. Resolve but to obey, and a conductor will be found. Go to the chapel; there pray for your sins and for mine. (*He leads her out and returns.*) — Sins, indeed! I break a dreadful vow, but I save the life of a parent; and the penance I will do for my perjury shall appal even the judges of blood.

Enter REYNOLD.

REY. Sir knight, the messenger of Count Roderic desires to speak with you.

GEO. Admit him.

Enter HUGO.

HUG. Count Roderic *of Maltingen greets you. He says he will this night hear the bat flutter and the owlet scream, and he bids me ask if thou also wilt listen to the music.

GEO. I understand him. I will be there.

HUG. And the count says to you, that he will not ransom your wounded squire, though you would downweigh his best horse with gold. But you may send him a confessor, for the count says he will need one.

GEO. Is he so near death?

HUG. Not as it seems to me. He is weak through loss of blood; but since his wound was dressed he can both stand and walk. Our count has a notable balsam, which has recruited him much.

GEO. Enough — I will send a priest. (*Exit* HUGO.) I fathom his plot. He would add another witness to the tale of Martin's guilt. But no priest shall approach him. Reynold, thinkest thou not we could send one of the troopers, disguised as a monk, to aid Martin in making his escape?

REY. Noble sir, the followers of your house are so well known to those of Maltingen, that I fear it is impossible.

GEO. Knowest thou of no stranger who might be employed? His reward shall exceed even his hopes.

REY. So please you — I think the minstrel could well execute such a commission; he is shrewd and cunning, and can write and read like a priest.

GEO. Call him. — (*Exit* REYNOLD.) If this fails, I must employ open force. Were Martin removed, no tongue can assert the bloody truth.

Enter MINSTREL.

GEO. Come hither, Minhold. Hast thou courage to undertake a dangerous enterprise?

BER. My life, sir knight, has been one scene of danger and of dread. I have forgotten how to fear.

GEO. Thy speech is above thy seeming. Who art thou?

BER. An unfortunate knight, obliged to shroud myself under this disguise.

GEO. What is the cause of thy misfortune?

BER. I slew, at a tournament, a prince, and was laid under the ban of the empire.

GEO. I have interest with the emperor. Swear to perform what task I shall impose on thee, and I will procure the recall of the ban.

BER. I swear.

GEO. Then take the disguise of a monk, and go with the follower of Count Roderic, as if to confess my wounded squire Martin. Give him thy dress, and remain in prison in his stead. Thy captivity shall be short, and I pledge my knightly word I will labor to execute my promise, when thou shalt have leisure to unfold thy history.

BER. I will do as you direct. Is the life of your squire in danger?

GEO. It is, unless thou canst accomplish his release.

BER. I will essay it. [*Exit.*

GEO. Such are the mean expedients to which George of Aspen must now resort. No longer can I debate with Roderic in the field. The depraved — the perjured knight must contend with him only in the arts of dissimulation and treachery. Oh, mother! mother! the most bitter consequence of thy crime has been the birth of thy first-born! But I must warn my brother of the impending storm. Poor Henry, how little can thy gay temper anticipate evil! What, ho there! (*Enter an Attendant.*) Where is Baron Henry?

ATT. Noble sir, he rode forth, after a slight refreshment, to visit the party in the field.

GEO. Saddle my steed; I will follow him.

ATT. So please you, your noble father has twice demanded your presence at the banquet.

GEO. It matters not — say that I have ridden forth to the Wolfshill. Where is thy lady?

Att. In the chapel, sir knight.

Geo. 'Tis well — saddle my bay-horse — (*apart*) for the last time.   [*Exit*.

ACT IV. — Scene I.

The wood of Griefenhaus, with the ruins of the Castle. A nearer view of the Castle than in Act Second, but still at some distance.

Enter Roderic, Wolfstein, *and Soldiers, as from a reconnoitring party*.

Wolf. They mean to improve their success, and will push their advantage far. We must retreat betimes, Count Roderic.

Rod. We are safe here for the present. They make no immediate motion of advance. I fancy neither George nor Henry are with their party in the wood.

Enter Hugo.

Hug. Noble sir, how shall I tell what has happened?

Rod. What?

Hug. Martin has escaped.

Rod. Villain, thy life shall pay it! (*Strikes at* Hugo — *is held by* Wolfstein.)

Wolf. Hold, hold, Count Roderic! Hugo may be blameless.

Rod. Reckless slave! how came he to escape?

Hug. Under the disguise of a monk's habit, whom by your orders we brought to confess him.

Rod. Has he been long gone?

Hug. An hour and more since he passed our sentinels, disguised as the chaplain of Aspen; but he walked so slowly and feebly, I think he cannot yet have reached the posts of the enemy.

Rod. Where is the treacherous priest?

Hug. He awaits his doom not far from hence.   [*Exit* Hugo.

Rod. Drag him hither. The miscreant that snatched the morsel of vengeance from the lion of Maltingen shall expire under torture.

Re-enter Hugo, *with* Bertram *and Attendants*.

Rod. Villain! what tempted thee, under the garb of a minister of religion, to steal a criminal from the hand of justice!

Ber. I am no villain, Count Roderic; and I only aided the escape of one wounded wretch whom thou didst mean to kill basely.

Rod. Liar and slave! thou hast assisted a murderer, upon whom justice had sacred claims.

Ber. I warn thee again, Count, that I am neither liar nor slave. Shortly I hope to tell thee I am once more thy equal.

Rod. Thou! Thou! —

Ber. Yes! the name of Bertram of Ebersdorf was once not unknown to thee.

Rod. (*astonished*). Thou Bertram! the brother of Arnolf of Ebersdorf, first husband of the Baroness Isabella of Aspen?

Ber. The same.

Rod. Who, in a quarrel at a tournament, many years since, slew a blood-relation of the emperor, and was laid under the ban?

Ber. The same.

Rod. And who has now, in the disguise of a priest, aided the escape of Martin, squire to George of Aspen?

Ber. The same — the same.

Rod. Then, by the holy cross of Cologne, thou hast set at liberty the murderer of thy brother Arnolf!

Ber. How! What! I understand thee not!

Rod. Miserable plotter! — Martin, by his own confession, as Wolfstein heard, avowed having aided Isabella in the murder of her husband. I had laid such a plan of vengeance as should have made all Germany shudder. And thou hast counteracted it — thou, the brother of the murdered Arnolf!

Ber. Can this be so, Wolfstein?

Wolf. I heard Martin confess the murder.

Ber. Then I am indeed unfortunate!

Rod. What, in the name of evil, brought thee here?

Ber. I am the last of my race. When I was outlawed, as thou knowest, the lands of Ebersdorf, my rightful inheritance, were declared forfeited, and the emperor bestowed them upon Rudiger when he married Isabella. I attempted to defend my domain, but Rudiger — Hell thank him for it — enforced the ban against me at the head of his vassals, and I was constrained to fly. Since then I have warred against the Saracens in Spain and Palestine.

ROD. But why didst thou return to a land where death attends thy being discovered?

BER. Impatience urged me to see once more the land of my nativity, and the towers of Ebersdorf. I came there yesterday, under the name of the minstrel Minhold.

ROD. And what prevailed on thee to undertake to deliver Martin?

BER. George, though I told not my name, engaged to procure the recall of the ban; besides, he told me Martin's life was in danger, and I accounted the old villain to be the last remaining follower of our house. But, as God shall judge me, the tale of horror thou hast mentioned I could not have even suspected. Report ran, that my brother died of the plague.

WOLF. Raised for the purpose, doubtless, of preventing attendance upon his sick-bed, and an inspection of his body.

BER. My vengeance shall be dreadful as its cause! The usurpers of my inheritance, the robbers of my honor, the murderers of my brother, shall be cut off, root and branch!

ROD. Thou art, then, welcome here; especially if thou art still a true brother to our invisible order.

BER. I am.

ROD. There is a meeting this night on the business of thy brother's death. Some are now come. I must despatch them in pursuit of Martin.

Enter HUGO.

HUG. The foes advance, sir knight.

ROD. Back! back to the ruins! Come with us, Bertram; on the road thou shalt hear the dreadful history.   [*Exeunt.*

From the opposite side enter GEORGE, HENRY, WICKERD, CONRAD, *and Soldiers.*

GEO. No news of Martin yet?

WIC. None, sir knight.

GEO. Nor the minstrel?

WIC. None.

GEO. Then he has betrayed me, or is prisoner — misery either way. Begone and search the wood, Wickerd.

[*Exeunt* WICKERD *and followers.*

HEN. Still this dreadful gloom on thy brow, brother?

GEO. Ay! what else?

HEN. Once thou thoughtest me worthy of thy friendship.

GEO. Henry, thou art young —

HEN. Shall I therefore betray thy confidence?

GEO. No! but thou art gentle and well-natured. Thy mind cannot even support the burden which mine must bear, far less wilt thou approve the means I shall use to throw it off.

HEN. Try me.

GEO. I may not.

HEN. Then thou dost no longer love me.

GEO. I love thee, and because I love thee, I will not involve thee in my distress.

HEN. I will bear it with thee.

GEO. Shouldst thou share it, it would be doubled to me!

HEN. Fear not, I will find a remedy.

GEO. It would cost thee peace of mind, here, and hereafter.

HEN. I take the risk.

GEO. It may not be, Henry. Thou wouldst become the confidant of crimes past — the accomplice of others to come.

HEN. Shall I guess?

GEO. I charge thee, no!

HEN. I must. Thou art one of the secret judges.

GEO. Unhappy boy! what hast thou said?

HEN. Is it not so?

GEO. Dost thou know what the discovery has cost thee?

HEN. I care not.

GEO. He who discovers any part of our mystery must himself become one of our number.

HEN. How so?

GEO. If he does not consent, his secrecy will be speedily ensured by his death. To that we are sworn — take thy choice!

HEN. Well, are you not banded in secret to punish those offenders whom the sword of justice cannot reach, or who are shielded from its stroke by the buckler of power?

GEO. Such is indeed the purpose of our fraternity; but the end is pursued through paths dark, intricate, and slippery with blood. Who is he that shall tread them with safety? Accursed be the hour in which I entered the labyrinth, and doubly accursed that in which thou too must lose the cheerful sunshine of a soul without a mystery!

HEN. Yet for thy sake will I be a member.

GEO. Henry, thou didst rise this morning a free man. No one could say to thee, "Why dost thou so?" Thou layest thee down to-night the veriest slave that ever tugged at an oar — the slave of men whose actions will appear to thee savage and incomprehensible, and whom thou must aid against the world, upon peril of thy throat.

HEN. Be it so. I will share your lot.

GEO. Alas, Henry! Heaven forbid! But since thou hast by a hasty word fettered thyself, I will avail myself of thy bondage. Mount thy fleetest steed, and hie thee this very night to the Duke of Bavaria. He is chief and paramount of our chapter. Show him this signet and this letter; tell him that matters will be this night discussed concerning the house of Aspen. Bid him speed him to the assembly, for he well knows the president is our deadly foe. He will admit thee a member of our holy body.

HEN. Who is the foe whom you dread?

GEO. Young man, the first duty thou must learn is implicit and blind obedience.

HEN. Well I shall soon return and see thee again.

GEO. Return, indeed, thou wilt; but for the rest — well! that matters not.

HEN. I go: thou wilt set a watch here?

GEO. I will. (HENRY *going.*) Return, my dear Henry; let me embrace thee, shouldst thou not see me again.

HEN. Heaven! what mean you?

GEO. Nothing. The life of mortals is precarious; and, should we not meet again, take my blessing and this embrace — and this — (*Embraces him warmly.*) And now haste to the duke. (*Exit* HENRY.) Poor youth, thou little knowest what thou hast undertaken. But if Martin has escaped, and if the duke arrives, they will not dare to proceed without proof.

Re-enter WICKERD *and followers.*

WIC. We have made a follower of Maltingen prisoner, Baron George, who reports that Martin has escaped.

GEO. Joy! joy! such joy as I can now feel! Set him free for the good news — and, Wickerd, keep a good watch in this spot all night. Send out scouts to find Martin, least he should not be able to reach Ebersdorf.

WIC. I shall, noble sir.

[*The kettle-drums and trumpets flourish as for setting the watch: the scene closes.*

SCENE II.

The Chapel at Ebersdorf, an ancient Gothic building.

ISABELLA *is discovered rising from before the altar, on which burn two tapers.*

ISA. I cannot pray. Terror and guilt have stifled devotion. The heart must be at ease — the hands must be pure when they are lifted to Heaven. Midnight is the hour of summons: it is now near. How can I pray, when I go resolved to deny a crime which every drop of my blood could not wash away! And my son! Oh! he will fall the victim of my crime! Arnolf! Arnolf! thou art dreadfully avenged! (*Tap at the door.*) The footstep of my dreadful guide. (*Tap again.*) My courage is no more. (*Enter* GERTRUDE *by the door.*) Gertrude! it only thou? (*Embraces her.*)

GER. Dear aunt, leave this awful place; it chills my very blood. My uncle sent me to call you to the hall.

ISA. Who is in the hall?

GER. Only Reynold and the family, with whom my uncle is making merry.

ISA. Sawest thou no strange faces?

GER. No; none but friends.

ISA. Art thou sure of that? Is George there?

GER. No, nor Henry; both have ridden out. I think they might have stayed one day at least. But come, aunt, I hate this place; it reminds me of my dream. See, yonder was the spot where methought they were burying you alive, below yon monument (*pointing*).

ISA. (*starting*). The monument of my first husband. Leave me, leave me, Gertrude. I follow in a moment. (*Exit* GERTRUDE.) Ay, here he lies! forgetful alike of his crimes and injuries! Insensible, as if this chapel had never rung with my shrieks, or the castle resounded to his parting groans! When shall I sleep so soundly? (*As she gazes on the monument, a figure muffled in black appears from behind it.*) Merciful God! is it a vision, such as has haunted my couch? (*It approaches: she goes on with mingled terror and resolution.*) Ghastly phantom, art thou the restless spirit of one who died in agony, or art thou the mysterious being that must guide me to the presence of the avengers of blood? (*Figure bends its head and beckons.*) — To-morrow! To-morrow! I cannot follow thee now! (*Figure shows a dagger from beneath its cloak.*) Compulsion! I understand thee: I will follow. (*She follows the figure a little way; he turns and wraps a black veil round her head, and takes her hand : then both exeunt behind the monument.*)

SCENE III.

The Wood of Griefenhaus. — *A watch-fire, round which sit* WICKERD, CONRAD, *and others, in their watch-cloaks.*

WIC. The night is bitter cold.

CON. Ay, but thou hast lined thy doublet well with old Rhenish.

WIC. True; and I'll give you warrant for it. (*Sings.*)

(RHEINWEIN LIED.)

What makes the troopers' frozen courage muster?
    The grapes of juice divine.

Upon the Rhine, upon the Rhine they cluster:
    Oh, blessed be the Rhine!

Let fringe and furs, and many a rabbit skin, sirs,
    Bedeck your Saracen;
He'll freeze without what warms our hearts within sirs,
    When the night-frost crusts the fen.

But on the Rhine, but on the Rhine they cluster,
    The grapes of juice divine,
That make our troopers' frozen courage muster;
    Oh, blessed be the Rhine!

CON. Well sung, Wickerd; thou wert ever a jovial soul.

Enter a trooper or two more.

WIC. Hast thou made the rounds, Frank?

FRANK. Yes, up to the hemlock marsh. It is a stormy night; the moon shone on the Wolfshill, and on the dead bodies with which to-day's work has covered it. We heard the spirit of the house of Maltingen wailing over the slaughter of its adherents: I durst go no farther.

WIC. Hen-hearted rascal! The spirit of some old raven, who was picking their bones.

CON. Nay, Wickerd; the churchmen say there are such things.

FRANK. Ay; and Father Ludovic told us last sermon, how the devil twisted the neck of ten farmers at Kletterbach, who refused to pay Peter's pence.

WIC. Yes, some church devil, no doubt.

FRANK. Nay, old Reynold says, that in passing, by midnight, near the old chapel at our castle, he saw it all lighted up, and heard a chorus of voices sing the funeral service.

ANOTHER SOLDIER. Father Ludovic heard the same.

WIC. Hear me, ye hare-livered boys! Can you look death in the face in battle, and dread such nursery bugbears? Old Reynold saw his vision in the strength of the grape. As for the chaplain, far be it from me to name the spirit which visits him; but I know what I know, when I found him confessing Bertrand's pretty Agnes in the chestnut grove.

CON. But, Wickerd, though I have often heard of strange tales, which I could not credit, yet there is one in our family so well attested, that I almost believe it. Shall I tell it you?

ALL SOLDIERS. Do! do tell it, gentle Conrad.

WIC. And I will take t'other sup of Rhenish to fence against the horrors of the tale.

CON. It is about my own uncle and god-father, Albert of Horsheim.

WIC. I have seen him — he was a gallant warrior.

CON. Well! He was long absent in the Bohemian wars. In an expedition he was benighted, and came to a lone house on the edge of a forest. He and his followers knocked repeatedly for entrance in vain. They forced the door, but found no inhabitants.

FRANK. And they made good their quarters?

CON. They did, and Albert retired to rest in an upper chamber. Opposite to the bed on which he threw himself was a large mirror. At midnight he was awaked by deep groans, he cast his eyes upon the mirror, and saw —

FRANK. Sacred Heaven! Heard you nothing?

WIC. Ay, the wind among the withered leaves. Go on, Conrad. Your uncle was a wise man.

CON. That's more than gray hairs can make other folks.

WIC. Ha! stripling, art thou so malapert? Though thou art Lord Henry's page, I shall teach thee who commands this party.

ALL SOLDIERS. Peace, peace, good Wickerd, let Conrad proceed.

CON. Where was I?

FRANK. About the mirror.

CON. True. My uncle beheld in the mirror the reflection of a human face, distorted and covered with blood. A voice pronounced articulately, "It is yet time." As the words were spoken, my uncle discerned in the ghastly visage the features of his own father.

SOLDIER. Hush! By St. Francis I heard a groan. (*They start up all but* WICKERD.)

WIC. The croaking of a frog, who has caught cold in this bitter night, and sings rather more hoarsely than usual.

FRANK. Wickerd, thou art surely no Christian. (*They sit down, and close round the fire.*)

CON. Well — my uncle called up his attendants, and they searched every nook of the chamber, but found nothing. So they covered the mirror with a cloth, and Albert was left alone; but hardly had he closed his eyes when the same voice proclaimed. "It is now too late:" the covering was drawn aside, and he saw the figure —

FRANK. Merciful Virgin! It comes. (*All rise.*)

WIC. Where? what?

CON. See yon figure coming from the thicket!

Enter MARTIN, *in the monk's dress, much disordered: his face is very pale and his steps slow.*

WIC. (*levelling his pike*). Man or devil, which thou wilt, thou shalt feel cold iron if thou budgest a foot nearer. (MARTIN *stops.*) Who art thou? What dost thou seek?

MAR. To warm myself at your fire. It is deadly cold.

WIC. See there, ye cravens, your apparition is a poor benighted monk: sit down, father. (*They place* MARTIN *by the fire.*) By heaven, it is Martin — our Martin! Martin, how fares it with thee? We have sought thee this whole night.

MAR. So have many others (*vacantly*).

CON. Yes, thy master.

MAR. Did you see him too?

CON. Whom? Baron George?

MAR. No! my first master, Arnolf of Ebersdorf.

WIC. He raves.

MAR. He passed me but now in the wood, mounted upon his old black steed; its nostrils breathed smoke and flame;

neither tree nor rock stopped him. He said, "Martin, thou wilt return this night to my service!"

WIC. Wrap thy cloak around him, Francis, he is distracted with cold and pain. Dost thou not recollect me, old friend?

MAR. Yes, you are the butler at Ebersdorf: you have the charge of the large gilded cup, embossed with the figures of the twelve apostles. It was the favorite goblet of my old master.

CON. By our Lady, Martin, thou must be distracted indeed, to think our master would intrust Wickerd with the care of the cellar.

MAR. I know a face so like the Apostle Judas on that cup. I have seen the likeness when I gazed on a mirror.

WIC. Try to go to sleep, dear Martin; it will relieve thy brain. (*Footsteps are heard in the wood.*) To your arms. (*They take their arms.*)

Enter two MEMBERS *of the Invisible Tribunals, muffled in their cloaks.*

CON. Stand! Who are you?

I MEM. Travellers benighted in the wood.

WIC. Are ye friends to Aspen or Maltingen?

I MEM. We enter not into their quarrel. We are friends to the right.

WIC. Then ye are friends to us, and welcome to pass the night by our fire.

2 MEM. Thanks. (*They approach the fire, and regard* MARTIN *very earnestly.*)

CON. Hear ye any news abroad?

2 MEM. None; but that oppression and villany are rife and rank as ever.

WIC. The old complaint.

I MEM. No! never did former age equal this in wickedness; and yet, as if the daily commission of enormities were not enough to blot the sun, every hour discovers crimes which have lain concealed for years.

CON. Pity the Holy Tribunal should slumber in its office.

2 MEM. Young man, it slumbers not. When criminals are ripe for its vengeance, it falls like the bolt of Heaven.

MAR. (*attempting to rise*). Let me be gone.

CON. (*detaining him*). Whither now, Martin?

MAR. To mass.

I MEM. Even now, we heard a tale of a villain, who, ungrateful as the frozen adder, stung the bosom that had warmed him into life.

MAR. Conrad, bear me off, I would be away from these men.

CON. Be at ease, and strive to sleep.

MAR. Too well I know — I shall never sleep again.

2 MEM. The wretch of whom we speak became, from revenge and lust of gain, the murderer of the master whose bread he did eat.

WIC. Out upon the monster!

I MEM. For nearly thirty years was he permitted to cumber the ground. The miscreant thought his crime was concealed; but the earth which groaned under his footsteps — the winds which passed over his unhallowed head — the stream which he polluted by his lips — the fire at which he warmed his blood-stained hands — every element bore witness to his guilt.

MAR. Conrad, good youth — lead me from hence, and I will show thee where, thirty years since, I deposited a mighty bribe. [*Rises.*

CON. Be patient, good Martin.

WIC. And where was the miscreant seized?

[*The two Members suddenly lay hands on* MARTIN, *and draw their daggers; the soldiers spring to their arms.*

I MEM. On this very spot.

WIC. Traitors, unloose your hold.

I MEM. In the name of the Invisible Judges, I charge ye, impede us not in our duty.

[*All sink their weapons and stand motionless.*

MAR. Help! help!

I MEM. Help him with your prayers.

[*He is dragged off. The scene shuts.*

ACT V. — Scene I.

The subterranean chapel of the Castle of Griefenhaus. It seems deserted, and in decay. There are four entrances, each defended by an iron portal. At each door stands a warder clothed in black, and masked, armed with a naked sword. During the whole scene they remain motionless on their posts. In the centre of the chapel is the ruinous altar, half sunk in the ground, on which lie a large book, a dagger, and a coil of ropes, beside two lighted tapers. Antique stone benches of different heights around the chapel. In the back scene is seen a dilapidated entrance into the sacristy, which is quite dark.

Various Members of the Invisible Tribunal enter by the four different doors of the chapel. Each whispers something as he passes the Warder, which is answered by an inclination of the head. The costume of the members is a long black robe, capable of muffling the face; some wear it in this manner; others have their faces uncovered, unless on the entrance of a stranger; they place themselves in profound silence upon the stone benches.

Enter Count Roderic, *dressed in a scarlet cloak of the same form with those of the other members. He takes his place on the most elevated bench.*

Rod. Warders, secure the doors! (*The doors are barred with great care.*) Herald, do thy duty!

    [*Members all rise — Herald stands by the altar.*

Her. Members of the Invisible Tribunal, who judge in secret, and avenge in secret, like the Deity, are your hearts free from malice, and your hands from blood-guiltiness?

    [*All the Members incline their heads.*

Rod. God pardon our sins of ignorance, and preserve us from those of presumption.

    [*Again the Members solemnly incline their heads.*

Her. To the east, and to the west, and to the north, and to the south, I raise my voice; wherever there is treason, wherever there is blood-guiltiness, wherever there is sacrilege, sorcery, robbery, or perjury, there let this curse alight, and pierce the marrow and the bone. Raise, then, your voices, and say with me, woe! woe unto offenders!

All. Woe! woe! [*Members sit down.*

Her. He who knoweth of an unpunished crime, let him stand forth as bound by his oath when his hand was laid upon the dagger and upon the cord, and call to the assembly for vengeance!

Mem. (*rises, his face covered*). Vengeance! vengeance! vengeance!

Rod. Upon whom dost thou invoke vengeance?

Accuser. Upon a brother of this order, who is forsworn and perjured to its laws.

Rod. Relate his crime.

Accu. This perjured brother was sworn, upon the steel and upon the cord, to denounce malefactors to the judgment-seat, from the four quarters of heaven, though it were the spouse of his heart, or the son whom he loved as the apple of his eye; yet did he conceal the guilt of one who was dear unto him; he folded up the crime from the knowledge of the tribunal; he removed the evidence of guilt, and withdrew the criminal from justice. What does his perjury deserve?

Rod. Accuser, come before the altar; lay thy hand upon the dagger and the cord, and swear to the truth of thy accusation.

Accu. (*his hand on the altar*). I swear!

Rod. Wilt thou take upon thyself the penalty of perjury, should it be found false?

Accu. I will.

Rod. Brethren, what is your sentence?

    [*The Members confer a moment in whispers — a silence.*

Eldest Mem. Our voice is, that the perjured brother merits death.

Rod. Accuser, thou hast heard the voice of the assembly; name the criminal.

Accu. George, Baron of Aspen.

    [*A murmur in the assembly.*

A Mem. (*suddenly rising*). I am ready, according to our holy laws, to swear, by the steel and the cord, that George of Aspen merits not this accusation, and that it is a foul calumny.

Accu. Rash man! gagest thou an oath so lightly?

Mem. I gage it not lightly. I proffer it in the cause of innocence and virtue.

Accu. What if George of Aspen should not himself deny the charge?

Mem. Then would I never trust man again.

Accu. Hear him, then, bear witness against himself. (*Throws back his mantle.*)

Rod. Baron George of Aspen?

Geo. The same — prepared to do penance for the crime of which he stands self-accused.

Rod. Still, canst thou disclose the name of the criminal whom thou hast rescued from justice; on that condition alone, thy brethren may spare thy life.

Geo. Thinkest thou I would betray for the safety of my life, a secret I have preserved at the breach of my word? — No! I have weighed the value of my obligation — I will not discharge it — but most willingly will I pay the penalty!

Rod. Retire, George of Aspen, till the assembly pronounce judgment.

Geo. Welcome be your sentence — I am weary of your yoke of iron. A light beams on my soul. Woe to those who seek justice in the dark haunts of mystery and of cruelty! She dwells in the broad blaze of the sun, and Mercy is ever by her side. Woe to those who would advance the general weal by trampling upon the social affections! they aspire to be more than men — they shall become worse than tigers. I go: better for me your altars should be stained with my blood, than my soul blackened with your crimes.

[*Exit* George, *by the ruinous door in the back scene, into the sacristy.*

Rod. Brethren, sworn upon the steel and upon the cord, to judge and to avenge in secret, without favor and without pity, what is your judgment upon George of Aspen, self-accused of perjury, and resistance to the laws of our fraternity.

[*Long and earnest murmurs in the assembly.*

Rod. Speak your doom.

Eldest Mem. George of Aspen has declared himself perjured; — the penalty of perjury is death.

Rod. Father of the secret judges — Eldest among those who avenge in secret — take to thee the steel and the cord; — let the guilty no longer cumber the land.

Eldest Mem. I am fourscore and eight years old. My eyes are dim, and my hand is feeble; soon shall I be called before the throne of my Creator; — how shall I stand there, stained with the blood of such a man?

Rod. How wilt thou stand before that throne, loaded with the guilt of a broken oath? The blood of the criminal be upon us and ours!

Eldest Mem. So be it, in the name of God!

[*He takes the dagger from the altar, goes slowly towards the back scene, and reluctantly enters the sacristy.*

Eldest Judge. (*from behind the scene*). Dost thou forgive me?

Geo. (*behind*). I do! (*He is heard to fall heavily.*)

[*Re-enter the old judge from the sacristy. He lays on the altar the bloody dagger.*

Rod. Hast thou done thy duty?

Eldest Mem. I have. (*He faints.*)

Rod. He swoons. Remove him.

[*He is assisted off the stage. During this, four members enter the sacristy and bring out a bier covered with a pall, which they place on the steps of the altar. A deep silence.*

Rod. Judges of evil, dooming in secret, and avenging in secret, like the Deity: God keep your thoughts from evil, and your hands from guilt.

Ber. I raise my voice in this assembly, and cry, vengeance! vengeance! vengeance!

Rod. Enough has this night been done — (*He rises and brings* Bertram *forward.*) Think what thou doest — George has fallen — it were murder to slay both mother and son.

Ber. George of Aspen was thy victim — a sacrifice to thy hatred and envy. I claim mine, sacred to justice and to my murdered brother. Resume thy place! — thou canst not stop the rock thou hast put in motion.

Rod. (*resumes his seat*). Upon whom callest thou for vengeance?

Ber. Upon Isabella of Aspen.

Rod. She has been summoned.

Herald. Isabella of Aspen, accused of murder by poison, I charge thee to appear, and stand upon thy defence.

[*Three knocks are heard at one of the doors — it is opened by the warder.*

Enter Isabella, *the veil still wrapped around her head, led by her conductor. All the members muffle their faces.*

Rod. Uncover her eyes.

[*The veil is removed.* Isabella *looks wildly round.*

Rod. Knowest thou, lady, where thou art?

Isa. I guess.

Rod. Say thy guess.

Isa. Before the avengers of blood.

Rod. Knowest thou why thou art called to their presence?

Isa. No.

Rod. Speak, accuser.

Ber. I impeach thee, Isabella of Aspen, before this awful assembly, of having murdered, privily and by poison, Arnolf of Ebersdorf, thy first husband.

Rod. Canst thou swear to the accusation?

Ber. (*his hand on the altar*). I lay my hand on the steel and the cord, and wear.

Rod. Isabella of Aspen, thou hast heard thy accusation. What canst thou answer?

Isa. That the oath of an accuser is no proof of guilt!

Rod. Hast thou more to say?

Isa. I have.

Rod. Speak on.

Isa. Judges invisible to the sun, and seen only by the stars of midnight! I stand before you, accused of an enormous, daring, and premeditated crime. I was married to Arnolf when I was only eighteen years old. Arnold was wary and jealous; ever suspecting me without a cause, unless it was because he had injured me. How then should I plan and perpetrate such a deed? The lamb turns not against the wolf, though a prisoner in his den.

Rod. Have you finished?

Isa. A moment. Years after years have elapsed without a whisper of this foul suspicion. Arnolf left a brother! though common fame had been silent, natural affection would have been heard against me — why spoke he not my accusation? Or has my conduct justified this horrible charge? No! awful judges, I may answer, I have founded cloisters, I have endowed hospitals. The goods that Heaven bestowed on me I have not held back from the needy. I appeal to you, judges of evil, can these proofs of innocence be downweighed by the assertion of an unknown and disguised, perchance a malignant accuser.

Ber. No longer will I wear that disguise. (*Throws back his mantle.*) Dost thou know me now?

Isa. Yes; I know thee for a wandering minstrel, relieved by the charity of my husband.

Ber. No, traitress! know me for Bertram of Ebersdorf, brother to him thou didst murder. Call her accomplice, Martin. Ha! turnest thou pale!

Isa. May I have some water? — (*Apart.*) Sacred Heaven! his vindictive look is so like. — [*Water is brought.*

A Mem. Martin died in the hands of our brethren.

Rod. Dost thou know the accuser, lady?

Isa. (*reassuming fortitude*). Let not the sinking of nature under this dreadful trial be imputed to the consciousness of guilt. I do know the accuser — know him to be outlawed for homicide, and under the ban of the empire: his testimony cannot be received.

ÉLDEST JUDGE. She says truly.

BER. (*to* RODERIC). Then I call upon thee and William of Wolfstein to bear witness to what you know.

ROD. Wolfstein is not in the assembly, and my place prevents me from being a witness.

BER. Then I will call another: meanwhile let the accused be removed.

ROD. Retire, lady. [ISABELLA *is led to the sacristy.*

ISA. (*in going off*). The ground is slippery. — Heavens! it is floated with blood!

[*Exit into the sacristy.*

ROD. (*apart to* BERTRAM). Whom dost thou mean to call? [BERTRAM *whispers.*

ROD. This goes beyond me. (*After a moment's thought.*) But be it so. Maltingen shall behold Aspen humbled in the dust. (*Aloud.*) Brethren, the accuser calls for a witness who remains without: admit him.

[*All muffle their faces.*

Enter RUDIGER, *his eyes bound or covered, leaning upon two members ; they place a stool for him, and unbind his eyes.*

ROD. Knowest thou where thou art, and before whom?

RUD. I know not, and I care not. Two strangers summoned me from my castle to assist, they said, at a great act of justice. I ascended the litter they brought, and I am here.

ROD. It regards the punishment of perjury and the discovery of murder. Art thou willing to assist us?

RUD. Most willing, as is my duty.

ROD. What if the crime regard thy friend?

RUD. I will hold him no longer so.

ROD. What if thine own blood?

RUD. I would let it out with my poniard.

ROD. Then canst thou not blame us for this deed of justice. Remove the pall.

[*The pall is lifted, beneath which is discovered the body of* GEORGE, *pale and bloody.* RUDIGER *staggers towards it.*

RUD. My George! my George! Not slain manly in battle, but murdered by legal assassins. Much, much may I mourn thee, my beloved boy; but not now, not now : never will I shed a tear for thy death till I have cleared thy fame. Hear me, ye midnight murderers, he was innocent (*raising his voice*) — upright as the truth itself. Let the man who dares gainsay me lift that gage. If the Almighty does not strengthen these frail limbs, to make good a father's quarrel, I have a son left, who will vindicate the honor of Aspen, or lay his bloody body beside his brother's.

ROD. Rash and insensible! Hear first the cause. Hear the dishonor of thy house.

ISA. (*from the sacristy*). Never shall he hear it till the author is no more!

[RUDIGER *attempts to rush toward the sacristy, but is prevented* ISABELLA *enters wounded, and throws herself on* GEORGE'S *body.*

ISA. Murdered for me — for me! my dear, dear son!

RUD. (*still held*). Cowardly villains, let me loose! Maltingen, this is thy doing! Thy face thou wouldst disguise thy deeds, thou canst not! I defy thee to instant and mortal combat!

ISA. (*looking up*). No! no! endanger not thy life! Myself! myself! could not bear thou shouldst know —— Oh! (*Dies.*)

RUD. Oh! let me go — let me but try to stop her blood, and I will forgive all.

ROD. Drag him off and detain him. The voice of lamentation must not disturb the stern deliberation of justice.

RUD. Bloodhound of Maltingen, well beseems thee thy base revenge. The marks of my son's lance are still on thy craven crest! Vengeance on the band of ye!

[RUDIGER *is dragged off to the sacristy.*

ROD. Brethren, we stand discovered. What is to be done to him who shall descry our mystery.

ÉLDEST JUDGE. He must become brother of our order, or die!

Rod. This man will never join us! He cannot put his hand into ours, which are stained with the blood of his wife and son: he must therefore die! (*Murmurs in the assembly.*) Brethren! I wonder not at your reluctance; but the man is powerful, has friends and allies to buckler his cause. It is over with us, and with our order, unless the laws are obeyed. (*Fainter murmurs.*) Besides, have we not sworn a deadly oath to execute these statutes? (*A dead silence.*) Take to thee the steel and the cord (*to the eldest judge*).

Eldest Judge. He has done no evil — he was the companion of my battle— I will not!

Rod. (*to another*). Do thou — and succeed to the rank of him who has disobeyed. Remember your oath! (*Member takes the dagger, and goes irresolutely forward: looks into the sacristy, and comes back.*)

Mem. He has fainted — fainted in anguish for his wife and his son: the bloody ground is strewn with his white hairs, torn by those hands that have fought for Christendom. I will not be your butcher. (*Throws down the dagger.*)

Ber. Irresolute and perjured! the robber of my inheritance, the author of my exile, shall die!

Rod. Thanks, Bertram. Execute the doom — secure the safety of the holy tribunal!

[Bertram *seizes the dagger, and is about to rush into the sacristy, when three loud knocks are heard at the door.*

All. Hold! hold!

[*The* Duke *of* Bavaria, *attended by many members of the Invisible Tribunal, enters, dressed in a scarlet mantle trimmed with ermine, and wearing a ducal crown.* — *He carries a rod in his hand.* — *All rise.* — *A murmur among the members, who whisper to each other,* " The Duke," " The Chief," *etc.*

Rod. The Duke of Bavaria! I am lost.

Duke. (*sees the bodies.*) I am too late — the victims have fallen.

Hen. (*who enters with the* Duke). Gracious Heaven! O George!

Rud. (*from the sacristy*). Henry, it is thy voice — save me!

[Henry *rushes into the sacristy.*

Duke. Roderic of Maltingen, descend from the seat which thou hast dishonored. (Roderic *leaves his place, which the* Duke *occupies.*) — Thou standest accused of having perverted the laws of our order; for that being a mortal enemy to the House of Aspen, thou hast abused thy sacred authority to pander to thy private revenge; and to this Wolfstein has been witness.

Rod. Chief among our circles, I have but acted according to our laws.

Duke. Thou hast indeed observed the letter of our statutes, and woe am I that they do warrant this night's bloody work! I cannot do unto thee as I would, but what I can I will. Thou hast not indeed transgressed our law, but thou hast wrested and abused it: kneel down, therefore, and place thy hands betwixt mine. (Roderic *kneels as directed.*) I degrade thee from thy sacred office. (*Spreads his hands as pushing* Roderic *from him.*) If after two days thou darest to pollute Bavarian ground by thy footsteps, be it at the peril of the steel and the cord. (Roderic *rises.*) I dissolve this meeting. (*All rise.*) Judges and condemners of others, God teach you knowledge of yourselves! (*All bend their heads* — Duke *breaks his rod and comes forward.*)

Rod. Lord Duke, thou hast charged me with treachery — thou art my liege lord — but who else dares maintain the accusation, lies in his throat.

Hen. (*rushing from the sacristy*). Villain! I accept thy challenge!

Rod. Vain boy! my lance shall chastise thee in the lists — there lies my gage.

Duke. Henry, on thy allegiance, touch it not. (*To* Roderic.) Lists shalt thou never more enter; lance shalt thou never more wield. (*Draws his sword.*) With this sword wast thou dubbed a knight;

and with this sword I dishonor thee — I thy prince — (*strikes him slightly with the flat of the sword*) — I take from thee the degree of knight, the dignity of chivalry. Thou art no longer a free German noble; thou art honorless and rightless; the funeral obsequies shall be performed for thee as for one dead to knightly honor and to fair fame; thy spurs shall be hacked from thy heels; thy arms baffled and reversed by the common executioner.

Go, fraudful and dishonored, hide thy shame in a foreign land! (RODERIC *shows a dumb expression of rage.*) Lay hands on Bertram of Ebersdorf: as I live, he shall pay the forfeiture of his outlawry. Henry, aid us to remove thy father from this charnel-house. Never shall he know the dreadful secret. Be it mine to soothe the sorrows, and to restore the honor of the House of Aspen.

(*Curtain slowly falls.*)

APPENDIX.

THE LAY OF THE LAST MINSTREL.

NOTE 1.
The feast was over in Branksome tower. —
P. 10.

In the reign of James I., Sir William Scott of Buccleuch, chief of the clan bearing that name, exchanged, with Sir Thomas Inglis of Manor, the estate of Murdiestone, in Lanarkshire, for one-half of the barony of Branksome, or Brankholm, lying upon the Teviot, about three miles above Hawick. He was probably induced to this transaction from the vicinity of Branksome to the extensive domain which he possessed in Ettrick Forest, and in Teviotdale. In the former district he held by occupancy the estate of Buccleuch, and much of the forest land on the river Ettrick. In Teviotdale, he enjoyed the barony of Eckford, by a grant from Robert II. to his ancestor, Walter Scott of Kirkurd, for the apprehending of Gilbert Ridderford, confirmed by Robert III., 3d May, 1424. Tradition imputes the exchange betwixt Scott and Inglis to a conversation, in which the latter — a man, it would appear, of a mild and forbearing nature — complained much of the injuries to which he was exposed from the English Borderers, who frequently plundered his lands of Branksome. Sir William Scott instantly offered him the estate of Murdiestone, in exchange for that which was subject to such egregious inconvenience. When the bargain was completed, he dryly remarked, that the cattle in Cumberland were as good as those of Teviotdale; and proceeded to commence a system of reprisals upon the English, which was regularly pursued by his successors. In the next reign, James II. granted to Sir Walter Scott of Branksome, and to Sir David, his son, the remaining half of the barony of Branksome, to be held in blanche for the payment of a red rose. The cause assigned for the grant is, their brave and faithful exertions in favor of the King against the house of Douglas, with whom James had been recently tugging for the throne of Scotland. This charter is dated the 2nd February, 1443; and, in the same month, part of the barony of Langholm, and many lands in Lanarkshire, were conferred upon Sir Walter and his son by the same monarch.

NOTE 2.
Nine-and-twenty knights of fame
Hung their shields in Branksome Hall. —
P. 10.

The ancient barons of Buccleuch, both from feudal splendor and from their frontier situation, retained in their household at Branksome, a number of gentlemen of their own name, who held lands from their chief, for the military service of watching and warding his castle.

NOTE 3.
——with Jedwood-axe at saddlebow. — P. 10.

"Of a truth," says Froissart, "the Scottish cannot boast great skill with the bow, but rather bear axes, with which, in time of need, they give heavy strokes." The Jedwood-axe was a sort of partisan, used by horsemen, as appears from the arms of Jedburgh, which bear a cavalier mounted and armed with this weapon. It is also called a Jedwood or Jeddart staff.

NOTE 4.
They watch, against Southern force and
* guile,*
* Lest Scroop, or Howard, or Percy's*
* powers,*
Threaten Branksome's lordly towers,
From Warkworth, or Naworth, or merry
* Carlisle.* — P. 11.

Branksome Castle was continually exposed to the attacks of the English, both from its situation and the restless military disposition of its inhabitants, who were seldom on good terms with their neighbors.

Note 5.

Bards long shall tell,
How Lord Walter fell! — P. 11.

Sir Walter Scott of Buccleuch succeeded to his grandfather, Sir David, in 1492. He was a brave and powerful baron, and Warden of the West Marches of Scotland. His death was the consequence of the feud betwixt the Scotts and Kerrs.

Note 6.

While Cessford owns the rule of Carr,
While Ettrick boasts the line of Scott,
The slaughter'd chiefs, the mortal jar,
The havock of the feudal war,
Shall never, never be forgot! — P. 11.

Among other expedients resorted to for stanching the feud betwixt the Scotts and the Kerrs, there was a bond executed in 1529, between the heads of each clan, binding themselves to perform reciprocally the four principal pilgrimages of Scotland, for the benefit of the souls of those of the opposite name who had fallen in the quarrel. But either this indenture never took effect, or else the feud was renewed shortly afterwards.

Note 7.

With Carr in arms had stood. — P. 11.

The family of Ker, Kerr, or Carr,* was very powerful on the Border. Their influence extended from the village of Preston-Grange, in Lothian, to the limits of England. Cessford Castle, now in ruins, the ancient baronial residence of the family, is situated near the village of Morebattle, within two or three miles of the Cheviot Hills. Tradition affirms that it was founded by Halbert, or Habby Kerr, a gigantic warrior, concerning whom many stories are current in Roxburghshire. The Duke of Roxburgh represents Ker of Cessford.

Note 8.

Lord Cranstoun. — P. 11.

The Cranstouns are an ancient Border family, whose chief seat was in Crailing, in Teviotdale. They were at this time at feud with the clan of Scott; for it appears that the Lady of Buccleuch, in 1557, beset the Laird of Cranstoun, seeking his life. Nevertheless, the same Cranstoun, or perhaps his son, was married to a daughter of the same lady.

* The name is spelt differently by the various families who bear it. Carr is selected, not as the most correct, but as the most poetical reading.

Note 9.

Of Bethune's line of Picardie. — P. 11.

The Bethunes were of French origin, and derived their name from a small town in Artois. There were several distinguished families of the Bethunes in the neighboring province of Picardy ; they numbered among their descendants the celebrated Duc de Sully, and the name was accounted among the most noble in France, while aught noble remained in that country.† The family of Bethune, or Beatoun, in Fife, produced three learned and dignified prelates : namely, Cardinal Beaton, and two successive Archbishops of Glasgow, all of whom flourished about the date of the romance. Of this family was descended Dame Janet Beaton, Lady Buccleuch, widow of Sir Walter Scott of Branksome. She was a woman of masculine spirit, as appeared from her riding at the head of her son's clan, after her husband's murder. She was believed by the superstition of the vulgar to possess supernatural knowledge. With this was mingled, by faction, the foul accusation of her having influenced Queen Mary to the murder of her husband. One of the placards, preserved in Buchanan's Detection, accuses of Darnley's murder " the Erle of Bothwell, Mr. James Balfour, the persoun of Fliske, Mr. David Chalmers, black Mr. John Spens, who was principal deviser of the murder ; and the Queen assenting thairto, throw the persuasion of the Erle Bothwell, and *the witchcraft of Lady Buckleuch*."

Note 10.

He learn'd the art that none may name,
In Padua, far beyond the sea. — P. 11.

Padua was long supposed by the Scottish peasants to be the principal school of necromancy. The Earl of Gowrie, slain at Perth, in 1600, pretended, during his studies in Italy, to have acquired some knowledge of the cabala. — See the examination of Wemyss of Bogie, before the Privy Council, concerning Gowrie's Conspiracy.

Note 11.

His form no darkening shadow traced
Upon the sunny wall. — P. 11.

The shadow of a necromancer is independent of the sun. Glycas informs us that Simon Magus caused his shadow to go before him, making people believe it was an

† This expression and sentiment were dictated by the situation of France, in the year 1803, when the poem was originally written. 1821.

attendant spirit. — HEYWOOD'S *Hierarchie*, p. 475. A common superstition was that when a class of students had made a certain progress in their mystic studies, they were obliged to run through a subterranean hall, where the devil literally caught the hindmost in the race, unless he crossed the hall so speedily that the arch-enemy could only grasp his shadow. Hence the old Scotch proverb, "De'il take the hindmost." Sorcerers were often fabled to have given their shadows to the fiend.

NOTE 12.

By wily turns, by desperate bounds,
Had baffled Percy's best blood-hounds. —
                                          P. 13.

The kings and heroes of Scotland, as well as the Border-riders, were sometimes obliged to study how to evade the pursuit of blood-hounds. Barbour informs us that Robert Bruce was repeatedly tracked by sleuth-dogs. On one occasion, he escaped by wading a bow-shot down a brook, and ascending into a tree by a branch which overhung the water; thus, leaving no trace on land of his footsteps, he baffled the scent.

A sure way of stopping the dog was to spill blood upon the track, which destroyed the discriminating fineness of his scent. A captive was sometimes sacrificed on such occasions. Henry the Minstrel tells a romantic story of Wallace, founded on this circumstance : — The hero's little band had been joined by an Irishman, named Fawdoun, or Fadzean, a dark, savage, and suspicious character. After a sharp skirmish at Black-Erne Side, Wallace was forced to retreat with only sixteen followers, the English pursuing with a Border blood-hound.

In the retreat, Fawdoun, tired, or affecting to be so, would go no farther, and Wallace, having in vain argued with him, in hasty anger, struck off his head, and continued the retreat. When the English came up, their hound stayed upon the dead body : —

> " The sleuth stopped at Fawdon, still she stood,
> Nor farther would, fra time she fund the
> blood."

NOTE 13.

But when Melrose he reach'd, 'twas silence
* all ;*
He meetly stabled his steed in stall,
And sought the convent's lonely wall. —
                                          P. 14.

The ancient and beautiful monastery of Melrose was founded in 1136 by King David I. It was destroyed by the English in 1322,

rebuilt by David Bruce, and again injured and effaced at the Reformation. Its ruins afford the finest specimen of Gothic architecture and Gothic sculpture which Scotland can boast. The stone of which it is built, though it has resisted the weather for so many ages, retains perfect sharpness, so that even the most minute ornaments seem as entire as when newly wrought.

NOTE 14.

When the buttress and buttress, alternately,
Seem framed of ebon and ivory ;
When silver edges the imagery,
And the scrolls that teach thee to live and
* die.*

* .   .   .   .   .*

Then view St. David's ruined pile. — P. 15.

The buttresses ranged along the sides of the ruins of Melrose Abbey, are, according to the Gothic style, richly carved and fretted, containing niches for the statues of saints, and labelled with scrolls, bearing appropriate texts of Scripture. Most of these statues have been demolished.

David I. of Scotland purchased the reputation of sanctity, by founding, and liberally endowing, not only the monastery of Melrose, but those of Kelso, Jedburgh, and many others ; which led to the well-known observation of his successor, that he was a *sore saint for the crown.*

NOTE 15.

And there the dying lamps did burn,
* Before thy low and lonely urn,*
O gallant Chief of Otterburne ! — P. 16.

The famous and desperate battle of Otterburne was fought 15th August, 1388, between Henry Percy, called Hotspur, and James, Earl of Douglas. Both these renowned rival champions were at the head of a chosen body of troops. Percy was made prisoner, and the Scots won the day through their gallant general. The Earl of Douglas was slain in the action. He was buried at Melrose, beneath the high altar.

NOTE 16.

—— dark Knight of Liddesdale ! — P. 16.

William Douglas, called the Knight of Liddesdale, flourished during the reign of David II., and was so distinguished by his valor, that he was called the Flower of Chivalry. Nevertheless, he tarnished his renown by the cruel murder of Sir Alexander Ramsay of Dalhousie, originally his friend and brother in arms. The King had conferred upon Ramsay the sheriffdom of Teviotdale, to which Douglas pretended some claim. In revenge of this preference, the Knight of Liddesdale came down upon Ramsay, while he was administering justice at Hawick, seized and carried him off to his remote and inaccessible castle of Hermitage, where he threw his unfortunate prisoner, horse and man, into a dungeon, leaving him to perish of hunger. King David, though incensed at such a high-handed outrage, was compelled to appoint Douglas his victim's successor.

NOTE 17.

—— *the wondrous Michael Scott.* — P. 17.

Sir Michael Scott of Balwearie flourished during the 13th century, and was one of the ambassadors sent to bring the maid of Norway to Scotland upon the death of Alexander III. By a poetical anachronism, he is here placed in a later era. He was a man of much learning, chiefly acquired in foreign countries. He wrote a commentary upon Aristotle, printed at Venice in 1496: and several treatises upon natural philosophy, from which he appears to have been addicted to the abstruse studies of judicial astrology, alchymy, physiognomy, and chiromancy. Hence he passed among his contemporaries for a skilful magician. Dempster informs us that he remembers to have heard in his youth that the magic books of Michael Scott were still in existence, but could not be opened without danger, on account of the malignant fiends who were thereby invoked.

Tradition varies concerning the place of his burial; some contend for Home Coltrame, in Cumberland; others for Melrose Abbey. But all agree that his books of magic were interred in his grave, or preserved in the convent where he died.

NOTE 18.

The words that cleft Eildon Hills in three. — P. 17.

Michael Scott was, once upon a time, much embarrassed by a spirit, for whom he was under the necessity of finding constant employment. He commanded him to build a *cauld*, or damhead, across the Tweed at Kelso; it was accomplished in one night, and still does honor to the infernal architect. Michael next ordered that Eildon Hill, which was then a uniform cone, should be divided into three. Another night was sufficient to part its summit into the three picturesque peaks which it now bears. At length the enchanter conquered this indefatigable demon by employing him in the hopeless and endless task of making ropes out of sea-sand.

NOTE 19.

The Baron's Dwarf his courser held. — P. 19.

The idea of Lord Cranstoun's Goblin Page is taken from a being called Gilpin Horner, who appeared, and made some stay, at a farm-house among the Border mountains.

NOTE 20.

All was delusion, naught was truth. — P. 22

Glamour, in the legends of Scottish superstition, means the magic power of imposing on the eyesight of the spectators, so that the appearance of an object shall be totally different from the reality. To such a charm the ballad of Johnny Fa' imputes the fascination of the lovely Countess, who eloped with that gipsy leader : —

" Sae soon as they saw her weel-far'd face,
They cast the *glamour* o'er her."

NOTE 21.

Until they came to a woodland brook ;
The running stream dissolved the spell. — P. 22.

It is a firm article of popular faith, that no enchantment can subsist in a living stream. Nay, if you can interpose a brook betwixt you and witches, spectres, or even fiends, you are in perfect safety. Burns's inimitable *Tam o' Shanter* turns entirely upon such a superstition.

NOTE 22.

He never counted him a man,
Would strike below the knee. — P. 23.

To wound an antagonist in the thigh or leg was reckoned contrary to the law of arms. In a tilt betwixt Gawain Michael, an English squire, and Joachim Cathore, a Frenchman, " they met at the speare poyntes rudely ; the French squyer justed right pleasantly ; the Englishman ran too lowe, for he strak the Frenchman depe into the thigh. Wherewith the Erle of Buckingham was right sore displeased, and so were all the other lords, and sayde how it was shamefully done." — FROISSART, vol i., chap. 366.

NOTE 23.

On many a cairn's gray pyramid,
Where urns of mighty chiefs lie hid. — P. 25.

The cairns, or piles of loose stones, which crown the summit of most of our Scottish hills, and are found in other remarkable situations, seem usually, though not universally, to have been sepulchral monuments. Six flat stones are commonly found in the centre, forming a cavity of greater or smaller dimensions, in which an urn is often placed. The author is possessed of one, discovered beneath an immense cairn at Roughlee, in Liddesdale. It is of the most barbarous construction ; the middle of the substance alone having been subjected to the fire, over which, when hardened, the artist had laid an inner and outer coat of unbaked clay, etched with some very rude ornament, his skill apparently being inadequate to baking the vase when completely finished. The contents were bones and ashes, and a quantity of beads made of coal. This seems to have been a barbarous imitation of the Roman fashion of sepulture.

NOTE 24.
For pathless marsh, and mountain cell,
The peasant left his lowly shed. — P. 26.

The morasses were the usual refuge of the Border herdsmen on the approach of an English army. — (*Minstrelsy of the Scottish Border*, vol. i., p. 393.) Caves, hewed in the most dangerous and inaccessible places, also afforded an occasional retreat. Such caverns may be seen in the precipitous banks of the Teviot at Sunlaws, upon the Ale at Ancram, upon the Jed at Hundalee, and in many other places upon the Border. The banks of the Eske, at Gorton and Hawthornden, are hollowed into similar recesses.

NOTE 25.
Watt Tinlinn. — P. 26.

This person was, in my younger days, the theme of many a fireside tale. He was a retainer of the Buccleuch family, and held for his Border service a small tower on the frontiers of Liddesdale. Watt was by profession a *sutor*, but by inclination and practice an archer and warrior. Upon occasion, the captain of Bowcastle, military governor of that wild district of Cumberland, is said to have made an incursion into Scotland, in which he was defeated, and forced to fly. Watt Tinlinn pursued him closely through a dangerous morass ; the captain, however, gained the firm ground ; and, seeing Tinlinn dismounted and floundering in the bog, used these words of insult. — "Sutor Watt, ye cannot sew your boots ; the heels *risp*, and the seams *rive*." * — "If I cannot sew," retorted Tinlinn, discharging a shaft, which nailed the captain's thigh to his saddle, "if I cannot sew, I can *yerk*." †

* *Risp*, creak. — *Rive*, tear.

† *Yerk*, to twitch, as shoemakers do, in securing the stitches of their work.

NOTE 26.
Belted Will Howard. — P. 27.

Lord William Howard, third son of Thomas, Duke of Norfolk, succeeded to Naworth Castle, and a large domain annexed to it, in right of his wife Elizabeth, sister of George Lord Dacre, who died without heirs male, in the 11th of Queen Elizabeth. By a poetical anachronism, he is introduced into the romance a few years earlier than he actually flourished. He was warden of the Western Marches ; and, from the rigor with which he repressed the Border excesses, the name of Belted Will Howard is still famous in our traditions.

NOTE 27.
Lord Dacre. — P. 27.

The well-known name of Dacre is derived from the exploits of one of their ancestors at the siege of Acre, or Ptolemais, under Richard Cœur de Lion.

NOTE 28.
The German Hackbut-men. — P. 27.

In the wars with Scotland, Henry VIII. and his successors employed numerous bands of mercenary troops. At the battle of Pinky there were in the English army six hundred hackbutters on foot, and two hundred on horseback, composed chiefly of foreigners. On the 27th of September, 1549, the Duke of Somerset, Lord Protector, writes thus to the Lord Dacre, warden of the West Marches: — "The Almains, in number two thousand, very valiant soldiers, shall be sent to you shortly from Newcastle, together with Sir Thomas Holcroft, and with the force of your wardenry (which we would were advanced to the most strength of horsemen that might be), shall make the attempt to Loughmaben, being of no such strength but that it may be skailed with ladders, whereof, beforehand, we would you caused secretly some number to be provided ; or else undermined with the pyke-axe, and so taken : either to be kept for the King's Majesty, or otherwise to be defaced, and taken from the profits of the enemy. And in like manner the house of Carlaverock to be used." — *History of Cumberland*, vol. i., Introd., p. lxi.

NOTE 29.
"*Ready, aye ready,*" *for the field.* — P. 27.

Sir John Scott of Thirlestane flourished in the reign of James V., and possessed the estates of Thirlestane, Gamescleuch, etc., lying upon the river of Ettrick, and extend-

ing to St. Mary's Loch, at the head of
Yarrow. It appears that when James had
assembled his nobility and their feudal followers, at Fala, with the purpose of invading
England, and was, as is well-known, disappointed by the obstinate refusal of his peers,
this baron alone declared himself ready to
follow the King wherever he should lead.
In memory of his fidelity, James granted to
his family a charter of arms, entitling them
to bear a border of fleurs-de-luce, similar to
the tressure in the royal arms, with a bundle
of spears for the crest: motto, *Ready, aye
ready.*

Note 30.

Their gathering word was Bellenden. —
P. 29.

Bellenden is situated near the head of
Borthwick water, and being in the centre of
the possessions of the Scotts, was frequently
used as their place of rendezvous and gathering word.

Note 31.

That he may suffer march-treason pain. —
P. 31.

Several species of offences, peculiar to the
Border, constituted what was called march-
treason. Among others, was the crime of
riding, or causing to ride, against the opposite country during the time of truce. Thus,
in an indenture made on the 25th day of
March, 1334, betwixt noble lords Sirs Henry
Percy, Earl of Northumberland, and Archibald Douglas, Lord of Galloway, a truce is
agreed upon until the 1st day of July, and it
is expressly accorded, "Gif ony stellis authir
on the ta part, or on the tothyr, that he shall
be hanget or heofdit; and gif ony company
stellis any gudes within the trieux before-
sayd, ane of that company sall be hanget or
heofdit, and the remanant sall restore the
gudys stolen in the dubble." — *History of
Westmoreland and Cumberland*, Introd., p.
xxxix.

Note 32.

Knighthood he took of Douglas' sword. —
P. 31.

The dignity of knighthood, according to
the original institution, had this peculiarity,
that it did not flow from the monarch, but
could be conferred by one who himself possessed it, upon any squire who, after due
probation, was found to merit the honor of
chivalry. Latterly, this power was confined
to generals, who were wont to create knights
bannerets after or before an engagement.

Note 33.

When English blood swell'd Ancram's ford.
— P. 31.

The battle of Ancram Moor, or Peniel-
heuch, was fought A.D. 1545. The English,
commanded by Sir Ralph Evers and Sir
Brian Latoun, were totally routed, and both
their leaders slain in the action. The Scottish army was commanded by Archibald
Douglas, Earl of Angus, assisted by the
Laird of Buccleuch and Norman Lesley.

Note 34.

*For who, in field or foray slack,
Saw the blanche lion e'er fall back.* —
P. 32.

This was the cognizance of the noble
house of Howard in all its branches. The
crest, or bearing of a warrior, was often
used as a *nomme de guerre.*

Note 35.

*The Bloody Heart blazed in the van,
Announcing Douglas, dreaded name.* —
P. 34.

The chief of this potent race of heroes,
about the date of the poem, was Archibald
Douglas, seventh Earl of Angus, a man of
great courage and activity. The Bloody
Heart was the well-known cognizance of the
House of Douglas, assumed from the time
of good Lord James, to whose care Robert
Bruce committed his heart, to be carried to
the Holy Land.

Note 36.

*And Swinton laid the lance in rest,
That tamed of yore the sparkling crest
Of Clarence's Plantagenet.* — P. 34.

At the battle of Beaugé, in France,
Thomas, Duke of Clarence, brother to
Henry V., was unhorsed by Sir John Swinton, of Swinton, who distinguished him by
a coronet set with precious stones, which he
wore around his helmet. The family of
Swinton is one of the most ancient in Scotland, and produced many celebrated warriors.

Note 37.

And shouting still, "A Home! a Home!"
— P. 34.

The Earls of Home, as descendants of the
Dunbars, ancient Earls of March, carried a
lion rampant, argent: but, as a difference,
changed the color of the shield from gules
to vert, in allusion to Greenlaw, their ancient possession. The slogan or war-cry of

this powerful family was, " A Home! a Home!" It was anciently placed in an escrol above the crest. The helmet is armed with a lion's head erased gules, with a cap of state gules, turned up ermine.

The Hepburns, a powerful family in East Lothian, were usually in close alliance with the Homes. The chief of this clan was Hepburn, Lord of Hailes : a family which terminated in the too famous Earl of Bothwell.

NOTE 38.

'Twixt truce and war, such sudden change
Was not infrequent, nor held strange,
In the old Border-day. — P. 35.

Notwithstanding the constant wars upon the Borders, and the occasional cruelties which marked the mutual inroads, the inhabitants on either side do not appear to have regarded each other with that violent and personal animosity which might have been expected. On the contrary, like the outposts of hostile armies, they often carried on something resembling friendly intercourse, even in the middle of hostilities; and it is evident, from various ordinances against trade and intermarriages, between English and Scottish Borderers, that the governments of both countries were jealous of their cherishing too intimate a connection.

NOTE 39.

—— on the darkening plain,
Loud hollo, whoop, or whistle ran,
As bands, their stragglers to regain,
Give the shrill watchword of their clan. —
P. 35.

Patten remarks, with bitter censure, the disorderly conduct of the English Borderers, who attended the Protector Somerset on his expedition against Scotland.

NOTE 40.

She wrought not by forbidden spell. —
P. 41.

Popular belief, though contrary to the doctrines of the Church, made a favorable distinction betwixt magicians and necromancers, or wizards : the former were supposed to command the evil spirits, and the latter to serve, or at least to be in league and compact with, those enemies of mankind. The arts of subjecting the demons were manifold ; sometimes the fiends were actually swindled by the magicians.*

* There are some amusing German and Irish tories to that effect.

NOTE 41.

A merlin sat upon her wrist,
Held by a leash of silken twist. — P. 41

A merlin, or sparrow-hawk, was actually carried by ladies of rank, as a falcon was, in time of peace, the constant attendant of a knight or baron. See LATHAM *on Falconry.* — Godscroft relates, that when Mary of Lorraine was regent she pressed the Earl of Angus to admit a royal garrison into his Castle of Tantallon. To this he returned no direct answer ; but, as if apostrophizing a goss-hawk, which sat on his wrist, and which he was feeding during the Queen's speech, he exclaimed, " The devil's in this greedy glede, she will never be full." Home's *History of the House of Douglas,* 1743, vol. ii., p. 131. Barclay complains of the common and indecent practice of bringing hawks and hounds into churches.

NOTE 42.

And princely peacock's gilded train,
And o'er the boar-head, garnish'd brave.
— P. 41.

The peacock, it is well known, was considered, during the times of chivalry, not merely as an exquisite delicacy, but as a dish of peculiar solemnity. After being roasted, it was again decorated with its plumage, and a sponge, dipped in lighted spirits of wine, was placed in its bill. When it was introduced on days of grand festival, it was the signal for the adventurous knights to take upon them vows to do some deed of chivalry, " before the peacock and the ladies." The boar's head was also a usual dish of feudal splendor. In Scotland it was sometimes surrounded with little banners displaying the colors and achievements of the baron at whose board it was served. — PINKERTON's *History,* vol. i., p. 432.

NOTE 43.

Smote, with his gauntlet, stout Hunthill. —
P. 41.

The Rutherfords of Hunthill were an ancient race of Border Lairds, whose names occur in history, sometimes as defending the frontier against the English, sometimes as disturbing the peace of their own country. Dickon Draw-the-sword was son to the ancient warrior, called in tradition the Cock of Hunthill, remarkable for leading into battle nine sons, gallant warriors, all sons of the aged champion.

Note 44.

—— *bit his glove.* — P. 41.

To bite the thumb, or the glove, seems not to have been considered, upon the Border, as a gesture of contempt, though so used by Shakespeare, but as a pledge of mortal revenge. It is yet remembered, that a young gentleman of Teviotdale, on the morning after a hard drinking-bout, observed that he had bitten his glove. He instantly demanded of his companion with whom he had quarrelled? And, learning that he had had words with one of the party, insisted on instant satisfaction, asserting that though he remembered nothing of the dispute, yet he was sure he never would have bit his glove unless he had received some unpardonable insult. He fell in the duel, which was fought near Selkirk, in 1721.

Note 45.

—— *old Albert Græme,*
The Minstrel of that ancient name. — P. 42.

" John Græme, second son of *Malice,* Earl of *Monteith,* commonly surnamed *John with the Bright Sword,* upon some displeasure risen against him at court, retired with many of his clan and kindred into the English Borders, in the reign of King Henry the Fourth, where they seated themselves; and many of their posterity have continued ever since. Mr. Sandford, speaking of them, says (which indeed was applicable to most of the Borderers on both sides), ' They were all stark moss-troopers and arrant thieves: both to England and Scotland outlawed; yet sometimes connived at, because they gave intelligence forth of Scotland, and would raise four hundred horse at any time upon a raid of the English into Scotland. A saying is recorded of a mother to her son (which is now become proverbial), *Ride, Rowley, hough's i' the pot:* that is, the last piece of beef was in the pot, and therefore it was high time for him to go and fetch more.' " — *Introduction to the History of Cumberland.*

Note 46.
Who has not heard of Surrey's fame? —
P. 43.

The gallant and unfortunate Henry Howard, Earl of Surrey, was unquestionably the most accomplished cavalier of his time; and his sonnets display beauties which would do honor to a more polished age. He was beheaded on Tower-hill in 1546; a victim to the mean jealousy of Henry VIII., who could not bear so brilliant a character near his throne.

The song of the supposed bard is founded on an incident said to have happened to the Earl in his travels. Cornelius Agrippa, the celebrated alchemist, showed him in a looking-glass the lovely Geraldine, to whose service he had devoted his pen and his sword. The vision represented her as indisposed, and reclining upon a couch, reading her lover's verses by the light of a waxen taper.

MARMION.

Note 1.

As when the Champion of the Lake
Enters Morgana's fated house,
Or in the Chapel Perilous,
Despising spells and demons' force,
Holds converse with the unburied corse.
— P. 53.

THE romance of the Morte Arthur contains a sort of abridgment of the most celebrated adventures of the Round Table; and, being written in comparatively modern language, gives the general reader an excellent idea of what romances of chivalry actually were. It has also the merit of being written in pure old English; and many of the wild adventures which it contains are told with a simplicity bordering upon the sublime. Several of these are referred to in the text; and I would have illustrated them by more full extracts, but as this curious work is about to be republished, I confine myself to the tale of the Chapell Perilous, and of the quest of Sir Launcelot after the Sangreal.

" Right so Sir Launcelot departed, and when he came to the Chapell Perilous, he alighted downe, and tied his horse to a little gate. And as soon as he was within the churchyard, he saw on the front of the chapell, many faire rich shields turned upside downe; and many of the shields Sir Launcelot had seene knights have before; with that he saw stand by him thirtie great knights, more, by a yard, than any man that ever he had seene, and all those grinned and gnashed at Sir Launcelot; and when he saw their countenance, hee dread them sore, and so put his shield afore him, and tooke his sword in his hand, ready to doe battaile; and they were all armed in black harneis, ready, with their shields and swords drawen. And when Sir Launcelot would have gone through them, they scattered on every side of him, and gave him the way; and therewith he waxed all bold, and entered into the chapell, and then hee saw no light but a dimme lampe burning, and then was he ware of a corps covered with a cloath of silke; then Sir Launcelot stooped downe, and cut a piece of that cloath away, and then it fared under him as the earth had quaked a little, whereof he was afeard, and then hee saw a faire sword lye by the dead knight, and that he gat in his hand, and hied him out of the chappell. As soon as he was in the chappell-yerd, all the knights spoke to him with a grimly voice, and said, 'Knight, Sir Launcelot, lay that sword from thee, or else thou shalt die.' — 'Whether I live or die,' said Sir Launcelot, 'with no great words get yee it againe, therefore fight for it and yee list.' Therewith he passed through them; and, beyond the chappell-yerd, there met him a faire damosell, and said, 'Sir Launcelot, leave that sword behind thee, or thou wilt die for it.' — 'I will not leave it,' said Sir Launcelot, 'for no threats.' — 'No?' said she, 'and ye did leave that sword, Queen Guenever should ye never see.' — 'Then were I a fool and I would leave this sword,' said Sir Launcelot. — 'Now, gentle knight,' said the damosell, 'I require thee to kiss me once.' — 'Nay,' said Sir Launcelot, 'that God forbid!' — 'Well, sir,' said she, 'and thou haddest kissed me thy life dayes had been done, but now, alas!' said she, 'I have lost all my labor; for I ordeined this chappell for thy sake, and for Sir Gawaine; and once I had Sir Gawaine within it; and at that time he fought with that knight which there lieth dead in yonder chappell, Sir Gilbert the bastard, and that time hee smote off Sir Gilbert the bastard's left hand. And so, Sir Launcelot, now I tell thee, that I have loved thee these seaven yeare; but there may no woman have thy love but Queene Guenever; but sithen I may not rejoyice thee to have thy body alive, I had kept no more joy in this world but to have had thy dead body; and I would have balmed it and served, and so have kept it in my life daies, and daily I should have clipped thee, and kissed thee, in the despite of Queen Guenever.' — 'Yee say well,' said Sir Launcelot; 'Jesus preserve me from your subtill

craft.' And therewith he took his horse and departed from her."

NOTE 2.

A sinful man, and unconfess'd,
He took the Sangreal's holy quest,
And, slumbering, saw the vision high,
He might not view with waking eye. —
P. 54.

One day, when Arthur was holding a high feast with his Knights of the Round Table, the Sangreal, or vessel out of which the last passover was eaten (a precious relic, which had long remained concealed from human eyes, because of the sins of the land), suddenly appeared to him and all his chivalry. The consequence of this vision was, that all the knights took on them a solemn vow to seek the Sangreal. But alas! it could only be revealed to a knight at once accomplished in earthly chivalry, and pure and guiltless of evil conversation. All Sir Launcelot's noble accomplishments were therefore rendered vain by his guilty intrigue with Queen Guenever or Ganore; and in his holy quest he encountered only such disgraceful disasters as that which follows : —

"But Sir Launcelot rode overthwart and endlong in a wild forest, and held no path but as wild adventure led him; and at the last he came unto a stone crosse, which departed two wayes, in wast land; and, by the crosse, was a stone that was of marble; but it was so dark, that Sir Launcelot might not well know what it was. Then Sir Launcelot looked by him, and saw an old chappell, and there he wend to have found people. And so Sir Launcelot tied his horse to a tree, and there he put off his shield, and hung it upon a tree, and then hee went unto the chappell doore, and found it wasted and broken. And within he found a faire altar, full richly arrayed with cloth of silk, and there stood a faire candlestick, which beare six great candles, and the candlesticke was of silver. And when Sir Launcelot saw this light, he had a great will for to enter into the chappell, but he could find no place where hee might enter. Then was hee passing heavie and dismaied. Then he returned, and came againe to his horse, and tooke off his saddle and his bridle, and let him pasture, und unlaced his helme, and ungirded his sword, and laid him downe to sleepe upon his shield, before the crosse.

"And so hee fell on sleepe; and, halfe waking and halfe sleeping, hee saw come by him two palfreys, both faire and white, the which beare a litter, therein lying a sicke knight. And when he was nigh the crosse, he there abode still. All this Sir Launcelot saw and beheld, for hee slept not verily, and hee heard him say, ' O sweete Lord, when shall this sorrow leave me, and when shall the holy vessel come by me, where through I shall be blessed, for I have endured thus long for little trespasse!' And thus a great while complained the knight, and allwaies Sir Launcelot heard it. With that Sir Launcelot saw the candlesticke, with the fire tapers, come before the crosse; but he could see no body that brought it. Also there came a table of silver, and the holy vessell of the Sancgreall, the which Sir Launcelot had seen before that time in King Petchour's house. And therewithall the sicke knight set him upright, and held up both his hands, and said, ' Faire sweete Lord, which is here within the holy vessell, take heede to mee, that I may bee hole of this great malady!' And therewith upon his hands, and upon his knees, he went so nigh, that he touched the holy vessell and kissed it: And anon he was hole, and then he said, ' Lord God, I thank thee, for I am healed of this malady.' Soo when the holy vessell had been there a great while, it went into the chappelle againe, with the candlesticke and the light, so that Sir Launcelot wist not where it became, for he was overtaken with sinne, that hee had no power to arise against the holy vessell, wherefore afterward many men said of him shame. But he tooke repentance afterward. Then the sicke knight dressed him upright, and kissed the crosse. Then anon his squire brought him his armes, and asked his lord how he did. ' Certainly,' said hee, ' I thanke God right heartily, for through the holy vessell I am healed: But I have right great mervaile of this sleeping knight, which hath had neither grace nor power to awake during the time that this holy vessell hath beene here present.' — ' I dare it right well say,' said the squire, ' that this same knight is defouled with some manner of deadly sinne, whereof he has never confessed.' — ' By my faith,' said the knight, ' whatsoever he be he is unhappie; for, as I deeme, hee is of the fellowship of the Round Table, the which is entred into the quest of the Sancgreall.' — ' Sir,' said the squire, ' here I have brought you all your armes, save your helme and your sword; and, therefore, by mine assent, now may ye take this knight's helme and his sword;' and so he did. And when he was cleane armed, he took Sir Launcelot's horse, for he was better than his owne, and so they departed from the crosse.

" Then anon Sir Launcelot awaked, and set himselfe upright, and he thought him

what hee had there seene, and whether it were dreames or not; right so he heard a voice that said, ' Sir Launcelot, more hardy than is the stone, and more bitter than is the wood, and more naked and bare than is the liefe of the fig-tree, therefore go thou from hence, and withdraw thee from this holy place;' and when Sir Launcelot heard this, he was passing heavy, and wist not what to doe. And so he departed sore weeping, and cursed the time that he was borne; for then he deemed never to have had more worship; for the words went unto his heart, till that he knew wherefore that hee was so called."

NOTE 3.

And Dryden, in immortal strain,
Had raised the Table Round again. — P. 54.

Dryden's melancholy account of his projected Epic Poem, blasted by the selfish and sordid parsimony of his patrons, is contained in an " Essay on Satire," addressed to the Earl of Dorset, and prefixed to the Translation of Juvenal. After mentioning a plan of supplying machinery from the guardian angels of kingdoms, mentioned in the Book of Daniel, he adds : —

" Thus, my lord, I have, as briefly as I could, given your lordship, and by you the world, a rude draught of what I have been long laboring in my imagination, and what I had intended to have put in practice; (though far unable for the attempt of such a poem ;) and to have left the stage, to which my genius never much inclined me, for a work which would have taken up my life in the performance of it. This, too, I had intended chiefly for the honor of my native country, to which a poet is particularly obliged. Of two subjects, both relating to it, I was doubtful whether I should choose that of King Arthur conquering the Saxons, which, being farther distant in time, gives the greater scope to my invention : or that of Edward the Black Prince, in subduing Spain and restoring it to the lawful prince, though a great tyrant, Don Pedro the Cruel; which, for the compass of time, including only the expedition of one year, for the greatness of the action and its answerable event, for the magnanimity of the English hero, opposed to the ingratitude of the person whom he restored, and for the many beautiful episodes which I had interwoven with the principal design, together with the characters of the chiefest English persons, (wherein, after Virgil and Spenser, I would have taken occasion to represent my living friends and patrons of the noblest families, and also shadowed the event of future ages in the succession of our imperial line), — with these helps, and those of the machines which I have mentioned, I might perhaps have done as well as some of my predecessors, or at least chalked out a way for others to amend my errors in a like design ; but being encouraged only with fair words by King Charles II., my little salary ill paid, and no prospect of future subsistence, I was then discouraged in the beginning of my attempt ; and now age has overtaken me, and want, a more insufferable evil, through the change of the times, has wholly disabled me."

NOTE 4.

Their theme the merry minstrels made,
Of Ascapart, and Bevis bold. — P. 54.

The "History of Bevis of Hampton" is abridged by my friend Mr. George Ellis, with that liveliness which extracts amusement even out of the most rude and unpromising of our old tales of chivalry. Ascapart, a most important personage in the romance, is thus described in an extract : —

" This geaunt was mighty and strong,
And full thirty foot was long.
He was bristled like a sow ;
A foot he had between each brow ;
His lips were great, and hung aside ;
His eyen were hollow, his mouth was wide ;
Lothly he was to look on than,
And liker a devil than a man.
His staff was a young oak,
Hard and heavy was his stroke."
Specimens of Metrical Romances,
vol. ii., p. 136.

I am happy to say that the memory of Sir Bevis is still fragrant in his town of Southampton ; the gate of which is sentinelled by the effigies of that doughty knight-errant and his gigantic associate.

NOTE 5.

Day set on Norham's castled steep,
And Tweed's fair river, broad and deep, etc.
— P. 54.

The ruinous castle of Norham (anciently called Ubbanford), is situated on the southern bank of the Tweed, about six miles above Berwick, and where that river is still the boundary between England and Scotland. The extent of its ruins, as well as its historical importance, shows it to have been a place of magnificence, as well as strength. Edward I. resided there when he was created umpire of the dispute concerning the Scottish succession. It was repeatedly taken and retaken during the wars between England and Scotland ; and, indeed, scarce

any happened in which it had not a principal share. Norham Castle is situated on a steep bank which overhangs the river. The repeated sieges which the castle had sustained rendered frequent repairs necessary. In 1164, it was almost rebuilt by Hugh Pudsey, Bishop of Durham, who added a huge keep or donjon ; notwithstanding which King Henry II., in 1174, took the castle from the bishop and committed the keeping of it to William de Neville. After this period it seems to have been chiefly garrisoned by the King, and considered as a royal fortress. The Greys of Chillingham Castle were frequently the castellans, or captains of the garrison ; yet, as the castle was situated in the patrimony of St. Cuthbert, the property was in the see of Durham till the Reformation. After that period it passed through various hands. At the union of the crowns, it was in the possession of Sir Robert Carey (afterwards Earl of Monmouth) for his own life, and that of two of his sons. After King James's accession, Carey sold Norham Castle to George Home, Earl of Dunbar, for £6,000. See his curious Memoirs, published by Mr. Constable of Edinburgh.

According to Mr. Pinkerton, there is, in the British Museum, Cal. B. 6, 216, a curious memoir of the Dacres on the State of Norham Castle in 1522, not long after the battle of Flodden. The inner ward, or keep, is represented as impregnable : " The provisions are three great vats of salt eels, forty-four kine, three hogsheads of salted salmon, forty quarters of grain, besides many cows and four hundred sheep, lying under the castle-wall nightly ; but a number of the arrows wanted feathers, and a good *Fletcher* (*i.e.* maker of arrows) was required." — *History of Scotland*, vol. ii., p. 201, note.

The ruins of the castle are at present considerable, as well as picturesque. They consist of a large shattered tower, with many vaults, and fragments of other edifices enclosed within an outward wall of great circuit.

NOTE 6.

The battled towers, the donjon keep. — P. 54.

It is perhaps unnecessary to remind my readers that the *donjon*, in its proper signification, means the strongest part of a feudal castle ; a high square tower, with walls of tremendous thickness, situated in the centre of the other buildings, from which, however, it was usually detached. Here, in case of the outward defences being gained, the garrison retreated to make their last stand.

The donjon contained the great hall and principal rooms of state for solemn occasions, and also the prison of the fortress; from which last circumstance we derive the modern and restricted use of the word *dungeon.* Ducange (*voce* DUNJO) conjectures plausibly, that the name is derived from these keeps being usually built upon a hill, which in Celtic is called DUN. Borlase supposes the word came from the darkness of the apartments in these towers, which were thence figuratively called Dungeons: thus deriving the ancient word from the modern application of it.

NOTE 7.

Well was he arm'd from head to heel,
In mail and plate of Milan steel.
— P. 55.

The artists of Milan were famous in the Middle Ages for their skill in armory, as appears from the following passage, in which Froissart gives an account of the preparations made by Henry, Earl of Hereford, afterwards Henry IV., and Thomas, Duke of Norfolk, Earl Marischal, for their proposed combat in the lists at Coventry: —
" These two lords made ample provision of all things necessary for the combat; and the Earl of Derby sent off messengers to Lombardy, to have armor from Sir Galeas, Duke of Milan. The Duke complied with joy, and gave the knight, called Sir Francis, who had brought the message, the choice of all his armor for the Earl of Derby. When he had selected what he wished for in plated and mail armor, the Lord of Milan, out of his abundant love for the Earl, ordered four of the best armorers in Milan to accompany the knight to England, that the Earl of Derby might be more completely armed." JOHNES' *Froissart*, vol. iv., p. 597.

NOTE 8.

Who checks at me, to death is dight.
— P. 55.

The crest and motto of Marmion are borrowed from the following story: — Sir David de Lindsay, first Earl of Crauford, was, among other gentlemen of quality, attended during a visit to London, in 1390, by Sir William Dalzell, who was, according to my authority, Bower, not only excelling in wisdom, but also of a lively wit. Chancing to be at the court, he there saw Sir Piers Courtenay, an English knight, famous for skill in tilting, and for the beauty of his person, parading the palace, arrayed in a new man-

tle, bearing for device an embroidered falcon, with this rhyme, —

" I bear a falcon, fairest of flight,
    Whoso pinches at her, his death is dight *
                              In graith." †

The Scottish knight, being a wag, appeared next day in a dress exactly similar to that of Courtenay, but bearing a magpie instead of the falcon, with a motto ingeniously contrived to rhyme to the vaunting inscription of Sir Piers: —

" I bear a pie picking at a peice,
    Whoso picks at her, I shall pick at his nese, ‡
                              In faith."

This affront could only be expiated by a joust with sharp lances. In the course, Dalzell left his helmet unlaced, so that it gave way at the touch of his antagonist's lance, and he thus avoided the shock of the encounter. This happened twice: in the third encounter the handsome Courtenay lost two of his front teeth. As the Englishman complained bitterly of Dalzell's fraud in not fastening his helmet, the Scottishman agreed to run six courses more, each champion staking in the hand of the King two hundred pounds, to be forfeited, if, on entering the list, any unequal advantage should be detected. This being agreed to, the wily Scot demanded that Sir Piers, in addition to the loss of his teeth, should consent to the extinction of one of his eyes, he himself having lost an eye in the fight of Otterburne. As Courtenay demurred to this equalization of optical powers, Dalzell demanded the forfeit; which, after much altercation, the King appointed to be paid to him, saying, he surpassed the English both in wit and valor. This must appear to the reader a singular specimen of the humor of that time. I suspect the Jockey Club would have given a different decision from Henry IV.

NOTE 9.

They hail'd Lord Marmion:
They hail'd him Lord of Fontenaye,
Of Lutterward, and Scrivelbaye,
Of Tamworth tower and town. — P. 56.

Lord Marmion, the principal character of the present romance, is entirely a fictitious personage. In earlier times, indeed, the family of Marmion, Lords of Fontenaye, in Normandy, was highly distinguished. Robert de Marmion, Lord of Fontenaye, a distinguished follower of the Conqueror, obtained a grant of the castle and town of Tamworth, and also of the manor of Scrivelby, in Lincolnshire. One or both of these noble possessions was held by the honorable

* Prepared.   † Armor.   ‡ Nose.

service of being the Royal Champion, as the ancestors of Marmion had formerly been to the Dukes of Normandy. But after the castle and demesne of Tamworth had passed through four successive barons from Robert, the family became extinct in the person of Philip de Marmion, who died in 20th Edward I. without issue male. He was succeeded in his castle of Tamworth by Alexander de Freville, who married Mazera, his granddaughter. Baldwin de Freville, Alexander's descendant, in the reign of Richard I., by the supposed tenure of his castle at Tamworth, claimed the office of Royal Champion, and to do the service appertaining; namely, on the day of coronation, to ride, completely armed, upon a barbed horse, into Westminster Hall, and there to challenge the combat against any who would gainsay the King's title. But this office was adjudged to Sir John Dymoke, to whom the manor of Scrivelby had descended by another of the co-heiresses of Robert de Marmion; and it remains in that family, whose representative is Hereditary Champion of England at the present day. The family and possessions of Freville have merged in the Earls of Ferrars. I have not, therefore, created a new family, but only revived the titles of an old one in an imaginary personage.

It was one of the Marmion family who, in the reign of Edward II., performed that chivalrous feat before the very castle of Norham, which Bishop Percy has woven into his beautiful ballad, "The Hermit of Warkworth." The story is thus told by Leland: —

"The Scottes cam yn to the marches of England, and destroyed the castles of Werk and Herbotel, and overran much of Northumberland marches.

"At this tyme, Thomas Gray and his friendes defended Norham from the Scottes.

"It were a wonderful processe to declare, what mischefes cam by hungre and asseges by the space of xi. years in Northumberland; for the Scottes became so proude, after they had got Berwick, that they nothing esteemed the Englishmen.

"About this tyme there was a great feste made yn Lincolnshir, to which came many gentlemen and ladies; and among them one lady brought a heaulme for a man of were, with a very riche creste of gold, to William Marmion, knight, with a letter of commandement of her lady, that he should go into the daungerest place in England, and ther to let the heaulme be seene and known as famous. So he went to Norham; whither, within 4 days of cumming, cam Philip Moubray,

guardian of Berwicke, having yn his bande 40 men of armes, the very flour of men of the Scottish marches.

"Thomas Gray, capitayne of Norham, seynge this, brought his garrison afore the barriers of the castel, behind whom cam William, richly arrayed, as al glittering in gold, and wearing the heaulme, his lady's present.

"Then said Thomas Gray to Marmion, 'Sir Knight, ye be cum hither to fame your helmet: mount up on yowr horse, and ryde lyke a valiant man to yowr foes even here at hand, and I forsake God if I rescue not thy body deade or alive or I myself wyl dye for it.'

"Whereupon he toke his cursere, and rode among the throng of ennemyes; the which layed sore stripes on him, and pulled him at the last out of his sadel to the grounde.

"Then Thomas Gray, with al the hole garrison, lette prick yn among the Scottes, and so wondid them and their horses, that they were overthrowan; and Marmion, sore beten, was horsid agayn, and, with Gray, persewed the Scottes yn chase. There were taken fifty horse of price; and the women of Norham brought them to the foote men to follow the chase."

NOTE 10.

Sir Hugh the Heron bold,
Baron of Twisel, and of Ford,
And Captain of the Hold. — P. 57.

Were accuracy of any consequence in a fictitious narrative, this castellan's name ought to have been William: for William Heron of Ford was husband to the famous Lady Ford, whose siren charms are said to have cost our James IV. so dear. Moreover, the said William Heron was, at the time supposed, a prisoner in Scotland, being surrendered by Henry VIII., on account of his share in the slaughter of Sir Robert Ker of Cessford. His wife, represented in the text as residing at the Court of Scotland, was, in fact, living in her own Castle at Ford. — See SIR RICHARD HERON'S curious *Genealogy of the Heron Family*.

NOTE 11.

James back'd the cause of that mock prince,
Warbeck, that Flemish counterfeit,
Who on the gibbet paid the cheat.
Then did I march with Surrey's power,
What time we razed old Ayton tower.
— P. 58.

The story of Perkin Warbeck, or Richard, Duke of York, is well known. In 1496 he was received honorably in Scotland; and

James IV., after conferring upon him in marriage his own relation, the Lady Catherine Gordon, made war on England in behalf of his pretensions. To retaliate an invasion of England, Surrey advanced into Berwickshire at the head of considerable forces, but retreated, after taking the inconsiderable fortress of Ayton.

NOTE 12.

—— *I trow,*
Norham can find you guides enow;
For here be some have pricked as far,
On Scottish ground, as to Dunbar;
Have drunk the monks of St. Bothan's ale,
And driven the beeves of Lauderdale:
Harried the wives of Greenlaw's goods,
And given them light to set their hoods.
— P. 58.

The garrisons of the English castles of Wark, Norham, and Berwick, were, as may be easily supposed, very troublesome neighbors to Scotland. Sir Richard Maitland of Ledington wrote a poem, called "The Blind Baron's Comfort;" when his barony of Blythe in Lauderdale was *harried* by Rowland Foster, the English captain of Wark, with his company, to the number of 300 men. They spoiled the poetical knight of 5,000 sheep, 200 nolt, 30 horses and mares; the whole furniture of his house of Blythe, worth 100 pounds Scots (8£. 6s. 8d.), and everything else that was portable.

NOTE 13.

The priest of Shoreswood — he could rein
The wildest war-horse in your train. — P. 58.

This churchman seems to have been akin to Welsh, the vicar of St. Thomas of Exeter, a leader among the Cornish insurgents in 1549. "This man," says Holinshed, "had many good things in him. He was of no great stature, but well set, and mightilie compact. He was a very good wrestler; shot well, both in the longbow and also in the crossbow; he handled his handgun and peece very well; he was a very good woodman, and a hardie, and such a one as would not give his head for the polling, or his beard for the washing. He was a companion in any exercise of activitie, and of a courteous and gentle behaviour. He descended of a good honest parentage, being borne at Peneverin in Cornwall; and yet, in this rebellion, an arch-captain and a principal doer." — Vol. iv., p. 958, 4to edition. This model of clerical talents had the misfortune to be hanged upon the steeple of his own church.

NOTE 14.

—— *that Grot where Olives nod,*
Where, darling of each heart and eye,
From all the youth of Sicily,
Saint Rosalie retired to God. — P. 59.

" Sante Rosalia was of Palermo, and born of a very noble family, and when very young abhorred so much the vanities of this world, and avoided the converse of mankind, resolving to dedicate herself wholly to God Almighty, that she, by divine inspiration, forsook her father's house, and never was more heard of, till her body was found in that cleft of a rock, on that almost inaccessible mountain, where now the chapel is built; and they affirm that she was carried up there by the hands of angels; for that place was not formerly so accessible (as now it is) in the days of the Saint: and even now it is a very bad, and steepy, and breakneck way. In this frightful place, this holy woman lived a great many years, feeding only on what she found growing on that barren mountain, and creeping into a narrow and dreadful cleft in a rock, which was always dropping wet, and was her place of retirement as well as prayer; having worn out even the rock with her knees in a certain place, which is now open'd on purpose to show it to those who come here. This chapel is very richly adorn'd; and on the spot where the Saint's dead body was discovered, which is just beneath the hole in the rock, which is open'd on purpose, as I said, there is a very statue of marble representing her in a lying posture, railed in all about with fine iron and brass work; and the altar, on which they say mass, is built just over it." — *Voyage to Sicily and Malta*, by Sir John Dryden (son to the poet), p. 107.

NOTE 15.

Friar John ——
Himself still sleeps before his beads
Have mark'd ten aves, and two creeds. —
P. 59.

Friar John understood the soporific virtue of his beads and breviary as well as his namesake in Rabelais. " But Gargantua could not sleep by any means, on which side soever he turned himself. Whereupon the monk said to him, 'I never sleep soundly but when I am at sermon or prayers. Let us therefore begin, you and I, the seven penitential psalms, to try whether you shall not quickly fall asleep.' The conceit pleased Gargantua very well; and, beginning the first of these psalms, as soon as they came to *Beati quorum*, they fell asleep, both the one and the other."

Note 16.

The summon'd Palmer came in place. —
P. 59.

A *Palmer*, opposed to a *Pilgrim*, was one who made it his sole business to visit different holy shrines ; travelling incessantly, and subsisting by charity : whereas the Pilgrim retired to his usual home and occupations, when he had paid his devotions at the particular spot which was the object of his pilgrimage. The Palmers seem to have been the *Quæstionarii* of the ancient Scottish canons 1242 and 1296.

Note 17.

To fair St. Andrew's bound,
Within the ocean-cave to pray,
Where good Saint Rule his holy lay,
From midnight to the dawn of day,
Sung to the billows' sound. — P. 60.

St. Regulus (*Scottice*, St. Rule), a monk of Patræ, in Achaia, warned by a vision, is said, A.D. 370, to have sailed westward, until he landed at Saint Andrews in Scotland, where he founded a chapel and tower. The latter is still standing, and, though we may doubt the precise date of its foundation, is certainly one of the most ancient edifices in Scotland. A cave, nearly fronting the ruinous castle of the Archbishops of St. Andrews, bears the name of this religious person. It is difficult of access ; and the rock in which it is hewed is washed by the German Ocean. It is nearly round, about ten feet in diameter, and the same in height. On one side is a sort of stone altar ; on the other an aperture into an inner den, where the miserable ascetic who inhabited this dwelling probably slept. At full tide, egress and regress are hardly practicable. As Regulus first colonized the metropolitan see of Scotland, and converted the inhabitants in the vicinity, he has some reason to complain, that the ancient name of Killrule (*Cella Reguli*) should have been superseded even in favor of the tutelar saint of Scotland. The reason of the change was, that St. Rule is said to have brought to Scotland the relics of St. Andrew.

Note 18.

—— Saint Fillan's blessed well,
Whose spring can frenzied dreams dispel,
And the crazed brain restore. — P. 60.

St. Fillan was a Scottish saint of some reputation. Although Popery is, with us, matter of abomination, yet the common people still retain some of the superstitions connected with it. There are in Perthshire several wells and springs dedicated to St.

Fillan, which are still places of pilgrimage and offerings, even among the Protestants. They are held powerful i . cases of madness ; and, in some of very late occurrence, lunatics have been left all night bound to the holy stone, in confidence that the saint would cure and unloose them before morning.

Note 19.

The scenes are desert now, and bare,
Where flourish'd once a forest fair. — P. 61.

Ettrick Forest, now a range of mountainous sheep-walks, was anciently reserved for the pleasure of the royal chase. Since it was disparked, the wood has been, by degrees, almost totally destroyed, although, wherever protected from the sheep, copses soon arise without any planting. When the King hunted there, he often summoned the array of the country to meet and assist his sport. Thus, in 1528, James V. " made proclamation to all lords, barons, gentlemen, landwardmen, and freeholders, that they should compear at Edinburgh, with a month's victuals, to pass with the king where he pleased, to danton the thieves of Tiviotdale, Annandale, Liddisdale, and other parts of that country ; and also warned all gentlemen that had good dogs to bring them, that he might hunt in the said country as he pleased : The whilk the Earl of Argyle, the Earl of Huntley, the Earl of Athole, and so all the rest of the gentlemen of the Highland, did, and brought their hounds with them in like manner, to hunt with the King, as he pleased.

" The second day of June the King past out of Edinburgh to the hunting, with many of the nobles and gentlemen of Scotland with him, to the number of twelve thousand men ; and then past to Meggitland, and hounded and hawked all the country and bounds ; that is to say, Crammat, Pappert-law, St. Mary-laws, Carlavirick, Chapel, Ewindoores, and Longhope. I heard say, he slew, in these bounds, eighteen score of harts." *

These huntings had, of course, a military character, and attendance upon them was a part of the duty of a vassal. The act for abolishing ward or military tenures in Scotland, enumerates the services of hunting, hosting, watching, and warding, as those which were in future to be illegal.

Taylor, the water-poet, has given an account of the mode in which these huntings were conducted in the Highlands of Scotland, in the seventeenth century, having

* PITSCOTTIE's *History of Scotland*, folio edition, p. 143.

been present at Braemar upon such an occasion : —

"There did I find the truly noble and right honorable lords, John Erskine, Earl of Mar ; James Stewart, Earl of Murray ; George Gordon, Earl of Engye, son and heir to the Marquess of Huntley ; James Erskine, Earl of Buchan ; and John, Lord Erskine, son and heir to the Earl of Mar, and their Countesses, with my much honored and my last assured and approved friend, Sir William Murray, knight of Abercarney, and hundreds of others, knights, esquires, and their followers ; all and every man in general, in one habit, as if Lycurgus had been there, and made laws of equality ; for once in the year, which is the whole month of August, and sometimes part of September, many of the nobility and gentry of the kingdom (for their pleasure) do come into these Highland countries to hunt ; where they do conform themselves to the habit of the Highlandmen, who, for the most part, speak nothing but Irish : and, in former time, were those people which were called the *Red-shanks*. Their habit is, — shoes, with but one sole a-piece ; stockings (which they call short hose), made of a warm stuff of divers colours, which they call tartan ; as for breeches, many of them, nor their forefathers, never wore any, but a jerkin of the same stuff that their hose is of ; their garters being bands or wreaths of hay or straw ; with a plaid about their shoulders ; which is a mantle of divers colours, much finer and lighter stuff than their hose ; with blue flat caps on their heads ; a handkerchief, knit with two knots, about their necks ; and thus are they attired. Now their weapons are — long bowes and forked arrows, swords, and targets, harquebusses, muskets, durks, and Lochaber axes. With these arms I found many of them armed for the hunting. As for their attire, any man, of what degree soever, that comes amongst them, must not disdain to wear it ; for, if they do, then they will disdain to hunt, or willingly to bring in their dogs ; but if men be kind unto them, and be in their habit, then are they conquered with kindness, and the sport will be plentiful. This was the reason that I found so many noblemen and gentlemen in those shapes. But to proceed to the hunting : —

"My good Lord of Mar having put me into that shape, I rode with him from his house, where I saw the ruins of an old castle, called the Castle of Kindroghit. It was built by King Malcolm Canmore (for a hunting-house), who reigned in Scotland, when Edward the Confessor, Harold, and Norman William, reigned in England. I speak of it, because it was the last house I saw in those parts ; for I was the space of twelve days after, before I saw either house, corn-field, or habitation for any creature but deer, wild horses, wolves, and such like creatures, — which made me doubt that I should never have seen a house again.

"Thus, the first day, we travelled eight miles, where there were small cottages built on purpose to lodge in, which they call Lonquhards. I thank my good Lord Erskine, he commanded that I should always be lodged in his lodging : the kitchen being always on the side of a bank : many kettles and pots boiling, and many spits turning and winding, with great variety of cheer, — as venison baked ; sodden, roast, and stewed beef ; mutton, goats, kid, hares, fresh salmon, pigeons, hens, capons, chickens, partridges, muir-coots, heath-cocks, caperkellies, and termagants ; good ale, sacke, white and claret, tent (or allegant), with most potent aquavitæ.

"All these, and more than these, we had continually in superfluous abundance, caught by falconers, fowlers, fishers, and brought by my lord's tenants and purveyors to victual our camp, which consisteth of fourteen or fifteen hundred men and horses. The manner of the hunting is this : Five or six hundred men do rise early in the morning, and they do disperse themselves divers ways, and seven, eight, or ten miles compass, they do bring, or chase in, the deer in many herds (two, three, or four hundred in a herd), to such or such a place, as the noblemen shall appoint them ; then, when day is come, the lords and gentlemen of their companies do ride or go to the said places, sometimes wading up to the middles, through burns and rivers ; and then, they being come to the place, do lie down on the ground till those foresaid scouts, which are called the Tinkhell, do bring down the deer ; but, as the proverb says of the bad cook, so these tinkhell men do lick their own fingers ; for, besides their bows and arrows, which they carry with them, we can hear, now and then, a harquebuss or a musket go off, which they do seldom discharge in vain. Then, after we had staid there three hours or thereabouts, we might perceive the deer appear on the hills round about us (their heads making a show like a wood), which, being followed close by the tinkhell, are chased down into the valley where we lay ; then all the valley. on each side, being waylaid with a hundred couple of strong Irish greyhounds, they are all let loose, as occasion serves, upon the herd of deer, that with dogs, guns, arrows, durks, and daggers, in the space of two hours, fourscore fat deer were slain; which after are disposed of, some one way, and some another, twenty and thirty miles, and more than enough left for us, to make merry withall at our rendezvous.

NOTE 20.

By lone Saint Mary's silent lake.
— P. 62.

This beautiful sheet of water forms the reservoir from which the Yarrow takes its source. It is connected with a smaller lake, called the Loch of the Lowes, and surrounded by mountains. In the winter it is still frequented by flights of wild swans; hence my friend Mr. Wordsworth's lines: —

" The swan on still St. Mary's Lake
   Floats double, swan and shadow."

Near the lower extremity of the lake are the ruins of Dryhope tower, the birthplace of Mary Scott, daughter of Philip Scott, of Dryhope, and famous by the traditional name of the Flower of Yarrow. She was married to Walter Scott of Harden, no less renowned for his depredations, than his bride for her beauty. Her romantic appellation was in later days, with equal justice, conferred on Miss Mary Lilias Scott, the last of the elder branch of the Harden family. The author well remembers the talent and spirit of the latter Flower of Yarrow, though age had then injured the charms which procured her the name. The words usually sung to the air of " Tweedside," beginning, " What beauties does Flora disclose," were composed in her honor.

NOTE 21.

—— in feudal strife, a foe,
Hath laid Our Lady's chapel low.
— P. 62.

The chapel of St. Mary of the Lowes (*de lacubus*) was situated on the eastern side of the lake, to which it gives name. It was injured by the clan of Scott, in a feud with the Cranstouns; but continued to be a place of worship during the seventeenth century. The vestiges of the building can now scarcely be traced; but the burial-ground is still used as a cemetery. A funeral, in a spot so very retired, has an uncommonly striking effect. The vestiges of the chaplain's house are yet visible. Being in a high situation, it commanded a full view of the lake, with the opposite mountain of Bourhope, belonging, with the lake itself, to Lord Napier. On the left hand is the tower of Dryhope, mentioned in a preceding note.

NOTE 22.

—— The Wizard's grave;
That Wizard Priest's, whose bones are thrust
From company of holy dust. — P. 63.

At one corner of the burial-ground of the demolished chapel, but without its precincts, is a small mound, called *Binram's Corse,* where tradition deposits the remains of a necromantic priest, the former tenant of the chaplainry.

NOTE 23.

Some ruder and more savage scene,
Like that which frowns round dark Lochskene. — P. 63.

Loch-skene is a mountain lake, of considerable size, at the head of the Moffat-water. The character of the scenery is uncommonly savage; and the earn, or Scottish eagle, has, for many ages, built its nest yearly upon an islet in the lake. Loch-skene discharges itself into a brook, which, after a short and precipitate course, falls from a cataract of immense height, and gloomy grandeur, called from its appearance, the " Gray Mare's Tail." The " Giant's Grave," afterwards mentioned, is a sort of trench, which bears that name, a little way from the foot of the cataract. It has the appearance of a battery, designed to command the pass.

NOTE 24.

——St. Cuthbert's Holy Isle. — P. 64.

Lindisfarne, an isle on the coast of Northumberland, was called Holy Island, from the sanctity of its ancient monastery, and from its having been the episcopal seat of the see of Durham during the early ages of British Christianity. A succession of holy men held that office; but their merits were swallowed up in the superior fame of St. Cuthbert, who was sixth Bishop of Durham, and who bestowed the name of his " patrimony " upon the extensive property of the see. The ruins of the monastery upon Holy Island betoken great antiquity. The arches are, in general, strictly Saxon, and the pillars which support them, short, strong, and massy. In some places, however, there are pointed windows, which indicate that the building has been repaired at a period long subsequent to the original foundation. The exterior ornaments of the building, being of a light sandy stone, have been wasted, as described in the text. Lindisfarne is not properly an island, but rather, as the venerable Bede has termed it, a semi-isle; for, although surrounded by the sea at full tide, the ebb leaves the sands dry between it and the opposite coast of Northumberland, from which it is about three miles distant.

NOTE 25.

—— in their convent cell,
A Saxon princess once did dwell,
The lovely Edelfled. — P. 66.

She was the daughter of King Oswy, who, in gratitude to Heaven for the great victory which he won in 655, against Penda, the Pagan King of Mercia, dedicated Edelfleda, then but a year old, to the service of God, in the monastery of Whitby, of which St. Hilda was then abbess. She afterwards adorned the place of her education with great magnificence.

NOTE 26.

—— of thousand snakes, each one
Was changed into a coil of stone,
When holy Hilda pray'd ;
They told, how sea-fowls' pinions fail,
As over Whitby's towers they sail. —
P. 66.

These two miracles are much insisted upon by all ancient writers who have occasion to mention either Whitby or St. Hilda. The relics of the snakes which infested the precincts of the convent, and were, at the abbess's prayer, not only beheaded, but petrified, are still found about the rocks, and are termed by Protestant fossilists, *Ammonitæ*.
The other miracle is thus mentioned by Camden : " It is also ascribed to the power of her sanctity, that these wild geese, which, in the winter, fly in great flocks to the lakes and rivers unfrozen in the southern parts, to the great amazement of every one, fall down suddenly upon the ground, when they are in their flight over certain neighboring fields hereabouts ; a relation I should not have made, if I had not received it from several credible men. But those who are less inclined to heed superstition attribute it to some occult quality in the ground, and to somewhat of antipathy between it and the geese, such as they say is betwixt wolves and scylla roots : For that such hidden tendencies and aversions, as we call sympathies and antipathies, are implanted in many things by provident Nature, for the preservation of them, is a thing so evident that everybody grants it." Mr. Charlton, in his History of Whitby, points out the true origin of the fable, from the number of sea-gulls that, when flying from a storm, often alight near Whitby ; and from the woodcocks, and other birds of passage, who do the same upon their arrival on shore, after a long flight.

NOTE 27.

His body's resting-place, of old,
How oft their Patron changed, they told. —
P. 66.

St. Cuthbert was, in the choice of his sepulchre, one of the most mutable and unreasonable saints in the Calendar. He died A.D. 688, in a hermitage upon the Farne Islands, having resigned the bishopric of Lindisfarne, or Holy Island, about two years before. His body was brought to Lindisfarne, where it remained until a descent of the Danes, about 793, when the monastery was nearly destroyed. The monks fled to Scotland with what they deemed their chief treasure, the relics of St. Cuthbert. The Saint was, however, a most capricious fellow-traveller, which was the more intolerable. as, like Sinbad's Old Man of the Sea, he journeyed upon the shoulders of his companions. They paraded him through Scotland for several years, and came as far west as Whithern, in Galloway, whence they attempted to sail for Ireland, but were driven back by tempests. He at length made a halt at Norham ; from thence he went to Melrose, where he remained stationary for a short time, and then caused himself to be launched upon the Tweed in a stone coffin, which landed him at Tilmouth, in Northumberland.
The resting-place of the remains of this Saint is not now matter of uncertainty. So recently as 17th May, 1827, 1,139 years after his death, their discovery and disinterment were effected. Under a blue stone in the middle of the shrine of St. Cuthbert, at the eastern extremity of the choir of Durham Cathedral, there was then found a walled grave, containing the coffins of the Saint. The first, or outer one, was ascertained to be that of 1541, the second of 1041 ; the third, or inner one, answering in every particular to the description of that of 698, was found to contain, not indeed, as had been averred then, and even until 1539, the incorruptible body, but the entire skeleton of the Saint ; the bottom of the grave being perfectly dry, free from offensive smell, and without the slightest symptom that a human body had ever undergone decomposition within its walls. The skeleton was found swathed in five silk robes of emblematic embroidery, the ornamental parts laid with gold leaf, and these again covered with a robe of linen. Beside the skeleton were also deposited several gold and silver *insignia*, and other relics of the Saint.
[Speaking of the burial of Cuthbert, Mr. Hartshorne says, " Aldhune was at that time

bishop of the, previously for a long period, wandering see of Lindisfarne. But we now hear no more of that ancient name as the seat of Episcopacy. A cathedral church, such as it was . . . was speedily erected upon the hill of Durham. This church was consecrated, with much magnificence and solemnity, in the year 999." — *History of Northumberland*, P. 221.]

Note 28.

Even Scotland's dauntless king and heir, etc.,
Before his standard fled. — P. 67.

Every one has heard, that when David I., with his son Henry, invaded Northumberland in 1136, the English host marched against them under the holy banner of St. Cuthbert; to the efficacy of which was imputed the great victory which they obtained in the bloody battle of Northallerton, or Cutonmoor. The conquerors were at least as much indebted to the jealousy and intractability of the different tribes who composed David's army: among whom, as mentioned in the text, were the Galwegians, the Britons of Strath-Clyde, the men of Teviotdale and Lothian, with many Norman and German warriors, who asserted the cause of the Empress Maud. See CHALMERS'S *Caledonia*, vol. i., p. 622; a most laborious, curious, and interesting publication, from which considerable defects of style and manner ought not to turn aside the Scottish antiquary.

Note 29.

'Twas he, to vindicate his reign,
Edged Alfred's falchion on the Dane,
And turn'd the Conqueror back again. — P. 67.

Cuthbert, we have seen, had no great reason to spare the Danes, when opportunity offered. Accordingly, I find, in Simeon of Durham, that the Saint appeared in a vision to Alfred, when lurking in the marshes of Glastonbury, and promised him assistance and victory over his heathen enemies; a consolation which, as was reasonable, Alfred, after the victory of Ashendown, rewarded by a royal offering at the shrine of the Saint. As to William the Conqueror, the terror spread before his army, when he marched to punish the revolt of the Northumbrians in 1096, had forced the monks to fly once more to Holy Island with the body of the Saint. It was, however, replaced before William left the north; and, to balance accounts, the Conqueror having intimated an indiscreet curiosity to view the Saint's body, he was, while in the act of commanding the shrine to be opened, seized with heat and sickness, accompanied with such a panic terror, that, notwithstanding there was a sumptuous dinner prepared for him, he fled without eating a morsel (which the monkish historian seems to have thought no small part both of the miracle and the penance), and never drew his bridle till he got to the river Tees.

Note 30.

Saint Cuthbert sits, and toils to frame.
The sea-born beads that bear his name. — P. 67.

Although we do not learn that Cuthbert was, during his life, such an artificer as Dunstan, his brother in sanctity, yet, since his death, he has acquired the reputation of forging those *Entrochi* which are found among the rocks of Holy Island, and pass there by the name of St. Cuthbert's Beads. While at this task, he is supposed to sit during the night upon a certain rock, and use another as his anvil. This story was perhaps credited in former days; at least the Saint's legend contains some not more probable.

Note 31.

Old Colwulf. — P. 67.

Ceolwulf, or Colwulf, King of Northumberland, flourished in the eighth century. He was a man of some learning; for the venerable Bede dedicates to him his " Ecclesiastical History." He abdicated the throne about 738, and retired to Holy Island, where he died in the odor of sanctity. Saint as Colwulf was, however, I fear the foundation of the penance vault does not correspond with his character; for it is recorded among his *memorabilia*, that, finding the air of the island raw and cold, he indulged the monks, whose rule had hitherto confined them to milk or water, with the comfortable privilege of using wine or ale. If any rigid antiquary insists on this objection, he is welcome to suppose the penance-vault was intended, by the founder, for the more genial purposes of a cellar.

Note 32.

Tynemouth's haughty Prioress. — P. 67.

That there was an ancient priory at Tynemouth is certain. Its ruins are situated on a high rocky point; and, doubtless, many a vow was made to the shrine by the distressed mariners who drove towards the iron-bound coast of Northumberland in stormy weather. It was anciently a nunnery; for Virca, abbess of Tynemouth, presented St. Cuthbert (yet alive) with a rare winding-sheet, in emulation of a holy lady called Tuda, who had sent him a coffin. But, as in the case of Whitby, and of Holy Island, the introduction of nuns at Tynemouth in the reign of Henry VIII. is an anachronism. The nunnery at Holy Island is altogether fictitious. Indeed, St. Cuthbert was unlikely to permit such an establishment; for, notwithstanding his accepting the mortuary gifts above mentioned, and his carrying on a visiting acquaintance with the Abbess of Coldingham, he certainly hated the whole female sex; and, in revenge of a slippery trick played to him by an Irish princess, he, after death, inflicted severe penances on such as presumed to approach within a certain distance of his shrine.

NOTE 33.

On those the wall was to enclose,
Alive within the tomb. — P. 69.

It is well known that the religious, who broke their vows of chastity, were subjected to the same penalty as the Roman vestals in a similar case. A small niche, sufficient to enclose their bodies, was made in the massive wall of the convent; a slender pittance of food and water was deposited in it, and the awful words, VADE IN PACE, were the signal for immuring the criminal. It is not likely that, in later times, this punishment was often resorted to; but among the ruins of the Abbey of Coldingham were some years ago discovered the remains of a female skeleton, which from the shape of the niche and position of the figure seemed to be that of an immured nun.

NOTE 34.

The village inn. — P. 73.

The accommodations of a Scottish hostelrie, or inn, in the sixteenth century, may be collected from Dunbar's admirable tale of "The Friars of Berwick." Simon Lawder, "the gay ostlier," seems to have lived very comfortably; and his wife decorated her person with a scarlet kirtle, and a belt of silk and silver, and rings upon her fingers; and feasted her paramour with rabbits, capons, partridges, and Bordeaux wine. At least, if the Scottish inns were not good, it was not for want of encouragement from the legislature; who, so early as the reign of James I., not only enacted that in all boroughs and fairs there be hostellaries, having stables and chambers, and provision for man and horse, but by another statute ordained that no man, travelling on horse or foot, should presume to lodge anywhere except in these hostellaries; and that no person, save innkeepers, should receive such travellers, under the penalty of forty shillings, for exercising such

hospitality. But, in spite of these provident enactments, the Scottish hostels are but indifferent, and strangers continue to find reception in the houses of individuals.

NOTE 35.

The death of a dear friend. — P. 76.

Among other omens to which faithful credit is given among the Scottish peasantry, is what is called the "dead-bell," explained by my friend James Hogg to be that tinkling in the ears which the country people regard as the secret intelligence of some friend's decease.

NOTE 36.

The Goblin Hall. — P. 77.

A vaulted hall under the ancient castle of Gifford or Yester (for it bears either name indifferently), the construction of which has from a very remote period been ascribed to magic. The Statistical Account of the Parish of Garvald and Baro gives the following account of the present state of this castle and apartment : — " Upon a peninsula formed by the water of Hopes on the east, and a large rivulet on the west, stands the ancient castle of Yester. Sir David Dalrymple, in his Annals, relates, that 'Hugh Gifford de Yester died in 1267; that in his castle there was a capacious cavern, formed by magical art, and called in the country Bo-Hall; i.e., Hobgoblin Hall.' A staircase of twenty-four steps led down to this apartment, which is a large and spacious hall, with an arched roof, and though it had stood for so many centuries, and been exposed to the external air for a period of fifty or sixty years, it is still as firm and entire as if it had only stood a few years. From the floor of this hall another staircase of thirty-six steps leads down to a pit which hath a communication with Hopes-water. A great part of the walls of this large and ancient castle are still standing. There is a tradition that the castle of Yester was the last fortification in this country that surrendered to General Gray, sent into Scotland by Protector Somerset." — *Statistical Account*, vol. xiii. I have only to add, that, in 1737, the Goblin Hall was tenanted by the Marquess of Tweeddale's falconer, as I learn from a poem by Boyse, entitled "Retirement," written upon visiting Yester. It is now rendered inaccessible by the fall of the stair.

NOTE 37.

There floated Haco's banner trim
Above Norweyan warriors grim. — P. 77.

In 1263, Haco, King of Norway, came into

the Frith of Clyde with a powerful armament, and made a descent at Largs, in Ayrshire. Here he was encountered and defeated, on the 2d October, by Alexander III. Haco retreated to Orkney, where he died soon after this disgrace to his arms. There are still existing, near the place of battle, many barrows, some of which, having been opened, were found, as usual, to contain bones and urns.

NOTE 38.

Upon his breast a pentacle. — P. 77.

" A pentacle is a piece of fine linen, folded with five corners, according to the five senses, and suitably inscribed with characters. This the magician extends towards the spirits which he invokes, when they are stubborn and rebellious, and refuse to be conformable unto the ceremonies and rites of magic." — See the discourses, etc., in Reginald Scott's *Discovery of Witchcraft*, ed. 1665, p. 66.

NOTE 39.

As born upon that blessed night,
When yawning graves and dying groan
Proclaim'd Hell's empire overthrown. —
P. 78.

It is a popular article of faith that those who are born on Christmas, or Good Friday, have the power of seeing spirits, and even of commanding them. The Spaniards imputed the haggard and downcast looks of their Philip II. to the disagreeable visions to which this privilege subjected him.

NOTE 40.

Yet still the knightly spear and shield
The Elfin warrior doth wield
Upon the brown hill's breast. — P. 79.

The following extract from the Essay upon the Fairy superstitions, in the " Minstrelsy of the Scottish Border," vol. ii., will show whence many of the particulars of the combat between Alexander III. and the Goblin Knight are derived : —

Gervase of Tilbury, *Otia Imperial. ap. Script. rer. Brunsvic.* (vol. i. p. 797), relates the following popular story concerning a fairy knight : " Osbert, a bold and powerful baron, visited a noble family in the vicinity of Wandelbury, in the bishopric of Ely. Among other stories related in the social circle of his friends, who, according to custom, amused each other by repeating ancient tales and traditions, he was informed, that if any knight, unattended, entered an adjacent plain by moonlight, and challenged an adversary to appear, he would be immediately encountered by a spirit in the form of a knight. Osbert resolved to make the experiment, and set out, attended by a single squire, whom he ordered to remain without the limits of the plain, which was surrounded by an ancient intrenchment. On repeating the challenge, he was instantly assailed by an adversary, whom he quickly unhorsed, and seized the reins of his steed. During this operation, his ghostly opponent sprung up, and darting his spear, like a javelin, at Osbert, wounded him in the thigh. Osbert returned in triumph with the horse, which he committed to the care of his servants. The horse was of a sable color, as well as his whole accoutrements, and apparently of great beauty and vigor. He remained with his keeper till cock-crowing, when, with eyes flashing fire, he reared, spurned the ground, and vanished. On disarming himself, Osbert perceived that he was wounded, and that one of his steel boots was full of blood." Gervase adds, that " as long as he lived, the scar of his wound opened afresh on the anniversary of the eve on which he encountered the spirit." Less fortunate was the gallant Bohemian knight, who, travelling by night with a single companion, " came in sight of a fairy host, arrayed under displayed banners. Despising the remonstrances of his friend, the knight pricked forward to break a lance with a champion, who advanced from the ranks apparently in defiance. His companion beheld the Bohemian overthrown, horse and man, by his aërial adversary ; and returning to the spot next morning, he found the mangled corpses of the knight and steed." — *Hierarchy of Blessed Angels*, p. 554.

Besides these instances of Elfin chivalry above quoted, many others might be alleged in support of employing fairy machinery in this manner. The forest of Glenmore, in the North Highlands, is believed to be haunted by a spirit called *Lham-dearg*, in the array of an ancient warrior, having a bloody hand, from which he takes his name. He insists upon those with whom he meets doing battle with him ; and the clergyman who makes up an account of the district, extant in the Macfarlane MS. in the Advocates' Library, gravely assures us, that, in his time, *Lham-dearg* fought with three brothers, whom he met in his walk, none of whom long survived the ghostly conflict. Barclay, in his " Euphormion," gives a singular account of an officer who had ventured, with his servant, rather to intrude upon a haunted house in a town in Flanders, than to put up with worse quarters elsewhere. After taking the usual precautions of providing fires, lights, and arms, they watched till midnight, when behold ! the severed arm of a man dropped from the ceiling; this was followed by the legs, the other arm, the trunk, and the head of the body, all separately. The members rolled together, united themselves in the presence of the astonished soldiers, and formed a gigantic warrior, who defied them both to combat. The blows, although they penetrated the body and amputated the limbs of their strange antagonist, had, as the reader may easily believe, little effect on an enemy who possessed such powers of self-union; nor did his efforts make more effectual impression upon them. How the combat terminated I do not exactly remember, and have not the book by me; but I think the spirit made to the intruders on his mansion the usual proposal that they should renounce their redemption; which being declined, he was obliged to retreat.

The northern champions of old were accustomed peculiarly to search for, and delight in, encounters with such military spectres. See a whole chapter on the subject, in BAR- THOLINUS, *De Causis contemptæ Mortis a Danis.* p. 253.

NOTE 41.

Close to the hut no more his own,
Close to the aid he sought in vain,
The morn may find the stiffen'd swain.
— P. 81.

I cannot help here mentioning that, on the night in which these lines were written, suggested, as they were, by a sudden fall of snow, beginning after sunset, an unfortunate man perished exactly in the manner here described, and his body was next morning found close to his own house. The accident happened within five miles of the farm of Ashestiel.

NOTE 42.

Forbes. — P. 81.

Sir William Forbes of Pitsligo, Baronet; unequalled, perhaps, in the degree of individual affection entertained for him by his friends, as well as in the general respect and esteem of Scotland at large. His "Life of Beattie," whom he befriended and patronized in life, as well as celebrated after his decease, was not long published before the benevolent and affectionate biographer was called to follow the subject of his narrative. This melancholy event very shortly succeeded the marriage of the friend, to whom this introduction is addressed, with one of Sir William's daughters.

NOTE 43.

Friar Rush. — P. 83.

Alias "Will o' the Wisp." This person-age is a strolling demon, or *esprit follet,* who, once upon a time, got admittance into a monastery as a scullion, and played the monks many pranks. He was also a sort of Robin Goodfellow and Jack o' Lantern. It is in allusion to this mischievous demon that Milton's clown speaks, —

"She was pinch'd, and pull'd, she said,
  And he by *Friar's Lantern* led."

"The history of Friar Rush" is of extreme rarity, and for some time, even the existence of such a book was doubted, although it is expressly alluded to by Reginald Scott, in his "Discovery of Witchcraft." I have perused a copy in the valuable library of my friend, Mr. Heber; and I observe from Mr. Beloe's "Anecdotes of Literature," that there is one in the excellent collection of the Marquess of Stafford.

NOTE 44. ·

Sir David Lindesay of the Mount,
Lord Lion King-at-arms. — P. 84.

The late elaborate edition of Sir David Lindesay's Works, by Mr. George Chalmers, has probably introduced him to many of my readers. It is perhaps to be regretted that the learned Editor had not bestowed more pains in elucidating his author, even although he should have omitted, or at least reserved, his disquisitions on the origin of the language used by the poet. But, with all its faults, his work is an acceptable present to Scottish antiquaries. Sir David Lindesay was well known for his early efforts in favor of the Reformed doctrines, and, indeed, his play, coarse as it now seems, must have had a powerful effect upon the people of his age. I am uncertain if I abuse poetical license by introducing Sir David Lindesay in the character of Lion-Herald, sixteen years before he obtained that office. At any rate, I am not the first who has been guilty of the anachronism; for the author of "Flodden Field" despatches *Dellamount,* which can mean nobody but Sir David de la Mont, to France, on the message of defiance from James IV. to Henry VIII. It was often an office imposed on the Lion King-at-arms to receive foreign ambassadors; and Lindesay himself did this honor to Sir Ralph Sadler in 1539-40. Indeed, the oath of the Lion, in its first article, bears reference to his frequent employment upon royal messages and embassies.

The office of heralds in feudal times being held of the utmost importance, the inauguration of the King-at-arms, who presided over their colleges, was proportionally solemn. In fact, it was the mimicry of a royal coronation, except that the unction was made with wine instead of oil. In Scotland, a namesake and kinsman of Sir David Lindesay, inaugurated in 1592, "was crowned by King James with the ancient crown of Scotland, which was used before the Scottish kings assumed a close crown ; " and on occasion of the same solemnity, dined at the King's table wearing the crown. It is probable that the coronation of his predecessor was not less solemn. So sacred was the herald's office, that in 1515, Lord Drummond was by Parliament declared guilty of treason, and his lands forfeited, because he had struck with his fist the Lion King-at-arms when he reproved him for his follies. Nor was he restored, but at the Lion's earnest solicitation.

Note 45.
Crichtoun Castle. — P. 85.

A large ruinous castle on the banks of the Tyne, about ten miles from Edinburgh. As indicated in the text, it was built at different times, and with a very differing regard to splendor and ·accommodation. The oldest part of the building is a narrow keep, or tower, such as formed the mansion of a lesser Scottish baron ; but so many additions have been made to it, that there is now a large courtyard, surrounded by buildings of different ages. The eastern front of the court is raised above a portico, and decorated with entablatures, bearing anchors. All the stones of this front are cut into diamond facets, the angular projections of which have an uncommonly rich appearance. The inside of this part of the building appears to have contained a gallery of great length and uncommon elegance. Access was given to it by a magnificent staircase, now quite destroyed. The soffits are ornamented with twining cordage and rosettes ; and the whole seems to have been far more splendid than was usual in Scottish castles. The castle belonged originally to the Chancellor, Sir William Crichton, and probably owed to him its first enlargement, as well as its being taken by the Earl of Douglas, who imputed to Crichton's counsels the death of his predecessor, Earl William, beheaded in Edinburgh Castle, with his brother, in 1440. It is said to have been totally demolished on that occasion ; but the present state of the ruin shows the contrary. In 1483 it was garrisoned by Lord Crichton, then its proprietor, against King James III., whose displeasure he had incurred by seducing his sister Margaret, in revenge, it is said, for the Monarch having dishonored his bed. From the Crichton family the castle passed to that of the Hepburns, Earls of Bothwell ; and when the forfeitures of Stewart, the last

Earl of Bothwell, were divided, the barony and Castle of Crichton fell to the share of the Earl of Buccleuch. They were afterwards the property of the Pringles of Clifton, and are now that of Sir John Callander, Baronet. It were to be wished the proprietor would take a little pains to preserve these splendid remains of antiquity, which are at present used as a fold for sheep, and wintering cattle ; although, perhaps, there are very few ruins in Scotland which display so well the style and beauty of ancient castle-architecture. The castle of Crichton has a dungeon vault, called the *Massy More*. The epithet, which is not uncommonly applied to the prisons of other old castles in Scotland, is of Saracenic origin. It occurs twice in the "*Epistolæ Itinerariæ*" of Tollius, " *Carcer subterraneus, sive, ut Mauri appellant,* MAZMORRA," p. 147 ; and again, " *Coguntur omnes Captivi sub noctem in ergastula subterranea, quæ Turcæ Algezerani vocant* MAZMORRAS," p. 243. The same word applies to the dungeons of the ancient Moorish castles in Spain, and serves to show from what nation the Gothic style of castle-building was originally derived.

Note 46.
Earl Adam Hepburn. — P. 85.

He was the second Earl of Bothwell, and fell in the field of Flodden, where, according to an ancient English poet, he distinguished himself by a furious attempt to retrieve the day : —

" Then on the Scottish part, right proud,
   The Earl of Bothwell then out brast,
And stepping forth, with stomach good,
   Into the enemies' throng he thrust ;
And *Bothwell ! Bothwell !* cried bold,
   To cause his souldiers to ensue ;
But there he caught a welcome cold,
   The Englishman straight down him threw.
Thus Haburn through his hardy heart
   His fatal fine in conflict found," etc.
          Flodden Field, a Poem ; edited by
            H. Weber. Edin., 1808.

Adam was grandfather to James, Earl of Bothwell, too well known in the history of Queen Mary.

Note 47.

For that a messenger from Heaven,
In vain to James had counsel given,
Against the English war. — P. 85.

This story is told by Pitscottie with characteristic simplicity : — " The King, seeing that France could get no support of him for that time, made a proclamation, full hastily, through all the realm of Scotland, both east and west, south and north, as well in the isles as in the firm land, to all manner of men, between sixty and sixteen years, that they should be ready, within twenty days, to pass with him, with forty days' victual, and to meet at the Burrow-muir of Edinburgh, and there to pass forward where he pleased. His proclamations were hastily obeyed, contrary to the Council of Scotland's will; but every man loved his prince so well that they would on no ways disobey him; but every man caused make his proclamation so hastily, conform to the charge of the King's proclamation.

" The King came to Lithgow, where he happened to be for the time at the Council, very sad and dolorous, making his devotion to God, to send him good chance and fortune in his voyage. In this meantime there came a man, clad in a blue gown, in at the kirk door, and belted about him in a roll of linen cloth; a pair of brotikings * on his feet, to the great of his legs; with all other hose and clothes conform thereto; but he had nothing on his head, but syde † red yellow hair behind, and on his haffets. ‡ which wan down to his shoulders; but his forehead was bald and bare. He seemed to be a man of two-and-fifty years, with a great pike-staff in his hand, and came first forward among the lords, crying and speiring § for the King, saying, he desired to speak with him. While at the last, he came where the priest was sitting in the desk at his prayers; but when he saw the King, he made him little reverence or salutation, but leaned down groffling on the desk before him, and said to him in this manner, as after follows:—'Sir King, my mother hath sent me to you, desiring you not to pass, at this time, where thou art purposed; for if thou does, thou wilt not fare well in thy journey, nor none that passeth with thee. Further, she bade thee mell ‖ with no woman, nor use their counsel, nor let them touch thy body, nor thou theirs; for, if thou do it, thou wilt be confounded and brought to shame'

" By this man had spoken thir words unto the King's grace, the evening song was near done, and the King paused on thir words, studying to give him an answer: but, in the meantime, before the King's eyes, and in the presence of all the lords that were about him for the time, this man vanished away, and could no ways be seen or comprehended, but vanished away as he had been a blink of the sun, or a whip of the whirlwind, and could no more be seen. I heard say, Sir David Lindesay, Lyon-herauld, and John Inglis the

* Buskins. ‡ Cheeks. ‖ Meddle.
† Long. § Asking.

marshal, who were, at that time, young men, and special servants to the King's grace, were standing presently beside the King, who thought to have laid hands on this man, that they might have speired further tidings at him: But all for nought; they could not touch him; for he vanished away betwixt them, and was no more seen."

Note 48.
The wild-buck bells.— P. 86.

I am glad of an opportunity to describe the cry of the deer by another word than *braying*, although the latter has been sanctified by the use of the Scottish metrical translation of the Psalms. *Bell* seems to be an abbreviation of bellow. This sylvan sound conveyed great delight to our ancestors, chiefly, I suppose, from association. A gentle knight in the reign of Henry VIII., Sir Thomas Wortley, built Wantley Lodge, in Wancliffe Forest, for the pleasure (as an ancient inscription testifies) of "listening to the hart's *bell.*"

Note 49.
June saw his father's overthrow.— P. 86.

The rebellion against James III. was signalized by the cruel circumstance of his son's presence in the hostile army. When the King saw his own banner displayed against him, and his son in the faction of his enemies, he lost the little courage he had ever possessed, fled out of the field, fell from his horse as it started at a woman and water-pitcher, and was slain, it is not well understood by whom. James IV., after the battle, passed to Stirling, and hearing the monks of the chapel-royal deploring the death of his father, their founder, he was seized with deep remorse, which manifested itself in severe penances. (See Note 56 on stanza ix. of canto v.) The battle of Sauchie-burn, in which James III. fell, was fought 18th June, 1488.

Note 50.
The Borough-moor. — P. 88.

The Borough, or Common Moor of Edinburgh, was of very great extent, reaching from the southern walls of the city to the bottom of Braid Hills. It was anciently a forest; and, in that state, was so great a nuisance, that the inhabitants of Edinburgh had permission granted to them of building wooden galleries, projecting over the street, in order to encourage them to consume the timber, which they seem to have done very effectually. When James IV. mustered the array of the kingdom there, in 1513, the Borough-moor was, according to Hawthornden, "a field spacious, and delightful by the shade of many stately and aged oaks." Upon that, and similar occasions, the royal standard is traditionally said to have been displayed from the Hare-Stane, a high stone, now built into the wall, on the left hand of the highway leading towards Braid, not far from the head of Burntsfield Links. The Hare-Stane probably derives its name from the British word *Har*, signifying an army.

Note 51.

—— in proud Scotland's royal shield,
The ruddy lion ramp'd in gold. — P. 89.

The well-known arms of Scotland. If you will believe Boethius and Buchanan, the double treasure round the shield, mentioned, *counter fleur-de-lysed or lingued and armed azure*, was first assumed by Achaius, King of Scotland, contemporary of Charlemagne, and founder of the celebrated League with France; but later antiquaries make poor Eochy, or Achy, little better than a sort of King of Brentford, whom old Grig (who has also swelled into Gregorius Magnus) associated with himself in the important duty of governing some part of the north-eastern coast of Scotland.

Note 52.

—— Caledonia's Queen is changed. — P. 91.

The Old Town of Edinburgh was secured on the north side by a lake, now drained, and on the south by a wall, which there was some attempt to make defensible even so late as 1745. The gates, and the greater part of the wall, have been pulled down, in the course of the late extensive and beautiful enlargement of the city. My ingenious and valued friend, Mr. Thomas Campbell, proposed to celebrate Edinburgh under the epithet here borrowed. But the "Queen of the North" has not been so fortunate as to receive from so eminent a pen the proposed distinction.

Note 53.

The cloth-yard arrows. — P. 92.

This is no poetical exaggeration. In some of the counties of England, distinguished for archery, shafts of this extraordinary length were actually used. Thus at the battle of Blackheath, between the troops of Henry VII., and the Cornish insurgents, in 1496, the bridge of Dartford was defended by a picked band of archers from the rebel army, "whose arrows," says Holinshed, "were in length a full cloth yard." The Scottish, according to Ascham, had a proverb, that every English archer carried

under his belt twenty-four Scots, in allusion to his bundle of unerring shafts.

Note 54

He saw the hardy burghers there
March arm'd on foot with faces bare. —
P. 93.

The Scottish burgesses were, like yeomen, appointed to be armed with bows and sheaves, sword, buckler, knife, spear, or a good axe instead of a bow, if worth £100 : their armor to be of white or bright harness. They wore *white hats*, i.e., bright steel caps, without crest or visor. By an act of James IV. their *weapon-schawings* are appointed to be held four times a year, under the aldermen or bailiffs.

Note 55.

On foot the yeoman too ——
Each at his back (a slender store)
His forty days' provision bore,
His arms were halbert, axe, or spear. —
P. 93.

Bows and quivers were in vain recommended to the peasantry of Scotland, by repeated statutes ; spears and axes seem universally to have been used instead of them. Their defensive armor was the plate-jack, hauberk, or brigantine ; and their missile weapons cross-bows and culverins. All wore swords of excellent temper, according to Patten ; and a voluminous handkerchief round their neck, "not for cold, but for cutting." The mace also was much used in the Scottish army. The old poem on the battle of Flodden mentions a band —

" Who manfully did meet their foes,
With leaden mauls, and lances long."

When the feudal array of the kingdom was called forth, each man was obliged to appear with forty days' provision. When this was expended, which took place before the battle of Flodden, the army melted away of course. Almost all the Scottish forces, except a few knights, men-at-arms, and the Border-prickers, who formed excellent light cavalry, acted upon foot.

Note 56.

A banquet rich, and costly wines,
To Marmion and his train. — P. 94.

In all transactions of great or petty importance, and among whomsoever taking place, it would seem that a present of wine was a uniform and indispensable preliminary. It was not to Sir John Falstaff alone that such an introductory preface was necessary, however well judged and acceptable on the part of Mr. Brook; for Sir Ralph Sadler, while on an embassy to Scotland in 1539-40, mentions, with complacency, "the same night came Rothesay (the herald so called) to me again, and brought me wine from the King, both white and red." — *Clifford's Edition*, p. 39.

NOTE 57.

—— *his iron-belt,*
That bound his breast in penance-pain,
In memory of his father slain. — P. 95.

Few readers need to be reminded of this belt, to the weight of which James added certain ounces every year that he lived. Pitscottie founds his belief that James was not slain in the battle of Flodden, because the English never had this token of the iron-belt to show to any Scottishman. The person and character of James are delineated according to our best historians. His romantic disposition, which led him highly to relish gayety, approaching to license, was, at the same time, tinged with enthusiastic devotion. These propensities sometimes formed a strange contrast. He was wont, during his fits of devotion, to assume the dress, and conform to the rules, of the order of Franciscans; and when he had thus done penance for some time in Stirling, to plunge again into the tide of pleasure. Probably, too, with no unusual inconsistency, he sometimes laughed at the superstitious observances to which he at other times subjected himself.

NOTE 58.

Sir Hugh the Heron's wife. — P. 95.

It has been already noticed (see note 10) that King James's acquaintance with Lady Heron of Ford did not commence until he marched into England. Our historians impute to the King's infatuated passion the delays which led to the fatal defeat of Flodden. The author of "The Genealogy of the Heron Family" endeavors, with laudable anxiety, to clear the Lady Ford from the scandal; that she came and went, however, between the armies of James and Surrey is certain. See PINKERTON'S *History* and the authorities he refers to, vol. ii., p. 99.

NOTE 59.

The fair Queen of France
Sent him a turquois ring and glove,
And charged him, as her knight and love,
For her to break a lance. — P. 95.

"Also the Queen of France wrote a love letter to the King of Scotland, calling him her love, showing him that she had suffered much rebuke in France for the defending of his honor. She believed surely that he

would recompense her again with some of his kingly support in her necessity; that is to say, that he would raise her an army, and come three foot of ground on English ground, for her sake. To that effect she sent him a ring off her finger, with fourteen thousand French crowns to pay his expenses." PITSCOTTIE, p. 110. — A turquois ring, probably this fatal gift, is, with James's sword and dagger, preserved in the College of Heralds, London.

NOTE 60.

Archibald Bell-the-Cat. — P. 97.

Archibald Douglas, Earl of Angus, a man remarkable for strength of body and mind, acquired the popular name of *Bell-the-Cat*, upon the following remarkable occasion: — James the Third, of whom Pitscottie complains that he delighted more in music, and "policies of building," than in hunting, hawking, and other noble exercises, was so ill advised as to make favorites of his architects and musicians, whom the same historian irreverently terms masons and fiddlers. His nobility, who did not sympathize in the King's respect for the fine arts, were extremely incensed at the honors conferred on those persons, particularly on Cochrane, a mason, who had been created Earl of Mar; and, seizing the opportunity, when, in 1482, the King had convoked the whole array of the country to march against the English, they held a midnight council in the church of Lauder, for the purpose of forcibly removing these minions from the King's person. When all had agreed on the propriety of this measure, Lord Gray told the assembly the apologue of the Mice, who had formed a resolution that it would be highly advantageous to their community to tie a bell round the cat's neck, that they might hear her approach at a distance; but which public measure unfortunately miscarried, from no mouse being willing to undertake the task of fastening the bell. "I understand the moral," said Angus, "and, that what we propose may not lack execution, I will *bell-the-cat.*"

NOTE 61.

Against the war had Angus stood,
And chafed his royal Lord. — P. 97.

Angus was an old man when the war against England was resolved upon. He earnestly spoke against that measure from its commencement; and, on the eve of the battle of Flodden, remonstrated so freely upon the impolicy of fighting, that the King said to him, with scorn and indignation, "if he was afraid he might go home." The Earl burst into tears at this insupportable insult, and retired accordingly, leaving his sons George, Master of Angus, and Sir William of Glenbervie, to command his followers. They were both slain in the battle, with two hundred gentlemen of the name of Douglas. The aged earl, broken-hearted at the calamities of his house and his country, retired into a religious house, where he died about a year after the field of Flodden.

NOTE 62.

Tantallon hold. — P. 97.

The ruins of Tantallon Castle occupy a high rock projecting into the German Ocean, about two miles east of North Berwick. The building formed a principal castle of the Douglas family, and when the Earl of Angus was banished, in 1527, it continued to hold out against James V. The King went in person against it, and for its reduction borrowed from the Castle of Dunbar, then belonging to the Duke of Albany, two great cannons, "Thrawn-mouth'd Meg and her Marrow;" also, "two great botcards, and two moyan, two double falcons, and four quarter falcons." Yet, notwithstanding all this apparatus, James was forced to raise the siege, and only afterwards obtained possession of Tantallon by treaty with the governor, Simon Panango. When the Earl of Angus returned from banishment, upon the death of James, he again obtained possession of Tantallon, and it actually afforded refuge to an English ambassador, under circumstances similar to those described in the text. This was no other than the celebrated Sir Ralph Sadler, who resided there for some time under Angus's protection, after the failure of his negotiations for matching the infant Mary with Edward VI.

NOTE 63.

Their motto on his blade. — P. 97.

A very ancient sword, in possession of Lord Douglas, bears among a great deal of flourishing, two hands pointing to a heart, which is placed betwixt them, and the date 1329, being the year in which Bruce charged the good Lord Douglas to carry his heart to the Holy Land.

NOTE 64.

—— *Martin Swart.* — P. 99.

A German general, who commanded the auxiliaries sent by the Duchess of Burgundy with Lambert Simnel. He was defeated and killed at Stokefield. The name of this German general is preserved by that of the field of battle, which is called, after him, Swartmoor. There were songs about him long current in England. — See Dissertation prefixed to RITSON'S *Ancient Songs*, 1792, p. lxi.

NOTE 65.

—— *The Cross.* — P. 100.

The Cross of Edinburgh was an ancient and curious structure. The lower part was an octagonal tower, sixteen feet in diameter, and about fifteen feet high. At each angle there was a pillar, and between them an arch, of the Grecian shape. Above these was a projecting battlement, with a turret at each corner, and medallions, of rude but curious workmanship, between them. Above this rose the proper Cross, a column of one stone, upwards of twenty feet high, surmounted with a unicorn. This pillar is preserved in the grounds of the property of Drum, near Edinburgh. The magistrates of Edinburgh in 1756, with consent of the Lords of Session, destroyed this curious monument under a wanton pretext that it encumbered the streets. From the Tower of the Cross, so long as it remained, the heralds published the acts of Parliament.

NOTE 66.

This awful summons came.
— P. 101.

This supernatural citation is mentioned by all our Scottish historians. It was, probably, like the apparition at Linlithgow, an attempt, by those averse to the war, to impose upon the superstitious temper of James IV.

NOTE 67.

One of his own ancestry.
Drove the Monks forth of Coventry.
P. 103.

This relates to the catastrophe of a real Robert de Marmion, in the reign of King Stephen, whom William of Newbury describes with some attributes of my fictitious hero. "*Homo bellicosus, ferocia, et astucia, fere nullo suo tempore impar.*" This Baron, having expelled the Monks from the church of Coventry, was not long of experiencing the Divine judgment, as the same monks, no doubt, termed his disaster. Having waged a feudal war with the Earl of Chester, Marmion's horse fell, as he charged in the van of his troop, against a body of the Earl's followers; the rider's thigh being broken by the fall, his head was cut off by a common foot-soldier, ere he could receive any succor. The whole story is told by William of Newbury.

Note 68.

—— *The savage Dane*
At Iol more deep the mead did drain. —

P. 104.

The Iol of the heathen Danes (a word still applied to Christmas in Scotland) was solemnized with great festivity. The humor of the Danes at table displayed itself by pelting each other with bones; and Torfæus tells a long and curious story, in the History of Hrolfe Kraka, of one Hottus, an inmate of the Court of Denmark, who was so generally assailed with these missiles, that he constructed, out of the bones with which he was overwhelmed, a very respectable intrenchment, against those who continued the raillery.

Note 69.

Who lists may in their mumming see
Traces of ancient mystery. — P. 105.

It seems certain that the *Mummers* of England, who (in Northumberland at least) used to go about in disguise to the neighboring houses, bearing the then useless ploughshare; and the *Guisards* of Scotland, not yet in total disuse, present, in some indistinct degree, a shadow of the old mysteries, which were the origin of the English drama. In Scotland (*me ipso teste*), we were wont, during my boyhood, to take the characters of the apostles, at least of Peter, Paul, and Judas Iscariot; the first had the keys, the second carried a sword, and the last the bag, in which the dole of our neighbors' plumcake was deposited. One played a champion, and recited some traditional rhymes; another was: —

"Alexander, King of Macedon,
Who conquer'd all the world but Scotland alone."

These, and many such verses, were repeated, but by rote, and unconnectedly. There was also, occasionally, I believe, a Saint George. In all, there was a confused resemblance of the ancient mysteries, in which the characters of Scripture, the Nine Worthies, and other popular personages, were usually exhibited.

Note 70.

The Highlander ——
Will, on a Friday morn, look pale,
If ask'd to tell a fairy tale. —

P. 106.

The *Daoine shi* , or *Men of Peace*, of the Scottish Highlanders, rather resemble the Scandinavian *Duergar* than the English Fairies. Notwithstanding their name, they are, if not absolutely malevolent, at least peevish, discontented, and apt to do mischief on slight provocation. The belief of their existence is deeply impressed on the Highlanders, who think they are particularly offended at mortals who talk to them, who wear their favorite color (green), or in any respect interfere with their affairs. This is especially to be avoided on Friday, when, whether as dedicated to Venus, with whom, in Germany, this subterraneous people are held nearly connected, or for a more solemn reason, they are more active, and possessed of greater power. Some curious particulars concerning the popular superstition of the Highlanders may be found in Dr. Graham's Picturesque Sketches of Perthshire.

Note 71.

The last lord of Franchémont. — P. 106.

The journal of the friend to whom the Fourth Canto of the Poem is inscribed, furnished me with the following account of a striking superstition.

" Passed the pretty little village of Franchémont (near Spaw), with the romantic ruins of the old castle of the Counts of that name. The road leads through many delightful vales on a rising ground; at the extremity of one of them stands the ancient castle, now the subject of many superstitious legends. It is firmly believed by the neighboring peasantry, that the last Baron of Franchémont deposited, in one of the vaults of the castle, a ponderous chest, containing an immense treasure in gold and silver, which, by some magic spell, was intrusted to the care of the Devil, who is constantly found sitting on the chest in the shape of a huntsman. Any one adventurous enough to touch the chest is instantly seized with the palsy. Upon one occasion, a priest of noted piety was brought to the vault : he used all the arts of exorcism to persuade his infernal majesty to vacate his seat, but in vain ; the huntsman remained immovable. At last, moved by the earnestness of the priest, he told him that he would agree to resign the chest, if the exorciser would sign his name with blood. But the priest understood his meaning, and refused, as by that act he would have delivered over his soul to the Devil. Yet if anybody can discover the mystic words used by the person who deposited the treasure, and pronounce them, the fiend must instantly decamp. I had many stories of a similar nature from a peasant, who had himself seen the Devil in the shape of a great cat."

NOTE 72.

—— the huge and sweeping brand
Which wont of yore, in battle fray,
His foeman's limbs to shred away,
As wood-knife lops the sapling spray.
                                    — P. 110.

The Earl of Angus had strength and personal activity corresponding to his courage. Spens of Kilspindie, a favorite of James IV., having spoken of him lightly, the Earl met him while hawking, and, compelling him to single combat, at one blow cut asunder his thigh-bone, and killed him on the spot. But ere he could obtain James's pardon for this slaughter, Angus was obliged to yield his castle of Hermitage, in exchange for that of Bothwell, which was some diminution to the family greatness. The sword with which he struck so remarkable a blow, was presented by his descendant James, Earl of Morton, afterwards Regent of Scotland, to Lord Lindesay of the Byres, when he defied Bothwell to single combat on Carberry Hill. See Introduction to the *Minstrelsy of the Scottish Border.*

NOTE 73.

And hopest thou hence unscathed to go? —
No! by St. Bride of Bothwell, no!
Up drawbridge, grooms! — what, Warder, ho!
Let the portcullis fall. — P. 111.

This ebullition of violence in the potent Earl of Angus is not without its example in the real history of the house of Douglas, whose chieftains possessed the ferocity with the heroic virtues of a savage state. The most curious instance occurred in the case of Maclellan, Tutor of Bomby, who, having refused to acknowledge the pre-eminence claimed by Douglas over the gentlemen and Barons of Galloway, was seized and imprisoned by the Earl, in his castle of the Thrieve, on the borders of Kirkcudbrightshire. Sir Patrick Gray, commander of King James the Second's guard, was uncle to the Tutor of Bomby, and obtained from the King a "sweet letter of supplication," praying the Earl to deliver his prisoner into Gray's hand. When Sir Patrick arrived at the castle, he was received with all the honor due to a favorite servant of the King's household; but while he was at dinner, the Earl, who suspected his errand, caused his prisoner to be led forth and beheaded. After dinner, Sir Patrick presented the King's letter to the Earl, who received it with great affection of reverence; "and took him by the hand, and led him forth to the green, where the gentleman was lying dead, and showed

him the manner, and said, ' Sir Patrick, you are come a little too late; yonder is your sister's son lying, but he wants his head: take his body, and do with it what you will.' — Sir Patrick answered again, with a sore heart, and said, ' My lord, if ye have taken from him his head, dispone upon the body as ye please;' and with that called for his horse, and leaped thereon; and when he was on horseback, he said to the Earl on this manner, ' My lord, if I live, you shall be rewarded for your labors that you have used at this time, according to your demerits.'

"At this saying the Earl was highly offended, and cried for horse. Sir Patrick, seeing the Earl's fury, spurred his horse, but he was chased near Edinburgh ere they left him; and had it not been his led horse was so tried and good he had been taken." — PITSCOTTIE'S *History*, p. 39.

NOTE 74.

A letter forged! — Saint Jude to speed!
Did ever knight so foul a deed! — P. 111.

Lest the reader should partake of the Earl's astonishment, and consider these crimes inconsistent with the manners of the period, I have to remind him of the numerous forgeries (partly executed by a female assistant) devised by Robert of Artois, to forward his suit against the Countess Matilda; which, being detected, occasioned his flight into England, and proved the remote cause of Edward the Third's memorable wars in France. John Harding, also, was expressly hired by Edward I. to forge such documents as might appear to establish the claim of fealty asserted over Scotland by the English monarchs.

NOTE 75.

Twisel Bridge. — P. 113.

On the evening previous to the memorable battle of Flodden, Surrey's headquarters were at Barmoor Wood, and King James held an inaccessible position on the ridge of Flodden-hill, one of the last and lowest eminences detached from the ridge of Cheviot. The Till, a deep and slow river, winded between the armies. On the morning of the 9th September, 1513, Surrey marched in a north-westerly direction, and crossed the Till, with his van and artillery, at Twisel-bridge, nigh where that river joins the Tweed, his rear-guard column passing about a mile higher, by a ford. This movement had the double effect of placing his army between King James and his supplies from Scotland, and of striking the Scottish monarch with surprise, as he seems to have relied on the depth of the river in his front. But as the passage, both over the bridge and through the ford, was difficult and slow, it seems possible that the English might have been attacked to great advantage while struggling with these natural obstacles. I know not if we are to impute James's forbearance to want of military skill, or to the romantic declaration which Pitscottie puts in his mouth, " that he was determined to have his enemies before him on a plain field," and therefore would suffer no interruption to be given, even by artillery, to their passing the river.

The ancient bridge of Twisel, by which the English crossed the Till, is still standing beneath Twisel Castle, a splendid pile of Gothic architecture rebuilt by Sir Francis Blake. Beneath a tall rock near the bridge is a plentiful fountain called St. Helen's Well.

NOTE 76.

Hence might they see the full array,
Of either host, for deadly fray. — P. 114.

The reader cannot here expect a full account of the battle of Flodden ; but, so far as is necessary to understand the romance, I beg to remind him, that, when the English army, by their skilful countermarch, were fairly placed between King James and his own country, the Scottish monarch resolved to fight ; and, setting fire to his tents, descended from the ridge of Flodden to secure the neighboring eminence of Brankstone, on which that village is built. Thus the two armies met, almost without seeing each other, when, according to the old poem, of " Flodden Field,"

" The English line stretch'd east and west,
And southward were their faces set ;
The Scottish northward proudly prest,
And manfully their foes they met."

The English army advanced in four divisions. On the right, which first engaged, were the sons of Earl Surrey ; namely, Thomas Howard, the Admiral of England, and Sir Edmund, the Knight Marshal of the army. Their divisions were separated from each other ; but, at the request of Sir Edmund, his brother's battalion was drawn very near to his own. The centre was commanded by Surrey in person ; the left wing by Sir Edward Stanley, with the men of Lancashire, and of the palatinate of Chester. Lord Dacre, with a large body of horse, formed a reserve. When the smoke, which the wind had driven between the armies, was somewhat dispersed, they perceived the Scots, who had moved down the hill in a similar

order of battle and in deep silence. The Earls of Huntly and of Home commanded their left wing, and charged Sir Edmund Howard with such success as entirely to defeat his part of the English right wing. Sir Edmund's banner was beaten down, and he himself escaped with difficulty to his brother's division. The Admiral, however, stood firm ; and Dacre advancing to his support with the reserve of cavalry, probably between the intervals of the divisions commanded by the brothers Howard, appears to have kept the victors in effectual check. Home's men, chiefly Borderers, began to pillage the baggage of both armies ; and their leader is branded by the Scottish historians with negligence or treachery. On the other hand, Huntly, on whom they bestow many encomiums, is said by the English historians to have left the field after the first charge. Meanwhile the Admiral, whose flank these chiefs ought to have attacked, availed himself of their inactivity, and pushed forward against another large division of the Scottish army in his front, headed by the Earls of Crawford and Montrose, both of whom were slain, and their forces routed. On the left, the success of the English was yet more decisive ; for the Scottish right wing, consisting of undisciplined Highlanders, commanded by Lennox and Argyle, was unable to sustain the charge of Sir Edward Stanley, and especially the severe execution of the Lancashire archers. The King and Surrey, who commanded the respective centres of their armies, were meanwhile engaged in close and dubious conflict. James, surrounded by the flower of his kingdom, and impatient of the galling discharge of arrows, supported also by his reserve under Bothwell, charged with such fury, that the standard of Surrey was in danger. At that critical moment, Stanley, who had routed the left wing of the Scottish, pursued his career of victory and arrived on the right flank, and in the rear of James's division, which, throwing itself into a circle, disputed the battle till night came on. Surrey then drew back his forces ; for the Scottish centre not having been broken, and their left wing being victorious, he yet doubted the event of the field. The Scottish army, however, felt their loss, and abandoned the field of battle in disorder, before dawn. They lost, perhaps, from eight to ten thousand men ; but that included the very prime of their nobility, gentry, and even clergy. Scarce a family of eminence but has an ancestor killed at Flodden ; and there is no province in Scotland, even at this day, where the battle is mentioned without a sensation of terror and sorrow. The English lost, also, a great number of men, perhaps within one-third of the vanquished, but they were of inferior note.

NOTE 77.

——*Brian Tunstall, stainless knight.*—
P. 114.

Sir Brian Tunstall, called in the romantic language of the time, Tunstall the Undefiled, was one of the few Englishmen of rank slain at Flodden. He figures in the ancient English poem, to which I may safely refer my readers; as an edition, with full explanatory notes, has been published by my friend, Mr. Henry Weber. Tunstall, perhaps, derived his epithet of *undefiled* from his white armor and banner, the latter bearing a white cock, about to crow, as well as from his unstained loyalty and knightly faith. His place of residence was Thurland Castle.

NOTE 78.

Reckless of life, he desperate fought,
And fell on Flodden plain;
And well in death his trusty brand,
Firm clench'd within his manly hand,
Beseem'd the monarch slain.—
P. 118.

There can be no doubt that King James fell in the battle of Flodden. He was killed, says the curious French Gazette, within a lance's length of the Earl of Surrey; and the same account adds, that none of his division were made prisoners, though many were killed; a circumstance that testifies the desperation of their resistance. The Scottish historians record many of the idle reports which passed among the vulgar of their day. Home was accused by the popular voice, not only of failing to support the King, but even of having carried him out of the field, and murdered him. And this tale was revived in my remembrance by an unauthenticated story of a skeleton, wrapped in a bull's hide, and surrounded with an iron chain, said to have been found in the well of Home Castle; for which, on inquiry, I could never find any better authority than the sexton of the parish having said that, *if the well were cleaned out, he would not be surprised at such a dis-*

covery. Home was the chamberlain of the King, and his prime favorite; he had much to lose (in fact did lose all) in consequence of James's death, and nothing earthly to gain by that event; but the retreat, or inactivity of the left wing which he commanded, after defeating Sir Edmund Howard, and even the circumstance of his returning unhurt, and loaded with spoil, from so fatal a conflict, rendered the propagation of any calumny against him easy and acceptable. Other reports gave a still more romantic turn to the King's fate, and averred, that James, weary of greatness, after the carnage among his nobles, had gone on a pilgrimage, to merit absolution for the death of his father, and the breach of his oath of amity to Henry. In particular, it was objected to the English, that they could never show the token of the iron belt, which, however, he was likely enough to have laid aside on the day of the battle, as encumbering his personal exertions. They produce a better evidence, the monarch's sword and dagger, which are still preserved in the Herald's College in London. Stowe has recorded a degrading story of the disgrace with which the remains of the unfortunate monarch were treated in his time. An unhewn column marks the spot where James fell, still called the King's Stone.

NOTE 79.

The fair cathedral storm'd and took.—
P. 118.

This storm of Lichfield cathedral, which had been garrisoned on the part of the King, took place in the Great Civil War. Lord Brook, who, with Sir John Gill, commanded the assailants, was shot with a musket-ball through the vizor of his helmet. The royalists remarked, that he was killed by a shot fired from St. Chad's cathedral, and upon St. Chad's Day, and received his death-wound in the very eye with which, he had said, he hoped to see the ruin of all the cathedrals in England. The magnificent church in question suffered cruelly upon this and other occasions; the principal spire being ruined by the fire of the besiegers.

THE LADY OF THE LAKE.

NOTE 1.

—— *the heights of Uam-Var,*
And roused the cavern, where, 'tis told,
A giant made his den of old. — P. 125.

UA-VAR, as the name is pronounced, or
more properly *Uaighmor*, is a mountain to
the north-east of the village of Callender in
Menteith, deriving its name, which signifies
the great den or cavern, from a sort of retreat among the rocks on the south side,
said, by tradition, to have been the abode of
a giant. In latter times, it was the refuge
of robbers and banditti, who have been only
extirpated within these forty or fifty years.
Strictly speaking, this stronghold is not a
cave, as the name would imply, but a sort of
small enclosure, or recess, surrounded with
large rocks, and open above head.

NOTE 2.

Two dogs of black Saint Hubert's breed,
Unmatch'd for courage, breath, and speed.
— P. 125.

" The hounds which we call Saint Hubert's hounds, are commonly all blacke, yet
neuertheless, the race is so mingled at these
days, that we find them of all colours. These
are the hounds which the abbots of St. Hubert haue always kept some of their race
or kind, in honour or remembrance of the
saint, which was a hunter with S. Eustace.
Whereupon we may conceiue that (by the
grace of God) all good huntsmen shall follow
them into paradise." — *The Noble Art of
Venerie or Hunting, translated and collected for the Use of all Noblemen and
Gentlemen.* Lond. 1611, 4to, p. 15.

NOTE 3.

For the death-wound and death-halloo,
Muster'd his breath, his whinyard drew.
— P. 126.

When the stag turned to bay, the ancient
hunter had the perilous task of going in
upon, and killing or disabling the desperate
animal. At certain times of the year this
was held particularly dangerous, a wound
received from a stag's horn being then
deemed poisonous, and more dangerous than
one from the tusks of a boar, as the old
rhyme testifies : —

" If thou be hurt with hart, it brings thee to thy
   bier,
   But barber's hand will boar's hurt heal, therefore thou need'st not fear."

At all times, however, the task was danger-

ous, and to be adventured upon wisely and
warily, either by getting behind the stag
while he was gazing on the hounds, or by
watching an opportunity to gallop roundly
in upon him, and kill him with a sword.

NOTE 4.

And now to issue from the glen,
No pathway meets the wanderer's ken,
Unless he climb, with footing nice,
A far projecting precipice. — P. 127.

Until the present road was made through
the romantic pass which I have presumptu-
ously attempted to describe in the preceding
stanzas, there was no mode of issuing out of
the defile called the Trosachs, excepting by
a sort of ladder, composed of the branches
and roots of trees.

NOTE 5.

To meet with Highland plunderers here,
Were worse than loss of steed or deer. —
                                    P. 129.

The clans who inhabited the romantic regions in the neighborhood of Loch Katrine,
were, even until a late period, much addicted
to predatory excursions upon their Lowland
neighbors.

NOTE 6.

A gray-hair'd sire, whose eye intent,
Was on the vision'd future bent. — P. 129.

If force of evidence could authorize us to
believe facts inconsistent with the general
laws of nature, enough might be produced in
favor of the existence of the second-sight.
It is called in Gaelic *Taishitaraugh*, from
Taish, an unreal or shadowy appearance ;
and those possessed of the faculty are called
Taishatrin, which may be aptly translated
visionaries. Martin, a steady believer in the
second-sight, gives the following account of
it : —

" The second-sight is a singular faculty of
seeing an otherwise invisible object without
any previous means used by the person that
used it for that end ; the vision makes such
a lively impression upon the seers, that they
neither see nor think of anything else, except the vision, as long as it continues ; and
then they appear pensive or jovial, according
to the object that was represented to them.

" At the sight of a vision, the eyelids of
the person are erected, and the eyes continue
staring until the object vanishes. This is obvious to others who are by when the persons
happen to see a vision, and occurred more

than once to my own observation, and to others that were with me.

"If a woman is seen standing at a man's left hand, it is a presage that she will be his wife, whether they be married to others, or unmarried at the time of the apparition.

"To see a spark of fire fall upon one's arm or breast, is a forerunner of a dead child to be seen in the arms of those persons; of which there are several fresh instances.

"To see a seat empty at the time of one's sitting in it, is a presage of that person's death soon after."— MARTIN's *Description of the Western Islands*, 1716, 8vo, p. 300, *et seq.*

To these particulars innumerable examples might be added, all attested by grave and credible authors. But, in despite of evidence which neither Bacon, Boyle, nor Johnson were able to resist, the *Taisch*, with all its visionary properties, seems to be now universally abandoned to the use of poetry. The exquisitely beautiful poem of Lochiel will at once occur to the recollection of every reader.

NOTE 7.

Here, for retreat in dangerous hour,
Some chief had framed a rustic bower.—
P. 130.

The Celtic chieftains, whose lives were continually exposed to peril, had usually, in the most retired spot of their domains, some place of retreat for the hour of necessity, which, as circumstances would admit, was a tower, a cavern, or a rustic hut, in a strong and secluded situation. One of these last gave refuge to the unfortunate Charles Edward, in his perilous wanderings after the battle of Culloden.

NOTE 8.

My sire's tall form might grace the part
Of Ferragus or Ascabart.— P. 130.

These two sons of Anak flourished in romantic fable. The first is well known to the admirers of Ariosto, by the name of Ferrau. He was an antagonist of Orlando, and was at length slain by him in single combat.

Ascapart, or Ascabart, makes a very material figure in the History of Bevis Hampton, by whom he was conquered. His effigies may be seen guarding one side of a gate at Southampton, while the other is occupied by Sir Bevis himself.

NOTE 9.

Though all unask'd his birth and name.
— P. 131.

The Highlanders, who carried hospitality to a punctilious excess, are said to have con-

sidered it as churlish to ask a stranger his name or lineage before he had taken refreshment. Feuds were so frequent among them, that a contrary rule would in many cases have produced the discovery of some circumstance which might have excluded the guest from the benefit of the assistance he stood in need of.

NOTE 10.

Morn's genial influence roused a minstrel
gray.
—— *Allan Bane.*— P. 132.

The Highland chieftains retained in their service the bard, as a family officer, to a late period.

NOTE 11.

—— *The Græme.*— P. 134.

The ancient and powerful family of Graham (which, for metrical reasons, is here spelt after the Scottish pronunciation) held extensive possessions in the counties of Dumbarton and Stirling. Few families can boast of more historical renown, having claim to three of the most remarkable characters in the Scottish annals. Sir John the Græme, the faithful and undaunted partaker of the labors and patriotic warfare of Wallace, fell in the unfortunate field of Falkirk, 1298. The celebrated Marquis of Montrose, in whom De Retz saw realized his abstract idea of the heroes of antiquity, was the second of these worthies. And, notwithstanding the severity of his temper, and the rigor with which he executed the oppressive mandates of the princes whom he served, I do not hesitate to name as a third, John Græme of Claverhouse, Viscount of Dundee, whose heroic death in the arms of victory may be allowed to cancel the memory of his cruelty to the nonconformists, during the reigns of Charles II. and James II.

NOTE 12.

This harp, which erst Saint Modan sway'd.
— P. 134.

I am not prepared to show that Saint Modan was a performer on the harp. It was, however, no unsaintly accomplishment; for Saint Dunstan certainly did play upon that instrument, which retaining, as was natural, a portion of the sanctity attached to its master's character, announced future events by its spontaneous sound.

NOTE 13.

Ere Douglasses, to ruin driven,
Were exiled from their native heaven.—
P. 134.

The downfall of the Douglasses of the

house of Angus during the reign of James
V. is the event alluded to in the text.

NOTE 14.

In Holy-Rood a knight he slew. — P. 135.

This was by no means an uncommon oc
currence in the Court of Scotland; nay, the
presence of the sovereign himself scarcely
restrained the ferocious and inveterate feuds
which were the perpetual source of bloodshed
among the Scottish nobility. The murder
of Sir William Stuart of Ochiltree, called
The Bloody, by the celebrated Francis, Earl
of Bothwell, may be mentioned among
many others. — JOHNSTONI *Historia Rerum
Britannicarum*, ab anno 1572 ad annum
1628. Amstelodami, 1655, fol. p. 135.

NOTE 15.

*The Douglas, like a stricken deer,
Disown'd by every noble peer.* — P. 135.

The exile state of this powerful race is not
exaggerated in this and subsequent passages.
The hatred of James against the race of
Douglas was so inveterate, that numerous as
their allies were, and disregarded as the regal
authority had usually been in similar cases,
their nearest friends, even in the most remote
parts of Scotland, durst not entertain them,
unless under the strictest and closest disguise.

NOTE 16.

—— *Maronnan's cell.* — P. 135.

The parish of Kilmaronock, at the eastern extremity of Loch Lomond, derives its
name from a cell or chapel dedicated to St.
Maronock, or Marnock, or Maronnan, about
whose sanctity very little is now remembered.
There is a fountain devoted to him in the
same parish; but its virtues, like the merits
of its patron, have fallen into oblivion.

NOTE 17.

—— *Bracklinn's thundering wave.* —
P. 135.

This is a beautiful cascade made by a
mountain stream called the Keltie, at a place
called the Bridge of Bracklinn, about a mile
from the village of Callender in Menteith.

NOTE 18.

For Tine-man forged by fairy lore. —
P. 136.

Archibald, the third Earl of Douglas, was
so unfortunate in all his enterprises, that he
acquired the epithet of TINE-MAN, because
he *tined*, or lost, his followers, in every battle
which he fought.

NOTE 19.

*Did, self-unscabbarded, foreshow
The footstep of a secret foe.* — P. 136.

The ancient warriors, whose hope and
confidence rested chiefly in their blades, were
accustomed to deduce omens from them, especially from such as was supposed to have
been fabricated by enchanted skill, of which
we have various instances in the romances
and legends of the time.

NOTE 20.

*Those thrilling sounds that call the might
Of old Clan-Alpine to the fight.* — P. 136.

The connoisseurs in pipe-music affect to
discover in a well-composed pibroch, the im-
itative sounds of march, conflict, flight, pursuit, and all the " current of a heady fight."

NOTE 21.

Roderigh Vich Alpine dhu, ho! ieroe! —
P. 137.

Roderick the Black, the descendant of
Alpine. Besides his ordinary name and surname, which were chiefly used in the intercourse with the Lowlands, every Highland
chief had an epithet expressive of his patriarchal dignity as head of the clan, and which
was common to all his predecessors, as Pharaoh to the kings of Egypt, or Arsaces to
those of Parthia, this name was usually a
patronymic, expressive of his descent from
the founder of the family. Thus the Duke
of Argyle is called MacCallum More, or the
Son of Colin the Great.

NOTE 22.

*And while the Fiery Cross glanced, like a
meteor, round.* — P. 142.

When a chieftain designed to summon his
clan upon any sudden or important emer-
gency, he slew a goat, and making a cross
of any light wood, seared its extremities in
the fire, and extinguished them in the blood
of the animal. This was called the *Fiery
Cross*, also *Crean Tarigh*, or the *Cross of
Shame*, because disobedience to what the
symbol implied, inferred infamy. It was delivered to a swift and trusty messenger, who
ran full speed with it to the next hamlet,
where he presented it to the principal person,
with a single word, implying the place of
rendezvous. He who received the symbol
was bound to send it forward with equal despatch to the next village; and thus it passed
with incredible celerity through all the district which owed allegiance to the chief, and
also among his allies and neighbors, if the
danger was common to them. At sight of the

Fiery Cross, every man, from sixteen years old to sixty, capable of bearing arms, was obliged instantly to repair, in his best weapons and accoutrements, to the place of rendezvous. He who failed to appear, suffered the extremities of fire and sword, which were emblematically denounced to the disobedient by the bloody and burnt marks upon this warlike signal. During the civil war of 1745-56, the Fiery Cross often made its circuit: and upon one occasion it passed through the whole district of Breadalbane, a tract of thirty-two miles, in three hours.

NOTE 23.

That monk, of savage form and face. — P. 143.

The state of religion in the Middle Ages afforded considerable facilities for those whose mode of life excluded them from regular worship, to secure, nevertheless, the ghostly assistance of confessors, perfectly willing to adapt the nature of their doctrine to the necessities and peculiar circumstances of their flock. Robin Hood, it is well known, had his celebrated domestic chaplain, Friar Tuck.

NOTE 24.

Of Brian's birth strange tales were told. — P. 143.

The legend which follows is not of the author's invention. It is possible he may differ from modern critics, in supposing that the records of human superstition, if peculiar to, and characteristic of, the country in which the scene is laid, are a legitimate subject of poetry. He gives, however, ready assent to the narrower proposition which condemns all attempts of an irregular and disordered fancy to excite terror, by accumulating a train of fantastic and incoherent horrors, whether borrowed from all countries and patched upon a narrative belonging to one which knew them not, or derived from the author's own imagination. In the present case, therefore, I appeal to the record which I have transcribed, with the variation of a very few words from the geographical collections made by the Laird of Macfarlane. I know not whether it be necessary to remark, that the miscellaneous concourse of youths and maidens on the night and on the spot where the miracle is said to have taken place, might, even in a credulous age, have somewhat diminished the wonder which accompanied the conception of Gilli-Doir-Magrevollich.

"There is bot two myles from Inverloghie, the church of Kilmalee, in Loghyeld. In an-cient tymes there was ane church builded upon ane hill, which was above this church, which doeth now stand in this toune; and ancient men doeth say, that there was a battell foughten on ane litle hill not the tenth part of a myle from this church, be certaine men which they did not know what they were. And long tyme thereafter, certaine herds of that toune, and of the next toune, called Unnatt, both wenches and youthes, did on a tyme conveen with others on that hill; and the day being somewhat cold, did gather the bones of the dead men that were slayne long tyme before in that place, and did make a fire to warm them. At last they did all remove from the fire, except one maid or wench, which was verie cold, and she did remaine there for a space. She being quyet-lie her alone, without anie other companie, took up her cloaths above her knees, or thereby to warm her; a wind did come and caste the ashes upon her, and she was conceived of ane man-chyld. Severall tymes thereafter she was verie sick, and at last she was knowne to be with chyld. And then her parents did ask at her the matter heiroff, which the wench could not weel answer which way to satisfie them. At last she resolved them with ane answer. As fortune fell upon her concerning this marvellous miracle, the chyld being borne, his name was called *Gilli-Doir-Maghrevollich*, that is to say, the *Black Child, Son to the Bones.* So called, his grandfather sent him to school, and so he was a good schollar, and godlie. He did build this church which doeth now stand in Lochyeld, called Kilmalee." — MACFAR-LANE, *ut supra,* ii. 188.

NOTE 25.

Yet ne'er again to braid her hair
The Virgin snood did Alice wear. — P. 143.

The *snood*, or riband, with which a Scottish lass braided her hair, had an emblematical signification, and applied to her maiden character. It was exchanged for the *curch*, *toy*, or coif, when she passed, by marriage, into the matron state. But if the damsel was so unfortunate as to lose pretensions to the name of maiden without gaining a right to that of matron, she was neither permitted to use the snood, nor advanced to the graver dignity of the curch. In old Scottish songs there occur many sly allusions to such misfortune; as in the old words to the popular tune of "Ower the muir amang the heather."

"Down amang the broom, the broom,
    Down amang the broom, my dearie,
The lassie lost her silken snood,
    That gard her greet till she was wearie."

NOTE 26.

The fatal Ben-Shie's boding scream. —
P. 144.

Most great families in the Highlands were supposed to have a tutelar, or rather a domestic spirit, attached to them, who took an interest in their prosperity, and intimated, by its wailings, any approaching disaster. A superstition of the same kind is, I believe, universally received by the inferior ranks of the native Irish.

NOTE 27.

Sounds, too, had come in midnight blast
Of charging steeds, careering fast
Along Benharrow's shingly side,
Where mortal horsemen ne'er might ride.
— P. 144.

A presage of the kind alluded to in the text is still believed to announce death to the ancient Highland family of M'Lean of Lochbuy. The spirit of an ancestor slain in battle is heard to gallop along a stony bank, and then to ride thrice around the family residence, ringing his fairy bridle, and thus intimating the approaching calamity.

NOTE 28.

—the dun deer's hide
On fleeter foot was never tied. — P. 145.

The present *brogue* of the Highlanders is made of half-dried leather, with holes to admit and let out the water; for walking the moors dry-shod is a matter altogether out of the question. The ancient buskin was still ruder, being made of undressed deer's hide, with the hair outwards; a circumstance which procured the Highlanders the well-known epithet of *Redshanks*.

NOTE 29.

The dismal coronach. — P. 146.

The *coronach* of the Highlanders, like the *ululatus* of the Romans, and the *ululoo* of the Irish, was a wild expression of lamentation, poured forth by the mourners over the body of a departed friend. When the words of it were articulate, they expressed the praises of the deceased, and the loss the clan would sustain by his death.

NOTE 30.

Not faster o'er thy heathery braes,
Balquidder, speeds the midnight blaze. —
P. 148.

It may be necessary to inform the southern reader, that the heath on the Scottish moorlands is often set fire to, that the sheep may have the advantage of the young herbage produced in room of the tough old heather plants. This custom (execrated by sportsmen) produces occasionally the most beautiful nocturnal appearances, similar almost to the discharge of a volcano. This simile is not new to poetry. The charge of a warrior, in the fine ballad of Hardyknute, is said to be " like fire to heather set."

NOTE 31.

——By many a bard, in Celtic tongue,
Has Coir-nan-Uriskin been sung. — P. 149.

This is a very steep and most romantic hollow in the mountain of Benvenue, overhanging the southeastern extremity of Loch Katrine. It is surrounded with stupendous rocks, and overshadowed with birch-trees, mingled with oaks, the spontaneous production of the mountain, even where its cliffs appear denuded of soil.

NOTE 32.

The Taghairm call'd ; by which, afar,
Our sires foresaw the events of war. —
P. 151.

The Highlanders, like all rude people, had various superstitious modes of inquiring into futurity. One of the most noted was the *Taghairm*, mentioned in the text. A person was wrapped up in the skin of a newly slain bullock, and deposited beside a waterfall, or at the bottom of a precipice, or in some other strange, wild, and unusual situation, where the scenery around him suggested nothing but subjects of horror. In this situation, he revolved in his mind the question proposed; and whatever was impressed upon him by his exalted imagination, passed for the inspiration of the disembodied spirits who haunt the desolate recesses.

NOTE 33.

——that huge cliff, whose ample verge
Tradition calls the Hero's Targe. — P. 152.

There is a rock so named in the Forest of Glenfinlas, by which a tumultuary cataract takes its course. This wild place is said in former times to have afforded refuge to an outlaw, who was supplied with provisions by a woman, who lowered them down from the brink of the precipice above. His water he procured for himself, by letting down a flagon tied to a string, into the black pool beneath the fall.

NOTE 34.

Which spills the foremost foeman's life,
That party conquers in the strife. — P. 152.

Though this be in the text described as a response of the Taghairm, or Oracle of the

Hide, it was of itself an augury frequently attended to. The fate of the battle was often anticipated in the imagination of the combatants, by observing which party first shed blood. It is said that the Highlanders under Montrose were so deeply imbued with this notion, that, on the morning of the battle of Tippermoor, they murdered a defenceless herdsman, whom they found in the fields, merely to secure an advantage of so much consequence to their party.

NOTE 35.

Why sounds yon stroke on beech and oak,
Our moonlight circle's screen?
Or who comes here to chase the deer,
Beloved of our Elfin Queen? — P. 154.

Fairies, if not positively malevolent, are capricious, and easily offended. They are, like other proprietors of the forest, peculiarly jealous of their rights of *vert* and *venison*. This jealousy was also an attribute of the northern *Duergar*, or dwarfs; to many of whose distinctions the fairies seem to have succeeded, if, indeed, they are not the same class of beings.

NOTE 36.

—— *who may dare on wold to wear*
The fairies' fatal green? — P. 154.

As the *Daoine Shi'*, or Men of Peace, wore green habits, they were supposed to take offence when any mortals ventured to assume their favorite color. Indeed, from some reason which has been, perhaps, originally a general superstition, *green* is held in Scotland to be unlucky to particular tribes and counties. The Caithness men, who hold this belief, allege as a reason, that their bands wore that color when they were cut off at the battle of Flodden; and for the same reason they avoid crossing the Ord on a Monday, being the day of the week on which their ill-omened array set forth. Green is also disliked by those of the name of Ogilvy; but more especially it is held fatal to the whole clan of Grahame. It is remembered of an aged gentleman of that name, that when his horse fell in a fox-chase, he accounted for it at once by observing, that the whipcord attached to his lash was of this unlucky color.

NOTE 37.

For thou wert christen'd man. — P. 154.

The elves were supposed greatly to envy the privileges acquired by Christian initiation, and they gave to those mortals who had fallen into their power a certain precedence, founded upon this advantageous distinction.

Tamlane, in the old ballad, describes his own rank in the fairy procession : —

> " For I ride on a milk-white steed,
> And aye nearest the town;
> Because I was a christen'd knight,
> They gave me that renown."

NOTE 38.

Who ever reck'd, where, how, or when,
The prowling fox was trapp'd or slain? —
P. 159.

St. John actually used this illustration when engaged in confuting the plea of law proposed for the unfortunate Earl of Strafford : " It was true we gave laws to hares and deer, because they are beasts of chase ; but it was never accounted either cruelty or foul play to knock foxes or wolves on the head as they can be found, because they are beasts of prey. In a word, the law and humanity were alike : the one being more fallacious, and the other more barbarous, than in any age had been vented in such an authority." — CLARENDON'S *History of the Rebellion.* Oxford, 1702, fol. vol. p. 183.

NOTE 39.

—— *his Highland cheer,*
The harden'd flesh of mountain deer. —
P. 159.

The Scottish Highlanders in former times, had a concise mode of cooking their venison, or rather of dispensing with cooking it, which appears greatly to have surprised the French whom chance made acquainted with it. The Vidame of Charters, when a hostage in England, during the reign of Edward VI., was permitted to travel into Scotland, and penetrated as far as to the remote Highlands (*au fin fond des Sauvages*). After a great hunting party, at which a most wonderful quantity of game was destroyed, he saw these *Scottish Savages* devour a part of their venison raw, without any further preparation than compressing it between two batons of wood, so as to force out the blood and render it extremely hard. This they reckoned a great delicacy ; and when the Vidame partook of it, his compliance with their taste rendered him extremely popular.

NOTE 40.

Not then claim'd sovereignty his due,
While Albany, with feeble hand,
Held borrow'd truncheon of command. —
P. 161.

There is scarcely a more disorderly period in Scottish history than that which succeeded the battle of Flodden, and occupied the mi nority of James V. Feuds of ancient standing broke out like old wounds, and every quarrel among the independent nobility, which occurred daily, and almost hourly, gave rise to fresh bloodshed.

NOTE 41.

——*I only meant*
To show the reed on which you leant,
Deeming this path you might pursue
Without a pass from Roderick Dhu.——

P. 163.

This incident, like some other passages in the poem, illustrative of the character of the ancient Gael, is not imaginary, but borrowed from fact. The Highlanders, with the inconsistency of most nations in the same state, were alternately capable of great exertions of generosity, and of cruel revenge and perfidy.

NOTE 42.

On Bochastle the mouldering lines,
Where Rome, the Empress of the world,
Of yore her eagle-wings unfurl'd.— P. 163.

The torrent which discharges itself from Loch Vennachar, the lowest and eastmost of the three lakes which form the scenery adjoining to the Trosachs, sweeps through a flat and extensive moor, called Bochastle. Upon a small eminence, called the *Dun* of Bochastle, and indeed on the plain itself, are some intrenchments, which have been thought Roman. There is, adjacent to Callender, a sweet villa, the residence of Captain Fairfoul, entitled the Roman Camp.

NOTE 43.

See, here, all vantageless I stand,
Arm'd, like thyself, with single brand.—

P. 163.

The duellists of former times did not always stand upon those punctilios respecting equality of arms, which are now judged essential to fair combat. It is true, that in former combats in the lists, the parties were, by the judges of the field, put as nearly as possible in the same circumstances. But in private duel it was often otherwise.

NOTE 44.

Ill fared it then with Roderick Dhu,
That on the field his targe he threw,
For train'd abroad his arms to wield,
Fitz-James's blade was sword and shield.—

P. 164.

A round target of light wood, covered with strong leather, and studded with brass or iron, was a necessary part of a Highlander's equipment. In charging regular troops, they received the thrust of the bayonet in this buckler, twisted it aside, and used the broadsword against the encumbered soldier. In the civil war of 1745, most of the front rank of the clans were thus armed; and Captain Grose informs us, that, in 1747, the privates of the 42d regiment, then in Flanders, were, for the most part, permitted to carry targets.—*Military Antiquities,* vol. i., p. 164.

NOTE 45.

The burghers hold their sports to-day.—

P. 166.

Every burgh of Scotland, of the least note, but more especially the considerable towns, had their solemn *play,* or festival, when feats of archery were exhibited, and prizes distributed to those who excelled in wrestling, hurling the bar, and the other gymnastic exercises of the period. Stirling, a usual place of royal residence, was not likely to be deficient in pomp upon such occasions, especially since James V. was very partial to them. His ready participation in these popular amusements was one cause of his acquiring the title of King of the Commons, or *Rex Plebeiorum,* as Lesley has latinized it. The usual prize to the best shooter was a silver arrow. Such a one is preserved at Selkirk and at Peebles.

NOTE 46.

Robin Hood. — P. 167.

The exhibition of this renowned outlaw and his band was a favorite frolic at such festivals as we are describing. This sporting, in which kings did not disdain to be actors, was prohibited in Scotland upon the Reformation, by a statute, of the 6th Parliament of Queen Mary, c. 61, A.D. 1555, which ordered, under heavy penalties, that, "na manner of person be chosen Robert Hude, nor Little John, Abbot of Unreason, Queen of May, nor otherwise." But in 1561, the "rascal multitude," says John Knox, "were stirred up to make a Robin Hude, whilk enormity was of many years left and damned by statute and act of Parliament; yet would they not be forbidden." Accordingly, they raised a very serious tumult, and at length made prisoners the magistrates who endeavored to suppress it, and would not release them till they extorted a formal promise that no one should be punished for his share of the disturbance. It would seem, from the complaints of the General Assembly of the Kirk, that these profane festivities were continued down to 1592.

NOTE 47.

Prize of the wrestling match, the King
To Douglas gave a golden ring. — P. 167.

The usual prize of a wrestling was a ram
and a ring, but the animal would have embarrassed my story. Thus, in the Cokes
Tale of Gamelyn, ascbribed to Chaucer : —

> "There happed to be there beside,
>   Tryed a wrestling;
> And therefore there was y-setten
>   A ram and als a ring."

NOTE 48.

These drew not for their fields the sword
Like tenants of a feudal lord,
Nor own'd the patriarchal claim
Of Chieftain in their leader's name;
Adventurers they. — P. 170.

The Scottish armies consisted chiefly of
the nobility and barons, with their vassals,
who held lands under them, for military service by themselves and their tenants. The
patriarchal influence exercised by the heads
of clans in the Highlands and borders was of
a different nature, and sometimes at vari-
ance with feudal principles. It flowed from
the *Patria Potestas*, exercised by the chieftain as representing the original father of
the whole name, and was often obeyed in
contradiction to the feudal superior.

NOTE 49.

Thou now hast glee-maiden and harp!
Get thee an ape, and trudge the land,
The leader of a juggler band. — P. 171.

The jongleurs, or jugglers, used to call in
the aid of various assistants, to render these
performances as captivating as possible. The
glee-maiden was a necessary attendant. Her
duty was tumbling and dancing ; and therefore the Anglo-Saxon version of St. Mark's
Gospel states Herodias to have vaulted or
tumbled before King Herod.

NOTE 50.

That stirring air that peals on high,
O'er Dermid's race our victory, —
Strike it. — P. 174.

There are several instances, at least in
tradition, of persons so much attached to
particular tunes as to require to hear them
on their deathbed. Such an anecdote is
mentioned by the late Mr. Riddel of Glen-
riddel, in his collection of Border tunes,
respecting an air called the " Dandling of
the Bairns," for which a certain Gallovidian
laird is said to have evinced this strong
mark of partiality. It is popularly told of

a famous freebooter, that he composed the
tune known by the name of Macpherson's
Rant, while under sentence of death, and
played it at the gallows-tree. Some spirited
words have been adapted to it by Burns. A
similar story is recorded of a Welsh bard,
who composed and played on his deathbed
the air called *Dafyddy Garregg Wen.*

NOTE 51.

Battle of Beal' an Duine. — P. 174.

A skirmish actually took place at a pass
thus called in the Trosachs, and closed with
the remarkable incident mentioned in the
text. It was greatly posterior in date to the
reign of James V.

NOTE 52.

And Snowdoun's Knight is Scotland's King.
— P. 178.

This discovery will probably remind the
reader of the beautiful Arabian tale of *Il
Bondocani.* Yet the incident is not borrowed from that elegant story, but from
Scottish tradition. James V., of whom we
are treating, was a monarch whose good
and benevolent intentions often rendered
his romantic freaks venial, if not respectable, since from his anxious attention to the
interests of the lower and most oppressed
class of his subjects he was, as we have seen,
popularly termed the *King of the Commons.*
For the purpose of seeing that justice was
regularly administered, and frequently from
the less justifiable motive of gallantry, he
used to traverse the vicinage of his several
palaces in various disguises. The two excellent comic songs, entitled, "The Gaber-
lunzie Man," and "We'll gae nae mair a
roving," are said to have been founded upon
the success of his amorous adventures when
travelling in the disguise of a beggar. The
latter is perhaps the best comic ballad in any
language.

NOTE 53.

——Stirling's tower
Of yore the name of Snowdoun claims. —
P. 178.

William of Worcester, who wrote about
the middle of the fifteenth century, calls
Stirling Castle Snowdoun. Sir David
Lindesay bestows the same epithet upon it
in his complaint of the Papingo : —

> "Adieu, fair Snawdoun, with thy towers high,
>   Thy chapel-royal, park, and table round;
> May, June, and July, would I dwell in thee,
>   Were I a man, to hear the birdis sound,
> Whilk doth againe thy royal rock rebound."

THE VISION OF DON RODERICK.

NOTE I.

And Cattraeth's glens with voice of tri-
umph rung,
And mystic Merlin harp'd, and gray-hair'd
Llywarch sung! — P. 181.

THIS locality may startle those readers who do not recollect that much of the ancient poetry preserved in Wales refers less to the history of the Principality to which that name is now limited, than to events which happened in the north-west of England and south-west of Scotland, where the Britons for a long time made a stand against the Saxons. The battle of Cattraeth, lamented by the celebrated Aneurin, is supposed, by the learned Dr. Leyden, to have been fought on the skirts of Ettrick Forest. It is known to the English reader by the paraphrase of Gray, beginning, —

" Had I but the torrent's might,
With headlong rage and wild affright," etc.

But it is not so generally known that the champions mourned in this beautiful dirge were the British inhabitants of Edinburgh, who were cut off by the Saxons of Deiria or Northumberland, about the latter part of the sixth century.

Llywarch, the celebrated bard and monarch, was prince of Argood in Cumberland; and his youthful exploits were performed upon the Border. Merlin Wyllt, or the Savage, bore the name of Caledonia, and hence is appropriated to Scotland. The spot in which he was buried, near Drumelzier on the Tweed, is still shown. See Pennycuick's " Description of Tweeddale," Edinburgh, 1715, vol. iv., p. 26.

NOTE 2.

Minchmore's haunted spring. — P. 182.

A belief in the existence and nocturnal revels of the fairies still lingers among the vulgar in Selkirkshire. A copious fountain upon the ridge of Minchmore, called the Cheesewell, is supposed to be sacred to these fanciful spirits, and it was customary to propitiate them by throwing in something upon passing it. A pin was the usual oblation; and the ceremony is still sometimes practised, though rather in jest than earnest.

NOTE 3.

the rude villager, his labor done,
In verse spontaneous chants some favor'd
name. — P. 182.

The flexibility of the Italian and Spanish languages, and perhaps the liveliness of their genius, renders these countries distinguished for the talent of improvisation, which is found even among the lowest of the people. It is mentioned by Baretti and other travellers.

NOTE 4.

kindling at the deeds of Græme. —
P. 182.

Over a name sacred for ages to heroic verse, a poet may be allowed to exercise some power. I have used the freedom, here and elsewhere, to alter the orthography of the name of my gallant countryman, in order to apprise the Southern reader of its legitimate sound ; — Grahame being, on the other side of the Tweed, usually pronounced as a dissyllable.

NOTE 5.

What ! will Don Roderick here till morn-
ing stay,
To wear in shrift and prayer the night
away?
And are his hours in such dull penance
past,
For fair Florinda's plunder'd charms to
pay? — P. 184.

Almost all the Spanish historians, as well as the voice of tradition, ascribe the invasion of the Moors to the forcible violation committed by Roderick upon Florinda, called by the Moors, Caba or Cava. She was the daughter of Count Julian, one of the Gothic monarch's principal lieutenants, who, when the crime was perpetrated, was engaged in the defence of Ceuta against the Moors. In his indignation at the ingratitude of his sovereign, and the dishonor of his daughter, Count Julian forgot the duties of a Christian and a patriot, and, forming an alliance with Musa, then the Caliph's lieutenant in Africa, he countenanced the invasion of Spain by a body of Saracens and Africans, commanded by the celebrated Tarik; the issue of which was the defeat and death of Roderick, and the occupation of almost the whole peninsula by the Moors. Voltaire, in his General History, expresses his doubts of this popular story, and Gibbon gives him some countenance; but the universal tradition is quite sufficient for the purposes of poetry. The Spaniards, in detestation of Florinda's memory, are said by Cervantes, never to bestow that name on any human female, reserving it for their dogs.

Note 6.

The Tecbir war-cry and the Lelie's yell. —
　　　　　　　　　　　　P. 186.

The Tecbir (derived from the words *Alla acbar*, God is most mighty), was the original war-cry of the Saracens. It is celebrated by Hughes in the Siege of Damascus : —

" We heard the Tecbir ; so these Arabs call
　Their shout of onset, when, with loud appeal,
　They challenge Heaven, as if demanding
　　　conquest."

The *Lelie*, well known to the Christians during the crusades, is the shout of *Alla illa Alla*, the Mahometan confession of faith. It is twice used in poetry by my friend Mr. W. Stewart Rose, in the romance of Partenopex, and in the Crusade of St. Lewis.

Note 7.

By Heaven, the Moors prevail ! the Christians yield ! —
*　Their coward leader gives for flight the sign !*
The sceptred craven mounts to quit the field —
Is not yon steed Orelia ? — Yes, 'tis mine !
　　　　　　　　　　　　— P. 187.

Count Julian, the father of the injured Florinda, with the connivance and assistance of Oppas, Archbishop of Toledo, invited, in 713, the Saracens into Spain. A considerable army arrived under the command of Tarik, or Tarif, who bequeathed the well-known name of Gibraltar (*Gibel al Tarik*, or the mountain of Tarik) to the place of his landing. He was joined by Count Julian, ravaged Andalusia, and took Seville. In 714 they returned with a still greater force, and Roderick marched into Andalusia at the head of a great army, to give them battle. The field was chosen near Xeres. [Roderick was defeated, and fled from the field of battle on his favorite steed Orelia. This famous and matchless charger was found riderless on the banks of the river Guadelite, with the King's upper garment, buskins, etc. It was supposed that in trying to swim the river he was drowned. But wild legions as to his after fate long prevailed in Spain. — See SOUTHEY's " Don Roderick." — ED.]

Note 8.

When for the light bolero ready stand,
*　The mozo blithe, with gay muchacha met.*
　　　　　　　　　　　　— P. 189.

The bolero is a very light and active dance, much practised by the Spaniards, in which castanets are always used. *Mozo* and *muchacha* are equivalent to our phrase of lad and lass.

Note 9.

While trumpets rang, and heralds cried,
*　" Castile ! " —* P. 191.

The heralds, at the coronation of a Spanish monarch, proclaim his name three times, and repeat three times the word *Castilla, Castilla, Castilla ;* which, with all other ceremonies, was carefully copied in the mock inauguration of Joseph Bonaparte.

Note 10.

High blazed the war, and long, and far, and wide. — P. 192.

Those who were disposed to believe that mere virtue and energy are able of themselves to work forth the salvation of an oppressed people, surprised in a moment of confidence, deprived of their officers, armies, and fortresses, who had every means of resistance to seek in the very moment when they were to be made use of, and whom the numerous treasons among the higher orders deprived of confidence in their natural leaders, — those who entertained this enthusiastic but delusive opinion may be pardoned for expressing their disappointment at the protracted warfare in the Peninsula. There are, however, another class of persons, who, having themselves the highest dread or veneration, or something allied to both, for the power of the modern Attila, will nevertheless give the heroical Spaniards little or no credit for the long, stubborn, and unsubdued resistance of three years to a power before whom their former well-prepared, well-armed, and numerous adversaries fell in the course of as many months. While these gentlemen plead for deference to Bonaparte, and crave

" Respect for his great place, and bid the devil
　Be duly honor'd for his burning throne,"

it may not be altogether unreasonable to claim some modification of censure upon those who have been long and to a great extent successfully resisting this great enemy of mankind. That the energy of Spain has not uniformly been directed by conduct equal to its vigor, has been too obvious ; that her armies, under their complicated disadvantages, have shared the fate of such as were defeated after taking the field with every possible advantage of arms and discipline, is surely not to be wondered at. But that a nation, under the circumstances of repeated discomfiture, internal treason, and the mismanagement incident to a temporary and hastily adopted government, should have wasted, by its stubborn, uniform, and prolonged resistance, myriads after myriads of those soldiers who had overrun the world — and some of its provinces should, like Galicia, after being abandoned by their allies, and overrun by their enemies, have recovered their freedom by their own unassisted exertions; that others, like Catalonia, undismayed by the treason which betrayed some fortresses, and the force which subdued others, should not only have continued their resistance, but have attained over their victorious enemy a superiority, which is even now enabling them to besiege and retake the places of strength which had been wrested from them, is a tale hitherto untold in the revolutionary war.

NOTE 11.

They won not Zaragoza, but her children's bloody tomb. — P. 192.

The interesting account of Mr. Vaughan * has made most readers acquainted with the first siege of Zaragoza. The last and fatal siege of that gallant and devoted city is detailed with great eloquence and precision in the " Edinburgh Annual Register " for 1809, — a work in which the affairs of Spain have been treated of with attention corresponding to their deep interest, and to the peculiar sources of information open to the historian. The following are a few brief extracts from this splendid historical narrative : —

" A breach was soon made in the mud walls, and then, as in the former siege, the war was carried on in the streets and houses; but the French had been taught by experience, that in this species of warfare the Zaragozans derived a superiority from the feeling and principle which inspired them and the cause for which they fought. The only means of conquering Zaragoza was to destroy it house by house, and street by street; and upon this system of destruction they proceeded. Three companies of miners, and eight companies of sappers, carried on this subterraneous war; the Spaniards, it is said, attempted to oppose them by countermines; these were operations to which they were wholly unused, and, according to the French statement, their miners were every day discovered and suffocated. Meantime, the bombardment was incessantly kept up. ' Within the last forty-eight hours,' said Palafox in a letter to his friend General Doyle, ' 6,000 shells have been thrown in. Two-thirds of the town are in ruins; but we shall perish under the ruins of the remaining third rather than surrender.' In the course of the siege, above 17,000 bombs were thrown at the town; the stock of powder with which Zaragoza

* " Narrative of the Siege of Zaragoza," by Richard Charles Vaughan, 1809. Mr. Vaughan was afterwards British Minister at Washington."

had been stored was exhausted; they had none at last but what they manufactured day by day; and no other cannon-balls than those which were shot into the town, and which they collected and fired back upon the enemy."

In the midst of these horrors and privations, the pestilence broke out in Zaragoza. To various causes, enumerated by the annalist, he adds, " scantiness of food, crowded quarters, unusual exertion of body, anxiety of mind, and the impossibility of recruiting their exhausted strength by needful rest, in a city which was almost incessantly bombarded, and where every hour their sleep was broken by the tremendous explosion of mines. There was now no respite, either by day or night, for this devoted city; even the natural order of light and darkness was destroyed in Zaragoza; by day it was involved in a red sulphureous atmosphere of smoke, which hid the face of heaven; by night the fire of cannons and mortars, and the flames of burning houses, kept it in a state of terrific illumination.

" When once the pestilence had begun, it was impossible to check its progress, or confine it to one quarter of the city. Hospitals were immediately established, — there were above thirty of them; as soon as one was destroyed by the bombardment, the patients were removed to another, and thus the infection was carried to every part of Zaragoza. Famine aggravated the evil; the city had probably not been sufficiently provided at the commencement of the siege, and of the provisions which it contained, much was destroyed in the daily ruin which the mines and bombs had effected. Had the Zaragozans and their garrison proceeded according to military rules, they would have surrendered before the end of January; their batteries had then been demolished, there were open breaches in many parts of their weak walls, and the enemy were already within the city. On the 30th, above sixty houses were blown up, and the French obtained possession of the monasteries of the Augustines and Las Monicas, which adjoined each other, two of the last defensible places left. The enemy forced their way into the church; every column, every chapel, every altar, became a point of defence, which was repeatedly attacked, taken, and retaken; the pavement was covered with blood, the aisles and body of the church strewed with the dead, who were trampled under foot by the combatants. In the midst of this conflict, the roof, shattered by repeated bombs, fell in; the few who were not crushed, after a short pause, which this tremendous shock, and their own unexpected escape, occasioned, renewed the fight with rekindled fury; fresh parties of the enemy poured in; monks and citizens, and soldiers, came to the defence, and the contest was continued upon the ruins, and the bodies of the dead and the dying." ——

Yet, seventeen days after sustaining these extremities, did the heroic inhabitants of Zaragoza continue their defence; nor did they then surrender until their despair had extracted from the French generals a capitulation, more honorable than has been granted to fortresses of the first order.

Who shall venture to refuse the Zaragozans the eulogium conferred upon them by the eloquence of Wordsworth! — " Most gloriously have the citizens of Zaragoza proved that the true army of Spain, in a contest of this nature, is the whole people. The same city has also exemplified a melancholy, yea, a dismal truth, yet consolatory and full of joy, — that when a people are called suddenly to fight for their liberty, and are sorely pressed upon, their best field of battle is the floors upon which their children have played; the chambers where the family of each man has slept (his own or his neighbors'), upon or under the roofs by which they have been sheltered; in the gardens of their recreation; in the street, or in the market-place; before the altars of their temples, and among their congregated dwellings, blazing or uprooted.

" The government of Spain must never forget Zaragoza for a moment. Nothing is wanting to produce the same effects everywhere, but a leading mind, such as that city was blessed with. In the latter contest this has been proved; for Zaragoza contained, at that time, bodies of men from almost all parts of Spain. The narrative of those two sieges should be the manual of every Spaniard. He may add it to the ancient stories of Numantia and Saguntum; let him sleep upon the book as a pillow, and, if he be a devout adherent to the religion of his country, let him wear it in his bosom for his crucifix to rest upon." — WORDSWORTH *on the Convention of Cintra.*

NOTE 12.

The Vault of Destiny. — P. 195.

Before finally dismissing the enchanted cavern of Don Roderick, it may be noticed, that the legend occurs in one of Calderon's plays, entitled *La Virgin del Sagrario.* The scene opens with the noise of the chase, and Recisundo, a predecessor of Roderick upon the Gothic throne, enters pursuing a stag.

The animal assumes the form of a man, and defies the King to enter the cave, which forms the bottom of the scene, and engage with him in single combat. The King accepts the challenge, and they engage accordingly, but without advantage on either side, which induces the Genie to inform Recisundo, that he is not the monarch for whom the adventure of the enchanted cavern is reserved, and he proceeds to predict the downfall of the Gothic monarchy, and of the Christian religion, which shall attend the discovery of its mysteries. Recisundo, appalled by these prophecies, orders the cavern to be secured by a gate and bolts of iron. In the second part of the same play, we are informed that Don Roderick had removed the barrier, and transgressed the prohibition of his ancestor, and had been apprised by the prodigies which he discovered of the approaching ruin of his kingdom.

NOTE 13.

While downward on the land his legions press,
Before them it was rich with vine and flock,
And smiled like Eden in her summer dress; —
Behind their wasteful march a reeking wilderness. — P. 195.

I have ventured to apply to the movements of the French army that sublime passage in the prophecies of Joel, which seems applicable to them in more respects than that I have adopted in the text. One would think their ravages, their military appointments, the terror which they spread among invaded nations, their military discipline, their arts of political intrigue and deceit, were distinctly pointed out in the following verses of Scripture:—

" 2. A day of darkness and of gloominesse, a day of clouds and of thick darkness, as the morning spread upon the mountains; a great people and a strong, there hath not been ever the like, neither shall be any more after it, even to the yeares of many generations. 3. A fire devoureth before them, and behind them a flame burneth; the land is as the Garden of Eden before them, and behinde them a desolate wilderness, yea and nothing shall escape them. 4. The appearance of them is as the appearance of horses; and as horsemen, so shall they runne. 5. Like the noise of chariots on the tops of mountains, shall they leap, like the noise of a flame of fire that devoureth the stubble, as a strong people set in battel array. 6. Before their face shall the people be much pained: all faces shall gather blacknesse. 7. They shall run like mighty men, they shall climb the wall like men of warre, and they shall march every one in his wayes, and they shall not break their ranks. 8. Neither shall one thrust another, they shall walk every one in his path: and when they fall upon the sword, they shall not be wounded. 9. They shall run to and fro in the citie; they shall run upon the wall, they shall climbe up upon the houses: they shall enter in at the windows like a thief. 10. The earth shall quake before them, the heavens shall tremble, the sunne and the moon shall be dark, and the starres shall withdraw their shining."

In verse 20th, also, which announces the retreat of the northern army, described in such dreadful colors, into "a land barren and desolate," and the dishonor with which God afflicted them for having "magnified themselves to do great things," there are particulars not inapplicable to the retreat of Massena; — Divine Providence having, in all ages, attached disgrace as the natural punishment of cruelty and presumption.

NOTE 14.

The rudest sentinel, in Britain born,
  With horror paused to view the havoc done,
Gave his poor crust to feed some wretch forlorn. — P. 196.

Even the unexampled gallantry of the British army in the campaign of 1810-11, although they never fought but to conquer, will do them less honor in history than their humanity, attentive to soften to the utmost of their power the horrors which war, in its mildest aspect, must always inflict upon the defenceless inhabitants of the country in which it is waged, and which, on this occasion, were tenfold augmented by the barbarous cruelties of the French. Soup-kitchens were established by subscription among the officers, wherever the troops were quartered for any length of time. The commissaries contributed the heads, feet, etc., of the cattle slaughtered for the soldiery: rice, vegetables, and bread, where it could be had, were purchased by the officers. Fifty or sixty starving peasants were daily fed at one of these regimental establishments, and carried home the relics to their famished households. The emaciated wretches, who could not crawl from weakness, were speedily employed in pruning their vines. While pursuing Massena, the soldiers evinced the same spirit of humanity, and in many instances, when reduced themselves to short allowance, from having outmarched their supplies, they shared their pittance with the starving in-

habitants, who had ventured back to view the ruins of their habitations, burnt by the retreating enemy, and to bury the bodies of their relations whom they had butchered. Is it possible to know such facts without feeling a sort of confidence, that those who so well deserve victory are most likely to attain it? — It is not the least of Lord Wellington's military merits, that the slightest disposition towards marauding meets immediate punishment. Independently of all moral obligation, the army which is most orderly in a friendly country, has always proved most formidable to an armed enemy.

NOTE 15.

Vain-glorious fugitive! — P. 196.

The French conducted this memorable retreat with much of the *fanfaronnade* proper to their country, by which they attempt to impose upon others, and perhaps on themselves, a belief that they are triumphing in the very moment of their discomfiture. On the 30th March, 1811, their rear-guard was overtaken near Pega by the British cavalry. Being well posted, and conceiving themselves safe from infantry (who were indeed many miles in the rear), and from artillery, they indulged themselves in parading their bands of music, and actually performed "God save the King." Their minstrelsy was, however, deranged by the undesired accompaniment of the British horse-artillery, on whose part in the concert they had not calculated. The surprise was sudden, and the rout complete; for the artillery and cavalry did execution upon them for about four miles, pursuing at the gallop as often as they got beyond the range of the guns.

NOTE 16.

Vainly thy squadrons hide Assuava's plain,
And front the flying thunders as they roar,
  With frantic charge and tenfold odds, in vain! — P. 196

In the severe action of Fuentes de Honoro, upon 5th May, 1811, the grand mass of the French cavalry attacked the right of the British position, covered by two guns of the horse-artillery, and two squadrons of cavalry. After suffering considerably from the fire of the guns, which annoyed them in every attempt at formation, the enemy turned their wrath entirely towards them, distributed brandy among their troopers, and advanced to carry the field-pieces with the desperation of drunken fury. They were in nowise checked by the heavy loss which they sustained in this daring attempt, but closed, and fairly mingled with the British cavalry, to whom they bore the proportion of ten to one. Captain Ramsay (let me be permitted to name a gallant countryman), who commanded the two guns, dismissed them at the gallop, and putting himself at the head of the mounted artillerymen, ordered them to fall upon the French, sabre-in-hand. This very unexpected conversion of artillerymen into dragoons, contributed greatly to the defeat of the enemy, already disconcerted by the reception they had met from the two British squadrons: and the appearance of some small re-enforcements, notwithstanding the immense disproportion of force, put them to absolute rout. A colonel or major of their cavalry, and many prisoners (almost all intoxicated), remained in our possession. Those who consider for a moment the difference of the services, and how much an artilleryman is necessarily and naturally led to identify his own safety and utility with abiding by the tremendous implement of war, to the exercise of which he is chiefly, if not exclusively, trained, will know how to estimate the presence of mind which commanded so bold a manœuvre, and the steadiness and confidence with which it was executed.

NOTE 17.

And what avails thee that, for Cameron slain,
Wild from his plaided ranks the yell was given.
— P. 196.

The gallant Colonel Cameron was wounded mortally during the desperate contest in the streets of the village called Fuentes de Honoro. He fell at the head of his native Highlanders, the 71st and 79th, who raised a dreadful shriek of grief and rage. They charged with irresistible fury, the finest body of French Grenadiers ever seen, being a part of Bonaparte's selected guard. The officer who led the French, a man remarkable for stature and symmetry, was killed on the spot. The Frenchman who stepped out of his rank to take aim at Colonel Cameron was also bayoneted, pierced with a thousand wounds, and almost torn to pieces by the furious Highlanders, who, under the command of Colonel Cadogan, bore the enemy out of the contested ground at the point of the bayonet. Massena pays my countrymen a singular compliment in his account of the attack and defence of this village, in which he says the British lost many officers, *and Scotch.*

NOTE 18.

O who shall grudge him Albuera's bays,
Who brought a race regenerate to the field
Roused them to emulate their fathers' praise,
Temper'd their headlong rage, their courage steel'd,
And raised fair Lusitania's fallen shield.
— P. 197.

Nothing during the war of Portugal seems, to a distinct observer, more deserving of praise, than the self-devotion of Field-Marshal Beresford, who was contented to undertake all the hazard of obloquy which might have been founded upon any miscarriage in the highly important experiment of training the Portuguese troops to an improved state of discipline. In exposing his military reputation to the censure of imprudence from the most moderate, and all manner of unutterable calumnies from the ignorant and malignant, he placed at stake the dearest pledge which a military man had to offer; and nothing but the deepest conviction of the high and essential importance attached to success can be supposed an adequate motive. How great the chance of miscarriage was supposed, may be estimated from the general opinion of officers of unquestioned talents and experience, possessed of every opportunity of information; how completely the experiment has succeeded, and how much the spirit and patriotism of our ancient allies had been underrated, is evident, not only from those victories in which they have borne a distinguished share, but from the liberal and highly honorable manner in which these opinions have been retracted. The success of this plan, with all its important consequences, we owe to the indefatigable exertions of Field-Marshal Beresford.

NOTE 19.

—— a race renown'd of old,
Whose war-cry oft has waked the battle-
swell.
* * * * * * *
——the conquering shout of Græme.—P. 198.

This stanza alludes to the various achievements of the warlike family of Græme, or Grahame. They are said, by tradition, to have descended from the Scottish chief, under whose command his countrymen stormed the wall built by the Emperor Severus between the Friths of Forth and Clyde, the fragments of which are still popularly called Græme's Dyke. Sir John the Græme, "the hardy, wight, and wise," is well known as the friend of Sir William Wallace. Alderne, Kilsythe, and Tibbermuir, were scenes of the victories of the heroic Marquis of Montrose. The pass of Killycrankie is famous for the action between King William's forces and the Highlanders in 1689,

" Where glad Dundee in faint huzzas expired."

It is seldom that one line can number so many heroes, and yet more rare when it can appeal to the glory of a living descendant in support of its ancient renown.

The allusions to the private history and character of General Grahame may be illustrated by referring to the eloquent and affecting speech of Mr. Sheridan, upon the vote of thanks to the Victors of Barosa.

ROKEBY.

Note 1.

On Barnard's towers, and Tees's stream, etc.
— P. 203.

" BARNARD'S CASTLE," saith old Leland, " standeth stately upon Tees." It is founded upon a very high bank, and its ruins impend over the river, including within the area a circuit of six acres and upwards. This once magnificent fortress derives its name from its founder, Barnard Baliol, the ancestor of the short and unfortunate dynasty of that name, which succeeded to the Scottish throne under the patronage of Edward I. and Edward III. Baliol's Tower, afterwards mentioned in the poem, is a round tower of great size, situated at the western extremity of the building. It bears marks of great antiquity, and was remarkable for the curious construction of its vaulted roof, which has been lately greatly injured by the operations of some persons, to whom the tower has been leased for the purpose of making patent shot! The prospect from the top of Baliol's Tower commands a rich and magnificent view of the wooded valley of the Tees.

Barnard Castle often changed masters during the Middle Ages. From John Baliol, the first King of Scotland of that family, it went by forfeiture to Edward I. It was held by the Beauchamps of Warwick, the Staffords of Buckingham, the Bishops of Durham, and by the Crown. Richard III. is said to have enlarged and strengthened its fortifications, and to have made it for some time his principal residence, for the purpose of bridling and suppressing the Lancastrian faction in the northern counties. The earls of West Moreland received it probably through marriage, and after the suppression of the rebellion in the twelfth year of Queen Elizabeth's reign, it reverted to the Crown, and was sold or leased to Car, Earl of Somerset, the guilty and unhappy favorite of James I. It was afterwards granted to Sir Henry Vane the Elder, and came finally into possession of the Earls of Darlington.

Note 2.

—— *no human ear,*
Unsharpen'd by revenge and fear,
Could e'er distinguish horse's clank. —
P. 204.

I have had occasion to remark, in real life, the effect of keen and fervent anxiety in giving acuteness to the organs of sense. My gifted friend, Miss Joanna Baillie, whose dramatic works display such intimate acquaintance with the operations of human passion, has not omitted this remarkable circumstance : —

" *De Montfort* (*off his guard*). 'Tis Rezenvelt: I heard his well-known foot,
From the first staircase mounting step by step.
   Freb. How quick an ear thou hast for distant sound!
I heard him not.
     (*De Montfort looks embarrassed, and is silent.*)"

Note 3.

The morion's plumes his visage hide,
And the buff-coat, an ample fold,
Mantles his form's gigantic mould. — P. 204.

The use of complete suits of armor was fallen into disuse during the Civil War, though they were still worn by leaders of rank and importance. "In the reign of King James I.," says our military antiquary, " no great alterations were made in the article of defensive armor, except that the buff-coat, or jerkin, which was originally worn under the cuirass, now became frequently a substitute for it, it having been found that a good buff leather would of itself resist the stroke of a sword ; this, however, only occasionally took place among the light-armed cavalry and infantry, complete suits of armor being still used among the heavy-horse. Buff-coats continued to be worn by the city-trained bands till within the memory of persons now living, so that defensive armor may, in some measure, be said to have terminated in the same materials with which it began ; that is, the skins of animals, or

leather." — GROSE'S *Military Antiquities.*
Lond., 1801, 4to, vol. ii., p. 323.

Of the buff-coats, which were worn over
the corslets, several are yet preserved; and
Captain Grose has given an engraving of one
which was used in the time of Charles I. by
Sir Francis Rhodes, Bart., of Balbrough-
Hall, Derbyshire. They were usually lined
with silk or linen, secured before by buttons,
or by a lace, and often richly decorated with
gold or silver embroidery.

NOTE 4.

On his dark face a scorching clime,
And toil, had done the work of time.

* * * * * *

Death had he seen by sudden blow,
By wasting plague, by tortures slow. —
P. 204.

In this character, I have attempted to
sketch one of those West Indian adventurers,
who, during the course of the seventeenth
century, were popularly known by the name,
of Buccaneers. The successes of the English
in the predatory incursions upon Spanish
America, during the reign of Elizabeth, had
never been forgotten; and, from that period
downward, the exploits of Drake and Raleigh
were imitated, upon a smaller scale indeed,
but with equally desperate valor, by small
bands of pirates, gathered from all nations,
but chiefly French and English. The en-
grossing policy of the Spaniards tended
greatly to increase the number of these freebooters, from whom their commerce and
colonies suffered, in the issue, dreadful
calamity.

The Windward Islands, which the Spanish
did not deem worthy their own occupation,
had been gradually settled by adventurers
of the French and English nations. After
Frederic of Toledo, acting under orders from
the Court of Madrid, had cruelly destroyed
these colonies, in 1630, the planters, rendered
desperate by persecution, began under the well-
known name of Buccaneers, or Bucaniers,
a retaliation both by piracy on sea and predatory descents on Spanish territory. See
either *Raynal,* or " The History of the
Bucaniers."

NOTE 5.

—— *On Marston heath*
Met, front to front, the ranks of death. —
P. 205.

The well known and desperate battle of
Long-Marston Moor, which terminated so
unfortunately for the cause of Charles, commenced under very different auspices. Prince
Rupert had marched with an army of

20,000 men for the relief of York, then besieged by Sir Thomas Fairfax, at the head
of the Parliamentary army, and the Earl of
Leven, with the Scottish auxiliary forces.
In this he is so completely succeeded, that
he compelled the besiegers to retreat to Mars
ton Moor, a large open plain, about eight
miles distant from the city. Thither they
were followed by the Prince, who had now
united to his army the garrison of York,
probably not less than ten thousand men
strong, under the gallant Marquis (then
Earl) of Newcastle. Whitelocke has recorded, with much impartiality, the following particulars of this eventful day : — " The
right wing of the Parliament was commanded
by Sir Thomas Fairfax, and consisted of all
his horse, and three regiments of the Scots
horse; the left wing was commanded by the
Earl of Manchester and Colonel Cromwell.
One body of their foot was commanded by
Lord Fairfax, and consisted of his foot, and
two brigades of the Scots foot for reserve;
and the main body of the rest of the foot was
commanded by General Leven.

" The right wing of the Prince's army was
commanded by the Earl of Newcastle; the
left wing by the Prince himself; and the
main body by General Goring, Sir Charles
Lucas, and Major-General Porter. Thus
were both sides drawn up into battalia.

" July 3d, 1644. In this posture both
armies faced each other, and about seven
o'clock in the morning the fight began between them. The Prince, with his left wing,
fell on the Parliament's right wing, routed
them, and pursued them a great way; the
like did General Goring, Lucas, and Porter,
upon the Parliament's main body. The
three generals, giving all for lost, hasted
out of the field, and many of their soldiers
fled, and threw down their arms; the King's
forces too eagerly following them, the victory, now almost achieved by them, was
again snatched out of their hands. For
Colonel Cromwell, with the brave regiment
of his countrymen, and Sir Thomas Fairfax,
having rallied some of his horse, fell upon
the Prince's right wing, where the Earl of
Newcastle was, and routed them; and the
rest of their companions rallying, they fell
altogether upon the divided bodies of Rupert
and Goring, and totally dispersed them, and
obtained a complete victory, after three
hours' fight.

" From this battle and the pursuit, some
reckon were buried 7,000 Englishmen; all
agree that above 3,000 of the Prince's men
were slain in the battle, besides those in the
chase, and 3,000 prisoners taken, many of
their chief officers, twenty-five pieces of ord-

nance, forty-seven colors, 10,000 arms, two wagons of carabins and pistols, 130 barrels of powder, and all their bag and baggage." WHITELOCKE'S *Memoirs*, fol. p. 89. Lond., 1682.

NOTE 6.

Monckton and Mitton told the news,
How troops of Roundheads choked the Ouse,
And many a bonny Scot aghast,
Spurring his palfrey northward, past,
Cursing the day when zeal or meed
First lured their Lesley o'er the Tweed. —
P. 208.

Monckton and Mitton are villages near the river Ouse, and not very distant from the field of battle. The particulars of the action were violently disputed at the time ; but the following extract, from the Manuscript History of the Baronial House of Somerville, is decisive as to the flight of the Scottish general, the Earl of Leven. The details are given by the author of the history on the authority of his father, then the representative of the family. This curious manuscript was published by consent of Lord Somerville.

"The order of this great battell, wherin both armies was neer of ane equall number, consisting, to the best calculatione, neer to threescore thousand men upon both sydes, I shall not take upon me to discryve ; albeit, from the draughts then taken upon the place, and information I receaved from this gentleman, who being then a volunteer, as having no command, had opportunitie and libertie to ryde from the one wing of the armie to the other, to view all ther several squadrons of horse and battallions of foot, how formed, and in what manner drawn up, with every other circumstance relating to the fight, and that both as to the King's armies and that of the Parliament's, amongst whom, untill the engadgment, he went from statione to statione to observe ther order and forme ; but that the descriptione of this battell, with the various success on both sides at the beginning, with the loss of the royal armie, and the sad effects that followed that misfortune as to his Majestie's interest, hes been so often done already by English authors, little to our commendatione, how justly I shall not dispute, seing the truth is, as our principall generall fled that night neer fourtie mylles from the place of the fight, that part of the armie where he commanded being totallie routed ; but it is as true, that much of the victorie is attributed to the good conduct of David Lesselie, lievetennent-generall of our horse. Cromwell himself, that minione of fortune, but

the rod of God's wrath, to punish eftirward three rebellious nations, disdained not to take orders from him, albeit then in the same qualitie of command for the Parliament, as being lievetennent-generall to the Earl of Manchester's horse, whom, with the assistance of the Scots' horse, haveing routed the Prince's right wing, as he had done that of the Parliament's. These two commanders of the horse upon that wing wisely restrained the great bodies of their horse from persuing these brocken troups, but, wheelling to the left-hand, falls in upon the naked flanks of the Prince's main battallion of foot, carying them doune with great violence ; nether mett they with any great resistance untill they came to the Marques of Newcastle his battallione of White Coats, who, first peppering them soundly with ther shott, when they came to charge, stoutly boor them up with their picks that they could not enter to break them. Here the Parliament's horse of that wing receaved ther greatest losse, and a stop for sometyme putt to ther hoped-for victorie ; and that only by the stout resistance of this gallant battallione, which consisted neer of four thousand foot, until at length a Scots regiment of dragouns, commanded by Collonell Frizeall, with other two, was brought to open them upon some hand, which at length they did, when all the ammunitione was spent. Having refused quarters, every man fell in the same order and ranke wherein he had foughten.

" Be this execution was done, the Prince returned from the persuite of the right wing of the Parliament's horse, which he had beatten and followed too farre, to the losse of the battell, which certanely, in all men's opinions, he might have caryed if he had not been too violent upon the pursuite ; which gave his enemies upon the left-hand opportunitie to disperse and cut doune his infantrie, who, having cleared the field of all the standing bodies of foot, wer now, with many [foot soldiers] of their oune, standing ready to receave the charge of his allmost spent horses, if he should attempt it ; which the Prince observeing, and seeing all lost, he retreated to Yorke with two thousand horse. Notwithstanding of this, ther was that night such a consternatione in the Parliament armies, that it's believed by most of those that wer there present, that if the Prince, haveing so great a body of horse inteire, had made ane onfall that night, or the ensueing morning be-tyme, he had carryed the victorie out of ther hands ; for it's certane, by the morning's light, he had rallyed a body of ten thousand men, whereof ther was neer three thousand gallant horse. These, with the assistance of the toune and garrisoune of Yorke, might have done much to have recovered the victory, for the losse of this battell in effect lost the King and his interest in the three kingdomes; his Majestie never being able eftir this to make head in the north, but lost his garrisons every day.

"As for Generall Lesselie, in the beginning of this flight haveing that part of the army quite brocken, whare he had placed himself, by the valour of the Prince, he imagined, and was confermed by the opinione of others then upon the place with him, that the battell was irrecoverably lost, seeing they wer fleeing upon all hands; theirfore they humblie intreated his excellence to reteir and wait his better fortune, which, without farder advyseing, he did; and never drew bridle untill he came the lenth of Leads, having ridden all that night with a cloak of *drap de berrie* about him, belonging to this gentleman of whom I write, then in his retinue, with many other officers of good qualitie. It was neer twelve the next day befor they had the certanety who was master of the field, when at length ther arryves ane express, sent by David Lesselie, to acquaint the general they had obtained a most glorious victory, and that the Prince, with his brocken troupes, was fled from Yorke. This intelligence was somewhat amazeing to these gentlemen that had been eye-witnesses to the disorder of the armie before ther retearing, and had then accompanyed the General in his flight; who, being much wearyed that evening of the battell with ordering of his armie, and now quite spent with his long journey in the night, had casten himselfe doune upon a bed to rest, when this gentleman comeing quyetly into his chamber, he awoke, and hastily cryes out, 'Lievetennent-collonell, what newes?'—'All is safe, may it please your Excellence; the Parliament's armie hes obtained a great victory;' and then delyvers the letter. The Generall, upon the hearing of this, knocked upon his breast, and sayes, 'I would to God I had dyed upon the place!' and then opens the letter, which, in a few lines, gave ane account of the victory, and in the close pressed his speedy returne to the armie, which he did the next day, being accompanyed some mylles back by this gentleman, who then takes his leave of him, and receaved at parting many expressions of kyndenesse, with promises that he would never be unmyndful of his care and respect towards him; and in the end he entreats him to present his service to all his friends and acquaintances in Scotland. Thereftir the Generall sets forward in his journey for the armie, as this

gentleman did for . . . in order to his transportatione for Scotland, where he arryved sex dayes eftir the fight of Mestoune Muir, and gave the first true account and descriptione of that great battell, wherein the Covenanters then gloryed soe much, that they impiously boasted the Lord had now signally appeared for his cause and people; it being ordinary for them, dureing the whole time of this warre, to attribute the greatness of their success to the goodness and justice of ther cause, untill Divine Justice trysted them with some crosse dispensatione, and then you might have heard this language from them, 'That it pleases the Lord to give his oune the heaviest end of the tree to bear, that the saints and the people of God must still be sufferers while they are here away, that the malignant party was God's rod to punish them for ther unthankfullnesse, which in the end he will cast into the fire;' with a thousand other expressions and Scripture citations, prophanely and blasphemously uttered by them to palliate ther villainie and rebellion."— *Memoires of the Somervilles.* — Edin., 1815.

NOTE 7.

With his barb'd horse, fresh tidings say,
Stout Cromwell has redeem'd the day. —
P. 208.

Cromwell, with his regiment of cuirassiers, had a principal share in turning the fate of the day at Marston Moor; which was equally matter of triumph to the Independents, and of grief and heart-burning to the Presbyterians and to the Scottish.

NOTE 8.

Do not my native dales prolong,
Of Percy Rede, the tragic song,
Train'd forward to his bloody fall
By Girsonfield, that treacherous Hall? —
P. 208.

In a poem entitled, "The Lay of the Reedwater Minstrel," Newcastle, 1809, this tale, with many others peculiar to the valley of the Reed, is commemorated:— "The particulars of the traditional story of Parcy Reed of Troughend, and the Halls of Girsonfield, the author had from a descendant of the family of Reed. From his account, it appears that Percival Reed, Esquire, a keeper of Reedsdale, was betrayed by the Halls (hence denominated the false-hearted Halls) to a band of moss-troopers of the name of Crosier, who slew him at Batinghope, near the source of the Reed.

"The Halls were, after the murder of Parcy Reed, held in such universal abhor rence and contempt by the inhabitants of Reedsdale, for their cowardly and treacherous behaviour, that they were obliged to leave the country." In another passage, we are informed that the ghost of the injured Borderer is supposed to haunt the banks of a brook called the Pringle. These Reeds of Troughend were a very ancient family, as may be conjectured from their deriving their surname from the river on which they had their mansion. An epitaph on one of their tombs affirms that the family held their lands of Troughend, which are situated on the Reed, nearly opposite to Otterburn, for the incredible space of nine hundred years.

NOTE 9.

And near the spot that gave me name,
The moated mound of Risingham,
Where Reed upon her margin sees
Sweet Woodburne's cottages and trees,
Some ancient sculptor's art has shown
An outlaw's image on the stone. — P. 208.

Risingham, upon the river Reed, near the beautiful hamlet of Woodburne, is an ancient Roman station, formerly called Habitancum. Camden says, that in his time the popular account bore, that it had been the abode of a deity, or giant, called Magon; and appeals, in support of this tradition, as well as to the etymology of Risingham, or Reisenham, which signifies, in German, the habitation of the giants, to two Roman altars taken out of the river, inscribed, DEO MOGONTI CADENORUM. About half a mile distant from Risingham, upon an eminence covered with scattered birch-trees, and fragments of rock, there is cut upon a large rock, in *alto relievo*, a remarkable figure, called Robin of Risingham, or Robin of Reedsdale. It presents a hunter, with his bow raised in one hand, and in the other what seems to be a hare. There is a quiver at the back of the figure, and he is dressed in a long coat, or kirtle, coming down to the knees, and meeting close, with a girdle bound round him. Dr. Horseley, who saw all monuments of antiquity with Roman eyes, inclines to think this figure a Roman archer: and certainly the bow is rather of the ancient size, than of that which was so formidable in the hand of the English archers of the Middle Ages. But the rudeness of the whole figure prevents our founding strongly upon mere inaccuracy of proportion. The popular tradition is, that it represents a giant, whose brother resided at Woodburn, and he himself at Risingham. It adds, that they subsisted by hunting, and that one of them, finding the game become too scarce to support them, poisoned his companion, in whose memory the monument was engraved. What strange and tragic circumstance may be concealed under this legend, or whether it is utterly apocryphal, it is now impossible to discover.

NOTE 10.

——Do thou revere
The statutes of the Buccaneer. — P. 208.

The "statutes of the Buccaneers" were, in reality, more equitable than could have been expected from the state of society under which they had been formed. They chiefly related, as may readily be conjectured, to the distribution and the inheritance of their plunder.

When the expedition was completed, the fund of prize-money acquired was thrown together, each party taking his oath that he had retained or concealed no part of the common stock. If any one transgressed in this important particular, the punishment was, his being set ashore on some desert key or island, to shift for himself as he could. The owners of the vessel had then their share assigned for the expenses of the outfit. These were generally old pirates, settled at Tobago, Jamaica, St. Domingo, or some other French or English settlement. The surgeon's and carpenter's salaries, with the price of provisions and ammunition, were also defrayed. Then followed the compensation due to the maimed and wounded, rated according to the damage they had sustained; as six hundred pieces of eight, or six slaves, for the loss of an arm or leg, and so in proportion.

"After this act of justice and humanity, the remainder of the booty was divided into as many shares as there were Buccaneers. The commander could only lay claim to a single share, as the rest; but they complimented him with two or three in proportion as he had acquitted himself to their satisfaction. When the vessel was not the property of the whole company, the person who had fitted it out, and furnished it with necessary arms and ammunition, was entitled to a third of all the prizes. Favor had never any influence in the division of the booty, for every share was determined by lot. Instances of such rigid justice as this are not easily met with, and they extended even to the dead. Their share was given to the man who was known to be their companion when alive, and therefore their heir. If the person who had been killed had no intimate, his part was sent to his relations, when they were known. If there were no friends nor relations, it was distributed in charity to the poor and to churches, which were to pray for the person in whose name these benefactions were given, the fruits of inhuman, but necessary piratical plunder." — RAYNAL'S *History of European Settlements in the East and West Indies, by Justamond.* Lond., 1776, 8vo, iii. p. 41.

NOTE 11.
The course of Tees. — P. 212.

The view from Barnard Castle commands the rich and magnificent valley of Tees. Immediately adjacent to the river, the banks are very thickly wooded ; at a little distance they are more open and cultivated ; but, being interspersed with hedge-rows, and with isolated trees of great size and age, they still retain the richness of woodland scenery. The river itself flows in a deep trench of solid rock, chiefly limestone and marble. The finest view of its romantic course is from a handsome modern-built bridge over the Tees, by the late Mr. Morritt of Rokeby. In Leland's time, the marble quarries seem to have been of some value. " Hard under the cliff by Egleston, is found on eche side of Tese very fair marble, wont to be taken up booth by marbelers of Barnardes Castelle and of Egleston, and partly to have been wrought by them, and partly sold onwrought to others." — *Itinerary.* Oxford, 1768, 8vo, p. 88.

NOTE 12.
Egliston's gray ruins. — P. 212.

The ruins of this abbey, or priory (for Tanner calls it the former, and Leland the latter), are beautifully situated upon the angle formed by a little dell called Thorsgill, at its junction with the Tees. A good part of the religious house is still in some degree habitable, but the church is in ruins. Egliston was dedicated to St. Mary and St. John the Baptist, and is supposed to have been founded by Ralph de Multon about the end of Henry the Second's reign. There were formerly the tombs of Rokeby, Bowes, and Fitz-Hugh.

NOTE 13.
—— *the mound,*
Raised by that Legion long renown'd,
Whose votive shrine asserts their claim,
Of pious, faithful, conquering fame. —
P. 212.

Close behind the George Inn at Greta Bridge, there is a well-preserved Roman encampment, surrounded with a triple ditch, lying between the river Greta and a brook called the Tutta. The four entrances are easily to be discerned. Very many Roman altars and monuments have been found in the vicinity, most of which are preserved at Rokeby by my friend Mr. Morritt. Among others is a small votive altar with the inscription LEG. VI. VIC. P.F.F., which has been rendered *Legio sexta, victrix, pia, fortis, fidelis.* (" The victorious Sixth Legion, full of reverence, gallantry, fidelity.")

NOTE 14.
Rokeby's turrets high. — P. 212.

This ancient manor long gave name to a family by whom it is said to have been possessed from the Conquest downward, and who are at different times distinguished in history. It was the Baron of Rokeby who finally defeated the insurrection of the Earl of Northumberland, *tempore Hen. IV.* See *Holinshed's Chronicles,* London, 1808, iii., p. 45. The Rokeby, or Rokesby, family continued to be distinguished until the great Civil War, when, having embraced the cause of Charles I., they suffered severely by fines and confiscations. The estate then passed from its ancient possessors to the family of the Robinsons, from whom it was purchased by the father of my valued friend, the present proprietor.

NOTE 15.
A stern and lone, yet lovely road,
As e'er the foot of Minstrel trode. — P. 213.

What follows is an attempt to describe the romantic glen, or rather ravine, through which the Greta finds a passage between Rokeby and Mortham ; the former situated upon the left bank of Greta, the latter on the right bank, about half a mile nearer to its junction with the Tees.

NOTE 16.
—— *tell*
*   *   *   *   *
How whistle rash bids tempests roar. —
P. 214.

That this is a general superstition is well known to all who have been on ship-board, or who have conversed with seamen. The most formidable whistler that I remember to have met with was the apparition of a certain Mrs. Leakey, who, about 1636, resided, we are told, at Mynehead, in Somerset, where her only son drove a considerable trade between that port and Waterford, and was owner of several vessels. This old gentlewoman was of a social disposition, and so acceptable to her friends, that they used to say to her and to each other, it were a pity such an excellent, good-natured old lady should die ; to which she was wont to reply, that whatever pleasure they might find in her company just now, they would not greatly like to see or converse with her after death, which nevertheless she was apt to think might happen. Accordingly, after her death and funeral, she began to appear to various persons by night and by noon-day, in her own house, in the town and fields, at sea and upon shore. So far had she departed from her former urbanity, that she is recorded to have kicked a doctor of medicine for his impolite negligence in omit-ting to hand her over a stile. It was also her humor to appear upon the quay, and call for a boat. But especially as soon as any of her son's ships approached the har-bor, "this ghost would appear in the same garb and likeness as when she was alive, and, standing at the mainmast, would blow with a whistle, and though it were never so great a calm, yet immediately there would arise a most dreadful storm, that would break, wreck, and drown ship and goods." When she had thus proceeded until her son had neither cash to freight a vessel, nor could have procured men to sail in it, she began to attack the persons of his family, and actu-ally strangled their only child in the cradle. The rest of her story, showing how the spectre looked over the shoulder of her daughter-in-law, while dressing her hair in the looking-glass, and how Mrs. Leakey the younger took courage to address her, and how the beldam despatched her to an Irish prelate, famous for his crimes and misfor-tunes, to exhort him to repentance, and to apprise him that otherwise he would be hanged, and how the bishop was satisfied with replying that if he was born to be hanged, he should not be drowned; — all these, with many more particulars, may be found at the end of one of John Dunton's publications, called Athenianism, London, 1710, where the tale is engrossed under the title of The Apparition Evidence.

NOTE 17.

Of Erick's cap and Elmo's light. — P. 214.

"This Ericus, King of Sweden, in his time was held second to none in the magi-cal art; and he was so familiar with the evil spirits, which he exceedingly adored, that which way soever he turned his cap, the wind would presently blow that way. From this occasion he was called Windy Cap; and many men belived that Regnerus, King of Denmark, by the conduct of this Ericus, who was his nephew, did happily extend his piracy into the most remote parts of the earth, and conquered many countries and fenced cities by his cunning, and at last was his coadjutor; that by the consent of the nobles, he should be chosen King of Sweden, which continued a long time with him very happily, until he died of old age."— OLAUS MAGNUS, *History of the Goths, Swedes, and Vandals,* Lond., 1658, fol. p. 45.

NOTE 18.

The Demon frigate. — P. 214.

This is an allusion to a well-known nauti-cal superstition concerning a fantastic vessel, called by sailors the Flying Dutchman, and supposed to be seen about the latitude of the Cape of Good Hope. She is distin-guished from earthly vessels by bearing a press of sail when all others are unable, from stress of weather, to show an inch of canvas. The cause of her wandering is not altogether certain; but the general account is, that she was originally a vessel loaded with great wealth, on board of which some horrid act of murder and piracy had been committed; that the plague broke out among the wicked crew who had perpetrated the crime, and that they sailed in vain from port to port, offering, as the price of shel-ter, the whole of their ill-gotten wealth; that they were excluded from every harbor, for fear of the contagion which was devour-ing them; and that, as a punishment of their crimes, the apparition of the ship still continues to haunt those seas in which the catastrophe took place, and is considered by the mariners as the worst of all possible omens.

NOTE 19.

—— by some desert isle or key. — P. 214.

What contributed much to the security of the Buccaneers about the Windward Islands, was the great number of little islets, called in that country *keys.* These are small sandy patches, appearing just above the surface of the ocean, covered only with a few bushes and weeds, but sometimes affording springs of water, and, in general, much frequented by turtle. Such little uninhabited spots afforded the pirates good harbors, either for refitting or for the purpose of ambush; they were occasionally the hiding-place of their treasure, and often afforded a shelter to themselves. As many of the atrocities which they practised on their prisoners were committed in such spots, there are some of these keys which even now have an indifferent reputation among seamen, and where they are with difficulty prevailed on to remain ashore at night, on account of the visionary terrors incident to places which have been thus contaminated.

Note 20.

Before the gate of Mortham stood. — P. 215.

The castle of Mortham, which Leland terms " Mr. Rokesby's Place, *in ripa citer.,* scant a quarter of a mile from Greta Bridge, and not a quarter of a mile beneath into Tees," is a picturesque tower, surrounded by buildings of different ages, now converted into a farm-house and offices. The battlements of the tower itself are singularly elegant, the architect having broken them at regular intervals into different heights; while those at the corners of the tower project into octangular turrets. They are also from space to space covered with stones laid across them, as in modern embrasures, the whole forming an uncommon and beautiful effect. The surrounding buildings are of a less happy form, being pointed into high and steep roofs. A wall with embrasures encloses the southern front, where a low portal arch affords an entry to what was the castle court. At some distance is most happily placed between the stems of two magnificent elms the monument alluded to in the text. It is said to have been brought from the ruins of Eglistone Priory, and, from the armory with which it is richly carved, appears to have been a tomb of the Fitz-Hughs.

The situation of Mortham is eminently beautiful, occupying a high bank, at the bottom of which the Greta winds out of the dark, narrow, and romantic dell, which the text has attempted to describe, and flows onward through a more open valley to meet the Tees about a quarter of a mile from the castle. Mortham is surrounded by old trees, happily and widely grouped with Mr. Morritt's new plantations.

Note 21.

There dig, and tomb your precious heap,
And bid the dead your treasure keep. —
            P. 216.

If time did not permit the Buccaneers to lavish away their plunder in their usual debaucheries, they were wont to hide it, with many superstitious solemnities, in the desert islands and keys which they frequented, and where much treasure, whose lawless owners perished without reclaiming it, is still supposed to be concealed. The most cruel of mankind are often the most superstitious; and these pirates are said to have had recourse to a horrid ritual, in order to secure an unearthly guardian to their treasures. They killed a negro or Spaniard, and buried him with the treasure, believing that his spirit would haunt the spot, and terrify away all intruders. I cannot produce any other authority on which this custom is ascribed to them than that of maritime tradition, which is, however, amply sufficient for the purposes of poetry.

Note 22.

The power   *   *   *
*   *   *   *   *
That unsubdued and lurking lies
To take the felon by surprise,
And force him, as by magic spell,
In his despite his guilt to tell. — P. 216.

All who are conversant with the administration of criminal justice, must remember many occasions in which malefactors appear to have conducted themselves with a species of infatuation, either by making unnecessary confidences respecting their guilt, or by sudden and involuntary allusions to circumstances by which it could not fail to be exposed. A remarkable instance occurred in the celebrated case of Eugene Aram. A skeleton being found near Knaresborough, was supposed, by the persons who gathered around the spot, to be the remains of one Clarke, who had disappeared some years bebefore, under circumstances leading to a suspicion of his having been murdered. One Houseman, who had mingled in the crowd, suddenly said, while looking at the skeleton, and hearing the opinion which was buzzed around, " That is no more Dan Clarke's bone than it is mine!" — a sentiment expressed so positively, and with such peculiarity of manner, as to lead all who heard him to infer that he must necessarily know where the real body had been interred. Accordingly, being apprehended, he confessed having assisted Eugene Aram to murder Clarke, and to hide his body in Saint Robert's Cave. It happened to the author himself, while conversing with a person accused of an atrocious crime, for the purpose of rendering him professional assistance upon his trial, to hear the prisoner, after the most solemn and reiterated protestations that he was guiltless, suddenly, and, as it were, involuntarily, in the course of communications, make such an admission as was altogether incompatible with innocence.

Note 23.

—— *Brackenbury's dismal tower.* — P. 218.

This tower has been already mentioned. It is situated near the north-eastern extremity of the wall which encloses Barnard Castle, and is traditionally said to have been the prison. By an odd coincidence, it bears a name which we naturally connect with im prisonment, from its being that of Sir Robert Brackenbury, lieutenant of the Tower of London under Edward IV. and Richard III.

NOTE 24.

Nobles and knights, so proud of late,
Must fine for freedom and estate.

    **   *   *   **

Right heavy shall his ransom be,
Unless that maid compound with thee. —
              P. 219.

After the battle of Marston Moor, the Earl of Newcastle retired beyond sea in disgust, and many of his followers laid down their arms, and made the best composition they could with the Committees of Parliament. Fines were imposed upon them in proportion to their estates and degrees of delinquency, and these fines were often bestowed upon such persons as had deserved well of the Commons. In some circumstances it happened, that the oppressed cavaliers were fain to form family alliances with some powerful person among the triumphant party.

NOTE 25.

The Indian, prowling for his prey,
Who hears the settlers track his way.—
              P. 219.

The patience, abstinence, and ingenuity exerted by the North-American Indians, when in pursuit of plunder or vengeance, is the most distinguished feature in their character; and the activity and address which they display in their retreat is equally surprising.

NOTE 26.

In Redesdale his youth had heard,
Each art her wily dalesmen dared,
When Rooken-edge, and Redswair high,
To bugle rung and bloodhound's cry. —
              P. 219.

" What manner of cattle-stealers they are that inhabit these valleys in the marches of both kingdoms, John Lesley, a Scotche man himself, and Bishop of Ross, will inform you. They sally out of their own borders in the night, in troops, through unfrequented by-ways and many intricate windings. All the day-time they refresh themselves and their horses in lurking holes they had pitched upon before, till they arrive in the dark in those places they have a design upon. As soon as they have seized upon the booty, they, in like manner, return home in the night, through blind ways, and fetching many a compass. The more skilful any captain is to pass through those wild deserts, crooked turnings, and deep precipices, in the

thickest mists, his reputation is the greater, and he is looked upon as a man of an excellent head. And they are so very cunning, that they seldom have their booty taken from them, unless sometimes when, by the help of blood-hounds following them exactly upon the track, they may chance to fall into the hands of their adversaries. When being taken, they have so much persuasive eloquence, and so many smooth, insinuating words at command, that if they do not move their judges, nay, and even their adversaries (notwithstanding the severity of their natures), to have mercy, yet they incite them to admiration and compassion."— CAMDEN's *Britannia*.

The inhabitants of the valleys of Tyne and Reed were, in ancient times, so inordinately addicted to these depredations, that in 1564, the Incorporated Merchant-adventurers of Newcastle made a law that none born in these districts should be admitted apprentice. The inhabitants are stated to be so generally addicted to rapine, that no faith should be reposed in those proceeding from " such lewde and wicked progenitors." This regulation continued to stand unrepealed until 1771. A beggar, in an old play, describes himself as " born in Redesdale, in Northumberland, and come of a wight-riding surname, called the Robsons, good honest men and true, *saving a little shifting for their living, God help them!* "—a description which would have applied to most Borderers on both sides.

Reidswair, famed for a skirmish to which it gives name, [see Border Minstrelsy, vol. ii., p. 15,] is on the very edge of the Carter Fell, which divides England from Scotland. The Rooken is a place upon Reedwater. Bertram, being described as a native of these dales, where the habits of hostile depredation long survived the union of the crowns, may have been, in some degree, prepared by education for the exercise of a similar trade in the wars of the Buccaneers.

NOTE 27.

Hiding his face, lest foemen spy
The sparkle of his swarthy eye. — P. 220.

After one of the recent battles, in which the Irish rebels were defeated, one of their most active leaders was found in a bog, in which he was immersed up to the shoulders, while his head was concealed by an impending ledge of turf. Being detected and seized, notwithstanding his precaution, he became solicitous to know how his retreat had been discovered. " I caught," answered the Sutherland Highlander, by whom he was taken, "the sparkle of your eye." Those who are accustomed to mark hares upon their form usually discover them by the same circumstance. Sir Walter Scott continued to be fond of coursing hares long after he had laid aside all other field sports, and he used to say jocularly, that he had more pleasure in being considered an excellent *finder*, than in all his reputation as a *trouveur*.

NOTE 28.

Here stood a wretch, prepared to change His soul's redemption for revenge. — P. 221.

It is agreed by all the writers upon magic and witchcraft, that revenge was the most common motive for the pretended compact between Satan and his vassals.

NOTE 29.

Of my marauding on the clowns Of Calverley and Bradford downs. — P. 222.

The troops of the King, when they first took the field, were as well disciplined as could be expected from circumstances. But as the circumstances of Charles became less favorable, and his funds for regularly paying his forces decreased, habits of military license prevailed among them in greater excess. Lacy the player, who served his master during the Civil War, brought out, after the Restoration, a piece called The Old Troop, in which he seems to have commemorated some real incidents which occurred in his military career. The names of the officers of the Troop sufficiently express their habits. We have Fleaflint Plundermaster-General, Captain Ferret-farm, and Quartermaster Burn-drop. The officers of the Troop are in league with these worthies, and connive at their plundering the country for a suitable share in the booty. All this was undoubtedly drawn from the life, which Lacy had an opportunity to study. The moral of the whole is comprehended in a rebuke given to the lieutenant, whose disorders in the country are said to prejudice the King's cause more than his courage in the field could recompense. The piece is by no means void of farcical humor.

NOTE 30.

——Brignall's woods, and Scargill's wave, E'en now, o'er many a sister cave. — P. 222.

The banks of the Greta, below Rutherford Bridge, abound in seams of grayish slate, which are wrought in some places to a very great depth, under ground, thus forming artificial caverns, which, when the seam has been exhausted, are gradually hidden by the underwood which grows in profusion upon the romantic banks of the river. In times of public confusion, they might be well adapted to the purposes of banditti.

NOTE 31.

When Spain waged warfare with our land. — P. 224.

There was a short war with Spain in 1625–26, which will be found to agree pretty well with the chronology of the poem. But probably Bertram held an opinion very common among the maritime heroes of the age, that, "there was no peace beyond the Line." The Spanish *guarda-costas* were constantly employed in aggressions upon the trade and settlements of the English and French; and, by their own severities, gave room for the system of buccaneering, at first adopted in self-defence and retaliation, and afterwards persevered in from habit and thirst of plunder.

NOTE 32.

—— our comrades' strife. — P. 225.

The laws of the Buccaneers, and their successors the Pirates, however severe and equitable, were, like other laws, often set aside by the stronger party. Their quarrels about the division of the spoil fill their history, and they as frequently arose out of mere frolic, or the tyrannical humor of their chiefs. An anecdote of Teach (called Blackbeard), shows that their habitual indifference for human life extended to their companions, as well as their enemies and captives.

"One night, drinking in his cabin with Hands, the pilot, and another man, Blackbeard, without any provocation, privately draws out a small pair of pistols, and cocks them under the table, which being perceived by the man, he withdrew upon deck, leaving Hands, the pilot, and the captain together. When the pistols were ready, he blew out the candles, and, crossing his hands, discharged them at his company. Hands, the master, was shot through the knee, and lamed for life; the other pistol did no execution." — JOHNSON's *History of Pirates.* Lond., 1733, 8vo, vol. i., p. 38.

NOTE 33.

Song. — Adieu for evermore. — P. 225.

The last verse of this song is taken from the fragment of an old Scottish ballad, of which I only recollected two verses when the first edition of Rokeby was published. Mr. Thomas Sheridan kindly pointed out to me an entire copy of this beautiful song, which seems to express the fortunes of some followers of the Stuart family : —

" It was a' for our rightful king
   That we left fair Scotland's strand,
It was a' for our rightful king
   That we e'er saw Irish land,
               My dear,
   That we e'er saw Irish land.

" Now all is done that man can do,
   And all is done in vain !
My love ! my native land, adieu !
   For I must cross the main,
               My dear,
   For I must cross the main.

" He turned him round and right about,
   All on the Irish shore,
He gave his bridle-reins a shake,
   With, Adieu for evermore,
               My dear !
   Adieu for evermore !

" The soldier frae the war returns,
   And the merchant frae the main,
But I hae parted wi' my love,
   And ne'er to meet again,
               My dear,
   And ne'er to meet again.

" When day is gone and night is come,
   And a' are boun' to sleep,
I think on them that's far awa'
   The lee-lang night, and weep,
               My dear,
   The lee-lang night, and weep."

Note 34.

Rere-cross on Stanmore. — P. 227.

Rere-cross, Ree-cross, or Roi-cross ; that is, the cross of the King, is the border mark between England and Scotland.

This is a fragment of an old cross, with its pediment, surrounded by an intrenchment, upon the very summit of the waste ridge of Stanmore, near a small house of entertainment. The situation of the cross, and the pains taken to defend it, seem to indicate that it was intended for a landmark of importance.

Note 35.

Hast thou lodged our deer ? — P. 227.

The duty of the ranger, or pricker, was first to lodge or harbor the deer, i.e., to discover his retreat, and then to make his report to his prince or master.

Note 36.

When Denmark's raven soar'd on high,
Triumphant thro' Northumbrian sky,
Till, hovering near, her fatal croak
Bade Reged's Britons dread the yoke. —
                                    P. 228.

About the year of God 866, the Danes,

under their celebrated leaders Inguar (more properly Agnar) and Hubba, sons, it is said, of the still more celebrated Regnar Lodbrog, invaded Northumberland, bringing with them the magical standard, so often mentioned in poetry, called REAFEN, or Rumfan, from its bearing the figure of a raven : —

" Wrought by the sisters of the Danish king,
   Of furious Ivar in a midnight hour :
While the sick moon at their enchanted song
   Wrapt in pale tempest, labor'd thro' the clouds,
The demons of destruction then, they say,
   Were all abroad, and mixing with the woof
Their baleful power : The sisters ever sung,
   ' Shake, standard, shake this ruin on our
      foes.' "

              THOMSON *and* MALLET'S *Alfred.*

The Danes renewed and extended their incursions, and began to colonize, establishing a kind of capital at York, from which they spread their conquests and incursions in every direction. Stanmore, which divides the mountains of Westmoreland and Cumberland, was probably the boundary of the Danish kingdom in that direction. The district to the west, known in ancient British history by the name of Reged, had never been conquered by the Saxons, and continued to maintain a precarious independence until it was ceded to Malcolm, King of Scots, by William the Conqueror, probably on account of its similarity in language and manners to the neighboring British kingdom of Strath-Clyde.

Upon the extent and duration of the Danish sovereignty in Northumberland, the curious may consult the various authorities quoted in the *Gesta et Vestigia Danorum extra Daniam,* tom. ii. p. 40. The most powerful of their Northumbrian leaders seems to have been Ivar, called, from the extent of his conquests, *Widfam ;* that is, *The Strider.*

Note 37.

Beneath the shade the Northmen came,
Fix'd on each vale a Runic name. — P. 228.

The heathen Danes have left several traces of their religion in the upper part of Teesdale. Balder-garth, which derives its name from the unfortunate son of Odin, is a tract of waste land, on the very ridge of Stanmore ; and a brook, which falls into the Tees near Barnard Castle, is named after the same deity. A field upon the banks of the Tees is also termed Woden-Croft, from the supreme deity of the Edda.

Note 38.

Who has not heard how brave O'Neale
In English blood imbrued his steel? —P. 229.

The O'Neale here meant, for more than

one succeeded to the chieftainship during the reign of Elizabeth, was Hugh, the grandson of Con O'Neale, called Con Bacco, or the Lame. His father, Matthew O'Kelly, was illegitimate, and, being the son of a blacksmith's wife, was usually called Matthew the blacksmith. His father, nevertheless, destined his succession to him; and he was created, by Elizabeth, Baron of Dungannon. Upon the death of Con Bacco, this Matthew was slain by his brother. Hugh narrowly escaped the same fate, and was protected by the English. Shane O'Neale, his uncle, called Shane Dymas, was succeeded by Turlough Lynogh O'Neale; after whose death Hugh, having assumed the chieftainship, became nearly as formidable to the English as any by whom it had been possessed. He rebelled repeatedly, and as often made submissions, of which it was usually a condition that he should not any longer assume the title of O'Neale; in lieu of which he was created Earl of Tyrone. But this condition he never observed longer than until the pressure of superior force was withdrawn. His baffling the gallant Earl of Essex in the field, and over-reaching him in a treaty, was the induction to that nobleman's tragedy. Lord Mountjoy succeeded in finally subjugating O'Neale; but it was not till the succession of James, to whom he made personal submission, and was received with civility at court.

NOTE 39.

But chief arose his victor pride,
When that brave Marshal fought and
died.

—P. 229.

The chief victory which Tyrone obtained over the English was in a battle fought near Blackwater, while he besieged a fort garrisoned by the English, which commanded the passes into his country.

Tyrone is said to have entertained a personal animosity against the knight-marshal, Sir Henry Bagnal, whom he accused of detaining the letters which he sent to Queen Elizabeth, explanatory of his conduct, and offering terms of submission. The river, called by the English, Blackwater, is termed in Irish, Avon-Duff, which has the same signification. Both names are mentioned by Spenser in his "Marriage of the Thames and the Medway." But I understand that his verses relate not to the Blackwater of Ulster, but to a river of the same name in the south of Ireland:—

"Swift Avon-Duff, which of the Englishmen
Is called Blackwater."

NOTE 40.

The Tanist he to great O'Neale. — P. 229.

"*Eudox.* What is that which you call Tanist and Tanistry? These be names and terms never heard of nor known to us.

"*Iren.* It is a custom amongst all the Irish, that presently after the death of one of their chiefe lords or captaines, they doe presently assemble themselves to a place generally appointed and knowne unto them, to choose another in his stead, where they do nominate and elect, for the most part not the eldest sonne, nor any of the children of the lord deceased, but the next to him in blood, that is, the eldest and worthiest, as commonly the next brother unto him, if he have any, or the next cousin, or so forth, as any is elder in that kindred or sept; and then next to them doe they chose the next of the blood to be Tanist, who shall next succeed him in the said captainry, if he live thereunto.

"*Eudox.* Do they not use any ceremony in the election, for all barbarous nations are commonly great observers of ceremonies and superstitious rites?

"*Iren.* They use to place him that shall be their captaine upon a stone, always reserved to that purpose, and placed commonly upon a hill. In some of which I have seen formed and engraven a foot, which they say was the measure of their first captaine's foot; whereon hee standing, receives an oath to preserve all the ancient former customes of the countrey inviolable, and to deliver up the succession peaceably to his Tanist, and then hath a wand delivered unto him by some whose proper office that is; after which, descending from the stone, he turneth himself round, thrice forwards and thrice backwards.

"*Eudox.* But how is the Tanist chosen?

"*Iren.* They say he setteth but one foot upon the stone, and receiveth the like oath that the captaine did."— SPENSER's *View of the State of Ireland,* apud *Works,* Lond., 1805, 8vo, vol. viii. p. 306.

The Tanist, therefore, of O'Neale, was the heir-apparent of his power. This kind of succession appears also to have regulated, in very remote times, the succession to the crown of Scotland. It would have been imprudent, if not impossible, to have asserted a minor's right of succession in those stormy days, when the principles of policy were summed up in my friend Mr. Wordsworth's lines:—

"—— the good old rule
Sufficeth them; the simple plan,
That they should take who have the power,
And they should keep who can."

NOTE 41.

With wild majestic port and tone,
Like envoy of some barbarous throne. —
P. 230.

The Irish chiefs, in their intercourse with the English, and with each other, were wont to assume the language and style of independent royalty.

NOTE 42.

His foster-father was his guide. — P. 230.

There was no tie more sacred among the Irish than that which connected the foster-father, as well as the nurse herself, with the child they brought up.

NOTE 43.

Great Nial of the Pledges Nine. — P. 231.

Neal Naighvallach, or Of the Nine Hostages, is said to have been Monarch of all Ireland during the end of the fourth or beginning of the fifth century. He exercised a predatory warfare on the coast of England and of Bretagne, or Armorica; and from the latter country brought off the celebrated Saint Patrick, a youth of sixteen, among other captives, whom he transported to Ireland. Neal derived his epithet from nine nations, or tribes, whom he held under his subjection, and from whom he took hostages.

NOTE 44.

Shane-Dymas wild. — P. 231.

This Shane-Dymas, or John the Wanton, held the title and power of O'Neale in the earlier part of Elizabeth's reign, against whom he rebelled repeatedly.

" This chieftain is handed down to us as the most proud and profligate man on earth. He was immoderately addicted to women and wine. He is said to have had 200 tuns of wine at once in his cellar at Dandram, but usquebaugh was his favorite liquor. He spared neither age nor condition of the fair sex. Altho' so illiterate that he could not write, he was not destitute of address, his understanding was strong, and his courage daring. He had 600 men for his guard; 4,000 foot, 1,000 horse for the field. He claimed superiority over all the lords of Ulster, and called himself king thereof." — CAMDEN.

When reduced to extremity by the English, and forsaken by his allies, this Shane-Dymas fled to Clandeboy, then occupied by a colony of Scottish Highlanders of the family of MacDonell. He was at first courteously received, but by degrees they began to quarrel about the slaughter of some of their friends whom Shane-Dymas had put to death, and advancing from words to deeds, fell upon him with their broadswords, and cut him to pieces. After his death a law was made that none should presume to take the name and title of O'Neale.

NOTE 45.

—— *Geraldine.* — P. 231.

The O'Neales were closely allied with this powerful and warlike family; for Henry Owen O'Neale married the daughter of Thomas Earl of Kildare, and their son Con-More married his cousin-german, a daughter of Gerald Earl of Kildare. This Con-More cursed any of his posterity who should learn the English language, sow corn, or build houses, so as to invite the English to settle in their country. Others ascribe this anathema to his son Con-Bacco. Fearflatha O'Gnive, bard to the O'Neales of Clannaboy, complains in the same spirit of the towers and ramparts with which the strangers had *disfigured* the fair sporting fields of Erin. — See WALKER'S *Irish Bards*, p. 140.

NOTE 46.

—— *his page, the next degree*
In that old time to chivalry. — P. 231.

Originally, the order of chivalry embraced three ranks : — 1. The Page; 2. The Squire; 3. The Knight ; — a gradation which seems to have been imitated in the mystery of freemasonry. But, before the reign of Charles I., the custom of serving as a squire had fallen into disuse, though the order of the page was still, to a certain degree, in observance. This state of servitude was so far from inferring anything degrading, that it was considered as the regular school for acquiring every quality necessary for future distinction.

NOTE 47.

Seem'd half abandon'd to decay. — P. 236.

The ancient castle of Rokeby stood exactly upon the site of the present mansion, by which a part of its walls is enclosed. It is surrounded by a profusion of fine wood, and the park in which it stands is adorned by the junction of the Greta and of the Tees. The title of Baron Rokeby of Armagh was, in 1777, conferred on the Right Reverend Richard Robinson, Primate of Ireland, descended of the Robinsons, formerly of Rokeby, in Yorkshire.

NOTE 48.

—— *The Felon Sow.* — P. 238.

The ancient minstrels had a comic as well as a serious strain of romance; and although the examples of the latter are by far the most numerous, they are, perhaps, the less valuable. The comic romance was a sort of parody upon the usual subjects of minstrel poetry. If the latter described deeds of heroic achievement, and the events of the battle, the tourney, and the chase, the former, as in the Tournament of Tottenham, introduced a set of clowns debating in the field, with all the assumed circumstances of chivalry. One of the very best of these mock romances, and which has no small portion of comic humor, is the Hunting of the Felon Sow of Rokeby by the Friars of Richmond.

NOTE 49.

The Filea of O'Neale was he. — P. 239.

The Filea, or Ollamh Re Dan, was the proper bard, or, as the name literally implies, poet. Each chieftain of distinction had one or more in his service, whose office was usually hereditary. The late ingenious Mr. Cooper Walker, has assembled a curious collection of particulars concerning this order of men, in his Historical Memoirs of the Irish Bards. There were itinerant bards of less elevated rank, but all were held in the highest veneration.

NOTE 50.

Ah, Clandeboy! thy friendly floor
Slieve-Donard's oak shall light no more. —
P. 239.

Clandeboy is a district of Ulster, formerly possessed by the sept of the O'Neales, and Slieve-Donard a romantic mountain in the same province. The clan was ruined after Tyrone's great rebellion, and their places of abode laid desolate. The ancient Irish, wild and uncultivated in other respects, did not yield even to their descendants in practising the most free and extended hospitality.

NOTE 51.

On Marwood Chase and Toller Hill. —
P. 239.

Marwood Chase is the old park extending along the Durham side of the Tees, attached to Barnard Castle. Toller Hill is an eminence on the Yorkshire side of the river, commanding a superb view of the ruins.

NOTE 52.

"And Scotland's vaunted Hawthornden,
And, silenced on Iernian shore,
M'Curtin's harp should charm no more."
— P. 240.

Drummond of Hawthornden was in the zenith of his reputation as a poet during the Civil War. He died in 1649, at the age of sixty-four. M'Curtin was hereditary Ollamh or bard of North Munster, and Filea to Donough, Earl of Thomond and President of Munster. When Lord Thomond joined Elizabeth's forces, M'Curtin satirized him in a poem in which he said, "How am I afflicted that the descendant of the great Brion Boiromh cannot furnish me with a theme worthy the honor and glory of his exalted race." The Earl vowed vengeance, and the bard fled to County Cork. But, once coming in Thomond's way, he pretended to be suddenly seized with the pangs of death. His wife, entering into the spirit of the comedy, bewailed him, and told the Earl that it was her husband's dying request to be pardoned. "That nobleman," says Walker, in his "Memoirs of the Irish Bards," "was moved to compassion, and not only declared that he most heartily forgave him, but opening his purse, presented the fair mourner with some pieces to inter him. This instance of his lordship's pity and generosity gave courage to the trembling bard; who suddenly springing up, recited an extemporaneous ode in praise of Donough, and re-entering into his service, became once more his favorite."

NOTE 53.

Littlecot[e] Hall. — P. 244.

This ballad is founded on a fact; — the horrible murder of an infant by Wild Dayrell, as he was called. He gave the house and lands as a bribe to the judge (Popham) in order to save his life. A few months after Dayrell broke his neck by a fall from his horse.

NOTE 54.

As thick a smoke these hearts have given
At Hallow-tide or Christmas-even. — P. 245.

Such an exhortation was, in similar circumstances, actually given to his followers by a Welsh chieftain.

NOTE 55.

O'er Hexham's altar hung my glove. —
P. 253.

This custom among the Redesdale and Tynedale Borderers of duelling, which often resulted in petty warfare, the contending parties mustering their adherents, was found and is mentioned in the interesting life of Barnard Gilpin.

"It happened that a quarrel of this kind was on foot when Mr. Gilpin was at Rothbury, in those parts. During the two or three first days of his preaching, the contending parties observed some decorum, and never appeared at church together. At length, however, they met. One party had been early at church, and just as Mr. Gilpin began his sermon, the other entered. They stood not long silent. Inflamed at the sight of each other, they began to clash their weapons, for they were all armed with javelins and swords, and mutually approached. Awed, however, by the sacredness of the place, the tumult in some degree ceased. Mr. Gilpin proceeded; when again the combatants began to brandish their weapons, and draw towards each other. As a fray seemed near, Mr. Gilpin stepped from the pulpit, went between them, and addressed the leaders, put an end to the quarrel, for the present, but could not effect an entire reconciliation. They promised him, however, that till the sermon was over they would make no more disturbance. He then went again into the pulpit, and spent the rest of the time in endeavoring to make them ashamed of what they had done. His behavior and discourse affected them so much, that, at his further entreaty, they promised to forbear all acts of hostility while he continued in the country. And so much respected was he among them, that whoever was in fear of his enemy used to resort where Mr. Gilpin was, esteeming his presence the best protection.

" One Sunday morning, coming to a church in those parts, before the people were assembled, he observed a glove hanging up, and was informed by the sexton that it was meant as a challenge to any one who should take it down. Mr. Gilpin ordered the sexton to reach it to him; but upon his utterly refusing to touch it, he took it down himself, and put it into his breast. When the people were assembled, he went into the pulpit, and, before he concluded his sermon, took occasion to rebuke them severely for these inhuman challenges. 'I hear,' saith he, 'that one among you hath hanged up a glove, even in this sacred place, threatening to fight any one who taketh it down : see, I have taken it down :' and, pulling out the glove, he held it up to the congregation, and then showed them how unsuitable such savage practices were to the profession of Christianity, using such persuasives to mutual love as he thought would most affect them." — *Life of Barnard Gilpin*, Lond., 1753, 8vo, p. 177.

Note 56.

A horseman arm'd, at headlong speed. — P. 256.

This, and what follows, is taken from a real achievement of Major Robert Philipson, called from his desperate and adventurous courage, Robin the Devil.

THE BRIDAL OF TRIERMAIN.

Note 1.

The Baron of Triermain. — P. 263.

Triermain was a fief of the Barony of Gilsland in Cumberland; it was possessed by a Saxon family at the time of the Conquest, but, " after the death of Gilmore, Lord of Tryermaine and Torcrossock, Hubert Vaux gave Tryermaine and Torcrossock to his second son, Ranulph Vaux; which Ranulph afterwards became heir to his elder brother Robert, the founder of Lanercost, who died, without issue. Ranulph, being Lord of all Gilsland, gave Gilmore's lands to his younger son, named Roland, and let the Barony descend to his eldest son Robert, son of Ranulph. Ronald had issue Alexander, and he Ranulph, after whom succeeded Robert, and they were named Rolands successively, that were lords thereof, until the reign of Edward the Fourth. That house

gave for arms, Vert [Argent, not vert], a bend dexter, chequy, or, and gules." — Burn's *Antiquities of Westmoreland and Cumberland*, vol. ii., p. 482.

Note 2.

He pass'd red Penrith's Table Round. — P. 264.

A circular intrenchment, about half a mile from Penrinth, is thus popularly termed. The circle within the ditch is about one hundred and sixty paces in circumference, with openings, or approaches, directly opposite to each other. As this ditch is on the inner side, it could not be intended for the purpose of defence, and it has reasonably been conjectured that the enclosure was designed for the solemn exercise of feats of chivalry, and the embankment around for the convenience of the spectators.

NOTE 3.

Mayburgh's mound.— P. 264.

Higher up the river Eamont than Arthur's Round Table, is a prodigious enclosure of great antiquity, formed by a collection of stones upon the top of a gently sloping hill, called Mayburgh. In the plain which it encloses there stands erect an unhewn stone of twelve feet in height. Two similar masses are said to have been destroyed during the memory of man. The whole appears to be a monument of Druidical times.

NOTE 4.

That sable tarn.— P. 265.

The small lake called Scales-tarn lies so deeply embossed in the recesses of the huge mountain called Saddleback, more poetically Glaramara, is of such great depth, and so completely hidden from the sun, that it is said its beams never reach it, and that the reflection of the stars may be seen at mid-day.

NOTE 5.

The terrors of Tintadgel's spear.— P. 266.

Tintadgel Castle, in Cornwall, is reported to have been the birthplace of King Arthur.

NOTE 6.

Scattering a shower of fiery dew.— P. 269.

The author has an indistinct recollection of an adventure, somewhat similar to that which is here ascribed to King Arthur, having befallen one of the ancient Kings of Denmark. The horn in which the burning liquor was presented to that Monarch, is said still to be preserved in the Royal Museum at Copenhagen.

NOTE 7.

The monarch, breathless and amazed,
Back on the fatal castle gazed—
Nor tower nor donjon could he spy,
Darkening against the morning sky.—
P. 269.

— " We now gained a view of the Vale of St. John's, a very narrow dell, hemmed in by mountains, through which a small brook makes many meanderings, washing little enclosures of grass-ground, which stretch up the rising of the hills. In the widest part of the dale you are struck with the appearance of an ancient ruined castle, which seems to stand upon the summit of a little mount, the mountains around forming an amphitheatre. The massive bulwark shows a front of various towers, and makes an awful, rude, and

Gothic appearance, with its lofty turrets and rugged battlements; we traced the galleries, the bending arches, the buttresses. The greatest antiquity stands characterized in its architecture : the inhabitants near it assert it is an antediluvian structure.

" The traveller's curiosity is roused, and he prepares to make a nearer approach, when that curiosity is put upon the rack by his being assured that, if he advances, certain genii who govern the place, by virtue of their supernatural art and necromacy, will strip it of all its beauties, and by enchantment transform the magic walls. The vale seems adapted for the habitation of such beings; its gloomy recesses and retirements look like the haunts of evil spirits. There was no delusion in the report; we were soon convinced of its truth; for this piece of antiquity, so venerable and noble in its aspect, as we drew near, changed its figure, and proved no other than a shaken massive pile of rocks, which stand in the midst of this little vale, disunited from the adjoining mountains, and have so much the real form and resemblance of a castle, that they bear the name of the Castle Rocks of St. John."
— HUTCHINSON'S *Excursion to the Lakes*, p. 121.

NOTE 8.

Twelve bloody fields, with glory fought.—
P. 270.

Arthur is said to have defeated the Saxons in twelve pitched battles, and to have achieved the other feats alluded to in the text.

NOTE 9.

The flower of chivalry.
There Galaad sat with manly grace,
Yet maiden meekness in his face;
There Morolt of the iron mace,
And love-lorn Tristrem there.—
P. 270.

The characters named in the stanza are all of them more or less distinguished in the romances which treat of King Arthur and his Round Table, and their names are strung together, according to the established customs of minstrels upon such occasions, for example, in the ballad of the Marriage of Sir Gawaine : —

" Sir Lancelot, Sir Stephen bolde,
 They rode with him that daye,
And foremost of the companye,
 There rode the stewarde Kaye.

" Soe did Sir Banier, and Sir Bore,
 And eke Sir Garratte keen,
Sir Tristrem, too, that gentle knight,
 To the forest, fresh and greene."

NOTE 10.

——*Lancelot, that evermore*
Look'd stolen-wise on the Queen. — P. 270.

Upon this delicate subject hear Richard Robinson, citizen of London, in his Assertion of King Arthur: " But as it is a thing sufficiently apparent that she (Guenever, wife of King Arthur) was beautiful, so it is a thing doubted whether she was chaste, yea or no. Truly, so far as I can with honestie, I would spare the impayred honour of noble women. But yet the truth of the historie pluckes me by the eare, and willeth not onely, but commandeth me to declare what the ancients have deemed of her. To wrestle or contend with so great authoritie were indeed unto mei a controversie, and that greate." — *Assertion of King Arthure.* Imprinted by John Wolfe, London, 1582.

NOTE 11.

There were two who loved their neighbors'
wives,
And one who loved his own. — P. 271.

" In our forefathers' tyme, when Papistrie, as a standyng poole, covered and overflowed all England, fewe books were read in our tongue, savying certaine bookes of chevalrie, as they said, for pastime and pleasure : which, as some say, were made in the monasteries, by idle monks or wanton chanons. As one, for example, La Morte d'Arthure ; the whole pleasure of which book standeth in two speciall poyntes, in open manslaughter and bold bawdrye; in which booke they be counted the noblest knightes that do kill most men without any quarrell, and commit foulest adoulteries by subtlest shiftes ; as Sir Lancelot with the wife of King Arthur, his master ; Sir Tristram, with the wife of King Marke, his uncle ; Sir Lamerocke, with the wife of King Lote, that was his own aunt. This is good stuffe for wise men to laugh at; or honest men to take pleasure at ; yet I know when God's Bible was banished the Court, and La Morte d'Arthure received into the Prince's chamber." — ASCHAM'S *Schoolmaster.*

NOTE 12.

Who won the cup of gold. — P. 271.

See the comic tale of the Boy and the Mantle, in the third volume of Percy's Reliques of Ancient Poetry, from the Breton or Norman original of which Ariosto is supposed to have taken his tale of the Enchanted Cup.

NOTE 13.

Whose logic is from Single-speech. — P. 275.

See " Parliamentary Logic, etc.," by the Hon. W. G. Hamilton (1808), commonly called " Single-Speech Hamilton."

NOTE TO THE POEM.

Scott composed this poem with the intention that the public should attribute it to his friend Mr. Erskine (Lord Kinedder). The joke succeeded ; but on the third edition being published, Lord Kinedder avowed the true author, the deception having gone further than either he or Scott intended. We mention this fact in order to explain the preface. — ED.

THE LORD OF THE ISLES.

NOTE 1.

Thy rugged halls, Artornish! rung —
                                    P. 291.

THE ruins of the Castle of Artornish are situated upon a promotory, on the Morven, or mainland side of the Sound of Mull, a name given to the deep arm of the sea which divides that island from the continent. The situation is wild and romantic in the highest degree, having on the one hand a high and precipitous chain of rocks overhanging the sea, and on the other the narrow entrance to the beautiful salt-water lake, called Loch Alline, which is in many places finely fringed with copsewood. The ruins of Artornish are not now very considerable, and consist chiefly of the remains of an old keep, or tower, with fragments of outward defences. But, in former days, it was a place of great consequence, being one of the principal strongholds, which the Lords of the Isles, during the period of their stormy independence, possessed upon the mainland of Argyleshire. It is almost opposite to the Bay of Aros, in the Island of Mull, where there was another castle, the occasional residence of the Lords of the Isles.

NOTE 2.

Rude Heiskar's seal through surges dark
Will long pursue the minstrel's bark. —
                                    P. 291.

The seal displays a taste for music, which

could scarcely be expected from his habits and local predilections. They will long follow a boat in which any musical instrument is played, and even a tune simply whistled has attractions for them. The Dean of the Isles says of Heiskar, a small, uninhabited rock, about twelve (Scottish) miles from the Isle of Uist, that an infinite slaughter of seals takes place there.

NOTE 3.

―― *a turret's airy head,*
Slender and steep, and battled round,
O'erlook'd, dark Mull! thy mighty Sound.
— P. 292.

The Sound of Mull, which divides that island from the continent of Scotland, is one of the most striking scenes which the Hebrides afford to the traveller. Sailing from Oban to Aros, or Tombermory, through a narrow channel, yet deep enough to bear vessels of the largest burden, he has on his left the bold and mountainous shores of Mull ; on the right those of that district of Argyleshire called Morven, or Morvern, successively indented by deep salt-water lochs, running up many miles inland. To the southeastward arise a prodigious range of mountains, among which Cruachan-Ben is pre-eminent. And to the northeast is the no less huge and picturesque range of the Ardnamurchan hills. Many ruinous castles, situated generally upon cliffs overhanging the ocean, add interest to the scene.

NOTE 4.

The heir of mighty Somerled. — P. 292.

Somerled was thane of Argyle and Lord of the Isles, about the middle of the twelfth century. He seems to have exercised his authority in both capacities, independent of the crown of Scotland, against which he often stood in hostility. He made various incursions upon the western lowlands during the reign of Malcolm IV., and seems to have made peace with him upon the terms of an independent prince, about the year 1157. In 1164 he resumed the war against Malcolm, and invaded Scotland with a large, but probably a tumultuary army, collected in the isles, in the mainland of Argyleshire, and in the neighboring provinces of Ireland. He was defeated and slain, in an engagement with a very inferior force, near Renfrew. This chieftain married a daughter of Olaus, King of Man. The Lords of the Isles descended from his eldest son, Ronald, and the Lords of Lorn from his second son, Dougal, whence they took their surname of Mac-Dougal.

NOTE 5.
Lord of the Isles. — P. 292.

The representative of this independent principality, for such it seems to have been, though acknowledging occasionally the pre-eminence of the Scottish crown, was, at the period of the poem, Angus, called Angus Og : but the name has been *euphoniæ gratia*, exchanged for that of Ronald, which frequently occurs in the genealogy. Angus was a protector of Robert Bruce, whom he received in his Castle of Dunnaverty, during the time of his greatest distress.

NOTE 6.
The House of Lorn. — P. 293.

The House of Lorn, as we observed in a former note, was, like the Lord of the Isles, descended from a son of Somerled, slain at Renfrew, in 1164. This son obtained the succession of his mainland territories, comprehending the greater part of the three districts of Lorn, in Argyleshire, and of course might rather be considered as petty princes than feudal barons. They assumed the patronymic appellation of MacDougal, by which they are distinguished in the history of the Middle Ages.

NOTE 7.

Awaked before the rushing prow,
The mimic fires of ocean glow,
Those lightnings of the wave.
— P. 295.

The phenomenon called by sailors Sea-fire, is one of the most beautiful and interesting which is witnessed in the Hebrides. At times the ocean appears entirely illuminated around the vessel, and a long train of lambent coruscations are perpetually bursting upon the sides of the vessel, or pursuing her wake through the darkness.

NOTE 8.

That keen knight, De Argentine. — P. 298.

Sir Egidius, or Giles de Argentine, was one of the most accomplished knights of the period. He had served in the wars of Henry of Luxemburg with such high reputation that he was, in popular estimation, the third worthy of the age. Those to whom fame assigned precedence over him were, Henry of Luxemburg himself, and Robert Bruce. Argentine had warred in Palestine, encountered thrice with the Saracens, and had slain two antagonists in each engagement ; — an easy matter, he said, for one Christian knight to slay two Pagan dogs.

Note 9.

" Fill me the mighty cup ! " he said,
" Erst own'd by royal Somerled." —

P. 298.

A Hebridean drinking cup of the most ancient and curious workmanship, has been long preserved in the Castle of Dunvegan, in Skye, the romantic seat of Mac-Leod of Mac-Leod, the chief of that ancient and powerful clan. The horn of Rorie More, preserved in the same family, and recorded by Dr. Johnson, is not to be compared with this piece of antiquity, which is one of the greatest curiosities in Scotland.

Note 10.

—— *" the rebellious Scottish crew,*
Who to Rath-Erin's shelter drew,
With Carrick's outlaw'd chief." —

P. 299.

It must be remembered by all who have read the Scottish history, that after he had slain Comyn at Dumfries, and asserted his right to the Scottish crown, Robert Bruce was reduced to the greatest extremity by the English and their adherents. He was crowned at Scone by the general consent of the Scottish barons, but his authority endured but a short time. According to the phrase said to have been used by his wife, he was for that year " a summer king, but not a winter one."

Note 11.

The Broach of Lorne. — P. 299.

Robert Bruce, after his defeat at Methven, being hard pressed by the English, endeavored, with the dispirited remnant of his followers, to escape from Breadalbane and the mountains of Perthshire into the Argyle-shire Highlands. But he was encountered and repulsed, after a very severe engagement, by the Lord of Lorn. Bruce's personal strength and courage were never displayed to greater advantage than in this conflict. There is a tradition in the family of the Mac-Dougals of Lorn, that their chieftain engaged in personal battle with Bruce himself, while the latter was employed in protecting the retreat of his men ; that Mac-Dougal was struck down by the king, whose strength of body was equal to his vigor of mind, and would have been slain on the spot, had not two of Lorn's vassals, a father and son, whom tradition terms Mac-Keoch, rescued him by seizing the mantle of the monarch, and dragging him from above his adversary. Bruce rid himself of these foes by two blows of his redoubted battle-axe, but was so closely pressed by the other followers of Lorn that he was forced to abandon the mantle, and broach which fastened it, clasped in the dying grasp of the Mac-Keochs. A studded broach, said to have been that which King Robert lost upon this occasion, was long preserved in the family of Mac-Dougal, and was lost in a fire which consumed their temporary residence.

Great art and expense were bestowed upon the broach which secured the plaid. Some were as broad as a platter, engraved with curious designs and decorated with crystals or more valuable stones.

Note 12.

When Comyn fell beneath the knife
Of that fell homicide the Bruce. — P. 296.

Vain Kirkpatrick's bloody dirk,
Making sure of murder's work. — P. 300.

Every reader must recollect that the proximate cause of Bruce's asserting his right to the crown of Scotland, was the death of John, called the Red Comyn. The causes of this act of violence, equally extraordinary from the high rank, both of the perpetrator and sufferer, and from the place where the slaughter was committed, are variously related by the Scottish and English historians, and cannot now be ascertained. The fact that they met at the high altar of the Minorites, or Greyfriar's Church in Dumfries, that their difference broke out into high and insulting language, and that Bruce drew his dagger and stabbed Comyn, is certain. Rushing to the door of the church, Bruce met two powerful barons, Kirkpatrick of Closeburn, and James de Lindsay, who eagerly asked him what tidings ? " Bad tidings," answered Bruce ; " I doubt I have slain Comyn." " Doubtest thou ? " said Kirkpatrick ; " I make sicker " (*i.e.* sure). With these words, he and Lindsay rushed into the church, and despatched the wounded Comyn. The Kirkpatricks of Closeburn assumed in memory of this deed, a hand holding a dagger, with the memorable words, " I make sicker."

Note 13.

Barendown fled fast away,
Fled the fiery De la Haye. — P. 300.

These knights are enumerated by Barbour among the small number of Bruce's adherents, who remained in arms with him after the battle of Methven.

NOTE 14.

*Was't not enough to Ronald's bower
I brought thee like a paramour.* — P. 303.

It was anciently customary in the Highlands to bring the bride to the house of the husband. Nay, in some cases, the complaisance was stretched so far that she remained there upon trial for a twelvemonth; and the bridegroom, even after this period of cohabitation, retained an option of refusing to fulfil his engagement. It is said that a desperate feud ensued between the clans of Mac-Donald of Sleate and Mac-Leod, owing to the former chief having availed himself of this license to send back to Dunvegan a sister or daughter of the latter. Mac-Leod, resenting the indignity, observed, that since there was no wedding bonfire, there should be one to solemnize the divorce. Accordingly, he burned and laid waste the territories of Mac-Donald, who retaliated, and a deadly feud, with all its accompaniments, took place in form.

NOTE 15.

*Since matchless Wallace first had been
In mock'ry crown'd with wreaths of green.* — P. 303.

Stow gives the following curious account of the trial and execution of this celebrated patriot: "William Wallace, who had ofttimes set Scotland in great trouble, was taken and brought to London, with great numbers of men and women wondering upon him. He was lodged in the house of William Delect, a citizen of London, in Fenchurch Street. On the morrow, being the eve of St. Bartholomew, he was brought on horseback to Westminster. John Legrave and Jeffrey, knights, the mayor, sheriffs, and aldermen of London, and many others, both on horseback and on foot, accompanying him, and in the great hall at Wesminster, he being placed on the south bench, crowned with laurel, for that he had said in times past that he ought to bear a crown in that hall, as it was commonly reported, and being impeached for a traitor by Sir Peter Malorie, the king's justice, he answered, that he was never traitor to the King of England, but for other things whereof he was accused, he confessed them; and was after headed and quartered." — STOW, *Chr.* p. 209. There is something singularly doubtful about the mode in which Wallace was taken. That he was betrayed to the English is indubitable; and popular fame charges Sir John Menteith with the indelible infamy. "Accursed," says Arnold Blair, "be the day of nativity of John de Menteith, and may his name be struck out of the book of life." But John de Menteith was all along a zealous favorer of the English interest, and was governor of Dumbarton Castle by commission from Edward the First; and therefore, as the accurate Lord Hailes has observed, could not be the friend and confidant of Wallace, as tradition states him to be. The truth seems to be, that Menteith, thoroughly engaged in the English interest, pursued Wallace closely, and made him prisoner through the treachery of an attendant, whom Peter Langtoft calls Jack Short. The infamy of seizing Wallace must rest, therefore, between a degenerate Scottish nobleman, the vassal of England, and a domestic, the obscure agent of his treachery; between Sir John Menteith, son of Walter, Earl of Menteith, and the traitor Jack Short.

NOTE 16.

*Was not the life of Athole shed,
To soothe the tyrant's sicken'd bed?* — P. 303.

John de Strathbogie, Earl of Athole, had attempted to escape out of the kingdom, but a storm cast him upon the coast, when he was taken, sent to London, and executed with circumstances of great barbarity, being first half strangled, then let down from the gallows while yet alive, barbarously dismembered, and his body burnt. It may surprise the reader to learn that this was a *mitigated* punishment; for in respect that his mother was a granddaughter of King John, by his natural son, Richard, he was not drawn on a sledge to execution, "that point was forgiven," and he made the passage on horseback. Matthew of Westminster tells us that King Edward, then extremely ill, received great ease from the news that his relative was apprehended. "*Quo audito, Rex Angliæ, etsi gravissimo morbo tunc langueret, levius tamen tulit dolorem*" To this singular expression the text alludes.

NOTE 17.

*While I the blessed cross advance,
And expiate this unhappy chance,
In Palestine with sword and lance.* — P. 304.

Bruce uniformly professed, and probably felt, compunction for having violated the sanctuary of the church by the slaughter of Comyn; and finally, in his last hours, in testimony of his faith, penitence, and zeal, he requested James Lord Douglas to carry his heart to Jerusalem, to be there desposited in the Holy Sepulchre.

Note 18.

De Bruce ! I rose with purpose dread
To speak my curse upon thy head.— P. 304.

So soon as the notice of Comyn's slaughter reached Rome, Bruce and his adherents were excommunicated. It was published first by the Archbishop of York, and renewed at different times, particularly by Lambyrton, Bishop of St. Andrews, in 1308, but it does not appear to have answered the purpose which the English monarch expected. Indeed, for reasons which it may be difficult to trace, the thunders of Rome descended upon the Scottish mountains with less effect than in more fertile countries. Probably the comparative poverty of the benefices occasioned that fewer foreign clergy settled in Scotland, and the interests of the native churchmen were linked with that of their country. Many of the Scottish prelates, Lambyrton the primate particularly, declared for Bruce, while he was yet under the ban of the church, though he afterwards again changed sides.

Note 19.

A hunted wanderer on the wild,
On foreign shores a man exiled. — P. 304.

This is not metaphorical. The echoes of Scotland did actually

" —— ring
With the bloodhounds that bay'd for her fugitive king."

A very curious and romantic tale is told by Barbour upon this subject, which may be abridged as follows : —

When Bruce had again got footing in Scotland, in the spring of 1306, he continued to be in a very weak and precarious condition, gaining, indeed, occasional advantages, but obliged to fly before his enemies whenever they assembled in force. Upon one occasion, while he was lying with a small party in the wilds of Cumnock, in Ayrshire, Aymer de Valence, Earl of Pembroke, with his inveterate foe, John of Lorn, came against him suddenly with eight hundred Highlanders, besides a large body of men-at-arms. They brought with them a slough-dog, or blood-hound, which, some say, had been once a favorite with the Bruce himself, and therefore was least likely to lose the trace.

Bruce, whose force was under four hundred men, continued to make head against the cavalry, till the men of Lorn had nearly cut off his retreat. Perceiving the danger of his situation, he acted as the celebrated and ill-requited Mina is said to have done in similar circumstances. He divided his force into three parts, appointed a place of rendezvous and commanded them to retreat by different routes. But when John of Lorn arrived at the spot where they divided, he caused the hound to be put upon the trace, which immediately directed him to the pursuit of that party which Bruce headed. This, therefore, Lorn pursued with his whole force, paying no attention to the others. The king again, subdivided his small body into three parts, and with the same result, for the pursuers attached themselves exclusively to that which he led in person. He then caused his followers to disperse, and retained only his foster-brother in his company. The slough-dog followed the trace, and, neglecting the others, attached himself and his attendants to the pursuit of the king. Lorn became convinced that his enemy was nearly in his power, and detached five of his most active attendants to follow him and interrupt his flight. They did so with all the agility of mountaineers. " What aid wilt thou make ? " said Bruce to his single attendant, when he saw the five men gain ground on him. " The best I can," replied his foster-brother. " Then," said Bruce, " here I make my stand." The five pursuers came up fast. The king took three to himself, leaving the other two to his foster-brother. He slew the first who encountered him ; but observing his foster-brother hard pressed, he sprung to his assistance, and despatched one of his assailants. Leaving him to deal with the survivor, he returned upon the other two, both of whom he slew before his foster-brother had despatched his single antagonist. When this hard encounter was over, with a courtesy, which in the whole work marks Bruce's character, he thanked his foster-brother for his aid. " It likes you to say so," answered his follower ; " but you yourself slew four of the five." — " True," said the king, " but only because I had better opportunity than you. They were not apprehensive of me when they saw me encounter three, so I had a moment's time to spring to thy aid, and to return equally unexpectedly upon my own opponents."

In the meanwhile Lorn's party approached rapidly, and the king and his foster-brother betook themselves to a neighboring wood. Here they sat down, for Bruce was exhausted by fatigue, until the cry of the slough-hound came so near that his foster-brother entreated Bruce to provide for his safety by retreating further. " I have heard," answered the king, " that whosoever will wade a bow-shot length down a running stream, shall make the slough-hound lose scent. Let us try the experiment, for were yon devilish hound silenced I should care little for the rest."

Lorn in the meanwhile advanced, and found the bodies of his slain vassals, over whom he made his moan, and threatened the most deadly vengeance. Then he followed the hound to the side of the brook down which the king had waded a great way. Here the hound was at fault, and John of Lorn, after long attempting in vain to recover Bruce's trace, relinquished the pursuit.

"Others," says Barbour, "affirm that upon this occasion the king's life was saved by an excellent archer who accompanied him, and who perceiving that they would be finally taken by means of the blood-hound hid himself in a thicket, and shot him with an arrow. In which way," adds the metrical biographer, "this escape happened I am uncertain, but at that brook the king escaped from his pursuers."

NOTE 20.

" Alas ! dear youth, the unhappy time,"
Answer'd the Bruce, "must bear the crime,
Since guiltier far than you,
Even I"—he paused: for Falkirk's woes
Upon his conscious soul arose. — P. 306.

I have followed the vulgar and inaccurate tradition, that Bruce fought against Wallace, and the array of Scotland, at the fatal battle of Falkirk. The story which seems to have no better authority than that of Blind Harry, bears, that having made much slaughter during the engagement, he sat down to dine with the conquerors without washing the filthy witness from his hands.

" Fasting he was, and had been in great need,
Blooded were all his weapons, and his weed ;
Southeron lords scorn'd him in terms rude,
And said, Behold yon Scot eats his own blood.

"Then, rued he sore, for reason bad be known,
That blood and land alike should be his own ;
With them he long was, ere he got away,
But contrair Scots he fought not from that
day."

The account given by most of our historians, of the conversation between Bruce and Wallace over the Garron River, is equally apocryphal. There is full evidence that Bruce was not at that time on the English side, nor present at the battle of Falkirk ; nay, that he acted as a guardian of Scotland, along with John Comyn, in the name of Baliol, and in opposition to the English.

NOTE 21.

These are the savage wilds that lie
North of Strathnardill and Dunskye. —
P. 307.

The extraordinary piece of scenery which I have here attempted to describe is, I think, unparalleled in any part of Scotland, at least in any which I have happened to visit. It lies just upon the frontier of the Laird of Mac-Leod's country, which is thereabouts divided from the estate of Mr. Mac-Allister of Strath-Aird, called Strathnardill by the Dean of the Isles.

NOTE 22.

And mermaid's alabaster grot,
Who bathes her limbs in sunless well,
Deep in Strathaird's enchanted cell. —
P. 311.

Imagination can hardly conceive anything more beautiful than the extraordinary grotto discovered not many years since upon the estate of Alexander Mac-Allister, Esq., of Strathaird. It has since been much and deservedly celebrated, and a full account of its beauties has been published by Dr. Mac-Leay of Oban. The general impression may perhaps be gathered from the following extract from a journal, which, written under the feelings of the moment, is likely to be more accurate than any attempt to recollect the impressions then received : — " The first entrance to this celebrated cave is rude and unpromising ; but the light of the torches, with which we were provided, was soon reflected from the roof, floor, and walls, which seem as if they were sheeted with marble, partly smooth, partly rough with frost-work and rustic ornaments, and partly seeming to be wrought into statuary. The floor forms a steep and difficult ascent, and might be fancifully compared to a sheet of water, which, while it rushed whitening and foaming down a declivity, had been suddenly arrested and consolidated by the spell of an enchanter. Upon attaining the summit of this ascent, the cave opens into a splendid gallery, adorned with the most dazzling crystallizations, and finally descends with rapidity to the brink of a pool of the most limpid water, about four or five yards broad. There opens beyond this pool a portal arch, formed by two columns of white spar, with beautiful chasing upon the sides, which promises a continuation of the cave. One of our sailors swam across, for there is no other mode of passing, and informed us (as indeed we partly saw by the light he carried) that the enchantment of Mac-Allister's cave terminates with this portal, a little beyond which there was only a rude cavern, speedily choked with stones and earth. But the pool, on the brink of which we stood, surrounded by the most fanciful mouldings, in a substance resembling white marble, and distinguished by the depth and purity of its waters, might have been the bathing grotto of a naiad. The groups of combined figures projecting, or embossed, by which the pool is surrounded, are exquisitely elegant and fanciful. A statuary might catch beautiful hints from the singular and romantic disposition of those stalactites. There is scarce a form or group on which active fancy may not trace figures or grotesque ornaments, which have been gradually moulded in this cavern by the dropping of the calcareous water hardening into petrifactions. Many of those fine groups have been injured by the senseless rage of appropriation of recent tourists; and the grotto had lost (I am informed), through the smoke of torches, something of that vivid silver tint which was originally one of its chief distinctions. But enough of beauty remains to compensate for all that may be lost." — Dr. Mac-Allister of Strathaird has, with great propriety, built up the exterior entrance to this cave, in order that strangers may enter properly attended by a guide, to prevent any repetition of the wanton and selfish injury which this singular scene has already sustained.

NOTE 23.

Yet to no sense of selfish wrongs,
Bear witness with me, Heaven, belongs
My joy o'er Edward's bier. — P. 314.

The generosity which does justice to the character of an enemy, often marks Bruce's sentiments, as recorded by the faithful Barbour. He seldom mentions a fallen enemy without praising such good qualities as he might possess. I shall only take one instance. Shortly after Bruce landed in Carrick, in 1306, Sir Ingram Bell, the English governor of Ayr, engaged a wealthy yeoman, who had hitherto been a follower of Bruce, to undertake the task of assassinating him. The king learned this treachery, as he is said to have done other secrets of the enemy, by means of a female with whom he had an intrigue. Shortly after he was possessed of this information, Bruce, resorting to a small thicket at a distance from his men, with only a single page to attend him, met the traitor, accompanied by two of his sons. They approached him with their wonted familiarity, but Bruce, taking his page's bow and arrow, commanded them to keep at a distance. As they still pressed forward with professions of zeal for his person and service, he, after a second warning, shot the father with the arrow; and being assaulted successively by the two sons, despatched first one, who was armed with an axe, then as the other charged him with a spear, avoided the thrust, struck the head from the spear, and

cleft the skull of the assassin with a blow of his two-handed sword.

NOTE 24.

And Ronin's mountains dark have sent
Their hunters to the shore. — P. 315.

Ronin (popularly called Rum, a name which a poet may be pardoned for avoiding if possible) is a very rough and mountainous island, adjacent to those of Eigg and Canna or Cannay. There is almost no arable ground upon it, so that, except in the plenty of the deer, which of course are now nearly extirpated, it still deserves the description bestowed by the arch-dean of the Isles: " Ronin, sixteen myle north-wast from the ile of Coll, lyes ane ile callit Ronin Ile, of sixteen myle long, and six in bredthe in the narrowest, ane forest of heigh mountains, an abundance of little deir in it, quhilk deir will never be slane dounewith, but the principal saittis man be in the height of the hill, because the deir will be callit upwart ay be the tainchell or without tynchel they will pass upwart perforce. In this ile will be gotten about Britane als many wild nests upon the plane mure as men pleasis to gadder, and yet by reason the fowls has few to start them except deir. This ile lyes from the west to the eist in lenth, and pertains to M'Kenabrey of Colla. Many solan geese are in this ile." — MONRO'S *Description of the Western Isles*, p. 18.

NOTE 25.

On Scooreigg next a warning light
Summon'd her warriors to the fight;
A numerous race, ere stern Macleod
O'er their bleak shores in vengeance strode.
— P. 315.

These, and the following lines of the stanza, refer to a dreadful tale of feudal vengeance, of which unfortunately there are relics that still attest the truth. Scoor-Eigg is a high peak in the centre of the small Isle of Eigg, or Egg. It is well known to mineralogists, as affording many interesting specimens, and to others whom chance or curiosity may lead to the island, for the astonishing view of the mainland and neighboring isles, which it commands. The following account is extracted from the poet's own journal kept during his tour through the Scottish Islands.

26th August, 1814.— At seven this morning we were in the sound which divides the Isle of Rum from that of Egg. The latter, although hilly and rocky, and traversed by a remarkably high and barren ridge, called Scoor-Rigg, has, in point of soil, a much more promising appearance. Southward of both lies the Isle of Muich, or Muck, a low and fertile island, and though the least, yet probably the most valuable of the three. We manned the boat and rowed along the shore of Egg in quest of a cavern, which had been the memorable scene of a horrid feudal vengeance. We had rounded more than half the island, admiring the entrance of many a bold natural cave, which its rocks exhibited, without finding that which we sought, until we procured a guide. Nor, indeed, was it surprising that it should have escaped the search of strangers, as there are no outward indications more than might distinguish the entrance of a fox-earth. This noted cave has a very narrow opening, through which one can hardly creep on his knees and hands. It rises steep and lofty within, and runs into the bowels of the rock to the depth of two hundred and fifty-five measured feet ; the height at the entrance may be about three feet, but rises within to eighteen or twenty, and the breadth may vary in the same proportion. The rude and stony bottom of this cave is strewed with the bones of men, women, and children, the sad relics of the ancient inhabitants of the island, two hundred in number, who were slain on the following occasion : — The Mac-Donalds of the Isle of Egg, a people dependent on Clan-Ranald, had done some injury to the Laird of Mac-Leod. The tradition of the isle says, that it was by a personal attack on the chieftain, in which his back was more broken. But that of the other isles bears more probably, that the injury was offered to two or three of the Mac-Leods, who, landing upon Eigg, and using some freedom with the young women, were seized by the islanders, bound hand and foot, and turned adrift in a boat which the wind and waves safely conducted to Skye. To avenge the offence given, Mac-Leod sailed with such a body of men as rendered resistance hopeless. The natives, fearing his vengeance, concealed themselves in this cavern, and, after a strict search, the Mac-Leods went on board their galleys, after doing what mischief they could, concluding the inhabitants had left the isle, and betaken themselves to the Long Island, or some of Clan-Ranald's other possessions. But next morning they espied from the vessels a man upon the island, and immediately landing again, they traced his retreat by the marks of his footsteps, a light snow being unhappily on the ground. Mac-Leod then surrounded the cavern, summoned the subterranean garrison, and demanded that the individuals who had offended him should be delivered up to him. This was peremptorily refused. The chieftain then caused his people to divert the course of a rill of water, which, falling over the entrance of the cave, would have prevented his purposed vengeance. He then kindled at the entrance of the cavern a huge fire, composed of turf and fern, and maintained it with unrelenting assiduity, until all within were destroyed by suffocation. The date of this dreadful deed must have been recent, if one may judge from the fresh appearance of those relics. I brought off, in spite of the prejudice of our sailors, a skull from among the numerous specimens of mortality which the cavern afforded. Before re-embarking we visited another cave, opening to the sea, but of a character entirely different, being a large open vault, as high as that of a cathedral, and running back a great way into the rock at the same height. The height and width of the opening gives ample light to the whole. Here, after 1745, when the Catholic priests were scarcely tolerated, the priest of Eigg used to perform the Roman Catholic service, most of the islanders being of that persuasion. A huge ledge of rocks rising about half-way up one side of the vault, served for altar and pulpit ; and the appearance of a priest and Highland congregation in such an extraordinary place of worship, might have engaged the pencil of Salvator."

NOTE 26.

Scenes sung by him who sings no more. —
P. 316.

The ballad entitled, "Macphail of Colonsay, and the Mermaid of Corrievrekin" [see Border Minstrelsy, vol. iv., p. 285], was composed by John Leyden, from a tradition which he found while making a tour through the Hebrides about 1801, soon before his fatal departure for India, where, after having made further progress in Oriental literature than any man of letters who had embraced those studies, he died a martyr to his zeal for knowledge, in the island of Java, immediately after the landing of our forces near Batavia, in August, 1811.

NOTE 27.

Up Tarbat's western lake they bore,
Then dragg'd their bark the isthmus o'er. —
P. 316.

The peninsula of Cantire is joined to South Knapdale by a very narrow isthmus ; formed by the western and eastern Loch of Tarbat. These two salt water lakes, or bays, encroach so far upon the land, and the extremities come so near to each other, that there is not above a mile of land to divide them.

NOTE 28.

The sun, ere yet he sunk behind
Ben-Ghoil, "the Mountain of the Wind,"
Gave his grim peaks a greeting kind,
And bade Loch Ranza smile. — P. 316.

Loch Ranza is a beautiful bay, on the northern extremity of Arran, opening towards East Tarbat Loch. It is well described by Pennant: "The approach was magnificent; a fine bay in front about a mile deep, having a ruined castle near the lower end, on a low far-projecting neck of land, that forms another harbor, with a narrow passage; but within has three fathom of water, even at the lowest ebb. Beyond is a little plain watered by a stream, and inhabited by the people of a small village. The whole is environed with a theatre of mountains; and in the background the serrated crags of Grianan-Athol soar above." — PENNANT'S *Tour to the Western Isles*, pp. 191, 192. Ben-Ghaoil, "the mountain of the winds," is generally known by its English, and less poetical, name of Goatfield.

NOTE 29.

Each to Loch Ranza's margin spring;
That blast was winded by the king! —
P. 318.

The passage in Barbour, describing the landing of Bruce, and his being recognized by Douglas and those of his followers who had preceded him, by the sound of his horn, is in the original singularly simple and affecting. The king arrived in Arran with thirty-three small row-boats. He interrogated a female if there had arrived any warlike men of late in that country. "Surely, sir," she replied, "I can tell you of many who lately came hither, discomfited the English governor, and blockaded his castle of Brodick. They maintain themselves in a wood at no great distance." The king, truly conceiving that this must be Douglas and his followers, who had lately set forth to try their fortune in Arran, desired the woman to conduct him to the wood. She obeyed.

" The king then blew his horn on high;
And gert * his men that were him by,
Hold them still, and all privy;
And syne again his horn blew he.
James of Dowglas heard him blow,
And at the last alone gan know,
And said, ' Soothly yon is the king;
I know long while since his blowing.'
The third time therewithal he blew,
And then Sir Robert Boid it knew;
And said, ' Yon is the king, but dread.
Go we forth till him, better speed.

* Caused.

Then went they till the king in hye,
And him inclined courteously.
And blithely welcomed them the king,
And was joyful of their meeting,
And kissed them; and speared † syne
How they had fared in hunting?
And they him told all, but lesing. ‡
Syne laud they God of their meeting,
Syne with the king till his harbourye
Went both joyfu' and jolly."

BARBOUR'S *Bruce*, Book v., pp. 115, 116.

NOTE 30.

—— *his brother blamed,*
But shared the weakness, while ashamed,
With haughty laugh his head he turn'd,
And dash'd away the tear he scorn'd —
P. 319.

The kind and yet fiery character of Edward Bruce is well painted by Barbour, in the account of his behavior after the battle of Bannockburn. Sir Walter Ross, one of the very few Scottish nobles who fell in that battle, was so dearly beloved by Edward, that he wished the victory had been lost, so Ross had lived.

NOTE 31.

Thou heard'st a wretched female plain
In agony of travail-pain,
And thou didst bid thy little band
Upon the instant turn and stand,
And dare the worst that foe might do,
Rather than, like a knight untrue,
Leave to pursuers merciless
A woman in her last distress. — P. 320.

This incident, which illustrates so happily the chivalrous generosity of Bruce's character, is one of the many simple and natural traits recorded by Barbour. It occurred during the expedition which Bruce made to Ireland, to support the pretensions of his brother Edward to the throne of that kingdom.

NOTE 32.

O'er chasms he pass'd where fractures wide
Craved wary eye and ample stride. —
P. 323.

The interior of the island of Arran abounds with beautiful Highland scenery. The hills, being very rocky and precipitous, afford some cataracts of great height, though of inconsiderable breadth. There is one pass over the river Machrai, renowned for the dilemma of a poor woman, who, being tempted by the narrowness of the ravine to step across, succeeded in making the first movement, but took fright when it became necessary to move the other foot, and remained in a pos-

† Asked.   ‡ Without falsehood.

ture equally ludicrous and dangerous, until some chance passenger assisted her to extricate herself. It is said she remained there some hours.

NOTE 33.

Old Brodick's gothic towers were seen,
From Hastings, late their English Lord,
Douglas had won them by the sword. —
P. 323.

Brodick or Brathwick Castle, in the Isle of Arran, is an ancient fortress, near an open roadstead called Brodick-Bay, and not far distant from a tolerable harbor, closed in by the Island of Lamlash. This important place had been assailed a short time before Bruce's arrival in the island. James Lord Douglas, who accompanied Bruce to his retreat in Rachrine, seems, in the spring of 1306, to have tired of his abode there, and set out accordingly, in the phrase of the times, to see what adventure God would send him. Sir Robert Boyd accompanied him; and his knowledge of the localities of Arran appears to have directed his course thither. They landed in the island privately, and appear to have laid an ambush for Sir John Hastings, the English governor of Brodwick, and surprised a considerable supply of arms and provisions, and nearly took the castle itself. Indeed, that they actually did so, has been generally averred by historians, although it does not appear from the narrative of Barbour. On the contrary, it would seem that they took shelter within a fortification of the ancient inhabitants, a rampart called *Tor an Schian.* When they were joined by Bruce, it seems probable that they gained Brodick Castle. At least tradition says that from the battlements of the tower he saw the supposed signal-fire on Turnberry-nook. . . . The castle is now much modernized, but has a dignified appearance, being surrounded by flourishing plantations.

NOTE 34.

Oft, too, with unaccustomed ears,
A language much unmeet he hears. —
P. 323.

Barbour, with great simplicity, gives an anecdote, from which it would seem that the vice of profane swearing, afterwards too general among the Scottish nation, was, at this time, confined to military men. As Douglas, after Bruce's return to Scotland, was roving about the mountainous country of Tweeddale, near the water of Line, he chanced to hear some persons in a farmhouse says, "*the devil.*" Concluding, from this hardy expression, that the house contained warlike guests, he immediately as-

sailed it, and had the good fortune to make prisoners Thomas Randolph, afterwards the famous Earl of Murray, and Alexander Stuart, Lord Bonkle. Both were then in the English interest, and had come into that country with the purpose of driving out Douglas. They afterwards ranked among Bruce's most zealous adherents.

NOTE 35.

Now ask you whence that wondrous light,
Whose fairy glow beguiled their sight !
It ne'er was known. — P. 326.

The following are the words of an ingenious correspondent, to whom I am obliged for much information respecting Turnberry and its neighborhood. " The only tradition now remembered of the landing of Robert the Bruce in Carrick, relates to the fire seen by him from the Isle of Arran. It is still generally reported, and religiously believed by many, that this fire was really the work of supernatural power, unassisted by the hand of any mortal being ; and it is said, that, for several centuries, the flame rose yearly, on the same hour of the same night of the year, on which the king first saw it from the turrets of Brodick Castle ; and some go so far as to say, that if the exact time were known, it would be still seen. That this superstitious notion is very ancient, is evident from the place where the fire is said to have appeared being called the Bogles' Brae, beyond the remembrance of man. In support of this curious belief, it is said that the practice of burning heath for the improvement of land was then unknown ; that a spunkie (Jack o'lanthorn) could not have been seen across the breadth of the Forth of Clyde, between Ayrshire and Arran ; and that the courier of Bruce was his kinsman, and never suspected of treachery." — Letter from Mr. Joseph Train, of Newton Stewart.

NOTE 36.

The Bruce hath won his father's hall ! —
P. 330.

I have followed the flattering and pleasing tradition, that the Bruce, after his descent upon the coast of Ayrshire, actually gained possession of his maternal castle. But the tradition is not accurate. The fact is, that he was only strong enough to alarm and drive in the outposts of the English garrison, then commanded, not by Clifford, as assumed in the text, but by Percy. Neither was Clifford slain upon this occasion, though he had several skirmishes with Bruce. He fell afterwards in the battle of Bannockburn. Bruce, after alarming the castle of

Turnberry, and surprising some part of the garrison, who were quartered without the walls of the fortress, retreated into the mountainous part of Carrick, and there made himself so strong, that the English were obliged to evacuate Turnberry, and at length the Castle of Ayr. Many of his benefactions and royal gifts attest his attachment to the hereditary followers of his house, in this part of the country.

NOTE 37.

When Bruce's banner had victorious flow'd,
O'er Loudoun's mountain, and in Ury's
vale. — P. 331.

The first important advantage gained by Bruce, after landing at Turnberry, was over Aymer de Valence, Earl of Pembroke, the same by whom he had been defeated near Methven. They met, as has been said, by 'appointment, at Loudonhill, in the west of Scotland. Pembroke sustained a defeat; and from that time Bruce was at the head of a considerable flying army. Yet he was subsequently obliged to retreat into Aberdeenshire, and was there assailed by Comyn, Earl of Buchan, desirous to avenge the death of his relative, the Red Comyn, and supported by a body of English troops under Philip de Mowbray. Bruce was ill at the time of a scrofulous disorder, but took horse to meet his enemies, although obliged to be supported on either side. He was victorious, and it is said that the agitation of his spirits restored his health.

NOTE 38.

When English blood oft deluged Douglas-
dale. — P. 331.

The " good Lord James of Douglas," during these commotions, often took from the English his own castle of Douglas ; but being unable to garrison it, contented himself with destroying the fortifications, and retiring into the mountains. As a reward to his patriotism, it is said to have been prophesied, that how often soever Douglas Castle should be destroyed, it should always again rise more magnificent from its ruins. Upon one of these occasions he used fearful cruelty, causing all the store of provisions, which the English had laid up in his castle, to be heaped together, bursting the wine and beer casks among the wheat and flour, slaughtering the cattle upon the same spot, and upon the top of the whole cutting the throats of the English prisoners. This pleasantry of the " good Lord James " is commemorated under the name of the *Douglas's Larder.*

NOTE 39.

And fiery Edward routed stout St. John. —
P. 331.

" John de St John, with 15,000 horsemen, had advanced to oppose the inroad of the Scots. By a forced march he endeavored to surprise them, but intelligence of his motions was timeously received. The courage of Edward Bruce, approaching to temerity, frequently enabled him to achieve what men of more judicious valor would never have attempted. He ordered the infantry, and the meaner sort of his army, to entrench themselves in strong narrow ground. He himself, with fifty horsemen well harnessed, issued forth under cover of a thick mist, surprised the English on their march, attacked and dispersed them." — DALRYMPLE's *Annals of Scotland,* quarto, Edinburgh, 1779, p. 25.

NOTE 40.

When Randolph's war-cry swell'd the south-
ern gale. — P. 331.

Thomas Randolph, Bruce's sister's son, a renowned Scottish chief, was in the early part of his life not more remarkable for consistency than Bruce himself. He espoused his uncle's party when Bruce first assumed the crown, and was made prisoner at the fatal battle of Methven, in which his relative's hopes appeared to be ruined. Randolph accordingly not only submitted to the English, but took an active part against Bruce ; appeared in arms against him : and in the skirmish where he was so closely pursued by the bloodhound, it is said his nephew took his standard with his own hand. But Randolph was afterwards made prisoner by Douglas in Tweeddale, and brought before King Robert. Some harsh language was exchanged between the uncle and nephew, and the latter was committed for a time to close custody. Afterwards, however, they were reconciled, and Randolph was created Earl of Moray about 1312. After this period he eminently distinguished himself, first by the surprise of Edinburgh Castle, and afterwards by many similar enterprises, conducted with equal courage and ability.

NOTE 41.

—— Stirling's towers,
Beleaguered by King Robert's powers ;
And they took term of truce. — P. 331.

When a long train of success, actively improved by Robert Bruce, had made him master of almost all Scotland, Stirling Castle continued to hold out. The care of the blockade was committed by the king to his brother Edward, who concluded a treaty with Sir Philip Mowbray, the governor, that he should surrender the fortress, if it were not succored by the King of England before St. John the Baptist's day. The King severely blamed his brother for the impolicy of a treaty, which gave time to the king of England to advance to the relief of the castle, with all his assembled forces, and obliged himself either to meet them in battle with an inferior force, or to retreat with dishonor. "Let all England come," answered the reckless Edward; "we will fight them were they more." The consequence was, of course, that each kingdom mustered its strength for the expected battle; and as the space agreed upon reached from Lent to Midsummer, full time was allowed for that purpose.

Note 42.

And Cambria, but of late subdued,
Sent forth her mountain multitude. —
P. 332.

Edward the First, with the usual policy of a conqueror, employed the Welsh, whom he had subdued, to assist him in his Scottish wars, for which their habits, as mountaineers, particularly fitted them. But this policy was not without its risks. Previous to the battle of Falkirk, the Welsh quarrelled with the English men-at-arms, and after bloodshed on both parts, separated themselves from his army, and the feud between them, at so dangerous and critical a juncture, was reconciled with difficulty. Edward II. followed his father's example in this particular, and with no better success. They could not be brought to exert themselves in the cause of their conquerors. But they had an indifferent reward for their forbearance. Without arms, and clad only in scanty dresses of linen cloth, they appeared naked in the eyes even of the Scottish peasantry; and after the rout of Bannockburn, were massacred by them in great numbers, as they retired in confusion towards their own country. They were under command of Sir Maurice de Berkeley.

Note 43.

And Connoght pour'd from waste and wood
Her hundred tribes, whose sceptre rude
Dark Eth O'Connor sway'd. — P. 332.

There is in the Fœdera an invitation to Eth O'Connor, chief of the Irish of Connaught, setting forth that the king was about to move against his Scottish rebels, and therefore requesting the attendance of all the force he could muster, either commanded by himself in person, or by some nobleman of his race. These auxiliaries were to be commanded by Richard de Burgh, Earl of Ulster.

Note 44.

The monarch rode along the van. — P. 334.

The English vanguard, commanded by the Earls of Gloucester and Hereford, came in sight of the Scottish army upon the evening of the 23d of June. Bruce was then riding upon a little palfrey in front of his foremost line, putting his host in order. It was then that the personal encounter took place betwixt him and Sir Henry de Bohun, a gallant English knight, the issue of which had a great effect upon the spirits of both armies.

Note 45.

Responsive from the Scottish host,
Pipe-clang and bugle-sound were toss'd. —
P. 336.

There is an old tradition, that the well-known Scottish tune of "Hey, tutti, taitti," was Bruce's march at the battle of Bannockburn. The late Mr. Ritson, no granter of propositions, doubts whether the Scots had any martial music, quotes Froissart's account of each soldier in the host bearing a little horn, on which, at the onset, they would make such a horrible noise, as if all the devils of hell had been among them. He observes, that these horns are the only music mentioned by Barbour, and concludes, that it must remain a moot point whether Bruce's army were cheered by the sound even of a solitary bagpipe. — *Historical Essay prefixed to Ritson's Scottish Songs.* — It may be observed in passing, that the Scottish of this period certainly observed some musical cadence, even in winding their horns, since Bruce was at once recognized by his followers from his mode of blowing. See Note 29, p. 750. But the tradition, true or false, has been the means of securing to Scotland one of the finest lyrics in the language, the celebrated war-song of Burns, — "Scots, wha hae wi' Wallace bled."

Note 46.

See where yon bare-foot Abbott stands,
And blesses them with lifted hands. —
P. 336.

"Maurice, abbot of Inchaffray, placing himself on an eminence, celebrated mass in sight of the Scottish army. He then passed along the front bare-footed, and bearing a crucifix in his hands, and exhorting the Scots, in few and forcible words, to combat for their rights and their liberty. The Scots kneeled down. 'They yield,' cried Edward; 'see, they implore mercy.' — 'They do,' answered Ingelram de Umfraville, 'but not ours. On that field they will be victorious, or die.'" — *Annals of Scotland*, vol. ii. p. 47.

NOTE 47.

Forth, Marshal, on the peasant foe!
We'll tame the terrors of their bow,
And cut the bow-string loose! —

P. 337.

The English archers commenced the attack with their usual bravery and dexterity. But against a force, whose importance he had learned by fatal experience, Bruce was provided. A small but select body of cavalry were detached from the right, under command of Sir Robert Keith. They rounded, as I conceive, the marsh called Milton bog, and, keeping the firm ground, charged the left flank and rear of the English archers. As the bowmen had no spears nor long weapons fit to defend themselves against horse, they were instantly thrown into disorder, and spread through the whole English army a confusion from which they never fairly recovered.

Although the success of this manœuvre was evident, it is very remarkable that the Scottish generals do not appear to have profited by the lesson. Almost every subsequent battle which they lost against England, was decided by the archers, to whom the close and compact array of the Scottish phalanx afforded an exposed and unresisting mark. The bloody battle of Halidoun-hill, fought scarcely twenty years afterwards, was so completely gained by the archers, that the English are said to have lost only one knight, one esquire, and a few foot-soldiers. At the battle of Neville's Cross, in 1346, where David II. was defeated and made prisoner, John de Graham, observing the loss which the Scots sustained from the English bowmen, offered to charge and disperse them, if a hundred men-at-arms were put under his command. "*But*, to confess the truth," says Fordun, "he could not procure a single horseman for the service proposed." Of such little use is experience in war, where its results are opposed by habit or prejudice.

NOTE 48.

Each braggart churl could boast before,
Twelve Scottish lives his baldric bore! —

P. 337.

Roger Ascham quotes a similar Scottish proverb, "whereby they give the whole praise of shooting honestly to Englishmen, saying thus, 'that every English archer beareth under his girdle twenty-four Scottes.' Indeed Toxophilus says before, and truly, of the Scottish nation, 'The Scottes surely be good men of warre in theyre owne feates as can be; but as for shootinge, they can neither use it to any profite, nor yet challenge it for any praise.'" — *Works of Ascham, edited by Bennet*, 4to, p. 110.

It is said, I trust incorrectly, by an ancient English historian, that the "good Lord James of Douglas," dreaded the superiority of the English archers so much, that when he made any of them prisoner, he gave him the option of losing the forefinger of his right hand, or his right eye, either species of mutilation rendering him incapable to use the bow. I have mislaid the reference to this singular passage.

NOTE 49.

Down! down! in headlong overthrow,
Horseman and horse, the foremost go. —

P. 337.

It is generally alleged by historians, that the English men-at-arms fell into the hidden snare which Bruce had prepared for them. Barbour does not mention the circumstance. According to his account, Randolph, seeing the slaughter made by the cavalry on the right wing among the archers, advanced courageously against the main body of the English, and entered into close combat with them. Douglas and Stuart, who commanded the Scottish centre, led their division also to the charge, and the battle, becoming general along the whole line, was obstinately maintained on both sides for a long space of time; the Scottish archers doing great execution among the English men-at-arms, after the bowmen of England were dispersed.

NOTE 50.

And steeds that shriek in agony. —

P. 337.

I have been told that this line requires an explanatory note; and, indeed, those who witness the silent patience with which horses submit to the most cruel usage, may be permitted to doubt, that in moments of sudden and intolerable anguish, they utter a most melancholy cry. Lord Erskine, in a speech made in the House of Lords, upon a bill for enforcing humanity towards animals, noticed this remarkable fact, in language which I will not mutilate by attempting to repeat it. It was my fortune, upon one occasion, to hear a horse, in a moment of agony, utter a thrilling scream, which I still consider the most melancholy sound I ever heard.

NOTE 51.

Lord of the Isles, my trust in thee
Is firm as Ailsa Rock;
Rush on with Highland sword and targe,
I with my Carrick spearmen charge. —
P. 338.

When the engagement between the main bodies had lasted some time, Bruce made a decisive movement by bringing up the Scottish reserve. It is traditionally said, that at this crisis, he addressed the Lord of the Isles in a phrase used as a motto by some of his descendants, "My trust is constant in thee." Barbour intimates that the reserve "assembled on one field," that is, on the same line with the Scottish forces already engaged, which leads Lord Hailes to conjecture that the Scottish ranks must have been much thinned by slaughter, since, in that circumscribed ground there was room for the reserve to fall into the line. But the advance of the Scottish cavalry must have contributed a good deal to form the vacancy occupied by the reserve.

NOTE 52.

To arms they flew, — axe, club, or spear, —
And mimic ensigns high they rear. —
P. 339.

The followers of the Scottish camp observed, from the Gillies' Hill in the rear, the impression produced upon the English army by the bringing up of the Scottish reserve, and prompted by the enthusiasm of the moment, or the desire of plunder, assumed, in a tumultuary manner, such arms as they found nearest, fastened sheets to tent-poles and lances, and showed themselves like a new army advancing to battle.

The unexpected apparition, of what seemed a new army, completed the confusion which already prevailed among the English, who fled in every direction, and were pursued with immense slaughter.

THE FIELD OF WATERLOO.

NOTE 1.

The peasant, at his labor blithe,
Plies the hook'd staff and shorten'd scythe.
— P. 343.

THE reaper in Flanders carries in his left hand a stick with an iron hook, with which he collects as much grain as he can cut at one sweep with a short scythe, which he holds in his right hand. They carry on this double process with great spirit and dexterity.

NOTE 2.

Pale Brussels! then what thoughts were thine. — P. 345.

It was affirmed by the prisoners of war, that Bonaparte had promised his army, in case of victory, twenty-four hours' plunder of the city of Brussels.

NOTE 3.

"On! On!" was still his stern exclaim. —
P. 345.

The characteristic obstinacy of Napoleon was never more fully displayed than in what we may be permitted to hope will prove the last of his fields. He would listen to no advice, and allow of no obstacles. An eye-witness has given the following account of his demeanor towards the end of the action: —

"It was near seven o'clock; Bonaparte, who till then had remained upon the ridge of the hill whence he could best behold what passed, contemplated with a stern countenance the scene of this horrible slaughter. The more that obstacles seemed to multiply, the more his obstinacy seemed to increase. He became indignant at these unforeseen difficulties; and, far from fearing to push to extremities an army whose confidence in him was boundless, he ceased not to pour down fresh troops, and to give orders to march forward — to charge with the bayonet — to carry by storm. He was repeatedly informed from different points, that the day went against him, and that the troops seemed to be disordered; to which he only replied, — '*En avant! En avant!*'

"One general sent to inform the Emperor that he was in a position which he could not maintain, because it was commanded by a battery, and requested to know, at the same time, in what way he should protect his division from the murderous fire of the English artillery. 'Let him storm the battery,' replied Bonaparte, and turned his back on the aide-de-camp who brought the message."

— Relation de la Bataille de Mont-St.-Jean. Par un Témoin Oculaire. Paris, 1815, 8vo, p. 51.

NOTE 4.

The fate their leader shunn'd to share.— P. 345.

It has been reported that Bonaparte charged at the head of his guards, at the last period of this dreadful conflict. This, however, is not accurate. He came down indeed to a hollow part of the high road, leading to Charleroi, within less than a quarter of a mile of the farm of La Haye Sainte, one of the points most fiercely disputed. Here he harangued the guards, and informed them that his preceding operations had destroyed the British infantry and cavalry, and that they had only to support the fire of the artillery, which they were to attack with the bayonet. This exhortation was received with shouts of *Vive l'Empereur,* which were heard over all our line, and led to an idea that Napoleon was charging in person. But the guards were led on by Ney; nor did Bonaparte approach nearer the scene of action than the spot already mentioned, which the rising banks on each side rendered secure from all such balls as did not come in a straight line. He witnessed the earlier part of the battle from places yet more remote, particularly from an observatory which had been placed there by the King of the Netherlands, some weeks before, for the purpose of surveying the country.[*] It is not meant to infer from these particulars that Napoleon showed, on that memorable occasion, the least deficiency in personal courage; on the contrary, he evinced the greatest composure and presence of mind during the whole action. But it is no less true that report has erred in ascribing to him any desperate efforts of valor for recovery of the battle; and it is remarkable, that during the whole carnage, none of his suite were either killed or wounded, whereas scarcely one of the Duke of Wellington's personal attendants escaped unhurt.

NOTE 5.

England shall tell the fight.— P. 345.

In riding up to a regiment which was hard pressed,[†] the Duke called to the men, "Sol-

[*] The mistakes concerning this observatory have been mutual. The English supposed it was erected for the use of Bonaparte: and a French writer affirms it was constructed by the Duke of Wellington.

[†] The 95th. The Duke's words were, "Stand fast, 95th — what will they say in England?"

diers, we must never be beat, — what will they say in England?" It is needless to say how this appeal was answered.

NOTE 6.

As plies the smith his clanging trade.— P. 346.

A private soldier of the 95th regiment compared the sound which took place immediately upon the British cavalry mingling with those of the enemy, to "*a thousand tinkers at work mending pots and kettles.*"

NOTE 7.

The British shock of levell'd steel.— P. 346.

No persuasion or authority could prevail upon the French troops to stand the shock of the bayonet. The Imperial Guards, in particular, hardly stood till the British were within thirty yards of them, although the French author, already quoted, has put into their mouths the magnanimous sentiment, "The Guards never yield — they die." The same author has covered the plateau, or eminence, of St. Jean, which formed the British position, with redoubts and retrenchments which never had an existence. As the narrative, which is in many respects curious, was written by an eye-witness, he was probably deceived by the appearance of a road and a ditch which run along part of the hill. It may be also mentioned, in criticising this work, that the writer mentions the Château of Hougomont to have been carried by the French, although it was resolutely and successfully defended during the whole action. The enemy, indeed, possessed themselves of the wood by which it is surrounded, and at length set fire to the house itself; but the British (a detachment of the Guards, under the command of Colonel Macdonnell, and afterwards of Colonel Home) made good the garden, and thus preserved, by their desperate resistance, the post which covered the return of the Duke of Wellington's right flank.

NOTE 8.

What bright careers 'twas thine to close.— P. 348.

Sir Thomas Picton, Sir William Ponsonby, Sir William de Lancy, and numberless gallant officers.

NOTE 9.

Laurels from the hand of Death.— P. 348.

Colonel Sir William de Lancey had married the beautiful Miss Hall, daughter of Sir James Hall, Bart., only two months before the Battle of Waterloo.

NOTE 10.

Gallant Miller's failing eye.—
P. 348.

Colonel Miller of the Guards, son of Sir William Miller, Lord Glenlee, when lying mortally wounded in the attack on the Bois de Bossu, desired to see once more the colors of his regiment. They were waved about his head, and he died declaring that he was satisfied.

NOTE 11.

And Cameron, in the shock of steel.—
P. 348.

Colonel Cameron of Fassiefern, fell at Quatre Bras, June 16, 1815, heading a charge of the 92d Highlanders.

NOTE 12.

And generous Gordon. — P. 348.

" Colonel the Honorable Sir Alexander Gordon "—brother to the Earl of Aberdeen —who fell by the side of the Duke in the heat of the action.

NOTE 13.

Fair Hougomont. — P. 348.

" Hougomont " — a château with a garden and wood round it. A post of great importance, valiantly held by the Guards during the battle.

GLENFINLAS.

NOTE 1.

How blazed Lord Ronald's beltane-tree.—
P. 388.

THE fires lighted by the Highlanders on the 1st of May, in compliance with the custom derived from the Pagan times, are termed *The Beltane-tree.* It is a festival celebrated with various superstitious rites, both in the north of Scotland and in Wales.

NOTE 2.

The seer's prophetic spirit found. — P. 388.

I can only describe the second sight, by adopting Dr. Johnson's definition, who calls it " An impression, either by the mind upon the eye, or by the eye upon the mind, by which things distant and future are perceived and seen as if they were present." To which I would only add, that the spectral appearances, thus presented, usually presage misfortune ; that the faculty is painful to those who suppose they possess it ; and that they usually acquire it while themselves under the pressure of melancholy.

NOTE 3.

Will good St. Oran's rule prevail. — P. 389.

St. Oran was a friend and follower of St. Columba, and was buried at Icolmkill. His pretensions to be a saint were rather dubious. According to the legend, he consented to be buried alive, in order to propitiate certain demons of the soil, who obstructed the attempts of Columba to build a chapel. Columba caused the body of his friend to be dug up, after three days had elapsed ; when Oran, to the horror and scandal of the assistants, declared that there was neither a God, a judgment, nor a future state ! He had no time to make further discoveries, for Columba caused the earth once more to be shovelled over him with the utmost despatch. The chapel, however, and the cemetery, was called *Relig Ouran ;* and, in memory of his rigid celibacy, no female was admitted to pay her devotions, or be buried in that place. This is the rule alluded to in the poem.

NOTE 4.

And thrice St. Fillan's powerful prayer.—
P. 391.

St. Fillan has given his name to many chapels, holy fountains, etc., in Scotland. He was, according to Camerarius, an Abbot of Pittenween, in Fife ; from which situation he retired, and died a hermit in the wilds of Glenurchy, A.D. 649. While engaged in transcribing the Scriptures, his left hand was observed to send forth such a splendor, as to afford light to that with which he wrote ; a miracle which saved many candles to the convent, as St. Fillan used to spend whole nights in that exercise. The 9th of January was dedicated to this saint, who gave his name to Kilfillan, in Renfrew, and St. Phileans, or Forgend, in Fife. Lesley, lib. 7, tells us, that Robert the Bruce was possessed of Fillan's miraculous and luminous arm, which he enclosed in a silver shrine, and had it carried at the head of his army. Previous to the battle of Bannockburn, the king's chaplain, a man of little faith, abstracted the relic, and deposited it in a place of security, lest it should fall into the hands of the English. But, lo! while Robert was addressing his prayers to the empty casket, it was observed to open and shut suddenly ; and, on inspection, the saint was found to have himself deposited his arm in the shrine as an assurance of victory. Such is the tale of Lesley. But though Bruce little needed that the arm of St. Fillan should assist his own, he dedicated to him, in gratitude, a priory at Killin, upon Loch Tay.

In the Scots Magazine for July, 1802, there is a copy of a very curious crown grant, dated 11th July, 1487, by which James III. confirms, to Malice Doire, an inhabitant of Strathfillan, in Perthshire, the peaceable exercise and enjoyment of a relic of St. Fillan, being apparently the head of a pastoral staff called the Quegrich, which he and his predecessors are said to have possessed since the days of Robert Bruce. As the Quegrich was used to cure diseases, this document is probably the most ancient patent ever granted for a quack medicine. The ingenious correspondent, by whom it is furnished, farther observes, that additional particulars, concerning St. Fillan, are to be found in BELLENDEN'S *Boece*, Book 4, folio ccxiii., and in PENNANT'S *Tour in Scotland*, 1772, pp. 11, 15.

THE EVE OF ST. JOHN.

NOTE I.

BATTLE OF ANCRAM MOOR. — P. 392.

LORD EVERS, and Sir Brian Latoun, during the year 1544, committed the most dreadful ravages upon the Scottish frontiers, compelling most of the inhabitants, and especially the men of Liddesdale, to take assurance under the King of England. Upon the 17th November, in that year, the sum total of their depredations stood thus, in the bloody ledger of Lord Evers : —

Towns, towers, barnekynes, paryshe churches, bastill houses, burned and destroyed — 192

Scots slain	403
Prisoners taken	816
Nolt (cattle)	10,386
Shepe	12,492
Nags and geldings	1296
Gayt	200
Bolls of corn	850

Insight gear, etc. (furniture), an incalculable quantity.

MURDIN'S *State Papers*, vol. i., p. 51.

For these services Sir Ralph Evers was made a Lord of Parliament. See a strain of exulting congratulation upon his promotion poured forth by some contemporary minstrel, in vol. 1., p. 417, *Scottish Minstrelsy*.

The King of England had promised to these two barons a feudal grant of the country, which they had thus reduced to a desert ; upon hearing which, Archibald Douglas, the seventh earl of Angus, is said to have sworn to write the deed of investiture upon their skins, with sharp pens and bloody ink, in resentment for their having defaced the tombs of his ancestors at Melrose. — GODSCROFT. In 1545, Lord Evers and Latoun again entered Scotland, with an army consisting of 3,000 mercenaries, 1,500 English Borderers, and 700 assured Scottish men, chiefly Armstrongs, Turnbulls, and other broken clans. In this second incursion, the English generals even exceeded their former cruelty. Evers burned the tower of Broomhouse, with its lady (a noble and aged woman, says Lesley), and her whole family. The English penetrated as far as Melrose, which they had destroyed last year, and which they now again pillaged. As they returned towards Jedburgh, they were followed by Angus at the head of 1,000 horse, who was shortly after joined by the famous Norman Lesley, with a body of Fife men. The English being probably unwilling to cross the Teviot while the Scots hung upon their rear, halted upon Ancram Moor, above the village of that name ; and the Scottish general was deliberating whether to advance or retire, when Sir Walter Scott [*] of Buccleuch came up at

[*] The Editor has found no instance upon record of this family having taken assurance with England. Hence, they usually suffered dreadfully from the English forays. In August, 1544 (the year preceding the battle), the whole lands belonging to Buccleuch, in West Teviotdale, were harried by Evers ; the outworks, or barmkin, of the Tower of Branxholm burned, eight Scots slain, thirty made prisoners, and an immense prey of horses, cattle, and sheep carried off. The lands upon Kale Water, belonging to the same chieftain, were also plundered, and much spoil obtained ; thirty Scots slain, and the Moss Tower (a fortress near Eskford) *smoked very sore*. Thus Buccleuch had a long account to settle at Ancram Moor. — MURDIN'S *State Papers*, pp. 45, 46.

full speed with a small but chosen body of his retainers, the rest of whom were near at hand. By the advice of this experienced warrior (to whose conduct Pitscottie and Buchanan ascribe the success of the engagement), Angus withdrew from the height which he occupied, and drew up his forces behind it, upon a piece of low, flat ground called Panier-heugh or, Paniel-heugh. The spare horses being sent to an eminence in their rear, appeared to the English to be the main body of the Scots in the act of flight. Under this persuasion, Evers and Latoun hurried precipitately forward, and having ascended the hill, which their foes had abandoned, were no less dismayed than astonished to find the phalanx of Scottish spearmen drawn up in firm array upon the flat ground below. The Scots, in their turn, became the assailants. A heron, roused from the marshes by the tumult, soared away betwixt the encountering armies. "O!" exclaimed Angus, "that I had here my white goss-hawk, that we might all yoke at once!"—GODSCROFT. The English, breathless and fatigued, having the setting sun and wind full in their faces, were unable to withstand the resolute and desperate charge of the Scottish lances. No sooner had they begun to waver, than their own allies, the assured Borderers, who had been waiting the event, threw aside their red crosses, and joining their countrymen, made a most merciless slaughter among the English fugitives, the pursuers calling upon each other to "remember Broomhouse!"—LESLEY, p. 478.

In the battle fell Lord Evers, and his son, together with Sir Brian Latoun, and 800 Englishmen, many of whom were persons of rank. A thousand prisoners were taken. Among these was a patriotic alderman of London, Read by name, who, having contumaciously refused to pay his portion of a benevolence, demanded from the city by Henry VIII., was sent by royal authority to serve against the Scots. These, at settling his ransom, he found still more exorbitant in their exactions than the monarch.—REDPATH'S *Border History*, p. 563.

Evers was much regretted by King Henry, who swore to avenge his death upon Angus, against whom he conceived himself to have particular grounds of resentment, on account of favors received by the earl at his hands. The answer of Angus was worthy of a Douglas, "Is our brother-in-law offended," * said he, "that I, as a good Scotsman, have avenged my ravaged country, and the defaced tombs of my ancestors, upon Ralph

---

Evers? They were better men than he, and I was bound to do no less. And will he take my life for that? Little knows King Henry the skirts of Kirnetable † I can keep myself there against all his English host."—GODSCROFT.

Such was the noted battle of Ancram Moor. The spot on which it was fought is called Lilyard's Edge, from an Amazonian Scottish woman of that name, who is reported, by tradition, to have distinguished herself in the same manner as Squire Witherington. ‡ The old people point out her monument, now broken and defaced. The inscription is said to have been legible within this century, and to have run thus:—

" Fair maiden Lylliard lies under this stane,
 Little was her stature, but great was her fame:
 Upon the English louns she laid mony thumps,
 And, when her legs were cutted off, she fought
     upon her stumps."
          Vide *Account of the Parish of Melrose.*

It appears, from a passage in Stowe, that an ancestor of Lord Evers held also a grant of Scottish lands from an English monarch. " I have seen," says the historian, " under the broad-seale of the said King Edward I., a manor called Ketnes, in the county of Forfare, in Scotland, and neere the furthest part of the same nation northward, given to John Ure and his heires, ancestor to the Lord Ure that now is, for his service done in these partes, with market, etc., dated at Lanercost, the 20th day of October, anno regis 34." STOWE'S *Annals*, p. 210. This grant, like that of Henry, must have been dangerous to the receiver.

NOTE 2.

A covering on her wrist. — P. 395.

There is an old and well-known Irish tradition that the bodies of certain spirits and devils are scorchingly hot, so that they leave upon anything they touch an impress as if of red-hot iron. It is related of one of Melancthon's relations, that a devil seized hold of her hand, which bore the mark of a burn to her dying day. The incident in the poem is of a similar nature— the ghost's hands " scorch'd like a fiery brand," leaving a burning impress on the table and the lady's wrist. Another class of fiends are reported to be icy cold, and to freeze the skin of any one with whom they come in contact.

NOTE 3.

That nun who ne'er beholds the day.—P. 395.

The circumstances of the nun, " who never

---

* Angus had married the widow of James IV., sister to King Henry VIII.

† Kirnetable, now called Cairntable, is a mountainous tract at the head of Douglasdale.

‡ See *Chevy Chase.*

saw the day," is not entirely imaginary. About fifty years ago, an unfortunate female wanderer took up her residence in a dark vault, among the ruins of Dryburgh Abbey, which, during the day, she never quitted. When night fell, she issued from this miserable habitation, and went to the house of Mr. Haliburton of Newmains, the Editor's great-grandfather, or to that of Mr. Erskine of Sheilfield, two gentlemen of the neighborhood. From their charity she obtained such necessaries as she could be prevailed upon to accept. At twelve, each night, she lighted her candle, and returned to her vault, assuring her friendly neighbors, that, during her absence, her habitation was arranged by a spirit, to whom she gave the uncouth name of *Fat lips;* describing him as a little man, wearing heavy iron shoes, with which he trampled the clay floor of the vault, to dispel the damps. This circumstance caused her to be regarded, by the well-informed, with compassion, as deranged in her understanding ; and, by the vulgar, with some degree of terror. The cause of her adopting this extraordinary mode of life she would never explain. It was, however, believed to have been occasioned by a vow, that, during the absence of a man to whom she was attached, she would never look upon the sun. Her lover never returned. He fell during the civil war of 1745-6, and she never more would behold the light of day.

The vault, or rather dungeon, in which this unfortunate woman lived and died, passes still by the name of the supernatural being, with which its gloom was tenanted by her disturbed imagination, and few of the neighboring peasants dare enter it by night. — Note of 1803.

CADYOW CASTLE.

NOTE 1.

—*sound the pryse!* — P. 397.

Pryse. — The note blown at the death of the game. — *In Caledonia olim frequens erat sylvestris quidam bos, nunc vero rarior, qui, colore candidissimo, jubam densam et demissam, instar leonis gestat, truculentus ac ferus ab humano genere abhorrens, ut quæcunque homines vel manibus contrectârint, vel halitu perflaverint, ab iis multos post dies omnino abstinuerunt. Ad hoc tanta audacia huic bovi indita erat, ut non solum irritatus equites furenter prosterneret, sed ne tantillum lacessitus omnes promiscue homines cornibus ac ungulis peteret ; ac canum, qui apud nos ferocissimi sunt, impetus plane contemneret. Ejus carnes cartilaginosæ, sed saporis suavissimi. Erat is olim per illam vastissimam Caledoniæ sylvam frequens, sed humana ingluvie jam assumptus tribus tantum locis est reliquus, Strivilingii, Cumbernaldiæ, et Kincarniæ.* — LESLÆUS Scotiæ Descriptio, p. 13.

NOTE 2.

Stern Claud replied. — P. 398.

Lord Claud Hamilton, second son of the Duke of Chatelherault, and commendator of the Abbey of Paisley, acted a distinguished part during the troubles of Queen Mary's reign, and remained unalterably attached to the cause of that unfortunate princess. He led the van of her army at the fatal battle of Langside, and was one of the commanders at the Raid of Stirling, which had so nearly given complete success to the Queen's faction. He was ancestor of the present Marquis of Abercorn.

NOTE 3.

Woodhouselee. — P. 398.

This barony, stretching along the banks of the Esk, near Auchendinny, belonged to Bothwellhaugh, in right of his wife. The ruins of the mansion, from which she was expelled in the brutal manner which occasioned her death, are still to be seen in a hollow glen beside the river. Popular report tenants them with the restless ghost of the Lady Bothwellhaugh ; whom, however, it confounds with Lady Anne Bothwell, whose *Lament* is so popular. This spectre is so tenacious of her rights, that, a part of the stones of the ancient edifice having been employed in building or repairing the present Woodhouselee, she has deemed it a part of her privilege to haunt that house also ; and, even of very late years, has excited considerable disturbance and terror among the domestics. This is a more remarkable vindication of the *rights of ghosts* as the present Woodhouselee, which gives his title to the Honorable Alexander Fraser Tytler, a senator of the College of Justice, is situated on the slope of the Pentland hills, distant at least four miles from her proper abode. She always appears in white, and with her child in her arms.

NOTE 4.

Drives to the leap his jaded steed. — P. 398.

Birrel informs us, that Bothwellhaugh, being closely pursued, "after that spur and wand had failed him, he drew forth his dagger, and strocke his horse behind, whilk caused the horse to leap a very brode stanke [i.e., ditch], by whilk means he escapit, and gat away from all the rest of the horses." — BIRREL'S *Diary*, p. 18.

NOTE 5.

From the wild Border's humbled side. — P. 398.

Murray's death took place shortly after an expedition to the Borders; which is thus commemorated by the author of the Elegy: —

" So having stablischt all things in this sort,
To Liddisdaill again he did resort,
Throw Ewisdail, Eskdail, and all the daills rode he,
And also lay three nights in Cannabie,
Whair na prince lay thir hundred yeiris before,
Nae thief durst stir, they did him feir sa sair;
And, that they suld na mair thair thift allege,
Threescore and twelf he brocht of thame in pledge,
Syne wardit thame, whilk maid the rest keep ordour;
Then mycht the rasch-bus keep ky on the Border."
Scottish Poems, 16th century, p. 232.

NOTE 6.

With hackbut bent. — P. 398.

Hackbuck bent — Gun cock'd. The carbine, with which the Regent was shot, is preserved at Hamilton Palace. It is a brass piece, of a middling length, very small in the bore, and, what is rather extraordinary, appears to have been rifled or indented in the barrel. It had a matchlock, for which a modern firelock has been injudiciously substituted.

NOTE 7.

The wild Macfarlane's plaided clan. — P. 398.

This clan of Lennox Highlanders were attached to the Regent Murray. Holinshed, speaking of the battle of Langside, says, " In this batyle the vallancie of an Heiland gentleman, named Macfarlane, stood the Regent's part in great steede; for, in the hottest brunte of the fighte, he came up with two hundred of his friendes and countrymen, and so manfully gave in upon the flankes of the

Queen's people, that he was a great cause of the disordering of them. This Macfarlane had been lately before, as I have heard, condemned to die, for some outrage by him committed, and obtayning pardon through suyte of the Countess of Murray, he recompensed that clemencie by this piece of service now at this batayle." Calderwood's account is less favorable to the Macfarlanes. He states that " Macfarlane, with his Highlandmen, fled from the wing where they were set. The Lord Lindsay, who stood nearest to them in the Regent's battle, said, ' Let them go! I shall fill their place better;' and so, stepping forward, with a company of fresh men, charged the enemy, whose spears were now spent, with long weapons, so that they were driven back by force, being before almost overthrown by the avaunt-guard and harquebusiers, and so were turned to flight." — CALDERWOOD'S *MS. apud* KEITH, p. 480. Melville mentions the flight of the vanguard, but states it to have been commanded by Morton, and composed chiefly of commoners of the barony of Renfrew.

NOTE 8.

Glencairn and stout Parkhead were nigh. — P. 398.

The Earl of Glencairn was a steady adherent of the Regent. George Douglas of Parkhead was a natural brother of the Earl of Morton, whose horse was killed by the same ball by which Murray fell.

NOTE 9.

*——haggard Lindesay's iron eye,
That saw fair Mary weep in vain.* — P. 398.

Lord Lindsay of the Byres was the most ferocious and brutal of the Regent's faction, and, as such, was employed to extort Mary's signature to the deed of resignation presented to her in Lochleven castle. He discharged his commission with the most savage rigor; and it is even said, that when the weeping captive, in the act of signing, averted her eyes from the fatal deed, he pinched her arm with the grasp of his iron glove.

NOTE 10.

So close the minions crowded nigh. — P. 399.

Not only had the Regent notice of the intended attempt upon his life, but even of the very house from which it was threatened. With that infatuation at which men wonder, after such events have happened, he deemed it would be a sufficient precaution to ride briskly past the dangerous spot. But even this was prevented by the crowd; so that Bothwellhaugh had time to take deliberate aim. — SPOTTISWOODE, p. 233. BUCHANAN.

THE GRAY BROTHER.

NOTE 1.
By blast of bugle free. — P. 401.

THE barony of Pennycuik, the property of Sir George Clerk, Bart., is held by a singular tenure ; the proprietor being bound to sit upon a large rocky fragment called the Buckstane, and wind three blasts of a horn, when the King shall come to hunt on the Borough Muir, near Edinburgh. Hence the family have adopted as their crest a demi-forester proper, winding a horn, with the motto, *Free for a Blast*. The beautiful mansion-house of Pennycuik is much admired, both on account of the architecture and surrounding scenery.

NOTE 2.
To Auchendinny's hazel shade. — P. 401.

Auchendinny, situated upon the Eske below Pennycuik, the present residence of the ingenious H. Mackenzie, Esq., author of the *Man of Feeling, etc.* Edition 1803.

NOTE 3.
Melville's beechy grove. — P. 401.

Melville Castle, the seat of the Right Honorable Lord Melville, to whom it gives the title of Viscount, is delightfully situated upon the Eske, near Lasswade.

NOTE 4.
Roslin's rocky glen. — P. 401.

The ruins of Roslin Castle, the baronial residence of the ancient family of St. Clair. The Gothic chapel, which is still in beautiful preservation, with the romantic and woody dell in which they are situated, belong to the Right Honorable the Earl of Rosslyn,

the representative of the former Lords of Roslin.

NOTE 5.
Dalkeith, which all the Virtues love. — P. 401.

The village and Castle of Dalkeith belonged of old to the famous Earl of Morton, but is now the residence of the noble family of Buccleuch. The park extends along the Eske, which is there joined by its sister stream of the same name.

NOTE 6.
Classic Hawthornden. — 401.

Hawthornden, the residence of the poet Drummond. A house of more modern date is enclosed, as it were, by the ruins of the ancient castle, and overhangs a tremendous precipice upon the banks of the Eske, perforated by winding caves, which in former times were a refuge to the oppressed patriots of Scotland. Here Drummond received Ben Jonson, who journeyed from London on foot in order to visit him. The beauty of this striking scene has been much injured of late years by the indiscriminate use of the axe. The traveller now looks in vain for the leafy bower,

"Where Jonson sat in Drummond's social shade."

Upon the whole, tracing the Eske from its source till it joins the sea at Musselburgh, no stream in Scotland can boast such a varied succession of the most beautiful scenery — 1803. . . . The beautiful scenery of Hawthornden has, since the above note was written, recovered all its former ornament of wood — 1833.

NOTE: P. 459.

Sir Walter Scott, while engaged in writing "Woodstock," noted in his journal, under date of March 24, 1826, that John Ballantyne was "clamorous for a motto." He adds : "It is foolish to encourage people to expect mottoes and such like decoramints. You have no success in finding them, and there is a disgrace in wanting them. It is like being in the habit of showing feats of strength, which you at length gain praise by accomplishing, while some shame occurs in failure."

It was while correcting the proof-sheets of "The Antiquary," that he was first led to adorn the chapters of his works with original verse. Lockhart thus described the occasion of it : —

"On one occasion he happened to ask John Ballantyne, who was sitting by him, to hunt for a particular passage in Beaumont and Fletcher. John did as he was bid, but did not succeed in discovering the lines. 'Hang it, Johnnie!' cried Scott, 'I believe I can make a motto sooner than you will find one.' He did so accordingly, and from that hour, whenever memory failed to suggest an appropriate epigraph, he had recourse to the inexhaustible mines of 'Old Play' or 'Old Ballad,' to which we owe some of the most exquisite verses that ever flowed from his pen."

" Each blank in faithless memory void
The poet's glowing thought supplied."

When, in 1822, Constable was compiling a volume of the poetry contained in Scott's Novels, Tales, and Romances the author wrote him :—

" It is odd to say, but nevertheless quite certain, that I do not know whether some of the things are original or not, and I wish you would devise some way of stating this in the title."

Constable finally adopted an explanatory note or advertisement written by Scott himself, which ran :—

" We believe by far the greater part of the poetry interspersed through these novels to be original compositions by the author. At the same time, the reader will find passages which are quoted from other authors, and very probably detect more of these than our more limited reading has enabled us to ascertain. Indeed, it is our opinion that some of the following poetry is neither entirely original nor altogether borrowed ; but consists, in some instances, of passages from other writers, which the author has not hesitated to alter considerably, or to adapt the quotation more explicitly and aptly to the matter in hand."

A glimpse of Scott in the very act of furnishing one of these extemporized mottoes is given in Lockhart's Life. It was one day in December, 1831, while visiting Mr. Cadell in Edinburgh, and saddening his friends by his strange apathy and unwonted silence, the effects of his malady, Ballantyne reminded him that a motto was wanted for one of the chapters of " Count Robert of Paris." " He looked out for a moment at the gloomy weather," says Lockhart, and penned the lines beginning, " The storm increases, 'tis no sunny shower," which he entitled, " The Deluge." (See p. 536).

Many of Scott's quotations have been located, and those that are undoubtedly the work of another author are omitted from this edition. Whenever there is room for doubt quotations are inserted.

INDEX OF FIRST LINES.